Morality and Moral Controversies

Morality and Moral Controversies, 10th Edition challenges students to critically assess today's leading moral, social, and political issues. As a comprehensive anthology, it provides students with the tools they need to understand the philosophical ideas that are currently shaping our world.

The 10th edition includes classic and contemporary readings in moral theory, the most current topics in applied ethics, and updated debates in social and political philosophy. As in the previous nine editions, the materials were selected for balance, timeliness, and accessibility after reviewing a vast range of possible articles from leading scholarly journals, mainstream periodicals, online posts, and book chapters. Hallmarks include carefully edited and philosophically relevant U.S. Supreme Court decisions, compelling readings, and contrasting points of view that reflect a broad ethical and political spectrum.

Upon completing this book, readers will be able to:

- Understand philosophical ideas that are shaping the world today.
- Apply various philosophical ideas to politics, religion, ethics, economics, personal relationships, medicine, the environment and climate change, warfare, and other areas.
- Appreciate how to construct, apply, and evaluate basic philosophical arguments.

Key updates to the 10th edition include:

- *All* material published in the actual book (in contrast to placing sections online behind a paywall, as was the case in earlier editions with a different publisher)
- New readings on:
  - autonomous warfare
  - self-driving cars
  - the right to health care
  - technology and privacy
  - the value of democracy
  - racial equality
  - immigration.

Steven Scalet is Professor of Philosophy at the University of Baltimore (UB), where he helped launch the Program in Philosophy, Law, and Ethics. Prior to working at UB, he directed the Program in Philosophy, Politics, and Law at Binghamton University (State University of New York, SUNY), and received the Chancellor's Award for Excellence in Teaching. Scalet received his Ph.D. in Philosophy and M.A. in Economics from the University of Arizona. Scalet is the author of *Markets, Ethics, and Business Ethics, 2nd Edition* (2018).

John Arthur (1946–2007) was a professor of philosophy with areas of specialization in legal theory, social ethics, and political philosophy. He authored several books, including *Race, Equality, and the Burdens of History* (2007). He taught at Binghamton University for eighteen years.

Morality and Moral Controversies

Readings in Moral, Social, and Political Philosophy

10th Edition

Steven Scalet, Editor
John Arthur, Co-Editor

Routledge
Taylor & Francis Group
NEW YORK AND LONDON

Tenth edition published 2019
by Routledge
52 Vanderbilt Avenue, New York, NY 10017

and by Routledge
2 Park Square, Milton Park, Abingdon, Oxon, OX14 4RN

Routledge is an imprint of the Taylor & Francis Group, an informa business

© 2019 Taylor & Francis

The right of Steven Scalet and John Arthur to be identified as the authors of the editorial material, and of the authors for their individual chapters, has been asserted in accordance with sections 77 and 78 of the Copyright, Designs and Patents Act 1988.

All rights reserved. No part of this book may be reprinted or reproduced or utilised in any form or by any electronic, mechanical, or other means, now known or hereafter invented, including photocopying and recording, or in any information storage or retrieval system, without permission in writing from the publishers.

Trademark notice: Product or corporate names may be trademarks or registered trademarks, and are used only for identification and explanation without intent to infringe.

Sixth edition published by Prentice Hall 2002
Ninth edition published by Routledge 2014

Library of Congress Cataloging-in-Publication Data
Names: Scalet, Steven, editor. | Arthur, John, 1946–2007, editor.
Title: Morality and Moral Controversies: Readings in Moral, Social, and Political Philosophy/Steven Scalet, editor; John Arthur, co-editor.
Description: 10 [edition]. | New York: Routledge, 2019.
Identifiers: LCCN 2018032897 (print) | LCCN 2018052077 (ebook) | ISBN 9781315222882 (ebk) | ISBN 9781138387997 (hbk) | ISBN 9780415789318 (pbk)
Subjects: LCSH: Ethics. | Social problems.
Classification: LCC BJ1025 (ebook) | LCC BJ1025 .M67 2018 (print) | DDC 170–dc23
LC record available at https://lccn.loc.gov/2018032897

ISBN: 978-1-138-38799-7 (hbk)
ISBN: 978-0-415-78931-8 (pbk)
ISBN: 978-1-315-22288-2 (ebk)

Typeset in Times New Roman
by Swales & Willis, Exeter, Devon, UK

Printed and bound in Great Britain by
TJ International Ltd, Padstow, Cornwall

Contents

PART I
Moral Thinking   1

1 Self-Interest, Altruism, Religion, and Conscience   3

Leviathan: Morality as Rational Advantage   3
THOMAS HOBBES

Morality and Rational Self-Interest   13
BARUCH BRODY

Divine Commands and the Social Nature of Obligation   23
ROBERT MERRIHEW ADAMS

Morality, Religion, and Conscience   32
JOHN ARTHUR

The Conscience of Huckleberry Finn   42
JONATHAN BENNETT

2 The Sources and Grounds of Morality   53

The Sources of Moral Ideas: Society, Custom, and Sympathy   53
EDWARD WESTERMARCK

Trying Out One's New Sword   55
MARY MIDGLEY

Morality Is Based on Sentiment   60
DAVID HUME

Morality and Normativity   67
MICHAEL J. PERRY

The Moral Instinct   77
STEVEN PINKER

3 Classical and Contemporary Theories of Morality   90

Nicomachean Ethics   90
ARISTOTLE

The Fundamental Principles of the Metaphysic of Morals — 98
IMMANUEL KANT

Utilitarianism — 110
JOHN STUART MILL

Intuitionism — 120
W. D. ROSS

Kant and Utilitarianism Contrasted — 125
ONORA O'NEILL

The Real and Alleged Problems of Utilitarianism — 131
RICHARD B. BRANDT

The Ethics of Care as Moral Theory — 140
VIRGINIA HELD

PART II
Life and Death — 149

4 Terrorism and Torture — 151

Is Terrorism Morally Distinctive? — 151
SAMUEL SCHEFFLER

Torture: The Case for Dirty Harry — 157
UWE STEINHOFF

Training Torturers: A Critique of the "Ticking Bomb" Argument — 167
JESSICA WOLFENDALE

5 War, Autonomous Machines, and the Arms Trade — 178

On the Morality of War — 178
RICHARD A. WASSERSTROM

The Morality of Pacifism — 190
CHEYNEY RYAN

When Is a Robot a Moral Agent? — 193
JOHN P. SULLINS

Autonomous Machines, Moral Judgment, and Acting for the Right Reasons — 202
DUNCAN PURVES, RYAN JENKINS, AND BRADLEY J. STRAWSER

Weapons, Security, and Oppression: A Normative Study of International Arms Transfers — 209
JAMES CHRISTENSEN

6 Capital Punishment — 217

The Death Penalty — 217
GREGG V. GEORGIA

Desert and Capital Punishment — 226
MARTIN PERLMUTTER

The Ultimate Punishment 236
ERNEST VAN DEN HAAG
Abolishing the Death Penalty Even for the Worst Murderers 242
HUGO ADAM BEDAU
Justice, Civilization, and the Death Penalty 253
JEFFREY H. REIMAN

7 Animals, Environmentalism, and Climate 261

All Animals Are Equal 261
PETER SINGER
Speciesism and the Idea of Equality 273
BONNIE STEINBOCK
People or Penguins 281
WILLIAM F. BAXTER
The Land Ethic: Animal Liberation and Environmentalism 287
J. BAIRD CALLICOTT
Two Kinds of Climate Justice: Avoiding Harm and Sharing Burdens 297
SIMON CANEY

8 Cloning and Abortion 307

The Ethics of Cloning-to-Produce-Children 307
THE PRESIDENT'S COUNCIL ON BIOETHICS
The Constitutional Right to Abortion 326
ROE V. WADE
A Defense of Abortion 332
JUDITH JARVIS THOMSON
On the Moral and Legal Status of Abortion 342
MARY ANNE WARREN
Abortion and the Concept of a Person 351
JANE ENGLISH
An Argument That Abortion Is Wrong 359
DON MARQUIS
Fathers and Fetuses 370
GEORGE W. HARRIS

9 Health Care and Deciding Who Should Live 380

The Medical Minimum: Zero 380
JAN NARVESON
A Right to Health Care 388
PAVLOS ELEFTHERIADIS
Requiring Medical Treatment 395
JFK MEMORIAL HOSPITAL V. HESTON

Death with Dignity Act — 398
GONZALES V. OREGON

Aging and the Ends of Medicine — 405
DANIEL CALLAHAN

The Survival Lottery — 413
JOHN HARRIS

PART III
Personal Relationships — 421

10 Love and Sex — 423

Duties Toward the Body in Respect to Sexual Impulse — 423
IMMANUEL KANT

Plain Sex — 428
ALAN H. GOLDMAN

Gay Basics: Some Questions, Facts, and Values — 438
RICHARD D. MOHR

What Is the Point of Love? — 450
CAROLYN PRICE

11 Family and Friendship — 462

Is Adultery Immoral? — 462
RICHARD A. WASSERSTROM

Licensing Parents — 471
HUGH LAFOLLETTE

Can Parents and Children Be Friends? — 480
JOSEPH KUPFER

Parents and Children as Friends — 490
KRISTJÁN KRISTJÁNSSON

What Do Grown Children Owe Their Parents? — 497
JANE ENGLISH

12 Personal Dimensions of Technology: Friendships, Self-Driving Cars, and Privacy — 503

Is Google Making Us Stupid? What the Internet Is Doing to Our Brains — 503
NICHOLAS CARR

Friendship in the Shadow of Technology — 510
LAURENCE THOMAS

Social Networking Sites and Our Lives — 517
PEW INTERNET AND AMERICAN LIFE PROJECT

Why Ethics Matters for Autonomous Cars — 522
PATRICK LIN

Inequality and Other Problems with Nozick's Libertarianism   810
JOHN RAWLS

Money and Commodities   815
MICHAEL WALZER

Property Rights and Eminent Domain   820
KELO V. CITY OF NEW LONDON

The Social Responsibility of Business Is to Increase Its Profits   825
MILTON FRIEDMAN

Rethinking the Social Responsibility of Business: A Debate   830
JOHN MACKEY AND MILTON FRIEDMAN

18 Race, Gender, and Affirmative Action   838

Separate but Equal?   838
BROWN V. BOARD OF EDUCATION

Rethinking the Problem of the Ghetto   841
TOMMIE SHELBY

Affirmative Action in Higher Education   850
GRUTTER V. BOLLINGER

Affirmative Action in Higher Education   863
GRATZ V. BOLLINGER

Reverse Discrimination   870
JAMES RACHELS

The Subjection of Women   873
JOHN STUART MILL AND HARRIET TAYLOR

Sexual Equality and Discrimination: Difference vs. Dominance   882
WILL KYMLICKA

Social Movements and the Politics of Difference   887
IRIS MARION YOUNG

Freedom, Conditioning, and the Real Woman   895
JANET RADCLIFFE RICHARDS

19 Immigration, National Boundaries, and Multiculturalism   909

An Overview of the Ethics of Immigration   909
JOSEPH H. CARENS

Immigration and Democratic Principles: On Carens' Ethics of Immigration   921
SARAH SONG

Immigration and Freedom of Association   924
CHRISTOPHER HEATH WELLMAN

Multiculturalism: A Liberal Perspective   930
JOSEPH RAZ

Reason Before Identity 939
AMARTYA SEN

Assimilation and Cultural Identity 947
WISCONSIN V. YODER

*Appendix: The Bill of Rights and the Fourteenth
    Amendment: A Transcription* 953

Part I

Moral Thinking

Chapter 1

Self-Interest, Altruism, Religion, and Conscience

The essays in this chapter consider what are often some of the first questions asked when people begin to study ethics. One is the connection between morality, on the one hand, and self-interest, on the other. Is morality opposed to self-interest, as some suppose, or is it in some sense to everyone's advantage? Another related question involves people's actual motives. While we sometimes think we act for the sake of morality, is it possible that this is mistaken and that ultimately our real motives are always selfish ones? These questions lead naturally to the topic of the last essays in the chapter: the connections, if any, between morality and religion, and the relationships between motives of sympathy for others and moral duty.

> ### READING: LEVIATHAN: MORALITY AS RATIONAL ADVANTAGE
>
> THOMAS HOBBES[*]
>
> Thomas Hobbes was born in 1588 when the approach of the Spanish Armada was threatening Britain. "Fear and I were born twins," he would later say, emphasizing his conviction that the need for security was the foundation of society and the basis of political obligation. He lived during a critical and difficult period of English history, which included struggles over the traditional authority of the church and the emerging role of modern science. He also saw radical political change, including the absolutism of the Stuart monarchy, the English civil war, and the abolition and subsequent restoration of the monarchy. He died just before constitutional government won its final victory. Hobbes served as tutor for Charles II, who gave Hobbes a pension after being restored to the throne. After publishing early works expressing antiroyalist attitudes, Hobbes was sent into exile, he was condemned in the House of Commons, and, even after he died, his books were burned at Oxford. He was suspected of atheism and, perhaps most important, he rejected the divine basis of political authority. God, he said, is beyond rational understanding; we can only know he exists as the first cause of the universe. Hobbes lived until the age of ninety-one, enjoying a life of travel, study, polemical controversy, and literary and philosophical activity. He was personally temperate, lively, and a loyal friend; he played tennis until the

[*] From Thomas Hobbes, *Leviathan* (1651).

age of seventy-five and attributed his lifelong good health to exercise and singing in bed. He wrote on a variety of subjects, but his most famous work by far is *Leviathan*, published in 1651.

Hobbes was heavily influenced by the new Galilean scientific method and thought that physical laws could account for human behavior, just as they do for all other phenomena. He sought to understand human beings (and politics) in accord with the new scientific methods.

Just before the selection reprinted here, Hobbes argued that the world, including human beings, is composed of material particles. Minds, he argued, are therefore no different from bodies; human "motion," such as walking, speaking, and other acts, is caused by our desires, appetites, and aversions. In this selection, Hobbes discusses reason and the human condition in a "state of nature," which refers to any situation where human beings live together without any overarching government, state, or socially enforced laws. Although the idea can be analyzed historically and empirically, it is most often understood as a hypothetical situation for constructing a broader philosophical argument.

The First Part: Of Man

Good. Evil. ...

Whatsoever is the object of any man's appetite or desire, that is it which he for his part calleth *good*: and the object of his hate and aversion, *evil*; and of his contempt, *vile* and *inconsiderable*. For these words of good, evil, and contemptible, are ever used with relation to the person that useth them: there being nothing simply and absolutely so ....

Deliberation

When in the mind of man, appetites, and aversions, hopes, and fears, concerning one and the same thing, arise alternately; and divers good and evil consequences of the doing, or omitting the thing propounded, come successively into our thoughts; so that sometimes we have an appetite to it; sometimes an aversion from it; sometimes hope to be able to do it; sometimes despair, or fear to attempt it; the whole sum of desires, aversions, hopes and fears continued till the thing be either done, or thought impossible, is that we call DELIBERATION ....

The Will

In *deliberation*, the last appetite, or aversion, immediately adhering to the action, or to the omission thereof, is that we call the WILL ....

Felicity

Continual success in obtaining those things which a man from time to time desireth, that is to say, continual prospering, is that men call FELICITY; I mean the felicity of this life. For there is no such thing as perpetual tranquility of mind,

*What Justifies Democracy? and Rule Over None II: Social Equality
and the Justification of Democracy*   675
NIKO KOLODNY

Are Charter Cities Legitimate?   684
RAHUL SAGAR

Political Morality and the Authority of Tradition   690
STEVEN WALL

Transnational Legal Sites and Democracy-Building   698
SEYLA BENHABIB

Social Movements   704
AVERY KOLERS

16   Liberty: Free Speech and Drug Use   712

Of the Liberty of Thought and Discussion   712
JOHN STUART MILL

*Powers in Public: Reactions, Responses, and Resistance to Offensive
Public Speech*   716
LAURA BETH NIELSEN

*The Social Benefits of Protecting Hate Speech and Exposing
Sources of Prejudice*   726
MARCUS SCHULZKE

Organized Protests and Free Speech   733
SNYDER V. PHELPS (WESTBORO BAPTIST CHURCH)

Nazi Marches   742
VILLAGE OF SKOKIE V. NATIONAL SOCIALIST PARTY

Do Corporations Have Freedom of Speech?   746
CITIZENS UNITED V. FEDERAL ELECTION COMMISSION

The Ethics of Smoking   764
ROBERT E. GOODIN

Addiction and Drug Policy   777
DANIEL SHAPIRO

*The Ethics of Addiction: An Argument in Favor of Letting Americans
Take Any Drug They Want*   784
THOMAS SZASZ

17   Economic Justice: Markets and Property   795

Of Justice   795
DAVID HUME

The Entitlement Theory   799
ROBERT NOZICK

Technology and New Challenges for Privacy   529
LESLIE P. FRANCIS

The Benefits of Being Watched   532
ANDREW OBERG

Privacy, Neuroscience, and Neuro-Surveillance   542
ADAM D. MOORE

PART IV
Political, Social, and Economic Relationships   555

13   The Ideal State   557

The Second Treatise of Government   557
JOHN LOCKE

Libertarian Justice   565
TIBOR R. MACHAN

On Liberty   579
JOHN STUART MILL

On Representative Government   589
JOHN STUART MILL

A Theory of Justice   596
JOHN RAWLS

14   Protests, Patriotism, and the Rule of Law   608

Flag Burning as Constitutionally Protected   608
TEXAS V. JOHNSON

Is Patriotism a Virtue?   612
ALASDAIR MACINTYRE

Patriotism as Bad Faith   619
SIMON KELLER

Frederick Douglass's Patriotism   634
BERNARD R. BOXILL

Letter from a Birmingham Jail   646
REV. MARTIN LUTHER KING, JR.

Crito   658
PLATO

Legitimate and Illegitimate Uses of Police Force   664
JOHN KLEINIG

15   Democracy: Foundations, Recent Contributions, and Global Challenges   674

Gettysburg Address (1863)   674
ABRAHAM LINCOLN

while we live here; because life itself is but motion, and can never be without desire, nor without fear, no more than without sense ....

Of the Natural Condition of Mankind as Concerning Their Felicity and Misery

Men by Nature Equal

Nature hath made men so equal, in the faculties of the body, and mind; as that though there be found one man sometimes manifestly stronger in body, or of quicker mind than another; yet when all is reckoned together, the difference between man, and man, is not so considerable, as that one man can thereupon claim to himself any benefit, to which another may not pretend, as well as he. For as to the strength of body, the weakest has strength enough to kill the strongest, either by secret machination, or by confederacy with others, that are in the same danger with himself.

And as to the faculties of the mind, setting aside the arts grounded upon words, and especially that skill of proceeding upon general, and infallible rules, called science; which very few have, and but in few things; as being not a native faculty, born with us: nor attained, as prudence, while we look after somewhat else, I find yet a greater equality amongst men, than that of strength. For prudence is but experience; which equal time, equally bestows on all men, in those things they equally apply themselves unto. That which may perhaps make such equality incredible, is but a vain conceit of one's own wisdom, which almost all men think they have in a greater degree, than the vulgar; that is, than all men but themselves, and a few others, whom by fame, or for concurring with themselves, they approve.

From Equality Proceeds Diffidence

From this equality of ability, ariseth equality of hope in the attaining of our ends. And therefore if any two men desire the same thing, which nevertheless they cannot both enjoy, they become enemies; and in the way to their end, which is principally their own conservation, and sometimes their delectation only, endeavor to destroy, or subdue one another. And from hence it comes to pass, that where an invader hath no more to fear, than another man's single power: if one plant, sow, build, or possess a convenient seat, others may probably be expected to come prepared with forces united, to dispossess, and deprive him, not only of the fruit of his labour, but also of his life, or liberty. And the invader again is in the like danger of another.

From Diffidence War

And from this diffidence of one another, there is no way for any man to secure himself, so reasonable, as anticipation; that is, by force, or wiles, to master the persons of all men he can, so long, till he see no other power great enough to endanger him: and this is no more than his own conservation requireth, and is generally allowed. Also because there be some, that taking pleasure in contemplating their own power in the acts of conquest, which they pursue farther than their security requires; if others, that otherwise would be glad to be at ease within modest bounds, should not by invasion increase their power, they would not be able, [for a] long time, by standing only on their defence, to subsist. And by consequence, such augmentation of dominion over men being necessary to a man's conservation, it ought to be allowed him.

Again, men have no pleasure, but on the contrary a great deal of grief, in keeping company, where there is no power able to overawe them all. For every man looketh that his companion should value him, at the same rate he sets upon himself: and upon all signs of contempt, or undervaluing, naturally endeavors, as far as he dares, (which amongst them that have no common power to keep them in quiet, is far enough to make them destroy each other), to extort a greater value from his contemners, by damage; and from others, by the example.

So that in the nature of man, we find three principal causes of quarrel. First, competition; secondly, diffidence; thirdly, glory.

The first, maketh men invade for gain; the second, for safety; and the third, for reputation. The first use violence, to make themselves masters of other men's persons, wives, children, and cattle; the second, to defend them; the third, for trifles, as a word, a smile, a different opinion, and any other sign of undervalue, either direct in their persons, or by reflection in their kindred, their friends, their nation, their profession, or their name.

Out of Civil States, There Is Always War of Every One Against Every One

Hereby it is manifest, that during the time men live without a common power to keep them all in awe, they are in that condition which is called war; and such a war, as is of every man, against every man. For WAR, consisteth not in battle only, or the act of fighting; but in a tract of time, wherein the will to contend by battle is sufficiently known: and therefore the notion of *time*, is to be considered in the nature of war; as it is in the nature of weather. For as the nature of foul weather, lieth not in a shower or two of rain; but in an inclination thereto of many days together: so the nature of war, consisteth not in actual fighting; but in the known disposition thereto, during all the time there is no assurance to the contrary. All other time is PEACE.

The Incommodities of Such a War

Whatsoever therefore is consequent to a time of war, where every man is enemy to every man; the same is consequent to the time, wherein men live without other security, than what their own strength, and their own invention shall furnish them withal. In such condition, there is no place for industry; because the fruit thereof is uncertain: and consequently no culture of the earth; no navigation, nor use of the commodities that may be imported by sea; no commodious building; no instruments of moving, and removing, such things as require much force; no knowledge of the face of the earth; no account of time; no arts; no letters; no society; and which is worst of all, continual fear, and danger of violent death; and the life of man, solitary, poor, nasty, brutish, and short.

It may seem strange to some man, that has not well weighed these things; that nature should thus dissociate, and render men apt to invade, and destroy one another: and he may therefore, not trusting to this inference, made from the passions, desire perhaps to have the same confirmed by experience. Let him therefore consider with himself, when taking a journey, he arms himself, and seeks to go well accompanied; when going to sleep, he locks his doors; when even in his house he locks his chests; and this when he knows there be laws, and public officers, armed, to revenge all injuries shall be done him; what opinion he has of his fellow-subjects, when he rides armed; of his fellow citizens, when he locks his doors; and of his children, and servants, when he locks his chests. Does he not there as much accuse mankind by his actions, as I do by my words? But neither of us accuse man's nature in it. The desires, and other passions of man, are in themselves no sin. No more are the actions, that proceed from those passions, till they know a law that forbids them: which till laws be made they cannot know: nor can any law be made, till they have agreed upon the person that shall make it.

It may peradventure be thought, there was never such a time, nor condition of war as this; and I believe it was never generally so, over all the world: but there are many places, where they live so now. For the savage people in many places of America, except the government of small families, the concord whereof dependeth on natural lust, have no government at all; and live at this day in that brutish manner, as I said before. Howsoever, it may be perceived what manner of life there would be, where there were no common power to fear, by the manner of life, which men that have formerly lived under a peaceful government, use to degenerate into, in a civil war.

But though there had never been any time, wherein particular men were in a condition of war one against another; yet in all times, kings, and persons of sovereign authority, because of their independency, are in continual jealousies, and in the state and posture of gladiators; having their weapons pointing, and their eyes fixed on one another; that is, their forts, garrisons, and guns upon the frontiers of their kingdoms; and continual spies upon their neighbours; which is a posture of war. But because they uphold thereby, the industry of their subjects; there does not follow from it, that misery, which accompanies the liberty of particular men.

In Such a War Nothing Is Unjust

To this war of every man, against every man, this also is consequent; that nothing can be unjust. The notions of right and wrong, justice and injustice have there no place. Where there is no common power, there is no law: where no law, no injustice. Force, and fraud, are in war the two cardinal virtues. Justice, and injustice are none of the faculties neither of the body, nor mind. If they were, they might be in a man that were alone in the world, as well as his senses, and passions. They are qualities, that relate to men in society, not in solitude. It is consequent also to the same condition, that there be no propriety, no dominion, no *mine* and *thine* distinct; but only that to be every man's, that he can get: and for so long, as he can keep it. And thus much for the ill condition, which man by mere nature is actually placed in; though with a possibility to come out of it, consisting partly in the passions, partly in his reason.

The Passions That Incline Men to Peace

The passions that incline men to peace, are fear of death; desire of such things as are necessary to commodious living; and a hope by their industry to obtain them.

And reason suggesteth convenient articles of peace, upon which men may be drawn to agreement. These articles, are they, which otherwise are called the Laws of Nature: whereof I shall speak more particularly.

Of the First and Second Natural Laws, and of Contracts

Right of Nature What

The RIGHT OF NATURE, which writers commonly call *jus naturale*, is the liberty each man hath, to use his own power, as he will himself, for the preservation of his own nature; that is to say, of his own life: and consequently, of doing any thing, which in his own judgment, and reason, he shall conceive to be the aptest means thereunto.

Liberty What

By LIBERTY, is understood, according to the proper signification of the word, the absence of external impediments: which impediments, may oft take away part of a man's power to do what he would; but cannot hinder him from using the power left him, according as his judgment, and reason shall dictate to him.

A Law of Nature What. Difference of Right and Law

A LAW OF NATURE, *lex naturalis*, is a precept or general rule, found out by reason, by which a man is forbidden to do that, which is destructive of his life, or taketh away the means of preserving the same; and to omit that, by which he thinketh it may be best preserved ....

Naturally Every Man Has Right to Every Thing. The Fundamental Law of Nature

And because the condition of man, as hath been declared [above], is a condition of war of every one against every one; in which case every one is governed by his own reason; and there is nothing he can make use of, that may not be a help unto him, in preserving his life against his enemies; it followeth, that in such a condition, every man has a right to every thing; even to one another's body. And therefore, as long as this natural right of every man to every thing endureth, there can be no security to any man, how strong or wise soever he be, of living out the time, which nature ordinarily alloweth men to live. And consequently it is a precept, or general rule of reason, *that every man, ought to endeavor peace, as far as he has hope of obtaining it; and when he cannot obtain it, that he may seek, and use, all helps, and advantages of war* ....

The Second Law of Nature

From this fundamental law of nature, by which men are commanded to endeavor peace, is derived this second law; *that a man be willing, when others are so too, as far-forth, as for peace, and defence of himself he shall think it necessary, to lay down this right to all things; and be contented with so much liberty against other men, as he would allow other men against himself.* For as long as every man holdeth this right, of doing any thing he liketh; so long are all men in the condition of war. But if other men will not lay down their right, as well as he; then there is no reason for anyone to divest himself of his; for that were to expose himself to prey, which no man is bound to, rather than to dispose himself to peace ....

Not All Rights Are Alienable

Whensoever a man transferreth his right, or renounceth it; it is either in consideration of some right reciprocally transferred to himself; or for some other good he hopeth for thereby. For it is a voluntary act: and of the voluntary acts of every man, the object is some *good to himself.* And therefore there be some rights, which no man can be understood by any words, or other signs, to have abandoned, or transferred. As first a man cannot lay down the right of resisting them, that assault him by force, to take away his life; because he cannot be understood to aim thereby, at any good to himself. The same may be said of wounds, and chains, and imprisonment; because there is no benefit consequent to such patience; as there is to the patience of suffering another to be wounded, or imprisoned ....

Covenants of Mutual Trust, When Invalid

If a covenant be made, wherein neither of the parties perform presently, but trust one another; in the condition of mere nature, which is a condition of war of every man against every man, upon any reasonable suspicion, it is void; but if there be a common power set over them both, with right and force sufficient to compel performance, it is not void. For he that performeth first, has no assurance the other will perform after; because the bonds of words are too weak to bridle men's ambition, avarice, anger, and other passions, without the fear of some coercive power; which in the condition of mere nature, where all men are equal, and judges of the justness of their own fears, cannot possibly be supposed. And therefore he which performeth first does but betray himself to his enemy; contrary to the right, he can never abandon, of defending his life, and means of living ....

Covenants Extorted by Fear Are Valid

Covenants entered into by fear, in the condition of mere nature, are obligatory. For example, if I covenant to pay a ransom, or service for my life, to an enemy; I am bound by it: for it is a contract, wherein one receiveth the benefit of life; the other is to receive money, or service for it; and consequently, where no other law, as in the condition of mere nature, forbiddeth the performance, the covenant is valid ....

Of Other Laws of Nature

The Third Law of Nature, Justice

From that law of nature, by which we are obliged to transfer to another, such rights, as being retained, hinder the peace of mankind, there followeth a third; which is this, *that men perform their covenants made:* without which, covenants are in vain, and but empty words; and the right of all men to all things remaining, we are still in the condition of war.

Justice and Injustice What

And in this law of nature, consisteth the fountain and original of JUSTICE. For where no covenant hath preceded, there hath no right been transferred, and every man has right to every thing; and consequently, no action can be unjust. But when a covenant is made, then to break it is unjust: and the definition of INJUSTICE, is no other than the not *performance of covenant*. And whatsoever is not unjust, is *just*.

Justice and Propriety Begin with the Constitution of Commonwealth

But because covenants of mutual trust, where there is a fear of not performance on either part, as hath been said in the former chapter, are invalid; though the original of justice be the making of covenants; yet injustice actually there can be none, till the cause of such fear be taken away; which while men are in the natural condition of war, cannot be done. Therefore before the names of just, and unjust can have place, there must be some coercive power, to compel men equally to the performance of their covenants, by the terror of some punishment, greater than the benefit they expect by the breach of their covenant; and to make good that propriety, which by mutual contract men acquire, in recompense of the universal right they abandon: and such power there is none before the erection of a commonwealth ....

Justice Not Contrary to Reason

The fool hath said in his heart, there is no such thing as justice; and sometimes also with his tongue: seriously alleging, that every man's conservation, and contentment, being committed to his own care, there could be no reason, why every man might not do what he thought conduced thereunto. He does not therein deny, that there are covenants; and that they are sometimes broken, sometimes kept; but he questioneth whether injustice, taking away the fear of God, may not sometimes stand with that reason, which dictateth to every man his own good ....

[I say that] in a condition of war, wherein every man to every man, for want of a common power to keep them all in awe, is an enemy, there is no man who can hope by his own strength, or wit, to defend himself from destruction without the help of confederates; where every one expects the same defence by the confederation, that any one else does: and therefore he which declares he thinks it reason to deceive those that help him, can in reason expect no other means of safety than what can be had from his own single power. He therefore that breaketh his covenant, and consequently declareth that he thinks he may with reason do so, cannot be received into any society, that unite themselves for peace and defence, but by the error of them that receive him; nor when he is received, be retained in it, without seeing the danger of their error; which errors a man cannot reasonably reckon upon as the means of his security: and therefore if he be left, or cast out of society he perisheth; and if he live in society, it is by the errors of other men, which he could not foresee, nor reckon upon; and consequently against the reason of his preservation ....

The Second Part: Of Commonwealth

Of the Causes, Generation, and Definition of a Commonwealth

The End of Commonwealth, Particular Security

The final cause, end, or design of men, who naturally love liberty, and dominion over others, in the introduction of that restraint upon themselves, in which we see them live in commonwealths, is the foresight of their own preservation, and of a more contented life thereby; that is to say, of getting themselves out from that miserable condition of war, which is necessarily consequent, as hath been shown, to the natural passions of men, when there is no visible power to keep them in awe, and tie them by fear of punishment to the performance of their covenants, and observation of those laws of nature set down [above].

Which Is Not to Be Had From the Law of Nature

For the laws of nature, as *justice, equality, modesty, mercy*, and, in sum, *doing to others, as we would be done to*, of themselves, without the terror of some power, to cause them to be observed, are contrary to our natural passions. that carry us to partiality, pride, revenge, and the like. And covenants, without the sword, are but words, and of no strength to secure a man at all. Therefore notwithstanding the laws of nature (which every one hath then kept, when he has the will to keep them, when he can do it safely) if there be no power erected or not great enough for our security; every man will, and may lawfully rely on his own strength and art, for caution against all other men. ... For if we could suppose a great multitude of men to consent in the observation of justice, and other laws of nature, without a common power to keep them all in awe; we might as well suppose all mankind to do the same; and then there neither would be, nor need to be any civil government, or commonwealth at all; because there would be peace without subjection ....

The Generation of a Commonwealth. The Definition of a Commonwealth

The only way to erect such a common power, as may be able to defend them from the invasion of foreigners, and the injuries of one another, and thereby to secure them in such sort, as that by their own industry, and by the fruits of the earth, they may nourish themselves and live contentedly; is, to confer all their power and strength upon one man, or upon one assembly of men, that may reduce all their wills, by plurality of voices, unto one will; which is as much as to say, to appoint one man, or assembly of men, to bear their person; and every one to own, and acknowledge himself to be author of whatsoever he that so beareth their person, shall act, or cause to be acted, in those things which concern the common peace and safety; and therein to submit their wills, every one to his will, and their judgments, to his judgment.

This is more than consent, or concord; it is a real unity of them all, in one and the same person, made by covenant of every man with every man, in such manner, as if every man should say to every man, *I authorize and give up my right of governing myself, to this man, or to this assembly of men, on this condition, that thou give up thy right to him, and authorize all his actions in like manner.* This done, the multitude so united in one person, is called a COMMONWEALTH, in Latin CIVITAS. This is the generation of that great LEVIATHAN, or rather, to speak more reverently, of that *mortal god*, to which we owe under the *immortal God*, our peace and defence. For by this authority, given him by every particular man in the commonwealth, he hath the use of so much power and strength conferred on him, that by terror thereof, he is enabled to form the wills of them all, to peace at home, and mutual aid against their enemies abroad. And in him consisteth the essence of the commonwealth; which, to define it, is *one person, of whose acts a great multitude, by mutual covenants one with another, have made themselves every one the author, to the end he may use the strength and means of them all, as he shall think expedient, for their peace and common defence.*

Of the Liberty of Subjects Liberty, What

LIBERTY, or FREEDOM, signifieth, properly, the absence of opposition; by opposition, I mean external impediments of motion; and may be applied no less to irrational, and inanimate creatures, than to rational. For whatsoever is so tied, or environed, as it cannot move but within a certain space, which space is determined by the opposition of some external body, we say it hath not liberty to go further ....

What It Is to Be Free

And according to this proper, and generally received meaning of the word, a FREEMAN, *is he that in those things, which by his strength and wit he is able to do, is not hindered to do what he has a will to.* ... [F]rom the use of the word *free-will*, no liberty can be inferred of the will, desire, or inclination, but the liberty of the man; which consisteth in this, that he finds no stop, in doing what he has the will, desire, or inclination to do.

Fear and Liberty Consistent

Fear and liberty are consistent; as when a man throweth his goods into the sea for *fear* the ship should sink, he doth it nevertheless very willingly, and may refuse to do it if he will: it is therefore the action of one that was *free*: so a man sometimes pays his debt, only for *fear* of imprisonment, which because nobody hindered him from detaining, was the action of a man at *liberty*. And generally all actions which men do in commonwealths, for *fear* of the law, are actions, which the doers had *liberty* to omit.

Liberty and Necessity Consistent

Liberty, and *necessity* are consistent: as in the water, that hath not only *liberty*, but a *necessity* of descending by the channel; so likewise in the actions which men voluntarily do: which, because they proceed from their will, proceed from *liberty*; and yet, because every act of man's will, and every desire, and inclination proceedeth from some cause, and that from another cause, in a continual chain, whose first link is the hand of God the first of all causes, proceed from *necessity*. So that to him that could see the connexion of those causes, the necessity of all men's voluntary actions, would appear manifest.

Review and Discussion Questions

1. Hobbes is often described as a "psychological egoist." What might that mean, given his understanding of human deliberation and motivation?
2. How does Hobbes understand felicity, or happiness?
3. Describe the state of nature. When does Hobbes think it would arise? What would life be like under it? In what sense are people free?
4. What are the laws of nature, according to Hobbes?
5. Explain how all of morality, not just politics, may be understood as an agreement for mutual advantage.
6. How does Hobbes respond to the "fool" who claims that justice is contrary to reason and that a rational person would act unjustly?
7. What is freedom, according to Hobbes? Do people have both freedom and free will? Explain.
8. Does Hobbes think morality applies in a state of war when there is no state or society? Explain.
9. Evaluate Hobbes's answer to question 8. Why do you agree or disagree?

READING: MORALITY AND RATIONAL SELF-INTEREST

BARUCH BRODY[*]

In this selection, Baruch Brody discusses the problem of whether morality conflicts with self-interest and whether it is rational for a person to follow the dictates of morality rather than self-interest. Then, in the final section, he assesses psychological egoism, the notion that however much people may appear to be acting unselfishly, it is self-interest that always motivates human action. Baruch Brody is the Andrew W. Mellon Professor in Humanities at Rice University.

The Conventional Answers

There is a variety of conventional attempts to meet this problem [of the possible conflict between self-interest and morality]. The simplest is the plain denial that it exists. Consider, for example, the familiar maxim "Honesty is the best policy." This and other such sayings essentially claim that, if we look at the matter fully, considering long-range as well as short-range considerations, we will see that our self-interest is best served by doing the right thing. There is clearly some truth to these maxims. There are cases in which doing the wrong action will clearly hurt us in the long run.

For example, many students know that it is often possible to get a good grade, with much less work, by cheating on an exam. And this dishonest course of action might at first seem to be in their self-interest. But look carefully at the long-range consequences of cheating. Suppose, for example, you really need to know the material you were being tested on at some later time, perhaps in another course, or outside of school. You may lose out then because you cheat

---

[*] From *Beginning Philosophy* by Baruch Brody. Copyright © 1977. Reprinted by permission of Prentice Hall, Inc.

now. Marital infidelity is another example. Many people have found they can be unfaithful to their spouses and "get away with it." The immediate pleasures obtained from doing so have made it seem as though this dishonest act is really in their self-interest. But again, one should carefully examine the long-range consequences, for example, the psychological effects on one's relationship with one's spouse. This might well reveal that faithfulness is really in one's true interest.

There may well be many such cases in which "honesty pays." But it would be rash to conclude that this is true in all cases. At first glance, in fact, it would seem that there are many cases in which the opposite is true. Consider some of your actions that you know to have been wrong. Did you really always lose because you did them? If you didn't lose, then wasn't it the smart thing to do? Why shouldn't we perform the wrong action in such cases?

Let's consider these questions more closely. First of all, does the fear of being caught and punished enter into the issue? Perhaps we shouldn't do the wrong action because the punishment we will receive for doing it outweighs any gain we receive. I suspect that this answer is widely believed. It seems, for example, to lie behind the belief that a strong system of criminal justice will deter crime. The trouble with this answer is that it assumes that we will always be caught and punished. It doesn't address itself to the cases in which we have a good chance of getting away with our wrongdoings. When the probability of being caught is low enough, and the gain from wrongdoing large enough, it would seem rational to gamble on getting away with the wrong action.

The moral training which many parents give their children unfortunately emphasizes just this possibility of being caught and punished. This leads children, not unreasonably, to conclude that there is an eleventh commandment: "Thou shall not get caught." Children conclude that being moral is appropriate only when there is little chance of getting away with being immoral. If we don't want children to draw that conclusion, we must train them otherwise. But we must be able to give them a different reason for behaving morally—so we return to our basic question.

Things would be very different, of course, if we knew that we would *always* be caught and punished. However, the opposite is true; all too often, we have a good chance of avoiding punishment, at least the ordinary forms of punishment. This last remark will suggest to many that there may be other forms of punishment, ones that always work, and that our problem can be solved if we will turn our attention to them.

What could these super-effective forms of punishment be? One is the internal pangs of conscience. After all, say some moralists, we always know when we do wrong, and our conscience bothers us about it. The reason then for doing the right action, even if we could get away with wrongdoing, is that we will be punished by our consciences for doing the wrong action. Another kind of punishment is divine retribution. According to some religious moralists, we shouldn't do wrong, even if we can get away with it, because God will always know about it. He will punish us, if not in this life, then in the afterlife.

There is no doubt that some wrongdoers suffer greatly from pangs of conscience. But as a general solution to the question of why one should be moral, this appeal to the pangs of conscience is insufficient because: (1) it does not apply to all people, since the voice of conscience seems to be weak in many people; (2) it does not apply to all cases, since in many cases one's conscience is not particularly bothered and the gain from wrongdoing may outweigh the slight stirrings of conscience; (3) it does not take into account the way our consciences come to terms with our shortcomings. As I think we all know from our own experience, we tend to find justifications for our shortcomings, especially when they are repeated. After a while, our consciences no longer bother us. It is this malleability of conscience that makes it an uncertain basis for doing the right action.

The appeal to divine punishment is a different matter. For if God does exist and does punish all evildoers, then we always have a powerful reason—and one based on self-interest—for doing the right action. However, most philosophers have not wanted to rest the case for being moral on our desire to avoid divine retribution. To begin with, no matter how sound that case may be logically, it does not seem to be psychologically effective. Perhaps this is because divine punishment seems so far away, belonging to some unknown existence after death. ... Perhaps most important, this type of argument would force us to re-evaluate our feelings about the nobility of moral behavior. If the reason for behaving morally is just to avoid punishment (even divine punishment), then we have no reason to treat moral self-sacrifice as a noble form of behavior.

This last point is extremely important, and we will examine other aspects of it later. ... But it has a special significance in the religious context, one that should be noted now. Let us begin with an example. Suppose that someone gives a very large sum of money to a noble cause. We would normally approve of that action and think highly of the person who gave the money. The action, so to speak, raises his moral worth. But now suppose that we discover that he gave the money because (1) he was promised even more in return if he gave it, and (2) he was told that he would be severely punished if he didn't give it. We would still be glad that he gave the money (it is good, after all, for the cause to have the funds). But we would no longer think so highly of the donor. The action no longer raises his moral worth in our view. Now when the religious person says we should act out of a fear of divine punishment and a desire for divine reward, that person is advocating that we all act with motives similar to those of our "pseudo-philanthropist." And this seems a terrible thing to advocate. In short, while religious moralists may believe that God will punish the evil and reward the good, they should oppose the view that these rewards and punishments give us our reason for behaving morally ....

Thomas Hobbes's Solution

Hobbes begins with a fundamental assumption about human nature: that human beings are essentially self-interested agents, each acting to obtain what he thinks is in his self-interest and prepared to harm other human beings in order to obtain it. Now this would be okay if there were enough goods to completely satisfy everyone. But since there are not, human beings compete for what is available and come into armed conflict with each other. Hobbes calls this state of human conflict the state of nature.

Now there are those who would say that Hobbes's picture of human nature is too bleak, and that he is not justified in supposing that human beings would actually behave in that way. Hobbes felt, however, that he could justify his pessimistic views by reference to facts that we could all observe.

> It may seem strong to some man that has not well weighed these things that Nature should thus dissociate and render men apt to invade and destroy one another; and he may therefore desire ... to have the same confirmed by experience. Let him, therefore, consider with himself: when taking a journey, he arms himself and seeks to go well accompanied; when going to sleep, he locks his doors; when even in his house he locks his chests: and this when he knows there be laws and public officers. ... Does he not there as much accuse mankind by his actions as I do by my words?
>
> (*Leviathan*, Chapter 13)

Now, said Hobbes, it is clear that no rational person would want to live in the state of nature. It would not be so bad if we could be sure of winning. But no person is so strong that he doesn't have to fear conflicts with other people (or groups of people). So the state of nature is something we should want to avoid.

The basic idea behind Hobbes's argument for acting morally is then very simple: the rational self-interested person should agree to abide by certain moral principles, which would regulate his relations with other human beings, in order to be able to live without this fear of conflict. Or, to put this point another way, if we are to live with other people, we must follow certain moral rules respecting the rights and interests of other people. Only in that way can people live in peace with one another.

Hobbes clearly has an important point. Even if we do give up something by behaving morally, and even if we would in a particular case gain by behaving immorally, we know that we would lose even more if everyone behaved immorally. And it is this knowledge that leads us to behave morally.

But isn't there a confusion here? Hobbes is right in saying that we would be better off if everyone behaved morally than if everyone pursued his own self-interest without regard to morality. But wouldn't *I* be better off if I could follow my own self-interest while others worried about morality? And if so, isn't it rational for me to do just that? Shouldn't I try to get away with advantageous acts of immorality while urging others to be moral?

[Imagine] an immoral but advantageous act—spreading a vicious lie in order to get a lucrative position. What would Hobbes say to a person considering such an act? Presumably, Hobbes would say to him that he would be better off if no one did that than if everyone did that sort of thing. And no doubt that claim of Hobbes is true. After all, if everyone went around spreading such lies, our would-be liar could certainly be harmed by them as well. But couldn't our person then reply to Hobbes by saying that he would gain if he spread such lies while others did not and that *that* is exactly what he hopes to do by surreptitiously spreading lies while encouraging others to be moral? How could Hobbes meet that reply?

Hobbes was very aware of such questions and problems. He preferred, however, to think of them as follows. Suppose that I decide to behave morally and not pursue my immediate self-interest. Suppose, for example, I decide not to spread the lie about my competitor. This will be fine if others also decide to behave that way; if, for example, my competitor also decides not to spread lies about me. But suppose that other people then decide to treat me immorally. Suppose my competitor decides to tell the lies about me, after all. Then I will really be in trouble. My interests will suffer greatly if I obey the restrictions of morality while others do not.

How, asked Hobbes, can I be sure that this won't happen? How can I take the chance of behaving morally when I know that others may decide not to follow suit?

Hobbes's own solution to all of these problems is that we should institute a very powerful state, one that has almost absolute power. This sort of state will ensure that everyone obeys the restrictions of morality.

> The only way to erect such a common power, as may be able to defend them from the invasion of foreigners, and the injuries of one another, and thereby to secure them in such sort as that by their own industry and by the fruits of the earth they may nourish themselves and live contentedly, is to confer all their strength and power upon one man, or upon one assembly of men, that they may reduce all their wills, by plurality of voices, onto one will.
> (*Leviathan*, Chapter 17)

There are many who feel that such a solution is unacceptable because we would have to give up too many of our liberties to the state. The price, they would say, is too high. And if we won't have Hobbes's state his solution apparently collapses. Some of these philosophers have claimed, however, that Hobbes's absolute state is not required to ensure moral behavior. Kurt Baier, for example, claimed that:

> [R]eason can support morality, only when the presumption about other people's behavior is reversed. Hobbes thought that this could be achieved only by the creation of an absolute ruler with absolute power to enforce his laws. We have already seen that this is not true and that it can also be achieved if people live in a society, that is, if they have common ways of life, which are taught to all members and somehow enforced by the group. Its members have reason to expect their fellows generally to obey its rules, that is, its religion, morality, customs, and law, even when doing so is not, on certain occasions, in their interest. Hence they too have reason to follow these rules.
> (*The Moral Point of View*, Chapter 7, Section 3)

This claim is not, however, entirely convincing. To begin with, it seems to be overly optimistic about the extent to which moral training and social pressure lead people to behave morally. Second, and more important, even if we could expect most people to behave morally in most cases, not all of our problems would be solved. It's true that we wouldn't need to worry about others cheating if we behaved morally. But the question would still remain as to why we should behave morally if we could get away with advantageous immoral acts. Without something like Hobbes's absolute government, there will be cases in which we could get away with advantageous immoralities. Baier doesn't really explain why we should not gain personal advantages by performing those actions.

More Radical Approaches

We have so far examined attempts to show that being moral is always in our self-interest. These we have found lacking. This leads us to wonder if it's even possible to connect morality and self-interest. Suppose that it's not. What does that mean?

There are philosophers who feel that this failure is not really very important. Some believe, in fact, that the whole attempt was a mistake. One such philosopher was H. A. Prichard. He wrote:

> A general but not very critical familiarity with the literature of Moral Philosophy might well lead to the remark that much of it is occupied with attempts either to prove that there is a necessary connexion between duty and interest or in certain cases even to exhibit the connexion as something self-evident. ... When we read the attempts referred to we naturally cannot help in a way wishing them to succeed; and we might express our wish in the form that we should all like to be able to believe that honesty is the best policy. At the same time we also cannot help feeling that somehow they are out of place, so that the real question is not so much whether they are successful, but whether they ought ever to have been made.
>
> (*Duty and Interest*, 1929, n.p.)

Philosophers like Prichard feel there is no need to prove that morality is identical with self-interest because we have reason to be moral even if it is not in our self-interest. ... Prichard and his followers believe that there are other reasons for acting morally. And, they say, since there are these other reasons, it is not very important if we cannot prove that morality is in our self-interest.

What are these other reasons? Prichard says, for one thing, that we want to do the right thing:

> We obviously are referring to a fact when we speak of someone as possessing a sense of duty and, again, a strong sense of duty. And if we consider what we are thinking of in these individuals whom we think of as possessing it, we find that we cannot exclude from it a desire to do what is a duty, as such, for its own sake, or, more simply, a desire to do what is a duty. ... If we admit the existence of a desire to do what is right, then there is no longer any reason for maintaining as a general thesis that in any case in which a man knows some action to be right, he must, if he is to be led to do it, be convinced that he will gain by doing it. For we shall be able to maintain that his desire to do what is right, if strong enough, will lead him to do the action in question in spite of any aversion from doing it which he may feel on account of its disadvantages.
>
> (Ibid.)

Other philosophers have said the reason is that we have a concern for the welfare of others. Francis Hutcheson, for example, said that the true reason for virtuous action is "some determination of our nature to study the good of others, or some instinct, antecedent to all reason from interest, which influences us to the love of others."

Let us return now to our case of the two competitors for the one job. According to Prichard, the one competitor should not spread the damaging lie about the other because doing so will fly in the face of his desire to do the right thing. According to Hutcheson, the one competitor should not spread the damaging lie about the other because doing so will fly in the face of his concern for the well-being of others.

This whole approach, if accepted, would certainly affect our ideas about moral training. We have already remarked that in the moral training of a child, it is a mistake to emphasize the personal benefits that come from being moral. If we do emphasize this, of course, we do not provide the child with a reason for being moral in cases where morality and self-interest conflict. Prichard's theory suggests, as an alternative, that moral training should develop in the child a desire to do the right thing. Hutcheson's views suggest that moral training should develop the child's concern for the well-being of others. John Stuart Mill envisaged just this kind of moral training.

> In an improving state of the human mind, the influences are constantly on the increase, which tend to generate in each individual a feeling of unity with all the rest; which, if perfect, would make him never think of, or desire, any beneficial condition for himself, in the benefits of which they are not included. If we now suppose this feeling of unity to be taught as a religion, and the whole force of education, of institutions, and of opinion, directed ... to make every person grow up from infancy surrounded on all sides both by the profession and the practice of it. I think that no one, who can realise this conception, will feel any misgiving about the sufficiency of the ultimate sanction.
>
> (*Utilitarianism*, Chapter 3)

The Prichard-Hutcheson view also helps explain an important fact about morality. Because of their motives, we often distinguish between two people who have performed the same action, praising one while not praising the other. A philanthropist who gives to gain public acclaim is not as praiseworthy as one who gives for truly charitable motives. Now if self-interest were really the only motive for human action, there could be no such distinction. All actions would be selfishly motivated and no one would deserve praise for moral behavior. But if Prichard or Hutcheson is right, we can distinguish those who deserve praise from those who do not. Those who act with motives other than self-interest will clearly be the ones deserving praise ....

We have seen attractive features in the views of Prichard and Hutcheson. They seem to provide us with a reason for being moral even against our own self-interest. They offer us an interesting approach to moral training and education. And they provide us with a satisfactory account of when actions and people are truly praiseworthy. There are, nevertheless, two large problems which they must face:

1   Assume that one of their theories is true. That means that we have at least two radically different types of motives: self-interest, on the one hand, and, on the other, duty or benevolence. How then are we to choose between them when they conflict? No doubt these theories provide us with a reason for being moral. But we are also left with a reason for being immoral. What rational basis is there for choosing between these reasons? Consider again the competitors for the job. If either Hutcheson or Prichard is right, then the competitors have a reason for not spreading the lie (concern for the "good of others," or the "desire to do what is right"). But they also have a reason for

spreading it (self-interest). So how shall they decide between these two reasons?

2. Are their theories correct? Do we ever really act from any motive other than self-interest? From our own experiences we all are painfully aware of people who seem to be acting from the loftiest of motives but who are really acting out of self-interest. Maybe that is true in all cases.

In the final sections we will deal with these two objections.

What Really Are Our Motives?

Let us begin with the second objection, which raises the question of human motives. Hutcheson and Prichard are attacking the thesis of *psychological egoism*, the view that the only reason or motive for any action is self-interest. They insist that there must be other reasons for human actions.

What arguments do they offer for their views? To begin with, they think that the truth of their views is something that we can experience in our own feelings. Thus, Hutcheson writes:

> But what will most effectually convince us of the truth on this point is reflection upon our own hearts, whether we have not a desire of the good of others, generally without any consideration or intention of obtaining these pleasant reflections on our own virtue.
>
> (*An Inquiry Into the Origin of Our Ideas of Beauty and Virtue*)

Secondly, they feel that we can see in the actions of others clear examples of actions not based on self-interest. Finally, they appeal to the fact that only their views explain (as we saw above) the fact that some people are praiseworthy.

Prichard and Hutcheson certainly recognize that those who act out of nonselfish motives are often motivated by self-interest, too. All that they want to claim is that this does leave a place open for the nonselfish motives:

> But it must be here observed that as all men have self-love as well as benevolence, these two principles may jointly excite a man to the same action, and then they are to be considered as two forces impelling the same body to motion. ... Thus if a man has such strong benevolence as would have produced an action without any views of self-interest, that such a man has also in view private advantage, along with public good, as the effect of his action, does in no way diminish the benevolence of the action. When he would not have produced so much public good had it not been for prospect of self-interest, then the effect of self-love is to be deducted, and his benevolence is proportioned to the remainder of good, which pure benevolence would have produced.
>
> (Hutcheson, op. cit.)

Many people are skeptical about these claims. They suggest that the only thing that we really desire is what is in our own self-interest. Such people offer three arguments for this view:

1   When we look at examples of supposedly nonselfish actions, we often find that they are motivated by hidden considerations of self-interest.
2   People who supposedly act from benevolent motives or from a sense of duty are really acting to obtain the pleasure of seeing others happy or the pleasure of feeling that they are virtuous. So they are really acting to obtain their own pleasure, and that is an act motivated by self-interest.
3   In any case, we act to satisfy our desires, whatever they are, and that makes our actions motivated by self-interest.

The first of these arguments has a great deal of intuitive appeal. After all, we have all been fooled that way. We have all admired people for their supposedly noble and generous actions only to discover the truly selfish motives that have moved them. Nevertheless, these experiences, while enough to make us somewhat skeptical about people's motives, are not enough to establish the general truth of egoism. They do not establish that people only act from selfish motives. And there is, after all, the evidence that Hutcheson and Prichard appeal to that suggests that egoism is not valid.

The second argument is more substantial. It concedes that there is some psychological truth in the Hutcheson-Prichard thesis, but it claims that the thesis distorts the nature of that truth. We are not moved, says the argument, by a desire to do what is right or to see others happy; what really moves us is the pleasure we get from thinking of ourselves as doing the right thing or from seeing others happy. Since it is this desire for our pleasure that moves us, egoism is still correct. This view was forcefully presented by Moritz Schlick:

> The idea of personal destruction is, in general, one of the most terrifying; not the most terrifying, for there are enough miseries in comparison with which death is felt as a soothing relief. Yet we observe, in life and history, acts of will whose fatal and miserable consequences are not only inevitable for the performer, but are clearly seen by him to be involved as the goal of his action. The martyr accepts pain and death for the sake of an idea, a friend gives his life or "happiness" for his friend. Can any one in earnest say of such persons that their decisions are determined by the motives which possess the most pleasant or the least unpleasant emotional tones?
>
> According to my firm conviction, one cannot say anything else if one would tell the truth, for such are the facts. Let us then try to analyze and understand the motive of heroism. The hero acts "for the sake of a cause"; he desires to carry out an idea or realize a definite goal. It is clear that the thought of his goal or that idea dominates his consciousness to such an extent that there is in it hardly room for any other thoughts. At least this holds in the case of inspiration, from which alone an heroic act can arise. It is true that the idea of his own painful destruction is present, but, however burdened with pain it may be in itself, it is inhibited and repressed by the predominant end-in-view, which finally triumphs in an "act of will," in an effort which becomes stronger and sharper the longer and more clearly the thought of the unavoidable catastrophe confronts him. What is the source of the astonishing force of the decisive end-in-view? Whence the power of this affect? Without doubt this is due to *emotion*. Inspiration is the greatest pleasure that can fall to the

lot of man. To be inspired by something means to be overcome by the greatest joy in the thought of it. The man who, under the stress of inspiration, decides to help a friend or save another creature from pain and destruction, whatever the cost, finds the thought of this act so profoundly joyful, so overwhelmingly pleasant that, at the moment, the idea of the preservation of his own life and the avoidance of pain cannot compare with it. And he who fights for a cause with such inspiration that he accepts all persecution and insult realizes his idea with such elevated pure joy that neither the thought of his miseries nor their actual pain can prevail aught against it. The notion of giving up his purpose because of pain is, for him, more unpleasant than the pain itself.

(*Problems of Ethics*, Chapter 2)

Nevertheless, this second argument does not really succeed. To begin with, even if its claims were true, we would still have a reason for acting morally. After all, the pleasure we get from thinking of ourselves as righteous or from seeing others happy is just as much a reason for doing the right action as Prichard's sense of duty or Hutcheson's sense of benevolence. But more important, there is evidence from both introspection and our observations of others to suggest that these claims are false. Hutcheson, for example, seems correct when he writes:

> Reflections in our minds again will best discover the truth. Many have never thought upon this connection; nor do we ordinarily intend the obtaining of any such pleasure when we do generous offices. We all often feel delight upon seeing others happy, but during our pursuit of their happiness we have no intention of obtaining this delight. We often feel the pain of compassion, but were our sole ultimate intention or desire the freeing of ourselves from this pain, would the deity offer us either wholly to blot out all memory of the person in distress, or to take away this connection, so that we should be easy during the misery of our friend, on the one hand, or on the other would relieve him from his misery, we should be as ready to choose the former way as the latter, since either of them would free us from our pain, which upon this scheme is the sole end proposed by the compassionate person. Don't we find in ourselves that our desire does not terminate upon the removal of our own pain? Were this our sole intention, we would run away, shut our eyes, or divert our thoughts from the miserable object, as the readiest way of removing our pain.

(Hutcheson, op. cit.)

The third of the arguments noted above rests on a common confusion. It supposes that if I do an action to satisfy some desire of mine, then, no matter what the nature of the desire, the action is based on self-interest. But this supposition is a mistake. A "self-interested action" is one done to satisfy certain interests of mine, or certain desires for my own happiness, and not merely one done to satisfy any desire.

This point can also be put as follows: Those who make this third objection have the following picture in mind:

self-interested	other
action done to satisfy a desire	action not done to satisfy a desire

Given this picture, and the plausible assumption that all actions satisfy a desire, they conclude that the "other" category is empty and that all actions are self-interested actions. The trouble with this argument is that they are working with the wrong picture. The correct picture of the distinction is rather this one:

self-interested	other
action done to satisfy a desire for my own well-being	action done to satisfy a desire for something other than my own well-being

Given this picture, we can agree that all actions are done to satisfy some desire of the agent and still claim that not all actions are self-interested. All we need to suppose is that the agent can have desires for something other than his own well-being. And this certainly seems reasonable.

Review and Discussion Questions

1. Why does Brody reject the conventional ideas about the conflict between self-interest and morality?
2. Why does Brody reject Hobbes's solution?
3. What are the radical solutions Brody suggests?
4. "To act morally when it is against your self-interest is irrational." How would Brody respond to this statement?
5. What distinction does Brody rely on to refute the position of the psychological egoist? Does he succeed? Why or why not?

READING: DIVINE COMMANDS AND THE SOCIAL NATURE OF OBLIGATION

ROBERT MERRIHEW ADAMS[*]

How should we understand the nature of obligations? As demands created from our own self-interest? As demands derived from our moral ideals? As demands

---

[*] Robert M. Adams, "Divine Commands and the Social Nature of Obligation," *Faith and Philosophy* 4 (1987): 262–275.

created by society? In this selection, Robert Merrihew Adams argues that in general obligations arise from relationships, and he analyzes what makes obligations a distinctive type of motive and demand. He then asks what type of relationships could create obligations that are "fully moral" rather than "pre-moral." He argues that fully moral obligations come from a relationship with a loving God who provides divine commands. Robert Merrihew Adams was a professor at Rutgers, UCLA, Yale University, Michigan, and Oxford, among others.

Divine command metaethics is a type of social theory of the nature of obligation ....

The central idea in divine command metaethics is the expansion of our vision of the social dimension of ethics to include God as the most important participant in our system of personal relationships. In this paper I will first try to show how facts about human relationships can fill some of the role that facts of obligation are supposed to play, specifically with regard to moral motivation (in Section 1) and guilt (in Section 2). Then (in Section 3) I will note certain problems that arise for social theories of obligation, and argue that they can be dealt with more adequately by a divine command theory ....

Section 1: How Social Requirements Motivate

It is essential to the point of any conception of obligation that obligations motivate—that having an obligation to do x is generally regarded as a reason for doing x. One problem about the nature of obligation is to understand this motivation.

This will not be much of a problem if we assume that one is obliged only to do things that one expects to have good results. Then the goodness of the results provides a reason, and one's desires for such good consequences a motive, for doing what one is obliged to do. Unfortunately, those who (like me) are not utilitarians cannot assume that obligations will always be so happily attuned to the value of expected results. We think we are sometimes obliged to tell the truth and to keep promises, for example, when we do not expect the consequences to be good. What would motivate us to do such a thing?

Even non-utilitarian moralists may not be satisfied with the reply that the conscientious agent has good enough reason for her action simply in the fact that it is right. This seems too abstract. John Rawls (certainly no utilitarian) writes,

> The doctrine of the purely conscientious act is irrational. This doctrine holds ... that the highest moral motive is the desire to do what is right and just simply because it is right and just, no other description being appropriate. ... But on this interpretation the sense of right lacks any apparent reason; it resembles a preference for tea rather than coffee.[1]

If we are to see the fact of having an obligation as itself a reason for action, we need a richer, less abstract understanding of the nature of obligation, in which we might find something to motivate us.

According to social theories of the nature of obligation, having an obligation to do something consists in being required (in a certain way, under certain circumstances), by another person or a group of persons, to do it. This opens more than one possibility for understanding obligations as reasons for action. One reason or motive for complying with a social requirement, of course, is that we fear punishment or retaliation for non-compliance. This is undoubtedly a real factor, which helps to keep morality (and other benign, and not so benign, social institutions) afloat. But here we are primarily interested in what *other* motives there may be for compliance.

The alternative explanation that I wish to pursue in this section is that *valuing one's social bonds* gives one, under certain conditions, a reason to do what is required of one by one's associates or one's community (and thus to fulfill obligations, understood as social requirements). ... The pattern of motivation to which I wish to call attention is one in which I value the relationship which I see myself as actually having, and my complying is an *expression* of my valuing and respecting the relationship. It is one in which I act primarily *out of* a valuing of the relationship, rather than with the obtaining or maintaining of the relationship as an *end.*

There are at least four aspects of the relational situation that matter motivationally with regard to compliance with social requirements.

1. It matters that the demand is actually made. It is a question here of what other people do in fact (reasonably or rightly) require of me, not just of what they could reasonably require ....

    Actual demands made on us in relationships that we value are undeniably real and motivationally strong. Most actual conscientiousness rests at least partly on people's sense of such demands. Our awareness of this source of moral motivation is reflected in appeals to "be a good citizen"—or, when in a foreign country, to "remember that you are a guest."

    The actual making of the demand is important, not only to the strength, but also to the character, of the motive. Not every good reason for doing something makes it intelligible that I should feel that I *have* to do it. This is one of the ways in which having even the best of reasons for doing something does not as such amount to having an obligation to do it. But the perception that something is demanded of me by other people, in a relationship that I value, does help to make it intelligible that I should feel that I have to do it.

2. It also matters motivationally how the individual who is subject to the demand is related, and feels related, to those persons who are making the demand. Let us assume, for purposes of this discussion, that the demand is made by a community ....

    A "community" is a group of people who live their lives to some extent—possibly a very limited extent—in common. To see myself as "belonging" to a community is to see the institution or other members of the group as "having something to say about" how I live and act—perhaps not about every department of my life, and only to a reasonable extent about any department of it, but it is part of the terms of the relationship that their demands on certain subjects are expected to have some weight with me. And valuing such a relationship—loving it or respecting it—implies some willingness to submit to reasonable demands of the community. One is willing to comply, not as a means of satisfying a desire *to* belong, but as an expression of one's sense that one *does* belong, and one's endorsement of that relationship.

3. It also matters what are the attributes of the demander. To put it crudely and simply, one will have more reason to comply with demands made by an individual or group that one admires than by one that one holds a mean

opinion of. If the demander is particularly impressive or admirable in any way—one will see more reason to comply than if the demander seems ill-informed, foolish, or in some other way contemptible.

4   Finally, it matters motivationally how the demandee evaluates the demand itself. ... Is the demand one which appeals to you, or one which disgusts or revolts you? Is it one which seems to be conducive to the things that you prize most, admire most, and so forth? You could ask that about your particular compliance, or you could ask it about general compliance, if that is what is being demanded. And what is the wider social significance of the demand? Is it an expression of a project or social movement that seems good or bad to you? No obligation concepts at all are employed in these questions; yet the answers to them both will and should affect the extent to which a social requirement gives you a reason for action ....

Section 2: Guilt and Relationship

The nature of obligations cannot be understood apart from the reactions that people have and are expected to have to the breach of an obligation; and central to these reactions is the notion of guilt. This is one of the main differences between obligations and other sorts of reasons for action. If I fail to do what I had the most reason to do, I am not necessarily guilty, and there is apt to be nothing offensive about my reacting quite light-heartedly to the lapse. But if I fail to do what I have an obligation to do, then (other things being equal) I am guilty, and a light-hearted reaction would normally be offensive.

The word "guilt" is not properly the name of a feeling, but of an objective moral condition which may rightly be recognized by others even if it is not recognized by the guilty person. However, feelings of guilt, and other reactions to guilt, may reasonably be taken as a source of understanding of the objective fact of guilt to which they point ....

In our first experience of guilt its principal significance was an action or attitude of ours that ruptured or strained our relationship with a parent. There did not have to be a failure of benevolence or a violation of a rule; perhaps we were even too young to understand rules. It was enough that something we did or expressed offended the parent, and seemed to threaten the relationship. This is the original context in which the obligation cluster of moral concepts and sentiments arise. We do not begin with a set of moral principles but with a relationship, actual in part and in part desired, which is immensely valued for its own sake. Everything that attacks or opposes that relationship seems to us bad.

Of course this starkly simple mentality is pre-moral. We do not really have obligation concepts until we can make some sort of distinction, among the things we do that strain relationships, between those in which we are at fault or wrong and those in which we are innocent or right (not to mention those in which we are partly wrong and partly right). We begin to grasp such a distinction as we learn such facts as the following: Not every demand or expectation laid on us by other people constitutes an obligation, but only demands made in certain ways in certain kinds of relationship (for instance, commands of one's parents and teachers), and expectations that arise in certain ways (for instance, from promises). An unexpressed wish is not a command. One is not guilty for anything one has not really done. The fact that somebody is angry does not necessarily imply that an obligation has been violated.

This development is compatible, however, with regarding obligations as a species of social requirement, and guilt as consisting largely in alienation from those who have required of us what we did not do. I believe it is not childish, but perceptive and correct, to persist in this way of thinking about obligation and guilt. This is a controversial position. It is generally agreed that learning about guilt begins in the way that I have indicated, and that the value we place on good relationships, not only with parents but also with peers, is crucial to moral development. But many moralists hold that in the highest stages of the moral life (perhaps not reached by many adults) the center of moral motivation is transplanted from the messy soil of concrete relationships to the pure realm of moral principles; and a corresponding development is envisaged for the sense of guilt. Thus John Rawls traces the development of the sense of justice from a "morality of authority" through a "morality of association" to a "morality of principles"; corresponding to these three stages, he speaks of "feelings of (authority) guilt," "feelings of (association) guilt," and "feeling of (principle) guilt"—only the last of these counting as "feelings of guilt in the strict sense."[2]

It is certainly possible to come to value—even to love—an ethical principle for its own sake, and this provides a motive for conforming to it. I doubt that this is ever the most powerful of ethical motives; but what I would emphasize here is that this way of relating to ethical principles has more to do with ideals than with obligations. To love truthfulness is one thing; to feel that one *has* to tell the truth is something else. Similarly, it seems to me that there is something wrong-headed about the idea of "principle guilt."

To be sure, there are *feelings* of guilt for the violation of a rule, where no person is seen as offended. But these are typically remnants of a morality of authority, and most plausibly understood as rooted in an internalization of childhood perceptions of requirements imposed by parents or other authority figures. They are part of a heteronomous, not an autonomous, reaction. The fact that the rule is seen as imposed on me, as something that I *have to* obey, is the ghost of my conception of it as sponsored by a person or persons who will be (understandably) offended if it is violated.

Feelings of "principle guilt," as Rawls conceives of them, are not like that. They are autonomous and based on one's valuing the rules, seeing them as expressing one's nature as a rational agent in a society of free and equal members. It is this non-compulsive, rational reaction to the breach of a personally valued principle that seems to me not to be a recognition of guilt, but of something different.

Suppose I have done something that is simply contrary to some principle that I believe in. It is not that I have done significant harm to anyone, or alienated myself from anyone. The situation does not call for apologies or reactions to anticipated or possible or appropriate anger, because there is no one (let's suppose not even God) who might be understandably angry with me about it. It does not seem either natural or appropriate for me to feel *guilty* in such a situation. Maybe someone is entitled to think less of me for the deed. Perhaps I will see less value in my own life on account of it. I may in this way be alienated from myself, though not from anyone else. But these are reasons for feeling ashamed or degraded, rather than for feeling guilty.[3] Guilt is not necessarily worse than degradation, but they are different. And I think a main point of difference between them is that, in typical cases, guilt involves alienation from someone else who required or expected of us what we were obligated to do and have not done.

Section 3: The Supreme Demander

Much can be understood about the nature of obligation in terms of human social relationships, as I have been trying to show. We even have a use for a notion of "an obligation" that can be understood purely sociologically, and therefore "naturalistically," in terms of a description of social practices such as commanding, promising, punishing, and apologizing, without any attempt to evaluate these practices as good or bad. This is a pre-moral notion in at least two ways.

1   It is not the notion of an obligation that is "overriding" in the way that fully moral obligation is. An obligation, in this sense, must give most participants in the social system *some reason* to do what it obliges them to do; but it need not override other considerations. So no understanding is presupposed here of the nature of such an overriding.
2   More fundamentally, the purely sociological notion is not the notion of a morally valid or binding obligation. It is just the notion of *an* obligation or duty, in the sense in which we can agree that Adolf Eichmann had *a* duty to arrange for the transportation of Jews to extermination camps. Certainly this was not a morally valid or binding duty at all, but it was in some sense *a* duty. It played a part in a system of social relationships such that there were superiors who, understandably (though immorally), would be angry if he did not do it, and in relation to who he would feel uncomfortable if he did not do it, even if they did not know of this omission. Obligations in this pre-moral sense can be good or bad; they can even be morally repugnant, as Eichmann's was.

The nature of obligation in the pre-moral sense does not need a divine command theory to explain it. That is a good thing, because divine command metaethics itself presupposes a pre-moral, sociological conception of obligation. It is the very core of a divine command theory to think of the divine/human relationship on the model of a social relationship in which authority, commands, obedience, loyalty, and belonging play a part. But we cannot really have these things without both the reality and the concept of an obligation, in some sense. A command imposes an obligation, or is the sort of thing that could impose an obligation. And one who obeys a command sees herself as fulfilling an obligation arising out of the command. There must therefore be some sort of obligation whose nature cannot without circularity be explained in terms of anyone's commands. What divine command metaethics is meant to explain is the nature of obligation, not in the minimal, pre-moral sense, but in a stronger, fully moral sense.

The earlier sections of this paper were meant to show something of the importance of interpersonal or social relationships for the nature of obligation in even a fully moral sense. The idea of trying to understand all obligation, including moral obligation, as constituted by some sort of social requirement has its attractions. As the Eichmann case makes clear, however, any acceptable account of the nature of moral obligation in terms of social requirements must incorporate some way of *evaluating* the requirements; and it may be doubted whether a descriptive sociological theory has the resources for the evaluation that is needed. In Section 1 I described some ways in which, without appealing to any criterion of obligation as such, an individual can evaluate, and would naturally be expected to evaluate, demands made on her by other people, or by her community. That sort of evaluation is subjective, however. Its subjectivity does not keep it from being important to the motivational significance of obligation. But a definition of moral obligation in terms of social requirements that "pass" that kind of evaluation would not ascribe to moral obligation the objectivity or interpersonal validity that it is supposed to have.

The need for a standard by which to evaluate them is not the only disadvantage of human social requirements as a basis for understanding the nature of moral obligation. They also fail to cover the whole territory of moral obligation. We find that there are situations in which we would say, at least retrospectively, that none of the existing human communities demanded as much as they should have, or that there was something that really ought to have been required that was not demanded by any community, or perhaps even by any human individual, in the situation.

Moral obligation seems therefore to need a source or standard that is superior to human social requirements. Can it be found? ... The attempt has certainly been made to find it, after all, in a human society, in some way both actual and ideal, to which we can be seen as belonging. Emile Durkheim's lectures on *Moral Education* present a great sociologist's fascinating development of this idea. But it seems pretty clear that no actual human society is going to come close to filling this bill. To put it crudely and simply, no actual human society is good enough for that.

Where else would we look for an ideal source of moral obligation? My proposal is that we look to the set of ideas on which Durkheim quite openly and frankly modeled his secular, sociological account of morality—that is, the theistic ideas. Durkheim, following in the steps of Comte, was turning theistic ethics inside out, as it were, to get his conception of society as the source of moral obligation. I suggest that we turn the idea right side out again, and think of God as the source. More precisely, my view is that commands or requirements[4] actually issued or imposed by a loving God are the supreme standard of moral obligation. I will argue that they have much of the significance of social requirements as a source of obligation.

The pivotal role of God's forgiveness in the ethical life of theists underlines the advantages of divine command metaethics for the understanding of *guilt*. If the supreme standard of ethical obligation is what is required by God, then a violation of it is an offense against a person and not just against a principle, and results in something that has the full relational significance of guilt, and not just of disgrace or degradation. This relational significance enriches the possibilities for dealing with guilt—most notably by helping us to understand ethical guilt, as something that can be removed by forgiveness.

Moreover, divine commands have the *motivational* significance of actual social requirements. I will point out four motivational features of divine command metaethics and of the divine commander corresponding (but in a different order) to the four motivational features of human social requirements discussed in Section 1 above.

1   One thing that matters to the motivational force of divine commands is how God is related to us. It matters that he is our creator. It matters that he loves us. It matters that God has entered into covenant with us; it matters that there is a history of relationship between God and the individual and between God and the religious community and that the divine commands play a significant role in this history, and are related to divine purposes that

we see being worked out in this history and having a certain importance for our lives. It matters that all of these things about the relationship are such that, seeing them, we have reason to value the relationship, rather than to be alienated from it.

2   It matters what God's attributes are. God is supremely knowledgeable and wise—he is omniscient, after all; and that is very important motivationally. It makes a difference if you think of commands as coming from someone who completely understands both us and our situation.

It matters not only that God is loving but also that he is just. "Just" is to be understood here in a sense that is quite naturalistic and largely procedural. We are applying to God a concept that has its original home in courts of law. Without any appeal to a standard of fully moral obligation we can recognize certain truths about justice: A just judge punishes people, if at all, only for things that they have actually done. Merit and demerit have some relevance to the way it is just to treat people. The just judge is interested in getting out, and acting in accordance with, the truth.

Another important attribute of God is that he is beautiful or wonderful. This is a point at which Durkheim understood religious ethics rather well, and tried to exploit it for his purposes. "The good," he wrote, "is society ... insofar as it is a reality richer than our own, to which we cannot attach ourselves without a resulting enrichment of our nature."[5] The religious root of this idea is obvious and requires no further comment, except to say that Durkheim is quite right in thinking that the richness, for us, of the being from which requirements proceed is a powerful motivating factor.

3   It matters, for the motivation strength of divine command metaethics, what it is that is demanded of us. And it matters how what is demanded relates to our valuings. It matters motivationally, for example, that we do not believe that God demands cruelty for its own sake. Here again in thinking of our valuings we do not have to presuppose a full panoply of obligation concepts. It is enough if in some sense we love kindness and feel revolted or disgusted at cruelty. God's requirements function as an objective standard of obligation; but our subjective valuings are important to the way in which the divine requirements fulfill this function.

It is undoubtedly important that in theistic ethics the divine legislation is generally seen as upholding the binding character of a large proportion of the "obligations" defined by human institutions and practices. The divine/human relationship is not simply a superior alternative to human society as a source of obligation. Rather, God is seen as the chief member of a more comprehensive social system or "family," which is reflected, though imperfectly, in actual human relationships. Thus the motivational significance of divine and human requirements is to a large extent integrated.

4   Finally, it matters that the requirements are actually imposed by God. Critics have argued that this does not really matter in divine command metaethics as I have expounded it. They suggest that all the work is being done by the stipulation that it is the demands of a *loving* God that bind—that really nothing would be lost if we just said that our overriding, fully moral obligation is constituted by what *would* be commanded by a loving God, whether there is one or not. I want to say why I think that that is not an adequate substitute.

My reasons on this point parallel my reasons for not being satisfied with an ideal, non-actual human authority as a source of moral obligation. First of all, I do not believe in the counterfactuals. I do not believe that there is a unique set of commands that would be issued by any loving God. There are some things that a loving God might command and might not command. In particular, among the things that I believe actually to be valid moral demands, there are some that I think might have been arranged differently by a God who would still be loving, and who would still satisfy the additional requirements of the metaethical theory. For example, a loving God could have commanded different principles regarding euthanasia from those that I believe are actually in force.

In the second place, even aside from any doubts about whether these counterfactuals about loving Gods are true, it seems to me that they are motivationally weak. They do not have anything like the motivational or reason-generating power of the belief that something actually is demanded of me by my loving creator and heavenly father. The latter belief is therefore one that metaethics cannot easily afford to exchange for the belief that such and such *would* have been demanded of me by a loving God.

Can the nature of moral obligation be adequately understood in terms of social requirements? Yes, if our system of social relationships includes God.[6]

Notes

1 John Rawls, *A Theory of Justice* (Cambridge, MA: Harvard University Press, 1971), p. 477f. This passage is quoted, with approval, in James Wallace, *Virtues and Vices* (Ithaca, NY and London: Cornell University Press, 1978), p. 116. What I have said thus far about utilitarian and nonutilitarian reasons for fulfilling an obligation largely follows Wallace's (much fuller) line of argument.
2 Rawls, *A Theory of Justice* (op. cit.), chs. 70–72, pp. 465, 470, and 474f.
3 It is significant that insofar as my reaction arises from my personally valuing a principle, or seeing it as expressing my nature, it does not seem to matter very much whether the principle is moral or aesthetic or intellectual. I could be degraded in my own eyes by doing something I regard as aesthetically or intellectually unworthy of me.
4 The possibility of speaking of divine "requirements" here, rather than always of "commands," may serve to suggest the diversity of ways (by no means limited to explicit injunctions in sacred texts) in which God's demands may be communicated.
5 Emile Durkheim, *L'education morale* (Paris: Félix Alcan, 1925), p. 110.
6 Some of my work on this material was supported by a sabbatical leave from UCLA and a fellowship at the Center of Theological Inquiry in Princeton, NJ; both are acknowledged with thanks. A version of the paper was presented to a summer institute on the philosophy of religion, sponsored by the National Endowment for the Humanities, at Western Washington University in 1986. I am grateful for the many comments received there, and to Marilyn McCord Adams for helpful discussion of a draft.

Review and Discussion Questions

1 Adams discusses four characteristics of being obligated that arise from being in relationships with other persons. What are these characteristics?
2 How does Adams analyze the nature of guilt? What is his criticism of the "principle guilt"?
3 Why does Adams believe that it's unconvincing that real obligation arises solely from within human society?
4 How would Brody or Hobbes respond to Adams's argument?

READING: MORALITY, RELIGION, AND CONSCIENCE

JOHN ARTHUR[*]

What is morality? Does it depend in some way on religion, and, if so, how? This essay first describes, then assesses, three different ways in which it has sometimes been thought that morality requires religion as its basis. The article concludes with a brief discussion of John Dewey's suggestion that "morality is social" and what that might imply about moral reflection and about moral education. John Arthur was professor of philosophy and director of the Program in Philosophy, Politics, and Law at Binghamton University, State University of New York.

The question I discuss in this paper was famously captured by a character in Dostoyevsky's novel *The Brothers Karamazov*: "Without God," said Ivan, "everything is permitted." I want to argue that this is wrong: there is in fact no important sense in which morality depends on religion. Yet, I will also argue, there do remain important other respects in which the two *are* related. In the concluding section I extend the discussion of the origins of morality beyond religion by considering the nature of conscience, the ways morality is "social," and the implications of these ideas for moral education. First, however, I want to say something about the subjects: just what are we referring to when we speak of morality and of religion?

I Morality and Religion

A useful way to approach the first question—the nature of morality—is to ask what it would mean for a society to exist without a social moral code. How would such people think and behave? What would that society look like? First, it seems clear that such people would never feel guilt or resentment. For example, the notions that I ought to remember my parents' anniversary, that he has a moral responsibility to help care for his children after the divorce, that she has a right to equal pay for equal work, and that discrimination on the basis of race is unfair would be absent in such a society. Notions of duty, rights, and obligations would not be present, except perhaps in the legal sense; concepts of justice and fairness would also be foreign to these people. In short, people would have no tendency to evaluate or criticize the behavior of others, nor to feel remorse about their own behavior. Children would not be taught to be ashamed when they steal or hurt others, nor would they be allowed to complain when others treat them badly. (People might, however, feel regret at a decision that didn't turn out as they had hoped; but that would only be because their expectations were frustrated, not because they feel guilty.)

---

[*] Slightly revised from a paper that originally appeared in *Contemporary Readings in Social and Political Ethics* ed. by Gary Brodsky, John Troyer, and David Vance. Copyright © 1995 by John Arthur (Buffalo, NY: Prometheus, 1984), pp. 46–52. Reprinted by permission Estate of John Arthur, Amy Shapiro, executor, ashapiro@hhk.com.

Such a society lacks a moral code. What, then, of religion? Is it possible that people lacking a morality would nonetheless have religious beliefs? It seems clear that it is possible. Suppose every day these same people file into their place of worship to pay homage to God (they may believe in many gods or in one all-powerful creator of heaven and earth). Often they can be heard praying to God for help in dealing with their problems and thanking Him for their good fortune. Frequently they give sacrifices to God, sometimes in the form of money spent to build beautiful temples and churches, other times by performing actions they believe God would approve such as helping those in need. These practices might also be institutionalized, in the sense that certain people are assigned important leadership roles. Specific texts might also be taken as authoritative, indicating the ways God has acted in history and His role in their lives or the lives of their ancestors.

To have a moral code, then, is to tend to evaluate (perhaps without even expressing it) the behavior of others and to feel guilt at certain actions when we perform them. Religion, on the other hand, involves beliefs in supernatural power(s) that created and perhaps also control nature, the tendency to worship and pray to those supernatural forces or beings, and the presence of organizational structures and authoritative texts. The practices of morality and religion are thus importantly different. One involves our attitudes toward various forms of behavior (lying and killing, for example), typically expressed using the notions of rules, rights, and obligations. The other, religion, typically involves prayer, worship, beliefs about the supernatural, institutional forms, and authoritative texts.

We come, then, to the central question: What is the connection, if any, between a society's moral code and its religious practices and beliefs? Many people have felt that morality is in some way dependent on religion or religious truths. But what sort of "dependence" might there be? In what follows I distinguish various ways in which one might claim that religion is necessary for morality, arguing against those who claim morality depends in some way on religion. I will also suggest, however, some other important ways in which the two are related, concluding with a brief discussion of conscience and moral education.

2 Religious Motivation and Guidance

One possible role which religion might play in morality relates to motives people have. Religion, it is often said, is necessary so that people will *do* right. Typically, the argument begins with the important point that doing what is right often has costs: refusing to shoplift or cheat can mean people go without some good or fail a test; returning a billfold means they don't get the contents. Religion is therefore said to be necessary in that it provides motivation to do the right thing. God rewards those who follow His commands by providing for them a place in heaven or by insuring that they prosper and are happy on earth. He also punishes those who violate the moral law. Others emphasize less self-interested ways in which religious motives may encourage people to act rightly. Since God is the creator of the universe and has ordained that His plan should be followed, they point out, it is important to live one's life in accord with this divinely ordained plan. Only by living a moral life, it is said, can people live in harmony with the larger, divinely created order.

The first claim, then, is that religion is necessary to provide moral motivation. The problem with that argument, however, is that religious motives are far from the only ones people have. For most of us, a decision to do the right thing (if that is our decision) is made for a variety of reasons: "What if I get caught? What if somebody sees me—what will he or she think? How will I feel afterwards? Will I regret it?" Or maybe the thought of cheating just doesn't arise. We were raised to be a decent person, and that's what we are—period. Behaving fairly and treating others well is more important than whatever we might gain from stealing or cheating, let alone seriously harming another person. So it seems clear that many motives for doing the right thing have nothing whatsoever to do with religion. Most of us, in fact, do worry about getting caught, being blamed, and being looked down on by others. We also may do what is right just because it's right, or because we don't want to hurt others or embarrass family and friends. To say that we need religion to act morally is mistaken; indeed, it seems to me that many of us, when it really gets down to it, don't give much of a thought to religion when making moral decisions. All those other reasons are the ones which we tend to consider, or else we just don't consider cheating and stealing at all. So far, then, there seems to be no reason to suppose that people can't be moral yet irreligious at the same time.

A second argument that is available for those who think religion is necessary to morality, however, focuses on moral guidance and knowledge rather than on people's motives. However much people may want to do the right thing, according to this view, we cannot ever know for certain what is right without the guidance of religious teaching. Human understanding is simply inadequate to this difficult and controversial task; morality involves immensely complex problems, and so we must consult religious revelation for help.

Again, however, this argument fails. First, consider how much we would need to know about religion and revelation in order for religion to provide moral guidance. Besides being sure that there is a God, we'd also have to think about which of the many religions is true. How can anybody be sure his or her religion is the right one? But even if we assume the Judeo-Christian God is the real one, we still need to find out just what it is He wants us to do, which means we must think about revelation.

Revelation comes in at least two forms, and not even all Christians agree on which is the best way to understand revelation. Some hold that revelation occurs when God tells us what He wants by providing us with His words: the Ten Commandments are an example. Many even believe, as evangelist Billy Graham once said, that the entire Bible was written by God using thirty-nine secretaries. Others, however, doubt that the "word of God" refers literally to the words God has spoken but believe instead that the Bible is a historical document, written by human beings, of the events or occasions in which God revealed Himself. It is an especially important document, of course, but nothing more than that. So on this second view revelation is not understood as *statements* made by God but rather as His *acts* such as leading His people from Egypt, testing Job, and sending His son as an example of the ideal life. The Bible is not itself revelation; it's the historical account of revelatory actions.

If we are to use revelation as a moral guide, then we must first know what is to count as revelation: words given us by God, historical events, or both? But even supposing that we could somehow answer those questions, the problems of relying on revelation are still not over since we still must interpret that revelation. Some feel, for example, that the Bible justifies various forms of killing, including war and capital punishment, on the basis of such statements as "An eye for an eye." Others, emphasizing such sayings as "Judge not lest ye be judged" and "Thou shalt not kill," believe the Bible demands absolute pacifism. How are we to know which interpretation is correct? It is likely, of course, that the answer people give to such religious questions will be influenced in part at least by their own moral beliefs: if capital punishment is thought to be unjust, for example, then an interpreter will seek to read the Bible in a way that is consistent with that moral truth. That is not, however, a happy conclusion for those wishing to rest morality on revelation, for it means that their understanding of what God has revealed is itself dependent on their prior moral views. Rather than revelation serving as a guide for morality, morality is serving as a guide for how we interpret revelation.

So my general conclusion is that far from providing a shortcut to moral understanding, looking to revelation for guidance often creates more questions and problems. It seems wiser under the circumstances to address complex moral problems like abortion, capital punishment, and affirmative action directly, considering the pros and cons of each side, rather than to seek answers through the much more controversial and difficult route of revelation.

3 The Divine Command Theory

It may seem, however, that we have still not really gotten to the heart of the matter. Even if religion is not necessary for moral motivation or guidance, it is often claimed, religion is necessary in another more fundamental sense. According to this view, religion is necessary for morality because without God there could be no right or wrong. God, in other words, provides the foundation or bedrock on which morality is grounded. This idea was expressed by Bishop R. C. Mortimer:

> God made us and all the world. Because of that He has an absolute claim on our obedience. ... From [this] it follows that a thing is not right simply because we think it is. It is right because God commands it.[1]

What Bishop Mortimer has in mind can be seen by comparing moral rules with legal ones. Legal statutes, we know, are created by legislatures; if the state assembly of New York had not passed a law limiting the speed people can travel, then there would be no such legal obligation. Without the statutory enactments, such a law simply would not exist. Mortimer's view, the *divine command theory*, would mean that God has the same sort of relation to moral law as the legislature has to statutes it enacts: without God's commands there would be no moral rules, just as without a legislature there would be no statutes.

Defenders of the divine command theory often add to this a further claim, that only by assuming God sits at the foundation of morality can we explain the objective difference between right and wrong. This point was forcefully argued by F. C. Copleston in a 1948 British Broadcasting Corporation radio debate with Bertrand Russell.

COPLESTON: ... The validity of such an interpretation of man's conduct depends on the recognition of God's existence, obviously. ... Let's take a look at the Commandant of the [Nazi] concentration camp at Belsen. That appears to you as undesirable and evil and to me too. To Adolph Hitler we suppose it appeared as something good and desirable. I suppose you'd have to admit that for Hitler it was good and for you it is evil.

RUSSELL: No, I shouldn't go so far as that. I mean, I think people can make mistakes in that as they can in other things. If you have jaundice you see things yellow that are not yellow. You're making a mistake.

COPLESTON: Yes, one can make mistakes, but can you make a mistake if it's simply a question of reference to a feeling or emotion? Surely Hitler would be the only possible judge of what appealed to his emotions.

RUSSELL: ... You can say various things about that; among others, that if that sort of thing makes that sort of appeal to Hitler's emotions, then Hitler makes quite a different appeal to my emotions.

COPLESTON: Granted. But there's no objective criterion outside feeling then for condemning the conduct of the Commandant of Belsen, in your view. ... The human being's idea of the content of the moral law depends certainly to a large extent on education and environment, and a man has to use his reason in assessing the validity of the actual moral ideas of his social group. But the possibility of criticizing the accepted moral code presupposes that there is an objective standard, that there is an ideal moral order, which imposes itself. ... It implies the existence of a real foundation of God.[2]

Against those who, like Bertrand Russell, seek to ground morality in feelings and attitudes, Copleston argues that there must be a more solid foundation if we are to be able to claim truly that the Nazis were evil. God, according to Copleston, is able to provide the objective basis for the distinction, which we all know to exist, between right and wrong. Without divine commands at the root of human obligations, we would have no real reason for condemning the behavior of anybody, even Nazis. Morality, Copleston thinks, would then be nothing more than an expression of personal feeling.

To begin assessing the divine command theory, let's first consider this last point. Is it really true that only the commands of God can provide an objective basis for moral judgments? Certainly many philosophers have felt that morality rests on its own perfectly sound footing, be it reason, human nature, or natural sentiments. It seems wrong to conclude, automatically, that morality cannot rest on anything but religion. And it is also possible that morality doesn't have any foundation or basis at all, so that its claims should be ignored in favor of whatever serves our own self-interest.

In addition to these problems with Copleston's argument, the divine command theory faces other problems as well. First, we would need to say much more about the relationship between morality and divine commands. Certainly the expressions "is commanded by God" and "is morally required" do not *mean* the same thing. People and even whole societies can use moral concepts without understanding them to make any reference to God. And while it is true that God (or any other moral being, for that matter) would tend to want others to do the right thing, this hardly shows that being right and being commanded by God are the same thing.

Parents want their children to do the right thing, too, but that doesn't mean parents, or anybody else, can make a thing right just by commanding it!

I think that, in fact, theists should reject the divine command theory. One reason is what it implies. Suppose we were to grant (just for the sake of argument) that the divine command theory is correct, so that actions are right just because they are commanded by God. The same, of course, can be said about those deeds that we believe are wrong. If God hadn't commanded us not to do them, they would not be wrong.

But now notice this consequence of the divine command theory. Since God is all-powerful, and since right is determined solely by His commands, is it not possible that He might change the rules and make what we now think of as wrong into right? It would seem that according to the divine command theory the answer is "yes": it is theoretically possible that tomorrow God would decree that virtues such as kindness and courage have become vices while actions that show cruelty and cowardice will henceforth be the right actions. (Recall the analogy with a legislature and the power it has to change law.) So now rather than it being right for people to help each other out and prevent innocent people from suffering unnecessarily, it would be right (God having changed His mind) to create as much pain among innocent children as we possibly can! To adopt the divine command theory therefore commits its advocate to the seemingly absurd position that even the greatest atrocities might be not only acceptable but morally required if God were to command them.

Plato made a similar point in the dialogue *Euthyphro*. Socrates is asking Euthyphro what it is that makes the virtue of holiness a virtue, just as we have been asking what makes kindness and courage virtues. Euthyphro has suggested that holiness is just whatever all the gods love.

SOCRATES: Well, then, Euthyphro, what do we say about holiness? Is it not loved by all the gods, according to your definition?
EUTHYPHRO: Yes.
SOCRATES: Because it is holy, or for some other reason?
EUTHYPHRO: No, because it is holy.
SOCRATES: Then it is loved by the gods because it is holy: it is not holy because it is loved by them?
EUTHYPHRO: It seems so.
SOCRATES: ... Then holiness is not what is pleasing to the gods, and what is pleasing to the gods is not holy as you say, Euthyphro. They are different things.
EUTHYPHRO: And why, Socrates?
SOCRATES: Because we are agreed that the gods love holiness because it is holy: and that it is not holy because they love it.[3]

This raises an interesting question: Why, having claimed at first that virtues are merely what is loved (or commanded) by the gods, would Euthyphro so quickly contradict this and agree that the gods love holiness *because* it's holy, rather than the reverse? One likely possibility is that Euthyphro believes that whenever the gods love something they do so with good reason, not without justification and arbitrarily. To deny this, and say that it is merely the gods' love that makes holiness a virtue, would mean that the gods have no basis for their attitudes, that they are arbitrary in what they love. Yet—and this is the crucial point—it's far from clear that a religious person would want to say that God is arbitrary in that way. If we say that it is simply God's loving something that makes it right, then what sense would it make to say God wants us to do right? All that could mean, it seems, is that God wants us to do what He wants us to do; He would have no reason for wanting it. Similarly, "God is good" would mean little more than "God does what He pleases." The divine command theory therefore leads us to the results that God is morally arbitrary, and that His wishing us to do good or even God's being just mean nothing more than that God does what He does and wants whatever He wants. Religious people who reject that consequence would also, I am suggesting, have reason to reject the divine command theory itself, seeking a different understanding of morality.

This now raises another problem, however. If God approves kindness because it is a virtue and hates the Nazis because they were evil, then it seems that God discovers morality rather than inventing it. So haven't we then identified a limitation on God's power, since He now, being a good God, must love kindness and command us not to be cruel? Without the divine command theory, in other words, what is left of God's omnipotence?

But why, we may ask, is such a limitation on God unacceptable? It is not at all clear that God really can do anything at all. Can God, for example, destroy Himself? Or make a rock so heavy that He cannot lift it? Or create a universe which was never created by Him? Many have thought that God cannot do these things but also that His inability to do them does not constitute a genuine limitation on His power since these are things that cannot be done at all: to do them would violate the laws of logic. Christianity's most influential theologian, Thomas Aquinas, wrote in this regard that "whatever implies contradiction does not come within the scope of divine omnipotence, because it cannot have the aspect of possibility. Hence it is more appropriate to say that such things cannot be done than that God cannot do them."[4]

How, then, ought we to understand God's relationship to morality if we reject the divine command theory? Can religious people consistently maintain their faith in God the Creator and yet deny that what is right is right because He commands it? I think the answer to this is "yes." Making cruelty good is not like making a universe that wasn't made, of course. It's a moral limit on God rather than a logical one. But why suppose that God's limits are only logical?

One final point about this. Even if we agree that God loves justice or kindness because of their nature, not arbitrarily, there still remains a sense in which God could change morality, even having rejected the divine command theory. That's because if we assume, plausibly I think, that morality depends in part on how we reason, what we desire and need, and the circumstances in which we find ourselves, then morality will still be under God's control since God could have constructed us or our environment very differently. Suppose, for instance, that he created us so that we couldn't be hurt by others or didn't care about freedom. Or perhaps our natural environment were created differently, so that all we would have to do is ask and anything we want would be given to us. If God had created either nature or us that way, then it seems likely our morality might also be different in important ways from the one we now think correct. In that sense, then, morality depends on God whether or not one supports the divine command theory.

4 On Dewey's Thought That "Morality Is Social"

I have argued here that religion is not necessary in providing moral motivation or guidance and against the divine command theory's claim that God is necessary for there to be morality at all. In this last section, I want first to look briefly at how religion and moral codes sometimes *do* influence each other. Then I will consider the development of moral conscience and the important ways in which morality might correctly be thought to be "social."

Nothing I have said so far means that morality and religion are independent of each other. But in what ways are they related, assuming I am correct in claiming morality does not *depend* on religion? First, of course, we should note the historical influence religions have had on the development of morality as well as on politics and law. Many of the important leaders of the abolitionist and civil rights movements were religious leaders, as are many current members of the pro-life movement. The relationship is not, however, one sided: morality has also influenced religion, as the current debate within the Catholic church over the role of women, abortion, and other social issues shows. In reality, then, it seems clear that the practices of morality and religion have historically each exerted an influence on the other.

But just as the two have shaped each other historically, so too do they interact at the personal level. I have already suggested how people's understanding of revelation, for instance, is often shaped by morality as they seek the best interpretations of revealed texts. Whether trying to understand a work of art, a legal statute, or a religious text, interpreters regularly seek to understand them in the best light—to make them as good as they can be, which requires that they bring moral judgment to the task of religious interpretation and understanding.

The relationship can go the other direction as well, however, as people's moral views are shaped by their religious training and beliefs. These relationships between morality and religion are often complex, hidden even from ourselves, but it does seem clear that our views on important moral issues, from sexual morality and war to welfare and capital punishment, are often influenced by our religious outlook. So not only are religious and moral practices and understandings historically linked, but for many religious people the relationship extends to the personal level—to their understanding of moral obligations as well as their sense of who they are and their vision of who they wish to be.

Morality, then, is influenced by religion (as is religion by morality), but morality's social character extends deeper even than that, I want to argue. First, of course, we possess a socially acquired language within which we think about our various choices and the alternatives we ought to follow, including whether a possible course of action is the right thing to do. Second, morality is social in that it governs relationships among people, defining our responsibilities to others and theirs to us. Morality provides the standards we rely on in gauging our interactions with family, lovers, friends, fellow citizens, and even strangers. Third, morality is social in the sense that we are, in fact, subject to criticism by others for our actions. We discuss with others what we should do and often hear from them concerning whether our decisions were acceptable. Blame and praise are a central feature of morality.

While not disputing any of this, John Dewey has stressed another, less obvious aspect of morality's social character. Consider then the following comments regarding the origins of morality and conscience in an article he titled "Morality Is Social":

> In language and imagination we rehearse the responses of others just as we dramatically enact other consequences. We foreknow how others will act, and the foreknowledge is the beginning of judgment passed on action. We know *with* them; there is conscience. An assembly is formed within our breast which discusses and appraises proposed and performed acts. The community without becomes a forum and tribunal within, a judgment-seat of charges, assessments and exculpations. Our thoughts of our own actions are saturated with the ideas that others entertain about them. ... Explicit recognition of this fact is a prerequisite of improvement in moral education. ... Reflection is morally indispensable.[5]

So Dewey's thought is that to consider matters from the moral point of view means we must think beyond ourselves, by which he means imagining how we as well as others might respond to various choices now being contemplated. To consider a decision from the *moral* perspective, says Dewey, requires that we envision an "assembly of others" that is "formed within our breast." That means, in turn, that morality and conscience cannot be sharply distinguished from our nature as social beings since conscience invariably brings with it, or constitutes, the perspective of the other. "Is this right?" and "What would this look like were I to have to defend it to others?" are not separable questions.[6]

It is important not to confuse Dewey's point here, however. He is *not* saying that what is right is finally to be determined by the reactions of actually existing other people, or even by the reaction of society as a whole. What is right or fair can never be finally decided by what is popular, and indeed might not meet the approval of any specific group. But what then might Dewey mean in speaking of such an "assembly of others" as the basis of morality? The answer is that rather than actual people or groups, the assembly Dewey envisions is hypothetical or "ideal." The "community without" is thus transformed into a "forum and tribunal within, a judgment-seat of charges, assessments and exculpations." So it is through the powers of our imagination that we can meet our moral responsibilities and exercise moral judgment, using these powers to determine what morality requires by imagining the reaction of Dewey's "assembly of others."

Morality is therefore *inherently* social in a variety of ways. It depends on socially learned language, is learned from interactions with others, and governs our interactions with others in society. But it also demands, as Dewey put it, that we know "with" others, envisioning for ourselves what their points of view would require along with our own. Conscience demands we occupy the positions of others.

Viewed in this light, God would play a role in a religious person's moral reflection and conscience since it is unlikely a religious person would wish to exclude God from the "forum and tribunal" that constitutes conscience. Rather, for the religious person conscience would almost certainly include the imagined reaction of God along with the reactions of others who might be affected by the action. Other people are also important, however, since it is often an open question just what God's reaction would be; revelation's meaning, as I have argued, is subject to interpretation. So it seems that for a religious person, morality and

God's will cannot be separated, though the connection between them is not the one envisioned by defenders of the divine command theory.

Which leads to my final point, about moral education. If Dewey is correct, then it seems clear there is an important sense in which morality not only can be taught but must be. Besides early moral training, moral thinking depends on our ability to imagine others' reactions and to imaginatively put ourselves into their shoes. "What would somebody (including, perhaps, God) think if this got out?" expresses more than a concern with being embarrassed or punished; it is also the voice of conscience and indeed of morality itself. But that would mean, thinking of education, that listening to others, reading about what others think and do, and reflecting within ourselves about our actions and whether we could defend them to others are part of the practice of morality itself. Morality cannot exist without the broader, social perspective introduced by others, and this social nature ties it, in that way, with education and with public discussion, both actual and imagined. "Private" moral reflection taking place independent of the social world would be no moral reflection at all. It follows that moral *education*, in the form of both studying others' moral ideas and subjecting our own to discussion and criticism, is not only possible, but essential.

Notes

1 R. C. Mortimer, *Christian Ethics* (London: Hutchinson's University Library, 1950), pp. 7–8.
2 This debate was broadcast on the *Third Program* of the British Broadcasting Corporation in 1948.
3 Plato, *Euthyphro*, trans. H. N. Fowler (Cambridge, MA: Harvard University Press, 1947).
4 Thomas Aquinas, *Summa Theologica*, Part 1, Q. 25, Art. 3.
5 John Dewey, "Morality Is Social," in *The Moral Writings of John Dewey*, rev. ed., ed. James Gouinlock (Amherst, NY: Prometheus Books, 1994), pp. 182–184.
6 Obligations to animals raise an interesting problem for this conception of morality. Is it wrong to torture animals only because other *people* could be expected to disapprove? Or is it that the animal itself would disapprove? Or, perhaps, duties to animals rest on sympathy and compassion while human moral relations are more like Dewey describes, resting on morality's inherently social nature and on the dictates of conscience viewed as an assembly of others.

Review and Discussion Questions

1 How does Arthur respond to those who argue that religion is necessary for moral motivation?
2 Arthur denies that religion is necessary for moral understanding or knowledge. Why does he think that?
3 How does the analogy with a legal system suggest that God may be necessary for there to be a right and a wrong?
4 Why does Arthur reject the divine command theory?
5 In what ways are morality and religion connected, according to Arthur?
6 "Morality is social," said John Dewey. What did he mean by that?
7 What is the significance of Dewey's idea for moral education? What would Dewey probably have thought about a class in ethics?
8 In footnote 6, Arthur raises the problem of humans' obligations to animals. How would you be inclined to answer the questions he asks there?

READING: THE CONSCIENCE OF HUCKLEBERRY FINN

JONATHAN BENNETT*

Sometimes a situation will arise in which a person feels a conflict between doing the right thing and sympathy for those who may be hurt as a result of meeting morality's demands. Here, Jonathan Bennett graphically illustrates this conflict in three surprising and fascinating examples: Huck Finn's conflict over whether to free his slave friend Jim; Nazi commander Himmler's feelings for the Jews and the duty he felt to kill them; and Jonathan Edwards's attitudes toward fallen people, who he thought were doomed to live in hell, and the justice of the wrathful God who condemns them. Bennett uses these examples to explore the relations between duty and sympathy as well as the wisdom of relying on our feelings when they conflict with duty. Jonathan Bennett is Professor of Philosophy Emeritus at Syracuse University.

In this paper,[1] I shall present not just the conscience of Huckleberry Finn but two others as well. One of them is the conscience of Heinrich Himmler. He became a Nazi in 1923; he served drably and quietly, but well, and was rewarded with increasing responsibility and power. At the peak of his career he held many offices and commands, of which the most powerful was that of leader of the S.S.—the principal police force of the Nazi regime. In this capacity, Himmler commanded the whole concentration-camp system, and was responsible for the execution of the so-called final solution of the Jewish problem. It is important for my purposes that this piece of social engineering should be thought of not abstractly but in concrete terms of Jewish families being marched to what they think are bathhouses, to the accompaniment of loudspeaker renditions of extracts from *The Merry Widow* and *Tales of Hoffman*, there to be choked to death by poisonous gases. Altogether, Himmler succeeded in murdering about four and a half million of them as well as several million gentiles, mainly Poles and Russians.

The other conscience to be discussed is that of the Calvinist theologian and philosopher Jonathan Edwards. He lived in the first half of the eighteenth century, and has a good claim to be considered America's first serious and considerable philosophical thinker. He was for many years a widely renowned preacher and Congregationalist minister in New England; in 1748, a dispute with his congregation led him to resign (he couldn't accept their view that unbelievers should be admitted to the Lord's Supper in the hope that it would convert them); for some years after that, he worked as a missionary, preaching to Indians through an interpreter; then, in 1758, he accepted the presidency of what is now Princeton University and within two months died from a smallpox inoculation. Along the way he wrote some first-rate philosophy: his book

---

* Excerpted from pp. 123–134, "The Conscience of Huckleberry Finn" by Jonathan Bennett, *Philosophy* 49 (1974). Copyright © 1974. Reprinted by permission of Cambridge University Press.

attacking the notion of free will is still sometimes read. Why I should be interested in Edwards's conscience will be explained in due course.

I shall use Heinrich Himmler, Jonathan Edwards, and Huckleberry Finn to illustrate different aspects of a single theme, namely the relationship between *sympathy* on the one hand and *bad morality* on the other.

All that I can mean by a "bad morality" is a morality whose principles I deeply disapprove of. When I call a morality bad, I cannot prove that mine is better; but when I here call any morality bad, I think you will agree with me that it is bad, and that is all I need.

There could be dispute as to whether the springs of someone's actions constitute a *morality*. I think, though, that we must admit that someone who acts in ways which conflict grossly with our morality may nevertheless have a morality of his own—a set of principles of action which he sincerely assents to, so that for him the problem of acting well or rightly or in obedience to conscience is the problem of conforming to those principles. The problem of conscientiousness can arise as acutely for a bad morality as for any other: rotten principles may be as difficult to keep as decent ones.

As for "sympathy": I use this term to cover every sort of fellow-feeling, as when one feels pity over someone's loneliness or horrified compassion over his pain or when one feels a shrinking reluctance to act in a way which will bring misfortune to someone else. These feelings must not be confused with *moral judgments*. My sympathy for someone in distress may lead me to help him or even to think that I ought to help him; but in itself it is not a judgment about what I ought to do but just a feeling for him in his plight. We shall get some light on the difference between feelings and moral judgments when we consider Huckleberry Finn.

Obviously, feelings can impel one to action, and so can moral judgments; and in a particular case sympathy and morality may pull in opposite directions. This can happen not just with bad moralities but also with good ones like yours and mine. For example, a small child, sick and miserable, clings tightly to his mother and screams in terror when she tries to pass him over to the doctor to be examined. If the mother gave way to her sympathy, that is to her feeling for the child's misery and fright, she would hold it close and not let the doctor come near, but don't we agree that it might be wrong for her to act on such a feeling? Quite generally, then, anyone's moral principles may apply to a particular situation in a way which runs contrary to the particular thrusts of fellow-feeling that he has in that situation. My immediate concern is with sympathy in relation to bad morality, but not because such conflicts occur only when the morality is bad.

Now, suppose that someone who accepts a bad morality is struggling to make himself act in accordance with it in a particular situation where his sympathies pull him another way. He sees the struggle as one between doing the right, conscientious thing, and acting wrongly and weakly, like the mother who won't let the doctor come near her sick, frightened baby. Since we don't accept this person's morality, we may see the situation very differently, thoroughly disapproving of the action he regards as the right one and endorsing the action which from his point of view constitutes weakness and backsliding.

Conflicts between sympathy and bad morality won't always be like this, for we won't disagree with every single dictate of a bad morality. Still, it can happen in the way I have described, with the agent's right action being our wrong one, and vice versa. That is just what happens in a certain episode in Chapter 16 of *The Adventures of Huckleberry Finn*, an episode which brilliantly illustrates how fiction can be instructive about real life.

Huck Finn has been helping his slave friend Jim to run away from Miss Watson, who is Jim's owner. In their raft-journey down the Mississippi River, they are near to the place at which Jim will become legally free. Now let Huck take over the story:

> Jim said it made him all over trembly and feverish to be so close to freedom. Well, I can tell you it made me all over trembly and feverish, too, to hear him, because I begun to get it through my head that he was most free—and who was to blame for it? Why, me. I couldn't get that out of my conscience, no how nor no way. It hadn't ever come home to me, before, what this thing was that I was doing. But now it did; and it stayed with me, and scorched me more and more. I tried to make out to myself that I warn't to blame, because I didn't run Jim off from his rightful owner; but it warn't no use, conscience up and say, every time: "But you knowed he was running for his freedom, and you could a paddled ashore and told somebody." That was so—I couldn't get around that, no way. That was where it pinched. Conscience says to me: "What had poor Miss Watson done to you, that you could see her nigger go off right under your eyes and never say one single word? What did that poor old woman do to you, that you could treat her so mean? ..." I got to feeling so mean and so miserable I most wished I was dead.

Jim speaks of his plan to save up to buy his wife, and then his children, out of slavery; and he adds that if the children cannot be bought he will arrange to steal them. Huck is horrified:

> Thinks I, this is what comes of my not thinking. Here was this nigger which I had as good as helped to run away, coming right out flat-footed and saying he would steal his children—children that belonged to a man I didn't even know; a man that hadn't ever done me no harm.
>
> I was sorry to hear Jim say that, it was such a lowering of him. My conscience got to stirring me up hotter than ever, until at last I says to it: "Let up on me—it ain't too late, yet—I'll paddle ashore at first light, and tell." I felt easy, and happy, and light as a feather, right off. All my troubles was gone.

This is bad morality all right. In his earliest years Huck wasn't taught any principles, and the only ones he has encountered since then are those of rural Missouri, in which slaveowning is just one kind of ownership and is not subject to critical pressure. It hasn't occurred to Huck to question those principles. So the action, to us abhorrent, of turning Jim in to the authorities presents itself clearly to Huck as the right thing to do.

For us, morality and sympathy would both dictate helping Jim to escape. If we felt any conflict, it would have both these on one side and something else on the other—greed for a reward, or fear of punishment. But Huck's morality conflicts with his sympathy, that is, with his unargued, natural feeling for his friend. The conflict starts when Huck sets off in the canoe toward the shore, pretending that he is going to reconnoitre, but really planning to turn Jim in:

> As I shoved off, [Jim] says: "Pooty soon I'll be a-shout'n for joy, en I'll say, it's all on accounts o' Huck I's a free man ... Jim won't ever forget you, Huck; you's de bes' fren' Jim's ever had; en you's de only fren' old Jim's got now."
>
> I was paddling off, all in a sweat to tell on him; but when he says this, it seemed to kind of take the tuck all out of me. I went along slow then, and I warn't right down certain whether I was glad I started or whether I warn't. When I was fifty yards off, Jim says:
>
> "Dah you goes, de ole true Huck; de on'y white genlman dat ever kep' his promise to ole Jim." Well, I just felt sick. But I says. I *got* to do it—I can't get *out* of it.

In the upshot, sympathy wins over morality. Huck hasn't the strength of will to do what he sincerely thinks he ought to do. Two men hunting for runaway slaves ask him whether the man on his raft is black or white:

> I didn't answer up prompt, I tried to, but the words wouldn't come. I tried, for a second or two, to brace up and out with it, but I warn't man enough—hadn't the spunk of a rabbit. I see I was weakening; so I just give up trying, and up and says: "He's white."

So Huck enables Jim to escape, thus acting weakly and wickedly—he thinks. In this conflict between sympathy and morality, sympathy wins.

One critic has cited this episode in support of the statement that Huck suffers "excruciating moments of wavering between honesty and respectability." That is hopelessly wrong, and I agree with the perceptive comment on it by another critic, who says:

> The conflict waged in Huck is much more serious: he scarcely cares for respectability and never hesitates to relinquish it, but he does care for honesty and gratitude—and both honesty and gratitude require that he should give Jim up. It is not, in Huck, honesty at war with respectability but love and compassion for Jim struggling against his conscience. His decision is for Jim and hell: a right decision made in the mental chains that Huck never breaks. His concern for Jim is and remains irrational. Huck finds many reasons for giving Jim up and none for stealing him. To the end Huck sees his compassion for Jim as a weak, ignorant, and wicked felony.[2]

That is precisely correct—and it can have that virtue only because Mark Twain wrote the episode with such unerring precision. The crucial point concerns reasons, which all occur on one side of the conflict. On the side of conscience we have principles, arguments, considerations, ways of looking at things:

> "It hadn't ever come home to me before what I was doing"
> "I tried to make out that I warn't to blame"
> "Conscience said 'But you knew ...' —I couldn't get around that"

> "What had poor Miss Watson done to you?"
> "This is what comes of my not thinking"
> "children that belonged to a man I didn't even know."

On the other side, the side of feeling, we get nothing like that. When Jim rejoices in Huck, as his only friend, Huck doesn't consider the claims of friendship or have the situation "come home" to him in a different light. All that happens is: "When he says this, it seemed to kind of take the tuck all out of me. I went along slow then, and I warn't right down certain whether I was glad I started or whether I warn't." Again, Jim's words about Huck's "promise" to him don't give Huck any reason for changing his plan: in his morality, promises to slaves probably don't count. Their effect on him is of a different kind: "Well, I just felt sick." And when the moment for final decision comes, Huck doesn't weigh up pros and cons: he simply *fails* to do what he believes to be right—he isn't strong enough, hasn't "the spunk of a rabbit." This passage in the novel is notable not just for its finely wrought irony, with Huck's weakness of will leading him to do the right thing, but also for its masterly handling of the difference between general moral principles and particular unreasoned emotional pulls.

Consider now another case of bad morality in conflict with human sympathy, the case of odious Himmler. Here, from a speech he made to some S.S. generals, is an indication of the content of his morality:

> What happens to a Russian, to a Czech, does not interest me in the slightest. What the nations can offer in the way of good blood of our type, we will take, if necessary by kidnapping their children and raising them here with us. Whether nations live in prosperity or starve to death like cattle interests me only in so far as we need them as slaves to our Kultur; otherwise it is of no interest to me. Whether 10,000 Russian females fall down from exhaustion while digging an antitank ditch interests me only in so far as the antitank ditch for Germany is finished.[3]

But has this a moral basis at all? And if it has, was there in Himmler's own mind any conflict between morality and sympathy? Yes there was. Here is more from the same speech:

> I also want to talk to you quite frankly on a very grave matter. ... I mean ... the extermination of the Jewish race. ... Most of you must know what it means when 100 corpses are lying side by side, or 500, or 1,000. To have stuck it out and at the same time—apart from exceptions caused by human weakness—to have remained decent fellows, that is what has made us hard. This is a page of glory in our history which has never been written and is never to be written.

Himmler saw his policies as being hard to implement while still retaining one's human sympathies—while still remaining a "decent fellow." He is saying that only the weak take the easy way out and just squelch their sympathies and is praising the stronger and more glorious course of retaining one's sympathies while acting in violation of them. In the same spirit, he ordered that when executions were carried out in concentration camps, those responsible "are to be influenced in such a way as to suffer no ill effect in their character and mental attitude." A year later he boasted that the S.S. had wiped out the Jews

> without our leaders and their men suffering any damage in their minds and souls. The danger was considerable, for there was only a narrow path between the Scylla of their becoming heartless ruffians unable any longer to treasure life, and the Charybdis of their becoming soft and suffering nervous breakdowns.

And there really can't be any doubt that the basis of Himmler's policies was a set of principles which constituted his morality—a sick, bad, wicked *morality*. He described himself as caught in "the old tragic conflict between will and obligation." And when his physician Kersten protested at the intention to destroy the Jews, saying that the suffering involved was "not to be contemplated," Kersten reports that Himmler replied:

> He knew that it would mean much suffering for the Jews. ... "It is the curse of greatness that it must step over dead bodies to create new life. Yet we must cleanse the soil or it will never bear fruit. It will be a great burden for me to bear."

This, I submit, is the language of morality.

So in this case, tragically, bad morality won out over sympathy. I am sure that many of Himmler's killers did extinguish their sympathies, becoming "heartless ruffians" rather than "decent fellows"; but not Himmler himself. Although his policies ran against the human grain to a horrible degree, he did not sandpaper down his emotional surfaces so that there was no grain there, allowing his actions to slide along smoothly and easily. He did, after all, bear his hideous burden and even paid a price for it. He suffered a variety of nervous and physical disabilities, including nausea and stomach convulsions, and Kersten was doubtless right in saying that these were "the expression of a psychic division which extended over his whole life."

This same division must have been present in some of those officials of the church who ordered heretics to be tortured so as to change their theological opinions. Along with the brutes and the cold careerists, there must have been some who cared and who suffered from the conflict between their sympathies and their bad morality.

In the conflict between sympathy and bad morality, then, the victory may go to sympathy, as in the case of Huck Finn, or to morality, as in the case of Himmler.

Another possibility is that the conflict may be avoided by giving up, or not ever having, those sympathies which might interfere with one's principles. That seems to have been the case with Jonathan Edwards. I am afraid that I shall be doing an injustice to Edwards's many virtues and to his great intellectual energy and inventiveness; for my concern is only with the worst thing about him—namely his morality, which was worse than Himmler's.

According to Edwards, God condemns some men to an eternity of unimaginably awful pain, though he arbitrarily spares others—"arbitrarily" because none deserve to be spared:

> Natural men are held in the hand of God over the pit of hell ...; they have deserved the fiery pit, and are already sentenced to it; and God is dreadfully provoked, his anger is as great towards them as to those that are actually suffering the executions of the fierceness of his wrath in hell; the devil is waiting for them, hell is gaping for them, the flames gather and flash about them, and would fain lay hold on them ...; and ... there are no means within reach that can be any security to them. ... All that preserves them is the mere arbitrary will, and uncovenanted unobliged forebearance of an incensed God.[4]

Notice that he says "they have deserved the fiery pit." Edwards insists that men *ought* to be condemned to eternal pain, and his position isn't that this is right because God wants it but rather that God wants it because it is right. For him, moral standards exist independently of God, and God can be assessed in the light of them (and of course found to be perfect). For example, he says:

> They deserve to be cast into hell; so that ... justice never stands in the way, it makes no objection against God's using his power at any moment to destroy them. Yea, on the contrary, justice calls aloud for an infinite punishment of their sins.

Elsewhere, he gives elaborate arguments to show that God is acting justly in damning sinners. For example, he argues that a punishment should be exactly as bad as the crime being punished: God is infinitely excellent, so any crime against him is infinitely bad, and so eternal damnation is exactly right as a punishment—it is infinite, but, as Edwards is careful also to say, it is "no more than infinite."

Of course, Edwards himself didn't torment the damned; but the question still arises of whether his sympathies didn't conflict with his *approval* of eternal torment. Didn't he find it painful to contemplate any fellow human's being tortured for ever? Apparently not:

> The God that holds you over the pit of hell, much as one holds a spider or some loathsome insect over the fire, abhors you, and is dreadfully provoked; ... he is of purer eyes than to bear to have you in his sight; you are ten thousand times so abominable in his eyes as the most hateful venomous serpent is in ours.

When God is presented as being as misanthropic as that, one suspects misanthropy in the theologian. This suspicion is increased when Edwards claims that "the saints in glory will ... understand how terrible the sufferings of the damned are; yet ... will not be sorry for [them]."[5] He bases this partly on a view of human nature whose ugliness he seems not to notice:

> The seeing of the calamities of others tends to heighten the sense of our own enjoyments. When the saints in glory, therefore, shall see the doleful state of the damned, how will this heighten their sense of the blessedness of their own state. ... When they shall see how miserable others of their fellow-creatures are ...; when they shall see the smoke of their torment, ... and hear

> their dolorous shrieks and cries, and consider that they in the mean time are in the most blissful state, and shall surely be in it to all eternity; how they will rejoice!

I hope this is less than the whole truth! His other main point about why the saints will rejoice to see the torments of the damned is that it is *right* that they should do so:

> The heavenly inhabitants ... will have no love nor pity to the damned. ... [This will not show] a want of a spirit of love in them ...; for the heavenly inhabitants will know that it is not fit that they should love [the damned] because they will know then, that God has no love to them, nor pity for them.

The implication that *of course* one can adjust one's feelings of pity so that they conform to the dictates of some authority—doesn't this suggest that ordinary human sympathies played only a small part in Edwards's life?

Huck Finn, whose sympathies are wide and deep, could never avoid the conflict in that way; but he is determined to avoid it, and so he opts for the only other alternative he can see—to give up morality altogether. After he has tricked the slave-hunters, he returns to the raft and undergoes a peculiar crisis:

> I got aboard the raft, feeling bad and low, because I knowed very well I had done wrong, and I see it warn't no use for me to try to learn to do right; a body that don't get *started* right when he's little, ain't got no show—when the pinch comes there ain't nothing to back him up and keep him to his work, and so he gets beat. Then I thought a minute, and says to myself, hold on—s'pose you'd a done right and give Jim up; would you feel better than what you do now? No, says I, I'd feel bad—I'd feel just the same way I do now. Well, then, says I, what's the use of you learning to do right, when it's troublesome to do right and ain't no trouble to do wrong, and the wages is just the same? I was stuck. I couldn't answer that. So I reckoned I wouldn't bother no more about it, but after this always do whichever come handiest at the time.

Huck clearly cannot conceive of having any morality except the one he has learned—too late, he thinks—from his society. He is not entirely a prisoner of that morality, because he does after all reject it; but for him that is a decision to relinquish morality as such; he cannot envisage revising his morality, altering its content in face of the various pressures to which it is subject, including pressures from his sympathies. For example, he does not begin to approach the thought that slavery should be rejected on moral grounds or the thought that what he is doing is not theft because a person cannot be owned and therefore cannot be stolen.

The basic trouble is that he cannot or will not engage in abstract intellectual operations of any sort. In Chapter 33 he finds himself "feeling to blame, somehow" for something he knows he had no hand in; he assumes that this feeling is a deliverance of conscience; and this confirms him in his belief that conscience shouldn't be listened to:

> It don't make no difference whether you do right or wrong, a person's conscience ain't got no sense, and just goes for him *anyway*. If I had a yaller dog and didn't know no more than a person's conscience does, I would poison him. It takes up more room than all the rest of a person's insides, and yet ain't no good, nohow.

That brisk, incurious dismissiveness fits well with the comprehensive rejection of morality back on the raft. But this is a digression.

On the raft, Huck decides not to live by principles, but just to do whatever "comes handiest at the time"—always acting according to the mood of the moment. Since the morality he is rejecting is narrow and cruel and his sympathies are broad and kind, the results will be good. But moral principles are good to have because they help to protect one from acting badly at moments when one's sympathies happen to be in abeyance. On the highest possible estimate of the role one's sympathies should have, one can still allow for principles as embodiments of one's best feelings, one's broadest and keenest sympathies. On that view, principles can help one across intervals when one's feelings are at less than their best, that is, through periods of misanthropy or meanness or self-centeredness or depression or anger.

What Huck didn't see is that one can live by principles and yet have ultimate control over their content. And one way such control can be exercised is by checking one's principles in the light of one's sympathies. This is sometimes a pretty straightforward matter. It can happen that a certain moral principle becomes untenable—meaning literally that one cannot hold it any longer—because it conflicts intolerably with the pity or revulsion or whatever that one feels when one sees what the principle leads to. One's experience may play a large part here: experiences evoke feelings, and feelings force one to modify principles. Something like this happened to the English poet Wilfred Owen, whose experiences in the First World War transformed him from an enthusiastic soldier into a virtual pacifist. I can't document his change of conscience in detail; but I want to present something which he wrote about the way experience can put pressure on morality.[6]

The Latin poet Horace wrote that it is sweet and fitting (or right) to die for one's country—*dulce et decorum est pro patria mori*—and Owen wrote a fine poem about how experience could lead one to relinquish that particular moral principle. He describes a man who is too slow donning his gas mask during a gas attack—"As under a green sea, I saw him drowning," Owen says. The poem ends like this:

> In all my dreams, before my helpless sight
> He plunges at me, guttering, choking, drowning.
> If in some smothering dreams you too could pace
> Behind the wagon that we flung him in,
> And watch the white eyes writhing in his face,
> His hanging face, like a devil's sick of sin;
> If you could hear, at every jolt, the blood
> Come gargling from the froth-corrupted lungs,
> Obscene as cancer, bitter as the cud
> Of vile, incurable sores on innocent tongues,—

> My friend, you would not tell with such high zest
> To children ardent for some desperate glory,
> The old Lie: Dulce et decorum est
> Pro patria mori.

There is a difficulty about drawing from all this a moral for ourselves. I imagine that we agree in our rejection of slavery, eternal damnation, genocide, and uncritical patriotic self-abnegation; so we shall agree that Huck Finn, Jonathan Edwards, Heinrich Himmler, and the poet Horace would have done well to bring certain of their principles under severe pressure from ordinary human sympathies. But then we can say this because we can say that all those are bad moralities, whereas we cannot look at our own moralities and declare them bad. This is not arrogance: it is obviously incoherent for someone to declare the system of moral principles that he accepts to be bad, just as one cannot coherently say of anything that one *believes* it but it is *false*.

Still, although I can't point to any of my beliefs and say "That is false," I don't doubt that some of my beliefs *are* false; and so I should try to remain open to correction. Similarly, I accept every single item in my morality—that is inevitable—but I am sure that my morality could be improved, which is to say that it could undergo changes which I should be glad of once I had made them. So I must try to keep my morality open to revision, exposing it to whatever valid pressures there are—including pressures from my sympathies.

I don't give my sympathies a blank check in advance. In a conflict between principle and sympathy, principles ought sometimes to win. For example, although I think it was right to take part in the Second World War on the Allied side, there were many ghastly individual incidents which might have led someone to doubt the rightness of his participation in that war. I think it would have been right for such a person to keep his sympathies in a subordinate place on those occasions, not allowing them to modify his principles in such a way as to make a pacifist of him.

Still, one's sympathies should be kept as sharp and sensitive and aware as possible, and not only because they can sometimes affect one's principles or one's conduct or both. Owen, at any rate, says that feelings and sympathies are vital even when they can do nothing but bring pain and distress. In another poem he speaks of the blessings of being numb in one's feelings: "Happy are the men who yet before they are killed/Can let their veins run cold," he says. These are the ones who do not suffer from any compassion which, as Owen puts it, "makes their feet/Sore on the alleys cobbled with their brother." He contrasts these "happy" ones, who "lose imagination," with himself and others "who with a thought besmirch/Blood over all our soul." Yet the poem's verdict goes against the "happy" ones. Owen does not say that they will act worse than the others whose souls are besmirched with blood because of their keen awareness of human suffering. He merely says that they are the losers because they have cut themselves off from the human condition:

> By choice they made themselves immune
> To pity and whatever moans in man
> Before the last sea and the hapless stars;
> Whatever mourns when many leave these shores;
> Whatever shares
> The eternal reciprocity of tears.

Notes

1. This paper began life as the Potter Memorial Lecture, given at Washington State University in Pullman, Washington, in 1972.
2. M. J. Sidnell, "Huck Finn and Jim," *The Cambridge Quarterly* 2 (1967): 203–211.
3. Quoted in William L. Shirer, *The Rise and Fall of the Third Reich* (New York: Simon and Schuster, 1960), pp. 937–938. Next quotation: Ibid., p. 966. All further quotations relating to Himmler are from Roger Manvell and Heinrich Fraenkel, *Heinrich Himmler* (London: Heinemann, 1965), pp. 132, 197, 184 (twice), 187.
4. Vergilius Ferm, ed., *Puritan Sage: Collected Writings of Jonathan Edwards* (New York: Library Publishers, 1953), p. 370. Next three quotations: Ibid., pp. 366, 294 ("no more than infinite"), 372.
5. This and the next two quotations are from "The End of the Wicked Contemplated by the Righteous: or, The Torments of the Wicked in Hell, No Occasion of Grief to the Saints in Heaven," from *The Works of President Edwards* (London, 1817), vol. IV, pp. 507–508, 511–512, and 509, respectively.
6. Extracts from "Dulce et Decorum Est" and "Insensibility" are from *The Collected Poems of Wilfred Owen*, ed. by C. Day Lewis. © Chatto & Windus Ltd. 1946, 1963. Reprinted by permission of The Owen Estate, Chatto & Windus Ltd., and New Directions Publishing Corporation.

Review and Discussion Questions

1. Describe the examples Bennett uses to illustrate how feelings and duty may conflict.
2. How does Bennett characterize the relationship between morality and sympathy? In light of his examples, do you agree with the role he gives to each?
3. Why does Bennett think Edwards's morality was worse than Himmler's?
4. Besides sympathy, what means are available to criticize our own or others' moral principles?

Essay and Paper Topics for Chapter 1

1. Discuss Hobbes's claim that morality is ultimately grounded in self-interest. Are the answers given by Brody adequate? If so, explain how; and if not, do later articles provide a better response?
2. How are morality and religion related, if they are? What are the most important contrasts between the perspectives of Arthur and Adams?
3. Are duty, self-interest, and sympathy opposed to one another, or can they be mutually supportive? Are there real conflicts between these motives or are they in the end only in apparent conflict? Explain.

Chapter 2

The Sources and Grounds of Morality

The essays in this chapter address questions that rest at the foundation of our thinking about morality and moral reasoning. Is it true, as some think, that moral ideas arise from and are limited by our culture? Is there a rational basis from which to criticize cultures? These questions lead to other perennial problems in moral theory, including the justification or grounds of our moral beliefs, moral truth, and the connections between morality and feelings. To what extent is morality best explained and understood through a scientific and evolutionary account of humanity? To what extent does understanding morality require additional claims about its authority derived from sources beyond what science could explain or discover?

READING: THE SOURCES OF MORAL IDEAS: SOCIETY, CUSTOM, AND SYMPATHY

EDWARD WESTERMARCK[*]

In this essay, Edward Westermarck begins by noting the importance of society and custom in teaching morality. Yet in many societies, it is also possible to take a critical stance toward traditional customs and practices, a stance that involves the intellect and reason. But despite this (limited) role of the intellect, Westermarck argues, it is the emotional constitution of people that shapes their sympathies and therefore their moral outlook. Reason plays only a limited role in determining moral convictions. Westermarck was a Finnish philosopher and sociologist.

Society is the school in which men learn to distinguish between right and wrong. The headmaster is Custom, and the lessons are the same for all. The first moral judgments were pronounced by public opinion; public indignation and public approval are the prototypes of the moral emotions. As regards questions of morality, there was, in early society, practically no difference of opinion; hence a character of universality, or objectivity, was from the very beginning attached to all moral judgments. And when, with advancing civilization, this unanimity was to some extent disturbed by individuals venturing to dissent from the opinions of the majority, the disagreement was largely due to facts which in no way affected the moral principle, but had reference only to its application.

---

[*] From Edward Westermarck, *The Origin and Development of the Moral Ideas* (1906).

Most people follow a very simple method in judging of an act. Particular modes of conduct have their traditional labels, many of which are learnt with language itself; and the moral judgment commonly consists simply in labelling the act according to certain obvious characteristics which it presents in common with others belonging to the same group. But a conscientious and intelligent judge proceeds in a different manner. He carefully examines all the details connected with the act, the external and internal conditions under which it was performed, its consequences, its motive; and, since the moral estimate in a large measure depends upon the regard paid to these circumstances, his judgment may differ greatly from that of the man in the street, even though the moral standard which they apply be exactly the same. But to acquire a full insight into all the details which are apt to influence the moral value of an act is in many cases anything but easy, and this naturally increases the disagreement. There is thus in every advanced society a diversity of opinion regarding the moral value of certain modes of conduct which results from circumstances of a purely intellectual character—from the knowledge or ignorance of positive facts—and involves no discord in principle.

Now it has been assumed by the advocates of various ethical theories that all the differences of moral ideas originate in this way, and that there is some ultimate standard which must be recognised as authoritative by everybody who understands it rightly. ... [A]ll disagreement as to questions of morals is attributed to ignorance or misunderstanding.

The influence of intellectual considerations upon moral judgments is certainly immense. We shall find that the evolution of the moral consciousness to a large extent consists in its development from the unreflecting to the reflecting, from the unenlightened to the enlightened. All higher emotions are determined by cognitions, they arise from "the presentation of determinate objective conditions"; and moral enlightenment implies a true and comprehensive presentation of those objective conditions by which the moral emotions, according to their very nature, are determined. Morality may thus in a much higher degree than, for instance, beauty be a subject of instruction and of profitable discussion, in which persuasion is carried by the representation of existing data. But although in this way many differences may be accorded, there are points in which unanimity cannot be reached even by the most accurate presentation of facts or the subtlest process of reasoning.

Whilst certain phenomena will almost of necessity arouse similar moral emotions in every mind which perceives them clearly, there are others with which the case is different. The *emotional constitution of man* does not present the same uniformity as the human intellect. Certain cognitions inspire fear in nearly every breast; but there are brave men and cowards in the world, independently of the accuracy with which they realise impending danger. Some cases of suffering can hardly fail to awaken compassion in the most pitiless heart; but the sympathetic dispositions of men vary greatly, both in regard to the beings with whose sufferings they are ready to sympathise, and with reference to the intensity of the emotion. The same holds good for the moral emotions. The existing diversity of opinion as to the rights of different classes of men, and of the lower animals, which springs from emotional differences, may no doubt be modified by a clearer insight into certain facts, but no perfect agreement can be expected as long as the conditions under which the emotional dispositions are formed remain unchanged. Whilst an enlightened mind *must* recognise the complete or relative irresponsibility of an animal, a child, or a mad-man, and *must* be influenced in its moral judgment by the motives of an act—no intellectual enlightenment, no scrutiny of facts, can decide how far the interests of the lower animals should be regarded when conflicting with those of men, or how far a person is bound, or allowed, to promote the welfare of his nation, or his own welfare, at the cost of that of other nations or other individuals. Professor Sidgwick's well-known moral axiom, "I ought not to prefer my own lesser good to the greater good of another," would, if explained to a Fuegian or a Hottentot, be regarded by him, not as self-evident, but as simply absurd; nor can it claim general acceptance even among ourselves. Who is that "Another" to whose greater good I ought not prefer my own lesser good? A fellow-countryman, a savage, a criminal, a bird, a fish—all without distinction? It will, perhaps, be argued that on this, and on all other points of morals, there would be general agreement, if only the moral consciousness of men were sufficiently developed. But then, when speaking of a "sufficiently developed" moral consciousness (beyond insistence upon a full insight into the governing facts of each case), we practically mean nothing else than agreement with our own moral convictions. The expression is faulty and deceptive, because, if intended to mean anything more, it presupposes an objectivity of the moral judgments which they do not possess, and at the same time seems to be proving what it presupposes. We may speak of an intellect as sufficiently developed to grasp a certain truth, because truth is objective; but it is not proved to be objective by the fact that it is recognised as true by a "sufficiently developed" intellect. The objectivity of truth lies in the recognition of facts as true by all who understand them *fully*, whilst the appeal to a *sufficient* knowledge assumes their objectivity. To the verdict of a perfect intellect, that is, an intellect which knows everything existing, all would submit; but we can form no idea of a moral consciousness which could lay claim to a similar authority ....

The presumed objectivity of moral judgments thus being a chimera, there can be no moral truth in the sense in which this term is generally understood. The ultimate reason for this is, that the moral concepts are based upon emotions, and that the contents of an emotion fall entirely outside the category of truth.

Review and Discussion Questions

1. What is the difference Westermarck sees between how people commonly think about moral issues and how a conscientious and intelligent judge approaches a moral question?
2. What explains the widespread phenomenon of moral disagreement, if not ignorance and misunderstanding?
3. Westermarck says that, in general, "higher emotions are determined by cognitions." Do you agree?
4. Do you share Westermarck's conclusion that much of morality rests on people's emotional constitutions? What else might it rest on? Explain your answer.

READING: TRYING OUT ONE'S NEW SWORD

MARY MIDGLEY[*]

Moral isolationism, according to Mary Midgley, is the familiar position that respect and tolerance demand that members of one culture should not criticize other

---

[*] Excerpted from pp. 69–75 in *Heart and Mind* by Mary Midgley. Copyright © 1981. Reprinted by permission of David Higham Associates Ltd.

cultures. Rejecting that position, she argues that it is little more than an internally inconsistent version of "immoralism." Nor, she claims, does it accurately describe the ways in which cultures are formed and changed. Using an ancient samurai custom as an example, she suggests various ways in which cultures can, in fact, be criticized. Mary Midgley is a British moral philosopher and taught philosophy at the University of Newcastle-upon-Tyne for twenty years; now retired, she spends much of her time writing about philosophy and culture.

All of us are, more or less, in trouble today about trying to understand cultures strange to us. We hear constantly of alien customs. We see changes in our lifetime which would have astonished our parents. I want to discuss here one very short way of dealing with this difficulty, a drastic way which many people now theoretically favor. It consists in simply denying that we can ever understand any culture except our own well enough to make judgments about it. Those who recommend this hold that the world is sharply divided into separate societies, sealed units, each with its own system of thought. They feel that the respect and tolerance due from one system to another forbids us ever to take up a critical position to any other culture. Moral judgment, they suggest, is a kind of coinage valid only in its country of origin.

I shall call this position "moral isolationism." I shall suggest that it is certainly not forced upon us, and indeed that it makes no sense at all. People usually take it up because they think it is a respectful attitude to other cultures. In fact, however, it is not respectful. Nobody can respect what is entirely unintelligible to them. To respect someone, we have to know enough about him to make a *favorable* judgment, however general and tentative. And we do understand people in other cultures to this extent. Otherwise a great mass of our most valuable thinking would be paralyzed.

To show this, I shall take a remote example, because we shall probably find it easier to think calmly about it than we should with a contemporary one, such as female circumcision in Africa or the Chinese Cultural Revolution. The principles involved will still be the same. My example is this. There is, it seems, a verb in classical Japanese which means "to try out one's new sword on a chance wayfarer." (The word is *tsujigiri*, literally "crossroads-cut.") A samurai sword had to be tried out because, if it was to work properly, it had to slice through someone at a single blow, from the shoulder to the opposite flank. Otherwise, the warrior bungled his stroke. This could injure his honor, offend his ancestors, and even let down his emperor. So tests were needed, and wayfarers had to be expended. Any wayfarer would do—provided, of course, that he was not another samurai. Scientists will recognize a familiar problem about the rights of experimental subjects.

Now, when we hear of a custom like this, we may well reflect that we simply do not understand it and therefore are not qualified to criticize it at all, because we are not members of that culture. But we are not members of any other culture either, except our own. So we extend the principle to cover all extraneous cultures, and we seem therefore to be moral isolationists. But this is, as we shall see, an impossible position. Let us ask what it would involve.

We must ask first: Does the isolating barrier work both ways? Are people in other cultures equally unable to criticize us? This question struck me sharply when I read a remark in *The Guardian* by an anthropologist about a South

American Indian who had been taken into a Brazilian town for an operation, which saved his life. When he came back to his village, he made several highly critical remarks about the white Brazilians' way of life. They may very well have been justified. But the interesting point was that the anthropologist called these remarks "a damning indictment of Western civilization." Now the Indian had been in that town about two weeks. Was he in a position to deliver a damning indictment? Would we ourselves be qualified to deliver such an indictment on the samurai, provided we could spend two weeks in ancient Japan? What do we really think about this?

My own impression is that we believe that outsiders can, in principle, deliver perfectly good indictments—only it usually takes more than two weeks to make them damning. Understanding has degrees. It is not a slapdash yes-or-no matter. Intelligent outsiders can progress in it and in some ways will be at an advantage over the locals. But if this is so, it must clearly apply to ourselves as much as anybody else.

Our next question is this: Does the isolating barrier between cultures block praise as well as blame? If I want to say that the samurai culture has many virtues, or to praise the South American Indians, am I prevented from doing *that* by my outside status? Now, we certainly do need to praise other societies in this way. But it is hardly possible that we could praise them effectively if we could not, in principle, criticize them. Our praise would be worthless if it rested on definite grounds, if it did not flow from some understanding. Certainly we may need to praise things which we do not *fully* understand. We say "there's something very good here, but I can't quite make out what it is yet." This happens when we want to learn from strangers. And we can learn from strangers. But to do this we have to distinguish between those strangers who are worth learning from and those who are not. Can we then judge which is which?

This brings us to our third question: What is involved in judging? Now plainly there is no question here of sitting on a bench in a red robe and sentencing people. Judging simply means forming an opinion and expressing it if it is called for. Is there anything wrong about this? Naturally, we ought to avoid forming—and expressing—*crude* opinions, like that of a simple-minded missionary, who might dismiss the whole samurai culture as entirely bad, because non-Christian. But this is a different objection. The trouble with crude opinions is that they are crude, whoever forms them, not that they are formed by the wrong people. Anthropologists, after all, are outsiders quite as much as missionaries. Moral isolationism forbids us to form *any* opinions on these matters. Its ground for doing so is that we don't understand them. But there is much that we don't understand in our own culture too. This brings us to our last question: If we can't judge other cultures, can we really judge our own? Our efforts to do so will be much damaged if we are really deprived of our opinions about other societies, because these provide the range of comparison, the spectrum of alternatives against which we set what we want to understand. We would have to stop using the mirror which anthropology so helpfully holds up to us.

In short, moral isolationism would lay down a general ban on moral reasoning. Essentially, this is the program of immoralism, and it carries a distressing logical difficulty. Immoralists like Nietzsche are actually just a rather specialized sect of moralists. They can no more afford to put moralizing out of business than smugglers can afford to abolish customs regulations. The power of moral judgment is, in fact, not a luxury, not a perverse indulgence of the self-righteous. It is a necessity. When we judge something to be bad or good, better or worse than something else, we are taking it as an example to aim at or avoid. Without opinions of this sort, we would have no framework of comparison for our own policy, no chance of profiting by other people's insights or mistakes. In this vacuum, we could form no judgments on our own actions.

Now it would be odd if *Homo sapiens* had really got himself into a position as bad as this—a position where his main evolutionary asset, his brain, was so little use to him. None of us is going to accept this skeptical diagnosis. We cannot do so, because our involvement in moral isolationism does not flow from apathy but from a rather acute concern about human hypocrisy and other forms of wickedness. But we polarize that concern around a few selected moral truths. We are rightly angry with those who despise, oppress, or steamroll other cultures. We think that doing these things is actually *wrong*. But this is itself a moral judgment. We could not condemn oppression and insolence if we thought that all our condemnations were just a trivial local quirk of our own culture. We could still less do it if we tried to stop judging altogether.

Real moral skepticism, in fact, could lead only to inaction, to our losing all interest in moral questions, most of all in those which concern other societies. When we discuss these things, it becomes instantly clear how far we are from doing this. Suppose, for instance, that I criticize the bisecting samurai, that I say his behavior is brutal. What will usually happen next is that someone will protest, will say that I have no right to make criticisms like that of another culture. But it is most unlikely that he will use this move to end the discussion of the subject. Instead, he will justify the samurai. He will try to fill in the background, to make me understand the custom, by explaining the exalted ideals of discipline and devotion which produced it. He will probably talk of the lower value which the ancient Japanese placed on individual life generally. He may well suggest that this is a healthier attitude than our own obsession with security. He may add, too, that the wayfarers did not seriously mind being bisected, that in principle they accepted the whole arrangement.

Now an objector who talks like this is implying that it *is* possible to understand alien customs. That is just what he is trying to make me do. And he implies, too, that if I do succeed in understanding them, I shall do something better than giving up judging them. He expects me to change my present judgment to a truer one—namely, one that is favorable. And the standards I must use to do this cannot just be samurai standards. They have to be ones current in my own culture. Ideals like discipline and devotion will not move anybody unless he himself accepts them. As it happens, neither discipline nor devotion is very popular in the West at present. Anyone who appeals to them may well have to do some more arguing to make *them* acceptable before he can use them to explain the samurai. But if he does succeed here, he will have persuaded us not just that there was something to be said for them in ancient Japan but that there would be here as well.

Isolating barriers simply cannot arise here. If we accept something as a serious moral truth about one culture, we can't refuse to apply it—in however different an outward form—to other cultures as well, wherever circumstances admit it. If we refuse to do this, we just are not taking the other culture seriously. This becomes clear if we look at the last argument used by my objector—that of justification by consent of the victim. It is suggested that sudden bisection is quite in order, *provided* that it takes place between consenting adults. I cannot now discuss how conclusive this justification is. What I am pointing out is simply that it can only work if we believe that *consent* can make such a transaction respectable—and this is a thoroughly modern and Western idea. It would probably never occur to a samurai; if it did, it would surprise him very much. It is *our* standard. In applying it, too, we are likely to make another typically Western demand. We shall ask for good factual evidence that the wayfarers actually do have this rather surprising taste—that they are really willing to be bisected. In applying Western standards in this way, we are not being confused or irrelevant. We are asking the questions which arise *from where we stand*, questions which we can see the sense of. We do this because asking questions which you can't see the sense of is humbug. Certainly we can extend our questioning by imaginative effort. We can come to understand other societies better. By doing so, we may make their questions our own or we may see that they are really forms of the questions which we are asking already. This is not impossible. It is just very hard work. The obstacles which often prevent it are simply those of ordinary ignorance, laziness, and prejudice.

If there were really an isolating barrier, of course, our own culture could never have been formed. It is no sealed box but a fertile jungle of different influences—Greek, Jewish, Roman, Norse, Celtic, and so forth, into which further influences are still pouring—American, Indian, Japanese, Jamaican, you name it. The moral isolationist's picture of separate, unmixable cultures is quite unreal. People who talk about British history usually stress the value of this fertilizing mix, no doubt rightly. But this is not just an odd fact about Britain. Except for the very smallest and most remote, all cultures are formed out of many streams. All have the problem of digesting and assimilating things which, at the start, they do not understand. All have the choice of learning something from this challenge, or, alternatively, of refusing to learn and fighting it mindlessly instead.

This universal predicament has been obscured by the fact that anthropologists used to concentrate largely on very small and remote cultures, which did not seem to have this problem. These tiny societies, which had often forgotten their own history, made neat, self-contained subjects for study. No doubt it was valuable to emphasize their remoteness, their extreme strangeness, their independence of our cultural tradition. This emphasis was, I think, the root of moral isolationism. But, as the tribal studies themselves showed, even there the anthropologists were able to interpret what they saw and make judgments—often favorable—about the tribesmen. And the tribesmen, too, were quite equal to making judgments about the anthropologists—and about the tourists and Coca-Cola salesmen who followed them. Both sets of judgments, no doubt, were somewhat hasty; both have been refined in the light of further experience. A similar transaction between us and the samurai might take even longer. But that is no reason at all for deeming it impossible. Morally as well as physically, there is only one world, and we all have to live in it.

Review and Discussion Questions

1 What is moral isolationism?
2 Why does Midgley reject moral isolationism?
3 What does respecting people require, according to Midgley? Do you agree?
4 Explain what Midgley means in saying there is only one world. Do you agree with her?
5 Different cultures could be compared in many ways, including their capacity to promote people's well-being, material prosperity, justice, goodness, knowledge, and others. How should they be compared from a moral point of view?

READING: MORALITY IS BASED ON SENTIMENT

DAVID HUME[*]

David Hume (1711–1776) was a towering figure of the Scottish Enlightenment. He lived in Edinburgh, where he wrote on a wide array of subjects, including epistemology, history, religion, science, ethics, and politics. Hume attended Edinburgh University until he was about fifteen. By the age of twenty-eight, he had already published his massive critical study of knowledge and morality titled *A Treatise of Human Nature*. Deeply disappointed by the book's reception, which, he wrote, "fell dead born from the press," Hume rewrote it as *An Enquiry Concerning Human Understanding* (1748) and *An Enquiry Concerning the Principles of Morals* (1751). He subsequently published *Political Discourses* (1752) and *The History of England* (1754), which won him wide acclaim.

Hume was an amiable, moderate man whose company was widely sought. His philosophy, however, was radically critical. Taking his lead from modern science, especially Newton, Hume sought to use the tools of scientific observation and philosophical argument together to understand human knowledge, religion, morality, and politics. As an empiricist, Hume believed that things that can be present to the mind (which he termed *perceptions*) are either impressions or ideas. Impressions occur whenever we feel an emotion or have an image of an external object; ideas are present whenever we reflect on impressions we have had. Ideas are therefore weaker than impressions, and all of our ideas are derived from sense impressions. Mathematics concerns itself merely with the relationships among our ideas.

Hume's key claim, then, is that reasoning can never motivate people, since it involves either the pure relations of ideas (mathematics) or the causes and effects of objects on other objects, including bodies. What does motivate us then must be our own feelings, which include our own pleasures and pains, of course, but also the sentiments we feel when thinking about the experiences of others. Values and morality are therefore sharply distinct from facts about the world or about mathematical ideas. Moral condemnation and approval arise from feelings alone, which are uniquely capable of motivating us to act. The selection discusses those

---

[*] From David Hume, *A Treatise of Human Nature* (1739–1740) and *An Enquiry Concerning the Principles of Morals* (1751).

issues about human motivation and concludes with a brief account of benevolence and its role in morality.

1 Reason Subordinate to Emotion

Nothing is more usual in philosophy, and even in common life, than to talk of the combat of passion and reason, to give the preference to reason, and assert that men are only so far virtuous as they conform themselves to its dictates. Every rational creature, it is said, is obliged to regulate his actions by reason; and if any other motive or principle challenge the direction of his conduct, he ought to oppose it, till it be entirely subdued, or at least brought to a conformity with that superior principle. On this method of thinking the greatest part of moral philosophy, ancient and modern, seems to be founded. ... [However,] I shall endeavor to prove *first*, that reason alone can never be a motive to any action of the will; and *secondly*, that it can never oppose passion in the direction of the will.

The understanding exerts itself after two different ways, as it judges from demonstration or probability; as it regards the abstract relations of our [mathematical] ideas, or those relations of objects, of which experience only gives us information. I believe it scarce will be asserted, and the first species of reasoning alone is ever the cause of any action. As its proper province is the world of ideas, and as the will always places us in that of realities, demonstration and volition seem, upon that account, to be totally removed from each other. Mathematics, indeed, are useful in all mechanical operations, and arithmetic in almost every art and profession: but it is not of themselves they have any influence. Mechanics are the art of regulating the motions of bodies *to some designed end or purpose*; and the reason why we employ arithmetic in fixing the proportions of numbers, is only that we may discover the proportions of their influence and operation. A merchant is desirous of knowing the sum total of his accounts with any person: why? but that he may learn what sum will have the same *effects* in paying his debt, and going to market, as all the particular articles taken together. Abstract or demonstrative reasoning, therefore, never influences any of our actions, but only as it directs our judgment concerning causes and effects; which leads us to the second operation of the understanding.

It is obvious that when we have the prospect of pain or pleasure from any object, we feel a consequent emotion of aversion or propensity, and are carried to avoid or embrace what will give us this uneasiness or satisfaction. It is also obvious that this emotion rests not here, but making us cast our view on every side, comprehends whatever objects are connected with its original one by the relation of cause and effect. Here then reasoning takes place to discover this relation; and according as our reasoning varies, our actions receive a subsequent variation. But it is evident in this case, that the impulse arises not from reason, but is only directed by it. It is from the prospect of pain or pleasure that the aversion or propensity arises towards any object: and these emotions extend themselves to the causes and effects of that object, as they are pointed out to us by reason and experience. It can never in the least concern us to know that such objects are causes, and such others effects, if both the causes and effects be indifferent to us. Where the objects themselves do not affect us, their connection can never give them any influence; and it is plain, that as reason is nothing but the discovery of this connection, it cannot be by its means that the objects are able to affect us.

Since reason alone can never produce any action, or give rise to volition, I infer, that the same faculty is as incapable of preventing volition, or of disputing the preference with any passion or emotion. This consequence is necessary ....

A passion is an original existence, or, if you will, modification of existence, and contains not any representative quality, which renders it a copy of any other existence or modification. When I am angry, I am actually possessed with the passion, and in that emotion have no more a reference to any other object, than when I am thirsty, or sick, or more than five foot high. It is impossible, therefore, that this passion can be opposed by, or be contradictory to truth and reason; since this contradiction consists in the disagreement of ideas, considered as copies, with those objects, which they represent ....

It is certain, there are certain calm desires and tendencies, which, although they be real passions, produce little emotion in the mind, and are more known by their effects than by the immediate feeling or sensation. These desires are of two kinds; either certain instincts originally implanted in our natures, such as benevolence and resentment, the love of life, and kindness to children; or the general appetite to good, and aversion to evil, considered merely as such. When any of these passions are calm, and cause no disorder in the soul, they are very readily taken for the determinations for reason, and are supposed to proceed from the same faculty, with that, which judges of truth and falsehood. Their nature and principles have been supposed the same, because their sensations are not evidently different.

Beside these calm passions, which often determine the will, there are certain violent emotions of the same kind, which have likewise a great influence on that faculty. When I receive any injury from another, I often feel a violent passion of resentment, which makes me desire his evil and punishment, independent of all considerations of pleasure and advantage to myself. When I am immediately threatened with any grievous ill, my fears, apprehensions, and aversions rise to a great height, and produce a sensible emotion.

The common error of metaphysicians has lain in ascribing the direction of the will entirely to one of these principles, and supposing the other to have no influence. Men often act knowingly against their interest: For which reason the view of the greatest possible good does not always influence them. Men often counteract a violent passion in prosecution of their interests and designs: It is not therefore the present uneasiness alone, which determines them. In general we may observe, that both these principles operate on the will; and where they are contrary, that either of them prevails, according to the *general* character or *present* disposition of the person. What we call strength of mind, implies the prevalence of the calm passions above the violent; although we may easily observe, there is no man so constantly possessed of this virtue, as never on any occasion to yield to the solicitations of passion and desire ....

According to [my] principle, which is so obvious and natural, it is only in two senses, that any affection can be called unreasonable. First, when a passion, such as hope or fear, grief or joy, despair or security, is founded on the supposition of the existence of objects, which really do not exist. Secondly, when in exerting any passion in action, we choose means insufficient for the designed end, and deceive ourselves in our judgment of causes and effects. Where a passion is neither founded on false suppositions, nor chooses means insufficient for the end, the understanding can neither justify nor condemn it. It is not contrary to reason to prefer the destruction of the whole world to the scratching of my finger. It is not contrary to reason for me to choose my total ruin to prevent the least uneasiness of an Indian or person wholly unknown to me. It is as little contrary to reason to prefer even my own acknowledged lesser good to my greater, and have a more ardent affection for the former than the latter. A trivial good may, from certain circumstances, produce a desire superior to what arises from the greatest and most valuable enjoyment; nor is there any thing more extraordinary in this, than in mechanics to see one pound weight raise up a hundred by the advantage of its situation. In short, a passion must be accompanied with some false judgment, in order to its being unreasonable; and even then it is not the passion, properly speaking, which is unreasonable, but the judgment.

The consequences are evident. Since a passion can never, in any sense, be called unreasonable, but when founded on a false supposition, or when it chooses means insufficient for the designed end, it is impossible, that reason and passion can ever oppose each other, or dispute for the government of the will and actions. The moment we perceive the falsehood of any supposition, or the insufficiency of any means, our passions yield to our reason without any opposition. I may desire any fruit as of an excellent relish; but whenever you convince me of my mistake, my longing ceases. I may will the performance of certain actions as means of obtaining any desired good; but as my willing of these actions is only secondary, and founded on the supposition, that they are causes of the proposed effect; as soon as I discover the falsehood of that supposition, they must become indifferent to me ....

2 Moral Distinctions Not Derived from Reason

It would be tedious to repeat all the arguments, by which I have proved, that reason is perfectly inert, and can never either prevent or produce any action or affection. It will be easy to recollect what has been said upon that subject. I shall only recall on this occasion one of these arguments, which I shall endeavor to render still more conclusive, and more applicable to the present subject.

Reason is the discovery of truth or falsehood. Truth or falsehood consists in an agreement or disagreement either to the *real* relations of ideas, or to *real* existence and matter of fact. Whatever, therefore, is not susceptible of this agreement or disagreement, is incapable of being true or false, and can never be an object of our reason. Now it is evident our passions, volitions, and actions, are not susceptible of any such agreement or disagreement; being original facts and realities, complete in themselves, and implying no reference to other passions, volitions, and actions. It is impossible, therefore, they can be pronounced either true or false, and be either contrary or conformable to reason.

This argument is of double advantage to our present purpose. For it proves *directly*, that actions do not derive their merit from a conformity to reason, nor their blame from a contrariety to it; and it proves the same truth more *indirectly*, by showing us, that as reason can never immediately prevent or produce any action by contradicting or approving of it, it cannot be the source of moral good and evil, which are found to have that influence. Actions may be laudable or blameable; but they cannot be reasonable or unreasonable: laudable or blameable, therefore, are not the same with reasonable or unreasonable. The merit and demerit of actions frequently contradict, and sometimes control our natural propensities. But reason has no such influence. Moral distinctions, therefore, are not the offspring of reason. Reason is wholly inactive, and can never be the source of so active a principle as conscience, or a sense of morals ....

Take any action allowed to be vicious: wilful murder, for instance. Examine it in all lights, and see if you can find that matter of fact, or real existence, which you call *vice*. In whichever way you take it, you find only certain passions, motives, volitions and thoughts. There is no other matter of fact in the case. The vice entirely escapes you, as long as you consider the object. You never can find it, till you turn your reflection into your own breast, and find a sentiment of disapprobation, which arises in you, towards this action. Here is a matter of fact; but it is the object of feeling, not of reason. It lies in yourself, not in the object. So that when you pronounce any action or character to be vicious, you mean nothing, but that from the constitution of your nature you have a feeling or sentiment of blame from the contemplation of it. Vice and virtue, therefore, may be compared to sounds, colours, heat and cold, which, according to modern philosophy, are not qualities in objects, but perceptions in the mind: and this discovery in morals, like that other in physics, is to be regarded as a considerable advancement of the speculative sciences; though, like that too, it has little or no influence on practice. Nothing can be more real, or concern us more, than our own sentiments of pleasure and uneasiness; and if these be favourable to virtue, and unfavourable to vice, no more can be requisite to the regulation of our conduct and behaviour.

I cannot forbear adding to these reasonings an observation, which may, perhaps, be found of some importance. In every system of morality, which I have hitherto met with, I have always remarked, that the author proceeds for some time in the ordinary way of reasoning, and establishes the being of a God, or makes observations concerning human affairs; when of a sudden I am surprised to find, that instead of the usual copulations of propositions, *is*, and *is not*, I meet with no proposition that is not connected with an *ought*, or an *ought not*. This change is imperceptible; but is, however, of the last consequence. For as this *ought*, or *ought not*, expresses some new relation or affirmation, it is necessary that it should be observed and explained; and at the same time that a reason should be given, for what seems altogether inconceivable, how this new relation can be a deduction from others, which are entirely different from it. But as authors do not commonly use this precaution, I shall presume to recommend it to the readers; and am persuaded, that this small attention would subvert all the vulgar systems of morality, and let us see, that the distinction of vice and virtue is not founded merely on the relations of objects, nor is perceived by reason.

3 Why Utility Pleases

... It has often been asserted, that, as every man has a strong connexion with society, and perceives the impossibility of his solitary subsistence, he becomes, on that account, favourable to all those habits or principles, which promote order in society, and insure to him the quiet possession of so inestimable a blessing. As much as we value our own happiness and welfare, as much must we applaud the practice of justice and humanity, by which alone the social confederacy can be maintained, and every man reap the fruits of mutual protection and assistance.

This deduction of morals from self-love, or a regard to private interest, is an obvious thought. ... [Yet] the voice of nature and experience seems plainly to oppose the selfish theory.

We frequently bestow praise on virtuous actions, performed in very distant ages and remote countries; where the utmost subtilty of imagination would not discover any appearance of self-interest, or find any connexion of our present happiness and security with events so widely separated from us.

A generous, a brave, a noble deed, performed by an adversary, commands our approbation; while in its consequences it may be acknowledged prejudicial to our particular interest ....

Usefulness is agreeable, and engages our approbation. This is a matter of fact, confirmed by daily observation. But, useful? For what? For somebody's interest, surely. Whose interest then? Not our own only: For our approbation frequently extends farther. It must, therefore, be the interest of those, who are served by the character of action approved of; and these we may conclude, however remote, are not totally indifferent to us ....

The human countenance, says Horace, borrows smiles or tears from the human countenance. Reduce a person to solitude, and he loses all enjoyment, except either of the sensual or speculative kind; and that because the movements of his heart are not forwarded by correspondent movements in his fellow-creatures. The signs of sorrow and mourning, though arbitrary, affect us with melancholy; but the natural symptoms, tears and cries and groans, never fail to infuse compassion and uneasiness. And if the effects of misery touch us in so lively a manner; can we be supposed altogether insensible or indifferent towards its causes; when a malicious or treacherous character and behaviour are presented to us? ....

In general, it is certain, that, wherever we go, whatever we reflect on or converse about, everything still presents us with the view of human happiness or misery, and excites in our breast a sympathetic movement of pleasure or uneasiness. In our serious occupations, in our careless amusements, this principle still exerts its active energy. ... We surely take into consideration the happiness and misery of others, in weighing the several motives of action, and incline to the former, where no private regards draw us to seek our own promotion or advantage by the injury of our fellow-creatures. And if the principles of humanity are capable, in many instances, of influencing our actions, they must, at all times, have *some* authority over our sentiments, and give us a general approbation of what is useful to society, and blame of what is dangerous or pernicious. The degrees of these sentiments may be the subject of controversy; but the reality of their existence, one should think, must be admitted in every theory or system. ... Sympathy, we shall allow, is much fainter than our concern for ourselves, and sympathy with persons remote from us much fainter than that with persons near and contiguous; but for this very reason it is necessary for us, in our calm judgments and discourse concerning the characters of men, to neglect all these differences, and render our sentiments more public and social. Besides, that we ourselves often change our situation in this particular, we every day meet with persons who are in a situation different from us, and who could never converse with us were we to remain constantly in that position and point of view, which is peculiar to ourselves. The intercourse of sentiments, therefore, in society and conversation, makes us form some general unalterable standard, by which we may approve or disapprove of characters and manners ....

It is sufficient for our present purpose, if it be allowed, what surely, without the greatest absurdity cannot be disputed, that there is some benevolence, however small, infused into our bosom; some spark of friendship for human kind; some particle of the dove kneaded into our frame, along with the elements of the wolf and serpent. Let these generous sentiments be supposed ever so weak; let them be insufficient to move even a hand or finger of our body, they must still direct the determinations of our mind, and where everything else is equal, produce a cool preference of what is useful and serviceable to mankind, above what is pernicious and dangerous. A *moral distinction*, therefore, immediately arises; a general sentiment of blame and approbation; a tendency, however faint, to the objects of the one, and a proportionable aversion to those of the other ....

Avarice, ambition, vanity, and all passions vulgarly, though improperly, comprised under the denomination of *self-love*, are here excluded from our theory concerning the origin of morals, not because they are too weak, but because they have not a proper direction for that purpose. The notion of morals implies some sentiment common to all mankind, which recommends the same object to general approbation, and makes every man, or most men, agree in the same opinion or decision concerning it. It also implies some sentiment, so universal and comprehensive as to extend to all mankind, and render the actions and conduct, even of the persons the most remote, an object of applause or censure, according as they agree or disagree with that rule of right which is established ....

When a man denominates another his *enemy*, his *rival*, his *antagonist*, his *adversary*, he is understood to speak the language of self-love, and to express sentiments, peculiar to himself, and arising from his particular circumstances and situation. But when he bestows on any man the [moral] epithets of *vicious* or *odious* or *depraved*, he then speaks another language and expresses sentiments, in which he expects all his audience to concur with him. He must here, therefore, depart from his private and particular situation, and must choose a point of view, common to him with others; he must move some universal principle of the human frame, and touch a string to which all mankind have an accord and symphony. If he mean, therefore, to express that this man possesses qualities, whose tendency is pernicious to society, he has chosen this common point of view, and has touched the principle of humanity, in which every man, in some degree, concurs. While the human heart is compounded of the same elements as at present, it will never be wholly indifferent to public good, nor entirely unaffected with the tendency of characters and manners. And though this affection of humanity may not generally be esteemed so strong as vanity or ambition, yet, being common to all men, it can alone be the foundation of morals, or of any general system of blame or praise.

Review and Discussion Questions

1. Hume says it is common to think of reason and passion or sentiments as in conflict. Why does he think passion cannot conflict with abstract relations of ideas?
2. Why does Hume think that the impulse to avoid a pain arises not from reason but from passion?
3. In what sense does Hume mean that a passion can never be called "unreasonable"?
4. What is the difference between "calm desires and tendencies" and "violent" ones?
5. In what sense does Hume think morality rests not on self-love but on benevolence?
6. In *The Theory of Moral Sentiments*, Adam Smith writes that "We can never survey our own sentiments and motives, we can never form any judgment concerning them, unless we remove ourselves, as it were, from our own natural station, and endeavour to view them as at a certain distance from us. But we can do this in no other way than by endeavouring to view them with the eyes of other people, or as other people are likely to view them. Whatever judgment we can form concerning them, accordingly, must always bear some secret reference, either to what are, or to what, upon a certain condition, would be, or to what, we imagine, ought to be the judgment of others. We endeavour to examine our *own* conduct, as we imagine any other fair and impartial spectator would examine it" (Whitefish, MT: Kessinger Publishing, 2010, p. 49). Discuss that idea in light of Hume's essay.

READING: MORALITY AND NORMATIVITY

MICHAEL J. PERRY[*]

In this essay, Michael Perry argues that there are many "moralities" and he focuses his attention on what he considers the distinctive morality of human rights. He provides a religious grounding that he believes is "ecumenical as among the three great monotheistic faiths," and he doubts that any secular grounding can provide conclusive reasons to believe in and live by the morality of human rights. Michael J. Perry is the Robert W. Woodruff Professor of Law at Emory University.

> The masses blink and say: "We are all equal. Man is but man, before God—we are all equal." Before God! But now this God has died.
> Friedrich Nietzsche[1]

> Few contemporary moral philosophers ... have really joined battle with Nietzsche about morality. By and large we have just gone on taking moral judgements for granted as if nothing had happened. We, the philosopher watchdogs, have mostly failed to bark.
> Philippa Foot[2]

---

[*] Perry, Michael, J. "Morality and Normativity," *Legal Theory* 13(3–4) (2007): 211–255. Reprinted with permission.

I Preliminaries

As we all know, there is not just one morality in the world; there are many. By a "morality," I mean a claim or set of claims to the effect that human beings, either some or all, should live a certain sort of life—"should" in the sense of "have conclusive reason to."

The morality Adolph Hitler espoused is radically different from the morality Mother Theresa espoused; nonetheless, each is a morality. "Hitler's 'morality' is not a morality," you reply, "because it is, to put it mildly, false. There is only one true morality, and Hitler's—least of all Hitler's—is not it!" To say that there are many moralities, however, is to say nothing about whether a particular morality—or indeed any morality—is true. (Moral skepticism, properly understood, is the position not that morality is false—again, there is not just one morality—but that every morality is false, that every claim or set of claims to the effect that human beings, some or all, have conclusive reason to live a certain sort of life is false.) There are many moralities—and the morality Hitler espoused is one of them ....

Of course, just as one can acknowledge that there are many moralities and reject every one of them as false, one can acknowledge that there are many moralities and affirm a particular morality as true—affirm as true, that is, the claim that one should live, that one has conclusive reason to live, the sort of life the morality claims one should live.

A morality may purport to be true for all human beings by claiming that all human beings have conclusive reason to live the sort of life it claims all human beings should live. Or a morality may purport to be true only for some human beings. Either way, a morality may be false in one sense but partly true in another: some, but only some, of the human beings for whom the morality purports to be true may have conclusive reason to live the sort of life the morality claims they should live. Conceivably, two (or more) moralities may both be true or both be partly true in this sense: one morality may be true for those or for some of those for whom it purports to be true, and another morality may be true for those or for some of those for whom it purports to be true ....

The "ground-of-normativity" question—as I call it—can be asked about any morality; to ask it about a particular morality is simply to ask whether (and for whom) the morality is true and, if so, why in virtue of what—it is true. Again, to say that a particular morality is true (for one) is to say that one should live—that one has conclusive reason to live—the sort of life the morality claims one should live; put another way, it is to say that one has conclusive reason to be(come) the sort of person who lives the sort of life the morality claims one should live. So to ask whether a particular morality is true is to ask what conclusive reason one has, if any, to live the sort of life the morality in question claims one should live. To ask the ground-of-normativity question about a particular morality is to ask what grounds the "should" in the morality's claim that one should live a certain sort of life; it is to ask why—in virtue of what—one should live that sort of life.

In the next section of this essay, I elaborate a particular—and particularly important—morality that I call the morality of human rights (because, as explained, it is the principal articulated morality that underlies the law of human rights). In Section III, I ask the ground-of-normativity question about the morality of human rights and then elaborate a religious response .... In Section IV [I explain] why one might be skeptical that there is a plausible secular response to the question (i.e., to the question asked about the morality of human rights). ... Finally, in Section VII I ask what difference it makes if there is no plausible secular response to the ground-of-normativity question.

II The Morality of Human Rights

Although it is only one morality among many, the morality of human rights has become the dominant morality of our time; indeed, unlike any morality before it, the morality of human rights has become a truly global morality. (Relatedly, the language of human rights has become the moral *lingua franca*.) Nonetheless, the morality of human rights is not well understood.

What does the morality of human rights hold? ....

According to the International Bill of Rights ... and also according to the constitutions of many liberal democracies, the morality of human rights consists of a twofold claim. The first part of the claim is that *each and every (born) human being has equal inherent dignity* ....

The second part of the claim is that *the inherent dignity of human beings has a normative force for us, in this sense: we should—every one of us—live our lives in accord with the fact that every human being has inherent dignity; that is, we should respect—we have conclusive reason to respect—the inherent dignity of every human being.*

There is another way to state the twofold claim that is the morality of human rights: Every human being has inherent dignity *and* is *"inviolable"*: not-to-be-violated. According to the morality of human rights, one can violate a human being either explicitly or implicitly. One violates a human being *explicitly* if one explicitly denies that she (or he) has inherent dignity.

(The Nazis explicitly denied that the Jews had inherent dignity.)[3] One violates a human being *implicitly* if one treats her as if she lacks inherent dignity, either by doing to her what one would not do to her or refusing to do for her what one would not refuse to do for her if one genuinely perceived her to have inherent dignity. (Even if the Nazis had not explicitly denied that the Jews had inherent dignity, they would have implicitly denied it: the Nazis did to the Jews what no one would have done to them who genuinely perceived the Jews to have inherent dignity.) In the context of the morality of human rights, to say that (1) every human being has inherent dignity and we should live our lives accordingly (namely, in a way that respects that dignity) is to say that (2) every human being has inherent dignity and is inviolable: not-to-be-violated in the sense of "violate" just indicated. To affirm the morality of human rights is to affirm the twofold claim that every human being has inherent dignity and is inviolable.

If it is true, why is it true—*in virtue of what* is it true—that every human being has inherent dignity and is inviolable? That the International Bill of Rights is (famously) silent on that question is not surprising, given the plurality of religious and nonreligious views that existed among those who bequeathed us the Universal Declaration and the two covenants.[4] Indeed, the claim that every human being has inherent dignity and is inviolable is deeply problematic for many secular thinkers, because the claim is difficult—perhaps to the point of impossible—to align with one of their fundamental convictions, what Bernard Williams called "Nietzsche's thought": "[T]here is not only no God, but no metaphysical order of any kind."[5]

III The Ground-of-Normativity Question: A Religious Response

> Only someone who is religious can speak seriously of the sacred, but such talk informs the thoughts of most of us whether or not we are religious, for it shapes our thoughts about the way in which human beings limit our will as does nothing else in nature. If we are not religious, we will often search for one of the inadequate expressions which are available to us to say what we hope will be a secular equivalent of it. We may say that all human beings are inestimably precious, that they are ends in themselves, that they are owed unconditional respect, that they possess inalienable rights, and, of course, that they possess inalienable dignity. In my judgment these are ways of trying to say what we feel a need to say when we are estranged from the conceptual resources we need to say it. Be that as it may: each of them is problematic and contentious. Not one of them has the simple power of the religious ways of speaking.
>
> Where does that power come from? Not, I am quite sure, from esoteric theological or philosophical elaborations of what it means for something to be sacred. It derives from the unashamedly anthropomorphic character of the claim that we are sacred because God loves us, his children.
>
> Raimond Gaita[6]

I said that the ground-of-normativity question can be asked about any morality. Let us ask it about the morality of human rights: Is the morality of human rights true (or at least partly true)? Do we (or at least some of us) have conclusive reason to live the sort of life the morality of human rights claims that we —every one of us—should live: *a life in which we strive never to violate any human being, never to treat any human being as if she lacks inherent dignity; a life in which we strive always to respect the inherent dignity of every human being?*

In this section, I elaborate an affirmative religious response—in particular, a Christian response—to the question. Of course, no one who is not a religious believer will find the response plausible; indeed, even many who are religious believers will not find the response plausible. Nonetheless, the religious (Christian) response I am about to elaborate is a[n] intelligible, coherent response to the ground-of-normativity question, a response that for many religious believers is conclusive reason to live the sort of life the morality of human rights claims they (and we) should live.

Imagine a religious believer named Sarah. Although she is a Christian, Sarah is sufficiently familiar with Judaism and Islam to know that her religious response to the ground-of-normativity question, which she is about to elaborate, is not one that just Christians (not all Christians, but many) affirm; many religious Jews and Muslims affirm it too. So, notwithstanding her Christian vocabulary and scriptural references, Sarah's religious response is ecumenical as among the three great monotheistic faiths.[7]

Sarah affirms that every human being has inherent dignity and that we should live our lives accordingly ....

Predictably, Sarah's affirmation provokes this question: Why—in virtue of what—does every human being have inherent dignity? Sarah gives a religious explanation. Speaking the words of the First Letter of John, Sarah says that "God is love." ("Whoever fails to love does not know God, because God is love." 1 John 4:8.[8] "God is love, and whoever remains in love remains in God and God in him." 1 John 4:16.) Moreover, God's act of creating and sustaining the universe is an act of love, and we human beings are the beloved children of God and sisters and brothers to one another. (As Hilary Putnam has noted, the moral image central to what Putnam calls the Jerusalem-based religions "stresse[s] equality and also fraternity, as in the metaphor of the whole human race as One Family, of all women and men as sisters and brothers.") Every human being has inherent dignity, says Sarah, in the sense that every human being is a beloved child of God and a sister/brother to every other human being.

Sarah is fully aware that she is speaking analogically, but that is the best anyone can do, she insists, in speaking about who/what God is ....

Sarah's explanation provokes a yet further question, about the ground of the normativity—of the "should"—in the claim that we should live our lives in a way that respects the inherent dignity of every human being:

I'll assume, for the sake of our discussion, that every human being has inherent dignity in the sense that every human being is a beloved child of God and a sister/brother to every other human being. So what? Why should it matter to me—to the way I live my life—that every human being has inherent dignity, that every human being is a beloved child of God and a sister/brother to me? Why should I respect—why should I want to be a person who respects—the inherent dignity of every human being?

In responding to this important question about the ground of normativity, Sarah—who "understands the authority of moral claims to be warranted not by divine dictates but by their contribution to human flourishing"[9]—states her belief that the God who loves us has created us to love one another ....

Given our created nature—given what we have been created for—the most fitting way of life for us human beings, the most deeply satisfying way of life of which we are capable, as children of God and sisters and brothers to one another, is one in which we embrace Jesus' "new" commandment, reported in John 13:34, to "love one another ... just as I have loved you."[10] ....

As it happens, Sarah embodies Jesus' extravagant counsel to "love one another just as I have loved you." She loves all human beings. Sarah loves even "the Other": she loves not only those for whom she has personal affection, or those with whom she works or has other dealings, or those among whom she lives; she loves even those who are most remote, who are unfamiliar, strange, alien, those who, because they are so distant or weak or both, will never play any concrete role, for good or ill, in Sarah's life. Sarah loves even those from whom she is most estranged and toward whom she feels most antagonistic: those whose ideologies and projects and acts she judges to be not merely morally objectionable but morally abominable. Sarah loves even her enemies; indeed, Sarah loves even those who have violated her, who have failed to respect her inherent dignity. Sarah is fond of quoting Graham Greene to her incredulous friends:

> When you visualized a man or a woman carefully, you could always begin to feel pity. ... When you saw the corners of the eyes, the shape of the mouth, how the hair grew, it was impossible to hate. Hate was just a failure of imagination.[11]

Such love—such a state of being, such an orientation in the world—is obviously an ideal. Moreover, it is for most human beings an extremely demanding ideal; for many persons it is also an implausible ideal.[12] Why should anyone embrace the ideal? Why should anyone want to be (or to become) such a person—a person who, like Sarah, loves even the Other? This is, existentially if not intellectually, the fundamental moral question for anyone: Why should I want to be the sort of person who makes the choices, who does the things, I am being told I should make and do?

And in fact, Sarah's interlocutor presses her with this question: "Why should I want to be the sort of person who, like you, loves the Other? What reason do I have to do *that*?" Because that is essentially the question about the ground of the normativity in the claim that we should live our lives in a way that respects the inherent dignity of every human being, Sarah is puzzled; she thought that she had already answered the question. Sarah patiently rehearses her answer, an answer that appeals ultimately to *one's commitment to one's own authentic well-being*:

> The most deeply satisfying way of life of which we are capable is one in which we "love one another just as I have loved you." By becoming persons who love one another, we fulfill—we perfect—our created nature and thereby achieve our truest, deepest, most enduring happiness.

It is now Sarah's turn to ask a question of her interlocutor: "What further reason could you possibly want for becoming (or remaining) the sort of person who loves the Other?"

When he was deliberating about how to live, St. Augustine asked, "What does anything matter, if it does not have to do with happiness?" His question requires explanation, because he is not advising selfishness nor the reduction of other people to utilities, and even qualification, because other things can have some weight. All the same, the answer he expects is obviously right: only a happy life matters conclusively. If I had a clear view of it, I could have no motive to decline it, I could regret nothing by accepting it, I would have nothing about which to deliberate further.[13]

A clarification may be helpful here. Does Sarah do what she does for the Other—for example, does she contribute to Bread for the World as a way of feeding the hungry—for a self-regarding reason? Does she do so, say, because it makes her happy to do so? No. Although feeding the hungry does make Sarah happy, that is not why she does it. Given the sort of person she is, the reason—the other-regarding reason—Sarah feeds the hungry is this: "The hungry are my sisters and brothers; I love them." Now, a different question: Why is Sarah committed to being the sort of person she is and why does she believe that everyone should want to be such a person? Pace Augustine, Sarah's answer to that question is self-regarding: "As persons who love one another, we fulfill our created nature and thereby achieve our truest, deepest, most enduring happiness." ....

It bears emphasis that Sarah does not believe that she should be the sort of person she is because God has issued a command to her to be that sort of person—a command that, because God is entitled to rule, to legislate, she is obligated to obey. For Sarah, God is not best understood in such terms ....

For Sarah, "[t]he Law of God is not what God legislates but what God is, just as the Law of Gravity is not what gravity legislates but what gravity is."[14] Sarah believes that because God is who God is, because the universe is what it is, and because we are who we are, and not because of anything commanded by God as supreme legislator, the most fitting way of life for us human beings—the most deeply satisfying way of life of which we are capable—is one in which we children of God, we sisters and brothers, "love one another just as I have loved you."

IV Is There a Plausible Secular Response?

Sarah is deeply skeptical that any secular ground can bear the weight of—that any secular worldview can embed—the twofold claim that every human being has inherent dignity and is inviolable ....

Australian philosopher Raimond Gaita, who is an atheist,[15] observes (in the passage that serves as the epigraph for the preceding section of this essay) that

> [i]f we are not religious, we will often search for one of the inadequate expressions which are available to us to say what we hope will be a secular equivalent of [the religious articulation that all human beings, as beloved children of God, are sacred] ....

I am not suggesting that morality cannot survive the death of God. There is, after all, not just one morality in the world; there are many. Nor am I suggesting that one cannot be good unless one believes in God. Many people who do not believe in God are good, even saintly, just as many people who believe in God—including many Christians, as Desmond Tutu has reminded us—are not good. Nonetheless, it is obscure to Sarah what ground one who is not a religious believer can give for the twofold claim that every human being has inherent dignity and that we should live our lives accordingly. It is especially obscure to her what ground a resolute atheist can give.

Imagine a cosmology according to which the universe is, finally and radically, meaningless ....

For one who believes that the universe is utterly bereft of transcendent meaning, why—in virtue of what—is it the case that every human being has inherent dignity and is inviolable? ....

Jeffrie Murphy, for example, insists that it is, for him, "very difficult—perhaps impossible—to embrace religious convictions," but he nonetheless claims that:

> the liberal theory of rights requires a doctrine of human dignity, preciousness and sacredness that cannot be utterly detached from a belief in God or at least from a world view that would be properly called religious in some metaphysically profound sense ... the idea that fundamental moral values may require [religious] convictions is not one to be welcomed with joy [by secular enthusiasts of the liberal theory of rights]. This idea generates tensions and appears to force choices that some of us would prefer not to make. *But it still might be true for all of that ....*[16]

VII So What If There Is No Plausible Response?

Assume, dear reader, that neither Sarah's nor any other religious response to the ground-of-normativity question that engages us here is plausible. Assume, too, that no secular response is plausible. So what? What difference does it make? ....

Richard Rorty would certainly reject Sarah's position because Rorty rejects any position, secular as well as religious, that relies on the idea of human nature:

> [H]istoricist thinkers [ever since Hegel] have denied[:] that there is such a thing as "human nature" or the "deepest level of the self." Their strategy has been to insist that socialization, and thus historical circumstance, goes all the way down, that there is nothing "beneath" socialization or prior to history which is definatory of the human. Such writers tell us that the question "What is it to be a human being?" should be replaced by questions like "What is it to inhabit a rich twentieth-century democratic society?"
>
> (*Contingency, Irony, and Solidarity* (Cambridge: Cambridge University Press, 1989), p. xiii)

Rorty writes approvingly of "this historicist turn," which, he says,

> has helped free us, gradually but steadily, from theology and metaphysics—from the temptation to look for an escape from time and chance. It has helped us substitute Freedom for Truth as the goal of thinking and of social progress.
>
> (Ibid.)

In his embrace of the cause of human rights, Rorty relies on what we may call "Eurocentric" sentiments: the sentiments of twenty-first-century North Americans and Western Europeans ....

For many of us who embrace the cause of human rights, the fundamental wrong done at Auschwitz and the other Nazi death camps, for example, was not that our local sentiments were offended, but that the normative order of the world was violated. Given Sarah's understanding of the normative order of the world, Auschwitz constitutes, for Sarah, a terrible violation of who God is, of what the universe is, and, in particular, of who we human beings are.

Now, we might be quite wrong to believe—it might be a false belief—that the world has a normative order one transgresses whenever one violates any human being. But if we are wrong, if our belief is false—at least, if we have no reason to be other than agnostic about the issue—and if we nonetheless coerce others and perhaps even, at the limit, kill others in the name of protecting the inherent dignity of human beings, then, pace Rorty, are we not coercing and killing in the name of nothing but our local sentiments and preferences, our Eurocentric human rights culture? Does Rorty want us to say something like this: "It's a brutal world out there. It's either them or us—either their sentiments and culture or ours. It's not that might makes right. It's that there is no right, only might. May our might, not theirs, prevail!" Rorty did once say something like that:

> [W]hen the secret police come, when the torturers violate the innocent, there is nothing to be said to them of the form "There is something within you which you are betraying. Though you embody the practices of a totalitarian society which will endure forever, there is something beyond those practices which condemns you."[17]

Against the background of Rorty's comments, let us ask: Should we who embrace the cause of human rights abandon "human rights foundationalism"; should we abandon the project of trying to ground, whether on religious or secular premises, the claim that every human being has inherent dignity and is inviolable? If we were to abandon the project of trying to ground that claim, what would we then be left with? Our Eurocentric sentiments and preferences? ("When the secret police come ....") How much weight these sentiments and preferences would be able to bear—and for how long—is an open question. Listen to the Polish poet and Nobel laureate, Czeslaw Milosz:

> What has been surprising in the post-Cold War period are those beautiful and deeply moving words pronounced with veneration in places like Prague and Warsaw, words which pertain to the old repertory of the rights of man and the dignity of the person.
>   I wonder at this phenomenon because maybe underneath there is an abyss. After all, those ideas had their foundation in religion, and I am not over-optimistic as to the survival of religion in a scientific-technological civilization. Notions that seemed buried forever have suddenly been resurrected. But how long can they stay afloat if the bottom is taken out?[18]

Perhaps some who have no ground—who find any religious ground implausible but can discern no plausible secular ground—are more confident about their conviction that every human being has inherent dignity and is inviolable than they would be about any possible ground for their conviction. ("I have reached bedrock and this is where my spade is turned.")[19] Perhaps some will say that they have no time to obsess about possible grounds for their conviction because they are too busy doing the important work of "changing the world." But still this question intrudes: If, as their (bedrock?) conviction holds, the Other, even the Other, truly does have inherent dignity and truly is inviolable, what else must be true; what must be true for it to be true that the Other has inherent dignity and is inviolable? That question brings us back to something I say above: the morality of human rights is deeply problematic for many secular thinkers because that morality is difficult—perhaps to the point of impossible—to align with one of their fundamental convictions, what Bernard Williams called "Nietzsche's thought": "[T]here is, not only no God, but no metaphysical order of any kind."[20]

Again, the point is not that morality cannot survive the death of God. There is not just one morality; there are many. The serious question is whether a particular morality—the morality of human rights—can survive the death (or deconstruction) of God. (Was it such a morality Nietzsche saw in the coffin at God's funeral?) Nietzsche's thought ("not only no God, but no metaphysical order of any kind") and the morality of human rights (every human being has inherent dignity and is inviolable) are deeply antithetical to one another. Which will prevail?

Notes

1. This passage—quoted in George Parkin Grant, *English Speaking Justice* 77 (1985)—appears in Friedrich Nietzsche, IV *Thus Spoke Zarathustra* ("On the Higher Man"), near the end of sec. 1.
2. Philippa Foot, *Natural Goodness* 103 (2001).
3. See Michael Burleigh & Wolfgang Wipperman, *The Racial State: Germany, 1933–1945* (1991); Johannes Morsink, *World War Two and the Universal Declaration*, 15 Hum. Rts. Q. 357, 363 (1993).
4. See Jacques Maritain, *Introduction*, in UNESCO, *Human Rights: Comments and Interpretation* 9–17 (1949). Maritain writes: "We agree about the rights but on condition that no one asks us why." Id. at 9. See also Youngjae Lee, *International Consensus as Persuasive Authority in the Eighth Amendment*, 156 U. Pa. L. Rev. (2007): "International human rights treaties are ... willfully silent about the reasons behind the norms that they adopt." However, Maritain is wrong: There was agreement *both* about "the rights" (actually, about some rights) and about a part of the "why": namely, that every human being has inherent dignity. Again, the Declaration explicitly refers in its preamble to "the inherent dignity ... of all members of the human family" and states in Article 1 that "[a]ll members of the human family are born free and equal in dignity and rights ... and should act towards one another in a spirit of brotherhood." So what Maritain should say is this: "We agree about the rights. We even agree about the inherent dignity—but on condition that no one asks us why every human being has inherent dignity."
5. Bernard Williams, "Republican and Galilean," *New York Review*, November 8, 1990, at 45, 48 (reviewing Charles Taylor, *Sources of the Self: The Making of Modern Identity* (1989)). Cf. John M. Rist, *Real Ethics: Rethinking the Foundations of Morality* (2002), at 2: "[Plato] came to believe that if morality, as more than 'enlightened' self-interest, is to be rationally justifiable, it must be established on metaphysical foundations."
6. Raimond Gaita, *A Common Humanity: Thinking about Love and Truth and Justice* 23–24 (2000).
7. If we listen carefully to what Sarah is about to say and if we refrain from imputing to Sarah standard Christian positions on theological issues Sarah does not address, such as the divinity of Jesus—we will not assume that Sarah identifies herself as a Christian in the conventional sense (though for all we know, she may).
8. The translations of biblical passages here and elsewhere in this book are those of *The New Jerusalem Bible* (1985).
9. See Jean Porter, *Nature as Reason: A Thomistic Theory of the Natural Law* (2005), at 144–145. Quoting Stephen Pope, *The Evolutionary Roots of Morality in Theological Perspective*, 33 Zygon 545, 554 (1998).
10. For Christians, the basic shape of the good life is indicated by the instruction given by Jesus at a Passover seder on the eve of his execution: "I give you a new commandment: love one another; you must love one another just as I have loved you." John 13:34. See also John 15:12, 17.
11. Graham Greene, *The Power and the Glory* (Penguin ed. 1940), at 131.
12. It seems to have been an implausible ideal for Ivan Karamazov:

> I have never been able to understand how it was possible to love one's neighbors. And I mean precisely one's neighbors, because I can conceive of the possibility of loving those who are far away. I read somewhere about a saint, John the Merciful, who, when a hungry frozen beggar came to him and asked him to warm him, lay down with him, put his arms around him, and breathed into the man's reeking mouth that was festering with the sores of some horrible disease. I am convinced that he did so in a state of frenzy, that it was a false gesture, that this act of love was dictated by some self-imposed penance. If I must love my fellow man, he had better hide himself, for no sooner do I see his face than there's an end to my love for him.

Fyodor Dostoevsky, *The Brothers Karamazov*, opening of ch. 5, IV (Constance Garnett trans., 1933).
13 Stephen Scott, *Motive and Justification*, 85 J. Phil. 479, 499 (1988).
14 John Dominic Crossan, *Case against Manifesto*, 5 Law Text Culture 129, 144 (2000).
15 See John Haldane, *The Greatest of These Is Love, as an Atheist Reminds Us*, The Tablet [London], December 9, 2000, at 1678.
16 Jeffrie Murphy, *Afterword: Constitutionalism, Moral Skepticism, and Religious Belief*, in Constitutionalism: The Philosophical Dimension 239, 248 (Alan S. Rosenbaum ed., 1988) (emphasis added).
17 Richard Rorty, *Consequences of Pragmatism* (1982), at xlii.
18 Czeslaw Milosz, *The Religious Imagination at 2000*, New Persp. Q., fall 1997, at 32.
19 Ludwig Wittgenstein, *Philosophical Investigations*, sec. 217 (1953), quoted in Hilary Putnam, *The Many Faces of Realism* (1987), at 85.
20 See *supra* note 6.

Review and Discussion Questions

1 What is the "ground-of-normativity" question that Perry analyzes in this essay?
2 What is "Sarah's" response to this question?
3 In what sense, if any, does Perry offer an argument that secular responses are not as conclusive as religious responses to the ground-of-normativity question?
4 Does the success of Perry's argument depend on a Christian perspective, or are those religious ideas merely an illustration of a more general argument? Explain.
5 Is Perry's argument essentially a psychological point about what motivates people? If it's more than that, what more is it?

READING: THE MORAL INSTINCT

STEVEN PINKER[*]

What is an evolutionary explanation of morality? In this essay, Steven Pinker explains what it means for human beings to have a moral sense on our best current understanding of evolutionary biology. He also examines how we should assess the significance of evolutionary explanations of morality. Steven Pinker is the Johnstone Family Professor of Psychology at Harvard University.

Which of the following people would you say is the most admirable: Mother Teresa, Bill Gates or Norman Borlaug? And which do you think is the least admirable? For most people, it's an easy question. Mother Teresa, famous for ministering to the poor in Calcutta, has been beatified by the Vatican, awarded the Nobel Peace Prize and ranked in an American poll as the most admired person of the twentieth century. Bill Gates, infamous for giving us the Microsoft dancing paper clip and the blue screen of death, has been decapitated in effigy in "I Hate Gates" Web sites and hit with a pie in the face. As for Norman Borlaug … who the heck is Norman Borlaug?

---

[*] Pinker, Steven, "The Moral Instinct," *New York Times Sunday Magazine*, January 13, 2008. Reprinted with permission.

Yet a deeper look might lead you to rethink your answers. Borlaug, father of the "Green Revolution" that used agricultural science to reduce world hunger, has been credited with saving a billion lives, more than anyone else in history. Gates, in deciding what to do with his fortune, crunched the numbers and determined that he could alleviate the most misery by fighting everyday scourges in the developing world like malaria, diarrhea and parasites. Mother Teresa, for her part, extolled the virtue of suffering and ran her well-financed missions accordingly: their sick patrons were offered plenty of prayer but harsh conditions, few analgesics and dangerously primitive medical care.

It's not hard to see why the moral reputations of this trio should be so out of line with the good they have done. Mother Teresa was the very embodiment of saintliness: white-clad, sad-eyed, ascetic and often photographed with the wretched of the earth. Gates is a nerd's nerd and the world's richest man, as likely to enter heaven as the proverbial camel squeezing through the needle's eye. And Borlaug, now ninety-three, is an agronomist who has spent his life in labs and nonprofits, seldom walking onto the media stage, and hence into our consciousness, at all.

I doubt these examples will persuade anyone to favor Bill Gates over Mother Teresa for sainthood. But they show that our heads can be turned by an aura of sanctity, distracting us from a more objective reckoning of the actions that make people suffer or flourish. It seems we may all be vulnerable to moral illusions the ethical equivalent of the bending lines that trick the eye on cereal boxes and in psychology textbooks. Illusions are a favorite tool of perception scientists for exposing the workings of the five senses, and of philosophers for shaking people out of the naïve belief that our minds give us a transparent window onto the world (since if our eyes can be fooled by an illusion, why should we trust them at other times?). Today, a new field is using illusions to unmask a sixth sense, the moral sense. Moral intuitions are being drawn out of people in the lab, on Web sites and in brain scanners, and are being explained with tools from game theory, neuroscience and evolutionary biology ....

The Moralization Switch

The starting point for appreciating that there *is* a distinctive part of our psychology for morality is seeing how moral judgments differ from other kinds of opinions we have on how people ought to behave. Moralization is a psychological state that can be turned on and off like a switch, and when it is on, a distinctive mind-set commandeers our thinking. This is the mind-set that makes us deem actions immoral ("killing is wrong"), rather than merely disagreeable ("I hate brussels sprouts"), unfashionable ("bell-bottoms are out") or imprudent ("don't scratch mosquito bites").

The first hallmark of moralization is that the rules it invokes are felt to be universal. Prohibitions of rape and murder, for example, are felt not to be matters of local custom but to be universally and objectively warranted. One can easily say, "I don't like brussels sprouts, but I don't care if you eat them," but no one would say, "I don't like killing, but I don't care if you murder someone."

The other hallmark is that people feel that those who commit immoral acts deserve to be punished. Not only is it allowable to inflict pain on a person who has broken a moral rule; it is wrong *not* to, to "let them get away with it." People are thus untroubled in inviting divine retribution or the power of the state to harm other people they deem immoral. Bertrand Russell wrote, "The infliction of cruelty with a good conscience is a delight to moralists. That is why they invented hell."

We all know what it feels like when the moralization switch flips inside us—the righteous glow, the burning dudgeon, the drive to recruit others to the cause. The psychologist Paul Rozin has studied the toggle switch by comparing two kinds of people who engage in the same behavior but with different switch settings. Health vegetarians avoid meat for practical reasons, like lowering cholesterol and avoiding toxins. Moral vegetarians avoid meat for ethical reasons: to avoid complicity in the suffering of animals. By investigating their feelings about meat-eating, Rozin showed that the moral motive sets off a cascade of opinions. Moral vegetarians are more likely to treat meat as a contaminant—they refuse, for example, to eat a bowl of soup into which a drop of beef broth has fallen. They are more likely to think that other people ought to be vegetarians, and are more likely to imbue their dietary habits with other virtues, like believing that meat avoidance makes people less aggressive and bestial.

Much of our recent social history, including the culture wars between liberals and conservatives, consists of the moralization or amoralization of particular kinds of behavior. Even when people agree that an outcome is desirable, they may disagree on whether it should be treated as a matter of preference and prudence or as a matter of sin and virtue. Rozin notes, for example, that smoking has lately been moralized. Until recently, it was understood that some people didn't enjoy smoking or avoided it because it was hazardous to their health. But with the discovery of the harmful effects of secondhand smoke, smoking is now treated as immoral. Smokers are ostracized; images of people smoking are censored; and entities touched by smoke are felt to be contaminated (so hotels have not only nonsmoking rooms but nonsmoking *floors*). The desire for retribution has been visited on tobacco companies, who have been slapped with staggering "punitive damages."

At the same time, many behaviors have been amoralized, switched from moral failings to lifestyle choices. They include divorce, illegitimacy, being a working mother, marijuana use and homosexuality. Many afflictions have been reassigned from payback for bad choices to unlucky misfortunes. There used to be people called "bums" and "tramps"; today they are "homeless." Drug addiction is a "disease"; syphilis was rebranded from the price of wanton behavior to a "sexually transmitted disease" and more recently a "sexually transmitted infection."

This wave of amoralization has led the cultural right to lament that morality itself is under assault, as we see in the group that anointed itself the Moral Majority. In fact there seems to be a Law of Conservation of Moralization, so that as old behaviors are taken out of the moralized column, new ones are added to it. Dozens of things that past generations treated as practical matters are now ethical battlegrounds, including disposable diapers, I.Q. tests, poultry farms, Barbie dolls and research on breast cancer. Food alone has become a minefield, with critics sermonizing about the size of sodas, the chemistry of fat, the freedom of chickens, the price of coffee beans, the species of fish and now the distance the food has traveled from farm to plate.

Many of these moralizations, like the assault on smoking, may be understood as practical tactics to reduce some recently identified harm. But whether an activity flips our mental switches to the "moral" setting isn't just a matter of how much harm it does. We don't show contempt to the man who fails to change the batteries in his smoke alarms or takes his family on a driving vacation, both of which multiply the risk they will die in an accident. Driving a gas-guzzling Hummer is reprehensible, but driving a gas-guzzling old Volvo is not; eating a Big Mac is unconscionable, but not imported cheese or crème brûlée. The reason for these double standards is obvious: people tend to align their moralization with their own lifestyles.

Reasoning and Rationalizing

It's not just the content of our moral judgments that is often questionable, but the way we arrive at them. We like to think that when we have a conviction, there are good reasons that drove us to adopt it. That is why an older approach to moral psychology, led by Jean Piaget and Lawrence Kohlberg, tried to document the lines of reasoning that guided people to moral conclusions. But consider these situations, originally devised by the psychologist Jonathan Haidt:

> Julie is traveling in France on summer vacation from college with her brother Mark. One night they decide that it would be interesting and fun if they tried making love. Julie was already taking birth-control pills, but Mark uses a condom, too, just to be safe. They both enjoy the sex but decide not to do it again. They keep the night as a special secret, which makes them feel closer to each other. What do you think about that—was it O.K. for them to make love?

> A woman is cleaning out her closet and she finds her old American flag. She doesn't want the flag anymore, so she cuts it up into pieces and uses the rags to clean her bathroom.

> A family's dog is killed by a car in front of their house. They heard that dog meat was delicious, so they cut up the dog's body and cook it and eat it for dinner.

Most people immediately declare that these acts are wrong and then grope to justify *why* they are wrong. It's not so easy. In the case of Julie and Mark, people raise the possibility of children with birth defects, but they are reminded that the couple were diligent about contraception. They suggest that the siblings will be emotionally hurt, but the story makes it clear that they weren't. They submit that the act would offend the community, but then recall that it was kept a secret. Eventually many people admit, "I don't know, I can't explain it, I just know it's wrong." People don't generally engage in moral reasoning, Haidt argues, but moral *rationalization*: they begin with the conclusion, coughed up by an unconscious emotion, and then work backward to a plausible justification.

The gap between people's convictions and their justifications is also on display in the favorite new sandbox for moral psychologists, a thought experiment devised by the philosophers Philippa Foot and Judith Jarvis Thomson called the Trolley

Problem. On your morning walk, you see a trolley car hurtling down the track, the conductor slumped over the controls. In the path of the trolley are five men working on the track, oblivious to the danger. You are standing at a fork in the track and can pull a lever that will divert the trolley onto a spur, saving the five men. Unfortunately, the trolley would then run over a single worker who is laboring on the spur. Is it permissible to throw the switch, killing one man to save five? Almost everyone says "yes."

Consider now a different scene. You are on a bridge overlooking the tracks and have spotted the runaway trolley bearing down on the five workers. Now the only way to stop the trolley is to throw a heavy object in its path. And the only heavy object within reach is a fat man standing next to you. Should you throw the man off the bridge? Both dilemmas present you with the option of sacrificing one life to save five, and so, by the utilitarian standard of what would result in the greatest good for the greatest number, the two dilemmas are morally equivalent. But most people don't see it that way: though they would pull the switch in the first dilemma, they would not heave the fat man in the second. When pressed for a reason, they can't come up with anything coherent, though moral philosophers haven't had an easy time coming up with a relevant difference, either.

When psychologists say "most people" they usually mean "most of the two dozen sophomores who filled out a questionnaire for beer money." But in this case it means most of the 200,000 people from a hundred countries who shared their intuitions on a Web-based experiment conducted by the psychologists Fiery Cushman and Liane Young and the biologist Marc Hauser. A difference between the acceptability of switch-pulling and man-heaving, and an inability to justify the choice, was found in respondents from Europe, Asia and North and South America; among men and women, blacks and whites, teenagers and octogenarians, Hindus, Muslims, Buddhists, Christians, Jews and atheists; people with elementary-school educations and people with Ph.D.'s.

Joshua Greene, a philosopher and cognitive neuroscientist, suggests that evolution equipped people with a revulsion to manhandling an innocent person. This instinct, he suggests, tends to overwhelm any utilitarian calculus that would tot up the lives saved and lost. The impulse against roughing up a fellow human would explain other examples in which people abjure killing one to save many, like euthanizing a hospital patient to harvest his organs and save five dying patients in need of transplants, or throwing someone out of a crowded lifeboat to keep it afloat.

By itself this would be no more than a plausible story, but Greene teamed up with the cognitive neuroscientist Jonathan Cohen and several Princeton colleagues to peer into people's brains using functional M.R.I. They sought to find signs of a conflict between brain areas associated with emotion (the ones that recoil from harming someone) and areas dedicated to rational analysis (the ones that calculate lives lost and saved).

When people pondered the dilemmas that required killing someone with their bare hands, several networks in their brains lighted up. One, which included the medial (inward-facing) parts of the frontal lobes, has been implicated in emotions about other people. A second, the dorsolateral (upper and outer-facing) surface of the frontal lobes, has been implicated in ongoing mental computation (including nonmoral reasoning, like deciding whether to get somewhere by plane or train).

And a third region, the anterior cingulate cortex (an evolutionarily ancient strip lying at the base of the inner surface of each cerebral hemisphere), registers a conflict between an urge coming from one part of the brain and an advisory coming from another.

But when the people were pondering a hands-off dilemma, like switching the trolley onto the spur with the single worker, the brain reacted differently: only the area involved in rational calculation stood out. Other studies have shown that neurological patients who have blunted emotions because of damage to the frontal lobes become utilitarians: they think it makes perfect sense to throw the fat man off the bridge. Together, the findings corroborate Greene's theory that our nonutilitarian intuitions come from the victory of an emotional impulse over a cost-benefit analysis.

A Universal Morality?

The findings of trolleyology—complex, instinctive and worldwide moral intuitions—led Hauser and John Mikhail (a legal scholar) to revive an analogy from the philosopher John Rawls between the moral sense and language. According to Noam Chomsky, we are born with a "universal grammar" that forces us to analyze speech in terms of its grammatical structure, with no conscious awareness of the rules in play. By analogy, we are born with a universal moral grammar that forces us to analyze human action in terms of its moral structure, with just as little awareness.

The idea that the moral sense is an innate part of human nature is not farfetched. A list of human universals collected by the anthropologist Donald E. Brown includes many moral concepts and emotions, including a distinction between right and wrong; empathy; fairness; admiration of generosity; rights and obligations; proscription of murder, rape and other forms of violence; redress of wrongs; sanctions for wrongs against the community; shame; and taboos.

The stirrings of morality emerge early in childhood. Toddlers spontaneously offer toys and help to others and try to comfort people they see in distress. And according to the psychologists Elliot Turiel and Judith Smetana, preschoolers have an inkling of the difference between societal conventions and moral principles. Four-year-olds say that it is not O.K. to wear pajamas to school (a convention) and also not O.K. to hit a little girl for no reason (a moral principle). But when asked whether these actions would be O.K. if the teacher allowed them, most of the children said that wearing pajamas would now be fine but that hitting a little girl would still not be.

Though no one has identified genes for morality, there is circumstantial evidence they exist. The character traits called "conscientiousness" and "agreeableness" are far more correlated in identical twins separated at birth (who share their genes but not their environment) than in adoptive siblings raised together (who share their environment but not their genes). People given diagnoses of "antisocial personality disorder" or "psychopathy" show signs of morality blindness from the time they are children. They bully younger children, torture animals, habitually lie and seem incapable of empathy or remorse, often despite normal family backgrounds. Some of these children grow up into the monsters who bilk elderly people out of their savings, rape a succession of women or shoot convenience-store clerks lying on the floor during a robbery.

Though psychopathy probably comes from a genetic predisposition, a milder version can be caused by damage to frontal regions of the brain (including the areas that inhibit intact people from throwing the hypothetical fat man off the bridge). The neuroscientists Hanna and Antonio Damasio and their colleagues found that some children who sustain severe injuries to their frontal lobes can grow up into callous and irresponsible adults, despite normal intelligence. They lie, steal, ignore punishment, endanger their own children and can't think through even the simplest moral dilemmas, like what two people should do if they disagreed on which TV channel to watch or whether a man ought to steal a drug to save his dying wife.

The moral sense, then, may be rooted in the design of the normal human brain. Yet for all the awe that may fill our minds when we reflect on an innate moral law within, the idea is at best incomplete ….

Could we be wired with an abstract spec sheet that embraces all the strange ideas that people in different cultures moralize?

The Varieties of Moral Experience

When anthropologists like Richard Shweder and Alan Fiske survey moral concerns across the globe, they find that a few themes keep popping up from amid the diversity. People everywhere, at least in some circumstances and with certain other folks in mind, think it's bad to harm others and good to help them. They have a sense of fairness: that one should reciprocate favors, reward benefactors and punish cheaters. They value loyalty to a group, sharing and solidarity among its members and conformity to its norms. They believe that it is right to defer to legitimate authorities and to respect people with high status. And they exalt purity, cleanliness and sanctity while loathing defilement, contamination and carnality.

The exact number of themes depends on whether you're a lumper or a splitter, but Haidt counts five—harm, fairness, community (or group loyalty), authority and purity—and suggests that they are the primary colors of our moral sense. Not only do they keep reappearing in cross-cultural surveys, but each one tugs on the moral intuitions of people in our own culture. Haidt asks us to consider how much money someone would have to pay us to do hypothetical acts like the following:

Stick a pin into your palm.

Stick a pin into the palm of a child you don't know. (Harm.)

Accept a wide-screen TV from a friend who received it at no charge because of a computer error.

Accept a wide-screen TV from a friend who received it from a thief who had stolen it from a wealthy family. (Fairness.)

Say something bad about your nation (which you don't believe) on a talk-radio show in your nation.

Say something bad about your nation (which you don't believe) on a talk-radio show in a foreign nation. (Community.)

Slap a friend in the face, with his permission, as part of a comedy skit.

Slap your minister in the face, with his permission, as part of a comedy skit. (Authority.)

Attend a performance-art piece in which the actors act like idiots for 30 minutes, including flubbing simple problems and falling down on stage.

Attend a performance-art piece in which the actors act like animals for 30 minutes, including crawling around naked and urinating on stage. (Purity.)

In each pair, the second action feels far more repugnant. Most of the moral illusions we have visited come from an unwarranted intrusion of one of the moral spheres into our judgments. A violation of community led people to frown on using an old flag to clean a bathroom. Violations of purity repelled the people who judged the morality of consensual incest and prevented the moral vegetarians and nonsmokers from tolerating the slightest trace of a vile contaminant. At the other end of the scale, displays of extreme purity lead people to venerate religious leaders who dress in white and affect an aura of chastity and asceticism.

The Genealogy of Morals

The five spheres are good candidates for a periodic table of the moral sense not only because they are ubiquitous but also because they appear to have deep evolutionary roots. The impulse to avoid harm, which gives trolley ponderers the willies when they consider throwing a man off a bridge, can also be found in rhesus monkeys, who go hungry rather than pull a chain that delivers food to them and a shock to another monkey. Respect for authority is clearly related to the pecking orders of dominance and appeasement that are widespread in the animal kingdom. The purity–defilement contrast taps the emotion of disgust that is triggered by potential disease vectors like bodily effluvia, decaying flesh and unconventional forms of meat, and by risky sexual practices like incest.

The other two moralized spheres match up with the classic examples of how altruism can evolve that were worked out by sociobiologists in the 1960s and 1970s and made famous by Richard Dawkins in his book *The Selfish Gene*. Fairness is very close to what scientists call reciprocal altruism, where a willingness to be nice to others can evolve as long as the favor helps the recipient more than it costs the giver and the recipient returns the favor when fortunes reverse. The analysis makes it sound as if reciprocal altruism comes out of a robotlike calculation, but in fact Robert Trivers, the biologist who devised the theory, argued that it is implemented in the brain as a suite of moral emotions. Sympathy prompts a person to offer the first favor, particularly to someone in need for whom it would go the furthest. Anger protects a person against cheaters who accept a favor without reciprocating, by impelling him to punish the ingrate or sever the relationship. Gratitude impels a beneficiary to reward those who helped him in the past. Guilt prompts a cheater in danger of being found out to repair the relationship by redressing the misdeed and advertising that he will behave better in the future (consistent with Mencken's definition of *conscience* as "the inner voice which warns us that someone might be looking"). Many experiments on who helps whom, who likes whom, who punishes whom and who feels guilty about what have confirmed these predictions.

Community, the very different emotion that prompts people to share and sacrifice without an expectation of payback, may be rooted in nepotistic altruism, the empathy and solidarity we feel toward our relatives (and which evolved because any gene that pushed an organism to aid a relative would have helped copies of itself sitting inside that relative). In humans, of course, communal feelings can be lavished on nonrelatives as well. Sometimes it pays people (in an evolutionary sense) to love their companions because their interests are yoked, like spouses with common children, in-laws with common relatives, friends with common tastes or allies with common enemies. And sometimes it doesn't pay them at all, but their kinship-detectors have been tricked into treating their groupmates as if they were relatives by tactics like kinship metaphors (*blood brothers, fraternities, the fatherland*), origin myths, communal meals and other bonding rituals.

Juggling the Spheres

All this brings us to a theory of how the moral sense can be universal and variable at the same time. The five moral spheres are universal, a legacy of evolution. But how they are ranked in importance, and which is brought in to moralize which area of social life—sex, government, commerce, religion, diet and so on—depends on the culture. Many of the flabbergasting practices in faraway places become more intelligible when you recognize that the same moralizing impulse that Western elites channel toward violations of harm and fairness (our moral obsessions) is channeled elsewhere to violations in the other spheres. Think of the Japanese fear of nonconformity (community), the holy ablutions and dietary restrictions of Hindus and Orthodox Jews (purity), the outrage at insulting the Prophet among Muslims (authority). In the West, we believe that in business and government, fairness should trump community and try to root out nepotism and cronyism. In other parts of the world this is incomprehensible—what heartless creep would favor a perfect stranger over his own brother?

The ranking and placement of moral spheres also divides the cultures of liberals and conservatives in the United States. Many bones of contention, like homosexuality, atheism and one-parent families from the right, or racial imbalances, sweatshops and executive pay from the left, reflect different weightings of the spheres. In a large Web survey, Haidt found that liberals put a lopsided moral weight on harm and fairness while playing down group loyalty, authority and purity. Conservatives instead place a moderately high weight on all five. It's not surprising that each side thinks it is driven by lofty ethical values and that the other side is base and unprincipled.

Reassigning an activity to a different sphere, or taking it out of the moral spheres altogether, isn't easy. People think that a behavior belongs in its sphere as a matter of sacred necessity and that the very act of questioning an assignment is a moral outrage. The psychologist Philip Tetlock has shown that the mentality of taboo—a conviction that some thoughts are sinful to think—is not just a superstition of Polynesians but a mind-set that can easily be triggered in college-educated Americans. Just ask them to think about applying the sphere of reciprocity to relationships customarily governed by community or authority. When Tetlock asked subjects for their opinions on whether adoption agencies should place children with the couples willing to pay the most, whether people should have the right to sell their organs and whether they should be able to buy their way out of jury duty, the subjects not only disagreed but felt personally insulted and were outraged that anyone would raise the question ....

Is Nothing Sacred?

.... The attempt to dissect our moral intuitions can look like an attempt to debunk them. Evolutionary psychologists seem to want to unmask our noblest motives as ultimately self-interested—to show that our love for children, compassion for the unfortunate and sense of justice are just tactics in a Darwinian struggle to perpetuate our genes. The explanation of how different cultures appeal to different spheres could lead to a spineless relativism, in which we would never have grounds to criticize the practice of another culture, no matter how barbaric, because "we have our kind of morality and they have theirs." And the whole enterprise seems to be dragging us to an amoral nihilism, in which morality itself would be demoted from a transcendent principle to a figment of our neural circuitry.

In reality, none of these fears are warranted, and it's important to see why not. The first misunderstanding involves the logic of evolutionary explanations. Evolutionary biologists sometimes anthropomorphize DNA for the same reason that science teachers find it useful to have their students imagine the world from the viewpoint of a molecule or a beam of light. One shortcut to understanding the theory of selection without working through the math is to imagine that the genes are little agents that try to make copies of themselves.

Unfortunately, the meme of the selfish gene escaped from popular biology books and mutated into the idea that organisms (including people) are ruthlessly self-serving. And this doesn't follow. Genes are not a reservoir of our dark unconscious wishes. "Selfish" genes are perfectly compatible with selfless organisms, because a gene's metaphorical goal of selfishly replicating itself can be implemented by wiring up the brain of the organism to do unselfish things, like being nice to relatives or doing good deeds for needy strangers. When a mother stays up all night comforting a sick child, the genes that endowed her with that tenderness were "selfish" in a metaphorical sense, but by no stretch of the imagination is *she* being selfish ....

Is Morality a Figment?

So a biological understanding of the moral sense does not entail that people are calculating maximizers of their genes or self-interest. But where does it leave the concept of morality itself?

Here is the worry. The scientific outlook has taught us that some parts of our subjective experience are products of our biological makeup and have no objective counterpart in the world. The qualitative difference between red and green, the tastiness of fruit and foulness of carrion, the scariness of heights and prettiness of flowers are design features of our common nervous system, and if our species had evolved in a different ecosystem or if we were missing a few genes, our reactions could go the other way. Now, if the distinction between right and wrong is also a product of brain wiring, why should we believe it is any more real than the distinction between red and green? And if it is just a collective hallucination, how could we argue that evils like genocide and slavery are wrong for everyone, rather than just distasteful to us?

Putting God in charge of morality is one way to solve the problem, of course, but Plato made short work of it 2,400 years ago. Does God have a good reason for designating certain acts as moral and others as immoral? If not—if his dictates are divine whims—why should we take them seriously? Suppose that God commanded us to torture a child. Would that make it all right, or would some other standard give us reasons to resist? And if, on the other hand, God was forced by moral reasons to issue some dictates and not others—if a command to torture a child was never an option—then why not appeal to those reasons directly?

This throws us back to wondering where those reasons could come from, if they are more than just figments of our brains. They certainly aren't in the physical world like wavelength or mass. The only other option is that moral truths exist in some abstract Platonic realm, there for us to discover, perhaps in the same way that mathematical truths (according to most mathematicians) are there for us to discover. On this analogy, we are born with a rudimentary concept of number, but as soon as we build on it with formal mathematical reasoning, the nature of mathematical reality forces us to discover some truths and not others. (No one who understands the concept of two, the concept of four and the concept of addition can come to any conclusion but that $2 + 2 = 4$.) Perhaps we are born with a rudimentary moral sense, and as soon as we build on it with moral reasoning, the nature of moral reality forces us to some conclusions but not others.

Moral realism, as this idea is called, is too rich for many philosophers' blood. Yet a diluted version of the idea—if not a list of cosmically inscribed Thou-Shalts, then at least a few If-Thens—is not crazy. Two features of reality point any rational, self-preserving social agent in a moral direction. And they could provide a benchmark for determining when the judgments of our moral sense are aligned with morality itself.

One is the prevalence of nonzero-sum games. In many arenas of life, two parties are objectively better off if they both act in a nonselfish way than if each of them acts selfishly. You and I are both better off if we share our surpluses, rescue each other's children in danger and refrain from shooting at each other, compared with hoarding our surpluses while they rot, letting the other's child drown while we file our nails or feuding like the Hatfields and McCoys. Granted, I might be a bit better off if I acted selfishly at your expense and you played the sucker, but the same is true for you with me, so if each of us tried for these advantages, we'd both end up worse off. Any neutral observer, and you and I if we could talk it over rationally, would have to conclude that the state we should aim for is the one in which we both are unselfish. These spreadsheet projections are not quirks of brain wiring, nor are they dictated by a supernatural power; they are in the nature of things.

The other external support for morality is a feature of rationality itself: that it cannot depend on the egocentric vantage point of the reasoner. If I appeal to you to do anything that affects me—to get off my foot, or tell me the time or not run me over with your car—then I can't do it in a way that privileges my interests over yours (say, retaining my right to run you over with my car) if I want you to take me seriously. Unless I am Galactic Overlord, I have to state my case in a way that would force me to treat you in kind. I can't act as if my interests are special just because I'm me and you're not, any more than I can persuade you that the spot I am standing on is a special place in the universe just because I happen to be standing on it.

Not coincidentally, the core of this idea—the interchangeability of perspectives—keeps reappearing in history's best-thought-through moral philosophies, including the Golden Rule (itself discovered many times); Spinoza's Viewpoint of Eternity; the Social Contract of Hobbes, Rousseau and Locke; Kant's Categorical Imperative; and Rawls's Veil of Ignorance. It also underlies Peter Singer's theory of the Expanding Circle—the optimistic proposal that our moral sense, though shaped by evolution to overvalue self, kin and clan, can propel us on a path of moral progress, as our reasoning forces us to generalize it to larger and larger circles of sentient beings.

Doing Better by Knowing Ourselves

Morality, then, is still something larger than our inherited moral sense, and the new science of the moral sense does not make moral reasoning and conviction obsolete. At the same time, its implications for our moral universe are profound.

At the very least, the science tells us that even when our adversaries' agenda is most baffling, they may not be amoral psychopaths but in the throes of a moral mind-set that appears to them to be every bit as mandatory and universal as ours does to us. Of course, some adversaries really are psychopaths, and others are so poisoned by a punitive moralization that they are beyond the pale of reason. (The actor Will Smith had many historians on his side when he recently speculated to the press that Hitler thought he was acting morally.) But in any conflict in which a meeting of the minds is not completely hopeless, a recognition that the other guy is acting from moral rather than venal reasons can be a first patch of common ground. One side can acknowledge the other's concern for community or stability or fairness or dignity, even while arguing that some other value should trump it in that instance. With affirmative action, for example, the opponents can be seen as arguing from a sense of fairness, not racism, and the defenders can be seen as acting from a concern with community, not bureaucratic power. Liberals can ratify conservatives' concern with families while noting that gay marriage is perfectly consistent with that concern.

The science of the moral sense also alerts us to ways in which our psychological makeup can get in the way of our arriving at the most defensible moral conclusions. The moral sense, we are learning, is as vulnerable to illusions as the other senses. It is apt to confuse morality per se with purity, status and conformity. It tends to reframe practical problems as moral crusades and thus see their solution in punitive aggression. It imposes taboos that make certain ideas indiscussible. And it has the nasty habit of always putting the self on the side of the angels ....

There are many other issues for which we are too quick to hit the moralization button and look for villains rather than bug fixes. What should we do when a hospital patient is killed by a nurse who administers the wrong drug in a patient's intravenous line? Should we make it easier to sue the hospital for damages? Or should we redesign the IV fittings so that it's physically impossible to connect the wrong bottle to the line?

And nowhere is moralization more of a hazard than in our greatest global challenge. The threat of human-induced climate change has become the occasion for a moralistic revival meeting. In many discussions, the cause of climate change is overindulgence (too many S.U.V.'s) and defilement (sullying the atmosphere), and the solution is temperance (conservation) and expiation (buying carbon offset coupons). Yet the experts agree that these numbers don't add up: even if every last American became conscientious about his or her carbon emissions, the effects on climate change would be trifling, if for no other reason than that two billion Indians and Chinese are unlikely to copy our born-again abstemiousness. Though voluntary conservation may be one wedge in an effective carbon-reduction pie, the other wedges will have to be morally boring, like a carbon tax and new energy technologies, or even taboo, like nuclear power and deliberate manipulation of the ocean and atmosphere. Our habit of moralizing problems, merging them with intuitions of purity and contamination, and resting content when we feel the right feelings, can get in the way of doing the right thing.

Far from debunking morality, then, the science of the moral sense can advance it, by allowing us to see through the illusions that evolution and culture have saddled us with and to focus on goals we can share and defend. As Anton Chekhov wrote, "Man will become better when you show him what he is like."

Review and Discussion Questions

1 What is Pinker's point in comparing Mother Teresa, Bill Gates, and Norman Borlaug?
2 What does Pinker mean by a "moralization switch"?
3 What is the Trolley Problem, and why does Pinker discuss this case?
4 Does evolutionary theory imply that humans are ultimately selfish? Explain.
5 What are the five "primary colors" of our moral sense, according to Pinker?
6 If morality can be explained by evolutionary theory, then what explains great variation in moral codes around the world? What is the relevance of language acquisition to this question?
7 Is morality objective on Pinker's account? Explain.

Essay and Paper Topics for Chapter 2

1 Applying the various essays in this chapter, write a brief essay on the nature of morality and its relationship with custom, with reason or intellect, and with feelings.
2 Describe whether you think morality is objective or subjective, being careful to define what you mean by those terms.
3 Write an essay comparing the views of Pinker and Perry.
4 How might Hume defend his claim that morality depends on sentiment against one of the authors who takes the opposite position?
5 Which author has the best response to Hobbes in Chapter 1? Explain which view makes the most sense to you, and why.
6 What grounds morality, if anything? What is this question asking, in your view?

Chapter 3

Classical and Contemporary Theories of Morality

The essays in this chapter include some of the most important historical and contemporary works in moral theory. Part A includes traditional philosophical theories. Part B provides more contemporary writings.

Part A: Classical Theories

The essays in this part include some of the most important writings in the history of philosophy. Each in its own way tries to provide a general, theoretical account of morality and moral argument. Topics include the grounds or justifications on which morality rests, the role of reason in morality, whether a single test for right and wrong exists, and what constitutes the ideal or best way of life. Selections range over great time and distance: from ancient Greece and Aristotle's *Nicomachean Ethics*, written more than 2,000 years ago, to England and Mill's nineteenth-century utilitarianism.

READING: NICOMACHEAN ETHICS

ARISTOTLE[*]

Aristotle (384–322 B.C.) was born in Stagira, a town near Macedonia. He went to Athens when he was seventeen years old and studied with Plato at the Academy for twenty years. When Plato died, Aristotle left Athens and traveled to Macedonia, where he tutored the young heir to the throne, who was later to become known as Alexander the Great. In 334 B.C., Aristotle returned to Athens and founded his own school, the Lyceum. When Alexander died in 323, there was strong anti-Macedonian feeling in Athens, and Aristotle left for Chalcis, where he died the next year at sixty-two. Aristotle studied and wrote about an astonishing range of subjects. No single person, it is often said, has ever founded and advanced so many fields of learning. Aristotle wrote separate treatises on physics, biology, logic, psychology, ethics, metaphysics, aesthetics, literary criticism, and political science. In the Middle Ages, he was known simply as "The Philosopher."

In this selection, taken from *Nicomachean Ethics*, Aristotle begins with a discussion of the study of ethics and of human nature and then turns to the

---

[*] From *Nicomachean Ethics*, trans. James E. C. Weldon (1892).

nature of *eudaimonia*—that is, well-being or happiness. To understand happiness, it is necessary to understand the natural purpose or function of humans, which Aristotle describes as activity in accordance with reason. In that sense, happiness is also an excellent, specifically virtuous activity. Virtues, he argues, are those habits and traits that allow people to live well in communities, and true happiness is not, contrary to popular opinion, merely a pleasure. Nor is happiness to be found in economic wealth, although living a virtuous and happy life requires at least some wealth and certainly brings pleasure to the one who is able to achieve it. Turning finally to the nature of the virtues, Aristotle first distinguishes intellectual from moral virtue, arguing that whereas intellectual virtues can be taught, moral virtues must be acquired through habit and require a certain sort of community if they are to be realized. Using examples such as courage and liberality, he argues that moral virtues can best be understood as a mean between extremes.

Book I: Happiness and the Good Life

Every art and every scientific inquiry, and similarly every action and purpose, may be said to aim at some good. Hence the good has been well defined as that at which all things aim. But it is clear that there is a difference in ends; for the ends are sometimes activities, and sometimes results beyond the mere activities. Where there are ends beyond the action, the results are naturally superior to the action.

As there are various actions, arts, and sciences, it follows that the ends are also various. Thus health is the end of the medical art, a ship of shipbuilding, victory of strategy, and wealth of economics. It often happens that a number of such arts or sciences combine for a single enterprise, as the art of making bridles and all such other arts as furnish the implements of horsemanship combine for horsemanship, and horsemanship and every military action for strategy; and in the same way, other arts or sciences combine for others. In all these cases, the ends of the master arts or sciences, whatever they may be, are more desirable than those of the subordinate arts or sciences, as it is for the sake of the former that the latter are pursued. It makes no difference to the argument whether the activities themselves are the ends of the action, or something beyond the activities, as in the above-mentioned sciences.

If it is true that in the sphere of action there is some end which we wish for its own sake, and for the sake of which we wish everything else, and if we do not desire everything for the sake of something else (for, if that is so, the process will go on ad infinitum, and our desire will be idle and futile), clearly this end will be good and the supreme good. Does it not follow then that the knowledge of this good is of great importance for the conduct of life? Like archers who have a mark at which to aim, shall we not have a better chance of attaining what we want? If this is so, we must endeavor to comprehend, at least in outline, what this good is, and what science or faculty makes it its object ....

As every science and undertaking aims at some good, what is in our view the good at which political science [including moral and political theory] aims, and what is the highest of all practical goods? As to its name there is, I may say, a general agreement. The masses and the cultured classes agree in calling it happiness, and conceive that "to live well" or "to do well" is the same thing as "to be happy." But as to what happiness is they do not agree, nor do the masses give the same account of it as the philosophers. The former take it to be something visible and palpable, such as pleasure, wealth, or honor; different people, however, give different definitions of it, and often even the same man gives different definitions at different times. When he is ill, it is health, when he is poor, it is wealth; if he is conscious of his own ignorance, he envies people who use grand language above his own comprehension. Some philosophers, on the other hand, have held that, besides these various goods, there is an absolute good which is the cause of goodness in them all. [These were members of Plato's school of thought.] It would perhaps be a waste of time to examine all these opinions; it will be enough to examine such as are most popular or as seem to be more or less reasonable.

.... Men's conception of the good or of happiness may be read in the lives they lead. Ordinary or vulgar people conceive it to be a pleasure, and accordingly choose a life of enjoyment. For there are, we may say, three conspicuous types of life, the sensual, the political, and, thirdly, the life of thought. Now the mass of men present an absolutely slavish appearance, choosing the life of brute beasts, but they have ground for so doing because so many persons in authority share the tastes of Sardanapalus. [A half-legendary ruler of ancient Assyria, whose name to the Greeks stood for the extreme of Far Eastern luxury and extravagance.] Cultivated and energetic people, on the other hand, identify happiness with honor, as honor is the general end of political life. But this seems too superficial an idea for our present purpose; for honor depends more upon the people who pay it than upon the person to whom it is paid, and the good we feel is something which is proper to a man himself and cannot be easily taken away from him. Men too appear to seek honor in order to be assured of their own goodness. Accordingly, they seek it at the hands of the sage and of those who know them well, and they seek it on the ground of their virtue; clearly then, in their judgment at any rate, virtue is better than honor. Perhaps then we might look on virtue rather than honor as the end of political life. Yet even this idea appears not quite complete; for a man may possess virtue and yet be asleep or inactive throughout life, and not only so, but he may experience the greatest calamities and misfortunes. Yet no one would call such a life a life of happiness, unless he were maintaining a paradox. But we need not dwell further on this subject, since it is sufficiently discussed in popular philosophical treatises. The third life is the life of thought ....

The life of money making is a life of constraint; and wealth is obviously not the good of which we are in quest; for it is useful merely as a means to something else. It would be more reasonable to take the things mentioned before—sensual pleasure, honor, and virtue—as ends than wealth, since they are things desired on their own account. Yet these too are evidently not ends, although much argument has been employed to show that they are ....

But leaving this subject for the present, let us revert to the good of which we are in quest and consider what it may be. For it seems different in different activities or arts; it is one thing in medicine, another in strategy, and so on. What is the good in each of these instances? It is presumably that for the sake of which all else is done. In medicine this is health, in strategy victory, in architecture a house, and so on. In every activity and undertaking it is the end, since it is for the sake of the end that all people do whatever else they do. If then there is an end for all our activity, this will be the good to be accomplished; and if there are several such ends, it will be these.

Our argument has arrived by a different path at the same point as before; but we must endeavor to make it still plainer. Since there are more ends than one, and some of these ends—for example, wealth, flutes, and instruments generally—we desire as means to something else, it is evident that not all are final ends. But the highest good is clearly something final. Hence if there is only one final end, this will be the object of which we are in search; and if there are more than one, it will be the most final. We call that which is sought after for its own sake more final than that which is sought after as a means to something else; we call that which is never desired as a means to something else more final than things that are desired both for themselves and as means to something else. Therefore, we call absolutely final that which is always desired for itself and never as a means to something else. Now happiness more than anything else answers to this description. For happiness we always desire for its own sake and never as a means to something else, whereas honor, pleasure, intelligence, and every virtue we desire partly for their own sakes (for we should desire them independently of what might result from them), but partly also as means to happiness, because we suppose they will prove instruments of happiness. Happiness, on the other hand, nobody desires for the sake of these things, nor indeed as a means to anything else at all ....

Perhaps, however, it seems a commonplace to say that happiness is the supreme good; what is wanted is to define its nature a little more clearly. The best way of arriving at such a definition will probably be to ascertain the function of man. For, as with a flute player, a sculptor, or any artist, or in fact anybody who has a special function or activity, his goodness and excellence seem to lie in his function, so it would seem to be with man, if indeed he has a special function. Can it be said that, while a carpenter and a cobbler have special functions and activities, man, unlike them, is naturally functionless? Or, as the eye, the hand, the foot, and similarly each part of the body has a special function, so may man be regarded as having a special function apart from all these? What, then, can this function be? It is not life; for life is apparently something that man shares with plants; and we are looking for something peculiar to him. We must exclude therefore the life of nutrition and growth. There is next what may be called the life of sensation. But this too, apparently, is shared by man with horses, cattle, and all other animals. There remains what I may call the active life of the rational part of man's being. Now this rational part is twofold; one part is rational in the sense of being obedient to reason, and the other in the sense of possessing and exercising reason and intelligence.

The function of man then is activity of soul in accordance with reason, or not apart from reason. Now, the function of a man of a certain kind, and of a man who is good of that kind—for example, of a harpist and a good harpist—are in our view the same in kind. This is true of all people of all kinds without exception, the superior excellence being only an addition to the function; for it is the function of a harpist to play the harp, and of a good harpist to play the harp well. This being so, if we define the function of man as a kind of life, and this life as an activity of the soul or a course of action in accordance with reason, and if the function of a good man is such activity of a good and noble kind, and if everything is well done when it is done in accordance with its proper excellence, it follows that the good of man is activity of soul in accordance with virtue, or, if there are more virtues than one, in accordance with the best and most complete virtue. But we must add the words "in a complete life." For as one swallow or one day does not make a spring, so one day or a short time does not make a man blessed or happy ....

Our account accords too with the view of those who hold that happiness is virtue or excellence of some sort; for activity in accordance with virtue is virtue. But there is plainly a considerable difference between calling the supreme good possession or use, a state of mind, or an activity. For a state of mind may exist without producing anything good—for example, if a person is asleep, or in any other way inert. Not so with an activity, since activity implies acting and acting well. As in the Olympic games it is not the most beautiful and strongest who receive the crown but those who actually enter the combat, for from those come the victors, so it is those who act that win rightly what is noble and good in life.

Their life too is pleasant in itself. For pleasure is a state of mind, and whatever a man is fond of is pleasant to him, as a horse is to a lover of horses, a show to a lover of spectacles, and, similarly, just acts to a lover of justice, and virtuous acts in general to a lover of virtue. Now most men find a sense of discord in their pleasures, because their pleasures are not all naturally pleasant. But the lovers of nobleness take pleasure in what is naturally pleasant, and virtuous acts are naturally pleasant. Such acts then are pleasant both to these persons and in themselves. Nor does the life of such persons need more pleasure attached to it as a sort of charm; it possesses pleasure in itself. For, it may be added, a man who does not delight in noble acts is not good; as nobody would call a man just who did not enjoy just action, or liberal who did not enjoy liberal action, and so on. If this is so, it follows that acts of virtue are pleasant in themselves. They are also good and noble, and good and noble in the highest degree, for the judgment of the virtuous man on them is right, and his judgment is as we have described. Happiness then is the best and noblest and pleasantest thing in the world ....

Still it is clear, as we said, that happiness requires the addition of external goods; for it is impossible, or at least difficult, to do noble deeds with no outside means. For many things can be done only through the aid of friends or wealth or political power; and there are some things the lack of which spoils our felicity, such as good birth, wholesome children, and personal beauty. For a man who is extremely ugly in appearance or low born or solitary and childless can hardly be happy; perhaps still less so, if he has exceedingly bad children or friends, or has had good children or friends and lost them by death. As we said, then, happiness seems to need prosperity of this kind in addition to virtue. For this reason some persons identify happiness with good fortune, though others do so with virtue ....

It is reasonable then not to call an ox or a horse or any other animal happy; for none of them is capable of sharing in this activity. For the same reason no child can be happy, since the youth of a child keeps him for the time being from such activity; if a child is ever called happy, the ground of felicitation is his promise, rather than his actual performance. For happiness demands, as we said, a complete virtue and a complete life. And there are all sorts of changes and chances in life, and the most prosperous of men may in his old age fall into extreme calamities, as Priam did in the heroic legends. [The disastrous fate of Priam, king of Troy, was part of the well-known Homeric tales.] And a person who has experienced such chances and died a miserable death, nobody calls happy ....

Now the events of chance are numerous and of different magnitudes. Small pieces of good fortune or the reverse do not turn the scale of life in any way, but great and numerous events make life happier if they turn out well, since they naturally give it beauty and the use of them may be noble and good. If, on the other hand, they turn out badly, they mar and mutilate happiness by causing pain and hindrances to many activities. Still, even in these circumstances, nobility shines out when a person bears with calmness the weight of accumulated misfortunes, not from insensibility but from dignity and greatness of spirit.

Then if activities determine the quality of life, as we said, no happy man can become miserable; for he will never do what is hateful and mean. For our idea of the truly good and wise man is that he bears all the chances of life with dignity and always does what is best in the circumstances, as a good general makes the best use of the forces at his command in war, or a good cobbler makes the best shoe with the leather given him, and so on through the whole series of the arts. If this is so, the happy man can never become miserable. I do not say that he will be fortunate if he meets such chances of life as Priam. Yet he will not be variable or constantly changing, for he will not be moved from his happiness easily or by ordinary misfortunes, but only by great and numerous ones; nor after them will he quickly regain his happiness. If he regains it at all, it will be only over a long and complete period of time and after great and notable achievement.

We may safely then define a happy man as one who is active in accord with perfect virtue and adequately furnished with external goods, not for some chance period of time but for his whole lifetime ....

Inasmuch as happiness is an activity of soul in accordance with complete or perfect virtue, it is necessary to consider virtue, as this will perhaps be the best way of studying happiness ....

Book II: Virtue and the Mean

Virtue then is twofold, partly intellectual and partly moral, and intellectual virtue is originated and fostered mainly by teaching; it therefore demands experience and time. Moral virtue on the other hand is the outcome of habit. From this fact it is clear that moral virtue is not implanted in us by nature, for a law of nature cannot be altered by habituation. Thus a stone, that naturally tends to fall downwards, cannot be habituated or trained to rise upwards. It is neither by nature then nor in defiance of nature that virtues are implanted in us. Nature gives us the capacity of receiving them, and that capacity is perfected by habit.

Again, if we take the various natural powers which belong to us, we first possess the proper faculties and afterwards display the activities. It is obviously so with the senses. Not by seeing frequently or hearing frequently do we acquire the sense of seeing or hearing; on the contrary, because we have the senses we make use of them; we do not get them by making use of them. But the virtues we get by first practicing them, as we do in the arts. For it is by doing what we ought to do when we study the arts that we learn the arts themselves; we become builders by building and harpists by playing the harp. Similarly, it is by doing just acts that we become just, by doing temperate acts that we become temperate, by doing brave acts that we become brave. The experience of states confirms this statement, for it is by training in good habits that lawmakers make the citizens good. This is the object all lawmakers have at heart; if they do not succeed in it, they fail of their purpose; and it makes the distinction between a good constitution and a bad one.

Again, the causes and means by which any virtue is produced and destroyed are the same. It is by our actions in dealing between man and man that we become either just or unjust. It is by our actions in the face of danger and by our training ourselves to fear or to courage that we become either cowardly or courageous. It is much the same with our appetites and angry passions. People become temperate and gentle, others licentious and passionate, by behaving in one or the other way in particular circumstances. In a word, moral states are the results of activities like the states themselves. It is our duty therefore to keep a certain character in our activities, since our moral states depend on the differences in our activities. So the difference between one and another training in habits in our childhood is not a light matter, but important, or rather, all-important.

Our present study is not, like other studies, purely theoretical in intention; for the object of our inquiry is not to know what virtue is but how to become good, and that is the sole benefit of it. We must, therefore, consider the right way of performing actions, for it is acts that determine the character of the resulting moral states.

That we should act in accordance with right reason is a common general principle, which may here be taken for granted ....

The first point to be observed is that in matters we are now considering deficiency and excess are both fatal. It is so, we see, in questions of health and strength. Too much or too little gymnastic exercise is fatal to strength. Similarly, too much or too little meat and drink is fatal to health, whereas a suitable amount produces, increases, and sustains it ....

It is the same with temperance, courage, and other moral virtues. A person who avoids and is afraid of everything and faces nothing becomes a coward; a person who is not afraid of anything but is ready to face everything becomes foolhardy. Similarly, he who enjoys every pleasure and abstains from none is licentious; he who refuses all pleasures, like a boor, is an insensible sort of person. For temperance and courage are destroyed by excess and deficiency but preserved by the mean ....

Every art then performs its function well, if it regards the mean and refers the works which it produces to the mean. This is the reason why it is usually said of successful works that it is impossible to take anything from them or to add anything to them, which implies that excess or deficiency is fatal to excellence but that the mean state ensures it. Good artists too, as we say, have an eye to the mean in their works. But virtue, like Nature herself, is more accurate and better than any art; virtue therefore will aim at the mean;—I speak of moral virtue, as it is moral virtue which is concerned with emotions and actions, and it is these which admit of excess and deficiency and the mean. Thus it is possible to go too far, or not to go far enough, in respect of fear, courage, desire, anger, pity, and pleasure and pain generally, and the excess and the deficiency are alike wrong; but to experience these emotions at the right times and on the right occasions and towards the right persons and for the right causes and in the right manner is the mean or the supreme good, which is characteristic of virtue. Similarly there may be excess, deficiency, or the mean, in regard to actions. But virtue is concerned with emotions and actions, and here excess is an error and deficiency a fault, whereas the mean is successful and laudable, and success and merit are both characteristics of virtue.

It appears then that virtue is a mean state, so far at least as it aims at the mean ....

On the other hand, there are many different ways of going wrong; for evil is in its nature infinite. [It] is easy to miss the mark but difficult to hit it. And so by reasoning excess and deficiency are characteristics of vice and the mean is a characteristic of virtue.

Virtue then is a state of deliberate moral purpose consisting in a mean that is relative to ourselves, the mean being determined by reason, or as a prudent man would determine it ....

But not every action or every emotion admits of a mean. There are some whose very name implies wickedness, as, for example, malice, shamelessness, and envy among the emotions, and adultery, theft, and murder among the actions. All these and others like them are marked as intrinsically wicked, not merely the excesses or deficiencies of them. It is never possible then to be right in them; they are always sinful. Right or wrong in such acts as adultery does not depend on our committing it with the right woman, at the right time, or in the right manner; on the contrary it is wrong to do it at all. It would be equally false to suppose that there can be a mean or excess of deficiency in unjust, cowardly, or licentious conduct ....

There are then three dispositions, two being vices, namely, excess and deficiency, and one virtue, which is the mean between them; and they are all in a sense morally opposed. Thus the brave man appears foolhardy compared with the coward, but cowardly compared with the foolhardy. Similarly, the temperate man appears licentious compared with the insensible man but insensible compared with the licentious; and the liberal man appears extravagant compared with the stingy man but stingy compared with the spendthrift. The result is that the extremes each denounce the mean as belonging to the other extreme; the coward calls the brave man foolhardy, and the foolhardy man calls him cowardly; and so on in other cases ....

That is why it is so hard to be good; for it is always hard to find the mean in anything; anybody can get angry—that is easy—and anybody can give or spend money, but to give it to the right person, to give the right amount of it, at the right time, for the right cause and in the right way, this is not what anybody can do, nor is it easy. That is why goodness is rare, praiseworthy, and noble. One who aims at the mean must begin by departing from the extreme, for of the two extremes one is more wrong than the other .... We must also note the weakness to which we are ourselves particularly prone, since different natures tend in different ways; and we may ascertain what our tendency is by observing our feelings of pleasure and pain. Then we must drag ourselves away towards the opposite extreme; for by pulling ourselves as far as possible from what is wrong we shall arrive at the mean.

In all cases we must especially be on our guard against the pleasant, or pleasure, for we are not impartial judges of pleasure ....

Undoubtedly [finding the mean] is a difficult task, especially in individual cases. It is not easy to determine the right matter, objects, occasion, and duration of anger. Sometimes we praise people who are deficient in anger, and call them gentle, and at other times we praise people who exhibit a fierce temper as high spirited. It is not however a man who deviates a little from goodness, but one who deviates a great deal, whether on the side of excess or of deficiency, that is blamed; for he is sure to call attention to himself. It is not easy to decide in theory how far and to what extent a man may go before he becomes blameworthy, but neither is it easy to define in theory anything else in the region of the senses; such things depend on circumstances, and our judgment of them depends on our perception.

98   Moral Thinking

> **Review and Discussion Questions**
>
> 1. What is the end or function of human beings, according to Aristotle?
> 2. How does Aristotle understand happiness? Why does he think it is the supreme good?
> 3. Why does Aristotle reject the pursuit of money or pleasure as the key to happiness?
> 4. Explain Aristotle's understanding of the nature of virtue and its connection with habit.
> 5. Explain the theory of the virtues as a mean between extremes. Give examples of the virtues.
> 6. Do you agree that happiness (or well-being) and virtue are connected? If not, what *is* the basis of happiness?

READING: THE FUNDAMENTAL PRINCIPLES OF THE METAPHYSIC OF MORALS

IMMANUEL KANT*

Immanuel Kant lived his entire life within a few miles of Konigsberg, in East Prussia, where he was born in 1724. Kant never married and was a man of remarkable organization and regularity of habits; it is even said that people would set their clocks based on his afternoon walks. Like Thomas Hobbes, he lived a long and very productive life, dying in 1804 at the age of eighty. Kant's writing has had and continues to have an immense impact on all areas of philosophy, from epistemology and ethics to metaphysics and political theory.

Rejecting both Aristotle, who believed it necessary to study closely human psychology and the nature of human happiness in order to understand morality, and utilitarians, who often believe sentiment and feeling to be at the root of morality, Kant argues that duty is based solely on reason. To be genuinely worthy, Kant argues, one must not just act *in accordance with* duty; one must also act *for duty's sake*. To do the right thing out of selfish motives (for fear of getting caught, for example) would not be to act for the sake of duty and, therefore, would not evidence the kind of value that actions done purely for the sake of duty do.

How then is one to know what duty requires? Kant argues that reason provides the foundation on which duty rests. An action is right, he claims, if it conforms to a moral rule that any agent must follow if he or she is to act rationally. That rule, which distinguishes right from wrong, is what Kant calls the *categorical* (that is, exceptionless) *imperative*; an imperative that Kant expresses as requiring that a person must never perform an act unless he or she can consistently will (or intend) that the maxim or principle that motivates the action could become a universal law. In this way, Kant argues, the categorical imperative constitutes the heart of the distinction between right and wrong—a distinction that any rational being can comprehend and act on.

Kant also speaks of a second formulation of the categorical imperative that he believes is equivalent to the first. The second formulation states that one must act so as to treat people as ends in themselves, never merely as means.

---

* From *Fundamental Principles of the Metaphysic of Morals* (1785), trans. Thomas K. Abbott (1873).

That second version, then, looks at actions from the perspective of the one acted upon rather than the agent. After discussing four examples of moral reasoning, Kant concludes with a description of what he terms the "kingdom of ends" as well as of human dignity and autonomy.

The Good Will

Nothing can possibly be conceived in the world, or even out of it, which can be called good without qualification, except a *good will*. Intelligence, wit, judgment, and the other talents of the mind, however they may be named, or courage, resolution, perseverance, as qualities of temperament, are undoubtedly good and desirable in many respects; but these gifts of nature may also become extremely bad and mischievous if the will which is to make use of them, and which, therefore, constitutes what is called *character*, is not good. It is the same with the *gifts of fortune*. Power, riches, honor, even health, and the general well-being and contentment with one's condition which is called *happiness*, inspire pride, and often presumption, if there is not a good will to correct the influence of these on the mind, and with this also to rectify the whole principle of acting, and adapt it to its end. The sight of a being who is not adorned with a single feature of a pure and good will, enjoying unbroken prosperity, can never give pleasure to an impartial rational spectator. Thus a good will appears to constitute the indispensable condition even of being worthy of happiness.

There are even some qualities which are of service to this good will itself, and may facilitate its action, yet which have no intrinsic unconditional value, but always presuppose a good will, and this qualifies the esteem that we justly have for them, and does not permit us to regard them as absolutely good. Moderation in the affections and passions, self-control, and calm deliberation are not only good in many respects, but even seem to constitute part of the intrinsic worth of the person; but they are far from deserving to be called good without qualification, although they have been so unconditionally praised by the ancients. For without the principles of a good will, they may become extremely bad; and the coolness of a villain not only makes him far more dangerous, but also directly makes him more abominable in our eyes than he would have been without it.

A good will is good not because of what it performs or effects, not by its aptness for the attainment of some proposed end, but simply by virtue of the volition—that is, it is good in itself, and considered by itself is to be esteemed much higher than all that can be brought about by it in favor of any inclination, nay, even of the sum-total of all inclinations. Even if it should happen that, owing to special disfavor of fortune, or the niggardly provision of a stepmotherly nature, this will should wholly lack power to accomplish its purpose, if with its greatest efforts it should yet achieve nothing, and there should remain only the good will (not, to be sure, a mere wish, but the summoning of all means in our power), then, like a jewel, it would still shine by its own light, as a thing which has its whole value in itself. Its usefulness or fruitlessness can neither add to nor take away anything from this value. It would be, as it were, only the setting to enable us to handle it the more conveniently in common commerce, or to attract to it the attention of those who are not yet connoisseurs, but not to recommend it to true connoisseurs, or to determine its value ....

The First Proposition of Morality

We have then to develop the notion of a will which deserves to be highly esteemed for itself, and is good without a view to anything further .... [Consider] that it is always a matter of duty that a tradesman should not overcharge an inexperienced purchaser; and wherever there is much commerce the prudent tradesman does not overcharge, but keeps a fixed price of everyone, so that a child buys of him as well as any other. Men are thus honestly served, but this is not enough to make us believe that the tradesman acted from duty and from principles of honesty: his own advantage required it. Accordingly the action was done neither from duty nor from direct inclination, but merely with a selfish view ....

On the other hand, it is a duty to maintain one's life; and, in addition, everyone also has a direct inclination to do so. But on this account the often anxious care which most men take for it has no intrinsic worth, and their maxim has no moral import. They preserve their life *as duty requires*, no doubt, but not *because duty requires*. On the other hand, if adversity and hopeless sorrow have completely taken away the relish for life; if the unfortunate one, strong in mind, indignant at his fate rather than desponding or dejected, wishes for death, and yet preserves his life without loving it—not from inclination of fear, but from duty—then his maxim has a moral worth ....

To be beneficent when we can is a duty; and besides this, there are many minds so sympathetically constituted that, without any other motive of vanity or self-interest, they find a pleasure in spreading joy around them, and can take delight in the satisfaction of others so far as it is their own work. But I maintain that in such a case an action of this kind, however proper, however amiable it may be, has nevertheless no true moral worth, but is on a level with other inclinations, for example, the inclination to honor, which, if it is happily directed to that which is in fact of public utility and accordant with duty, and consequently honorable, deserves praise and encouragement, but not esteem. For the maxim[1] lacks the moral import, namely, that such actions be done *from duty*, not from inclination. Put the case that the mind of that philanthropist was clouded by sorrow of his own, extinguishing all sympathy with the lot of others, and that while he still has the power to benefit others in distress, he is not touched by their trouble because he is absorbed with his own; and now suppose that he tears himself out of this dead insensibility and performs the action without any inclination to it, but simply from duty, then ... has his action its genuine moral worth .... It is just in this that the moral worth of the character is brought out which is incomparably the highest of all, namely, that he is beneficent, not from inclination, but from duty ....

It is in this manner, undoubtedly, that we are to understand those passages of Scripture in which we are commanded to love our neighbour, even our enemy. For love, as an affection, cannot be commanded, but beneficence for duty's sake may. This is *practical* love, and not *pathological*—a love that is seated in the will, and not in the propensities of feeling—in principles of action and not of tender sympathy; and it is this love alone which can be commanded.

The Second and Third Propositions of Morality

The second proposition is: That an action done from duty derives its moral worth, *not from the purpose* which is to be attained by it, but from the maxim by which it is determined, and therefore does not depend on the realization of the object of the action, but merely on the *principle of volition* by which the action has taken place, without regard to any object of desire. It is clear from what precedes that the purposes which we may have in view in our actions, or their effects regarded as ends and springs of the will, cannot give to actions any unconditional or moral worth. In what, then, can their worth lie if it is not to consist in the will and in reference to its expected effect? It cannot lie anywhere but in the *principle of the will* without regard to the ends which can be attained by the action ....

The third proposition, which is a consequence of the two preceding, I would express thus: *Duty is the necessity of acting from respect for the law.* I may have *inclination* for an object as the effect of my proposed action, but I cannot have respect for it just for this reason that it is an effect and not an energy of will. Similarly, I cannot have *respect* for inclination, whether my own or another's; I can at most, if my own, approve it; if another's, sometimes even love it, that is, look on it as favorable to my own interest. It is only what is connected with my will as a principle, by no means as an effect—what does not sub-serve my inclination, but overpowers it, or at least in case of choice excludes it from its calculation—in other words, simply the law of itself, which can be an object of respect, and hence a command. Now an action done from duty must wholly exclude the influence of inclination, and with it every object of the will, so that nothing remains which can determine the will except objectively the *law*, and subjectively *pure respect* for this practical law, and consequently the maxim[2] that I should follow this law even to the thwarting of all my inclinations.

Thus the moral worth of an action does not lie in the effect expected from it, nor in any principle of action which requires to borrow its motive from this expected effect. For all these effects—agreeableness of one's condition, and even the promotion of the happiness of others—could have been also brought about by other causes, so that for this there would have been no need of the will of a rational being; whereas it is in this alone that the supreme and unconditional good can be found. The pre-eminent good which we call moral can therefore consist in nothing else than *the conception of law* in itself, *which certainly is only possible in a rational being*, in so far as this conception, and not the expected effect, determines the will. This is a good which is already present in the person who acts accordingly, and we have not to wait for it to appear first in the result.

The Supreme Principle of Morality: The Categorical Imperative

But what sort of law can that be the conception of which must determine the will, even without paying any regard to the effect expected from it, in order that this will may be called good absolutely and without qualification? As I have deprived the will of every impulse which could arise to it from obedience to any law, there remains nothing but the universal conformity of its actions to law in general, which alone is to serve the will as a principle, that is, I am never to act otherwise than so *that I could also will that my maxim should become a universal law.* Here, now, it is the simple conformity to law in general, without assuming any particular law applicable to certain actions, that serves the will as its principle, and must so serve it if duty is not to be a vain delusion and a chimerical notion. The common reason of men in its practical judgments perfectly coincides with this, and always has in view the principle here suggested. Let the question be, for example: may I when in distress make a promise with the intention not to keep it? I readily distinguish here between the two significations which the question may have: whether it is prudent or whether it is right to make a false promise. The former may undoubtedly often be the case. I see clearly indeed that it is not enough to extricate myself from a present difficulty by means of this subterfuge, but it must be well considered whether there may not hereafter spring from this lie much greater inconvenience than that from which I now free myself, and as, with all my supposed *cunning*, the consequences cannot be so easily foreseen but that credit once lost may be much more injurious to me than any mischief which I seek to avoid at present, it should be considered whether it would not be more *prudent* to act herein according to a universal maxim, and to make it a habit to promise nothing except with the intention of keeping it. But it is soon clear to me that such a maxim will still only be based on the fear of consequences. Now it is a wholly different thing to be truthful from duty, and to be so from apprehension of injurious consequences. In the first case, the very notion of the action already implies a law for me; in the second case, I must first look about elsewhere to see what results may be combined with it which would affect myself. For to deviate from the principle of duty is beyond all doubt wicked; but to be unfaithful to my maxim of prudence may often be very advantageous to me, although to abide by it is certainly safer. The shortest way, however, and an unerring one, to discover the answer to this question whether a lying promise is consistent with duty, is to ask myself, Should I be content that my maxim (to extricate myself from difficulty by a false promise) should hold good as a universal law, for myself as well as for others; and should I be able to say to myself, "Every one may make a deceitful promise when he finds himself in a difficulty from which he cannot otherwise extricate himself"? Then I presently become aware that, while I can will the lie, I can by no means will that lying should be a universal law. For with such a law there would be no promises at all, since it would be in vain to allege my intention in regard to my future actions to those who would not believe this allegation, or if they over-hastily did so, would pay me back in my own coin. Hence my maxim, so soon as it should be made a universal law, would necessarily destroy itself.

I do not, therefore, need any far-reaching penetration to discern what I have to do in order that my will may be morally good. Inexperienced in the course of the world, incapable of being prepared for all its contingencies, I only ask myself; Canst thou also will that thy maxim should be a universal law? If not, then it must be rejected, and that not because of a disadvantage accruing from it to myself or even to others, but because it cannot enter as a principle into a possible universal legislation, and reason extorts from me immediate respect for such legislation. I do not indeed as yet *discern* on what this respect is based (this the philosopher may inquire), but at least I understand this—that it is an estimation of the worth which far outweighs all worth of what is recommended by inclination, and that the necessity of acting from pure respect for the practical law is what constitutes duty, to which every other motive must give place because it is the condition of a will being good *in itself*, and the worth of such a will is above everything.

Thus, then, without quitting the moral knowledge of common human reason, we have arrived at its principle. And although, no doubt, common men do not conceive it in such an abstract and universal form, yet they always have it really before their eyes and use it as the standard of their decision. Here it would be easy to show how, with this compass in hand, men are well able to distinguish, in every case that occurs, what is good, what bad, conformably to duty or inconsistent with it ....

Imperatives: Hypothetical and Categorical

Everything in nature works according to laws. Rational beings alone have the faculty of acting according *to the conception of laws*, that is according to principles, *i.e.*, have a *will*. Since the deduction of actions from principles requires *reason*, the will is nothing but practical reason .... The conception of an objective principle, in so far as it is obligatory for a will, is called a command (of reason), and the formula of the command is called an Imperative.

All imperatives are expressed by the word *ought* [or *shall*], and thereby indicate the relation of an objective law of reason to a will, which from its subjective constitution is not necessarily determined by it (an obligation) ....

Now all *imperatives* command either *hypothetically* or *categorically*. The former represent the practical necessity of a possible action as means to something else that is willed (or at least which one might possibly will). The categorical imperative would be that which represented an action as necessary of itself without reference to another end, that is, as objectively necessary ....

If now the action is good only as a means to *something else*, then the imperative is *hypothetical*; if it is conceived as good *in itself* and consequently as being necessarily the principle of a will which of itself conforms to reason, then it is *categorical* ....

Accordingly the hypothetical imperative only says that the action is good for some purpose, *possible or actual*. In the first case it is a *problematical*, in the second an *assertorial* practical principle. The categorical imperative which declares an action to be objectively necessary in itself without reference to any purpose, that is, without any other end, is valid as an *apodictic* (practical) principle ....

First Formulation of the Categorical Imperative: Universal Law

When I conceive a hypothetical imperative, in general I do not know beforehand what it will contain until I am given the condition. But when I conceive a categorical imperative, I know at once what it contains. For as the imperative contains besides the law only the necessity that the maxims shall conform to this law, while the law contains no conditions restricting it, there remains nothing but the general statement that the maxim of the action should conform to a universal law, and it is this conformity alone that the imperative properly represents as necessary.

There is therefore but one categorical imperative, namely, this: *Act only on that maxim whereby thou canst at the same time will that it should become a universal law.*

Now if all imperatives of duty can be deduced from this one imperative as from their principle, then, although it should remain undecided whether what is called duty is not merely a vain notion, yet at least we shall be able to show what we understand by it and what this notion means ....

Four Illustrations

We will now enumerate a few duties, adopting the usual division of them into duties to ourselves and to others, and into perfect and imperfect duties.

1. A man reduced to despair by a series of misfortunes feels wearied of life, but is still so far in possession of his reason that he can ask himself whether it would not be contrary to his duty to himself to take his own life. Now he inquires whether the maxim of his action could become a universal law of nature. His maxim is: From self-love I adopt it as a principle to shorten my life when its longer duration is likely to bring more evil than satisfaction. It is asked then simply whether this principle founded on self-love can become a universal law of nature. Now we see at once that a system of nature of which it should be a law to destroy life by means of the very feeling whose special nature it is to impel to the improvement of life would contradict itself, and therefore could not exist as a system of nature; hence that maxim cannot possibly exist as a universal law of nature, and consequently would be wholly inconsistent with the supreme principle of all duty.

2. Another finds himself forced by necessity to borrow money. He knows that he will not be able to repay it, but sees also that nothing will be lent to him unless he promises stoutly to repay it in a definite time. He desires to make this promise, but he has still so much conscience as to ask himself: Is it not unlawful and inconsistent with duty to get out of a difficulty in this way? Suppose, however, that he resolves to do so, then the maxim of his action would be expressed thus: When I think myself in want of money, I will borrow money and promise to repay it, although I know that I never can do so. Now this principle of self-love or of one's own advantage may perhaps be consistent with my whole future welfare; but the question now is, Is it right? I change then the suggestion of self-love into a universal law, and state the question thus: How would it be if my maxim were a universal law? Then I see at once that it could never hold as a universal law of nature, but would necessarily contradict itself. For supposing it to be a universal law that everyone when he thinks himself in a difficulty should be able to promise whatever he pleases, with the purpose of not keeping his promise, the promise itself would become impossible, as well as the end that one might have in view in it, since no one would consider that anything was promised to him, but would ridicule all such statements as vain pretenses.

3. A third finds in himself a talent which with the help of some culture might make him a useful man in many respects. But he finds himself in comfortable circumstances and prefers to indulge in pleasure rather than to take pains in enlarging and improving his happy natural capacities. He asks, however, whether his maxim of neglect of his natural gifts, besides agreeing with his inclination to indulgence, agrees also with what is called duty. He sees then

that a system of nature could indeed subsist with such a universal law, although men (like the South Sea islanders) should let their talents rest and resolve to devote their lives merely to idleness, amusement, and propagation of their species—in a word, to enjoyment; but he cannot possibly will that this should be a universal law of nature, or be implanted in us as such by a natural instinct. For, as a rational being, he necessarily wills that his faculties be developed, since they serve him, and have been given him, for all sorts of possible purposes.

4 A fourth, who is in prosperity, while he sees that others have to contend with great wretchedness and that he could help them, thinks: What concern is it of mine? Let everyone be as happy as Heaven pleases, or as he can make himself; I will take nothing from him nor even envy him, only I do not wish to contribute anything to his welfare or to his assistance in distress! Now no doubt, if such a mode of thinking were a universal law, the human race might very well subsist, and doubtless even better than in a state in which everyone talks of sympathy and good-will, or even takes care occasionally to put it into practice, but, on the other side, also cheats when he can, betrays the rights of men, or otherwise violates them. But although it is possible that a universal law of nature might exist in accordance with that maxim, it is impossible *to will* that such a principle should have the universal validity of a law of nature. For a will which resolved this would contradict itself, inasmuch as many cases might occur in which one would have need of the love and sympathy of others, and in which, by such a law of nature, sprung from his own will, he would deprive himself of all hope of the aid he desires.

These are a few of the many actual duties, or at least what we regard as such, which obviously fall into two classes on the one principle that we have laid down. We must be *able to will* that a maxim of our action should be a universal law. This is the canon of the moral appreciation of the action generally. Some actions are of such a character that their maxim cannot without contradiction be even *conceived* as a universal law of nature, far from it being possible that we should *will* that it *should* be so. In others, this intrinsic impossibility is not found, but still it is impossible to *will* that their maxim should be raised to the universality of a law of nature, since such a will would contradict itself ....

Second Formulation of the Categorical Imperative: Humanity as End in Itself

The will is conceived as a faculty of determining oneself to action *in accordance with the conception of certain laws*. And such a faculty can be found only in rational beings. The ends which a rational being proposes to himself at pleasure as *effects* of his actions are all only relative, for it is only their relation to the particular desires of the subject that gives them their worth, which therefore cannot furnish principles universal and necessary for all rational beings and every volition, that is to say practical laws. Hence all these relative ends can give only hypothetical imperatives. Supposing, however, that there were something *whose existence* has *in itself* an absolute worth, something which, being *an end in itself*, could be a source of definite laws, then in this and this alone would lie the source of a possible categorical imperative, *i.e.*, a practical law ....

Now I say: man and generally any rational being exists as an end in himself, *not merely as a means* to be arbitrarily used by this or that will, but in all his actions, whether they concern himself or other rational beings, must be always regarded at the same time as an end. All objects of the inclinations have only a conditional worth; for if the inclinations and the wants founded on them did not exist, then their object would be without value. Thus the worth of any object which is *to be acquired* by our action is always conditional. Beings whose existence depends not on our will but on nature's, have nevertheless, if they are nonrational beings, only a relative value as means, and are therefore called *things*; rational beings, on the contrary, are called *persons*, because their very nature points them out as ends in themselves, that is, as something which must not be used merely as means, and so far therefore restricts freedom of action (and is an object of respect). These, therefore, are not merely subjective ends whose existence has a worth *for us* as an effect of our action, but *objective ends*, that is, things whose existence is an end in itself—an end, moreover, for which no other can be substituted, which they should sub-serve *merely* as means, for otherwise nothing whatever would possess *absolute worth* ....

If then there is a supreme practical principle or, in respect of the human will, a categorical imperative, it must be one which, being drawn from the conception of that which is necessarily an end for everyone because it is *an end in itself*, constitutes an objective principle of will, and can therefore serve as a universal practical law. The foundation of this principle is: *rational nature exists as an end in itself*. Man necessarily conceives his own existence as being so: so far then this is a *subjective* principle of human actions. But every other rational being regards its existence similarly, just on the same rational principle that holds for me: so that it is at the same time an objective principle, from which as a supreme practical law all laws of the will must be capable of being deduced. Accordingly the practical imperative will be as follows: *So act as to treat humanity, whether in thine own person or in that of any other, in every case as an end withal, never as means only*. We will now inquire whether this can be practically carried out ....

The Kingdom of Ends

The conception of the will of every rational being as one which must consider itself as giving in all the maxims of its will universal laws, so as to judge itself and its actions from this point of view—this conception leads to another which depends on it and is very fruitful, namely that of a *kingdom of ends*.

By a *kingdom* I understand the union of different rational beings in a system by common laws. Now since it is by laws that ends are determined as regards their universal validity, hence, if we abstract from the personal differences of rational beings and likewise from all the content of their private ends, we shall be able to conceive all ends combined in a systematic whole (including both rational beings as ends in themselves, and also the special ends which each may propose to himself), that is to say, we can conceive a kingdom of ends, which on the preceding principles is possible.

For all rational beings come under the *law* that each of them must treat itself and all others *never merely as means*, but in every case *at the same time as ends in themselves.* Hence results a systematic union of rational beings by common objective laws, *i.e.,* a kingdom which may be called a kingdom of ends, since what these laws have in view is just the relation of these beings to one another as ends and means. It is certainly only an ideal.

A rational being belongs as a *member* to the kingdom of ends when although giving universal laws in it he is also himself subject to these laws. He belongs to it *as sovereign,* when while giving laws he is not subject to the will of any other.

A rational being must always regard himself as giving laws in a kingdom of ends which freedom of the will makes possible, whether it be as member or as sovereign. He cannot, however, maintain the latter position merely by the maxims of his will, but only in case he is a completely independent being without wants and with unrestricted power adequate to his will.

Morality consists then in the reference of all action to the legislation which alone can render a kingdom of ends possible. This legislation must be capable of existing in every rational being, and of emanating from his will, so that the principle of this will, is never to act on any maxim which could not without contradiction be also a universal law, and accordingly always so to act *that the will could at the same time regard itself as giving in its maxims universal laws.* If now the maxims of rational beings are not by their own nature coincident with this objective principle, then the necessity of acting on it is called practical obligation, *i.e., duty.* Duty does not apply to the sovereign in the kingdom of ends, but it does to every member of it and to all in the same degree.

The practical necessity of acting on this principle, *i.e.,* duty, does not rest at all on feelings, impulses, or inclinations, but solely on the relation of rational beings to one another, a relation in which the will of a rational being must always be regarded as *legislative* ....

In the kingdom of ends everything has either Value or Dignity. Whatever has a value can be replaced by something else which is *equivalent*; whatever on the other hand is above all value, and therefore admits of no equivalent, has a dignity.

Whatever has reference to the general inclinations and wants of mankind has a *market value*; whatever without presupposing a want, corresponds to a certain taste, that is to a satisfaction in the mere purposeless play of our faculties, has a *fancy value*; but that which constitutes the condition under which alone anything can be an end in itself, this has not merely a relative worth, *i.e.,* value, but an intrinsic worth, that is, *dignity.*

Now morality is the condition under which alone a rational being can be an end in himself, since by this alone is it possible that he should be a legislating member in the kingdom of ends. Thus morality, and humanity as capable of it, is that which alone has dignity. Skill and diligence in labour have a market value; wit, lively imagination, and humour have a fancy value; on the other hand, fidelity to promises, benevolence from principle (not from instinct) have an intrinsic worth. Neither nature nor art contains anything which in default of these it could put in their place, for their worth consists not in the effects which spring from them, not in the use and advantage which they secure, but in the disposition of mind, that is the maxims of the will which are ready to manifest themselves in such actions, even though they should not have the desired effect. These actions also need no recommendation from any subjective taste or sentiment, that they may be looked on with immediate favour and satisfaction: they need no immediate propensities or feeling for them; they exhibit the will that performs them as an object of an immediate respect, and nothing but reason is required to *impose* them on the will; not to *flatter* it into them, which in the case of duties would be a contradiction. This estimation therefore shows that the worth of such a disposition is dignity, and places it infinitely above all value, with which it cannot for a moment be brought into comparison or competition without as it were violating its sanctity.

What then is it which justifies virtue or the morally good disposition, in making such lofty claims? It is nothing less than the privilege it secures to the rational being of participating in the giving of universal laws, by which it qualifies him to be a member of a possible kingdom of ends, a privilege to which he was already destined by his own nature as being an end in himself, and on that account legislating in the kingdom of ends; free as regards all laws of physical nature, and obeying those only which he himself gives, and by which his maxims can belong to a system of universal law, to which at the same time he submits himself. For nothing has any worth except what the law assigns it. Now the legislation itself which assigns the worth of everything, must for that very reason possess dignity, that is an unconditional incomparable worth, and the word *respect* alone supplies a becoming expression for the esteem which a rational being must have for it. *Autonomy* then is the basis of the dignity of human and of every rational nature ....

The Autonomy of the Will

Autonomy of the will is the property that the will has of being a law to itself (independently of any property of the objects of volition). The principle of autonomy is this: Always choose in such a way that in the same volition the maxims of the choice are at the same time present as universal law.

If the will seeks the law that is to determine it anywhere but in the fitness of its maxims for its own legislation of universal laws, and if it thus goes outside of itself and seeks this law in the character of any of its objects, then heteronomy always results. The will in that case does not give itself the law, but the object does so because of its relation to the will. This relation, whether it rests on inclination or on representations of reason, admits only of hypothetical imperatives: I ought to do something because I will something else. On the other hand, the moral, and hence categorical, imperative says that I ought to act in this way or that way, even though I did not will something else ....

The Concept of Freedom Is the Key That Explains the Autonomy of the Will

The will is a kind of causality belonging to living beings in so far as they are rational, and *freedom* would be this property of such causality that it can be efficient, independently of foreign causes determining it; just as physical necessity is the property that the causality of all rational beings has of being determined to activity by the influence of foreign causes ....

What else then can freedom of the will be but autonomy, that is, the property of the will to be a law to itself? But the proposition: The will is in every action a law to itself, only expresses the principle to act on no other maxim than that which can also have as an object itself as a universal law. Now this is precisely the formula of the categorical imperative and is the principle of morality, so that a free will and a will subject to moral laws are one and the same ....

Freedom Must Be Presupposed as a Property of the Will of All Rational Beings

It is not enough to predicate freedom of our own will, from whatever reason, if we have not sufficient grounds for predicating the same of all rational beings. For as morality serves as a law for us only because we are rational beings, it must also hold for all rational beings. Now I say every being that cannot act except under the idea of freedom is just for that reason in a practical point of view really free, that is to say, all laws which are inseparably connected with freedom have the same force for him as if his will had been shown to be free in itself by a proof theoretically conclusive. (I adopt this method of assuming freedom merely as an idea which rational beings suppose in their actions, in order to avoid the necessity of proving it in theory. The form is sufficient for my purpose; for even though the speculative proof should not be made out, yet a being that cannot act except with the idea of freedom is bound by the same laws that would oblige a being who is actually free.) Now I affirm that we must attribute to every rational being which has a will that it has also the idea of freedom and acts entirely under this idea. For in such a being we conceive a reason that is practical, that is, has causality in reference to its objects. It must regard itself as the author of its principles independent of foreign influences. Consequently, as practical reason or as the will of a rational being it must regard itself as free, that is to say, the will of such a being cannot be a will of its own except under the idea of freedom. This idea must therefore in a practical point of view be ascribed to every rational being.

Notes

1. A *maxim* is the subjective principle of volition. The objective principle (*i.e.*, that which would also serve subjectively as a practical principle to all rational beings if reason had full power over the faculty of desire) is the practical law.
2. A maxim is a subjective principle of action, and must be distinguished from the objective principle, namely, practical law. The former contains the practical rule set by reason according to the conditions of the subject (often its ignorance or its inclinations), so that it is the principle on which the subject acts; but the law is the objective principle valid for every rational being, and is the principle which it *ought to act*—that is, an imperative.

Review and Discussion Questions

1. What distinguishes acting from inclination and acting from duty? Which reflects genuine moral worth? Why?
2. How do hypothetical and categorical imperatives differ?

3 Describe the two versions Kant gives of the categorical imperative. Give an example of how the categorical imperative is applied.
4 What does Kant mean by a *maxim*?
5 Explain what Kant means by *autonomy*. Are persons autonomous?
6 Explain how Kant would respond to those who emphasize the role of emotions and feelings in morality.

READING: UTILITARIANISM

JOHN STUART MILL[*]

John Stuart Mill (1806–1873) had an unusual childhood, by almost any standard. His father, James Mill, who was a friend of the economist David Ricardo and the legal theorist John Austin, was among the most devoted followers of Jeremy Bentham, the utilitarian philosopher. James developed a plan for the education of his son, John Stuart, that included a rigorous tutoring program and the isolation of the boy from other children. Young John was a brilliant student. By the age of three, he had begun learning Greek. At eight, he learned Latin and pursued mathematics and history. By the age of twelve, he was studying logic and political economy, and at fifteen, he studied law at University College, London, with John Austin.

At twenty-four, Mill began a lifelong friendship and intellectual collaboration with Harriet Taylor. Although they were close companions, Harriet Taylor remained married for two decades. When her husband John Taylor died, she and John Stuart Mill were married. The two then withdrew from "insipid society" and the gossip they had endured for years; they lived happily for seven years until her death. Mill served briefly as a member of Parliament and died in France (where he had bought a house near the cemetery in which Harriet was buried).

Mill's influence has been tremendous; he wrote important books on logic, philosophy of science, and economics, as well as on ethics and political philosophy. *The Subjection of Women* remains a classic, as is *On Liberty*, his brilliant statement of the justification and limits of government and of freedom of speech. In the following selections from *Utilitarianism*, Mill explains utilitarian moral theory, responds to critics, and explores the theory's philosophical basis.

General Remarks

On the present occasion, I shall attempt to contribute something towards the understanding and appreciation of the Utilitarian or Happiness theory, and towards such proof as it is susceptible of. It is evident that this cannot be proof in the ordinary and popular meaning of the term. Questions of ultimate ends are not amenable to direct proof. We are not, however, to infer that its acceptance or rejection must depend on blind impulse, or arbitrary choice. Considerations may be presented

---

[*] From John Stuart Mill, *Utilitarianism* (1861).

capable of determining the intellect either to give or withhold its assent to the doctrine; and this is equivalent of proof.

What Utilitarianism Is

The creed which accepts as the foundation of morals *utility* or the *greatest happiness principle* holds that actions are right in proportion as they tend to promote happiness, wrong as they tend to produce the reverse of happiness. By "happiness" is intended pleasure, and the absence of pain; by "unhappiness," pain, and the privation of pleasure. To give a clear view of the moral standard set up by the theory, much more requires to be said; in particular, what things it includes in the ideas of pain and pleasure, and to what extent this is left an open question. But these supplementary explanations do not affect the theory of life on which this theory of morality is grounded—namely, that pleasure, and freedom from pain, are the only things desirable as ends; and that all desirable things (which are as numerous in the utilitarian as in any other scheme) are desirable either for the pleasure inherent in themselves, or as means to the promotion of pleasure and the prevention of pain.

Now such a theory of life excites in many minds, and among them in some of the most estimable in feeling and purpose, inveterate dislike. To suppose that life has (as they express it) no higher end than pleasure—no better and nobler object of desire and pursuit—they designate as utterly mean and groveling; as a doctrine worthy only of swine ....

[But it] is quite compatible with the principle of utility to recognize the fact, that some *kinds* of pleasure are more desirable and more valuable than others. It would be absurd that while, in estimating all other things, quality is considered as well as quantity, the estimation of pleasures should be supposed to depend on quantity alone.

If I am asked what I mean by difference of quality in pleasures, or what makes one pleasure more valuable than another merely as a pleasure, except its being greater in amount, there is but one possible answer. Of two pleasures, if there be one to which all or almost all who have experience of both give a decided preference, irrespective of any feeling of moral obligation to prefer it, that is the more desirable pleasure. If one of the two is, by those who are competently acquainted with both, placed so far above the other that they prefer it, even though knowing it to be attended with a greater amount of discontent, and would not resign it for any quantity of the other pleasure which their nature is capable of, we are justified in ascribing to the preferred enjoyment a superiority in quality, so far outweighing quantity as to render it, in comparison, of small account.

Now it is an unquestionable fact that those who are equally acquainted with, and equally capable of appreciating and enjoying, both, do give a most marked preference to the manner of existence which employs their higher faculties. Few human creatures would consent to be changed into any of the lower animals, for a promise of the fullest allowance of a beast's pleasures; no intelligent human being would consent to be a fool; no instructed person would be an ignoramus; no person of feeling and conscience would be selfish and base, even though they should be persuaded that the fool, the dunce, or the rascal is better satisfied with his lot than they are with theirs. They would not resign what they possess more than he for the most complete satisfaction of all the desires which they have in common with him. If they ever fancy they would, it is only in cases of unhappiness so extreme, that to escape from it they would exchange their lot for almost any other, however undesirable in their own eyes. A being of higher faculties requires more to make him happy, is capable probably of more acute suffering, and certainly accessible to it at more points, than one of an inferior type; but in spite of these liabilities, he can never really wish to sink into what he feels to be a lower grade of existence. We may give what explanation we please of this unwillingness: we may attribute it to pride, a name which is given indiscriminately to some of the most and to some of the least estimable feelings of which mankind are capable; we may refer it to the love of liberty and personal independence, an appeal to which was with the Stoics one of the most effective means for the inculcation of it; to the love of power, or to the love of excitement, both of which do really enter into and contribute to it: but its most appropriate appellation is a sense of dignity, which all human beings possess in one form or other, and in some, though by no means in exact, proportion to their higher faculties, and which is so essential a part of the happiness of those in whom it is strong, that nothing which conflicts with it could be, otherwise than momentarily, an object of desire to them ....

From this verdict of the only competent judges I apprehend there can be no appeal. On a question which is the best worth having of two pleasures, or which of two modes of existence is the most grateful to the feelings, apart from its moral attributes and from its consequences, the judgment of those who are qualified by knowledge of both, or, if they differ, that of the majority among them, must be admitted as final. And there need be the less hesitation to accept this judgment respecting the quality of pleasures, since there is no other tribunal to be referred to even on the question of quantity. What means are there of determining which is the acutest of two pains, or the intensest of two pleasurable sensations, except the general suffrage of those who are familiar with both? Neither pains nor pleasures are homogeneous, and pain is always heterogeneous with pleasure. What is there to decide whether a particular pleasure is worth purchasing at the cost of a particular pain, except the feelings and judgment of the experienced? When, therefore, those feelings and judgment declare the pleasures derived from the higher faculties to be preferable in kind, apart from the question of intensity, to those of which the animal nature, disjoined from the higher faculties, is susceptible, they are entitled on this subject to the same regard ....

Though it is only in a very imperfect state of the world's arrangements that anyone can best serve the happiness of others by the absolute sacrifice of his own, yet so long as the world is in that imperfect state, I fully acknowledge that the readiness to make such a sacrifice is the highest virtue which can be found in man. I will add that in this condition of the world, paradoxical as the assertion may be, the conscious ability to do without happiness gives the best prospect of realizing such happiness as is attainable. For nothing except that consciousness can raise a person above the chances of life, by making him feel that, let fate and fortune do their worst, they have not power to subdue him ....

The utilitarian morality does recognize in human beings the power of sacrificing their own greatest good for the good of others. It only refuses to admit that the sacrifice is itself a good. A sacrifice which does not increase, or tend to increase, the sum total of happiness, it considers as wasted ....

The assailants of utilitarianism seldom have the justice to acknowledge, that the happiness which forms the utilitarian standard of what is right in conduct is not the agent's own happiness but that of all concerned. As between his own happiness and that of others, utilitarianism requires him to be as strictly impartial as a disinterested and benevolent spectator. In the golden rule of Jesus of Nazareth, we read the complete spirit of the ethics of utility. "To do as you would be done by," and "to love your neighbor as yourself," constitute the ideal perfection of utilitarian morality. As the means of making the nearest approach to this ideal, utility would enjoin, first, that laws and social arrangements should place the happiness or (as speaking practically, it may be called) the interest of every individual as nearly as possible in harmony with the interest of the whole; and, secondly, that education and opinion, which have so vast a power over human character, should so use that power as to establish in the mind of every individual an indissoluble association between his own happiness and the good of the whole, especially between his own happiness and the practice of such modes of conduct, negative and positive, as regard for the universal happiness prescribes; so that not only he may be unable to conceive the possibility of happiness to himself, consistent with the conduct opposed to the general good, but also that a direct impulse to promote the general good may be in every individual one of the habitual motives of action, and the sentiments connected therewith may fill a large and prominent place in every human being's sentient existence ....

We not uncommonly hear the doctrine of utility inveighed against as a *godless* doctrine. If it be necessary to say anything at all against so mere an assumption, we may say that the question depends upon what idea we have formed of the moral character of the Deity. If it be a true belief that God desires, above all things, the happiness of his creatures, and that this was his purpose in their creation, utility is not only not a godless doctrine, but more profoundly religious than any other. If it be meant that utilitarianism does not recognize the revealed will of God as the supreme law of morals, I answer that a utilitarian who believes in the perfect goodness and wisdom of God necessarily believes that whatever God has thought fit to reveal on the subject of morals must fulfill the requirements of utility in a supreme degree ....

Again, defenders of utility often find themselves called upon to reply to such objections as this—that there is not time, previous to action, for calculating and weighing the effects of any line of conduct on the general happiness. This is exactly as if anyone were to say that it is impossible to guide our conduct by Christianity because there is not time, on every occasion on which anything has to be done, to read through the Old and New Testaments. The answer to the objection is that there has been ample time, namely, the whole past duration of the human species. During all that time mankind have been learning by experience the tendencies of actions; on which experience all the prudence as well as all the morality of life are dependent .... The corollaries from the principle of utility, like the precepts of every practical art, admit of indefinite improvement, and, in a progressive state of the human mind, their improvement is perpetually going on.

But to consider the rules of morality as improvable is one thing; to pass over the intermediate generalization entirely and endeavor to test each individual action directly by the first principle is another. It is a strange notion that the acknowledgment of a first principle is inconsistent with the admission of secondary ones. To inform a traveler respecting the place of his ultimate destination is not to forbid the use of landmarks and direction-posts on the way.

The proposition that happiness is the end and aim of morality does not mean that no road ought to be laid down to that goal, or that persons going thither should not be advised to take one direction rather than another. Men really ought to leave off talking a kind of nonsense on this subject, which they would neither talk nor listen to on other matters of practical concernment. Nobody argues that the art of navigation is not founded on astronomy, because sailors cannot wait to calculate the Nautical Almanack. Being rational creatures, they go to sea with it ready calculated; and all rational creatures go out upon the sea of life with their minds made up on the common questions of right and wrong, as well as on many of the far more difficult questions of wise and foolish. And this, as long as foresight is a human quality, it is to be presumed they will continue to do. Whatever we adopt as the fundamental principle of morality, we require subordinate principles to apply it by ....

There exists no moral system under which there do not arise unequivocal cases of conflicting obligation. These are real difficulties, the knotty points both in the theory of ethics and in the conscientious guidance of personal conduct. They are overcome practically, with greater or with less success, according to the intellect and virtue of the individual; but it can hardly be pretended that anyone will be the less qualified for dealing with them, from possessing an ultimate standard to which conflicting rights and duties can be referred. If utility is the ultimate source of moral obligations, utility may be invoked to decide between them when their demands are incompatible. Though the application of the [utilitarian] standard may be difficult, it is better than none at all; while in other systems, the moral laws all claiming independent authority, there is no common umpire entitled to interfere between them; their claims to precedence one over another rest on little better than sophistry, and, unless determined, as they generally are, by the unacknowledged influence of consideration of utility, afford a free scope for the action of personal desires and partialities. We must remember that only in these cases of conflict between secondary principles is it requisite that first principles should be appealed to. There is no case of moral obligation in which some secondary principle is not involved; and if only one, there can seldom be any real doubt which one it is, in the mind of any person by whom the principle itself is recognized.

Of What Sort of Proof the Principle of Utility Is Susceptible

It has already been remarked that questions of ultimate ends do not admit of proof, in the ordinary acceptation of the term. To be incapable of proof by reasoning is common to all first principles; to the first premises of our knowledge, as well as to those of our conduct. But the former, being matters of fact, may be the subject of a direct appeal to the faculties which judge of fact—namely, our senses, and our internal consciousness. Can an appeal be made to the same faculties on questions of practical ends? Or by what other faculty is cognizance taken of them?

Questions about ends are, in other words, questions about what things are desirable. The utilitarian doctrine is, that happiness is desirable, and the only thing desirable, as an end; all other things being only desirable as means to that end. What ought to be required of this doctrine—what conditions is it requisite that the doctrine should fulfill—to make good its claim to be believed?

The only proof capable of being given that an object is visible, is that people actually see it. The only proof that a sound is audible, is that people hear it: and so of the other sources of our experience. In like manner, I apprehend, the sole evidence it is possible to produce that anything is desirable, is that people do actually desire it. If the end which the utilitarian doctrine proposes to itself were not, in theory and in practice, acknowledged to be an end, nothing could ever convince any person that it was so. No reason can be given why the general happiness is desirable, except that each person, so far as he believes it to be attainable, desires his own happiness. This, however, being a fact, we have not only all the proof which the case admits of, but all which it is possible to require, that happiness is a good: that each person's happiness is a good to that person, and the general happiness, therefore, a good to the aggregate of all persons. Happiness has made out its title as one of the ends of conduct, and consequently one of the criteria of morality.

But it has not, by this alone, proved itself to be the sole criterion. To do that, it would seem, by the same rule, necessary to show, not only that people desire happiness, but that they never desire anything else. Now it is palpable that they do desire things which, in common language, are decidedly distinguished from happiness. They desire, for example, virtue, and the absence of vice, no less really than pleasure and the absence of pain. The desire of virtue is not as universal, but it is as authentic a fact, as the desire of happiness. And hence the opponents of the utilitarian standard deem that they have a right to infer that there are other ends of human action besides happiness, and that happiness is not the standard of approbation and disapprobation ….

The ingredients of happiness are very various, and each of them is desirable in itself, and not merely when considered as swelling an aggregate. The principle of utility does not mean that any given pleasure, as music, for instance, or any given exemption from pain, as for example health, is to be looked upon as means to a collective something termed happiness, and to be desired on that account. They are desired and desirable in and for themselves; besides being a means, they are part of the end. Virtue, according to the utilitarian doctrine, is not naturally and originally part of the end, but is capable of becoming so; and in those who live disinterestedly it has become so, and is desired and cherished, not as a means to happiness, but as part of their happiness.

To illustrate this further, we may remember that virtue is not the only thing originally a means, and which if it were not a means to anything else would be and remain indifferent, but which by association with what it is a means to comes to be desired for itself, and that too with the utmost intensity. What, for example, shall we say of the love of money? There is nothing originally more desirable about money than about any heap of glittering pebbles. Its worth is solely that of the things which it will buy; the desires for other things than itself, which it is a means of gratifying. Yet the love of money is not only one of the strongest moving forces of human life, but money is, in many cases, desired in and for itself; the desire to possess it is often stronger than the desire to use it, and goes on increasing when all the desires which point to ends beyond it, to be compassed by it, are falling off. It may, then, be said truly that money is desired not for the sake of an end, but as part of the end. From being a means to happiness, it has come to be itself a principal ingredient of the individual's conception of happiness. The same may be said of the majority of the great objects of human life: power, for example, or fame, except that to each of these there is a certain amount of immediate pleasure annexed, which has at least the semblance of being naturally inherent in them—a thing which cannot be said of money ....

It results from the preceding considerations that there is in reality nothing desired except happiness. Whatever is desired otherwise than as a means to some end beyond itself, and ultimately to happiness, is desired as itself a part of happiness, and is not desired for itself until it has become so ....

We have now, then, an answer to the question, of what sort of proof the principle of utility is susceptible. If the opinion which I have now stated is psychologically true—if human nature is so constituted as to desire nothing which is not either a part of happiness or a means of happiness—we can have no other proof, and we require no other, that these are the only things desirable. If so, happiness is the sole end of human action, and the promotion of it the test by which to judge of all human conduct; from whence it necessarily follows that it must be the criterion of morality, since a part is included in the whole ....

On the Connection Between Justice and Utility

In all ages of speculation, one of the strongest obstacles to the reception of the doctrine that Utility or Happiness is the criterion of right and wrong, has been drawn from the idea of Justice ....

To throw light upon this question, it is necessary to attempt to ascertain what is the distinguishing character of justice, or of injustice: ....

In the first place it is mostly considered unjust to deprive anyone of his personal liberty, his property, or any other thing which belongs to him by law. Here, therefore, is one instance of the application of the terms just and unjust in a perfectly definite sense, namely, that it is just to respect, unjust to violate, the *legal rights* of any one ....

Secondly, the legal rights of which he is deprived, may be rights which *ought* not to have belonged to him; in other words, the law which confers on him these rights, may be a bad law .... When, however, a law is thought to be unjust, it seems to be regarded as being so in the same way in which a breach of law is unjust, namely, by infringing somebody's right; which, as it cannot in this case be a legal right ... is called a moral right. We may say, therefore, that a second case of injustice consists in taking or withholding from any person that to which he has *a moral right*.

Thirdly, it is universally considered just that each person should obtain that (whether good or evil) which he *deserves*; and unjust that he should obtain a good, or be made to undergo an evil, which he does not deserve .... Speaking in a general way, a person is understood to deserve good if he does right, evil if he does wrong; and in a more particular sense, to deserve good from those to whom he does or has done good, and evil from those to whom he does or has done evil ....

Fourthly, it is confessedly unjust to *break faith* with any one: to violate an engagement, either express or implied, or disappoint expectations raised by our own conduct, at least if we have raised those expectations knowingly and voluntarily ....

Fifthly, it is, by universal admission, inconsistent with justice to be *partial*—to show favor or preference to one person over another in matters in which favor and preference do not apply ....

Among the many diverse applications of the term "justice" it is a matter of some difficulty to seize the mental link which holds them together .... In our survey of the various popular acceptations of justice, the term appeared generally to involve the idea of a personal right—a claim on the part of one or more individuals, like that which the law gives when it confers a proprietary or other legal right. Whether the injustice consists in depriving a person of a possession, or in breaking faith with him, or in treating him worse than he deserves, or worse than other people who have no greater claims—in each case the supposition implies two things: a wrong done, and some assignable person who is wronged. Injustice may also be done by treating a person better than others; but the wrong in this case is to his competitors, who are also assignable persons. It seems to me that this feature in the case—a right in some person, correlative to the moral obligation—constitutes the specific difference between justice and generosity or beneficence. Justice implies something which is not only right to do, and wrong not to do, but which some individual person can claim from us as his moral right. No one has a moral right to our generosity or beneficence because we are not morally bound to practice those virtues toward any given individual ....

[T]he idea of justice supposes two things; a rule of conduct, and a sentiment which sanctions the rule. The first must be supposed common to all mankind, and intended for their good. The other (the sentiment) is a desire that punishment may be suffered by those who infringe the rule. There is involved, in addition, the conception of some definite person who suffers by the infringement; whose rights (to use the expression appropriated to the case) are violated by it. And the sentiment of justice appears to me to be, the animal desire to repel or retaliate a hurt or damage to oneself, or to those with whom one sympathizes, widened so as to include all persons, by the human capacity of enlarged sympathy, and the human conception of intelligent self-interest. From the latter elements, the feeling derives its morality; from the former, its peculiar impressiveness, and energy of self-assertion.

I have, throughout, treated the idea of a *right* residing in the injured person, and violated by the injury, not as a separate element in the composition of the idea and sentiment, but as one of the forms in which the other two elements clothe themselves. These elements are, a hurt to some assignable person or persons on the one hand, and a demand for punishment on the other. An examination of our own minds, I think, will show, that these two things include all that we mean when we speak of violation of a right. When we call anything a person's right, we mean that he has a valid claim on society to protect him in the possession of it, either by the force of law, or by that of education and opinion. If he has what we consider a sufficient claim, on whatever account, to have something guaranteed to him by society, we say that he has a right to it. If we desire to prove that anything does not belong to him by right, we think this done as soon as it is admitted that society ought not to take measures for securing it to him, but should leave him to chance, or to his own exertions. Thus, a person is said to have a right to what he can earn in fair professional competition; because society ought not to allow any other person to hinder him from endeavouring to earn in that manner as much as he can. But he has not a right to three hundred a year, though he may happen to be earning it; because society is not called on to provide that he shall earn that sum. On the contrary, if he owns ten thousand pounds three per cent, stock, he *has* a right to three hundred a year; because society has come under an obligation to provide him with an income of that amount.

To have a right, then, is, I conceive, to have something which society ought to defend me in the possession of. If the objector goes on to ask, why it ought? I can give him no other reason than general utility. If that expression does not seem to convey a sufficient feeling of the strength of the obligation, nor to account for the peculiar energy of the feeling, it is because there goes to the composition of the sentiment, not a rational only but also an animal element—the thirst for retaliation; and this thirst derives its intensity, as well as its moral justification, from the extraordinarily important and impressive kind of utility which is concerned. The interest involved is that of security, to everyone's feelings the most vital of all interests ....

We are continually informed that utility is an uncertain standard, which every different person interprets differently, and that there is no safety but in the immutable, ineffaceable, and unmistakable dictates of justice, which carry their evidence in themselves. Not only have different nations and individuals different notions of justice, but in the mind of one and the same individual, justice is not some one rule, principle, or maxim but many which do not always coincide in their dictates, and, in choosing between which, he is guided either by some extraneous standard or by his own personal predilections.

For instance, there are some who say that it is unjust to punish anyone for the sake of example to others. Others maintain the extreme reverse, contending that to punish persons who have attained years of discretion for their own benefit, is despotism and injustice since, if the matter is solely their own good, no one has a right to control their own judgment of it; but that they may justly be punished to prevent evil to others ....

To escape these and other difficulties, a favorite contrivance has been the fiction of a contract whereby at some unknown period all members of society engaged to obey the laws and consented to be punished for any disobedience to them, thereby giving to their legislators the right, which it is assumed they would not otherwise have had, of punishing them, either for their own good or for that of the society. This happy thought was considered to get rid of the whole difficulty and to legitimate the infliction of punishment, in virtue of another received maxim of justice—that is not unjust which is done with the consent of the person who is supposed to be hurt by it. I need hardly remark that, even if consent were not a mere fiction, this maxim is not superior in authority to others which it is brought in to supersede. It is, on the contrary, an instructive specimen of the loose and irregular matter in which supposed principles of justice grow up ....

Again, ... how many conflicting conceptions of justice come to light in discussing the proper apportionment of punishment to offenses. [One is] an eye for an eye, a tooth for a tooth. [Others think] it should be measured by the moral guilt of the culprit, [or] what amount of punishment is necessary to deter the offense .... Who shall decide between these appeals to conflicting principles of justice? Each, from his own point of view, is unanswerable; and any choice between them, on grounds of justice, must be perfectly arbitrary. Social utility alone can decide the preference.

Review and Discussion Questions

1. Some have argued that the intensity and duration of a pain or pleasure matter, not its inherent nature. Mill rejects that. What does he mean in claiming that some pleasures are higher than others? What argument does Mill give for that conclusion?
2. Does Mill believe that people should think specifically in each case about what would maximize utility when deciding what to do, or does he think that they should rely on other standards or attitudes? Explain.
3. Discuss Mill's "proof" of the utility principle.
4. When people come to desire things for their own sake, those things become part of their happiness, says Mill. Is that consistent with his earlier discussion of pleasure and happiness? Explain.
5. Explain the issues that Mill thinks are questions of justice, indicating which features these have in common.
6. Contrast Mill's approach with the social contract theory. Why does Mill reject the social contract in favor of the utility principle?
7. Explain how Mill understands moral rights. Are they universally applicable in all societies? Explain.
8. Philosopher Robert Nozick has raised an important question about value. Imagine, he suggests, that there existed an "experience machine" that would provide any experimental state you wanted. Such experiences could include great pleasures, wonderful accomplishments, important relationships, or anything else that you wanted to experience. The only catch is that it is all done via computers attached to the brain. The question, then, is whether there would be anything valuable to you that you would miss if your life took place entirely in the machine. How would Mill answer that question? What do you think the answer is?

Essay and Paper Topics for Part A: Classical Theories

1. Compare the different ways that Aristotle and Mill understand human happiness or well-being. Which view seems closer to the truth? Explain.
2. Write an essay on the idea of impartiality and its role in moral theory, using two of the authors you have read in this chapter.
3. Discuss the following claim: Utilitarians such as Mill emphasize the role of sympathy in thinking about morality, while Kant emphasizes reason. In fact, however, we need both.
4. Some people say that morality is most importantly about how we should act. Others say that more important for morality is our motivations and intentions. Still others argue that the most important insight is that morality is about forming a good character over a lifetime apart from analyzing any particular personal motives or actions. Drawing on the insights from these readings, what is your assessment?

Part B: Contemporary Perspectives

These essays in Part B represent a sampling of contemporary reflections and new development from the moral theories presented in Part A in this chapter. The first essay, by W. D. Ross, discusses the nature of duty and the "intuitions" on which it rests. The next, by Onora O'Neill, offers a perspective on the dispute between utilitarians such as Mill, on one hand, and the ethics of Kant, on the other, while at the same time giving her own interpretation and defense of Kant. Richard Brandt defends utilitarianism, while Virginia Held criticizes traditional theory from a feminist perspective and explains the importance of contemporary feminism for developing new directions in ethical theory.

READING: INTUITIONISM

W. D. ROSS*

In this selection, W. D. Ross offers an account of morality that is different from the moral theories already discussed (perhaps he may even be said to reject moral theory entirely) but that also, he argues, provides an accurate picture of both the nature of morality and its ultimate justification. Central to Ross's account is the distinction between *prima facie* duties such as keeping promises and being truthful, on one hand, and our actual duty in a particular situation, on the other. After identifying the different origins of *prima facie* duties, Ross then discusses the basis or grounding of moral knowledge. W. D. Ross (1877–1971) taught philosophy at Oxford University.

When a plain man fulfils a promise because he thinks he ought to do so, it seems clear that he does so with no thought of its total consequences, still less with any opinion that these are likely to be the best possible. He thinks in fact much more of the past than of the future. What makes him think it right to act in a certain way is the fact that he has promised to do so—that and, usually, nothing more .... It may be said that besides the duty of fulfilling promises I have and recognize a duty of relieving distress, and that when I think it right to do the latter at the cost of not doing the former, it is not because I think I shall produce more good [as utilitarians claim] but because I think it the duty which is in the circumstances more of a duty. This account surely corresponds ... closely with what we really think in such a situation ....

[Utilitarianism] ... seems to simplify unduly our relations to our fellows. It says, in effect, that the only morally significant relation in which my neighbours stand to me is that of being possible beneficiaries by my action. They do stand in this relation to me, and this relation is morally significant. But they may also stand to me in the relation of promisee to promiser, of creditor to debtor, of wife to husband, of child to parent, of friend to friend, of fellow countryman to fellow countryman, and the like; and each of these relations is the foundation of a *prima facie* duty, which is more or less incumbent on me according to the circumstances of the case. When I am in a situation, as perhaps I always am, in which more than one of these *prima facie* duties is incumbent on me, what I have to do is to study the situation as fully as I can until I form the considered opinion (it is never more) that in the circumstances one of them is more incumbent than any other; then I am bound to think that to do this *prima facie* duty is my duty *sans phrase* in the situation.

I suggest "*prima facie* duty" or "conditional duty" as a brief way of referring to the characteristic (quite distinct from that of being a duty proper) which an act has, in virtue of being of a certain kind (e.g., the keeping of a promise), of being an act which would be a duty proper if it were not at the same time of another kind which is morally significant. Whether an act is a duty proper or actual duty depends on *all* the morally significant kinds it is an instance of ....

---

* From W. D. Ross, *The Right and the Good* (1930), published by Oxford University Press.

There is nothing arbitrary about these *prima facie* duties. Each rests on a definite circumstance which cannot seriously be held to be without moral significance. Of *prima facie* duties I suggest, without claiming completeness or finality for it, the following division.

(1) Some duties rest on previous acts of my own. These duties seem to include two kinds, (*a*) those resting on a promise or what may fairly be called an implicit promise, such as the implicit undertaking not to tell lies which seems to be implied in the act of entering into conversation (at any rate by civilized men), or of writing books that purport to be history and not fiction. These may be called the duties of fidelity. (*b*) Those resting on a previous wrongful act. These may be called the duties of reparation. (2) Some rest on previous acts of other men, i.e. services done by them to me. These may be loosely described as the duties of gratitude. (3) Some rest on the fact or possibility of a distribution of pleasure or happiness (or of the means thereto) which is not in accordance with the merit of the persons concerned; in such cases there arises a duty to upset or prevent such a distribution. These are the duties of justice. (4) Some rest on the mere fact that there are other beings in the world whose condition we can make better in respect of virtue, or of intelligence, or of pleasure. These are the duties of beneficence. (5) Some rest on the fact that we can improve our own condition in respect of virtue or of intelligence. These are the duties of self-improvement. (6) I think that we should distinguish from (4) the duties that may be summed up under the title of "not injuring others." No doubt to injure others is incidentally to fail to do them good; but it seems to me clear that non-maleficence is apprehended as a duty distinct from that of beneficence, and as a duty of a more stringent character. It will be noticed that this alone among the types of duty has been stated in a negative way. All attempts might no doubt be made to state this duty, like the others, in a positive way. It might be said that it is really the duty to prevent ourselves from acting either from an inclination to harm others or from an inclination to seek our own pleasure, in *doing* which we should incidentally harm them. But on reflection it seems clear that the primary duty here is the duty not to harm others, this being a duty whether or not we have an inclination that if followed would lead to our harming them; and that when we have such an inclination the primary duty not to harm others gives rise to a consequential duty to resist the inclination. The recognition of this duty of non-maleficence is the first step of the way to the recognition of the duty of beneficence; and that accounts for the prominence of the commands "thou shalt not kill," "thou shalt not commit adultery," "thou shalt not steal," "thou shalt not bear false witness," in so early a code as the Decalogue. But even when we have come to recognize the duty of beneficence, it appears to me that the duty of non-maleficence is recognized as a distinct one, and as *prima facie* more binding. We should not in general consider it justifiable to kill one person in order to keep another alive or to steal from one in order to give alms to another ....

If the objection is made, that the catalogue of duties is an unsystematic one resting on no logical principle, it may be replied, first, that it makes no claim to being ultimate. It is a *prima facie* classification of the duties which reflection on our moral convictions seems actually to reveal. And if these convictions are, as I would claim that they are, of the nature of knowledge, and if I have not misstated them, the list will be a list of authentic conditional duties, correct as far as it goes though not necessarily complete ....

It may, again, be objected that our theory that there are these various and often conflicting types of *prima facie* duty leaves us with no principle upon which to discern what is our actual duty in particular circumstances. But ... why should two sets of circumstances, or one set of circumstances, *not* possess different characteristics, any one of which makes a certain act our *prima facie* duty? When I ask what it is that makes me in certain cases sure that I have a *prima facie* duty to do so and so, I find that it lies in the fact that I have made a promise; when I ask the same question in another case, I find the answer lies in the fact that I have done a wrong. And if on reflection I find (as I think I do) that neither of these reasons is reducible to the other, I must not on any *a priori* ground assume that such a reduction is possible ....

In actual experience [*prima facie* duties] are compounded together in highly complex ways. Thus, for example, the duty of obeying the laws of one's country arises partly (as Socrates contends in the *Crito*) from the duty of gratitude for the benefits one has received from it; partly from the implicit promise to obey which seems to be involved in permanent residence in a country whose laws we know we are *expected* to obey, and still more clearly involved when we ourselves invoke the protection of its laws (this is the truth underlying the doctrine of the social contract); and partly (if we are fortunate in our country) from the fact that its laws are potent instruments for the general good.

Or again, the sense of a general obligation to bring about (so far as we can) a just apportionment of happiness to merit is often greatly reinforced by the fact that many of the existing injustices are due to a social and economic system which we have, not indeed created, but taken part in and assented to; the duty of justice is then reinforced by the duty of reparation.

It is necessary to say something by way of clearing up the relation between *prima facie* duties and the actual or absolute duty to do one particular act in particular circumstances. If, as almost all moralists except Kant are agreed, and as most plain men think, it is sometimes right to tell a lie or to break a promise, it must be maintained that there is a difference between *prima facie* duty and actual or absolute duty. When we think ourselves justified in breaking, and indeed morally obliged to break, a promise in order to relieve some one's distress, we do not for a moment cease to recognize a *prima facie* duty to keep our promise, and this leads us to feel, not indeed shame or repentance, but certainly compunction, for behaving as we do, we recognize, further, that it is our duty to make up somehow to the promisee for the breaking of the promise. We have to distinguish from the characteristic of being our duty that of tending to be our duty. Any act that we do contains various elements in virtue of which it falls under various categories. In virtue of being the breaking of a promise, for instance, it tends to be wrong; in virtue of being an instance of relieving distress it tends to be right. Tendency to be one's duty may be called a parti-resultant attribute, i.e. one which belongs to an act in virtue of some one component in its nature. *Being* one's duty is a totiresultant attribute, one which belongs to an act in virtue of its whole nature and of nothing less than this ....

Something should be said of the relation between our apprehension of the *prima facie* rightness of certain types of act and our mental attitude towards particular acts. It is proper to use the word "apprehension" in the former case and not in the latter. That an act, *qua* fulfilling a promise, or *qua* effecting a just distribution of good, or *qua* returning services rendered, or *qua* promoting the good of others, or *qua* promoting the virtue or insight of the agent, is *prima facie* right, is self-evident; not in the sense that it is evident from the beginning of our lives, or as soon as we attend to the proposition for the first time, but in the sense that when we have reached sufficient mental maturity and have given sufficient attention to the proposition it is evident without any need of proof, or of evidence beyond itself. It is self-evident just as a mathematical axiom, or the validity of a form of inference, is evident. The moral order expressed in these propositions is just as much part of the fundamental nature of the universe (and, we may add, of any possible universe in which there were moral agents at all) as is the spatial or numerical structure expressed in the axioms of geometry or arithmetic. In our confidence that these propositions are true there is involved the same trust in our reason that is involved in our confidence in mathematics and we should have no justification for trusting it in the latter sphere and distrusting it in the former. In both cases we are dealing with propositions that cannot be proved, but that just as certainly need no proof ....

Our judgments about our actual duty in concrete situations have none of the certainty that attaches to our recognition of the general principles of duty. A statement is certain, i.e. is an expression of knowledge, only in one or other of two cases: when it is either self-evident, or a valid conclusion from self-evident premises. And our judgments about our particular duties have neither of these characters. (1) They are not self-evident. Where a possible act is seen to have two characteristics, in virtue of one of which it is *prima facie* right, and in virtue of the other *prima facie* wrong, we are (I think) well aware that we are not certain whether we ought or ought not to do it; that whether we do it or not, we are taking a moral risk. We come in the long run, after consideration, to think one duty more pressing than the other, but we do not feel certain that it is so. And though we do not always recognize that a possible act has two such characteristics, and though there *may* be cases in which it has not, we are never certain that any particular possible act has not, and therefore never certain that is right, nor certain that it is wrong. For, to go no further in the analysis, it is enough to point out that any particular act will in all probability in the course of time contribute to the bringing about of good or of evil for many human beings, and thus have a *prima facie* rightness or wrongness of which we know nothing. (2) Again, our judgments about our particular duties are not logical conclusions from self-evident premises. The only possible premises would be the general principles stating their *prima facie* rightness or wrongness *qua* having the different characteristics they do have; and even if we could (as we cannot) apprehend the extent to which an act will tend on the one hand, for example, to bring about advantages for our benefactors, and on the other hand to bring about disadvantages for fellow men who are not our benefactors, there is no principle by which we can draw the conclusion that it is on the whole right or on the whole wrong. In this respect the judgment as to the rightness of a particular act is just like the judgment as to the beauty of a ...

natural object or work of art. A poem is, for instance, in respect of certain qualities beautiful and in respect of certain others not beautiful, and our judgment as to the degree of beauty it possesses on the whole is never reached by logical reasoning from the apprehension of its particular beauties or particular defects. Both in this and in the moral case we have more or less probable opinions which are not logically justified conclusions from the general principles that are recognized as self-evident.

There is therefore much truth in the description of the right act as a fortunate act. If we cannot be certain that it is right, it is our good fortune if the act we do is the right act. This consideration does not, however, make the doing of our duty a mere matter of chance. There is a parallel here between the doing of duty and the doing of what will be to our personal advantage. We never *know* what act will in the long run be to our advantage. Yet it is certain that we are more likely in general to secure our advantage if we estimate to the best of our ability the probable tendencies of our actions in this respect, than if we act on caprice. And similarly we are more likely to do our duty if we reflect to the best of our ability on the *prima facie* rightness or wrongness of various possible acts in virtue of the characteristics we perceive them to have, than if we act without reflection. With this greater likelihood we must be content ....

In what has preceded, a good deal of use has been made of "what we really think" about moral questions .... It might be said that this is in principle wrong; that we should not be content to expound what our present moral consciousness tells us but should aim at a criticism of our existing moral consciousness in the light of theory. Now I do not doubt that the moral consciousness of men has in detail undergone a good deal of modification as regards the things we think right, at the hands of moral theory. But ... we have to ask ourselves whether we really *can* get rid of our view that promise-keeping has a bindingness independent of productiveness of maximum good. In my own experience I find that I cannot, in spite of a very genuine attempt to do so, and I venture to think that most people will find the same, and that just because they cannot lose the sense of special obligation, they cannot accept as self-evident, or even as true, the theory which would require them to do so ....

I would maintain, in fact, that what we are apt to describe as "what we think" about moral questions contains a considerable amount that we do not think but know, and that this forms the standard by reference to which the truth of any moral theory has to be tested, instead of having itself to be tested by reference to any theory. I hope that I have in what precedes indicated what in my view these elements of knowledge are that are involved in our ordinary moral consciousness.

It would be a mistake to found a natural science on "what we really think," i.e. on what reasonably thoughtful and well-educated people think about the subjects of the science before they have studied them scientifically. For such opinions are interpretations, and often misinterpretations, of sense-experience; and the man of science must appeal from these to sense-experience itself, which furnishes his real data. In ethics no such appeal is possible. We have no more direct way of access to the facts about rightness and goodness and about what things are right or good, than by thinking about them; the moral convictions of thoughtful and well-educated people are the data of ethics just as sense-perceptions are the data of a natural science. Just as some of the latter have to be rejected as illusory, so have some of the former; but as the latter are rejected only when they are in conflict with other more accurate sense-perceptions, the former are rejected only when they are in conflict with other convictions which stand better the test of reflection. The existing body of moral convictions of the best people is the cumulative product of the moral reflection of many generations, which has developed an extremely delicate power of appreciation of moral distinctions, and this the theorist cannot afford to treat with anything other than the greatest respect. The verdicts of the moral consciousness of the best people are the foundation on which he must build; though he must first compare them with one another and eliminate any contradictions they may contain.

Review and Discussion Questions

1 What does Ross mean by *prima facie* duties, and how does he distinguish them from actual duties?
2 What are the five types of *prima facie* duties?
3 How, according to Ross, do we know which are our *prima facie* duties? Does his answer to that question pay adequate attention, in your opinion, to the role that society plays in inculcating moral attitudes? Does his answer pay adequate attention to the diversity of moral attitudes among different peoples?

READING: KANT AND UTILITARIANISM CONTRASTED

ONORA O'NEILL[*]

Onora O'Neill's description of the dispute between Kantian and utilitarian philosophers is useful not only because it provides a valuable review of Kant's ethical theory and how it differs from utilitarianism, but also for its criticisms of utilitarianism. In this selection, she focuses in particular on the requirement that persons be treated as ends in themselves, and on the value of human life. Onora O'Neill is a crossbench member of the House of Lords, taught philosophy at Cambridge University, and has written widely on political philosophy, ethics, and other areas of philosophy.

Kant's moral theory has acquired the reputation of being forbiddingly difficult to understand and, once understood, excessively demanding in its requirements. I don't believe that this reputation has been wholly earned, and I am going to try to undermine it …. I shall try to reduce some of the difficulties …. [And then] I shall compare Kantian and utilitarian approaches and assess their strengths and weaknesses. The main method by which I propose to avoid some of the difficulties of Kant's moral theory is by explaining only one part of the theory. This does not seem to me to be an irresponsible approach in this case. One of the things that makes

---

[*] Onora O'Neill, "A Simplified Account of Kant's Ethics," in Tom Regan (ed.), *Matters of Life and Death* (New York: McGraw-Hill, 1986).

Kant's moral theory hard to understand is that he gives a number of different versions of the principle that he calls the Supreme Principle of Morality, and these different versions don't look at all like one another. They also don't look at all like the utilitarians' Greatest Happiness Principle. But the Kantian principle is supposed to play a similar role in arguments about what to do.

Kant calls his Supreme Principle the *Categorical Imperative*; its various versions also have sonorous names. One is called the Formula of Universal Law; another is the Formula of the Kingdom of Ends. The one on which I shall concentrate is known as the *Formula of the End in Itself*. To understand why Kant thinks that these picturesquely named principles are equivalent to one another takes quite a lot of close and detailed analysis of Kant's philosophy. I shall avoid this and concentrate on showing the implications of this version of the Categorical Imperative.

The Formula of the End in Itself

Kant states the Formula of the End in Itself as follows:

> Act in such a way that you always treat humanity, whether in your own person or in the person of any other, never simply as a means but always at the same time as an end.[1]

To understand this we need to know what it is to treat a person as a means or as an end. According to Kant, each of our acts reflects one or more *maxims*. The maxim of the act is the principle on which one sees oneself as acting. A maxim expresses a person's policy, or if he or she has no settled policy, the principle underlying the particular intention or decision on which he or she acts. Thus, a person who decides "This year I'll give 10 percent of my income to famine relief" has as a maxim the principle of tithing his or her income for famine relief. In practice, the difference between intentions and maxims is of little importance, for given any intention, we can formulate the corresponding maxim by deleting references to particular times, places, and persons. In what follows I shall take the terms "maxim" and "intention" as equivalent. Whenever we act intentionally, we have at least one maxim and can, if we reflect, state what it is. (There is of course room for self-deception here—"I'm only keeping the wolf from the door" we may claim as we wolf down enough to keep ourselves overweight, or, more to the point, enough to feed someone else who hasn't enough food.)

When we want to work out whether an act we propose to do is right or wrong, according to Kant, we should look at our maxims and not at how much misery or happiness the act is likely to produce and whether it does better at increasing happiness than other available acts. We just have to check that the act we have in mind will not use anyone as a mere means and, if possible, that it will treat other persons as ends in themselves.

Using Persons as Mere Means

To use someone as a *mere means* is to involve them in a scheme of action *to which they could not in principle consent*. Kant does not say that there is anything wrong about using someone as a means. Evidently we have to do so in any cooperative scheme of action. If I cash a check I use the teller as a means, without whom I could not lay my hands on the cash; the teller in turn uses me as a means to earn his or her living. But in this case, each party consents to her or his part in the transaction. Kant would say that though they use one another as means, they do not use one another as *mere* means. Each person assumes that the other has maxims of his or her own and is not just a thing or a prop to be manipulated.

But there are other situations where one person uses another in a way to which the other could not in principle consent. For example, one person may make a promise to another with every intention of breaking it. If the promise is accepted, then the person to whom it was given must be ignorant of what the promisor's intention (maxim) really is. If one knew that the promisor did not intend to do what he or she was promising, one would, after all, not accept or rely on the promise. It would be as though there had been no promise made. Successful false promising depends on deceiving the person to whom the promise is made about what one's real maxim is. And since the person who is deceived doesn't know that real maxim, he or she can't in principle consent to his or her part in the proposed scheme of action. The person who is deceived is, as it were, a prop or a tool—a mere means—in the false promisor's scheme. A person who promises falsely treats the acceptor of the promise as a prop or a thing and not as a person. In Kant's view, it is this that makes false promising wrong.

One standard way of using others as mere means is by deceiving them. By getting someone involved in a business scheme or a criminal activity on false pretenses, or by giving a misleading account of what one is about, or by making a false promise or a fraudulent contract, one involves another in something to which he or she in principle cannot consent, since the scheme requires that he or she doesn't know what is going on. Another standard way of using others as mere means is by coercing them. If a rich or powerful person threatens a debtor with bankruptcy unless he or she joins in some scheme, then the creditor's intention is to coerce; and the debtor, if coerced, cannot consent to his or her part in the creditor's scheme. To make the example more specific: If a moneylender in an Indian village threatens not to renew a vital loan unless he is given the debtor's land, then he uses the debtor as a mere means. He coerces the debtor, who cannot truly consent to this "offer he can't refuse." (Of course, the outward form of such transactions may look like ordinary commercial dealings, but we know very well that some offers and demands couched in that form are coercive.)

In Kant's view, acts that are done on maxims that require deception or coercion of others and so cannot have the consent of those others (for consent precludes both deception and coercion) are wrong. When we act on such maxims, we treat others as mere means, as things rather than as ends in themselves. If we act on such maxims, our acts are not only wrong but unjust: such acts wrong the particular others who are deceived or coerced.

Treating Persons as Ends in Themselves

Duties of justice are, in Kant's view (as in many others'), the most important of our duties. When we fail in these duties, we have used some other or others as mere means. But there are also cases where, though we do not use others as mere means, still we fail to use them as ends in themselves in the fullest possible way. To treat someone as an end in him or herself requires in the first place that one not use him or her as mere means, that one respects each as a rational person with his or her own maxims. But beyond that, one may also seek to foster others' plans and maxims by sharing some of their ends. To act beneficently is to seek others' happiness, therefore to intend to achieve some of the things that those others aim at with their maxims. If I want to make others happy, I will adopt maxims that not merely do not manipulate them but that foster some of their plans and activities. Beneficent acts try to achieve what others want. However, we cannot seek everything that others want; their wants are too numerous and diverse, and, of course, sometimes incompatible. It follows that beneficence has to be selective.

There is then quite a sharp distinction between the requirements of justice and of beneficence in Kantian ethics. Justice requires that we act on *no* maxims that use others as mere means. Beneficence requires that we act on *some* maxims that foster others' ends, though it is a matter for judgment and discretion which of their ends we foster. Some maxims no doubt ought not to be fostered because it would be unjust to do so. Kantians are not committed to working interminably through a list of happiness-producing and misery-reducing acts; but there are some acts, whose obligatoriness utilitarians may need to debate as they try to compare total outcomes of different choices, to which Kantians are stringently bound. Kantians will claim that they have done nothing wrong if none of their acts is unjust and that their duty is complete if in addition their life plans have in the circumstances been reasonably beneficent.

In making sure that they meet all the demands of justice, Kantians do not try to compare all available acts and see which has the best effects. They consider only the proposals for action that occur to them and check that these proposals use no other as mere means. If they do not, the act is permissible; if omitting the act would use another as mere means, the act is obligatory. Kant's theory has less scope than utilitarianism. Kantians do not claim to discover whether acts whose maxims they don't know fully are just. They may be reluctant to judge others' acts or policies that cannot be regarded as the maxim of any person or institution. They cannot rank acts in order of merit. Yet the theory offers more precision than utilitarianism when data are scarce. One can usually tell whether one's act would use others as mere means, even when its impact on human happiness is thoroughly obscure.

The Limits of Kantian Ethics: Intentions and Results

Kantian ethics differs from utilitarian ethics both in its scope and in the precision with which it guides action. Every action, whether of a person or of an agency, can be assessed by utilitarian methods, provided only that information is available about all the consequences of the act. The theory has unlimited scope, but, owing to lack of data, often lacks precision. Kantian ethics has a more restricted scope. Since it assesses actions by looking at the maxims of agents, it can only assess intentional acts. This means that it is most at home in assessing individuals' acts; but it can be extended to assess acts of agencies that (like corporations and governments and student unions) have decision-making procedures. It can do nothing to assess patterns of action that reflect no intention or policy, hence it cannot assess the acts of groups lacking decision-making procedures, such as the student movement, the women's movement, or the consumer movement.

It may seem a great limitation of Kantian ethics that it concentrates on intentions to the neglect of results. It might seem that all conscientious Kantians have to do is to make sure that they never intend to use others as mere means and that they sometimes intend to foster others' ends. And, as we all know, good intentions sometimes lead to bad results, and correspondingly, bad intentions sometimes do not harm, or even produce good. [Some philosophers have argued] that the good intentions of those who feed the starving lead to dreadful results in the long run. If some traditional arguments in favor of capitalism are right, the greed and selfishness of the profit motive have produced unparalleled prosperity for many.

But such discrepancies between intentions and results are the exception and not the rule. For we cannot just *claim* that our intentions are good and do what we will. Our intentions reflect what we expect the immediate results of our action to be. Nobody credits the "intentions" of a couple who practice neither celibacy nor contraception but still insist "we never mean to have (more) children." Conception is likely (and known to be likely) in such cases. Where people's expressed intentions ignore the normal and predictable results of what they do, we infer that (if they are not amazingly ignorant) their words do not express their true intentions. The Formula of the End in Itself applies to the intentions on which one acts—not to some prettified version that one may avow. Provided this intention—the agent's real intention—uses no other as mere means, he or she does nothing unjust. If some of his or her intentions foster others' ends, then he or she is sometimes beneficent. It is therefore possible for people to test their proposals by Kantian arguments even when they lack the comprehensive causal knowledge that utilitarianism requires. Conscientious Kantians can work out whether they will be doing wrong by some act even though it blurs the implications of the theory. If we peer through the blur, we see that the utilitarian view is that lives may indeed be sacrificed for the sake of a greater good even when the persons are not willing. There is nothing wrong with using another as a mere means provided that the end for which the person is so used is a happier result than could have been achieved any other way, taking into account the misery the means have caused. In utilitarian thought, persons are not ends in themselves. Their special moral status derives from their being means to the production of happiness. Human life has therefore a high though derivative value, and one life may be taken for the sake of greater happiness in other lives or for ending of misery in that life. Nor is there any deep difference between ending a life for the sake of others' happiness by not helping (e.g., by triaging) and doing so by harming. Because the distinction between justice and beneficence is not sharply made within utilitarianism, it is not possible to say that triaging is a matter of not benefiting, while other interventions are a matter of injustice.

Utilitarian moral theory has then a rather paradoxical view of the value of human life. Living, conscious humans are (along with other sentient beings) necessary for the existence of everything utilitarians value. But it is not their being alive but the state of their consciousness that is of value. Hence, the best results may require certain lives to be lost—by whatever means—for the sake of the total happiness and absence of misery that can be produced.

Kant and Respect for Persons

Kantians reach different conclusions about human life. Human life is valuable because humans (and conceivably other beings, e.g., angels or apes) are the bearers of rational life. Humans are able to choose and to plan. This capacity and its exercise are of such value that they ought not to be sacrificed for anything of lesser value. Therefore, no one rational or autonomous creature should be treated as mere means for the enjoyment or even the happiness of another. We may in Kant's view justifiably—even nobly—risk or sacrifice our lives for others. For in doing so we follow our own maxim and nobody uses us as mere means. But no others may use either our lives or our bodies for a scheme that they have either coerced or deceived us into joining. For in doing so they would fail to treat us as rational beings; they would use us as mere means and not as ends in ourselves.

It is conceivable that a society of Kantians, all of whom took pains to use no other as mere means, would end up with less happiness or with fewer persons alive than would some societies of complying utilitarians. For since the Kantians would be strictly bound only to justice, they might without wrong-doing be quite selective in their beneficence and fail to maximize either survival rates or happiness or even to achieve as much of either as a strenuous group of utilitarians, who know that their foresight is limited and that they may cause some harm or fail to cause some benefit. But they will not cause harms that they can foresee without this being reflected in their intentions.

Utilitarianism and Respect for Life

From the differing implications that Kantian and utilitarian moral theories have for our actions towards those who do or may suffer famine, we can discover two sharply contrasting views of the value of human life. Utilitarians value happiness and the absence or reduction of misery. As a utilitarian one ought (if conscientious) to devote one's life to achieving the best possible balance of happiness over misery. If one's life plan remains in doubt, this will be because the means to this end are often unclear. But whenever the causal tendency of acts is clear, utilitarians will be able to discern the acts they should successively do in order to improve the world's balance of happiness over unhappiness.

This task is not one for the faint-hearted. First, it is dauntingly long, indeed interminable. Second, it may at times require the sacrifice of happiness, and even of lives, for the sake of a greater happiness. Such sacrifice may be morally required not only when the person whose happiness or even whose life is at stake volunteers to make the sacrifice. It may be necessary to sacrifice some lives for the sake of others. As our control over the means of ending and preserving human life has increased, analogous dilemmas have arisen in many areas for utilitarians. Should life be preserved at the cost of pain when modern medicine makes this possible? Should life be preserved without hope of consciousness? Should triage policies, because they may maximize the number of survivors, be used to determine who should be left to starve? Should population growth be fostered wherever it will increase the total of human happiness—or on some views so long as average happiness is not reduced? All these questions can be fitted into utilitarian frameworks and answered *if* we have the relevant information. And sometimes the answer will be that human happiness demands the sacrifice of lives, including the sacrifice of unwilling lives. Further, for most utilitarians, it makes no difference if the unwilling sacrifices involve acts of injustice to those whose lives are to be lost. It might, for example, prove necessary for maximal happiness that some persons have their allotted rations, or their hard-earned income, diverted for others' benefit. Or it might turn out that some generations must sacrifice comforts or liberties and even lives to rear "the fabric of felicity" for their successors. On the other hand, nobody will have been made an instrument of others' survival or happiness in the society of complying Kantians.

Note

1 This standard formulation can be found, for example, in *Groundwork of the Metaphysic of Morals* (New York: Harper Perennial, 2009), p. 96.

Review and Discussion Questions

1 Which of the versions of Kant's categorical imperative does O'Neill discuss? Give examples of how people might fail to live up to that principle by treating others as mere means.
2 How, exactly, does O'Neill understand the requirement that we treat people as ends? How does promise-keeping illustrate this?
3 O'Neill distinguishes sharply between duties of justice and duties of beneficence. What is that distinction, according to her?
4 Why do you think O'Neill says that Kant offers more precision than do utilitarians? Do you agree? Explain.
5 What specific practical differences are there in the demands that utilitarians and Kantians make of people, according to O'Neill?

READING: THE REAL AND ALLEGED PROBLEMS OF UTILITARIANISM

RICHARD B. BRANDT[*]

In this essay, noted utilitarian philosopher Richard Brandt defends one version of utilitarianism—specifically, rule-utilitarianism—against a range of criticisms. Brandt begins by distinguishing *rule*-utilitarianism from *act*-utilitarianism, a distinction he traces to John Stuart Mill. In his view, the right act is the one that would be permitted by a moral system or code that is "optimal" for society. But, Brandt wonders, how then are we to understand the concept of an agent's "society"? The second genuine puzzle for utilitarians involves the notion of social benefit or utility: Are only pleasant experiences intrinsically good, or are there other things also inherently good such as knowledge, love, or virtue? The third problem is how the rule-utilitarian would respond to the suggestion that we have a stronger obligation to refrain from harming others than to refrain from helping them, even though (let's assume) the consequences of both are

[*] Richard B. Brandt, April 1983. *The Real and Alleged Problems of Utilitarianism. Hastings Center Report* 13, no. 2. Copyright © 1983 The Hastings Center. Reprinted by permission of the publisher.

identical. In answering this, Brandt is led to consider in more detail the notion of an optimal moral code and its connection with conventional morality and actual duty. He concludes with a brief discussion of why his view is not open to charges of utopianism, since it asks people to follow an optimal moral code whether or not others are likely to do so. Richard Brandt was Professor of Philosophy at the University of Michigan.

Everybody believes that some actions, or types of action, are morally right or wrong; or that it is a person's moral obligation to do, or to avoid doing, these actions. Many philosophers, however, have wanted to introduce some order into this chaos of opinions, and have sought to find a small number of fundamental principles of right and wrong from which all justified moral beliefs can be deduced, given relevant factual information. A few philosophers—among them Immanuel Kant, with his famous "categorical imperative," and recently John Rawls, with his emphasis on justice—have thought that we can make do with just one fundamental principle. The oldest of such one-principle theories, which has shown vitality and appeal for philosophers for thousands of years, is utilitarianism, the view that the benefit or harm done by an act, or class of actions, or prohibition of an act-type, determines whether it is wrong or right morally. If acts of incest or homosexual contact or deceit are wrong, for example, it is because the acts or practice or traits of character they involve have impact for good or ill, happiness or unhappiness.

Unfortunately from the point of view of simplicity, there are different kinds of utilitarianism. One of them is "act-utilitarianism"—the thesis that a particular act is right if, and only if, no other act the agent could perform at the time would have, or probably would have (on the agent's evidence), better consequences. Such important philosophers as G. E. Moore, Henry Sidgwick, and Bertrand Russell advocated this view at about the turn of the century. A second form, which is older and probably more influential among philosophers at present, is "rule-utilitarianism"; its thesis is roughly that an act is morally right if, and only if, it would be as beneficial to have a moral code permitting that act as to have any moral code that is similar but prohibits the act. There are other types of utilitarianism, but these two seem most important now ....

[U]tilitarian reflection is prominent in the field of medicine; for instance, in the literature on the "autonomy" to be granted patients in decisions about treatment, or on what physicians should tell seriously ill patients about their prospects .... Utilitarian reflections are also prominent in recent analyses of U.S. foreign policy, including policy about immigration, although of course some writers take different approaches. The recent report of a Congressional Select Committee on immigration policy is full of talk about the impact of a liberal policy on unemployment in the U.S., about the alleged long-range negative noneconomic cost of a society culturally more heterogeneous than at present, of the human cost of refusing admission to refugees or the poverty-stricken hoping for a better life in America, and so on. Some form of utilitarian-type thinking pervades most present reflection about public affairs and policymaking in this country.

Philosophers who criticize utilitarianism usually center their fire on the first form of the theory (act-utilitarianism). Unfortunately they often imply, if not state, that this criticism disposes of utilitarianism in all its forms. This is a mistake. Adherents of rule-utilitarianism are themselves quite critical of act-utilitarianism, although the theories are fairly closely related, especially when evaluation of a long-range public policy is the issue.

In what follows I shall discuss rule-utilitarianism, since it seems to me more plausible. The choice is not eccentric; despite the number of thoughtful advocates today of act-utilitarianism I believe most philosophers who advocate utilitarianism today are in the rule-utilitarian camp. Another reason for concentrating on rule-utilitarianism is that some of its problems have not received comparable attention.

What Is Rule-Utilitarianism?

... [R]ule-utilitarianism as a theory of *action*—not of right laws—goes back at least as far as Richard Cumberland in 1672. Bishop Berkeley, in his *Passive Obedience* (1712), was the first to distinguish clearly between the two forms of utilitarianism, and he opted for the second. More specifically, he asserted that we are not morally bound to do whatever we believe will produce most good or happiness, but we are morally bound to follow certain moral laws prohibiting or enjoining certain types of action—these being God's laws as identified by revelation or natural reason. These laws have been selected by God because, in his benevolence, he wants the happiness of mankind and knows that following these laws will maximize it. God, incidentally, also lets it be known that it will not be to the long-range interest of anyone to infringe his laws; so the theory provides motivation to do what is right. Now, if the part about God is deleted from Berkeley's view, what remains is the skeleton of much of the kind of rule-utilitarianism I wish to discuss. This is the view roughly held by J. S. Mill; we of course have to flesh out the account a bit.

First, we have to think of the morality of a society: that is, of people in the society mostly sharing certain aversions to or desires for (partly as a matter of innate or learned benevolence, but partly as a result of a process of motivational learning we need not try to specify) certain types of actions. These presumably will include aversions to hurting others, telling lies, and breaking promises. But there are also learned dispositions to experience guilt in case we act contrary to these aversions and disapproval of others when they act contrary. We also admire others who do what we say is above and beyond the call of duty. Further, we disapprove of, and are averse to, various kinds of acts in different degrees: we would not commit murder and we disapprove intensely of anyone who does (without excuse); we also don't like it very much when a person brushes off a request for a match, but our disapproval is slight, and we feel only mild aversion to doing the same thing. Consciences are also equipped with a system of excuses; we don't feel guilty, or at least don't disapprove so vigorously of others, if we believe infractions are the result of certain conditions, say, ignorance, insanity, extreme fear, and so on.

This motivational description of conscience may not be appealing, but most of it appears in Mill's third chapter, and to some extent in the fifth chapter, of *Utilitarianism*. To my mind that *is* conscience, and the morality of a society is nothing more than the consciences of its members; or, if you like, the conscience of the average person.

If this is what a morality—or moral code—is, what is a "rule-utilitarian"? A rule-utilitarian thinks that right actions are the kind permitted by the moral code [that is] optimal for the society of which the agent is a member. An optimal code is one designed to maximize welfare or what is good (thus, utility). This leaves open the possibility that a particular right act by itself may not maximize benefit.

This definition does not imply anything about what a utilitarian means by "right" or "optimal" or about how a utilitarian will justify the main thesis. Utilitarians need not have any particular account of the meaning of these terms, and they need not offer any particular justification of their thesis; they can simply advocate the utilitarian principle.

On the rule-utilitarian view, then, to find what is morally right or wrong we need to find which actions would be permitted by a moral system that is "optimal" for the agent's society.

The First Real Puzzle

The last phrase in this definition raises the first "problem" or "puzzle" I wish to discuss—for an agent's society will comprise various subgroups, and it could be that the moral code optimal for one may not be optimal for others. For instance, perhaps the moral code comprising the consciences of physicians and lawyers should be more clearly articulated in certain areas than the moral code of the general public. There is no reason to burden the general public with, say, aversion to refusing to treat patients who cannot pay or breaches of confidentiality. Remember that we have to include the learning-costs in a cost-benefit analysis of a moral system. That being so, perhaps the rule-utilitarian must recognize special moralities for groups like physicians who, unlike the general public, meet certain problems regularly and need to respond to them intuitively without long inference from general principles. Similarly, it is possible that the morality optimal for children is not the morality optimal for adults. Rule-utilitarians, then, may be free to think that the moral codes justified for physicians, lawyers, children, bishops, and university students will differ. The identification of such possible special codes is part of the subject matter of "professional ethics."

This conception raises a difficult question that I shall not try to answer. Could the optimal moral code for a physician or a politician or an army officer direct a person to do something incompatible with what the optimal code for the general public would prescribe for the same situation? Presumably we *do* think that the optimal code for one society might lead to behavior incompatible with behavior required by the optimal code for another society. If that is possible, what is the really right thing to do when these codes conflict? For a rule-utilitarian who thinks that the actions of governments may be morally right or wrong, there is a related question. Must we talk of an "optimal moral code" for governments? Can we think of governments as quasi-persons, and talk of an optimal conscience for them? Or may we talk not of the acts of governments being right or wrong, but only of the morally right or wrong acts of office-holders or politicians? Rule-utilitarians should think more about this ....

The Second Puzzle

The rule-utilitarian, then, says that right action is action permitted by the moral code for society that would maximize net benefit or utility. But what is meant to count as benefit or utility? The traditional answer has been: pleasure, hedonic tone (positive or negative), or happiness. So said Bentham, Mill, and the earlier theological utilitarians. Now many philosophers argue that this is not what we should try to maximize, and that anyone who thinks this way is taking a crude view of human nature. What then should we add? J. L. Mackie suggests in *Ethics: Inventing Right and Wrong* (1977):

> liberty of thought and discussion, thought and discussion themselves, understanding of all sorts of things, including ourselves and other human beings, a self-reliant, enterprising, and experimental spirit and way of life, artistic creation and craftsmanship of any sort, the enjoyment and appreciation of beauty, and general participatory self-government both in smaller institutions and in the determination of large scale social policies and laws.
>
> (p. 150)

He says this in criticism of utilitarianism of all kinds. Is utilitarianism in all its forms committed to a hopelessly narrow view of what is good?

There is no *logical* connection between either act- or rule-utilitarianism and hedonism, and none between a deontological ethics and nonhedonism. True, the utilitarian says we are to identify right action by appeal to maximizing net benefit or utility, but he leaves the definition of these terms open. Indeed, one can say we should maximize what is intrinsically good, and go on to say, as "ideal utilitarians" like Moore and Rashdall did, that various states of affairs quite different from pleasure are intrinsically good—say, knowledge, virtue, and friendship. One could then say, as these ideal utilitarians did, that the right action is fixed by maximizing the intrinsically good and then propose that one can make justified comparative judgments about the intrinsic worth of knowledge, virtue, and the like so as to determine, roughly, when the good is being maximized.

However, this heterogeneity of intrinsic goods should surely be avoided, if possible. For different persons, with different intuitions about how intrinsically good some of these things are, can come out in very different places in their estimates of the total goodness that one action or moral code is likely to produce, as compared with another. So philosophers have wanted to find a view that does not rely so much on intuitions. This is one consideration that makes hedonism attractive; for the hedonist holds that only one sort of thing is good in itself, so the question of which code or action maximizes the good can be reduced to a factual question of how much enjoyment is produced. But there is another theory that avoids both reliance on intuitions and the alleged narrowness of the hedonist view. This is the view that "utility" is to be defined not in terms of pleasure but of *satisfaction of desires* or *interest*. Whereas the hedonist says state of affairs X is better than state of affairs Y if it contains more pleasure, the desire-satisfactionist says X is better than Y if there is more preference for X over Y than for Y over X. This last sounds a bit complex, but many people who have observed betting behavior think that cardinal numbers can be assigned to a person's desires: if so, then, if the strengths among different persons' desires can be compared and we can determine how many people prefer X over Y (or Y over X) and by how much, we have a way to aggregate preferences of a society. So ideally (just as does the traditional hedonist view, assuming pleasures can be measured), the interest-satisfaction theory provides a way to identify which policy or behavior would maximize desire-satisfaction.

Thus hedonism and the desire theory have emerged as leading contenders for a conception of utility suited for a simple maximizing theory of right and wrong conduct—simple in the sense that essentially there is only one sort of thing that is good in itself. The second theory is probably more popular today, for one or more of three reasons. First, it allows many things to be good—anything wanted for itself. Second, it seems easier to measure the strength of desires than an amount of pleasure. Third, the desire theory may seem more democratic; it goes on the basis of what people actually want, not on the basis of what will give them happiness—we are not to deny people what they want just because we think it will make them happier in the long run.[1]

From a practical point of view, the two theories are not all that different, since there is a close relation between desire and pleasure. People want to attain pleasant states and avoid unpleasant ones, other things being equal. Further, other things being equal, getting what one wants is pleasant and not getting it is unpleasant. So there is a close connection between desire and pleasure, but the implications of the two theories are not identical.

Though I shall not attempt here to adjudicate between these theories, I want to make three remarks. First, to avoid misunderstanding, the hedonistic theory must obviously make up its mind what pleasure is. I myself think that some element of experience or activity is pleasant if it makes the person, at the time, want to continue or repeat it simply for itself and not for extraneous reasons. This view has been called a "motivational" theory of pleasure. If we accept this, we will recognize that not only physical sensations are pleasant: a person can thoroughly enjoy reading a book, solving a crossword puzzle, or even writing a philosophy paper. This leads to my second point. Some critics ... have argued that utilitarianism, in its hedonist form, is very narrow in its conclusions about what is to be maximized, or what is good. But when we start surveying the various items philosophers have characterized as good, like knowledge, or friendship and love, or relationships of trust, or qualities of character like courage or fair-mindedness, we need to ask whether all of these do not make life more pleasant, and whether we would be much interested in them if they didn't. The critic may reply that of course all these things add to happiness, but they would be worthwhile in themselves even if they didn't. But if the critic takes this line, the point is much harder to establish, and one is left feeling that the happiness theory is not so narrow after all.

Such criticisms are, of course, blunted if we adopt the desire theory of utility, for then the utilitarian can say that anything judged intrinsically good by the anti-hedonist is something people desire. Hence the utilitarian will consider it one of the things to be maximized.

My third comment refers to some difficulties in the desire theory. I don't think we really want to maximize satisfaction of desire in general. People desire all sorts of things that it is idiotic to desire. At most we should want to maximize the satisfaction of those desires that people *would* have if they were fully informed about everything that might make them change their desires. Call this the "informed desire" theory. Even so, I doubt that we want to maximize desire-satisfaction as such; mostly we are concerned to help people get what they want because we think it will make them happy, whereas not getting it will sadden or frustrate them. There is a further complicated point that I cannot develop. People's desires are continually changing. So which desires should one try to satisfy at any time? Only the unchanging desires? The desires the person has now but won't have later? Desires the person will have at the time he is to get what he now wants? It is very difficult to find any convincing formulation.

The utilitarian, then, has to decide upon his conception of the "utility" which, when maximized, is the test of right and wrong. He ought to think more about this choice. But the charge that the utilitarian is committed to a crude or narrow view of what is good seems manifestly mistaken.

The Third Puzzle

For the sake of simplicity let us assume from here on that we are opting for a hedonist conception of "utility." Let us think of pleasure as being measurable. So that the basic unit is a "hedon-moment"—an experience, for one minute, with a pleasure level of plus one. We shall speak of "hedon-moments" having a negative value when the pleasure level is negative. An experience for one minute with a hedonic tone of level plus two would be two hedon-moments, just as an experience for two minutes with hedonic tone or level plus one. And so on.

Given these concepts, we might say that moral system A produces more utility than moral system B if and only if the net balance of hedon-moments from getting A current in the society and keeping it there would be, or would probably be, greater than the net balance from getting B into place and keeping it there. When a system A is more satisfactory in this sense than any other system, we can say that A is the optimal moral system, and that its content fixes which acts are morally right or wrong ....

[Some] writers believe that we have more of an obligation to avoid harming another person by an amount A than we have to do something that would raise the utility level of another person by the same amount A. They also believe that we have some obligation to act to reduce the misery of another, at least when the cost to ourselves is not very great; but we do not have a comparable obligation to bring about an equal improvement in the well-being of another who is already above the misery range. In the latter case there is *no* obligation to act at all, or at most a weak one. It is generally thought that an act-utilitarian theory cannot recognize such distinctions. How about a rule-utilitarian theory? ....

Here we have to go back to the theory of justification, which I have been avoiding. I think we have to inquire what kind of moral code a person would support for the society in which he or she expects to live. Here I am talking about a person who is fully rational, fully informed, and has that degree of benevolence a fully informed person would have. Others might say we have to find the moral principles that fully informed, impartial, but otherwise normal people would subscribe to. Still others might say we have to find the principles that reflect our carefully considered moral "intuitions." The reader may object that thinking all this out would require a lifetime, but the form of rule-utilitarianism stated above may not need any amendment for the range of cases about which the reader has to make practical decisions.

The Alleged Problems

I now take leave of puzzles, thought about which might lead us to some refinements of rule-utilitarianism, and turn to just plain objections that have been raised against rule-utilitarianism in any form. The ones I shall discuss are related, and together they may be viewed as variations on a charge of Utopianism.

In order to appraise these objections, I must expand still more the conception of an "optimal" moral code. The term does not refer to a set of rules that would do most good if everyone conformed to them all the time. The meaning is more complex. Recall that "a moral code" is a set of desires or aversions directed at certain types of acts and the disposition to feel guilty about not conforming to these desires or aversions as well as to disapprove of such failure to conform on the part of others when they have no excuse. Now these dispositions may vary both in their intensity and in their prevalence in a given society. The more intense and widespread an aversion to a certain sort of behavior, the less frequent the behavior is apt to be. But the more intense and widespread, the greater the cost of teaching the rule and keeping it alive, the greater the burden on the individual, and so on.

The "optimality" of a moral code encompasses both the benefits of reduced objectionable behavior and the long-term cost. So the moral code optimal for a given society is that whole system with a given degree of average intensity and spread among the population, for each of its components, that comes out best in a cost-benefit analysis. Needless to say, like the law, the optimal moral code normally will not produce 100 percent compliance with all its rules; that would be too costly. It may do so in small homogeneous populations: physical violence is unheard of on the Hopi reservation. But mostly not. According to our conception, the rule-utilitarian believes that an act is prima facie obligatory if and only if (and to the degree that) such an optimal code would build in some degree of moral aversion to not performing it.

The first objection to this view is that it would be harmful for some people to live according to the optimal code in a society where the optimal code is not widespread, for so doing could be either pointless or injurious. For instance, the optimal moral code might call for no one ever to carry a lethal weapon, whereas living by such a code would not be a good idea, these critics say, in a society where most persons are trigger-happy gun-carrying demons. Furthermore, it is especially incoherent for a utilitarian to advocate behaving in such a counterproductive way: his basic thesis is that utility is the point of morality, but here the rule-utilitarian seems to be advocating behavior that is likely to be harmful.

There is an adequate reply to this objection: it has not been shown that such harmful requirements would ever appear in an optimal moral code. In the gun-carrying society, an optimal moral code would surely give directions to be prepared to defend one's self and one's family but of course to defend only. The rule might be: "Never carry a gun when it can be done at no personal risk; otherwise carry a gun but use it only in self-defense." (An actual moral code would rarely include injunctions as specific as this, but it might if a rule were aimed at meeting a specific problem about which more abstract principles were not much help.) An optimal moral code may not always provide for doing the very best possible thing in every situation; morality is a blunt instrument, like the law. But no proof has been offered that an optimal code would prescribe doing seriously harmful things as a result of the optimal moral code not being widely accepted in the society. True, an optimal code might well tell one to keep a promise when few others are doing so, and this might do little immediate good; but at least it would be a step in building a convention of promise-keeping ....

[Another] objection has been raised: whereas it might be nice for people to act in accordance with an optimal moral code when that code is not widely accepted, one cannot seriously claim that it is their moral obligation. Some critics say it may be morally obligatory to do what will in fact do most good in an actual situation even when the conventional moral code doesn't call for that and that it may even be obligatory to act in accordance with an optimal moral code if there is good reason to think that so doing would seriously tend to usher the optimal code into the status of being conventional. But, these critics say, just to live by an optimal moral code for no further reason is not one's moral obligation. To this objection there are adequate retorts. We may begin by asking what the ground rules are supposed to be for deciding that one does or doesn't really have a moral obligation to do something. Doubtless answering this question adequately would lead us back to the theory of the meaning and justification of moral beliefs. But suppose it can be shown that what one is morally obligated to do is what an impartial, informed, otherwise normal person would demand of one morally or what would be demanded by a moral system that rational, fully informed people with a rational degree of benevolence would support in preference to other moral systems and to no system at all. And suppose that these conceptions lead to the conclusion that it is obligatory to follow an optimal moral code. Then it is hard to see why one must ... start over and do something more in order to show that it is morally obligatory to follow the requirements of the optimal code.

Furthermore, we do not believe that a person has no obligation to do things which the moral code current in his society does not demand. We do not believe that a person has no obligation to be kind to suffering animals, or to prisoners in a prison camp in wartime, just because other people don't or because conventional morality doesn't demand it. Are moral reformers never correct when they martyr themselves in order to discharge their moral obligations as they see them? We must make at least two concessions. First, we must agree that if one lives according to a moral code that demands more than the traditional moral codes, one is doing something that it would not be disgraceful not to do—assuming that to act disgracefully is to fall a bit below the normal level. Second, I agree that the normal social sanctions for behaving morally are absent if one is living up to a standard that conventional morality does not require. Indeed, one may sometimes *incur* moral sanctions for living in accordance with an optimal code, for instance if one insists on treating persons of another race as social equals in a place where such behavior is frowned upon ....

Note

1 Actually, one could argue with some force that Mill, who is supposed to be a hedonist, was straddling the two. For he takes the odd view that virtue and wealth are *parts* of happiness. He has often been accused of confusion here, and doubtless he was confused. What he had good reason for saying was only that people *want* things like money and virtue, and may be made unhappy by not obtaining them. Could he have confused being desired and being pleasant? On a later page he seems to confirm such a confusion by saying that "desiring a thing and finding it pleasant ... are two different modes of naming the same psychological fact" (*Utilitarianism*, Ch. 4).

Review and Discussion Questions

1 What is "rule-utilitarianism," and how does Brandt distinguish it from "act-utilitarianism"?
2 How does Brandt propose to understand the notion of a society or group?

3 Describe the different answers to the question of what it would mean to maximize net benefit or utility. Which view does Brandt adopt?
4 Explain Brandt's theory of justification of morality, including the notion of an "optimal" moral code.
5 Explain why Brandt's view might be thought "utopian" and his responses to the charge.

READING: THE ETHICS OF CARE AS MORAL THEORY

VIRGINIA HELD[*]

In this essay, Virginia Held discusses how traditional moral theories are inadequate for capturing the full range of our moral concerns and how they devalue the important role of caring relationships for ethics. Virginia Held is Distinguished Professor of Philosophy at the Graduate School of the City University of New York.

The ethics of care is only a few decades old.[1] Some theorists do not like the term "care" to designate this approach to moral issues and have tried substituting "the ethic of love," or "relational ethics," but the discourse keeps returning to "care" as the so far more satisfactory of the terms considered, though dissatisfactions with it remain. The concept of care has the advantage of not losing sight of the work involved in caring for people and of not lending itself to the interpretation of morality as ideal but impractical to which advocates of the ethics of care often object. Care is both value and practice.

By now, the ethics of care has moved far beyond its original formulations, and any attempt to evaluate it should consider much more than the one or two early works so frequently cited. It has been developed as a moral theory relevant not only to the so-called private realms of family and friendship but to medical practice, law, political life, the organization of society, war, and international relations.

The ethics of care is sometimes seen as a potential moral theory to be substituted for such dominant moral theories as Kantian ethics, utilitarianism, or Aristotelian virtue ethics. It is sometimes seen as a form of virtue ethics. It is almost always developed as emphasizing neglected moral considerations of at least as much importance as the considerations central to moralities of justice and rights or of utility and preference satisfaction. And many who contribute to the understanding of the ethics of care seek to integrate the moral considerations, such as justice, which other moral theories have clarified, satisfactorily with those of care, though they often see the need to reconceptualize these considerations.

Features of the Ethics of Care

Some advocates of the ethics of care resist generalizing this approach into something that can be fitted into the form of a moral theory. They see it as a mosaic of

---

[*] Virginia Held, "The Ethics of Care as Moral Theory," Chapter 1 in *The Ethics of Care: Personal, Political and Global* (Oxford: Oxford University Press, 2006), pp. 9–28. Reprinted by permission.

insights and value the way it is sensitive to contextual nuance and particular narratives rather than making the abstract and universal claims of more familiar moral theories.[2] Still, I think one can discern among various versions of the ethics of care a number of major features.

First, the central focus of the ethics of care is on the compelling moral salience of attending to and meeting the needs of the particular others for whom we take responsibility. Caring for one's child, for instance, may well and defensibly be at the forefront of a person's moral concerns. The ethics of care recognizes that human beings are dependent for many years of their lives, that the moral claim of those dependent on us for the care they need is pressing, and that there are highly important moral aspects in developing the relations of caring that enable human beings to live and progress. All persons need care for at least their early years. Prospects for human progress and flourishing hinge fundamentally on the care that those needing it receive, and the ethics of care stresses the moral force of the responsibility to respond to the needs of the dependent. Many persons will become ill and dependent for some periods of their later lives, including in frail old age, and some who are permanently disabled will need care the whole of their lives. Moralities built on the image of the independent, autonomous, rational individual largely overlook the reality of human dependence and the morality for which it calls. The ethics of care attends to this central concern of human life and delineates the moral values involved ....

Second, in the epistemological process of trying to understand what morality would recommend and what it would be morally best for us to do and to be, the ethics of care values emotion rather than rejects it. Not all emotion is valued, of course, but in contrast with the dominant rationalist approaches, such emotions as sympathy, empathy, sensitivity, and responsiveness are seen as the kind of moral emotions that need to be cultivated not only to help in the implementation of the dictates of reason but to better ascertain what morality recommends.[3] Even anger may be a component of the moral indignation that should be felt when people are treated unjustly or inhumanely, and it may contribute to (rather than interfere with) an appropriate interpretation of the moral wrong. This is not to say that raw emotion can be a guide to morality; feelings need to be reflected on and educated. But from the care perspective, moral inquiries that rely entirely on reason and rationalistic deductions or calculations are seen as deficient.

The emotions that are typically considered and rejected in rationalistic moral theories are the egoistic feelings that undermine universal moral norms, the favoritism that interferes with impartiality, and the aggressive and vengeful impulses for which morality is to provide restraints. The ethics of care, in contrast, typically appreciates the emotions and relational capabilities that enable morally concerned persons in actual interpersonal contexts to understand what would be best. Since even the helpful emotions can often become misguided or worse—as when excessive empathy with others leads to a wrongful degree of self-denial or when benevolent concern crosses over into controlling domination—we need an *ethics* of care, not just care itself. The various aspects and expressions of care and caring relations need to be subjected to moral scrutiny and *evaluated*, not just observed and described.

Third, the ethics of care rejects the view of the dominant moral theories that the more abstract the reasoning about a moral problem the better because the more likely to avoid bias and arbitrariness, the more nearly to achieve impartiality. The ethics of care respects rather than removes itself from the claims of particular others with whom we share actual relationships ....[4]

Annette Baier considers how a feminist approach to morality differs from a Kantian one and Kant's claim that women are incapable of being fully moral because of their reliance on emotion rather than reason. She writes,

> Where Kant concludes "so much the worse for women," we can conclude "so much the worse for the male fixation on the special skill of drafting legislation, for the bureaucratic mentality of rule worship, and for the male exaggeration of the importance of independence over mutual interdependence ...."[5]

A fourth characteristic of the ethics of care is that like much feminist thought in many areas, it reconceptualizes traditional notions about the public and the private. The traditional view, built into the dominant moral theories, is that the household is a private sphere beyond politics into which government, based on consent, should not intrude ....

Dominant moral theories have seen "public" life as relevant to morality while missing the moral significance of the "private" domains of family and friendship. Thus the dominant theories have assumed that morality should be sought for unrelated, independent, and mutually indifferent individuals assumed to be equal. They have posited an abstract, fully rational "agent as such" from which to construct morality,[6] while missing the moral issues that arise between interconnected persons in the contexts of family, friendship, and social groups. In the context of the family, it is typical for relations to be between persons with highly unequal power who did not choose the ties and obligations in which they find themselves enmeshed. For instance, no child can choose her parents yet she may well have obligations to care for them. Relations of this kind are standardly noncontractual, and conceptualizing them as contractual would often undermine or at least obscure the trust on which their worth depends. The ethics of care addresses rather than neglects moral issues arising in relations among the unequal and dependent, relations that are often laden with emotion and involuntary, and then notices how often these attributes apply not only in the household but in the wider society as well. For instance, persons do not choose which gender, racial, class, ethnic, religious, national, or cultural groups to be brought up in, yet these sorts of ties may be important aspects of who they are and how their experience can contribute to moral understanding.

A fifth characteristic of the ethics of care is the conception of persons with which it begins. This will be dealt with in the next section.

The Critique of Liberal Individualism

The ethics of care usually works with a conception of persons as relational, rather than as the self-sufficient independent individuals of the dominant moral theories ....

Every person starts out as a child dependent on those providing us care, and we remain interdependent with others in thoroughly fundamental ways throughout our lives. That we can think and act as if we were independent depends on a network of social relations making it possible for us to do so. And our relations are part of what constitute our identity. This is not to say that we cannot become autonomous; feminists have done much interesting work developing an alternative conception of autonomy in place of the liberal individualist one.[7] Feminists have much experience rejecting or reconstituting relational ties that are oppressive. But it means that from the perspective of an ethics of care, to construct morality *as if* we were Robinson Crusoes, or, to use Hobbes's image, mushrooms sprung from nowhere, is misleading.[8] As Eva Kittay writes, this conception fosters the illusion that society is composed of free, equal, and independent individuals who can choose to associate with one another or not. It obscures the very real facts of dependency for everyone when they are young, for most people at various periods in their lives when they are ill or old and infirm, for some who are disabled, and for all those engaged in unpaid "dependency work."[9] And it obscures the innumerable ways persons and groups are interdependent in the modern world ....

Justice and Care

.... An ethic of justice focuses on questions of fairness, equality, individual rights, abstract principles, and the consistent application of them. An ethic of care focuses on attentiveness, trust, responsiveness to need, narrative nuance, and cultivating caring relations. Whereas an ethic of justice seeks a fair solution between competing individual interests and rights, an ethic of care sees the interests of carers and cared-for as importantly intertwined rather than as simply competing. Whereas justice protects equality and freedom, care fosters social bonds and cooperation ....

My own suggestions for integrating care and justice are to keep these concepts conceptually distinct and to delineate the domains in which they should have priority.[10] In the realm of law, for instance, justice and the assurance of rights should have priority, although the humane considerations of care should not be absent. In the realm of the family and among friends, priority should be given to expansive care, though the basic requirements of justice surely should also be met. But these are the clearest cases; others will combine moral urgencies. Universal human rights (including the social and economic ones as well as the political and civil) should certainly be respected, but promoting care across continents may be a more promising way to achieve this than mere rational recognition. When needs are desperate, justice may be a lessened requirement on shared responsibility for meeting needs, although this rarely excuses violations of rights. At the level of what constitutes a society in the first place, a domain within which rights are to be assured and care provided, appeal must be made to something like the often weak but not negligible caring relations among persons that enable them to recognize each other as members of the same society. Such recognition must eventually be global; in the meantime, the civil society without which the liberal institutions of justice cannot function presume a background of some degree of caring relations rather than of merely competing individuals .... Furthermore, considerations of care provide a more fruitful basis than considerations of justice for deciding much about how society should be structured, for instance, how extensive or how restricted markets should be .... And in the course of protecting the rights that ought to be recognized, such as those to basic necessities, policies that express the caring of the community for all its members will be better policies than those that grudgingly, though fairly, issue an allotment to those deemed unfit.

Care is probably the most deeply fundamental value. There can be care without justice: There has historically been little justice in the family, but care and life have gone on without it. There can be no justice without care, however, for without care no child would survive and there would be no persons to respect ....

The Feminist Background

The ethics of care has grown out of the constructive turmoil of the phase of feminist thought and the rethinking of almost all fields of inquiry that began in the United States and Europe in the late 1960s. During this time, the bias against women in society and in what was taken to be knowledge became a focus of attention.

Feminism is a revolutionary movement. It aims to overturn what many consider the most entrenched hierarchy there is: the hierarchy of gender. Its fundamental commitment is to the equality of women, although that may be interpreted in various ways. A most important achievement of feminism has been to establish that the experience of women is as important, relevant, and philosophically interesting as the experience of men. The feminism of the late twentieth century was built on women's experience.

Experience is central to feminist thought, but what is meant by experience is not mere empirical observation, as so much of the history of modern philosophy and as analytic philosophy tend to construe it. Feminist experience is what art and literature as well as science deal with. It is the lived experience of feeling as well as thinking, of performing actions as well as receiving impressions, and of being aware of our connections with other persons as well as of our own sensations. And by now, for feminists, it is not the experience of what can be thought of as women as such, which would be an abstraction, but the experience of actual women in all their racial and cultural and other diversity.[11]

The feminist validation of women's experience has had important consequences in ethics. It has led to a fundamental critique of the moral theories that were (and to a large extent still are) dominant and to the development of alternative, feminist approaches to morality. For instance, in the long history of thinking about the human as Man, the public sphere from which women were excluded was seen as the source of the distinctively human, moral, and creative. The Greek conception of the polis illustrated this view, later reflected strongly in social contract theories. As the realm of economic activity was added after industrialization to that of the political, artistic, and scientific to compose what was seen as human, transformative, and progressive, the private sphere of the household continued to be thought of as natural, a realm where the species is reproduced, repetitively replenishing the biological basis of life.

The dominant moral theories when the feminism of the late twentieth century appeared on the scene were Kantian moral theory and utilitarianism. These were the theories that, along with their relevant metaethical questions, dominated the literature in moral philosophy and the courses taught to students.[12] They were also the moral outlooks that continued to have a significant influence outside philosophy in the field of law, one of the few areas that had not banished moral questions in favor of purportedly value-free psychology and social science.

These dominant moral theories can be seen to be modeled on the experience of men in public life and in the marketplace. When women's experience is thought to be as relevant to morality as men's, a position whose denial would seem to be biased, these moralities can be seen to fit very inadequately the morally relevant experience of women in the household. Women's experience has typically included cultivating special relationships with family and friends, rather than primarily dealing impartially with strangers, and providing large amounts of caring labor for children and often for ill or elderly family members. Affectionate sensitivity and responsiveness to need may seem to provide better moral guidance for what should be done in these contexts than do abstract rules or rational calculations of individual utilities ....

Within traditional moral philosophy, debates have been extensive and complex concerning the relative merits of deontological or Kantian moral theory as compared with the merits of the various kinds of utilitarian or consequentialist theory and of the contractualism that can take a more Kantian or a more utilitarian form. But from the newly asserted point of view of women's experience of moral issues, what may be most striking about all of these is their similarity. Both Kantian moralities of universal, abstract moral laws, and utilitarian versions of the ethics of Bentham and Mill advocating impartial calculations to determine what will produce the most happiness for the most people have been developed for interactions between relative strangers. Contractualism treats interactions between mutually disinterested individuals. All require impartiality and make no room at the foundational level for the partiality that connects us to those we care for and to those who care for us. Relations of family, friendship, and group identity have largely been missing from these theories, though recent attempts, which I find unsuccessful, have been made to handle such relations within them.

Although their conceptions of reason differ significantly, with Kantian theory rejecting the morality of instrumental reasoning and utilitarian theory embracing it, both types of theory are rationalistic. Both rely on one very simple supreme and universal moral principle: the Kantian categorical imperative, or the utilitarian principle of utility, in accordance with which everyone ought always to act. Both ask us to be entirely impartial and to reject emotion in determining what we ought to do. Though Kantian ethics enlists emotion in carrying out the dictates of reason, and utilitarianism allows each of us to count ourselves as one among all whose pain or pleasure will be affected by an action, for both kinds of theory we are to disregard our emotions in the epistemological process of figuring out what we ought to do. These characterizations also hold for contractualism.

These theories generalize from the ideal contexts of the state and the market, addressing the moral decisions of judges, legislators, policy makers, and citizens. But because they are *moral* theories rather than merely political or legal or economic theories, they extend their recommendations to what they take to be *all* moral decisions about how we ought to act in any context in which moral problems arise.

In Margaret Walker's assessment, these are idealized "theoretical-juridical" accounts of actual moral practices. They invoke the image of "a fraternity of independent peers invoking laws to deliver verdicts with authority."[13] Fiona Robinson asserts that in dominant moral theories, values such as autonomy, independence, noninterference, self-determination, fairness, and rights are given priority, and there is a "systematic devaluing of notions of interdependence, relatedness, and positive involvement" in the lives of others.[14] The theoretical-juridical accounts, Walker shows, are presented as appropriate for "the" moral agent, as recommendations for how "we" ought to act, but their canonical forms of moral judgment are the judgments of those who resemble "a judge, manager, bureaucrat, or gamesman."[15] They are abstract and idealized forms of the judgments made by persons who are dominant in an established social order. They do not represent the moral experiences of women caring for children or aged parents, or of minority service workers providing care for minimal wages. And they do not deal with the judgments of groups who must rely on communal solidarity for survival ....

The ethics of care builds concern and mutual responsiveness to need both the personal and the wider social level. Within social relations in which we care enough about each other to form a social entity, we may agree for limited purposes to imagine each other as liberal individuals and to adopt liberal policies to maximize individual benefits. But we should not lose sight of restricted and artificial aspects of such conceptions. The ethics of care offers a view of both the more immediate and the more distant human relationships on which satisfactory societies can be built. It provides new theory with which to develop new practices and can perhaps offer greater potential for making progress than is contained in the views of traditional moral theory.

Notes

1 I use the term "ethics" to suggest that there are multiple versions of this ethic, though they all have much in common, making it understandable that some prefer "the ethic of care." I use "the ethics of care" as a collective and singular noun. Some moral philosophers have tried to establish a definitional distinction between "ethics" and "morality"; I think such efforts fail, and I use the terms more or less interchangeably, though I certainly distinguish between the moral or ethical beliefs groups of people in fact have and moral or ethical recommendations that are justifiable or admirable.

2 See, for example, Annette C. Baier, *Moral Prejudices: Essays on Ethics* (Cambridge, MA: Harvard University Press, 1994), esp. Chap. 1; Peta Bowden, *Caring: Gender Sensitive Ethics* (London: Routledge, 1997); and Margaret Urban Walker, "Feminism, Ethics, and the Question of Theory," *Hypatia: A Journal of Feminist Philosophy* 7 (1992): 23–38.

3 See, for example, Baier, *Moral Prejudices*; Virginia Held, *Feminist Morality: Transforming Culture, Society, and Politics* (Chicago, IL: University of Chicago Press, 1993); Diana Tietjens Meyers, *Subjection and Subjectivity* (New York: Routledge, 1994); and Margaret Urban Walker, *Moral Understandings: A Feminist Study in Ethics* (New York: Routledge, 1998).

4 See, for example, Seyla Benhabib, *Situating the Self: Gender, Community, and Postmodernism in Contemporary Ethics* (New York: Routledge, 1992); Marilyn Friedman, *What Are Friends For? Feminist Perspectives on Personal Relationships* (Ithaca, NY: Cornell University Press, 1993); Held, *Feminist Morality*; and Eva Feder Kittay, *Love's Labor: Essays on Women, Equality, and Dependency* (New York: Routledge, 1999).

5 Baier, *Moral Prejudices*, p. 26.

6 Good examples are Stephen L. Darwall, *Impartial Reason* (Ithaca, NY: Cornell University Press, 1983), and David Gauthier, *Morals by Agreement* (Oxford: Oxford University Press, 1986).

7 See, for example, Diana T. Meyers, *Self, Society, and Personal Choice* (New York: Columbia University Press, 1989); Grace Clement, *Care, Autonomy, and Justice*

(Boulder, CO: Westview Press, 1996); Diana T. Meyers, ed., *Feminists Rethink the Self* (Boulder, CO: Westview Press, 1997); and Catriona Mackenzie and Natalie Stoljar, eds., *Relational Autonomy: Feminist Perspectives on Autonomy, Agency, and the Social Self* (New York: Oxford University Press, 2000). See also Marina Oshana, "Personal Autonomy and Society." *Journal of Social Philosophy* 29(1) (spring 1998): 81–102.

8 This image is in Thomas Hobbes's *The Citizen: Philosophical Rudiments Concerning Government and Society*, ed. B. Gert (Garden City, NY: Doubleday, 1972), p. 205. For a contrasting view, see Sibyl Schwarzenbach, "On Civic Friendship." *Ethics* 107(1) (1996): 97–128.
9 Kittay, *Love's Labor*.
10 See Held, *Rights and Goods*.
11 See, for example, Elizabeth V. Spelman, *Inessential Woman* (Boston, MA: Beacon Press, 1988); Sara Lucia Hoagland, *Lesbian Ethics: Toward New Value* (Palo Alto, CA: Institute of Lesbian Studies, 1989); Patricia Hill Collins, *Black Feminist Thought: Knowledge, Consciousness, and the Politics of Empowerment* (Boston, MA: Unwin Hyman, 1990); Patricia J. Williams, *The Alchemy of Race and Rights* (Cambridge, MA: Harvard University Press, 1991); and Uma Narayan, *Dislocating Cultures: Identities, Traditions and Third World Women* (New York: Routledge, 1997).
12 I share Stephen Darwall's view that normative ethics and metaethics are highly interrelated and cannot be clearly separated. See his *Philosophical Ethics*, esp. Chap. 1.
13 Walker, *Moral Understandings*, p. 1.
14 Robinson, *Globalizing Care*, p. 7.
15 Walker, *Moral Understandings*, p. 21.

Review and Discussion Questions

1 What are the core features of the ethics of care?
2 What is Virginia Held's critique of traditional moral theories? Do you agree?
3 How does the focus on justice contrast with the focus on caring, according to Held? What is the relationship between justice and caring, in your view? Can you describe a scenario where demands of justice and caring conflict? What is the appropriate resolution?
4 What are the "domains" of justice and caring, according to Held? Do you agree with her analysis?
5 What is the feminist background for the ethics of care, and how would you characterize the significance of this background for understanding and applying an ethics of care?

Essay and Paper Topics for Part B: Contemporary Theories

1 Discuss the utilitarian moral theory in light of O'Neill's or Ross's criticisms. In your essay, be sure to consider how the utilitarian philosopher might best respond to the criticisms and why you do or do not think that such a response is adequate.
2 Is Brandt guilty of any of the charges Held makes against traditional philosophy or does he successfully avoid them?
3 Compare Ross's view of moral truth and objectivity with that of one other philosopher.
4 In what senses does morality change with the times, and in what senses, if any, is it changeless? Draw on two authors from this chapter or preceding chapters to support your views.
5 How does the ethics of care compare and contrast with the other approaches to moral theory?

Part II

Life and Death

Chapter 4

Terrorism and Torture

We begin discussions of life and death in this chapter by examining questions about terrorism and torture. The first essay examines different perspectives about what terrorism is, and the other two essays examine whether torture can be justified in the face of grave threats.

READING: IS TERRORISM MORALLY DISTINCTIVE?

SAMUEL SCHEFFLER[*]

It is sometimes said that one man's terrorist is another man's freedom fighter. Should we take that to mean that the word *terrorist* is devoid of any real meaning and is simply a way to describe one's enemies? Scheffler argues against this broad use of the term. What counts as "terrorism" is specific and distinctive, he maintains. Samuel Scheffler is University Professor and Professor of Philosophy and Law at New York University.

The term "terrorism" may by now have become too ideologically freighted to have any analytic value. If the term is to be an aid to understanding, two opposed but complementary ways of employing it will have to be resisted. On the one hand, there is the tendency, among the representatives and defenders of governments facing violent threats from non-state groups and organizations, to use the term to refer to all forms of political violence perpetrated by non-state actors. On the other hand, there is the tendency, among the representatives and defenders of non-state actors engaged in political violence, to insist that "the real terrorists" are the officials or the military forces of those states with which they are locked in conflict. Under the combined influence of these two tendencies, the word "terrorism" is in danger of becoming little more than a pejorative term used to refer to the tactics of one's enemies.

In this paper, I will proceed on the assumption that the concept of terrorism retains more content than that, and that we recognize a use of the term in which it

---

[*] Abridged from "Is Terrorism Morally Distinctive?" by Samuel Scheffler, *The Journal of Political Philosophy* 14(1) (2006): 1–17. Copyright © 2006 by Samuel Scheffler. Published by Blackwell Publishing Ltd. Reprinted by permission of Copyright Clearance Center on behalf of the publisher. Some footnotes omitted.

refers to a special kind of phenomenon or class of phenomena .... A number of contemporary writers on terrorism have found it natural to situate their discussions in relation to the traditional theory of the just war.[1] For my purposes, it will be helpful to begin instead with the pre-eminent philosopher of fear in our tradition, Thomas Hobbes. It is striking that, in his famous catalogue of the "incommodities" of the state of nature, Hobbes describes fear as the worst incommodity of all. The state of nature, he says, is characterized by a war of "every man against every man," and such a war comprises not merely actual battles but an extended "tract of time" in which "the will to contend by battle is sufficiently known."[2] This means that, in the war of every man against every man, a condition of general insecurity prevails for an extended period. "In such condition," he says,

> there is no place for industry, because the fruit thereof is uncertain; and consequently no culture of the earth; no navigation, nor use of the commodities that may be imported by sea; no commodious building; no instruments of moving and removing such things as require much force; no knowledge of the face of the earth; no account of time; no arts; no letters; no society; *and which is worst of all, continual fear, and danger of violent death.* And the life of man, solitary, poor, nasty, brutish, and short.
> (Ch. 13, para. 9, pp. 95–6, emphasis added)

Hobbes makes at least three points in this passage and the surrounding text that are relevant to our topic. First, there is his insistence on how bad a thing fear is. Continual fear—not momentary anxiety but the grinding, unrelenting fear of imminent violent death—is unspeakably awful. It is, he suggests, worse than ignorance. It is worse than the absence of arts, letters and social life. It is worse than being materially or culturally or intellectually impoverished. Fear dominates and reduces a person. A life of continual fear is scarcely a life at all. Someone who is in the grip of chronic terror is in a state of constant distress; he "hath his heart all the day long gnawed on by fear of death, poverty, or other calamity and has no repose, nor pause of his anxiety, but in sleep" (Ch. 12, para. 5, p. 82).

The second point is that fear is incompatible with social life. On the one hand, sustained fear undermines social relations, so that in addition to being worse than various forms of poverty and deprivation it also contributes to them, by destroying the conditions that make wealth and "commodious living" possible. Fearful people lead "solitary" lives. Alone with their fears, trusting no one, they cannot sustain rewarding forms of interpersonal exchange. On the other hand, the establishment of society offers relief from fear and, in Hobbes' view, it is to escape from fear that people form societies. The fear of death, he says, is the first of "the passions that incline men to peace" (Ch. 13, para. 14, p. 97). Indeed, and this is the third point, it is *only* within a stable political society that the miserable condition of unremitting fear can be kept at bay. In addition to being incompatible with social life, sustained fear is the inevitable fate of pre-social human beings.

Terrorists take these Hobbesian insights to heart. In a familiar range of cases, at least, they engage in violence against some people in order to induce fear or terror in others, with the aim of destabilizing or degrading (or threatening to destabilize or degrade) an existing social order .... I will call these "the standard cases." I do so in part on the boringly etymological ground that these cases preserve the link between the idea of terrorism and the root concept of terror. But I will also go on to argue—indeed, it is my primary thesis—that the etymology points us to something morally interesting which might otherwise be easier to overlook.

In "the standard cases," terrorists undertake to kill or injure a more or less random group of civilians or noncombatants; in so doing, they aim to produce fear within some much larger group of people, and they hope that this fear will in turn erode or threaten to erode the quality or stability of an existing social order .... The fear that terrorism produces may, for example, erode confidence in the government, depress the economy, distort the political process, reduce associational activity and provoke destructive changes in the legal system ....

Terrorist violence may, of course, have many other aims as well, even in the standard cases. The terrorists may hope that their violent acts will attract publicity for their cause, or promote their personal ambitions, or provoke a response that will widen the conflict, or enhance their prestige among those they claim to represent, or undermine their political rivals, or help them to achieve a kind of psychological or metaphysical liberation. Nor need they conceive of their actions exclusively in instrumental terms. They may also be seeking to express their rage. Or they may believe that their victims are not in the relevant sense innocent, despite being civilians or noncombatants, and they may think of themselves as administering forms of deserved punishment or retribution.

There are many other respects in which what I am calling standard cases of terrorism can differ from one another. But they all have the following minimum features: (1) the use of violence against civilians or noncombatants, (2) the intention that this use of violence should create fear in others, including other civilians and noncombatants, and (3) the further intention that this fear should destabilize or degrade an existing social order, or at any rate that it should raise the specter of such destabilization or degradation. The destabilization or degradation of the social order may itself have many different aims. Among other things, it may be intended (a) as a prelude to the imposition of a different social order or the reconstitution of the existing order on different terms, (b) as a way of effecting some change in the policy of an existing state or society, (c) as a form of deserved punishment, and hence as an end in itself, or (d) as some combination of these.

What makes terrorism of the standard kind possible is the corrosive power of fear. As Hobbes suggests, sustained or continual fear is a regressive force both individually and socially. It can induce the unraveling of an individual's personality and, as we have already seen, its cumulative effects on large numbers of people can degrade the social order and diminish the quality of social life. Its capacity to achieve these effects is enhanced by the infectiousness of fear, the fact that it can so easily be transmitted from one person to another .... In this age of instant communication, moreover, the capacity of terrorist acts to cause fear, and to exploit the phenomena of mutual reinforcement and intensification, is greatly increased. The news media can be counted on to provide graphic coverage of each terrorist outrage, so that a bomb blast anywhere can generate fear and insecurity everywhere. These attitudes in turn become newsworthy and are dutifully reported by the media, thus contributing to the syndrome of mutual reinforcement.

I said earlier that, in the standard cases, terrorist violence is usually directed against a "more or less random" group of civilians or noncombatants .... In this way, the appearance of randomness is used to exploit the psychic economy of identification in such a way as to maximize the spread of fear.

This is not to say that it is always easy to achieve one's aims using terrorist tactics. In fact, it is usually difficult for terrorist acts to destabilize an otherwise stable social order. This is not merely because such acts can backfire, and reduce support for the terrorists' goals. Nor is it merely because of the large armies, police forces and intelligence services that stable societies normally have available to fight those who employ terrorism. Just as important is the fact that stable societies, and individuals raised in such societies, have substantial social and psychological resources with which to resist the destructive effects of fear. People can be remarkably tenacious in their determination to preserve the lives they have made for themselves in society, and if fear can be infectious so too can courage and the determination to persevere in the face of great danger. These too have mutually reinforcing and intensifying effects.

But terrorism does not need to destabilize a social order altogether in order to transform and degrade it and, as we have seen, often such transformation and degradation will suffice to enable those who employ terrorist tactics to achieve some or all of their aims. The problem is that living with fear can have corrosive effects even for those who are courageous and determined to persevere. One might put the point provocatively and say that courage itself—or the need to sustain it over long periods of time—can be corrosive. Living each day with the vivid awareness that one's children may be killed whenever they leave home, or that a decision to meet one's friends at a restaurant or café may result in violent death, or that an ordinary bus ride on a sunny day may end with lumps of flesh raining down on a previously peaceful neighborhood, exacts a cost. Nor is this true only if one yields to one's fears and keeps one's children at home, gives up socializing and avoids public transportation. It is also true if one grits one's teeth and resolves to carry on as normal. People often say, in explaining their determination to maintain a normal routine in the face of terrorist activities or threats, that to do otherwise would be to "give the terrorists what they want." This is not wrong, but it understates the problem. Maintaining one's normal routine does not suffice to preserve normalcy. Terrorism undermines normalcy almost by definition. One cannot, simply through an act of will, immunize oneself against the effects of continual fear and danger on one's state of mind or on the quality of one's life. These effects are distressingly easy for groups that use terrorist tactics to achieve and distressingly difficult for the members of targeted populations to avoid.

This is one reason why terrorism is so popular, even if it is not always ultimately successful. Apologists for terror often claim that it is the weapon of the weak, who have no other tools available for fighting back against their oppressors. This may be true in some circumstances. As far as I can see, however, those who engage in terrorism rarely invest much time in exploring the availability of other tools. All too often terrorism is the tool of choice simply because the perceived advantages it offers are so great. It costs relatively little in money and manpower. It has immediate effects and generates extensive and highly sensationalized publicity for one's cause. It affords an emotionally satisfying outlet for feelings of rage and the desire for vengeance. It induces an acute sense of vulnerability in all those who identify with its immediate victims. And insofar as those victims are chosen randomly from among some very large group, the class of people who identify with them is maximized, so that an extraordinary number of people are given a vivid sense of the potential costs of resisting one's demands. Figuratively and often literally, terrorism offers the biggest bang for one's buck.

If what I have said to this point is on the right track, then it does seem that terrorism is morally distinctive, at least insofar as it conforms to the pattern of what I have been calling the "standard cases." In these cases, at least, it differs from other kinds of violence directed against civilians and noncombatants. By this I do not mean that it is worse, but rather that it has a different moral anatomy. By analogy: humiliation is morally distinctive, and so too are torture, slavery, political oppression and genocide. One can investigate the moral anatomy of any of these evils without taking a position on where it stands in an overall ranking of evils. Many people are pluralists about the good. We can be pluralists about the bad as well.

In the "standard cases," some people are killed or injured (the primary victims), in order to create fear in a larger number of people (the secondary victims), with the aim of destabilizing or degrading the existing social order for everyone. The initial act of violence sets off a kind of moral cascade: death or injury to some, anxiety and fear for many more, the degradation or destabilization of the social order for all. Nor is this simply a cascade of harms. It is, instead, a chain of intentional abuse, for those who employ terrorist tactics do not merely produce these harms, they intentionally aim to produce them. The primary victims are used—their deaths and injuries are used—to terrify others, and those others are used—their fear and terror are used—to degrade and destabilize the social order ....

As I noted at the outset, the term "terrorism" is sometimes used, by representatives and defenders of governments facing violent threats from non-state groups and organizations, to refer to all forms of political violence perpetrated by non-state actors. This makes it impossible by definition for states to engage in terrorism. Although I have not endorsed this—or any other—definition, my narrow focus on the standard cases and my emphasis on terrorism's destabilizing aims may seem to imply that it can only be the tactic of insurgents or other non-state actors. But this is not in fact a consequence of my view. States can certainly employ terrorist tactics in the manner I have described as a way of destabilizing other societies. They can do this in wartime, through the use of such tactics as "terror bombing," or in peacetime, through covert operations targeting another country's civilian population. And domestically, a government might use such tactics in order to create a limited degree of instability, with the aim of discrediting its opponents or generating increased support for repressive policies. Of course, it is crucial in such cases that the government should not appear to be the perpetrator of the terrorist acts, since its aim is precisely to ascribe those acts to others. Still, the fact remains that governments can engage in terrorism both against other societies and, with the qualification just mentioned, domestically as well ....

Conclusion

The title of this paper poses a question. The answer that has emerged from my discussion is as follows. Terrorism is morally distinctive insofar as it seeks to exploit the nexus of violence and fear in such a way as to degrade or destabilize an existing social order. Terrorist acts may have many functions other than the degradation of the social order, and the degradation of the social order may itself be intended to serve different purposes. But insofar as it conforms to the "standard" pattern I have described, terrorism has a morally distinctive character, whatever other functions and purposes individual instances of it may also serve. If, as is often the case, the term is applied more widely, then one consequence may be that terrorism so understood is not always morally distinctive. For example ... many philosophers now believe the term should be taken to refer to any politically motivated violence that is directed against civilians or noncombatants .... This usage makes the distinctive character of the "standard cases" easier to overlook. And the distinctiveness of those cases will certainly be easier to overlook if terrorism is defined instead as political violence that is perpetrated by non-state actors ....

I do not take these considerations as reasons for insisting on a definition of terrorism that limits it to the standard cases. But I do think that the word "terrorism" is morally suggestive precisely because "terror" is its linguistic root, and that if we define the term in a way that effaces or even breaks the connection between terrorism and terror ... then we are liable to miss some of the moral saliences toward which the word "terrorism" gestures. The currency of that particular word, which adds to the already rich vocabulary we have for describing violence of various kinds, testifies to the power of fear and to the peculiar moral reactions evoked by its deliberate use for political ends. It is perfectly possible that, under the pressure of ideology or confusion or convenience, our usage of the term may evolve in such a way that it applies in some cases where fear plays no role and does not apply in some of what I have been calling the standard cases. Indeed, this may already have happened. But then we will need to find other ways of reminding ourselves of how bad a thing fear is, of the diabolical ways in which it can be provoked and exploited for political purposes, and of the specific character of our moral reactions when that happens.

Notes

1 The pioneering contemporary revival of just war theory is, of course, Michael Walzer's *Just and Unjust Wars* (New York: Basic Books, 1977).
2 Thomas Hobbes, *Leviathan*, Chapter 13, paragraph 8. Quotation taken from the edition edited by A. P. Martinich (Peterborough, ON: Broadview Press, 2002), p. 95. Subsequent references, including chapter, paragraph, and page number in the Martinich edition, will be given parenthetically in the text.

Review and Discussion Questions

1 Are there problems with Scheffler's account of terrorism?
2 How do you think Scheffler would respond to someone who believes that one person's terrorist is another person's freedom fighter?
3 What difference does it make to analyze how people conceive of terrorism?

READING: TORTURE: THE CASE FOR DIRTY HARRY

UWE STEINHOFF[*]

In this selection, Uwe Steinhoff argues that the use of torture is morally justified in a much larger range of cases than most people might initially accept. Uwe Steinhoff is Associate Professor at the Department of Politics and Public Administration at the University of Hong Kong, and Senior Research Associate in the University of Oxford Changing Character of War Programme.

What is so bad about torturing people, anyway? People also kill people. Soldiers kill people, policemen kill people, doctors kill people, executioners kill people and ordinary people kill people. Some of these killings are justified. So why shouldn't it be justified in some cases to torture people? After all, being killed seems to be worse than being tortured. Even most of the tortured people seem to see it this way; otherwise they would kill themselves in order to escape further torture (yes, some do, but they are only few). So, if killing is sometimes justified, torture too must sometimes be justified.

Henry Shue thinks that this is a weak argument. Referring in particular to the legitimate killing of people in war, he states:

> Even if one grants that killing someone in combat is doing him or her a greater harm than torturing him or her ... it by no means follows that there could not be a justification for the greater harm that was not applicable to the lesser harm. Specifically, it would matter if some killing could satisfy other moral constraints (besides the constraint of minimizing harm) which no torture could satisfy.[1]

The moral constraint he has in mind is the prohibition of assaults upon the defenceless. However, it can be doubted whether this is a valid constraint at all. Shue's idea that it is valid is based on the fact that one "of the most basic principles for the conduct of war (*jus in Bello*) rests on the distinction between combatants and noncombatants and requires that insofar as possible, violence not be directed at noncombatants."[2] One fundamental function of this distinction, according to Shue, is to try to make a terrible combat fair. No doubt, the opportunities may not have been anywhere near equal—it would be impossible to restrict wars to equally matched opponents. But at least none of the parties to the combat were defenceless.[3]

To be sure, Shue admits that this "invokes a simplified, if not romanticized, portrait of warfare," but he explains that

> the point now is not to attack or defend the efficacy of the principle of warfare that combat is more acceptable morally if restricted to official combatants, but to

---

[*] Copyright © 2006 by *Journal of Applied Philosophy*. Reprinted by permission of Copyright Clearance Center on behalf of the publisher. Some footnotes omitted.

notice one of its moral bases, which, I am suggesting, is that it allows for a "fair fight" by means of protecting the utterly defenceless from assault.[4]

It is true that the fact that the prohibition of assaults upon the defenceless is not always obeyed in war does not pose any problem for Shue's argument. What does pose a problem, however, is that this principle is no *jus in Bello* principle at all, and it does not, *pace* Shue, underlie the principled distinction between combatants and noncombatants.[5] This can be seen quite easily. Suppose an army that possesses superior artillery advances upon the enemy trenches. It has two options. It can shell the enemy trenches from a safe distance with artillery fire. The enemy would be entirely defenceless against such an attack; his weapons do not have the range for fighting back. (This was pretty much the situation in the first and the second Iraq wars.) Or it can advance without shelling the enemy first. Here the enemy would be able to fire upon the advancing troops and to inflict heavy casualties. The point now is that there is simply no article in the laws of war (and no constraint in just war theory, for that matter) that would rule out the first option as such. Of course, if the objectives of the war could be achieved without shelling the enemy in its death-trap trenches *and* without inflicting higher casualties on one's own forces, this alternative course of action would have to be adopted. But the reason for this is the principle of proportionality. An alleged principle of the immunity of the defenceless plays no role here.

To be sure, I do not deny that there is something fishy about attacking the defenceless. What is fishy about it might be captured very well in this passage:

> The pilot of a fighter-bomber or the crew of a man-of-war from which the Tomahawk rockets are launched are beyond the reach of the enemy's weapons. War has lost all features of the classical duel situation here and has approached, to put it cynically, certain forms of pest control.[6]

Judged from a traditional warrior's code of honour, a code that emphasises, among other things, courage, there is nothing honourable in killing off defenceless enemies (whether it is therefore already *dis*honourable is yet another question). But honour and morality are not the same, and honour and the laws of war are not either. In short, the prohibition of assaults upon the defenceless is neither an explicit nor an implicit principle of the laws of war or of just war theory.

Moreover, it is not even clear what should be unfair about killing the defenceless in war in the first place. If the rules of war allowed both sides to kill, for example, defenceless prisoners of war, where is the unfairness? Both sides are in the same situation. And if the laws of war allowed the torture of POWs, the same would be true. Invoking principles of fairness does not deliver an argument against either of the two practices.

David Sussman has recently attempted to give another explanation of why torture, allegedly, "bears an especially high burden of justification, greater in degree and different in kind from even that of killing."[7] However, he also cautions that this "is not to say that when torture is wrong, it is worse that [sic] wrongful acts of maiming and killing" or that

> it is more important for us to prevent torture than it is to prevent murder, or that torturers should be condemned or punished more severely than murderers.

> The moral differences between torture, killing, and maiming may not always make a difference in such third-personal contexts.[8]

But why, then, should torture bear an "especially high burden of justification"? Does it bear such a higher burden only in second-person or first-person contexts? But what is that supposed to mean? That whereas one does not need a better justification for allowing others to torture or for not condemning torturers than for allowing others to kill or for not condemning killers, one does need a better justification for torturing (and perhaps also for risking being tortured) than for killing? Sussman argues that:

> [T]orture forces its victim into the position of colluding against himself through his own affects and emotions, so that he experiences himself as simultaneously powerless and yet actively complicit in his own violation. So construed, torture turns out to be not just an extreme form of cruelty, but the pre-eminent instance of a kind of forced self-betrayal, more akin to rape than other kinds of violence characteristic of warfare or police action.[9]

He elaborates:

> What the torturer does is to take his victim's pain, and through it his victim's body, and make it begin to express the torturer's will.[10]
>
> .... Torture does not merely insult or damage its victim's agency, but rather turns such agency against itself, forcing the victim to experience herself as helpless yet complicit in her own violation. This is not just an assault on or violation of the victim's autonomy but also a perversion of it, a kind of systematic mockery of the basic moral relations that an individual bears both to others and to herself. Perhaps this is why torture seems qualitatively worse than other forms of brutality or cruelty.[11]

But all this can hardly explain the alleged difference between "third-personal" and other contexts. In fact, it would seem rather natural to assume that, if torture isn't worse than killing from a third-person perspective, it isn't so from a second- or first-person perspective either. If Sussman sees this differently, the high burden of justification, it appears, would be on him.

Conversely, assume a dictator confronts prisoner A with the following choice—to either kill one of ten prisoners or to torture one of them for two hours (all these prisoners are innocent and have no special relation to the first prisoner).[12] If A refuses to choose and to act on his choice, all ten prisoners will be killed. If he decided to choose (and it seems plain to me that he is justified in choosing even though he may not be obliged to do so), should the prisoner facing the choice rather kill one prisoner than torture one of them for two hours? This is to be strongly doubted. On the other hand, there can hardly be any doubt that the ten prisoners would prefer him to opt for torture if he asked them what to do—to refuse to choose, to choose to kill or to choose to torture. He is not permitted to ask them (if he did, all ten prisoners would be killed). However, in light of the fact that it is reasonable to assume that they would prefer two hours of torture to being killed for good, he should honour that preference if he decides to choose. It seems, then, that torture is easier to justify than killing even from a first-person perspective.

Moreover, the feature that in Sussman's eyes makes torture so bad is by no means unique to torture. We find it, in fact, even in armed robbery. If a robber points a gun at a victim and threatens to kill him if the victim does not give his money to the robber, the robber, if successful, also turns the victim's agency against the victim himself. He makes the victim's fear express his, the robber's, will; and the victim, in handing over the money for fear of death, is "complicit" in his own violation.

It is important to note here that the victim will also normally not react to the threat with a utility/risk-calculation, i.e. with rational deliberation. If, especially at night in a dark alley, one has a gun pointed at one's head and hears: "Give me your f ... money or I'll f ... kill you," one will hardly engage in deliberations of this kind:

> The probability that his threat is meant seriously lies around x; my options to defend myself or to escape are this and that, with this and that probability of success; if, on the other hand, I give him the money, this will cost me certainly y money units, which in turn leads with probability z to my not being able to pay in time for this and that thing, which in turn ... and therefore I will ....

Rather, many people threatened with deadly violence will think: "Oh my God, he wants to shoot me, he wants to shoot me ... I'll give him the money!" thus, the sudden death threat and the perceived time pressure will in many if not most cases severely disturb the ability to deliberate rationally if they do not completely undermine it. In short, fear may overwhelm one as pain overwhelms the victim of torture. There may be differences of degree but no qualitative ones. Besides, at least some forms of torture will undermine the ability of some torture victims to think rationally less than some forms of death threat would of some threatened people.

Thus, Sussman is not able to show that there is a higher burden of justification on torture than on killing. Conversely, thought experiments like those of the ten prisoners strongly suggest that it is the other way around.

Of course, it is true that *emotional reactions* to displays of torture, for example in movies, are much stronger than those to displays of killing. And I suspect that much of the conviction that torture is somehow more terrible than death is sustained by these immediate emotional reactions. In fact, however, little of moral relevance follows from them. After all, the emotional reactions to scenes involving large amounts of faeces or cockroaches, for example, are mostly also stronger than to scenes involving killing, at least when it is a quick killing. When the killing is prolonged the reactions are stronger, but they are then prompted by the displayed suffering—sometimes simply in the form of fear—not by the impending death itself. The point is that *we simply cannot empathise with the dead*. There is nothing we can empathise *with*. We do not know how it is to be dead, and there is certainly no possibility to *feel* dead (in any non-metaphorical sense). We do know, however, what it is to feel *pain*. Therefore, if we see how pain is inflicted on another person, we can feel quite literally *compassion*. There is no such compassion possible with the dead (we can only feel sorry for them, but that is a completely different and far less intense feeling). In other words, our emotional reactions to displays of torture or killing respectively are distorted by certain limits of empathy. What are not distorted are our emotional reactions to the prospect of our *own* death. Most of us fear it more than torture (that is limited in time). Whether killing is worse than torturing, then, should be measured against the preferences of people facing the alternatives of torture (over a certain limited time) and death—most prefer torture. To measure it against emotional reactions to displays of torture would by way of extension also mean that it is better to shoot someone dead than to push him into a bathtub filled with cockroaches. But such an implication obviously reduces the premise to absurdity.

Thus, it seems the argument in defence of torture given at the beginning is not such a weak one after all. We can now slightly rephrase it in the light of our findings: If it is permissible to kill a defenceless enemy combatant in order to avoid own casualties, why should it not be permissible to torture a defenceless terrorist in order to avoid own casualties?

One might try to answer this by saying that the enemy soldiers in my example may be defenceless in the situation in which they are shelled or attacked with missiles, but that they *still pose a threat*—they threaten our advancing troops, which is precisely the reason why we take them out by artillery or rockets. The detained terrorist, on the other hand, does not pose a threat anymore. For what can he do?

Sanford Levinson states that "the defender of torture would dispute the premise that the captured prisoner is no longer a threat, at least if the prisoner possesses important information about the future conduct of his fellow terrorists."[13] The case of the defender of torture can be made much stronger, however, if we take the infamous ticking bomb case. The terrorist has somewhere hidden a bomb that will, if it goes off, kill a high number of innocents (maybe it is even a nuclear bomb that would destroy one of the ten biggest cities in the world). He does not want to say where it is. Would it not be justified to torture him in order to make him disclose the vital information and find the bomb in time to disable it?

Some might be inclined to argue that *withholding* vital information (i.e. an omission) couldn't reasonably be described as a threat. Perhaps, perhaps not. However, people culpably posing a threat and aggressors are not the only persons that can be legitimately killed. For it seems, as Phillip Montague has pointed out, that, in cases in which one cannot save oneself from the negative consequences of another person's acts in any other way than by diverting or inflicting them on this person, one is justified in doing so. Montague states the following conditions for this:

> (i) individuals $X_1 \ldots X_n$ are situated so that harm will unavoidably befall some but not all of them; (ii) that they are so situated is the fault of some but not all members of the group; (iii) the nature of the harm is independent of the individuals who are harmed; (iv) Y, who is not necessarily included in $X_1 \ldots X_n$ is in a position to determine who will be harmed.[14]

The inflicting of harm (for example in the form of an attack or in the form of torture) on a certain person, thus, is not legitimised here by a *present* aggression but by the person's culpably causing the threat of harm. This cause can lie in the past. Montague adduces the example of a doctor who wishes for the death of a cardiac patient and therefore swallows the pacemaker the patient needs. The only chance to get the pacemaker quickly enough to save the patient's life is to perform a hasty operation on the doctor, which, however, would be fatal to him. Hence, one faces here a situation in which either the innocent patient or the malicious doctor has to die. However, if one of the two has to die anyway and one has to decide who it is going to be, then one clearly should, says Montague, decide against the person who has culpably brought about this situation. That seems to be a pretty reasonable stance, and I agree with him. The application to the case of the terrorist who has hidden a bomb to kill innocents is obvious.

It even suffices when the bomb would kill only *one* innocent. We do not have to assume a ticking nuclear bomb, killing thousands or even millions. Consider the Dirty Harry case. In the Don Siegel movie *Dirty Harry* someone kidnaps a female child and puts her in a place where she will suffocate if not rescued in time. There is not much time left, according to the very claims of the kidnapper. The police officer Harry (Clint Eastwood) is to deliver the ransom to the kidnapper. When they finally meet at night in a park, the kidnapper knocks Harry down with his gun and tells him that he will let the girl die anyway. He also tells Harry that he wants him to know that before he kills him too. In the moment he is about to shoot Harry, who lies defenceless and badly beaten to his feet, Harry's partner interferes (and is shot). The kidnapper can escape, wounded. Harry pursues him. Finally he corners him, and the kidnapper raises his arms to surrender. Harry shoots him in the leg. The kidnapper is frightened to death, tells Harry not to kill him and that he has rights. Harry asks him where the girl is. The kidnapper talks only about his rights. Harry sees the kidnapper's leg wound and puts his foot on it, torturing the kidnapper. The camera retreats. In the next scene, the girl is saved.

The Dirty Harry case, it seems to me, is a case of morally justified torture. But isn't the kidnapper right? Does not even he have rights? Yes, he has, but in these circumstances he does not have the right not to be tortured. Again, the situation is analogous to self-defence. The aggressor does not lose all of his rights, but his right to life weighs less than the innocent defender's right to life. The aggressor culpably brings about a situation where one of the two—he or the defender—will die. It is only just and fair that the harm that will befall in this situation upon one of the two is diverted to the person who is responsible for the harm—the aggressor. In the Dirty Harry case, the kidnapper brings about a situation where a person is tortured or will continue to be tortured until death (being slowly suffocated in a small hole *is* torture). It is only just and fair that this harm befalls the person responsible for the situation—the kidnapper. Moreover, the choice is made even easier by the fact that being tortured for a small period of time is better than being tortured until death. Harry made the right decision.

Two replies might be made at this point. The first one—repeated like a litany by certain opponents of torture—is that interrogative torture simply does not work. That, however, is simply wrong. Sometimes interrogative torture does work, and the torturer gets the information he was looking for.[15]

Well, one might say, but at least interrogative torture is not very reliable. Apart from the fact that even that is not so clear, it would not even help. Consider the following case: An innocent person is being attacked by an aggressor, who fires a deadly weapon at him (and misses him at first but keeps firing). The attacked person's only possibility to save his life is by using the One-Million-Pains-To-One-Kill-Gun that he happens to have with him. On average, you have to pull the trigger of this gun one million times in order to have one immediately incapacitating projectile come out of it (it incapacitates through the infliction of unbearable pain). All the other times it fires projectiles that only ten seconds after hitting a human target cause the target unbearable pain. Thus, firing this gun at the aggressor will certainly cause the aggressor unbearable pain, but the probability that it will save the life of the defender is only 1:1,000,000. I must admit that I cannot even begin to make sense of the suggestion that, given these odds, the defender should not use the gun against the aggressor. Yes, the pain inflicted by the weapon on the aggressor is extremely unlikely to secure the survival of the defender, but there still *is* a chance that it will, so why should the *defender* forgo this chance for the benefit of the *aggressor*? Obviously, there is no reason (at least none that I could see). Again, the application to the torture of ticking bomb terrorists and Dirty Harry kidnappers is obvious.

What is the second reply? Richard H. Weisberg takes issue with the example of the ticking bomb case:

> [T]he hypothetical itself lacks the virtues of intelligence, appropriateness, and especially sophistication. Here, as in *The Brothers Karamazov—pace* Sandy Levinson—it is the complex rationalizers who wind up being more naive than those who speak strictly, directly, and simply against injustice. "You can't know whether a person knows where the bomb is," explains Cole in a recent piece in the *Nation*, "or even if they're telling the truth. Because of this, you wind up sanctioning torture in general."[16]

To begin with, by allowing torture in the ticking bomb case one does *not* necessarily wind up sanctioning it in general. Killing (of certain people) is sanctioned in war but not in general. The actual second reply I was referring to, however, is *that you do not know whether you have the right person*. (That you do not know whether the person speaks the truth is simply the first reply. We have already dealt with it.) But what does it mean: "You don't know"? Does it mean you do not know for certain? If not knowing for certain whether you have the right person would be sufficient reason not to harm that person, we would not only have to abstain from self-defence but also from punishment. You *never* know for certain!

Take the example of a man who draws a gun in front of a head of state and aims at him. The bodyguards simply cannot know (for certain) whether this person wants to shoot, they cannot even know whether it is a real gun. Maybe the "attacker" is only a retard with a water pistol. So the bodyguards of the head of state (whom we want to assume innocent) should not shoot at such a person who, for all they *can* know, seems to be attacking the person they are to protect? Actually, if shooting (and probably killing) him is the only way to make sure that he is not able to pull the trigger, they *should* shoot him.

One might say that this person, even if he does not really want to shoot and has no real gun, at least *feigns* an attack, and this makes him liable to counter-attack. Whoever credibly feigns an attack on another person cannot later, after having suffered from severe countermeasures, complain that he "only" feigned it. He shouldn't have feigned it at all. We can, however, have a comparable situation with a terrorist. If a person says to other persons that he is going to build a powerful bomb to blow up a kindergarten and has the necessary skills and buys the necessary chemicals, he had better not, when the security service storms his hideout where he is surrounded by his bomb-making equipment, sneeringly say: "You are too late. I have already planted the bomb. It will go off in 12 hours and kill hundreds of children." If he then is tortured by the security service, which wants to find out where the bomb is, he is not, it seems, in a particularly good position to complain about that *even if he has not planted a bomb*. Moreover, even if a real or supposed terrorist has not made that particularly threatening statement, hanging around with the wrong people in the wrong situations can also make you liable to attack. Suppose an innocent woman is hunted by a mob. Maybe they do not like her skin colour, her ethnic group, her religion or whatever. The mob has already killed other people for the same reason. She hides with the hand grenade she fortunately has, behind a bush. Suddenly one of the group sees her, points his finger at her, shouts "There she is," and the armed members of the group raise their guns to shoot at her. Not all members of the group have guns. Some are unarmed and shout: "Kill her, kill her!" Others do not even shout but sneer, foaming at the mouth (I am not talking about completely innocent people, who just "happen" to be there for no fault of their own). The only way she can save herself is to throw the grenade at the mob, which will kill all of them, including the unarmed ones. Is she justified in doing so? I would think so. Being a member of certain groups that collectively undertake aggressive acts or intentionally pose a threat to innocent people makes one liable to severe countermeasures. Consequently, a member of a terrorist group might be liable to torture in the ticking bomb case, even if he does not know where the bomb is.

It helps, by the way, very little to aver at this point that torture is simply not compatible with liberalism. David Luban, for example, claims that torture aims "to strip away from its victim all the qualities of human dignity that liberalism prizes" and that "torture is a microcosm, raised to the highest level of intensity, of the tyrannical political relationships that liberalism hates the most."[17] However, prisons are also "microcosms" of tyranny; yet, most liberals do not find them incompatible with liberalism. Where is the difference? Maybe it lies in the fact that in torture tyranny is "raised to the highest level." But, first, it is far from clear that one hour of torture is more tyrannical than 15 years of prison. Second, even if torture were more tyrannical than prison, and liberalism abhorred tyranny, there remained still the fact that liberalism can accommodate quite intense forms of tyranny, such as incarceration for life (or for a decade and more). Why should it not also be able to accommodate the most extreme form of tyranny? "Because it is the most extreme form" is in itself no answer to this question.

More importantly, liberalism is not so much about "dignity"—which is a quite elusive concept, anyway (in particular, I deny that the dignity of the culpable aggressor is violated by Dirty Harry's action any more than it would be violated by Dirty Harry's killing him in self-defence)—but about liberty. It is called liberalism, not "dignism." It is also not about just anybody's liberty. It is about the liberty of the innocent. This is why there is no particular problem in liberalism to kill aggressors or to deprive them of their liberty if this is the only way to protect innocent people from these aggressors. The core value of the liberal state is the protection of the liberty and the rights of *innocent* individuals against *aggressors*. The state can be such an aggressor, but the state can and must also protect against other aggressors. To keep Dirty Harry in the situation described from torturing the kidnapper, therefore, would run against the liberal state's own *raison d'être*. The state would help the aggressor, not the victim; it would help the aggressor's tyranny over the innocent and therefore actually abet the relationship it hates the most.

Since my description of the core value of liberalism, as I submit, is at least as plausible as Luban's (and I think it is historically much more plausible), the appeal to liberalism cannot help absolute opponents of torture. To claim that liberalism "correctly understood" absolutely prohibits torture simply engages in an attempt of persuasive definition and begs the question. Besides, why could liberalism, "correctly understood," not be wrong?

But—speaking about the innocent—what about the risk of torturing a completely *innocent* person, a person that made itself *not* liable? Yes, that risk exists, as it does in the case of punishment. In the latter case, the risk of punishing innocent persons has to be weighed against the risk of not at all punishing the non-innocent and of not at all deterring potential criminals. In the case of interrogative torture in the context of a ticking bomb situation, the risk of torturing an innocent person has to be weighed against the risk of letting other innocent persons die in an explosion. If the weighing process in the former case can justify punishment, it is unclear why the weighing process in the latter case could not sometimes justify torture. If the odds are high enough, it does. In fact, the justification in the latter case might even be easier—easier at least than justifying capital punishment, for death, as already noted, is worse than torture (at least for most people who are confronted with a decision between their death and being tortured for a limited time). It might even be easier than justifying incarceration for one or two decades, for it is not clear that many persons would not prefer some hours or even days of torture to that alternative.

To sum up the discussion so far: A compelling argument for an absolute *moral* prohibition of torture cannot be made. Under certain circumstances torture can be justified. *Justified*, not only excused. I emphasise this because some philosophers claim that situations of so-called necessity or emergency can only *excuse* torture (and some other extreme measures) ....

No doubt, an absolutist opponent of torture will not be particularly impressed by the argument offered so far. In fact, absolutists normally (although perhaps not always) do not even try to refute the arguments adduced against their absolutist positions; they tend to just persistently and dramatically reaffirm their positions. The writer and poet Ariel Dorfman is a good example:

> I can only pray that humanity will have the courage to say no, no to torture, no to torture under any circumstance whatsoever, no to torture, no matter who the enemy, what the accusation, what sort of fear we harbor; no to torture no matter what kind of threat is posed to our safety; no to torture anytime, anywhere; no to torture anyone; no to torture.[18]

Moral absolutism is a dangerous and mistaken view. If, for example, humanity would face the choice (maybe posed by some maniac with the ultimate weapon or by an alien race, or what have you) between being exterminated or torturing one particularly bad man (let us say Idi Amin) for an hour or a day, it is far from clear why any person in his right mind—both intellectually *and* morally—should pray that humanity said "no to torture."[19] And what, by the way, if the choice is between all human beings (that includes children) being *tortured* by the alien race or only one particularly bad man being tortured by some humans? Consequences count; they cannot simply be ignored for the benefit of some allegedly absolute rule, especially if they might be catastrophic. *Fiat justitia, pereat mundus* is an irrational and immoral maxim.

To say it again: A compelling argument for an absolute *moral* prohibition of torture cannot be made ....

Notes

1. H. Shue, "Torture" in S. Levinson (ed.) *Torture: A Collection* (Oxford: Oxford University Press, 2004), pp. 49–60, at p. 49.
2. Ibid.
3. Ibid., pp. 50f.
4. Ibid., p. 51.
5. Henry Shue has meanwhile in conversation distanced himself somewhat from drawing a parallel between the prohibition of torture and *jus in bello* requirements.
6. H. Münkler, *Die neuen Kriege* (Reinbek bei Hamburg: Rowohlt, 2003), p. 234, my translation.
7. D. Sussman, "What's wrong with torture?" *Philosophy and Public Affairs* 33, 1 (2005): 4.
8. Ibid., n. 10.
9. Ibid., p. 4.
10. Ibid., p. 21.
11. Ibid., p. 30.
12. The example is a variant of Bernard Williams's famous example of Jim and the twenty Indians.
13. S. Levinson, "The debate on torture: war on virtual states," *Dissent* (Summer) (2003): 79–90, at pp. 83f.
14. P. Montague, "The morality of self-defense: a reply to Wasserman," *Philosophy and Public Affairs* 18 (1989): 81–89, at pp. 81f. Ryan advocates a similar position to Montague's. See C. C. Ryan, "Self-defense, pacifism, and the possibility of killing," *Ethics* 93 (1984): 508–524, at pp. 515ff.
15. See S. Levinson, "Contemplating torture: an introduction," in Levinson (2004) op. cit., pp. 23–43, at pp. 33ff., and the further references there.
16. R. H. Weisberg, "Loose professionalism," in Levinson (2004) op. cit., pp. 299–305, at p. 304.
17. D. Luban (2005) "Liberalism and the unpleasant question of torture," http://ethics.stanford.edu/newsletter/_old/december/Liberalism%20and%20the%20Unpleasant%20 Question%20Question%20of%20Torture.doc, accessed on 2 October 2005, electronic resource. A comparable argument is put forward by K. Seth, "Too close to the rack and the screw: constitutional constraints on torture in the war on terror," *University of Pennsylvania Journal of Constitutional Law* 6 (2003–2004): 278–325.
18. A. Dorfman, "The tyranny of terror: is torture inevitable in our century and beyond?" in Levinson (2004) op. cit., pp. 3–18, at p. 17.
19. Torturing this person would, of course, be a case of self-preservation and not of self- or other-defence (or something close to it) as in the Dirty Harry case.

Review and Discussion Questions

1. Are there any good counterarguments to Steinhoff's position(s)? What are they?
2. Steinhoff defends the position that accepting the moral justification of torture does not imply support for laws justifying torture. What do you think? Explain your answer.

READING: TRAINING TORTURERS: A CRITIQUE OF THE "TICKING BOMB" ARGUMENT

JESSICA WOLFENDALE[*]

Torturing requires torturers. This fact leads Jessica Wolfendale to consider the institutional implications of moral arguments that purportedly justify torture. Professor Wolfendale teaches at the Center for Applied Philosophy and Public Ethics at the University of Melbourne.

Suppose a fanatic, perfectly willing to die rather than collaborate in the thwarting of his own scheme, has set a hidden nuclear device to explode in the heart of Paris. There is no time to evacuate the innocent people or even the movable art treasures—the only hope of preventing tragedy is to torture the perpetrator, find the device, and deactivate it.[1]

1 Introduction

The war against terrorism has re-ignited the debate about the permissibility of torture. Once again we are hearing variations of the "ticking bomb" argument in support of the use of torture against terrorism suspects. Terrorism is claimed to pose such an extreme threat that the prohibition against torture cannot be maintained. We are involved in a new kind of war in which the ordinary moral constraints cannot apply. In the words of Cofer Black, former head of the U.S. Counterterrorism Center: "There was a before 9/11, and there was an after 9/11 ... After 9/11 the gloves come off."[2]

Variations of the ticking bomb argument have been put forward by writers such as Alan Dershowitz and Mark Bowden.[3] These variations have involved detailed discussions about the exact conditions under which the torture of terrorism suspects might be justified. Most often these arguments are put forward as utilitarian justifications for overriding the prohibition against torture, but sometimes they take the form of self-defense arguments or arguments from necessity.[4] In every case, however, one crucial issue has been missing from the analysis of these arguments: permitting torture means permitting torturers.

In this paper I argue that the scope and kind of training necessary to produce the torturer needed in the ticking bomb scenario raises serious questions about the legitimacy of these kinds of arguments for the use of torture ....

2 The Ticking Bomb Torturer

In the standard ticking bomb scenario, a suspect has been caught who possesses information that must be obtained quickly in order to avert huge civilian casualties.

---

[*] Jessica Wolfendale, "Training Torturers—A Critique of the 'Ticking Bomb' Argument," *Social Theory and Practice* 32(2) (April 2006). Copyright © 2006 by Florida State University. Reprinted by permission of the publisher.

Most ticking bomb scenarios do not explain *how* the suspect was identified or caught. As Jean Maria Arrigo notes, a lack of such explanation is problematic. To have identified the key terrorist, know how and where to capture him, and to be sure that he has the relevant information requires an already well established and comprehensive intelligence network involving "informants, electronic surveillance networks, and undercover agents."[5] The proponent of the ticking bomb argument must therefore be sure that the relevant information cannot be found through these (already formidable) intelligence resources. However, for the purposes of this argument we will give the supporter of the ticking bomb argument the benefit of the doubt and assume that despite the vast array of intelligence resources, the only way to find out where the bomb is hidden is to interrogate the suspect. The suspect to be interrogated is usually a fanatical terrorist willing to die for his cause—someone unlikely to be intimidated by mere threats of violence and who may well be prepared for torture.

Under these conditions, the ticking bomb torturer must be able to extract the required information in the shortest time possible without killing the suspect. The torturer must be an expert in interrogational torture—excessively sadistic torture or torture for the purposes of punishment, dehumanization, or deterring others is generally agreed to be impermissible. Given these constraints, what kind of training would the ticking bomb torturer require?

Perhaps the ticking bomb torturer would not need any particular skills or training. There are numerous examples of ordinary people who have massacred, tortured, raped, and committed other atrocities without any special training. Stanley Milgram's famous experiments on obedience to authority demonstrated clearly that many of us will obey orders to harm another if those orders are given by a legitimate (or apparently legitimate) authority figure.[6]

It is true that ordinary people have the capacity to commit horrendous acts of violence without any particular training. However, the ticking bomb scenario requires far more than the infliction of extreme violence. The aim of the torture and the constraints on the kind of torture that may be used require a very particular kind of torturer. Unlike deterrent or dehumanizing torture, interrogational torture requires finesse, skill, and discipline. Given the importance of the information that is required from the suspect, the ticking bomb torturer needs to be *already* trained in effective interrogational torture. It would not do to take an ordinary soldier and make him torture a terrorist suspect at the last minute. One has only to look at the incompetence of the guards at Abu Ghraib (they took *photos*) to see the danger of allowing mere amateurs to torture prisoners. The problems with allowing untrained police or soldiers to torture suspects is illustrated in this quote from the commander of a military police unit in Baghdad. A Military Intelligence officer requested this commander to "keep the detainees awake around the clock." The commander refused, because while the Military Intelligence officers had received training, "my soldiers don't know how to do it. And when you ask an eighteen-year-old kid to keep someone awake, and he doesn't know how to do it, he's going to get creative."[7]

The ticking bomb scenario is far too serious to permit torturers to "get creative" with the suspect. The good interrogational torturer needs to be entirely in control of the process of torture. He must be able to torture whoever is placed in front of him without flinching and without hesitation. However, he cannot be sadistic or overly brutal. Such a person would not have the discipline or skills to extract the information without killing the captive. The need for discipline, skill, and control is emphasized in real-life torturer training manuals. The Khmer Rouge Manual for Torture makes the need for discipline quite clear: "The purpose of torturing is to get their responses. It's not something we do for the fun of it."[8] Sadism and lack of discipline undermine the effectiveness of torture.

But torture requires more than practical skills; it requires immense strength of mind. Torturers need to be trained to manage the psychological stress associated with torturing. To gain a realistic understanding of how the ticking bomb torturer should be trained, we can usefully look at how real-life torturers are trained. After all, supporters of the ticking bomb case should consider all the relevant real-life consequences of training torturers if they are to derive a realistic understanding of the ticking bomb scenario.

3 The Training of Torturers

In the real world, most torturers are soldiers or military policemen who have been trained in elite military units.[9] For example, torturers in South America, Greece, Myanmar, South Africa, and Ireland all were part of elite military units charged with gathering intelligence and other covert operations.[10] Ronald Crelinsten describes these units as having "exalted reputations within the military or police command structure. If their existence is known to the public, they are often highly respected and/or highly feared."[11] These units, such as Kopassus in Indonesia, the Greek ESA (Army Police Corps), Special Air Services in Australia and the U.K., the U.S. Army's Delta Force and the Green Berets,[12] are renowned for the covert nature of their operations (they are sometimes called "secret armies"[13]) and for the extremely harsh training new recruits must undergo.[14] In fact, the severity of these units' training contributes to their exalted reputations and becomes a significant mark of pride for those who make it through ....

3.1 Basic Training in the Elite Military Units

Special Forces training includes many features besides interrogation training: survival skills, reconnaissance, rescue operations, jungle training as well as counter-terrorism and counter-insurgency training.[15] I will focus on survival training, as it is during such training that interrogation skills and interrogation/capture survival skills are taught.

Survival training refers to a gamut of different training exercises. The U.S. *Survive, Evade, Resist, Escape* course at the John F. Kennedy Special Warfare Center and School encapsulates many of the techniques found in the Special Forces training programs of other countries. The aim of this kind of training is

> to give students the skill to survive and evade capture or, if captured, to resist interrogation or exploitation and plan their escape. The course includes a classroom phase, a field phase and a resistance training laboratory which simulates the environment of a prisoner of war camp.[16]

In the "resistance training laboratory" trainees undergo a highly realistic re-creation of the experience of being captured and interrogated by the enemy. What such re-creations involve can be seen in the British SAS training course. Trainees receive lessons and lectures in interrogation techniques from people who have been POWs, tortured or have other experiences .... At the end [of the training] every SAS man has to withstand interrogation training. The men are blindfolded, put in stress positions and interrogated for over 48 hours. White noise (sound) is also used. After a week on the run, cold, dehydrated and exhausted, the mind sometimes starts to play tricks and reality becomes blurred.[17]

It is worth noting that the techniques of forced standing ("stress positions"), noise bombardment, and blindfolding are commonly recognized torture techniques—they form part of the "five techniques" used by the British in 1971 in Ireland, techniques that were declared by the European Commission on Human Rights to meet the definition of torture.[18] The Green Beret course instructors deny that such training constitutes torture. However, when these techniques are applied to *others* they clearly *do* constitute torture.[19] ...

In summary, the training process of these specialized units involves intense, highly stressful, and often brutal exercises. Aside from the more conventional weapons and fitness training, trainees are subjected to the techniques of psychological torture, a process which is extremely distressing and humiliating and can result in dissociation and deep anxiety. Despite the severity of this training and the suffering that it can cause to trainees, this training is very effective in desensitizing trainees to the infliction and the endurance of suffering. New trainees become desensitized to their own suffering, and when they in their turn play the "torturer" in the stress inoculation training they learn to be desensitized to the infliction of pain. This desensitization reduces soldiers' empathetic reaction to physical suffering and thereby makes the infliction of pain and humiliation on the enemy psychologically easier. Given that the ticking bomb torturer might have to inflict incredibly brutal tortures without flinching, he must be thoroughly desensitized to the infliction of pain and must not be hampered by feelings of empathy or sympathy for the suspect —in the ticking bomb scenario there would be no time for hesitation ....

Torturers, if they are to be effective and efficient, must "feel nothing" about what they are doing. But desensitization to the infliction of suffering is not sufficient to make torturers "feel nothing" when they torture suspects. Torturers must also develop the right attitude towards their work; they need to be able to torture with a minimum of emotional engagement. Studies on real-life torturers demonstrate that this is best achieved by adopting the discourse of professionalism.

3.2 Turning Torture Into a Profession

The following quotes from real-life torturers demonstrate the view of torture as a profession:

> "I'm here," the officer, whose name was Massini, told [the] prisoner. "I'm a serious professional. After the revolution, I will be at your disposal to torture whom you like."[20]

> "I don't use ... violence outside the standard of my conscience as a human being. I'm a conscientious professional. I know what to do and when to do it."[21]

"We didn't operate on anger or sadism or anything like that .... It became a function. It became part of the job. It became standard operating procedure."[22]

Professionalism discourse is used to legitimize and normalize torture. This occurs in two ways. First, the elite military units represent the pinnacle of military training and attract soldiers by appealing to the military's professional ideals. Members of these units are encouraged to see themselves as the most professional of soldiers carrying out the unpleasant duties necessary to protect the nation from terrorism and other threats. The appeal to professionalism provides a veneer of legitimacy to the use of torture by tying justifications for the use of torture to the professional goals of the military and by appealing directly to the torturer's professional pride.

Second, the characterization of torture as a profession contributes to what the sociologist Herbert Kelman calls "routinization."[23] Torture becomes a routine job subject to role-specific professional standards and justifications. The language of professionalism aids this process by reconfiguring the act of torture from a brutal act of violence against another human being to what Kelman calls the "routine application of specialized knowledge and skills."[24]

Martha Huggins argues that the language of professionalism disembodies violence by removing all reference to the infliction of violence on an actual human body.[25] This is evident in the fact that torture is almost never called by that name; it is always "interrogation."[26] Even the names of different torture methods are euphemistic: "operating table," "safe house" (torture center), "the grill," and "the submarine."[27] Even the term "torture lite" is intended to reduce awareness of what this kind of torture actually does to the victims.[28]

The routinization of torture, aided by the language of professionalism, encourages torturers to adopt an extreme form of professional detachment ....

This kind of detachment was also used in Auschwitz to inure new doctors to the unpleasant tasks they had to perform. Robert Lifton describes the experiences of new doctors:

> Newcomers ... "suffered initially" at the selections, but "then it got to be routine—like all other routines in Auschwitz." ... Most SS doctors underwent ... an extraordinary individual-psychological shift from revulsion to acceptance.[29]

Like good Nazi doctors, professional torturers do not get emotionally involved in their work. Unlike the poorly trained Abu Ghraib guards, they are not sadistic or filled with hatred but govern their work by strict professional standards. Good torturers must overcome feelings such as distress, revulsion, and doubt. They must, like the Nazi doctors, move from "revulsion to acceptance." Indeed, being able to overcome such feelings comes to be seen as a sign of toughness, discipline, and strength of character—another mark of pride for the elite soldiers who must carry out the dirty work of torture ....

3.3 Dehumanization

Torture victims are often humiliated, filthy, terrified, and naked and this significantly aids the torturers' perception of them as sub-human. Crelinsten notes that "[I]t has often been reported that the screams of torture victims no longer sound human. The irony is that, to the torturer, this only reinforces their dehumanization."[30] Indeed, torture techniques such as hooding, sleep deprivation, denial of toilet facilities, and personal humiliations deliberately aim to make torture victims feel and look less than human, therefore making it easier for torturers to treat them as if they *were* less than human ....

Indeed, through the dehumanizing process of torture, torturers not only find the act of torture psychologically easier, but can also come to feel that the victims somehow deserve their own suffering—a belief evident in the following quote from a U.S. soldier involved in the abuse of prisoners in Iraq. While watching two prisoners being forced to masturbate and simulate oral sex, this soldier commented: "Look what these animals do when you leave them alone for two seconds."[31] The victims' suffering and humiliation (caused solely by the torture) comes to be seen as evidence of their sub-human qualities—evidence that justifies treating them as sub-humans. Believing that the victims "deserve it"—are "animals"—combined with the "neutral" language of professionalism clearly contributes to a belief in the lessening of moral responsibility for harming them ....

There are good reasons why such training would result in the most effective ticking bomb torturer. The time constraints on the ticking bomb scenario mean that the torturer cannot be concerned about the suspect's guilt or the moral justifications for the use of torture—any hesitation could have devastating consequences. If the ticking bomb torturer is trained in the ways I have described he will find it far easier to torture the suspect without suffering from moral and emotional qualms. He must be able to do his work without being overcome with distress or revulsion, and this means that he must already be accustomed to inflicting suffering and he must be immune to the victim's distress. The ticking bomb torturer, if he is to be effective, must also accept his orders without question; he must be able to rest assured that the burden of responsibility lies with the authorities and that they have sufficient reason to require his talents. Adopting the discourse of professionalism will make such obedience easier because it will allow the torturer to restrict his moral concerns to how well he carries out his professional duties rather than whether the use of his professional skills is morally justified. In the words of the Khmer Rouge manual ... "it is necessary to avoid any question or hesitancy or halfheartedness of not daring to do torture."[32] There is too much at stake in the ticking bomb scenario to risk having an ill-prepared novice for a torturer. The ideal ticking bomb torturer needs to be the most consummate professional, and this is best achieved by the combination of the training found in Special Forces units and the use of the discourse of professionalism.

4 What's Wrong with Training Torturers?

Supporters of the ticking bomb argument could admit that the ticking bomb torturer might need the kind of training I have described if he is to have the best chance of success. They may also admit that the need for this training has not been fully discussed before and that this training seems, at the very least, quite harsh. But should the supporter of the ticking bomb argument be concerned about the need for torturer training or is this training just another consideration easily outweighed by the magnitude of the threat in the ticking bomb scenario? ....

By encouraging torturers not to concern themselves with the moral justifications for the use of torture, the combination of the Special Forces training and the discourse of professionalism instill dispositions of unreflective obedience. Because torturers are trained to obey orders without thinking, they are very unlikely to question whether a particular order is justified—the question of the actual guilt of the suspect is beyond their professional jurisdiction. A consequence of this is that torturers are very unlikely to restrict their professional activities only to cases that meet the stringent criteria of the ticking bomb scenario. This problem is not merely a hypothetical possibility that might occur when professional torturers are trained; it is occurring now and has occurred many times in the past. Amnesty International has identified over 150 countries that use torture,[33] and the United States government has been using torture in Guantanamo Bay and elsewhere.[34] In the vast majority of these cases the use of torture would never be justified under the ticking bomb argument. Instead, the use of torture in the real world is most often what sociologists Herbert Kelman and V. Lee Hamilton call a "crime of obedience"—a crime that occurs when individuals perform acts of severe violence against others, simply because such acts were ordered by an authority.[35] This is hardly surprising given that torturers are trained in ways that make obedience to illegal and immoral orders quite likely, and given that the "profession" of torture is given a veneer of legitimization by appeals to the military's professional ideals. Torturers are taught to see torture as a professional job that requires the toughest, most professional soldiers. Torturers worldwide are obeying illegal and immoral orders to torture because that is what they are trained to do. Yet the ticking bomb scenario requires these kinds of torturers—torturers who are quite *deliberately* trained not to question the morality of torture. I turn now to what a supporter of the ticking bomb argument might say in response.

5 Objections

The supporter of the ticking bomb argument may claim that *of course* the use of torture for immoral purposes should be avoided and *of course* the use of torture by the 150 countries mentioned by Amnesty International is probably both illegal and immoral. But, they may argue, training torturers for the ticking bomb scenario would be different. Trained torturers would not be given the order to torture unless the ticking bomb scenario actually arose. The fact that torture and torturers are used for many immoral purposes in the real world does not mean that there is anything wrong with training torturers per se. It's just the way torturers are used that is problematic.

The problem with this objection is straightforward. The use of torture and torturers for illegal and immoral purposes is not accidental; it is not a result of "bad apple" torturers who sell their services to immoral causes. The illegal and immoral use of torture is directly connected to how torturers are trained. The training of torturers—training that would be needed for the ticking bomb torturer—produces dispositions closely linked to crimes of obedience because it produces individuals who are very likely to obey illegal and immoral orders. Unless the ticking bomb supporter can guarantee that such orders would never be given, then they must admit that training torturers is likely to lead (and has led to) crimes of obedience. The ticking bomb argument relies on the assumption that the order to torture would only ever be given in legitimate (highly specified) circumstances and that torturers, despite their training, would know—somehow—that such orders were justified. However, there is no evidence that the use of torture would or could be restricted to such highly unusual circumstances, and there is ample evidence that torture is very frequently used for purposes that would never fit the ticking bomb criteria. In three years of research I have not found a single example of authorities who used torture only in ticking bomb cases.

A second response that a supporter of the ticking bomb argument could make would be to take into consideration the effects of training torturers and tighten the requirements that must be met before the use of torture would be justified in the ticking bomb scenario. They might claim that it is *possible* to imagine a case of torture that managed to avoid all the consequences listed above and fulfilled the necessary criteria and problematic epistemological requirements of the ticking bomb scenario. There might be a hypothetical situation in a hypothetical world where the threat was sufficiently great, and where there was no alternative but to use torture, very little evidence that the use of torture and torturers would become widespread, no infliction of excessive pain, and little or no likelihood of long-term or widespread institutional changes. Now, if such a situation were in fact possible I would be happy to admit that the use of torture might be justified. Indeed, even those who believed torture to be wrong pro tanto might concede that torture would be morally permissible if such a situation arose. Does this mean that my argument against the supporter of the ticking bomb justification has failed?

I have two responses to this objection. First, I do not believe that such a hypothetical scenario is possible. The interrogational torture needed for the ticking bomb scenario cannot effectively be achieved without a trained torturer who is able and willing to obey his orders without question. It is therefore *im*possible for me to imagine a situation in which such an act of torture could take place without the training I described and without torture also being used worldwide in illegal and immoral cases.

Second, I am just not interested in the permissibility of torture in *any* possible world or hypothetical example. I am interested in the actual arrangements needed for even isolated instances of torture to occur. Because the ticking bomb argument is used in debates about the permissibility of torture on terrorism suspects in *this* world, supporters of the ticking bomb argument cannot rely on purely hypothetical cases to support their claims. Moral arguments about the use of torture must take into consideration what permitting torture involves in reality, not in a purely hypothetical example. That torture might be justified in a hypothetical example in a hypothetical world gives absolutely no reason to think that it can be justified (or legalized) in *this* world. Henry Shue makes the same point:

> Does the possibility that torture might be justifiable in some of the rarefied situations which can be imagined provide any reason to consider relaxing the legal prohibitions against it? Absolutely not. The distance between the situations which much be concocted in order to have a plausible case of morally permissible torture and the situations which actually occur is, if anything, further reason why the existing prohibitions against torture should remain.[36]

Given the pain and suffering caused by torture, supporters of the ticking bomb argument have a positive moral duty to consider whether permitting torture in the war against terrorism could be restricted only to cases that met the ticking bomb criteria. Whatever should be the case in an ideal world in which torture and torturers would only be used in legitimate ticking bomb scenarios, in this world torture and torturers are overwhelmingly used in ways that would never meet the criteria of the ticking bomb scenario.[37] Therefore, in order to answer the question that prompted the debate about torture in the first place—whether we should permit the torture of terrorism suspects—supporters of the ticking bomb argument need to explain how the mere possibility of a ticking bomb case arising justifies a use of torture that requires training torturers in a way that deliberately instils dispositions linked to crimes of obedience, crimes that cause and have caused immense suffering to millions of people worldwide.

6 Conclusion

.... As we have seen from current and past uses of torture, the training of torturers—the way they would need to be trained in the ticking bomb scenario—is connected to the illegal and immoral use of torture on a vast scale. In this world torture causes far more suffering than it has ever prevented. The mere possibility of a ticking bomb scenario arising is not sufficient to justify such massive suffering. In this world, it is impossible to contain the use of torture and the use of torturers within the limits of the ticking bomb scenario.

Notes

1 Henry Shue, "Torture," *Philosophy and Public Affairs* 7 (1978): 124–43, p. 141.
2 Quoted in Major William D. Casebeer, "Torture Interrogation of Terrorists: A Theory of Exceptions (with Notes, Cautions, and Warnings)" (paper presented at the Joint Services Conference on Professional Ethics, Washington, DC, 2003). Last accessed 15 February 2005 at www.usafa.af.mil/jscope/JSCOPE03/Casebeer03.html.
3 See Alan Dershowitz, "Want to Torture? Get a Warrant." Last accessed 21 March 2005 at www.sfgate.com/cgibin/article.cgi?file=/chronicle/archive/2002/01/22/ED5329.DTL; and Mark Bowden, "Torture, if it saves lives, may be a necessary evil." Last accessed 21 March 2005 at www.philly.com/mld/inquirer/news/special_packages/sunday_review/3015768.htm.
4 For example, on pages 39–43 of the infamous "torture memo" prepared by the United States Justice Department, the memo presented two defenses for interrogation methods that "crossed the line" from harsh treatment to torture, a defense from necessity (torture is necessary to prevent a greater evil) and a defense based on justified self-defense and defense of others. For the full text of the memo, see http://news.findlaw.com/nytimes/docs/doj/bybee80102mem.pdf, last accessed 13 September 2005.
5 Jean Maria Arrigo, "A utilitarian argument against torture interrogation of terrorists," *Science and Engineering Ethics* 10 (2004): 1–30, at p. 12.
6 See Stanley Milgram, *Obedience to Authority: An Experimental View* (London: Tavistock Publications, 1974). In his most famous experiment, where the victim was audible but not visible, 62.5% of subjects were fully obedient and continued administering electric shocks even after the subject had demanded to be released from the experiment (p. 36).
7 Seymour M. Hersh, *Chain of Command: The Road from 9/11 to Abu Ghraib* (New York: HarperCollins, 2004), p. 34.
8 Ronald D. Crelinsten, "In their own words: the world of the torturer," in Ronald D. Crelinsten and Alex P. Schmid (eds.), *The Politics of Pain: Torturers and Their Masters* (Boulder, CO: Westview Press, 1993), pp. 35–65, at p. 37.
9 Crelinsten, "In their own words," pp. 58–60.

10 There have been several studies of the South American torturers. In "In their own words," Crelinsten quotes from studies of torturers from Brazil, Uruguay, and Chile (pp. 58–60). For a study of the Greek torturers, see Janice T. Gibson and Mika Haritos-Fatouros, "The education of a torturer; there is a cruel method to the madness of teaching people to torture. Almost anyone can learn it," *Psychology Today* 20 (1986): 50–58.
11 Crelinsten, "In their own words," p. 45.
12 Entries from Richard M. Bennett, *Elite Forces: An Encyclopedia of the World's Most Formidable Secret Armies* (London: Virgin Books, 2003).
13 This phrase comes from the title of Bennett's book.
14 Website for the British Special Air Service. Last accessed 15 February 2005 at www.geocities.com/sascenter/train.html. For example, only 1 in 4 trainees complete the training course for the Green Berets. Statistics from the John F. Kennedy Special Warfare Center and School website. Last accessed 14 February 2005 at www.training.sfahq.com/survival_training.htm.
15 For example, see the websites for the British SAS and John F. Kennedy Special Warfare Center and School.
16 Website for John F. Kennedy Special Warfare Center and School.
17 Website for British Special Air Service.
18 John Conroy, *Unspeakable Acts, Ordinary People: The Dynamics of Torture* (New York: Alfred A. Knopf, 2000), p. 6. The European Commission of Human Rights found that these techniques constituted torture.
19 Detainees from the Guantanamo Bay military camp have claimed that while in detention they were "forcibly injected, denied sleep and forced to stand for hours in painful positions" (Tania Branigan, "Former terror detainees accuse U.S. of ill-treatment," *The Age*, 20 August 2003, p. 9).
20 Quoted in Crelinsten, "In their own words," p. 56.
21 Martha Huggins, "Legacies of authoritarianism: Brazilian torturers' and murderers' reformulation of memory," *Latin American Perspectives* 27 (2000): 57–78, p. 63.
22 Conroy, *Unspeakable Acts*, p. 92.
23 Herbert C. Kelman, "The social context of torture: policy process and authority structure," in Crelinsten and Schmid (eds.), *The Politics of Pain*, p. 30.
24 Ibid., p. 31.
25 Huggins, "Legacies of authoritarianism," p. 61.
26 Crelinsten, "In their own words," p. 40.
27 Ibid., p. 41.
28 Bowden uses the term "torture lite" to differentiate physical torture from psychological torture, which he claims (entirely without argument) is not "real" torture but merely "coercion" ("Torture … may be a necessary evil," p. 4). Studies of torture survivors have shown that the effects of so-called "torture lite" techniques are just as if not more devastating to the victims as the effects of physical torture. See, for example, Stefan Priebe and Michael Bauer, "Inclusion of psychological torture in PTSD Criterion A," *The American Journal of Psychiatry* 152 (1995): 1691–92; Mark Van Ommeren et al., "Psychiatric disorders among tortured Bhutanese refugees in Nepal," *Archives of General Psychiatry* 58 (2001): 475–82; and M. Basoglu et al., "Factors related to long-term traumatic stress responses in survivors of torture in Turkey," *Journal of the American Medical Association* 272 (1994): 357–63.
29 Robert Jay Lifton, *The Nazi Doctors: Medical Killing and the Psychology of Genocide* (New York: Basic Books, 1986), pp. 194–95.
30 Crelinsten, "In their own words," p. 41.
31 Hersh, *Chain of Command*, p. 24.
32 Crelinsten, "In their own words," p. 37.
33 *Amnesty International*, "Stop torture." Accessed 17 August 2005 at www.amnestyusa.org/stoptorture/index.do.
34 There is substantial evidence that torture has been used at Guantanamo Bay, in Afghanistan, and elsewhere. This evidence derives not only from the testimony of prisoners but also from the statements of soldiers and interrogators who have worked in or witnessed the treatment of prisoners in Afghanistan, Guantanamo Bay, and Iraq. Human Rights Watch has

documented abuse in prisons in Afghanistan and elsewhere (see "Abuse: systematic and chronic," accessed 20 December 2005 at http://hrw.org/english/docs/2005/10/07/usint11839_txt.htm. An Amnesty International report issued in October 2004 found that "senior U.S. military and civilian officials had set a climate, both through words and actions, conducive to torture and ill-treatment" (Amnesty International, "Guantanamo and beyond: the continuing pursuit of unchecked executive power," accessed 20 December 2005 at http://web.amnesty.org/library/index/ENGAMR510632005. See also the Amnesty International report "The human rights scandal at Guantanamo Bay," accessed 20 December 2005 at http://web.amnesty.org/library/index/ENGIOR410242004. Hersh has also documented the evidence of torture at Guantanamo Bay in *Chain of Command*. For example, a CIA analyst sent to Guantanamo Bay in 2002 interviewed over 30 prisoners and concluded that "we were committing war crimes in Guantanamo" (p. 2).

35 Herbert C. Kelman and V. Lee Hamilton, *Crimes of Obedience: Towards a Social Psychology of Authority and Responsibility* (New Haven, CT: Yale University Press, 1989), p. 46.
36 Shue, "Torture," p. 143.
37 Another consistent consequence of permitting torture is the expansion of the pool of torture victims. As far back as the Spanish Inquisition, when torture has been authorized by the governing authorities the pool of permissible torture victims was not limited to those directly involved or clearly possessing guilty knowledge, but came to include those merely suspected of involvement or of knowing someone who was involved (Kelman, "The social context of torture," p. 27). Arrigo's analysis similarly concludes that, historically, dragnet interrogations are the norm ("A utilitarian argument," p. 12).

Review and Discussion Questions

1 What objections to her argument does Wolfendale consider?
2 Are you convinced by Wolfendale's responses to those objections? Why or why not?
3 Has Wolfendale argued that torture is morally impermissible, legally impermissible, or both?
4 Steinhoff and Wolfendale have seemingly different methods for establishing whether a moral argument "succeeds." How would you describe the difference?

Essay and Paper Topics for Chapter 4

1 "Torture should be permitted under extreme circumstances." How do you assess this statement? How would you answer the person who offers what you think is the best argument against your conclusion?
2 Offer three useful definitions of terrorism, including Scheffler's account as one of the three. Contrast the choices and defend which view is best.
3 What is the debate between Steinhoff and Wolfendale and which argumentative strategy is more compelling for analyzing the morality of torture?

Chapter 5

War, Autonomous Machines, and the Arms Trade

Questions about the morality of war and morality within war have been part of the human experience from the earliest writings of history. The first two essays explore the most basic questions of moral justifications regarding war. The next two engage with the explosive growth of new technologies in robotic and autonomous warfare and focus on whether or how it can be appropriate to regard an autonomous machine as a moral agent. The last essay raises moral concerns with the arms trade.

READING: ON THE MORALITY OF WAR

RICHARD A. WASSERSTROM[*]

When is war justified, if at all? And what are the moral limits on how wars should be fought? Some say war *itself* is simply beyond the bounds of morality; if not everything is fair in love, at least it is in war. In this essay, Richard A. Wasserstrom discusses both the question of applying morality to war and the various issues that arise as one begins to think about the justification of war as well as the rules governing how wars should be fought. He also weighs the issues surrounding killing innocents. Richard A. Wasserstrom is Professor of Philosophy Emeritus at the University of California at Santa Cruz.

I War and Moral Nihilism

Before we examine the moral criteria for assessing war, we must examine the claim that it is not possible to assess war in moral terms. ... For want of a better name for this general view, I shall call it moral nihilism in respect to war. If it is correct, there is, of course, no point in going further.

During the controversy over the rightness of the Vietnam War there have been any number of persons, including a large number in the university, who have claimed that in matters of war (but not in other matters) morality has no place. The war in Vietnam may, they readily concede, be stupid, unwise, or against the

---

[*] From Richard A. Wasserstrom, "On the Morality of War: A Preliminary Inquiry," *Stanford Law Review* 21(7) (June 1969): 1627–1656. Copyright © 1969 by the Board of Trustees of Leland Stanford Junior University. Reprinted by permission of the *Stanford Law Review* and the author. Some footnotes omitted.

best interests of the United States, but it is neither immoral nor unjust—not because it is moral or right, but because these descriptions are *in this context* either naive or meaningless or inapplicable.

Nor is this view limited to the Vietnam War. Consider, for example, the following passage from a speech given only a few years ago by Dean Acheson:

> [T]hose involved in the Cuban crisis of October, 1962, will remember the irrelevance of the supposed moral considerations brought out in the discussions. Judgment centered about the appraisal of dangers and risks, and weighing of the need for decisive and effective action against considerations of prudence; the need to do enough, against the consequences of doing too much. Moral talk did not bear on the problem. Nor did it bear upon the decision of those called upon to advise the President in 1949 whether and with what degree or urgency to press the attempt to produce a thermonuclear weapon. A respected colleague advised me that it would be better that our nation and people should perish rather than be party to a course so evil as producing that weapon. I told him that on the Day of Judgment his view might be confirmed and that he was free to go forth and preach the necessity for salvation. It was not, however, a view which I would entertain as a public servant.[1]

Whatever may be the correct exegesis of this text, I want to treat it as illustrative of the position that morality has no place in the assessment of war. There are several things worth considering in respect to such a view. In the first place, the claim that in matters of war morality has no place is ambiguous. To put it somewhat loosely, the claim may be descriptive, or it may be analytic, or it may be prescriptive. Thus, it would be descriptive if it were merely the factual claim that matters relating to war uniformly turn out to be decided on grounds of national interest or expediency rather than by appeal to what is moral. This claim I will not consider further; it is an empirical one better answered by students of American (and foreign) diplomatic relations.

It would be a prescriptive claim were it taken to assert that matters relating to war ought always be decided by appeal to (say) national interest rather than an appeal to the moral point of view. For reasons which have yet to be elucidated, on this view the moral criteria are capable of being employed but it is undesirable to do so. I shall say something more about this view in a moment.

The analytic point is not that morality ought not be used, but rather that it cannot. On this view the statement "The United States is behaving immorally in the way it is waging war in Vietnam" (or, "in waging war in Vietnam") is not wrong but meaningless.

What are we to make of the analytic view? As I have indicated, it could, of course, be advanced simply as an instance of a more sweeping position concerning the general meaninglessness of the moral point of view. What I find particularly interesting, though, is the degree to which this thesis is advanced as a special view about war and not as a part of a more general claim that all morality is meaningless.

I think that there are at least [three] reasons why this special view may be held. First, the accusation that one's own country is involved in an immoral war is personally very threatening. For one thing, if the accusation is well-founded it may be thought to imply that certain types of socially cooperative behavior are forbidden to the citizen and that other kinds of socially deviant behavior are obligatory upon him. Yet, in a time of war it is following just this sort of dictate that will be treated more harshly by the actor's own government. Hence the morally responsible citizen is put in a most troublesome moral dilemma. If his country is engaged in an immoral war then he may have a duty to oppose and resist; yet opposition and resistance will typically carry extraordinarily severe penalties.

The pressure is, I suspect, simply too great for many of us. We are unwilling to pay the fantastically high personal price that goes with the moral point of view, and we are equally unwilling to plead guilty to this most serious charge of immorality. So we solve the problem by denying the possibility that war can be immoral. The relief is immediate; the moral "heat" is off. If war cannot be immoral, then one's country cannot be engaged in an immoral war but only a stupid or unwise one. And whatever one's obligation to keep one's country from behaving stupidly or improvidently, they are vastly less stringent and troublesome than obligations imposed by the specter of complicity in an immoral war. We may, however, pay a price for such relief since we obliterate the moral distinctions between the Axis and the Allies in World War II at the same time as the distinctions between the conduct of the United States in 1941–45 and the conduct of the United States in 1967–68 in Vietnam.

Second, I think the view that moral judgments are meaningless sometimes seems plausible because of the differences between personal behavior and the behavior of states. There are not laws governing the behavior of states in the same way in which there are positive laws governing the behavior of citizens. International law is a troublesome notion just because it is both like and unlike our concept of positive law.

Now, how does skepticism about the law-like quality of international law lead to the claim that it is impossible for war to be either moral or immoral? It is far from obvious. Perhaps it is because there is at least one sense of justice that is intimately bound up with the notion of rule-violation; namely, that which relates justice to the following of rules and to the condemnation and punishment of those who break rules. In the absence of positive laws governing the behavior of states, it may be inferred (although I think mistakenly) that it is impossible for states to behave either justly or unjustly. But even if justice can be said to be analyzable solely in terms of following rules, morality certainly cannot. Hence the absence of international laws cannot serve to make the moral appraisal of war impossible.

More plausible is the view that says there can be no moral assessment of war just because there is, by definition, no morality in war. If war is an activity in which anything goes, moral judgments on war are just not possible.

To this there are two responses. To begin with, it is not, as our definitional discussion indicates, a necessary feature of war that it be an activity in which everything is morally permissible. There is a difference between the view that war is unique because killing and violence are morally permissible in contexts and circumstances where they otherwise would not be and the view that war is unique because everything is morally permissible.

A less absolutist argument for the absurdity of discussing the morality of war might be that at least today the prevailing (although not necessary) conception of war is one that as a practical matter rules out no behavior on moral grounds. After all, if flame throwers are deemed perfectly permissible, if the bombing of cities is applauded and not condemned, and if thermonuclear weapons are part of the arsenal of each of the major powers, then the remaining moral prohibitions on the conduct of war are sufficiently insignificant to be ignored.

The answer to this kind of an argument requires, I believe, that we distinguish the question of what is moral in war from that of the morality of war or of war generally. Paradoxically, the more convincing the argument from war's conduct, the stronger is the moral argument *against* engaging in war at all. For the more it can be shown that engaging in war will inevitably lead to despicable behavior to which no moral predicates are deemed applicable, the more this also constitutes an argument against bringing such a state of affairs into being.

There is still another way to take the claim that in matters of war morality has no place. That is what I have called the prescriptive view: that national interest ought to determine policies in respect to war, not morality. This is surely one way to interpret the remarks of Dean Acheson reproduced earlier. It is also, perhaps, involved in President Truman's defense of the dropping of the atomic bomb on Hiroshima. What he said was this:

> Having found the bomb, we have to use it. We have used it against those who attacked us without warning at Pearl Harbor, against those who have starved and beaten and executed American prisoners of war, against those who have abandoned all pretense of obeying international laws of warfare. We have used it in order to shorten the agony of war, in order to save the lives of thousands and thousands of young Americans.[2]

Although this passage has many interesting features, I am concerned only with President Truman's insistence that the dropping of the bomb was justified because it saved the lives "of thousands and thousands of young Americans."

Conceivably, this is merely an elliptical way of saying that on balance fewer lives were lost through the dropping of the bomb and the accelerated cessation of hostilities than through any alternative course of conduct. Suppose, though, that this were not the argument. Suppose, instead, that the justification were regarded as adequate provided only that it was reasonably clear that fewer *American* lives would be lost than through any alternative course of conduct. Thus, to quantify the example, we can imagine someone maintaining that Hiroshima was justified because 20,000 fewer Americans died in the Pacific theater than would have died if the bomb had not been dropped. And this is justified even though 30,000 more Japanese died than would have been killed had the war been fought to an end with conventional means. Thus, even though 10,000 more people died than would otherwise have been the case, the bombing was justified because of the greater number of American lives saved.

On this interpretation, the argument depends upon valuing the lives of Americans higher than the lives of persons from other countries. As such, is there anything to be said for the argument? Its strongest statement, and the only one that I shall consider, might go like this: Truman was the President of the United States and as such had an obligation always to choose that course of conduct that appeared to offer the greatest chance of maximizing the interests of the United States. As President, he was obligated to prefer the lives of American soldiers over those from any other country, and he was obligated to prefer them just because they were Americans and he was their President.

Some might prove such a point by drawing an analogy to the situation of a lawyer or a parent or a corporation executive. A lawyer has a duty to present his client's case in the fashion most calculated to ensure his client's victory, and he has this obligation irrespective of the objective merits of his client's case. Similarly, we are neither surprised nor dismayed when a parent prefers the interests of his child over those of other children. A parent qua parent is certainly not behaving immorally when he acts so as to secure satisfactions for his child, again irrespective of the objective merits of the child's needs or wants. And, mutatis mutandis, a corporate executive has a duty to maximize profits for his company. Thus, as public servants, Dean Acheson and Harry Truman had no moral choice but to pursue those policies that appeared to them to be in the best interest of the United States. And to a lesser degree, all persons qua citizens of the United States have a similar, if slightly more attenuated, obligation. Therefore, morality has no real place in war.

The analogy, however, must not stop halfway. It is certainly both correct and important to observe that public officials, like parents, lawyers, and corporate executives, do have special moral obligations that are imposed by virtue of the position or role they fill. A lawyer does have a duty to prefer his client's interests in a way that would be improper were the person anyone other than a client. And the same sort of duty, I think, holds for a parent, an executive, a President, and a citizen in their respective roles. The point becomes distorted, however, when it is supposed that such an obligation always, under all circumstances, overrides any and all other obligations that the person might have. The case of the lawyer is instructive. While he has an obligation to attend to his client's interests in very special ways, there are many other things that it is impermissible for the lawyer to do in furtherance of his client's interests—irrespective, this time, of how significantly they might advance that interest.

The case for the President, or for public servants generally, is similar. While the President may indeed have an obligation to prefer and pursue the national interests, this obligation could only be justifiable—could only be a moral obligation—if it were enmeshed in a comparable range of limiting and competing obligations. If we concede that the President has certain obligations to prefer the national interest that no one else has, we must be equally sensitive to the fact that the President also has some of the same obligations to other persons that all other men have—if for no other reason than that all persons have the right to be treated or not treated in certain ways. So whatever special obligations the President may have cannot by themselves support the view that in war morality ought to have no place.

But the major problem with the national-interest argument is its assumption that the national interest not only is something immutable and knowable but also that it limits national interest to narrowly national concerns. It is parochial to suppose that the American national interest really rules out solicitude for other states in order to encourage international stability.

Finally, national interest as a goal must itself be justified. The United States' position of international importance may have imposed on it a duty of more than national concern. The fact that such a statement has become hackneyed by constant use to justify American interference abroad should not blind us to the fact that it may be viable as an argument for a less aggressive international responsibility.

2 Assessing the Morality of Wars

If we turn now to confront more directly the question of the morality of wars, it is evident that there is a variety of different perspectives from which, or criteria in terms of which, particular wars may be assessed. First, to the extent to which the model of war as a game continues to have a place, wars can be evaluated in terms of the degree to which the laws of war—the rules for initiating and conducting war—are adhered to by the opposing countries. Second, the rightness or wrongness of wars is often thought to depend very much upon the cause for which a war is fought. And third, there is the independent justification for a war that is founded upon an appeal of some kind to a principle of self-defense.

In discussing the degree to which the laws of war are followed or disregarded, there are two points that should be stressed. First, a skepticism as to the meaningfulness of any morality *within* war is extremely common. The gnomic statement is Sherman's: "War is hell." The fuller argument depends upon a rejection of the notion of war as a game. It goes something like this. War is the antithesis of law or rules. It is violence, killing, and all of the horror they imply. Even if moral distinctions can be made in respect to such things as the initiation and purposes of a war, it is absurd to suppose that moral distinctions can be drawn once a war has begun. All killing is bad, all destruction equally wanton.

Now there does seem to me to be a fairly simple argument of sorts that can be made in response. Given the awfulness of war, it nonetheless appears plausible to discriminate among degrees of awfulness. A war in which a large number of innocent persons are killed is, all other things being equal, worse than one in which only a few die. A war in which few combatants are killed is, *ceteris paribus*, less immoral than one in which many are killed. And more to the point, perhaps, any unnecessary harm to others is surely unjustifiable. To some degree, at least, the "laws of war" can be construed as attempts to formalize these general notions and to define instances of unnecessary harm to others.

The second criterion, the notion of the cause that can be invoked to justify a war, may involve two quite different inquiries. On the one hand, we may intend the sense in which cause refers to the *consequences* of waging war, to the forward-looking criteria of assessment. Thus, when a war is justified as a means by which to make the world safe for democracy or on the grounds that a failure to fight now will lead to a loss of confidence on the part of one's allies or as necessary to avoid fighting a larger, more destructive war later, when these sorts of appeals are made, the justification is primarily consequential or forward-looking in character. Here the distinction between morality and prudence—never a very easy one to maintain in international relations—is always on the verge of collapse. On the other hand, a war may be evaluated through recourse to what may be termed backward-looking criteria. Just as in the case of punishment or blame where what happened in the past is relevant to the justice of punishing or blaming someone, so in the case of war, what has already happened is, on this view, relevant to the justice or rightness of the war that is subsequently waged. The two backward-looking criteria that are most frequently invoked in respect to war are the question of whether the war involved a violation of some prior promise, typically expressed in the form of a treaty or concord.

Two sorts of assertions are often made concerning the role of the treaty in justifying resort to war. First, if a country has entered into a treaty not to go to war and if it violates that treaty, it is to be condemned for, in effect, having broken its promise. And second, if a country has entered into a treaty in which it has agreed to go to war under certain circumstances and if those circumstances come to pass, then the country is at least justified in going to war—although it is not in fact obligated to do so.

Once again ... it is clear that treaties can be relevant but not decisive factors. This is so just because it is sometimes right to break our promises and sometimes wrong to keep them. The fact that a treaty is violated at best tends to make a war unjust or immoral in some degree, but it does not necessarily render the war unjustified.

The other backward-looking question, that of aggression, is often resolved by concluding that under no circumstances is the initiation of a war of aggression justified. This is a view that Americans and America have often embraced. Such a view was expounded at Nuremberg by Mr. Justice Jackson when he said:

> [T]he wrong for which their [the German] fallen leaders are on trial is not that they lost the war, but that they started it. And we must not allow ourselves to be drawn into a trial of the causes of war, for our position is that no grievances or policies will justify resort to aggressive war. ... Our position is that whatever grievances a nation may have, however objectionable it finds that *status quo*, aggressive warfare is an illegal means for settling those grievances or for altering those conditions.[3]

A position such as this is typically thought to imply two things: (1) the initiation of war is never justifiable; (2) the warlike response to aggressive war is justifiable. Both views are troublesome.

To begin with, it is hard to see how the two propositions go together very comfortably. Conceivably, there are powerful arguments against the waging of aggressive war. Almost surely, though, the more persuasive of these will depend, at least in part, on the character of war itself—on such things as the supreme importance of human life or the inevitable injustices committed in every war. If so, then the justifiability of meeting war with war will to that degree be called into question.

To take the first proposition alone, absent general arguments about the unjustifiability of all war, it is hard to see how aggressive war can be ruled out in a wholly a priori fashion. Even if we assume that no problems are presented in determining what is and is not aggression, it is doubtful that the quality of aggression could always be morally decisive in condemning the war. Would a war undertaken to free innocent persons from concentration camps or from slavery always be unjustifiable just because *it was aggressive*? Surely this is to rest too much upon only one of a number of relevant considerations.

From a backward-looking point of view, the claim that a warring response to aggressive war is always justified is even more perplexing.

In order to understand the force of the doctrine of self-defense when invoked in respect to war and to assess its degree of legitimate applicability, it is necessary that we look briefly at self-defense as it functions as a doctrine of municipal criminal law.

[W]hat is important is that we keep in mind two of the respects in which the law qualifies resort to the claim of self-defense. On one hand, the doctrine cannot be invoked successfully if the intended victim could have avoided the encounter through a reasonable escape or retreat unless the attack takes place on one's own property. And on the other hand, the doctrine requires that no more force be employed than is reasonably necessary to prevent the infliction of comparable harm.

Now how does all of this apply to self-defense as a justification for engaging in war? In the first place, to the extent to which the basic doctrine serves as an excuse, the applicability to war seems doubtful. While it may make sense to regard self-defense of one's person as a natural, instinctive response to an attack, it is only a very anthropomorphic view of countries that would lead us to elaborate a comparable explanation here.

In the second place, it is not even clear that self-defense can function very persuasively as a justification. For it to do so it might be necessary, for example, to be able to make out a case that countries die in the same way in which persons do or that a country can be harmed in the same way in which a person can be. Of course, persons in the country can be harmed and killed by war, and I shall return to this point in a moment, but we can also imagine an attack in which none of the inhabitants of the country will be killed or even physically harmed unless they fight back. But the country as a separate political entity might nonetheless disappear. Would we say that this should be regarded as the equivalent of human death? That it is less harmful? More harmful? These are issues to which those who readily invoke the doctrine of self-defense seldom address themselves.

Even if we were to decide, however, that there is no question but that a country is justified in relying upon a doctrine of self-defense that is essentially similar to that which obtains in the criminal law, it would be essential to observe the constraints that follow. Given even the unprovoked aggressive waging of war by one country against another, the doctrine of self-defense could not be invoked by the country so attacked to justify waging unlimited defensive war or insisting upon unconditional surrender. Each or both of these responses might be justifiable, but not simply because a country was wrongly attacked. It would, instead, have to be made out that something analogous to retreat was neither possible nor appropriate and, even more, that no more force was used than was reasonably necessary to terminate the attack.

There is, to be sure, an answer to this. The restrictions that the criminal law puts upon self-defense are defensible, it could be maintained, chiefly because we have a municipal police force, municipal laws, and courts. If we use no more than reasonable force to repel attacks, we can at least be confident that the attacker will be apprehended and punished and, further, that we live in a society in which this sort of aggressive behavior is deterred by a variety of means. It is the absence of such a context that renders restrictions on an international doctrine of self-defense inappropriate.

I do not think this answer is convincing. It is relevant to the question of what sorts of constraints will be operative on the behavior of persons and countries, but it is not persuasive as to the invocation of *self-defense* as a justification for war. To use more force than is reasonably necessary to defend oneself is, in short, to do more than defend oneself. If such non-self-defensive behavior is to be justified, it must appeal to some different principle or set of principles.

There are, therefore, clearly cases in which a principle of self-defense does appear to justify engaging in a war: at a minimum, those cases in which one's country is attacked in such a way that the inhabitants are threatened with deadly force and in which no more force than is reasonably necessary is employed to terminate the attack.

3 War and Innocents

The strongest argument against war is that which rests upon the connection between the morality of war and the death of innocent persons. The specter of thermonuclear warfare makes examination of this point essential; yet the problem was both a genuine and an urgent one in the pre-atomic days of air warfare, particularly during the Second World War.

The argument based upon the death of innocent persons goes something like this: Even in war innocent people have a right to life and limb that should be respected. It is no less wrong and no more justifiable to kill innocent persons in war than at any other time. Therefore, if innocent persons are killed in a war, that war is to be condemned.

The argument can quite readily be converted into an attack upon all modern war. Imagine a thoroughly unprovoked attack upon another country—an attack committed, moreover, from the worst of motives and for the most despicable of ends. Assume too, for the moment, that under such circumstances there is nothing immoral about fighting back and even killing those who are attacking. Nonetheless, if in fighting back innocent persons will be killed, the defenders will be acting immorally. However, given any war fought today, innocent persons will inevitably be killed. Therefore, any war fought today will be immoral.

There are a variety of matters that require clarification before the strength of this argument can be adequately assessed. In particular, there are four questions that must be examined: (1) What is meant by "innocence" in this context? (2) Is it plausible to suppose that there are any innocents? (3) Under what circumstances is the death of innocent persons immoral? (4) What is the nature of the connection between the immorality of the killing of innocent persons and the immorality of the war in which this killing occurs?

It is anything but clear what precisely is meant by "innocence" or "the innocent" in an argument such as this. One possibility would be that all noncombatants are innocent. But then, of course, we would have to decide what was meant by "noncombatants." Here we might be tempted to claim that noncombatants are all of those persons who are not in the army—not actually doing the fighting; the combatants are those who are. There are, however, serious problems with this position. For it appears that persons can be noncombatants in this sense and yet indistinguishable in any apparently relevant sense from persons in the army. Thus, civilians may be manufacturing munitions, devising new weapons, writing propaganda, or doing any number of other things that make them indistinguishable from many combatants vis-à-vis their relationship to the war effort.

A second possibility would be to focus upon an individual's causal connection with the attempt to win the war rather than on his status as soldier or civilian. In this view, only some noncombatants would be innocent and virtually no combatants would be. If the causal connection is what is relevant, meaningful distinctions might be made among civilians. One might distinguish between those whose activities or vocations help the war effort only indirectly, if at all, and those whose activities are more plausibly described as directly beneficial. Thus, the distinctions would be between a typical grocer or a tailor, on the one hand, and a worker in an armaments plant, on the other. Similarly, children, the aged, and the infirm would normally not be in a position to play a role causally connected in this way with the waging of war.

There are, of course, other kinds of possible causal connections. In particular, someone might urge that attention should also be devoted to the existence of a causal connection between the individual's civic behavior and the war effort. Thus, for example, a person's voting behavior or the degree of his political opposition to the government or his financial contributions to the war effort might all be deemed to be equally relevant to his status as an innocent.

Still a fourth possibility, closely related to those already discussed, would be that interpretation of innocence concerned with culpability rather than causality per se. On this view a person would properly be regarded an innocent if he could not fairly be held responsible for the war's initiation or conduct. Clearly, the notion of culpability is linked in important ways with that of causal connection, but they are by no means identical. So it is quite conceivable, for example, that under some principles of culpability, many combatants might not be culpable and some noncombatants might be extremely culpable, particularly if culpability were to be defined largely in terms of state of mind and enthusiasm for the war. Thus, an aged or infirm person who cannot do very much to help the war effort but is an ardent proponent of its aims and objectives might be more culpable (and less innocent in this sense) than a conscriptee who is firing a machine gun only because the penalty for disobeying the command to do so is death.

But we need not propose an airtight definition of "innocence" in order to answer the question of whether, in any war, there will be a substantial number of innocent persons involved. For irrespective of which sense or senses of innocence are ultimately deemed most instructive or important, it does seem clear that there will be a number of persons in any country (children are probably the clearest example) who will meet any test of innocence that is proposed.

The third question enumerated earlier is: Under what circumstances is the death of innocent persons immoral? One possible view is that which asserts simply that it is unimportant which circumstances bring about the death of innocent persons. As long as we know that innocent persons will be killed as a result of war, we know all we need to know to condemn any such war.

Another, and perhaps more plausible, view is that which regards the death of innocent persons as increasingly unjustifiable if it was negligently, recklessly, knowingly, or intentionally brought about. Thus, if a country engages in acts of war with the intention of bringing about the death of children, perhaps to weaken the will of the enemy, it would be more immoral than if it were to engage in acts of war aimed at killing combatants but which through error also kill children.

A different sort of problem arises if someone asks how we are to differentiate the deaths of children in war from, for example, the deaths of children that accompany the use of highways or airplanes in times of peace. Someone might, that is, argue that we permit children to ride in cars on highways and to fly in airplanes even though we know that there will be accidents and that as a result of these accidents innocent children will die. And since we know this to be the case, the situation appears to be indistinguishable from that of engaging in acts of war where it is known that the death of children will be a direct, although not intended, consequence.

I think that there are three sorts of responses that can be made to an objection of this sort. In the first place, in a quite straight-forward sense, the highway does not, typically, cause the death of the innocent passenger; the careless driver or the defective tire does. But it is the intentional bombing of the heavily populated city that does cause the death of the children who live in the city.

In the second place, it is one thing to act where one knows that certain more or less identifiable persons will be killed (say, bombing a troop camp when one knows that those children who live in the vicinity of the camp will also be killed) and quite another thing to engage in conduct in which all one can say is that it can be predicted with a high degree of confidence that over a given period of time a certain number of persons (including children) will be killed.

In the third place, there is certainly a difference in the two cases in respect to the possibility of deriving benefits from the conduct. That is to say, when a highway is used, one is participating in a system or set of arrangements in which benefits are derived from that use (even though risks, and hence costs, are also involved). It is not easy to see how a similar sort of analysis can as plausibly be proposed in connection with typical acts of war.

The final and most important issue that is raised by the argument concerning the killing of the innocent in time of war is that of the connection between the immorality of the killing of innocent persons and the immorality of the war in which this killing occurs. Writers in the area often fail to discuss the connection.

Miss Anscombe puts the point this way:

> [I]t is murderous to attack [the innocent] or make them a target for an attack which [the attacker] judges will help him toward victory. For murder is the deliberate killing of the innocent, whether for its own sake or as a means to some further end.[4]
>
> ("War and Murder" in *Nuclear Weapons: A Catholic Response* (1961), p. 49)

It is likely that Miss Anscombe means to assert an absolutist view here—that there are no circumstances under which the intentional killing of innocent persons, even in time of war, can be justified. It is always immoral to do so. At least their arguments are phrased in absolutist terms. If this is the view that they intend to defend, it is, I think, a hard one to accept. This is so just because it ultimately depends upon too complete a rejection of the relevance of consequences to the moral character of action. It also requires too rigid a dichotomy between acts and omissions. It seems to misunderstand the character of our moral life to claim that, no matter what the consequences, the intentional killing of an innocent person could never be justifiable—even, for example, if a failure to do so would bring about the death of many more innocent persons.

My own view is that as a theoretical matter an absolutist position is even less convincing here. Given the number of criteria that are relevant to the moral assessment of any war and given the great number of persons involved in and the extended duration of most wars, it would be false to the complexity of the issues to suppose that so immediately simple a solution were possible.

But having said all of this, the *practical*, as opposed to the theoretical, thrust of the argument is virtually unabated. If wars were conducted, or were likely to be conducted, so as to produce only the occasional intentional killing of the innocent, that would be one thing. We could then say with some confidence that on this ground at least wars can hardly be condemned out of hand. Unfortunately, though, mankind no longer lives in such a world and, as a result, the argument from the death of the innocent has become increasingly more convincing. The intentional, or at least knowing, killing of the innocent on a large scale became a practically necessary feature of war with the advent of air warfare. And the genuinely indiscriminate killing of very great numbers of innocent persons is the dominant legacy of the birth of thermonuclear weapons. At this stage, the argument from the death of the innocent moves appreciably closer to becoming a decisive objection to war. For even if we reject, as I have argued we should, both absolutist interpretations of the argument, the core of truth that remains is the insistence that in war, no less than elsewhere, the knowing killing of the innocent is an evil that throws up the heaviest of justificatory burdens. My own view is that in any major war that can or will be fought today, none of those considerations that can sometimes justify engaging in war will in fact come close to meeting this burden. But even if I am wrong, the argument from the death of the innocent does, I believe, make it clear both where the burden is and how unlikely it is today to suppose that it can be honestly discharged.

Notes

1 D. Acheson, "Ethics in International Relations Today," in *The Vietnam Reader*, ed. M. Raskin and B. Fall (1965), p. 13.
2 Address to the Nation by President Harry S. Truman, August 9, 1945, quoted in R. Tucker, *The Just War* (1960), pp. 21–22, n. 14.
3 Quoted in R. Tucker, supra note 2, p. 12.
4 "War and Murder" in Nuclear Weapons: A Catholic Response (1961), p. 49.

Review and Discussion Questions

1 Describe and evaluate the argument that warfare is amoral.
2 How does Wasserstrom argue that morality *is* relevant for assessing war?
3 What considerations does Wasserstrom think could justify war? Describe the limitations of each.
4 "War is wrong because it inevitably means the deaths of innocents." How does Wasserstrom assess this argument?
5 Under what circumstances would it be right to say that a war is unjust?
6 What is the best way to characterize the general structure of Wasserstrom's argument?

READING: THE MORALITY OF PACIFISM

CHEYNEY RYAN[*]

In this selection from his longer article "Self-Defense, Pacifism, and the Possibility of Killing," Cheyney Ryan describes the pacifist's position as requiring respect for other human beings and an appreciation of the bond shared by all. Far from a simple disagreement, he argues, the dispute between the pacifist and those who would commit violent acts is a deep, intractable one to which people must pay close attention. Cheyney Ryan is Emeritus Professor of Law and Philosophy at the University of Oregon and a fellow at the Oxford Institute for Ethics, Law and Armed Conflict.

George Orwell tells how early one morning [during the Spanish Civil War] he ventured out with another man to snipe at the fascists from the trenches outside their encampment. After having little success for several hours, they were suddenly alerted to the sound of Republican airplanes overhead. Orwell writes,

> At this moment a man, presumably carrying a message to an officer, jumped out of the trench and ran along the top of the parapet in full view. He was half-dressed and holding up his trousers with both hands as he ran. I refrained from shooting at him. It is true that I am a poor shot and unlikely to hit a running man at a hundred yards. Still, I did not shoot partly because of that detail about the trousers. I had come here to shoot "Fascists"; but a man who is holding up his trousers isn't a "Fascist", he is *visibly a fellow creature*, similar to yourself, and you don't feel like shooting him.[1]

Orwell was not a pacifist, but the problem he finds in this particular act of killing is akin to the problem which the pacifist finds in all acts of killing. That problem, the example suggests, takes the following form.

The problem with shooting the half-clothed man does not arise from the rights involved, nor is it dispensed with by showing that, yes indeed, you are justified (by your rights) in killing him. But this does not mean, as some have suggested to me, that the problem is therefore not a *moral* problem at all ("sheer sentimentality" was an objection raised by one philosopher ex-marine). Surely if Orwell had gleefully blasted away here, if he had not at least felt the tug of the other's "fellow-creaturehood," then this would have reflected badly, if not on his action, then on *him*, as a human being. The problem, in the Orwell case, is that the man's dishabille made inescapable the fact that he was a "fellow creature" and in so doing it stripped away the labels and denied the distance so necessary to murderous actions (it is not for nothing that armies give us stereotypes in thinking about the enemy). The problem, I am tempted to say, involves not so much the justification as the *possibility* of killing in such circumstances ("How could you bring yourself to

---

[*] Abridged from Cheyney Ryan, "Self-Defense, Pacifism, and the Possibility of Killing," *Ethics* (April 1, 1983).

do it?" is a natural response to one who felt no problem in such situations). And therein lies the clue to the pacifist impulse.

The pacifist's problem is that he cannot create, or does not wish to create, the necessary distance between himself and another to make the act of killing possible. Moreover, the fact that others obviously can create that distance is taken by the pacifist to reflect badly on them; they move about in the world insensitive to the half-clothed status which all humans, qua fellow creatures, share. This latter point is important to showing that the pacifist's position is indeed a moral position and not just a personal idiosyncrasy. What should now be evident is the sense in which that moral position is motivated by a picture of the personal relationship and outlook one should maintain toward others, regardless of the actions they might take toward you. It is fitting in this regard that the debate over self-defense should come down to a personal relationship, the "negative bond" between Aggressor and Defender. For even if this negative bond renders killing in self-defense permissible, the pacifist will insist that the deeper bonds of fellow-creaturehood should render it impossible. That such an outlook will be branded by others as sheer sentimentality comes to the pacifist as no surprise.

I am aware that this characterization of the pacifist's outlook may strike many as obscure, but the difficulties in characterizing that outlook themselves reflect, I think, how truly fundamental the disagreement between the pacifist and the non-pacifist really is. That disagreement far transcends the familiar problems of justice and equity; it is no surprise that the familiar terms should fail us. As to the accuracy of this characterization, I would offer as indirect support the following example of the aesthetic of fascism, which I take to be at polar ends from that of pacifism, and so illustrative in contrast of the pacifist outlook:

> War is beautiful because it establishes man's dominion over the subjugated machinery by means of gas masks, terrifying megaphones, flame throwers, and small tanks. War is beautiful because it initiates the dreamt-of metalization of the human body. War is beautiful because it enriches the flowering meadow with the fiery orchids of machine guns.[2]

What the fascist rejoices in the pacifist rejects, in toto—the "metalization of the human body," the insensitivity to fellow-creaturehood which the pacifist sees as the presupposition of killing.

This account of the pacifist's position suggests some obvious avenues of criticism of the more traditional sort. One could naturally ask whether killing necessarily presupposes objectification and distance, as the pacifist feels it does. It seems to me, though, that the differences between the pacifist and the non-pacifist are substantial enough that neither side is likely to produce a simple "refutation" along such lines which the other conceivably could, or logically need, accept. If any criticism of pacifism is to be forthcoming which can make any real claim to the pacifist's attention, it will be one which questions the consistency of his conclusions with what I have described as his motivating impulse. Let me suggest how such a criticism might go.

If the pacifist's intent is to acknowledge through his attitudes and actions the other person's status as a fellow creature, the problem is that violence, and even killing, are at times a means of acknowledging this as well, a way of bridging the distance between oneself and another person, a way of acknowledging one's *own* status as a person. This is one of the underlying themes of Hegel's account of conflict in the master–slave dialectic, and the important truth it contains should not be lost in its seeming glorification of conflict. That the refusal to allow others to treat one as an object is an important step to defining one's own integrity is a point well understood by revolutionary theorists such as Fanon. It is a point apparently lost to pacifists like Gandhi, who suggested that the Jews in the Warsaw Ghetto would have made the superior moral statement by committing collective suicide, since their resistance proved futile anyway. What strikes us as positively bizarre in the pacifist's suggestion, for example, that we *not* defend our loved ones when attacked is not the fact that someone's rights might be abused by our refusal to so act. Our real concern is what the refusal to intervene would express about our relationships and ourselves, for one of the ways we acknowledge the importance of a relationship is through our willingness to take such actions, and that is why the problem in such cases is how we can bring ourselves *not* to intervene (how is passivity possible).

The willingness to commit violence is linked to our love and estimation for others, just as the capacity for jealousy is an integral part of affection. The pacifist may respond that this is just a sociological or psychological fact about how our community links violence and care, a questionable connection that expresses thousands of years of macho culture. But this connection is no *more* questionable than that which views acts of violence against an aggressor as expressing hatred or indifference or objectification. If the pacifist's problem is that he cannot consistently live out his initial impulse—the posture he wishes to assume toward others requires that he commit violence and that he not commit violence—does this reflect badly on his position? Well, if you find his goals attractive it may well reflect badly on the position—or *fix*—we are all in. Unraveling the pacifist's logic may lead us to see that our world of violence and killing is one in which regarding some as people requires that we regard others as things and that this is not a fact that can be excused or absolved through the techniques of moral philosophy. If the pacifist's error arises from the desire to smooth this all over by hewing to one side of the dilemma, he is no worse than his opponent, whose "refutation" of pacifism serves to dismiss those very intractable problems of violence of which pacifism is the anxious expression. As long as this tragic element in violence persists, pacifism will remain with us as a response; we should not applaud its demise, for it may well mark that the dilemmas of violence have simply been forgotten.

Impatients will now ask: So do we kill or don't we? It should be clear that I do not have the sort of answer to this question that a philosopher, at least, might expect. One can attend to the problems involved in either choice, but the greatest problem is that the choice does not flow naturally from a desire to acknowledge in others and in ourselves their importance and weaknesses and worth.

Notes

1 George Orwell, "Looking Back on the Spanish Civil War," in *A Collection of Essays by George Orwell* (New York: Doubleday, 1954), p. 199.
2 Marinetti, a founder of Futurism, cited in Walter Benjamin's essay, "The Work of Art in the Age of Mechanical Reproduction," Illuminations (New York: Schocken Books, 1969), p. 241.

Review and Discussion Questions

1. Describe the point of the example that begins the essay.
2. Ryan seems to suggest that the choice between self-defense or not acting in self-defense does not really get at the question that the pacifist wants to address. How do you make sense of this position? How does the structure of his argument differ from Wasserstrom's approach?
3. How might Wasserstrom respond to the pacifist's position?

READING: WHEN IS A ROBOT A MORAL AGENT?

JOHN P. SULLINS[*]

In this article John Sullins considers whether robots can have moral agency and the conditions under which they can be morally responsible for the results of their activity. John Sullins is Professor of Philosophy at Sonoma State University.

Abstract

In this paper I argue that in certain circumstances robots can be seen as real moral agents. A distinction is made between persons and moral agents such that it is not necessary for a robot to have personhood in order to be a moral agent. I detail three requirements for a robot to be seen as a moral agent. The first is achieved when the robot is significantly autonomous from any programmers or operators of the machine. The second is when one can analyze or explain the robot's behavior only by ascribing to it some predisposition or "intention" to do good or harm. And finally, robot moral agency requires the robot to behave in a way that shows an understanding of responsibility to some other moral agent. Robots with all of these criteria will have moral rights as well as responsibilities regardless of their status as persons.

Robots have been a part of our work environment for the past few decades but they are no longer limited to factory automation. The additional range of activities they are being used for is growing. Robots are now automating a wide range of professional activities such as: aspects of the healthcare industry, white collar office work, search and rescue operations, automated warfare, and the service industries.

A subtle, but far more personal, revolution has begun in home automation as robot vacuums and toys are becoming more common in homes around the world. As these machines increase in capability and ubiquity, it is inevitable that they will impact our lives ethically as well as physically and emotionally. These impacts will be both positive and negative and in this paper I will address the moral status of robots and how that status, both real and potential, should affect the way we design and use these technologies.

---

[*] John P. Sullins, "When Is a Robot a Moral Agent?" *International Review of Information Ethics* 6(12) (2006): 23–30.

Morality and Human Robot Interactions

As robotics technology becomes more ubiquitous, the scope of human robot interactions will grow. At the present time, these interactions are no different than the interactions one might have with any piece of technology, but as these machines become more interactive they will become involved in situations that have a moral character that may be uncomfortably similar to the interactions we have with other sentient animals. An additional issue is that people find it easy to anthropomorphize robots and this will enfold robotics technology quickly into situations where, if the agent were a human rather than a robot, the situations would easily be seen as moral situations. A nurse has certain moral duties and rights when dealing with his or her patients. Will these moral rights and responsibilities carry over if the caregiver is a robot rather than a human?

We have three possible answers to this question. The first possibility is that the morality of the situation is just an illusion. We fallaciously ascribe moral rights and responsibilities to the machine due to an error in judgment based merely on the humanoid appearance or clever programming of the robot. The second option is that the situation is pseudo-moral. That is, it is partially moral but the robotic agents involved lack something that would make them fully moral agents. And finally, even though these situations may be novel, they are nonetheless real moral situations that must be taken seriously. In this paper I will argue for this latter position as well as critique the positions taken by a number of other researches on this subject.

Morality and Technologies

To clarify this issue it is important to look at how moral theorists have dealt with the ethics of technology use and design. The most common theoretical schema is the standard user, tool, and victim model. Here the technology mediates the moral situation between the actor who uses the technology and the victim. In this model we typically blame the user, not the tool, when a person using some tool or technological system causes harm.

If a robot is simply a tool, then the morality of the situation resides fully with the users and/or designers of the robot. If we follow this reasoning, then the robot is not a moral agent. At best the robot is an instrument that advances the moral interests of others.

But this notion of the impact of technology on our moral reasoning is much too simplistic. If we expand our notion of technology a little, I think we can come up with an already existing technology that is much like what we are trying to create with robotics yet challenges the simple view of how technology impacts ethical and moral values. For millennia humans have been breeding dogs for human uses and if we think of technology as a manipulation of nature to human ends, we can comfortably call domesticated dogs a technology. This technology is naturally intelligent and probably has some sort of consciousness as well; furthermore, dogs can be trained to do our bidding, and in these ways, dogs are much like the robots we are striving to create. For the sake of this argument, let's look at the example of guide dogs for the visually impaired.

This technology does not comfortably fit the standard model described above. Instead of the *tool/user* model we have a complex relationship between the trainer, the guide dog, and the blind person for whom the dog is trained to help. Most of us would see the moral good of helping the visually impaired person with a loving and loyal animal expertly trained. But where should we affix the moral praise? In fact, both the trainer and the dog seem to share it. We praise the skill and sacrifice of the trainers and laud the actions of the dog as well.

An important emotional attachment is formed between all the agents in this situation but the attachment of the two human agents is strongest towards the dog and we tend to speak favorably of the relationships formed with these animals using terms identical to those used to describe healthy relationships with other humans.

The website for the organization Guide Dogs for the Blind quotes the American Veterinary Association to describe the human animal bond as:

> The human–animal bond is a mutually beneficial and dynamic relationship between people and other animals that is influenced by the behaviors that are essential to the health and well-being of both; this includes but is not limited to emotional, psychological, and physical interaction of people, other animals, and the environment.[1]

Certainly, providing guide dogs for the visually impaired is morally praiseworthy, but is a good guide dog morally praiseworthy in itself? I think so. There are two sensible ways to believe this. The least controversial is to consider things that perform their function well have a moral value equal to the moral value of the actions they facilitate. A more contentious claim is the argument that animals have their own wants, desires, and states of well-being, and this autonomy, though not as robust as that of humans, is nonetheless advanced enough to give the dog a claim for both moral rights and possibly some meagre moral responsibilities as well.

The question now is whether the robot is correctly seen as just another tool or if it is something more like the technology exemplified by the guide dog. Even at the present state of robotics technology, it is not easy to see on which side of this disjunct reality lies.

No robot in the real world, or that of the near future, is, or will be, as cognitively robust as a guide dog. But even at the modest capabilities robots have today some have more in common with the guide dog than a simple tool like a hammer.

Categories of Robotic Technologies

It is important to realize that there are currently two distinct varieties of robotics technologies that have to be distinguished in order to make sense of the attribution of moral agency to robots.

There are telerobots and there are autonomous robots. Each of these technologies has a different relationship to moral agency.

Telerobots

Telerobots are remotely controlled machines that make only minimal autonomous decisions. This is probably the most successful branch of robotics at this time since they do not need complex artificial intelligence to run; its operator provides the intelligence for the machine. The famous NASA Mars Rovers are controlled in this way, as are many deep-sea exploration robots. Telerobotic surgery will soon become a reality, as may telerobotic nurses. These machines are also beginning to see action in search and rescue as well as battlefield applications including remotely controlled weapons platforms such as the Predator drone and the SWORD, which is possibly the first robot deployed to assist infantry in a close fire support role.

Obviously, these machines are being employed in morally charged situations. With the relevant actors interacting in this way:

$$\text{Operator} \rightarrow \text{Robot} \rightarrow \text{Victim}$$

The ethical analysis of telerobots is somewhat similar to that of any technical system where the moral praise or blame is to be borne by the designers, programmers, and users of the technology. Since humans are involved in all the major decisions that the machine makes, they also provide the moral reasoning for the machine.

But, for the robot to be a moral agent, it is necessary that the machine have a significant degree of autonomous ability to reason and act on those reasons. So we will now look at machines that attempt to achieve just that.

Autonomous Robots

For the purposes of this paper, autonomous robots present a much more interesting problem. Autonomy is a notoriously thorny philosophical subject. A full discussion of the meaning of "autonomy" is not possible here, nor is it necessary, as I will argue in a later section of this paper. I use the term "autonomous robots" in the same way that roboticists use the term (see Arkin, 2009; Lin et al., 2008), and I am not trying to make any robust claims for the autonomy of robots. Simply, autonomous robots must be capable of making at least some of the major decisions about their actions using their own programming. This may be simple and not terribly interesting philosophically, such as the decisions a robot vacuum makes to decide exactly how it will navigate a floor that it is cleaning. Or, they may be much more robust and require complex moral and ethical reasoning such as when a future robotic caregiver must make a decision as to how to interact with a patient in a way that advances both the interests of the machine and the patient equitably. Or, they may be somewhere in-between these exemplar cases.

The programmers of these machines are somewhat responsible for the actions of such machines, but not entirely so. Much as one's parents are a factor, but not the exclusive cause, in one's own moral decision making. This means that the machine's programmers are not to be seen as the only locus of moral agency in robots. This leaves the robot itself as a possible location for a certain amount of moral agency. Since moral agency is found in a web of relations, other agents such as the programmers, builders, and marketers of the machines, as well as other robotic and software agents, and the users of these machines, all form a community of interaction. I am not trying to argue that robots are the only locus of moral agency in such a community, only that in certain situations they can be seen as fellow moral agents in that community.

The obvious objection here is that moral agents must be persons, and the robots of today are certainly not persons. Furthermore, this technology is unlikely to challenge our notion of personhood for some time to come. So in order to maintain the claim that robots can be moral agents I will now have to argue that personhood is not required for moral agency. To achieve that end I will first look at what others have said about this.

Philosophical Views on the Moral Agency of Robots

There are four possible views on the moral agency of robots. The first is that robots are not now moral agents but might become them in the future. Daniel Dennett supports this position and argues in his essay, "When HAL Kills, Who Is to Blame?" that a machine like the fictional HAL can be considered a murderer because the machine has mens rea, or a guilty state of mind, which includes: motivational states of purpose, cognitive states of belief, or a non-mental state of negligence (Dennett, 1998). But to be morally culpable, they also need to have "higher order intentionality," meaning that they can have beliefs about beliefs and desires about desires, beliefs about its fears about its thoughts about its hopes, and so on (1998). Dennett does not believe we have machines like that today. But he sees no reason why we might not have them in the future.

The second position one might take on this subject is that robots are incapable of becoming moral agent now or in the future. Selmer Bringsjord makes a strong stand on this position. His dispute with this claim centers on the fact that robots will never have an autonomous will since they can never do anything that they are not programmed to do (Bringsjord, 2007). Bringsjord shows this with an experiment using a robot named PERI, which his lab uses for experiments. PERI is programmed to make a decision to either drop a globe, which represents doing something morally bad, or holding on to it, which represents an action that is morally good. Whether or not PERI holds or drops the globe is decided entirely by the program it runs, which in turn was written by human programmers. Bringsjord argues that the only way PERI can do anything surprising to the programmers requires that a random factor be added to the program, but then its actions are merely determined by some random factor, not freely chosen by the machine, therefore PERI is no moral agent (Bringsjord, 2007).

There is a problem with this argument. Since we are all the products of socialization and that is a kind of programming through memes, then we are no better off than PERI. If Bringsjord is correct, then we are not moral agents either, since our beliefs, goals, and desires are not strictly autonomous, since they are the products of culture, environment, education, brain chemistry, etc. It must be the case that the philosophical requirement for robust free will, whatever that turns out to be, demanded by Bringsjord, is a red herring when it comes to moral agency. Robots may not have it, but we may not have it either, so I am reluctant to place it as a necessary condition for moral agency.

A closely related position to the above argument is held by Bernhard Irrgang who claims that, "[i]n order to be morally responsible, however, an act needs a participant, who is characterized by personality or subjectivity" (Irrgang, 2006).

As he believes it is not possible for non-cyborg robots to attain subjectivity, it is impossible for robots to be called to account for their behavior. Later I will argue that this requirement is too restrictive and that full subjectivity is not needed.

The third possible position is the view that we are not moral agents but robots are. Interestingly enough at least one person actually held this view. In a paper written a while ago but only recently published, Joseph Emile Nadeau claims that an action is a free action if and only if it is based on reasons fully thought out by the agent. He further claims that only an agent that operates on a strictly logical theorem prover can thus be truly free (Nadeau, 2006). If free will is necessary for moral agency and we as humans have no such apparatus operating in our brain, then using Nadeau's logic, we are not free agents. Robots on the other hand are programmed this way explicitly so if we built them, Nadeau believes they would be the first truly moral agents on earth (Nadeau, 2006).[2]

The fourth stance that can be held on this issue is nicely argued by Luciano Floridi and J. W. Sanders of the Information Ethics Group at the University of Oxford (2004). They argue that the way around the many apparent paradoxes in moral theory is to adopt a "mind-less morality" that evades issues like free will and intentionality since these are all unresolved issues in the philosophy of mind that are inappropriately applied to artificial agents such as robots.

They argue that we should instead see artificial entities as agents by appropriately setting levels of abstraction when analyzing the agents (2004). If we set the level of abstraction low enough we can't even ascribe agency to ourselves since the only thing an observer can see are the mechanical operations of our bodies, but at the level of abstraction common to everyday observations and judgments this is less of an issue. If an agent's actions are interactive and adaptive with their surroundings through state changes or programming that is still somewhat independent from the environment the agent finds itself in, then that is sufficient for the entity to have its own agency (2004). When these autonomous interactions pass a threshold of tolerance and cause harm we can logically ascribe a negative moral value to them; likewise the agents can hold a certain appropriate level of moral consideration themselves, in much the same way that one may argue for the moral status of animals, environments, or even legal entities such as corporations (Floridi and Sanders, paraphrased in Sullins, 2005).

My views build on the fourth position and I will now argue for the moral agency of robots, even at the humble level of autonomous robotics technology today.

The Three Requirements of Robotic Moral Agency

In order to evaluate the moral status of any autonomous robotic technology, one needs to ask three questions of the technology under consideration:

- Is the robot significantly autonomous?
- Is the robot's behavior intentional?
- Is the robot in a position of responsibility?

These questions have to be viewed from a reasonable level of abstraction, but if the answer is "yes" to all three, then the robot is a moral agent.

Autonomy

The first question asks if the robot could be seen as significantly autonomous from any programmers, operators, and users of the machine. I realize that "autonomy" is a difficult concept to pin down philosophically. I am not suggesting that robots of any sort will have radical autonomy; in fact I seriously doubt human beings have that quality. I mean to use the term "autonomy," in the engineering sense implying that the machine is not under the direct control of any other agent or user. The robot must not be a telerobot or be temporarily behaving as one. If the robot does have this level of autonomy, then the robot has a practical independent agency. If this autonomous action is effective in achieving the goals and tasks of the robot, then we can say the robot has effective autonomy. The more effective autonomy the machine has, meaning the more adept it is in achieving its goals and tasks, then the more agency we can ascribe to it. When that agency[3] causes harm or good in a moral sense, we can say the machine has moral agency.

Autonomy as described is not sufficient in itself to ascribe moral agency. Thus entities such as bacteria, or animals, ecosystems, computer viruses, simple artificial life programs, or simple autonomous robots, all of which exhibit autonomy as I have described it, are not to be seen as responsible moral agents simply on account of possessing this quality. They may very credibly be argued to be agents worthy of moral consideration, but if they lack the other two requirements argued for next, they are not robust moral agents for whom we can credibly demand moral rights and responsibilities equivalent to those claimed by capable human adults.

It might be the case that the machine is operating in concert with a number of other machines or software entities. When that is the case we simply raise the level of abstraction to that of the group and ask the same questions of the group. If the group is an autonomous entity, then the moral praise or blame is ascribed at that level. We should do this in a way similar to what we do when describing the moral agency of groups of humans acting in concert.

Intentionality

The second question addresses the ability of the machine to act "intentionally." Remember, we do not have to prove the robot has intentionality in the strongest sense, as that is impossible to prove without argument for humans as well. As long as the behavior is complex enough that one is forced to rely on standard folk psychological notions of predisposition or "intention" to do good or harm, then this is enough to answer in the affirmative to this question. If the complex interaction of the robot's programming and environment causes the machine to act in a way that is morally harmful or beneficial, and the actions are seemingly deliberate and calculated, then the machine is a moral agent.

There is no requirement that the actions really are intentional in a philosophically rigorous way, nor that the actions are derived from a will that is free on all levels of abstraction. All that is needed is that, at the level of the interaction between the agents involved, there is a comparable level of personal intentionality and free will between all the agents involved.

Responsibility

Finally, we can ascribe moral agency to a robot when the robot behaves in such a way that we can only make sense of that behavior by assuming it has a responsibility to some other moral agent(s).

If the robot behaves in this way and it fulfills some social role that carries with it some assumed responsibilities, and only way we can make sense of its behavior is to ascribe to it the "belief" that it has the duty to care for its patients, then we can ascribe to this machine the status of a moral agent.

Again, the beliefs do not have to be real beliefs; they can be merely apparent. The machine may have no claim to consciousness, for instance, or a soul, a mind, or any of the other somewhat philosophically dubious entities we ascribe to human specialness. These beliefs, or programs, just have to be motivational in solving moral questions and conundrums faced by the machine.

For example, robotic caregivers are being designed to assist in the care of the elderly. Certainly a human nurse is a moral agent. When and if a [nurse-like] machine carries out those same duties, it will be a moral agent, if it is autonomous as described above, behaves in an intentional way, and whose programming is complex enough that it understands its role in the responsibility of the health care system that it is operating in towards the patient under its direct care.

This would be quite a machine and not something that is currently on offer. Any machine with less capability would not be a full moral agent, though it may still have autonomous agency and intentionality; these qualities would make it deserving of moral consideration, meaning that one would have to have a good reason to destroy it or inhibit its actions, but we would not be required to treat it as a moral equal and any attempt by humans who might employ these lesser capable machines as if they were fully moral agents should be avoided.

Some critics of this position have argued that my position "unnecessarily complicates the issue of responsibility assignment for immoral actions" (Arkin, 2007, p. 10). But I would counter that it is going to be some time before we meet mechanical entities that we recognize as moral equals but we have to be very careful that we pay attention to how these machines are evolving and grant that status the moment it is deserved. Long before that day, though, complex robot agents will be partially capable of making autonomous moral decisions and these machines will present vexing problems. Especially when machines are used in police work and warfare where they will have to make decisions that could result in tragedies. Here we will have to treat the machines the way we might do for trained animals such as guard dogs. The decision to own and operate them is the most significant moral question and the majority of the praise or blame for the actions of such machines belongs to the owners and operators of these robots.

Conversely, it is logically possible, though not probable in the near term, that robotic moral agents may be more autonomous, have clearer intentions, and a more nuanced sense of responsibility than most human agents. In that case this moral status may exceed our own. How could this happen? The philosopher Eric Dietrich argues that as we are more and more able to mimic the human mind computationally, we need simply forgo programming the nasty tendencies evolution has given us and instead implement "only those that tend to produce the grandeur of humanity[;] we will have produced the better robots of our nature and made the world a better place" (Dietrich, 2001).

There are further extensions of this argument that are possible. Non-robotic systems such as software "bots" are directly implicated, as is the moral status of corporations. It is also obvious that these arguments could be easily applied to the questions regarding the moral status of animals and environments. As I argued earlier, domestic and farmyard animals are the closest technology we have to what we dream robots will be like. So these findings have real world applications outside robotics to animal welfare and rights, but I will leave that argument for a future paper.

Conclusions

Robots are moral agents when there is a reasonable level of abstraction under which we must grant that the machine has autonomous intentions and responsibilities. If the robot can be seen as autonomous from many points of view, then the machine is a robust moral agent, possibly approaching or exceeding the moral status of human beings.

Thus it is certain that if we pursue this technology, then future highly complex interactive robots will be moral agents with the corresponding rights and responsibilities, but even the modest robots of today can be seen to be moral agents of a sort under certain, but not all, levels of abstraction and are deserving of moral consideration.

Notes

1 Retrieved from the website Guide Dogs for the Blind: www.guidedogs.com/about-mission.html#Bond.
2 One could counter this argument from a computationalist standpoint by acknowleding that it is unlikely we have a theorem prover in our biological brain, but in the virtual machine formed by our mind, anyone trained in logic most certainly does have a theorem prover of sorts, meaning that there are at least some human moral agents.
3 Meaning: self-motivated, goal-driven behavior.

References

Arkin, Ronald (2007): Governing Lethal Behavior: Embedding Ethics in a Hybrid Deliberative/Reactive Robot Architecture, U.S. Army Research Office Technical Report GIT-GVU-07-11. Retrieved from: www.cc.gatech.edu/ai/robot-lab/onlinepublications/formalizationv35.pdf.
Arkin, Ronald (2009): *Governing Lethal Behavior in Autonomous Robots*, Chapman & Hall/CRC.
Bringsjord, Selmer (2007): *Ethical Robots: The Future Can Heed Us*, AI and Society (online).
Dennett, Daniel (1998): When HAL Kills, Who's to Blame? Computer Ethics. In: Stork, David, eds. *HAL's Legacy: 2001's Computer as Dream and Reality*, MIT Press.
Dietrich, Eric (2001): Homo Sapiens 2.0: Why We Should Build the Better Robots of Our Nature. *Journal of Experimental and Theoretical Artificial Intelligence*, Volume 13, Issue 4, pp. 323–328.
Floridi, Luciano and Sanders, J. W. (2004): On the Morality of Artificial Agents. *Minds and Machines*, Volume 14, Issue 3, pp. 349–379.
Irrgang, Bernhard (2006): Ethical Acts in Robotics. *Ubiquity*, Volume 7, Issue 34 (September 5, 2006–September 11, 2006). www.acm.org/ubiquity.

Lin, Patrick, Bekey, George, and Abney, Keith (2008): Autonomous Military Robotics: Risk, Ethics, and Design, US Department of Navy, Office of Naval Research, Retrieved from: http://ethics.calpoly.edu/ONR_report.pdf.

Nadeau, Joseph Emile (2006): Only Androids Can Be Ethical. In: Ford, Kenneth, and Glymour, Clark, eds. *Thinking about Android Epistemology*, MIT Press, pp. 241–248.

Sullins, John (2005): Ethics and Artificial Life: From Modeling to Moral Agents. *Ethics and Information Technology*, Volume 7, pp. 139–148.

Review and Discussion Questions

1 What is the thesis of Sullins's essay?
2 What is his distinction between a telerobot and an autonomous robot?
3 Sullins believes that comparing autonomous robots to guide dogs is a revealing analogy. Do you agree? What is the point of the analogy?
4 What are the four views on the moral agency of robots that Sullins discusses?
5 What are Sullins's three requirements of robotic moral agency? How do you assess this discussion?

READING: AUTONOMOUS MACHINES, MORAL JUDGMENT, AND ACTING FOR THE RIGHT REASONS

DUNCAN PURVES, RYAN JENKINS, AND BRADLEY J. STRAWSER[*]

The authors argue against the development of weapons that can make targeting decisions of life and death "on their own." They argue that machines lack the capacities for moral judgments and acting for the right reasons. Duncan Purves is Assistant Professor of Philosophy at the University of Florida. Ryan Jenkins is Assistant Professor of Philosophy at California Polytechnic State University at San Luis Obispo. Bradley J. Strawser is Associate Professor of Philosophy in the Defense Analysis Department at the Naval Postgraduate School.

Modern weapons of war have undergone precipitous technological change over the past generation and the future portends even greater advances. Of particular interest are so-called "autonomous weapon systems" (henceforth, AWS), that will someday purportedly have the ability to make life and death targeting decisions "on their own." Many have strong moral intuitions against such weapons, and public concern over AWS is growing. A coalition of several non-governmental organizations, for example, has raised the alarm through their highly publicized "Campaign to Stop Killer Robots" in an effort to enact an international ban on fully autonomous weapons. Despite the strong and widespread sentiments against such weapons, however, proffered philosophical arguments against AWS are often found lacking in substance.

---

[*] Abridged from "Autonomous Machines, Moral Judgment, and Acting for the Right Reasons" by Duncan Purves, Ryan Jenkins, and Bradley J. Strawser, *Ethical Theory and Moral Practice* 18 (2015): 851–872. Reprinted by permission of Springer Science and Media. Footnotes omitted.

We propose that the prevalent moral aversion to AWS is supported by a pair of compelling objections. First, we argue that even a sophisticated robot is not the kind of thing that is capable of replicating human moral judgment. This conclusion follows if human moral judgment is not codifiable, i.e., it cannot be captured by a list of rules. Moral judgment requires either the ability to engage in wide reflective equilibrium, the ability to perceive certain facts *as* moral considerations, moral imagination, or the ability to have moral experiences with a particular phenomenological character. Robots cannot in principle possess these abilities, so robots cannot in principle replicate human moral judgment. If robots cannot in principle replicate human moral judgment then it is morally problematic to deploy AWS with that aim in mind. Second, we then argue that even if it is possible for a sufficiently sophisticated robot to make "moral decisions" that are extensionally indistinguishable from (or better than) human moral decisions, these "decisions" could not be made for the right reasons. This means that the "moral decisions" made by AWS are bound to be morally deficient in at least one respect even if they are extensionally indistinguishable from human ones. ...

There are several reasons philosophers accept that the exercise of moral judgment is necessary for proper moral decision making. For example, many philosophers deny that moral principles are codifiable. The *codifiability thesis* is the claim that the true moral theory could be captured in universal rules that the morally uneducated person could competently apply in any situation. The *anti-codifiability thesis* is simply the denial of this claim, which entails that some moral judgment on the part of the agent is necessary. The *locus classicus* of this view is McDowell (1979). There, McDowell introduces the anti-codifiability thesis when arguing against an impoverished view of the moral deliberation of a virtuous agent. (The details of the view he is criticizing need not worry us.) He writes:

> This picture fits only if the virtuous person's views about how, in general, one should behave are susceptible of codification, in principles apt for serving as major premises in syllogisms of the sort envisaged. But to an unprejudiced eye *it should seem quite implausible that any reasonably adult moral outlook admits of any such codification.* As Aristotle consistently says, the best generalizations about how one should behave hold only for the most part. If one attempted to reduce one's conception of what virtue requires to a set of rules, then, however subtle and thoughtful one was in drawing up the code, cases would inevitably turn up in which a mechanical application of the rules would strike one as wrong ....
>
> (1979: 336, emphasis added)

.... We wish to remain agnostic on the particular species of judgment that is required to successfully follow the true moral theory. It may be that the exercise of moral judgment has a necessary phenomenal character or "what-it's-like." It could be that successfully following the true moral theory requires a kind of practical wisdom. It could be that a kind of wide reflective equilibrium is needed, which requires us to strike the right balance between general moral principles and our moral intuitions. All that is required for our argument against AWS is that one of these accounts of moral judgment, or something similar, offers the right picture of moral judgment.

Second, whatever the kind of moral judgment that is required to successfully follow the true moral theory, an artificial intelligence will never be able to replicate it. However artificial intelligence is created, it must be the product of a discrete list of instructions provided by humans. There is thus no way for artificial intelligence to replicate human moral judgment, given our first premise....

Furthermore, take the possible requirements of moral judgment considered above: phenomenal quality, phronesis, and wide reflective equilibrium. Only a minority of philosophers of mind believe that AI could have phenomenal consciousness—most are skeptical or uncommitted. If AI cannot be conscious in this way, and if this kind of consciousness is what moral judgment requires, then AI will never be able to engage in moral judgment. ...

Hence, we could never trust an artificial intelligence to make a moral decision, and so we should expect them to make significant moral mistakes. For example, it would be far easier to make AI carry out immoral or criminal orders than it is to get human soldiers to carry out such orders. If an AWS cannot make moral judgments, they cannot resist an immoral order in the way that a human soldier might, because they are incapable of evaluating the deontic status of the order. It is not just that an AWS would be more prone to making moral mistakes. Rather, we argue, they could not in principle discern the correct answer. Unless the true moral theory is codifiable, artificial intelligence can never be trusted to make sound moral decisions. [The authors survey some initial responses and objections and then continue their discussion as follows—Ed. note]

.... what if the anti-codifiability thesis is false? What if computers could become as good as or better than humans at making moral decisions or, indeed, could become perfect at making moral decisions? ....

[However, o]ur second objection to the deployment of AWS supposes that AI could become as good as or better than humans at making moral decisions, but contends that their decisions would be morally deficient in the following respect: they could not be made for the *right reasons*. ...

To help make this point, consider the following case, Racist Soldier.

> Imagine a racist man who viscerally hates all people of a certain ethnicity and longs to murder them, but he knows he would not be able to get away with this under normal conditions. It then comes about that the nation-state of which this man is a citizen has a just cause for war: they are defending themselves from invasion by an aggressive, neighboring state. It so happens that this invading state's population is primarily composed of the ethnicity that the racist man hates. The racist man joins the army and eagerly goes to war, where he proceeds to kill scores of enemy soldiers of the ethnicity he so hates. Assume that he abides by the *jus in bello* rules of combatant distinction and proportionality, yet not for moral reasons. Rather, the reason for every enemy soldier he kills is his vile, racist intent.

We contend that it would be wrong to deploy the Racist Soldier, other things being equal, knowing his racist tendencies and desires. That is, if we had a choice between deploying either Racist Soldier or another soldier who would not kill for such reasons, and both would accomplish the military objective, we would have a strong moral reason to choose the non-racist soldier. The likely explanation for this is that, while Racist Soldier abides by the constraints of *jus in bello*, he is *acting for the wrong reasons*. We believe this judgment can be extended to AWS. Just as it would be wrong to deploy the Racist Soldier, it would be wrong to deploy AWS to the theater of war because AWS would not be acting for the right reasons in making decisions about life and death. ...

AI mimics human moral behavior, but cannot take a moral consideration such as a child's suffering to be a reason for acting. AI cannot be *motivated* to act morally; it simply manifests an automated response which is entirely determined by the list of rules that it is programmed to follow. Therefore, AI cannot act *for* reasons, in this sense. Because AI cannot act for reasons, it cannot act for the *right* reasons.

One may here object that *Racist Soldier* shows only that it is wrong to act for the *wrong* reasons. It does not establish the positive claim, asserted above, that there is something morally problematic about *failing* to act for the *right* reasons. As we have just suggested, it is not the case that the AI is acting for the wrong reasons (as the racist soldier is), but rather the AI is not acting for any reasons *at all*. This means that if our argument against the deployment of AI is to work, we must establish the positive claim that failing to act for the right reasons is morally problematic as well.

In response, consider a modified version of *Racist Soldier* above, *Sociopathic Soldier*.

> Imagine a sociopath who is completely unmoved by the harm he causes to other people. He is not a sadist; he does not derive pleasure from harming others. He simply does not take the fact that an act would harm someone as a reason against performing the act. In other words, he is incapable of acting for moral reasons. It then comes about that the nation-state of which this man is a citizen has a just cause for war: they are defending themselves from invasion by an aggressive, neighboring state. It so happens that the man joins the army (perhaps due to a love of following orders) and eagerly goes to war, where he proceeds to kill scores of enemy soldiers without any recognition that their suffering is morally bad. He is effective precisely because he is unmoved by the harm that he causes and because he is good at following direct orders. Assume that he abides by the classic *jus in bello* rules of combatant distinction and proportionality, yet not for moral reasons. No, the sociopathic soldier is able to operate effectively in combat precisely because of his *inability* to act for moral reasons.

Most who think it would be morally problematic to deploy the racist soldier in virtue of the fact that he would be acting for the *wrong* reasons will also think it would be clearly morally problematic to deploy the sociopathic soldier over a non-sociopathic soldier. If there is a moral problem with deploying the sociopathic soldier, however, it is most plausibly derived from the fact that he would *fail* to act for the *right* reasons. But we have already established that AWS cannot, in principle, act *for* reasons in the relevant sense, and thus that they cannot act for the right reasons. The actions performed by AWS in war will therefore be morally problematic in the same way as the sociopath soldier: neither of them acts for the right reasons in killing enemy combatants. ...

We appreciate that the application of the criterion of right intention to soldiers engaged *in war* might seem out of place in the just war tradition. However, this would overlook the views of prominent early members of the tradition, such as Augustine and Aquinas, who take the intentions of combatants to be relevant to the justice of resorting to war. Augustine enumerates the "real evils of war" as

> love of violence, revengeful cruelty, fierce and implacable enmity, wild resistance, and the lust of power, and such like ... it is generally to punish these things, when force is required to inflict the punishment, that, in obedience to God or some lawful authority, good men undertake wars ....
>
> (1887: n.p.)

.... Prominent contemporary just war theorists have agreed. Thomas Nagel (1972: 139), Robert Sparrow (2007: 67–68), and Peter Asaro (2012) have acknowledged the plausibility of this view—with roots in the historical just war tradition—that intentions matter morally not just for policymakers *ad bellum* but for soldiers *in bello* as well. ...

We close this section by acknowledging important limitations of the above argument—and perhaps any argument—against AWS. We have only attempted to show that there is something seriously morally deficient about the way that AWS go about making decisions about ending human lives. In other words, we have defended the existence of a powerful *pro tanto* moral reason not to deploy AWS in war. We have not shown that this reason is *decisive* in the face of all countervailing moral considerations. For example, if deploying AWS in a particular conflict can be expected to reduce civilian casualties from 10,000 to 1000, this consideration might very well override the fact that AWS would not act for the right reasons in achieving this morally desirable result. Indeed, if AWS prove to be sufficiently superior to traditional armed forces at achieving morally desirable aims in war, then there may not be *any* moral objection strong enough to render their deployment morally impermissible. Still, until we are confident in such a marked superiority, we consider this *pro tanto* reason to pose a significant obstacle to their deployment.

Non-Weaponized Autonomous Technology

Any account of the permissibility of autonomous weapons systems will risk prohibiting the use of autonomous decision-making technologies that most people view as neutral or morally good. While many of us tend to have a significant moral aversion to the thought of autonomous weapon systems, most have no such similar moral aversion to non-weaponized autonomous systems such as driverless cars. In fact, for many people, the opposite is true: many of us hold that non-weaponized future autonomous technology holds the potential for great good in the world. While the prospect of driverless cars raises interesting ethical challenges of its own, virtually no one is inclined to posit that driverless cars are on the same shaky moral ground as autonomous weapons. Yet this—lumping driverless cars and AWS together—seems to follow from all the contingent and responsibility-based objections to AWS currently on offer. Thus we have to be careful not to throw out the baby with the bathwater. ...

Our response is twofold. First, AWS are designed with the *purpose* of making moral decisions about human life and death, whereas driverless cars are intended for a wholly different (and peaceful) purpose. If they should end up making moral decisions about life and death, it is merely foreseen but not intended. Return to the racist soldier case. Only suppose that, instead of deploying Racist Soldier to the front lines of combat where we know he will encounter (and kill) members of the group he hates, we deploy him to a different front where his exposure to members of the group he hates is very unlikely. This seems morally acceptable even if there is a small chance that he will still encounter and kill a member of that group in this different front, despite our efforts to avoid this result. Were this to happen, it would be regrettable, but this circumstance would have been merely foreseen but not intended. Morally, we have made a very different—and less worrisome— choice than if we had purposefully put him somewhere with the intention that he kill people.

Though the moral significance of the distinction between intending and foreseeing is firmly entrenched in just war theory, its moral significance is controversial among contemporary ethicists. Our second reply rests on less controversial ground. Notice that AWS will, as a matter of fact, constantly make life-and-death decisions regarding humans, if they are doing their job. That is, the probability of AWS making life-and-death moral decisions is very high given that the capacity to make such decisions is the explicit reason for which they are deployed and put into use. These decisions can be expected to be radically less common with driverless cars, since that is not the reason they would be put into use. ...

Unlike AWS, driverless cars, and some forms of autonomous missile defense systems, are not deployed with the intention that they will make life-and-death decisions. Nor are they nearly as *likely* as AWS to need to make life-and-death decisions. We find these two responses to be at least partially satisfying in conjunction. Even if the responses fail to maintain a hard moral distinction between weaponized and non-weaponized AWS, however, we are not ultimately concerned about our argument ruling out driverless cars and other autonomous systems. We ought to meet a high bar before deploying artificial intelligences of any kind that could make morally serious decisions—especially those concerning life and death. It is plausible that no autonomous system could meet this bar.

Conclusion

Imagining a future of autonomous weapons like those we describe above poses other challenges. Suppose autonomous weapons become genuine moral decision makers, i.e., they become agents. If all agents—even artificially intelligent ones— have equal moral worth, then a strong motivation for deploying AWS in place of human soldiers, i.e., the preservation of morally important life, becomes moot.

Suppose, as many virtue theorists do, that acting for the right reasons is a necessary constituent of a good life. If, as we maintain, AWS and other AI cannot act for the right reasons, then bringing them into existence would mean bringing into existence an agent while denying it the possibility of a good life.

There is also a *Meno* problem for moral machines. A sufficiently advanced artificial intelligence could seem radically alien, and have an equally exotic conscience. Intelligent machines whose moral decisions differ from ours could seem to some to be moral monsters and to others to be moral saints. Judging which of these appraisals is correct will be challenging, but it could well determine the future of the human race.

Suppose this problem is less threatening than it seems and that autonomous weapons eventually become *much better* than humans at making moral decisions. Wouldn't it then—obviously—become obligatory to actually *surrender* our moral decision making to AI? This would include not merely decisions made *in* war, but decisions over whether to go to war. Why should we have human parliaments and congresses, so notoriously bad at making moral decisions, when we could have the AI make such decisions for us? And, at that point, it's worth asking: why stop at employing AWS in times of war? Indeed, some will think that decisions made about healthcare policies or economic distribution and the like are morally more important than even decisions about war, as it is possible that significantly more people are affected by such actions. Why stop there? Rather, we could be obligated to "outsource" *all* of our morally important decisions to AI, even personal ones such as decisions about where to live, what career to pursue, whom to marry, and so forth. After all, all of these decisions can easily have consequences that are morally significant. Some people, of course, will be perfectly happy with such a vision. Others confess a deep-seated discomfort with the idea; a discomfort the source of which we have been at pains to investigate. Whatever that reason is that counts against us surrendering all of our moral autonomy to AI, it also counts against us deploying AWS.

It could be that we are uncomfortable with AWS making decisions so easily, in the same way we are uncomfortable with deploying the psychopathic soldier, even supposing he performs all the right actions. We regard with great pity those who have their autonomy co-opted by or outsourced to someone else, since we view autonomy as a supremely important good for humans. There is something truly disturbing about someone whose life is entirely determined by decisions that are outside of his immediate control. Could we be obligated to enter this pitiable state? If we are resistant, it could be that we ultimately believe that grappling with difficult moral issues is one of the things that gives human life meaning.

References

Asaro, P. (2012) On Banning Autonomous Weapon Systems: Human Rights, Automation, and the Dehumanization of Lethal Decision-Making. *International Review of the Red Cross* 94(886): 687–709.
Augustine (1887) Contra Faustum Manichaeum. In: Schaff (ed.) *From Nicene and Post-Nicene Fathers*, first series, vol. 4. Christian Literature Publishing Co, Buffalo.
McDowell, J. (1979) Virtue and Reason. *Monist* 62(3): 331–350.
Nagel, T. (1972) War and Massacre. *Philosophy & Public Affairs* 1(2): 123–144.
Sparrow, R. (2007) Killer Robots. *Journal of Applied Philosophy* 24(1): 62–77.

Review and Discussion Questions

1 What is the anti-codifiability thesis? If this thesis is true, why would it be impossible for machines to replicate moral judgment?
2 What is required to make sound moral judgments, in your view? If it is something more than accurately applying the correct set of rules, what is that capacity?

3 What do the examples of the "Racist Soldier" and "Sociopathic Soldier" show, according to the authors?
4 Do soldiers' intentions matter in the conduct of war from a moral point of view?
5 Do the authors' arguments imply that driverless cars should be prohibited? How do they respond to this question? Do you agree with their analysis?
6 How do the authors end their essay? If autonomous machines are morally responsible agents, then what? Is Sullins likely to agree or disagree with that analysis?

READING: WEAPONS, SECURITY, AND OPPRESSION: A NORMATIVE STUDY OF INTERNATIONAL ARMS TRANSFERS

JAMES CHRISTENSEN[*]

James Christensen considers whether all arms trade ought to be prohibited and argues instead that states can legitimately sell and transfer arms to other states. He argues, however, that this practice has important moral limitations. James Christensen is Lecturer in Political Theory at the University of Essex, United Kingdom.

Since the terrorist attacks of September 11, 2001, the US government has drastically ramped up arms sales to oppressive regimes regarded as valuable allies in the "war on terror", and in the years since the Arab Spring large quantities of weapons have been transferred to rebel groups seeking to topple despotic rulers. It is thus important to question whether such transfers can be justified. ...

I

It is natural to feel instinctively uneasy about the existence of markets in weapons, and some activists call for the arms trade to be completely abolished. While this stance is, perhaps, understandable, it is, I think, ultimately misguided: an ethically defensible arms trade is possible. The first step in my argument for this claim is to note that all persons have a right to security, or, perhaps more accurately, that all persons have a cluster of security rights: rights not to be assaulted, tortured, raped, killed, and so forth. In short, all persons have a right to *physical safety* .... The right to security generates a variety of correlative duties. For now, notice that it puts states under a duty to protect the security of their citizens. The next important step in the argument is to point out that, in order to discharge this duty, states need weapons (or at least that in all realistically imaginable scenarios they need weapons). Without weapons, states would be unable to protect their citizens from armed aggressors (armed criminals, terrorist groups, belligerent regimes, etc.).

---

[*] Abridged from "Weapons, Security, and Oppression: A Normative Study of International Arms Transfers" by James Christensen, *Journal of Political Philosophy* 23(1) (2015): 23–39. Reprinted by permission of Wiley-Blackwell. Some footnotes omitted.

Weapons enable states to both deter and repel such threats, and thus to protect their citizens' security.

It might be said that, in theory, states could protect their citizens' right to security not by acquiring weapons with which to deter and repel armed aggressors, but rather by bringing about the worldwide abolition of weapons. There are multiple reasons for dismissing this claim. First, and most obviously, bringing about the worldwide abolition of weapons is not an option that is realistically available to states. Second, even if states agreed to mutual disarmament, there would always be the very real possibility that certain states would secretly retain their arsenals. And, third, even if mutual disarmament was achieved at time T, there would always be the very real possibility that certain states would (perhaps secretly) rearm at time T + n. When a state disarms, it leaves itself and its citizens vulnerable, even if other states have also agreed to disarm.

Now, some states lack the capacity to produce their own weapons, or at least to produce weapons of adequate quality and in sufficient quantities. Consequently, in order to acquire weapons of adequate quality and in sufficient quantities, and to discharge their duty to protect the safety of their citizens, such states must import weapons from abroad. If these states were unable to import weapons—if no international trade in weapons was permitted—they would not be able to ensure the security of their citizens. Blocking all international arms transfers would penalize states which lack the capacity to produce their own weapons, and unjustifiably jeopardize the security of the people who live in those states. ...

For most of the 20th century, the largest arms exporters mainly sold weapons to other economically developed countries, most of which, by virtue of being economically developed, presumably either possessed or could acquire the capacity to produce weapons of adequate quality and in sufficient quantities.[1] The argument presented above does not explicitly vindicate these kinds of transfers, but it does provide the resources needed to do so. It establishes that weapons have a legitimate function, namely, they enable states to discharge their duty to protect the security of their citizens. And if weapons have a legitimate function, it is hard to see why trade in weapons would only be morally permissible when it consists in transfers to states which lack the capacity to produce weapons of their own. If a state possesses the capacity to produce its own weapons, but has a comparative disadvantage in weapons manufacturing, it makes sense for that state to purchase weapons from abroad and to devote the resources it would have otherwise used to manufacture weapons to alternative lines of production. ...

The arms trade, then, can be justified by appeal to the right to security. States are permitted to purchase weapons either because doing so is (i) necessary to protect their citizens' security, or (ii) the most efficient way of protecting their citizens' security. And in order for a state to be able to purchase weapons, others must be permitted to sell weapons. ...

So far, I have defended the moral permissibility of (a form of) the arms trade by appealing to the value of security. But that same value can be used to identify moral limits to the arms trade .... All weapons are designed to incapacitate, injure, or kill, and so all weapons pose a threat to individuals' physical safety. But some weapons pose an unacceptably large threat to individuals who have not made themselves liable to attack, and who are thus not permissible targets. Paradigmatic examples of such weapons include land mines and nerve gas, both of which kill and maim indiscriminately. These weapons pose a threat which is either spatially- or temporally-extended to an unusual and excessive degree. Nerve gas generates harms which are highly diffuse; it can travel large distances and kill non-combatants far from the battlefield. The threat posed by landmines has a shorter range, but extends far into the future: people continue to be killed and dismembered by unexploded mines long after hostilities have ceased. Ammunition containing depleted uranium, which was used extensively by British and US forces in Iraq and the Balkans, also potentially falls into this category. Upon impact, depleted uranium shells release radioactive particles which are potentially cancer-causing, persist in the environment for decades, and can travel far from the site where they were originally released.[2] ...

Let us now consider limits imposed by the right to security on the range of appropriate recipients of arms transfers. ... Some states ... behave in an aggressive and provocative manner, waging unjust wars, arming militant groups attempting to overthrow legitimate governments, and supplying weapons to terrorist organizations. Sometimes they engage in terroristic activity themselves.[3]

Some states violate the security rights of their own citizens. Some fail to provide an adequate degree of security, while others actively deprive their citizens of their security. Their police and military forces kill unarmed protesters, torture dissidents, beat prisoners, rape civilians, and engage in various other violent crimes. For many individuals, the very agent that is duty-bound to protect them represents the primary threat to their security. ...

When a state arms such regimes it facilitates, and thus becomes complicit in, those regimes' crimes. States are therefore morally required to refrain from arming such regimes. ... The proposition is, I think, intuitive enough, but it is vulnerable to a number of objections. I will focus on defending the claim that states must refrain from selling (and must prevent their citizens from selling) weapons to regimes which oppress their own citizens, but most of what I say also applies to states which aggress against other countries.

II

The claim that states must refrain from arming oppressive regimes can be resisted in the following manner. ... [S]tates can sometimes enhance the security of their citizens by providing weapons to oppressive regimes, because such regimes are sometimes willing to contribute to the suppression of terrorist threats. When states can enhance the security of their citizens in this way, they are duty-bound to transfer arms to oppressive regimes.

This argument can be used to defend recent US foreign policy decisions. Since the terrorist attacks of September 11, 2001, the US has increased arms supplies to a variety of oppressive regimes on the grounds that those regimes, if well equipped, can play a valuable role in the "war on terror", and thereby positively contribute to the security of US citizens. ... I will identify four problems which the claim faces.

The first problem the argument encounters concerns its empirical claim that states can enhance the security of their citizens—and, more specifically, reduce the threat they face from terrorism—by arming certain oppressive regimes. In a recent discussion of trade-offs between security and liberty, Jeremy Waldron argues that those who recommend curtailing civil liberties in order to reduce the threat to security posed by terrorist organizations must show that the curtailments they propose will actually have a positive impact upon security.[4]... This will not be easy.

A second problem concerns the argument's normative claim that states have a duty to arm oppressive regimes when doing so enhances the security of their citizens. This claim is problematic because the right to security is not plausibly conceived of as a right to be *maximally* secure. ... To illustrate this point, consider the duties imposed upon a mother by her child's right to security. The mother may be able to enhance her child's security by hiring a guard to patrol the perimeter of their house; hiring a security guard might reduce the probability that a dangerous intruder will break in and pose a threat to the child. Moreover, hiring a security guard might not be financially burdensome (suppose the mother is quite wealthy), and we can stipulate that hiring a security guard would not violate anyone's rights (or wrong anyone in any other way). Still, provided that the probability of a house invasion is already low—suppose the mother and child live in a reasonably safe neighbourhood, and other reasonable security precautions are taken (an intruder alarm has been installed, doors and windows are locked at night, etc.)—it just does not seem plausible to claim that the child's right imposes upon her mother a *duty* to hire a security guard. By hiring a security guard the mother goes *beyond* the call of duty; she provides her child with more than the *adequate* degree of security to which her child is entitled. The upshot of these considerations is this: in order to show that the right to security imposes upon states a duty to transfer arms to oppressive regimes, it is not sufficient to show that such transfers will have a positive impact on security; rather, what must be shown is that arming oppressive regimes will ensure that people enjoy the adequate degree of security that the right to security is a right to. ...

A third problem is that, in order to vindicate the provision of weapons to oppressive regimes, it must be shown that there are not acceptable alternative methods for generating the extra security which such provision offers. Given that states have at their disposal a wide variety of strategies for protecting their citizens from terrorist attacks, many of which appear less morally problematic than arming oppressive regimes, it is incumbent upon proponents of the latter option to explain why the available alternatives are unacceptable or insufficient.

The final problem is also the most serious. ... This duty is not plausibly conceived of as a duty to provide the relevant quantity of security *whatever it takes*, but rather as a duty to provide that quantity of security *if and when it can be provided through morally permissible means*.

Consider an analogy. Suppose I am expected to attend a close friend's wedding, and that, on the way to the ceremony, I get caught in a traffic jam. As a result of the delay, I can only get to the wedding on time by driving at dangerously high speeds and running red lights. Clearly I am not permitted to drive at dangerously high speeds and run red lights. The set of options morally available to me is not expanded by the fact that the normal option set is too restrictive to enable me to get to the wedding on time. Moreover, provided that I allowed myself a reasonable amount of time to travel to the wedding, and that the traffic jam could not have reasonably been foreseen, I think we should deny that by arriving late to the wedding I have violated a duty to my friend. If I had a duty to be on time, then clearly my late arrival would constitute a violation of that duty. But we should deny that

I had such a duty, and say instead that I had a duty to *pursue a morally permissible course of action which could reasonably be expected to get me to the wedding on time*. (When we say that one has a duty to be on time to a friend's wedding, it is, I suggest, this more nuanced duty that we actually have in mind. The shorter phrase is convenient shorthand.) I would violate that duty if I carelessly failed to leave myself enough time to travel to the wedding, or if I chose to take a particular route in the knowledge that there were likely to be delays along that route, and was late as a result. But I would also violate that duty if, after being innocently delayed by a traffic jam which I could not have reasonably anticipated, I proceeded to drive at dangerously high speeds and run red lights, thereby recklessly endangering other motorists and pedestrians. Similarly, by arming oppressive regimes a state violates its duty to provide a particular quantity of security if and when that quantity can be provided through morally permissible means.

Now, it might be objected that, in the case I described, driving dangerously fast and running red lights is impermissible because the harms it inflicts (including risks) are disproportionate to the harms I was trying to avoid (the disappointment my friend would feel if I missed his wedding). But, it might be argued, dangerous driving would be permissible in a case in which the harms (including risks) it inflicts were proportional to the harms the driver sought to prevent. Suppose there is a man in my car who will die unless he receives immediate medical attention. In such a scenario, it seems that I would be morally permitted to drive in a manner which imposes upon other motorists and pedestrians a degree of risk that is higher than that which could permissibly be imposed in less exceptional circumstances. Analogously, it might be argued, it is permissible for a state to inflict the harms associated with arming an oppressive regime when those harms are proportional to the expected harms it seeks to prevent befalling its own citizens, and the harms the US inflicts, or contributes to inflicting, when it arms oppressive regimes are proportional to the expected harms it seeks to prevent—namely, the harms which its citizens would suffer if they fell victim to a terrorist attack.

I do not find this argument convincing. ... Consider a child who will die unless she receives a heart transplant. If the child's mother kills someone in order to give that person's heart to her child, the harms she inflicts are proportional to the harms she aims to prevent. But no one would think it anything but obvious that the mother acts impermissibly.

The thought underlying this conviction is that, except perhaps in the most exceptional of circumstances, it is simply impermissible to inflict certain, serious, harms upon innocent individuals, even if, by inflicting such harms, one could prevent comparable harms from befalling others. Do the harms generated by weapons transfers to oppressive regimes fall into this category? I think that, at least in certain (not unrepresentative) cases, our answer to this question must be affirmative. One country which received large quantities of US weapons in the aftermath of 9/11 is Uzbekistan, a country presided over by an authoritarian regime which is regularly accused of serious human rights abuses.[5] Here is a short excerpt from the US State Department's 2006 Human Rights Report for that country:

> The government's human rights record, already poor, continued to worsen during the year. Citizens did not have the right in practice to change their

government through peaceful and democratic means. Security forces routinely tortured, beat, and otherwise mistreated detainees under interrogation to obtain confessions or incriminating information. In several cases, authorities subjected human rights activists and other critics of the regime to forced psychiatric *treatment*. Human rights activists and journalists who criticized the government were subject to harassment, arbitrary arrest, politically motivated prosecution, and physical attack. The government generally did not take steps to investigate or punish the most egregious cases of abuse .... The government continued to refuse to authorize an independent international investigation of the alleged killing of numerous unarmed civilians during the violent disturbances of May 2005.[6]

Elaborating, the report notes that "torture and abuse were systematic", and that methods used by security forces included "suffocation, electric shock, deprivation of food and water, and sexual abuse ...". Security forces were accused of abusing human rights activists by "dropping them onto concrete floors, forcing needles under their fingernails, suffocating them with gas masks, and burning their skin with lighted cigarettes".[7]

It is hard to imagine anyone denying that these are serious harms. Moreover, weapons transfers contribute to these serious harms in at least four ways: first, they provide tools with which security forces coerce, maim, and kill; second, they increase the power of the state relative to internal dissidents; third, they increase the power of the state relative to members of the international community which may wish to intervene to protect basic rights; fourth, arms transfers constitute a form of international cooperation, and thus demonstrate that such cooperation is not contingent upon respect for basic rights: they counteract any verbal exhortations made by the exporting state, and reveal that opportunities for cooperation will be forthcoming irrespective of whether basic rights are respected. With these considerations in mind, I resubmit my original claim: states are morally required to refrain from selling weapons to oppressive regimes. [The author considers additional objections in Section III—Ed. note.]

IV

.... In this section I consider the moral permissibility of transferring arms to rebel groups waging revolutionary war against oppressive regimes. A concern for the security rights of those ruled by oppressive regimes gives us a prima facie reason to welcome the overthrow of those regimes, and to support the groups attempting to overthrow them. But that same concern also casts doubt on the strategy of supporting those groups by arming them. ...

If supporting a rebel group is to be permissible, it seems clear that several conditions, adapted from traditional just war theory, must be satisfied: the rebel group must have a just cause—the aim of the group cannot be to overthrow one oppressive regime and replace it with another; the harms which will occur if the rebels, with outside assistance, continue to fight must be proportional to the harms which the war effort can be expected to prevent; the war must be necessary—alternative means of getting rid of the regime must be unavailable; and it must be reasonable to expect that the rebel group, at least if it receives outside help, will not deliberately inflict violence upon non-combatants. These conditions will be relevant in what follows.

Arming a rebel group might be impermissible even if supporting it in other ways is not. This might be true for a variety of reasons, but I shall focus on one. Arming rebel groups has a notable shortcoming which some other means of support do not share, namely, the advantages conferred by certain forms of support can be terminated at any time, but the advantages conferred by the provision of weapons cannot. ... It cannot simply ask for its weapons back. It can refuse to provide additional weapons, of course, but there is little it can do about the weapons it has already sent: it lost control of those the second they entered rebel hands. ... [A]t time T it might be reasonable to believe that the rebel group one is contemplating supporting will not deliberately inflict violence upon non-combatants, but at time T + n it might became painfully clear that that belief was unfounded. ... Such a scenario is not at all improbable. ...

Intervening in revolutions is fraught with difficulty, and all methods of support have attendant risks. It is, nevertheless, important to emphasize the dangers associated with the provision of arms, for that strategy is often perceived to be superior to more direct forms of military intervention which tend to be eschewed when possible on the grounds that they put troops in harm's way, upset the electorate, and are extremely expensive. The US has recently supplied weapons to rebel forces in Syria but has resisted calls for other types of action. The upshot of the considerations adduced here is that providing arms should not be regarded as an unproblematic way of assisting rebel groups which is necessarily preferable to other available methods. By transferring weapons to a rebel group, states provide that group with the means to violate the security rights of their fellow countrymen and countrywomen. ...

V

We have seen that the arms trade has an important role to play in ensuring that the right to security is protected. But we have also seen that the right to security generates duties to restrict the arms trade in significant ways. Weapons which pose a disproportionately large threat to non-combatants must not be traded, and weapons should not be sold to oppressive regimes. We also saw that while we may have good reasons to support rebel groups attempting to overthrow oppressive regimes, supporting such groups by arming them is, from a moral perspective, highly problematic.

Notes

1 Rachel Stohl and Suzette Grillot, *The International Arms Trade* (Cambridge: Polity Press, 2009), p. 22.
2 Sandra S. Wise et al., "Particulate Depleted Uranium Is Cytotoxic and Clastogenic to Human Lung Cells", *Chemical Research in Toxicology*, 20 (2007), 815–820; Randall R. Parrish et al., "Depleted Uranium Contamination by Inhalation Exposure and Its Detection After ~ 20 Years: Implications for Human Health Assessment", *Science of the Total Environment*, 390 (2008), 58–68.
3 On terrorist states, see Robert E. Goodin, *What's Wrong with Terrorism?* (Cambridge: Polity Press, 2006), ch. 4.

4 Waldron, *Torture, Terror and Trade-Offs* (New York: Oxford University Press, 2010), pp. 44–45.
5 Stohl and Grillot, *International Arms Trade*, p. 35.
6 US Department of State, "Uzbekistan", 2006 Country Reports on Human Rights Practices, March 6, 2007; available at www.state.gov/j/drl/rls/hrrpt/2006/78848.htm.
7 Ibid.

Review and Discussion Questions

1 Is there anything inherently wrong with a market in weapons?
2 Christensen says: no. What is his argument and do you agree with it?
3 What is his argument for concluding that states must refrain from selling weapons to states that are oppressive?
4 What are the counterarguments that he considers, and what are his responses?
5 What is Christensen's view about states that arm rebel groups?

Essay and Paper Topics for Chapter 5

1 Drawing on Ryan's essay, what is the most coherent pacifist position that is responsive to Wasserstrom's arguments?
2 "The use of robotics in warfare adds no new fundamental questions about the ethics of war. New technologies simply introduce variations on the same age-old questions." Assess.
3 What is the best argument for prohibiting the arms trade? Can it withstand Christensen's counterargument?

Chapter 6

Capital Punishment

The next topic related to issues of life and death is about a continuing controversy: capital punishment. The first selection is taken from the U.S. Supreme Court's opinion that held that executions are not unconstitutional violations of the Eighth Amendment's ban on cruel and unusual punishment. That case is followed by two articles, one by Martin Perlmutter and the other by Ernest van den Haag, that defend capital punishment. Perlmutter discusses the justification of executions from a utilitarian and retributivist perspective, while van den Haag replies to the arguments of capital punishment's critics. Next, Hugo Adam Bedau argues that capital punishment should be abolished in all circumstances. Finally, Jeffrey Reiman argues that the death penalty, like torture, is simply beyond the pale of what civilized societies should do to their own.

READING: THE DEATH PENALTY

GREGG V. GEORGIA[*]

The Eighth Amendment to the U.S. Constitution says in part that no "cruel and unusual punishment" shall be inflicted. But what, precisely, does that mean? Some examples are clear enough, for instance drawing and quartering, burning at the stake, and other extreme forms of mutilation or torture. But what about executions? The Supreme Court has consistently held that the meaning of "cruel and unusual" is not fixed but instead must be adjusted as society evolves. In this case, the question before the Court is whether executions for murder are unconstitutional. In an earlier case, *Furman v. Georgia* (1972), the Court overturned a death sentence in part because the specific procedures that were used made imposition of the penalty "arbitrary." A minority of the justices had also argued in *Furman* that executions per se were unconstitutional. In this opinion, the Court again considers both questions: the constitutionality of executions and the constitutionality of the procedures by which it is determined who shall die. In doing so, it also considers the important philosophical issues surrounding punishment and its justification.

---

[*] *Gregg v. Georgia* 428 U.S. 153 (1976).

Mr. Justice Stewart, with Justices Powell and Stevens Concurring

We address initially the basic contention that the punishment of death for the crime of murder is, under all circumstances, "cruel and unusual" in violation of the Eighth and Fourteenth Amendments of the Constitution. [Later in] this opinion, we will consider the sentence of death imposed under the Georgia statutes at issue in this case.

The substantive limits imposed by the Eighth Amendment on what can be made criminal and punished were discussed in *Robinson v. California* (1962). The Court found unconstitutional a state statute that made the status of being addicted to a narcotic drug a criminal offense. It held, in effect, that it is "cruel and unusual" to impose any punishment at all for the mere status of addiction. The cruelty in the abstract of the actual sentence imposed was irrelevant: "Even one day in prison would be a cruel and unusual punishment for the 'crime' of having a common cold." *Id.*, at 667. Most recently, in *Furman v. Georgia*, ... three Justices in separate concurring opinions found the Eighth Amendment applicable to procedures employed to select convicted defendants for the sentence of death.

It is clear from the foregoing precedents that the Eighth Amendment has not been regarded as a static concept. As Mr. Chief Justice Warren said, in an oft-quoted phrase, "[t]he Amendment must draw its meaning from the evolving standards of decency that mark the progress of a maturing society." Thus, an assessment of contemporary values concerning the infliction of a challenged sanction is relevant to the application of the Eighth Amendment. As we develop below more fully, ... this assessment does not call for a subjective judgment. It requires, rather, that we look to objective indicia that reflect the public attitude toward a given sanction.

But our cases also make clear that public perceptions of standards of decency with respect to criminal sanctions are not conclusive. A penalty also must accord with "the dignity of man," which is the "basic concept underlying the Eighth Amendment." *Trop v. Dulles*. This means, at least, that the punishment not be "excessive." When a form of punishment in the abstract (in this case, whether capital punishment may ever be imposed as a sanction for murder) rather than in the particular (the propriety of death as a penalty to be applied to a specific defendant for a specific crime) is under consideration, the inquiry into "excessiveness" has two aspects. First, the punishment must not involve the unnecessary and wanton infliction of pain. Second, the punishment must not be grossly out of proportion to the severity of the crime.

The imposition of the death penalty for the crime of murder has a long history of acceptance both in the United States and in England. The common law rule imposed a mandatory death sentence on all convicted murderers. ... And the penalty continued to be used into the twentieth century by most American States, although the breadth of the common law rule was diminished, initially by narrowing the class of murders to be punished by death and subsequently by widespread adoption of laws expressly granting juries the discretion to recommend mercy ....

It is apparent from the text of the Constitution itself that the existence of capital punishment was accepted by the Framers. At the time the Eighth Amendment was ratified, capital punishment was a common sanction in every State. Indeed, the

First Congress of the United States enacted legislation providing death as the penalty for specified crimes ....

The most marked indication of society's endorsement of the death penalty for murder is the legislative response to *Furman*. The legislatures of at least thirty-five States have enacted new statutes that provide for the death penalty for at least some crimes that result in the death of another person. And the Congress of the United States, in 1974, enacted a statute providing the death penalty for aircraft piracy that results in death. These recently adopted statutes have attempted to address the concerns expressed by the Court in *Furman* primarily (i) by specifying the factors to be weighed and the procedures to be followed in deciding when to impose a capital sentence, or (ii) by making the death penalty mandatory for specified crimes ....

[H]owever, the Eighth Amendment demands more than that a challenged punishment be acceptable to contemporary society. The Court also must ask whether it comports with the basic concept of human dignity at the core of the Amendment. ... Although we cannot "invalidate a category of penalties because we deem less severe penalties adequate to serve the ends of penology," *Furman v. Georgia*, ... at 451 (Powell, J., dissenting), the sanction imposed cannot be so totally without penological justification that it results in the gratuitous infliction of suffering ....

The death penalty is said to serve two principal social purposes: retribution and deterrence of capital crimes by prospective offenders.[1]

In part, capital punishment is an expression of society's moral outrage at particularly offensive conduct. This function may be unappealing to many, but it is essential in an ordered society that asks its citizens to rely on legal processes rather than self-help to vindicate their wrongs.

> The instinct for retribution is part of the nature of man, and channeling that instinct in the administration of criminal justice serves an important purpose in promoting the stability of a society governed by law. When people begin to believe that organized society is unwilling or unable to impose upon criminal offenders the punishment they "deserve," then there are sown the seeds of anarchy—of self-help, vigilante justice, and lynch law.
>
> (*Furman v. Georgia*, ... at 308; Stewart, J., concurring)

"Retribution is no longer the dominant objective of the criminal law," *Williams v. New York* (1949), but neither is it a forbidden objective nor one inconsistent with our respect for the dignity of men. ... Indeed, the decision that capital punishment may be the appropriate sanction in extreme cases is an expression of the community's belief that certain crimes are themselves so grievous an affront to humanity that the only adequate response may be the penalty of death.

Statistical attempts to evaluate the worth of the death penalty as a deterrent to crimes by potential offenders have occasioned a great deal of debate. The results simply have been inconclusive ....

Although some of the studies suggest that the death penalty may not function as a significantly greater deterrent than lesser penalties, there is no convincing empirical evidence either supporting or refuting this view. We may nevertheless assume safely that there are murderers, such as those who act in passion, for whom the threat of death has little or no deterrent effect. But for many others, the death penalty undoubtedly is a significant deterrent. There are carefully contemplated murders, such as murders for hire; where the possible penalty of death may well enter into the cold calculus that precedes the decision to act.[2] And there are some categories of murder, such as murder by a life prisoner, where other sanctions may not be adequate.

The value of capital punishment as a deterrent of crime is a complex factual issue the resolution of which properly rests with the legislatures, which can evaluate the results of statistical studies in terms of their own local conditions and with a flexibility of approach that is not available to the courts. ... Indeed, many of the post-*Furman* statutes reflect just such a responsible effort to define those crimes and those criminals for which capital punishment is most probably an effective deterrent.

In sum, we cannot say that the judgment of the Georgia Legislature that capital punishment may be necessary in some cases is clearly wrong. Considerations of federalism, as well as respect for the ability of a legislature to evaluate, in terms of its particular State, the moral consensus concerning the death penalty and its social utility as a sanction, require us to conclude, in the absence of more convincing evidence, that the infliction of death as a punishment for murder is not without justification and thus is not unconstitutionally severe.

Finally, we must consider whether the punishment of death is disproportionate in relation to the crime for which it is imposed. There is no question that death as a punishment is unique in its severity and irrevocability ....

When a defendant's life is at stake, the Court has been particularly sensitive to ensure that every safeguard is observed. ... But we are concerned here only with the imposition of capital punishment for the crime of murder, and when a life has been taken deliberately by the offender, we cannot say that the punishment is invariably disproportionate to the crime. It is an extreme sanction, suitable to the most extreme of crimes.

We hold that the death penalty is not a form of punishment that may never be imposed, regardless of the circumstances of the offense, regardless of the character of the offender, and regardless of the procedure followed in reaching the decision to impose it.

We now consider whether Georgia may impose the death penalty on the petitioner in this case. ... Because of the uniqueness of the death penalty, *Furman* held that it could not be imposed under sentencing procedures that created a substantial risk that it would be inflicted in an arbitrary and capricious manner. Mr. Justice White concluded that "the death penalty is exacted with great infrequency even for the most atrocious crimes and there is no meaningful basis for distinguishing the few cases in which it is imposed from the many cases in which it is not." *Id.*, at 313 (concurring). Indeed, the death sentences examined by the Court in *Furman* were

> cruel and unusual in the same way that being struck by lightning is cruel and unusual. For, of all the people convicted of [capital crimes], many just as reprehensible as these, the petitioners [in *Furman* were] among a capriciously selected random handful upon whom the sentence of death has in fact been imposed. ... [T]he Eighth and Fourteenth Amendments cannot tolerate the infliction of a sentence of death under legal systems that permit this unique penalty to be so wantonly and so freakishly imposed.
>
> (*Id.*, at 309–310; Stewart, J., concurring)

In summary, the concerns expressed in *Furman* that the penalty of death not be imposed in an arbitrary or capricious manner can be met by a carefully drafted statute that ensures that the sentencing authority is given adequate information and guidance. As a general proposition these concerns are best met by a system that provides for a bifurcated proceeding at which the sentencing authority is apprised of the information relevant to the imposition of sentence and provided with standards to guide its use of the information ....

The basic concern of *Furman* centered on those defendants who were being condemned to death capriciously and arbitrarily. Under the procedures before the Court in that case, sentencing authorities were not directed to give attention to the nature or circumstances of the crime committed or to the character or record of the defendant. Left unguided, juries imposed the death sentence in a way that could only be called freakish. The new Georgia sentencing procedures, by contrast, focus the jury's attention on the particularized nature of the crime and the particularized characteristics of the individual defendant. While the jury is permitted to consider any aggravating or mitigating circumstances, it must find and identify at least one statutory aggravating factor before it may impose a penalty of death. In this way the jury's discretion is channeled. No longer can a jury wantonly and freakishly impose the death sentence; it is always circumscribed by the legislative guidelines. In addition, the review function of the Supreme Court of Georgia affords additional assurance that the concerns that prompted our decision in *Furman* are not present to any significant degree in the Georgia procedure applied here.

For the reasons expressed in this opinion, we hold that the statutory system under which Gregg was sentenced to death does not violate the Constitution. Accordingly, the judgment of the Georgia Supreme Court is affirmed.

It is so ordered.

Mr. Justice Brennan, Dissenting

The Cruel and Unusual Punishments Clause "must draw its meaning from the evolving standards of decency that mark the progress of a maturing society."[3] ...

In *Furman v. Georgia*, ... I read "evolving standards of decency" as requiring focus upon the essence of the death penalty itself and not primarily or solely upon the procedures under which the determination to inflict the penalty upon a particular person was made. I there said:

> From the beginning of our Nation, the punishment of death has stirred acute public controversy. Although pragmatic arguments for and against the punishment have been frequently advanced, this longstanding and heated controversy cannot be explained solely as the result of differences over the practical wisdom of a particular government policy. At bottom, the battle has been waged on moral grounds. The country has debated whether a society for which the dignity of the individual is the supreme value can, without a fundamental inconsistency, follow the practice of deliberately putting some of its members to death. In the United States, as in other nations of the western world, "the struggle about this punishment has been one between ancient and deeply rooted beliefs in retribution, atonement or vengeance on the one hand, and, on the other, beliefs in the personal value and

dignity of the common man that were born of the democratic movement of the eighteenth century, as well as beliefs in the scientific approach to an understanding of the motive forces of human conduct, which are the result of the growth of the sciences of behavior during the nineteenth and twentieth centuries." It is this essentially moral conflict that forms the backdrop for the past changes in and the present operation of our system of imposing death as a punishment for crime.

(*Id.*, at 296)[4]

That continues to be my view. For the Clause forbidding cruel and unusual punishments under our constitutional system of government embodies in unique degree moral principles restraining the punishments that our civilized society may impose on those persons who transgress its laws. Thus, I too say:

> For myself, I do not hesitate to assert the proposition that the only way the law has progressed from the days of the rack, the screw and the wheel is the development of moral concepts, or, as stated by the Supreme Court the application of "evolving standards of decency." ...[5]

This Court inescapably has the duty, as the ultimate arbiter of the meaning of our Constitution, to say whether, when individuals condemned to death stand before our Bar, "moral concepts" require us to hold that the law has progressed to the point where we should declare that the punishment of death, like punishments on the rack, the screw, and the wheel, is no longer morally tolerable in our civilized society. ... I emphasize only that foremost among the "moral concepts" recognized in our cases and inherent in the Clause is the primary moral principle that the State, even as it punishes, must treat its citizens in a manner consistent with their intrinsic worth as human beings—a punishment must not be so severe as to be degrading to human dignity. A judicial determination whether the punishment of death comports with human dignity is therefore not only permitted but compelled by the Clause ....

The fatal constitutional infirmity in the punishment of death is that it treats

> members of the human race as nonhumans, as objects to be toyed with and discarded. [It is] thus inconsistent with the fundamental premise of the Clause that even the vilest criminal remains a human being possessed of common human dignity.

(*Id.*, at 273)

As such it is a penalty that "subjects the individual to a fate forbidden by the principle of civilized treatment guaranteed by the [Clause]." I therefore would hold, on that ground alone, that death is today a cruel and unusual punishment prohibited by the Clause. "Justice of this kind is obviously no less shocking than the crime itself, and the new 'official' murder, far from offering redress for the offense committed against society, adds instead a second defilement to the first."[6]

Mr. Justice Marshall, Dissenting

In *Furman* I concluded that the death penalty is constitutionally invalid for two reasons. First, the death penalty is excessive. ... And second, the American people, fully informed as to the purposes of the death penalty and its liabilities, would in my view reject it as morally unacceptable ....

Since the decision in *Furman*, the legislatures of thirty-five States have enacted new statutes authorizing the imposition of the death sentence for certain crimes, and Congress has enacted a law providing the death penalty for air piracy resulting in death. ... I would be less than candid if I did not acknowledge that these developments have a significant bearing on a realistic assessment of the moral acceptability of the death penalty to the American people. But if the constitutionality of the death penalty turns, as I have urged, on the opinion of an *informed* citizenry, then even the enactment of new death statutes cannot be viewed as conclusive. In *Furman*, I observed that the American people are largely unaware of the information critical to a judgment on the morality of the death penalty, and concluded that if they were better informed they would consider it shocking, unjust, and unacceptable. ... A recent study, conducted after the enactment of the post-*Furman* statutes, has confirmed that the American people know little about the death penalty, and that the opinions of an informed public would differ significantly from those of a public unaware of the consequences and effects of the death penalty.[7]

Even assuming, however, that the post-*Furman* enactment of statutes authorizing the death penalty renders the prediction of the views of an informed citizenry an uncertain basis for a constitutional decision, the enactment of those statutes has no bearing whatsoever on the conclusion that the death penalty is unconstitutional because it is excessive. An excessive penalty is invalid under the Cruel and Unusual Punishments Clause "even though popular sentiment may favor" it. ... The inquiry here, then, is simply whether the death penalty is necessary to accomplish the legitimate legislative purposes in punishment, or whether a less severe penalty—life imprisonment —would do as well ....

The two purposes that sustain the death penalty as nonexcessive in the Court's view are general deterrence and retribution. In *Furman*, I canvassed the relevant data on the deterrent effect of capital punishment. ... The state of knowledge at that point, after literally centuries of debate, was summarized as follows by a United Nations Committee:

> It is generally agreed between the retentionists and abolitionists, whatever their opinions about the validity of comparative studies of deterrence, that the data which now exist show no correlation between the existence of capital punishment and lower rates of capital crime.[8]

The available evidence, I concluded in *Furman*, was convincing that "capital punishment is not necessary as a deterrent to crime in our society." *Id.*, at 353 ....

The other principal purpose said to be served by the death penalty is retribution. ... It is this notion that I find to be the most disturbing aspect of today's unfortunate decisions.

The concept of retribution is a multifaceted one, and any discussion of its role in the criminal law must be undertaken with caution. On one level, it can be said that the notion of retribution or reprobation is the basis of our insistence that only those who have broken the law be punished, and in this sense the notion is quite obviously central to a just system of criminal sanctions. But our recognition that retribution plays a crucial role in determining who may be punished by no means requires approval of retribution as a general justification for punishment.[9] It is the question whether retribution can provide a moral justification for punishment—in particular, capital punishment—that we must consider.

My Brothers Stewart, Powell, and Stevens offer the following explanation of the retributive justification for capital punishment:

> The instinct for retribution is part of the nature of man, and channeling that instinct in the administration of criminal justice serves an important purpose in promoting the stability of a society governed by law. When people begin to believe that organized society is unwilling or unable to impose upon criminal offenders the punishment they "deserve," then there are sown the seeds of anarchy—of self-help, vigilante justice, and lynch law.[10]

This statement is wholly inadequate to justify the death penalty. As my Brother Brennan stated in *Furman*, "[t]here is no evidence whatever that utilization of imprisonment rather than death encourages private blood feuds and other disorders." ... at 303 (concurring opinion). It simply defies belief to suggest that the death penalty is necessary to prevent the American people from taking the law into their own hands.

In a related vein, it may be suggested that the expression of moral outrage through the imposition of the death penalty serves to reinforce basic moral values —that it marks some crimes as particularly offensive and therefore to be avoided. The argument is akin to a deterrence argument, but differs in that it contemplates the individual's shrinking from antisocial conduct not because he fears punishment, but because he has been told in the strongest possible way that the conduct is wrong. This contention, like the previous one, provides no support for the death penalty. It is inconceivable that any individual concerned about conforming his conduct to what society says is "right" would fail to realize that murder is "wrong" if the penalty were simply life imprisonment.

The foregoing contentions—that society's expression of moral outrage through the imposition of the death penalty preempts the citizenry from taking the law into its own hands and reinforces moral values—are not retributive in the purest sense. They are essentially utilitarian in that they portray the death penalty as valuable because of its beneficial results. These justifications for the death penalty are inadequate because the penalty is, quite clearly I think, not necessary to the accomplishment of those results.

There remains for consideration, however, what might be termed the purely retributive justification for the death penalty—that the death penalty is appropriate, not because of its beneficial effect on society, but because the taking of the murderer's life is itself morally good. Some of the language of the opinion of my Brothers Stewart, Powell, and Stevens ... appears positively to embrace this notion of retribution for its own sake as a justification for capital punishment. They state:

> [T]he decision that capital punishment may be the appropriate sanction in extreme cases is an expression of the community's belief that certain crimes are themselves so grievous an affront to humanity that the only adequate response may be the penalty of death.[11]

They then quote with approval from Lord Justice Denning's remarks before the British Royal Commission on Capital Punishment:

> The truth is that some crimes are so outrageous that society insists on adequate punishment, because the wrongdoer deserves it, irrespective of whether it is a deterrent or not.[12]

Of course, it may be that these statements are intended as no more than observations as to the popular demands that it is thought must be responded to in order to prevent anarchy. But the implication of the statements appears to me to be quite different, that society's judgment that the murderer "deserves" death must be respected not simply because the preservation of order requires it, but because it is appropriate that society make the judgment and carry it out. It is this latter notion, in particular, that I consider to be fundamentally at odds with the English Amendment. ... The mere fact that the community demands the murderer's life in return for the evil he has done cannot sustain the death penalty, for as Justices Stewart, Powell, and Stevens remind us, "the Eighth Amendment demands more than that a challenged punishment be acceptable to contemporary society." To be sustained under the Eighth Amendment, the death penalty must "comport with the basic concept of human dignity at the core of the Amendment," *Id.*; the objective in imposing it must be "[consistent] with our respect for the dignity of [other] men." Under these standards, the taking of life "because the wrongdoer deserves it" surely must fall, for such a punishment has as its very basis the total denial of the wrongdoer's dignity and worth.

The death penalty, unnecessary to promote the goal of deterrence or to further any legitimate notion of retribution, is an excessive penalty forbidden by the Eighth and Fourteenth Amendments. I respectfully dissent from the Court's judgment upholding the sentences of death imposed upon the petitioners in these cases.

Notes

1 Another purpose that has been discussed is the incapacitation of dangerous criminals and the consequent prevention of crimes that they may otherwise commit in the future.
2 Other types of calculated murders, apparently occurring with increasing frequency, include the use of bombs or other means of indiscriminate killings, the extortion murder of hostages or kidnap victims, and the execution-style killing of witnesses to a crime.
3 *Trop v. Dulles*, 356 U.S. 86, 101 (1958) (plurality opinion of Warren, C.J.).
4 Quoting T. Sellin, *The Death Penalty*, A Report for the Model Penal Code Project of the American Law Institute 15 (1959).
5 *Novak v. Beto*, 453 F. 2d 661, 672 (CA5 1971) (Tuttle, J., concurring in part and dissenting in part).
6 A. Camus, *Reflections on the Guillotine* 5–6 (Fridtjof-Karla Pub. 1960).
7 Sarat and Vidmar, "Public Opinion, the Death Penalty, and the English Amendment: Testing the Marshall Hypothesis," 1976 *Wis. L. Rev.* 171.
8 United Nations, Department of Economic and Social Affairs, *Capital Punishment*, pt. II, 159, p. 123 (1968).
9 See, *e.g.*, H. Hart, *Punishment and Responsibility* 8–10, 71–83 (1968); H. Packer, *Limits of the Criminal Sanction* 38–39, 66 (1968).
10 Ante at 428 U.S. 183, quoting from *Furman v. Georgia,* supra at 408 U.S. 308 (STEWART, J., concurring).
11 Ante at 428 U.S. 184 (footnote omitted).
12 Ante at 428 U.S. 184 n. 30.

Review and Discussion Questions

1 How would you define *punishment*? How is it different from taxation?
2 The Supreme Court states that the Eighth Amendment means that punishment cannot be "excessive." What two reasons do the justices who defend executions give to prove that capital punishment is not excessive?
3 How do the two dissenters respond to the argument that executions are not excessive punishment?
4 Besides not being excessive, the death penalty must also be compatible with society's "evolving standards of decency." Why does Justice Stewart think it is not incompatible?
5 Why do the dissenters think executions are not compatible with evolving standards of decency? How does Justice Marshall respond to Justice Stewart's point about what state legislatures had done after the *Furman* decision?
6 Consider the following argument: the death penalty must deter, no matter what statistics say, because almost everybody would prefer life in prison to execution. Do you agree with this argument?

READING: DESERT AND CAPITAL PUNISHMENT

MARTIN PERLMUTTER[*]

Martin Perlmutter argues that the utilitarian approach to punishment, emphasizing the usefulness of deterrence, protection, and rehabilitation, is inadequate, primarily because it views punishment as "forward-looking." Rather, he claims, the proper focus of punishment is on the past; people are punished for past wrongdoing. If the wrongdoing is serious enough, he argues, then capital punishment is appropriate and the wrongdoer deserves death. Perlmutter concludes by arguing that, in a sense, the criminal has a right to be punished—that to fail to do so treats him or her as less than a person. Martin Perlmutter is Professor of Philosophy at the University of Charleston, South Carolina.

> "Shall we receive good at the hand of God and shall we not receive evil?" In all this Job did not sin with his lips.
>
> (Job 2:10)

Punishment is a form of harm or deprivation; in punishing somebody, we are making that person worse off than he was before. And since it seems that we have a *prima facie* obligation not to make others worse off, the practice of punishment needs a justification in virtue of which that *prima facie* obligation is overridden. Why are we entitled to harm persons when we punish them?

There are two general answers to this question. The first looks to the future and to the overall consequences of inflicting the harm; it maintains that one is entitled to make a person worse off if the consequences of doing so outweigh the harm done. Inflicting harm is justified when the harm done is part of a larger chain in which that harm results in yet greater good. The good produced by the harm might be the rehabilitation of the offender, the protection of others from the offender, or

---

[*] Copyright © 1992 by Martin Perlmutter. Reprinted by permission of the author.

the deterrence of other future offenders. This answer is utilitarian; it looks to future goods, which outweigh the present harm, as the justification of the present harm. The second looks to the past and to the past deeds of the offender; it maintains that one is entitled to make a person worse off if that person's past deeds are such that he deserves to be punished. Just as it is fitting to reward someone who does well with some goods, whether those be a trophy, a better job, or a salary increase, so it is appropriate to deprive someone who does poorly of those same goods. Of course, it would be nice if good consequences proceeded from the punishment, just as it would be nice if good consequences proceeded from giving the trophy to the winner rather than to the loser, but good consequences, like rehabilitation, protection, or deterrence, are not in any way integral to punishment. This answer is the retributive view of punishment; it looks to past deeds in virtue of which the harm is deserved as justification of the harm.[1]

In this paper I will argue that punishment focuses on the past; it is thus a retributive concept. Just as the concepts "praise," "blame," and, more importantly, "desert" have a backward focus, so too "punishment" looks to the past. The justification of punishment is another matter. I will argue that the practice of punishment is justified, because the individual who did the wrong also "chose" the punishment; in punishing the wrongdoer, we are honoring that individual's choice. The justification of punishment is to be found in the broader notion of desert, another backward-looking concept. I will also argue that capital punishment is defensible; there are some crimes that are so serious, so offensive to the moral community, that their perpetrators deserve death for committing them. As Justice Stewart points out in *Gregg v. Georgia*,

> the decision that capital punishment may be the appropriate sanction in extreme cases is an expression of the community's belief that certain crimes are themselves so grievous an affront to humanity that the only adequate response may be the penalty of death.

Finally, as a postscript, I will make some general remarks about treating somebody as a person. In doing so, I will try to make sense of the seemingly absurd Hegelian view that "in punishment the offender is honored as a rational being, since the punishment is looked on as his right."

1 The Concept of Punishment

Before we ask questions about the justification of punishment, we should be clear about what punishment is. Otherwise, we would not know whether or not it is punishment that we are justifying. So, for example, justifying the reform or rehabilitation of an offender might not be a difficult task, but it would be a justification of punishment only if punishment were essentially a reformative or rehabilitative notion.

There are two features of punishment that are essential to it. First, punishment is inflicting harm; nothing can count as punishment unless it is a deprivation or causes pain or suffering to the person on whom it is inflicted. This is not quite right since a person might prefer his punishment to the alternatives available to him; on occasion, a drunkard might prefer a warm cell with a mattress to the cold outside, and a child might rather be banished to his room than continue to play with his friends. The intention in punishing, however, is to do harm; in punishing somebody, we intend to make the person worse off than he would be without the punishment.[2] So punishment must involve pain or other consequences normally considered unpleasant.

Not every case of making a person worse off, however, is an instance of punishment. Confining a person who has an infectious disease, hitting somebody just for the fun of it, and taxing the wealthy might well be instances of harming persons, but they are not cases of punishment, even if they were deprivations that we were justified in imposing. For a deprivation to be a punishment, it has to be associated with past wrongdoing. A heavily taxed wealthy person would be overstating his case if he complained that he was being punished for being wealthy, for there is no presumption of any past wrongdoing in his case.

Second, then, a person may be punished if and only if there is some presumption of past wrongdoing. Again, this is a conceptual requirement; it is part of the meaning of "punishment." Imposing harm is not punishment unless the imposition of the harm is connected with a supposed past wrongdoing.

This connection between wrongdoing and the imposition of harm is so strong that some have maintained a conceptual link between them. It has been claimed that the very concept of wrongdoing must contain a reference to punishment; that is, an act is an instance of wrongdoing if and only if the agent is subject to punishment for performing it. In legal contexts, a natural home for the discussion of punishment, such a view has had some currency. An act is a legal offense just in case there is a sanction that attaches to performing it; a rule of law requires that a person perform or forbear from performing some act and promises harm in case of noncompliance. As a more general thesis, however, it is false; wrongdoing or offense cannot have liability to punishment in its explication, for there are many offenses that do not subject the offender to any penalty. Punishment, however, does require reference to both harm and wrongdoing.

The imposition of harm and past wrongdoing are closely related. The harm imposed is in virtue of the past wrongdoing; the person deserves to suffer because he committed an offense. It is appropriate that the person suffer harm or deprivation because of the person's past deeds; had the person not done wrong, he would not have deserved the suffering. This is central to punishment.

The connection can be seen in the nature of rules, whether they be the regulations of baseball, the laws of society, or the rules of bridge. Rules are constitutive of baseball, society, and bridge. The rules define the practice, they distribute the benefits and the burdens, and they determine acceptable behavior within the practice. In violating a rule, the person is competing unfairly; that is an improper way of gaining an advantage. Throwing a spitball, stealing a car, or surreptitiously signaling the ace of spades are all unacceptable ways of getting ahead. Persons who attempt to benefit by violating a rule are subject to a penalty for so doing because they are benefiting from the practice but are participating unfairly in it. Typically, there are procedures for determining whether the rule has been violated, what the penalty should be, and who should administer the penalty.

The legitimate domain of punishment is restricted to special relationships. A state can legitimately punish its citizens, it is within a parent's province to punish his or her child, and a teacher has the authority to punish his or her students.

So too the tournament director at bridge, the umpire, and the baseball commissioner. Not everyone, however, is entitled to punish, even in response to past wrongdoing. As a general rule, a citizen cannot punish the state, a child cannot punish a parent, and a student cannot punish a teacher.

Although blame is similar to punishment in many ways—in blaming a person, we are causing that person a limited sort of harm in virtue of a past wrongdoing—blame is more general than punishment in this way.[3] The legitimate domain of blame is not restricted to special relationships. While it may be morally unacceptable to blame somebody, though he is blameworthy, that unacceptability is in virtue of considerations of the future. On occasion, the bad consequences of expressing the blame make such expressions unacceptable even to someone who is blameworthy. It might be unacceptable to blame somebody for past deeds if that person is on his deathbed, it might be silly for you to blame somebody if doing so would upset you a great deal, and there might be no point to blaming somebody who would enjoy the loss of your esteem. In each of these cases, it might be morally unacceptable or imprudent to blame him, even though he is blameworthy. But it is not a question of authority; blame, unlike punishment, is not restricted to special relationships. Each of these three cases would be a paradigmatic instance of blaming, just as a morally unacceptable case of telling the truth would be a paradigmatic instance of truth-telling.

2 A Utilitarian Critique of Punishment

A utilitarian might focus on the analogy of punishment to blame to argue that though punishment has a backward focus, the moral acceptability of inflicting the harm must derive from the future consequences of the harm inflicted. If it is morally unacceptable to express blame to a person on his deathbed, though the person is blameworthy, then blameworthiness is not sufficient for the moral acceptability of blaming. And it is forward-looking considerations that make expressing the blame morally unacceptable; that is, since nothing good will be accomplished by expressing the blame and somebody will be worse off for it, the blame should not be expressed. Similarly, in punishment, past wrongdoing is not sufficient for the moral acceptability of inflicting the harm. Even if inflicting harm requires past wrongdoing for it to be punishment, it requires good consequences for it to be morally acceptable. As a result, in the utilitarian view, it is the consequences of inflicting harm that determine whether or not it is morally acceptable to inflict the harm, though it is backward-looking considerations that determine whether or not it is punishment. Just as taxing the wealthy might be a morally acceptable way of harming the wealthy only if the consequences justify it, so too fining a traffic offender is morally acceptable only if the consequences justify it. Of course, taxing the wealthy is not based on past wrongdoing, so it is not punishment, whereas fining the traffic offender is punishment. But whether or not inflicting harm is punishment is only a detail and does not speak to the moral acceptability of inflicting it.

This utilitarian view is general and not restricted to punishment. According to it, one should always do what has the best consequences. What has already happened is relevant only insofar as the future is concerned. The fact that a person has committed an offense might be a reason for inflicting harm on the person, but only in virtue of the future benefits of the harm. Thus, a past offense might serve as evidence for future offenses and future offenses are to be avoided, so it might be best to protect his future victims by imprisoning him. Or it might be best to discourage future offenders by inflicting harm on this offender for this offense. But unless there is a justification in the future, it would be morally unacceptable to inflict the harm. For if there were no such future benefits, then, all things considered, in punishing one is increasing the amount of suffering in the world and that is morally unacceptable.

This utilitarian challenge might require abandoning the practice of punishment. If punishment involves intending to make a person worse off because of past wrongdoing, then the only utilitarian defense of punishment could be deterrence. For reform of the offender or protection of society from the offender's future offenses does not involve intentionally making the offender worse off any more than curing a person of an infectious disease involves that intention. Were we able to cure a person of a disease without inconveniencing the victim, one would surely do so. Similarly, if reform were the aim of punishment, punishment would not necessarily involve making the offender worse off, even temporarily. The same holds true for societal protection as an aim of punishment; it too does not necessarily involve making a person worse off. Deterrence fares a little better, but even it does not require actually inflicting the harm as opposed to merely appearing to others to inflict the harm. Punishment necessarily involves harm or deprivation, whereas reform, deprivation, and even deterrence do not.

An example might help. Suppose my son lies to me and suppose also that I am persuaded that I have no evidence that sending him to his room will do any more good than not sending him to his room. I might still think that he deserves to be punished for what he did and send him to his room, thereby inflicting harm on him for what he did. A utilitarian would claim that I should not have done it, for no good will result from my harming my son in this way. If he is right, it is not because he has a different theory of punishment which yields a different result in this case. Rather, it is because punishment is not justified; it is because, in his view, I am not entitled to inflict harm unless a greater good will result. The utilitarian is giving a critique of punishment, not an alternative theory of punishment.

Even if the utilitarian does not provide an alternative theory of punishment, he might be right in his critique of punishment. My punishing my son for lying might be morally unacceptable, because reform, protection, or deterrence is not gained by it. It might be morally unacceptable to do anything whose foreseeable consequences involve more harm than good. And if it is, then the practice of punishment ought to be abandoned.

3 A Critique of Utilitarianism

The utilitarian contention ignores the fact that many of our moral concepts are backward-looking. Most often, we are morally required to do things because of what happened in the past. It is that which makes social contract theories appealing; we are obligated to behave in accordance with an implicit contract, something which we already tacitly agreed to do. More simply, though, we are required to keep a promise because we made it, we are required to award the prize to the winner because he won the race, and we are required to repay a debt because we borrowed the money. Frequently, it is the past and not the future which determines the moral acceptability of an action. Of course, keeping a promise has consequences for the practice of promise-keeping, and the fact that a promise was made also has consequences, since the promise created expectations. But what makes it right to keep a promise is the past fact that a promise was made. So, the well-known example of a secret promise to a dying man to deliver a hoard of money, which he entrusts to me, to his already rich son is relevant. It is the promise, and not the consequences, which makes it right to give his son the money.

The utilitarian is correct in recognizing that, on occasion, we are morally required to look to the future and that the future sometimes affects what it is morally acceptable to do, even in the case of backward-looking concepts. Thus, though a promise was made, perhaps to meet somebody for lunch, it would be morally unacceptable to do so if it would result in somebody's death, because of the need to rush somebody to the hospital. But in cases such as this, it is not *merely* minimizing harm or maximizing benefit that is operative. Rather, a rational person would not expect the promise to be kept to him in a case such as this. The commitment involved in promises does not create an obligation in such a case.

So even though the utilitarian contention about maximizing benefits and minimizing harm has some plausibility, it does not conform to our everyday moral intuitions about what is morally acceptable. Of course, a utilitarian might urge that it is unreasonable to take the past as seriously as we do. But until we become persuaded by such urgings, and it is not clear that we should become persuaded by them, we should continue to take our everyday moral notions seriously and reject the utilitarian contention. Promises should be kept because they were made, debts should be repaid because they were incurred, and awards should be given because they are deserved. Moral notions such as these show that the past plays a much larger role in justifying behavior than a utilitarian acknowledges.

The notion of desert is central to punishment. What a person deserves is most often determined by what he has done. Does a person ever deserve to have harm inflicted on him for what he has done? The answer seems straightforward. On occasion, when a person knowingly and intentionally does wrong, he should be punished for what he did. In much the same way as a person occasionally deserves to be blamed, deserves the loss of another's esteem, a person occasionally deserves to have harm inflicted upon him.

Even a view which emphasizes deterrence as the rationale for inflicting the harm requires such a notion of desert. Otherwise, harming an innocent person to deter others would be morally acceptable. A plausible deterrence view must insist that in doing wrong a person made it acceptable to have harm inflicted upon himself, thereby deterring others. That is, he deserves the harm; the punishment is morally acceptable because of the past misdeed. So even a theory which emphasizes deterrence requires a retributive underpinning.

4 Capital Punishment

The view that the severity of the punishment should be determined by the severity of the crime is a natural extension of the retributive view that punishment is a person's due in virtue of the wrong that the person committed. That is, the crime should not only legitimate that the person be punished, but it should also determine the extent of the punishment. Simply put, the more serious the crime, the more severe the penalty.

Lex talionis, literally the law of retaliation, is the custom of inflicting a similar injury on the person who injures another. The person who causes another to lose an eye must himself lose an eye; the person who murders another must himself be put to death. That was a common practice of punishment in earlier societies and is included in the Biblical corpus of laws (Exodus 21:23–25, for example). Most often, *lex talionis* is inapplicable, since most wrongs do not have analogous injuries applicable to the offender. But the view that the severity of the offense should determine the severity of the punishment remains a plausible view, one which many of us intuitively accept. The U.S. Supreme Court used this principle as a negative test when it upheld the death penalty in *Gregg v. Georgia:* "The punishment must not be grossly out of proportion to the severity of the crime."

Of course, one cannot grade wrongs with mathematical precision and there is no scientific procedure for ranking punishments. But some wrongs are worse than others. Missing an appointment altogether is worse than being five minutes late; robbing a bank is worse than not feeding a parking meter; marking the deck of cards is worse than neglecting to inform one's opponents of a bridge convention; and intentionally losing a baseball game is worse than questioning an umpire's third-strike call. More generally, a third offense is worse than a first offense, a premeditated act is worse than an impulsive or negligent one; and an altogether self-interested criminal act is worse than a criminal act designed to benefit another. Punishments are more easily ranked. A thousand-dollar fine is worse than a hundred-dollar fine; ten years in prison is worse than one year in prison; and solitary confinement is worse than imprisonment in a minimum-security detention facility.

Are there any limits on the appropriate punishments? Is life imprisonment, capital punishment, bodily mutilation, or castration beyond the pale of acceptable punishment? Two issues need to be separated. First, the appropriateness of the punishment for the particular crime. Life imprisonment would be too severe a penalty for a parking violation, even though life imprisonment might be appropriate for other offenses. Second, the appropriateness of the punishment for any crime.[4] Some harms are unacceptable because they are not the sorts of thing that persons are ever entitled to do, even as a punishment. Maiming, bodily mutilation, and torture seem to be disqualified for this reason.

Clearly, there are cultural factors which are relevant as response to these questions. How serious the crime and what punishments are compatible with conceptions of human dignity vary from culture to culture. And there are objective criteria which can be used to determine both issues. Sexual relations between consenting adults is generally allowed in our culture but is a serious wrong in others. In our cultural setting, bodily mutilation is a form of humiliation that is unacceptable; it is not compatible with our fundamental standards of human dignity and decency. Nobody should be allowed to mutilate another, even as a response to a serious crime (such as mutilating another). Imprisonment, even for a long term, is different, since our society clearly thinks that imprisonment is an appropriate response to wrongdoing. Depriving a person of his liberty is an acceptable response to wrongdoing; bodily mutilation is not.

A person might reasonably prefer an unacceptable punishment to an acceptable one. Having one's hand cut off or being castrated seems less severe as a punishment than life imprisonment; a person might well prefer a life without a hand or a life without some sexual pleasures to a life without liberty, even though our society allows the latter as a punishment and disallows the former. The issue is not a matter of preference or severity; the punishment has to accord with human dignity. In our society, bodily integrity and privacy are important values that preclude maiming, bodily mutilation, or castration.

What about capital punishment? Again, we need to separate two questions. First, is death too severe a penalty to impose for any offense? Are there any crimes that are so serious that death is an appropriate penalty for them? Second, is capital punishment compatible with our views of human dignity and decency?

In our society, murder is a crime for which death is a fitting punishment. Not only does murder result in the death of another, it undermines the very fabric of a moral community. A murderer should be altogether and completely cut off from the moral community which he sought to undermine. The murderer caused death and deserves death in response. Life imprisonment is not adequate because it makes the criminal a dependent of the community, a ward of the community he sought to undermine. The murderer's only claim is that he be treated in a way that is compatible with society's standards of human dignity.

Others might want to restrict capital punishment to other crimes—to mass murder, to the killing of a police officer, or to political assassination. There is no scientific way to determine what crimes are so egregious that capital punishment is appropriate for them and I need not argue for the appropriateness of capital punishment for any particular crime. But I do want to insist that if our standards of decency allow death as an acceptable punishment, then there are some crimes that warrant it as a punishment.

But does our view of human dignity allow for capital punishment? The legislature of most every state has enacted new statutes authorizing the death penalty for certain crimes, the Congress has made air piracy punishable by death, and the Supreme Court has ruled that the death penalty is not cruel and unusual punishment. Surveys indicate that the vast majority of Americans support the death penalty for some crimes, and seemingly rational persons occasionally choose death when their life prospects are sufficiently grim. So there is excellent evidence that capital punishment is not humiliating in an unacceptable way and that capital punishment is compatible with standards of human dignity.

5 Punishment and Desert

We are now in a position to understand the Hegelian view that "in punishment the offender is honored as a rational being, since the punishment is looked on as his right" (Hegel's Philosophy of Right, Section 100). If the offender deserves to be punished in virtue of his past wrongdoing, then if we do not punish him, we should have some reason for not treating him as he deserves. If we are in no way excusing what he did but merely exempting him from the harm, then we are not dealing with him as he deserves. In choosing to do wrong and in realizing the consequences of what he did, he brought the punishment upon himself. In punishing him, we are respecting his choice. The punishment is his due in much the same way as the prize is the due of the winner. If we refused the winner the prize merely because we did not want him to benefit, then we would be acting illegitimately by not giving him his desert. So too with punishment. In punishment we are honoring the integrity of the agent by giving him his due.

The right to be punished is a strange sort of right. Rights are generally associated with what is in one's interest, so we must say that it is in the offender's interest to be punished. Pain or suffering is undesirable, however, so people will ordinarily not claim their right to be punished. Nevertheless, persons do have an interest in being treated as persons, as genuine members of the moral community. Such treatment requires that one's choices are honored and that one is dealt with in a manner appropriate to those choices. The right to be punished, then, is derivative on the right to be treated as a person. Just as persons deserve to be rewarded, so too persons deserve to be punished. Both rewarding and punishing are instances of respecting persons.

On occasion, it is more appropriate to use a therapy model than the model of honoring the integrity of human beings. Wrongdoing is occasionally pathological and should be dealt with much as one deals with other pathological conditions. If the agent is himself a victim, then it is appropriate to treat him as a victim in the way that a therapy model does. If kleptomania is a disease, then the person should be treated for it, not punished for it. So one might treat the person for this illness much as one would treat a person for a cancer. In treating a person in this way, however, one is treating him as a victim, not as an agent; one is not respecting his choices; and one is not honoring him as a human being.

Most often, the therapy model is inappropriate. When it is inappropriate, the person as a moral agent has a right to be punished, not treated. It is demeaning to have our choices treated as if they were something over which we have no control. It is in our interest to be treated as a person, as an autonomous moral agent; we ordinarily do want our choices to be respected as emanating from us, rather than to be dealt with as symptoms of an ailment over which we have no control.

A deathbed scenario is sometimes used to criticize this retributive view. Should we punish a person on his deathbed for a past wrongdoing? The retributive view suggests that we should, that in doing so we are honoring his choices as a human being, and that he deserves the punishment in virtue of the wrong that he did. A utilitarian disagrees. He thinks that such treatment is inhumane, that respecting him as a human being requires that we forgo the punishment.

The correct answer depends on how the person on his deathbed is viewed. If the only interest, or the overwhelming interest, that we associate with a dying person is a peaceful death, then we should not punish him. A dying person would require special treatment in virtue of that dominant interest. If he wants a promise to be made, even an unreasonable promise, it might be best to make it, later to break it. If he is blameworthy, it might be unacceptable to blame him. It might even be acceptable to lie to him about his prospects for survival. But insofar as we are entitled to do all these things, we are compromising his status as a full-fledged member of the moral community. If the pressing interest to die comfortably and untroubled overrides his generally more important interest to be treated as a person, then our ordinary moral discourse fails. It is not, however, because we respect him as a person that we are willing to do these things. Rather, it is because his situation is so dire that it demands that his immediate needs be met. Issues of desert are overwhelmed by issues of immediate need.

Most often, however, it is desert that determines the moral acceptability of behavior. Occasionally, what one deserves is for harm to be inflicted. On those occasions, one deserves to be punished; it is one's right as a person.

Notes

1. These two general answers do get a bit more complex. For the utilitarian might go on to maintain that inflicting harm can only be punishment if it is in virtue of a past deed that the harm is inflicted. Taking from the wealthy to feed starving children might be a morally acceptable way of harming the wealthy, but it is a conceptual mistake to view it as a punishment. Inflicting harm to prevent yet greater harm or to produce beneficial consequences might be morally acceptable, but it is not punishment unless it is backward-looking enough so that it is inflicted in virtue of some past misdeed. And the retributivist might not want to be saddled with punishing a person when no possible earthly benefit will derive from it. It seems severe to inflict harm on another in those cases when absolutely nothing will be gained from it, except perhaps a balancing of the moral scales. So punishment may become a bit backward-looking for the utilitarian and a bit forward-looking for the retributivist.

    Thus, both views, when modified, seem to agree that both backward-looking and forward-looking considerations are relevant for determining the moral acceptability of punishment. Yet the focus of the two views is different. For the retributivist thinks that it is the past wrongdoing which makes inflicting harm morally acceptable, whereas the utilitarian maintains that inflicting harm can be made morally acceptable only by considering the future consequences of the harm. Thus, the retributivist is not committed to the view that inflicting the harm is morally acceptable only if doing so produces better consequences than not inflicting it, for he believes that the justification lies in the past.

2. Again, this will not do. A judge might realize that the drunken defendant prefers the warm cell yet punish him by sentencing him to a night in jail. Presumably, a night in jail is normally considered less pleasant than not spending a night in jail, even if it is not so in every case. In legal contexts, the penalty is determined by what is normally considered harmful or unpleasant.

3. There are two features associated with blame that need to be distinguished. First, there is blameworthiness. Blameworthiness is wholly backward-looking, focusing exclusively on the agent and his past deeds. Blameworthiness is analogous to responsibility, another backward-looking concept. Second, there is expressing the blame, typically to the blameworthy person. On occasion, it is morally unacceptable to express blame, though blame is appropriate. The deathbed case might be such a case. Clearly, the fact that a man is dying does not affect his blameworthiness, for it has nothing whatever to do with his being accountable for his past misdeeds.

4. In his provocative essay "Why I Am Not a Christian," Bertrand Russell criticizes Christ's teaching of hell. He says, "I do not myself feel that any person who is really profoundly humane can believe in everlasting punishment." For Russell, eternal damnation is always an inappropriate punishment, never deserved by any misdeed. He thinks it altogether too severe.

Review and Discussion Questions

1. Explain why Perlmutter thinks that utilitarians miss the point of punishment.
2. Why does Perlmutter think that to punish someone is to honor that person while failing to punish may show disrespect?
3. Retributivists take the view that the *degree* of punishment should match the degree of moral blameworthiness of the act. How would such a view of punishment treat attempted crimes as compared with successful ones? Is that a reasonable approach?
4. How might a retributivist be expected to view punishment of drunk drivers? Drivers who kill when drunk? Drivers who kill after falling asleep?

5 Are there ever cases in which we should punish people who are not morally blameworthy? Explain.
6 Do utilitarians ignore the fact that some moral concepts are "backward-looking," as Perlmutter says? How might Mill respond to that claim? Is his response adequate?
7 What is Perlmutter's position regarding capital punishment? What is your assessment of this position?
8 Some people argue that punishment is necessary so that people are treated as equals. Explain whether or how a claim about equality is relevant to Perlmutter's argument.

READING: THE ULTIMATE PUNISHMENT

ERNEST VAN DEN HAAG[*]

Ernest van den Haag is among capital punishment's best-known and most enthusiastic supporters. In this essay, he reviews the case on behalf of executions, beginning with the topic of its "maldistribution" among those who deserve it. He then discusses the concern that it is applied incorrectly to those who are innocent, whether it deters crime, its cost to society and to the executed, and whether it "brutalizes" society. He concludes with a brief discussion of capital punishment's supposed excessiveness and with Justice Brennan's claim that it "degrades" and is inconsistent with "human dignity." Ernest van den Haag was Professor of Jurisprudence and Public Policy at Fordham University.

The death penalty is our harshest punishment.[1] It is irrevocable: it ends the existence of those punished instead of temporarily imprisoning them. Further, although not intended to cause physical pain, execution is the only corporal punishment still applied to adults.[2] These singular characteristics contribute to the perennial, impassioned controversy about capital punishment.

I Distribution

Consideration of the justice, morality, or usefulness of capital punishment is often conflated with objections to its alleged discriminatory or capricious distribution among the guilty. Wrongly so. If capital punishment is immoral *in se*, no distribution among the guilty could make it moral. If capital punishment is moral, no distribution would make it immoral. Improper distribution cannot affect the quality of what is distributed, be it punishments or rewards. Discriminatory or capricious distribution thus could not justify abolition of the death penalty. Further, maldistribution inheres no more in capital punishment than in any other punishment.

Maldistribution between the guilty and the innocent is, by definition, unjust. But the injustice does not lie in the nature of the punishment. Because of the finality of the death penalty, the most grievous maldistribution occurs when it is imposed upon

---

[*] Ernest van den Haag, "The Ultimate Punishment: A Defense," *Harvard Law Review* 99 (1986): 1662–1669.

the innocent. However, the frequent allegations of discrimination and capriciousness refer to maldistribution among the guilty and not to the punishment of the innocent.

Maldistribution of any punishment among those who deserve it is irrelevant to its justice or morality. Even if poor or black convicts guilty of capital offenses suffer capital punishment and other convicts equally guilty of the same crimes do not, a more equal distribution, however desirable, would merely be more equal. It would not be more just to the convicts under sentence of death.

Punishments are imposed on persons, not on racial or economic groups. Guilt is personal. The only relevant question is: Does the person to be executed deserve the punishment? Whether or not others who deserved the same punishment, whatever their economic or racial group, have avoided execution is irrelevant. If they have, the guilt of the executed convicts would not be diminished, nor would their punishment be less deserved. To put the issue starkly, if the death penalty were imposed on guilty blacks but not on guilty whites or if it were imposed by a lottery among the guilty, this irrationally discriminatory or capricious distribution would neither make the penalty unjust nor cause anyone to be unjustly punished, despite the undue impunity bestowed on others.[3]

Equality, in short, seems morally less important than justice. And justice is independent of distributional inequalities. The ideal of equal justice demands that justice be equally distributed, not that it be replaced by equality. Justice requires that as many of the guilty as possible be punished, regardless of whether others have avoided punishment. To let these others escape the deserved punishment does not do justice to them or to society. But it is not unjust to those who could not escape.

These moral considerations are not meant to deny that irrational discrimination, or capriciousness, would be inconsistent with constitutional requirements. But I am satisfied that the Supreme Court has in fact provided for adherence to the constitutional requirement of equality as much as is possible. Some inequality is indeed unavoidable as a practical matter in any system.[4] But *ultra posse nemo obligatur* (nobody is bound beyond ability).

Recent data reveal little direct racial discrimination in the sentencing of those arrested and convicted of murder.[5] The abrogation of the death penalty for rape has eliminated a major source of racial discrimination. Concededly, some discrimination based on the race of murder victims may exist; yet this discrimination affects criminal victimizers in an unexpected way. Murderers of whites are thought more likely to be executed than murderers of blacks. Black victims, then, are less fully vindicated than white ones. However, because most black murderers kill blacks, black murderers are spared the death penalty more often than are white murderers. They fare better than most white murderers.[6] The motivation behind unequal distribution of the death penalty may well have been to discriminate against blacks, but the result has favored them. Maldistribution is thus a straw man for empirical as well as analytical reasons.

II Miscarriages of Justice

In a recent survey, Professors Hugo Adam Bedau and Michael Radelet found that 7,000 persons were executed in the United States between 1900 and 1985 and that 25 were innocent of capital crimes.[7] Among the innocents they list Sacco and Vanzetti as well as Ethel and Julius Rosenberg. Although their data may be questionable, I do not doubt that, over a long enough period, miscarriages of justice will occur even in capital cases.

Despite precautions, nearly all human activities, such as trucking, lighting, or construction, cost the lives of some innocent bystanders. We do not give up these activities, because the advantages, moral or material, outweigh the unintended losses. Analogously, for those who think the death penalty just, miscarriages of justice are offset by the moral benefits and the usefulness of doing justice. For those who think the death penalty unjust even when it does not miscarry, miscarriages can hardly be decisive.

III Deterrence

Despite much recent work, there has been no conclusive statistical demonstration that the death penalty is a better deterrent than are alternative punishments.[8] However, deterrence is less than decisive for either side. Most abolitionists acknowledge that they would continue to favor abolition even if the death penalty were shown to deter more murders than alternatives could deter.[9] Abolitionists appear to value the life of a convicted murderer or, at least, his nonexecution more highly than they value the lives of the innocent victims who might be spared by deterring prospective murderers.

Deterrence is not altogether decisive for me either. I would favor retention of the death penalty as retribution even if it were shown that the threat of execution could not deter prospective murderers not already deterred by the threat of imprisonment.[10] Still, I believe the death penalty, because of its finality, is more feared than imprisonment and deters some prospective murderers not deterred by the threat of imprisonment. Sparing the lives of even a few prospective victims by deterring their murderers is more important than preserving the lives of convicted murderers because of the possibility, or even the probability, that executing them would not deter others. Whereas the lives of the victims who might be saved are valuable, that of the murderer has only negative value because of his crime. Surely the criminal law is meant to protect the lives of potential victims in preference to those of actual murderers.

Murder rates are determined by many factors; neither the severity nor the probability of the threatened sanction is always decisive. However, for the long run, I share the view of Sir James Fitzjames Stephen:

> Some men, probably, abstain from murder because they fear that if they committed murder they would be hanged. Hundreds of thousands abstain from it because they regard it with horror. One great reason why they regard it with horror is that murderers are hanged.[11]

Penal sanctions are useful in the long run for the formation of the internal restraints so necessary to control crime. The severity and finality of the death penalty is appropriate to the seriousness and the finality of murder.[12]

IV Incidental Issues: Cost, Relative Suffering, Brutalization

Many nondecisive issues are associated with capital punishment. Some believe that the monetary cost of appealing a capital sentence is excessive.[13] Yet most comparisons of the cost of life imprisonment with the cost of execution, apart from their dubious relevance, are flawed at least by the implied assumption that life prisoners will generate no judicial costs during their imprisonment. At any rate, the actual monetary costs are trumped by the importance of doing justice.

Others insist that a person sentenced to death suffers more than his victim suffered and that this (excess) suffering is undue according to the *lex talionis* (rule of retaliation).[14] We cannot know whether the murderer on death row suffers more than his victim suffered; however, unlike the murderer, the victim deserved none of the suffering inflicted. Further, the limitations of the *lex talionis* were meant to restrain private vengeance, not the social retribution that has taken its place. Punishment—regardless of the motivation—is not intended to revenge, offset, or compensate for the victim's suffering or to be measured by it. Punishment is to vindicate the law and the social order undermined by the crime. This is why a kidnapper's penal confinement is not limited to the period for which he imprisoned his victim, nor is a burglar's confinement meant merely to offset the suffering or the harm he caused his victim, nor is it meant only to offset the advantage he gained.[15]

Another argument ... is that by killing a murderer, we encourage, endorse, or legitimize unlawful killing. Yet although all punishments are meant to be unpleasant, it is seldom argued that they legitimize the unlawful imposition of identical unpleasantness. Imprisonment is not thought to legitimize kidnapping; neither are fines thought to legitimize robbery. The difference between murder and execution, or between kidnapping and imprisonment, is that the first is unlawful and undeserved, the second is lawful and deserved punishment for an unlawful act. The physical similarities of the punishment to the crime are irrelevant. The relevant difference is not physical but social.[16]

V Justice, Excess, Degradation

We threaten punishments in order to deter crime. We impose them not only to make the threats credible but also as retribution (justice) for the crimes that were not deterred. Threats and punishments are necessary to deter, and deterrence is a sufficient practical justification for them. Retribution is an independent moral justification.[17] Although penalties can be unwise, repulsive, or inappropriate and those punished can be pitiable, in a sense the infliction of legal punishment on a guilty person cannot be unjust. By committing the crime, the criminal volunteered to assume the risk of receiving a legal punishment that he could have avoided by not committing the crime. The punishment he suffers is the punishment he voluntarily risked suffering and therefore it is no more unjust to him than any other event for which one knowingly volunteers to assume the risk. Thus, the death penalty cannot be unjust to the guilty criminal.[18]

There remain, however, two moral objections. The penalty may be regarded as always excessive as retribution and always morally degrading. To regard the death penalty as always excessive, one must believe that no crime—no matter how heinous—could possibly justify capital punishment. Such a belief can be neither corroborated nor refuted; it is an article of faith.

Alternatively, or concurrently, one may believe that everybody, the murderer no less than the victim, has an imprescriptible (natural?) right to life. The law therefore should not deprive anyone of life. I share Jeremy Bentham's view that any such "natural and imprescriptible rights" are "nonsense upon stilts."[19]

Justice Brennan has insisted that the death penalty is "uncivilized," "inhuman," inconsistent with "human dignity" and, with "the sanctity of life,"[20] that it "treats members of the human race as nonhumans, as objects to be toyed with and discarded,"[21] that it is "uniquely degrading to human dignity"[22] and "by its very nature, [involves] a denial of the executed person's humanity."[23] Justice Brennan does not say why he thinks execution "uncivilized." Hitherto most civilizations have had the death penalty, although it has been discarded in Western Europe, where it is currently unfashionable probably because of its abuse by totalitarian regimes.

By "degrading," Justice Brennan seems to mean that execution degrades the executed convicts. Yet philosophers, such as Immanuel Kant and G. W. F. Hegel, have insisted that when deserved, execution, far from degrading the executed convict, affirms his humanity by affirming his rationality and his responsibility for his actions. They thought that execution, when deserved, is required for the sake of the convict's dignity. (Does not life imprisonment violate human dignity more than execution by keeping alive a prisoner deprived of all autonomy?)

Common sense indicates that it cannot be death—our common fate—that is inhuman. Therefore, Justice Brennan must mean that death degrades when it comes not as a natural or accidental event, but as a deliberate social imposition. The murderer learns through his punishment that his fellow men have found him unworthy of living; that because he has murdered, he is being expelled from the community of the living. This degradation is self-inflicted. By murdering, the murderer has so dehumanized himself that he cannot remain among the living. The social recognition of his self-degradation is the punitive essence of execution. To believe, as Justice Brennan appears to, that the degradation is inflicted by the execution reverses the direction of causality.

Execution of those who have committed heinous murders may deter only one murder per year. If it does, it seems quite warranted. It is also the only fitting retribution for murder I can think of.

Notes

1. Some writers ... have thought that life imprisonment is more severe .... However, the overwhelming majority of both abolitionists and of convicts under death sentence prefer life imprisonment to execution.
2. For a discussion of the sources of opposition to corporal punishment, see E. van den Haag, *Punishing Criminals* (1975), 195–206.
3. Justice Douglas, concurring in *Furman v. Georgia*, 408 U.S. 238 (1972), wrote that "a law which ... reaches that [discriminatory] result in practice has no more sanctity than a law which in terms provides the same." *Id.* at 256 (Douglas, J., concurring). Indeed, a law legislating this result "in terms" would be inconsistent with the "equal protection of the laws" provided by the Fourteenth Amendment, as would the discriminatory result reached in practice. But that result could be changed by changing the distributional practice. Thus, Justice Douglas notwithstanding, a discriminatory result does not make the death penalty unconstitutional, unless the penalty ineluctably must produce that result to an unconstitutional degree.
4. The ideal of equality, unlike the ideal of retributive justice (which can be approximated separately in each instance), is clearly unattainable unless all guilty persons are

apprehended, and thereafter tried, convicted, and sentenced by the same court, at the same time. Unequal justice is the best we can do; it is still better than the injustice, equal or unequal, which occurs if, for the sake of equality, we deliberately allow some who could be punished to escape.

5 See Bureau of Justice Statistics, U.S. Dept. of Justice, Bulletin No. NCJ-98, 399, *Capital Punishment 1984*, at 9 (1985); Johnson, *The Executioner's Bias, Nat'l Rev.*, November 15, 1985, at 44.
6 It barely need be said that any discrimination *against* (for example, black murderers of whites) must also be discrimination *for* (for example, black murderers of blacks).
7 Bedau & Radelet, *Miscarriages of Justice in Potentially Capital Cases* (1st draft, October 1985) (on file at Harvard Law School Library).
8 For a sample of conflicting views on the subject, see Baldus and Cole, "A Comparison of the Work of Thorsten Sellin and Isaac Ehrlich on the Deterrent Effect of Capital Punishment" *Yale L.J.* 85 (1975): 170; Bowers and Pierce, "Deterrence or Brutalization: What Is the Effect of Executions?" *Crime & Delinq.* 26 (1980): 453; Bowers and Pierce, "The Illusion of Deterrence in Isaac Ehrlich's Research on Capital Punishment" *Yale L.J.* 285 (1975): 187; Ehrlich, "Fear of Deterrence: A Critical Evaluation of the 'Report of the Panel on Research on Deterrent and Incapacitative Effects,'" *J. Legal Stud.* 6 (1977): 293; Ehrlich, "The Deterrent Effect of Capital Punishment: A Question of Life and Death" *Am. Econ. Rev.* (1975): 397, 415–16; Ehrlich and Gibbons, "On the Measurement of the Deterrent Effect of Capital Punishment and the Theory of Deterrence" *J. Legal Stud.* 6 (1977): 35.
9 For most abolitionists, the discrimination argument *see supra* is similarly nondecisive: they would favor abolition even if there could be no racial discrimination.
10 If executions were shown to increase the murder rate in the long run, I would favor abolition. Sparing the innocent victims who would be spared, *ex hypothesi*, by the non-execution of murderers would be more important to me than the execution, however just, of murderers. But although there is a lively discussion of the subject, no serious evidence exists to support the hypothesis that executions produce a higher murder rate. *Cf.* Phillips, "The Deterrent Effect of Capital Punishment: New Evidence on an Old Controversy," *Am. J. Soc.* 86, no. 139 (1980) (arguing that murder rates drop immediately after executions of criminals).
11 H. Gross, *A Theory of Criminal Justice* (1979) 489 (attributing this passage to Sir James Fitzjames Stephen).
12 *Weems v. United States*, 217 U.S. 349 (1910), suggests that penalties be proportionate to the seriousness of the crime—a common theme of the criminal law. Murder, therefore, demands more than life imprisonment, if, as I believe, it is a more serious crime than other crimes punished by life imprisonment. In modern times, our sensibility requires that the range of punishments be narrower than the range of crimes—but not so narrow as to exclude the death penalty.
13 *Cf.* Kaplan, "Administering Capital Punishment" *U. Fla. L. Rev.* 36 (1984): 177, 178, 190–91 (noting the high cost of appealing a capital sentence).
14 For an example of this view, see A. Camus, *Reflections on the Guillotine* (1959), 24–30. On the limitations allegedly imposed by the *lex talionis*, see Reiman, "Justice, Civilization, and the Death Penalty; Answering van den Haag" *Phil. & Pub. Aff.* 14 (1985): 115, 119–34.
15 Thus restitution (a civil liability) cannot satisfy the punitive purpose of penal sanctions, whether the purpose be retributive or deterrent.
16 Some abolitionists challenge: if the death penalty is just and serves as a deterrent, why not televise executions? The answer is simple. The death even of a murderer, however well deserved, should not serve as public entertainment. It so served in earlier centuries. But in this respect our sensibility has changed for the better, I believe. Further, television unavoidably would trivialize executions, wedged in, as they would be, between game shows, situation comedies, and the like. Finally, because televised executions would focus on the physical aspects of the punishment rather than the nature of the crime and the suffering of the victim, a televised execution would present the murderer as the victim of the state. Far from communicating the moral significance of the

execution, television would shift the focus to the pitiable fear of the murderer. We no longer place in cages those sentenced to imprisonment to expose them to public view. Why should we so expose those sentenced to execution?

17 See van den Haag, "Punishment as a Device for Controlling the Crime Rate," *Rutgers L. Rev.* 33 (1981): 706, 710 (explaining why the desire for retribution, although independent, would have to be satisfied even if deterrence were the only purpose of punishment).

18 An explicit threat of punitive action is necessary to the justification of any legal punishment: *nulla poena sine lege* (no punishment without [preexisting] law). To be sufficiently justified, the threat must in turn have a rational and legitimate purpose. "Your money or your life" does not qualify, nor does the threat of an unjust law, nor, finally, does a threat that is altogether disproportionate to the importance of its purpose. In short, preannouncement legitimizes the threatened punishment only if the threat is warranted. But this leaves a very wide range of justified threats. Furthermore, the punished person is aware of the penalty for his actions and thus volunteers to take the risk even of an unjust punishment. His victim, however, did not volunteer to risk anything. The question whether any self-inflicted injury—such as a legal punishment—ever can be unjust to a person who knowingly risked it is a matter that requires more analysis than is possible here.

19 *The Works of Jeremy Bentham* 105 (J. Bowring ed. 1972). However, I would be more polite about prescriptible natural rights, which Bentham described as "simple nonsense." *Id.* (It does not matter whether natural rights are called "moral" or "human" rights as they currently are by most writers.)

20 *The Death Penalty in America* 256–63 (H. Bedau ed., 3rd ed. 1982) quoting *Furman v. Georgia*, 408 U.S. 238, 286, 305 (1972) (Brennan, J., concurring).

21 *Id.* at 272–73; see also *Gregg v. Georgia*, 428 U.S. 153, 230 (1976) (Brennan, J., dissenting).

22 *Furman v. Georgia*, 408 U.S. 238, 291 (1972) (Brennan, J., concurring).

23 *Id.* at 290.

Review and Discussion Questions

1 How does van den Haag respond to those who would reject capital punishment because it falls disproportionately on minorities and the poor? How does he respond to those who would reject capital punishment because it sometimes leads to executions of innocents?
2 Why does van den Haag believe capital punishment deters criminals?
3 How does the author respond to Justice Brennan's claim that executions violate "human dignity"?

READING: ABOLISHING THE DEATH PENALTY EVEN FOR THE WORST MURDERERS

HUGO ADAM BEDAU[*]

In this essay Bedau argues that the death penalty should be abolished—that there are no conditions in modern society today that justify the use of the death penalty. He first considers various arguments that defend this view but that he

---

[*] Hugo A. Bedau, "Abolishing the Death Penalty Even for the Worst Murderers," Chapter 9 in *Killing As Punishment: Reflections on the Death Penalty in America* (Boston, MA: Northeastern University Press, 2004), pp. 158–178.

does not support, and then he offers his own defense of this position. Hugo Adam Bedau is an Emeritus Professor of Philosophy at Tufts University.

I

In the wake of the execution of Timothy McVeigh, convicted in June 1997 for his role in the murderous bombing of the Federal Building in Oklahoma City two years earlier, it is timely to ask this question: Who has the better of the argument, those who believe that some offenders (such as McVeigh) ought to be punished by being put to death, or those who believe that no one ought to be executed (not even McVeigh) and instead should be sentenced to long-term imprisonment?

To focus the question and keep the discussion relevant to the current scene, we can put aside the status of the death penalty for nonhomicidal crimes, for at least two reasons: First, the paradigm crime punishable by death has always been murder ("a life for a life"). It is also now settled constitutional law that nonhomicidal crimes such as rape and armed robbery are no longer subject to the punishment of death, as they had been only a generation ago.[1] Second, we need not discuss whether the death penalty is the appropriate punishment for *all* homicides. A mandatory death penalty for those convicted of killing another person would require abolishing the distinction between murder and manslaughter and between first- and second-degree murder; it would also require abolishing prosecutorial, judicial, and executive discretion in capital cases. Even if those considerations were not persuasive, the Supreme Court has decreed that mandatory death penalties, even for first-degree murder committed by a person under life sentence for murder, are unconstitutional.[2]

For these reasons it is plausible to argue that the only issue worth discussing is whether the majority of the public (some 65 to 70% at the present time)[3] is right in approving the death penalty for some murderers; or whether the minority (to which I belong) is right in defending absolute, exceptionless abolition.

We must concede from the start that a pick-and-choose death penalty policy has much to recommend it. It is typical of the contingencies acknowledged by modern morality where issues of life and death are concerned to shun principles that admit of no exceptions. (Thus, most of us do not favor laws prohibiting all abortions, or prohibiting all physician-assisted suicides.) But the absolute abolitionist position by definition allows no exceptions, which has a crucial consequence for the overall argument. It requires that we leave aside issues of great practical importance in the contemporary debate over the death penalty, such as the relatively greater economic costs of our current death penalty systems when compared with a system of long-term imprisonment; the unfairness—arbitrariness and discrimination—with which the death penalty is administered; and the risk of convicting, sentencing to death, and executing the innocent. These issues have been discussed elsewhere,[4] and they provide powerful objections to the death penalty in our society (just as they are the primary factors in the call for a national moratorium on executions by the House of Delegates of the American Bar Association).[5] Nevertheless, objections on these grounds are largely irrelevant from my current perspective, because it is possible to imagine an ideal world of criminal justice in which such deep-seated flaws and costs would not arise or, if they did, could be remedied without abolishing the death penalty. In that case, we would still be left with the need to explain whether and why we nevertheless oppose all executions.[6]

II

I propose to look first at the most popular moral grounds on which absolute abolitionists rest their case and see whether they can bear the weight placed on them.

The Value of Life[7]

Some abolitionists hold that human life (if not all life) has infinite value or worth[8] and so must be respected and protected accordingly. It follows from this belief that death is the greatest disvalue and murder the gravest wrong. It also follows that even murderers must be treated in light of the value of their lives, a value not erased (even if severely marred) by the harm and injustice their lethal violence has caused the innocent. And that supposedly rules out the death penalty.

But does it? As an empirical claim in any ordinary sense of "value," the value of a murderer's life is often (though by no means always) open to question. How much value, or potentiality for value, can we reasonably assign to the future life of the worst murderers—the sociopathic serial murderer, or the cold-hearted terrorist multiple murderer, or the unreformed and unreformable recidivist murderer—the Hannibal Lectors of fiction (*The Silence of the Lambs*) and the Ted Bundys and Timothy McVeighs of real life? ....

I do not want to suggest, much less argue (although some might), that all or even most of the nearly four thousand persons currently on the death rows of American prisons[9] are persons whose lives are essentially worthless or valueless (that is, as judged by society). I wouldn't know how to carry out in a responsible manner a systematic measurement of the worth or value of any human life as judged from society's point of view, especially if doing so were to allow for the possibility that some lives turn out to be worthless or valueless. All but the most prejudiced observers will concede that some (perhaps most) murderers retain more than a shred of human dignity and that some can redeem themselves in their own eyes and in ours at least to some extent. But that is not enough for the purposes of the present argument. What must be shown is that this is true of *all* the worst murderers, and I hesitate to endorse any such sweeping empirical claim. Even if one grants (as I do) that convicted murderers do not cease to be persons by virtue of their terrible crimes,[10] this hardly seems enough to establish the value of the life of each such offender.

Of course, the doctrine that even the worst murderer's life has some value (enough to outweigh all its disvalue) may not be an empirical claim at all. Instead, it may be a disguised normative judgment expressing moral disapproval of all executions. In that case, there is only a verbal difference between asserting (1) *every murderer's life has some value* (and enough to outweigh all disvalues), and (2) *we ought not to execute even the worst of the murderers*. To be sure, assertion (2) looks like the conclusion of an argument in which assertion (1) figures as a premise. But if the two assertions differ only verbally, then an appeal to assertion (1) does not advance the argument for assertion (2); instead, it tacitly begs the question. The only way to tell whether there really is a difference in meaning between assertion (2) and assertion (1) is to defend the one without implicitly relying on the other; but that is a task too large to undertake here.

If we regard assertion (2) as a genuine empirical claim, then our task is to establish this claim in a convincing manner on a case-by-case basis. Whether that can be done I do not know.[11] I doubt that it is unreasonable to be cautious, if not skeptical. (Caution is especially recommended in light of what we know about the sociopathy of most of the worst murderers: about how they got that way, and what is necessary—albeit not always sufficient—to bring about fundamental change in their lives.)[12]

Pending the completion of that task in a persuasive manner, I suggest that the default position for abolitionists who wish to rely on the value or worth of all human life is to insist that this value—of each and every person's life as judged by that person—puts the burden of argument on those who favor sentencing to death and killing persons without their informed voluntary consent.[13] Imposing the burden of argument in this manner is not only a minimalist strategy for the abolitionist; it is also fair and essential. The friends of the death penalty cannot reasonably reject or even contest this burden. Surely, there is no question that those who favor deliberately killing other persons *always* bear the burden of the argument. A serious discussion of life-and-death issues is impossible on any other assumption. This means that we must start from the somewhat paradoxical proposition that for the purposes of punishment under law, society must assume everyone's life is valuable, and that our lives have equal value, even though some seem to have little or no value.[14]

The Right to Life[15]

Some abolitionists (especially those influenced by Amnesty International and other human rights organizations) would say that we are morally forbidden to take the life of any murderer because even the murderer has an inalienable human right to life and that sentencing to death and executing a person violates that right. This argument has the merit of leaving aside empirical questions of the sort raised by the appeal to the value of human life. Instead, this argument plainly rests on a normative proposition about our rights.

But is the argument sound? Defenders of the death penalty typically reply (as John Locke did three centuries ago)[16] that even if the right to life is "natural" and "inalienable," the murderer *forfeits* his life (or, in some versions of this objection, his right to life), and so putting him to death at most infringes—and does not violate—that right. Most friends of the death penalty will agree that murderers, even if guilty and convicted, do not forfeit every right; they still have rights to due process of law and to equal protection of the law. Hence, lynching a convicted guilty murderer is itself a crime, even in a jurisdiction that authorizes the death penalty. But murderers do forfeit the one right that really matters, the right to life. Or so defenders of the death penalty will typically insist.

What reply do absolute abolitionists have to this objection? They cannot attack the general idea that rights can be forfeited, because that idea seems to be a perfectly ordinary even if tacit feature of any theory or doctrine of rights. For example, the Universal Declaration of Human Rights insists that everyone has a "right to liberty"; but it does not follow from this right that it is always wrong to deliberately deprive a person of liberty, as we do when we imprison a convicted offender. This amounts to conceding that under appropriate conditions persons can forfeit their right to liberty.[17]

Absolute abolitionists who resist the temptation to reject out of hand the doctrine of forfeiture of rights are likely to yield to the temptation to insist that whatever may be true of rights in general, the right to life cannot be forfeited—because it is an *absolute* right. That is, the right to life prevails over every other moral consideration that might be thought to compete with or override it. But here there is surely a problem. At best, I think, this is true only when we are referring to the right to life of the innocent. Consider the rationale of the use of lethal force in self-defense (or third-party defense).[18] Few abolitionists will deny that we have the right to act in self-defense to avoid becoming an undeserving victim of another's aggression. All but extreme pacifists will go on to grant that if the only way to prevent someone (oneself or another) from being the innocent victim of an unprovoked and uninvited act of apparently lethal intention is to use lethal force first, then in that sort of case one may kill the aggressor. Further, few abolitionists will insist that the police or other custodians of public order must never use lethal violence.

But once the use of lethal force is granted to be acceptable in such cases, the abolitionist is clearly not regarding the right to life as absolute. At most it is the right to life of the innocent that deserves unqualified respect, not the right to life of the guilty. Abolitionists who reason in this way thus cannot consistently use this right as a shield against deliberate and intentional lethal harm in all cases or as a stick with which to beat down claims by death penalty supporters who believe that even this right can be forfeited ....[19]

Perhaps at this point some absolute abolitionists will want to shift from relying on rights to relying upon the sanctity of human life. Such a shift not only puts aside any worry about empirical questions concerning the value of human life; it also has the advantage of making it difficult and perhaps impossible to make sense of forfeiting the sanctity of one's life by committing a terrible crime (even a crime that violates the sanctity of the innocent victim's life). In this respect sanctity has the edge on rights. But these advantages are purchased at a price: The sanctity of human life can be explained and defended only within a sectarian religious framework; one cannot appeal to the sanctity of human life in isolation from a whole host of related ideas and beliefs that do not have universal appeal. What is needed, I suggest, is a secular norm of universal application, which is exactly what the value of human life and the right to life attempt to provide.

General Social Utility[20]

Some oppose the death penalty on utilitarian grounds, arguing that the general welfare is better served by adopting and acting on a rule that forbids killing anyone in the name of punishment. All of us, whether or not we are utilitarians, agree that some enforceable rule prohibiting deliberately killing persons is necessary; we all agree that homicide is a crime unless excused or justified; we also agree that the ideal civilized society is one in which all rational persons would live without anyone murdering anyone; and we also agree that government officials and their agents, as well as private citizens, have committed inexcusable and unjustifiable homicide. (Think, respectively, of the federal government's attack on the Waco compound of the Branch Davidians in 1993, and the bombing of the Federal Building in Oklahoma City in 1995.) Can these agreements best be recognized and enforced by utilitarian reasoning?

Perhaps they can, but they fall well short of what is necessary to rule out all recourse to the death penalty. A utilitarian is very likely to consider certain cases, given the facts, as exceptions to any rule that absolutely prohibits killing other human beings in the name of punishment. Even the abolitionist founders of utilitarianism, notably Jeremy Bentham[21] and (to a lesser degree) J. S. Mill,[22] thought that the death penalty was appropriate in a narrow range of cases; so did Cesare Beccaria[23] before them and the American pragmatist Sidney Hook[24] in our own day.

To see how a utilitarian (or a pragmatist) would reason, consider the following kind of case (variations on this argument were voiced by some who favored the death sentence for McVeigh). Terrorist acts causing great loss of innocent life have been committed against a tolerably just government, and the chief offenders have been captured, tried, convicted, and now await sentencing. There is every reason to believe that many of their co-ideologists remain at large, scattered across the nation, and that the leaders awaiting sentencing will continue to inspire terrorist attacks as long as they remain alive. Doesn't the most plausible reading of the political facts support putting these convicted terrorists to death (perhaps even by public execution), in order to reduce the likelihood of further rebellion and harmful disorder? Why risk society's precarious security just to avoid putting to death dangerous terrorists who are clearly guilty?[25] In the wake of September 11, 2001, would not most Americans reason in precisely this way regarding the terrorist bombers of that day?

Reasoning of this sort is bound to attract utilitarians; it is always just a question of time and circumstances before the utilitarian opponent of the death penalty caves in and agrees that, yes, in this or that special (hypothetical or genuine) case, we can reasonably predict worse overall consequences for society if we do not put convicted felons to death and instead keep them in prison until their natural death. Utilitarians can easily oppose most death penalty laws—and Beccaria, Bentham, Mill, and Sidney Hook did; but I doubt that any utilitarian (or pragmatist) can oppose such laws and their application in *all* cases ....

Cruel and Unusual Punishment[26]

The Eighth Amendment in our Bill of Rights forbids "cruel and unusual punishment," and the Universal Declaration of Human Rights similarly forbids "torture, cruel, inhumane, or degrading punishment." Most abolitionists regard the death penalty as a violation of these principles.[27] This is not the place to argue the point; let us suppose they are correct. Whence do these constitutional principles derive their authority? Why ought we to respect them, especially given the awful and boundlessly cruel nature of many crimes (especially those committed by the worst murderers)?

[W]e might say we simply accept as intuitively sound the authority of these principles prohibiting cruelty; they are fundamental, non-derivative moral axioms governing our political thinking and our policy making. This answer will, of course, prove to have no persuasive effect on two groups of death penalty supporters: those who do not share this intuition in the first place; and those who do but who deny that these principles rule out the death penalty in all cases (especially if it is administered humanely and scrupulously).[28] Most of today's friends of the death penalty fall into the latter class. Few of them will seriously deny that we must accept some upper bound to permissible severity in punishment under law. But that still leaves considerable room for disagreement over just where to draw that upper bound—and in particular over which side of that boundary the death penalty falls ....

Of course, I have not exhausted all that moral reflection has to offer in defending a policy of absolute prohibition of the death penalty.[29] But perhaps I have said enough to cause some to conclude that absolute abolitionism is a policy insufficiently supported by sound moral principles (such as those reviewed above), reason, and experience. Those who believe this will view abolitionists as in the grip of an obsession against state authority to kill some prisoners and against exercising that authority in their names and on their behalf. This leads us to ask: Is it fair to impute stubborn irrationality and dogmatic sentimentality to those who are absolute abolitionists? I hope not, and I think not. There is another view to take of the prohibition against any killing as punishment, one that fastens on setting the upper bound of severity in punishment by reference to this question: Does the severity of the punishment under discussion exceed what is necessary to achieve whatever legitimate goals a system of punishment under law has in the first place? I think this question reorients the entire discussion in the right direction, and I now turn to the task of elaborating this perspective.

III

The argument I am about to present is ... consequentialist (without being utilitarian). Formulated in the context of American constitutional law, jurists would call it a "substantive due process" argument.[30] Political theorists will recognize its central principle as a familiar one in classic liberal political theory. The principle in question is that government must use "the least restrictive means to achieve a compelling state interest." In a somewhat fuller statement it can be formulated this way: Society, acting through the authority of its government, must not enact and enforce policies that impose more restrictive—invasive, harmful, violent—interference with human liberty, privacy, and autonomy than are absolutely necessary as the means to achieve legitimate and important social objectives. Anyone who takes this principle seriously, as I shall try to show, ought to oppose the death penalty in all cases because that penalty—at least in a society such as ours—violates this principle.

To reach that conclusion, one must accept the three propositions that constitute the argument. First, one must believe that the punishment of crime is a legitimate social objective, or (as I prefer) at least a necessary condition of achieving legitimate social objectives; otherwise, using severe sanctions and threatening serious deprivations in the name of punishment will not be warranted. Second, one must believe that the death penalty is much more severe, more invasive, less remediable, more violent than the usual alternative punishment, some form of long-term imprisonment. Third, one must believe that the death penalty is never necessary to achieve valid social objectives because other, less severe forms of punishment, such as constraints on an offender's liberty, privacy, and autonomy through long-term imprisonment, are sufficient.

These three propositions are of very different character. On what evidence and reasoning is each based? As to the first (punishment is a valid state objective), even opponents of current systems of imprisonment agree that some form of punishment is appropriate for the government to impose on convicted offenders, that the threat of punishment is an appropriate measure for society to use as a general deterrent, and that grave crimes call for severe punishment. Only the most radically pacific opponents of the death penalty rest their opposition on a general repudiation of punishment under law. So the friends and the enemies of capital punishment ought to be able to agree on the first proposition.

They are likely to divide, however, on a neglected distinction in this context of some importance. Is punishment as such really a valid state objective? Does punishment (including the threat of punishment) for its own sake, quite apart from its consequences, constitute a goal or purpose of society? I suggest that it doesn't. I also suggest that punishment is generally thought to be a valid state objective because advocating punishment as a *means* to certain valid ends is confused with advocating punishment as an *end* in itself. The relevant and valid state objective is a society tolerably free of violent crime; so it is crime reduction, not punishment infliction, that ought to preoccupy our policy makers. If so, then severe punishment (including the threat thereof) is defensible only to the extent that it is necessary to that end. (On this point, utilitarians have always been correct.) Were other measures to suffice or be reasonably believed to suffice to control crime, punishment under law in a tolerably just constitutional democracy would immediately be put into question. It would be vulnerable to the objection that punishment serves no valid purpose and instead has become pointless cruelty ....[31]

At present, however, this issue is moot because society does not have at its disposal fully effective nonpunitive methods of social control, and so one cannot argue that punishment (including especially the credible threat thereof) is unnecessary.

As to the second proposition (death is a more severe punishment than long-term imprisonment), those in the best position to judge—prisoners on death row and prisoners under life sentence who were, or might have been, sentenced to death—show by their behavior that they overwhelmingly believe death is a worse punishment than prison. Very few death row prisoners dismiss their lawyers and reject appeals and clemency hearings;[32] very few death row prisoners try to commit suicide, and fewer still try until they succeed.[33] As for the judgment of others, defenders of capital punishment typically believe that it is both a better deterrent and a fitting retribution, because it is the more severe punishment of the two. Abolitionists also agree that death is the more severe punishment; few if any are on record favoring life in prison because the death penalty is not severe enough. So I suggest we agree about the relative severity of the two modes of punishment and accept the second of my three propositions.

The third proposition (punishment by death is never necessary to achieve valid state objectives) is the one that is the most controversial. The argument for it must be an empirical one because the proposition itself is empirical. One source of disagreement here is lack of familiarity with the relevant evidence and unwillingness to accept the necessary inferences. (I shall ignore here the question of which side has the burden of argument and will proceed as if the abolitionist did.) The best version of the argument for this proposition goes like this: Anyone who studies the century and more of experience without the death penalty in American abolitionist jurisdictions must conclude that these jurisdictions have controlled criminal homicide and managed their criminal justice system, including their maximum security prisons with life-term violent offenders, at least as effectively as have neighboring death penalty jurisdictions. The public has not responded to abolition with riot and lynching; the police have not become habituated to excessive use of lethal force; prison guards, staff, and visitors are not at greater risk; surviving victims of murdered friends and loved ones have not found it more difficult to adjust to their grievous loss.[34]

If, in short, there is any argument for restoring the death penalty in America's abolition jurisdictions, it is not an argument rooted in the failures of long-term imprisonment as a general deterrent or incapacitation. It is not an argument from the insufficiency of retribution. It is not an argument from the destructive social behaviors inspired by abolition. And it is not an argument from the unmanageable dangers that a handful of the worst murderers present to public safety. So, what Michigan and Wisconsin did in abolishing the death penalty over a century ago, Ohio and Illinois could have done—and could do tomorrow if they wanted to. So could the rest of the nation.[35]

That completes the sketch of the general structure of the substantive due process argument against the death penalty; I think it carries the day.

Notes

1 *Coker v. Georgia*, 433 U.S. 584 (1977), and *Eberhard v. Georgia*, 433 U.S. 917 (1977). The constitutionality of nonhomicidal capital crimes as defined in the Anti-Terrorism and Effective Death Penalty Act, enacted by Congress in 1995, has yet to be decided.
2 *Woodson v. North Carolina*, 428 U.S. 280 (1976), and *Sumner v. Shuman*, 483 U.S. 66 (1987).
3 Phoebe C. Ellsworth & Samuel R. Gross, "Hardening of Attitudes: Americans' Views on the Death Penalty", *J. Soc. Issues* 50 (1994): 19–52, reprinted in *The Death Penalty in America: Current Controversies* (Hugo Adam Bedau ed., 1997).
4 See Bedau, *supra*; also International Commission of Jurists, *Administration or the Death Penalty in the United States* (1996); Raymond Paternoster, *Capital Punishment in America* (1991); Welsh S. White, *The Death Penalty in the Nineties: An Examination of the Modern System of Capital Punishment* (1991); and Amnesty International, *United States of America: The Death Penalty* (1987).
5 See *N.Y. Times*, February 4, 1997, at A20.
6 See David Dolinko, Foreword: How to Criticize the Death Penalty, *J. Crim. L. & Criminology* 77 (1986): 546, where this point is forcefully made.
7 For a general discussion of the value of human life, see John Kleinig, *Valuing Life* (1991). Kleinig does not address the question of differential valuation of human lives or of how to measure the value of a person's life (nor does he dismiss these questions as unanswerable or as nonsense).
8 Immanual Kant distinguished between the "relative worth" or "price" and the "intrinsic worth" or "dignity" of all persons. The former could vary from person to person and from time to time, but not the latter, all rational creatures were forever equal in dignity. See Kant, *Grounding for the Metaphysics of Morals* 40–41 (1785: trans. J. W. Ellington, 1981). This did not prevent Kant from arguing that murderers must be put to death; for a critical discussion, see Marvin Henberg, *Retribution: Evil for Evil in Ethics, Law, and Literature* i 58 (1990).
9 NAACP Legal Defense and Educational Fund, Inc., Death Row U.S.A. (Winter 1998), reports 3,365 person awaiting execution of a death sentence.

10 See Hugo Adam Bedau, Thinking about the Death Penalty as a Cruel and Unusual Punishment, *U.C. Davis L. Rev.* 18 (1985): 873, 921–23, reprinted in Hugo Adam Bedau, *Death Is Different: Studies in the Morality, Law, and Politics of Capital Punishment* 126–27 (1987).
11 Jeffrie Murphy discusses the possibility of human beings who are not moral persons because of the sociopathy; see his *Moral Death: A Kantian Essay on Psychopathy* 82 Ethics 284 (1972), reprinted in his *Retribution, Justice, and Therapy* 128–43 (1979). Murphy does not confuse clarifying this concept with arguing for its application in actual cases.
12 See in general John Gilligan, *Violence: Our Deadly Epidemic and Its Causes* (1996).
13 I insert this qualification so as to leave open the possibility that forms of euthanasia or assisted suicide may be morally acceptable.
14 The Supreme Court's decision in *Payne v. Tennessee*, 501 U.S. 808 (1991), which permits victim impact testimony during the sentencing phase of a capital trial, in effect repudiates this assumption of moral equality, because it invites testimony designed to show that the victim is someone exceptional, and so the killer deserves the exceptional punishment of death.
15 The right to life has yet to receive the lengthy treatment that it deserves. For some recent suggestions, see Susan Uniacke, *Permissible Killing: The Self-Defense Justification of Homicide* 209–18 (1994).
16 John Locke, *The Second Treatise of Government* (1690), in *Two Treatises of Governments*, §§ 23, 172 (Peter Laslett ed., 1963). For an influential modern moralist who takes the same line (without expressly leaning on Locke), see W. D. Ross, *The Right and the Good* 60 (1934).
17 Neglect by contemporary defenders of human rights to face the problems raised by traditional and commonplace claims that any right can be forfeited is nothing short of astounding; for further discussion see my article The Precarious Sovereignty of Rights, *Phil. Exchange* 5–16 (1997–1998), and Uniacke, *supra* note 15.
18 For a general discussion of self-defense and related issues, *see* Uniacke, *supra* note 15.
19 For fuller discussion of the issues in this paragraph, see Bedau, *supra*.
20 For representative contemporary utilitarian moral theory, see Geoffrey Scarre, *Utilitarianism* (1996); Richard B. Brandt, *Morality, Utilitarianism, and Rights* (1991); Anthony Quinton, *Utilitarianism* (2nd ed. 1989); J. J. C. Smart & Bernard Williams, *Utilitarianism: For and Against* (1973). None of these sources, however, offers any extended discussion of a utilitarian theory of punishment
21 Jeremy Bentham, *The Rationale or Punishment* (1830), reprinted in *The Works of Jeremy Bentham* 388 (John Bowring ed., 1838). See also my Bentham's Utilitarian Critique of the Death Penalty, *J. Crim. L. & Criminology* 74 (1983): 1033 reprinted in my *Death Is Different, supra* note 10, at 64–91.
22 J. S. Mill, *Speech in Favor of Capital Punishment* (1868), reprinted in *Philosophical Perspectives on Punishment* 271 (Gertrude Ezorsky ed., 1972).
23 Cesare Beccaria, *On Crimes and Punishments and Other Writings* (1764; Richard Bellamy ed., 1995).
24 Sidney Hook, The Death Sentence, in *The Death Penalty in America: An Anthology* 146 (Hugo Adam Bedau ed., 1964).
25 For my part, I reject this argument for reasons well stated by Thomas Perry Thornton, Terrorism and the Death Penalty, reprinted in *The Death Penalty in America* 181 (Hugo Adam Bedau ed., 3d ed. 1982), and by James Corcoran, McVeigh Gets a Last Chance: To Be a Martyr, *Boston Globe,* June 22, 1997, at D4. The position of the Catholic Church as set out in the papal encyclical *Evangelium Vitae* (1995) contemplates the possibility of the need to make a terrorist exception to complete abolition of the death penalty, but it implies that in actual fact modern nations do not need to do it.
26 Unfortunately, there is no comprehensive study of this clause in the Eighth Amendment. Larry Charles Berkson, *The Concept of Cruel and Unusual Punishment* (1975), provides little more than a digest of cases and statutes, when what is needed is a much deeper and broader theoretical account. For a fuller discussion of Berkson's book, see my review in *J. Crim. L. & Criminology* 68 (1977): 167–68.

27 Why the death penalty is a violation of the Eighth Amendment has yet to receive the thorough treatment it needs. Raoul Berger, in his *Death Penalties: The Supreme Court's Obstacle Course* (1982), vigorously argued against that idea and thereby provoked vigorous criticism among most of his reviewers. See, for example, my review in *Mich. L Rev.* 81 (Mar. 1983): 1152. See also my Thinking about the Death Penalty, *supra* note 10. On the death penalty as a violation of the UDHR and related norms of international law, see William A. Schabas, *The Death Penalty as Cruel Treatment and Torture: Capital Punishment Challenged in the World's Courts* (1996).

28 Today, lethal injection is widely defended on these grounds; it may well be true that this method of execution is superior to the legal alternatives (lethal gas, hanging, firing squad, electrocution) and yet still open to objection. For a recent discussion, see Schabas, *The Abolition of the Death Penalty in International Law* (Cambridge University Press, 3d ed., 2003), pp. 197–200.

29 For other discussions of the morality (or, rather, the immorality) of capital punishment, see my Capital Punishment, in *Matters of Life and Death: New Essays in Moral Philosophy* 160 (Tom Regan ed., 3rd ed. 1993), and my earlier essay Objections to the Death Penalty from the Moral Point of View, 58 *Rev.* Internat. *De droit penal* 557 (1987). See also Jeffrey Reiman, Justice, Civilization, and the Death Penalty, *Phil, & Pub. Affairs* 14 (1985): 115, reprinted in his *Critical Moral Liberalism: Theory and Practice* (1997); Carl Wellman, *Morals and Ethics* 244 (2nd ed. 1988); Stephen Nathanson, *An Eye for an Eye: The Morality of Punishing by Death* (1987); Richard Wasserstrom, Capital Punishment as Punishment: Some Theoretical Issues and Objections, *Midwest Stud, in Phil.* 7 (1982): 473; Thomas Hurka, Rights and Capital Punishment, *Dialogue* 21 (1982): 647; and H. L. A. Hart, Murder and the Principles of Punishment: England and the United States, *Nw. U. L. Rev.* 52 (1957): 433, reprinted in his *Punishment and Responsibility: Essays in the Philosophy of Law* (1968).

30 Elsewhere I have suggested that this argument has merit as an interpretation of the Eighth Amendment.

31 Elsewhere I have explored further the issues of this paragraph; see my Punitive Violence and Its Alternatives, in *Justice, Law, and Violence* 193 (James B. Brady & Newton Garver eds., 1991).

32 NAACP Legal Defense Fund, *supra*, at 7–15, reporting forty-seven "volunteers" for execution between 1973 and 1997. The total number of persons sentenced to death during these years is not less than five thousand.

33 *Id.*, reporting fifty-one suicides among death row convicts from 1973 through 1997. Attempted suicides are not reported.

34 We lack generally available reports and discussions of the prison behavior of life-term convicted murderers in the prisons of American abolition jurisdictions. In taking the position I do in the text, I am relying mainly on the absence of evidence to the contrary. Thus, at the symposium to celebrate 150 years without the death penalty in Michigan, held in May 1996 at the Thomas M. Cooley Law School in Lansing, Michigan, the state officials and local scholars who spoke on the occasion made no mention of problems in prison management that they believed would have been solved if only Michigan had had the death penalty. See especially Eugene G. Wanger, Historical Reflections on Michigan's Abolition of the Death Penalty, *Thomas M. Cooley L. Rev.* 13 (1996): 755.

35 Is it reasonable to believe that the death penalty could be abolished tomorrow in the Death Belt across the South (from the Carolinas to Arizona) without troubling social repercussions? One might well doubt that it could be. There is no sign in these states of the political leadership needed to make abolition acceptable to the general public as a humane and rational change in punitive policy. The political climate for the past generation, in which the death penalty has received rabid support, makes legislative or judicial abolition (or extensive executive clemency) all but impossible in these jurisdictions. In other death penalty states it is a different story. In New York, for example, beginning in 1977 gubernatorial vetos of death penalty legislation prevented its revival, and without public disorder, until 1995. Were New York's legislature or highest court tomorrow to repeal the death penalty or declare it unconstitutional under the state

constitution (either is highly unlikely), I am confident the return to abolition could be managed without adverse social effects.

Review and Discussion Questions

1 Bedau surveys several arguments that death penalty abolitionists use to defend their case. What are these arguments?
2 How does Bedau critique each of these arguments? Do you agree with his critiques? What more should be debated regarding these arguments, in your view?
3 Given that Bedau rejects various abolitionist arguments, he writes, "This leads us to ask: Is it fair to impute stubborn irrationality and dogmatic sentimentality to those who are absolute abolitionists? I hope not, and I think not." What is his argument in favor of the abolition of capital punishment?
4 Compare and contrast Bedau's argument with the other abolitionist arguments that he rejects. Is it a better argument in your view? Why or why not?

READING: JUSTICE, CIVILIZATION, AND THE DEATH PENALTY

JEFFREY H. REIMAN[*]

It is often assumed that if the death penalty is deserved, then it follows that it should be administered. Jeffrey Reiman disputes this claim, arguing instead that like torture, capital punishment should not be administered because of how horrible it is. He then goes on to assess the central claims made by Ernest van den Haag in defense of capital punishment. Jeffrey Reiman is William Fraser McDowell Professor Emeritus of Philosophy and Social Philosophy at American University.

Civilization, Pain, and Justice

[F]rom the fact that something is justly deserved, it does not automatically follow that it should be done, since there may be other moral reasons for not doing it such that, all told, the weight of moral reasons swings the balance against proceeding. The same argument can be given for the justice of the death penalty for murderers proves the justice of beating assaulters, raping rapists, and torturing torturers. Nonetheless, I believe, and suspect that most would agree, that it would not be right for us to beat assaulters, rape rapists, or torture torturers, *even though it were their just deserts*—and even if this were the only way to make them suffer as much as they had made their victims suffer. Calling for the abolition of the death penalty, though it be just, then, amounts to urging that as a society we place execution in the same category of sanction as beating, raping, and torturing and treat it as something it would not be right for us to do to offenders, *even if it were their just deserts* ....

---

[*] Jeffrey H. Reiman, "Justice, Civilization, and the Death Penalty," *Philosophy and Public Affairs* 14 (Spring 1985): 134–148. Copyright © 1985. Reprinted by permission of Blackwell Publishing Ltd., a company of John Wiley & Sons, Inc.

Progress in civilization is characterized by a lower tolerance for one's own pain and that suffered by others. And this is appropriate, since, via growth in knowledge, civilization brings increased power to prevent or reduce pain and, via growth in the ability to communicate and interact with more and more people, civilization extends the circle of people with whom we empathize.[1] If civilization is characterized by lower tolerance for our own pain and that of others, then publicly refusing to do horrible things to our fellows both signals the level of our civilization *and, by our example, continues the work of civilizing.* And this gesture is all the more powerful if we refuse to do horrible things to those who deserve them. I contend then that the more things we are able to include in this category, the more civilized we are and the more *civilizing.* Thus we gain from including torture in this category, and if execution is especially horrible, we gain still more by including it ….

What can be said of reducing the horrible things that we do to our fellows even when deserved? First of all, given our vulnerability to pain, it seems clearly a gain. Is it, however, an unmitigated gain? That is, would such a reduction ever amount to a loss? It seems to me that there are two conditions under which it would be a loss, namely, if the reduction made our lives more dangerous or if not doing what is justly deserved were a loss in itself. Let us leave aside the former, since, as I have already suggested and as I will soon indicate in greater detail, I accept that if some horrible punishment is necessary to deter equally or more horrible acts, then we may have to impose the punishment. Thus my claim is that reduction in the horrible things we do to our fellows is an advance in civilization *as long as our lives are not thereby made more dangerous* and that it is only then that we are called upon to extend that reduction as part of the work of civilization. Assuming then, for the moment, that we suffer no increased danger by refraining from doing horrible things to our fellows when they justly deserve them, does such refraining to do what is justly deserved amount to a loss?

It seems to me that the answer to this must be that refraining to do what is justly deserved is only a loss where it amounts to doing an injustice. But such refraining to do what is just is not doing what is unjust, unless what we do instead falls below the bottom end of the range of just punishments. Otherwise, it would be unjust to refrain from torturing torturers, raping rapists, or beating assaulters. In short, I take it that if there is no injustice in refraining from torturing torturers, then there is no injustice in refraining to do horrible things to our fellows generally, when they deserve them, as long as what we do instead is compatible with believing that they do deserve them. And thus that if such refraining does not make our lives more dangerous, then it is no loss, and given our vulnerability to pain, it is a gain. Consequently, reduction in the horrible things we do to our fellows, when not necessary to our protection, is an advance in civilization that we are called upon to continue once we consciously take upon ourselves the work of civilization.

To complete the argument, however, I must show that execution is horrible enough to warrant its inclusion alongside torture. Against this it will be said that execution is not especially horrible since it only hastens a fate that is inevitable for us. I think that this view overlooks important differences in the manner in which people reach their inevitable ends. I contend that execution is especially horrible, and it is so in a way similar to (though not identical with) the way in which torture is especially horrible. I believe we view torture as especially awful because of two of its features, which also characterize execution: intense pain and the spectacle of one human being completely subject to the power of another. This latter is separate from the issue of pain since it is something that offends us about unpainful things such as slavery (even voluntarily entered) and prostitution (even voluntarily chosen as an occupation).[2] Execution shares this separate feature, since killing a bound and defenseless human being enacts the total subjugation of that person to his fellows. I think, incidentally, that this accounts for the general uneasiness with which execution by lethal injection has been greeted. Rather than humanizing the event, it seems only to have purchased a possible reduction in physical pain at the price of increasing the spectacle of subjugation with no net gain in the attractiveness of the death penalty. Indeed, its net effect may have been the reverse.

In addition to the spectacle of subjugation, execution, even by physically painless means, is also characterized by a special and intense psychological pain that distinguishes it from the loss of life that awaits us all. Interesting in this regard is the fact that although we are not terribly squeamish about the loss of life itself, allowing it in war, self-defense, as a necessary cost of progress, and so on, we are, as the extraordinary hesitance of our courts testifies, quite reluctant to execute. I think this is because execution involves the most psychologically painful features of deaths. We normally regard death from human causes as worse than death from natural causes, since a humanly caused shortening of life lacks the consolation of unavoidability. And we normally regard death whose coming is foreseen by its victim as worse than sudden death, because a foreseen death adds to the loss of life the terrible consciousness of that impending loss. As a humanly caused death whose advent is foreseen by its victim, an execution combines the worst of both.

Thus far, by analogy with torture, I have argued that execution should be avoided because of how horrible it is to the one executed. But there are reasons of another sort that follow from the analogy with torture. Torture is to be avoided not only because of what it says about *what* we are willing to do to our fellows, but also because of what it says about *us* who are willing to do it. To torture someone is an awful spectacle not only because of the intensity of pain imposed but because of what is required to be able to impose such pain on one's fellows. The tortured body cringes, using its full exertion to escape the pain imposed upon it—it literally begs for relief with its muscles as it does with its cries. To torture someone is to demonstrate a capacity to resist this begging, and that in turn demonstrates a kind of hard-heartedness that a society ought not parade.

And this is true not only of torture but of all severe corporal punishment. Indeed, I think this constitutes part of the answer to the puzzling question of why we refrain from punishments like whipping, even when the alternative (some months in jail versus some lashes) seems more costly to the offender. Imprisonment is painful to be sure, but it is a reflective pain, one that comes with comparing what is to what might have been, and that can be temporarily ignored by thinking about other things. But physical pain has an urgency that holds body and mind in a fierce grip. Of physical pain, as Orwell's Winston Smith recognized, "you could only wish one thing: that it should stop."[3] Refraining from torture in particular and corporal punishment in general, we both refuse to put a fellow human being in this grip *and* refuse to show our ability to resist this wish. The death penalty is the last corporal punishment used officially in the modern world. And it is corporal not only because administered via the body but because the pain of foreseen, humanly administered death strikes us with the urgency that characterizes intense physical pain, causing grown men to cry, faint, and lose control of their bodily functions. There is something to be gained by refusing to endorse the hardness of heart necessary to impose such a fate.

By placing execution alongside torture in the category of things we will not do to our fellow human beings even when they deserve them, we broadcast the message that totally subjugating a person to the power of others *and* confronting him with the advent of his own humanly administered demise is too horrible to be done by civilized human beings to their fellows even when they have earned it: too horrible to do, and too horrible to be capable of doing. And I contend that broadcasting this message loud and clear would in the long run contribute to the general detestation of murder and be, to the extent to which it worked itself into the hearts and minds of the populace, a deterrent. In short, refusing to execute murderers though they deserve it both reflects and continues the taming of the human species that we call civilization. Thus, I take it that the abolition of the death penalty, though it is just punishment for murder, is part of the civilizing mission of modern states.

Civilization, Safety, and Deterrence

Earlier I said that judging a practice too horrible to do even to those who deserve it does not exclude the possibility that it could be justified if necessary to avoid even worse consequences. Thus, were the death penalty clearly proven a better deterrent to the murder of innocent people than life in prison, we might have to admit that we had not yet reached a level of civilization at which we could protect ourselves without imposing this horrible fate on murderers, and thus we might have to grant the necessity of instituting the death penalty.[4] But this is far from proven. The available research by no means clearly indicates that the death penalty reduces the incidence of homicide more than life imprisonment does. Even the econometric studies of Isaac Ehrlich, which purport to show that each execution saves seven or eight potential murder victims, have not changed this fact, as is testified to by the controversy and objections from equally respected statisticians that Ehrlich's work has provoked.[5]

Conceding that it has not been proven that the death penalty deters more murders than life imprisonment, van den Haag has argued that neither has it been proven that the death penalty does *not* deter more murders, and thus we must follow common sense which teaches that the higher the cost of something, the fewer people will choose it, and therefore at least some potential murderers who would not be deterred by life imprisonment will be deterred by the death penalty. ... Those of us who recognize how commonsensical it was, and still is, to believe that the sun moves around the earth, will be less willing than Professor van den Haag to follow common sense here, especially when it comes to doing something awful to our fellows. Moreover, there are good reasons for doubting common sense on this matter. Here are four:

1   From the fact that one penalty is more feared than another, it does not follow that the more feared penalty will deter more than the less feared, unless we know that the less feared penalty is not fearful enough to deter everyone who

can be deterred—and this is just what we don't know with regard to the death penalty. Though I fear the death penalty more than life in prison, I can't think of any act that the death penalty would deter me from that an equal likelihood of spending my life in prison wouldn't deter me from as well. Since it seems to me that whoever would be deterred by a given likelihood of death would be deterred by an *equal* likelihood of life behind bars, I suspect that the commonsense argument only seems plausible because we evaluate it unconsciously assuming that potential criminals will face larger likelihoods of death sentences than of life sentences. If the likelihoods were equal, it seems to me that where life imprisonment was improbable enough to make it too distant a possibility to worry much about, a similar low probability of death would have the same effect. After all, we are undeterred by small likelihoods of death every time we walk the streets. And if life imprisonment were sufficiently probable to pose a real deterrent threat, it would pose as much of a deterrent threat as death. And this is just what most of the research we have on the comparative deterrent impact of execution versus life imprisonment suggests.

2   In light of the fact that roughly 500 to 700 suspected felons are killed by the police in the line of duty every year and the fact that the number of privately owned guns in America is substantially larger than the number of households in America, it must be granted that anyone contemplating committing a crime *already* faces a substantial risk of ending up dead as a result. It's hard to see why anyone *who is not already deterred by this* would be deterred by the addition of the more distant risk of death after apprehension, conviction, and appeal. Indeed, this suggests that people consider risks in a much crueler way than van den Haag's appeal to common sense suggests—which should be evident to anyone who contemplates how few people use seatbelts (14% of drivers, on some estimates) when it is widely known that wearing them can spell the difference between life (outside prison) and death.

3   Van den Haag has maintained that deterrence doesn't work only by means of cost-benefit calculations made by potential criminals. It works also by the lesson about the wrongfulness of murder that is slowly learned in a society that subjects murderers to the ultimate punishment. ... But if I am correct in claiming that the refusal to execute even those who deserve it has a civilizing effect, then the refusal to execute also teaches a lesson about the wrongfulness of murder. My claim here is admittedly speculative, but no more so than van den Haag's to the contrary. And my view has the added virtue of accounting for the failure of research to show an increased deterrent effect from executions *without having to deny the plausibility of van den Haag's commonsense argument that at least some additional potential murderers will be deterred by the prospect of the death penalty.* If there is a deterrent effect from *not executing*, then it is understandable that while executions will deter some murderers, this effect will be balanced out by the weakening of the deterrent effect of not executing, such that no net reduction in murders will result. And this, by the way, also disposes of van den Haag's argument that in the absence of knowledge one way or the other on the deterrent effect of executions, we should execute murderers rather than risk the lives of innocent people whose murders might have been deterred if we had. If there is a deterrent effect of not executing, it follows that we risk innocent lives either way. And if this is so, it

4. Those who still think that van den Haag's commonsense argument for executing murderers is valid will find that the argument proves more than they bargained for. Van den Haag maintains that in the absence of conclusive evidence on the relative deterrent impact of the death penalty versus life imprisonment, we must follow common sense and assume that if one punishment is more fearful than another, it will deter some potential criminals not deterred by the less fearful punishment. Since people sentenced to death will almost universally try to get their sentences changed to life in prison, it follows that death is more fearful than life imprisonment and thus that it will deter some additional murderers. Consequently, we should institute the death penalty to save the lives these additional murderers would have taken. But, since people sentenced to be tortured to death would surely try to get their sentences changed to simple execution, the same argument proves that death by torture will deter still more potential murderers. Consequently, we should institute death by torture to save the lives these additional murderers would have taken. Anyone who accepts van den Haag's argument is then confronted with a dilemma: until we have conclusive evidence that capital punishment is a greater deterrent to murder than life imprisonment, we must grant *either* that we should not follow common sense and not impose the death penalty *or* we should follow common sense and torture murderers to death. In short, either we must abolish the electric chair or reinstitute the rack. Surely, this is the *reductio ad absurdum* of van den Haag's commonsense argument.

seems that the only reasonable course of action is to refrain from imposing what we know is a horrible fate.

Conclusion: History, Force, and Justice

I believe that, taken together, these arguments prove that we should abolish the death penalty though it is a just punishment for murder. Let me close with an argument of a different sort. When you see the lash fall upon the backs of Roman slaves or the hideous tortures meted out in the period of the absolute monarchs, you see more than mere cruelty at work. Surely you suspect that there is something about the injustice of imperial slavery and royal tyranny that requires the use of extreme force to keep these institutions in place. That is, for reasons undoubtedly related to those that support the second part of Durkheim's first law of penal evolution, we take the amount of force a society uses against its own people as an inverse measure of its justness. And though no more than a rough measure, it is a revealing one nonetheless, because when a society is limited in the degree of force it can use against its subjects, it is likely to have to be a juster society, since it will have to gain its subjects' cooperation by offering them fairer terms than it would have to if it could use more force. From this we cannot simply conclude that reducing the force used by our society will automatically make our society more just—but I think we can conclude that it will have this tendency, since it will require us to find means other than force for encouraging compliance with our institutions, and this is likely to require us to make those institutions as fair to all as possible. Thus, I hope that America will pose itself the challenge of winning its citizens' cooperation by justice rather than force and that when future historians look back on the twentieth century, they will find us with countries like France and England and Sweden that have abolished the death penalty rather than with those like South Africa and the Soviet Union and Iran that have retained it—with all that this suggests about the countries involved.

Notes

1 Van den Haag writes that our ancestors "were not as repulsed by physical pain as we are. The change has to do not with our greater smartness or moral superiority but with a new outlook pioneered by the French and American revolutions [namely, that assertion of human equality and with it 'universal identification'], and by such mundane things as the invention of anesthetics, which make pain much less of an everyday experience" (Ernest van den Haag and John P. Conrad, *The Death Penalty: A Debate* [New York: Plenum Press, 1983], p. 215; cf. van den Haag's *Punishing Criminals* [New York: Basic Books, 1975], pp. 196–206).
2 I am not here endorsing this view of voluntarily entered slavery or prostitution. I mean only to suggest that it is *the belief* that these relations involve the extreme subjugation of one person to the power of another that is at the basis of their offensiveness. What I am saying is quite compatible with finding that this belief is false with respect to voluntarily entered slavery or prostitution.
3 George Orwell, *1984* (New York: New American Library, 1983; originally published in 1949), p. 197.
4 I say "might" here to avoid the sticky question of just how effective a deterrent the death penalty would have to be to justify overcoming our scruples about executing. It is here that the other considerations often urged against capital punishment—discrimination, irrevocability, the possibility of mistake, and so on—would play a role. Omitting such qualifications, however, my position might crudely be stated as follows: *Just desert limits what a civilized society may do to deter crime, and deterrence limits what a civilized society may do to give criminals their just deserts.*
5 Issac Ehrlich, "The Deterrent Effect of Capital Punishment: A Question of Life or Death," *Am. Econ. Rev.* 65 (June 1975): 397–417. For reactions to Ehrlich's work, see Alfred Blumstein, Jacqueline Cohen, and Daniel Nagin, eds., *Deterrence and Incapacitation: Estimating the Effects of Criminal Sanctions on Crime Rates* (Washington, DC: National Academy of Sciences, 1978), esp. pp. 59–63 and 336–60; Brian E. Forst, "The Deterrent Effect on Capital Punishment: A Cross-State Analysis," *Minnesota Law Rev.* 61 (May 1977): 743–67; Deryck Beyleveld, "Ehrlich's Analysis of Deterrence," *Brit. J. Criminol.* 22 (April 1982): 101–23; and Isaac Ehrlich, "On Positive Methodology, Ethics and Polemics in Deterrence Research," *Brit. J. Criminol.* 22 (April 1982): 124–39. Much of the criticism of Ehrlich's work focuses on the fact that he found a deterrence impact of executions in the period from 1933–1969, which includes the period 1963–1969, a time when hardly any executions were carried out and crime rates rose for reasons that are arguably independent of the existence or nonexistence of capital punishment. When the 1963–1969 period is excluded, no significant deterrent effect shows. Prior to Ehrlich's work, research on the comparative deterrent impact of the death penalty versus life imprisonment indicated no increase in the incidence of homicide in states that abolished the death penalty and no greater incidence of homicide in states without the death penalty compared to similar states with the death penalty. See Thorsten Sellin, *The Death Penalty* (Philadelphia, PA: American Law Institute, 1959).

Review and Discussion Questions

1 How does Reiman understand social progress?
2 Explain why Reiman thinks that the failure to abolish capital punishment signifies a low level of civilization. What analogy does he make to substantiate his claim?
3 Describe each of Reiman's responses to van den Haag's argument that capital punishment deters.

Essay and Paper Topics for Chapter 6

1. Suppose we do not know whether capital punishment deters criminals. Is it better, all things considered, if we assume that it does deter and we are wrong, or if we assume it does not deter and we are wrong? Explain your answer.
2. On balance, do you think that capital punishment is justified or that it should be abolished? What argument poses the strongest challenge to your conclusion? How do you respond to it?
3. Compare the moral issues raised by killing in war and capital punishment. Might a person take the view that capital punishment is unjustified whereas killing in war is acceptable? Or should people who oppose capital punishment also be pacifists?
4. Drawing on the general moral theories from Part I that you found most reasonable, write an essay in which you discuss how, from the point of view of that theory, you would evaluate the position of at least two authors in this chapter.

Chapter 7

Animals, Environmentalism, and Climate

We assume that human lives are valuable and worth protecting; but what about other forms of life? Are species themselves important, for example? Are ecosystems in general valuable for their own sake? Essays in this chapter consider when and why nonhuman life is worthy of moral consideration and whether or not that value depends ultimately on satisfying human wants or needs. In addition, what is the best philosophical grounding for caring about the environment? The last essay contributes to recent debates about climate change.

READING: ALL ANIMALS ARE EQUAL

PETER SINGER[*]

In this influential essay, taken from his book *Animal Liberation*, Peter Singer argues that equality applies to animals as well as to humans and that our ordinary attitudes toward nonhuman animals betray a bias toward our species that is rather like the attitudes of a racist or sexist. Both our eating habits and our use of animals in experiments are, he argues, morally wrong. Peter Singer is the Ira W. DeCamp Professor of Bioethics at Princeton University, and a Laureate Professor at the Centre for Applied Philosophy and Public Ethics at the University of Melbourne.

"Animal Liberation" may sound more like a parody of other liberation movements than a serious objective. The idea of "The Rights of Animals" actually was once used to parody the case for women's rights. When Mary Wollstonecraft, a forerunner of today's feminists, published her *Vindication of the Rights of Women* in 1792, her views were widely regarded as absurd, and before long an anonymous publication appeared entitled *A Vindication of the Rights of Brutes*. The author of this satirical work (now known to have been Thomas Taylor, a distinguished Cambridge philosopher) tried to refute Mary Wollstonecraft's arguments by showing that they could be carried one stage further. If the argument for equality was sound when applied to women, why should it not be applied to dogs, cats, and horses? The reasoning seemed to hold for these "brutes" too; yet to hold that brutes had rights was manifestly absurd; therefore the reasoning by which this

---

[*] From *Animal Liberation* by Peter Singer. Copyright © 1977. Published by Avon Books. Reprinted by permission.

conclusion had been reached must be unsound, and if unsound when applied to brutes, it must also be unsound when applied to women, since the very same arguments had been used in each case.

I Sexual and Racial Equality

In order to explain the basis of the case for the equality of animals, it will be helpful to start with an examination of the case for the equality of women .... The extension of the basic principle of equality from one group to another does not imply that we must treat both groups in exactly the same way or grant exactly the same rights to both groups. Whether we should do so will depend on the nature of the members of the two groups. The basic principle of equality does not require equal or identical *treatment;* it requires equal *consideration.* Equal consideration for different beings may lead to different treatment and different rights ....

When we say that all human beings, whatever their race, creed, or sex, are equal, what is it that we are asserting? Those who wish to defend hierarchical, inegalitarian societies have often pointed out that by whatever test we choose, it simply is not true that all humans are equal. Like it or not, we must face the fact that humans come in different shapes and sizes; they come with different moral capacities, different intellectual abilities, different amounts of benevolent feeling and sensitivity to the needs of others, different abilities to communicate effectively, and different capacities to experience pleasure and pain. In short, if the demand for equality were based on the actual equality of all human beings, we would have to stop demanding equality.

Still, one might cling to the view that the demand for equality among human beings is based on the actual equality of different races and sexes. Although, it may be said, humans differ as individuals, there are no such differences between races and sexes *as such.* From the mere fact that a person is black or a woman we cannot infer anything about that person's intellectual or moral capacities. This, it may be said, is why racism and sexism are wrong. The white racist claims that whites are superior to blacks, but this is false .... The opponent of sexism would say the same: a person's sex is no guide to his or her abilities, and this is why it is unjustifiable to discriminate on the basis of sex.

The existence of individual variations that cut across the lines of race or sex, however, provides us with no defense at all against a more sophisticated opponent of equality, one who proposes that, say, the interests of all those with IQ scores below 100 be given less consideration than the interests of those with ratings over 100 ....

There is a second important reason why we ought not to base our opposition to racism and sexism on any kind of actual equality, even the limited kind that asserts that variations in capacities and abilities are spread evenly between the different races and sexes: we can have no absolute guarantee that these capacities and abilities really are distributed evenly, without regard to race or sex, among human beings. So far as actual abilities are concerned, there do seem to be certain measurable differences between both races and sexes. These differences do not, of course, appear in each case, but only when averages are taken. More important still, we do not yet know how much of these differences is really due to different genetic endowments of the different races and sexes and how much is due to poor schools, poor housing, and other factors that are the result of past and continuing discrimination. Perhaps all the important differences will eventually prove to be environmental rather than genetic. Anyone opposed to racism and sexism will certainly hope that this will be so, for it will make the task of ending discrimination a lot easier; nevertheless it would be dangerous to rest the case against racism and sexism on the belief that all significant differences are environmental in origin. The opponent of, say, racism who takes this line will be unable to avoid conceding that *if* differences in ability do after all prove to have some genetic connection with race, racism would in some way be defensible.

Fortunately there is no need to pin the case for equality to one particular outcome of a scientific investigation. The appropriate response to those who claim to have found evidence of genetically based differences in ability between the races or sexes is not to stick to the belief that the genetic explanation must be wrong, whatever evidence to the contrary may turn up: instead we should make it quite clear that the claim to equality does not depend on intelligence, moral capacity, physical strength, or similar matters of fact. Equality is a moral idea, not an assertion of fact. There is no logically compelling reason for assuming that a factual difference in ability between two people justifies any difference in the amount of consideration we give to their needs and interests. *The principle of equality of human beings is not a description of an alleged actual equality among humans: it is a prescription of how we should treat humans.*

Jeremy Bentham, the founder of the reforming utilitarian school of moral philosophy, incorporated the essential basis of moral equality into his system of ethics by means of the formula: "Each to count for one and none for more than one." In other words, the interests of every being affected by an action are to be taken into account and given the same weight as the like interests of any other being. A later utilitarian, Henry Sidgwick, put the point in this way: "The good of any one individual is of no more importance, from the point of view (if I may say so) of the Universe, than the good of any other."

It is an implication of this principle of equality that our concern for others and our readiness to consider their interests ought not to depend on what they are like or on what abilities they may possess. Precisely what this concern or consideration requires us to do may vary according to the characteristics of those affected by what we do: concern for the well-being of a child growing up in America would require that we teach him to read; concern for the well-being of a pig may require no more than that we leave him alone with other pigs in a place where there is adequate food and room to run freely. But the basic element—the taking into account of the interests of the being, whatever those interests may be—must, according to the principle of equality, be extended to all beings, black or white, masculine or feminine, human or nonhuman.

Thomas Jefferson, who was responsible for writing the principle of the equality of men into the American Declaration of Independence, saw this point. It led him to oppose slavery even though he was unable to free himself fully from his slaveholding background. He wrote in a letter to the author of a book that emphasized the notable intellectual achievements of Negroes in order to refute the then-common view that they had limited intellectual capacities:

> Be assured that no person living wishes more sincerely than I do, to see a complete refutation of the doubts I have myself entertained and expressed on the grade of understanding allotted to them by nature, and to find that they are on a par with ourselves but whatever be their degree of talent it is no measure of their rights. Because Sir Isaac Newton was superior to others in understanding, he was not therefore lord of the property or person of others.[1]

Similarly when in the 1850s the call for women's rights was raised in the United States, a remarkable black feminist named Sojourner Truth made the same point in more robust terms at a feminist convention:

> [T]hey talk about this thing in the head; what do they call it? ["Intellect," whispered someone near by.] That's it. What's that got to do with women's rights or Negroes' rights? If my cup won't hold but a pint and yours holds a quart, wouldn't you be mean not to let me have my little half-measure full?[2]

It is on this basis that the case against racism and the case against sexism must both ultimately rest; and it is in accordance with this principle that the attitude that we may call "speciesism," by analogy with racism, must also be condemned.

2 Speciesism and the Equality of Animals

Speciesism—the word is not an attractive one, but I can think of no better term—is a prejudice or attitude of bias toward the interests of members of one's own species and against those of members of other species. It should be obvious that the fundamental objections to racism and sexism made by Thomas Jefferson and Sojourner Truth apply equally to speciesism. If possessing a higher degree of intelligence does not entitle one human to use another for his own ends, how can it entitle humans to exploit nonhumans for the same purpose?[3]

Many philosophers and other writers have proposed the principle of equal consideration of interests, in some form or other, as a basic moral principle, but not many of them have recognized that this principle applies to members of other species as well as to our own. Jeremy Bentham was one of the few who did realize this. In a forward-looking passage written at a time when black slaves had been freed by the French but in the British dominions were still being treated in the way we now treat animals, Bentham wrote:

> The day *may* come when the rest of the animal creation may acquire those rights which never could have been withholden from them but by the hand of tyranny. The French have already discovered that the blackness of the skin is no reason why a human being should be abandoned without redress to the caprice of a tormentor. It may one day come to be recognized that the number of the legs, the villosity of the skin, or the termination of the *os sacrum* are reasons equally insufficient for abandoning a sensitive being to the same fate. What else is it that should trace the insuperable line? Is it the faculty of reason, or perhaps the faculty of discourse? But a full-grown horse or dog is beyond comparison a more rational, as well as a more conversable animal, than an infant of a day or a week or even a month, old. But suppose they

were otherwise, what would it avail? The question is not, Can they *reason?* nor Can they *talk?* but, Can they *suffer?*[4]

In this passage Bentham points to the capacity for suffering as the vital characteristic that gives a being the right to equal consideration. The capacity for suffering—or, more strictly, for suffering and/or enjoyment or happiness—is not just another characteristic like the capacity for language or higher mathematics. Bentham is not saying that those who try to mark "the insuperable line" that determines whether the interests of a being should be considered happen to have chosen the wrong characteristic. By saying that we must consider the interests of all beings with the capacity for suffering or enjoyment, Bentham does not arbitrarily exclude from consideration any interests at all—as those who draw the line with reference to the possession of reason or language do. The capacity for suffering and enjoyment is *a prerequisite for having interests at all*, a condition that must be satisfied before we can speak of interests in a meaningful way. It would be nonsense to say that it was not in the interests of a stone to be kicked along the road by a schoolboy. A stone does not have interests because it cannot suffer. Nothing that we can do to it could possibly make any difference to its welfare. A mouse, on the other hand, does have an interest in not being kicked along the road, because it will suffer if it is.

If a being suffers, there can be no moral justification for refusing to take that suffering into consideration. No matter what the nature of the being, the principle of equality requires that its suffering be counted equally with the like suffering—insofar as rough comparisons can be made—of any other being. If a being is not capable of suffering or of experiencing enjoyment or happiness, there is nothing to be taken into account. So the limit of sentience (using the term as a convenient if not strictly accurate shorthand for the capacity to suffer and/or experience enjoyment) is the only defensible boundary of concern for the interests of others. To mark this boundary by some other characteristic like intelligence or rationality would be to mark it in an arbitrary manner. Why not choose some other characteristic, like skin color?

The racist violates the principle of equality by giving greater weight to the interests of members of his own race when there is a clash between their interests and the interests of those of another race. The sexist violates the principle of equality by favoring the interests of his own sex. Similarly, the speciesist allows the interests of his own species to override the greater interests of members of other species. The pattern is identical in each case.

Most human beings are speciesists. Ordinary human beings—not a few exceptionally cruel or heartless humans, but the overwhelming majority of humans—take an active part in, acquiesce in, and allow their taxes to pay for practices that require the sacrifice of the most important interests of members of other species in order to promote the most trivial interests of our own species ....

3 Speciesism in Practice

For the great majority of human beings, especially in urban, industrialized societies, the most direct form of contact with members of other species is at mealtimes: we eat them. In doing so, we treat them purely as means to our ends. We regard their life and well-being as subordinate to our taste for a particular kind of dish. I say "taste" deliberately—this is purely a matter of pleasing our palate. There can be no defense of eating flesh in terms of satisfying nutritional needs, since it has been established beyond doubt that we could satisfy our need for protein and other essential nutrients far more efficiently with a diet that replaced animal flesh by soy beans, or products derived from soy beans, and other high-protein vegetable products.[5]

It is not merely the act of killing that indicates what we are ready to do to other species in order to gratify our tastes. The suffering we inflict on the animals while they are alive is perhaps an even clearer indication of our speciesism than the fact that we are prepared to kill them.[6] In order to have meat on the table at a price that people can afford, our society tolerates methods of meat production that confine sentient animals in cramped, unsuitable conditions for the entire duration of their lives. Animals are treated like machines that convert fodder into flesh, and any innovation that results in a higher "conversion ratio" is liable to be adopted. As one authority on the subject has said, "cruelty is acknowledged only when profitability ceases."[7] So hens are crowded four or five to a cage with a floor area of twenty inches by eighteen inches, or around the size of a single page of the *New York Times*. The cages have wire floors, since this reduces cleaning costs, though wire is unsuitable for the hens' feet; the floors slope, since this makes the eggs roll down for easy collection, although this makes it difficult for the hens to rest comfortably. In these conditions all the birds' natural instincts are thwarted: they cannot stretch their wings fully, walk freely, dust-bathe, scratch the ground, or build a nest. Although they have never known other conditions, observers have noticed that the birds vainly try to perform these actions. Frustrated at their inability to do so, they often develop what farmers call "vices," and peck each other to death. To prevent this, the beaks of young birds are often cut off.

This kind of treatment is not limited to poultry. Pigs are now also being reared in cages inside sheds. These animals are comparable to dogs in intelligence and need a varied, stimulating environment if they are not to suffer from stress and boredom. Anyone who kept a dog in the way in which pigs are frequently kept would be liable to prosecution, in England at least, but because our interest in exploiting pigs is greater than our interest in exploiting dogs, we object to cruelty to dogs while consuming the produce of cruelty to pigs. Of the other animals, the condition of veal calves is perhaps worst of all, since these animals are so closely confined that they cannot even turn around or get up and lie down freely. In this way they do not develop unpalatable muscle. They are also made anemic and kept short of roughage to keep their flesh pale, since white veal fetches a higher price; as a result, they develop a craving for iron and roughage and have been observed to gnaw wood off the sides of their stalls and lick greedily at any rusty hinge that is within reach.

Since, as I have said, none of these practices cater to anything more than our pleasures of taste, our practice of rearing and killing other animals in order to eat them is a clear instance of the sacrifice of the most important interests of other beings in order to satisfy trivial interests of our own. To avoid speciesism we must stop this practice, and each of us has a moral obligation to cease supporting the practice. Our custom is all the support that the meat industry needs. The decision to cease giving it that support may be difficult, but it is no more difficult than it would have been for a white Southerner to go against the traditions of his society and free his slaves; if we do not change our dietary habits, how can we censure those slaveholders who would not change their own way of living?

The same form of discrimination may be observed in the widespread practice of experimenting on other species in order to see if certain substances are safe for human beings or to test some psychological theory about the effect of severe punishment on learning or to try out various new compounds just in case something turns up. People sometimes think that all this experimentation is for vital medical purposes and so will reduce suffering overall. This comfortable belief is very wide of the mark. Drug companies test new shampoos and cosmetics that they are intending to put on the market by dropping them into the eyes of rabbits, held open by metal clips, in order to observe what damage results. Food additives, like artificial colorings and preservatives, are tested by what is known as the "LD50"—a test designed to find the level of consumption at which 50 percent of a group of animals will die. In the process, nearly all of the animals are made very sick before some finally die and others pull through. If the substance is relatively harmless, as it often is, huge doses have to be force-fed to the animals, until in some cases sheer volume or concentration of the substance causes death.

Much of this pointless cruelty goes on in the universities. In many areas of science, nonhuman animals are regarded as an item of laboratory equipment to be used and expended as desired. In psychology laboratories, experimenters devise endless variations and repetitions of experiments that were of little value in the first place. To quote just one example, from the experimenter's own account in a psychology journal: at the University of Pennsylvania, Perrin S. Cohen hung six dogs in hammocks with electrodes taped to their hind feet. Electric shock of varying intensity was then administered through the electrodes. If the dog learned to press its head against a panel on the left, the shock was turned off, but otherwise it remained on indefinitely. Three of the dogs, however, were required to wait periods varying from 2 to 7 seconds while being shocked before making the response that turned off the current. If they failed to wait, they received further shocks. Each dog was given from 26 to 46 "sessions" in the hammock, each session consisting of 80 "trials" or shocks, administered at intervals of one minute. The experimenter reported that the dogs, who were unable to move in the hammock, barked or bobbed their heads when the current was applied. The reported findings of the experiment were that there was a delay in the dogs' responses that increased proportionately to the time the dogs were required to endure the shock, but a gradual increase in the intensity of the shock had no systematic effect in the timing of the response. The experiment was funded by the National Institutes of Health, and the United States Public Health Service.[8]

In this example, and countless cases like it, the possible benefits to mankind are either nonexistent or fantastically remote, while the certain losses to members of other species are very real. This is, again, a clear indication of speciesism ....

4 The Value of Lives: Humans and Nonhumans

If I give a horse a hard slap across its rump with my open hand, the horse may start, but it presumably feels little pain. Its skin is thick enough to protect it against a mere slap. If I slap a baby in the same way, however, the baby will cry and presumably does feel pain, for its skin is more sensitive. So it is worse to slap a baby than a horse, if both slaps are administered with equal force. But there must be some kind of blow—I don't know exactly what it would be, but perhaps a blow with a heavy stick—that would cause the horse as much pain as we cause a baby by slapping it with our hand. That is what I mean by "the same amount of pain," and if we consider it wrong to inflict that much pain on a baby for no good reason, then we must, unless we are speciesists, consider it equally wrong to inflict the same amount of pain on a horse for no good reason.

There are other differences between humans and animals that cause other complications. Normal adult human beings have mental capacities which will, in certain circumstances, lead them to suffer more than animals would in the same circumstances. If, for instance, we decided to perform extremely painful or lethal scientific experiments on normal adult humans kidnapped at random from public parks for this purpose, every adult who entered a park would become fearful that he would be kidnapped. The resultant terror would be a form of suffering additional to the pain of the experiment. The same experiments performed on nonhuman animals would cause less suffering, since the animals would not have the anticipatory dread of being kidnapped and experimented upon. This does not mean, of course, that it would be right to perform the experiment on animals, but only that there is a reason, which is not speciesist, for preferring to use animals rather than normal adult humans, if the experiment is to be done at all. It should be noted, however, that this same argument gives us a reason for preferring to use human infants—orphans perhaps—or retarded humans for experiments rather than adults, since infants and retarded humans would also have no idea of what was going to happen to them. So far as this argument is concerned, nonhuman animals and infants and retarded humans are in the same category; and if we use this argument to justify experiments on nonhuman animals, we have to ask ourselves whether we are also prepared to allow experiments on human infants and retarded adults; and if we make a distinction between animals and these humans, on what basis can we do it, other than a bare-faced—and morally indefensible—preference for members of our own species?

There are many areas in which the superior mental powers of normal adult humans make a difference: anticipation, more detailed memory, greater knowledge of what is happening, and so on. Yet these differences do not all point to greater suffering on the part of the normal human being. Sometimes an animal may suffer more because of his more limited understanding. If, for instance, we are taking prisoners in wartime, we can explain to them that while they must submit to capture, search, and confinement they will not otherwise be harmed and will be set free at the conclusion of hostilities. If we capture a wild animal, however, we cannot explain that we are not threatening its life. A wild animal cannot distinguish an attempt to overpower and confine from an attempt to kill; the one causes as much terror as the other.

It may be objected that comparisons of the sufferings of different species are impossible to make and that for this reason when the interests of animals and humans clash the principle of equality gives no guidance. It is probably true that comparisons of suffering between members of different species cannot be made precisely, but precision is not essential. Even if we were to prevent the infliction of suffering on animals only when it is quite certain that the interests of humans will not be affected to anything like the extent that animals are affected, we would be forced to make radical changes in our treatment of animals that would involve our diet; the farming methods we use, experimental procedures in many fields of science; our approach to wildlife and to hunting, trapping, and the wearing of furs; and areas of entertainment like circuses, rodeos, and zoos. As a result, a vast amount of suffering would be avoided.

So far I have said a lot about the infliction of suffering on animals but nothing about killing them. This omission has been deliberate. The application of the principle of equality to the infliction of suffering is, in theory at least, fairly straightforward. Pain and suffering are bad and should be prevented or minimized, irrespective of the race, sex, or species of the being that suffers. How bad a pain is depends on how intense it is and how long it lasts, but pains of the same intensity and duration are equally bad, whether felt by humans or animals.

The wrongness of killing a being is more complicated. I have kept, and shall continue to keep, the question of killing in the background because in the present state of human tyranny over other species, the more simple, straightforward principle of equal consideration of pain or pleasure is a sufficient basis for identifying and protesting against all the major abuses of animals that humans practice. Nevertheless, it is necessary to say something about killing.

Just as most humans are speciesists in their readiness to cause pain to animals when they would not cause a similar pain to humans for the same reason, so most humans are speciesists in their readiness to kill other animals when they would not kill humans. We need to proceed more cautiously here, however, because people hold widely differing views about when it is legitimate to kill humans, as the continuing debates over abortion and euthanasia attest. Nor have moral philosophers been able to agree on exactly what it is that makes it wrong to kill humans and under what circumstances killing a human being may be justifiable.

Let us consider first the view that it is always wrong to take an innocent human life. We may call this the "sanctity-of-life" view. People who take this view oppose abortion and euthanasia. They do not usually, however, oppose the killing of nonhumans—so perhaps it would be more accurate to describe this view as the "sanctity of *human* life" view.

The belief that human life, and only human life, is sacrosanct is a form of speciesism. To see this, consider the following example.

Assuming that, as sometimes happens, an infant has been born with massive and irreparable brain damage. The damage is so severe that the infant can never be any more than a "human vegetable," unable to talk, recognize other people, act independently of others, or develop a sense of self-awareness. The parents of the infant, realizing that they cannot hope for any improvement in their child's condition and being in any case unwilling to spend, or ask the state to spend, the thousands of dollars that would be needed annually for proper care of the infant, ask the doctor to kill the infant painlessly.

Should the doctor do what the parents ask? Legally, he should not, and in this respect the law reflects the sanctity-of-life view. The life of every human being is sacred. Yet people who would say this about the infant do not object to the killing of nonhuman animals. How can they justify their different judgments? Adult chimpanzees, dogs, pigs, and many other species far surpass the brain-damaged infant in their ability to relate to others, act independently, be self-aware, and any other capacity that could reasonably be said to give value to life. With the most intensive care possible, there are retarded infants who can never achieve the intelligence level of a dog. Nor can we appeal to the concern of the infant's parents, since they themselves, in this imaginary example (and in some actual cases), do not want the infant kept alive.

The only thing that distinguishes the infant from the animal in the eyes of those who claim it has a "right to life" is that it is, biologically, a member of the species *Homo sapiens*, whereas chimpanzees, dogs, and pigs are not. But to use *this* difference as the basis for granting a right to life to the infant and not to the other animals is, of course, pure speciesism.[9] It is exactly the kind of arbitrary difference that the most crude and overt kind of racist uses in attempting to justify racial discrimination.

This does not mean that to avoid speciesism we must hold that it is as wrong to kill a dog as it is to kill a normal human being. The only position that is irredeemably speciesist is the one that tries to make the boundary of the right to life run exactly parallel to the boundary of our own species. Those who hold the sanctity-of-life view do this because while distinguishing sharply between humans and other animals they allow no distinctions to be made within our own species, objecting to the killing of the severely retarded and the hopelessly senile as strongly as they object to the killing of normal adults.

To avoid speciesism, we must allow that beings which are similar in all relevant respects have a similar right to life—and mere membership in our own biological species cannot be a morally relevant criterion for this right. Within these limits we could still hold that, for instance, it is worse to kill a normal adult human with a capacity for self-awareness and the ability to plan for the future and have meaningful relations with others than it is to kill a mouse, which presumably does not share all of these characteristics; or we might appeal to the close family and other personal ties which humans have but mice do not have to the same degree; or we might think that it is the consequences for other humans, who will be put in fear of their own lives, that makes the crucial difference; or we might think it is some combination of these factors, or other factors altogether.

Whatever criteria we choose, however, we will have to admit that they do not follow precisely the boundary of our own species. We may legitimately hold that there are some features of certain beings which make their lives more valuable than those of other beings; but there will surely be some nonhuman animals whose lives, by any standards, are more valuable than the lives of some humans. A chimpanzee, dog, or pig, for instance, will have a higher degree of self-awareness and a greater capacity for meaningful relations with others than a severely retarded infant or someone in a state of advanced senility. So if we base the right to life on these characteristics we must grant these animals a right to life as good as, or better than, such retarded or senile humans.

Now this argument cuts both ways. It could be taken as showing that chimpanzees, dogs, and pigs, along with some other species, have a right to life and we commit a grave moral offense whenever we kill them, even when they are old and suffering and our intention is to put them out of their misery. Alternatively, one could take the argument as showing that the severely retarded and hopelessly senile have no right to life and may be killed for quite trivial reasons, as we now kill animals.

Since my focus here is on ethical questions concerning animals and not on the morality of euthanasia, I shall not attempt to settle this issue finally. I think it is reasonably clear, though, that while both of the positions just described avoid speciesism, neither is entirely satisfactory. What we need is some middle position which would avoid speciesism but would not make the lives of the retarded and senile as cheap as the lives of pigs and dogs now are nor make the lives of pigs and dogs so sacrosanct that we think it wrong to put them out of hopeless misery. What we must do is bring nonhuman animals within our sphere of moral concern and cease to treat their lives as expendable for whatever trivial purposes we may have. At the same time, once we realize that the fact that a being is a member of our own species is not in itself enough to make it always wrong to kill that being, we may come to reconsider our policy of preserving human lives at all costs, even when there is no prospect of a meaningful life or of existence without terrible pain.

I conclude, then, that a rejection of speciesism does not imply that all lives are of equal worth. While self-awareness, intelligence, the capacity for meaningful relations with others, and so on are not relevant to the question of inflicting pain —since pain is pain, whatever other capacities beyond the capacity to feel pain the being may have—these capacities may be relevant to the question of taking life. It is not arbitrary to hold that the life of a self-aware being, capable of abstract thought, of planning for the future, of complex acts of communication, and so on, is more valuable than the life of a being without these capacities. To see the difference between the issues of inflicting pain and taking life, consider how we would choose within our own species. If we had to choose to save the life of a normal human or a mentally defective human, we would probably choose to save the life of the normal human; but if we had to choose between preventing pain in the normal human or the mental defective—imagine that both have received painful but superficial injuries and we only have enough painkiller for one of them—it is not nearly so clear how we ought to choose. The same is true when we consider other species. The evil of pain is, in itself, unaffected by the other characteristics of the being that feels the pain; the value of life is affected by these other characteristics.

Normally this will mean that if we have to choose between the life of a human being and the life of another animal we should choose to save the life of the human, but there may be special cases in which the reverse holds true, because the human being in question does not have the capacities of a normal human being ....

5 A Distinctive Human Dignity?

[The] idea of a distinctive human dignity and worth has a long history. Contemporary philosophers have cast off its original metaphysical and religious shackles and freely invoke the idea of human dignity without feeling any need to justify the idea at all. Why should we not attribute "intrinsic dignity" or "intrinsic worth" to ourselves? Why should we not say that we are the only things in the universe that have intrinsic value? ....

The truth is that the appeal to the intrinsic dignity of human beings appears to solve the egalitarian philosopher's problems only as long as it goes unchallenged.

Once we ask why it should be that all humans—including infants, mental defectives, criminal psychopaths, Hitler, Stalin, and the rest—have some kind of dignity or worth that no elephant, pig, or chimpanzee can ever achieve, we see that this question is as difficult to answer as our original request for some relevant fact that justifies the inequality of humans and other animals. In fact, these two questions are really one: talk of intrinsic dignity or moral worth does not help, because any satisfactory defense of the claim that all and only humans have intrinsic dignity would need to refer to some relevant capacities or characteristics that only human beings have, in virtue of which they have this unique dignity or worth. To introduce ideas of dignity and worth as a substitute for other reasons for distinguishing humans and animals is not good enough. Fine phrases are the last resource of those who have run out of arguments.

Notes

1 Letter to Henri Gregoire, February 25, 1809.
2 Reminiscences by Francis D. Gage, from Susan B. Anthony, *The History of Woman Suffrage*, vol. 1; the passage is to be found in the extract in Leslie Tanner, ed., *Voices from Women's Liberation* (New York: Signet, 1970).
3 I owe the term *speciesism* to Richard Ryder.
4 *Introduction to the Principles of Morals and Legislation* (1789), Chapter 17.
5 In order to produce 1 lb. of protein in the form of beef or veal, we must feed 21 lbs. of protein to the animal. Other forms of livestock are slightly less inefficient, but the average ratio in the U.S. is still 1:8. It has been estimated that the amount of protein lost to humans in this way is equivalent to 90 percent of the annual world protein deficit. For a brief account, see Frances Moore Lappe, *Diet for a Small Planet* (New York: Friends of the Earth/Ballantine, 1971), pp. 4–11.
6 Although one might think that killing a being is obviously the ultimate wrong one can do to it, I think that the infliction of suffering is a clearer indication of speciesism because it might be argued that at least part of what is wrong with killing a human is that most humans are conscious of their existence over time and have desires and purposes that extend into the future. Of course, if one took this view, one would have to hold that killing a human infant or mental defective is not in itself wrong and is less serious than killing certain higher mammals that probably do have a sense of their own existence over time.
7 Ruth Harrison, *Animal Machines* (London: Stuart, 1964). This book provides an eye-opening account of intensive farming methods for those unfamiliar with the subject.
8 *Journal of the Experimental Analysis of Behavior* 13, no. 1 (1970). Any recent volume of this journal, or of other journals in the field, such as the *Journal of Comparative and Physiological Psychology*, will contain reports of equally cruel and trivial experiments.
9 I am here putting aside religious views, for example the doctrine that all and only humans have immortal souls or are made in the image of God. Historically these views have been very important and no doubt are partly responsible for the idea that human life has a special sanctity. Logically, however, these religious views are unsatisfactory, since a reasoned explanation of why it should be that all humans and no nonhumans have immortal souls is not offered. This belief too, therefore, comes under suspicion as a form of speciesism. In any case, defenders of the "sanctity of life" view are generally reluctant to base their position on purely religious doctrines, since these doctrines are no longer as widely accepted as they once were.

Review and Discussion Questions

1 What reasons does Singer give for rejecting the idea that human equality rests on factual similarities?

2 What does Singer think human equality does mean? What are the implications of that for our treatment of animals?
3 Describe the practices that most clearly demonstrate our speciesism.
4 What facts about humans might you point to in defending the notion that a living human has rights that other animals lack?
5 Suppose a meat-eater argued that although factory farms do involve some suffering, the animals are still better off for having lived. How would that claim, if true, affect Singer's argument for vegetarianism?
6 Describe what you think would be the implications of Singer's position for euthanasia and abortion.

READING: SPECIESISM AND THE IDEA OF EQUALITY

BONNIE STEINBOCK[*]

Bonnie Steinbock rejects Peter Singer's attack on "speciesism," defending instead the view that membership in the human species is in itself morally important. Human beings, she claims, have important characteristics that warrant treating us differently from nonhuman animals even though, she admits, animal suffering is also morally important. Bonnie Steinbock is Professor of Philosophy Emeritus at Albany University, State University of New York.

Most of us believe that we are entitled to treat members of other species in ways which would be considered wrong if inflicted on members of our own species. We kill them for food, keep them confined, use them in painful experiments. The moral philosopher has to ask what relevant difference justifies this difference in treatment. A look at this question will lead us to reexamine the distinctions which we have assumed make a moral difference.

It has been suggested by Peter Singer[1] that our current attitudes are "speciesist," a word intended to make one think of "racist" or "sexist." The idea is that membership in a species is in itself not relevant to moral treatment, and that much of our behavior and attitudes toward nonhuman animals is based simply on this irrelevant fact.

There is, however, an important difference between racism or sexism and "speciesism." We do not subject animals to different moral treatment simply because they have fur and feathers but because they are in fact different from human beings in ways that could be morally relevant. It is false that women are incapable of being benefited by education, and therefore that claim cannot serve to justify preventing them from attending school. But this is not false of cows and dogs, even chimpanzees. Intelligence is thought to be a morally relevant capacity because of its relation to the capacity for moral responsibility.

What is Singer's response? He agrees that nonhuman animals lack certain capacities that human animals possess and that this may justify different *treatment*.

---

[*] Excerpted from pp. 247–256. "Speciesism and the Idea of Equality" by Bonnie Steinbock, *Philosophy* 53 (April 1978). Copyright © 1978 The Royal Institute of Philosophy. Reprinted by permission of Cambridge University Press.

But it does not justify giving less consideration to their needs and interests. According to Singer, the moral mistake which the racist or sexist makes is not essentially the factual error of thinking that blacks or women are inferior to white men. For even if there were no factual error, even if it were true that blacks and women are less intelligent and responsible than whites and men, this would not justify giving less consideration to their needs and interests. It is important to note that the term "speciesism" is in one way like, and in another way unlike, the terms "racism" and "sexism." What the term "speciesism" has in common with these terms is the reference to focusing on a characteristic which is, in itself, irrelevant to moral treatment. And it is worth reminding us of this. But Singer's real aim is to bring us to a new understanding of the idea of equality. The question is, On what do claims to equality rest? The demand for *human* equality is a demand that the interests of all human beings be considered equally unless there is a moral justification for not doing so. But why should the interests of all human beings be considered equally? In order to answer this question, we have to give some sense to the phrase, "All men (human beings) are created equal." Human beings are manifestly *not* equal, differing greatly in intelligence, virtue, and capacities. In virtue of what can the claim to equality be made?

It is Singer's contention that claims to equality do not rest on factual equality. Not only do human beings differ in their capacities, but it might even turn out that intelligence, the capacity for virtue, etc., are not distributed evenly among the races and sexes:

> The appropriate response to those who claim to have found evidence of genetically based differences in ability between the races or sexes is not to stick to the belief that the genetic explanation must be wrong, whatever evidence to the contrary may turn up; instead we should make it quite clear that the claim to equality does not depend on intelligence, moral capacity, physical strength, or similar matters of fact. Equality is a moral ideal, not a simple assertion of fact. There is no logically compelling reason for assuming that a factual difference in ability between two people justifies any difference in the amount of consideration we give to satisfying their needs and interests. The principle of equality of human beings is not a description of an alleged actual equality among humans: it is a prescription of how we should treat humans.[2]

Insofar as the subject is human equality, Singer's view is supported by other philosophers. Bernard Williams, for example, is concerned to show that demands for equality cannot rest on factual equality among people, for no such equality exists.[3] The only respect in which all men are equal, according to Williams, is that they are all equally men. This seems to be a platitude, but Williams denies that it is trivial. Membership in the species *Homo sapiens* in itself has no special moral significance, but rather the fact that all men are human serves as a *reminder* that being human involves the possession of characteristics that are morally relevant. But on what characteristics does Williams focus? Aside from the desire for self-respect (which I will discuss later), Williams is not concerned with uniquely human capacities. Rather, he focuses on the capacity to feel pain and the capacity to feel affection. It is in virtue of these capacities, it seems, that the idea of equality is to be justified.

Apparently Richard Wasserstrom has the same idea as he sets out the racist's "logical and moral mistakes" in "Rights, Human Rights and Racial Discrimination."[4] The racist fails to acknowledge that the black person is as capable of suffering as the white person. According to Wasserstrom, the reason why a person is said to have a right not to be made to suffer acute physical pain is that we all do in fact value freedom from such pain. Therefore, if anyone has a right to be free from suffering acute physical pain, everyone has this right, for there is no possible basis of discrimination. Wasserstrom says,

> For, if all persons do have equal capacities of these sorts and if the existence of these capacities is the reason for ascribing these rights to anyone, then all persons ought to have the right to claim equality of treatment in respect to the possession and exercise of these rights.[5]

The basis of equality, for Wasserstrom as for Williams, lies not in some uniquely human capacity, but rather in the fact that all human beings are alike in their capacity to suffer. Writers on equality have focused on this capacity, I think, because it functions as some sort of lowest common denominator, so that whatever the other capacities of a human being, he is entitled to equal consideration because, like everyone else, he is capable of suffering.

If the capacity to suffer is the reason for ascribing a right to freedom from acute pain, or a right to well-being, then it certainly looks as though these rights must be extended to animals as well. This is the conclusion Singer arrives at. The demand for human equality rests on the equal capacity of all human beings to suffer and to enjoy well-being. But if this is the basis of the demand for equality, then this demand must include all beings which have an equal capacity to suffer and enjoy well-being. That is why Singer places at the basis of the demand for equality not intelligence or reason but sentience. And equality will mean not equality of treatment but "equal consideration of interests." The equal consideration of interests will often mean quite different treatment, depending on the nature of the entity being considered. (It would be as absurd to talk of a dog's right to vote, Singer says, as to talk of a man's right to have an abortion.)

It might be thought that the issue of equality depends on a discussion of rights. According to this line of thought, animals do not merit equal consideration of interests because, unlike human beings, they do not, or cannot, have rights. But I am not going to discuss rights, important as the issue is. The fact that an entity does not have rights does not necessarily imply that its interests are going to count for less than the interests of entities which are right-bearers. According to the view of rights held by H. L. A. Hart and S. I. Benn, infants do not have rights, nor do the mentally defective, nor do the insane, insofar as they all lack certain minimal conceptual capabilities for having rights.[6] Yet it certainly does not seem that either Hart or Benn would agree that therefore their interests are to be counted for less or that it is morally permissible to treat them in ways in which it would not be permissible to treat right-bearers. It seems to mean only that we must give different sorts of reasons for our obligations to take into consideration the interests of those who do not have rights.

We have reasons concerning the treatment of other people which are clearly independent of the notion of rights. We would say that it is wrong to punch someone because doing that infringes his rights. But we could also say that it is wrong because doing that hurts him, and that is, ordinarily, enough of a reason not to do it. Now this particular reason extends not only to human beings but to all sentient creatures. One has a *prima facie* reason not to pull the cat's tail (whether or not the cat has rights) because it hurts the cat. And this is the only thing, normally, which is relevant in this case. The fact that the cat is not a "rational being," that it is not capable of moral responsibility, that it cannot make free choices or shape its life—all of these differences from us have nothing to do with the justifiability of pulling its tail. Does this show that rationality and the rest of it are irrelevant to moral treatment?

I hope to show that this is not the case. But first I want to point out that the issue is not one of cruelty to animals. We all agree that cruelty is wrong, whether perpetrated on a moral or nonmoral, rational or nonrational agent. Cruelty is defined as the infliction of unnecessary pain or suffering. What is to count as necessary or unnecessary is determined, in part, by the nature of the end pursued. Torturing an animal is cruel, because although the pain is logically necessary for the action to be torture, the end (deriving enjoyment from seeing the animal suffer) is monstrous. Allowing animals to suffer from neglect or for the sake of large profits may also be thought to be unnecessary and therefore cruel. But there may be some ends, which are very good (such as the advancement of medical knowledge), which can be accomplished by subjecting animals to pain in experiments. Although most people would agree that the pain inflicted on animals used in medical research ought to be kept to a minimum, they would consider pain that cannot be eliminated "necessary" and therefore not cruel. It would probably not be so regarded if the subjects were nonvoluntary human beings. Necessity, then, is defined in terms of human benefit, but this is just what is being called into question. The topic of cruelty to animals, while important from a practical viewpoint, because much of our present treatment of animals involves the infliction of suffering for no good reason, is not very interesting philosophically. What is philosophically interesting is whether we are justified in having different standards of necessity for human suffering and for animal suffering.

Singer says, quite rightly I think, "If a being suffers, there can be no moral justification for refusing to take that suffering into consideration."[7] But he thinks that the principle of equality requires that no matter what the nature of the being, its suffering be counted equally with the like suffering of any other being. In other words, sentience does not simply provide us with reasons for acting; it is the only relevant consideration for equal consideration of interests. It is this view that I wish to challenge.

I want to challenge it partly because it has such counterintuitive results. It means, for example, that feeding starving children before feeding starving dogs is just like a Catholic charity's feeding hungry Catholics before feeding hungry non-Catholics. It is simply a matter of taking care of one's own, something which is usually morally permissible. But whereas we would admire the Catholic agency which did not discriminate, but fed all children, first come, first served, we would feel quite differently about someone who had this policy for dogs and children. Nor is this, it seems to me, simply a matter of a sentimental preference for our own species. I might feel much more love for my dog than for a strange child—and yet I might feel morally obliged to feed the child before I fed my dog. If

I gave in to the feelings of love and fed my dog and let the child go hungry, I would probably feel guilty. This is not to say that we can simply rely on such feelings. Huck Finn felt guilty at helping Jim escape, which he viewed as stealing from a woman who had never done him any harm. But while the existence of such feelings does not settle the morality of an issue, it is not clear to me that they can be explained away. In any event, their existence can serve as a motivation for trying to find a rational justification for considering human interests above nonhuman ones.

However, it does seem to me that this requires a justification. Until now, common sense (and academic philosophy) have seen no such need. Benn says,

> No one claims equal consideration for all mammals—human beings count, mice do not, though it would not be easy to say why not …. Although we hesitate to inflict unnecessary pain on sentient creatures, such as mice or dogs, we are quite sure that we do not need to show good reasons for putting human interests before theirs.[8]

I think we do have to justify counting our interests more heavily than those of animals. But how? Singer is right, I think, to point out that it will not do to refer vaguely to the greater value of human life, to human worth and dignity:

> Faced with a situation in which they see a need for some basis for the moral gulf that is commonly thought to separate humans and animals, but can find no concrete difference that will do this without undermining the equality of humans, philosophers tend to waffle. They resort to high-sounding phrases like "the intrinsic dignity of the human individual." They talk of "the intrinsic worth of all men" as if men had some worth that other beings do not have or they say that human beings, and only human beings, are "ends in themselves," while "everything other than a person can only have value for a person." … Why should we not attribute "intrinsic dignity" or "intrinsic worth" to ourselves? Why should we not say that we are the only things in the universe that have intrinsic value? Our fellow human beings are unlikely to reject the accolades we so generously bestow upon them and those to whom we deny the honour are unable to object.[9]

Singer is right to be skeptical of terms like "intrinsic dignity" and "intrinsic worth." These phrases are no substitute for a moral argument. But they may point to one. In trying to understand what is meant by these phrases, we may find a difference or differences between human beings and nonhuman animals that will justify different treatment while not undermining claims for human equality. While we are not compelled to discriminate among people because of different capacities, if we can find a significant difference in capacities between human and nonhuman animals, this could serve to justify regarding human interests as primary. It is not arbitrary or smug, I think, to maintain that human beings have a different moral status from members of other species because of certain capacities which are characteristic of being human. We may not all be equal in these capacities, but all human beings possess them to some measure, and nonhuman animals do not. For example, human beings are normally held to be responsible for what they do. In recognizing that someone is responsible for his or her actions, you accord that person a respect which is reserved for those possessed of moral autonomy or capable of achieving such autonomy. Secondly, human beings can be expected to reciprocate in a way that nonhuman animals cannot. Nonhuman animals cannot be motivated by altruistic or moral reasons; they cannot treat you fairly or unfairly. This does not rule out the possibility of an animal being motivated by sympathy or pity. It does rule out altruistic motivation in the sense of motivation due to the recognition that the needs and interests of others provide one with certain reasons for acting.[10] Human beings are capable of altruistic motivation in this sense. We are sometimes motivated simply by the recognition that someone else is in pain and that pain is a bad thing, no matter who suffers it. It is this sort of reason that I claim cannot motivate an animal or any entity not possessed of fairly abstract concepts. (If some nonhuman animals do possess the requisite concepts—perhaps chimpanzees who have learned a language—they might well be capable of altruistic motivation.) This means that our moral dealings with animals are necessarily much more limited than our dealings with other human beings. If rats invade our houses, carrying disease and biting our children, we cannot reason with them, hoping to persuade them of the injustice they do us. We can only attempt to get rid of them. And it is this that makes it reasonable for us to accord them a separate and not equal moral status, even though their capacity to suffer provides us with some reason to kill them painlessly, if this can be done without too much sacrifice of human interests. Thirdly, as Williams points out, there is the "desire for self-respect": "a certain human desire to be identified with what one is doing, to be able to realize purposes of one's own, and not to be the instrument of another's will unless one has willingly accepted such a role."[11] Some animals may have some form of this desire, and to the extent that they do, we ought to consider their interest in freedom and self-determination. (Such considerations might affect our attitudes toward zoos and circuses.) But the desire for self-respect *per se* requires the intellectual capacities of human beings, and this desire provides us with special reasons not to treat human beings in certain ways. It is an affront to the dignity of a human being to be a slave (even if a well-treated one); this cannot be true for a horse or a cow. To point this out is of course only to say that the justification for the treatment of an entity will depend on the sort of entity in question. In our treatment of other entities, we must consider the desire for autonomy, dignity, and respect, but only where such a desire exists. Recognition of different desires and interests will often require different treatment, a point Singer himself makes.

But is the issue simply one of different desires and interests justifying and requiring different treatment? I would like to make a stronger claim, namely, that certain capacities, which seem to be unique to human beings, entitle their possessors to a privileged position in the moral community. Both rats and human beings dislike pain, and so we have a *prima facie* reason not to inflict pain on either. But if we can free human beings from crippling diseases, pain, and death through experimentation which involves making animals suffer, and if this is the only way to achieve such results, then I think that such experimentation is justified because human lives are more valuable than animal lives. And this is because of certain capacities and abilities that normal human beings have which animals apparently do not and which human beings cannot exercise if they are devastated by pain or disease.

My point is not that the lack of the sorts of capacities I have been discussing gives us a justification for treating animals just as we like, but rather that it is these differences between human beings and nonhuman animals which provide a rational basis for different moral treatment and consideration. Singer focuses on sentience alone as the basis of equality, but we can justify the belief that human beings have a moral worth that nonhuman animals do not, in virtue of specific capacities and without resorting to "high-sounding phrases."

Singer thinks that intelligence, the capacity for moral responsibility, for virtue, etc., are irrelevant to equality, because we would not accept a hierarchy based on intelligence any more than one based on race. We do not think that those with greater capacities ought to have their interests weighed more heavily than those with lesser capacities, and this, he thinks, shows that differences in such capacities are irrelevant to equality. But it does not show this at all. Kevin Donaghy argues (rightly, I think) that what entitles us human beings to a privileged position in the moral community is a certain minimal level of intelligence, which is a prerequisite for morally relevant capacities.[12] The fact that we would reject a hierarchical society based on degree of intelligence does not show that a minimal level of intelligence cannot be used as a cut-off point justifying giving greater consideration to the interests of those entities which meet this standard.

Interestingly enough, Singer concedes the rationality of valuing the lives of normal human beings over the lives of nonhuman animals.[13] We are not required to value equally the life of a normal human being and the life of an animal, he thinks, but only their suffering. But I doubt that the value of an entity's life can be separated from the value of its suffering in this way. If we value the lives of human beings more than the lives of animals, this is because we value certain capacities that human beings have and animals do not. But freedom from suffering is, in general, a minimal condition for exercising these capacities, for living a fully human life. So valuing human life more involves regarding human interests as counting for more. That is why we regard human suffering as more deplorable than comparable animal suffering.

But there is one point of Singer's which I have not yet met. Some human beings (if only a very few) are less intelligent than some nonhuman animals. Some have less capacity for moral choice and responsibility. What status in the moral community are these members of our species to occupy? Are their interests to be considered equally with ours? Is experimenting on them permissible where such experiments are painful or injurious but somehow necessary for human wellbeing? If it is certain of our capacities which entitle us to a privileged position, it looks as if those lacking those capacities are not entitled to a privileged position. To think it is justifiable to experiment on an adult chimpanzee but not on a severely mentally incapacitated human being seems to be focusing on membership in a species where that has no moral relevance. (It is being "speciesist" in a perfectly reasonable use of the word.) How are we to meet this challenge? ....

I doubt that anyone will be able to come up with a concrete and morally relevant difference that would justify, say, using a chimpanzee in an experiment rather than a human being with less capacity for reasoning, moral responsibility, etc. Should we then experiment on the severely retarded? Utilitarian considerations aside (the difficulty of comparing intelligence between species, for example), we feel a special obligation to care for the handicapped members of our own species, who cannot survive in this world without such care. Nonhuman animals manage very well, despite their "lower intelligence" and lesser capacities; most of them do not require special care from us. This does not, of course, justify experimenting on them. However, to subject to experimentation those people who depend on us seems even worse than subjecting members of other species to it. In addition, when we consider the severely retarded, we think, "That could be me." It makes sense to think that one might have been born retarded but not to think that one might have been born a monkey. And so, although one can imagine one's self in the monkey's place, one feels a closer identification with the severely retarded human being. Here we are getting away from such things as "morally relevant differences" and talking about something much more difficult to articulate, namely, the role of feeling and sentiment in moral thinking. We would be horrified by the use of the retarded in medical research. But what are we to make of this horror? Has it moral significance or is it "mere" sentiment, of no more importance than the sentiment of whites against blacks? It is terribly difficult to know how to evaluate such feelings.[14] I am not going to say more about this, because I think that the treatment of severely incapacitated human beings does not pose an insurmountable objection to the privileged-status principle. I am willing to admit that my horror at the thought of experiments being performed on severely mentally incapacitated human beings in cases in which I would find it justifiable and preferable to perform the same experiments on nonhuman animals (capable of similar suffering) may not be a moral emotion. But it is certainly not wrong of us to extend special care to members of our own species, motivated by feelings of sympathy, protectiveness, etc. If this is speciesism, it is stripped of its tone of moral condemnation. It is not racist to provide special care to members of your own race; it is racist to fall below your moral obligation to a person because of his or her race. I have been arguing that we are morally obliged to consider the interests of all sentient creatures but not to consider those interests equally with human interests. Nevertheless, even this recognition will mean some radical changes in our attitude toward and treatment of other species.[15]

Notes

1. Peter Singer, *Animal Liberation* (New York: Avon Books, 1977).
2. Singer, *Animal Liberation*, p. 5.
3. Bernard Williams, "The Idea of Equality," in *Philosophy, Politics and Society* (Second Series), ed. Laslett and Runciman (Blackwell, 1962), pp. 110–13, reprinted in *Moral Concepts*, ed. Feinberg (Oxford, 1970), pp. 153–71.
4. Richard Wasserstrom, "Rights, Human Rights, and Racial Discrimination," *Journal of Philosophy* 61, no. 20 (1964), reprinted in *Human Rights*, ed. A. I. Melden (Wadsworth, 1970), pp. 96–110.
5. Ibid., p. 106.
6. H. L. A. Hart, "Are There Any Natural Rights?" *Philosophical Review* 64 (1955), and Stanley I. Benn, "Abortion, Infanticide, and Respect for Persons," in *The Problem of Abortion*, ed. Feinberg (Wadsworth, 1973), pp. 92–104.
7. Singer, *Animal Liberation*, p. 9.
8. Stanley I. Benn, "Equality, Moral and Social," in *The Encyclopedia of Philosophy* 3 (1967), no. 40.
9. Singer, *Animal Liberation*, pp. 266–67.
10. This conception of altruistic motivation comes from Thomas Nagel's *The Possibility of Altruism* (Oxford, 1970).

11 Williams, "The Idea of Equality," p. 157.
12 Kevin Donaghy, "Singer on Speciesism," *Philosophic Exchange* (Summer 1974).
13 Singer, *Animal Liberation*, p. 22.
14 We run into the same problem when discussing abortion. Of what significance are our feelings toward the unborn when discussing its status? Is it relevant or irrelevant that it looks like a human being?
15 I would like to acknowledge the help of, and offer thanks to, Professor Richard Arneson of the University of California, San Diego; Professor Sidney Gendin of Eastern Michigan University; and Professor Peter Singer of Monash University, all of whom read and commented on earlier drafts of this paper.

Review and Discussion Questions

1 How does Steinbock distinguish racism and sexism from speciesism?
2 Describe how Peter Singer understands equality and the relevance of that understanding to how we should treat animals. Why does Steinbock reject Singer's understanding of equality?
3 Why does Steinbock think it is acceptable to treat a human being's interests more seriously than those of nonhuman animals?
4 How might Singer respond to Steinbock's claim that it may be correct to give mentally defective humans greater moral concern than nonhuman animals? Is that response adequate? Explain.

READING: PEOPLE OR PENGUINS

WILLIAM F. BAXTER[*]

What sorts of beings have moral standing and deserve moral consideration? How is that standing to be determined? In this essay, William F. Baxter opens the discussion by arguing that the key question that always needs to be addressed is: What are our goals? Instead of seeking simply to protect natural life, he argues, we must constantly be aware of other competing values and make choices accordingly. Baxter thus defends what he terms a *cost-benefit* approach to nature and the environment—a view that, he argues, is sound from the perspective of nature as well as of human beings. It is also, he claims, the only approach that is realistic. The soundest policy is to take account of only the needs and interests of people, not penguins or pine trees. Nature itself has no independent moral standing and will receive sufficient protection through a wise, human-centered ethic. The question always to be asked is therefore what is the optimal amount of pollution, not how pollution can be eliminated. William F. Baxter was the William Benjamin Scott and Luna M. Scott Professor of Law at Stanford University.

I start with the modest proposition that in dealing with pollution, or indeed with any problem, it is helpful to know what one is attempting to accomplish. Agreement on how and whether to pursue a particular objective, such as pollution control, is not

---

[*] From William F. Baxter, *People or Penguins: The Case for Optimal Pollution.* Copyright © 1974, by Columbia University Press. Reprinted by permission of the publisher.

possible unless some more general objective has been identified and stated with reasonable precision. We talk loosely of having clean air and clean water, of preserving our wilderness areas, and so forth. But none of these is a sufficiently general objective: each is more accurately viewed as a means rather than as an end.

With regard to clean air, for example, one may ask, "How clean?" and "What does clean mean?" It is even reasonable to ask, "Why have clean air?" Each of these questions is an implicit demand that a more general community goal be stated—a goal sufficiently general in its scope and enjoying sufficiently general assent among the community of actors that such "why" questions no longer seem admissible with respect to that goal.

If, for example, one states as a goal the proposition that "every person should be free to do whatever he wishes in contexts where his actions do not interfere with the interests of other human beings," the speaker is unlikely to be met with a response of "why?" The goal may be criticized as uncertain in its implications or difficult to implement, but it is so basic a tenet of our civilization—it reflects a cultural value so broadly shared, at least in the abstract—that the question "why" is seen as impertinent or imponderable or both.

I do not mean to suggest that everyone would agree with the "spheres-of-freedom" objective just stated. Still less do I mean to suggest that a society could subscribe to four or five such general objectives that would be adequate in their coverage to serve as testing criteria by which all other disagreements might be measured. One difficulty in the attempt to construct such a list is that each new goal added will conflict, in certain applications, with each prior goal listed; and thus each goal serves as a limited qualification on prior goals.

Without any expectation of obtaining unanimous consent to them, let me set forth four goals that I generally use as ultimate testing criteria in attempting to frame solutions to problems of human organization. My position regarding pollution stems from these four criteria. If the criteria appeal to you and any part of what appears hereafter does not, our disagreement will have a helpful focus: Which of us is correct, analytically, in supposing that his position on pollution would better serve these general goals? If the criteria do not seem acceptable to you, then it is to be expected that our more particular judgments will differ, and the task will then be yours to identify the basic set of criteria upon which your particular judgments rest.

My criteria are as follows:

1 The spheres-of-freedom criterion stated above.
2 Waste is a bad thing. The dominant feature of human existence is scarcity—our available resources, our aggregate labors, and our skill in employing both have always been, and will continue for some time to be, inadequate to yield to every man all the tangible and intangible satisfactions he would like to have. Hence, none of those resources or labors or skills should be wasted—that is, employed so as to yield less than they might yield in human satisfactions.
3 Every human being should be regarded as an end rather than as a means to be used for the betterment of another. Each should be afforded dignity and regarded as having an absolute claim to an evenhanded application of such rules as the community may adopt for its governance.

4 Both the incentive and the opportunity to improve his share of satisfactions should be preserved to every individual. Preservation of incentive is dictated by the "no-waste" criterion and enjoins against the continuous, totally egalitarian redistribution of satisfactions or wealth; but subject to that constraint, everyone should receive, by continuous redistribution if necessary, some minimal share of aggregate wealth so as to avoid a level of privation from which the opportunity to improve his situation becomes illusory.

The relationship of these highly general goals to the more specific environmental issues at hand may not be readily apparent, and I am not yet ready to demonstrate their pervasive implications. But let me give one indication of their implications. Recently scientists have informed us that use of DDT in food production is causing damage to the penguin population. For the present purposes let us accept that assertion as an indisputable scientific fact. The scientific fact is often asserted as if the correct implication—that we must stop agricultural use of DDT—followed from the mere statement of the fact of penguin damage. But plainly it does not follow if my criteria are employed.

My criteria are oriented to people, not penguins. Damage to penguins or sugar pines or geological marvels is, without more, simply irrelevant. One must go further, by my criteria, and say: penguins are important because people enjoy seeing them walk about rocks; and furthermore, the well-being of people would be less impaired by halting use of DDT than by giving up penguins. In short, my observations about environmental problems will be people-oriented, as are my criteria. I have no interest in preserving penguins for their own sake.

It may be said by way of objection to this position that it is very selfish of people to act as if each person represented one unit of importance and nothing else was of any importance. It is undeniably selfish. Nevertheless, I think it is the only tenable starting place for analysis for several reasons. First, no other position corresponds to the way most people really think and act—i.e., corresponds to reality.

Second, this attitude does not portend any massive destruction of nonhuman flora and fauna, for people depend on them in many obvious ways, and they will be preserved because and to the degree that humans do depend on them.

Third, what is good for humans is, in many respects, good for penguins and pine trees—clean air, for example. So that humans are, in these respects, surrogates for plant and animal life.

Fourth, I do not know how we could administer any other system. Our decisions are either private or collective. Insofar as Mr. Jones is free to act privately, he may give such preferences as he wishes to other forms of life: he may feed birds in winter and do with less himself, and he may even decline to resist an advancing polar bear on the ground that the bear's appetite is more important than those portions of himself that the bear may choose to eat. In short, my basic premise does not rule out private altruism to competing life forms. It does rule out, however, Mr. Jones's inclination to feed Mr. Smith to the bear, however hungry the bear, however despicable Mr. Smith.

Insofar as we act collectively, on the other hand, only humans can be afforded an opportunity to participate in the collective decisions. Penguins cannot vote now and are unlikely subjects for the franchise—pine trees more unlikely still. Again, each individual is free to cast his vote so as to benefit sugar pines if that is his inclination. But many of the more extreme assertions that one hears from some conservationists amount to tacit assertions that they are specially appointed representatives of sugar pines and hence that their preferences should be weighted more heavily than the preferences of other humans who do not enjoy equal rapport with "nature." The simplistic assertion that agricultural use of DDT must stop at once because it is harmful to penguins is of that type.

Fifth, if polar bears or pine trees or penguins, like men, are to be regarded as ends rather than means, if they are to count in our calculus of social organization, someone must tell me how much each one counts, and someone must tell me how these life forms are to be permitted to express their preferences, for I do not know either answer. If the answer is that certain people are to hold their proxies, then I want to know how those proxy-holders are to be selected: self-appointment does not seem workable to me.

Sixth, and by way of summary of all the foregoing, let me point out that the set of environmental issues under discussion—although they raise very complex technical questions of how to achieve any objective—ultimately raise a normative question: what ought we to do? Questions of ought are unique to the human mind and world—they are meaningless as applied to a nonhuman situation.

I reject the proposition that we ought to respect the "balance of nature" or to "preserve the environment" unless the reason for doing so, express or implied, is the benefit of man.

I reject the idea that there is a "right" or "morally correct" state of nature to which we should return. The word "nature" has no normative connotation. Was it "right" or "wrong" for the earth's crust to heave in contortion and create mountains and seas? Was it "right" for the first amphibian to crawl up out of the primordial ooze? Was it "wrong" for plants to reproduce themselves and alter the atmospheric composition in favor of oxygen? For animals to alter the atmosphere in favor of carbon dioxide both by breathing oxygen and eating plants? No answers can be given to these questions because they are meaningless questions.

All this may seem obvious to the point of being tedious, but much of the present controversy over environment and pollution rests on tacit normative assumptions about just such nonnormative phenomena: that it is "wrong" to impair penguins with DDT but not to slaughter cattle for prime rib roasts; that it is wrong to kill stands of sugar pines with industrial fumes but not to cut sugar pines and build housing for the poor. Every man is entitled to his own preferred definition of Walden Pond, but there is no definition that has any moral superiority over another, except by reference to the selfish needs of the human race.

From the fact that there is no normative definition of the natural state, it follows that there is no normative definition of clean air or pure water—hence no definition of polluted air—or of pollution—except by reference to the needs of man. The "right" composition of the atmosphere is one which has some dust in it and some lead in it and some hydrogen sulfide in it—just those amounts that attend a sensibly organized society thoughtfully and knowledgeably pursuing the greatest possible satisfaction for its human members.

The first and most fundamental step toward solution of our environmental problems is a clear recognition that our objective is not pure air or water but rather some optimal state of pollution. That step immediately suggests the question: How do we define and attain the level of pollution that will yield the maximum possible amount of human satisfaction?

Low levels of pollution contribute to human satisfaction but so do food and shelter and education and music. To attain ever-lower levels of pollution, we must pay the cost of having less of these other things. I contrast that view of the cost of pollution control with the more popular statement that pollution control will "cost" very large numbers of dollars. The popular statement is true in some senses, false in others; sorting out the true and false senses is of some importance. The first step in that sorting process is to achieve a clear understanding of the difference between dollars and resources. Resources are the wealth of our nation; dollars are merely claim checks upon those resources. Resources are of vital importance; dollars are comparatively trivial.

Four categories of resources are sufficient for our purposes: at any given time, a nation, or a planet if you prefer, has a stock of labor, of technological skill, of capital goods, and of natural resources (such as mineral deposits, timber, water, land, etc.). These resources can be used in various combinations to yield goods and services of all kinds—in some limited quantity. The quantity will be larger if they are combined efficiently, smaller if combined inefficiently. But in either event the resource stock is limited, the goods and services that they can be made to yield are limited; even the most efficient use of them will yield less than our population, in the aggregate, would like to have.

If one considers building a new dam, it is appropriate to say that it will be costly in the sense that it will require x hours of labor, y tons of steel and concrete, and z amount of capital goods. If these resources are devoted to the dam, then they cannot be used to build hospitals, fishing rods, schools, or electric can openers. That is the meaningful sense in which the dam is costly.

Quite apart from the very important question of how wisely we can combine our resources to produce goods and services is the very different question of how they get distributed—who gets how many goods? Dollars constitute the claim checks which are distributed among people and which control their share of national output. Dollars are nearly valueless pieces of paper except to the extent that they do represent claim checks to some fraction of the output of goods and services. Viewed as claim checks, all the dollars outstanding during any period of time are worth, in the aggregate, the goods and services that are available to be claimed with them during that period—neither more nor less.

It is far easier to increase the supply of dollars than to increase the production of goods and services—printing dollars is easy. But printing more dollars doesn't help because each dollar then simply becomes a claim to fewer goods, i.e., becomes worth less.

The point is this: many people fall into error upon hearing the statement that the decision to build a dam, or to clean up a river, will cost $X million. It is regrettably easy to say: "It's only money. This is a wealthy country, and we have lots of money." But you cannot build a dam or clean a river with $X million—unless you also have a match, you can't even make a fire. One builds a dam or cleans a river by diverting labor and steel and trucks and factories from making one kind of goods to making another. The cost in dollars is merely a shorthand way of describing the extent of the diversion necessary. If we build a dam for $X million, then we must recognize that we will have $X million less housing and food and medical care and electric can openers as a result.

Similarly, the costs of controlling pollution are best expressed in terms of the other goods we will have to give up to do the job. This is not to say the job should not be done. Badly as we need more housing, more medical care, more can openers, and more symphony orchestras, we could do with somewhat less of them, in my judgment at least, in exchange for somewhat cleaner air and rivers. But that is the nature of the trade-off, and analysis of the problem is advanced if that unpleasant reality is kept in mind. Once the trade-off relationship is clearly perceived, it is possible to state in a very general way what the optimal level of pollution is. I would state it as follows:

People enjoy watching penguins. They enjoy relatively clean air and smog-free vistas. Their health is improved by relatively clean water and air. Each of these benefits is a type of good or service. As a society we would be well advised to give up one washing machine if the resources that would have gone into that washing machine can yield greater human satisfaction when diverted into pollution control. We should give up one hospital if the resources thereby freed would yield more human satisfaction when devoted to elimination of noise in our cities. And so on, trade-off by trade-off, we should divert our productive capacities from the production of existing goods and services to the production of a cleaner, quieter, more pastoral nation up to—and no further than—the point at which we value more highly the next washing machine or hospital that we would have to do without than we value the next unit of environmental improvement that the diverted resources would create.

Now this proposition seems to me unassailable but so general and abstract as to be unhelpful—at least unadministerable in the form stated. It assumes we can measure in some way the incremental units of human satisfaction yielded by very different types of goods. The proposition must remain a pious abstraction until I can explain how this measurement process can occur. But I insist that the proposition stated describes the result for which we should be striving—and again, that it is always useful to know what your target is even if your weapons are too crude to score a bull's-eye.

Review and Discussion Questions

1 What are the basic tests or criteria Baxter uses to assess human decisions and organizations?
2 What are the reasons Baxter gives for thinking that his is the best approach to environmental issues?
3 Why does Baxter speak of the optimal amount of pollution instead of its elimination?
4 How, specifically, would Singer respond to this essay? How would Baxter respond to Singer?
5 Would Steinbock be likely to agree or disagree with Baxter? Explain.
6 Compare Baxter's view of nature with that of people who criticize homosexuality as "unnatural."

READING: THE LAND ETHIC: ANIMAL LIBERATION AND ENVIRONMENTALISM

J. BAIRD CALLICOTT*

J. Baird Callicott first distinguishes three philosophical positions: *ethical humanists*, who defend the special status of humans; *humane moralists* (like Peter Singer), who reject the notion of a special status for human beings in favor of animal liberation; and defenders of the "*land ethic*" (as represented by Aldo Leopold in his book *A Sand County Almanac*), who focus on the good of the "biotic community" as a whole. Each position offers its own account of what is valuable, but it is the land ethic, Callicott argues, that is the most creative, interesting, and practical of the alternatives. This environmentalist position also offers a different perspective on questions such as hunting and meat-eating, as well as on the value of nonanimal life.

In the ensuing years after Callicott wrote his influential article, he sought to correct and clarify Leopold's land ethic, which can be given moderate or extreme interpretations. Callicott now endorses a moderate interpretation of Leopold's views. For example, when you reach the point in the article where Callicott writes, "A thing is right when it tends to preserve the integrity, stability, and beauty of the biotic community. It is wrong when it tends otherwise," pause to consider how you might interpret the word "when." It could mean "if," identifying a sufficient condition for what is right, such that *other* situations could also be right; or it could mean "if and only if," identifying necessary and sufficient conditions of what is right, at the exclusion of other values or outcomes. In private communication with this editor and in his public responses, Callicott rejects an extreme interpretation of this maxim, (interpreted as "if and only if"), and argues that Leopold himself supported the more moderate position—that the land ethic is an accretion to previous layers of ethics, not a replacement. After reading the article below, see http://jbcallicott.weebly.com/introductory-palinode.html for more information about Callicott's views, his responses to critics, and his continuing commitment to the need for a new holistic environmental ethic.

J. Baird Callicott is University Distinguished Research Professor Emeritus at the University of North Texas.

Environmental Ethics and Animal Liberation

Partly because it is so new to Western philosophy (or at least heretofore only scarcely represented), *environmental ethics* has no precisely fixed conventional definition in glossaries of philosophical terminology. Aldo Leopold, however, is universally recognized as the father or founding genius of recent environmental ethics. His "land ethic" has become a modern classic and may be treated as the standard example, the paradigm case, as it were, of what an environmental ethic is. *Environmental ethics* then can be defined ostensively by using Leopold's land

---

* From J. Baird Callicott, "Animal Liberation: A Triangular Affair," *Environmental Ethics* 2(4) (Winter 1980): 311–338. Reprinted by permission.

ethic as the exemplary type. I do not mean to suggest that all environmental ethics should necessarily conform to Leopold's paradigm, but the extent to which an ethical system resembles Leopold's land ethic might be used, for want of anything better, as a criterion to measure the extent to which it is or is not of the environmental sort.

It is Leopold's opinion, and certainly an overall review of the prevailing traditions of Western ethics, both popular and philosophical, generally confirms it, that traditional Western systems of ethics have not accorded moral standing to nonhuman beings.[1] Animals and plants, soils and waters, which Leopold includes in his community of ethical beneficiaries, have traditionally enjoyed no moral standing, no rights, no respect, in sharp contrast to human persons whose rights and interests ideally must be fairly and equally considered if our actions are to be considered "ethical" or "moral." One fundamental and novel feature of the Leopold land ethic, therefore, is the extension of direct ethical considerability from people to nonhuman natural entities.

At first glance, the recent ethical movement usually labeled "animal liberation" or "animal rights" seems to be squarely and centrally a kind of environmental ethics. The more uncompromising among the animal liberationists have demanded equal moral consideration on behalf of cows, pigs, chickens, and other apparently enslaved and oppressed nonhuman animals. The theoreticians of this new hyper-egalitarianism have coined such terms as *speciesism* (on analogy with *racism* and *sexism*) and *human chauvinism* (on analogy with male chauvinism) and have made animal liberation seem, perhaps not improperly, the next and most daring development of political liberalism. Aldo Leopold also draws upon metaphors of political liberalism when he tells us that his land ethic "changes the role of *Homo sapiens* from conqueror of the land community to plain member and citizen of it."[2] For animal liberationists, it is as if the ideological battles for equal rights and equal consideration for women and for racial minorities have been all but won, and the next and greatest challenge is to purchase equality, first theoretically and then practically, for all (actually only some) animals, regardless of species. This more rhetorically implied than fully articulated historical progression of moral rights from fewer to greater numbers of "persons" (allowing that animals may also be persons), as advocated by animal liberationists, also parallels Leopold's scenario in "The Land Ethic" of the historical extension of "ethical criteria" to more and more "fields of conduct" and to larger and larger groups of people during the past 3,000 or so years.[3] As Leopold develops it, the land ethic is a cultural "evolutionary possibility," the next "step in a sequence."[4] For Leopold, however, the next step is much more sweeping, much more inclusive than the animal liberationists envision, since it "enlarges the boundaries of the [moral] community to include soils, waters, [and] plants" as well as animals.[5] Thus, the animal liberation movement *could* be construed as partitioning Leopold's perhaps undigestible and totally inclusive environmental ethic into a series of more assimilable stages: today animal rights, tomorrow equal rights for plants, and after that full moral standing for rocks, soil, and other earthy compounds, and perhaps sometime in the still more remote future, liberty and equality for water and other elementary bodies.

Put just this way, however, there is something jarring about such a graduated progression in the exfoliation of a more inclusive environmental ethic, something that seems absurd. A more or less reasonable case might be made for rights for some animals, but when we come to plants, soils, and waters, the frontier between plausibility and absurdity appears to have been crossed. Yet there is no doubt that Leopold sincerely proposes that *land* (in his inclusive sense) be ethically regarded. The beech and chestnut, for example, have in his view as much "biotic right" to life as the wolf and the deer, and the effects of human actions on mountains and streams for Leopold is an ethical concern as genuine and serious as the comfort and longevity of brood hens.[6] In fact, Leopold to all appearances never considered the treatment of brood hens on a factory farm or steers in a feedlot to be a pressing moral issue. He seems much more concerned about the integrity of the farm wood-lot and the effects of clear-cutting steep slopes on neighboring streams.

Animal liberationists put their ethic into practice (and display their devotion to it) by becoming vegetarians, and the moral complexities of vegetarianism have been thoroughly debated in the recent literature as an adjunct issue to animal rights. (No one however has yet expressed, as among Butler's Erewhonians, qualms about eating plants, though such sentiments might be expected to be latently present, if the rights of plants are next to be defended.) Aldo Leopold, by contrast, did not even condemn hunting animals, let alone eating them, nor did he personally abandon hunting, for which he had had an enthusiasm since boyhood, upon becoming convinced that his ethical responsibilities extended beyond the human sphere ....

The urgent concern of animal liberationists for the suffering of *domestic* animals, toward which Leopold manifests an attitude which can only be described as indifference, and the urgent concern of Leopold, on the other hand, for the disappearance of species of plants as well as animals and for soil erosion and stream pollution appear to be symptoms not only of very different ethical perspectives but profoundly different cosmic visions as well. The neat similarities, noted at the beginning of this discussion, between the environmental ethic of the animal liberation movement and the classical Leopoldian land ethic appear in light of these observations to be rather superficial and to conceal substrata of thought and value which are not at all similar. The theoretical foundations of the animal liberation movement and those of the Leopoldian land ethic may even turn out not to be companionable, complementary, or mutually consistent. The animal liberationists may thus find themselves not only engaged in controversy with the many conservative philosophers upholding *apartheid* between man and "beast," but also faced with an unexpected dissent from another, very different, system of environmental ethics. Animal liberation and animal rights may well prove to be a triangular rather than, as it has so far been represented in the philosophical community, a polar controversy.

Ethical Humanism and Humane Moralism

The orthodox response of "ethical humanism" (as this philosophical perspective may be styled) to the suggestion that nonhuman animals should be accorded moral standing is that such animals are not worthy of this high perquisite. Only human beings are rational or capable of having interests or possess *self*-awareness or have linguistic abilities or can represent the future, it is variously argued. These essential attributes taken singly or in various combinations make people somehow exclusively deserving of moral consideration. The so-called lower animals, it is insisted, lack the crucial qualification for ethical considerability and so may be treated (albeit humanely, according to some, so as not to brutalize man) as things or means, not as persons or as ends.

The theoreticians of the animal liberation movement ("humane moralists," as they may be called) typically reply as follows. Not all human beings qualify as worthy of moral regard according to the various criteria specified. Therefore, by parity of reasoning, human persons who do not so qualify as moral patients may be treated, as animals often are, as mere things or means (e.g., used in vivisection experiments, disposed of if their existence is inconvenient, eaten, hunted, etc., etc.). But the ethical humanists would be morally outraged if irrational and inarticulate infants, for example, were used in painful or lethal medical experiments or if severely retarded people were hunted for pleasure. Thus, the double dealing, the hypocrisy, of ethical humanism appears to be exposed. Ethical humanism, though claiming to discriminate between worthy and unworthy ethical patients on the basis of objective criteria impartially applied, turns out after all, it seems, to be *speciesism*, a philosophically indefensible prejudice (analogous to racial prejudice) against animals ....

The humane moralists, for their part, insist upon *sentience* (*sensibility* would have been a more precise word choice) as the only relevant capacity a being need possess to enjoy full moral standing. If animals, they argue, are conscious entities who, though deprived of reason, speech, forethought, or even *self-awareness* (however that may be judged) are capable of suffering, then their suffering should be as much a matter of ethical concern as that of our fellow human beings, or strictly speaking, as our very own .... As a *moral* agent, I should not consider my pleasure and pain to be of greater consequence in determining a course of action than that of other persons. Thus, by the same token, if animals suffer pain—and among philosophers, only strict Cartesians would deny that they do—then we are morally obliged to consider their suffering as much an evil to be minimized by conscientious moral agents as human suffering. Certainly actions of ours which contribute to the suffering of animals, such as hunting them, butchering and eating them, experimenting on them, etc., are on these assumptions morally reprehensible. Hence, a person who regards himself or herself as not aiming in life to live most selfishly, conveniently, or profitably but rightly and in accord with practical principle, if convinced by these arguments, should, among other things, cease to eat the flesh of animals, to hunt them, to wear fur and leather clothing and bone ornaments and other articles made from the bodies of animals, to eat eggs and drink milk if the animal producers of these commodities are retained under inhumane circumstances and to patronize zoos (as sources of psychological if not physical torment of animals). On the other hand, since certain very simple animals are almost certainly insensible to pleasure and pain, they may and indeed should be treated as morally inconsequential. Nor is there any *moral* reason why trees should be respected or rivers or mountains or anything which is, though living or tributary to life processes, unconscious. The humane moralists, like the moral humanists, draw a firm distinction between those beings worthy of moral consideration and those not. They simply insist upon a different but quite definite cut-off point on the spectrum of natural entities and accompany their criterion with arguments to show that it is more ethically defensible (granting certain assumptions) and more consistently applicable than that of the moral humanists.

The First Principle of the Land Ethic

.... But what about the third (and certainly minority) party to the animal liberation debate? What sort of reasonable and coherent moral theory would at once urge that animals (and plants and soils and waters) be included in the same class with people as beings to whom ethical consideration is owed and yet not object to some of them being slaughtered (whether painlessly or not) and eaten, others hunted, trapped, and in various other ways seemingly cruelly used? Aldo Leopold provides a concise statement of what might be called the categorical imperative or principal precept of the land ethic: "A thing is right when it tends to preserve the integrity, stability, and beauty of the biotic community. It is wrong when it tends otherwise."[7] What is especially noteworthy, and that to which attention should be directed in this proposition, is the idea that the good of the biotic *community* is the ultimate measure of the moral value, the rightness or wrongness, of actions. Thus, to hunt and kill a white-tailed deer in certain districts may not only be ethically permissible, it might actually be a moral requirement, necessary to protect the local environment, taken as a whole, from the disintegrating effects of a cervid population explosion. On the other hand, rare and endangered animals like the lynx should be especially nurtured and preserved. The lynx, cougar, and other wild feline predators, from the neo-Benthamite perspective (if consistently and evenhandedly applied) should be regarded as merciless, wanton, and incorrigible murderers of their fellow creatures, who not only kill, it should be added, but cruelly toy with their victims, thus increasing the measure of pain in the world. From the perspective of the land ethic, predators generally should be nurtured and preserved as critically important members of the biotic communities to which they are native. Certain plants, similarly, may be overwhelmingly important to the stability, integrity, and beauty of biotic communities, while some animals, such as domestic sheep (allowed perhaps by egalitarian and humane herdspersons to graze freely and to reproduce themselves without being harvested for lamb and mutton) could be a pestilential threat to the natural floral community of a given locale. Thus, the land ethic is logically coherent in demanding at once that moral consideration be given to plants as well as to animals and yet in permitting animals to be killed, trees felled, and so on. In every case, the effect upon ecological systems is the decisive factor in the determination of the ethical quality of actions.

The Land Ethic and the Ecological Point of View

.... Since ecology focuses upon the relationships between and among things, it inclines its students toward a more holistic vision of the world. Before the rather recent emergence of ecology as a science, the landscape appeared to be, one might say, a collection of objects, some of them alive, some conscious, but all the same, an aggregate, a plurality of separate individuals. With this "atomistic" representation of things, it is no wonder that moral issues might be understood as competing and mutually contradictory clashes of the "rights" of separate individuals, each separately pursuing its "interests." Ecology has made it possible to apprehend the same landscape as an articulate unity (without the least hint of mysticism or ineffability). Ordinary organic bodies have articulated and discernible parts (limbs, various organs, myriad cells); yet because of the character of the network of relations among those parts, they form in a perfectly familiar sense a second-order whole. Ecology makes it possible to see land, similarly, as a unified system of integrally related parts, as, so to speak, a third-order organic whole.

Another analogy that has helped ecologists to convey the particular holism which their science brings to reflective attention is that land is integrated as a human community is integrated. The various parts of the "biotic community" (individual animals and plants) depend upon one another *economically* so that the system as such acquires distinct characteristics of its own. Just as it is possible to characterize and define collectively peasant societies; agrarian communities; industrial complexes; capitalist, communist, and socialist economic systems; and so on, ecology characterizes and defines various biomes as desert, savanna, wetland, tundra, woodland, etc., communities, each with its particular "professions," "roles," or "niches."

Now we may think that among the duties we as moral agents have toward ourselves is the duty of self-preservation, which may be interpreted as a duty to maintain our own organic integrity. It is not uncommon in historical moral theory, further, to find that in addition to those peculiar responsibilities we have in relation both to ourselves and to other persons severally, we also have a duty to behave in ways that do not harm the fabric of society per se. The land ethic, in similar fashion, calls our attention to the recently discovered integrity—in other words, the unity—of the biota and posits duties binding upon moral agents in relation to that whole .... Hence, the representation of the natural environment as, in Leopold's terms, "one humming community" (or, less consistently in his discussion, a third-order organic being) brings into play, whether rationally or not, those stirrings of conscience which we feel in relation to delicately complex, functioning social and organic systems ....

Ethical Holism

.... An environmental ethic which takes as its *summum bonum* the integrity, stability, and beauty of the biotic community is not conferring moral standing on something else besides plants, animals, soils, and waters. Rather, the former, the good of the community as a whole, serves as a standard for the assessment of the relative value and relative ordering of its constitutive parts and therefore provides a means of adjudicating the often mutually contradictory demands of the parts considered separately for equal consideration. If diversity does indeed contribute to stability (a classical "law" of ecology), then specimens of rare and endangered species, for example, have a prima facie claim to preferential consideration from the perspective of the land ethic. Animals of those species, which, like the honeybee, function in ways critically important to the economy of nature, moreover, would be granted a greater claim to moral attention than psychologically more complex and sensitive ones, say rabbits and moles, which seem to be plentiful, globally distributed, reproductively efficient, and only routinely integrated into the natural economy. Animals and plants, mountains, rivers, seas, the atmosphere are the *immediate* practical beneficiaries of the land ethic.

The well-being of the biotic community, the biosphere as a whole, cannot be logically separated from their survival and welfare.

.... Is a healthy biotic community something we value because we are so utterly and (to the biologically well-informed) so obviously dependent upon it not only for our happiness but for our very survival or may we also perceive it disinterestedly as having an independent worth? Leopold insists upon a noninstrumental value for the biotic community and, mutatis mutandis, for its constituents. According to Leopold, collective enlightened self-interest on the part of human beings does not go far enough; the land ethic in his opinion (and no doubt this reflects his own moral intuitions) requires "love, respect, and admiration for land, and a high regard for its value." The land ethic, in Leopold's view, creates "obligations over and above self-interest." And "obligations have no meaning without conscience, and the problem we face is the extension of the social conscience from people to land."[8] If, in other words, any genuine ethic is possible, if it is possible to value *people* for the sake of themselves, then it is equally possible to value land in the same way ....

The biospheric perspective does not exempt *Homo sapiens* from moral evaluation in relation to the well-being of the community of nature taken as a whole. The preciousness of individual deer, as of any other specimen, is inversely proportional to the population of the species. Environmentalists, however reluctantly and painfully, do not omit to apply the same logic to their own kind. As omnivores, the population of human beings should, perhaps, be roughly twice that of bears, allowing for differences of size. A global population of more than 4 billion persons and showing no signs of an orderly decline presents an alarming prospect to humanists, but it is at present a global disaster (the more per capita prosperity, indeed, the more disastrous it appears) for the biotic community .... Edward Abbey in his enormously popular *Desert Solitaire* bluntly states that he would sooner shoot a man than a snake.[9] Abbey may not be simply depraved; this is perhaps only his way of dramatically making the point that the human population has become so disproportionate from the biological point of view that if one had to choose between a specimen of *Homo sapiens* and a specimen of a rare even if unattractive species, the choice would be moot ....

Reappraising Domesticity

Among the last philosophical remarks penned by Aldo Leopold before his untimely death in 1948 is the following: "Perhaps such a shift of values [as implied by the attempt to weld together the concepts of ethics and ecology] can be achieved by reappraising things unnatural, tame, and confined in terms of things natural, wild, and free."[10] ...

The "shift of values" which results from our "reappraising things unnatural, tame, and confined in terms of things natural, wild, and free" is especially dramatic when we reflect upon the definitions of *good* and *evil* espoused by Bentham and Mill and uncritically accepted by their contemporary followers. Pain and pleasure seem to have nothing at all to do with good and evil if our appraisal is taken from the vantage point of ecological biology. Pain in particular is primarily information. In animals, it informs the central nervous system of stress, irritation, or trauma in outlying regions of the organism. A certain level of pain under optimal organic circumstances is indeed desirable as an indicator of exertion—of the degree of exertion needed to maintain fitness, to stay "in shape," and of a level of exertion beyond which it would be dangerous to go. An arctic wolf in pursuit of a caribou may experience pain in her feet or chest because of the rigors of the chase. There is nothing bad or wrong in that. Or consider a case of injury. Suppose that a person in the course of a wilderness excursion sprains an ankle. Pain informs him or her of the injury and, by its intensity, the amount of further stress the ankle may endure in the course of getting to safety. Would it be better if pain were not experienced upon injury or, taking advantage of recent technology, anaesthetized? Pleasure appears to be, for the most part (unfortunately it is not always so), a reward accompanying those activities which contribute to organic maintenance, such as the pleasures associated with eating, drinking, grooming, and so on or those which contribute to social solidarity like the pleasures of dancing, conversation, teasing, etc., or those which contribute to the continuation of the species, such as the pleasures of sexual activity and of being parents. The doctrine that life is the happier the freer it is from pain and that the happiest life conceivable is one in which there is continuous pleasure uninterrupted by pain is biologically preposterous. A living mammal which experienced no pain would be one which had a lethal dysfunction of the nervous system. The idea that pain is evil and ought to be minimized or eliminated is as primitive a notion as that of a tyrant who puts to death messengers bearing bad news on the supposition that thus his well-being and security is improved.

More seriously still, the value commitments of the humane movement seem at bottom to betray a world-denying or rather a life-loathing philosophy. The natural world as actually constituted is one in which one being lives at the expense of others. Each organism, in Darwin's metaphor, struggles to maintain its own organic integrity. The more complex animals seem to experience (judging from our own case, and reasoning from analogy) appropriate and adaptive psychological accompaniments to organic existence. There is a palpable passion for self-preservation. There are desire, pleasure in the satisfaction of desires, acute agony attending injury, frustration, and chronic dread of death. But these experiences are the psychological substance of living. To live is to be anxious about life, to feel pain and pleasure in a fitting mixture, and sooner or later to die. That is the way the system works. If nature as a whole is good, then pain and death are also good. Environmental ethics in general require people to play fair in the natural system. The neo-Benthamites have in a sense taken the uncourageous approach. People have attempted to exempt themselves from the life/death reciprocities of natural processes and from ecological limitations in the name of a prophylactic ethic of maximizing rewards (pleasure) and minimizing unwelcome information (pain). To be fair, the humane moralists seem to suggest that we should attempt to project the same values into the nonhuman animal world and to widen the charmed circle, no matter that it would be biologically unrealistic to do so or biologically ruinous if, per impossible, such an environmental ethic were implemented.

There is another approach. Rather than imposing our alienation from nature and natural processes and cycles of life on other animals, we human beings could reaffirm our participation in nature by accepting life as it is given without a sugar coating. Instead of imposing artificial legalities, rights, and so on on nature, we might take the opposite course and accept and affirm natural biological laws, principles, and limitations in the human personal and social spheres. Such appears to have been the posture toward life of tribal peoples in the past. The chase was relished with its dangers, rigors, and hardships as well as its rewards: animal flesh was respectfully consumed; a tolerance for pain was cultivated; virtue and magnanimity were prized; lithic, floral, and faunal spirits were worshipped; population was routinely optimized by sexual continency, abortion, infanticide, and stylized warfare; and other life forms, although certainly appropriated, were respected as fellow players in a magnificent and awesome, if not altogether idyllic, drama of life. It is impossible today to return to the symbiotic relationship of Stone Age man to the natural environment, but the ethos of this (by far the longest) era of human existence could be abstracted and integrated with a future human culture seeking a viable and mutually beneficial relationship with nature. Personal, social, and environmental *health* would, accordingly, receive a premium value rather than comfort, self-indulgent pleasure, and anesthetic insulation from pain ....

.... This means, among other things, the reappraisal of the comparatively recent values and concerns of "civilized" *Homo sapiens* in terms of those of our "savage" ancestors. Civilization has insulated and alienated us from the rigors and challenges of the natural environment. The hidden agenda of the humane ethic is the imposition of the anti-natural prophylactic ethos of comfort and soft pleasure on an even wider scale. The land ethic, on the other hand, requires a shrinkage, if at all possible, of the domestic sphere; it rejoices in a recrudescence of wilderness and a renaissance of tribal cultural experience.

The converse of those goods and evils, axiomatic to the humane ethic, may be illustrated and focused by the consideration of a single issue raised by the humane morality: a vegetarian diet. Savage people seem to have had, if the attitudes and values of surviving tribal cultures are representative, something like an intuitive grasp of ecological relationships and certainly a morally charged appreciation of eating. There is nothing more intimate than eating, more symbolic of the connectedness of life, and more mysterious. What we eat and how we eat is by no means an insignificant ethical concern.

From the ecological point of view, for human beings universally to become vegetarians is tantamount to a shift of trophic niche from omnivore with carnivorous preferences to herbivore .... The human population would probably, as past trends overwhelmingly suggest, expand in accordance with the potential thus afforded. The net result would be fewer nonhuman beings and more human beings, who, of course, have requirements of life far more elaborate than even those of domestic animals, requirements which would tax other "natural resources" (trees for shelter, minerals mined at the expense of topsoil and its vegetation, etc.) more than under present circumstances. A vegetarian human population is therefore *probably* ecologically catastrophic.

Meat-eating as implied by the foregoing remarks may be more *ecologically* responsible than a wholly vegetable diet. Meat, however, purchased at the supermarket, externally packaged and internally laced with petrochemicals, fattened in feedlots, slaughtered impersonally, and, in general, mechanically processed from artificial insemination to microwave roaster, is an affront not only to physical metabolism and bodily health but to conscience as well. From the perspective of the land ethic, the immoral aspect of the factory farm has to do far less with the suffering and killing of non-human animals than with the monstrous transformation of living things from an organic to a mechanical mode of being ....

The land ethic, with its ecological perspective, helps us to recognize and affirm the organic integrity of self and the untenability of a firm distinction between self and environment. On the ethical question of what to eat, it answers not vegetables instead of animals but organically as opposed to mechanicochemically produced food. Purists like Leopold prefer, in his expression, to get their "meat from God," i.e., to hunt and consume wildlife and to gather wild plant foods and thus to live within the parameters of the aboriginal human ecological niche. Second best is eating from one's own orchard, garden, henhouse, pigpen, and barnyard. Third best is buying or bartering organic foods from one's neighbors and friends.

Conclusion

.... The debate over animal liberation, in short, should be conceived as triangular, not polar, with land ethics or environmental ethics, the third and, in my judgment, the most creative, interesting, and practicable alternative. Indeed, from this third point of view, moral humanism and humane moralism appear to have much more in common with one another than either have with environmental or land ethics. On reflection, one might even be led to suspect that the noisy debate between these parties has served to drown out the much deeper challenge to "business-as-usual" ethical philosophy represented by Leopold and his exponents and to keep ethical philosophy firmly anchored to familiar modern paradigms.

Notes

1 Aldo Leopold, *A Sand County Almanac* (New York: Oxford University Press, 1949), pp. 202–3.
2 Ibid., p. 204.
3 Ibid., pp. 201–3.
4 Ibid., p. 203.
5 Ibid., p. 204.
6 Ibid., p. 221 (trees); pp. 129–33 (mountains); p. 209 (streams).
7 Ibid., pp. 224–5.
8 Ibid., pp. 223 and 209.
9 Edward Abbey, *Desert Solitaire* (New York: Ballantine Books, 1968), p. 20.
10 Leopold, *Sand County Almanac*, p. ix.

Review and Discussion Questions

1 How does Callicott think environmental ethics differs from animal liberation (humane moralism)?
2 What is the first principle of the land ethic?
3 What does Callicott mean by saying that animal liberationists such as Bentham are "bluntly reductive"?
4 How does the environmental ethic differ from moral humanism?
5 Describe the reasons that seem to lead Callicott to conclude that the environmental ethic is superior to the others.
6 What practical implications do Callicott and you see from the adoption of the land ethic as opposed to animal liberation?

READING: TWO KINDS OF CLIMATE JUSTICE: AVOIDING HARM AND SHARING BURDENS

SIMON CANEY[*]

Simon Caney argues that people and institutions have duties to prevent climate change. He analyzes what these duties entail, and he justifies these duties through the idea that power implies responsibilities. Simon Caney is Professor of Political Theory at the University of Warwick.

I Two Kinds of Climate Justice

The overwhelming majority of climate scientists hold that humanity is facing the prospect of severe climate change and the Assessment Reports of the Intergovernmental Panel on Climate Change (IPCC) contain some stark warnings. In the IPCC's Fourth Assessment Report, the "best estimate" of the increase in global mean temperatures in the period between 1980–1999 and 2080–2099 ranged from 1.8°C (B1 scenario) and 4.0°C (A1F1 scenario). If we consider the "likely range" of temperature increases in this period, we see that the figures range from between a 1.1°C increase (B1) and 6.4°C increase (A1F1).[1] These changes—and the sea level rises and severe weather events associated with climate change—will have disastrous effects on human and non-human life.

One can distinguish between two ways of thinking about climate justice. One starts by focusing on how the burden of combating the problem should be shared fairly among the duty-bearers. An agent's responsibility, then, is to do her fair share. Its concern is with what I shall term *Burden-Sharing Justice*. A number of principles of burden-sharing justice have been proposed and assessed. Three, in particular, have been suggested—the principle that those who have caused the problem should bear the burden; the principle that those who have the ability to pay should bear the burden; and the principle that those who have benefited from the activities that cause climate change should bear the burden.

One might, however, look at the issue from a second point of view. This second perspective takes as its starting point the imperative to prevent climate change, and it works back from this to deduce who should do what. Its focus is primarily on ensuring that the catastrophe is averted (or at least minimised within reason). This perspective is concerned with the potential victims—those whose entitlements are threatened—and it ascribes responsibilities to others to uphold these entitlements. This approach focuses on what I shall term *Harm Avoidance Justice*.

…. Climate change poses serious existential threats to many people's lives and to the very existence of some communities. Its effects will be extremely harmful, possibly catastrophic, for millions of people. Given this, I think we have reason to focus on what would most effectively prevent the onset of dangerous climate change, and then consider what responsibilities would follow from that.[2] My aim

---

[*] Adapted from "Two Kinds of Climate Justice: Avoiding Harm and Sharing Burdens" by Simon Caney, *Journal of Political Philosophy* (2014). Reprinted by permission of Wiley-Blackwell. Some footnotes omitted.

in this paper, then, is to develop a normative account of climate change that takes as its starting point the assumption that it is of paramount importance that humanity avoids dangerous climate change ....

II Prioritizing Prevention I

The first prevention-oriented approach I wish to consider is that set out by Eric Posner and David Weisbach in their book *Climate Change Justice* (2010). Posner and Weisbach start from a commitment to preventing dangerous climate change and argue that to realize this commitment we must adopt what they term "International Paretianism". Their claim is nicely encapsulated in the following passage:

> Any treaty must satisfy what we shall call the principle of International Paretianism: all states must believe themselves better off by their lights as a result of the climate treaty. International Paretianism is not an ethical principle but a pragmatic constraint: in the state system, treaties are not possible unless they have the consent of all states, and states only enter treaties that serve their interests.[3]

Broken down into its constituent parts, Posner and Weisbach's argument is as follows:

(P1) It is necessary to have a climate treaty with which major emitters comply.
(P2) To be feasible an effective climate treaty must serve the interests of high emitting states (from "Feasibility" to "Pareto Superiority")

Therefore,

(C) A climate treaty must serve the interests of high emitting states.

....

Posner and Weisbach's argument gains whatever credibility it might possess because they present their claim in the passive mood. They write, for example, that "only a treaty that satisfies International Paretianism—that is, that advances the interests of all states relative to the status quo—is feasible". But this *passive* way of putting it is misleading. Treaties are agreed to by *agents* and we need to examine it from their point of view. From the point of view of the members of a high emitting political community, it is just not true that it is not possible for them to sign up to a treaty that leaves them worse off. They can.

Posner and Weisbach might make two replies. First, they might protest that they are not using "feasible" to mean "is possible". Rather, they might argue, they are using "feasible" to mean "is likely to happen" or, perhaps, "will happen". This, however, does not help their case for the same argument applies against this.

....

From the external point of view, it is defensible to argue that "concessions need to be made to high emitters because without that they are not *likely to* comply (or *will not* comply)". But if a high emitting country like the USA simply says "this treaty needs to reward us because unless it does so then we are not likely to comply" (or, just, "we will not comply"), then it is hard to see why this counts as a justification at all. It is a prediction of expected behaviour and perhaps a threat.

Pointing out that a proposed obligation is not possible is relevant. But saying that, though it is possible for one to do X, one *is not likely to comply* with it (or, more baldly, one *will not comply with it*) has no argumentative power. To posit that "ought" implies "can" is reasonable (if not uncontroversial), but to claim that "ought" implies either "is likely to" or "will" is obviously implausible. [Ed. Note: The author surveys and rejects a second preventative approach in Section III that would push the costs of combatting climate change to future generations as compensation for the sacrifices that emitters would make today.]

....

IV Prioritizing Prevention 3

Having criticised two approaches that might both appear to help us make progress in preventing dangerous change, I shall now outline and then defend my own prevention-oriented approach. The two preceding accounts have both sought to minimize the sacrifices that need to be made ....

My account starts from the recognition that, even if some costs can be passed on, some sacrifices have to be made. Given this, we cannot just assume that agents will comply with their duties to mitigate and enable adaptation to climate change. Unless one thinks that agents will spontaneously comply with such burdensome responsibilities—and our experience of human nature and the inconclusive nature of the negotiations on climate change for the last two decades have surely taught us that such a belief would be naïve in the extreme—anyone serious about preventing climate change (and thus avoiding harm) needs to reflect on how to respond to current and future non-compliance.

There are two distinct kinds of response to this challenge. To elaborate on these it is, however, necessary to distinguish here between two kinds of responsibility—what can be termed *first-order* and *second-order responsibilities*. First-order responsibilities, as I employ that term, are responsibilities that certain agents have to perform (or omit) certain actions. In the context of addressing climate change these *first-order* responsibilities include responsibilities to mitigate climate change (through reducing emissions and maintaining greenhouse gas sinks), to enable adaption, and to compensate people for harm done. *Second*-order responsibilities, by contrast, refer to responsibilities that some have to ensure that agents comply with their *first-order responsibilities* ....

A Task Delineation

As noted above, if our aim is to avert dangerous climate change, then it makes sense to commence our analysis with an account of what needs to be done to achieve this goal. In order to do this, we need to specify the content of the *second-order responsibilities* required to avert dangerous climate change. Without claiming to be exhaustive, one might identify at least six kinds of action that agents can perform.

The first, is <u>enforcement</u>: those who have (or could have) the political power to set up enforcement mechanisms may have a responsibility to do so. To give one example, Joseph Stiglitz has proposed that the WTO should employ trade sanctions against states that do not make an appropriate reduction in greenhouse gas emissions.[4] In addition to enforcing compliance (or, perhaps, as an alternative to doing this), one might also compel an agent to disclose its level of greenhouse gas emissions ….

A second type of second-order course of action is incentivization. Whereas enforcement imposes a burden on non-compliers, incentivization offers benefits to them in exchange for compliance. Organizations like the WTO and EU can, and do, insist that those belonging to them, and those seeking to join, must satisfy certain criteria. Such organizations can thus withhold membership (and, therefore, the benefits of such membership) from states that do not comply with their mitigation and adaptation responsibilities.

A third type of second-order action is what we might term enablement. By this I mean the capacity to enable others to engage in mitigation or adaptation. For example, some agents' willingness to comply with their first-order responsibilities to reduce their greenhouse gas emissions may be undermined because low-carbon alternatives may be difficult to find (or, in a variation on this, because the low-carbon alternatives are quite expensive). Given this, one way that some can affect whether agents comply with *first-order responsibilities* to mitigate is by: (a) facilitating scientific research (into clean technologies, new energy sources, and ways of increasing energy efficiency); and (b) transferring these scientific innovations widely so that people may reduce emissions more easily. For example, one way to enable agents to comply is by designing urban spaces so that people can move around (between their homes, workplaces, schools, and leisure activities) in ways which do not involve emitting high levels of greenhouse gases.

….

Consider now a fourth kind of second-order policy. Some agents can influence the behaviour of others by creating norms that discourage high emissions lifestyles (or, alternatively, that foster a commitment to adaptation). To employ a term coined by Cass Sunstein, some can act as "norm entrepreneurs".[5] Norms can be tremendously influential for they define what options count as appropriate and what not. To take two recent examples, attitudes towards smoking in confined spaces and attitudes to drink-driving have changed dramatically in the UK in the last thirty to forty years ….

Consider now a fifth kind of second-order policy—namely undermining resistance to effective climate policies. As Naomi Oreskes and Erik Conway have convincingly argued in *Merchants of Doubt*, oil companies have sought to spread misinformation about the nature, extent, and causes of global warming.[6] In addition to this, it has been persuasively argued that media representations of climate change are often misleading, and hence that the public understanding of climate science is often poor and out of line with the scientific consensus.[7] One service that some (in the media) can provide is to give an accurate portrayal of the state of climate science, reporting the levels of agreement on the existence of anthropogenic climate change, as well as including the areas of considerable uncertainty ….

To this list we can also add civil disobedience. Citizens can discourage, impede, and even prevent their governments from engaging in activities which increase emissions above an acceptable level by engaging in civil disobedience. They can—and often do—seek to block the construction of new motorways and new airports (or new runways at existing airports). By doing so they prevent, or at least obstruct, the ability of governments to default on their *first-order responsibilities* ....

B Kinds of Actors

Given this an account of what needs to be done, the next logical step is to consider who has the capacity to perform these tasks. To do so we might refer to each of the tasks presented above and then infer from this who can do what. Doing this will confirm that some actors that one might expect would have *second-order responsibilities* (such as governments and international institutions) can indeed play a pivotal role. However, it will also draw attention to the contribution that other less obvious actors can make.

If we begin, for example, with enforcement then the relevant agents of justice clearly include political actors such as states and international institutions like the WTO, the IMF and the World Bank. Furthermore, and in line with my response to Posner and Weisbach, it also implies that citizens can play a kind of enforcement role for they can punish governments that fail to put in place environmental policies. In addition to this, powerful agents can create new institutions with enforcement powers.

A similarly conventional picture emerges if we consider incentivization. Again, we can see that governments and international institutions can play a significant role. As noted above, membership of the organizations like the European Community and the World Trade Organization is often extremely beneficial, and given this, such organizations can use this to induce compliance by stipulating that those joining their organizations must honour certain environmental standards.

If we examine other tasks, however, we arrive at less conventional answers. Consider enablement for example. As I noted above, one important kind of enablement is technological innovation and diffusion. Given this, research councils, university science departments (who often have large research budgets), and corporations all have a capacity to make a significant contribution by orienting their research capacities to promoting these goals. As I also noted above, the layout of cities and towns can make a significant difference to the emissions that result from transportation. Given this, it follows that urban planners have a significant role to play—not a conclusion that has been stressed by the existing literature on climate ethics.

Reflecting on other tasks also reveals the role that can be played by other actors that one might not immediately consider to be potential agents of justice. For example, if we turn now to norm-creation, we can see that a significant role can be played by figures as diverse as church leaders, poets, novelists, charismatic individuals, and gifted communicators. To see the potential role played by communicators think, for example, of the influential science writer Rachel Carson, whose work, *Silent Spring* ([1962] 1965), chronicled the impacts of pesticides and had an enormous galvanising impact on environmentalism.

If we turn now to consider undermining resistance, we can also see that those who can communicate the findings of climate science effectively—such as climate scientists and science journalists—have an important role to play. We might think here, for example, of the role played by scientists like James Hansen. Also, those who are highly trusted—especially those who are regarded as reliable by communities which tend to resist climate change initiatives—can perform a vital function.

Reflection on who can discharge *second-order responsibilities* thus reveals the role that a wide variety of very different actors can play—including not just government departments, but also journalists, scientists, writers, research councils, churches, urban planners, officials responsible for demographic policy, and charismatic individuals ....

V The Power/Responsibility Principle

Section IV sought to introduce the idea of *second-order responsibilities* and to flesh out the kinds of *tasks* that need to be performed and the *agents* who can best perform them. It did not, however, give any argument as to why the agents designated in Section IV have this kind of responsibility. It was primarily descriptive.

My aim in this section is to address this lacuna and provide a justification of why the kinds of agents specified in Section IV have a duty to undertake *second-order responsibilities* ....

The dictum that "with power comes responsibility" is often voiced, especially in times of crisis. For example, Franklin Roosevelt wrote in his "Jefferson Day Address" that "[t]oday we have learned in the agony of war that great power involves great responsibility".[8] Similar sentiments were echoed by Winston Churchill who famously said that "[t]he price of greatness is responsibility".[9] The phrase has entered into popular consciousness.

For all this, the precise principle I am invoking has rarely received philosophical analysis. In *The Idea of Justice*, Amartya Sen affirms what looks like a similar principle. He refers to what he terms the "obligation of effective power".[10] However, when he explicates this it becomes clear that he simply means the capacity to aid people, which is not quite the principle I am analysing. A related point can be made with reference to David Miller's analysis of responsibilities. Miller refers to what he terms "the principle of *capacity*" which he defines as stating "that remedial responsibilities ought to be assigned according to the capacity of each agent to discharge them".[11] Again this is an important principle, but it does not distinguish between different ways of having a capacity to help others. Consider, for example, the oft-invoked principle that burdens of mitigating climate change and enabling adaptation should be borne by those with the greatest ability to pay (the "Ability to Pay" Principle). This is a kind of capacity principle. However, it is quite distinct from the Power/Responsibility Principle for two reasons. First the Power/Responsibility Principle—unlike the Ability to Pay Principle—is focused on *second-order responsibilities*. Furthermore, and even more importantly, many of those who have the power to make a difference do not have that power because of their access to financial resources and thus their ability to pay. The sources of their power may lie in their role in the political process (e.g., politicians or urban planners), or their knowledge and expertise (e.g., those capable of scientific innovations), or their powers of persuasion (e.g., norm entrepreneurs). The Power/Responsibility Principle is, thus, a distinct kind of capacity principle. Furthermore, as we shall see soon, it rests on a distinct kind of justification.

Why should we accept it? I shall not seek to provide a general account of when this principle applies and why. I shall, however, try to show why it applies in this context and thus why, given the prospect of dangerous climate change, those who can take up *second-order responsibilities* and thereby promote the ideal of *Harm Avoidance* have, modulo certain conditions, a duty to do so. My claim appeals to the following highly plausible assumptions.

1   Emergency. First, humanity faces a prospect of disastrous harms. To refer again to the IPCC, its Fourth Assessment Report chronicles severe threats to life (from heat stress, extreme precipitation, and storm surges), health (with increased exposure to several infectious diseases), access to water and to food (resulting in malnutrition and hunger) ....
2   Effectiveness. Second, certain agents can reduce, or severely limit, the chances of these dire outcomes ....
3   A Crucial and Privileged Causal Role. In addition to this, the agents identified in the previous section do not simply have the capacity to effect change. It is also the case that they have a capacity that many others lack. Their action is, thus, crucial in the sense that if disaster is to be averted, these kinds of agents must act ....
4   No Sufficiently Weighty Countervailing Considerations. The final step maintains that the second-order agents listed in the preceding section do not, in general, have countervailing responsibilities that take priority. I suspect that this is the most contentious step in my argument.

....

Let us turn now to consider ways that someone might resist the above argument, especially step [4]. First, someone might say that some of those designated second-order agents might have countervailing obligations. For example, it is commonly asserted that governments have a special responsibility to their own citizens to promote their interests.

In reply: This is plausible, but such responsibilities are clearly not absolute. We recognize that when a great deal is at stake such special responsibilities can be overridden. For example, I may have a special responsibility to keep a promise to meet someone, but if on my way there I encounter someone in great need and, if it is the case not only that I can play an effective role but my contribution is critical, then we recognize that this should take priority. Second, many second-order agents will not have countervailing responsibilities. For example, research scientists, church leaders, and charismatic individuals will not generally have fiduciary responsibilities that require them to abstain from the actions I described. In addition to this, governments with vulnerable populations will have a fiduciary responsibility to induce compliance with mitigation responsibilities. Finally, governments may have responsibilities that converge with mitigation policies—for example, a responsibility to improve air quality may call for a reduction in emissions and thus converge with mitigation policies.

A critic might then press a second objection. They might say that undertaking *second-order responsibilities* may impose excessive costs on the duty-bearers. Three points can be made in reply. First, it is worth noting that for many of the second-order agents I specified above, complying with their second-order responsibilities (as listed in IV.A) imposes little or no cost on the actor. Consider, for example, political organizations that can insist that new members meet certain environmental standards if they are to join. In many cases this imposes no burden on the organization: rather what they are doing is making a decision that might impose a cost on the would-be member. Or consider spokespersons for influential social organizations (like churches): their affirmation of environmental goals need not generate any extra cost on them. Or consider urban planners: they can ensure that built up areas be designed in such a way as to facilitate the use of cycling, to minimize sprawl, and to ensure that housing, schools, recreation, and shops are close to each other. This might conceivably impose costs on some, but the key point is that it does not impose costs on the urban planners ….

A second point can also be made to the "excessive cost" concern, namely that, in some of the cases under consideration, those being asked to perform *second-order responsibilities* may be being asked to perform tasks that they are already obligated to perform. For example, it is arguable that journalists have a duty to report the existing degree of consensus concerning climate change.

This leaves a third point. Some costs will no doubt remain …. In determining how much sacrifice the putative bearers of *second-order responsibilities* should bear, it is worth noting three further considerations. First, the costs on second-order agents are likely to be small when compared to the costs of inaction. Second, it is instructive to make a comparison with other cases where there is a call for sacrifices. Consider, for example, humanitarian intervention. Very few reject humanitarian intervention out of hand in all cases, and where some do, it is often because of practical concerns about whether such interventions succeed. But humanitarian intervention frequently results in deaths of troops on the intervening side. This prompts the following thought: If we are willing to send some to their death to defend others, then can we reasonably object to imposing non-lethal sacrifices on people to defend similarly important interests (in life, physical integrity, health, and subsistence)? Third, it is worth noting that those who take up *second-order responsibilities* might be able to seek compensation for their efforts at a later date. Their position can be contrasted with the victims of climate change because if action is not undertaken, then they may have very meagre (sometimes non-existent) capacities to seek compensation.

Thus neither way of arguing that there are overwhelming countervailing considerations seems promising. Given this then: *since* there is a prospect of disastrous effects on people's lives and *since* some agents not only can play an effective role, but their action is critical to avoiding these disastrous impacts; and, finally, *since* these agents lack compelling countervailing reasons for action we are, I think, driven to the conclusion that those agents with the power to discharge *second-order responsibilities* have a duty to do so ….

VI Concluding Remarks

It is time now to conclude. I have argued that we should examine the ethical challenges posed by climate change from two different perspectives—what I have termed *Burden-Sharing Justice* and *Harm Avoidance Justice*. Much of the normative analysis of the responsibilities relating to climate change has focused solely on *Burden-Sharing Justice*. My aim in this article has been to examine what an approach that prioritizes avoiding harm would look like. In doing so, I have examined two approaches which attempt to do this, but found both wanting because neither recognizes that averting dangerous climate change requires that some make sacrifices. Acknowledging the need for some sacrifices entails that we take seriously the need to create and sustain an institutional context which induces people to comply with their duties to mitigate and to enable adaptation. It calls, that is, for an account of second-order responsibilities.

Such responsibilities, so I have argued, should be guided by what I term the Power/Responsibility Principle where this asserts that, under certain circumstances, those with the power to ensure that agents comply with their first-order responsibilities have a responsibility to use their power to protect people from the existential threats posed by climate change. This principle differs in its *application, nature*, and *justification* from those principles commonly invoked in discussions of climatic responsibilities. It differs in its *application* for it is directed towards second-order responsibilities, not first-order ones; it differs in its *nature* because, as I argued above, it cannot be assimilated to common principles such as the Ability to Pay Principle or the Polluter Pays Principle; and, it differs in its *justification* because it can be grounded (as I have done here) on a commitment to avoiding catastrophe, rather than appeals to equitable burden-sharing.

The Power/Responsibility Principle takes us out of a realm where the focus is just on responsibilities to reduce emissions and to engage in adaptation, for it also provides an account of the more explicitly political responsibilities that are needed if we are to avoid severe climatic changes.

Notes

1 Susan Solomon et al. (eds.), *Climate Change 2007: The Physical Science Basis. Contribution of Working Group I to the Fourth Assessment Report of the Intergovernmental Panel on Climate Change* (Cambridge: Cambridge University Press, 2007), p. 70.
2 I am indebted here to a presentation by Robert Goodin at the conference on "Political Thought and the Environment" (University of Cambridge, 25 May 2012), which similarly emphasized the importance of adopting this perspective.
3 Eric A. Posner and David Weisbach, *Climate Change Justice* (Princeton, NJ: Princeton University Press, 2010), p. 6, footnote omitted.
4 Joseph E. Stiglitz, *Making Globalization Work* (London: Allen Lane, 2006), pp. 176–8.
5 See Cass R. Sunstein, "Social norms and social roles", *Columbia Law Review*, 96 (1996), 903–68, p. 909.
6 See Naomi Oreskes and Erik M Conway, *Merchants of Doubt: How a Handful of Scientists Obscured the Truth on Issues from Tobacco Smoke to Global Warming* (New York: Bloomsbury Press, 2010), Ch. 6.
7 See Maxwell T. Boykoff, *Who Speaks for the Climate?* (New York: Cambridge University Press, 2011).
8 See http://georgiainfo.galileo.usg.edu/FDRspeeches/FDRspeech45-1.htm. Roosevelt did not deliver this speech because he died before he was scheduled to give it.
9 David M. Kennedy, *The American People in World War II*. Volume II: *Freedom from Fear*. New York: Oxford University Press, 1999), p. 255.
10 Amartya Sen, *The Idea of Justice* (London: Penguin, 2009), p. 205: cf. pp. 205–7, 271.
11 David Miller, "Distributing responsibilities", *Journal of Political Philosophy*, 9 (2001), 453–71, p. 460.

Review and Discussion Questions

1 What is the distinction between the approaches that Simon Caney calls "burden-sharing" and "harm avoidance" justice? Which approach does he pursue in this essay and why?

2. Some argue that addressing climate change must appeal to people's self-interest to be realistic and ought to require no sacrifices. How does he critique Posner's and Weisbach's argument?
3. What is the distinction between first-order and second-order responsibilities?
4. Of all the second-order responsibilities that he lists, which are the most interesting to you and why?
5. Beyond merely describing this list of responsibilities, he provides an argument to justify why various people and institutions have duties to fulfill these responsibilities. What is that justification?
6. What are two objections to his account and how does he respond to those objections? Can you devise further objections and consider responses?

Essay and Paper Topics for Chapter 7

1. How might Singer respond to Callicott's argument? Is that response adequate?
2. Which of Callicott's three positions is closest to Steinbock's? How might she respond to Callicott's essay?
3. "Hunting is consistent with being an environmentalist." How do you assess this statement?
4. What are the most significant comparisons and contrasts across the first four essays?
5. Using a general moral theory from Part I that you found most reasonable, write an essay in which you discuss how that theory would evaluate the position of two philosophers you have read on moral obligations to animals and to nature.
6. How would each of the first four authors analyze the morality of climate change?

Chapter 8

Cloning and Abortion

The essays in this chapter represent a broad range of views on two of the most controversial moral and legal issues in the United States: cloning and abortion. This chapter begins with a debate about the ethics of cloning-to-produce-children. The President's Council on Bioethics produced this influential analysis of the ethics of cloning. The essays on abortion raise three issues. The first, and most often discussed, is the moral status of the fetus. The second question involves women's rights and political domination. Can a pregnant woman legitimately get an abortion based on her right to control her body? A third set of questions involves fathers: might the father legitimately demand that the mother not get an abortion?

> ### READING: THE ETHICS OF CLONING-TO-PRODUCE-CHILDREN
>
> THE PRESIDENT'S COUNCIL ON BIOETHICS
>
> In 2002, the President's Council on Bioethics released the document *Human Cloning and Human Dignity: An Ethical Inquiry*. The purpose of the report was to advise the president on important developments in biomedical science and to encourage national debate about this controversial topic. The Council distinguished arguments about the ethics of cloning-to-produce-children from arguments about the ethics of cloning-for-biomedical-research. This selection from the report focuses on the former: ethical arguments for and against cloning people. They ultimately conclude that cloning people ought to be banned.
>
> We will begin [this chapter] by formulating the best moral case for cloning-to-produce-children describing both the specific purposes it might serve and the philosophic and moral arguments made in its favor. From there we will move to the moral case against cloning-to-produce-children. Beginning with the safety objections that have dominated the debate thus far, we will show how these concerns ultimately point beyond themselves toward broader ethical concerns. Chief among these is how cloning-to-produce-children would challenge the basic nature of human procreation and the meaning of having children. We shall also consider cloning's effects on human identity, how it might move procreation toward a form of manufacture or toward eugenics, and how it could distort family relations and affect society as a whole.

The Case for Cloning-to-Produce-Children

Arguments in defense of cloning-to-produce-children often address questions of reproduction, but they tend to focus on only a relatively narrow sliver of the goods and principles involved. This certainly does not mean that such arguments lack merit. Indeed, some of the arguments in favor of cloning-to-produce-children appeal to the deepest and most meaningful of our society's shared values.

Purposes

In recent years, in anticipation of cloning-to-produce-children, proponents have articulated a variety of possible uses of a perfected technology: providing a "biologically related child" for an infertile couple; permitting reproduction for single individuals or same-sex couples; avoiding the risk of genetic disease; securing a genetically identical source of organs or tissues perfectly suitable for transplantation; "replacing" a loved spouse or child who is dying or has died; obtaining a child with a genotype of one's own choosing (including one's own genotype); replicating individuals of great genius, talent, or beauty, or individuals possessing traits that are for other reasons attractive to the cloners; and creating sets of genetically identical humans who might have special advantages in highly cooperative ventures in both war and peace.[1] The desire to control or select the genomes of children-to-be through cloning has charmed more than a few prospective users, in the United States and around the world.

Although we appreciate that a perfected technology, once introduced for one purpose, might then be used for any of these purposes, we shall examine further only those stated purposes that seem to us to merit serious consideration.

To Produce Biologically Related Children

Human cloning would allow individuals or couples with fertility problems to have biologically related children. For example, if a man could not produce sperm, cloning would allow him to have a child who is "biologically related" to him. In addition, it would allow married couples with fertility problems to avoid using donor gametes, and therefore avoid raising children with genetic inheritances from outside the marriage.

To Avoid Genetic Disease

Human cloning could allow couples at risk of generating children with genetic disease to have healthy children. For example, if both parents carried one copy of a recessive gene for the same heritable disorder, cloning might allow them to ensure that their child does not inherit the known genetic disease (without having to resort to using donor gametes or practicing preimplantation or prenatal genetic diagnosis and elimination of afflicted embryos or fetuses).

To Obtain "Rejection-Proof" Transplants

Human cloning could produce ideal transplant donors for people who are sick or dying. For example, if no genetic match could be found for a sick child needing a kidney or bone marrow transplant, and the parents had planned to have another child, cloning could potentially serve the human goods of beginning a new life and saving an existing one.

To "Replicate" a Loved One

Human cloning would allow parents to "replicate" a dead or dying child or relative. For example, one can imagine a case in which a family—mother, father, and child—is involved in a terrible car accident in which the father dies instantly and the child is critically injured. The mother, told that her child will soon die, decides that the best way to redeem the tragedy is to clone her dying child. This would allow her to preserve a connection with both her dead husband and her dying child, to create new life as a partial human answer to the grievous misfortune of her child's untimely death, and to continue the name and biological lineage of her deceased husband.

To Reproduce Individuals of Great Genius, Talent, or Beauty

Human cloning would allow families or society to reproduce individuals of great genius, talent, or beauty, where these traits are presumed to be based on the individuals' desirable or superior genetic makeups. For example, some admirers of great athletes, musicians, or mathematicians, believing that the admired attributes are the result of a superior genetic endowment, might want to clone these distinguished individuals. Just as the cloning of cattle is being promoted as a means of perpetuating champion milk- or meat-producing cows, so cloning-to-produce-children has been touted as a means of perpetuating certain "superior" human exemplars.

Arguments

The purposes or reasons for cloning-to-produce-children are, as they are stated, clearly intelligible on their face. When challenged, the defenders of these purposes often appeal to larger moral and political goods. These typically fall within the following three categories: human freedom, existence, and well-being.

The Goodness of Human Freedom

Strictly speaking, the appeal to human freedom is not so much a defense of cloning itself as it is of the *right* to practice it, asserted against those who seek to prohibit it. No one, we suspect, would say that he wanted to clone himself or anyone else in order to be free or to vindicate the goodness of liberty. Nevertheless, human freedom is a defense often heard in support of a "right" to clone.

Those who defend cloning-to-produce-children on the grounds of human freedom make two kinds of arguments. The first is that because individuals in pluralistic societies have different definitions of the good life and of right and wrong, society must protect individual freedom to choose against the possible tyranny of the majority. This means securing and even expanding the rights of individuals to make choices so long as their choices do not directly infringe on the rights (and especially the physical safety) of other rights-bearing citizens. In *Eisenstadt v. Baird* (1972), the United States Supreme Court enunciated what has been called a principle of reproductive freedom: "If the right to privacy means anything, it is the right of the individual, married or single, to be free from unwarranted governmental intrusion into matters so affecting a person as a decision whether to bear or beget a child."[2] Defenders of cloning-to-produce-children argue that, in the event that the physical risks to mother and future child were shown to be ethically acceptable, the use of this new reproductive technology would fall under the protective umbrella of reproductive freedom.

A second defense of human cloning on the grounds of freedom is the claim that human existence is by its very nature "open-ended," "indeterminate," and "unpredictable." Human beings are always remaking themselves, their values, and their ways of interacting with one another. New technologies are central to this open-ended idea of human life, and to shut down such technologies simply because they change the "traditional" ways of doing things is unjustifiable. As constitutional scholar Laurence Tribe has argued in reference to human cloning:

> A society that bans acts of human creation that reflect unconventional sex roles or parenting models (surrogate motherhood, in vitro fertilization, artificial insemination, and the like) for no better reason than that such acts dare to defy "nature" and tradition (and to risk adding to life's complexity) is a society that risks cutting itself off from vital experimentation and risks sterilizing a significant part of its capacity to grow.[3]

The Goodness of Existence

Like the appeal to freedom, the appeal to the goodness of existence is not an argument *for* cloning, but an argument *against* opponents who speak up in the name of protecting the cloned child-to-be against the harms connected with its risky and strange origins as a clone. This argument asserts that attempts to produce children through cloning, like *any* attempt to produce a child, will directly benefit the cloned-child-to-be, since without the act of cloning the child in question would not exist. Existence itself, it is argued, is the first "interest" that makes all other interests—including the interests of safety and well-being—possible. Even taking into account the possibility of serious genetic or developmental disorders, this position holds that a cloned individual, once born, would prefer existence as a clone to no existence at all. There is also a serious corollary about how, in the absence of a principle that values existence *as such*, we will and should regard and treat people born with disabilities or deformities: opponents of cloning might appear in a position of intolerance—of saying to cloned individuals, "Better for us (and for you) had you never existed."

The Goodness of Well-Being

The third moral argument for cloning-to-produce-children is that it would contribute in certain cases to the fulfillment of human goods that are widely honored and deeply rooted in modern democratic society. These human goods include the health of newborn and existing children, reproductive possibilities for infertile couples, and the possibility of having a biologically related child. In all these circumstances, human cloning could relieve existing suffering and sorrow or prevent them in the future. Those who take this position do not necessarily defend human cloning-to-produce-children as such. Rather, they argue that a moral and practical line can be drawn between cloning-to-produce-children that serves the "therapeutic" aims of health (for the cloned child-to-be, for the infertile couple, or for an existing child) and the "eugenic" aims of producing or mass-producing superior people.

Some people argue more broadly that an existing generation has a responsibility to ensure, to the extent possible, the genetic quality and fitness of the next generation. Human cloning, they argue, offers a new method for human control and self-improvement, by allowing families to have children free of specific genetic diseases or society to reproduce children with superior genetic endowments. It also provides a new means for gaining knowledge about the age-old question of nature versus nurture in contributing to human achievement and human flourishing, and to see how clones of great geniuses measure up against the "originals."

Critique and Conclusion

While we as a Council acknowledge merit in some of the arguments made for cloning-to-produce-children, we are generally not persuaded by them. The fundamental weakness of the proponents' case is found in their incomplete view of human procreation and families, and especially the place and well-being of children. Proponents of cloning tend to see procreation primarily as the free exercise of a parental right, namely, a right to satisfy parental desires for self-fulfillment or a right to have a child who is healthy or "superior." Parents seek to overcome obstacles to reproduction, to keep their children free of genetic disease or disorder, and to provide them with the best possible genetic endowment. The principles guiding such prospective parents are freedom (for themselves), control (over their child), and well-being (both for themselves and what they imagine is best for their child). Even taken together, these principles provide at best only a partial understanding of the meaning and entailments of human procreation and child-rearing. In practice, they may prove to undermine the very goods that the proponents of cloning aim to serve, by undermining the unconditional acceptance of one's offspring that is so central to parenthood.

There are a number of objections—or at the very least limitations—to viewing cloning-to-produce-children through the prism of rights. Basic human rights are usually asserted on behalf of the human individual agent: for example, a meaningful right *not to be prevented* from bearing a child can be asserted for each individual against state-mandated sterilization programs. But the act of procreation is not an act involving a single individual. Indeed, until human cloning arrives, it continues to be impossible for any one person to procreate alone. More important, there is a crucial third party involved: the child, whose centrality to the activity exposes the insufficiency of thinking about procreation in terms of rights.

After all, rights are limited in the following crucial way: they cannot be ethically exercised at the expense of the rights of another. But the "right to reproduce" cannot be ethically exercised without at least considering the child that such exercise will bring into being and who is at risk of harm and injustice from the exercise. This obligation cannot be waived by an appeal to the absolutist argument of the goodness of existence. Yes, existence is a primary good, but that does not diminish the ethical significance of knowingly and willfully putting a child in grave physical danger in the very act of giving that child existence. It is certainly true that a life with even severe disability may well be judged worth living by its bearer: "It is better to have been born as I am than not to be here at all." But if his or her disability was caused by behavior that could have been avoided by parents (for example, by not drinking or using drugs during pregnancy, or, arguably, by not cloning), many would argue that they should have avoided it. A post-facto affirmation of existence by the harmed child would not retroactively excuse the parental misconduct that caused the child's disability, nor would it justify their failure to think of the child's well-being as they went about exercising their "right to procreate." Indeed, procreation is, by its very nature, a limitation of absolute rights, since it brings into existence another human being toward whom we have responsibilities and duties.

In short, the right to decide "*whether* to bear or beget a child" does not include a right to have a child *by whatever means*. Nor can this right be said to imply a corollary—the right to decide what *kind* of child one is going to have. There are at least some circumstances where reproductive freedom must be limited to protect the good of the child (as, for instance, with the ban on incest). Our society's commitment to freedom and parental authority by no means implies that all innovative procedures and practices should be allowed or accepted, no matter how bizarre or dangerous.

Proponents of cloning, when they do take into account the interests of the child, sometimes argue that this interest justifies and even requires thoroughgoing parental control over the procreative process. Yet this approach, even when well-intentioned, may undermine the good of the child more than it serves the child's best interests. For one thing, cloning-to-produce-children of a desired or worthy sort overlooks the need to restrain the parental temptation to total mastery over children. It is especially morally dubious for this project to go forward when we know so little about the unforeseen and unintended consequences of exercising such genetic control. In trying by cloning to circumvent the risk of genetic disease or to promote particular traits, it is possible—perhaps likely that new risks to the cloned child's health and fitness would be inadvertently introduced (including the forgoing of genetic novelty, a known asset in the constant struggle against microbial and parasitic diseases). Parental control is a double-edged sword, and proponents seem not to acknowledge the harms, both physical and psychological, that may befall the child whose genetic identity is selected in advance.

The case for cloning in the name of the child's health and well-being is certainly the strongest and most compelling. The desire that one's child be free from a given genetic disease is a worthy aspiration. We recognize there may be some unusual or extreme cases in which cloning might be the best means to serve this moral good, if other ethical obstacles could somehow be overcome. (A few of us also believe that the desire to give a child "improved" or "superior" genetic equipment is not necessarily to be condemned.) However, such aspirations could endanger the personal, familial, and societal goods supported by the character of human procreation. We are willing to grant that there may be exceptional cases in which cloning-to-produce-children is morally defensible; however, that being said, we would also argue that such cases do not justify the harmful experiments and social problems that might be entailed by engaging in human cloning. Hard cases are said to make bad law. The same would be true for succumbing to the rare, sentimentally appealing case in which cloning seems morally plausible.[4]

Finally, proponents do not adequately face up to the difficulty of how "well-being" is to be defined. Generally, they argue that these matters are to be left up to the free choices of parents and doctors. But this means that the judgments of "proper" and "improper" will be made according to subjective criteria alone, and under such circumstances, it will be almost impossible to rule out certain "improvements" as unacceptable.

In the sections that follow, we shall explain more fully why Members of the Council are not convinced by the arguments for cloning-to-produce-children, even in the most defensible cases. To see why this is so, we need to consider cloning-to-produce-children from the broadest possible moral perspective, beginning with ethical questions regarding experiments on human subjects. What we hope to show is that the frequently made safety arguments strike deeper than we usually realize, and that they point beyond themselves toward more fundamental moral objections to cloning-to-produce-children.

The Case against Cloning-to-Produce-Children

The Ethics of Human Experimentation

We begin with concerns regarding the safety of the cloning procedure and the health of the participants ....

In initiating this analysis, there is perhaps no better place to start than the long-standing international practice of regulating experiments on human subjects. After all, the cloning of a human being, as well as all the research and trials required before such a procedure could be expected to succeed, would constitute experiments on the individuals involved—the egg donor, the birthing mother, and especially the child-to-be. It therefore makes sense to consider the safety and health concerns that arise from cloning-to-produce-children in light of the widely shared ethical principles that govern experimentation on human subjects.

Since the Second World War, various codes for the ethical conduct of human experimentation have been adopted around the world. These codes and regulations were formulated in direct response to serious ethical lapses and violations committed by research scientists against the rights and dignity of individual human beings. Among the most important and widely accepted documents to emerge were the Nuremberg Code of 1947[5] and the Helsinki Declaration of 1964.[6] Influential in the United States is also the Belmont Report, published in 1978 by the National Commission for the Protection of Human Subjects of Biomedical and Behavioral Research.[7] ...

It would be a mistake to view these codes in narrow or procedural terms, when in fact they embody society's profound sense that human beings are not to be treated as experimental guinea pigs for scientific research. Each of the codes was created to address a specific disaster involving research science—whether the experiments conducted by Nazi doctors on concentration camp prisoners, or the Willowbrook scandal in which mentally retarded children were infected with hepatitis, or the Tuskegee scandal in which underprivileged African-American men suffering from syphilis were observed but not treated by medical researchers—and each of the codes was an attempt to defend the inviolability and dignity of all human beings in the face of such threats and abuses. More simply stated, the codes attempt to defend the weak against the strong and to uphold the equal dignity of all human beings. In taking up the application of these codes to the case of cloning-to-produce-children, we would suggest that the proper approach is not simply to discover specific places where human cloning violates this or that stipulation of this or that code, but to grapple with how such cloning offends the spirit of these codes and what they seek to defend.

The ethics of research on human subjects suggest three sorts of problems that would arise in cloning-to-produce-children: (1) problems of safety; (2) a special problem of consent; and (3) problems of exploitation of women and the just distribution of risk. We shall consider each in turn.

Problems of Safety

First, cloning-to-produce-children is not now safe. Concerns about the safety of the individuals involved in a cloning procedure are shared by nearly everyone on all sides of the cloning debate. Even most proponents of cloning-to-produce-children generally qualify their support with a caveat about the safety of the procedure. Cloning experiments in other mammals strongly suggest that cloning-to-produce-children is, at least for now, far too risky to attempt.[8] Safety concerns revolve around potential dangers to the cloned child, as well as to the egg donor and the woman who would carry the cloned child to birth.

(a) Risks to the child. Risks to the cloned child-to-be must be taken especially seriously, both because they are most numerous and most serious and because—unlike the risks to the egg donor and birth mother—they cannot be accepted knowingly and freely by the person who will bear them. In animal experiments to date, only a small percentage of implanted clones have resulted in live births, and a substantial portion of those live-born clones have suffered complications that proved fatal fairly quickly. Some serious though nonfatal abnormalities in cloned animals have also been observed, including substantially increased birth-size, liver and brain defects, and lung, kidney, and cardiovascular problems.[9]

Longer-term consequences are of course not known ....

(b) Risks to the egg donor and the birth mother. Accompanying the threats to the cloned child's health and well-being are risks to the health of the egg donors. These include risks to her future reproductive health caused by the hormonal treatments required for egg retrieval and general health risks resulting from the necessary superovulation.[10]

Animal studies also suggest the likelihood of health risks to the woman who carries the cloned fetus to term. The animal data suggest that late-term fetal losses and spontaneous abortions occur substantially more often with cloned fetuses than in natural pregnancies ....

(c) An abiding moral concern. Because of these risks, there is widespread agreement that, at least for now, attempts at cloning-to-produce-children would constitute unethical experimentation on human subjects and are therefore impermissible ....

Past discussions of this subject have often given the impression that the safety concern is a purely temporary one that can be allayed in the near future, as scientific advances and improvements in technique reduce the risks to an ethically acceptable level. But this impression is mistaken, for considerable safety risks are likely to be enduring, perhaps permanent. If so, there will be abiding ethical difficulties *even with efforts aimed at making human cloning safe.*

The reason is clear: .... If experiments to learn how to clone a child are ever to be ethical, the degree of risk to that child-to-be would have to be extremely low, arguably no greater than for children-to-be who are conceived from union of egg and sperm. It is extremely unlikely that this moral burden can be met, not for decades if at all.

In multiple experiments involving six of the mammalian species cloned to date, more than 89 percent of the cloned embryos transferred to recipient females did not come to birth, and many of the live-born cloned animals are or become abnormal.[11] If success means achieving normal and healthy development not just at birth but throughout the life span, there is even less reason for confidence. The oldest cloned mammal (Dolly) is only six years old and has exhibited unusually early arthritis. [Ed. note. Dolly was euthanized at age six on February 15, 2003.] The reasons for failure in animal cloning are not well understood. Also, no nonhuman primates have been cloned. It will be decades (at least) before we could obtain positive evidence that cloned primates might live a normal healthy (primate) life.

Even a high success rate in animals would not suffice by itself to make human trials morally acceptable. In addition to the usual uncertainties in jumping the gap from animal to human research, cloning is likely to present particularly difficult problems of interspecies difference. Animal experiments have already shown substantial differences in the reproductive success of identical cloning techniques used in different species.[12] ...[13]

Can a highly reduced risk of deformity, disease, and premature death in animal cloning, coupled with the inherently unpredictable risk of moving from animals to humans, ever be low enough to meet the ethically acceptable standard set by reproduction begun with egg and sperm? The answer, as a matter of necessity, can never be better than "Just possibly." Given the severity of the possible harms involved in human cloning, and given that those harms fall on the very vulnerable child-to-be, such an answer would seem to be enduringly inadequate.

Similar arguments, it is worth noting, were made before the first attempts at human in vitro fertilization. People suggested that it would be unethical experimentation even to try to determine whether IVF could be safely done. And then, of course, IVF was accomplished. Eventually, it became a common procedure, and today the moral argument about its safety seems to many people beside the point. Yet the fact of success in that case does not establish precedent in this one, nor does it mean that the first attempts at IVF were not in fact unethical experiments upon the unborn, despite the fortunate results.

Be this as it may, the case of cloning is genuinely different. With IVF, assisted fertilization of egg by sperm immediately releases a developmental process, linked to the sexual union of the two gametes, that nature has selected over millions of years for the entire mammalian line. But in cloning experiments to produce children, researchers would be transforming a sexual system into an asexual one, a change that requires major and "unnatural" reprogramming of donor DNA if there is to be any chance of success. They are neither enabling nor restoring a natural process, and the alterations involved are such that success in one species cannot be presumed to predict success in another ....

It therefore appears to us that, given the dangers involved and the relatively limited goods to be gained from cloning-to-produce-children, conducting experiments in an effort to make cloning-to-produce-children safer would itself be an unacceptable violation of the norms of the ethics of research. *There seems to be no ethical way to try to discover whether cloning-to-produce-children can become safe, now or in the future.*

A Special Problem of Consent

A further concern relating to the ethics of human research revolves around the question of consent. Consent from the cloned child-to-be is of course impossible to obtain, and because no one consents to his or her own birth, it may be argued that concerns about consent are misplaced when applied to the unborn. But the issue is not so simple. For reasons having to do both with the safety concerns raised above and with the social, psychological, and moral concerns to be addressed below, an attempt to clone a human being would potentially expose a cloned individual-to-be to great risks of harm, quite distinct from those accompanying other sorts of reproduction. Given the risks, and the fact that consent cannot be obtained, the ethically correct choice may be to avoid the experiment. The fact that those engaged in cloning cannot ask an unconceived child for permission places a burden on the cloners, not on the child. Given that anyone considering creating a cloned child must know that he or she is putting a newly created human life at exceptional risk, the burden on the would-be cloners seems clear: they must make a compelling case why the procedure should not be avoided altogether.[14]...

Problems of Exploitation of Women and Just Distribution of Risk

Cloning-to-produce-children may also lead to the exploitation of women who would be called upon to donate oocytes. Widespread use of the techniques of cloning-to-produce-children would require large numbers of eggs. Animal models suggest that several hundred eggs may be required before one attempt at cloning can be successful. The required oocytes would have to be donated, and the process of making them available would involve hormonal treatments to induce superovulation. If financial incentives are offered, they might lead poor women especially to place themselves at risk in this way (and might also compromise the voluntariness of their "choice" to make donations). Thus, research on cloning-to-produce-children could impose disproportionate burdens on women, particularly low-income women.

Conclusion

These questions of the ethics of research—particularly the issue of physical safety—point clearly to the conclusion that cloning-to-produce-children is unacceptable. ... [W]e conclude that the problem of safety is not a temporary ethical concern. It is rather an enduring moral concern that might not be surmountable and should thus preclude work toward the development of cloning techniques to produce children ....

For some people, the discussion of ethical objections to cloning-to-produce-children could end here. Our society's established codes and practices in regard to human experimentation by themselves offer compelling reasons to oppose indefinitely attempts to produce a human child by cloning. But there *is* more to be said.

First, ... [t]he ethical objection based on lack of safety is *not* really an objection to cloning *as such*. Indeed, it may in time become a vanishing objection should people be allowed to proceed—despite insuperable ethical objections such as the ones we have just offered—with experiments to perfect the technique.[15] Should this occur, the ethical assessment of cloning-to-produce-children would need to address itself to the merits (and demerits) of cloning itself ....

How should these issues be raised, and within what moral framework? Some, but by no means all, of the deepest moral concerns connected to human cloning could be handled by developing a richer consideration of the ethics of human experimentation. Usually—and regrettably—we apply the ethical principles governing research on human subjects in a utilitarian spirit, weighing benefits versus harms, and moreover using only a very narrow notion of "harm." ...

The form of bioethical inquiry we are attempting here will make every effort not to truncate the moral meaning of our actions and practices by placing them on the Procrustean bed of utilitarianism. To be sure, the ethical principles governing human research are highly useful in efforts to protect vulnerable individuals against the misconduct or indifference of the powerful. But a different frame of reference is needed to evaluate the human meaning of innovations that may affect the lives and humanity of everyone, vulnerable or not.

Of the arguments developed below, some are supported by most Council Members, while other arguments are shared by only some Members. Even among the arguments they share, different Members find different concerns to be weightier. Yet we all believe that the arguments presented in the sections that follow are worthy of consideration in the course of trying to assess *fully* the ethical issues involved. We have chosen to err on the side of inclusion rather than exclusion of arguments because we acknowledge that concerns now expressed by only a few may turn out in the future to be more important than those now shared by all. Our fuller assessment begins with an attempt to fathom the deepest meaning of human procreation and thus necessarily the meaning of raising children. Our analysis will then move onto questions dealing with the effects of cloning on individuals, family life, and society more generally.

The Human Context: Procreation and Child-Rearing

Were it to take place, cloning-to-produce-children would represent a challenge to the nature of human procreation and child-rearing. Cloning is, of course, not only a means of procreation. It is also a technology, a human experiment, and an exercise of freedom, among other things. But cloning would be most unusual, consequential, and most morally important as a new way of bringing children into the world and a new way of viewing their moral significance.

We begin with the salient fact that a child *is not made, but begotten*. Procreation is not making but the outgrowth of doing. A man and woman give themselves in love to each other, setting their projects aside in order to do just that. Yet a child results, arriving on its own, mysterious, independent, yet the fruit of the embrace.[16] Even were the child wished for, and consciously so, he or she is the issue of their love, not the product of their wills; the man and woman in no way produce or choose a *particular* child, as they might buy a particular car. Procreation can, of course, be assisted by human ingenuity (as with IVF). In such cases, it may become harder to see the child solely as a gift bestowed upon the parents' mutual self-giving and not to some degree as a product of their parental wills. Nonetheless, because it is still sexual reproduction, the children born with the help of IVF begin—as do all other children—with a certain genetic independence of their parents. They replicate neither their fathers nor their mothers, and this is a salutary reminder to parents of the independence they must one day grant their children and for which it is their duty to prepare them.

Gifts and blessings we learn to accept as gratefully as we can. Products of our wills we try to shape in accord with our desires. Procreation as traditionally understood invites acceptance, rather than reshaping, engineering, or designing the next generation. It invites us to accept limits to our control over the next generation. It invites us even—to put the point most strongly—to think of the child as one who is not simply our own, our possession. Certainly, it invites us to remember that the child does not exist simply for the happiness or fulfillment of the parents ....

This concern can be expressed not only in language about the relation between the generations but also in the language of equality. The things we make are not just like ourselves; they are the products of our wills, and their point and purpose are ours to determine. But a begotten child comes into the world just as its parents once did, and is therefore their equal in dignity and humanity.

The character of sexual procreation shapes the lives of children as well as parents. By giving rise to genetically new individuals, sexual reproduction imbues all human beings with a sense of individual identity and of occupying a place in this world that has never belonged to another ....

Social identity, like genetic identity, is in significant measure tied to these biological facts. Societies around the world have structured social and economic responsibilities around the relationship between the generations established through sexual procreation, and have developed modes of child-rearing, family responsibility, and kinship behavior that revolve around the natural facts of begetting ....

A proper regard for the profundity of human procreation (including child-rearing and parent-child relations) is, in our view, indispensable for a full assessment of the ethical implications of cloning-to-produce-children.

Identity, Manufacture, Eugenics, Family, and Society

Keeping in mind our general observations about procreation, we proceed to examine a series of specific ethical issues and objections to cloning human children: (1)

problems of identity and individuality; (2) concerns regarding manufacture; (3) the prospect of a new eugenics; (4) troubled family relations; and (5) effects on society.

Problems of Identity and Individuality

Cloning-to-produce-children could create serious problems of identity and individuality. This would be especially true if it were used to produce multiple "copies" of any single individual, as in one or another of the seemingly far-fetched futuristic scenarios in which cloning is often presented to the popular imagination. Yet questions of identity and individuality could arise even in small-scale cloning, even in the (supposedly) most innocent of cases, such as the production of a single cloned child within an intact family. Personal identity is, we would emphasize, a complex and subtle psychological phenomenon, shaped ultimately by the interaction of many diverse factors. But it does seem reasonably clear that cloning would at the very least present a unique and possibly disabling challenge to the formation of individual identity.

Cloned children may experience concerns about their distinctive identity not only because each will be genetically essentially identical to another human being, but also because they may resemble in appearance younger versions of the person who is their "father" or "mother." Of course, our genetic makeup does not by itself determine our identities. But our genetic uniqueness is an important source of our sense of who we are and how we regard ourselves. It is an emblem of independence and individuality. It endows us with a sense of life as a never-before-enacted possibility. Knowing and feeling that nobody has previously possessed our particular gift of natural characteristics, we go forward as genetically unique individuals into relatively indeterminate futures.

These new and unique genetic identities are rooted in the natural procreative process. A cloned child, by contrast, is at risk of living out a life overshadowed in important ways by the life of the "original"—general appearance being only the most obvious ....

It may reasonably be argued that genetic individuality is not an indispensable human good, since identical twins share a common genotype and seem not to be harmed by it. But this argument misses the context and environment into which even a single human clone would be born. Identical twins have as progenitors two biological parents and are born together, before either one has developed and shown what his or her potential—natural or otherwise—may be. Each is largely free of the burden of measuring up to or even knowing in advance the genetic traits of the other, because both begin life together and neither is yet known to the world. But a clone is a genetic near-copy of a person who is already living or has already lived. This might constrain the clone's sense of self in ways that differ in kind from the experience of identical twins. Everything about the predecessor—from physical height and facial appearance, balding patterns and inherited diseases, to temperament and native talents, to shape of life and length of days, and even cause of death—will appear before the expectant eyes of the cloned person, always with at least the nagging concern that there, notwithstanding the grace of God, go I. The crucial matter, again, is not simply the truth regarding the extent to which genetic identity actually shapes us—though it surely does shape us to some extent. What matters is the cloned individual's *perception* of the significance of the "precedent life" and the way that perception cramps and limits a sense of self and independence.

Concerns Regarding Manufacture

The likely impact of cloning on identity suggests an additional moral and social concern: the transformation of human procreation into human manufacture, of begetting into making ....

To this point, parents have the right and the power to decide *whether* to have a child. With cloning, parents acquire the power, and presumably the right, to decide *what kind* of a child to have. Cloning would thus extend the power of one generation over the next—and the power of parents over their offspring—in ways that open the door, unintentionally or not, to a future project of genetic manipulation and genetic control.

Of course, there is no denying that we have already taken steps in the direction of such control. Preimplantation genetic diagnosis of embryos and prenatal diagnosis of fetuses—both now used to prevent the birth of individuals carrying genes for genetic diseases—reflect an only conditional acceptance of the next generation. With regard to *positive* selection for desired traits, some people already engage in the practice of sex selection, another example of conditional acceptance of offspring. But these precedents pale in comparison to the degree of control provided by cloning and, in any case, do not thereby provide a license to proceed with cloning. It is far from clear that it would be wise to proceed still farther in our attempts at control ....

Why does this matter? It matters because human dignity is at stake. In natural procreation, two individuals give life to a new human being whose endowments are not shaped deliberately by human will, whose being remains mysterious, and the open-endedness of whose future is ratified and embraced. Parents beget a child who enters the world exactly as they did—as an unmade gift, not as a product. Children born of this process stand equally beside their progenitors as fellow human beings, not beneath them as made objects. In this way, the uncontrolled beginnings of human procreation endow each new generation and each new individual with the dignity and freedom enjoyed by all who came before ....

Even were cloning to be used solely to remedy infertility, the decision to clone the (sterile) father would be a decision, willy-nilly, that the child-to-be should be the near-twin of his "father." Anyone who would clone merely to ensure a "biologically related child" would be dictating a very specific form of biological relation: genetic virtual identity. In every case of cloning-to-produce-children, scientists or parents would set out to produce specific individuals for particular reasons. The procreative process could come to be seen increasingly as a means of meeting specific ends, and the resulting children would be products of a designed manufacturing process, products over whom we might think it proper to exercise "quality control." Even if, in any given case, we were to continue to think of the cloned child as a gift, *the act itself teaches a different lesson*, as the child becomes the continuation of a parental project. We would learn to receive the next generation less with gratitude and surprise than with control and mastery.

One possible result would be the industrialization and commercialization of human reproduction. Manufactured objects become commodities in the marketplace, and their manufacture comes to be guided by market principles and financial concerns. When the "products" are human beings, the "market" could become a profoundly dehumanizing force. Already there is commerce in egg donation for IVF, with ads offering large sums of money for egg donors with high SAT scores and particular physical features.

The concerns expressed here do not depend on cloning becoming a widespread practice. The introduction of the terms and ideas of production into the realm of human procreation would be troubling regardless of the scale involved; and the adoption of a market mentality in these matters could blind us to the deep moral character of bringing forth new life. Even were cloning children to be rare, the moral harms to a society that accepted it could be serious.

Prospect of a New Eugenic

For some of us, cloning-to-produce-children also raises concerns about the prospect of eugenics or, more modestly, about genetic "enhancement." We recognize that the term "eugenics" generally refers to attempts to improve the genetic constitution of a particular political community or of the human race through general policies such as population control, forced sterilization, directed mating, or the like. It does not ordinarily refer to actions of particular individuals attempting to improve the genetic endowment of their own descendants. Yet, although cloning does not in itself point to public policies by which the state would become involved in directing the development of the human gene pool, this might happen in illiberal regimes, like China, where the government already regulates procreation.[17] And, in liberal societies, cloning-to-produce-children could come to be used privately for individualized eugenic or "enhancement" purposes: in attempts to alter (with the aim of improving) the genetic constitution of one's own descendants—and, indirectly, of future generations ....

Cloning can serve the ends of individualized enhancement either by avoiding the genetic defects that may arise when human reproduction is left to chance or by preserving and perpetuating outstanding genetic traits. In the future, if techniques of genetic enhancement through more precise genetic engineering became available, cloning could be useful for perpetuating the enhanced traits and for keeping any "superior" manmade genotype free of the flaws that sexual reproduction might otherwise introduce.

"Private eugenics" does not carry with it the dark implications of state despotism or political control of the gene pool that characterized earlier eugenic proposals and the racist eugenic practices of the twentieth century. Nonetheless, it could prove dangerous to our humanity. Besides the dehumanizing prospects of the turn toward manufacture that such programs of enhancement would require, there is the further difficulty of the lack of standards to guide the choices for "improvement." To this point, biomedical technology has been applied to treating diseases in patients and has been governed, on the whole, by a commonsense view of health and disease. To be sure, there are differing views about how to define "health." And certain cosmetic, performance-enhancing, or hedonistic uses of biomedical techniques have already crossed any plausible boundary between therapy and enhancement, between healing the sick and "improving" our powers.[18] Yet, for the most part, it is by some commonsense views of health that we judge who is in need of medical treatment and what sort of treatment might be most appropriate. Even today's practice of a kind of "negative" eugenics—through prenatal genetic diagnosis and abortion of fetuses with certain genetic abnormalities—is informed by the desire to promote health.

The "positive" eugenics that could receive a great boost from human cloning, especially were it to be coupled with techniques of precise genetic modification, would not seek to restore sick human beings to natural health. Instead, it would seek to alter humanity, based upon subjective or arbitrary ideas of excellence. The effort may be guided by apparently good intentions: to improve the next generation and to enhance the quality of life of our descendants. But in the process of altering human nature, we would be abandoning the standard by which to judge the goodness or the wisdom of the particular aims. We would stand to lose the sense of what is and is not human.

The fear of a new eugenics is not, as is sometimes alleged, a concern born of some irrational fear of the future or the unknown. Neither is it born of hostility to technology or nostalgia for some premodern pseudo-golden age of superior naturalness. It is rather born of the rational recognition that once we move beyond therapy into efforts at enhancement, we are in uncharted waters without a map, without a compass, and without a clear destination that can tell us whether we are making improvements or the reverse ....

Troubled Family Relations

Cloning-to-produce-children could also prove damaging to family relations, despite the best of intentions. We do not assume that cloned children, once produced, would not be accepted, loved, or nurtured by their parents and relatives. On the contrary, we freely admit that, like any child, they might be welcomed into the cloning family. Nevertheless, the cloned child's place in the scheme of family relations might well be uncertain and confused. The usually clear designations of father and brother, mother and sister, would be confounded. A mother could give birth to her own genetic twin, and a father could be genetically virtually identical to his son. The cloned child's relation to his or her grandparents would span one and two generations at once. Every other family relation would be similarly confused. There is, of course, the valid counter-argument that holds that the "mother" could easily be defined as the person who gives birth to the child, regardless of the child's genetic origins, and for social purposes that may serve to eliminate some problems. But because of the special nature of cloning-to-produce-children, difficulties may be expected.

The crucial point is not the *absence* of the natural biological connections between parents and children. The crucial point is, on the contrary, the *presence* of a unique, one-sided, and replicative biological connection to only *one* progenitor. As a result, family relations involving cloning would differ from all existing family arrangements, including those formed through adoption or with the aid of IVF. A great many children, after all, are adopted, and live happy lives in loving families, in the absence of any biological connections with their parents. Children conceived by artificial insemination using donor sperm and by various IVF techniques may have unusual relationships with their genetic parents, or no genetic relationships at all. But all of these existing arrangements attempt in important ways to emulate the model of the natural family (at least in its arrangement of the generations), while cloning runs contrary to that model.

What the exact effects of cloning-to-produce-children might be for families is highly speculative, to be sure, but it is still worth flagging certain troubling possibilities and risks. The fact that the cloned child bears a special tie to only one parent may complicate family dynamics. As the child developed, it could not help but be regarded as specially akin to only one of his or her parents. The sins or failings of the father (or mother), if reappearing in the cloned child, might be blamed on the progenitor, adding to the chances of domestic turmoil. The problems of being and rearing an adolescent could become complicated should the teenage clone of the mother "reappear" as the double of the woman the father once fell in love with. Risks of competition, rivalry, jealousy, and parental tension could become heightened.[19]...

For all these reasons, the cloning family differs from the "natural family" or the "adoptive family." By breaking through the natural boundaries between generations, cloning could strain the social ties between them.

Effects on Society

The hazards and costs of cloning-to-produce-children may not be confined to the direct participants. The rest of society may also be at risk. The impact of human cloning on society at large may be the least appreciated, but among the most important, factors to consider in contemplating the morality of this activity.

Cloning is a human activity affecting not only those who are cloned or those who are clones, but also the entire society that allows or supports such activity. For insofar as the society *accepts* cloning-to-produce-children, to that extent the society may be said to *engage* in it. A society that allows dehumanizing practices —especially when given an opportunity to try to prevent them—risks becoming an accomplice in those practices. (The same could be said of a society that allowed even a few of its members to practice incest or polygamy.) Thus the question before us is whether cloning-to-produce-children is an activity that we, *as a society*, should engage in. In addressing this question, we must reach well beyond the rights of individuals and the difficulties or benefits that cloned children or their families might encounter. We must consider what kind of a society we wish to be, and, in particular, what forms of bringing children into the world we want to encourage and what sorts of relations between the generations we want to preserve.

Cloning-to-produce-children could distort the way we raise and view children, by carrying to full expression many regrettable tendencies already present in our culture. We are already liable to regard children largely as vehicles for our own fulfillment and ambitions. The impulse to create "designer children" is present today—as temptation and social practice. The notion of life as a gift, mysterious and limited, is under siege. Cloning-to-produce-children would carry these tendencies and temptations to an extreme expression. It advances the notion that the child is but an object of our sovereign mastery.

A society that clones human beings thinks about human beings (and especially children) differently than does a society that refuses to do so. It could easily be argued that we have already in myriad ways begun to show signs of regarding our children as projects on which we may work our wills. Further, it could be argued that we have been so desensitized by our earlier steps in this direction that we do not recognize this tendency as a corruption. While some people contend that cloning-to-produce-children would not take us much further down a path we have already been traveling, we would emphasize that the precedent of treating children as projects cuts two ways in the moral argument. Instead of using this precedent to justify taking the next step of cloning, the next step might rather serve as a warning and a mirror in which we may discover reasons to reconsider what we are already doing. Precisely because the stakes are so high, precisely because the new biotechnologies touch not only our bodies and minds but also the very idea of our humanity, we should ask ourselves how we as a society want to approach questions of human dignity and flourishing.

Conclusion

Cloning-to-produce-children may represent a forerunner of what will be a growing number of capacities to intervene in and alter the human genetic endowment. No doubt, earlier human actions have produced changes in the human gene pool: to take only one example, the use of insulin to treat diabetics who otherwise would have died before reproducing has increased the genes for diabetes in the population. But different responsibilities accrue when one sets out to make such changes prospectively, directly, and deliberately. To do so without regard for the likelihood of serious unintended and unanticipated consequences would be the height of hubris. Systems of great complexity do not respond well to blunt human intervention, and one can hardly think of a more complex system—both natural and social—than that which surrounds human reproduction and the human genome. Given the enormous importance of what is at stake, we believe that the so-called "precautionary principle" should be our guide in this arena. This principle would suggest that scientists, technologists, and, indeed, all of us should be modest in claiming to understand the many possible consequences of any profound alteration of human procreation, especially where there are not compelling reasons to proceed. Lacking such understanding, no one should take action so drastic as the cloning of a human child. In the absence of the necessary human wisdom, prudence calls upon us to set limits on efforts to control and remake the character of human procreation and human life.

It is not only a matter of prudence. Cloning-to-produce-children would also be an *injustice* to the cloned child—from the imposition of the chromosomes of someone else, to the intentional deprivation of biological parents, to all of the possible bodily and psychological harms that we have enumerated in this chapter. It is ultimately the claim that the cloned child would be seriously wronged—and not only harmed in body—that would justify government intervention. It is to this question—the public policy question of what the government should and can do to prevent such injustice—that we will turn in Chapter 7. But, regarding the ethical assessment, Members of the Council are in unanimous agreement that cloning-to-produce-children is not only unsafe but also morally unacceptable and ought not to be attempted.[20]

Notes

1. Lederberg, J. "Experimental genetics and human evolution" *The American Naturalist*, September–October 1966.
2. Supreme Court of the United States. *Eisenstadt v. Baird*, 405 US 438, 1972.
3. Tribe, L. "On not banning cloning for the wrong reasons" in Nussbaum, M., and C. R. Sunstein eds., *Clones and Clones: Facts and Fantasies about Human Cloning*. New York: Norton, 1998, p. 321.
4. Consider the following analogy: We would not allow a rare sympathetic case for brother-sister marriage—where, say, the two children were separated at birth and later fell in love, ignorant of their kinship—to overturn the taboo on incest. Whatever their merit, the goals of well-being and health do not outweigh the moral and social harms that cloning would entail.
5. Nuremberg Report. *Trials of War Criminals before the Nuremberg Military Tribunals under Control Council Law No. 10*, Vol. 2. Washington, DC: Government Printing Office, 1949, pp. 181–182.
6. Helsinki Declaration. 18th World Medical Association General Assembly *Ethical Principles for Medical Research Involving Human Subjects*, adopted in Helsinki, Finland, June 1964, and amended in October 1975, October 1983, September 1989, October 1996, and October 2000.
7. Belmont Report. The National Commission for the Protection of Human Subjects of Biomedical and Behavioral Research. *The Belmont Report: Ethical Principles and Guidelines for the Protection of Human Subjects of Research*. Bethesda, MD: Government Printing Office, 1978.
8. See, for instance, Chapter 4 of the present report, as well as Chapter 3 of the NAS Report: National Academy of Sciences. *Scientific and Medical Aspects of Human Reproduction Cloning*. Washington, DC: National Academy Press, 2002.
9. These issues are discussed in the NAS Report (3–2) as well as in Wilmut, I., Roslin Institute, Scotland. "Application of animal cloning data to human cloning," paper presented at *Workshop: Scientific and Medical Aspects of Human Cloning*, National Academy of Sciences, Washington, DC, August 7, 2001; and Hill, J., Cornell University. "Placental defects in nuclear transfer (cloned) animals," paper presented at *Workshop: Scientific and Medical Aspects of Human Cloning*, National Academy of Sciences, Washington, DC, August 7, 2001.
10. See, for instance, Rimington, M., et al. "Counseling patients undergoing ovarian stimulation about the risks of ovarian hyper-stimulation syndrome." *Human Reproduction*, 14: 2921–2922, 1999; and Wakeley, K., and E. Grendys. "Reproductive technologies and risk of ovarian cancer." *Current Opinion in Obstetrics and Gynecology*, 12: 43–47, 2000.
11. NAS Report, Figure 3.
12. See for instance the NAS Report, Appendix B, Tables 1, 3, and 4.
13. It is of course true that there is always uncertainty about moving from animal to human experimentation or therapy. But in the usual case, what justifies the assumption of this added unknown risk is that the experimental subject is a likely beneficiary of the research, either directly or indirectly. And where this is not the case, risk may be assumed if there is informed and voluntary consent. Neither of these conditions applies for the child-to-be in human cloning experiments.
14. The argument made in this paragraph is not unique to cloning. There may be other circumstances in which prospective parents, about to impose great risk of harm on a prospective child-to-be, might bear a comparable burden.
15. Such improvements in technique could result in part from the practice of cloning-for-biomedical-research, were it to be allowed to go forward.
16. We are, of course, well aware that many children are conceived in casual, loveless, or even brutal acts of sexual intercourse, including rape and incest.
17. According to official Chinese census figures for 2000, more than 116 male births were recorded for every 100 female births. It is generally believed that this is the result of the widespread use of prenatal sex selection and China's one-child policy, though it

should be noted that even in a country such as South Korea, which has no such policy, the use of prenatal sex selection has skewed the sex ratio in favor of males.
18 One thinks of certain forms of plastic surgery or recreational uses of euphoriant drugs, and the uses in athletics and schools of performance-enhancing drugs, such as anabolic steroids, erythropoietin, and Ritalin.
19 And there might be special complications in the event of divorce. Does the child rightfully or more naturally belong to the "genetic parent"? How would a single parent deal with a child who shares none of her genes but carries 100 percent of the genes of the person she chose to divorce? Whether such foreseeable complications would in fact emerge is, of course, an empirical question that cannot be answered in advance. But knowledge of the complexities of family life lead us not to want to dismiss them.
20 Not surprisingly, some of us feel more strongly than others about this conclusion. One or two of us might someday be willing to see cloning-to-produce-children occur in the rare defensible case, but then only if means were available to confine its use to such cases.

Review and Discussion Questions

1 The writers of this report believe that the ethical case against cloning people is much stronger than the ethical case for cloning people. Do you agree? Explain.
2 What is the strongest argument on each side of the debate?
3 Are there important arguments about the ethics of cloning people that are missing from this report? What are they?

READING: THE CONSTITUTIONAL RIGHT TO ABORTION

ROE V. WADE[*]

Few constitutional cases have created more controversy, both moral and legal, than abortion. *Roe v. Wade* is the famous Supreme Court decision that guarantees women the right to get an abortion. The case began in August 1969 when Norma McCorvey discovered she was pregnant. Too poor to travel from Texas to California, the nearest state where abortions were legal, she sought help. A friend introduced her to two recent law school graduates, Sarah Weddington and Linda Coffee, and the three decided to challenge the constitutionality of Texas's law forbidding abortion. Norma McCorvey never got her abortion, nor did she see her baby girl again after leaving the hospital. Hoping to remain anonymous, she became Jane Roe for the purposes of the lawsuit she was bringing against Henry Wade, district attorney for Dallas County, Texas. Four years later, the Supreme Court took the controversial step of extending the right to privacy to include the right to get an abortion. Justice Blackmun wrote the majority opinion in this famous case; Justice White wrote a dissenting opinion. Justice Blackmun continued for years after this decision to get hate mail and threats; once, a pro-life advocate fired a bullet into his house.

---

[*] *Roe v. Wade* 410 U.S. 113 (1973). Some citations and footnotes omitted.

Justice Blackmun Delivered the Opinion of the Court

Three reasons have been advanced to explain historically the enactment of criminal abortion laws in the nineteenth century and to justify their continued existence.

It has been argued occasionally that these laws were the product of a Victorian social concern to discourage illicit sexual conduct. Texas, however, does not advance this justification in the present case ....

A second reason is concerned with abortion as a medical procedure. When most criminal abortion laws were first enacted, the procedure was a hazardous one for the woman ....

Modern medical techniques have altered this situation. Appellants and various *amici* refer to medical data indicating that abortion in early pregnancy, that is, prior to the end of first trimester, although not without its risk, is now relatively safe. ... The State has a legitimate interest in seeing to it that abortion, like any other medical procedure, is performed under circumstances that insure maximum safety for the patient. This interest obviously extends at least to the performing physician and his staff, to the facilities involved, to the availability of aftercare, and to adequate provision for any complication or emergency that might arise. The prevalence of high mortality rates at illegal "abortion mills" strengthens, rather than weakens, the State's interest in regulating the conditions under which abortions are performed. Moreover, the risk to the woman increases as her pregnancy continues. Thus the State retains a definite interest in protecting the woman's own health and safety when an abortion is proposed at a late stage of pregnancy.

The third reason is the State's interest—some phrase it in terms of duty—in protecting prenatal life. Some of the argument for this justification rests on the theory that a new human life is present from the moment of conception. The State's interest and general obligation to protect life then extends, it is argued, to prenatal life. Only when the life of the pregnant mother herself is at stake, balanced against the life she carries within her, should the interest of the embryo or fetus not prevail. Logically, of course, a legitimate state interest in this area need not stand or fall on acceptance of the belief that life begins at conception or at some other point prior to live birth. In assessing the State's interest, recognition may be given to the less rigid claim that as long as at least *potential* life is involved, the State may assert interests beyond the protection of the pregnant woman alone.

Parties challenging state abortion laws have sharply disputed in some courts the contention that a purpose of these laws, when enacted, was to protect prenatal life. ... There is some scholarly support for this view of original purpose. The few state courts called upon to interpret their laws in the nineteenth and early twentieth centuries did focus on the State's interest in protecting the woman's health rather than in preserving the embryo and fetus ....

The Constitution does not explicitly mention any right of privacy. In a line of decisions, however, ... the Court has recognized that a right of personal privacy, or a guarantee of certain areas or zones of privacy, does exist under the Constitution ....

This right of privacy, whether it be founded in the Fourteenth Amendment's concept of personal liberty and restrictions upon state action, as we feel it is, or, as the District Court determined, in the Ninth Amendment's reservation of rights to the people, is broad enough to encompass a woman's decision whether or not to terminate her pregnancy. The detriment that the State would impose upon the pregnant woman by denying this choice altogether is apparent. Specific and direct harm medically diagnosable even in early pregnancy may be involved. Maternity, or additional offspring, may force upon the woman a distressful life and future. Psychological harm may be imminent. Mental and physical health may be taxed by child care. There is also the distress, for all concerned, associated with the unwanted child, and there is the problem of bringing a child into a family already unable, psychologically and otherwise, to care for it. In other cases, as in this one, the additional difficulties and continuing stigma of unwed motherhood may be involved. All these are factors the woman and her responsible physician necessarily will consider in consultation.

On the basis of elements such as these, appellants and some *amici* argue that the woman's right is absolute and that she is entitled to terminate her pregnancy at whatever time, in whatever way, and for whatever reason she alone chooses. With this we do not agree. Appellant's arguments that Texas either has no valid interest at all in regulating the abortion decision, or no interest strong enough to support any limitation upon the woman's sole determination, is unpersuasive. The Court's decisions recognizing a right of privacy also acknowledge that some state regulation in areas protected by that right is appropriate. As noted above, a state may properly assert important interests in safeguarding health, in maintaining medical standards, and in protecting potential life. At some point in pregnancy, these respective interests become sufficiently compelling to sustain regulation of the factors that govern the abortion decision. The privacy right involved, therefore, cannot be said to be absolute. In fact, it is not clear to us that the claim asserted by some *amici* that one has an unlimited right to do with one's body as one pleases bears a close relationship to the right of privacy previously articulated in the Court's decisions ....

Where certain "fundamental rights" are involved, the Court has held that regulation limiting these rights may be justified only by a "compelling state interest," ... and that legislative enactments must be narrowly drawn to express only the legitimate state interests at stake ....

A. The appellee and certain *amici* argue that the fetus is a "person" within the language and meaning of the Fourteenth Amendment. In support of this they outline at length and in detail the well-known facts of fetal development. If this suggestion of personhood is established, the appellant's case, of course, collapses, for the fetus' right to life is then guaranteed specifically by the Amendment. The appellant conceded as much on reargument. On the other hand, the appellee conceded on reargument that no case should be cited that holds that a fetus is a person within the meaning of the Fourteenth Amendment.

The Constitution does not define "person" in so many words. ... But in nearly all these instances, the use of the word is such that it has application only postnatally. None indicates with any assurance that it has any possible prenatal application.[1]

All this, together with our observation, *supra*, that throughout the major portion of the nineteenth century prevailing legal abortion practices were far freer than they are today, persuades us that the word "person," as used in the Fourteenth Amendment, does not include the unborn ....

This conclusion, however, does not of itself fully answer the contentions raised by Texas, and we pass on to other considerations.

B. The pregnant woman cannot be isolated in her privacy. She carries an embryo and, later, a fetus, if one accepts the medical definitions of the developing young in the human uterus ....

Texas urges that, apart from the Fourteenth Amendment, life begins at conception and is present throughout pregnancy, and that, therefore, the State has a compelling interest in protecting that life from and after conception. We need not resolve the difficult question of when life begins. When those trained in the respective disciplines of medicine, philosophy, and theology are unable to arrive at any consensus, the judiciary, at this point in the development of man's knowledge, is not in a position to speculate as to the answer.

It should be sufficient to note briefly the wide divergence of thinking on this most sensitive and difficult question. There has always been strong support for the view that life does not begin until live birth. This was the belief of the Stoics. It appears to be the predominant, though not the unanimous, attitude of the Jewish faith. It may be taken to represent also the position of a large segment of the Protestant community, insofar as that can be ascertained; organized groups that have taken a formal position on the abortion issue have generally regarded abortion as a matter for the conscience of the individual and her family. As we have noted, the common law found greater significance in quickening. Physicians and their scientific colleagues have regarded that event with less interest and have tended to focus either upon conception or upon live birth or upon the interim point at which the fetus becomes "viable," that is, potentially able to live outside the mother's womb, albeit with artificial aid. Viability is usually placed at about seven months (28 weeks) but may occur earlier, even at 24 weeks. The Aristotelian theory of "mediate animation," that held sway throughout the Middle Ages and the Renaissance in Europe, continued to be official Roman Catholic dogma until the nineteenth century, despite opposition to this "ensoulment" theory from those in the Church who would recognize the existence of life from the moment of conception. The latter is now, of course, the official belief of the Catholic Church. As one of the briefs *amicus* discloses, this is a view strongly held by many non-Catholics as well, and by many physicians. Substantial problems for precise definition of this view are posed, however, by new embryological data that purport to indicate that conception is a "process" over time, rather than an event, and by new medical techniques such as menstrual extraction, the "morning-after" pill, implantation of embryos, artificial insemination, and even artificial wombs.

In areas other than criminal abortion the law has been reluctant to endorse any theory that life, as we recognize it, begins before live birth or to accord legal rights to the unborn except in narrowly defined situations and except when the rights are contingent upon live birth. For example, the traditional rule of tort law had denied recovery for prenatal injuries even though the child was born alive. That rule has been changed in almost every jurisdiction. In most States recovery is said to be permitted only if the fetus was viable, or at least quick, when the injuries were sustained, though few courts have squarely so held. ... [U]nborn children have been recognized as acquiring rights or interests by way of inheritance or other devolution of property, and have been represented by guardians ....

In view of all this, we do not agree that, by adopting one theory of life, Texas may override the rights of the pregnant woman that are at stake. We repeat, however, that the State does have an important and legitimate interest in preserving and protecting the health of the pregnant woman, whether she be a resident of the State or a non-resident who seeks medical consultation and treatment there, and that it has still another important and legitimate interest in protecting the potentiality of human life. These interests are separate and distinct. Each grows in substantiality as the woman approaches term and, at a point during pregnancy, each becomes "compelling."

With respect to the State's important and legitimate interest in the health of the mother, the "compelling" point, in the light of present medical knowledge, is at approximately the end of the first trimester. This is so because of the now established medical fact, referred to above, that until the end of the first trimester mortality in abortion is less than mortality in normal childbirth. It follows that, from and after this point, a State may regulate the abortion procedure to the extent that the regulation reasonably relates to the preservation and protection of maternal health. Examples of permissible state regulation in this area are requirements as to the qualifications of the person who is to perform the abortion; as to the licensure of that person; as to the facility in which the procedure is to be performed, that is, whether it must be a hospital or may be a clinic or some other place of less-than-hospital status; as to the licensing of the facility; and the like.

This means, on the other hand, that, for the period of pregnancy prior to this "compelling" point, the attending physician, in consultation with his patient, is free to determine, without regulation by the State, that in his medical judgment the patient pregnancy should be terminated. If that decision is reached, the judgment may be effectuated by an abortion free of interference by the State.

With respect to the State's important and legitimate interest in potential life, the "compelling" point is at viability. This is so because the fetus then presumably has the capability of meaningful life outside the mother's womb. State regulation protective of fetal life after viability thus has both logical and biological justifications. If the State is interested in protecting fetal life after viability, it may go so far as to proscribe abortion during that period except when it is necessary to preserve the life or health of the mother.

Measured against these standards, Art. 1196 of the Texas Penal Code, in restricting legal abortions to those "procured or attempted by medical advice for the purpose of saving the life of the mother," sweeps too broadly. The statute makes no distinction between abortions performed early in pregnancy and those performed later, and it limits to a single reason, "saving" the mother's life, the legal justification for the procedure. The statute, therefore, cannot survive the constitutional attack made upon it here.

Mr. Justice White, ... Dissenting

At the heart of the controversy in these cases are those recurring pregnancies that pose no danger whatsoever to the life or health of the mother but are nevertheless unwanted for any one or more of a variety of reasons—convenience, family planning, economics, dislike of children, the embarrassment of illegitimacy, etc. The common claim before us is that for any one of such reasons, or for no reason at all, and without asserting or claiming any threat to life or health, any woman is entitled to an abortion at her request if she is able to find a medical advisor willing to undertake the procedure.

The Court for the most part sustains this position: During the period prior to the time the fetus becomes viable, the Constitution of the United States values the convenience, whim or caprice of the putative mother more than the life or potential life of the fetus; the Constitution, therefore, guarantees the right to an abortion as against any state law or policy seeking to protect the fetus from an abortion not prompted by more compelling reasons of the mother.

With all due respect, I dissent. I find nothing in the language or history of the Constitution to support the Court's judgment. The Court simply fashions and announces a new constitutional right for pregnant mothers and, with scarcely any reason or authority for its action, invests that right with sufficient substance to override most existing state abortion statutes. The upshot is that the people and the legislatures of the 50 States are constitutionally disentitled to weigh the relative importance of the continued existence and development of the fetus on the one hand against a spectrum of possible impacts on the mother on the other hand. As an exercise of raw judicial power, the Court perhaps has authority to do what it does today; but in my view its judgment is an improvident and extravagant exercise of the power of judicial review which the Constitution extends to this Court.

The Court apparently values the convenience of the pregnant mother more than the continued existence and development of the life or potential life which she carries. Whether or not I might agree with that marshalling of values, I can in no event join the Court's judgment because I find no constitutional warrant for imposing such an order of priorities on the people and legislatures of the States. In a sensitive area such as this, involving as it does issues over which reasonable men may easily and heatedly differ, I cannot accept the Court's exercise of its clear power of choice by interposing a constitutional barrier to state efforts to protect human life and by investing mothers and doctors with the constitutionally protected right to exterminate it. This issue, for the most part, should be left with the people and to the political processes the people have devised to govern their affairs.

It is my view, therefore, that the Texas statute is not constitutionally infirm because it denies abortions to those who seek to serve only their convenience rather than to protect their life or health ....

Note

1 When Texas urges that a fetus is entitled to Fourteenth Amendment protection as a person, it faces a dilemma. Neither in Texas nor in any other State are all abortions prohibited. Despite broad proscription, an exception always exists. The exception contained in Art. 1196, for an abortion procured or attempted by medical advice for the purpose of saving the life of the mother, is typical. But if the fetus is a person who is not to be deprived of life without due process of law, and if the mother's condition is the sole determinant, does not the Texas exception appear to be out of line with the

Amendment's command? There are other inconsistencies between Fourteenth Amendment status and the typical abortion statute. It has already been pointed out that in Texas the woman is not a principal or an accomplice with respect to an abortion upon her. If the fetus is a person, why is the woman not a principal or an accomplice? Further, the penalty for criminal abortion specified by Art. 1195 is significantly less than the maximum penalty for murder prescribed by Art. 1257 of the Texas Penal Code. If the fetus is a person, may the penalties be different?

Review and Discussion Questions

1 According to Justice Blackmun, what have been the states' reasons for preventing abortion?
2 Why does the Court reject the view that a fetus is a "person" within the meaning of the Constitution?
3 Explain the trimester approach taken by Justice Blackmun in this case.
4 On what basis does Justice White dissent?
5 Does Blackmun's majority opinion successfully avoid the issue of the moral status of a fetus, as he suggests? Explain.

READING: A DEFENSE OF ABORTION

JUDITH JARVIS THOMSON[*]

It has seemed to many people that abortion obviously involves taking the life of an innocent human being. At conception, it is claimed, life is started, and it is undeniably human since it has a human genetic code. Indeed, each of us could trace our own development to such a point. Nor can it be doubted that the organism living inside the mother is alive, just like every other cell in the body. Only this one, it is argued, is different, because if left alone it will likely develop to the point of birth and childhood. Finally, the argument concludes, there is nothing else that occurs after conception that could possibly justify saying that before it occurred the human organism could be killed but not afterward. Birth, for example, amounts to no more than a change of location and the start of respiration and digestion, and neither location nor being on one's own respirative and digestive systems is necessary to be a living person, as we know from visiting any hospital. Viability, similarly, means nothing more than that the fetus is developed enough to survive on its own systems—a fact that we know, from seeing others who depend on such systems, is not the test for a being's status as a living human being. So only conception (the argument concludes) provides a morally significant point in the continuous development of a person. And since abortion involves killing such a person, it is impermissible.

This article, one of the best known in recent philosophical writing, is an attempt to answer this argument while leaving intact the claim that the fetus is a person. Employing an ingenious set of analogies, including one about a kidnapped violinist,

---

[*] Abridged from "A Defense of Abortion" by Judith Jarvis Thompson, *Philosophy and Public Affairs* 1(1) (1971): 47–66. Copyright © 1971. Reprinted by permission of Blackwell Publishing Ltd., a company of John Wiley & Sons, Inc.

Thomson argues that even assuming the fetus is a living person with a right to life, a mother's right to her body allows her to get an abortion in all but the most extreme circumstances. Judith Jarvis Thomson is Professor of Philosophy Emeritus at Massachusetts Institute of Technology.

Most opposition to abortion relies on the premise that the fetus is a human being, a person, from the moment of conception. The premise is argued for, but, as I think, not well. Take, for example, the most common argument. We are asked to notice that the development of a human being from conception through birth into childhood is continuous; then it is said that to draw a line, to choose a point in this development and say "before this point the thing is not a person, after this point it is a person" is to make an arbitrary choice, a choice for which in the nature of things no good reason can be given. It is concluded that the fetus is, or anyway that we had better say it is, a person from the moment of conception. But this conclusion does not follow. Similar things might be said about the development of an acorn into an oak tree, and it does not follow that acorns are oak trees or that we had better say they are. Arguments of this form are sometimes called "slippery slope arguments"—the phrase is perhaps self-explanatory—and it is dismaying that opponents of abortion rely on them so heavily and uncritically.

I am inclined to agree, however, that the prospects for "drawing a line" in the development of the fetus look dim. I am inclined to think also that we shall probably have to agree that the fetus has already become a human person well before birth. Indeed, it comes as a surprise when one first learns how early in its life it begins to acquire human characteristics. By the tenth week, for example, it already has a face, arms and legs, fingers and toes; it has internal organs, and brain activity is detectable. On the other hand, I think that the premise is false; that the fetus is not a person from the moment of conception. A newly fertilized ovum, a newly implanted clump of cells, is no more a person than an acorn is an oak tree. But I shall not discuss any of this. For it seems to me to be of great interest to ask what happens if, for the sake of argument, we allow the premise. How, precisely, are we supposed to get from there to the conclusion that abortion is morally impermissible? Opponents of abortion commonly spend most of their time establishing that the fetus is a person and hardly any time explaining the step from there to the impermissibility of abortion. Perhaps they think the step too simple and obvious to require much comment. Or perhaps instead they are simply being economical in argument. Many of those who defend abortion rely on the premise that the fetus is not a person but only a bit of tissue that will become a person at birth, and why pay out more arguments than you have to? Whatever the explanation, I suggest that the step they take is neither easy nor obvious, that it calls for closer examination than it is commonly given, and that when we do give it this closer examination we shall feel inclined to reject it.

I propose, then, that we grant that the fetus is a person from the moment of conception. How does the argument go from here? Something like this, I take it. Every person has a right to life. So the fetus has a right to life. No doubt the mother has a right to decide what shall happen in and to her body; everyone would grant that. But surely a person's right to life is stronger and more stringent than the mother's right to decide what happens in and to her body, and so outweighs it. So the fetus may not be killed; an abortion may not be performed.

It sounds plausible. But now let me ask you to imagine this. You wake up in the morning and find yourself back to back in bed with an unconscious violinist. A famous unconscious violinist. He has been found to have a fatal kidney ailment, and the Society of Music Lovers has canvassed all the available medical records and found that you alone have the right blood type to help. They have therefore kidnapped you, and last night the violinist's circulatory system was plugged into yours so that your kidneys can be used to extract poisons from his blood as well as your own. The director of the hospital now tells you,

> Look, we're sorry the Society of Music Lovers did this to you—we would never have permitted it if we had known. But still, they did it, and the violinist now is plugged into you. To unplug you would be to kill him. But never mind, it's only for nine months. By then he will have recovered from his ailment and can safely be unplugged from you.

Is it morally incumbent on you to accede to this situation? No doubt it would be very nice of you if you did, a great kindness. But do you have to accede to it? What if it were not nine months, but nine years? Or longer still? What if the director of the hospital says,

> Tough luck, I agree, but you've now got to stay in bed, with the violinist plugged into you, for the rest of your life. Because remember this. All persons have a right to life, and violinists are persons. Granted you have a right to decide what happens in and to your body, but a person's right to life outweighs your right to decide what happens in and to your body. So you cannot ever be unplugged from him.

I imagine you would regard this as outrageous, which suggests that something really is wrong with that plausible-sounding argument I mentioned a moment ago.

In this case, of course, you were kidnapped; you didn't volunteer for the operation that plugged the violinist into your kidneys. Can those who oppose abortion on the ground I mentioned make an exception for a pregnancy due to rape? Certainly. They can say that persons have a right to life only if they didn't come into existence because of rape; or they can say that all persons have a right to life but that some have less of a right to life than others, in particular, that those who come into existence because of rape have less. But these statements have a rather unpleasant sound. Surely the question of whether you have a right to life at all, or how much of it you have, shouldn't turn on the question of whether or not you are the product of a rape. And in fact the people who oppose abortion on the ground I mentioned do not make this distinction and hence do not make an exception in case of rape.

Nor do they make an exception for a case in which the mother has to spend the nine months of her pregnancy in bed. They would agree that would be a great pity, and hard on the mother; but all the same, all persons have a right to life, the fetus is a person, and so on. I suspect, in fact, that they would not make an exception for a case in which, miraculously enough, the pregnancy went on for nine years, or even the rest of the mother's life.

Some won't even make an exception for a case in which continuation of the pregnancy is likely to shorten the mother's life; they regard abortion as impermissible even to save the mother's life. Such cases are nowadays very rare, and many opponents of abortion do not accept this extreme view. All the same, it is a good place to begin: a number of points of interest come out in respect to it.

I The Extreme Anti-Abortion View

Let us call the view that abortion is impermissible even to save the mother's life "the extreme view." I want to suggest first that it does not issue from the argument I mentioned earlier without the addition of some fairly powerful premises. Suppose a woman has become pregnant and now learns that she has a cardiac condition such that she will die if she carries the baby to term. What may be done for her? The fetus, being a person, has a right to life, but as the mother is a person too, so has she a right to life. Presumably they have an equal right to life. How is it supposed to come out that an abortion may not be performed? If mother and child have an equal right to life, shouldn't we perhaps flip a coin? Or should we add to the mother's right to life her right to decide what happens in and to her body, which everybody seems to be ready to grant—the sum of her rights now outweighing the fetus's right to life?

The most familiar argument here is the following. We are told that performing the abortion would be directly killing the child, whereas doing nothing would not be killing the mother but only letting her die. Moreover, in killing the child, one would be killing an innocent person, for the child has committed no crime and is not aiming at his mother's death. ... If directly killing an innocent person is murder, and thus is impermissible, then the mother's directly killing the innocent person inside her is murder and thus is impermissible. But it cannot seriously be thought to be murder if the mother performs an abortion on herself to save her life. It cannot seriously be said that she must refrain, that she *must* sit passively by and wait for her death. Let us look again at the case of you and the violinist. There you are, in bed with the violinist, and the director of the hospital says to you,

> It's all most distressing, and I deeply sympathize, but you see this is putting an additional strain on your kidneys, and you'll be dead within the month. But you *have* to stay where you are all the same. Because unplugging you would be directly killing an innocent violinist, and that's murder, and that's impermissible.

If anything in the world is true, it is that you do not commit murder, you do not do what is impermissible, if you reach around to your back and unplug yourself from the violinist to save your life.

The main focus of attention in writings on abortion has been on what a third party may or may not do in answer to a request from a woman for an abortion. This is in a way understandable. Things being as they are, there isn't much a woman can safely do to abort herself. So the question asked is what a third party may do, and what the mother may do, if it is mentioned at all, is deduced, almost as an afterthought, from what it is concluded that third parties may do. But it seems to me that to treat the matter in this way is to refuse to grant to the mother that very status of person which is so firmly insisted on for the fetus. For we cannot simply read off what a person may do from what a third party may do. Suppose you find yourself trapped in a tiny house with a growing child. I mean a very tiny house and a rapidly growing child—you are already up against the wall of the house and in a few minutes you'll be crushed to death. The child on the other hand won't be crushed to death; if nothing is done to stop him from growing he'll be hurt, but in the end he'll simply burst open the house and walk out a free man. Now I could well understand it if a bystander were to say, "There's nothing we can do for you. We cannot choose between your life and his, we cannot be the ones to decide who is to live, we cannot intervene." But it cannot be concluded that you too can do nothing, that you cannot attack it to save your life. However innocent the child may be, you do not have to wait passively while it crushes you to death. Perhaps a pregnant woman is vaguely felt to have the status of [a] house, to which we don't allow the right of self-defense. But if the woman houses the child, it should be remembered that she is a person who houses it.

I should perhaps stop to say explicitly that I am not claiming that people have a right to do anything whatever to save their lives. I think, rather, that there are drastic limits to the right of self-defense. If someone threatens you with death unless you torture someone else to death, I think you have not the right, even to save your life, to do so. But the case under consideration here is very different. In our case there are only two people involved, one whose life is threatened and one who threatens it. Both are innocent: the one who is threatened is not threatened because of any fault, the one who threatens does not threaten because of any fault. For this reason we may feel that we bystanders cannot intervene. But the person threatened can.

In sum, a woman surely can defend her life against the threat to it posed by the unborn child, even if doing so involves its death. And this shows that the extreme view of abortion is false, and so we need not canvass any other possible ways of arriving at it from the argument I mentioned at the outset.

The extreme view could of course be weakened to say that while abortion is permissible to save the mother's life, it may not be performed by a third party, but only by the mother herself. But this cannot be right either. For what we have to keep in mind is that the mother and the unborn child are not like two tenants in a small house which has, by an unfortunate mistake, been rented to both: the mother owns the house. The fact that she does adds to the offensiveness of deducing that the mother can do nothing from the supposition that third parties can do nothing. But it does more than this: it casts a bright light on the supposition that third parties can do nothing. Certainly it lets us see that a third party who says "I cannot choose between you" is fooling himself if he thinks this is impartiality. If Jones has found and fastened on a certain coat, which he needs to keep from freezing but which Smith also needs to keep him from freezing, then it is not impartiality that says "I cannot choose between you" when Smith owns the coat. Women have said again and again, "This body is my body!" and they have reason to feel angry, reason to feel that it has been like shouting into the wind. Smith, after all, is hardly likely to bless us if we say to him, "Of course it's your coat, anybody would grant that it is. But no one may choose between you and Jones who is to have it."

We should really ask what it is that says "no one may choose" in the face of the fact that the body that houses the child is the mother's body. It may be simply a failure to appreciate this fact. But it may be something more interesting, namely the sense that one has a right to refuse to lay hands on people, even where it would be just and fair to do so, even where justice seems to require that somebody do so. Thus justice might call for somebody to get Smith's coat back from Jones, and yet you have a right to refuse to be the one to lay hands on Jones, a right to refuse to do physical violence to him. This, I think, must be granted. But then what should be said is not "no one may choose," but only "I cannot choose," and indeed not even this, but "I will not act," leaving it open that somebody else can or should, and in particular that anyone in a position of authority, with the job of securing people's rights, both can and should. So this is no difficulty. I have not been arguing that any given third party must accede to the mother's request that he perform an abortion to save her life, but only that he may ....

2 The Right to Life

Where the mother's life is not at stake, the argument I mentioned at the outset seems to have a much stronger pull. "Everyone has a right to life, so the unborn person has a right to life." And isn't the child's right to life weightier than anything other than the mother's own right to life, which she might put forward as ground for an abortion?

This argument treats the right to life as if it were unproblematic. It is not, and this seems to me to be precisely the source of the mistake.

For we should now, at long last, ask what it comes to, to have a right to life. In some views, having a right to life includes having a right to be given at least the bare minimum one needs for continued life. But suppose that what in fact is the bare minimum a man needs for continued life is something he has no right at all to be given? If I am sick unto death and the only thing that will save my life is the touch of Henry Fonda's cool hand on my fevered brow, then all the same, I have no right to be given the touch of Henry Fonda's cool hand on my fevered brow. It would be frightfully nice of him to fly in from the West Coast to provide it. It would be less nice, though no doubt well meaning, if my friends flew out to the West Coast and carried Henry Fonda back with them. But I have no right at all against anybody that he should do this for me. Or again, to return to the story I told earlier, the fact that for continued life that violinist needs the continued use of your kidneys does not establish that he has a right to be given the continued use of your kidneys. He certainly has no right against you that you should give him continued use of your kidneys. For nobody has any right to use your kidneys unless you give him such a right; and nobody has the right against you that you shall give him this right—if you do allow him to go on using your kidneys, this is a kindness on your part and not something he can claim from you as his due. Nor has he any right against anybody else that *they* should give him continued use of your kidneys. Certainly he had no right against the Society of Music Lovers that they should plug him into you in the first place. And if you now start to unplug yourself, having learned that you will otherwise have to spend nine years in bed with him, there is nobody in the world who must try to prevent you in order to see to it that he is given something he has a right to be given.

Some people are rather stricter about the right to life. In their view, it does not include the right to be given anything but amounts to, and only to, the right not to be killed by anybody. But here a related difficulty arises. If everybody is to refrain from killing that violinist, then everybody must refrain from doing a great many different sorts of things. Everybody must refrain from slitting his throat, everybody must refrain from shooting him—and everybody must refrain from unplugging you from him. But does he have a right against everybody that they shall refrain from unplugging you from him? To refrain from doing this is to allow him to continue to use your kidneys. It could be argued that he has a right against us that we should allow him to continue to use your kidneys. That is, while he had no right against us that we should give him the use of your kidneys, it might be argued that he anyway has a right against us that we shall not now intervene and deprive him of the use of your kidneys. I shall come back to third-party interventions later. But certainly the violinist has no right against you that you shall allow him to continue to use your kidneys. As I said, if you do allow him to use them, it is a kindness on your part, and not something you owe him ....

.... I am arguing only that having a right to life does not guarantee having either a right to be given the use of or a right to be allowed continued use of another person's body—even if one needs it for life itself. So the right to life will not serve the opponents of abortion in the very simple and clear way in which they seem to have thought it would.

3 The Right to Live and Use the Mother's Body

There is another way to bring out the difficulty. In the most ordinary sort of case, to deprive someone of what he has a right to is to treat him unjustly. Suppose a boy and his small brother are jointly given a box of chocolates for Christmas. If the older boy takes the box and refuses to give his brother any of the chocolates, he is unjust to him, for the brother has been given a right to half of them. But suppose that, having learned that otherwise it means nine years in bed with that violinist, you unplug yourself from him. You surely are not being unjust to him, for you gave him no right to use your kidneys and no one else can have given him any such right. But we have to notice that in unplugging yourself, you are killing him; and violinists, like everybody else, have a right to life, and thus in the view we were considering just now, the right not to be killed. So here you do what he supposedly has a right you shall not do, but you do not act unjustly to him in doing it.

The emendation which may be made at this point is this: the right to life consists not in the right not to be killed but rather in the right not to be killed unjustly. This runs a risk of circularity, but never mind; it would enable us to square the fact that the violinist has a right to life with the fact that you do not act unjustly toward him in unplugging yourself, thereby killing him. For if you do not kill him unjustly, you do not violate his right to life, and so it is no wonder you do him no injustice.

But if this emendation is accepted, the gap in the argument against abortion stares us plainly in the face: it is by no means enough to show that the fetus is a person and to remind us that all persons have a right to life—we need to be shown also that killing the fetus violates its right to life, i.e., that abortion is unjust killing. And is it?

I suppose we may take it as a datum that in a case of pregnancy due to rape the mother has not given the unborn person a right to the use of her body for food and shelter. Indeed, in what pregnancy could it be supposed that the mother has given the unborn person such a right? It is not as if there were unborn persons drifting about the world to whom a woman who wants a child says, "I invite you in."

But it might be argued that there are other ways one can have acquired a right to the use of another person's body than by having been invited to use it by that person. Suppose a woman voluntarily indulges in intercourse, knowing of the chance it will issue in pregnancy, and then she does become pregnant; is she not in part responsible for the presence, in fact the very existence, of the unborn person inside her? No doubt she did not invite it in. But doesn't her partial responsibility for its being there itself give it a right to the use of her body? If so, then her aborting it would be more like the boy's taking away the chocolates and less like your unplugging yourself from the violinist—doing so would be depriving it of what it does have a right to and thus would be doing it an injustice.

And then, too, it might be asked whether or not she can kill it even to save her own life: if she voluntarily called it into existence, how can she now kill it, even in self-defense?

The first thing to be said about this is that it is something new. Opponents of abortion have been so concerned to make out the independence of the fetus in order to establish that it has a right to life, just as its mother does, that they have tended to overlook the possible support they might gain from making out that the fetus is *dependent* on the mother in order to establish that she has a special kind of responsibility for it, a responsibility that gives it rights against her which are not possessed by any independent person—such as an ailing violinist who is a stranger to her.

On the other hand, this argument would give the unborn person a right to its mother's body only if her pregnancy resulted from a voluntary act, undertaken in full knowledge of the chance a pregnancy might result from it. It would leave out entirely the unborn person whose existence is due to rape. Pending the availability of some further argument, then, we would be left with the conclusion that unborn persons whose existence is due to rape have no right to the use of their mothers' bodies and thus that aborting them is not depriving them of anything they have a right to and hence is not unjust killing.

And we should also notice that it is not at all plain that this argument really does go even as far as it purports to. For there are cases and cases, and the details make a difference. If the room is stuffy and I therefore open a window to air it and a burglar climbs in, it would be absurd to say,

> Ah, now he can stay, she's given him a right to the use of her house—for she is partially responsible for his presence there, having voluntarily done what enabled him to get in, in full knowledge that there are such things as burglars, and that burglars burgle.

It would be still more absurd to say this if I had had bars installed outside my windows, precisely to prevent burglars from getting in and a burglar got in only because of a defect in the bars. It remains equally absurd if we imagine it is not a burglar who climbs in but an innocent person who blunders or falls in. Again, suppose it were like this: people-seeds drift about in the air like pollen, and if you open your windows, one may drift in and take root in your carpets or upholstery. You don't want children, so you fix up your windows with fine mesh screens, the very best you can buy. As can happen, however, and on very, very rare occasions does happen, one of the screens is defective, and a seed drifts in and takes root. Does the person-plant who now develops have a right to the use of your house? Surely not—despite the fact that you voluntarily opened your windows, you knowingly kept carpets and upholstered furniture, and you knew that screens were sometimes defective. Someone may argue that you are responsible for its rooting, that it does have a right to your house, because after all you could have lived out your life with bare floors and furniture or with sealed windows and doors. But this won't do—for by the same token anyone can avoid a pregnancy due to rape by having a hysterectomy, or anyway by never leaving home without a (reliable!) army.

It seems to me that the argument we are looking at can establish at most that there are some cases in which the unborn person has a right to the use of its mother's body and therefore some cases in which abortion is unjust killing. There is room for much discussion and argument as to precisely which, if any. But I think we should sidestep this issue and leave it open, for at any rate the argument certainly does not establish that all abortion is unjust killing.

4 Rights and Their Limits

There is room for yet another argument here, however. We surely must all grant that there may be cases in which it would be morally indecent to detach a person from your body at the cost of his life. Suppose you learn that what the violinist needs is not nine years of your life but only one hour: all you need do to save his life is to spend one hour in that bed with him. Suppose also that letting him use your kidneys for that one hour would not affect your health in the slightest. Admittedly you were kidnapped. Admittedly you did not give anyone permission to plug him into you. Nevertheless it seems to me plain you *ought* to allow him to use your kidneys for that hour—it would be indecent to refuse.

Again, suppose pregnancy lasted only an hour and constituted no threat to life or health. And suppose that a woman becomes pregnant as a result of rape. Admittedly she did not voluntarily do anything to bring about the existence of a child. Admittedly she did nothing at all which would give the unborn person a right to the use of her body. All the same, it might well be said, as in the newly emended violinist story, that she *ought* to allow it to remain for that hour—that it would be indecent for her to refuse ....

Suppose that the box of chocolates I mentioned earlier was given only to the older boy. There he sits, stolidly eating his way through the box, his small brother watching enviously. Here we are likely to say "You ought not to be so mean. You ought to give your brother some of those chocolates." My own view is that it just does not follow from the truth of this that the brother has any right to any of the chocolates. If the boy refuses to give his brother any, he is greedy, stingy, callous—but not unjust. ... Take the case of Henry Fonda again. I said earlier that I had no right to the touch of his cool hand on my fevered brow, even though I needed it to save my life. I said it would be frightfully nice of him to fly in from the West Coast to provide me with it but that I had no right against him that he should do so. But suppose he isn't on the West Coast. Suppose he has only to walk across the room, place a hand briefly on my brow—and lo, my life is saved. Then surely he *ought* to do it, it would be indecent to refuse ....

So my own view is that even though you ought to let the violinist use your kidneys for the one hour he needs, we should not conclude that he has a right to do so—we would say that if you refuse, you are, like the boy who owns all the chocolates and will give none away, self-centered and callous, indecent in fact, but not unjust. And similarly, that even supposing a case in which a woman pregnant due to rape ought to allow the unborn person to use her body for the hour he needs, we should not conclude that he has a right to do so; we should conclude that she is self-centered, callous, indecent, but not unjust, if she refuses. The complaints are no less grave; they are just different. ... [But] nobody is morally *required* to make large sacrifices, of health, of all other interests and concerns, of all other duties and commitments, for nine years, or even for nine months, in order to keep a person alive.

5 The Good Samaritan and the Responsibilities of Parents

We have in fact to distinguish between two kinds of Samaritan: the Good Samaritan and what we might call the Minimally Decent Samaritan. ... The Good Samaritan went out of his way, at some cost to himself, to help one in need of it. ... These things are a matter of degree, of course, but there is a difference, and it comes out perhaps most clearly in the story of Kitty Genovese, who, as you will remember, was murdered while thirty-eight people watched or listened and did nothing at all to help her. A Good Samaritan would have rushed out to give direct assistance against the murderer. Or perhaps we had better allow that it would have been a Splendid Samaritan who did this, on the ground that it would have involved a risk of death for himself. But the thirty-eight not only did not do this, they did not even trouble to pick up a phone to call the police. Minimally Decent Samaritanism would call for doing at least that, and their not having done it was monstrous. ... It seems plain that it was not morally required of any of the thirty-eight that he rush out to give direct assistance at the risk of his own life and that it is not morally required of anyone that he give long stretches of his life—nine years or nine months—to sustain the life of a person who has no special right (we were leaving open the possibility of this) to demand it ....

What we should ask is not whether anybody should be compelled by law to be a Good Samaritan, but whether we must accede to a situation in which somebody is being compelled—by nature, perhaps—to be a Good Samaritan. ... There you are, you were kidnapped, and nine years in bed with that violinist lie ahead of you. You have your own life to lead. You are sorry, but you simply cannot see giving up so much of your life to the sustaining of his. You cannot extricate yourself and ask us to do so. I should have thought that—in light of his having no right to the use of your body—it was obvious that we do not have to accede to your being forced to give up so much. We can do what you ask. There is no injustice to the violinist in our doing so ....

It may be said that what is important is not merely the fact that the fetus is a person, but that it is a person for whom the woman has a special kind of responsibility issuing from the fact that she is its mother. ... Surely we do not have any such "special responsibility" for a person unless we have assumed it, explicitly or implicitly. If a set of parents do not try to prevent pregnancy, do not obtain an abortion, but rather take it home with them, then they have assumed responsibility for it and have given it rights, and they cannot *now* withdraw support from it at the cost of its life because they now find it difficult to go on providing for it. But if they have taken all reasonable precautions against having a child, they do not simply by virtue of their biological relationship to the child who comes into existence have a special responsibility for it ....

I have argued that you are not morally required to spend nine months in bed sustaining the life of that violinist; but to say this is by no means to say that if when you unplug yourself there is a miracle and he survives, you then have a right to turn around and slit his throat. You may detach yourself even if this costs him his life; you have no right to be guaranteed his death by some other means if unplugging yourself does not kill him. There are some people who will feel dissatisfied by this feature of my argument. A woman may be utterly devastated by the thought of a child, a bit of herself, put out for adoption and never seen or heard of again. ... All the same, I agree that the desire for the child's death is not one which anybody may gratify, should it turn out to be possible to detach a child alive.

At this place, however, it should be remembered that we have only been pretending throughout that the fetus is a human being from the moment of conception. A very early abortion is surely not the killing of a person, and so is not dealt with by anything I have said.

Review and Discussion Questions

1 How does Thomson understand the right to life? Why shouldn't the fetus's having such a right prevent the mother from getting an abortion?
2 Suppose the violinist needed your kidneys for only five minutes. Does Thomson think you should allow him to use them? Why?
3 "Abortions almost always occur in cases in which the mother voluntarily had sex, so the violinist analogy doesn't apply." How does Thomson respond to this claim? Is her response adequate?
4 Suppose you found a baby in your mountain cabin just after the winter snows arrived. Should you now let it share your cabin (to which, let's assume, you have a right) for nine months if the only alternative is to put it outside to die? Is this situation a good analogy to abortion?
5 Is it important that it is her own child the mother kills, whereas the violinist is a stranger? Explain how Thomson understands this issue. Do you agree?

READING: ON THE MORAL AND LEGAL STATUS OF ABORTION

MARY ANNE WARREN[*]

In this essay, Mary Anne Warren begins by discussing Judith Jarvis Thomson's defense of abortion. Finding that defense inadequate, Warren concludes that the status of the

---

[*] From *The Monist*, 1973. Copyright © 1973 *The Monist*, La Salle, IL 61301. Reprinted by permission.

fetus is of central importance in assessing abortion. Warren's approach rests on a fundamental distinction that, if she is correct, would undermine the traditional pro-life position that life begins at conception and that no other event after conception can carry the moral weight needed to say that before then killing is justified, beyond those rare cases when both the mother and baby will die. It is crucial, according to Warren, to distinguish between a biological human being, on one hand, and a member of the "moral community" whose members enjoy full and equal moral rights, on the other. Merely being a member of the species *Homo sapiens* is not, she argues, sufficient to qualify as a moral person. Warren then goes on to discuss the circumstances in which a being should be regarded as having full moral rights; what, she asks, are the criteria for "person-hood"? In the last sections of her essay, Warren explores some of the consequences of her theory. Even very late abortions do not take the life of a person, she contends, nor is it relevant that a (merely) potential person is killed in abortions since its rights cannot outweigh the rights of already existing women. Mary Anne Warren is a retired Professor of Philosophy at San Francisco State University.

We will be concerned with both the moral status of abortion, which for our purposes we may define as the act which a woman performs in voluntarily terminating, or allowing another person to terminate, her pregnancy, and the legal status which is appropriate for this act. I will argue that while it is not possible to produce a satisfactory defense of a woman's right to obtain an abortion without showing that a fetus is not a human being, in the morally relevant sense of that term, we ought not to conclude that the difficulties involved in determining whether or not a fetus is human make it impossible to produce any satisfactory solution to the problem of the moral status of abortion. For it is possible to show that, on the basis of intuitions which we may expect even the opponents of abortion to share, a fetus is not a person and hence not the sort of entity to which it is proper to ascribe full moral rights.

Of course, while some philosophers would deny the possibility of any such proof,[1] others will deny that there is any need for it, since the moral permissibility of abortion appears to them to be too obvious to require proof. But the inadequacy of this attitude should be evident from the fact that both the friends and the foes of abortion consider their position to be morally self-evident. Because pro-abortionists have never adequately come to grips with the conceptual issues surrounding abortion, most, if not all, of the arguments which they advance in opposition to laws restricting access to abortion fail to refute or even weaken the traditional anti-abortion argument, i.e., that a fetus is a human being and therefore abortion is murder.

These arguments are typically of one of two sorts. Either they point to the terrible side effects of the restrictive laws, e.g., the deaths due to illegal abortions, and the fact that it is poor women who suffer the most as a result of these laws, or else they state that to deny a woman access to abortion is to deprive her of her right to control her own body. Unfortunately, however, the fact that restricting access to abortion has tragic side effects does not, in itself, show that the restrictions are unjustified, since murder is wrong regardless of the consequences of prohibiting it; and the appeal to the right to control one's body [such as Thomson's] which is generally construed as a property right, is at best a rather feeble argument for the permissibility of abortion. Mere ownership does not give me the right to kill innocent people whom I find on my property, and indeed I am apt to be held responsible if such people injure themselves while on my property. It is equally unclear that I have any moral right to expel an innocent person from my property when I know that doing so will result in his death.

Furthermore, it is probably inappropriate to describe a woman's body as her property, since it seems natural to hold that a person is something distinct from her property, but not from her body. Even those who would object to the identification of a person with his body, or with the conjunction of his body and his mind, must admit that it would be very odd to describe, say, breaking a leg, as damaging one's property and much more appropriate to describe it as injuring *oneself*. Thus it is probably a mistake to argue that the right to obtain an abortion is in any way derived from the right to own and regulate property.

But however we wish to construe the right to abortion, we cannot hope to convince those who consider abortion a form of murder of the existence of any such right unless we are able to produce a clear and convincing refutation of the traditional anti-abortion argument, and this has not, to my knowledge, been done. With respect to the two most vital issues which that argument involves, i.e., the humanity of the fetus and its implication for the moral status of abortion, confusion has prevailed on both sides of the dispute.

Thus, both pro-abortionists and anti-abortionists have tended to abstract the question of whether abortion is wrong to that of whether it is wrong to destroy a fetus, just as though the rights of another person were not necessarily involved. This mistaken abstraction has led to the almost universal assumption that if a fetus is a human being, with a right to life, then it follows immediately that abortion is wrong (except perhaps when necessary to save the woman's life) and that it ought to be prohibited. It has also been generally assumed that unless the question about the status of the fetus is answered, the moral status of abortion cannot possibly be determined ....

The question which we must answer in order to produce a satisfactory solution to the problem of the moral status of abortion is this: How are we to define the moral community, the set of beings with full and equal moral rights, such that we can decide whether a human fetus is a member of this community or not? What sort of entity, exactly, has the inalienable rights to life, liberty, and the pursuit of happiness? Jefferson attributed these rights to all *men*, and it may or may not be fair to suggest that he intended to attribute them *only* to men. Perhaps he ought to have attributed them to all human beings. If so, then we arrive, first, at the problem of defining what makes a being human, and, second, at the equally vital question ... namely, What reason is there for identifying the moral community with the set of all human beings, in whatever way we have chosen to define that term?

On the Definition of "Human"

One reason why this vital second question is so frequently overlooked in the debate over the moral status of abortion is that the term "human" has two distinct, but not often distinguished, senses. This fact results in a slide of meaning, which serves to conceal the fallaciousness of the traditional argument that since (1) it is wrong to kill innocent human beings, and (2) fetuses are innocent human beings, then (3) it is wrong to kill fetuses. For if "human" is used in the same sense in both (1) and (2), then whichever of the two senses is meant, one of these premises is question-begging. And if it is used in two different senses, then of course the conclusion doesn't follow.

Thus, (1) is a self-evident moral truth[2] and avoids begging the question about abortion only if "human being" is used to mean something like "a full-fledged member of the moral community." (It may or may not also be meant to refer exclusively to members of the species *Homo sapiens.*) We may call this the *moral* sense of "human." It is not to be confused with what we will call the *genetic* sense, i.e., the sense in which *any* member of the species is a human being and no member of any other species could be. If (1) is acceptable only if the moral sense is intended, (2) is non-question-begging only if what is intended is the genetic sense.

In "Deciding Who Is Human," Noonan argues for the classification of fetuses with human beings by pointing to the presence of the full genetic code and the potential capacity for rational thought.[3] It is clear that what he needs to show, for his version of the traditional argument to be valid, is that fetuses are human in the moral sense, the sense in which it is analytically true that all human beings have full moral rights. But in the absence of any argument showing that whatever is genetically human is also morally human, and he gives none, nothing more than genetic humanity can be demonstrated by the presence of the human genetic code. And, as we will see, the *potential* capacity for rational thought can at most show that an entity has the potential for *becoming* human in the moral sense.

Defining the Moral Community

Can it be established that genetic humanity is sufficient for moral humanity? I think that there are very good reasons for not defining the moral community in this way. I would like to suggest an alternative way of defining the moral community, which I will argue for only to the extent of explaining why it is, or should be, self-evident. The suggestion is simply that the moral community consists of all and only *people*, rather than all and only human beings,[4] and probably the best way of demonstrating its self-evidence is by considering the concept of personhood, to see what sorts of entity are and are not persons, and what the decision that a being is or is not a person implies about its moral rights.

What characteristics entitle an entity to be considered a person? This is obviously not the place to attempt a complete analysis of the concept of personhood, but we do not need such a fully adequate analysis just to determine whether and why a fetus is or isn't a person. All we need is a rough and approximate list of the most basic criteria of personhood and some idea of which, or how many, of these an entity must satisfy in order to properly be considered a person.

In searching for such criteria, it is useful to look beyond the set of people with whom we are acquainted and ask how we would decide whether a totally alien being was a person or not. (For we have no right to assume that genetic humanity is necessary for personhood.) Imagine a space traveler who lands on an unknown planet and encounters a race of beings utterly unlike any he has ever seen or heard of. If he wants to be sure of behaving morally toward these beings, he has to somehow decide whether they are people, and hence have full moral rights, or whether they are the sort of thing which he need not feel guilty about treating as, for example, a source of food.

How should he go about making this decision? If he has some anthropological background, he might look for such things as religion, art, and the manufacturing of tools, weapons, or shelters, since these factors have been used to distinguish our human from our prehuman ancestors in what seems to be closer to the moral than the genetic sense of "human." And no doubt he would be right to consider the presence of such factors as good evidence that the alien beings were people and morally human. It would, however, be overly anthropocentric of him to take the absence of these things as adequate evidence that they were not, since we can imagine people who have progressed beyond, or evolved without ever developing, these cultural characteristics.

I suggest that the traits which are most central to the concept of personhood, or humanity in the moral sense, are, very roughly, the following:

1. consciousness (of objects and events external and/or internal to the being), and in particular the capacity to feel pain;
2. reasoning (the *developed* capacity to solve new and relatively complex problems);
3. self-motivated activity (activity which is relatively independent of either genetic or direct external control);
4. the capacity to communicate, by whatever means, messages of an indefinite variety of types, that is, not just with an indefinite number of possible contents but on indefinitely many possible topics;
5. the presence of self-concepts and self-awareness, either individual, or racial, or both.

Admittedly, there are apt to be a great many problems involved in formulating precise definitions of these criteria, let alone in developing universally valid behavioral criteria for deciding when they apply. But I will assume that both we and our explorer know approximately what (1)–(5) mean and that he is also able to determine whether or not they apply. How, then, should he use his findings to decide whether or not the alien beings are people? We needn't suppose that an entity must have *all* of these attributes to be properly considered a person; (1) and (2) alone may well be sufficient for personhood, and quite probably (1)–(3) are sufficient. Neither do we need to insist that any one of these criteria is *necessary* for personhood, although once again (1) and (2) look like fairly good candidates for necessary conditions, as does (3), if "activity" is construed so as to include the activity of reasoning.

All we need to claim to demonstrate that a fetus is not a person is that any being which satisfies *none* of (1)–(5) is certainly not a person. I consider this claim to be so obvious that I think anyone who denied it and claimed that a being which satisfied none of (1)–(5) was a person all the same would thereby demonstrate that he had no notion at all of what a person is—perhaps because he had confused the concept of a person with that of genetic humanity. If the opponents of abortion were to deny the appropriateness of these five criteria, I do not know what further arguments would convince them. We would probably have to admit that our conceptual schemes were indeed irreconcilably different and that our dispute could not be settled objectively.

I do not expect this to happen, however, since I think that the concept of a person is one which is very nearly universal (to people) and that it is common to both pro-abortionists and anti-abortionists, even though neither group has fully realized the relevance of this concept to the resolution of their dispute. Furthermore, I think that on reflection even the anti-abortionists ought to agree not only that (1)–(5) are central to the concept of personhood but also that it is a part of this concept that all and only people have full moral rights. The concept of a person is in part a moral concept; once we have admitted that x is a person we have recognized, even if we have not agreed to respect, x's right to be treated as a member of the moral community. It is true that the claim that x is a *human being* is more commonly voiced as part of an appeal to treat x decently than is the claim that x is a person, but this is either because "human being" is here used in the sense which implies personhood or because the genetic and moral senses of "human" have been confused.

Now if (1)–(5) are indeed the primary criteria of personhood, then it is clear that genetic humanity is neither necessary nor sufficient for establishing that an entity is a person. Some human beings are not people, and there may well be people who are not human beings. A man or woman whose consciousness has been permanently obliterated but who remains alive is a human being which is no longer a person; defective human beings, with no appreciable mental capacity, are not and presumably never will be people; and a fetus is a human being which is not yet a person, and which therefore cannot coherently be said to have full moral rights. Citizens of the next century should be prepared to recognize highly advanced, self-aware robots or computers, should such be developed, and intelligent inhabitants of other worlds, should such be found, as people in the fullest sense and to respect their moral rights. But to ascribe full moral rights to an entity which is not a person is as absurd as to ascribe moral obligations and responsibilities to such an entity.

Fetal Development and the Right to Life

Two problems arise in the application of these suggestions for the definition of the moral community to the determination of the precise moral status of a human fetus. Given that the paradigm example of a person is a normal adult human being, then (1) How like this paradigm, in particular how far advanced since conception, does a human being need to be before it begins to have a right to life by virtue not of being fully a person as of yet, but of being *like* a person? and (2) To what extent, if any, does the fact that a fetus has the *potential* for becoming a person endow it with some of the same rights? Each of these questions requires some comment.

In answering the first question, we need not attempt a detailed consideration of the moral rights of organisms which are not developed enough, aware enough, intelligent enough, etc., to be considered people but which resemble people in some respects. It does seem reasonable to suggest that the more like a person, in the relevant respects, a being is, the stronger is the case for regarding it as having a right to life, and indeed the stronger its right to life is. Thus we ought to take seriously the suggestion that, insofar as "the human individual develops biologically in a continuous fashion ... the rights of a human person might develop in the same way."[5] But we must keep in mind that the attributes which are relevant in determining whether or not an entity is enough like a person to be regarded as having some of the same moral rights are no different from those which are relevant to determining whether or not it is fully a person—i.e., are no different from (1)–(5)—and that being genetically human or having recognizably human facial and other physical features or detectable brain activity or the capacity to survive outside the uterus are simply not among these relevant attributes.

Thus it is clear that even though a seven- or eight-month fetus has features which make it apt to arouse in us almost the same powerful protective instinct as is commonly aroused by a small infant, nevertheless it is not significantly more personlike than is a very small embryo. It is *somewhat* more personlike; it can apparently feel and respond to pain, and it may even have a rudimentary form of consciousness, insofar as its brain is quite active. Nevertheless, it seems safe to say that it is not fully conscious, in the way that an infant of a few months is, and that it cannot reason or communicate messages of indefinitely many sorts, does not engage in self-motivated activity, and has no self-awareness. Thus, in the *relevant* respects, a fetus, even a fully developed one, is considerably less personlike than is the average mature mammal, indeed the average fish. And I think that a rational person must conclude that if the right to life of a fetus is to be based upon its resemblance to a person, then it cannot be said to have any more right to life than, let us say, a newborn guppy (which also seems to be capable of feeling pain), and that a right of that magnitude could never override a woman's right to obtain an abortion, at any stage of her pregnancy.

There may, of course, be other arguments in favor of placing legal limits upon the stage of pregnancy in which an abortion may be performed. Given the relative safety of the new techniques of artificially inducing labor during the third trimester, the danger to the woman's life or health is no longer such an argument. Neither is the fact that people tend to respond to the thought of abortion in the later stages of pregnancy with emotional repulsion, since mere emotional responses cannot take the place of moral reasoning in determining what ought to be permitted. Nor, finally, is the frequently heard argument that legalizing abortion, especially late in the pregnancy, may erode the level of respect for human life, leading, perhaps, to an increase in unjustified euthanasia and other crimes. For this threat, if it is a threat, can be better met by educating people to the kinds of moral distinctions which we are making here than by limiting access to abortion (which limitation may, in its disregard for the rights of women, be just as damaging to the level of respect for human rights).

Thus, since the fact that even a fully developed fetus is not personlike enough to have any significant right to life on the basis of its personlikeness shows that no legal restrictions upon the stage of pregnancy in which an abortion may be performed can be justified on the grounds that we should protect the rights of the older fetus and since there is no other apparent justification for such restrictions, we may conclude that they are entirely unjustified. Whether or not it would be *indecent* (whatever that means) for a woman in her seventh month to obtain an abortion just to avoid having to postpone a trip to Europe, it would not, in itself, be *immoral*, and therefore it ought to be permitted.

Potential Personhood and the Right to Life

We have seen that a fetus does not resemble a person in any way which can support the claim that it has even some of the same rights. But what about its *potential*, the fact that if nurtured and allowed to develop naturally it will very probably become a person? Doesn't that alone give it at least some right to life? It is hard to deny that the fact that an entity is a potential person is a strong prima facie reason for not destroying it; but we need not conclude from this that a potential person has a right to life by virtue of that potential. It may be that our feeling that it is better, other things being equal, not to destroy a potential person is better explained by the fact that potential people are still (felt to be) an invaluable resource, not to be lightly squandered. Surely if every speck of dust were a potential person, we would be much less apt to conclude that every potential person has a right to become actual.

Still, we do not need to insist that a potential person has no right to life whatever. There may be something immoral, and not just imprudent, about wantonly destroying potential people, when doing so isn't necessary to protect anyone's rights. But even if a potential person does have some prima facie right to life, such a right could not possibly outweigh the right of a woman to obtain an abortion, since the rights of any actual person invariably outweigh those of any potential person whenever the two conflict. Since this may not be immediately obvious in the case of a human fetus, let us look at another case.

Suppose that our space explorer falls into the hands of an alien culture, whose scientists decide to create a few hundred thousand or more human beings by breaking his body into its component cells and using these to create fully developed human beings with, of course, his genetic code. We may imagine that each of these newly created men will have all of the original man's abilities, skills, knowledge, and so on, and will also have an individual self-concept; in short, that each of them will be a bona fide (though hardly unique) person. Imagine that the whole project will take only seconds and that its chances of success are extremely high and that our explorer knows all of this and also knows that these people will be treated fairly. I maintain that in such a situation he would have every right to escape if he could and thus to deprive all of these potential people of their potential lives; for his right to life outweighs all of theirs together, in spite of the fact that they are all genetically human, all innocent, and all have a very high probability of becoming people very soon if only he refrains from acting.

Indeed, I think he would have a right to escape even if it were not his life which the alien scientists planned to take but only a year of his freedom or, indeed, only a day. Nor would he be obligated to stay if he had gotten captured (thus bringing all these people-potentials into existence) because of his own carelessness or even if he had done so deliberately, knowing the consequences. Regardless of how he got captured, he is not morally obligated to remain in captivity for *any* period of time for the sake of permitting any number of potential people to come into actuality, so great is the margin by which one actual person's right to liberty outweighs whatever right to life even a hundred thousand potential people have. And it seems reasonable to conclude that the rights of a woman will outweigh by a similar margin whatever right to life a fetus may have by virtue of its potential personhood.

Thus, neither a fetus's resemblance to a person nor its potential for becoming a person provides any basis whatever for the claim that it has any significant right to life. Consequently, a woman's right to protect her health, happiness, freedom, and even her life[6] by terminating an unwanted pregnancy will always override whatever right to life it may be appropriate to ascribe to a fetus, even a fully developed one. And thus, in the absence of any overwhelming social need for every possible child, the laws which restrict the right to obtain an abortion or limit the period of pregnancy during which an abortion may be performed are a wholly unjustified violation of a woman's most basic moral and constitutional rights.

Notes

1 For example, Roger Wertheimer, who in "Understanding the Abortion Argument" (*Philosophy and Public Affairs,* 1, no. 1 [Fall 1971], 67–95), argues that the problem of the moral status of abortion is insoluble, in that the dispute over the status of the fetus is not a question of fact at all but only a question of how one responds to the facts.
2 Of course, the principle that it is (always) wrong to kill innocent human beings is in need of many other modifications, e.g., that it may be permissible to do so to save a greater number of other innocent human beings, but we may safely ignore these complications here.
3 Noonan, J., "Deciding who is human," *Natural Law Forum* 13: 135, 1968.
4 From here on, we will use "human" to mean genetically human, since the moral sense seems closely connected to, and perhaps derived from, the assumption that genetic humanity is sufficient for membership in the moral community.
5 Hayes, T. L., "A Biological View," *Commonweal* 85: 677–678 (March 17, 1967), quoted by Daniel Callahan in *Abortion, Law, Choice, and Morality* (London: Macmillan, 1970).
6 That is, insofar as the death rate for the woman is higher for childbirth than for early abortion.

Review and Discussion Questions

1 How does Warren answer those who defend the right to an abortion based on the "terrible side effects" of anti-abortion laws?
2 How does Warren respond to those who defend abortion on the ground that the woman owns her body?
3 Explain the biological or genetic sense of the term *human*, indicating how Warren thinks that sense differs from the moral sense of the term.
4 On what basis does Warren think a human fetus is not a moral person?
5 How does Warren respond to those who argue that even if a fetus isn't a person, it is still a potential one and for that reason should not be killed?
6 Do you agree that, in theory at least, it is possible for there to be a "person" who is not a biological human? Explain, indicating the significance of that position for abortion.
7 When, in the course of your development, would Warren say you became a moral "person"?
8 In response to those who point out her view might justify infanticide, Warren has responded that it does not because (a) other people, besides the mother, would like to raise the infant themselves and (b) others also value infants and would prefer they not be killed. Are those responses adequate, in your opinion? Explain.
9 "One virtue of Warren's approach is that it solves not only the abortion problem but also helps resolve cases in which a human being has become a 'human vegetable' and therefore should not be kept alive." Explain that comment, indicating whether or not you agree.

READING: ABORTION AND THE CONCEPT OF A PERSON

JANE ENGLISH[*]

The writer of the preceding essay, like most people generally, assumes that the abortion controversy depends in large measure on the concept of a person: If a fetus is a person, it is almost always wrong to get an abortion; if it is not a person, then abortion is almost always acceptable. Jane English doubts that this approach—thinking about the nature of a person—is the right one. The concept of a person includes a family of characteristics, she argues, and it cannot provide an answer to the legitimacy of abortion. English then discusses the senses in which it may, or may not, be true that the woman is entitled to get an abortion out of self-defense and concludes with some thoughts about morality in general, including the importance of our psychology in our attitudes toward babies, other persons, and animals. Jane English was Professor of Philosophy at the University of North Carolina.

The abortion debate rages on. Yet the two most popular positions seem to be clearly mistaken. Conservatives maintain that a human life begins at conception and that therefore abortion must be wrong because it is murder. But not all killings of humans are murders. Most notably, self-defense may justify even the killing of an innocent person.

Liberals, on the other hand, are just as mistaken in their argument that since a fetus does not become a person until birth, a woman may do whatever she pleases in and to her own body. First, you cannot do as you please with your own body if it affects other people adversely.[1] Second, if a fetus is not a person, that does not imply that you can do to it anything you wish. Animals, for example, are not persons, yet to kill or torture them for no reason at all is wrong.

At the center of the storm has been the issue of just when it is between ovulation and adulthood that a person appears on the scene. Conservatives draw the line at conception, liberals at birth. In this paper, I first examine our concept of a person and conclude that no single criterion can capture the concept of a person and no sharp line can be drawn. Next I argue that if a fetus is a person, abortion is still justifiable in many cases; and if a fetus is not a person, killing it is still wrong in many cases. To a large extent, these two solutions are in agreement. I conclude that our concept of a person cannot and need not bear the weight that the abortion controversy has thrust upon it.

I

The several factions in the abortion argument have drawn battle lines around various proposed criteria for determining what is and what is not a person. For

---

[*] Jane English, "Abortion and the Concept of a Person," *Canadian Journal of Philosophy* 5 (October 1975): 233–243. Reprinted with permission of the *Canadian Journal of Philosophy* and the Jane English Memorial Fund at the University of North Carolina.

example, Mary Anne Warren[2] lists five features (capacities for reasoning, self-awareness, complex communications, etc.) as her criteria for personhood and argues for the permissibility of abortion because a fetus falls outside this concept. Baruch Brody[3] uses brain waves. Michael Tooley[4] picks having a concept of self as his criterion and concludes that infanticide and abortion are justifiable, while the killing of adult animals is not. On the other side, Paul Ramsey[5] claims a certain gene structure is the defining characteristic. John Noonan[6] prefers conceived-of-humans and presents counterexamples to various other candidate criteria. For instance, he argues against viability as the criterion because the newborn and infirm would then be nonpersons, since they cannot live without the aid of others. He rejects any criterion that calls upon the sorts of sentiments a being can evoke in adults on the grounds that this would allow us to exclude other races as nonpersons if we could just view them sufficiently unsentimentally.

These approaches are typical: foes of abortion propose sufficient conditions for personhood which fetuses satisfy, while friends of abortion counter with necessary conditions for personhood which fetuses lack. But these both presuppose that the concept of a person can be captured in a straightjacket of necessary and/or sufficient conditions.[7] Rather, "person" is a cluster of features, of which rationality, having a self-concept, and being conceived of humans are only a part.

What is typical of persons? Within our concept of a person we include, first, certain biological factors: descended from humans, having a certain genetic makeup; having a head, hands, arms, eyes; capable of locomotion, breathing, eating, sleeping. There are psychological factors: sentience, perception, having a concept of self and of one's own interests and desires, the ability to use tools, the ability to use language or symbol systems, the ability to joke, to be angry, to doubt. There are rationality factors: the ability to reason and draw conclusions, the ability to generalize and to learn from past experience, the ability to sacrifice present interests for greater gains in the future. There are social factors: the ability to work in groups and respond to peer pressures; the ability to recognize and consider as valuable the interests of others; seeing oneself as among "other minds"; the ability to sympathize, encourage, love; the ability to evoke from others the responses of sympathy, encouragement, love; the ability to work with others for mutual advantage. Then there are legal factors: being subject to the law and protected by it, having the ability to sue and enter contracts, being counted in the census, having a name and citizenship, the ability to own property, inherit, and so forth.

Now the point is not that this list is incomplete or that you can find counterinstances to each of its points. People typically exhibit rationality, for instance, but someone who was irrational would not thereby fail to qualify as a person. On the other hand, something could exhibit the majority of these features and still fail to be a person, as an advanced robot might. There is no single core of necessary and sufficient features which we can draw upon with the assurance that they constitute what really makes a person; there are only features that are more or less typical.

This is not to say that no necessary or sufficient conditions can be given. Being alive is a necessary condition for being a person, and being a U.S. senator is sufficient. But rather than falling inside a sufficient condition or outside a necessary one, a fetus lies in the penumbra region where our concept of a person is not so simple. For this reason I think a conclusive answer to the question whether a fetus is a person is unattainable.

Here we might note a family of simple fallacies that proceed by stating a necessary condition for personhood and showing that a fetus has that characteristic. This is a form of the fallacy of affirming the consequent. For example, some have mistakenly reasoned from the premise that a fetus is human (after all, it is a human fetus rather than, say, a canine fetus) to the conclusion that it is a human. Adding an equivocation on "being," we get the fallacious argument that since a fetus is something both living and human, it is a human being.

Nonetheless, it does seem clear that a fetus has very few of the above family of characteristics, whereas a newborn baby exhibits a much larger proportion of them—and a two-year-old has even more. Note that one traditional anti-abortion argument has centered on pointing out the many ways in which a fetus resembles a baby. They emphasize its development ("It already has ten fingers ...") without mentioning its dissimilarities to adults (it still has gills and a tail). They also try to evoke the sort of sympathy on our part that we only feel toward other persons ("Never to laugh ... or feel the sunshine?"). This all seems to be a relevant way to argue, since its purpose is to persuade us that a fetus satisfies so many of the important features on the list that it ought to be treated as a person. Also note that a fetus near the time of birth satisfies many more of these factors than a fetus in the early months of development. This could provide reason for making distinctions among the different stages of pregnancy, as the U.S. Supreme Court has done.[8]

Historically, the time at which a person had been said to come into existence has varied widely. Muslims date personhood from fourteen days after conception. Some medievals followed Aristotle in placing ensoulment at forty days after conception for a male fetus and eighty days for a female fetus.[9] In European common law since the seventeenth century, abortion was considered the killing of a person only after quickening, the time when a pregnant woman first feels the fetus move on its own. Nor is this variety of opinions surprising. Biologically, a human being develops gradually. We shouldn't expect there to be any specific time or sharp dividing point when a person appears on the scene.

For these reasons I believe our concept of a person is not sharp or decisive enough to bear the weight of a solution to the abortion controversy. To use it to solve that problem is to clarify *obscurum per obscurius*.

II

Next let us consider what follows if a fetus is a person after all. Judith Jarvis Thomson's landmark article, "A Defense of Abortion,"[10] correctly points out that some additional argumentation is needed at this point in the conservative argument to bridge the gap between the premise that a fetus is an innocent person and the conclusion that killing it is always wrong. To arrive at this conclusion, we would need the additional premise that killing an innocent person is always wrong. But killing an innocent person is sometimes permissible, most notably in self-defense. Some examples may help draw out our intuitions or ordinary judgments about self-defense.

Suppose a mad scientist, for instance, hypnotized innocent people to jump out of the bushes and attack innocent passersby with knives. If you are so attacked, we agree you have a right to kill the attacker in self-defense if killing him is the only way to protect your life or to save yourself from serious injury. It does not seem to matter here that the attacker is not malicious but himself an innocent pawn, for your killing of him is not done in a spirit of retribution but only in self-defense.

How severe an injury may you inflict in self-defense? In part this depends upon the severity of the injury to be avoided: you may not shoot someone merely to avoid having your clothes torn. This might lead one to the mistaken conclusion that the defense may only equal the threatened injury in severity; that to avoid death you may kill, but to avoid a black eye you may only inflict a black eye or the equivalent. Rather, our laws and customs seem to say that you may create an injury somewhat, but not enormously, greater than the injury to be avoided. To fend off an attack whose outcome would be as serious as rape, a severe beating, or the loss of a finger, you may shoot; to avoid having your clothes torn, you may blacken an eye.

Aside from this, the injury you may inflict should only be the minimum necessary to deter or incapacitate the attacker. Even if you know he intends to kill you, you are not justified in shooting him if you could equally well save yourself by the simple expedient of running away. Self-defense is for the purpose of avoiding harms rather than equalizing harms.

Some cases of pregnancy present a parallel situation. Though the fetus is itself innocent, it may pose a threat to the pregnant woman's wellbeing, life prospects, or health, mental or physical. If the pregnancy presents a slight threat to her interests, it seems self-defense cannot justify abortion. But if the threat is on a par with a serious beating or the loss of a finger, she may kill the fetus that poses such a threat, even if it is an innocent person. If a lesser harm to the fetus could have the same defensive effect, killing it would not be justified. It is unfortunate that the only way to free the woman from the pregnancy entails the death of the fetus (except in very late stages of pregnancy). Thus, a self-defense model supports Thomson's point that the woman has a right only to be freed from the fetus, not a right to demand its death.[11]

The self-defense model is most helpful when we take the pregnant woman's point of view. In the pre-Thomson literature, abortion is often framed as a question for a third party: do you, a doctor, have a right to choose between the life of the woman and that of the fetus? Some have claimed that if you were a passerby who witnessed a struggle between the innocent hypnotized attacker and his equally innocent hypnotized victim, you would have no reason to kill either in defense of the other. They have concluded that the self-defense model implies that a woman may attempt to abort herself but that a doctor should not assist her. I think the position of the third party is somewhat more complex. We do feel some inclination to intervene on behalf of the victim rather than the attacker, other things being equal. But if both parties are innocent, other factors come into consideration. You would rush to the aid of your husband whether he was attacker or attackee. If a hypnotized famous violinist were attacking a skid row bum, we would try to save the individual who is of more value to society. These considerations would tend to support abortion in some cases.

But suppose you are a frail senior citizen who wishes to avoid being knifed by one of these innocent hypnotics, so you have hired a bodyguard to accompany you. If you are attacked, it is clear we believe that the bodyguard, acting as your agent, has a right to kill the attacker to save you from a serious beating. Your rights of self-defense are transferred to your agent. I suggest that we should similarly view the doctor as the pregnant woman's agent in carrying out a defense that she is physically incapable of accomplishing herself.

Thanks to modern technology, the cases are rare in which a pregnancy poses as clear a threat to a woman's bodily health as an attacker brandishing a switchblade. How does self-defense fare when more subtle, complex, and long-range harms are involved?

To consider a somewhat fanciful example, suppose you are a highly trained surgeon when you are kidnapped by the hypnotic attacker. He says he does not intend to harm you but to take you back to the mad scientist who, it turns out, plans to hypnotize you to have a permanent mental block against all your knowledge of medicine. This would automatically destroy your career, which would in turn have a serious adverse impact on your family, your personal relationships and your happiness. It seems to me that if the only way you can avoid this outcome is to shoot the innocent attacker, you are justified in so doing. You are defending yourself from a drastic injury to your life prospects. I think it is no exaggeration to claim that unwanted pregnancies (most obviously among teenagers) often have such adverse lifelong consequences as the surgeon's loss of livelihood.

Several parallels arise between various views on abortion and the self-defense model. Let's suppose further that these hypnotized attackers only operate at night, so that it is well known that they can be avoided completely by the considerable inconvenience of never leaving your house after dark. One view is that since you could stay home at night, therefore if you go out and are selected by one of these hypnotized people, you have no right to defend yourself. This parallels the view that abstinence is the only acceptable way to avoid pregnancy. Others might hold that you ought to take along some defense such as Mace which will deter the hypnotized person without killing him, but that if this defense fails, you are obliged to submit to the resulting injury, no matter how severe it is. This parallels the view that contraception is all right but abortion is always wrong, even in cases of contraceptive failure.

A third view is that you may kill the hypnotized person only if he will actually kill you, but not if he will only injure you. This is like the position that abortion is permissible only if it is required to save a woman's life. Finally we have the view that it is all right to kill the attacker, even if only to avoid a very slight inconvenience to yourself and even if you knowingly walked down the very street where all these incidents have been taking place without taking along any Mace or protective escort. If we assume that a fetus is a person, this is the analogue of the view that abortion is always justifiable "on demand."

The self-defense model allows us to see an important difference that exists between abortion and infanticide, even if a fetus is a person from conception. Many have argued that the only way to justify abortion without justifying infanticide would be to find some characteristic of personhood that is acquired at birth. Michael Tooley, for one, claims infanticide is justifiable because the really significant characteristics of a person are acquired some time after birth. But all such approaches look to characteristics of the developing human and ignore the relation between the fetus and the woman. What if, after birth, the presence of an infant or the need to support it posed a grave threat to the woman's sanity or life prospects? She could escape this threat by the simple expedient of running away. So a solution that does not entail the death of the infant is available. Before birth, such solutions are not available because of the biological dependence of the fetus on the woman. Birth is the crucial point not because of any characteristics the fetus gains but because after birth the woman can defend herself by a means less drastic than killing the infant. Hence, self-defense can be used to justify abortion without necessarily thereby justifying infanticide.

III

On the other hand, supposing a fetus is not after all a person, would abortion always be morally permissible? Some opponents of abortion seem worried that if a fetus is not a full-fledged person, then we are justified in treating it in any way at all. However, this does not follow. Nonpersons do get some consideration in our moral code, though of course they do not have the same rights as persons have (and in general they do not have moral responsibilities) and though their interests may be overridden by the interests of persons. Still, we cannot just treat them in any way at all.

Treatment of animals is a case in point. It is wrong to torture dogs for fun or to kill wild birds for no reason at all. It is wrong period, even though dogs and birds do not have the same rights persons do. However, few people think it is wrong to use dogs as experimental animals, causing them considerable suffering in some cases, provided that the resulting research will probably bring discoveries of great benefit to people. And most of us think it is all right to kill birds for food or to protect our crops. People's rights are different from the consideration we give to animals, then, for it is wrong to experiment on people, even if others might later benefit a great deal as a result of their suffering. You might volunteer to be a subject, but this would be supererogatory [more than is morally required]; you certainly have a right to refuse to be a medical guinea pig.

But how do we decide what you may or may not do to nonpersons? This is a difficult problem, one for which I believe no adequate account exists. You do not want to say, for instance, that torturing dogs is all right whenever the sum of its effects on people is good—when it doesn't warp the sensibilities of the torturer so much that he mistreats people. If that were the case, it would be all right to torture dogs if you did it in private or if the torturer lived on a desert island or died soon afterward, so that his actions had no effect on people. This is an inadequate account, because whatever moral consideration animals get, it has to be indefeasible, too. It will have to be a general proscription of certain actions, not merely a weighing of the impact on people on a case-by-case basis.

Rather, we need to distinguish two levels on which consequences of actions can be taken into account in moral reasoning. ... An ethical theory must operate by generating a set of sympathies and attitudes toward others which reinforce the functioning of that set of moral principles. Our prohibition against killing people operates by means of certain moral sentiments, including sympathy, compassion, and guilt. But if these attitudes are to form a coherent set, they carry us further: we tend to perform supererogatory actions, and we tend to feel similar compassion toward personlike nonpersons.

It is crucial that psychological facts play a role here. Our psychological constitution makes it the case that for our ethical theory to work, it must prohibit certain treatment of nonpersons which are significantly personlike. If our moral rules allowed people to treat some personlike nonpersons in ways we do not want people to be treated, this would undermine the system of sympathies and attitudes that makes the ethical system work. ... Thus it makes sense that it is those animals whose appearance and behavior are most like those of people that get the most consideration in our moral scheme.

It is because of "coherence of attitudes," I think, that the similarity of a fetus to a baby is very significant. A fetus one week before birth is so much like a newborn baby in our psychological space that we cannot allow any cavalier treatment of the former while expecting full sympathy and nurturative support for the latter. Thus, I think that anti-abortion forces are indeed giving their strongest arguments when they point to the similarities between a fetus and a baby and when they try to evoke our emotional attachment to and sympathy for the fetus. An early horror story from New York about nurses who were expected to alternate between caring for six-week premature infants and disposing of viable 24-week aborted fetuses is just that—a horror story. These beings are so much alike that no one can be asked to draw a distinction and treat them so very differently.

Remember, however, that in the early weeks after conception, a fetus is very much unlike a person. It is hard to develop these feelings for a set of genes which doesn't yet have a head, hands, beating heart, response to touch, or the ability to move by itself. Thus it seems to me that the alleged "slippery slope" between conception and birth is not so very slippery. In the early stages of pregnancy, abortion can hardly be compared to murder for psychological reasons, but in the latest stages it is psychologically akin to murder.

Another source of similarity is the bodily continuity between fetus and adult. Bodies play a surprisingly central role in our attitudes toward persons. One has only to think of the philosophical literature on how far physical identity suffices for personal identity or Wittgenstein's remark that the best picture of the human soul is the human body. Even after death, when all agree the body is no longer a person, we still observe elaborate customs of respect for the human body; like people who torture dogs, necrophiliacs are not to be trusted with people.[12] So it is appropriate that we show respect to a fetus as the body continuous with the body of a person. This is a degree of resemblance to persons that animals cannot rival.

Michael Tooley also utilizes a parallel with animals. He claims that it is always permissible to drown newborn kittens and draws conclusions about infanticide.[13] But it is only permissible to drown kittens when their survival would cause some hardship. Perhaps it would be a burden to feed and house six more cats or to find other homes for them. The alternative of letting them starve produces even more suffering than the drowning. Since the kittens get their rights secondhand, so to speak, via the need for coherence in our attitudes, their interests are often overridden by the interests of full-fledged persons. But if their survival would be no inconvenience to people at all, then it is wrong to drown them, contra Tooley.

Tooley's conclusions about abortion are wrong for the same reason. Even if a fetus is not a person, abortion is not always permissible, because of the resemblance of a fetus to a person. I agree with Thomson that it would be wrong for a woman who is seven months pregnant to have an abortion just to avoid having to postpone a trip to Europe. In the early months of pregnancy, when the fetus hardly resembles a baby at all, then, abortion is permissible whenever it is in the interests of the pregnant woman or her family. The reasons would only need to outweigh the pain and inconvenience of the abortion itself. In the middle months, when the fetus comes to resemble a person, abortion would be justifiable only when the continuation of the pregnancy or the birth of the child would cause harms—physical, psychological, economic, or social—to the woman. In the late months of pregnancy, even on our current assumption that a fetus is not a person, abortion seems to be wrong except to save a woman from significant injury or death.

The Supreme Court has recognized similar gradations in the alleged slippery slope stretching between conception and birth. To this point, the present paper has been a discussion of the moral status of abortion only, not its legal status. In view of the great physical, financial, and sometimes psychological costs of abortion, perhaps the legal arrangement most compatible with the proposed moral solution would be the absence of restrictions, that is, so-called abortion on demand.

So I conclude, first, that application of our concept of a person will not suffice to settle the abortion issue. After all, the biological development of a human being is gradual. Second, whether a fetus is a person or not, abortion is justifiable early in pregnancy to avoid modest harms and seldom justifiable late in pregnancy except to avoid significant injury or death.

Notes

1. We also have paternalistic laws which keep us from harming our own bodies even when no one else is affected. Ironically, anti-abortion laws were originally designed to protect pregnant women from a dangerous but tempting procedure.
2. Warren, M. A., "On the moral and legal status of abortion," *Monist* 57 (1973): 43–61.
3. Brody, B., "Fetal humanity and the theory of essentialism," in Baker, R. and F. Elliston eds., *Philosophy and Sex*. Buffalo, NY, 1975.
4. Tooley, M., "Abortion and infanticide," *Philosophy and Public Affairs* 1, 1971.
5. Ramsey, P. "The morality of abortion" in Rachels, J. ed., *Moral Problems*. New York, 1971.
6. Noonan, J., "Abortion and the Catholic church: a summary history," *Natural Law Forum* 12: 125–131, 1967.
7. Wittgenstein has argued against the possibility of so capturing the concept of a game; *Philosophical Investigations* (New York, 1958), §66–71.
8. Not because the fetus is partly a person and so has some of the rights of persons but rather because of the rights of personlike nonpersons ....
9. Aristotle himself was concerned, however, with the different question of when the soul takes form. For historical data, see Jimmye Kimmey, "How the abortion laws happened," *Ms.* 1 (April 1973) 48ff and John Noonan, "Abortion and the Catholic church."
10. Thomson, J. J., "A defense of abortion," *Philosophy and Public Affairs* 1, 1971.
11. Ibid.
12. On the other hand, if they can be trusted with people, then our moral customs are mistaken. It all depends on the facts of psychology.
13. Tooley, "Abortion and infanticide."

Review and Discussion Questions

1. What is the "typical" approach to the abortion question, according to English?
2. In what ways does English think a fetus resembles a person? In what ways does it not?
3. What conclusion does English reach about the attempt to solve the abortion question by asking if the fetus is a person?

4 Explain English's reasoning about self-defense and its relevance to the abortion controversy.
5 Suppose you were Judith Jarvis Thomson. Write an essay explaining whether and in what ways you either agree or disagree with English's essay.
6 Compare Michael Tooley's position on the nature of a person with other articles in this chapter. What problems do you see with Tooley's position? How might he respond?
7 What does English mean by "coherence of attitudes"? What is the importance of such coherence in attitudes for how we treat fetuses, according to English?

READING: AN ARGUMENT THAT ABORTION IS WRONG

DON MARQUIS[*]

After a brief critical discussion of Thomson's defense of abortion, Don Marquis develops an approach to the abortion question that first looks at the broader question of why it is wrong to kill, say, the readers of this book. The reason why standard murder is wrong, he claims, is that it deprives the victim of a future, just as abortion deprives another human being of a future. After giving four reasons why we should accept the "future like our own" theory, he concludes by responding to three objections to the position he has presented. Don Marquis is Emeritus Professor of Philosophy at the University of Kansas.

The purpose of this essay is to set out an argument for the claim that abortion, except perhaps in rare instances, is seriously wrong.[1] One reason for these exceptions is to eliminate from consideration cases whose ethical analysis should be controversial and detailed for clear-headed opponents of abortion. Such cases include abortion after rape and abortion during the first fourteen days after conception, when there is an argument that the fetus is not definitely an individual. Another reason for making these exceptions is to allow for those cases in which the permissibility of abortion is compatible with the argument of this essay. Such cases include abortion when continuation of a pregnancy endangers a woman's life and abortion when the fetus is anencephalic. When I speak of the wrongness of abortion in this essay, a reader should presume the above qualifications. I mean by an abortion an action intended to bring about the death of a fetus for the sake of the woman who carries it. (Thus, as is standard on the literature on this subject, I eliminate spontaneous abortions from consideration.) I mean by a fetus a developing human being from the time of conception to the time of birth. (Thus, as is standard, I call embryos and zygotes fetuses.)

The argument of this essay will establish that abortion is wrong for the same reason as killing a reader of this essay. I shall just assume, rather than establish, that killing you is seriously wrong. I shall make no attempt to offer a complete ethics of killing.

---

[*] "An Argument That Abortion Is Wrong" (pp. 91–102) by Don Marquis from *Ethics in Practice: An Anthology*, 1st edition by Hugh Lafollette. Copyright © 1997 by Blackwell Publishers Ltd. Reprinted by permission of Blackwell Publishing Ltd.

Finally, I shall make no attempt to resolve some very fundamental and difficult general philosophical issues into which this analysis of the ethics of abortion might lead.

Why the Debate Over Abortion Seems Intractable

Symmetries that emerge from the analysis of the major arguments on either side of the abortion debate may explain why the abortion debate seems intractable. Consider the following standard anti-abortion argument: fetuses are both human and alive. Humans have the right to life. Therefore, fetuses have the right to life. Of course, women have the right to control their own bodies, but the right to life overrides the right of a woman to control her own body. Therefore, abortion is wrong ....

Thomson's View

Judith Thomson (1971) has argued that even if one grants (for the sake of argument only) that fetuses have the right to life, this argument fails. Thomson invites you to imagine that you have been connected while sleeping, bloodstream to bloodstream, to a famous violinist. The violinist, who suffers from a rare blood disease, will die if disconnected. Thomson argues that you surely have the right to disconnect yourself. She appeals to our intuition that having to lie in bed with a violinist for an indefinite period is too much for morality to demand. She supports this claim by noting that the body being used is your body, not the violinist's body. She distinguishes the right to life, which the violinist clearly has, from the right to use someone else's body when necessary to preserve one's life, which it is not at all obvious the violinist has. Because the case of pregnancy is like the case of the violinist, one is no more morally obligated to remain attached to a fetus than to remain attached to the violinist.

It is widely conceded that one can generate from Thomson's vivid case the conclusion that abortion is morally permissible when a pregnancy is due to rape (Warren, 1973, 49; Steinbock, 1992, 79). But this is hardly a general right to abortion. Do Thomson's more general theses generate a more general right to an abortion? Thomson draws our attention to the fact that in a pregnancy, although a fetus uses a woman's body as a life-support system, a pregnant woman does not use a fetus's body as a life-support system. However, an opponent of abortion might draw our attention to the fact that in an abortion the life that is lost is the fetus's, not the woman's. This symmetry seems to leave us with a standoff.

Thomson points out that a fetus's right to life does not entail its right to use someone else's body to preserve its life. However, an opponent of abortion might point out that a woman's right to use her own body does not entail her right to end someone else's life in order to do what she wants with her body. In reply, one might argue that a pregnant woman's right to control her own body doesn't come to much if it is wrong for her to take any action that ends the life of the fetus within her. However, an opponent of abortion can argue that the fetus's right to life doesn't come to much if a pregnant woman can end it when she chooses. The consequence of all of these symmetries seems to be a standoff. But if we have the standoff, then one might argue that we are left with a conflict of rights: a fetal right to life versus the right of a woman to control her own body. One might then argue that the right to life seems to be a stronger right than the right to control one's own body in the case of abortion because the loss of one's life is a greater loss than the loss of the right to control one's own body in one respect for nine months. Therefore, the right to life overrides the right to control one's own body and abortion is wrong. Considerations like these have suggested to both opponents of abortion and supporters of choice that a Thomsonian strategy for defending a general right to abortion will not succeed. In fairness, one must note that Thomson did not intend her strategy to generate a general moral permissibility of abortion.

Do Fetuses Have the Right to Life?

The above considerations suggest that whether abortion is morally permissible boils down to the question of whether fetuses have the right to life. An argument that fetuses either have or lack the right to life must be based upon some general criterion for having or lacking the right to life. Opponents of abortion, on the one hand, look around for the broadest possible plausible criterion so that fetuses will fall under it. This explains why classic arguments against abortion appeal to the criterion of being human. This criterion appears plausible: the claim that all humans, whatever their race, gender, religion, or *age*, have the right to life seems evident enough. In addition, because the fetuses we are concerned with don't, after all, belong to another species, they are clearly human. Thus, the syllogism that generates the conclusion that fetuses have the right to life is apparently sound.

On the other hand, those who believe abortion is morally permissible wish to find a narrow, but plausible, criterion for possession of the right to life so that fetuses will fall outside of it. This explains, in part, why the standard pro-choice arguments in the philosophical literature appeal to the criterion of being a person (Warren, 1973). [Reprinted earlier—Ed. note.] This criterion appears plausible: the claim that only persons have the right to life seems evident enough. Furthermore, because fetuses are neither rational nor possess the capacity to communicate in complex ways nor possess a concept of self that continues through time, no fetus is a person. Thus, the syllogism needed to generate the conclusion that no fetus possesses the right to life is apparently sound. Given that no fetus possesses the right to life, a woman's right to control her own body easily generates the general right to abortion. The existence of two apparently defensible syllogisms which support contrary conclusions helps to explain why partisans on both sides of the abortion dispute often regard their opponents as either morally depraved or mentally deficient.

Which syllogism should we reject? The anti-abortion syllogism is usually attacked by attacking its major premise: the claim that whatever is biologically human has the right to life. This premise is subject to scope problems because the class of the biologically human includes too much: human cancer-cell cultures are biologically human, but they do not have the right to life. Moreover, this premise also is subject to moral relevance problems: the connection between the biological and the moral is merely assumed. It is hard to think of a good *argument* for such a connection. If one wishes to consider the category of human a moral category, as some people find it plausible to do in other contexts, then one is left with no way of showing that the fetus is fully human without begging the question. Thus, the classic anti-abortion argument appears subject to fatal difficulties.

These difficulties with the classic anti-abortion argument are well known and thought by many to be conclusive. The symmetrical difficulties with the classic pro-choice syllogism are not as well recognized. The pro-choice syllogism can be attacked by attacking its major premise: only persons have the right to life. This premise is subject to scope problems because the class of persons includes too little: infants, the severely retarded, and some of the mentally ill seem to fall outside the class of persons as the supporter of choice understands the concept. The premise is also subject to moral relevance problems: being a person is understood by the pro-choicer as having certain psychological attributes. If the pro-choicer questions the connection between the biological and the moral, the opponent of abortion can question the connection between the psychological and the moral. If one wishes to consider "person" a moral category, as is often done, then one is left with no way of showing that the fetus is not a person without begging the question ....

The argument of this section has attempted to establish, albeit briefly, that the classic anti-abortion argument and the pro-choice argument favored by most philosophers both face problems that are mirror images of one another. A standoff results. The abortion debate requires a different strategy.

The "Future Like Ours" Account of the Wrongness of Killing

Why do the standard arguments in the abortion debate fail to resolve the issue? The general principles to which partisans in the debate appeal are either truisms most persons would affirm in the absence of much reflection or very general moral theories. All are subject to major problems. A different approach is needed.

Opponents of abortion claim that abortion is wrong because abortion involves killing someone like us, a human being who just happens to be very young. Supporters of choice claim that ending the life of a fetus is not in the same moral category as ending the life of an adult human being. Surely this controversy cannot be resolved in the absence of an account of what it is about killing us that makes killing us wrong. On the one hand, if we know what property we possess that makes killing us wrong, then we can ask whether fetuses have the same property. On the other hand, suppose that we do not know what it is about us that makes killing us wrong. If this is so, we do not understand even easy cases in which killing is wrong. Surely we will not understand the ethics of killing fetuses, for if we do not understand easy cases, then we will not understand hard cases. Both pro-choicer and anti-abortionist agree that it is obvious that it is wrong to kill us. Thus, a discussion of what it is about us that makes killing us not only wrong but seriously wrong seems to be the right place to begin a discussion of the abortion issue.

Who is primarily wronged by a killing? The wrong of killing is not primarily explained in terms of the loss to the family and friends of the victim. Perhaps the victim is a hermit. Perhaps one's friends find it easy to make new friends. The wrong of killing is not primarily explained in terms of the brutalization of the killer. The great wrong to the victim explains the brutalization, not the other way around. The wrongness of killing us is understood in terms of what killing does to us. Killing us imposes on us the misfortune of premature death. That misfortune underlies the wrongness.

Premature death is a misfortune because when one is dead, one has been deprived of life. This misfortune can be more precisely specified. Premature death cannot deprive me of my past life. That part of my life is already gone. If I die tomorrow or if I live thirty more years my past life would be no different. It has occurred on either alternative. Rather than my past, my death deprives me of my future, of the life that I would have lived if I live out my natural life span.

The loss of a future biological life does not explain the misfortune of death. Compare two scenarios: in the former, I now fall into a coma from which I do not recover until my death in thirty years. In the latter, I die now. The latter scenario does not seem to describe a greater misfortune than the former.

The loss of our future conscious life is what underlies the misfortune of premature death. Not any future conscious life qualifies, however. Suppose that I am terminally ill with cancer. Suppose also that pain and suffering would dominate my future conscious life. If so, then death would not be a misfortune for me.

Thus, the misfortune of premature death consists of the loss to us of the future goods of consciousness. What are these goods? Much can be said about this issue, but a simple answer will do for the purposes of this essay. The goods of life are whatever we get out of life. The goods of life are those items toward which we take a "pro" attitude. They are completed projects of which we are proud, the pursuit of our goals, aesthetic enjoyments, friendships, intellectual pursuits, and physical pleasures of various sorts. The goods of life are what make life worth living. In general, what makes life worth living for one person will not be the same as what makes life worth living for another. Nevertheless, the list of goods in each of our lives will overlap. The lists are usually different in different stages of our lives.

What makes the goods of my future good for me? One possible, but wrong, answer is my desire for those goods now. This answer does not account for those aspects of my future life that I now believe I will later value but about which I am wrong. Neither does it account for those aspects of my future that I will come to value but which I don't value now. What is valuable to the young may not be valuable to the middle-aged. What is valuable to the middle-aged may not be valuable to the old. Some of life's values for the elderly are best appreciated by the elderly. Thus, it is wrong to say that the value of my future to me is just what I value now. What makes my future valuable to me are those aspects of my future that I will (or would) value when I will (or would) experience them, whether I value them now or not.

It follows that a person can believe that she will have a valuable future and be wrong. Furthermore, a person can believe that he will not have a valuable future and also be wrong. This is confirmed by our attitude toward many of the suicidal. We attempt to save the lives of the suicidal and to convince them that they have made an error in judgment. This does not mean that the future of an individual obtains value from the value that others confer on it. It means that, in some cases, others can make a clearer judgment of the value of a person's future *to that person* than the person herself. This often happens when one's judgment concerning the value of one's own future is clouded by personal tragedy.

Thus, what is sufficient to make killing us wrong, in general, is that it causes premature death. Premature death is a misfortune. Premature death is a misfortune, in general, because it deprives an individual of a future of value. An individual's future will be valuable to that individual if that individual will come, or would come, to value it. We know that killing us is wrong. What makes killing us wrong, in general, is that it deprives us of a future of value. Thus, killing someone is wrong, in general, when it deprives her of a future like ours. I shall call this "a FLO."

Arguments in Favor of the FLO Theory

At least four arguments support this FLO account of the wrongness of killing.

The Considered-Judgment Argument

The FLO account of the wrongness of killing is correct because it fits with our considered judgment concerning the nature of the misfortune of death. The analysis of the previous section is an exposition of the nature of this considered judgment. This judgment can be confirmed. If one were to ask individuals with AIDS or with incurable cancer about the nature of their misfortune, I believe that they would say or imply that their impending loss of an FLO makes their premature death a misfortune. If they would not, then the FLO account would plainly be wrong.

The Worst-of-Crimes Argument

The FLO account of the wrongness of killing is correct because it explains why we believe that killing is one of the worst of crimes. My being killed deprives me of more than my being robbed or beaten or harmed in some other way because my being killed deprives me of all of the value of my future, not merely part of it. This explains why we make the penalty for murder greater than the penalty for other crimes.

As a corollary, the FLO account of the wrongness of killing also explains why killing an adult human being is justified only in the most extreme circumstances, only in circumstances in which the loss of life to an individual is outweighed by a worse outcome if that life is not taken. Thus, we are willing to justify killing in self-defense, killing in order to save one's own life, because one's loss if one does not kill in that situation is so very great. We justify killing in a just war for similar reasons. We believe that capital punishment would be justified if, by having such an institution, fewer premature deaths would occur. The FLO account of the wrongness of killing does not entail that killing is always wrong. Nevertheless, the FLO account both explains why killing is one of the worst of crimes and, as a corollary, why the exceptions to the wrongness of killing are so very rare. A correct theory of the wrongness of killing should have these features.

The Appeal-to-Cases Argument

The FLO account of the wrongness of killing is correct because it yields the correct answers in many life-and-death cases that arise in medicine and have interested philosophers.

Consider medicine first. Most people believe that it is not wrong deliberately to end the life of a person who is permanently unconscious. Thus, we believe that it is not wrong to remove a feeding tube or a ventilator from a permanently comatose patient knowing that such a removal will cause death. The FLO account of the wrongness of killing explains why this is so. A patient who is permanently unconscious cannot have a future that she would come to value, whatever her values. Therefore, according to the FLO theory of the wrongness of killing, death could not, *ceteris paribus*, be a misfortune to her. Therefore, removing the feeding tube or ventilator does not wrong her.

By contrast, almost all people believe that it is wrong, *ceteris paribus*, to withdraw medical treatment from patients who are temporarily unconscious. The FLO account of the wrongness of killing also explains why this is so. Furthermore, these two unconsciousness cases explain why the FLO account of the wrongness of killing does not include present consciousness as a necessary condition for the wrongness of killing.

Consider now the issue of the morality of legalizing active euthanasia. Proponents of active euthanasia argue that if a patient faces a future of intractable pain and wants to die, then, *ceteris paribus*, it would not be wrong for a physician to give him medicine that she knows would result in his death. This view is so universally accepted that even the strongest *opponents* of active euthanasia hold it. The official Vatican view is that it is permissible for a physician to administer to a patient morphine sufficient (although no more than sufficient) to control his pain even if she foresees that the morphine will result in his death. Notice how nicely the FLO account of the wrongness of killing explains this unanimity of opinion. A patient known to be in severe intractable pain is presumed to have a future without positive value. Accordingly, death would not be a misfortune for him and an action that would (foreseeably) end his life would not be wrong.

Contrast this with the standard emergency medical treatment of the suicidal. Even though the suicidal have indicated that they want to die, medical personnel will act to save their lives. This supports the view that it is not the mere *desire* to enjoy a FLO which is crucial to our understanding of the wrongness of killing. *Having* a FLO is what is crucial to the account, although one would, of course, want to make an exception in the case of fully autonomous people who refuse life-saving medical treatment. Opponents of abortion can, of course, be willing to make an exception for fully autonomous fetuses who refuse life support.

The FLO theory of the wrongness of killing also deals correctly with issues that have concerned philosophers. It implies that it would be wrong to kill (peaceful) persons from outer space who come to visit our planet even though they are biologically utterly unlike us. Presumably, if they are persons, then they would have futures that are sufficiently like ours so that it would be wrong to kill them. The FLO account of the wrongness of killing shares this feature with the personhood views of the supporters of choice. Classical opponents of abortion who locate the wrongness of abortion somehow in the biological humanity of a fetus cannot explain this.

The FLO account does not entail that there is another species of animals whose members ought not be killed. Neither does it entail that it is permissible to kill any nonhuman animal. On the one hand, a supporter of animals' rights might argue that since some nonhuman animals have a future of value, it is wrong to kill them also, or at least it is wrong to kill them without a far better reason than we usually have for killing nonhuman animals. On the other hand, one might argue that the futures of nonhuman animals are not sufficiently like ours for the FLO account to entail that it is wrong to kill them. Since the FLO account does not specify which properties a future of another individual must possess so that killing that individual is wrong, the FLO account is indeterminate with respect to this issue. The fact that the FLO account of the wrongness of killing does not give a determinate answer to this question is not a flaw in the theory. A sound ethical account should yield the right answers in the obvious cases; it should not be required to resolve every disputed question.

A major respect in which the FLO account is superior to accounts that appeal to the concept of person is the explanation the FLO account provides of the wrongness of killing infants. There was a class of infants who had futures that include a class of events that are identical to the futures of the readers of this essay. Thus, reader, the FLO account explains why it was as wrong to kill you when you were an infant as it is to kill you now. This account can be generalized to almost all infants. Notice that the wrongness of killing infants can be explained in the absence of an account of what makes a future of an individual sufficiently valuable so that it is wrong to kill that individual. The absence of such an account explains why the FLO account is indeterminate with respect to the wrongness of killing nonhuman animals.

If the FLO account is the correct theory of the wrongness of killing, then because abortion involves killing fetuses and fetuses have FLOs for exactly the same reasons that infants have FLOs, abortion is presumptively seriously immoral. This inference lays the necessary groundwork for a fourth argument in favor of the FLO account that shows that abortion is wrong.

The Analogy-With-Animals Argument

Why do we believe it is wrong to cause animal suffering? We believe that in our own case and in the case of other adults and children, suffering is a misfortune. It would be as morally arbitrary to refuse to acknowledge that animal suffering is wrong as it would be to refuse to acknowledge that the suffering of persons of another race is wrong. It is, on reflection, suffering that is a misfortune, not the suffering of white males or the suffering of humans. Therefore, infliction of suffering is presumptively wrong no matter on whom it is inflicted and whether it is inflicted on persons or nonpersons. Arbitrary restrictions on the wrongness of suffering count as racism or speciesism. Not only is this argument convincing on its own, but it is the only way of justifying the wrongness of animal cruelty. Cruelty toward animals is clearly wrong. [This famous argument is due to Singer (1979)—Ed. note.]

The FLO account of the wrongness of abortion is analogous. We believe that in our own case and the cases of other adults and children, the loss of a future of value is a misfortune. It would be as morally arbitrary to refuse to acknowledge that the loss of a future of value to a fetus is wrong as to refuse to acknowledge that the loss of a future of value to Jews (to take a relevant twentieth-century example) is wrong. It is, on reflection, the loss of a future of value that is a misfortune, not the loss of a future of value to adults or loss of a future of value to non-Jews. To deprive someone of a future of value is wrong no matter on whom the deprivation is inflicted and no matter whether the deprivation is inflicted on persons or nonpersons. Arbitrary restrictions on the wrongness of this deprivation count as racism, genocide or ageism. Therefore, abortion is wrong. This argument that abortion is wrong should be convincing because it has the same form as the argument for the claim that causing pain and suffering to nonhuman animals is wrong. Since the latter argument is convincing, the former argument should be also. Thus, an analogy with animals supports the thesis that abortion is wrong.

Replies to Objections

The four arguments in the previous section establish that abortion is, except in rare cases, seriously immoral. Not surprisingly, there are objections to this view. There are replies to the [three] most important objections to the FLO argument for the immorality of abortion.

The Potentiality Objection

The FLO account of the wrongness of abortion is a potentiality argument. To claim that a fetus *has* a FLO is to claim that a fetus now has the potential to be in a state of a certain kind in the future. It is not to claim that all ordinary fetuses *will* have FLOs. Fetuses who are aborted, of course, will not. To say that a standard fetus has a FLO is to say that a standard fetus either will have or would have a life it will or would value. To say that a standard fetus would have a life it would value is to say that it will have a life it will value if it does not die prematurely. The truth of this conditional is based upon the nature of fetuses (including the fact that they naturally age), and this nature concerns their potential.

Some appeals to potentiality in the abortion debate rest on unsound inferences. For example, one may try to generate an argument against abortion by arguing that because persons have the right to life, potential persons also have the right to life. Such an argument is plainly invalid as it stands. The premise one needs to add to make it valid would have to be something like: "If X's have the right to Y, then potential X's have the right to Y." This premise is plainly false. Potential presidents don't have the rights of the presidency; potential voters don't have the right to vote.

In the FLO argument, potentiality is not used in order to bridge the gap between adults and fetuses, as is done in the argument in the above paragraph. The FLO theory of the wrongness of killing adults is based upon the adult's potentiality to have a future of value. Potentiality is in the argument from the very beginning. Thus, the plainly false premise is not required. Accordingly, the use of potentiality in the FLO theory is not a sign of an illegitimate inference.

The Argument from Interests

A second objection to the FLO account of the immorality of abortion involves arguing that even though fetuses have FLOs, nonsentient fetuses do not meet the minimum conditions for having any moral standing at all because they lack interests. Steinbock (1992, 5) has presented this argument clearly:

> Beings that have moral status must be capable of caring about what is done to them. They must be capable of being made, if only in a rudimentary sense,

happy or miserable, comfortable or distressed. Whatever reasons we may have for preserving or protecting nonsentient beings, these reasons do not refer to their own interests. For without conscious awareness, beings cannot have interests. Without interests, they cannot have a welfare of their own. Without a welfare of their own, nothing can be done for their sake. Hence, they lack moral standing or status.

Medical researchers have argued that fetuses do not become sentient until after twenty-two weeks of gestation (Steinbock, 1992, 50). If they are correct, and if Steinbock's argument is sound, then we have both an objection to the FLO account of the wrongness of abortion and a basis for a view of abortion minimally acceptable to most supporters of choice.

Steinbock's conclusion conflicts with our settled moral beliefs. Temporarily unconscious human beings are nonsentient, yet no one believes that they lack either interests or moral standing. Accordingly, neither conscious awareness nor the capacity for conscious awareness is a necessary condition for having interests.

The counterexample of the temporarily unconscious human being shows that there is something internally wrong with Steinbock's argument. The difficulty stems from an ambiguity. One cannot *take* an interest in something without being capable of caring about what is done to it. However, something can be *in* someone's interest without that individual being capable of caring about it, or about anything. Thus, life support can be *in* the interests of a temporarily unconscious patient even though the temporarily unconscious patient is incapable of *taking* an interest in that life support. If this can be so for the temporarily unconscious patient, then it is hard to see why it cannot be so for the temporarily unconscious (that is, nonsentient) fetus who requires placental life support. Thus, the objection based on interests fails ....

The Contraception Objection

The strongest objection to the FLO argument for the immorality of abortion is based on the claim that because contraception results in one less FLO, the FLO argument entails that contraception, indeed, abstention from sex when conception is possible is immoral. Because neither contraception nor abstention from sex when conception is possible is immoral, the FLO account is flawed.

There is a cogent reply to this objection.

If the argument of the early part of this essay is correct, then the central issue concerning the morality of abortion is the problem of whether fetuses are individuals who are members of the class of individuals whom it is seriously presumptively wrong to kill. The properties of being human and alive, of being a person, and of having a FLO are criteria that participants in the abortion debate have offered to mark off the relevant class of individuals. The central claim of this essay is that having a FLO marks off the relevant class of individuals. A defender of the FLO view could, therefore, reply that since at the time of contraception there is no individual to have a FLO, the FLO account does not entail that contraception is wrong. The wrong of killing is primarily a wrong to the individual who is killed; at the time of contraception there is no individual to be wronged.

However, someone who presses the contraception objection might have an answer to this reply. She might say that the sperm and egg are the individuals deprived of a FLO at the time of contraception. Thus, there are individuals whom contraception deprives of a FLO and if depriving an individual of a FLO is what makes killing wrong, then the FLO theory entails that contraception is wrong.

There is also a reply to this move. In the case of abortion, an objectively determinate individual is the subject of harm caused by the loss of a FLO. This individual is a fetus. In the case of contraception, there are far more candidates. (See Norcross, 1990.) Let us consider some possible candidates in order of the increasing number of individuals harmed: (1) The single harmed individual might be the combination of the particular sperm and the particular egg that would have united to form a zygote if contraception had not been used. (2) The two harmed individuals might be the particular sperm itself, and, in addition, the ovum itself that would have physically combined to form the zygote. (This is modeled on the double homicide of two persons who would otherwise in a short time fuse. (1) is modeled on harm to a single entity some of whose parts are not physically contiguous, such as a university.) (3) The many harmed individuals might be the millions of *combinations* of sperm and released ovum whose (small) chances of having a FLO were reduced by the successful contraception. (4) The even larger class of harmed individuals (larger by one) might be the class consisting of all of the individual sperm in an ejaculate and, in addition, the individual ovum released at the time of the successful contraception. (1) through (4) are all candidates for being the subject(s) of harm in the case of successful contraception or abstinence from sex. Which should be chosen? Should we hold a lottery? There seems to be no nonarbitrarily determinate subject of harm in the case of successful contraception. But if there is no such subject of harm, then no determinate thing was harmed. If no determinate thing was harmed, then (in the case of contraception) no wrong has been done. Thus, the FLO account of the wrongness of abortion does not entail that contraception is wrong.

Conclusion

This essay contains an argument for the view that, except in unusual circumstances, abortion is seriously wrong. Deprivation of a FLO explains why killing adults and children is wrong. Abortion deprives fetuses of FLOs. Therefore, abortion is wrong. This argument is based on an account of the wrongness of killing that is a result of our considered judgment on the nature of the misfortune of premature death. It accounts for why we regard killing as one of the worst of crimes. It is superior to alternative accounts of the wrongness of killing that are intended to provide insight into the ethics of abortion. This account of the wrongness of killing is supported by the way it handles cases in which our moral judgments are settled. This account has an analogue in the most plausible account of the wrongness of causing animals to suffer. This account makes no appeal to religion. Therefore, the FLO account shows that abortion, except in rare instances, is seriously wrong.

Note

1 This essay is an updated version of a view that first appeared in the *Journal of Philosophy* (1989). This essay incorporates attempts to deal with the objections of McInerney (1990), Norcross (1990), Shirley (1995), Steinbock (1992), and Paske (1994) to the original version of the view.

Bibliography

Marquis, D. B. "Why Abortion Is Immoral." *Journal of Philosophy* 86(4) (1989): 183–202.

McInerney, P. "Does a Fetus Already Have a Future Like Ours?" *Journal of Philosophy* 87 (1990): 264–268.

Norcross, A. "Killing, Abortion, and Contraception: A Reply to Marquis." *Journal of Philosophy* 87 (1990): 268–277.

Paske, G. "Abortion and the Neo-Natal Right to Life: A Critique of Marquis's Futurist Argument" in *The Abortion Controversy: A Reader*, ed. L. P. Pojman and F. J. Beckwith (Boston, MA: Jones and Bartlett, 1994): 343–353.

Sacred Congregation for the Propagation of the Faith *Declaration on Euthanasia* (Vatican City, 1980).

Shirley, E. S. "Marquis' Argument against Abortion: A Critique." *Southwest Philosophy Review* 11 (1995): 79–89.

Singer, P. "Not for Humans Only: The Place of Nonhumans in Environmental Issues" in *Ethics and Problems of the 21st Century*, ed. K. E. Goodpaster and K. M. Sayre (South Bend, IN: Notre Dame University Press, 1979).

Steinbock, B. *Life before Birth: The Moral and Legal Status of Embryos and Fetuses* (New York: Oxford University Press, 1992).

Warren, M. A. "On the Moral and Legal Status of Abortion." *Monist* 57 (1973): 43–61.

Review and Discussion Questions

1 Why does Marquis reject Thomson's defense of abortion?
2 Describe the "future like ours" account of why killing a human being is wrong.
3 What are the four reasons Marquis gives in support of the FLO theory?
4 Explain why Marquis does not believe his theory rests on a mistaken premise about the value of potential persons.
5 Warren claims that without consciousness, beings cannot have interests. How does Marquis respond to that claim?
6 Who is right on the interests question in your view? Explain.
7 How does Marquis answer those who claim that his FLO position leads to the absurd conclusion that contraception and even abstention from sex are wrong and therefore that the FLO argument must be rejected?

READING: FATHERS AND FETUSES

GEORGE W. HARRIS[*]

In his essay, George Harris looks at an issue that has, he points out, been largely ignored in discussions about abortion: the interests and desires of the father. Is it wrong, he asks, for a woman to get an abortion on the ground that it wrongs the father? Using five very different cases as illustrations, Harris argues that the central moral issue involves how to respect the autonomy of the father, and in that light he considers how abortion decisions affect the father's legitimate interests. George W. Harris is Chancellor Professor of Philosophy Emeritus at the College of William and Mary.

---

[*] Abridged from "Fathers and Fetuses" by George W. Harris, *Ethics* 96 (1986). Copyright © 1986 by the University of Chicago Press. Reprinted by permission of Copyright Clearance Center on behalf of the publisher.

Conspicuously absent from most discussions of the abortion issue are considerations of third-party interests, especially those of the father. A survey of the literature reveals an implicit assumption by most writers that the issue is to be viewed as a two-party conflict—the rights of the fetus versus the rights of the mother—and that an adequate analysis of the balance of these rights is sufficient to determine the conditions under which abortion is morally permissible. I shall argue, however, that in some cases it would be morally impermissible for a woman to have an abortion because it would be a wrongful harm to the father and a violation of his autonomy. Moreover, I shall argue for this on principles that I believe require a strong stand on women's rights.

I

The issue I wish to discuss then is whether or not it would ever be morally wrong for a woman to have an abortion on the grounds that it would be a wrong done to the father. I leave aside the issue of the rights of the fetus since I do not consider here whether abortion under the circumstances raised might be wrong on other grounds.

Consider then the following cases which are arranged to elucidate the moral considerations involved in the analysis. The extreme cases 1 and 5 are included not so much for their intrinsic importance but because of the light they shed on the analysis of cases 2, 3, and 4. Now, to the cases.

Case 1

Karen, a healthy twenty-five-year-old woman, becomes pregnant as the result of being raped by a man with severe psychological problems. After therapy and significant improvement in his mental health, the man recognizes what he has done and is willing to accept liability for the harms he has caused and even punishment should the victim deem it necessary. His only plea is that Karen carry the fetus to term and then give it to him if she does not care to raise the child herself. Unable, however, to dissociate the fetus from the trauma of the rape, Karen decides to abort.

Case 2

Jane and Jack, two attractive, healthy individuals, meet at a party given by mutual friends. During the weeks and months that follow, a casual but pleasant sexual relationship develops between them. As a result, Jane becomes pregnant. But after learning of the pregnancy, Jack reveals that he is a moderately serious Catholic and from a combined sense of guilt, responsibility, and parental instinct proposes that they be married. Jane, on the other hand, being neither Catholic nor desirous of a husband, decides to abort. Respecting her religious differences and her right to marry whomever she pleases, Jack offers to pay all of Jane's medical expenses, to take complete responsibility for the child after it is born, and to pay her a large sum of money to carry the fetus to term. Jane nonetheless decides to proceed with the abortion.

Case 3

Susan and Charles, both in perfect health, are in the fifth year of their marriage. Aside from his love for Susan, the prospect of raising a family is the most important thing in Charles's life—more important than career, possessions, sports, or any of the other things thought to be of the utmost importance to men. Susan, on the other hand, is secretly ambivalent about having children due to her indecisiveness between having a career and having a family. But because of her love for Charles and the fear of causing him what she believes might be unnecessary anxiety, she allows him to believe that her reluctance is only with when rather than with whether to have children. And despite reasonable efforts at birth control, Susan becomes pregnant just at a point at which her career takes a significant turn for the better. In the situation, it is a career rather than children that she wants, and she decides to have an abortion. Distraught, Charles tries to dissuade her by offering to forgo his own career and to take on the role traditionally reserved for mothers, but to no avail.

Case 4

Michelle and Steve, like Susan and Charles, are also in the fifth year of their marriage. And Steve, like Charles, is equally and similarly desirous of a family. Michelle, however, knows all along that she does not want children but avoids discussing the issue with Steve, allowing him to think that the beginning of their family is just a matter of time. She believes that eventually she can disabuse him of the values of family life in favor of a simple life together. But due to the unpleasantness of broaching the subject, Michelle procrastinates and accidentally becomes pregnant. And despite Steve's expectations, his pleas, and his offer to take on the major responsibilities of raising the child, Michelle decides to abort.

Case 5

Anne is a man-hater. Resentment brought on in part by traditional male chauvinistic attitudes toward women has led her to stereotype all men as little more than barbarians. Mark is a reasonably decent man who, like Charles and Steve, desires very much to be a parent. After meeting Mark, Anne devises a plan to vicariously vent her rage through Mark on the entire male sex. Carefully playing the role of a conventionally attractive woman with traditional life plans, she sets out to seduce Mark. Soon he falls in love with her and, thinking that he has met the ideal mate, proposes marriage. She accepts and after the wedding convinces Mark that if they are to have a happy married life and a healthy environment in which to raise children he must give up his lucrative realty business and the house he inherited from his parents. Valuing his life with Anne and the prospects of a family more than his career, he sells the business at a considerable loss and takes a less lucrative job. He also sells his home and buys another, again at a considerable financial loss. Finally, Anne becomes pregnant. Initially, she plays the adorable expectant mother, intentionally heightening Mark's expectations. But later she has an abortion. Relishing Mark's horror, she further reveals her scheme and explains that his pain and loss are merely the just deserts of any man for the things that men have done to women.

In all these cases, the issue is this: if we assume that all the men could be acceptable parents and that the pregnancies are physically normal, would any of the abortions by the woman in these cases constitute a moral wrong done to any of the men? In the following sections, I shall argue that only in the third, fourth, and fifth cases is a wrongful harm done to the father and that only in the fourth and fifth cases would it be morally impermissible for the woman to proceed with the abortion. By a "wrongful harm," I shall mean a harm that could reasonably have been avoided. I shall argue that in the cases where abortion is claimed to be morally impermissible, it is so on the grounds that it violates the father's autonomy; that is, it invades the man's morally legitimate interest in self-determination. The Kantian notion of treating persons as ends—as autonomous agents in pursuit of morally legitimate interests—underlies my argument. Its role will become clearer as the argument proceeds.

II

Much of the analysis presented here turns on the issue of when it is morally significant to say that the fetus is the father's as well as the mother's. One of the things that a woman can do without violating her interest in the autonomous control of her own body is to have a baby. I do not mean that she can do this alone but that, with the cooperation of a man, she can become pregnant as a matter of unencumbered choice. And though things are a bit more difficult for a man, one of the things he can do with his body, in cooperation with a woman, is to bring new life into the world. The interest in autonomy and the interest in procreation are therefore quite compatible and are common to both women and men. The significance of this, I believe, is that when a man and a woman autonomously decide to become parents together, a harm done to the fetus by a third party without the consent of both parents is a prima facie wrong done both to the man and to the woman because it is an interference with his autonomy as well as with hers. Moreover, a harm done to the fetus is a harm done to the man as well as to the woman because the fetus is both the object and the result of his pursuing a morally legitimate interest, that is, the interest in procreation. To harm the fetus, then, is to invade the morally legitimate interest in procreation of both the father and the mother and thereby to interfere with the man's as well as the woman's autonomy. Further exploration of these observations, I believe, is crucial to the analysis of the cases already presented.

In the first case, Karen's abortion, whatever its moral standing relative to the fetus, is not a wrong done to the man who raped her. This is true despite the fact that the man was not in control of his behavior and therefore was not responsible for his actions. The biological connection between the fetus and the father in this case is not sufficient to establish that the fetus is a morally legitimate object of interest for the man. The reason is obvious. Although procreation is a morally legitimate interest that men can have, the pursuit of this interest is restricted by the requirement that men respect the autonomy of women in this regard. And since the fetus was forced upon Karen by the man, she is not required to view the fetus as a legitimate object of interest for him. The fetus then is his only in a biological sense. Any harm done to the fetus is therefore neither a violation of his autonomy nor a harm done to him by Karen. It is important to note, however, that she could decide to keep it without violating her own or anyone else's autonomy. And this makes the fetus hers in a way that it is not the man's.

Similarly, in the second case, the fetus is Jane's in a way that it is not Jack's. The reasons, however, are slightly different than in the first case. Although Jane and Jack here each autonomously decide to pursue the interests in sex, neither has decided to pursue an interest in procreation. The fact that Jack has neglected to reveal his beliefs about abortion vitiates any claim he has that a harm done to the fetus is a violation of his autonomous pursuit of procreation. Rather, he has left it to Jane to assume that his only interest is in the pleasure of sex with her, and it is only this interest that she has a moral obligation to honor in terms of his autonomy. Had she promised him love and a family in order to have sex with him, she would have violated his autonomy both in regard to his interest in sex with love and his interest in procreation. Neither of these has occurred here. But though Jane is free from considerations of Jack's autonomy in deciding whether to abort or to keep the fetus, she could decide to keep it without violating her own sense of autonomy. It is this fact that makes the fetus hers in a way that it is not Jack's. Yet by parity of reasoning, Jack is equally free from any responsibility to Jane in terms of the fetus should she decide to keep it. For, like Jane he has not given his consent to the use of his body for the pursuit of her interest in procreation. He could, however, autonomously decide to take on the responsibility for the fetus. But she could not lay claim to a violation of her autonomy if he did not so choose. Had he promised her love and a family in order to have sex with her, he would have violated her autonomy in regard to her interest in sex with love and her interest in procreation. But since he has done neither of these, she has no valid claim that the fetus is a moral liability for him.[1] Thus the pursuit of casual sex can be quite compatible with the principle of autonomy; it is nonetheless morally perilous for both men and women.

In the third case, Charles is the victim of a wrongful harm and his autonomy has been violated. Due to the fact that both men and women have a morally legitimate interest in procreation, couples have an obligation to each other to be forthright and informative about their desires and reservations about family planning. Such forthrightness is necessary if each is to pursue morally legitimate interests without violating the autonomy of the other. Susan, in this case, has clearly been negligent in this responsibility to Charles. She has allowed him to believe that his sex life with her is more than casual and includes more than an expression of his love for her; it is, in part, a legitimate pursuit of his interest in procreation.

Moreover, he has not violated her autonomy as the rapist did with Karen in the first case. Consequently, the fetus is a morally legitimate object of interest for him, and to harm it is to harm Charles—a harm that could reasonably have been avoided by Susan had she told him about her reservations and informed him that should a pregnancy occur she might very well decide in favor of abortion. And it is no excuse that she had not led Charles to believe that she would carry through with any pregnancy, for she has led him to believe that she would carry through with some pregnancy and has now made a decision that thwarts any such expectation. As a result of Susan's negligence, then, the abortion causes a wrongful harm to Charles and is a violation of his autonomy because the fetus is his as well as hers.

But does it follow from this that the abortion is morally impermissible for Susan? The abortion would be morally impermissible if and only if she has a moral obligation to carry the fetus to term. And the issue we are considering here is whether she has such an obligation to Charles. By withholding important information relevant to her own interest in procreation, she has violated his autonomy in regard to two of his legitimate interests—his interest in procreation and his interest in respecting her autonomy in regard to procreation. Therefore, since the fetus is the result of his pursuing a morally legitimate interest in a morally legitimate way with due respect for her autonomy, the fetus is his as well as hers and she has a prima facie obligation to him not to harm it. What considerations then could possibly absolve her of her obligation to Charles?

The answer cannot be found in ranking the interest in a career over an interest in procreation; I cannot see that a career is a more legitimate means of self-determination than procreation or vice versa. Rather, I believe that the answer can be found in Susan's general interest in the control of her own body when compared with the nature of her negligence. To undertake a pregnancy is a serious investment of a woman's bodily and psychological resources—an undertaking that is not similarly possible for a man. The fetus then is a threat to the mother's autonomy in a way that it is not to the father's. And though Susan is responsible for being forthright about such matters, it is certainly understandable for a woman, as it is for a man, to be undecided about how to rank an interest in a career versus an interest in a possible family. Moreover, it is understandable, though far from mature or laudable, for a person to find it difficult to talk with his or her spouse about such matters when the spouse has strong desires for a family. To say that Susan has an obligation to carry his fetus to term in this case and to sacrifice the control of her own body is, it seems to me, to overestimate the fault of her negligence by not allowing for understandable weaknesses in regard to the responsibilities of autonomy. But we must be careful not to underestimate it. She has caused Charles a serious harm, and she has violated his autonomy. For that, she is guilty.

The fourth case is much like the third, except the violation of Steve's autonomy and the consequent wrongful harm are done with deceit rather than negligence. The burden to overcome the prima facie obligation not to harm the fetus is therefore stronger for Michelle than it was for Susan because Michelle could have been expected more reasonably to have avoided the harm. Again it is understandable, though neither mature nor laudable, for a person who is deeply in love with someone with significantly different life plans, perhaps as a result of self-deception, to think that the other person can be brought around to seeing things the other way. But it is not excusable. Surely, given the importance the interest in procreation plays in the lives of some people, a normal adult can be expected on the grounds of the other person's autonomy to be honest in such situations. If so, then in the absence of countervening moral considerations it would be a wrong to Steve for Michelle to have the abortion.

The fifth case involves malicious deceit with the intent to cause harm. Only a crazed ideologue could think that the harm caused Mark is not wrongful. And only someone who thinks that men have no legitimate moral interest in procreation could think that Anne's plan does not involve a violation of his autonomy. The fetus is clearly a morally legitimate object of interest for him and therefore his as well as hers. To harm the fetus then is a prima facie harm done to Mark. And given the extent of his sacrifices, the intensity of his expectations, and the depravity of Anne's intentions, it is difficult to see how the general interest in the autonomous control of one's own body could ever be morally significant enough to allow a woman like Anne to culminate the harm she has planned by having the abortion unless the fetus seriously threatened her most fundamental welfare. To think that the general interest in the autonomous control of one's body allows a woman this kind of freedom is to sanctify female autonomy and to trivialize male autonomy—the mirror image of the chauvinism Anne claims to despise. Assuming then that Anne is physically healthy and the pregnancy is not a threat to her fundamental welfare, for her to abort is morally wrong. She has an obligation to Mark to carry through with the pregnancy ....

III

Someone might argue, however, that the wrongs in these cases can be accounted for on moral grounds that are independent of special considerations of the father or the fetus. The negligence of Susan, the deceit of Michelle, the malice of Anne all—it might be argued—are wrongs independent of abortion, and there is nothing special about abortion amid these wrongs.

Certainly negligence, deceit, and malice are wrongs independent of abortion, but it does not follow from this that there is nothing special about the wrongs here. Susan, Michelle, and Anne would, respectively, be guilty of negligence, deceit, and malice even had Charles, Steve, and Mark turned out unknowingly to be sterile. But the fact that the men were not sterile and the fact that the women did become pregnant make possible an additional wrong that is special to the abortion issue and that involves fathers and fetuses. The nonmalicious deceit of Michelle illustrates this well. Had Steve been unknowingly sterile, Michelle would have wronged him by lying to him, but she would not have wrongfully harmed him. In fact, the particular harm Anne planned to inflict upon Mark would have been impossible had he been sterile. And had he been knowingly sterile, Anne could not have violated his autonomy by invading an interest that was impossible for him to pursue. Nonetheless, she would have wronged him in other ways. The fact that these other wrongs can affect a man's legitimate interest in procreation gives them special significance here. It might also be objected that one disquieting implication of the argument is that abortion would be said to constitute a "wrongful harm" to anyone and anything that has a "morally legitimate interest" in it. So, for example, in an underpopulated country like Norway or Australia, society might have a morally legitimate interest in childbearing, and every woman opting for an abortion might be said to do a "wrongful harm to society." Or grandparents might have a "morally legitimate" interest in grandchildren being born; and a woman aborting would be said to have done a "wrongful harm" to the would-be grandparents.[2]

Certainly these results are unacceptable, but I do not believe that they are consistent with the concept of autonomy I have in mind here. We might distinguish between interests that are prima facie morally legitimate and those that are morally legitimate *simpliciter* or legitimate after all moral considerations are in. An interest that is prima facie morally legitimate is one that in itself is a morally permissible interest to have. The interest in sex and the interest in procreation are two such interests, as are the interest in grandparents having grandchildren and the interest of a country in having a larger population. But one way in which prima facie morally legitimate interests can fail to be morally legitimate *simpliciter* is for a person who has these interests to pursue them in ways that are morally illegitimate.

Assume that the rapist has an interest in sex (which is doubtful, at least that it is his primary interest). This interest fails to be morally legitimate *simpliciter* when the pursuit of it invades the morally legitimate interest his victim has in her choice of sexual partners. And it is the primacy of the importance of individual choice and its moral legitimacy that is at the heart of the concept of autonomy employed here. Thus, a prima facie morally legitimate interest can fail to be morally legitimate *simpliciter* if it is pursued in a way that does not respect the autonomy of others to pursue their morally legitimate interests. So like the rapist who has an interest in sex, there is nothing wrong with what the country wants in wanting a larger population or in what potential grandparents want in wanting grandchildren. These interests become morally illegitimate, however, when the autonomy of the women involved is violated by the rapist, the country, or the grandparents in the pursuit of their interests. And it is the importance of autonomy to my argument that prevents the disquieting implication.

A final objection might be that too much of the argument turns on the extremity and implausibility of case 5. There is an ambiguity, however, in the charge of "implausibility." On the one hand, it might mean that the case is far-fetched in that cases like it are not at all likely to occur. Or on the other hand, it might mean that the analysis of the case is either unconvincing or that it sheds no light on the other cases. The first construal of the charge renders it irrelevant. We hope that there are and will be no such cases. But this is beside the point. If the analysis of the case can be defended against the charge of implausibility of the second kind, the case serves to shed light on moral issues in other contexts. This is what Judith Jarvis Thomson's violinist example [is] designed to do.[3] And no one thinks that these examples are implausible on the grounds that they are unlikely to occur. Those who think these examples are implausible think so on the grounds that they are misleading or otherwise uninformative in terms of analysis. The objection then turns on the second construal of the charge.

That the analysis is unconvincing might be argued either by claiming that Anne has not wronged Mark or that the wrong is independent of the abortion issue. Since I do not believe that anyone would upon reflection seriously claim the former and since I have already addressed the latter claim, the second charge must turn on the claim that the case fails to illuminate the issues in other contexts. But I believe that it does illuminate the issues of other cases. Most important, it establishes that a serious wrong that a woman can do to a man is to harm him by killing his fetus, and it shows how this might involve other wrongs that are done with intentional malice. Once these two points are established, the issue naturally arises as to whether the wrong of harming a man by killing his fetus might be done in other ways involving other wrongs that are not accompanied by malicious intent. I have argued that abortion constitutes a wrongful harm in cases involving negligence and nonmalicious deceit. Viewed from this perspective, cases 3 and 4 are illuminated by case 5. And viewed from this perspective, we can see that there are other ways—ways that are more likely to occur—in which we can wrong others by failing to take their autonomy and their interest seriously than just in cases where we intentionally and maliciously set out to do so. The latter cases are easy to recognize; the former are not always. Being alive to this is important, and that is why cases 3 and 4 and perhaps other more subtle ones are most important in the analysis.

IV

I have spoken about the rights of autonomy. It is time now to say something about its responsibilities. On any plausible view of the importance of autonomy, anyone who claims to have a right that others respect his or her autonomy must recognize the obligation to take seriously the autonomy of others. Men and women in their relations with each other as members of the opposite sex have not always done this. Let me briefly mention two ways in which men and women have failed in this responsibility.

The first has to do with equality. If the interest in procreation and the interest in, say, a career are equally legitimate, then a man cannot consistently require a woman with whom he is involved to take seriously his interest in a family if he does not take seriously her interest in a career. It is notoriously true that many men are chauvinistic in this regard. But by the same token, a woman cannot consistently require a man with whom she is involved to take seriously her interest in a career if she does not take seriously his interest in a family. This does not mean that she must have children with him, but it does mean that in working out her relationship with him she must grant that men have as legitimate an interest in being parents as do women. I am not sure that many women—or for that matter that many men—are emotionally prepared to admit this. Although we are making some progress in thinking that women have an equal right to a career as men and that men have equal obligations in child rearing as women, we are still hesitant to think that a man could be an equal to a woman in parenthood.

The second way in which men and women have failed to take each other's autonomy seriously involves forthrightness. Men, it is said with some justification, are unwilling to talk about their feelings. This often puts an unfair burden on the woman with whom a man is involved to understand what his interests are, and without adequate information regarding his interests, the woman is poorly positioned to respect his autonomy in regard to those interests. Thus one aspect of the responsibility to be forthright involves letting the other person know what your interests are so that your autonomy can be respected. This was Jack's failure in case 2.

Another aspect of the responsibility to be forthright has to do with allowing the other person to make an informed choice. Certainly it is an interference with another person's autonomy to purposefully provide them with or knowingly allow them to believe erroneous information relevant to their choices. This is what Susan, Michelle, and Anne have done in the cases considered. Such motivation to be less than forthright is not always selfish, but it is almost always a failure to take autonomy seriously.

V

To summarize: In order for a man to lay claim to the fetus being his in a sense that the mother is obligated to respect, the fetus must be the result of his pursuing the legitimate interest in procreation in a morally legitimate way. In cases 1 and 2, the men—in different ways—have not satisfied the requirement of acting in a way that is consistent with the responsibilities of autonomy. It would therefore not be a wrong done to these men for Karen and Jane to have their abortions. However, when a man has satisfied the requirements of autonomy in regard to the interest in procreation both in regard to himself and to his sexual partner, the woman has a prima facie obligation to him not to harm the fetus. And unless there is some countervening moral consideration to override this prima facie obligation, the abortion of the fetus is morally impermissible. I have argued that the latter is true in cases 4 and 5.

Notes

1 These observations do not contradict the practice of the courts in holding liable for support men who have simply become uninterested in their wives and children. What is being maintained is that the fact that a man is the biological father of a child is not sufficient either to give him rights to the child or to put him under an obligation to it or to the mother.
2 I owe this objection to Robert Goodin. The grandparents case was also mentioned to me by James F. Hill.
3 See Thomson, J. J., "A defense of abortion," *Philosophy and Public Affairs* 1: 46–66, 1971 [reprinted earlier].

Review and Discussion Questions

1 Is Harris right in thinking that in case 1, the woman has no responsibility to respect the man's autonomy? Explain.
2 Why in case 2 does Harris think that Jack's autonomy is not violated by an abortion and that the fetus is Jane's?
3 Discuss case 3, indicating why the fetus belongs to both and whether there are reasons showing that nonetheless Susan may get an abortion.
4 Why in case 4 is it wrong for Michelle to have an abortion?
5 Why is Anne obligated not to get an abortion, according to Harris?
6 Harris thinks that we should respect others' autonomy if we want them to respect ours and that this includes respecting their legitimate interests in being parents. Discuss this claim, indicating whether you agree and why.

Essay and Paper Topics for Chapter 8

1 Discuss Thomson's defense of abortion in light of the criticisms of it given by Warren and Marquis. How might Thomson respond to those criticisms? Do you think her responses would be adequate?
2 Compare the positions of Warren, English, and Marquis on the moral status or importance of the fetus. Which of the three seems the most reasonable to you? Explain why, indicating what problems you see with the others and the strength of the position you think most reasonable.
3 Discuss whether anti-abortion laws have political and social consequences for women and their role in society. What do you believe the consequences are? Are the consequences an important argument that should be considered in thinking about abortion rights? Explain.
4 Laws have traditionally included the "maternal presumption," which means that the law assumes mothers, rather than fathers, should be given custody of children after a divorce. Does that presumption make sense, in light of the ideal of gender equality? How do you think Harris would respond to the maternal presumption? Might a feminist disagree? Explain.
5 "Cloning oneself ought to be a matter of individual choice, just as abortion ought to be a matter of individual choice." How do you assess this statement?

Chapter 9

Health Care and Deciding Who Should Live

Advances in medical care pose some of the most difficult choices people must make. Sometimes the issues are personal: how to understand the value of life, how long to extend one's life with the help of medical care, and whether one should be able to end one's life in the face of terminal illness. The rapidly rising costs of medical care also force social questions about the proper distribution of scarce medical resources. Essays in this chapter discuss these issues and more. They begin with debate about whether health care is a right. Next is a famous legal case in which the court considered whether or not a woman could be given life-saving medical help against her family's will and without her consent. Another case is about Oregon's Death with Dignity Act, which pitted the state of Oregon, which allows medically prescribed assisted suicide, against the federal government, which hoped to exert its authority to restrict this practice. Who should have the authority to decide about the value and continuation of life? The two final essays probe how we should think about limited resources in the face of pressing medical needs and expenses and what bearing, if any, people's rights and values should have on this discussion.

READING: THE MEDICAL MINIMUM: ZERO

JAN NARVESON[*]

Jan Narveson argues against any positive rights to health care or any governmental mandate for supplying a minimal level of health care for people. Jan Narveson is Distinguished Professor Emeritus at the University of Waterloo, Canada.

I The Issue

.... "Is there a natural or moral right to [adequate] health care access or does the government have a moral duty to provide it?"

It is nice to have an occasional philosophical question that can be answered forthrightly. The answer to the latter question is: No.

---

[*] Adapted from "The Medical Minimum: Zero" in *Journal of Medicine and Philosophy* 36 (2011): 558–571. Reprinted by permission of Oxford University Press. Note omitted.

That is not the answer that any current politicians, or almost any current academics, would supply on this matter, and getting to it from widely shared premises, although in my judgment perfectly possible, is not the work of a moment. For the contrary conviction has the sanction of political correctness at present, and this in turn is very much promoted by the atmosphere of welfare democracy. But evidently, some survey of the ground is necessary for this purpose.

Let us begin with some important definitions. When there is talk of the government, or perhaps "society," "securing access" to this "adequate level of health care," the most obvious interpretation of those words is that the government will tax people in order to fund the supply of that level of care to *all Americans* (or, if it is some other country, then *all citizens of that country*). In the current terminology of political philosophy, this is equivalent to proclaiming that all Americans have the *right* against their government—which means, of course, to all their fellow Americans, since that is where the money comes from—to that level of care.

Those sorts of rights—rights that others, on pain of punishment, are to provide to the right holder with something in the way of a good or service that is advantageous to the recipient—are what we nowadays call a "positive right." The use of the term "right" is in fact systematically ambiguous, for in addition to positive rights there are what have come to be called, somewhat unsatisfactorily, *negative* rights. These are rights that others not do certain things to the right holder: especially, that those other people refrain from damaging, injuring, or depriving the person in question of what he or she is said to have a right to. That we have a negative right to our health is something no one would surely deny: for to say this is simply to say that others *may not damage our health*—make us sick, injure us, or, at the extreme, kill us. (Not, at any rate, without the consent of the person to whom this is done, as might happen. ...)

Recent critics (such as Holmes and Sunstein, *The Cost of Rights* [Stephen and Sunstein, 2000]) have pointed out what is true enough, that if government *supplies* the right in the sense of *guaranteeing* it, then no rights will be costless: there will be costs not only of positive rights, which is obvious, but also of negative ones—providing protection from robbers and murderers via a public police force, for example, or more obvious yet, national defense.

But as an attempt to derail the force of this distinction between positive and negative rights, this argument is misguided. For the distinction is not a distinction between two kinds of goods *supplied by governments*. It is a purely moral distinction between two sorts of actions/inactions that our fellow men may be claimed to owe us: namely, between their doing things for us, for example, supplying things to us, which of course requires cost and exertion on their part, and their not doing things to us, especially not *harming* us, which normally and in principle requires nothing from them. (To take my favorite classroom example: all of us at this very moment, and almost all the time, are completely fulfilling the right of all 7 or so billions of people on this planet *not to be molested* by us. No government outlays or impositions are required, on the face of it, to make it the case that Jones does not do x, nor are any outlays by Jones himself, normally. On the other hand, if each of us in the world is entitled to Jones's help in saving our lives if they need saving, then we are, almost all of us, in for a great deal of cost and effort, very likely, or, at the least, of expenditure, to induce those who would provide the care in question to provide it.)

....

But to see the impact of this distinction on the present case—if we suppose that we all have a negative right to health, what that means is simply a right that our fellows *not worsen our health*: not make us sick, not disable or otherwise injure us, and especially, not kill us. To be sure, this will not always be a right we can adequately fulfill by sheer inaction. Public washrooms these days abjure us to wash our hands, and those who do not can spread diseases that could easily have been prevented by the hand washing in question. And washing hands does take some effort. But of course, you can avoid spreading disease by not coming in contact with anybody either and that requires no effort, as such—though for most of us, it would require a level of self-denial for others' company that we would much rather not subject ourselves to. Broadly speaking, the point is that negative rights are a coherent concept and that there is a striking difference, typically enormous, between them and the positive rights that these philosophers have been at pains to deny.

Of course, the important question is whether anything morally important hangs on this distinction. Are there good arguments why we should think that our fellows should have negative rights and similarly good ones against crediting them with a significant array of positive rights? It is familiar stuff to claim that there cannot be arguments for basic ethical beliefs, of which this, of course, is an example. But I deny this. There need to be, and there can be, arguments for all moral views, and in the case of the present distinction, I think, there are very good ones indeed.

To see that there can be requires a further essential distinction. We are talking here about *morals*. We are not talking about *general personal values*. I am exceedingly fond of classical music, but that is not a moral value, though it certainly is a value. I am against murder and that is a moral value. What is the difference? Essentially, this: that morals are *rules for everybody*: they are what everybody is to do, not just what I am to do. They are about what I am to do only insofar as that is a deduction from what everybody may or should or must do. We all have a right to listen to whatever sort of music we like (not a positive right, of course: we ought to pay those who sing for us!); but from this nothing follows about which particular music I should listen to and when, if any at all. On the other hand, we all have a general right to life, if we have committed no capital offenses against anyone, and from this, it does follow that I am not to murder this particular person at this particular time, that one at that time, and so on.

....

.... Rights are what we morally are allowed to *compel* each other to respect if compulsion should be needed to elicit the respect in question.

All that is merely analysis in hopes of clarifying what is at issue. The question now is, what are rights or more generally moral claims based on—or are there any at all? By this time, there are various nonstarters that deserve discussion in textbooks but must be brushed aside quickly here. For example, talk of duties imposed by god, Nature, or the state or discerned by unique intuitive judgments is simply not on anymore (Narveson, 2010, 161–7). It is absurd and arrogant for A to claim that B has various duties because of what A's religious beliefs require or because of A's intuitions. And as to states, complex arguments are required—but, in brief, all *fascist* type theories must go: if a state can "impose" a duty on us, it is because we humans have, somehow, interests and values such that they make it rational for us to create a state that does that kind of imposing. And showing that is no easy matter (Narveson, 2008). In any case, any such claim is circular: the state may do what it does if and only if the right moral theory says that people have moral requirements or rights such that they may also create, or should support, a state that does that kind of imposing. We are then back to the question of what that right moral theory is, and the attempt to invoke the state to help out is shown to be useless.

So what we are left with is that individuals in society, related to each other. What there is to go on is individuals and their interests—their wants, their desires, their satisfactions, their goals—plus the fact of there being a great many others, each with their various interests, etc., and yet each of them with a unique bundle of interests, at least some of which bring them into conflict with their fellows. There is also the fact of our abilities, powers, skills, and talents, which vary enormously.

What each of us simply wants of our fellows is of little interest as such. (Why one's fellows ought to be disposed to satisfy one's desires, after all, is a bit of a puzzler.) What we collectively want, however, would be of great interest if we can manage to say what that is. But one thing it is not is something like *the general welfare*. Some of us want that, some do not; many are indifferent. We do not unite behind things like that. We can, however, unite behind what is in the *common* interest and especially behind any general requirements that can be seen to be what we need to impose on each other if we are to live the satisfactory lives we are each variously trying to live.

Now, the case for a general and generous allotment of negative rights is, I think, clear to the point of being simply overwhelming. If I propose to get my way by force, then you will be rational to resist, especially because, as Hobbes insists, we are probably not much different in strength and especially in our ability to rally others around to help if it comes to that. Nobody wants to be injured, killed, or robbed. We all do well both to disapprove of such actions and also to take measures, if need be, to deal with those who would propose to do such things.

But now we can get back to proposals about positive rights. Minimal income, minimal education, minimal medical care? Really? Is there a real claim that we will all rationally unite behind the proposal to *require* contributions from all—and specifically all our fellow countrypersons in the particular nation-state we happen to live in—for those purposes? That there is not is at least suggested by the fact that these claimed duties do not extend beyond the borders of political states. Governments want to impose such things, of course. But the fact that governments want us to do x falls well short of assuring that x is right. (Fascism in moral theory surely does not merit serious discussion.)

More plausibly, at first sight, there is an *insurance argument*: maybe we would all do well to contribute to a fund which would pay for anybody's medical care if needed, up to some level (hence, the relevant "minimum"). Here the problem is in the "maybe." Maybe we would—but maybe we would not. If we would, why would we do well to do so? Society contains a range of people in respect of the ability to produce what is socially useful. So-called social insurance looks like a bad investment from the point of view of producers. Insurance that actually is insurance—that is, where the individual is responding rationally to risks—is of course often a good idea, which is why wealthy societies are awash in insurance companies. But compulsory society-wide insurance is another matter. Those who find it obvious that such things are justified should engage in some real analysis and argument instead of just proclaiming it—as is, overwhelmingly, the current tendency.

We are, in short, safe in asserting the Humean natural rights: security of persons and possessions, recognition of transfers by consent (only), and reliability of contracts. None of these assures or even makes it particularly plausible that we should impose on all who can pay the duty of providing these various goods and services to persons who cannot produce enough to pay for them themselves. Charitable assistance to our fellows in time of need, yes. But compulsory assistance, as with taxation? Not obviously. Appeals to "insurance" cash in on an obviously good idea: most of us want insurance against some things. But as soon as it is made compulsory, the idea loses its appeal. We can see why insurance purchases might be a good idea, but if they are, then we will choose to take out that kind of insurance and make those payments. Compulsion takes the steam out of its appeal. Indeed, it is a familiar contradiction of the welfare state to argue: "Hey, this is such a good thing that of course you want it! Therefore, we will make you take it." The conclusion is inconsistent with its premise. If we think it that good, we will buy it of our own free will. If we must be compelled to take it, then evidently we do not think it is all that good.

Ordinary insurance does not cover nonparticipants. Now, there is no reason why it could not. There could be a company that offers a policy such that we pay 10% more in order to provide benefits of specified kinds for specified sets of persons who, perhaps, cannot afford them on their own. Some people would take such a policy, just as some people pay more for their coffee at Starbucks in order, as they suppose, to benefit the people who picked the beans back in Guatemala or wherever. That is perfectly OK. But suppose the government starts requiring us to have our coffee there. Or forbids importation of coffee made by people ready to take less pay in order to get a competitive advantage? That is a lot less obviously "OK."

Square one in this discussion, of course, should be occupied by some thought on the matter of rights. When people talk of a right to a decent minimum, etc., what do they have in mind? In context, it is clear that current discussions among academics in the United States in particular have in mind the "amount" of health care that your fellow citizens may be *required*, in the form of taxation, to purchase for you. It is presumed, in brief, that we have what is now known as a "positive right" against our fellow citizens to some amount of health care—the only real question being, how much? (That is certainly the standard assumption in Canada, where I live.) But the presumption has to be challenged. We may insist that to that particular question, there is only one plausible answer: None. This, one gathers, is not an acceptable answer in current discussions—unsurprisingly to students of government and political processes. But any other answer needs to tell us why people should be compelled to pay for other people's health care at the proposed level. We will say considerably more about that shortly.

A quick word should also be addressed to the word "natural" in our question. There is a special point about medical care, which is that until recently there essentially was no such thing. Persons presenting themselves as medical doctors, until not so much more than a century ago, knew so little about their art that, we are told, they were more likely to make their patients' conditions worse than better. Apart from rudimentary bandaging and elementary setting of broken limbs, essentially none of the familiar services we expect of modern doctors or hospitals would possibly have been supplied prior to about 1800. Thus, if there was a "natural right" to a "decent minimum" of health care, this would have the property—odd among rights—that it could not have been catered to for most of human history. Are we to say that all those people, in the presence of the sick or injured, were, alas, violating the rights of their putative patients? And if not, then what are we to say if we think to support this notion? Perhaps, that all persons everywhere have a right that those who can supply medical care do so—with the recognition that, until recently, that was essentially no one. Thus, for long, the positive version would in practice have coincided with the negative version by default. But today, of course, with our vast resources of medical knowledge and equipment and people ready and able to use these resources, things are much different. A positive right to medical care in today's world would be a right to something that can indeed be supplied. The question is whether that supply may properly be *compelled*.

II Rights: The Bearing of the Negative–Positive Distinction

By now, the distinction between negative and positive rights is fairly generally understood. A negative right is a right entailing a negative duty on those upon whom it falls—that is, a duty not to do certain things. The relevant persons are to *refrain* from acts that would prevent or substantially interfere with the right holder's voluntary performance of the act to which he is being said to have a right to do. A positive right, on the other hand, goes beyond the negative type in that it requires others not only to refrain from interfering but in fact, if need be, to render assistance up to some level (needing to be specified). It is a duty to do, not just to refrain.

So on our main question, it does have to be pointed out that there is a clear construal of rights, the negative type, on which a right of this kind is surely uncontroversial: of course people have the right to seek out health care on terms agreeable both to the parties from whom we would get it and to ourselves. It is a right to liberty: a right that no one may prevent people from making such purely voluntary arrangements as they can to advance their interests. This uncontested right, in short, is part and parcel of the view that we have negative rights: the right that others *not prevent*, not *interfere*, with our actions in the area of concern. That is the case with most other sorts of insurance, including life insurance: we decide how much, if any, to take out and with whom. ...

....

The distinction of negative and positive rights is not one of those how-many-angels-on-the-point-of-the-needle questions that some theorists allege. On the contrary, it makes all the difference, in this case (as in virtually all): between self-administered charity or voluntary insurance on the one hand and centrally enforced supposed entitlement on the other. The trend of the time is toward the latter, with clangorous appeals to political and politicized audiences. The appeals in question are notoriously question-begging: few nowadays ask whether; they ask only how much. But surely the first thing to settle should be the whether question: whether we have the entitlement in question at all. In the absence of a good case for the latter, the default, surely, is the former. Voluntary actions, so long as they are peaceable, need no justification. Compulsory impositions do.

....

III Insurance

Among those voluntary actions needing no justification would, of course, be contributions toward the care of others and, for that matter, toward research aimed at discovering cures or preventions of various diseases and other afflictions. The remaining possibility is, of course, formation of an insurance group, whose members pay an agreed fee in return for a range of services if those should be required.

.... But this does not bridge the gap between that choice and *requirements*, to pay, mandatorily, for health care for *everyone else*. ...

An argument is needed for any such program, then. And what might it be? Some assert, rather cavalierly, that there is a *human right* (of this positive type) to health care. Now, for one thing, they perhaps have not appreciated the implication of that view: namely, that we are all responsible for the health care of everyone—all 7 billion of us. If we suppose, as we should, that most of them are quite unable to pay for anything at all close to American standards, the implication looms large that America would be stuck with a health care bill considerably in excess of its gross national product, huge though that is. Very few advocates of government-provided health care are ready to swallow that implication. Their proposals tend to be confined in their reach to citizens or residents of their own country: people on the other side of the national boundary are not covered, despite being at least equally in need of care. Thus, the proposal that there is a positive human right to such care does not, at least, reflect the realistic spectrum of political opinion. Nor of any other kind of opinion short of the slightly lunatic, one would think.

....

But the main point is that on the most reasonable view of people, such a supposed right is not justifiable. We are not our brothers' keepers (especially when they are altogether unrelated). We are, of course, responsible for injury to others—contrary to the semantic skullduggery of the famous Biblical character—but this does not easily extend to being responsible for the care of their health.

All that said, the plausibility of health insurance, for many people, is clear enough. What kind of insurance? Basically, of course, whatever they choose. But not a type that is thrust upon them by somebody else.

At any rate, let us imagine our way into a regime of health insurance—what might it best be like?

First, it should be very sensitive to its status as *insurance*. In principle, and normally, insurance is voluntary: you decide whether to buy it and how much, in negotiation with providers or fellow members of insurance groups. But, second, insofar as any case is to be made for compulsory insurance, such insurance is best understood as insuring against the risk that unforeseeable or uncontrollable external factors present, such as ambient viruses or subtle genetic environmental features that affect the human genome. Thus, the bad habits of many people that leave them with heart disease, lung cancer, and so on should not obviously be insurable or, perhaps better, should be insurable only at actuarially derived higher premiums. No one should be in the position that his fellows can exact payments from others for avoidable, voluntarily imposed risks. Thus, smokers, persons with dangerous lifestyles, or persons with bad diets should pay more. Those who cannot afford this cannot afford their lifestyles—so why, then, should others be paying for them? The force of this restriction should not be underestimated. It has been plausibly claimed that by far the majority of major causes of death currently—heart attacks, diabetes, stroke, and many cancers—would be avoided by modest attention to exercise and diet and avoidance of smoking (and a few other things). An insurance policy that provided cover for emergencies but greatly increased costs for those who insist on being overweight, smoking, or prolonged inactivity would be rational. Those who adhere to known guidelines in respect of a healthy lifestyle can have modest health care costs even in today's expensive world. But involuntary, collective health care systems provide little or no incentive for such savings. So the question is: why should those who take reasonable care be stuck with the costs of those who do not? Others may, of course, take pity on them, but the exaction of charity is a contradiction in terms, as well as bad social policy. Normal people have considerable reserves of charitable sentiment, and those sentiments do impel them to philanthropy if they can afford it. The United States has been the world's leader in private charitable giving, by a very large magnitude, for a very long time, and it is to that resource we should turn for dealing with the unfortunate who are also financially unfortunate. But why should other people in general be saddled with expensive mandatory "health plans" for their irresponsible neighbors?

....

Those who participate in current discussions of "health care policy" assume, on the contrary, that it does not matter how or why people came to be in whatever unfortunate medical condition they are in—the government has the right, and of course the duty, given that right—to impose taxes on all of us to relieve those conditions to some level or other. And then it is just a question of how much the taxpayer can be expected to be willing to part with, as measured by who will win which elections in which this has become a major issue.

Those assumptions are pretty obviously wrong in every way. First, many people care little about their health: drug users, people who eat huge amounts of foods known to be likely to shorten their life expectancy significantly, and so on. Second, and more generally, all of us have interests such that we are willing, with perfect rationality, to expend less of our time, energy, and money on trying to maintain an advanced state of physical health than we are in promoting those interests. And third, both of the first two are clearly the subject of huge variation among people. ...

So the correct answer to the question addressed, to repeat, is: None. There is no level of health such that governments have any business compelling anyone to bring it about that everyone enjoys at least that level of health and certainly that they have access to a given level of "health care." Nor is there one standard health insurance policy that would plainly be best for everyone. ...

References

Berlin, I. 1969. "Two Concepts of Liberty." In *Four essays on liberty*, 1–32. New York: Oxford University Press.

Narveson, J. 2008. *You and the state.* Lanham, MD: Rowman & Littlefield.
Narveson, J. 2010. *This is ethical theory.* Chicago, IL: Open Court.
Stephen, L. H., and C. Sunstein. 2000. *The cost of rights: Why liberty depends on taxes.* New York: Norton.

Review and Discussion Questions

1. What definitions does Narveson introduce and what question does he wish to address?
2. Why does Narveson think it is justified to believe that people have negative rights to health care but not justified to believe that people have positive rights to health care? Do you agree with this form of justification?
3. If voluntary health insurance schemes are justifiable, why aren't mandatory health insurance schemes also justifiable?

READING: A RIGHT TO HEALTH CARE

PAVLOS ELEFTHERIADIS*

Pavlos Eleftheriadis believes that a moral right to health care is more complex than a basic right, such as a right to free speech, but that does not imply we don't have a public right to living in a society with an available health care system. He argues that we do. Pavlos Eleftheriadis is Professor of Public Law and a Fellow of Mansfield College at the University of Oxford.

Do we have a legal and moral right to health care against others? There are international conventions and institutions that say emphatically yes, and they summarize this in the expression of "the right to health," which is an established part of the international human rights canon. The International Covenant on Social and Economic Rights outlines this as "the right of everyone to the enjoyment of the highest attainable standard of physical and mental health," but declarations such as this remain tragically unfulfilled. According to recent figures, roughly two billion people lack access to essential drugs or to primary health care. Millions are afflicted by infections and illnesses that are easily avoidable or treatable. In the developing world many children die or grow stunted and damaged for lack of available treatments. Tropical diseases receive little or no attention by the major pharmaceutical companies' research departments. Is this a massive violation of the right to health? And if so, why does it attract so little attention? Is it because our supposed commitment to human rights and the rule of law is hypocritical and hollow? Or is it because the right to health is a special case of a right, so that these tragedies are no violation at all? Jennifer Prah Ruger summarized this puzzle when she wrote: "one would be hard pressed to find a more controversial or nebulous human right than the right to health."[1] ....

---

* Adapted from "A Right to Health Care" by Pavlos Eleftheriadis, *Journal of Law, Medicine, and Ethics* (Summer 2012): 268–285. Reprinted by permission of Wiley-Blackwell. Some footnotes omitted.

I

This is a complex subject that touches on deep and unresolved issues of ethics, medicine, and law. At its heart lies the terrifying and universal fact of human vulnerability. An external event, say an earthquake, a financial collapse or a war, can destroy our lives at an instant. This sets health apart from the different issue of poverty.[2] Our health is certain, one way or another, to give way. The awareness that this vulnerability is common to every man and woman in the world gives rise to common sentiments of sympathy and compassion and to ethical thinking itself.

Health is not entirely a matter of luck. Suffering an illness or an injury is a matter of luck, even when the social determinants of health change the probabilities. But health care is not a matter of luck. Medical care can reverse the effects of, say, a broken leg, a malignant tumor or an HIV infection, which could otherwise kill us. Our doctors can also give us a clear diagnosis, helping us plan whatever time we have to live. But effective health care is a matter of very complex cooperative processes, including networks of education, professional regulation, information, expertise and commerce. Such networks connect persons across the globe. One's survival may thus depend on a medicine produced in India, shipped to one's country on a Greek ship, administered in London by a Ghanaian doctor who was educated in Germany and being paid by an insurance company based in France, financed by another company based in New York.

Medical resources are of course finite. They are part of a cooperative project that makes everyone better off and some of us much better off in that it saves them from certain death or long suffering. Because the benefits and costs are a result of cooperation, we need to find a fair way of distributing them. Here we are exactly at the heart of what Rawls calls the "circumstances of justice."[3]

....

The simple expression "a right to health" seems to deny this complexity. It invites the thought that the "human right to health" is a kind of moral fundamental that prevents further balancing or assessment or indeed resorting to the uncertainties of the political process. When we say, for example, that there is a right to freedom of speech, we do not ask how much such freedom each one of us should enjoy nor do we wish to see the issue decided by a parliament. We assume that everyone should enjoy it equally and that in case one does not, a court will vindicate them according to ordinary processes of the rule of law. When we criticize a government for the use of torture, for example, we are indifferent to the distribution of suffering among its unlucky people. There is no defense that torture is equally applied to all or that it has been approved by the dominant political forces of the day.

This kind of categorical and institutional duty that normally accompanies rights seems impossible in the case of health. We accept that differences in health and health care are a fact of ordinary life ....

II

I start with a summary of the right to health as seen by the leading documents and institutions of international law. These are not offered as philosophical arguments nor should they be read in that light, but I find them extremely useful and informative. They are conclusions of practice and experience, reached in diplomatic conferences by seasoned practitioners. They express a common consensus among representatives of different cultures and systems. So they address all of the problems that are likely to be faced in practice by international organizations, governments, or non-governmental organizations in the course of providing assistance in health care in the developing world. Such statements can be significant starting points, both as to the questions and as to the answers likely to occupy any theoretical account.[4]

Perhaps the boldest statement of the human right to health is to be found in the Constitution of the World Health Organization: "The enjoyment of the highest attainable standard of health is one of the fundamental rights of every human being without distinction of race, religion, political belief, economic or social condition."[5] The Universal Declaration of Human Rights had used slightly different terminology. Article 25(1) reads:

> Everyone has the right to a standard of living adequate for the health and well-being of himself and of his family, including food, clothing, housing and medical care and necessary social services, and the right to security in the event of unemployment, sickness, disability, widowhood, old age or other lack of livelihood in circumstances beyond his control.

There is a more careful emphasis here on medical and other care, rather than health itself.

The International Covenant on Economic, Social, and Cultural Rights of 1966 in its Article 12 returned to health, not health care, as the required standard:

1. The States Parties to the present Covenant recognize the right of everyone to the enjoyment of the highest attainable standard of physical and mental health.
2. The steps to be taken by the States Parties to the present Covenant to achieve the full realization of this right shall include those necessary for:

    a   The provision for the reduction of the still birth rate and of infant mortality and for the healthy development of the child;
    b   The improvement of all aspects of environmental and industrial hygiene;
    c   The prevention, treatment and control of epidemic, endemic, occupational and other diseases;
    d   The creation of conditions which would assure to all medical service and medical attention in the event of sickness.

This more ambitious account of the right to health is subject to a number of general qualifications that apply to all social and economic rights. In article 1 the Covenant recognizes the right of peoples to "freely pursue their economic, social and cultural development." This must suggest that peoples have a great deal of freedom to determine the place of health relative to all other aims, economic, social, and cultural.

Two further general qualifications are that all the rights protected by this Covenant are to be "progressively achieved" subject to "available resources" according to article 2:

> Each State Party to the present Covenant undertakes to take steps, individually and through international assistance and co-operation, especially economic and technical, to the maximum of its available resources, with a view to achieving

progressively the full realization of the rights recognized in the present Covenant by all appropriate means, including particularly the adoption of legislative measures.

This provision is to be contrasted to the equivalent Article 2 of the International Covenant on Civil and Political Rights, under which the obligations to respect civil and political rights are immediate:

Each State Party to the present Covenant undertakes to respect and to ensure to all individuals within its territory and subject to its jurisdiction the rights recognized in the present Covenant, without distinction of any kind, such as race, colour, sex, language, religion, political or other opinion, national or social origin, property, birth or other status.

These qualifications make the right to health very different to the rights against torture or against religious discrimination. First, the right to health does not outline distinct actions that the government is to perform or avoid. There is neither a concrete negative nor a positive duty, e.g., not to inflict intentional pain and suffering, or not to discriminate on grounds of religion. Instead, the Covenant outlines general *goals or aims* that are to be achieved "progressively" and at a large scale. Second, the requirements do not concern conduct toward specific individuals, e.g., the potential victims of torture or religious discrimination. Instead, they are addressed to a population as a whole. The provisions concern general public policies that will produce broad benefits for all. This is true for example in the expression "the creation of conditions which would assure to all medical service and medical attention in the event of sicknesses." Third, the aims and goals to be achieved are not categorical but conditional on what is achievable or what is possible under available resources. What is achievable will depend on some kind of balancing of health against other values and priorities.

.... I do not think anyone can deny the wisdom of the advice contained in these statements. .... But to what extent do they ground duties corresponding to a human *right*? ....

[Ed. note: Sections III–V not included.]

VI

.... We know that human vulnerability makes health essential to any view of human flourishing. Our moral intuitions call for some special treatment of health care as a response to a common condition of vulnerability. On the other hand we know that health care, like food and education, can be bought and sold and its eventual distribution may properly be a matter of unintended consequences of personal choice, investment or risk-taking. It is a service like all others. If we follow the human rights canon and insist on the reality of a human right to health, then we take an unrealistically rigid view of duties of health care. The current inequality of health care in the world will be looked at as a massive human rights violation. If, on the other hand, we offer an entirely open-ended account of the right to health giving great leeway to states and corporations, then we risk weakening the idea of rights to a breaking point. For if the health disasters we observe in the world are not a violation to a right to health, then what is? We shall need to explain how any right may fail to have the categorical and peremptory nature of the right to free speech or the right against torture. This is then our puzzle. We want to both assert and deny the right to health. If rights have a categorical and peremptory role in moral reasoning, then there cannot be a right to health. But if there is no right to health, then the moral urgency of this aspect of human vulnerability is ignored ....

VII

.... Philosophers such as Kant, Rawls, and Waldron argue that there is a natural duty of justice, owed to all fellow human beings, to act in such a way as to set up, or support and maintain legitimate public institutions of law and government.[6] Here is then the link with personal codes of conduct. The natural duty of justice sits alongside other natural or basic duties we owe to others. This is an inter-personal duty and when properly discharged it gives rise to a new domain of social action: the political domain. The natural duty of justice requires that the structures of law and government have a public component and a system of jurisdiction ....

We have thus arrived at some important distinctions between personal duties of conduct and public duties enforceable through civil and criminal justice. The distinction is key in understanding the idea of a basic right to health. We are clearly drawn to the idea that helping others is a relevant consideration in personal relations. We cannot live a moral life while ignoring the vulnerability of other human beings, simply because we happen to be luckier than they. So we have both moral duties not to injury or exploit them and moral duties to come to their aid, when we can do so without risk to ourselves. There are all sorts of things we should not do to others and there are all sorts of vulnerabilities, physical, emotional, or economic that we are tempted but morally required not to exploit. These forms of imposition and oppression are all wrong, according to simple principles of conduct. They are wrong because they are humiliating,[7] but it does not follow that exactly the same moral duties can be translated to legal duties, properly enforced by a system of jurisdiction. Some judgments that we are expected to make as moral agents, for example about value or culture, may not be possible to share with others. ...

Benevolence, however, is not therefore excluded from the law, but it now works in different ways. It finds expression in ways that can be public and intelligible by all. ... If we are fellow citizens, then we are responsible for the benefits and burdens that result from our mutual co-operation. This is a special political responsibility. To put it another way, the creation of public institutions makes it possible for us to influence—and perhaps radically so—the lives of our fellow human beings. This creates a new moral responsibility for the results of our association. Rawls has called this the problem of social justice and argued that it is here that distributive justice becomes important. A just civil condition must consider itself responsible for the distribution of benefits and burdens among its members, and this must include health and health care.

.... We cannot determine who will or will not be ill, but we can determine the pattern of distribution of health care. We must do so by means of a public system of distribution of health care in the domestic case. In a society of autonomous but vulnerable human beings, this must be one of the natural duties of justice, since without it we are all exposed to intolerable inequalities between the lucky and the unlucky. Systems of health care ensure not simply that we look after the needy but also that all members of our political society can take our place in a society of equals. The key is not suffering as such, but the risk of humiliation and exploitation, which would destroy the ideal of equal citizenship. Conceived in this way, the basic rights to health care are not private law rights to aid or assistance against other persons, but public rights to have a system of health care that is available to all, instituted by our collective decision-making.

What could the content of a public right to a health care system be? Any institutional protection of equal liberty and equal citizenship has to take into account the fact of continuous human vulnerability. It can do so without fixing in any stable way the permanent elements of "basic need." Instead, the key idea is the equal liberty of persons conceived as citizens. If we are to live as equal members in a political community, then our institutions need to institute processes by which we are protected from the risk of suffering and vulnerability that would make it impossible for us to live as equal members. Given that we know that some of us will be unlucky and needy because of ill health at some point in their lives, we must make sure that we institute some common system of protection.

Health is an area that presents a dangerous asymmetry. Some of us will be extremely vulnerable because of ill health. Others will be able to routinely rescue us from this helplessness. Their power derives from the skills they possess or the drugs they can provide or the equipment they control. This asymmetry can lead to awful exploitation and oppression. Here lies, I believe, the special moral importance of health and health care. We do not need to define standards for the decent provision of medical care very accurately in the context of constitutional law or general moral thinking. They will depend on each society's particular economic outlook, its patterns of inequality, and its practices of care. However, the content of the principles is defined by a concern to protect everyone from domination and humiliation due to our common vulnerability. Health duties are therefore relational and not absolute. Their guiding idea is equal citizenship not equal distribution of goods and burdens.

If we define the right to health care as a public political right in this way, then we have vindicated our first intuition, that health care must be the subject of a basic or natural duty of justice. We can thus confirm the moral content of some of the existing documents of the international human rights canon. We can distinguish between the most essential obligations of health care of the kind outlined by General Comment 14, which distinguishes explicitly between "core" and other obligations.[8] Core obligations include access to essential drugs, water and sanitation and the setting up of a national public health strategy, which must exhibit care for all. These are the things whose lack causes not only suffering and pain but also humiliation and exploitation. This is why such matters are moral fundamentals. Other matters could perhaps be left to "progressive realization" according to available resources.

....

It follows also that what goes beyond these core obligations of public law must be open to the distributive choices that are, in principle, open to the political process. Such issues are not constitutional essentials and need not figure in a list of basic or human rights. Their failure does not indicate manifest wrongness. We may thus take most of the standards and principles outlined by the international documents on the right to health as not strictly speaking manifestations of a basic right to health, but of the general political imperative to pursue just and fair public policy. ...

.... Health care is important, but it is also another economic activity. So our second intuition is also to be vindicated. Not everything about health is reducible to a right to health. The puzzle is resolved once we distinguish between basic moral and constitutional rights with relational content (on the basis of equal liberty and citizenship) and ordinary institutional or legislative rights with distributive content (on the basis of democratic decision-making).

Notes

1 J. Prah Ruger, *Health and Social Justice* (Oxford: Oxford University Press, 2010).
2 See now the extremely useful essays collected in T. Pogge, ed., *Freedom from Poverty as a Human Right: Who Owes What to the Very Poor?* (Oxford: Oxford University Press, 2008).
3 J. Rawls, *A Theory of Justice*, revised edition (Oxford: Oxford University Press, 1999).
4 For very useful overviews. see the essays collected in A. Clapham and M. Robinson, *Realising the Human Right to Health* (Zurich: Rüffer and Rub, 2009) and S. Gruskin, M. Grodin, G. J. Annas and S. P. Marks, eds., *Perspectives on Health and Human Rights* (New York and London: Routledge, 2005).
5 Constitution of the World Health Organization, 1946/2006. There is an ongoing debate on the adequacy of this definition in light of its maximal ambition. See, for example, the more focused attempt at linking health with the ability of a person to adapt to his or her physical circumstances offered by M. Huber et al., "Health: How Should We Define It?" *BMJ* 343 (2011): d4163.
6 Kant, *Metaphysics of Morals*, 6:306, in Immanuel Kant, *Practical Philosophy*, trans. and ed. by M. J. Gregor (Cambridge: Cambridge University Press, 1996): 450; J. Rawls, *A Theory of Justice*, rev. ed. (Oxford: Oxford University Press, 1999): 99 (the text is identical to the 1971 edition at 115); J. Waldron, "Special Ties and Natural Duties," *Philosophy and Public Affairs* 22 (1993): 3.
7 For some illuminating reflections on humiliation and poverty, see A. Margalit, *The Decent Society*, trans. by Naomi Goldblum (Cambridge, MA: Harvard University Press, 1996): at 225–231. Onora O'Neill puts the point as a principle rejecting "injury." See O'Neill, *Towards Justice and Virtue: A Constructive Account of Practical Reasoning* (Cambridge: Cambridge University Press, 1996), at 164–183.
8 General comment 14 includes a provision for "core obligations" which State parties must satisfy, including "the right of access to health facilities, goods and services on a non-discriminatory basis, especially for vulnerable or marginalized groups, access to basic shelter, housing and sanitation, an adequate supply of safe and potable water, essential drugs, as from time to time defined under the WHO Action Programme on Essential Drugs, the equitable distribution of all health facilities, goods and services and implementing a national public health strategy and plan of action, on the basis of epidemiological evidence, addressing the health concerns of the whole population." This list leaves out important components of modern health care, such as all chronic care, rehabilitative care, recostructive care (including transplants), cosmetic surgery and psychological services.

Review and Discussion Questions

1 How does Eleftheriadis believe that the claim of a right to free speech, or a right against torture or discrimination, is different from a claim about the right to health?
2 What do leading documents in international law say about the right to health?
3 Eleftheriadis writes, "We want to both assert and deny the right to health." Why does he believe this?
4 Does Eleftheriadis's defense of a right to health care vindicate this tension? What is his defense?

READING: REQUIRING MEDICAL TREATMENT

JFK MEMORIAL HOSPITAL V. HESTON[*]

Legal paternalism is the position that legal coercion may be used to protect individuals from self-inflicted harm; it therefore implies that sometimes the state knows the interests of individual citizens better than they do. The following case, argued before the New Jersey Supreme Court, concerns a young woman who for religious reasons refused a blood transfusion deemed medically necessary to save her life.

The Opinion of the Court Was Delivered by Weintraub, C.J.

Delores Heston, age 22 and unmarried, was severely injured in an automobile accident. She was taken to the plaintiff's hospital where it was determined that she would expire unless operated upon for a ruptured spleen and that if operated upon she would expire unless whole blood was administered. Miss Heston and her parents are Jehovah's Witnesses and a tenet of their faith forbids blood transfusions. Miss Heston insists she expressed her refusal to accept blood, but the evidence indicates she was in shock on admittance to the hospital and in the judgment of the attending physicians and nurses was then or soon became disoriented and incoherent. Her mother remained adamant in her opposition to a transfusion, and signed a release of liability for the hospital and medical personnel. Miss Heston did not execute a release; presumably she could not. Her father could not be located.

Death being imminent, plaintiff on notice to the mother made application at 1:30 A.M. to a judge of the Superior Court for the appointment of a guardian for Miss Heston with directions to consent to transfusions as needed to save her life. At the hearing, the mother and her friends thought a certain doctor would pursue surgery without a transfusion, but the doctor, in response to the judge's telephone call, declined the case. The court appointed a guardian with authority to consent to blood transfusions "for the preservation of the life of Delores Heston." Surgery was performed at 4:00 A.M. the same morning. Blood was administered. Miss Heston survived.

Defendants then moved to vacate the order. Affidavits were submitted by both sides. The trial court declined to vacate the order. This appeal followed. We certified it before argument in the Appellate Division.

The controversy is moot. Miss Heston is well and no longer in plaintiff's hospital. The prospect of her return at some future day in like circumstances is too remote to warrant a declaratory judgment as between the parties. Nonetheless, the public interest warrants a resolution of the cause, and for that reason we accept the issue. ...

In *Perricone*, we sustained an order for compulsory blood transfusion for an infant despite the objection of the parents who were Jehovah's Witnesses. In *Raleigh Fitkin-Paul Morgan Memorial Hospital v. Anderson, N.J.* (1964), it

---

[*] *JFK Memorial Hospital v. Heston* 58 N.J. 576.

appeared that both the mother, a Jehovah's Witness, and the child she was bearing would die if blood were not transfused should she hemorrhage. We held that a blood transfusion could be ordered if necessary to save the lives of the mother and the unborn child. We said:

> We have no difficulty in so deciding with respect to the infant child. The more difficult question is whether an adult may be compelled to submit to such medical procedures when necessary to save his life. Here we think it is unnecessary to decide that question in broad terms because the welfare of the child and the mother are so intertwined and inseparable that it would be impracticable to attempt to distinguish between them with respect to the sundry factual patterns which may develop. The blood transfusions (including transfusions made necessary by the delivery) may be administered if necessary to save her life or the life of her child, as the physician in charge at the time may determine.

The case at hand presents the question we thus reserved in *Raleigh Fitkin-Paul Morgan Memorial Hospital.*

It seems correct to say there is no constitutional right to choose to die. Attempted suicide was a crime at common law and was held to be a crime under N.J.S.A. 2A:85–1. It is now denounced as a disorderly persons offense. N.J.S.A. 2A:170–25.6. Ordinarily nothing would be gained by a prosecution, and hence the offense is rarely charged. Nonetheless the Constitution does not deny the State an interest in the subject. It is commonplace for the police and other citizens, often at great risk to themselves, to use force or stratagem to defeat efforts at suicide, and it could hardly be said that thus to save someone from himself violated a right of his under the Constitution subjecting the rescuer to civil or penal consequences.

Nor is constitutional right established by adding that one's religious faith ordains his death. Religious beliefs are absolute, but conduct in pursuance of religious beliefs is not wholly immune from governmental restraint. *Mountain Lakes Bd. of Educ.* v. *Maas, N.J.* (1960) (vaccination of children); *Bunn* v. *North Carolina* (1949) (the use of snakes in a religious ritual); *Baer* v. *City of Bend, Or.* (1956) (fluoridation of drinking water). Of immediate interest is *Reynolds* v. *United States* (1878), in which it was held that Congress could punish polygamy in a territory notwithstanding that polygamy was permitted or demanded by religious tenet, and in which the Court said:

> Laws are made for the government of actions, and while they cannot interfere with mere religious belief and opinions, they may with practices. Suppose one believed that human sacrifices were a necessary part of religious worship, would it be seriously contended that the civil government under which he lived could not interfere to prevent a sacrifice? Or if a wife religiously believed it was her duty to burn herself upon the funeral pile of her dead husband, would it be beyond the power of the civil government to prevent her carrying her belief into practice?

Complicating the subject of suicide is the difficulty of knowing whether a decision to die is firmly held. Psychiatrists may find that beneath it all a person bent on self-destruction is hoping to be rescued, and most who are rescued do not repeat the attempt, at least not at once. Then, too, there is the question whether in any event the person was and continues to be competent (a difficult concept in this area) to choose to die. And of course there is no opportunity for a trial of these questions in advance of intervention by the State or a citizen.

Appellant suggests there is a difference between passively submitting to death and actively seeking it. The distinction may be merely verbal, as it would be if an adult sought death by starvation instead of a drug. If the State may interrupt one mode of self-destruction, it may with equal authority interfere with the other. It is arguably different when an individual, overtaken by illness, decides to let it run a fatal course. But unless the medical option itself is laden with the risk of death or of serious infirmity, the State's interest in sustaining life in such circumstances is hardly distinguishable from its interest in the case of suicide.

Here we are not dealing with deadly options. The risk of death or permanent injury because of a transfusion is not a serious factor. Indeed, Miss Heston did not resist a transfusion on that basis. Nor did she wish to die. She wanted to live, but her faith demanded that she refuse blood even at the price of her life. The question is not whether the State could punish her for refusing a transfusion. It may be granted that it would serve no State interest to deal criminally with one who resisted a transfusion on the basis of religious faith. The question is whether the State may authorize force to prevent death or may tolerate the use of force by others to that end. Indeed, the issue is not solely between the State and Miss Heston, for the controversy is also between Miss Heston and a hospital and staff who did not seek her out and upon whom the dictates of her faith will fall as a burden.

Hospitals exist to aid the sick and the injured. The medical and nursing professions are consecrated to preserving life. That is their professional creed. To them, a failure to use a simple, established procedure in the circumstances of this case would be malpractice, however the law may characterize that failure because of the patient's private convictions. A surgeon should not be asked to operate under the strain of knowing that a transfusion may not be administered even though medically required to save this patient. The hospital and its staff should not be required to decide whether the patient is or continues to be competent to make a judgment upon the subject, or whether the release tendered by the patient or a member of his family will protect them from civil responsibility. The hospital could hardly avoid the problem by compelling the removal of a dying patient, and Miss Heston's family made no effort to take her elsewhere.

When the hospital and staff are thus involuntary hosts and their interests are pitted against the belief of the patient, we think it reasonable to resolve the problem by permitting the hospital and its staff to pursue their functions according to their professional standards. The solution sides with life, the conservation of which is, we think, a matter of State interest. A prior application to a court is appropriate if time permits it, although in the nature of the emergency the only question that can be explored satisfactorily is whether death will probably ensue if medical procedures are not followed. If a court finds, as the trial court did, that death will likely follow unless a transfusion is administered, the hospital and the physician should be permitted to follow that medical procedure.

For the reasons already given, we find that the interest of the hospital and its staff, as well as the State's interest in life, warranted the transfusion of blood under the circumstances of this case. The judgment is accordingly affirmed.

Review and Discussion Questions

1. On what ground does the court reach its opinion that Delores Heston should be given the transfusion?
2. If the woman's reasons were not based on established religious doctrine, do you think the courts would have had so much difficulty with these decisions? Would you? Explain.

READING: DEATH WITH DIGNITY ACT

GONZALES V. OREGON[*]

In 1994, Oregon voters approved a ballot measure called the Oregon Death with Dignity Act. This law allows physicians, within certain safeguards, to prescribe lethal doses of drugs at the request of terminally ill patients. This law created national controversy and led the U.S. attorney general to ban physicians from prescribing these drugs through the authority of a federal regulation that every prescription for a controlled substance in the United States must be for a legitimate medical purpose. The attorney general held that prescribing lethal drugs was not a legitimate medical purpose. In a 6 to 3 ruling, the Supreme Court decided that the attorney general could not overrule the state law. The case goes to the question of who has the authority to decide what counts as a legitimate medical purpose.

Justice Kennedy Delivered the Opinion of the Court

The question before us is whether the Controlled Substances Act allows the United States Attorney General to prohibit doctors from prescribing regulated drugs for use in physician-assisted suicide, notwithstanding a state law permitting the procedure. As the Court has observed, "Americans are engaged in an earnest and profound debate about the morality, legality, and practicality of physician-assisted suicide." *Washington v. Glucksberg*, 521 U.S. 702, 735 (1997). The dispute before us is in part a product of this political and moral debate, but its resolution requires an inquiry familiar to the courts: interpreting a federal statute to determine whether Executive action is authorized by, or otherwise consistent with, the enactment.

In 1994, Oregon became the first State to legalize assisted suicide when voters approved a ballot measure enacting the Oregon Death with Dignity Act (ODWDA). ... ODWDA, which survived a 1997 ballot measure seeking its repeal, exempts from civil or criminal liability state-licensed physicians who, in compliance with the specific safeguards in ODWDA, dispense or prescribe a lethal dose of drugs upon the request of a terminally ill patient.

---

[*] *Gonzales v. Oregon* 546 U.S. (2006).

The drugs Oregon physicians prescribe under ODWDA are regulated under a federal statute, the Controlled Substances Act (CSA or Act). ... The CSA allows these particular drugs to be available only by a written prescription from a registered physician. In the ordinary course the same drugs are prescribed in smaller doses for pain alleviation.

A November 9, 2001 Interpretive Rule issued by the Attorney General addresses the implementation and enforcement of the CSA with respect to ODWDA. It determines that using controlled substances to assist suicide is not a legitimate medical practice and that dispensing or prescribing them for this purpose is unlawful under the CSA. The Interpretive Rule's validity under the CSA is the issue before us.

I

We turn first to the text and structure of the CSA. Enacted in 1970 with the main objectives of combating drug abuse and controlling the legitimate and illegitimate traffic in controlled substances, the CSA creates a comprehensive, closed regulatory regime criminalizing the unauthorized manufacture, distribution, dispensing, and possession of substances classified in any of the Act's five schedules. ... A 1971 regulation promulgated by the Attorney General requires that every prescription for a controlled substance "be issued for a legitimate medical purpose by an individual practitioner acting in the usual course of his professional practice." 21 CFR § 1306.04(a) (2005).

To prevent diversion of controlled substances with medical uses, the CSA regulates the activity of physicians. ... The Attorney General may deny, suspend, or revoke this registration if, as relevant here, the physician's registration would be "inconsistent with the public interest." §824(a)(4); §822(a)(2) ....

Oregon voters enacted ODWDA in 1994. For Oregon residents to be eligible to request a prescription under ODWDA, they must receive a diagnosis from their attending physician that they have an incurable and irreversible disease that, within reasonable medical judgment, will cause death within six months. Attending physicians must also determine whether a patient has made a voluntary request, ensure a patient's choice is informed, and refer patients to counseling if they might be suffering from a psychological disorder or depression causing impaired judgment. A second "consulting" physician must examine the patient and the medical record and confirm the attending physician's conclusions. Oregon physicians may dispense or issue a prescription for the requested drug, but may not administer it.

The reviewing physicians must keep detailed medical records of the process leading to the final prescription .... Physicians who dispense medication pursuant to ODWDA must also be registered with both the State's Board of Medical Examiners and the federal Drug Enforcement Administration (DEA). In 2004, 37 patients ended their lives by ingesting a lethal dose of medication prescribed under ODWDA ....

In 1997, Members of Congress concerned about ODWDA invited the DEA to prosecute or revoke the CSA registration of Oregon physicians who assist suicide. They contended that hastening a patient's death is not legitimate medical practice, so prescribing controlled substances for that purpose violates the CSA. ... Attorney

General Reno considered the matter and concluded that the DEA could not take the proposed action ....

In 2001, John Ashcroft was appointed Attorney General ....

On November 9, 2001, without consulting Oregon or apparently anyone outside his Department, the Attorney General issued an Interpretive Rule announcing his intent to restrict the use of controlled substances for physician-assisted suicide. Incorporating the legal analysis of a memorandum he had solicited from his Office of Legal Counsel, the Attorney General ruled

> assisting suicide is not a "legitimate medical purpose" within the meaning of 21 CFR 1306.04 (2001), and that prescribing, dispensing, or administering federally controlled substances to assist suicide violates the Controlled Substances Act. Such conduct by a physician registered to dispense controlled substances may "render his registration ... inconsistent with the public interest" and therefore subject to possible suspension or revocation under 21 U. S. C. 824(a)(4). The Attorney General's conclusion applies regardless of whether state law authorizes or permits such conduct by practitioners or others and regardless of the condition of the person whose suicide is assisted.
>
> (66 Fed. Reg. 56608 (2001))

There is little dispute that the Interpretive Rule would substantially disrupt the ODWDA regime. Respondents contend, and petitioners do not dispute, that every prescription filled under ODWDA has specified drugs classified under Schedule II. A physician cannot prescribe the substances without DEA registration, and revocation or suspension of the registration would be a severe restriction on medical practice ....

In response the State of Oregon, joined by a physician, a pharmacist, and some terminally ill patients, all from Oregon, challenged the Interpretive Rule in federal court. The United States District Court for the District of Oregon entered a permanent injunction against the Interpretive Rule's enforcement ....

II

Executive actors often must interpret the enactments Congress has charged them with enforcing and implementing. The parties before us are in sharp disagreement both as to the degree of deference we must accord the Interpretive Rule's substantive conclusions and whether the Rule is authorized by the statutory text at all ....

The Government does not suggest that its interpretation turns on any difference between the statutory and regulatory language. The CSA allows prescription of drugs only if they have a "currently accepted medical use," 21 U. S. C. §812(b); requires a "medical purpose" for dispensing the least controlled substances of those on the schedules, §829(c); and, in its reporting provision, defines a "valid prescription" as one "issued for a legitimate medical purpose," §830(b)(3)(A)(ii). Similarly, physicians are considered to be acting as practitioners under the statute if they dispense controlled substances "in the course of professional practice." §802(21). The regulation uses the terms "legitimate medical purpose" and "the course of professional practice," *ibid.*, but this just repeats two statutory phrases and attempts to summarize the others. It gives little or no instruction on a central issue in this case: Who decides whether a particular activity is in "the course of professional practice" or done for a "legitimate medical purpose"? ...

The Attorney General has rulemaking power to fulfill his duties under the CSA. The specific respects in which he is authorized to make rules, however, instruct us that he is not authorized to make a rule declaring illegitimate a medical standard for care and treatment of patients that is specifically authorized under state law ....

.... If the Attorney General's argument were correct, his power to deregister necessarily would include the greater power to criminalize even the actions of registered physicians, whenever they engage in conduct he deems illegitimate ....

The importance of the issue of physician-assisted suicide, which has been the subject of an "earnest and profound debate" across the country, *Glucksberg*, 521 U.S., at 735, makes the oblique form of the claimed delegation all the more suspect. Under the Government's theory, moreover, the medical judgments the Attorney General could make are not limited to physician-assisted suicide. Were this argument accepted, he could decide whether any particular drug may be used for any particular purpose, or indeed whether a physician who administers any controversial treatment could be deregistered ....

In deciding whether the CSA can be read as prohibiting physician-assisted suicide, we look to the statute's text and design. The statute and our case law amply support the conclusion that Congress regulates medical practice insofar as it bars doctors from using their prescription-writing powers as a means to engage in illicit drug dealing and trafficking as conventionally understood. Beyond this, however, the statute manifests no intent to regulate the practice of medicine generally. The silence is understandable given the structure and limitations of federalism, which allow the States "'great latitude under their police powers to legislate as to the protection of the lives, limbs, health, comfort, and quiet of all persons.'" *Medtronic, Inc. v. Lohr*, 518 U.S. 470, 475 (1996) (quoting *Metropolitan Life Ins. Co. v. Massachusetts*, 471 U.S. 724, 756 (1985)).

The structure and operation of the CSA presume and rely upon a functioning medical profession regulated under the States' police powers ....

Oregon's regime is an example of the state regulation of medical practice that the CSA presupposes. Rather than simply decriminalizing assisted suicide, ODWDA limits its exercise to the attending physicians of terminally ill patients, physicians who must be licensed by Oregon's Board of Medical Examiners. The statute gives attending physicians a central role, requiring them to provide prognoses and prescriptions, give information about palliative alternatives and counseling, and ensure patients are competent and acting voluntarily. Any eligible patient must also get a second opinion from another registered physician, and the statute's safeguards require physicians to keep and submit to inspection detailed records of their actions ....

.... A prescription, the Government argues, necessarily implies that the substance is being made available to a patient for a legitimate medical purpose. The statute, in this view, requires an anterior judgment about the term "medical" or "medicine." The Government contends ordinary usage of these words ineluctably refers to a healing or curative art, which by these terms cannot embrace the intentional hastening of a patient's death. It also points to the teachings of Hippocrates, the positions of prominent medical organizations, the Federal Government, and the judgment of the 49 States that have not legalized physician-assisted suicide as further support for the proposition that the practice is not legitimate medicine ....

On its own, this understanding of medicine's boundaries is at least reasonable. The primary problem with the Government's argument, however, is its assumption that the CSA impliedly authorizes an Executive officer to bar a use simply because it may be inconsistent with one reasonable understanding of medical practice ....

The background principles of our federal system belie the notion that Congress would use such an obscure grant of authority to regulate areas traditionally supervised by the States' police power. ... [W]e conclude the CSA's prescription requirement does not authorize the Attorney General to bar dispensing controlled substances for assisted suicide in the face of a state medical regime permitting such conduct.

IV

The Government, in the end, maintains that the prescription requirement delegates to a single Executive officer the power to effect a radical shift of authority from the States to the Federal Government to define general standards of medical practice in every locality. The text and structure of the CSA show that Congress did not have this far-reaching intent to alter the federal-state balance and the congressional role in maintaining it.

The judgment of the Court of Appeals is *Affirmed.*

Justice Scalia, with Whom Chief Justice Roberts and Justice Thomas Join, Dissenting

Virtually every relevant source of authoritative meaning confirms that the phrase "legitimate medical purpose" does not include intentionally assisting suicide. "Medicine" refers to "[t]he science and art dealing with the prevention, cure, or alleviation of disease." Webster's Second 1527. The use of the word "legitimate" connotes an *objective* standard of "medicine," and our presumption that the CSA creates a uniform federal law regulating the dispensation of controlled substances. ... Virtually every medical authority from Hippocrates to the current American Medical Association (AMA) confirms that assisting suicide has seldom or never been viewed as a form of "prevention, cure, or alleviation of disease," and (even more so) that assisting suicide is not a "legitimate" branch of that "science and art." See OLC Memo, App. to Pet. for Cert. 113a–130a ....

In the face of this "overwhelming weight of authority," the Court's admission that "[o]n its own, this understanding of medicine's boundaries is *at least reasonable,*" *ante,* at 26 (emphasis added), tests the limits of understatement. The only explanation for such a distortion is that the Court confuses the *normative* inquiry of what the boundaries of medicine *should be*—which it is laudably hesitant to undertake—with the *objective* inquiry of what the accepted definition of "medicine" *is.* The same confusion is reflected in the Court's remarkable statement that "[t]he primary problem with the Government's argument ... is its assumption that the CSA impliedly authorizes an Executive officer to bar a use simply because it may be inconsistent with *one reasonable understanding* of medical practice." *Ibid.* (emphasis added). The fact that many in Oregon believe that the boundaries of "legitimate medicine" *should be* extended to include assisted suicide does not change the fact that the overwhelming weight of authority (including the 47 States that condemn physician-assisted suicide) confirms that they have not yet been so extended ....

The Court contends that the phrase "legitimate medical purpose" *cannot* be read to establish a broad, uniform federal standard for the medically proper use of controlled substances. *Ante*, at 22. But it also rejects the most plausible alternative proposition, urged by the State, that any use authorized under state law constitutes a "legitimate medical purpose." (The Court is perhaps leery of embracing this position because the State candidly admitted at oral argument that, on its view, a State could exempt from the CSA's coverage the use of morphine to achieve euphoria.) Instead, the Court reverse-engineers an approach somewhere between a uniform national standard and a state-by-state approach, holding (with no basis in the CSA's text) that "legitimate medical purpose" refers to *all* uses of drugs unrelated to "addiction and recreational abuse." *Ante*, at 27. Thus, though the Court pays lipservice to state autonomy, see *ante*, 23–24, its standard for "legitimate medical purpose" is in fact a hazily defined *federal* standard based on its purposive reading of the CSA, and extracted from obliquely relevant sections of the Act ....

Third, §821 also gives the Attorney General authority to promulgate rules and regulations "relating to the ... control of the ... dispensing of controlled substances." As discussed earlier, it is plain that the *ordinary* meaning of "control" must apply to §821, so that the plain import of the provision is to grant the Attorney General rulemaking authority ....

The Court nevertheless holds that this triply unambiguous delegation cannot be given full effect because "the design of the statute," *ante*, at 18, evinces the intent to grant the Secretary of Health and Human Services exclusive authority over scientific and medical determinations. This proposition is not remotely plausible. ... Rather, ... [i]t is entirely reasonable to think (as Congress evidently did) that it would be easier for the Attorney General occasionally to make judgments about the legitimacy of medical practices than it would be for the Secretary [of Health and Human Services] to get into the business of law enforcement. It is, in other words, perfectly consistent with an intelligent "design of the statute" to give the Nation's chief law enforcement official, not its chief health official, broad discretion over the substantive standards that govern registration and deregistration. That is *especially* true where the contested "scientific and medical" judgment at issue has to do with the legitimacy of physician-assisted suicide, which ultimately rests, not on "science" or "medicine," but on a naked value judgment. It no more depends upon a "quintessentially medical judgmen[t]," *ante*, at 20, than does the legitimacy of polygamy or eugenic infanticide. And it requires no particular *medical* training to undertake the objective inquiry into how the continuing traditions of Western medicine have consistently treated this subject ....

In concluding to the contrary, the Court merely presents the conclusory assertion that "it is doubtful the Attorney General could cite the 'public interest' or 'public health' to deregister a physician simply because he deemed a controversial practice permitted by state law to have an illegitimate medical purpose." *Ante*, at 17. But why on earth not?—especially when he has interpreted the relevant statutory factors in advance to give fair warning that such a practice is "inconsistent with the public interest." The Attorney General's discretion to determine the public interest in this area is admittedly broad—but certainly no broader than other congressionally conferred Executive powers that we have upheld in the past ....

The Court's decision today is perhaps driven by a feeling that the subject of assisted suicide is none of the Federal Government's business. It is easy to sympathize with that position. The prohibition or deterrence of assisted suicide is certainly not among the enumerated powers conferred on the United States by the Constitution, and it is within the realm of public morality (*bonos mores*) traditionally addressed by the so-called police power of the States. But then, neither is prohibiting the recreational use of drugs or discouraging drug addiction among the enumerated powers. From an early time in our national history, the Federal Government has used its enumerated powers, such as its power to regulate interstate commerce, for the purpose of protecting public morality—for example, by banning the interstate shipment of lottery tickets, or the interstate transport of women for immoral purposes. See *Hoke* v. *United States*, 227 U.S. 308, 321–323 (1913); *Lottery Case*, 188 U.S. 321, 356 (1903). Unless we are to repudiate a long and well-established principle of our jurisprudence, using the federal commerce power to prevent assisted suicide is unquestionably permissible. The question before us is not whether Congress *can* do this, or even whether Congress *should* do this; but simply whether Congress *has* done this in the CSA. I think there is no doubt that it has. If the term "*legitimate* medical purpose" has any meaning, it surely excludes the prescription of drugs to produce death.

For the above reasons, I respectfully dissent from the judgment of the Court.

Justice Thomas, Dissenting

When Angel Raich and Diane Monson challenged the application of the Controlled Substances Act (CSA), to their purely intrastate possession of marijuana for medical use as authorized under California law, a majority of this Court (a mere seven months ago) determined that the CSA effectively invalidated California's law because "the CSA is a comprehensive regulatory regime specifically designed to regulate which controlled substances can be utilized for medicinal purposes, *and in what manner*." *Gonzales* v. *Raich*, 545 U.S. _____, _____, (2005). The majority employed unambiguous language, concluding that the "manner" in which controlled substances can be utilized "for medicinal purposes" is one of the "core activities regulated by the CSA." *Id.*, at _____. And, it described the CSA as "creating a comprehensive framework for regulating the production, distribution, and possession of ... 'controlled substances,'" including those substances that "'have a useful and legitimate medical purpose,'" in order to "foster the beneficial use of those medications" and "to prevent their misuse." *Id.*, at _____ (slip op., at 21).

Today the majority beats a hasty retreat from these conclusions ....

While the scope of the CSA and the Attorney General's power thereunder are sweeping, and perhaps troubling, such expansive federal legislation and broad grants of authority to administrative agencies are merely the inevitable and inexorable consequence of this Court's Commerce Clause and separation-of-powers jurisprudence.

I agree with limiting the applications of the CSA in a manner consistent with the principles of federalism and our constitutional structure. ... But that is now water over the dam. ... Such considerations have little, if any, relevance where, as here, we are merely presented with a question of statutory interpretation, and not the extent of constitutionally permissible federal power. ... Accordingly, I respectfully dissent.

Review and Discussion Questions

1 What are "legitimate medical purposes" according to this Court?
2 What is an alternative definition that is consistent with prescribing lethal drugs to terminally ill patients? Which definition is better? Explain.
3 Who should decide what counts as a legitimate medical purpose: terminally ill individuals, the medical profession, hospitals, state-by-state laws, federal law, or some other body?

READING: AGING AND THE ENDS OF MEDICINE

DANIEL CALLAHAN[*]

Medical costs are skyrocketing, both in terms of real dollars and as a percentage of our total expenditures. At the same time that the elderly are consuming ever-greater amounts of our health care resources, the poor, and especially children, often suffer from malnutrition and a lack of even basic health care, including vaccinations. In this essay, Daniel Callahan addresses the problems of health care for the elderly, arguing that those who have lived a natural life span should be denied expensive new medical technologies. This leads Callahan to consider the objectives of medicine along with the notion of what constitutes a natural life span. Daniel Callahan is Director of the International Program of the Hastings Center.

In October of 1986, Dr. Thomas Starzl of the Presbyterian University Hospital in Pittsburgh successfully transplanted a liver into a 76-year-old woman. The typical cost of such an operation is over $200,000. He thereby accelerated the extension to the elderly of the most expensive and most demanding form of high-technology medicine. Not long after that, Congress brought organ transplantation under Medicare coverage, thus guaranteeing an even greater extension of this form of lifesaving care to older age groups.

This is, on the face of it, the kind of medical progress we have long grown to hail a triumph of medical technology and a newfound benefit to be provided by an established entitlement program. But now an oddity. At the same time those events were taking place, a parallel government campaign for cost containment was under way, with a special targeting of health care to the aged under the Medicare program.

It was not hard to understand why. In 1980, the 11% of the population over age 65 consumed some 29% of the total American health care expenditures of $219.4 billion. By 1986, the percentage of consumption by the elderly had increased to 31% and total expenditures to $450 billion. Medicare costs are projected to rise from $75 billion in 1986 to $114 billion in the year 2000, and in real not inflated dollars.

---

[*] Reprinted with permission of the author and the publisher from *Annals of the New York Academy of Sciences* 530 (June 15, 1988): 125–132.

There is every incentive for politicians, for those who care for the aged, and for those of us on the way to becoming old to avert our eyes from figures of that kind. We have tried as a society to see if we can simply muddle our way through. That, however, is no longer sufficient. The time has come, I am convinced, for a full and open reconsideration of our future direction. We cannot for much longer continue on our present course. Even if we could find a way to radically increase the proportion of our health care dollar going to the elderly, it is not clear that that would be a good social investment.

Is it sensible, in the face of a rapidly increasing burden of health care costs for the elderly, to press forward with new and expensive ways of extending their lives? Is it possible to even hope to control costs while, simultaneously, supporting the innovative research that generates ever-new ways to spend money? These are now unavoidable questions. Medicare costs rise at an extraordinary pace, fueled by an ever-increasing number and proportion of the elderly. The fastest-growing age group in the United States are those over the age of 85, increasing at a rate of about 10% every two years. By the year 2040, it has been projected that the elderly will represent 21% of the population and consume 45% of all health care expenditures. Could costs of that magnitude be borne?

Yet even as this intimidating trend reveals itself, anyone who works closely with the elderly recognizes that the present Medicare and Medicaid programs are grossly inadequate in meeting the real and full needs of the elderly. They fail, most notably, in providing decent long-term care and medical care that does not constitute a heavy out-of-pocket drain. Members of minority groups and single or widowed women are particularly disadvantaged. How will it be possible, then, to keep pace with the growing number of elderly in even providing present levels of care, much less in ridding the system of its present inadequacies and inequities—and, at the same time, furiously adding expensive new technologies?

The straight answer is that it will not be possible to do all of those things and that, worse still, it may be harmful to even try. It may be harmful because of the economic burdens it will impose on younger age groups and because of the skewing of national social priorities too heavily toward health care that it is coming to require. But it may also be harmful because it suggests to both the young and the old that the key to a happy old age is good health care. That may not be true.

It is not pleasant to raise possibilities of that kind. The struggle against what Dr. Robert Butler aptly and brilliantly called "ageism" in 1968 has been a difficult one. It has meant trying to persuade the public that not all the elderly are sick and senile. It has meant trying to convince Congress and state legislatures to provide more help for the old. It has meant trying to educate the elderly themselves to look upon their old age as a time of new, open possibilities. That campaign has met with only partial success. Despite great progress, the elderly are still subject to discrimination and stereotyping. The struggle against ageism is hardly over.

Three major concerns have, nonetheless, surfaced over the past few years. They are symptoms that a new era has arrived. The first is that an increasingly large share of health care is going to the elderly in comparison with benefits for children. The federal government, for instance, spends six times as much on health care for those over 65 as for those under 18. As the demographer Samuel Preston observed in a provocative 1984 presidential address to the Population Association of America:

> There is surely something to be said for a system in which things get better as we pass through life rather than worse. The great leveling off of age curves of psychological distress, suicide and income in the past two decades might simply reflect the fact that we have decided in some fundamental sense that we don't want to face futures that become continually bleaker. But let's be clear that the transfers from the working-age population to the elderly are also transfers away from children, since the working ages bear far more responsibility for childrearing than do the elderly.[1]

Preston's address had an immediate impact. The mainline aging advocacy groups responded with pained indignation, accusing Preston of fomenting a war between the generations. But led by Dave Durenberger, Republican Senator from Minnesota, it also stimulated the formation of Americans for Generational Equity (AGE), an organization created to promote debate on the burden to future generations, but particularly the Baby Boom generation, of "our major social insurance programs."[2] These two developments signaled the outburst of a struggle over what has come to be called "Intergenerational equity" that is only now gaining momentum.

The second concern is that the elderly dying consume a disproportionate share of health care costs. Stanford economist Victor Fuchs has noted:

> At present, the United States spends about 1% of the gross national product on health care for elderly persons who are in their last year of life. ... One of the biggest challenges facing policy makers for the rest of this century will be how to strike an appropriate balance between care of the [elderly] dying and health services for the rest of the population.[3]

The third concern is summed up in an observation by Jerome L. Avorn, M.D., of the Harvard Medical School:

> With the exception of the birth-control pill, each of the medical-technology interventions developed since the 1950s has its most widespread impact on people who are past their fifties – the further past their fifties, the greater the impact.[4]

Many of these interventions were not intended for the elderly. Kidney dialysis, for example, was originally developed for those between the age of 15 and 45. Now some 30% of its recipients are over 65.

These three concerns have not gone unchallenged. They have, on the contrary, been strongly resisted, as has the more general assertion that some form of rationing of health care for the elderly might become necessary. To the charge that the elderly receive a disproportionate share of resources, the response has been that what helps the elderly helps every other age group. It both relieves the young of the burden of care for elderly parents they would otherwise have to bear and, since they too will eventually become old, promises them similar care when they come to need it. There is no guarantee, moreover, that any cutback in health care for the elderly would result in a transfer of the savings directly to the young. Our system is not that rational or that organized. And why, others ask, should we contemplate restricting care for the elderly when we wastefully spend hundreds of millions of dollars on an inflated defense budget?

The charge that the elderly dying receive a large share of funds hardly proves that it is an unjust or unreasonable amount. They are, after all, the most in need. As some important studies have shown, moreover, it is exceedingly difficult to know that someone is dying; the most expensive patients, it turns out, are those who are expected to live but who actually die. That most new technologies benefit the old more than the young is perfectly sensible: most of the killer diseases of the young have now been conquered.

These are reasonable responses. It would no doubt be possible to ignore the symptoms that the raising of such concerns represents and to put off for at least a few more years any full confrontation with the overpowering tide of elderly now on the way. There is little incentive for politicians to think about, much less talk about, limits of any kind on health care for the aged; it is a politically hazardous topic. Perhaps also, as Dean Guido Calabresi of the Yale Law School and his colleague Philip Bobbitt observed in their thoughtful 1978 book *Tragic Choices*, when we are forced to make painful allocation choices, "Evasion, disguise, temporizing ... [and] averting our eyes enables us to save some lives even when we will not save all."[5]

Yet however slight the incentives to take on this highly troubling issue, I believe it is inevitable that we must. Already rationing of health care under Medicare is a fact of life, though rarely labeled as such. The requirement that Medicare recipients pay the first $500 of the costs of hospital care, that there is a cutoff of reimbursement of care beyond 60 days, and a failure to cover long-term-care, are nothing other than allocation and cost-saving devices. As sensitive as it is to the votes of the elderly, the Reagan administration only grudgingly agreed to support catastrophic health care costs of the elderly (a benefit that will not, in any event, help many of the aged). It is bound to be far more resistant to long-term care coverage, as will any administration.

But there are other reasons than economics to think about health care for the elderly. The coming economic crisis provides a much-needed opportunity to ask some deeper questions. Just what is it that we want medicine to do for us as we age? Earlier cultures believed that aging should be accepted and that it should be in part a time of preparation for death. Our culture seems increasingly to reject that view, preferring instead, it often seems, to think of aging as hardly more than another disease to be fought and rejected. Which view is correct? To ask that question is only to note that disturbing puzzles about the ends of medicine and the ends of aging lie behind the more immediate financing worries. Without some kind of answer to them, there is no hope of finding a reasonable, and possibly even a humane, solution to the growing problem of health care for the elderly.

Let me put my own view directly. The future goal of medicine in the care of the aged should be that of improving the quality of their life, not in seeking ways to extend that life. In its longstanding ambition to forestall death, medicine has in the care of the aged reached its last frontier. That is hardly because death is absent elsewhere—children and young adults obviously still die of maladies that are open to potential cure—but because the largest number of deaths (some 70%) now occur among those over the age of 65, with the highest proportion in those over

85. If death is ever to be humbled, that is where the essentially endless work remains to be done. But however tempting that challenge, medicine should now restrain its ambition at that frontier. To do otherwise will, I believe, be to court harm to the needs of other age groups and to the old themselves.

Yet to ask medicine to restrain itself in the face of aging and death is to ask more than it, or the public that sustains it, is likely to find agreeable. Only a fresh understanding of the ends and meaning of aging, encompassing two conditions, are likely to make that a plausible stance. The first is that we—both young and old—need to understand that it is possible to live out a meaningful old age that is limited in time, one that does not require a compulsive effort to turn to medicine for more life to make it bearable. The second condition is that, as a culture, we need a more supportive context for aging and death, one that cherishes and respects the elderly while at the same time recognizing that their primary orientation should be to the young and the generations to come, not to their own age group. It will be no less necessary to recognize that in the passing of the generations lies the constant reinvigoration of biological life.

Neither of these conditions will be easy to realize. Our culture has, for one thing, worked hard to redefine old age as a time of liberation, not decline. The terms "modern maturity" or "prime time" have, after all, come to connote a time of travel, new ventures in education and self-discovery, the ever-accessible tennis court or golf course, and delightfully periodic but gratefully brief visits from well-behaved grandchildren.

This is, to be sure, an idealized picture. Its attraction lies not in its literal truth but as a widely-accepted utopian reference point. It projects the vision of an old age to which more and more believe they can aspire and which its proponents think an affluent country can afford if it so chooses. That it requires a medicine that is single-minded in its aggressiveness against the infirmities of old age is of a piece with its hopes. But as we have come to discover, the costs of that kind of war are prohibitive. No matter how much is spent the ultimate problem will still remain: people age and die. Worse still, by pretending that old age can be turned into a kind of endless middle age, we rob it of meaning and significance for the elderly themselves. It is a way of saying that old age can be acceptable only to the extent that it can mimic the vitality of the younger years.

There is a plausible alternative: that of a fresh vision of what it means to live a decently long and adequate life, what might be called a natural life span. Earlier generations accepted the idea that there was a natural life span—the biblical norm of three score years and ten captures that notion (even though, in fact, that was a much longer life span than was then typically the case). It is an idea well worth reconsidering and would provide us with a meaningful and realizable goal. Modern medicine and biology have done much, however, to wean us away from that kind of thinking. They have insinuated the belief that the average life span is not a natural fact at all but instead one that is strictly dependent upon the state of medical knowledge and skill. And there is much to that belief as a statistical fact: the average life expectancy continues to increase, with no end in sight.

But that is not what I think we ought to mean by a natural life span. We need a notion of a full life that is based on some deeper understanding of human need and sensible possibility, not the latest state of medical technology or medical possibility. We should instead think of a natural life span as the achievement of a life long enough to accomplish for the most part those opportunities that life typically affords people and which we ordinarily take to be the prime benefits of enjoying a life at all—that of loving and living, of raising a family, of finding and carrying out work that is satisfying, of reading and thinking, and of cherishing our friends and families.

If we envisioned a natural life span that way, then we could begin to intensify the devising of ways to get people to that stage of life and to work to make certain they do so in good health and social dignity. People will differ on what they might count as a natural life span; determining its appropriate range for social policy purposes would need extended thought and debate. My own view is that it can now be achieved by the late 70s or early 80s.

That many of the elderly discover new interests and new facets of themselves late in life—my mother took up painting in her 70s and was selling her paintings up until her death at 86—does not mean that we should necessarily encourage a kind of medicine that would make that the norm. Nor does it mean that we should base social and welfare policy on possibilities of that kind. A more reasonable approach is to ask how medicine can help most people live out a decently long life and how that life can be enhanced along the way.

A longer life does not guarantee a better life—there is no inherent connection between the two. No matter how long medicine enabled people to live, death at any time—at age 90, or 100, or 110—would frustrate some possibility, some as-yet-unrealized goal. There is sadness in that realization, but not tragedy. An easily preventable death of a young child is an outrage. The death from an incurable disease of someone in the prime of young adulthood is a tragedy. But death at an old age, after a long and full life, is simply sad, a part of life itself.

As it confronts aging, medicine should have as its specific goal that of averting premature death, understood as death prior to a natural life span, and the relief of suffering thereafter. It should pursue those goals in order that the elderly can finish out their years with as little needless pain as possible and with as much vigor as can be generated in contributing to the welfare of younger age groups and to the community of which they are a part. Above all, the elderly need to have a sense of the meaning and significance of their stage in life, one that is not dependent for its human value on economic productivity or physical vigor.

What would a medicine oriented toward the relief of suffering rather than the deliberate extension of life be like? We do not yet have a clear and ready answer to that question, so longstanding, central, and persistent has been the struggle against death as part of the self-conception of medicine. But the hospice movement is providing us with much helpful evidence. It knows how to distinguish between the relief of suffering and the extension of life. A greater control by the elderly over their dying—and particularly a more readily respected and enforceable right to deny aggressive life-extending treatment—is a long-sought, minimally necessary goal.

What does this have to do with the rising cost of health care for the elderly? Everything. The indefinite extension of life combined with a never-satisfied improvement in the health of the elderly is a recipe for monomania and limitless spending. It fails to put health in its proper place as only one among many human goods. It fails to accept aging and death as part of the human condition. It fails to present to younger generations a model of wise stewardship.

How might we devise a plan to limit health care for the aged under public entitlement programs that is fair, humane, and sensitive to their special requirements and dignity? Let me suggest three principles to undergird a quest for limits. First, government has a duty, based on our collective social obligations to each other, to help people live out a natural life span but not actively to help medically extend life beyond that point. Second, government is obliged to develop under its research subsidies and pay for, under its entitlement programs, only that kind and degree of life-extending technology necessary for medicine to achieve and serve the end of a natural life span. The question is not whether a technology is available that can save the life of someone who has lived out a natural life span, but whether there is an obligation for society to provide them with that technology. I think not. Third, beyond the point of natural life span, government should provide only the means necessary for the relief of suffering, not life-extending technology. By proposing that we use age as a specific criterion for the limitation of life-extending health care, I am challenging one of the most revered norms of contemporary geriatrics: that medical need and not age should be the standard of care. Yet the use of age as a principle for the allocation of resources can be perfectly valid, both a necessary and legitimate basis for providing health care to the elderly. There is not likely to be any better or less arbitrary criterion for the limiting of resources in the face of the open-ended possibilities of medical advancement in therapy for the aged.

Medical "need," in particular, can no longer work as an allocation principle. It is too elastic a concept, too much a function of the state of medical art. A person of 100 dying from congestive heart failure "needs" a heart transplant no less than someone who is 30. Are we to treat both needs as equal? That is not economically feasible or, I would argue, a sensible way to allocate scarce resources. But it would be required by a strict need-based standard.

Age is also a legitimate basis for allocation because it is a meaningful and universal category. It can be understood at the level of common sense. It is concrete enough to be employed for policy purposes. It can also, most importantly, be of value to the aged themselves if combined with an ideal of old age that focuses on its quality rather than its indefinite extension.

I have become impressed with the philosophy underlying the British health care system and the way it meets the needs of the old and the chronically ill. It has, to begin with, a tacit allocation policy. It emphasizes improving the quality of life through primary care medicine and well-subsidized home care and institutional programs for the elderly rather than through life-extending acute care medicine. The well-known difficulty in getting dialysis after 55 is matched by like restrictions on access to open heart surgery, intensive care units, and other forms of expensive technology. An undergirding skepticism toward technology makes that a viable option. That attitude, together with a powerful drive for equity, "explains," as two commentators have noted, "why most British put a higher value on primary care for the population as a whole than on an abundance of sophisticated technology for the few who may benefit from it."[6]

That the British spend a significantly smaller proportion of their GNP (6.2%) on health care than Americans (10.8%) for an almost identical outcome in health status is itself a good advertisement for its priorities. Life expectancies are, for men, 70.0 years in the U.S. and 70.4 years in Great Britain; and, for women, 77.8

in the U.S. and 76.7 in Great Britain. There is, of course, a great difference in attitudes in the U.S. and Britain, and our individualism and love of technology stand in the way of a quick shift of priorities.

Yet our present American expectations about aging and death, it turns out, may not be all that reassuring. How many of us are really so certain that high-technology American medicine promises us all that much better an aging and death, even if some features appear improved and the process begins later than in earlier times? Between the widespread fear of death in an impersonal ICU, cozened about machines and invaded by tubes, on the one hand, or wasting away in the back ward of a nursing home, on the other, not many of us seem comforted.

Once we have reflected on those fears, it is not impossible that most people could be persuaded that a different, more limited set of expectations for health care could be made tolerable. That would be all the more possible if there was a greater assurance than at present that one could live out a full life span, that one's chronic illnesses would be better supported, and that long-term care and home care would be given a more powerful societal backing than is now the case. Though they would face a denial of life-extending medical care beyond a certain age, the old would not necessarily fear their aging any more than they now do. They would, on the contrary, know that a better balance had been struck between making our later years as good as possible rather than simply trying to add more years.

This direction would not immediately bring down the costs of care of the elderly; it would add new costs. But it would set in place the beginning of a new understanding of old age, one that would admit of eventual stabilization and limits. The time has come to admit we cannot go on much longer on the present course of open-ended health care for the elderly. Neither confident assertions about American affluence nor tinkering with entitlement provisions and cost-containment strategies will work for more than a few more years. It is time for the dream that old age can be an infinite and open frontier to end and for the unflagging, but self-deceptive, optimism that we can do anything we want with our economic system to be put aside.

The elderly will not be served by a belief that only a lack of resources or better financing mechanisms or political power stand between them and the limitations of their bodies. The good of younger age groups will not be served by inspiring in them a desire to live to an old age that will simply extend the vitality of youth indefinitely, as if old age is nothing but a sign that medicine has failed in its mission. The future of our society will not be served by allowing expenditures on health care for the elderly endlessly and uncontrollably to escalate, fueled by a false altruism that thinks anything less is to deny the elderly their dignity. Nor will it be served by that pervasive kind of self-serving that urges the young to support such a crusade because they will eventually benefit from it also.

We require instead an understanding of the process of aging and death that looks to our obligation to the young and to the future, that recognizes the necessity of limits and the acceptance of decline and death, and that values the old for their age and not for their continuing youthful vitality. In the name of accepting the elderly and repudiating discrimination against them, we have mainly succeeded in pretending that, with enough will and money, the unpleasant part of old age can be abolished. In the name of medical progress we have carried out a relentless war against death and decline, failing to ask in any probing way if that will give us a better society for all age groups.

The proper question is not whether we are succeeding in giving a longer life to the aged. It is whether we are making of old age a decent and honorable time of life. Neither a longer lifetime nor more life-extending technology is the way to that goal. The elderly themselves ask for greater financial security, for as much self-determination and independence as possible, for a decent quality of life and not just more life, and for a respected place in society.

The best way to achieve those goals is not simply to say more money and better programs are needed, however much they have their important place. We would do better to begin with a sense of limits, of the meaning of the human life cycle, and of the necessary coming and going of the generations. From that kind of starting point, we could devise a new understanding of old age.

Notes

1 S. H. Preston. 1984. "Children and the Elderly: Divergent Paths for America's Dependents." *Demography* 21: 491–495.
2 Americans for Generational Equity. Case Statement. May 1986.
3 V. R. Fuchs. 1984. "Though Much Is Taken: Reflections on Aging, Health, and Medical Care." *Milbank Mem. Fund Q.* 62: 464–465.
4 J. L. Avorn. 1986. "Medicine, Health, and the Geriatric Transformation." *Daedalus* 115: 211–225.
5 G. Calabresi, & P. Bobbitt. 1978. *Tragic Choices*. W. W. Norton. New York.
6 F. H. Miller, & G. A. H. Miller. 1986. "The Painful Prescription: A Procrustean Perspective." *N. Engl. J. Med.* 314: 1385.

Review and Discussion Questions

1 Describe the problems with health care that Callahan identifies.
2 What should be the goal of medicine for the aged, according to Callahan?
3 What principles does Callahan recommend for limiting public health care for the aged?
4 What argument might you give in response to Callahan's proposals?

READING: THE SURVIVAL LOTTERY

JOHN HARRIS[*]

Life-saving transplantable organs, which many people need to live, are scarce. People sometimes die because they can't get them. In this essay, John Harris proposes a lottery in which people are randomly chosen to donate their healthy organs so that others can live. What, Harris asks, would be objectionable about such a system, given that the "donors" are chosen at random and everybody has the same chance of being sacrificed? Harris then discusses, and answers, various objections to the proposal.

---

[*] Excerpted from pp. 87–95, "The Survival Lottery" by John Harris, *Philosophy* 50 (1975). Copyright © 1975. Reprinted by permission of Cambridge University Press.

John Harris is the Lord Alliance Professor of Bioethics and Director of the Institute for Science, Ethics and Innovation, University of Manchester, England.

Let us suppose that organ transplant procedures have been perfected; in such circumstances, if two dying patients could be saved by organ transplants, then, if surgeons have the requisite organs in stock and no other needy patients but nevertheless allow their patients to die, we would be inclined to say, and be justified in saying, that the patients died because the doctors refused to save them. But if there are no spare organs in stock and none otherwise available, the doctors have no choice; they cannot save their patients and so must let them die. In this case, we would be disinclined to say that the doctors are in any sense the cause of their patients' deaths. But let us further suppose that the two dying patients, Y and Z, are not happy about being left to die. They might argue that it is not strictly true that there are no organs which could be used to save them. Y needs a new heart and Z new lungs. They point out that if just one healthy person were to be killed, his organs could be removed and both of them be saved. We and the doctors would probably be alike in thinking that such a step, while technically possible, would be out of the question. We would not say that the doctors were killing their patients if they refused to prey upon the healthy to save the sick. And because this sort of surgical Robin Hoodery is out of the question, we can tell Y and Z that they cannot be saved and that when they die they will have died of natural causes and not of the neglect of their doctors. Y and Z do not agree, however; they insist that if the doctors fail to kill a healthy man and use his organs to save them, then the doctors will be responsible for their deaths.

Many philosophers have for various reasons believed that we must not kill even if by doing so we could save life. They believe that there is a moral difference between killing and letting die. On this view, to kill A so that Y and Z might live is ruled out because we have a strict obligation not to kill but a duty of some lesser kind to save life. A. H. Clough's dictum "Thou shalt not kill but need'st not strive officiously to keep alive" expresses bluntly this point of view. The dying Y and Z may be excused for not being much impressed by Clough's dictum. They agree that it is wrong to kill the innocent and are prepared to agree to an absolute prohibition against so doing. They do not agree, however, that A is more innocent than they are. Y and Z might go on to point out that the currently acknowledged right of the innocent not to be killed, even where their deaths might give life to others, is just a decision to prefer the lives of the fortunate to those of the unfortunate. A is innocent in the sense that he has done nothing to deserve death, but Y and Z are also innocent in this sense. Why should they be the ones to die simply because they are so unlucky as to have diseased organs? Why, they might argue, should their living or dying be left to chance when in so many other areas of human life we believe that we have an obligation to ensure the survival of the maximum number of lives possible?

Y and Z argue that if a doctor refuses to treat a patient, with the result that the patient dies, he has killed that patient as sure as shooting and that, in exactly the same way, if the doctors refuse Y and Z the transplants that they need, then their refusal will kill Y and Z, again as sure as shooting. The doctors, and indeed the society which supports their inaction, cannot defend themselves by arguing that they are neither expected nor required by law or convention to kill so that lives may be saved (indeed, quite the reverse), since this is just an appeal to custom or authority. A man who does his own moral thinking must decide whether, in these circumstances, he ought to save two lives at the cost of one, or one life at the cost of two. The fact that so-called "third parties" have never before been brought into such calculations, have never before been thought of as being involved, is not an argument against their now becoming so. There are, of course, good arguments against allowing doctors simply to haul passersby off the streets whenever they have a couple of patients in need of new organs. And the harmful side effects of such a practice in terms of terror and distress to the victims, the witnesses, and society generally would give us further reasons for dismissing the idea. Y and Z realize this and have a proposal, which they will shortly produce, which would largely meet objections to placing such power in the hands of doctors and eliminate at least some of the harmful side effects.

In the unlikely event of their feeling obliged to reply to the reproaches of Y and Z, the doctors might offer the following argument: they might maintain that a man is only responsible for the death of someone whose life he might have saved, if, in all the circumstances of the case, he ought to have saved the man by the means available. This is why a doctor might be a murderer if he simply refused or neglected to treat a patient who would die without treatment, but not if he could only save the patient by doing something he ought in no circumstances to do—kill the innocent. Y and Z readily agree that a man ought not to do what he ought not to do, but they point out that if the doctors, and for that matter society at large, ought on balance to kill one man if two can thereby be saved, then failure to do so will involve responsibility for the consequent deaths. The fact that Y and Z's proposal involves killing the innocent cannot be a reason for refusing to consider their proposal, for this would just be a refusal to face the question at issue and so avoid having to make a decision as to what ought to be done in circumstances like these. It is Y and Z's claim that failure to adopt their plan will also involve killing the innocent, rather more of the innocent than the proposed alternative.

To back up this last point, to remove the arbitrariness of permitting doctors to select their donors from among the chance passersby outside hospitals, and the tremendous power this would place in doctors' hands, to mitigate worries about side effects and lastly to appease those who wonder why poor old A should be singled out for sacrifice, Y and Z put forward the following scheme: they propose that everyone be given a sort of lottery number. Whenever doctors have two or more dying patients who could be saved by transplants, and no suitable organs have come to hand through "natural" deaths, they can ask a central computer to supply a suitable donor. The computer will then pick the number of a suitable donor at random and he will be killed so that the lives of two or more others may be saved. No doubt if the scheme were ever to be implemented, a suitable euphemism for "killed" would be employed. Perhaps we would begin to talk about citizens being called upon to "give life" to others. With the refinement of transplant procedures, such a scheme could offer the chance of saving large numbers of lives that are now lost. Indeed, even taking into account the loss of the lives of donors, the numbers of untimely deaths each year might be dramatically reduced, so much so that everyone's chance of living to a ripe old age might be increased. If this were to be the consequence of the adoption of such a scheme, and it might well be, it could not be dismissed lightly. It might of course be objected that it is likely that more old people will need transplants to prolong their lives than will the young, and so the scheme would inevitably lead to a society dominated by the old. But if such a society is thought objectionable, there is no reason to suppose that a program could not be designed for the computer that would ensure the maintenance of whatever is considered to be an optimum age distribution throughout the population.

Suppose that interplanetary travel revealed a world of people like ourselves, but who organized their society according to this scheme. No one was considered to have an absolute right to life or freedom from interference, but everything was always done to ensure that as many people as possible would enjoy long and happy lives. In such a world, a man who attempted to escape when his number was up or who resisted on the grounds that no one had a right to take his life might well be regarded as a murderer. We might or might not prefer to live in such a world, but the morality of its inhabitants would surely be one that we could respect. It would not be obviously more barbaric or cruel or immoral than our own.

Y and Z are willing to concede one exception to the universal application of their scheme. They realize that it would be unfair to allow people who have brought their misfortune on themselves to benefit from the lottery. There would clearly be something unjust about killing the abstemious B so that W (whose heavy smoking has given him lung cancer) and X (whose drinking has destroyed his liver) should be preserved to overindulge again.

What objections could be made to the lottery scheme? A first straw to clutch at would be the desire for security. Under such a scheme, we would never know when we would hear *them* knocking at the door. Every post might bring a sentence of death, every sound in the night might be the sound of boots on the stairs. But, as we have seen, the chances of actually being called upon to make the ultimate sacrifice might be slimmer than is the present risk of being killed on the roads, and most of us do not lie trembling abed, appalled at the prospect of being dispatched on the morrow. The truth is that lives might well be more secure under such a scheme.

If we respect individuality and see every human being as unique in his own way, we might want to reject a society in which it appeared that individuals were seen merely as interchangeable units in a structure, the value of which lies in its having as many healthy units as possible. But of course Y and Z would want to know why A's individuality was more worthy of respect than theirs.

Another plausible objection is the natural reluctance to play God with men's lives, the feeling that it is wrong to make any attempt to re-allot the life opportunities that fate has determined, that the deaths of Y and Z would be "natural," whereas the death of anyone killed to save them would have been perpetrated by men. But if we are able to change things, then to elect not to do so is also to determine what will happen in the world.

Neither does the alleged moral difference between killing and letting die afford a respectable way of rejecting the claims of Y and Z. For if we really want to counter proponents of the lottery, if we really want to answer Y and Z and not just put them off, we cannot do so by saying that the lottery involves killing and object to it for that reason, because to do so would, as we have seen, just beg the question as to whether the failure to save as many people as possible might not also amount to killing.

To opt for the society which Y and Z propose would be then to adopt a society in which saintliness would be mandatory. Each of us would have to recognize a binding obligation to give up his own life for others when called upon to do so. In such a society, anyone who reneged upon this duty would be a murderer. The most promising objection to such a society, and indeed to any principle which required us to kill A in order to save Y and Z, is, I suspect, that we are committed to the right of self-defense. If I can kill A to save Y and Z, then he can kill me to save P and Q, and it is only if I am prepared to agree to this that I will opt for the lottery or be prepared to agree to a man's being killed if doing so would save the lives of more than one other man. Of course, there is something paradoxical about basing objections to the lottery scheme on the right of self-defense since, *ex hypothesi*, each person would have a better chance of living to a ripe old age if the lottery scheme were to be implemented. Nonetheless, the feeling that no man should be required to lay down his life for others makes many people shy away from such a scheme, even though it might be rational to accept it on prudential grounds and perhaps even mandatory on utilitarian grounds. Again, Y and Z would reply that the right of self-defense must extend to them as much as to anyone else, and while it is true that they can only live if another man is killed, they would claim that it is also true that if they are left to die, then someone who lives on does so over their dead bodies.

It might be argued that the institution of the survival lottery has not gone far to mitigate the harmful side effects in terms of terror and distress to victims, witnesses, and society generally that would be occasioned by doctors simply snatching passersby off the streets and disorganizing them for the benefit of the unfortunate. Donors would after all still have to be procured, and this process, however it was carried out, would still be likely to prove distressing to all concerned. The lottery scheme would eliminate the arbitrariness of leaving the life-and-death decisions to the doctors and remove the possibility of such terrible power falling into the hands of any individuals, but the terror and distress would remain. The effect of having to apprehend presumably unwilling victims would give us pause. Perhaps only a long period of education or propaganda could remove our abhorrence. What this abhorrence reveals about the rights and wrongs of the situation is, however, more difficult to assess. We might be inclined to say that only monsters could ignore the promptings of conscience so far as to operate the lottery scheme. But the promptings of conscience are not necessarily the most reliable guide. In the present case, Y and Z would argue that such promptings are mere squeamishness, an overnice self-indulgence that costs lives. Death, Y and Z would remind us, is a distressing experience whenever and to whomever it occurs, so the less it occurs the better. Fewer victims and witnesses will be distressed as part of the side effects of the lottery scheme than would suffer as part of the side effects of not instituting it.

Lastly, a more limited objection might be made, not to the idea of killing to save lives but to the involvement of "third parties." Why, so the objection goes, should we not give X's heart to Y or Y's lungs to X, the same number of lives being thereby preserved and no one else's life set at risk? Y and Z's reply to this objection differs from their previous line of argument. To amend their plan so that the involvement of so-called "third parties" is ruled out would, Y and Z claim, violate their right to equal concern and respect with the rest of society. They argue that such a proposal would amount to treating the unfortunate who need new organs as a class within society whose lives are considered to be of less value than those of its more fortunate members. What possible justification could there be for singling out one group of people whom we would be justified in using as donors but not another? The idea in the mind of those who would propose such a step must be something like the following: since Y and Z cannot survive, since they are going to die in any event, there is no harm in putting their names into the lottery, for the chances of their dying cannot thereby be increased and will in fact almost certainly be reduced. But this is just to ignore everything that Y and Z have been saying. For if their lottery scheme is adopted, they are not going to die anyway—their chances of dying are no greater and no less than those of any other participant in the lottery whose number may come up. This ground for confining selection of donors to the unfortunate therefore disappears. Any other ground must discriminate against Y and Z as members of a class whose lives are less worthy of respect than those of the rest of society.

It might more plausibly be argued that the dying who cannot themselves be saved by transplants, or by any other means at all, should be the priority selection group for the computer program. But how far off must death be for a man to be classified as "dying"? Those so classified might argue that their last few days or weeks of life are as valuable to them (if not more valuable) than the possibly longer span remaining to others. The problem of narrowing down the class of possible donors without discriminating unfairly against some subclass of society is, I suspect, insoluble.

Such is the case for the survival lottery. Utilitarians ought to be in favor of it, and absolutists cannot object to it on the ground that it involves killing the innocent, for it is Y and Z's case that any alternative must also involve killing the innocent. If the absolutist wishes to maintain his objection, he must point to some morally relevant difference between positive and negative killing. This challenge opens the door to a large topic with a whole library of literature, but Y and Z are dying and do not have time to explore it exhaustively. In their own case, the most likely candidate for some feature which might make this moral difference is the malevolent intent of Y and Z themselves. An absolutist might well argue that while no one intends the deaths of Y and Z, no one necessarily wishes them dead or aims at their demise for any reason, they do mean to kill A (or have him killed). But Y and Z can reply that the death of A is no part of their plan, they merely wish to use a couple of his organs, and if he cannot live without them ... *tant pis*! None would be more delighted than Y and Z if artificial organs would do as well and so render the lottery scheme otiose.

One form of absolutist argument perhaps remains. This involves taking an Orwellian stand on some principle of common decency. The argument would then be that even to enter into the sort of "macabre" calculations that Y and Z propose displays a blunted sensibility, a corrupted and vitiated mind. Forms of this argument have recently been advanced by Noam Chomsky *(American Power and the New Mandarins)* and Stuart Hampshire *(Morality and Pessimism)*. The indefatigable Y and Z would of course deny that their calculations are in any sense "macabre," and would present them as the most humane course available in the circumstances. Moreover they would claim that the Orwellian stand on decency is the product of a closed mind and not susceptible to rational argument. Any reasoned defense of such a principle must appeal to notions like respect for human life, as Hampshire's argument in fact does, and these Y and Z could make conformable to their own position.

Can Y and Z be answered? Perhaps only by relying on moral intuition, on the insistence that we do feel there is something wrong with the survival lottery and our confidence that this feeling is prompted by some morally relevant difference between our bringing about the death of A and our bringing about the deaths of Y and Z. Whether we could retain this confidence in our intuitions if we were to be confronted by a society in which the survival lottery operated, was accepted by all, and was seen to save many lives that would otherwise have been lost it would be interesting to know.

There would of course be great practical difficulties in the way of implementing the lottery. In so many cases it would be agonizingly difficult to decide whether or not a person had brought his misfortune on himself. There are numerous ways in which a person may contribute to his predicament, and the task of deciding how far, or how decisively, a person is himself responsible for his fate would be formidable. And in those cases where we can be confident that a person is innocent of responsibility for his predicament, can we acquire this confidence in time to save him? The lottery scheme would be a powerful weapon in the hands of someone willing and able to misuse it. Could we ever feel certain that the lottery was safe from unscrupulous computer programmers? Perhaps we should be thankful that such practical difficulties make the survival lottery an unlikely consequence of the perfection of transplants. Or perhaps we should be appalled.

It may be that we would want to tell Y and Z that the difficulties and dangers of their scheme would be too great a price to pay for its benefits. It is as well to be clear, however, that there is also a high, perhaps an even higher, price to be paid for the rejection of the scheme. That price is the lives of Y and Z and many like them, and we delude ourselves if we suppose that the reason why we reject their plan is that we accept the sixth commandment.

Acknowledgment

Thanks are due to Ronald Dworkin, Jonathan Glover, M. J. Inwood, and Anne Seller for helpful comments.

Review and Discussion Questions

1 Describe the lottery system that Harris imagines. What problem(s) or objections is it meant to overcome?
2 How does Harris answer those who might claim the lottery system would be "playing God"?
3 Why does Harris think that the distinction between killing and allowing to die cannot be used to criticize the lottery?
4 What does Harris propose to do about people who need the organs because their own actions have destroyed their health?
5 Harris thinks that he has answered those who worry that the lottery would have too many bad side effects. How does he answer them? Are his answers adequate?
6 Would it matter if the survival lottery were chosen by a democratic vote? How could it be fairly chosen, since the risks vary with age as well as health?

Essay and Paper Topics for Chapter 9

1. Is there a right to health care? Draw on any of the moral theories in Chapter 3.
2. Drawing on any of the readings in this chapter, what is your position on the ethics of euthanasia and how do you defend it?
3. Using the essay by Daniel Callahan in this chapter as a point of reference, discuss how medical resources should be distributed.
4. Use both Supreme Court cases in this chapter and any other relevant arguments offered throughout this book to defend your view about who should have the authority to decide about controversial and medically important health care decisions.

Part III

Personal Relationships

Chapter 10

Love and Sex

Love, sexual relationships, and sexual morality are oft-discussed, intensely personal, emotional, and profoundly important topics to most people. Should sex be limited to marriage? What is sex, ideally? Merely an intense pleasurable experience? An expression of love? Essays in this chapter begin with Kant's famous discussion of sexual duty, followed by a series of different perspectives on the nature of sex, homosexuality, and the point of love.

READING: DUTIES TOWARD THE BODY IN RESPECT TO SEXUAL IMPULSE

IMMANUEL KANT*

In this reading, Immanuel Kant discusses the nature of the "sexual impulse" and people's needs to control it, as well as his views on marriage. Kant sees sexual desire as threatening people's higher, rational nature, and in particular the requirement that we respect ourselves and others by acting only on principles we can will to become universal laws. Specifically, he thinks some sexual practices violate the fundamental ethical principle that we must never treat another person merely as a means, but always as an end. Prostitution, concubinage, and extramarital sex are all, Kant argues, inconsistent with this most fundamental of moral requirements. He then goes on to describe the moral basis of marriage and the morality of homosexuality. Kant's biography can be found in Chapter 3.

Amongst our inclinations there is one which is directed towards other human beings. They themselves, and not their work and services, are its Objects of enjoyment. It is true that man has no inclination to enjoy the flesh of another—except, perhaps, in the vengeance of war, and then it is hardly a desire—but none the less there does exist an inclination which we may call an appetite for enjoying another human being. We refer to sexual impulse. Man can, of course, use another human being as an instrument for his service; he can use his hands, his feet, and even all his powers; he can use him for his own purposes with the other's consent. But

---

* From pp. 162–172 in *Lectures in Ethics* by Immanuel Kant, translated by Louis Infield. Copyright © 1963. Published by Methuen & Company. Reprinted by permission of Taylor & Francis Books UK.

there is no way in which a human being can be made an Object of indulgence for another except through sexual impulse. This is in the nature of a sense, which we can call the sixth sense; it is an appetite for another human being. We say that a man loves someone when he has an inclination towards another person. If by this love we mean true human love, then it admits of no distinction between types of persons, or between young and old. But a love that springs merely from sexual impulse cannot be love at all, but only appetite. Human love is goodwill, affection, promoting the happiness of others and finding joy in their happiness. But it is clear that, when a person loves another purely from sexual desire, none of these factors enter into the love. Far from there being any concern for the happiness of the loved one, the lover, in order to satisfy his desire and still his appetite, may even plunge the loved one into the depths of misery. Sexual love makes of the loved person an Object of appetite; as soon as that appetite has been stilled, the person is cast aside as one casts away a lemon which has been sucked dry. Sexual love can, of course, be combined with human love and so carry with it the characteristics of the latter, but taken by itself and for itself, it is nothing more than appetite. Taken by itself it is a degradation of human nature; for as soon as a person becomes an Object of appetite for another, all motives of moral relationship cease to function, because as an Object of appetite for another a person becomes a thing and can be treated and used as such by every one. This is the only case in which a human being is designed by nature as the Object of another's enjoyment. Sexual desire is at the root of it; and that is why we are ashamed of it, and why all strict moralists, and those who had pretensions to be regarded as saints, sought to suppress, and extirpate it. It is true that without it a man would be incomplete; he would rightly believe that he lacked the necessary organs, and this would make him imperfect as a human being; none the less men made pretence on this question and sought to suppress these inclinations because they degraded mankind.

Because sexuality is not an inclination which one human being has for another as such, but is an inclination for the sex of another, it is a principle of the degradation of human nature, in that it gives rise to the preference of one sex to the other, and to the dishonouring of that sex through the satisfaction of desire. The desire which a man has for a woman is not directed towards her because she is a human being, but because she is a woman; that she is a human being is of no concern to the man; only her sex is the object of his desire. Human nature is thus subordinated. Hence it comes that all men and women do their best to make not their human nature but their sex more alluring and direct their activities and lusts entirely towards sex. Human nature is thereby sacrificed to sex. If then a man wishes to satisfy his desire, and a woman hers, they stimulate each other's desire; their inclinations meet, but their object is not human nature but sex, and each of them dishonours the human nature of the other. They make of humanity an instrument for the satisfaction of their lusts and inclinations, and dishonour it by placing it on a level with animal nature. Sexuality, therefore, exposes mankind to the danger of equality with the beasts. But as man has this desire from nature, the question arises how far he can properly make use of it without injury to his manhood. How far may persons allow one of the opposite sex to satisfy his or her desire upon them? Can they sell themselves, or let themselves out on hire, or by some other contract allow use to be made of their sexual faculties? Philosophers generally point out the harm done by this inclination and the ruin it brings to the body or to the commonwealth, and they believe that, except for the harm it does, there would be nothing contemptible in such conduct in itself. But if this were so, and if giving vent to this desire was not in itself abominable and did not involve immorality, then any one who could avoid being harmed by them could make whatever use he wanted of his sexual propensities. For the prohibitions of prudence are never unconditional; and the conduct would in itself be unobjectionable, and would only be harmful under certain conditions. But in point of fact, there is in the conduct itself something which is contemptible and contrary to the dictates of morality. It follows, therefore, that there must be certain conditions under which alone the use of the *facultates sexuales* would be in keeping with morality. There must be a basis for restraining our freedom in the use we make of our inclinations so that they conform to the principles of morality. We shall endeavour to discover these conditions and this basis. Man cannot dispose over himself because he is not a thing; he is not his own property; to say that he is would be self-contradictory; for in so far as he is a person he is a Subject in whom the ownership of things can be vested, and if he were his own property, he would be a thing over which he could have ownership. But a person cannot be a property and so cannot be a thing which can be owned, for it is impossible to be a person and a thing, the proprietor and the property.

Accordingly, a man is not at his own disposal. He is not entitled to sell a limb, not even one of his teeth. But to allow one's person for profit to be used by another for the satisfaction of sexual desire, to make of oneself an Object of demand, is to dispose over oneself as over a thing and to make of oneself a thing on which another satisfies his appetite, just as he satisfies his hunger upon a steak. But since the inclination is directed towards one's sex and not towards one's humanity, it is clear that one thus partially sacrifices one's humanity and thereby runs a moral risk. Human beings are, therefore, not entitled to offer themselves, for profit, as things for the use of others in the satisfaction of their sexual propensities. In so doing they would run the risk of having their person used by all and sundry as an instrument for the satisfaction of inclination. This way of satisfying sexuality is *vaga libido* [prostitution], in which one satisfies the inclinations of others for gain. It is possible for either sex. To let one's person out on hire and to surrender it to another for the satisfaction of his sexual desire in return for money is the depth of infamy. The underlying moral principle is that man is not his own property and cannot do with his body what he will. The body is part of the self; in its togetherness with the self it constitutes the person; a man cannot make of his person a thing, and this is exactly what happens in *vaga libido*. This manner of satisfying sexual desire is, therefore, not permitted by the rules of morality. But what of the second method, namely *concubinatus* [sex outside marriage]? Is this also inadmissible? In this case both persons satisfy their desire mutually and there is no idea of gain, but they serve each other only for the satisfaction of sexuality. There appears to be nothing unsuitable in this arrangement, but there is nevertheless one consideration which rules it out. Concubinage consists in one person surrendering to another only for the satisfaction of their sexual desire whilst retaining freedom and rights in other personal respects affecting welfare and happiness. But the person who so surrenders is used as a thing; the desire is still directed only towards sex and not towards the person as a human being. But it is obvious that to surrender part of oneself is to surrender the whole, because a human being is a unity. It is not possible to have the disposal of a part only of a person without having at the same time a right of disposal over the whole person, for each part of a person is integrally bound up with the whole. But concubinage does not give me a right of disposal over the whole person but only over a part, namely the *organa sexualia.* It presupposes a contract. This contract deals only with the enjoyment of a part of the person and not with the entire circumstances of the person. Concubinage is certainly a contract, but it is one-sided; the rights of the two parties are not equal. But if in concubinage I enjoy a party of a person, I thereby enjoy the whole person; yet by the terms of the arrangement I have not the rights over the whole person, but only over a part; I, therefore, make the person into a thing. For that reason this method of satisfying sexual desire is also not permitted by the rules of morality. The sole condition on which we are free to make use of our sexual desire depends upon the right to dispose over the person as a whole—over the welfare and happiness and generally over all the circumstances of that person. If I have the right over the whole person, I have also the right over the part and so I have the right to use the person's *organa sexualia* for the satisfaction of sexual desire. But how am I to obtain these rights over the whole person? Only by giving that person the same rights over the whole of myself. This happens only in marriage. Matrimony is an agreement between two persons by which they grant each other reciprocal rights, each of them undertaking to surrender the whole of their person to the other with a complete right to disposal over it. We can now apprehend by reason how a *commercium sexuale* [sexual relationship] is possible without degrading humanity and breaking the moral laws. Matrimony is the only condition in which use can be made of one's sexuality. If one devotes one's person to another, one devotes not only sex but the whole person; the two cannot be separated. If, then, one yields one's person, body and soul, for good and ill and in every respect, so that the other has complete rights over it, and if the other does not similarly yield himself in return and does not extend in return the same rights and privileges, the arrangement is one-sided. But if I yield myself completely to another and obtain the person of the other in return, I win myself back; I have given myself up as the property of another, but in turn I take that other as my property, and so win myself back again in winning the person whose property I have become. In this way the two persons become a unity of will. Whatever good or ill, joy or sorrow befall either of them, the other will share in it. Thus sexuality leads to a union of human beings, and in that union alone its exercise is possible. This condition of the use of sexuality, which is only fulfilled in marriage, is a moral condition. But let us pursue this aspect further and examine the case of a man who takes two wives. In such a case each wife would have but half a man, although she would be giving herself wholly and ought in consequence to be entitled to the whole man. To sum up: *vaga libido* is ruled out on moral grounds; the same applies to concubinage; there only remains matrimony, and in matrimony polygamy is ruled out also for moral reasons; we, therefore, reach the conclusion that the only feasible arrangement is that of monogamous marriage. Only under that condition can I indulge my *facultas sexualis.* We cannot here pursue the subject further.

Crimina carnis [crimes of the flesh] are contrary to self-regarding duty because they are against the ends of humanity. They consist in abuse of one's sexuality. Every form of sexual indulgence, except in marriage, is a misuse of sexuality, and so a *crimen carnis*. Adultery cannot take place except in marriage; it signifies a breach of marriage. Just as the engagement to marry is the most serious and most inviolable engagement between two persons and binds them for life, so also is adultery the greatest breach of faith that there can be, because it is disloyalty to an engagement than which there can be none more important. For this reason adultery is cause for divorce. Another cause is incompatibility and inability to be at one, whereby unity and concord of will between the two persons is impossible.

Uses of sexuality which are contrary to natural instinct and to animal nature are *crimina carnis contra naturam*. First amongst them we have onanism [masturbation]. This is abuse of the sexual faculty without any object, the exercise of the faculty in the complete absence of any object of sexuality. The practice is contrary to the ends of humanity and even opposed to animal nature. By it man sets aside his person and degrades himself below the level of animals. A second *crimen carnis contra naturam* is intercourse between *sexus homogenii* [same sex], in which the object of sexual impulse is a human being but there is homogeneity instead of heterogeneity of sex, as when a woman satisfies her desire on a woman, or a man on a man. This practice too is contrary to the ends of humanity; for the end of humanity in respect of sexuality is to preserve the species without debasing the person; but in this instance the species is not being preserved (as it can be by a *crimen carnis secundum naturam*), but the person is set aside, the self is degraded below the level of the animals, and humanity is dishonoured. The third *crimen carnis contra naturam* occurs when the object of the desire is in fact of the opposite sex but is not human. Such is sodomy, or intercourse with animals. This, too, is contrary to the ends of humanity and against our natural instinct. It degrades mankind below the level of animals, for no animal turns in this way from its own species. All *crimina carnis contra naturam* degrade human nature to a level below that of animal nature and make man unworthy of his humanity. He no longer deserves to be a person. From the point of view of duties towards himself such conduct is the most disgraceful and the most degrading of which man is capable. Suicide is the most dreadful, but it is not as dishonourable and base as the *crimina carnis contra naturam*. These vices make us ashamed that we are human beings and, therefore, capable of them.

Review and Discussion Questions

1 What is the difference between true human love and sexual desire, according to Kant?
2 Kant says that sex can subordinate another human being by treating her (or him) not as a human being but as a sexual creature. Explain what you think he might mean.
3 Explain how Kant seems to understand the nature of persons: Are we minds, bodies, or both? What does he mean when he says we are "not at our own disposal"?
4 In what way does sex outside marriage or concubinage presuppose a contract that deals "only with a part of the person"? How can people gain "rights over the whole person," according to Kant? What does he mean by that phrase?
5 Explain Kant's objection to homosexuality. How might it be argued that homosexual relations are compatible with, rather than contrary to, Kant's view of the legitimate use of our sexual faculties?
6 Kant writes elsewhere that polygamy is ruled out because the contract is unequal: One person gives up more than the other. In marriage, however, he thinks the relationship is reciprocal and therefore acceptable. Explain why Kant would think that, given his general moral view.

READING: PLAIN SEX

ALAN H. GOLDMAN*

Critical of Kant and various defenders of the means–end conception of sex, Goldman offers an alternative "plain fact" understanding of human sexuality. Rather than serving another goal, such as reproduction or the expression of love, sex in Goldman's view is something far simpler: the desire for physical contact. Goldman concludes with discussions of the nature of love and of sexual perversion. Alan H. Goldman is the Kenan Professor of Humanities Emeritus at the College of William and Mary.

1 Sex as the Desire for Physical Contact

I shall suggest here that sex continues to be misrepresented in recent writings, at least in philosophical writings, and I shall criticize the predominant form of analysis which I term "means–end analysis." Such conceptions attribute a necessary external goal or purpose to sexual activity, whether it be reproduction, the expression of love, simple communication, or interpersonal awareness. They analyze sexual activity as a means to one of these ends, implying that sexual desire is a desire to reproduce, to love or be loved, or to communicate with others. All definitions of this type suggest false views of the relation of sex to perversion and morality by implying that sex which does not fit one of these models or fulfill one of these functions is in some way deviant or incomplete.

The alternative, simpler analysis with which I will begin is that sexual desire is desire for contact with another person's body and for the pleasure which such contact produces; sexual activity is activity which tends to fulfill such desire of the agent. This definition in terms of the general goal of sexual desire appears preferable to an attempt to more explicitly list or define specific sexual activities, for many activities such as kissing, embracing, massaging, or holding hands may or may not be sexual, depending upon the context and more specifically upon the purposes, needs, or desires into which such activities fit. The generality of the definition also represents a refusal (common in recent psychological texts) to overemphasize orgasm as the goal of sexual desire or genital sex as the only norm of sexual activity (this will be hedged slightly in the discussion of perversion below).

Central to the definition is the fact that the goal of sexual desire and activity is the physical contact itself, rather than something else which this contact might express. By contrast, what I term "means–end analyses" posit ends which I take to be extraneous to plain sex, and they view sex as a means to these ends.

This initial [plain-sex] analysis may seem to some either over- or underinclusive. It might seem too broad in leading us to interpret physical contact as sexual desire in activities such as football and other contact sports. In these cases, however, the desire is not for contact with another body per se, it is not directed toward a particular person for that purpose, and it is not the goal of the activity—

---

* Abridged from "Plain Sex" by Alan H. Goldman, *Philosophy and Public Affairs* 6(3) (1977): 267–287. Copyright © 1977. Reprinted by permission of Blackwell Publishing Ltd., a company of John Wiley & Sons, Inc.

the goal is winning or exercising or knocking someone down or displaying one's prowess. If the desire is purely for contact with another specific person's body, then to interpret it as sexual does not seem an exaggeration. A slightly more difficult case is that of a baby's desire to be cuddled and our natural response in wanting to cuddle it. In the case of the baby, the desire may be simply for the physical contact, for the pleasure of the caresses. If so, we may characterize this desire, especially in keeping with Freudian theory, as sexual or protosexual. It will differ nevertheless from full-fledged sexual desire in being more amorphous, not directed outward toward another specific person's body. It may also be that what the infant unconsciously desires is not physical contact per se but signs of affection, tenderness, or security, in which case we have further reason for hesitating to characterize its wants as clearly sexual. The intent of our response to the baby is often the showing of affection, not the pure physical contact, so that our definition in terms of action which fulfills sexual desire *on the part of the agent* does not capture such actions, whatever we say of the baby. (If it is intuitive to characterize our response as sexual as well, there is clearly no problem here for my analysis.) The same can be said of signs of affection (or in some cultures polite greeting) among men or women: these certainly need not be homosexual when the intent is only to show friendship, something extrinsic to plain sex although valuable when added to it.

Our definition of sex in terms of the desire for physical contact may appear too narrow in that a person's personality, not merely her or his body, may be sexually attractive to another, and in that looking or conversing in a certain way can be sexual in a given context without bodily contact. Nevertheless, it is not the contents of one's thoughts per se that are sexually appealing but one's personality as embodied in certain manners of behavior. Furthermore, if a person is sexually attracted by another's personality, he or she will desire not just further conversation, but actual sexual contact. While looking at or conversing with someone can be interpreted as sexual in given contexts, it is so when intended as preliminary to, and hence parasitic upon, elemental sexual interest. Voyeurism or viewing a pornographic movie qualifies as a sexual activity, but only as an imaginative substitute for the real thing (otherwise a deviation from the norm as expressed in our definition). The same is true of masturbation as a sexual activity without a partner.

This characterization of sex as an intensely pleasurable physical activity and acute physical desire may seem to some to capture only its barest level. But it is worth distinguishing and focusing upon this least common denominator in order to avoid the false views of sexual morality and perversion which emerge from thinking that sex is essentially something else.

2 The Reproductive Model

We may turn then to what sex is not, to the arguments regarding supposed conceptual connections between sex and other activities which it is necessary to conceptually distinguish. The most comprehensible attempt to build an extraneous purpose into the sex act identifies that purpose as reproduction, its primary biological function. While this may be "nature's" purpose, it certainly need not be ours (the analogy with eating, while sometimes overworked, is pertinent here).

While this identification may once have had a rational basis which also grounded the identification of the value and morality of sex with that applicable to reproduction and childrearing, the development of contraception rendered the connection weak. Methods of contraception are by now so familiar and so widely used that it is not necessary to dwell upon the changes wrought by these developments in the concept of sex itself and in a rational sexual ethic dependent upon that concept. In the past, the ever-present possibility of children rendered the concepts of sex and sexual morality different from those required at present. There may be good reasons, if the presence and care of both mother and father are beneficial to children, for restricting reproduction to marriage. Insofar as society has a legitimate role in protecting children's interests, it may be justified in giving marriage a legal status, although this question is complicated by the fact (among others) that children born to single mothers deserve no penalties. In any case, the point here is simply that these questions are irrelevant at the present time to those regarding the morality of sex and its potential social regulation. (Further connections with marriage will be discussed below.)

3 The Sex-Love Model

Before discussing further relations of means–end analyses to false or inconsistent sexual ethics and concepts of perversion, I turn to [another example of means–end analysis]. One common position views sex as essentially an expression of love or affection between the partners. It is generally recognized that there are other types of love besides sexual, but sex itself is taken as an expression of one type, sometimes termed "romantic" love. Various factors again ought to weaken this identification. First, there are other types of love besides that which it is appropriate to express sexually, and "romantic" love itself can be expressed in many other ways. I am not denying that sex can take on heightened value and meaning when it becomes a vehicle for the expression of feelings of love or tenderness, but so can many other usually mundane activities such as getting up early to make breakfast on Sunday, cleaning the house, and so on. Second, sex itself can be used to communicate many other emotions besides love, and, as I will argue below, can communicate nothing in particular and still be good sex.

On a deeper level, an internal tension is bound to result from an identification of sex, which I have described as a physical-psychological desire, with love as a long-term, deep emotional relationship between two individuals. As this type of relationship, love is permanent, at least in intent, and more or less exclusive. A normal person cannot deeply love more than a few individuals even in a lifetime. We may be suspicious that those who attempt or claim to love many love them weakly if at all. Yet fleeting sexual desire can arise in relation to a variety of other individuals one finds sexually attractive. It may even be, as some have claimed, that sexual desire in humans naturally seeks variety, while this is obviously false of love. For this reason, monogamous sex, even if justified, almost always represents a sacrifice or the exercise of self-control on the part of the spouses, while monogamous love generally does not. There is no such thing as casual love in the sense in which I intend the term "love." It may occasionally happen that a spouse falls deeply in love with someone else (especially when sex is conceived in terms of love), but this is relatively rare in comparison to passing sexual desires for others; and while the former often indicates a weakness or fault in the marriage relation, the latter does not.

If love is indeed more exclusive in its objects than is sexual desire, this explains why those who view sex as essentially an expression of love would again tend to hold a repressive or restrictive sexual ethic. As in the case of reproduction, there may be good reasons for reserving the total commitment of deep love to the context of marriage and family—the normal personality may not withstand additional divisions of ultimate commitment and allegiance. There is no question that marriage itself is best sustained by a deep relation of love and affection; and even if love is not naturally monogamous, the benefits of family units to children provide additional reason to avoid serious commitments elsewhere which weaken family ties. It can be argued similarly that monogamous sex strengthens families by restricting and at the same time guaranteeing an outlet for sexual desire in marriage. But there is more force to the argument that recognition of a clear distinction between sex and love in society would help avoid disastrous marriages which result from adolescent confusion of the two when sexual desire is mistaken for permanent love and would weaken damaging jealousies which arise in marriages in relation to passing sexual desires. The love and affection of a sound marriage certainly differs from the adolescent romantic variety, which is often a mere substitute for sex in the context of a repressive sexual ethic.

In fact, the restrictive sexual ethic tied to the means–end analysis in terms of love again has failed to be consistent. At least it has not been applied consistently, but forms part of the double standard which has curtailed the freedom of women. It is predictable in light of this history that some women would now advocate using sex as another kind of means, as a political weapon or as a way to increase unjustly denied power and freedom. The inconsistency in the sexual ethic typically attached to the sex-love analysis, according to which it has generally been taken with a grain of salt when applied to men, is simply another example of the impossibility of tailoring a plausible moral theory in this area to a conception of sex which builds in conceptually extraneous factors.

I am not suggesting here that sex ought never to be connected with love or that it is not a more significant and valuable activity when it is. Nor am I denying that individuals need love as much as sex and perhaps emotionally need at least one complete relationship which encompasses both. Just as sex can express love and take on heightened significance when it does, so love is often naturally accompanied by an intermittent desire for sex. But again, love is accompanied appropriately by desires for other shared activities as well. What makes the desire for sex seem more intimately connected with love is the intimacy which is seen to be a natural feature of mutual sex acts. Like love, sex is held to lay one bare psychologically as well as physically. Sex is unquestionably intimate, but beyond that the psychological toll often attached may be a function of the restrictive sexual ethic itself rather than a legitimate apology for it. The intimacy involved in love is psychologically consuming in a generally healthy way, while the psychological tolls of sexual relations, often including embarrassment as a correlate of intimacy, are too often the result of artificial sexual ethics and taboos. The intimacy involved in both love and sex is insufficient in any case in light of previous points to render a means–end analysis in these terms appropriate.

4 Platonic Morality

I have now criticized various types of analysis sharing or suggesting a common means–end form. The reproductive model brands oral-genital sex a deviation but cannot account for kissing or holding hands; the sex-love model makes most sexual desire seem degrading or base. [Its defenders] ... condemn extramarital sex on the sound but irrelevant grounds that reproduction and deep commitment are best confined to family contexts. The romanticization of sex and the confusion of sexual desire with love operate in both directions: sex outside the context of romantic love is repressed; once it is repressed, partners become more difficult to find and sex becomes romanticized further, out of proportion to its real value for the individual.

What these analyses share in addition to a common form is accordance with and perhaps derivation from the Platonic-Christian moral tradition, according to which the animal or purely physical element of humans is the source of immorality, and plain sex in the sense I defined it is an expression of this element, hence in itself to be condemned. All the analyses examined seem to seek a distance from sexual desire itself in attempting to extend it conceptually beyond the physical. The love ... [analysis seeks] refinement or intellectualization of the desire; plain physical sex becomes vulgar, and too straightforward sexual encounters without an aura of respectable cerebral communicative content are to be avoided. [Robert] Solomon explicitly argues that sex cannot be a "mere" appetite, his argument being that if it were, subway exhibitionism and other vulgar forms would be pleasing.[1] This fails to recognize that sexual desire can be focused or selective at the same time as being physical. Lower animals are not attracted by every other member of their species, either. Rancid food forced down one's throat is not pleasing, but that certainly fails to show that hunger is not a physical appetite. Sexual desire lets us know that we are physical beings and, indeed, animals; this is why traditional Platonic morality is so thorough in its condemnation. Means–end analyses continue to reflect this tradition, sometimes unwittingly. They show that in conceptualizing sex it is still difficult, despite years of so-called revolution in this area, to free ourselves from the lingering suspicion that plain sex as physical desire is an expression of our "lower selves," that yielding to our animal natures is subhuman or vulgar.

5 Sex and Morality

Having criticized these analyses for the sexual ethics and concepts of perversion they imply, it remains to contrast my account along these lines. To the question of what morality might be implied by my analysis, the answer is that there are no moral implications whatever. Any analysis of sex which imputes a moral character to sex acts in themselves is wrong for that reason. There is no morality intrinsic to sex, although general moral rules apply to the treatment of others in sex acts as they apply to all human relations. We can speak of a sexual ethic as we can speak of a business ethic without implying that business in itself is either moral or immoral or that special rules are required to judge business practices which are not derived from rules that apply elsewhere as well. Sex is not in itself a moral category, although like business it invariably places us into relations with others in which moral rules apply. It gives us opportunity to do what is otherwise recognized as wrong, to harm others, deceive them, or manipulate them against their wills. Just as the fact that an act is sexual in itself never renders it wrong or adds to its wrongness if it is wrong on other grounds (sexual acts toward minors are wrong on other grounds [for example]), so no wrong act is to be excused because done from a sexual motive. If a "crime of passion" is to be excused, it would have to be on grounds of temporary insanity rather than sexual context (whether insanity does constitute a legitimate excuse for certain actions is too big a topic to argue here). Sexual motives are among others which may become deranged, and the fact that they are sexual has no bearing in itself on the moral character, whether negative or exculpatory, of the actions deriving from them. Whatever might be true of war, it is certainly not the case that all's fair in love or sex.

Our first conclusion regarding morality and sex is therefore that no conduct otherwise immoral should be excused because it is sexual conduct, and nothing in sex is immoral unless condemned by rules which apply elsewhere as well. The last clause requires further clarification. Sexual conduct can be governed by particular rules relating only to sex itself. But these precepts must be implied by general moral rules when these are applied to specific sexual relations or types of conduct. The same is true of rules of fair business, ethical medicine, or courtesy in driving a car. In the latter case, particular acts on the road may be reprehensible, such as tailgating or passing on the right, which seem to bear no resemblance as actions to any outside the context of highway safety. Nevertheless their immorality derives from the fact that they place others in danger, a circumstance which, when avoidable, is to be condemned in any context. This structure of general and specifically applicable rules describes a reasonable sexual ethic as well. To take an extreme case, rape is always a sexual act and it is always immoral. A rule against rape can therefore be considered an obvious part of sexual morality which has no bearing on nonsexual conduct. But the immorality of rape derives from its being an extreme violation of a person's body, of the right not to be humiliated, and of the general moral prohibition against using other persons against their wills, not from the fact that it is a sexual act.

The application elsewhere of general moral rules to sexual conduct is further complicated by the fact that it will be relative to the particular desires and preferences of one's partner (these may be influenced by and hence in some sense include misguided beliefs about sexual morality itself). This means that there will be fewer specific rules in the area of sexual ethics than in other areas of conduct, such as driving cars, where the relativity of preference is irrelevant to the prohibition of objectively dangerous conduct. More reliance will have to be placed upon the general moral rule, which in this area holds simply that the preferences, desires, and interests of one's partner or potential partner ought to be taken into account. This rule is certainly not specifically formulated to govern sexual relations; it is a form of the central principle of morality itself. But when applied to sex, it prohibits certain actions, such as molestation of children, which cannot be categorized as violations of the rule without at the same time being classified as sexual. I believe this last case is the closest we can come to an action which is wrong *because* it is sexual, but even here its wrongness is better characterized as deriving from the detrimental effects such behavior can have on the future emotional and sexual life of the naive victims and from the fact that such behavior therefore involves manipulation of innocent persons without regard for their interests. Hence, this case also involves violation of a general moral rule which applies elsewhere as well.

Aside from faulty conceptual analyses of sex and the influence of the Platonic moral tradition, there are two more plausible reasons for thinking that there are moral dimensions intrinsic to sex acts per se. The first is that such acts are normally intensely pleasurable. According to a hedonistic, utilitarian moral theory they therefore should be at least prima facie morally right, rather than morally neutral in themselves. To me this seems incorrect and reflects unfavorably on the ethical theory in question. The pleasure intrinsic to sex acts is a good, but not, it seems to me, a good with much positive moral significance. Certainly I can have no duty to pursue such pleasure myself, and while it may be nice to give pleasure of any form to others, there is no ethical requirement to do so, given my right over my own body. The exception relates to the context of sex acts themselves, when one partner derives pleasure from the other and ought to return the favor. This duty to reciprocate takes us out of the domain of hedonistic utilitarianism, however, and into a Kantian moral framework, the central principles of which call for just such reciprocity in human relations. Since independent moral judgments regarding sexual activities constitute one area in which ethical theories are to be tested, these observations indicate here, as I believe others indicate elsewhere, the fertility of the Kantian, as opposed to the utilitarian, principle in reconstructing reasoned moral consciousness.

It may appear from this alternative Kantian viewpoint that sexual acts must be at least prima facie wrong in themselves. This is because they invariably involve at different stages the manipulation of one's partner for one's own pleasure, which might appear to be prohibited on the formulation of Kant's principle which holds that one ought not to treat another as a means to such private ends. A more realistic rendering of this formulation, however, one which recognizes its intended equivalence to the first universalizability principle [the principle requiring we act only on a maxim whereby we can at the same time will that it should become a universal law], admits no such absolute prohibition. Many human relations, most economic transactions for example, involve using other individuals for personal benefit. These relations are immoral only when they are one-sided, when the benefits are not mutual, or when the transactions are not freely and rationally endorsed by all parties. The same holds true of sexual acts. The central principle governing them is the Kantian demand for reciprocity in sexual relations. In order to comply with the second formulation of the categorical imperative, one must recognize the subjectivity of one's partner. Even in an act which by its nature "objectifies" the other, one recognizes a partner as a subject with demands and desires by yielding to those desires, by allowing oneself to be a sexual object as well, by giving pleasure or ensuring that the pleasures of the acts are mutual. It is this kind of reciprocity which forms the basis for morality in sex, which distinguishes right acts from wrong in this area as in others. (Of course, prior to sex acts one must gauge their effects upon potential partners and take these longer-range interests into account.)

6 Love

I suggested earlier that in addition to generating confusion regarding the rightness or wrongness of sex acts, false conceptual analyses of the means–end form cause confusion about the value of sex to the individual. My account recognizes the satisfaction of desire and the pleasure this brings as the central psychological function of the sex act for the individual. Sex affords us a paradigm of pleasure but not a cornerstone of value. For most of us it is not only a needed outlet for desire but also the most enjoyable form of reaction we know. Its value is nevertheless easily mistaken by being confused with that of love, when it is taken as essentially an expression of that emotion. Although intense, the pleasures of sex are brief and repetitive rather than cumulative. They give values to the specific acts which generate them, but not the lasting kind of value which enhances one's whole life. The briefness of these pleasures contributes to their intensity (or perhaps their intensity makes them necessarily brief), but it also relegates them to the periphery of most rational plans for the good life.

By contrast, love typically develops over a long-term relation; while its pleasures may be less intense and physical, they are of more cumulative value. The importance of love to the individual may well be central in a rational system of value. And it has perhaps an even deeper moral significance relating to the identification with the interests of another person, which broadens one's possible relationships with others as well. Marriage is again important in preserving this relation between adults and children, which seems as important to the adults as it is to the children in broadening concerns which have a tendency to become selfish. Sexual desire, by contrast, is desire for another which is nevertheless essentially self-regarding. Sexual pleasure is certainly a good for the individual, and for many it may be necessary in order for them to function in a reasonably cheerful way. But it bears little relation to those other values just discussed, to which some analyses falsely suggest a conceptual connection.

7 Perverted Sex

While my initial analysis lacks moral implications in itself, as it should, it does suggest by contrast a concept of sexual perversion. Since the concept of perversion is itself a sexual concept, it will always be defined relative to some definition of normal sex; and any conception of the norm will imply a contrary notion of perverse forms. The concept suggested by my account again differs sharply from those implied by the means–end analyses examined above. Perversion does not represent a deviation from the reproductive function (or kissing would be perverted), from a loving relationship (or most sexual desire and many heterosexual acts would be perverted), or from efficiency in communicating (or unsuccessful seduction attempts would be perverted). It is a deviation from a norm, but the norm in question is merely statistical. Of course, not all sexual acts that are statistically unusual are perverted—a three-hour continuous sexual act would be unusual but not necessarily abnormal in the requisite sense. The abnormality in question must relate to the *form of the desire* itself in order to constitute sexual perversion; for example, desire, not for contact with another but for merely looking, for harming or being harmed, for contact with items of clothing. This concept of sexual abnormality is that suggested by my definition of normal sex in terms of its typical desire. However, not all unusual desires qualify either, only those with the typical physical sexual effects upon the individual who satisfies them. These effects, such as erection in males, were not built into the original definition of sex in terms of sexual desire, for they do not always occur in activities that are properly characterized as sexual, say, kissing for the pleasure of it. But they do seem to bear a close relation to the definition of activities as perverted. (For those who consider only genital sex sexual, we could build such symptoms into a narrower definition, then speak of sex in a broad sense as well as "proper" sex.)

Solomon [disagrees] with this statistical notion of perversion. For [him] the concept is evaluative rather than statistical. I do not deny that the term "perverted" is often used evaluatively (and purely emotively, for that matter), or that it has a negative connotation for the average speaker. I do deny that we can find a norm other than that of statistically usual desire, against which all and only activities that properly count as sexual perversions can be contrasted. Perverted sex is simply abnormal sex, and if the norm is not to be an idealized or romanticized extraneous end or purpose, it must express the way human sexual desires usually manifest themselves. Of course not all norms in other areas of discourse need be statistical in this way. Physical health is an example of a relatively clear norm which does not seem to depend upon the numbers of healthy people. But the concept in this case achieves its clarity through the connection of physical health with other clearly desirable physical functions and characteristics, for example, living longer. In the case of sex, that which is statistically abnormal is not necessarily incapacitating in other ways, and yet these abnormal desires with sexual effects upon their subject do count as perverted to the degree to which their objects deviate from usual ones. The connotations of the concept of perversion beyond those connected with abnormality or statistical deviation derive more from the attitudes of those likely to call certain acts perverted than from specifiable features of the acts themselves. These connotations add to the concept of abnormality that of *sub*normality, but there is no norm against which the latter can be measured intelligibly in accord with all and only acts intuitively called perverted.

The only proper evaluative norms relating to sex involve degrees of pleasure in the acts and moral norms, but neither of these scales coincides with statistical degrees of abnormality, according to which perversion is to be measured. The three parameters operate independently (this was implied for the first two when it was held above that the pleasure of sex is a good, but not necessarily a moral good). Perverted sex may be more or less enjoyable to particular individuals than normal sex, and more or less moral, depending upon the particular relations involved. Raping a sheep may be more perverted than raping a woman, but certainly not more condemnable morally.[2] It is nevertheless true that the evaluative connotations attaching to the term "perverted" derive partly from the fact that most people consider perverted sex highly immoral. Many such acts are forbidden by long-standing taboos, and it is sometimes difficult to distinguish what is forbidden from what is immoral. Others, such as sadistic acts, are genuinely immoral, but again not at all because of their connection with sex or abnormality. The principles which condemn these acts would condemn them equally if they were common and nonsexual. It is not true that we properly could continue to consider acts perverted which were found to be very common practice across societies. Such acts, if harmful, might continue to be condemned properly as immoral, but it was just shown that the immorality of an act does not vary with its degree of perversion. If not harmful, common acts previously considered abnormal might continue to be called perverted for a time by the moralistic minority; but the term when applied to such cases would retain only its emotive negative connotation without consistent logical criteria for application. It would represent merely prejudiced moral judgments.

To adequately explain why there is a tendency to so deeply condemn perverted acts would require a treatise in psychology beyond the scope of this paper. Part of the reason undoubtedly relates to the tradition of repressive sexual ethics and false conceptions of sex; another part to the fact that all abnormality seems to disturb and fascinate us at the same time. The former explains why sexual perversion is more abhorrent to many than other forms of abnormality; the latter indicates why we tend to have an emotive and evaluative reaction to perversion in the first place. It may be, as has been suggested according to a Freudian line,[3] that our uneasiness derives from latent desires we are loathe to admit, but this thesis takes us into psychological issues I am not competent to judge. Whatever the psychological explanation, it suffices to point out here that the conceptual connection between perversion and genuine or consistent moral evaluation is spurious and again suggested by misleading means–end idealizations of the concept of sex.

The position I have taken in this paper against those concepts is not totally new. Something similar to it is found in Freud's view of sex, which of course was genuinely revolutionary, and in the body of writings deriving from Freud to the present time. But in his revolt against romanticized and repressive conceptions, Freud went too far—from a refusal to view sex as merely a means to a view of it as the end of all human behavior, although sometimes an elaborately disguised end. This pansexualism led to the thesis (among others) that repression was indeed an inevitable and necessary part of social regulation of any form, a strange consequence of a position that began by opposing the repressive aspects of the means–end view. Perhaps the time finally has arrived when we can achieve a reasonable middle ground in this area, at least in philosophy if not in society.

Notes

1 Robert Solomon, "Sex and Perversion," *Philosophy and Sex*, R. Baker and F. Eliiston, eds. (Buffalo, NY: Prometheus, 1975).
2 The example is like one from Sara Ruddick, "Better Sex," in *Philosophy and Sex*, ed. Robert Baker and Frederick Elliston (New York: Prometheus Books, 1975), p. 96.
3 See Michael Slote, "Inapplicable Concepts and Sexual Perversion," in Baker and Elliston, *Philosophy and Sex*, pp. 261–267.

Review and Discussion Questions

1 What is the plain-sex view that Goldman defends? How does he contrast it with means–end views?
2 Why does Goldman reject the reproductive and the sex-love models?
3 On what grounds does Goldman reject Kant's account of sexual morality?
4 Discuss Goldman's understanding of perversion and its connection with morality. Why does he think people tend to condemn perversion?
5 Compare Goldman's understanding of love with that of Kant. Which one seems most reasonable to you? Why do you think that?

READING: GAY BASICS: SOME QUESTIONS, FACTS, AND VALUES

RICHARD D. MOHR[*]

In this essay, Richard Mohr surveys the wide array of issues surrounding homosexuality. He begins with a discussion of some of the important facts about homosexuals and homosexuality, including a discussion of the most prominent stereotypes, which, he points out, are in fact contradictory. He then reviews different forms of discrimination experienced by gays, considers arguments that homosexuality is wrong, and concludes with a discussion of social policies that affect gays. Richard D. Mohr is Professor Emeritus of Philosophy and Classics at the University of Illinois.

Over the last decade, gay men and lesbians have begun to make steady progress in getting our issues debated—in the courts, at City Hall, in state houses, in Congress, and by the White House. But there remain structural impediments to lesbians and gay men making consistent progress in shepherding our interests across these debates on into public policy, social practice, and law. Ironically, just as the progress that gays have made to date has largely been cultural, so too are the undertows that trip up further progress. These undertows include: the persistence of anti-gay stereotypes; a belief held by some that discrimination against gays is slight and so not a major social worry; a widespread belief, sometimes religiously based, that gays are somehow immoral, perverse, even willfully perverse; and a fear that changing social policies concerning lesbians and gay men will usher in other, undesirable, possibly cataclysmic changes. This essay seeks to address these problems and allay these fears.

Increasingly the average American knows someone who is lesbian or gay. In 1985, only one in five Americans claimed to have a friend or acquaintance who was a lesbian or gay man.[1] In 2004, forty percent of Americans claimed to have a close friend or family member who was a gay man or lesbian. If the question was expanded to ask after acquaintances as well, then sixty-nine percent of Americans claimed to know a lesbian or gay male.[2] This is important progress. Even so, much, perhaps most, of America's experience with gay men and lesbians is not first-hand, but mediated—has cultural rather than personal sources. First among these cultural sources are stereotypes that warp people's perception of lesbians and gay men, and can even swamp or erase the benefits of first-hand experience. For people tend to hold onto stereotypes even when their own circle includes friends who directly contradict the stereotype.

Mainstream media—television first among them—abound in portrayals of gay people (particularly gay men) that reinforce stereotypes rather than undercut them, especially in the absence of any programming that presents a hearty number of ordinary gay people. For example, cultural critics have argued that *Queer as Folk* reinforces the stereotype of gay men as aggressively promiscuous, while *Queer Eye for the Straight Guy* reinforces the stereotype of gay men as flighty ditzes.

To their credit, these two television programs have helped to de-fang the term "queer" and even launch it into some areas of mainstream circulation with

---

[*] Excerpted from pp. 17–36 in *The Long Arc of Justice* by Richard Mohr. Copyright © 2005 by Columbia University Press. Reprinted by permission of Columbia University Press.

a positive valance. But the shows also may be seen as emblems of the two oddly-contradictory stereotypes of gay people that still persist in our culture. On the one hand, gay people are seen as confused about their gender identity: lesbians are females who want to be, or at least look and act like, men—thus, the aspersions *bull dykes* and *diesel dykes*; while gay men are males who want to be, or at least look and act like, women—thus the aspersions *queen, fairy, nance, limp-wrist, nelly, sissy,* and *auntie.* These stereotypes of mismatches between biological sex and socially defined gender roles provide the fodder for ethnic-like jokes, which, though derisive, basically view lesbians and gay men as ridiculous: "How many fags does it take to change a light bulb?" Answer: "Eight—one to replace it and seven to scream 'Faaaaaabulous!'"

The other set of stereotypes casts gays as a pervasive, sinister, conspiratorial threat. The core stereotype here is that of gay people—especially gay men—as sex-crazed maniacs, and very likely child-molesters, but in any case vampire-like creatures which aggressively spread around a corruptive contagion. These stereotypes carry with them fears of the very destruction of family and civilization itself. The contradiction between these two images is obvious: something that is essentially ridiculous can hardly have such a staggering and menacing effect. Something must be afoot.

Clarifying the nature of stereotypes can help make sense of this incoherent amalgam. Stereotypes are not simply false generalizations from a skewed sample of cases examined.

[Stereotypes] have an active role in how a person takes in the world. They are part of the apparatus, lenses, if you will, through which the mind perceives the world. If you look through a lens with a tree painted on it, you see a tree everywhere. If you look through a pink lens, the world is pink. The lens filters out other colors. Stereotypes determine what we take to be "the facts," to be good evidence, sound ideas, even logical arguments. For they screen out any fact, idea, or argument that disagrees with what a person believes already.

Stereotypes can literally cause a person to see things. Consider, for example, the initial round of gay weddings in San Francisco during February 2004. When newly hitched lesbian and gay couples would emerge from City Hall, well-wishers in the plaza below would shout hurrahs. A week into these weddings, the Austrian-born Governor of California was in town for a state Republican convention. Two days later he reported to NBC's "Meet the Press" on the gay marriages he thought he had seen: "All of a sudden we see riots and we see protest and we see people clashing. The next thing we know is there's injured or there's dead people."[3] The *New York Times* reported of the very same events: "The San Francisco police reported no violence related to the same-sex marriage certificates." The stereotype of gays as destroyers of civilization made the governor see jubilation as civilization destroyed—anarchy. The stereotype caused the governor to project onto experience something he already believed and then use the stereotype-manipulated experience to reinforce beliefs he held already linking gays and anarchy—beliefs he felt so confident about that he would trot them out onto national television.

On this understanding of stereotypes, as culturally implanted lenses with a social agenda in mind, it is easy to see how the main anti-gay stereotypes operate in society's conception of itself. Stereotypes about gays as gender-confused reinforce powerful gender roles that are still prevalent in American society. These stereotypes condemn the possibility of choosing a social role independent of one's biological sex—a possibility that might threaten many guiding social divisions, both domestic and commercial. Blurred would be the socially sex-linked distinctions between breadwinner and homemaker, boss and secretary, doctor and nurse, protector and protected, even God and His world. The accusations "fag" and "dyke" serve in significant part to keep women in their place and to prevent men from breaking ranks and ceding away theirs.

The stereotypes of gays as destroyers of civilization function to displace (possibly irresolvable) social problems from their actual source to a remote and (society hopes) manageable one. For example, the stereotype of the gay person as child-molester functions to give the traditionally-defined family unit a false sheen of innocence. It keeps the unit from being examined too closely for incest, child abuse, wife-battering, and the terrorizing of women and children by a father's constant threats. The stereotype teaches that the problems of the family are alien to it, not internal to it.

If this account of stereotypes holds, society has been profoundly immoral. For its treatment of gays is a grand scale rationalization, a moral sleight-of-hand. The problem is not that society's usual standards of evidence and procedure in decision-making have been misapplied to gays. Rather, when it comes to gays, the standards themselves have simply been ruled out of court and disregarded in favor of mechanisms that encourage unexamined fear and hatred.

Discrimination

Partly because lots of people still suppose they don't personally know any gay people, and partly because of the on-going effects of stereotypes, society at large is not fully aware of the many ways in which lesbians and gay men are still subject to discrimination. Contributing to this ignorance is the difficulty for gay people, as an invisible minority, even to complain of discrimination, especially workplace discrimination. For if one is gay, to register a complaint would suddenly target oneself as a stigmatized person, and so, especially in the absence of any protection against discrimination, would simply invite more discrimination. So, discrimination against lesbians and gay men, like rape, goes seriously under-reported. Even so, known discrimination is widespread.

Annual studies by the National Gay and Lesbian Task Force have consistently found that over ninety percent of gay men and lesbians have been victims of violence or harassment in some form on the basis of their sexual orientation. Greater than one in five gay men and nearly one in ten lesbians have been punched, hit, or kicked; a quarter of all gays have had objects thrown at them; a third have been chased; a third have been sexually harassed, and nearly one-seventh have been spit on, all just for being perceived to be gay.

The most extreme form of anti-gay violence is queerbashing—where groups of young men target a person who they suppose is a gay man and beat and kick him unconscious and sometimes to death amid a torrent of taunts and slurs. In July 1999 at Fort Campbell, Kentucky, Private Calvin Glover goaded Private Barry Winchell into a fistfight. Glover lost the fistfight to Winchell, a soldier widely perceived in the barracks to be gay. The next night, a third soldier egged on and taunted Glover to defend his lost manhood—after all what could be more humiliating than to be beaten by a sissy?—and so Glover clubbed Winchell to death with a baseball bat as he slept. Glover got a life sentence, the friend twelve and a half years.[4]

But many queerbashing cases never reach the courts. Those that do are frequently marked by inequitable procedures and results. Judges will describe queerbashers as "just All-American Boys." In a particular disturbing case from the 1980s, a District of Columbia judge handed suspended sentences to queerbashers whose victim had been stalked, beaten, stripped at knife point, slashed, kicked, threatened with castration, and pissed on, because the judge thought the bashers were good boys at heart—they went to a religious prep school.[5] Current-day queerbashing functions somewhat similarly to past lynchings of blacks—to keep a whole stigmatized group in line. As with lynchings, society has routinely averted its eyes, giving its permission or even tacit approval to violence and harassment. These inequitable procedures show that the life and liberty of gays, like those of blacks, count for less than the life and liberty of members of the dominant culture.

There has been some progress on this front over the last decade. Thanks to the nationwide publicity given to the particularly brutal, Crucifixion-invoking murder of Matthew Shepard in Laramie, Wyoming, in October 1998, and to the subsequent trials and convictions of his assailants and their accomplices, queerbashers have had more difficulty mounting successful defenses which argue that their actions were a form of justified self-defense.[6] In such so-called "homosexual panic" defenses, the killer would simply claim his act was an understandable, automatic response to a sexual overture. It was the victim's fault; he provoked his own death. In the Shepard case, the judge barred the defense team from presenting such a defense, since it turns on and re-enforces prejudices against gays.[7] This ruling has set a judicial pattern for the rest of the country.

Still, as long as the stereotype of gays as child-molesters lives, many will believe, at least subconsciously, that when gays are attacked, they are just getting what they deserve. And young males can still find "out there" in popular culture lots of support for the violence they direct against gay men. In February 2001, the white rap artist Eminem won three Grammy Awards, including best rap album, for his *Marshall Mathers LP*, which had sold 5.2 million copies in just two months after its May 2000 release.[8] Of the record's eighteen tracks, thirteen belittle gay men and lesbians, one portrays gay men as child-molesters, one ridicules gay marriage, many include threats of lethal violence against gay men and lesbians ("My words are like a dagger that'll stab you in the head whether you're a fag or les"), often with a side-appeal to a "homosexual panic" justification ("You faggots keep eggin me on til I have you at knifepoint"). The tracks culminate in a genocidal fantasy: "You faggots can vanish to volcanic ash. And re-appear in hell with a can of gas, and a match."

Where young males are violent by government order, gay men and lesbians are also discriminated against. Lesbians and gay men are barred from military service. Until 1993, the bar was a Department of Defense directive that could have been changed by the President or Joint Chiefs of Staff. That year, it became a federal statute which can now be reversed only if Congress passes a new law or the federal courts declare the ban unconstitutional—something they have shown no inclination to do.

In 1996, Congress passed the so-called Defense of Marriage Act, which prevents the federal government from giving legal recognition to any same-sex marriages and permits states to do the same. By the Spring of 2004, thirty-eight states had taken up the federal offer and passed laws barring both in-state same-sex marriages and the recognition of those from out-of-state. A 1997 report which the Government Accounting Office researched and published in response to a request from the U.S. House Judiciary Committee found 1,049 federal laws which provide benefits, rights, and privileges only to those who are married.[9] By barring gays from military service and from marrying, governments do more than directly withhold rights and benefits from gays; they also set a precedent favoring discrimination in the private sector.

The federal government no longer has a blanket ban on gay employment in the CIA, FBI, National Security Agency, and the State Department—though these agencies continue to defend in the courts a right to discriminate and continue to take sexual orientation into account in making case-by-case hiring decisions.[10] State and local governments regularly fire gay teachers, policemen, firemen, social workers, and anyone who has contact with the public. Further, state licensing laws (though frequently honored only in the breach) officially bar gays from a vast array of occupations and professions—everything from doctors, lawyers, accountants, and nurses to hairdressers, morticians, even used-car dealers. Though gay sexual acts are now constitutionally protected, states still take them as marks of immoral personalities and so as making one unfit for whole swaths of employment opportunities. In its 2003 case, *Lawrence v. Texas* that declared sodomy laws unconstitutional, the Supreme Court punted on a perfect opportunity to block this whole line of discriminatory thinking.[11]

Gays are subject to discrimination in a wide variety of other ways, including private-sector employment, public accommodations, housing, child custody, adoption, and zoning regulations that bar "nonrelated" couples from living together.

Discrimination and the absorption by gay men and lesbians of society's traditional hatred of them interact to impede and, for some, block altogether the ability to create and maintain significant personal relations with loved ones. Every facet of life is affected by discrimination. Only the most compelling reasons could justify it.

Morality

Many people and, as noted, many states think society's treatment of gays is justified because they think gays are immoral. To evaluate this claim, different senses of "moral" must be distinguished. Sometimes "morality" just means the values generally held by members of a society—its mores, norms, and customs. On this understanding, gays are probably not moral: lots of people hate them, and social customs are designed to register widespread disapproval of gays. The problem here is that this sense of morality is merely a descriptive one. On this understanding, every society has a morality—even Nazi society, which had racism and mob rule as central features of its "morality" understood in this sense. What is needed in order to use the notion of morality to praise or condemn behavior is a sense of morality that is prescriptive or normative.

As the Nazi example makes clear, the fact that a lot of people in a society say something is good, even over eons, does not make it so. The rejection of the long history of socially approved and state-enforced slavery is another good example of this principle at work. Slavery would be wrong even if nearly everyone liked it. If the only justification for viewing gays as immoral is that most people dislike or disapprove of them, then consistency and fairness require that one abandon the belief.

Furthermore, recent historical and anthropological research has shown that opinion about gays has been by no means universally negative. It has varied widely even within the larger part of the Christian era and even within the Church itself.[12] There are even current societies—most notably in Papua New Guinea—where compulsory homosexual behavior is integral to the rites of male maturity.[13] Within the last forty years, American society has undergone a grand turnabout from deeply ingrained, near total condemnation to near total acceptance on two emotionally charged "moral" or "family" issues—contraception and divorce. Society holds its current descriptive morality of gays not because it has to, but because it chooses to.

Clearly, popular opinion and custom are not enough to ground moral condemnation of homosexuality. Religious arguments are also frequently used to condemn homosexuality. Such arguments usually proceed along two lines. One claims that the condemnation is a direct revelation of God, usually through the Bible. The other sees condemnation in God's plan as manifested in nature; homosexuality (it is claimed) is "contrary to nature."

One of the more remarkable discoveries of recent gay research is that the Bible may not be as univocal in its condemnation of homosexuality as many have believed. Christ never mentions homosexuality. Recent interpreters of the Old Testament have pointed out that the story of Lot at Sodom is probably intended to condemn inhospitality rather than homosexuality. Further, some of the Old Testament condemnations of homosexuality seem simply to be ways of tarring those of the Israelites' opponents who happen to accept homosexual practices when the Israelites themselves did not. If so, the condemnation is merely a quirk of history and rhetoric rather than a moral precept.

What does seem clear is that those who regularly cite the Bible to condemn an activity like homosexuality do so by reading it selectively. Do clergy who cite what they take to be condemnations of homosexuality in Leviticus maintain in their lives all the hygienic, dietary, and marital laws of Leviticus? If they cite the story of Lot at Sodom to condemn homosexuality, do they also cite the story of Lot in the Cave to condone incestuous rape? It seems then not that the Bible is being used to ground condemnations of homosexuality as much as society's dislike of homosexuality is being used to interpret the Bible.[14]

Even if a consistent portrait of condemnation could be gleaned from the Bible, what social significance should it be given? One of the guiding principles of society, enshrined in the Constitution as a check against government, is that decisions affecting social policy are not made on religious grounds. The Religious Right has been successful in defunding gay safe-sex literature and gay art, and in blocking the introduction of gay materials into school curriculums. If the real ground of the alleged immorality invoked by governments to discriminate against gays is religious (as it seems to be in these cases), then one of the major commitments of our nation is violated. Religious belief is a fine guide around which a person might organize his or her own life, but an awful instrument around which to organize someone else's life.

In the second kind of religious argument, people try to justify society's treatment of lesbians and gay men by saying they are unnatural.[15] Though the accusation of unnaturalness looks whimsical when taken as a general explanation of immorality, it is usually delivered with venom of forethought when applied to homosexuality. It carries a high emotional charge, usually expressing disgust and evincing queasiness. Probably it is nothing but an emotional charge. For people get equally disgusted and queasy at all sorts of things that are perfectly natural and that can hardly be fit subjects for moral condemnation. Two typical examples in current American culture are some people's responses to mothers' breastfeeding in public and to women who do not shave body hair. And nearly everyone thinks the idea of their own parents having sex, especially the sex that had them, is gross, gross, gross. But surely it's both perfectly natural and morally permissible. In like manner, people fling the term "unnatural" against gays in the same breath and with the same force as when they call gays "sick" and "gross." To explain his March 2004 vote in the Georgia House of Representatives for an amendment to the Georgia constitution barring gay marriage, the Rev. Randal Mangham emoted, "I don't appreciate having to explain to my nine-year-old why two big husky guys are kissing."[16] When people have strong emotional reactions, as they do in these cases, without being able to give good reasons for them, they can hardly be thought of as operating morally; more likely they are obsessed and manic.

Finally, people sometimes attempt to establish the authority for a moral obligation to use bodily parts in a certain fashion simply by claiming that moral laws are natural laws and vice versa. On this account, inanimate objects and plants are good in that they follow natural laws by necessity, animals follow them by instinct, and persons follow them by a rational will. People are special in that they must first discover the laws that govern them. Now, even if a person believes the view—dubious in the post-Newtonian, post-Darwinian world—that natural laws in the usual sense ($e = mc^2$, for instance) have some moral content, it is not at all clear how he or she is to discover the laws in nature that apply to people.

On the one hand, if one looks to people themselves for a model—and looks hard enough—one finds amazing variety, including homosexual relations as a social ideal (as in upper-class sixth-century Athens) and even as socially mandatory (as in some Melanesian initiation rites today). When one looks to people, one is simply unable to strip away the layers of social custom, history, and taboo in order to see what's really there to any degree more specific than that people are the creatures who make over their world and are capable of abstract thought. Or as Hannah Arendt put it, human beings are the creatures whose nature it is to have no nature.[17] That this is so should raise doubts that neutral principles are to be found in human nature that will condemn homosexuality.

Choice

But (it might be asked) aren't gays willfully the way they are? Social scientists have found that people who believe being gay is something fixed in a person's basic constitution are much more likely to support gay rights than people who think that being gay is something that one can cast off, in the way one could cease being a liar, thief, or Elvis fan. And it is widely conceded that if sexual orientation is something over which an individual—for whatever reason—has virtually no control, then discrimination against gays is presumptively wrong, as it is against racial and ethnic classes. Indeed most of the popular debate on lesbian and gay issues has turned on this very issue. Groups like Parents and Friends of Lesbians and Gays (PFLAG) doggedly believe that being gay is biologically determined, while most fundamentalists believe that being gay is a form of habitual sinning that, like a penchant for sweets or alcohol, can be given up with effort.

Attempts to answer the question whether or not sexual orientation is something that is reasonably thought to be within one's own control usually appeal simply to various claims of the biological or "mental" sciences. But the ensuing debate over genes, hormones, hypothalamuses, twins, early childhood development, and the like is as unnecessary as it is currently inconclusive.[18] All that is needed to answer the question is to look at the actual experience of lesbians and gay men in recent society and it becomes fairly clear that sexual orientation is not likely a matter of choice.

On the one hand, the "choice" of the gender of a sexual partner does not seem to express a trivial desire which might as easily be fulfilled by a simple substitution of the desired object. Picking the gender of a sex partner is decidedly dissimilar, that is, to such activities as picking a flavor of ice cream. If an ice cream parlor is out of one's flavor, one simply picks another. And if people were persecuted, threatened with jail terms, shattered careers, loss of family and housing and the like for eating, say, rocky road ice cream, no one would ever eat it. Everyone would pick another easily available flavor. That gay people abided in being gay even in the face of such persecution in the recent past suggests that being gay is not a matter of easy choice.

On the other hand, even if establishing a sexual orientation is not like making a relatively trivial choice, perhaps it is relevantly like making the central and serious life-choices by which individuals try to establish themselves as being of some type or having some occupation. Again, if one examines gay experience, or at least gay male experience, this seems not to be the case. For one virtually never sees anyone setting out to become a homosexual, in the way one does see people setting out to become doctors, lawyers, and bricklayers. One does not find gays-to-be picking some end—"At some point in the future, I want to become a homosexual"—and then set about planning and acquiring the ways and means to that end, in the way one does see people deciding that they want to become lawyers, and then sees them plan what courses to take and what sort of temperaments, habits, and skills to develop in order to become lawyers. Typically gays-to-be simply find themselves having homosexual encounters and yet, at least initially, resisting the identification of being homosexual. Such a person even very likely resists having such encounters, but ends up having them anyway. Only with time, luck, and personal effort, but sometimes never, does the person gradually come to accept her or his orientation, to view it as a given material condition of life, coming as materials do with certain capacities and limitations. The person begins to act in accordance with his or her orientation and its capacities, seeing its actualization as a requisite for an integrated personality and as a central component of personal well-being. As a result, the experience of coming out to oneself has for gays the basic structure of a discovery, not the structure of a choice. And far from signaling immorality, coming out to others affords one of the few remaining opportunities in ever more bureaucratic, technological, and socialistic societies to manifest courage.

To be fair, not a few lesbian feminists believe that being a lesbian is a choice, in particular a political choice.[19] This view, at least, has to hurdle the fact that sexual arousal is something that comes over a person. It is a passion, not an act of will, like pulling a lever in a voting booth. So with this caveat, even this lesbian feminist stance differs from the fundamentalists' view that homosexuality is a (bad) habit, one caused by sexual pleasure that, in their view, rivets the initial sexual desire to the soul and so turns it into a conditioned response, an inclination, a propensity.

Social Change

How would society at large be changed if gays were socially accepted? Suggestions to change social policy with regard to gays are invariably met with claims that to do so would invite the destruction of civilization itself. After all isn't that what did Rome in? Actually, Rome's decay paralleled not the flourishing of homosexuality but its repression under the later Christianized emperors.

Still, the charge that gays are bent on destroying civilization is surprisingly persistent. In 1989, the U.S. Navy offered up a theory of a gay suicide bomber to explain the explosion of a gun-turret on the U.S.S. Iowa that killed forty-seven sailors. The Navy alleged that one of the dead, Clayton Hartwig, was a suicidal closet-case, who blew up himself and his fellow sailors to cover up the shame he felt at being gay. The charge turned out to be baseless.[20] When in 1999 Vermont's Supreme Court ruled that the state had, in one way or another, to give same-sex couples rights and benefits identical to those given different-sex married couples, Republican Presidential candidate and long-time "family values" advocate Gary L. Bauer said that the decision was "worse than terrorism."[21] Two days after the September 11, 2001 terrorist attacks on the Pentagon and World Trade Center, the Rev. Jerry Falwell declared on Pat Robertson's religious television program "The 700 Club" that gay rights proponents and abortion providers have "got to take a lot of the blame for this because God will not be mocked," that these groups had so weakened America's morality that God "lifted the curtain of protection" from around the country allowing the terrorists in: "I point the finger in their face and say, 'you helped this happen'."[22] If the U.S. Navy, Gary Bauer, and Jerry Falwell laid such charges against any other group, Jews, for instance, everyone would recognize the charges as blood libels.

But even so, predictions of American civilization's imminent demise have been as premature as they have been frequent. Civilization has shown itself to be rather resilient here, in large part because of the country's traditional commitments to respect for privacy, to individual liberties, and especially to people minding their own business. These all give society an open texture and the flexibility to try out things to see what works. And because of this, we now need not speculate about what changes reforms in gay social policy might bring to society at large. For many reforms have already been tried.

By the time the Supreme Court declared sodomy laws unconstitutional in 2003, two-thirds of the states had through their own legislative or judicial branches decriminalized same-sex sex acts. Empirical studies have shown that there was no increase in other crimes in these states.

Neither has the passage of legislation barring discrimination against gays ushered in the end of civilization. Over one hundred counties and municipalities, including some of the country's largest cities (like Chicago, Los Angeles, and New York City) have passed such statutes barring discrimination in housing, employment and public accommodations, as have, by 2003, fourteen states: Wisconsin, Massachusetts, Connecticut, Hawaii, New Jersey, Vermont, Minnesota, New Hampshire, Nevada, Rhode Island, Maryland, New York, New Mexico and California. Four of these states—Minnesota, Rhode Island, New Mexico and California—also protect "gender identity," which is to say a person's being or being perceived as transsexual, transgendered, transvestite, or ambiguously gendered. Again, no more brimstone has fallen in any of these places than elsewhere.

Berkeley, California, in 1984, followed by a couple dozen other cities including New York, have passed "domestic partner" legislation giving same-sex couples at least some of the same rights to city benefits that heterosexually married couples have, and yet Berkeley has not become more weird than it already was. In 2000, Vermont, prompted by a decision of its Supreme Court the previous year, passed "civil-union" legislation giving gay and lesbian couples all the same rights and obligations as heterosexually married couples. In 2003 and 2004 respectively, California and New Jersey gave same-sex couples access to the core rights and obligations of marriage through legislation establishing "domestic partnership" registries. Most of northern European countries have instituted civil-union arrangements for same-sex couples—Denmark in 1989 and later Finland, France, Germany, Greenland, Iceland, Norway, and Sweden. In 2000, the Netherlands, followed by Belgium, gave lesbian and gay couples access to marriage in full.[23] Also in 2000, Brazil gave same-sex couples the right to inherit each other's pension and social security benefits.[24] The highest courts in three Canadian provinces have legalized gay marriage there—Ontario (2003), British Columbia (2003), and Quebec (2004).[25] In April 2004, the newly elected, left-of-center Prime Minister of Spain—yes, the country that brought you the Inquisition—announced his country would follow Belgium and the Netherlands by providing same-sex couples access to civil marriage.[26] England and Wales are inching toward civil unions for same-sex couples.[27]

In November of 2003, Massachusetts' highest court ruled that by May 17, 2004 the state had to start issuing marriage licenses to gay and lesbian couples. It then fortified its ruling in February 2004 by clarifying that a separate-but-equal civil-union arrangement for gay and lesbian couples, like Vermont's, would not pass constitutional muster as a substitute for same-sex couples having access to marriage.[28] On May 17, 2004, 1700 same-sex couples took out marriage licenses in the Commonwealth.[29]

In the private sector, a number of major universities (including Harvard, Stanford, the University of Chicago, and Southern Methodist University) are offering their employees domestic partnership benefits, as are, in increasing numbers, large and even conservative corporations, like Walt Disney Studios, Mobil Oil, Merrill Lynch, Delta Airlines, Boeing, General Motors, Ford, Coors Brewing, even Wal-Mart.[30] Between 1992 and 2004, the number of Fortune 500 companies doing so shot up from 12 to over 200.[31]

One virtually unnoticed area of private-sector progress has occurred in the most surprising of quarters—the insurance industry. Surprising, because insurance companies are inherently conservative institutions. Their well-being and very existence depend upon the usual, the normal, the average, the steady, the predictable. Only cats hate change more. Yet during the 1990s, most insurance carriers began offering domestic partner benefits under group coverage. It used to be that companies and towns with domestic partnership statutes were unable to find any insurer at all willing to carry their health policies. Now they have the luxury of competitive bids. The Allstate Insurance Co, a division of Sears, now writes homeowners policies for same-sex couples that are identical to those for heterosexually married couples. The Prudential Insurance Company, the nation's largest life insurance carrier, began offering its employees domestic partnership benefits in 1999. The same year, the conservative Chubb Group of Insurance Companies blitzed the mailboxes of gay and lesbian yuppie couples across the nation with six-color brochures inviting them to insure their art and antiques with Chubb, a provider of "major funding" for PBS's *Antiques Roadshow*. On the last page, the brochure offers seven bulleted reasons why the Chubb Group is "gay friendly"—its phrase. This private-sector progress is leading rather than following general governmental trends.

Seemingly hysterical predictions that the American family would collapse if such reforms would pass have proven false, just as the same dire predictions that the availability of divorce would lessen the ideal and desirability of marriage proved unfounded. Indeed if current discrimination, which drives gays into hiding and into anonymous relations, ended, far from seeing gays destroying American families, one would see gays forming them. Studies have found that virtually all gay men and lesbians express a desire to have a permanent lover. Yet, society makes gay coupling difficult. It is hard for people to live together as couples without having their sexual orientation perceived in the public realm, which in turn targets them for discrimination. Sharing a life in hiding is even more constricting than life in a small nuclear family. Members of nongay couples are here asked to imagine what it would take to erase every trace of their own sexual orientation for even just one week.

Still, if nothing else, the groundswell of gay marriages made suddenly possible by San Francisco's and Portland, Oregon's municipal and county disobedience in the Spring of 2004 show how committed to commitment gays are. Nearly one hundred percent of the same-sex couples issued licenses in San Francisco between February 12th and March 11th when California's Supreme Court suspended the issuing of them—3,955 out of 4,037 couples—subsequently returned to City Hall to register their licenses with the city after solemnization, showing that the city-hall celebrations were not publicity stunts, mere political acts, or cases of people being swept up in the moment.[32] During the seven weeks of March–April 2004 in which Multnomah County (Portland), Oregon, issued marriage licenses to same-sex couples, 6000 people availed themselves of the opportunity.[33]

Society makes gay coupling difficult, but those lesbian and gay male couples who have survived the odds show that the structure of more usual couplings is not a matter of destiny, but of personal responsibility. The so-called basic unit of society turns out not to be a unique immutable atom, but can adopt different parts and be adapted to different needs.

If discrimination ceased, gay men and lesbians would enter the mainstream of the human community openly and with self-respect. The energies that the typical gay person wastes in the anxiety of leading a day-to-day existence of systematic disguise would be released for use in personal flourishing. From this release would be generated the many spin-off benefits that accrue to a society when its individual members thrive.

Society would be richer for accepting another aspect of human diversity. Families with gay members would develop relations based on truth, trust, and openness rather than lies, embarrassment, or fear. And the heterosexual majority would be better off for knowing that they are no longer trampling their gay friends and neighbors.

Finally and perhaps paradoxically, in extending to gay men and lesbians the rights and benefits it has reserved for its dominant culture, America would confirm its deeply held vision of itself as a morally progressing nation, a nation itself advancing and serving as a beacon for others—especially with regard to human rights. The words with which our national pledge ends—"with liberty and justice for all"—are not a description of the present, but a call for the future. America is a nation prone to a prophetic political rhetoric which believes that morality is principled, not arbitrary, and that justice is more than the transient massings of a collective will. It is this vision that led the black civil rights movement to its successes. Those senators and representatives who opposed that movement and its centerpiece, the 1964 Civil Rights Act on obscurantist grounds, but who lived long enough and were noble enough came in time to express their heartfelt regret and shame at what they had done. It is to be hoped and someday to be expected that those who now grasp at anything to oppose the extension of that which is best about America to lesbians and gay men will one day feel the same.

Notes

1 *Newsweek*, August 12, 1985, p. 23 (Gallup Poll).
2 *Washington Post*, March 8, 2004 (*Washington Post—ABC Poll*); *Los Angeles Times*, April 10, 2004 (*Los Angeles Times* Poll).
3 *New York Times*, February 23, 2004, p. 14.
4 *New York Times*, January 10, 2000, p. 11.
5 *Washington Post*, May 15, 1984, p. 1.
6 *New York Times*, November 5, 1999, p. 1.
7 *New York Times*, November 2, 1999, p. 14.
8 "Rapper's Hate-Filled Lyrics Anger Some," *USA Today*, July 27, 2000.
9 "1,049 Laws Benefit Married Couples, GAO Says," *The Washington Blade*, February 21, 1997.
10 *New York Times*, December 12, 1993, p. 19.
11 *Lawrence v. Texas*, 539 U.S. 558 (2003).
12 John Boswell, *Christianity, Social Tolerance and Homosexuality* (Chicago, IL: University of Chicago Press, 1980), Chapter 4.
13 Gilbert Herdt, *Guardians of the Flute* (New York: McGraw-Hill, 1981).
14 Leviticus 18:22, 21:3 (condemnations of same-sex sex acts); Leviticus 11:1–47, 15:19–27 (dietary and hygienic codes); Genesis 19:1–25 (Lot at Sodom), 19:30–38 (Lot in Cave).
15 See, generally, Robert P. George, ed., *Natural Law Theory: Contemporary Essays* (Oxford: Oxford University Press, 1992).
16 *New York Times*, April 1, 2004, p. 1.
17 Hannah Arendt, *The Human Condition* (Chicago, IL: University of Chicago Press, 1958), Chapter 1.
18 See Edward Stein, *The Mismeasure of Desire* (New York: Oxford University Press, 2001).

19 See Claudia Card, *Lesbian Choices* (New York: Columbia University Press, 1995); Cheshire Calhoun, *Feminism, the Family, and the Politics of the Closet* (Oxford: Oxford University Press, 2000).
20 *The (Cleveland) Plain Dealer*, November 11, 1999, p. 1B.
21 *Baker v. State*, 170 Vt. 194; 744 A.2d 864 (1999); *New York Times*, December 28, 1999, p. 18.
22 *New York Times*, September 14, 2001, p. 13.
23 *New York Times*, December 20, 2000, p. 6.
24 *New York Times*, June 10, 2000, p. 6.
25 *New York Times*, March 20, 2004, p. 5.
26 *New York Times*, June 22, 2004, p. 5.
27 *New York Times*, December 7, 2002, p. 8; "Britain Proposes 'Gay Marriage' Plan," *Irish Examiner*.com, April 1, 2004, www.examiner.ie/pport/web/Full_Story/did-sgFJqm3hrTI3csg0aewFBADppk.asp (accessed June 22, 2004).
28 *Goodridge v. Dept. of Public Health*, 798 N.E.2d 941 (Mass. 2003); *In re Opinions of the Justices to the Senate*, 802 N.E.2d 565 (Mass. 2004).
29 *New York Times*, May 23, 2004, Section 4, p. 2.
30 *New York Times*, September 26, 2000, Section 3, p. 2.
31 *New York Times*, February 29, 2004, Section 2, p. 1.
32 *New York Times*, March 18, 2004, p. 21; *News Gazette* (Champaign, IL), Associated Press wire story (San Francisco), March 18, 2004, p. E1.
33 *New York Times*, April 21, 2004, p. 19.

Review and Discussion Questions

1 What are the leading gay stereotypes, according to Mohr?
2 How are stereotypes more pernicious than mere false generalizations?
3 In what ways does Mohr argue gays experience discrimination? Is it important, in this connection, that according to Mohr sexual orientation is not chosen?
4 How does Mohr respond to the argument that homosexuality is immoral?
5 What social and public policy changes have occurred recently, and what are the consequences?

READING: WHAT IS THE POINT OF LOVE?

CAROLYN PRICE[*]

Carolyn Price develops an account of what it means to love someone. She believes that love should be grounded in good reasons, which depends on the function of love. She defends her view against various objections and calls her view a "relationship theory" of love. Carolyn Price is a Senior Lecturer in Philosophy at the Open University in the United Kingdom.

In what follows, I shall be concerned only with personal love: for example, romantic or parental love. I shall focus on paradigm cases of personal love: that is, cases in which one person loves another for an extended period of time.

---

[*] Adapted from "What Is the Point of Love?" by Carolyn Price, *International Journal of Philosophical Studies* 20(2) (2012): 217–237. Reprinted by permission of Routledge, Taylor & Francis. Footnotes omitted.

I shall begin by identifying three assumptions that I shall make in what follows. None of these assumptions are unusual .... Nevertheless, they are all open to question, and I do not have space to defend them in detail here. Hence, my question might be rephrased as follows: given these three assumptions, how might we best develop a relationship theory of love?

First, I shall assume that love characteristically implies certain kinds of motivation or concern. I shall assume that the lover characteristically:

1   Harbours a concern for the welfare of the beloved;
2   Wants to spend time with their beloved, to share activities and experiences, exchange affection, and so on;
3   Wants their love to be reciprocated.

Secondly, I shall assume that love is not just a set of concerns: it also involves an evaluation of the beloved or of one's relationship with them. ... Suppose, for example, that Harry harbours loving concerns for his neighbour Jan, but that he experiences these concerns as inexplicable urges or whims: he does not think of Jan as special to him in any way. As well as being puzzling, this does not look like a case of love. Love requires that Harry values Jan, that he regards her as precious or important in some sense. As we shall see, however, there is room for dispute about the nature of this evaluation.

My third assumption is that love answers to reasons or grounds. This is a particularly controversial claim, and some theorists have developed "no reasons" theories of love. However, the claim that love *never* answers to reasons is open to question. Certainly, there seem to be cases in which love is properly described as unjustified or groundless: for example, cases in which someone loves a partner who is abusive or charmless. Of course, this does not by itself establish that love *always* requires justification, as I shall assume here. However, I believe that my account provides some of the materials that might be needed to defend this assumption. In particular, some possible counterexamples to this claim disappear once we recognise the diversity of considerations that can constitute grounds for love.

Some Questions about Love

Before considering how we might develop a relationship theory, I shall raise some questions about love. ...

(A) A Question about Lovability

Suppose that Addie is asked by a friend what she loves about Joe and that, in response, she comes up with the following list:

a   His sense of humour
b   His kindness
c   His lop-sided grin
d   His panache on the tennis court
e   His passion for Roman mosaics
f   His incurable untidiness

According to Addie, then, this is a list of Joe's lovable qualities—the qualities for which she loves Joe.

Perhaps the most striking feature of Addie's list is its diversity: it concerns Joe's appearance, his character, skills, habits, and interests. Some of the items on the list are relatively predictable; others are highly idiosyncratic. Indeed, looking at Addie's list, we might be tempted to conclude that someone can be loved for just about anything. Nevertheless, as Gabriele Taylor points out (1976: p. 154), there do seem to be *some* limitations on what we can love someone for: it is hard to make sense of the idea that Addie might love Joe for being deadly boring or unremittingly tiresome. This poses a puzzle: why are some qualities intelligibly lovable, but not others? What is it that links the apparently disparate items on Addie's list?

We might start with the thought that Joe's lovable qualities are his *positive* qualities. But this does not seem to be true of all the items on the list: untidiness does not seem to be a positive quality. Conversely, Joe may have positive qualities that do not belong on the list: perhaps Joe's dedication to his career is a positive, but not a lovable quality. The point can be brought out more clearly if we contrast love with admiration: Addie might admire Joe for his dedication to his career without loving him for it; she might love him for his untidiness without admiring him for it. What is the difference, then, between an admirable quality and a lovable one?

(B) A Question about Justification

To answer this question about lovability, we need first to address a prior question: what does it mean to say that Addie loves Joe *for* his lovable qualities? The most straightforward answer is that Joe's lovable qualities constitute Addie's *reasons* or *grounds* for loving him. But not all theorists take this view: as we shall see, Kolodny denies that love is ever justified by the personal qualities of the beloved. Before we can resolve the puzzle of lovability, then, we need to understand what kinds of consideration can constitute grounds for love.

As we have just seen, we might start by assuming that Addie's love for Joe is justified by his lovable qualities. Indeed, it might be suggested that this is true of all cases of love: love is always a response to the lovable personal qualities of the beloved (Taylor, 1976; Lamb, 1996). However, as Kolodny (2003: p. 139) points out, there is at least one exception to this claim. Consider Joe's love for his newborn daughter, Maia. Given Maia's age, it is implausible that Joe's love depends on her personal qualities: Joe loves Maia simply because she is his daughter.

It might be suggested that what this case shows is that we should abandon the assumption that love always answers to reasons or grounds: a father's love for his newborn daughter requires no justification. But this seems odd: it is not as if Joe's love is just a matter of taste or personal preference; on the contrary, his love for Maia seems wholly appropriate and justified. Plausibly, it is justified by the fact that Maia is Joe's daughter. If this is right, the conclusion to draw is not that love does not always require grounds, but that grounds for love are not confined to the personal qualities of the beloved: the existence of a familial relationship between the subject and the beloved can constitute grounds for love.

This raises some further questions, however. If a familial relationship can constitute grounds for love, might this be true of other kinds of relationship too? If so, what kinds of relationship might justify love, and why? Should we assume that Joe's love for Maia and Addie's love for Joe are justified in different ways? Or is there just one kind of justification for love? If love can be justified in more than one way, might there be yet other kinds of justification for love?

(C) A Puzzle about Love's Concerns

It might be suggested that we can answer these questions by considering the concerns that help to constitute love: grounds for love, perhaps, are grounds to harbour just these concerns (Taylor, 1976: p. 157). This looks like a promising strategy. However, the claim that love is partly constituted by these concerns produces a puzzle of its own. Why should love involve just these concerns? Why does love not motivate Addie to appreciate Joe from a distance, to imitate him, or simply to congratulate him? These are questions that a theory of love should be expected to answer.

...

Introducing Emotional Attitudes

Suppose that Addie is indignant about the government's decision to expand her local airport. We might take this to imply that Addie is, right now, fuming about the decision. Alternatively, we might take it to imply that Addie is disposed to become angry about the government's decision whenever the topic crops up. However, there is a third possibility. Suppose that Addie is so infuriated by the government's decision that she cannot stop thinking about it. Even after several weeks, it comes spontaneously to mind: she is inclined to raise it in conversations with friends and to check the internet for the latest news. She joins a campaign group and begins to think of herself as an environmental campaigner.

In this third scenario, Addie's indignation is not a passing episode of emotion that will fade away after a time. Rather, it has grown into something that may last a lifetime, shaping her plans and values, perhaps even her sense of who she is. On the other hand, it does not seem to be a dispositional state. Admittedly, it may involve certain dispositions: for example, she may be disposed to become frustrated when the decision is not reversed. But there is something else: an active propensity to think about the issue, to keep an eye out for developments, and to take account of it in her plans.

In what follows, I shall use the term "emotional attitude" to refer to an enduring psychological state of this kind.

Addie's indignant attitude seems to involve a number of elements:

1 She evaluates the government's decision as stupid and unfair.
2 She is motivated to redress the situation, as a matter of priority.
3 She harbours a number of emotional dispositions with respect to it.
4 She has an active propensity to attend to the issue.

It is possible to envisage other types of emotional attitude: for example, Addie might harbour a fearful attitude towards her neighbour's dog, an admiring attitude towards her sister, or a jealous attitude towards Joe. These emotional attitudes will involve a similar mix of evaluation and concern, together with an active propensity to attend to the situation.

Emotional Attitudes, Belief and Justification

I have suggested that an emotional attitude is characteristically generated and sustained by an evaluation of some kind. I have not yet said, however, what I take an emotional evaluation to be. I am going to suggest that emotional evaluations are not beliefs, but intentional states of a distinctive kind. There are several (oft-rehearsed) reasons for taking this view. I shall mention two of them here.

First, an emotional response can conflict with a belief. In harbouring a jealous attitude to Joe, for example, Addie may experience their relationship as under threat; yet, despite a parade of jealous thoughts, she may not actually believe that it is. What someone feels, then, seems to be distinct from what they believe.

It might be objected that this is too quick: perhaps Addie holds two contradictory beliefs. But if this is Addie's situation, she should be able to resolve the conflict either by suspending judgement or by examining the available evidence to reach a final verdict. A conflict between emotion and belief, however, can persist long after the subject has reached a considered judgement on the issue: changing an emotional response is often a much more extended and indirect process than revising a belief. Like many other philosophers of emotion, I take this to suggest that emotion and belief involve different processes of evaluation.

Secondly, emotional responses and evaluative beliefs do not draw on the same sources of information: in particular, emotional responses seem to be particularly dependent on perception and imagination. One might hear all the grisly details of a car accident and judge that it was a dreadful event. And yet one might not experience it as distressing until one sees, or perhaps imagines, what has happened. I take it that this offers further support to the claim that emotional responses are not sustained by beliefs, but by intentional states of a distinctive kind.

It is important not to overstretch this point. I am not denying that an emotional response will characteristically involve certain beliefs. Indeed, it is compatible with what I have said that emotional attitudes necessarily involve beliefs. Emotional attitudes involve beliefs in at least two different ways: first, as we have seen, an emotional attitude directs the subject's attention to certain aspects of the situation and motivates the subject to respond to it in certain ways: as a result, emotional attitudes involve certain characteristic trains of thought, and these may well carry conviction when the subject thinks them. Addie, for example, may well assent to her jealous thoughts as they form in her mind; it is only when she examines them more closely that she dismisses them as false. (In dismissing her thoughts, however, she need not have dismissed her jealousy: she may still be strongly disposed to have those thoughts, and she may have to expend some effort to keep them at bay.) Emotional attitudes, then, are partly constituted by thoughts and beliefs. Secondly, nothing I have said rules out the possibility that a subject's background beliefs will play a significant role in explaining why they respond emotionally in particular ways to particular situations. Addie's jealousy, for example, may depend in part on her beliefs about Joe's action; about certain social conventions; about the attitudes of potential rivals; and so on. These beliefs may help to explain Addie's jealous attitude, even if, in the end, she believes that there is no genuine threat to her relationship with Joe.

There is, then, much more to be said about the relationship between emotion and belief. The claim I am making here is quite specific: I am claiming that the evaluation that directly sustains an emotional attitude is not itself an evaluative belief. That this is so, I have suggested, explains why one's emotional evaluation of the situation can sometimes clash with one's evaluative beliefs about it; and why one's emotional response and one's evaluative beliefs sometimes appear to draw on different sources of information.

The claim that emotional evaluations are not beliefs might prompt us to wonder what standards of justification apply to them. Indeed, it might be suggested that emotional evaluations should be classed with perceptual states, as states that can be assessed as accurate or inaccurate, but not as justified or unjustified. I take it, however, that emotional evaluations do answer to standards of justification, and that, in this respect, they are closer to beliefs than to perceptual states. The difference, I would suggest, has to do with the educability of our emotional responses: it is possible, if not always easy, to reshape our emotional susceptibilities to get rid of emotional responses that are disproportionate or misplaced. We can do this, for example, by desensitising ourselves to certain cues or by finding different ways to interpret a certain kind of situation. Because we can educate our emotional sensibilities in this way, there is some point in evaluating the cues that prompt our emotional responses; in other words, there is some point in asking whether our emotional responses are well or poorly grounded.

I take it, then, that emotional evaluations do answer to standards of justification. Nevertheless, this does not imply that they answer to the *same* standards of justification as evaluative beliefs. Indeed, some theorists of emotion explicitly deny this. In particular, Patricia Greenspan has suggested that emotional evaluations answer to weaker standards than beliefs. While a belief answers to all the evidence the subject possesses, she argues, an emotional response may be justified provided that it has some evidential support: emotional responses, she suggests "are 'all-out ' reactions to *portions* of the evidence" (Greenspan, 1988: pp. 87–8, her italics). I shall return to this suggestion towards the end of the paper.

I have suggested that emotional attitudes are not underpinned by beliefs, but by evaluations of a distinctive kind. Because our emotional sensibilities are educable, there is some purpose in asking whether an emotional evaluation is well or poorly grounded. Nevertheless, there is no need to assume that emotional evaluations answer to the same standards as evaluative beliefs.

Emotional Attitudes and Function

There is one final point to be made before I return to the subject of love. I have suggested that emotional attitudes are complex psychological processes, which follow recognisable patterns. Each pattern of emotion can be seen as a response to a specific kind of event: for example, indignation is a response to injustice; fear is a response to a threat; sorrow is a response to loss, and so on. Moreover, in many cases, emotions can be seen as functioning to help the subject to cope with the situation: for example, Addie's indignation helps her to deal with the injustice by motivating her to redress it; fear helps her to deal with a threat by motivating her to escape from it, and so on.

The idea that emotions serve functions has a long history. In recent years, theorists interested in the evolutionary origins of emotions have argued that our emotional capacities evolved to help us to deal with challenges that commonly faced our ancestors (Tooby and Cosmides, 1990: pp. 407–8; Ekman, 1992: p. 171). In contrast, social constructivists argue that our emotional capacities are acquired through learning, and that they serve significant social functions (Averill, 1980). For the purposes of this discussion, I do not need to take a view on whether our emotional capacities are inherited, or learned, or both. What matters is the claim on which all these theorists agree: that many, if not all, emotions serve functions.

This is significant for the following reason: understanding what it is that an emotion functions to do enables us to explain why it takes the form it does. For example, the fact that Addie's indignant attitude motivates her to seek redress makes sense, given that the function of indignation is to enable the subject to respond appropriately to an injustice. This is not an intentional explanation: it does not appeal to what indignant people characteristically believe or value; nor does it appeal to the content of an indignant evaluation. Instead, it is a functional explanation: it appeals to the function of indignation to explain why it takes the form that it does.

Love as an Emotional Attitude

Love, I would suggest, is best understood as an emotional attitude. Certainly, Addie's love for Joe has much in common with her indignant attitude. Love is characteristically an enduring state. It involves both an evaluation and a set of concerns. Moreover, as has often been pointed out, love also seems to imply an active propensity to pay attention to the beloved. Indeed, in loving Joe, Addie can be expected to pay attention to him in many ways: by dwelling on his lovable qualities; by noticing how he is; by taking an interest in what he thinks and does; by taking account of him in making plans. Hence, her loving concerns for Joe are *active* concerns, which play a prominent role in her life. This attentional element ties love to (other) emotional attitudes and to emotional phenomena more broadly.

Again, there are reasons to deny that the evaluation that sustains love is a belief. First, people sometimes seem to love against their better judgement: they go on loving someone despite believing that they are abusive and unfaithful, or that their relationship is damaging or futile. In these cases, there seems to be a gap between what the subject feels and what the subject believes. Furthermore, while biographical research might lead me to believe that someone whom I have never met is a very lovable person, or that I share a significant familial relationship with them, this kind of second-hand knowledge does not seem sufficient for love. Love characteristically requires personal acquaintance and interaction with the beloved. In this respect, too, love is similar to (other) emotional responses such as fear or distress. There are good reasons, then, to classify love as an emotional attitude.

A New Relationship Theory of Love

If love is an emotional attitude, what difference does it make? Earlier, I suggested that understanding the function of an emotional response can help us to understand why it takes the form that it does. The availability of this kind of explanation is crucial in what follows. It is crucial because it suggests a new way of understanding the relationship claim. We can understand it as a claim about the function or purpose of love:

> R3 Love is an emotional attitude, the function of which is to foster an intense personal relationship between the subject and the beloved.

... I shall understand the term "personal relationship" to refer to a complex, reciprocal relationship, which might include not only mutual interest, appreciation and concern, but also friendly and intimate interaction. Some personal relationships are characteristically intense, in the sense that they involve strong mutual concern and interest and regular and intimate interaction. Parent/child relationships, romantic partnerships and close friendships are examples of intense personal relationships. If R3 is correct, the function of love is to foster an intense personal relationship of this kind.

Secondly, R3 does not presuppose that a personal relationship already exists between the subject and the beloved: fostering a relationship might be a matter of establishing a new relationship, or restoring one that has died. Indeed, the claim that a loving attitude has the function to foster an intense personal relationship leaves it open that, in some cases, love fails to fulfil this function. Thirdly, R3 is not a claim about what the subject believes: for, as we have seen, an emotional attitude need not depend on the subject's beliefs. ...

Lovability and Justification

In loving Joe, Addie evaluates him as a lovable person. R3 implies that this will be appropriate, provided that Joe is someone with whom it would be fitting for Addie to pursue a close personal relationship. This should not be taken to imply that, in loving Joe, Addie believes that Joe is such a person. If I were to claim this, my account would be open to the charge of over-intellectualisation. My claim is not about what Addie must believe, but only about the circumstances under which it is appropriate for Addie to respond to Joe as lovable—that is, to care about his welfare, to seek his company, and so on. ...

... there is no reason to deny that some of Joe's personal qualities might constitute grounds for love. Indeed, it seems reasonably obvious why Joe's kindness or sense of humour might provide grounds for Addie's love. It is also possible to see why his untidiness might also be relevant: perhaps it gives Addie an opportunity to tease him in a way that she (and hopefully he) enjoys. In contrast, it is hard to see how someone's being unremittingly tiresome could constitute grounds for sustaining a personal relationship with them. Again, we can appeal to R3 to explain why not all positive qualities constitute grounds for love: for example, perhaps Joe's dedication to his career has no impact (or perhaps a negative impact) on the relationship that he shares with Addie. ...

Nevertheless, R3 does not imply that personal qualities are the only grounds for love. R3 can also allow that the nature of the relationship between two people can constitute grounds for love. That two people have a close familial relationship, or that they already share a relationship of mutual concern, or that they find fulfilment in each other's company might all constitute strong grounds for a loving appraisal, given R3.

Indeed, I take it that R3 leaves scope to recognise yet other kinds of justification for love. In particular, I take it that grounds for love can include past events: that Joe supported Addie through a difficult time, or that they have achieved something valuable together might also constitute grounds for love. This may be, in part, because Joe's behaviour on these occasions provides particularly strong evidence of his lovable qualities or of his continuing concern for Addie. But another possibility is that these experiences have demonstrated the worth of the relationship itself, or increased the value of the relationship by fostering a shared outlook on life. In some cases, past events might justify continuing love, even though the subject is now estranged from the beloved.

This version of the relationship theory, then, licenses a relatively liberal interpretation of what might constitute grounds for love. In part, this is because R3 assumes a relatively inclusive conception of a personal relationship. But it is also because it does not presuppose that love must be founded on a relationship that already exists. Rather, it claims that love functions to foster a relationship in the future. Hence, although it allows that there are cases (familial love, say) in which love is grounded on an existing relationship, it can also allow that here are cases (unrequited love) in which there is, as yet, no relationship at all.

Love's Concerns

Love, I have suggested, implies a number of motivations: in loving Joe, Addie will have a concern for his welfare; she will want to spend time with him; and she will want Joe to reciprocate her concerns. Given R3, it is not difficult to explain why this should be: these motivations and the behaviour they generate help Addie to sustain an intense personal relationship with Joe. For, first, they partly constitute that relationship. And secondly, they encourage Joe to reciprocate in kind.

In making this claim, I am not suggesting that Addie herself must believe that her relationship with Joe is worth fostering; nor am I claiming that fostering their relationship is something that she consciously sets out to do. Of course, Addie may have such beliefs and goals: but if so, they will be the result of conscious reflection on the value of her relationship with Joe and its importance to her. On my account, this is something distinct from Addie's love. To say that Addie loves Joe implies that she wants to spend time with him, and that she wants him to care for her in return. But these concerns do not depend on her belief that she shares a valuable relationship with Joe. Indeed, as we have seen, she might want these things despite believing that her relationship with Joe is damaging or futile. If we want to explain why Addie has these concerns, the best thing to say is simply that they are part and parcel of her love for Joe. On this account, then, there is a clear distinction between acting out of love and acting from a considered appreciation of the value of a relationship.

If this is right, R3 has no role in explaining Addie's loving actions: Addie's loving actions are explained, simply, by her love. R3 becomes relevant only when we ask a more general question: why does love imply concerns of these kinds? In other words, we can appeal to R3 to resolve the puzzle of love's concerns. The explanation offered is a functional, not an intentional one: it implies nothing about the beliefs or values of the subject. Love's concerns make sense, given the function of love.

Love without Hope

.... I shall end by considering a case that might be thought to pose some difficulties for my account. As we shall see, the case raises some broader issues, and as a result, I cannot resolve it decisively here. Instead, my aim is to explore the case, and to indicate my preferred response.

Suppose that Zack loves Helen, with whom he has shared a close relationship for many years. Recently, Helen has suffered a massive stroke, leaving her paralysed and aphasic, unable to recognise Zack, to remember their life together, or to respond to his presence. She is no longer the witty and active woman with whom Zack fell in love. As he comes to understand the situation, Zack is seized by grief and compassion for Helen. Yet he also continues to love her.

This is, of course, a case of unrequited love. However ... there is no hope that Zack's love will be returned. Hence, Helen is no longer a person with whom Zack should—or even could—pursue an intense personal relationship. It might be thought, then, that my account implies that Zack's love is unjustified. On the face of it, though, this seems rather harsh: certainly, Zack's love seems perfectly intelligible.

In considering this case, we need to bear some distinctions in mind. First, we need to distinguish between the claim that Zack has good grounds to love Helen and the claim that his love fits the situation. Just as a belief may be justified by the evidence and yet false, an emotional response may be well-grounded and yet misplaced. Secondly, we should bear in mind that the claim that Zack continues to love Helen might be interpreted in two ways. One possibility is that Zack continues to love Helen as she *was*; in other words, that he remembers her with love. Another possibility is that he loves her as she is now.

The possibility that Zack remembers Helen with love raises no special difficulty for my account. Memories commonly produce emotional responses: one can remember a success with pride, or a clanger with embarrassment. There is no general reason to suppose that such emotional responses are redundant or out of place. ...

But what about the possibility that Zack continues to love Helen as she is now? Certainly, there is no reason to deny, on my account, that Zack has grounds to love Helen as she is. Admittedly, Zack's love cannot be justified by the personal qualities that Helen now has; or by the relationship that now exists between them. But it might well be justified by their history—by the experiences and achievements that they have shared. Given the length and intensity of their relationship, it is likely that Zack has many such grounds for loving Helen as she is.

It might be objected, though, that this is not enough to show that Zack's love is fully justified: for whatever grounds Zack has to love Helen, they will be outweighed by the fact that (as Zack knows) Helen can never again return his love. Hence, on my account, the objection goes, Zack's continuing love for Helen cannot be justified *overall*. The issue here depends on the standards of justification that apply to emotional evaluations. A belief, certainly, is supposed to answer to all the evidence that the subject possesses. As I mentioned earlier, however, we do not need to assume that emotional evaluations answer to the same standards as beliefs. ...

On my account, then, we can allow that Zack has strong grounds to love Helen; and perhaps even that his love for her is fully justified. There is, then, nothing puzzling or gratuitous about his feelings. But a further question remains: on my account, can Zack's love be said to fit the situation? I take it that the answer to this question is "no". For whatever grounds Zack has to love Helen, the fact remains that she is no longer someone with whom Zack can sustain an intense personal relationship. The mismatch between his feelings and the situation will be reflected in the inevitable frustration of his loving desires for interaction and reciprocity. Zack's compassion and grief better fit the situation as it is now.

Nevertheless, there is an important proviso here: there are significant continuities between Zack's love for Helen and the compassion and grief he also feels. First, these new responses are predicated on his love for her as she was. This is particularly obvious in the case of grief; but Zack's compassion, too, is likely to be shaped by his loving appreciation of the person that she was. Compassion and grief are not love; but in this case, they manifest love. Moreover, these emotions overlap with love in important ways: grief, for example, implies an evaluation of its object as precious and important; while compassion implies a concern for their welfare. Hence, Zack's appreciation of Helen and his concern for her welfare—both central elements in his love for her—will remain as apt as they were.

My account does imply, then, that Zack's love for Helen as she is does not fit the situation. Simply to state that, however, risks overlooking other important features of the case. In particular, Zack has strong grounds for his loving evaluation of Helen. Moreover, even if Zack's love is misplaced, his appreciation of her as she was and his continuing concern for her welfare are not.

Conclusion

I have argued that the relationship claim is best understood, not as a claim about the subject's beliefs, but as a claim about the function of love. The function of love, I have suggested, is to foster an intense personal relationship between the subject and the beloved. By adopting this version of the relationship claim, we can explain love's concerns, while maintaining a distinction between acting out of love and acting from an intellectual appreciation of the value of one's relationship with them; and we can explain how love is justified, while recognising the diversity of possible grounds for love. Underpinning this version of the relationship theory is a conception of love as a complex emotional attitude, irreducible to the subject's beliefs and desires.

References

Averill, J. (1980) 'A Constructivist View of Emotion', in R. Plutchik and H. Kellerman (eds) *Theories of Emotion*, New York: Academic Press, pp. 306–312.

Ekman, P. (1992) 'An Argument for Basic Emotions', *Cognition and Emotion* 6 (3/4): 169–200.

Greenspan, P. (1988) *Emotions and Reasons: An Enquiry into Emotional Justification*, London: Routledge.
Kolodny, N. (2003) 'Love as Valuing a Relationship', *Philosophical Review* 112 (2): 135–189.
Lamb, R. (1996) 'Love and Rationality', in R. E. Lamb (ed.) *Love Analyzed*, Boulder, CO: Westview Press, pp. 23–48.
Taylor, G. (1976) 'Love', *Proceedings of the Aristotelian Society* 76: 147–164.
Tooby, J. and L. Cosmides (1990) 'The Past Explains the Present: Emotional Adaptations and the Structure of Ancestral Environments', *Ethology and Sociobiology* 11: 375–424.

Review and Discussions Questions

1 What are Price's assumptions for her analysis and what questions does she think any successful theory of love must answer? Are these the assumptions and questions that you would pose to frame a discussion of love? Why or why not?
2 What is the distinction between having an emotion and having an "emotional attitude" in the sense that Price discusses?
3 How is an emotional attitude not quite like a belief or a visual perception, though it shares some commonalities with each?
4 Does love have a function? What is Price's analysis? Do you agree with this analysis?
5 Can you describe a case of love that showcases Price's analysis well, and a case of love that is difficult for her analysis to explain?

Essay and Paper Topics for Chapter 10

1 Compare and critically assess the different views on sex and sexuality defended in this chapter.
2 Discuss the nature of and the relationships among sex and love.
3 What is the point of love?

Chapter 11

Family and Friendship

Contemporary society has undergone, and continues to undergo, remarkable changes in attitudes toward marriage, family, and friendship. These changes take many forms and raise many issues. They include the nature of marriage and the duty of fidelity, the obligations of parenthood, and how to conceive of a healthy relationship between parents and children.

READING: IS ADULTERY IMMORAL?

RICHARD A. WASSERSTROM*

Richard Wasserstrom considers various reasons that might be given for supposing adultery is wrong, including claims that it involves promise-breaking and deception. He concludes with a discussion of the importance of fidelity as a support for the institution of marriage and whether adultery may be wrong just because it constitutes an attack on marriage. Richard Wasserstrom is Professor of Philosophy Emeritus at the University of California, Santa Cruz.

I propose in this paper to think about the topic of sexual morality and to do so in the following fashion. I shall consider just one kind of behavior that is often taken to be a case of sexual immorality—adultery. I am interested in pursuing at least two questions. First, I want to explore the question of in what respects adulterous behavior falls within the domain of morality at all: for this surely is one of the puzzles one encounters when considering the topic of sexual morality. It is often hard to see on what grounds much of the behavior is deemed to be either moral or immoral, for example, private homosexual behavior between consenting adults. I have purposely selected adultery because it seems a more plausible candidate for moral assessment than many other kinds of sexual behavior.

The second question I want to examine is that of what is to be said about adultery without being especially concerned to stay within the area of morality. I shall endeavor, in other words, to identify and to assess a number of the major arguments that might be advanced against adultery. I believe that they are the chief

---

* © 1975 by Richard A. Wasserstrom, in *Philosophy and Sex* ed. by R. Baker and F. Ellison (Buffalo, NY: Prometheus Books, 1975), pp. 207–221. Reprinted by permission of the author.

arguments that would be given in support of the view that adultery is immoral, but I think they are worth considering even if some of them turn out to be nonmoral arguments and considerations.

A number of the issues involved seem to me to be complicated and difficult. In a number of places I have at best indicated where further philosophical exploration is required without having successfully conducted the exploration myself. The paper may very well be more useful as an illustration of how one might begin to think about the subject of sexual morality than as an elucidation of important truths about the topic.

Before I turn to the arguments themselves, there are two preliminary points that require some clarification. Throughout the paper I shall refer to the immorality of such things as breaking a promise, deceiving someone, etc. In a very rough way, I mean by this that there is something morally wrong that is done in doing the action in question. I mean that the action is, in a strong sense of "prima facie," prima facie wrong or unjustified. I do not mean that it may never be right or justifiable to do the action, just that the fact that it is an action of this description always does count against the rightness of the action. I leave entirely open the question of what it is that makes actions of this kind immoral in this sense of "immoral."

The second preliminary point concerns what is meant or implied by the concept of adultery. I mean by "adultery" any case of extramarital sex, and I want to explore the arguments for and against extramarital sex, undertaken in a variety of morally relevant situations. Someone might claim that the concept of adultery is conceptually connected with the concept of immorality and that to characterize behavior as adulterous is already to characterize it as immoral or unjustified in the sense described above. There may be something to this. Hence the importance of making it clear that I want to talk about extramarital sexual relations. If they are always immoral, this is something that must be shown by argument. If the concept of adultery does in some sense entail or imply immorality, I want to ask whether that connection is a rationally based one. If not all cases of extramarital sex are immoral (again, in the sense described above), then the concept of adultery should either be weakened accordingly or restricted to those classes of extramarital sex for which the predication of immorality is warranted.

One argument for the immorality of adultery might go something like this: what makes adultery immoral is that it involves the breaking of a promise, and what makes adultery seriously wrong is that it involves the breaking of an important promise. For, so the argument might continue, one of the things the two parties promise each other when they get married is that they will abstain from sexual relationships with third persons. Because of this promise, both spouses quite reasonably entertain the expectation that the other will behave in conformity with it. Hence, when one of the parties has sexual intercourse with a third person, he or she breaks that promise about sexual relationships which was made when the marriage was entered into and defeats the reasonable expectations of exclusivity entertained by the spouse.

In many cases, the immorality involved in breaching the promise relating to extramarital sex may be a good deal more serious than that involved in the breach of other promises. This is so because adherence to this promise may be of much greater importance to the parties than is adherence to many of the other promises given or received by them in their life-time. The breaking of this promise may be much more hurtful and painful than is typically the case.

Why is this so? To begin with, it may have been difficult for the nonadulterous spouse to have kept the promise. Hence that spouse may feel the unfairness of having restrained himself or herself in the absence of reciprocal restraint having been exercised by the adulterous spouse. In addition, the spouse may perceive the breaking of the promise as an indication of a kind of indifference on the part of the adulterous spouse. If you really cared about me and my feelings—the spouse might say—you would not have done this to me. And third, and related to the above, the spouse may see the act of sexual intercourse with another as a sign of affection for the other person and as an additional rejection of the nonadulterous spouse as the one who is loved by the adulterous spouse. It is not just that the adulterous spouse does not take the feelings of the spouse sufficiently into account, the adulterous spouse also indicates through the act of adultery affection for someone other than the spouse. I will return to these points later. For the present, it is sufficient to note that a set of arguments can be developed in support of the proposition that certain kinds of adultery are wrong just because they involve the breach of a serious promise which, among other things, leads to the intentional infliction of substantial pain by one spouse upon the other.

Another argument for the immorality of adultery focuses not on the existence of a promise of sexual exclusivity but on the connection between adultery and deception. According to this argument, adultery involves deception. And because deception is wrong, so is adultery.

Although it is certainly not obviously so, I shall simply assume in this paper that deception is always immoral. Thus the crucial issue for my purposes is the asserted connection between extramarital sex and deception. Is it plausible to maintain, as this argument does, that adultery always does involve deception and is on that basis to be condemned?

The most obvious person on whom deceptions might be practiced is the non-participating spouse, and the most obvious thing about which the nonparticipating spouse can be deceived is the existence of the adulterous act. One clear case of deception is that of lying. Instead of saying that the afternoon was spent in bed with A, the adulterous spouse asserts that it was spent in the library with B or on the golf course with C.

There can also be deception even when no lies are told. Suppose, for instance, that a person has sexual intercourse with someone other than his or her spouse and just does not tell the spouse about it. Is that deception? It may not be a case of lying if, for example, the spouse is never asked by the other about the situation. Still, we might say, it is surely deceptive because of the promises that were exchanged at marriage. As we saw earlier, these promises provide a foundation for the reasonable belief that neither spouse will engage in sexual relationships with any other persons. Hence the failure to bring the fact of extramarital sex to the attention of the other spouse deceives that spouse about the present state of the marital relationship.

Adultery, in other words, can involve both active and passive deception. An adulterous spouse may just keep silent or, as is often the fact, the spouse may engage in an increasingly complex way of life devoted to the concealment of the facts from the nonparticipating spouse. Lies, half-truths, clandestine meetings, and the like may become a central feature of the adulterous spouse's existence. These are things that can and do happen, and when they do they make the case against adultery an easy one. Still, neither active nor passive deception is inevitably a feature of an extramarital relationship.

It is possible, though, that a more subtle but pervasive kind of deceptiveness is a feature of adultery. It comes about because of the connection in our culture between sexual intimacy and certain feelings of love and affection. The point can be made indirectly at first by seeing that one way in which we can, in our culture, mark off our close friends from our mere acquaintances is through the kinds of intimacies that we are prepared to share with them. I may, for instance, be willing to reveal my very private thoughts and emotions to my closest friends or to my wife but to no one else. My sharing of these intimate facts about myself is from one perspective a way of making a gift to those who mean the most to me. Revealing these things and sharing them with those who mean the most to me is one means by which I create, maintain, and confirm those interpersonal relationships that are of most importance to me.

Now in our culture, it might be claimed, sexual intimacy is one of the chief currencies through which gifts of this sort are exchanged. One way to tell someone—particularly someone of the opposite sex—that you have feelings of affection and love for them is by sharing with them sexual behaviors that one doesn't share with the rest of the world. This way of measuring affection was certainly very much a part of the culture in which I matured. It worked something like this. If you were a girl, you showed how much you liked someone by the degree of sexual intimacy you would allow. If you liked a boy only a little, you never did more than kiss—and even the kiss was not very passionate. If you liked the boy a lot and if your feeling was reciprocated, necking, and possibly petting, was permissible. If the attachment was still stronger and you thought it might even become a permanent relationship, the sexual activity was correspondingly more intense and more intimate, although whether it would ever lead to sexual intercourse depended on whether the parties (and particularly the girl) accepted fully the prohibition on nonmarital sex. The situation of the boy was related, but not exactly the same. The assumption was that males did not naturally link sex with affection in the way in which females did. However, since women did, males had to take this into account. That is to say, because a woman would permit sexual intimacies only if she had feelings of affection for the male and only if those feelings were reciprocated, the male had to have and express those feelings, too, before sexual intimacies of any sort would occur.

The result was that the importance of a correlation between sexual intimacy and feelings of love and affection was taught by the culture and assimilated by those growing up in the culture. The scale of possible positive feelings toward persons of the opposite sex ran from casual liking at the one end to the love that was deemed essential to and characteristic of marriage at the other. The scale of possible sexual behavior ran from brief, passionless kissing or hand-holding at the one end to sexual intercourse at the other. And the correlation between the two scales was quite precise. As a result, any act of sexual intimacy carried substantial meaning with it, and no act of sexual intimacy was simply a pleasurable set of bodily sensations. Many such acts were, of course, more pleasurable to the participants because they were a way of saying what the participants' feelings were. And sometimes they were less pleasurable for the same reason. The point is, however, that in any event sexual activity was much more than mere bodily enjoyment. It was not like eating a good meal, listening to good music, lying in the sun, or getting a pleasant back rub. It was behavior that meant a great deal concerning one's feelings for persons of the opposite sex in whom one was most interested and with whom one was most involved. It was among the most authoritative ways in which one could communicate to another the nature and degree of one's affection.

If this sketch is even roughly right, then several things become somewhat clearer. To begin with, a possible rationale for many of the rules of conventional sexual morality can be developed. If, for example, sexual intercourse is associated with the kind of affection and commitment to another that is regarded as characteristic of the marriage relationship, then it is natural that sexual intercourse should be thought properly to take place between persons who are married to each other. And if it is thought that this kind of affection and commitment is only to be found within the marriage relationship, then it is not surprising that sexual intercourse should only be thought to be proper within marriage.

Related to what has just been said is the idea that sexual intercourse ought to be restricted to those who are married to each other as a means by which to confirm the very special feelings that the spouses have for each other. Because the culture teaches that sexual intercourse means that the strongest of all feelings for each other are shared by the lovers, it is natural that persons who are married to each other should be able to say this is so to each other in this way. Revealing and confirming verbally that these feelings are present is one thing that helps to sustain the relationship; engaging in sexual intercourse is another.

In addition, this account would help to provide a framework within which to make sense of the notion that some sex is better than other sex. As I indicated earlier, the fact that sexual intimacy can be meaningful in the sense described tends to make it also the case that sexual intercourse can sometimes be more enjoyable than at other times. On this view, sexual intercourse will typically be more enjoyable where the strong feelings of affection are present than it will be where it is merely "mechanical." This is so in part because people enjoy being loved, especially by those whom they love. Just as we like to hear words of affection, so we like to receive affectionate behavior. And the meaning enhances the independently pleasurable behavior.

More to the point, moreover, an additional rationale for the prohibition on extramarital sex can now be developed. For given this way of viewing the sexual world, extramarital sex will almost always involve deception of a deeper sort. If the adulterous spouse does not in fact have the appropriate feelings of affection for the extramarital partner, then the adulterous spouse is deceiving that person about the presence of such feelings. If, on the other hand, the adulterous spouse does have the corresponding feelings for the extramarital partner but not toward the nonparticipating spouse, the adulterous spouse is very probably deceiving the nonparticipating spouse about the presence of such feelings toward that spouse. Indeed, it might be argued, whenever there is no longer love between the two persons who are married to each other, there is deception just because being married implies both to the participants and to the world that such a bond exists. Deception is inevitable, the argument might conclude, because the feelings of affection that ought to accompany any act of sexual intercourse can only be held toward one other person at any given time in one's life. And if this is so, then the adulterous spouse always deceives either the partner in adultery or the nonparticipating spouse about the existence of such feelings. Thus extramarital sex involves deception of this sort and is for this reason immoral even if no deception vis-à-vis the occurrence of the act of adultery takes place.

What might be said in response to the foregoing arguments? The first thing that might be said is that the account of the connection between sexual intimacy and feelings of affection is inaccurate. Not inaccurate in the sense that no one thinks of things that way, but in the sense that there is substantially more divergence of opinion than that account suggests. For example, the view I have delineated may describe reasonably accurately the concepts of the sexual world in which I grew up, but it does not capture the sexual *Weltanschauung* of today's youth at all. Thus, whether or not adultery implies deception in respect to feelings depends very much on the persons who are involved and the way they look at the "meaning" of sexual intimacy.

Second, the argument leaves to be answered the question of whether it is desirable for sexual intimacy to carry the sorts of messages described above. For those persons for whom sex does have these implications, there are special feelings and sensibilities that must be taken into account. But it is another question entirely whether any valuable end—moral or otherwise—is served by investing sexual behavior with such significance. That is something that must be shown and not just assumed. It might, for instance, be the case that substantially more good than harm would come from a kind of demystification of sexual behavior: one that would encourage the enjoyment of sex more for its own sake and one that would reject the centrality both of the association of sex with love and of love with only one other person.

I regard these as two of the more difficult, unresolved issues that our culture faces today in respect to thinking sensibly about the attitudes toward sex and love that we should try to develop in ourselves and in our children. Much of the contemporary literature that advocates sexual liberation of one sort or another embraces one or the other of two different views about the relationship between sex and love.

One view holds that sex should be separated from love and affection. To be sure, sex is probably better when the partners genuinely like and enjoy each other. But sex is basically an intensive, exciting sensuous activity that can be enjoyed in a variety of suitable settings with a variety of suitable partners. The situation in respect to sexual pleasure is no different from that of the person who knows and appreciates fine food and who can have a very satisfying meal in any number of good restaurants with any number of congenial companions. One question that must be settled here is whether sex can be so demystified; another, more important question is whether it would be desirable to do so. What would we gain and what might we lose if we all lived in a world in which an act of sexual intercourse was no more or less significant or enjoyable than having a delicious meal in a nice setting with a good friend? The answer to this question lies beyond the scope of this paper.

The second view seeks to drive the wedge in a different place. It is not the link between sex and love that needs to be broken; rather, on this view, it is the connection between love and exclusivity that ought to be severed. For a number of the reasons already given, it is desirable, so this argument goes, that sexual intimacy continue to be reserved to and shared with only those for whom one has very great affection. The mistake lies in thinking that any "normal" adult will only have those feelings toward one other adult during his or her lifetime—or even at any time in his or her life. It is the concept of adult love, not ideas about sex that, on this view, needs demystification. What are thought to be both unrealistic and unfortunate are the notions of exclusivity and possessiveness that attach to the dominant conception of love between adults in our and other cultures. Parents of four, five, six, or even ten children can certainly claim and sometimes claim correctly that they love all of their children, that they love them all equally, and that it is simply untrue to their feelings to insist that the numbers involved diminish either the quantity or the quality of their love. If this is an idea that is readily understandable in the case of parents and children, there is no necessary reason why it is an impossible or undesirable ideal in the case of adults. To be sure, there is probably a limit to the number of intimate, "primary" relationships that any person can maintain at any given time without the quality of the relationship being affected. But one adult ought surely to be able to love two, three, or even six other adults at any one time without that love being different in kind or degree from that of the traditional, monogamous, lifetime marriage. And as between the individuals in these relationships, whether within a marriage or without, sexual intimacy is fitting and good.

The issues raised by a position such as this one are also surely worth exploring in detail and with care. Is there something to be called "sexual love" which is different from parental love or the nonsexual love of close friends? Is there something about love in general that links it naturally and appropriately with feelings of exclusivity and possession? Or is there something about sexual love, whatever that may be, that makes these feelings especially fitting here? Once again the issues are conceptual, empirical, and normative all at once: What is love? How could it be different? Would it be a good thing or a bad thing if it were different?

Suppose, though, that having delineated these problems we were now to pass them by. Suppose, moreover, we were to be persuaded of the possibility and the desirability of weakening substantially either the links between sex and love or the links between sexual love and exclusivity. Would it not then be the case that adultery could be free from all of the morally objectionable features described so far? To be more specific, let us imagine that a husband and wife have what is today sometimes characterized as an "open marriage." Suppose, that is, that they have agreed in advance that extramarital sex is—under certain circumstances—acceptable behavior for each to engage in. Suppose that as a result there is no impulse to deceive each other about the occurrence or nature of any such relationships and that no deception in fact occurs. Suppose, too, that there is no deception in respect to the feelings involved between the adulterous spouse and the extramarital partner. And suppose, finally, that one or the other or both of the spouses then has sexual intercourse in circumstances consistent with these understandings. Under this description, so the argument might conclude, adultery is simply not immoral. At a minimum, adultery cannot very plausibly be condemned either on the ground that it involves deception or on the ground that it requires the breaking of a promise.

The remaining argument seeks to justify the prohibition by virtue of the role that it plays in the development and maintenance of nuclear families. The argument, or set of arguments, might, I believe, go something like this.

Consider first a far-fetched nonsexual example. Suppose a society were organized so that after some suitable age—say, 18, 19, or 20—persons were forbidden to eat anything but bread and water with anyone but their spouse. Persons might still choose in such a society not to get married. Good food just might not be very important to them because they have underdeveloped taste buds. Or good food might be bad for them because there is something wrong with their digestive system. Or good food might be important to them, but they might decide that the enjoyment of good food would get in the way of the attainment of other things that were more important. But most persons would, I think, be led to favor marriage in part because they preferred a richer, more varied, diet to one of bread and water. And they might remain married because the family was the only legitimate setting within which good food was obtainable. If it is important to have society organized so that persons will both get married and stay married, such an arrangement would be well suited to the preservation of the family and the prohibitions relating to food consumption could be understood as fulfilling that function.

It is obvious that one of the more powerful human desires is the desire for sexual gratification. The desire is a natural one, like hunger and thirst, in the sense that it need not be learned in order to be present within us and operative upon us. But there is in addition much that we do learn about what the act of sexual intercourse is like. Once we experience sexual intercourse ourselves—and in particular once we experience orgasm—we discover that it is among the most intensive, short-term pleasures of the body.

Because this is so, it is easy to see how the prohibition upon extramarital sex helps to hold marriage together. At least during that period of life when the enjoyment of sexual intercourse is one of the desirable bodily pleasures, persons will wish to enjoy those pleasures. If one consequence of being married is that one is prohibited from having sexual intercourse with anyone but one's spouse, then the spouses in a marriage are in a position to provide an important source of pleasure for each other that is unavailable to them elsewhere in the society.

The point emerges still more clearly if this rule of sexual morality is seen as of a piece with the other rules of sexual morality. When this prohibition is coupled, for example, with the prohibition on nonmarital sexual intercourse, we are presented with the inducement both to get married and to stay married. For if sexual intercourse is only legitimate within marriage, then persons seeking that gratification which is a feature of sexual intercourse are furnished explicit social directions for its attainment: namely marriage.

Nor, to continue the argument, is it necessary to focus exclusively on the bodily enjoyment that is involved. Orgasm may be a significant part of what there is to sexual intercourse, but it is not the whole of it. We need only recall the earlier discussion of the meaning that sexual intimacy has in our own culture to begin to see some of the more intricate ways in which sexual exclusivity may be connected with the establishment and maintenance of marriage as the primary heterosexual love relationship. Adultery is wrong, in other words, because a prohibition on extramarital sex is a way to help maintain the institutions of marriage and the nuclear family.

Now I am frankly not sure what we are to say about an argument such as this one. What I am convinced of is that like the arguments discussed earlier, this one also reveals something of the difficulty and complexity of the issues that are involved. So what I want now to do—in the brief and final portion of this paper—is to try to delineate with reasonable precision what I take several of the fundamental, unresolved issues to be.

The first is whether this last argument is an argument for the *immorality* of extramarital sexual intercourse. What does seem clear is that there are differences between this argument and the ones considered earlier. The earlier arguments condemned adulterous behavior because it was behavior that involved breaking of a promise, taking unfair advantage, or deceiving another. To the degree to which the prohibition on extramarital sex can be supported by arguments which invoke considerations such as these, there is little question but that violations of the prohibition are properly regarded as immoral. And such a claim could be defended on one or both of two distinct grounds. The first is that things like promise-breaking and deception are just wrong. The second is that adultery involving promise-breaking or deception is wrong because it involves the straightforward infliction of harm on another human being—typically the nonadulterous spouse—who has a strong claim not to have that harm so inflicted.

The argument that connects the prohibition on extramarital sex with the maintenance and preservation of the institution of marriage is an argument for the instrumental value of the prohibition. To some degree this counts, I think, against regarding all violations of the prohibition as obvious cases of immorality. This is so partly because hypothetical imperatives are less clearly within the domain of morality than are categorical ones and even more because instrumental prohibitions are within the domain of morality only if the end they serve or the way they serve it is itself within the domain of morality.

What this should help us see, I think, is the fact that the argument that connects the prohibition on adultery with the preservation of marriage is at best seriously incomplete. Before we ought to be convinced by it, we ought to have reasons for believing that marriage is a morally desirable and just social institution. And this is not quite as easy or obvious a task as it may seem to be. For the concept of marriage is both a loosely structured and a complicated one. There may be all sorts of intimate, interpersonal relationships which will resemble but not be identical with the typical marriage relationship presupposed by the traditional sexual morality. There may be a number of distinguishable sexual and loving arrangements which can all legitimately claim to be called *marriages*. The prohibitions of the traditional sexual morality may be effective ways to maintain some marriages and ineffective ways to promote and preserve others. The prohibitions of the traditional sexual morality may make good psychological sense if certain psychological theories are true, and they may be purveyors of immense psychological mischief if other psychological theories are true. The prohibitions of the traditional sexual morality may seem obviously correct if sexual intimacy carries the meaning that the dominant culture has often ascribed to it, and they may seem equally bizarre when sex is viewed through the perspective of the counterculture. Irrespective of whether instrumental arguments of this sort are properly deemed moral arguments, they ought not to fully convince anyone until questions like these are answered.

Review and Discussion Questions

1 Describe the various ways that adultery may involve deception.

2 How might one argue that adultery is wrong based on the importance of marriage? Does Wasserstrom accept this argument? Explain why or why not.
3 Suppose adultery does weaken the marriage institution. Does that mean it is wrong? Are people obligated never to weaken a useful institution?
4 Is passive deception always wrong? Explain, using examples, and then indicate if you think this is a problem for Wasserstrom's position.
5 Is Wasserstrom's argument relevant to the discussions of the nature of sex in Chapter 10? Explain.

READING: LICENSING PARENTS

HUGH LAFOLLETTE[*]

Undertaking to raise a child is an act with vast consequences, for good or ill—far greater than those that result from driving a car, for example. Yet society requires a license to make certain that people are at least minimally capable of driving safely, let alone practice medicine and law or give psychological counseling. Why, then, shouldn't parenting be an activity that also requires some sort of assurances of minimal competence? Hugh LaFollette argues that it should and that neither the theoretical nor the practical objections that might be brought against licensing parents are sufficiently strong to justify allowing people to have children when they are incapable of raising them competently. Hugh LaFollette holds the Cole Chair in Ethics at the University of South Florida.

In this essay I shall argue that the state should require all parents to be licensed. My main goal is to demonstrate that the licensing of parents is theoretically desirable, though I shall also argue that a workable and just licensing program actually could be established.

My strategy is simple. After developing the basic rationale for the licensing of parents, I shall consider several objections to the proposal and argue that these objections fail to undermine it. I shall then isolate some striking similarities between this licensing program and our present policies on the adoption of children. If we retain these adoption policies—as we surely should—then, I argue, a general licensing program should also be established. Finally, I shall briefly suggest that the reason many people object to licensing is that they think parents, particularly biological parents, own or have natural sovereignty over their children.

Regulating Potentially Harmful Activities

Our society normally regulates a certain range of activities; it is illegal to perform these activities unless one has received prior permission to do so. We require

---

[*] Abridged from "Licensing Parents" by Hugh LaFollette, *Philosophy and Public Affairs* 9(2) (1980): 182–197. Copyright © 1980. Reprinted by permission of Blackwell Publishing Ltd., a company of John Wiley & Sons, Inc.

automobile operators to have licenses. We forbid people from practicing medicine, law, pharmacy, or psychiatry unless they have satisfied certain licensing requirements.

Society's decision to regulate just these activities is not ad hoc. The decision to restrict admission to certain vocations and to forbid some people from driving is based on an eminently plausible, though not often explicitly formulated, rationale. We require drivers to be licensed because driving an auto is an activity which is potentially harmful to others, safe performance of the activity requires a certain competence, and we have a moderately reliable procedure for determining that competence. The potential harm is obvious: incompetent drivers can and do maim and kill people. The best way we have of limiting this harm without sacrificing the benefits of automobile travel is to require that all drivers demonstrate at least minimal competence. We likewise license doctors, lawyers, and psychologists because they perform activities which can harm others. Obviously they must be proficient if they are to perform these activities properly, and we have moderately reliable procedures for determining proficiency. Imagine a world in which everyone could legally drive a car, in which everyone could legally perform surgery, prescribe medications, dispense drugs, or offer legal advice. Such a world would hardly be desirable.

Consequently, any activity that is potentially harmful to others and requires certain demonstrated competence for its safe performance is subject to regulation—that is, it is theoretically desirable that we regulate it. If we also have a reliable procedure for determining whether someone has the requisite competence, then the action is not only subject to regulation but ought, all things considered, to be regulated.

It is particularly significant that we license these hazardous activities, even though denying a license to someone can severely inconvenience and even harm that person. Furthermore, available competency tests are not 100 percent accurate. Denying someone a driver's license in our society, for example, would inconvenience that person acutely. In effect, that person would be prohibited from working, shopping, or visiting in places reachable only by car. Similarly, people denied vocational licenses are inconvenienced, even devastated. We have all heard of individuals who had the "lifelong dream" of becoming physicians or lawyers, yet were denied that dream. However, the realization that some people are disappointed or inconvenienced does not diminish our conviction that we must regulate occupations or activities that are potentially dangerous to others. Innocent people must be protected even if it means that others cannot pursue activities they deem highly desirable.

Furthermore, we maintain licensing procedures even though our competency tests are sometimes inaccurate. Some people competent to perform the licensed activity (for example, driving a car) will be unable to demonstrate competence (they freeze up on the driver's test). Others may be incompetent, yet pass the test (they are lucky or certain aspects of competence—for example, the sense of responsibility—are not tested). We recognize clearly—or should recognize clearly—that no test will pick out all and only competent drivers, physicians, lawyers, and so on. Mistakes are inevitable. This does not mean we should forget that innocent people may be harmed by faulty regulatory procedures. In fact, if the procedures are sufficiently faulty, we should cease regulating that activity entirely until more reliable tests are available. I only want to emphasize here that tests need not be perfect. Where moderately reliable tests are available, licensing procedures should be used to protect innocent people from incompetents.

These general criteria for regulatory licensing can certainly be applied to parents. First, parenting is an activity potentially very harmful to children. The potential for harm is apparent: each year more than half a million children are physically abused or neglected by their parents.[1] Many millions more are psychologically abused or neglected—not given love, respect, or a sense of self-worth. The results of this maltreatment are obvious. Abused children bear the physical and psychological scars of maltreatment throughout their lives. Far too often they turn to crime.[2] They are far more likely than others to abuse their own children.[3] Even if these maltreated children never harm anyone, they will probably never be well-adjusted, happy adults. Therefore, parenting clearly satisfies the first criterion of activities subject to regulation.

The second criterion is also incontestably satisfied. A parent must be competent if he is to avoid harming his children; even greater competence is required if he is to do the "job" well. But not everyone has this minimal competence. Many people lack the knowledge needed to rear children adequately. Many others lack the requisite energy, temperament, or stability. Therefore, child-rearing manifestly satisfies both criteria of activities subject to regulation. In fact, I daresay that parenting is a paradigm of such activities since the potential for harm is so great (both in the extent of harm any one person can suffer and in the number of people potentially harmed) and the need for competence is so evident. Consequently, there is good reason to believe that all parents should be licensed. The only ways to avoid this conclusion are to deny the need for licensing any potentially harmful activity; to deny that I have identified the standard criteria of activities which should be regulated; to deny that parenting satisfies the standard criteria; to show that even though parenting satisfies the standard criteria there are special reasons why licensing parents is not theoretically desirable; or to show that there is no reliable and just procedure for implementing this program.

While developing my argument for licensing I have already identified the standard criteria for activities that should be regulated, and I have shown that they can properly be applied to parenting. One could deny the legitimacy of regulation by licensing, but in doing so one would condemn not only the regulation of parenting but also the regulation of drivers, physicians, druggists, and doctors. Furthermore, regulation of hazardous activities appears to be a fundamental task of any stable society.

Thus only two objections remain. In the next section I shall see if there are any special reasons why licensing parents is not theoretically desirable. Then, in the following section, I shall examine several practical objections designed to demonstrate that even if licensing were theoretically desirable, it could not be justly implemented.

Theoretical Objections to Licensing

Licensing is unacceptable, someone might say, since people have a right to have children, just as they have rights to free speech and free religious expression. They do not need a license to speak freely or to worship as they wish. Why? Because they have a right to engage in these activities. Similarly, since people have a right to have children, any attempt to license parents would be unjust.

This is an important objection since many people find it plausible, if not self-evident. However, it is not as convincing as it appears. The specific rights appealed to in this analogy are not without limitations. Both slander and human sacrifice are prohibited by law; both could result from the unrestricted exercise of freedom of speech and freedom of religion. Thus, even if people have these rights, they may sometimes be limited in order to protect innocent people. Consequently, even if people had a right to have children, that right might also be limited in order to protect innocent people, in this case children. Secondly, the phrase "right to have children" is ambiguous; hence, it is important to isolate its most plausible meaning in this context. Two possible interpretations are not credible and can be dismissed summarily. It is implausible to claim either that infertile people have rights to be *given* children or that people have rights to intentionally create children biologically without incurring any subsequent responsibility to them.

A third interpretation, however, is more plausible, particularly when coupled with observations about the degree of intrusion into one's life that the licensing scheme represents. On this interpretation, people have a right to rear children if they make good-faith efforts to rear procreated children the best way they see fit. One might defend this claim on the ground that licensing would require too much intrusion into the lives of sincere applicants.

Undoubtedly one should be wary of unnecessary governmental intervention into individuals' lives. In this case, though, the intrusion would not often be substantial, and when it is, it would be warranted. Those granted licenses would face merely minor intervention; only those denied licenses would encounter marked intrusion. This encroachment, however, is a necessary side effect of licensing parents—just as it is for automobile and vocational licensing. In addition, as I shall argue in more detail later, the degree of intrusion arising from a general licensing program would be no more than, and probably less than, the present (and presumably justifiable) encroachment into the lives of people who apply to adopt children. Furthermore, since some people hold unacceptable views about what is best for children (they think children should be abused regularly), people do not automatically have rights to rear children just because they will rear them in a way they deem appropriate.

Consequently, we come to a somewhat weaker interpretation of this right claim: a person has a right to rear children if he meets certain minimal standards of child-rearing. Parents must not abuse or neglect their children and must also provide for the basic needs of the children. This claim of right is certainly more credible than the previously canvassed alternatives, though some people might still reject this claim in situations where exercise of the right would lead to negative consequences; for example, to overpopulation. More to the point, though, this conditional right is compatible with licensing. On this interpretation one has a right to have children only if one is not going to abuse or neglect them. Of course, the very purpose of licensing is just to determine whether people *are* going to abuse or neglect their children. If the determination is made that someone will maltreat children, then that person is subject to the limitations of the right to have children and can legitimately be denied a parenting license.

In fact, this conditional way of formulating the right to have children provides a model for formulating all alleged rights to engage in hazardous activities. Consider, for example, the right to drive a car. People do not have an unconditional right to drive, although they do have a right to drive if they are competent. Similarly, people do not have an unconditional right to practice medicine; they have a right only if they are demonstrably competent. Hence, denying a driver's or physician's license to someone who has not demonstrated the requisite competence does not deny that person's rights. Likewise, on this model, denying a parenting license to someone who is not competent does not violate that person's rights.

Of course, someone might object that the right is conditional on actually being a person who will abuse or neglect children, whereas my proposal only picks out those we can reasonably predict will abuse children. Hence, this conditional right would be incompatible with licensing.

There are two ways to interpret this objection, and it is important to distinguish these divergent formulations. First, the objection could be a way of questioning our ability to predict reasonably and accurately whether people would maltreat their own children. This is an important practical objection, but I will defer discussion of it until the next section. Second, this objection could be a way of expressing doubt about the moral propriety of the prior restraint licensing requires. A parental licensing program would deny licenses to applicants judged to be incompetent even though they had never maltreated any children. This practice would be in tension with our normal skepticism about the propriety of prior restraint.

Despite this healthy skepticism, we do sometimes use prior restraint. In extreme circumstances we may hospitalize or imprison people judged insane, even though they are not legally guilty of any crime, simply because we predict they are likely to harm others. More typically, though, prior restraint is used only if the restriction is not terribly onerous and the restricted activity is one which could lead easily to serious harm. Most types of licensing (for example, those for doctors, drivers, and druggists) fall into this latter category. They require prior restraint to prevent serious harm, and generally the restraint is minor—though it is important to remember that some individuals will find it oppressive. The same is true of parental licensing. The purpose of licensing is to prevent serious harm to children. Moreover, the prior restraint required by licensing would not be terribly onerous for many people. Certainly the restraint would be far less extensive than the presumably justifiable prior restraint of, say, insane criminals. Criminals preventively detained and mentally ill people forcibly hospitalized are denied most basic liberties, while those denied parental licenses would be denied only that one specific opportunity. They could still vote, work for political candidates, speak on controversial topics, and so on. Doubtless some individuals would find the restraint onerous. But when compared to other types of restraint currently practiced, and when judged in light of the severity of harm maltreated children suffer, the restraint appears *relatively* minor.

Furthermore, we could make certain, as we do with most licensing programs, that individuals denied licenses are given the opportunity to reapply easily and repeatedly for a license. Thus, many people correctly denied licenses (because they are incompetent) would choose (perhaps it would be provided) to take counseling or therapy to improve their chances of passing the next test. On the other hand, most of those mistakenly denied licenses would probably be able to demonstrate in a later test that they would be competent parents.

Consequently, even though one needs to be wary of prior restraint, if the potential for harm is great and the restraint is minor relative to the harm we are trying to prevent—as it would be with parental licensing—then such restraint is justified. This objection, like all the theoretical objections reviewed, has failed.

Practical Objections to Licensing

I shall now consider five practical objections to licensing. Each objection focuses on the problems or difficulties of implementing this proposal. According to these objections, licensing is (or may be) theoretically desirable; nevertheless, it cannot be efficiently and justly implemented.

The first objection is that there may not be, or we may not be able to discover, adequate criteria of "a good parent." We simply do not have the knowledge, and it is unlikely that we could ever obtain the knowledge, that would enable us to distinguish adequate from inadequate parents.

Clearly there is some force to this objection. It is highly improbable that we can formulate criteria that would distinguish precisely between good and less-than-good parents. There is too much we do not know about child development and adult psychology. My proposal, however, does not demand that we make these fine distinctions. It does not demand that we license only the best parents; rather it is designed to exclude only the very bad ones. This is not just a semantic difference, but a substantive one. Although we do not have infallible criteria for picking out good parents, we undoubtedly can identify bad ones—those who will abuse or neglect their children. Even though we could have a lively debate about the range of freedom a child should be given or the appropriateness of corporal punishment, we do not wonder if a parent who severely beats or neglects a child is adequate. We know that person isn't. Consequently, we do have reliable and usable criteria for determining who is a bad parent; we have the criteria necessary to make a licensing program work.

The second practical objection to licensing is that there is no reliable way to predict who will maltreat their children. Without an accurate predictive test, licensing would be not only unjust but also a waste of time. Now I recognize that as a philosopher (and not a psychologist, sociologist, or social worker), I am on shaky ground if I make sweeping claims about the present or future abilities of professionals to produce such predictive tests. Nevertheless, there are some relevant observations I can offer.

Initially, we need to be certain that the demands on predictive tests are not unreasonable. For example, it would be improper to require that tests be 100 percent accurate. Procedures for licensing drivers, physicians, lawyers, druggists, etc., plainly are not 100 percent (or anywhere near 100 percent) accurate. Presumably we recognize these deficiencies yet embrace the procedures anyway. Consequently, it would be imprudent to demand considerably more exacting standards for the tests used in licensing parents.

In addition, from what I can piece together, the practical possibilities for constructing a reliable predictive test are not all that gloomy. Since my proposal does not require that we make fine-line distinctions between good and less-than-good parents but rather that we weed out those who are potentially very bad, we can use existing tests that claim to isolate relevant predictive characteristics—whether a person is violence-prone, easily frustrated, or unduly self-centered. In fact, researchers at Nashville General Hospital have developed a brief interview questionnaire which seems to have significant predictive value. Based on their data, the researchers identified 20 percent of the interviewees as a "risk group"—those having great potential for serious problems. After one year they found "the incidence of major breakdown in parent–child interaction in the risk group was approximately four to five times as great as in the low risk group."[4] We also know that parents who maltreat children often have certain identifiable experiences; for example, most of them were themselves maltreated as children. Consequently, if we combined our information about these parents with certain psychological test results, we would probably be able to predict with reasonable accuracy which people will maltreat their children.

However, my point is not to argue about the precise reliability of present tests. I cannot say emphatically that we now have accurate predictive tests. Nevertheless, even if such tests are not available, we could undoubtedly develop them. For example, we could begin a longitudinal study in which all potential parents would be required to take a specified battery of tests. Then these parents could be "followed" to discover which ones abused or neglected their children. By correlating the test scores with information on maltreatment, a usable, accurate test could be fashioned. Therefore, I do not think that the present unavailability of such tests (if they are unavailable) would count against the legitimacy of licensing parents.

The third practical objection is that even if a reliable test for ascertaining who would be an acceptable parent were available, administrators would unintentionally misuse that test. These unintentional mistakes would clearly harm innocent individuals. Therefore, so the argument goes, this proposal ought to be scrapped. This objection can be dispensed with fairly easily unless one assumes there is some special reason to believe that more mistakes will be made in administering parenting licenses than in other regulatory activities. No matter how reliable our proceedings are, there will always be mistakes. We may license a physician who, through incompetence, would cause the death of a patient; or we may mistakenly deny a physician's license to someone who would be competent. But the fact that mistakes are made does not and should not lead us to abandon attempts to determine competence. The harm done in these cases could be far worse than the harm of mistakenly denying a person a parenting license. As far as I can tell, there is no reason to believe that more mistakes will be made here than elsewhere.

The fourth proposed practical objection claims that any testing procedure will be intentionally abused. People administering the process will disqualify people they dislike or people who espouse views they dislike from rearing children.

The response to this objection is parallel to the response to the previous objection, namely, that there is no reason to believe that the licensing of parents is more likely to be abused than driver's license tests or other regulatory procedures. In addition, individuals can be protected from prejudicial treatment by pursuing appeals available to them. Since the licensing test can be taken on numerous occasions, the likelihood of the applicant's working with different administrative personnel increases and therefore the likelihood decreases that intentional abuse could ultimately stop a qualified person from rearing children. Consequently, since the probability of such abuse is not more than, and may even be less than, the intentional abuse of judicial and other regulatory authority, this objection does not give us any reason to reject the licensing of parents.

The fifth objection is that we could never adequately, reasonably, and fairly enforce such a program. That is, even if we could establish a reasonable and fair way of determining which people would be inadequate parents, it would be difficult, if not impossible, to enforce the program. How would one deal with violators and what could we do with babies so conceived? There are difficult problems here, no doubt, but they are not insurmountable. We might not punish parents at all—we might just remove the children and put them up for adoption. However, even if we are presently uncertain about the precise way to establish a just and effective form of enforcement, I do not see why this should undermine my licensing proposal. If it is important enough to protect children from being maltreated by parents, then surely a reasonable enforcement procedure can be secured. At least we should assume one can be unless someone shows that it cannot.

An Analogy with Adoption

So far I have argued that parents should be licensed. Undoubtedly many readers find this claim extremely radical. It is revealing to notice, however, that this program is not as radical as it seems. Our moral and legal systems already recognize that not everyone is capable of rearing children well. In fact, well-entrenched laws require adoptive parents to be investigated—in much the same ways and for much the same reasons as in the general licensing program advocated here. For example, we do not allow just anyone to adopt a child; nor do we let someone adopt without first estimating the likelihood of the person's being a good parent. In fact, the adoptive process is far more rigorous than the general licensing procedures I envision. Prior to adoption the candidates must first formally apply to adopt a child. The applicants are then subjected to an exacting home study to determine whether they really want to have children and whether they are capable of caring for and rearing them adequately. No one is allowed to adopt a child until the administrators can reasonably predict that the person will be an adequate parent. The results of these procedures are impressive. Despite the trauma children often face before they are finally adopted, they are five times less likely to be abused than children reared by their biological parents.[5]

Nevertheless we recognize, or should recognize, that these demanding procedures exclude some people who would be adequate parents. The selection criteria may be inadequate; the testing procedures may be somewhat unreliable. We may make mistakes. Probably there is some intentional abuse of the system. Adoption procedures intrude directly in the applicants' lives. Yet we continue the present adoption policies because we think it better to mistakenly deny some people the opportunity to adopt than to let just anyone adopt.

Once these features of our adoption policies are clearly identified, it becomes quite apparent that there are striking parallels between the general licensing program I have advocated and our present adoption system. Both programs have the same aim—protecting children. Both have the same drawbacks and are subject to the same abuses. The only obvious dissimilarity is that the adoption requirements are *more* rigorous than those proposed for the general licensing program. Consequently, if we think it is so important to protect adopted children, even though people who want to adopt are less likely than biological parents to maltreat their children, then we should likewise afford the same protection to children reared by their biological parents.

I suspect, though, that many people will think the cases are not analogous. The cases are relevantly different, someone might retort, because biological parents have a natural affection for their children and the strength of this affection makes it unlikely that parents would maltreat their biologically produced children.

Even if it were generally true that parents have special natural affections for their biological offspring, that does not mean that all parents have enough affection to keep them from maltreating their children. This should be apparent given the number of children abused each year by their biological parents. Therefore, even if there is generally such a bond, that does not explain why we should not have licensing procedures to protect children of parents who do not have a sufficiently strong bond. Consequently, if we continue our practice of regulating the adoption of children, and certainly we should, we are rationally compelled to establish a licensing program for all parents.

However, I am not wedded to a strict form of licensing. It may well be that there are alternative ways of regulating parents which would achieve the desired results—the protection of children—without strictly prohibiting nonlicensed people from rearing children. For example, a system of tax incentives for licensed parents and protective-services scrutiny of nonlicensed parents might adequately protect children. If it would, I would endorse the less drastic measure. My principal concern is to protect children from maltreatment by parents. I begin by advocating the more strict form of licensing since that is the standard method of regulating hazardous activities.

I have argued that all parents should be licensed by the state. This licensing program is attractive not because state intrusion is inherently judicious and efficacious, but simply because it seems to be the best way to prevent children from being reared by incompetent parents. Nonetheless, even after considering the previous arguments, many people will find the proposal a useful academic exercise, probably silly, and possibly even morally perverse. But why? Why do most of us find this proposal unpalatable, particularly when the arguments supporting it are good and the objections to it are philosophically flimsy?

I suspect the answer is found in a long-held, deeply ingrained attitude toward children, repeatedly reaffirmed in recent court decisions, and present, at least to some degree, in almost all of us. The belief is that parents own, or at least have natural sovereignty over, their children. It does not matter precisely how this belief is described, since on both views parents legitimately exercise extensive and virtually unlimited control over their children. Others can properly interfere with or criticize parental decisions only in unusual and tightly prescribed circumstances—for example, when parents severely and repeatedly abuse their children. In all other cases, the parents reign supreme.

This belief is abhorrent and needs to be supplanted with a more child-centered view. Why? Briefly put, this attitude has adverse effects on children and on the adults these children will become. Parents who hold this view may well maltreat the children. If these parents happen to treat their children well, it is only because they want to, not because they think their children deserve or have a right to good treatment. Moreover, this belief is manifestly at odds with the conviction that parents should prepare children for life as adults. Children subject to parents who perceive children in this way are unlikely to be adequately prepared for adulthood. Hence, to prepare children for life as adults and to protect them from maltreatment, this attitude toward children must be dislodged. As I have argued, licensing is a viable way to protect children. Furthermore, it would increase the likelihood that more children will be adequately prepared for life as adults than is now the case.

Notes

1 The statistics on the incidence of child abuse vary. Probably the most recent detailed study (Saad Nagi, *Child Maltreatment in the United States* [Columbia University Press, 1977]) suggests that between 400,000 and 1 million children are abused or neglected each year. Other experts claim the incidence is considerably higher. [Little has changed over time, with more recent data estimating over 700,000 victims of child abuse in 2009 alone (http://childhelpinfocenter.org/index.php?option=com_content&task=view&id=38&Itemid=50; last accessed 10/17/2012)—Ed. note.]
2 According to the National Committee for the Prevention of Child Abuse, more than 80 percent of incarcerated criminals were, as children, abused by their parents ....
3 "A review of the literature points out that abusive parents were raised in the same style that they have recreated in the pattern of rearing children." ... R. J. Gelles, "Child Abuse as Psychopathology—A Sociological Critique and Reformulation," *American Journal of Orthopsychiatry* 43, no. 4 (1973): 618–19.
4 The research gathered by Altemeir was reported by Ray Helfer in "Review of the Concepts and a Sampling of the Research Relating to Screening for the Potential to Abuse and/or Neglect One's Child." Helfer's paper was presented at a workshop sponsored by the National Committee for the Prevention of Child Abuse, 3–6 December 1978.
5 .... According to a study by David Gil (*Violence against Children* [Cambridge, MA: Harvard University Press, 1970]) only 4 percent of abused children were abused by adoptive parents. Since at least 2 percent of the children in the United States are adopted (*Encyclopedia of Social Work*, National Association of Social Workers, New York, 1977), that means the rate of abuse by biological parents is five times that of adoptive parents.

Review and Discussion Questions

1 What provides the motivation behind LaFollette's proposal? Is his concern warranted?
2 Describe LaFollette's response to the claim that parents have a right to raise children.
3 Describe the practical objections LaFollette discusses, along with his response to each.
4 On balance, do you think LaFollette's arguments are sufficiently sound to overcome the objections he considers? Explain.

READING: CAN PARENTS AND CHILDREN BE FRIENDS?

JOSEPH KUPFER[*]

Joseph Kupfer believes that parents and children cannot be friends and argues that the ideal relationship between parents and children should be conceived in different terms. Joseph Kupfer is University Professor of Philosophy at Iowa State University.

---

* Abridged from "Can Parents and Children Be Friends?" by Joseph Kupfer, *American Philosophical Quarterly* 27(1) (January 1990). Copyright © 1990 by *American Philosophical Quarterly*. Reprinted by permission of North American Philosophical Publications.

It is often said by layman and philosopher alike that ideally children should grow up to be friends with their parents. Growing up and out of the one-sided dependency characteristic of the early phases of their relationship, adult children should become companions to their parents. There ought to be a mutual caring and counsel. This emphasis on friendship reflects the fact that young children become adults able to contribute to their parents' lives in ways comparable to what their parents have done for them. It also reflects the undesirability of the apparent alternatives to friendship: estrangement, continued child-dependence, or mere civility.

Part of the difficulty is that we don't have a word or clear concept to capture the ideal parent–adult child relationship, and "friendship" does indeed come closest to what it should be. How else to describe the affection, respect, and give and take into which the relationship should evolve? In what follows I argue that parents and their adult children cannot become the "true" or "complete" friends they might be with peers. Contrary to an increasingly popular view, it is a mistake to turn to friendship as an ideal by which parents and children should orient or govern their relationships (or philosophers should theorize about them).[1] Fundamental features of the ideal parent–adult child relationship keep it from developing into full-blown friendship. While peers may fail to become ideal friends, it isn't for the same reasons that parents and their grown children can't. The obstacles between parents and children are built into the structure of the relationship.

On the other hand, parents and adult children can enjoy a relationship rich in qualities that are lacking in the best of friendships. As we shall see, the structural features which prevent complete friendship are also responsible for these goods unique to parents and their adult children. The ideal parent–adult child relationship and complete friendship complement one another because each possesses values and virtues which the other lacks. For the most part, I shall be neglecting the large areas of overlap, areas in which parents and adult children can enjoy a kind of friendship that is quite worthwhile in its own right. I will be purposely pressing the features which differentiate these two important relationships.

Obviously, the following discussion assumes certain parameters to the family structure; however, these wouldn't seem to make the remarks "historical" in a narrow sense. For certain historical periods such as Victorian England, a discussion such as this one would be unnecessary since the very idea of parents and adult children being friends would be laughable. It is precisely in a society such as ours where children have considerable freedom and rights, not to mention power, and where parents too often strive to be youthful, that the idea of their being friends can take hold. In showing that parents and adult children can't be ideal friends even in middle-class America, I do make assumptions which need not hold for all societies.

For one thing, I assume that the parents[2] are primarily responsible for rearing their children. In a society where child-rearing responsibility is diffused throughout the community, as in a Kibbutz, parents and adult children might be able to establish a genuine friendship. In the idealization of the parent–adult child relationship presented here, I also assume that the parents do an excellent job of rearing their children. The thrust of this is that to the extent that parents are ideal parents they cannot enter into an ideal friendship with their grown children. Since my claim is not a logical one it is of course *possible* for parents and adult children to form a complete friendship, just as it is possible to change one's voice pattern or handwriting. However, I hope that the analysis offered here of both the parent–child[3] relationship and ideal friendship relegates that possibility to the merely logical.

I

Parents and adult children cannot become true friends for two reasons. Their relationship lacks the equality friendship requires, and they are not sufficiently independent or separate from one another.[4] Both the inequality and lack of independence from one another result from the distinctive history of the relationship ....

.... The inequality which prevents their friendship is inequality in autonomy. By autonomy I mean the ability to be self-determining: to choose for oneself on the basis of one's own values and beliefs. The autonomous person takes into account the opinions and advice of others, but reaches conclusions and decisions based on critical reflection of the matters at hand. Adult children are not necessarily less autonomous than their parents *per se*, or in general. Rather, they are less autonomous than their parents in the relationship. Although a grown child may generally be more autonomous than her parents, in interaction with them she cannot be. Adult children can't quite "be themselves," at least not all of the selves they've become apart from their parents. Adult children's thoughts and actions are not as free as their parents' *in the context of their relationship*. Moreover, adult children cannot affect their parents in as fundamental ways as parents influenced them when young. This claim about unequal autonomy is what I shall now try to develop and defend. First, let me briefly suggest why equal autonomy is characteristic of true friendship.

Ideal friendship requires equal autonomy in the relationship for several reasons. Without it, there will be unequal influence and power. One friend will be making more of the decisions or having more impact on the decisions at which they mutually arrive. The less autonomous friend will offer less of the resistance and counterpoise upon which the best friendships stay balanced. As a consequence, the friendship of unequal autonomy will tend toward inequality in dependency, with one friend needing or relying disproportionately on the other. The more autonomous party to the relationship will receive less from the friendship, at least in terms of advice, criticism, and alternative perspective. These are important goods inherent to friendship, and their unequal enjoyment is a detriment to complete friendship.

In addition, the lack of equality in autonomy is likely to constrain the mutual and full self-disclosure at work in ideal friendships. The less autonomous friend may be inhibited from revealing too much, lest he become too dependent on the other. The more autonomous friend may be reluctant to confide deeply out of lack of respect for the other friend's judgment or doubts about her willingness to respond with independent conviction. For these and related reasons, equality in autonomy seems ingredient to the best of friendships.

To see why grown children can't be as autonomous as their parents within the relationship ... we should make much of the obvious—the parent helps *shape* who and what the young child is. Where the parent developed into an adult independently of the child, the young child grows up under the parent's influence and care. The physical, psychological, and social dependence of the child translates into an ontological inequality; the parent simply is more responsible for the being or identity of the young child than the other way around. Bringing the child into the world, raising her, taking part in her successes and failures, the parent contributes to the young child's identity in ways which she cannot reciprocate. While the parent may be changed dramatically *as a result* of rearing a child, the parent is not shaped *by* the child. The parent authors change in the young child, exerting control, both intentional and unwitting, over her development ....

The inequality in autonomy between parent and young child has an epistemological dimension as well as an ontological one. The parent witnesses the young child's coming-to-be. Consequently, he possesses intimate knowledge of the young child's development, including knowledge of the child before she knows herself. This gives the parent special access to the young child's personal identity which the child does not and can never enjoy with respect to the parent. The parent is, literally, an "authority" on the child, at least her childhood. When the young child is old enough to realize it, she knows that this person enjoys a unique knowledge of her ....

II

But why must this history of unequal autonomy in the relationship prevent equality later on, when child is grown up? It is because this history endures in the identities of the parent and adult child in at least two ways: in their self-concepts, and in their habits and attitudes toward each other. ... Our degree of autonomy in general depends upon our self-concept. For example, people who see themselves as able to carry out choices effectively or who have strong body images, tend to exercise greater control over their lives than those who do not. Because it includes the history of the unequal relationship with the parent, the adult child's self-concept limits the degree to which she can function autonomously with the parent.

It might be objected here that such a self-concept reflects an immature adult child suffering from a pathological dependency on the parent. ... The role I ascribe to the history of the unequal exercise of autonomy, however, is not confined to adult children who can't grow up. The self-concept of the healthy, mature adult child has a place for the parent as one who has helped make her autonomous. As such, the parent should (in the best of cases) be seen as a moral authority: teaching right and wrong; exemplifying virtues; displaying moral judgment in helping the young child through quandaries and conflicts. ... We should bear in mind that the specifics of the history of unequal autonomy need not be remembered in order to influence the child's self-concept, and so its impact cannot be reduced simply to memory of dependency.[5]

The history of the unequal autonomy affects the adult child in another way, besides informing her self-concept. It also fosters enduring habits and attitudes toward the parents which persist into the child's adulthood. Some of these enter into her self-concept, but not all. These habits and attitudes help constitute who we are. Such attitudes as respect and loyalty, as well as habits of deference and accommodation engendered in youth persist into adulthood ....

.... Of course, it may be *possible* to break the habits, dismantle our attitudes toward our parents, even rearrange our self-concept. But not without rebuilding our very selves. The self-concept, together with these habits and attitudes, critically defines who we are.

What has been said about the impact of unequal autonomy on the self-concept, habits, and attitudes of grown children reciprocally holds for parents as well. The parent's sense of self is informed in a complementary way by the history of unequal autonomy. The parent sees himself as provider and protector, teacher and guardian of the young child. Most people include the role of "parent" (but not child) in their self-concept. For it is, after all, something of an occupation: an arduous, rewarding job that becomes part of our self-understanding. A large component of this self-concept hinges on the ontological and epistemological discrepancy discussed above ....

How does the inequality in autonomy between parents and their adult children manifest itself in less than complete friendship? A few examples of behavior that is appropriate in a peer friendship but not for a parent in relation to his grown child should vivify the position being advanced. Consider a parent complaining to his grown child about the other parent; telling sexual stories or jokes; or, an unmarried parent going with the adult child to socialize with others in sexually oriented ways. While usually acceptable in a peer friendship, these sorts of behavior seem somehow out of place in the parent–adult child relationship. But why?

The answer has to do with the authority enjoyed by the parent. As the "author of his being," the young child's parent possesses an authority over her which does not just disappear once the child is grown up. The parent is ideally a moral authority *for* the young child: one to whom the child looks for insight and advice. And this, too, is likely to carry over into the child's adulthood ....

III

Let us now take up the second obstacle to complete friendship between parents and grown children: their lack of independence from one another.[6] ...

The young child grows up by means of the parent's help, in the shade of parental direction and protection. From earliest memory, the parent was "there." Much of the way the young child comes to understand herself and world is through her parent's eyes. They shape and color what the young child takes to be important or trivial, noble or banal. Moreover, this influence doesn't just disappear when the child reaches adulthood. Parental tastes and values, opinions and principles, inform the grown child's outlook.

On the other hand, a sizable portion of the parent's adult life is spent raising his young child. The energy and attention bestowed upon their young children, as much as physical resemblance, encourages parents to see their children as temporal extensions of themselves. As noted earlier, parents identify themselves *as* parents, like an occupation or religion. Seeing ourselves in our children, love of them is to some extent self-love (so argues Aristotle). Even though the parent is formed independently of the child, much of his identity is nonetheless tied to the adult child's.

Part of the delight in a complete friendship turns upon the way two people discover and grow into each other's lives, but parents and adult children cannot develop in quite this fresh way because their lives have been entwined since the child's beginning. Neither one can really "discover" an independently existing other. They are virtually too close to have the independence needed for friendship. Here it is not a matter of the independence of autonomy, of self-determination. Rather, it is the independence of identity. The union which characterizes true friendship presupposes separateness. Only the truly separate are capable of overcoming their separateness while yet remaining "other." The parent–adult child union precludes the degree of separateness needed.

.... In the ideal relationship, the parent gradually lets go and the adult child finally fends for herself. However, although they may discover particular things about one another as they go their separate ways, neither brings the wholly separate baggage *to* the relationship the way friends do. As a result, they don't discover each other as beings with independent histories and different values to be learned. As a result, parents and adult children don't encounter one another as sufficiently *different*.

The intimacy we ought to enjoy with our parents keeps us too close. Not in a sick loss of identity or independence, but in the enmeshing of lived life: meals taken, plans hatched, disappointments suffered. Ours is a common history peopled with crises, stories, and other family members—all along, right from the child's beginning. Intimacy and love, sharing and caring, aren't won or earned between parents and children. They evolve. But they are earned with friends. Establishing and maintaining friendships are achievements at which we must work. We prove ourselves before and to prospective friends. We woo them ....

IV

If the ideal parent–adult child relationship is less than a full-blown friendship so does it also contain valuable qualities which are missing from friendship. The very conditions which stand in the way of complete friendship (lack of independence from one another and inequality in autonomy) also enable the parent–adult child relationship to be uniquely fulfilling. These rewards, therefore, complement those inherent in true friendship. Let's begin with what we were just discussing: the lack of separateness between parents and children. Viewed positively, this can be construed as "identification."

By "identification" I mean feeling and thinking of another as part of one's self. Who we are is partly defined not just by our relationship to this person, but by the person's life itself. The other's well-being and suffering is experienced as constitutive of our well-being and suffering ....

The parent–adult child relationship involves mutual identification. However, parents seem to identify more with their children, probably because of the asymmetrical influence they enjoy in shaping their children's natures. In what follows, therefore, the emphasis will be on the effect on both parent and adult child of the *parent's* identification with the child. To the extent that the adult child does identify with the parent, the pattern developed here would then naturally apply in that direction as well.

How does this identification enrich their relationship in a way that eludes friendship? Because of mutual identification, parents and adult children experience a "doubling" of the adult child's fortune. Parents rejoice doubly in their grown children's success or good luck. They are glad for the adult child but also for themselves, as if their own good. Parents bask in a kind of reflected success the way a coach partakes of her athlete's victory or an editor his writer's triumph. Even some of the parents' self-esteem may be bound up in their grown children's accomplishments or the lack of them. It makes sense to speak of parents taking pride in their children in a way that it doesn't for friends. Of course, friends are glad for one another and receive pleasure, but they don't seem to take pride *in* one another's achievements.[7]

At the same time, the adult child delights in bringing her parents joy through her accomplishments. Parental satisfaction doubles her own. The fact that parents' successes don't typically have this impact on their children reflects the asymmetry in the extent of their respective identifications. Because *our* accomplishments don't afford our friends such great delight, moreover, we can't relish them in this double way through friendship.[8]

The identification between parents and their grown children is also the basis for a negative doubling. Although not itself desirable, it attests to the deep identification responsible for the multiplication of joy noted above. When adult children suffer failure or bad fortune, their parents anguish doubly. They are sorry for their adult children but also suffer on their behalf the way friends don't. Parents take on their grown children's loss or disappointment.

Congruently, an adult child's unhappiness over her own misfortune extends beyond herself to the sadness it brings her parents. Of course friends grieve with us, as Aristotle says, but parents don't just grieve with us; they also grieve for us. Maybe that is the difference. Friends are with us, consoling and restoring our confidence or hope. But while parents also offer support, they need consoling themselves (which *their* friends, in turn, provide) ....

I think that the difference between parents and friends with regard to this "doubling" effect of identification is underscored by the example of grandchildren. Grandchildren obviously bring joy directly to the grandparents. But grandparents also delight in their adult children's own enjoyment of these grandchildren. Grown children, in turn, take pleasure in "presenting" their parents with grandchildren, and savor their parents' enjoyment of their offspring. This just doesn't seem a plausible part of the structure of friendship. Friends certainly can enjoy one another's children and become very close to them. But they don't have the kind of vested interest in their welfare that grandparents do. We neither delight in our friends' children the way the children's grandparents do nor do we take such great pleasure in our friends' own enjoyment of their children ....

The parent–adult child relationship is also uniquely enriched by its characteristic types of love and their attendant qualities. The love between parents and their adult children is not necessarily better than that between friends, just importantly different from it. Perhaps because of the sense of their grown children as an extension of themselves, parents (ideally) feel an "unconditional" love for their children: a love that is untouched by accomplishments or failure, kindness or callousness. A love with no strings, which embraces the child's sheer existence even as an adult. Of course parents want their children to do well and usually feel pride or admiration when they do terrific things. But these sentiments are over and above the sort of love I am talking about.[9]

One way this unconditional love is exhibited is through parents' solicitousness of their children. Parents communicate a readiness to help their adult children and, within limits, find satisfaction in being a continuing source of wisdom and support. Because they feel the parents' love as unconditional, children may be able to request and accept help from parents that they can't from friends. Granted that we ask favors from friends we won't of our parents, surely we also feel more comfortable turning to our parents for certain *sorts* of help. Most plausible is the help that seems to be an extension of their role as nurturer and provider, such as nursing the adult child through an illness or lending her a substantial amount of money.

The adult child's love for her parents is, in the ideal, not quite this unconditional sort. The adult child's love is built on that primitive intimacy and attachment of which we earlier spoke. This affectionate attachment is the basis for the more consciously motivated love that the young child comes to feel. Loving our parents involves loving a protecting, nurturing, unconditionally *loving* authority. Even though the adult child should need less parental protection and nurturance, these qualities continue to define the object of her love. It is a love for an unequal, for one who took care of us and did so gladly. We love those who make us secure, and to the extent that our parents love us unconditionally as adults, we are also secure in that love.

An adult child's love for her parents is grounded in a particular kind of gratitude. Doubtless, the love and care we receive from our parents engenders a gratitude which is at first unreflective, one which grows up with us. A more reflective gratitude involves recognition of all the good things our parents have done for us, including the nurturance and love just mentioned. I think that this gratitude develops most fully out of reflection on our self-love. Just as the parent's love for the child extends his self-love, so is the child's gratitude-filled love for the parent a *product* of her self-love. Because we love ourselves, we love our parents for helping us be worth loving. We give credit to our parent for our good character, our loving nature, our ability to function autonomously. In appreciating ourselves we ideally come to appreciate our parents' contribution to who and what we are. This appreciation takes the form of gratitude-love.

.... There may be more to an adult child's love for her parents, for instance, she may love them for such virtues as patience or wit. But it is the gratitude for helping shape our identities that I am calling attention to here because that is what distinguishes love for parents most sharply from friendship love ....

Gratitude-love can also be more directly expressed toward our parents. Because they are so responsible for who we are, it is fitting for us to take care of them. While we may also take care of friends, even out of gratitude, it is not structurally part of the relationship. It is contingently connected to the friendship in a way that taking care of our parents is not. Taking care of our parents returns us to our origins by mirroring their nurturance of us. In this return to our origins we return to our parents as only *we* can: returning their unconditional love with our gratitude-love.

There is one more way in which the love between parents and grown children enhances the relationship in a unique way. Our parents' unconditional love for us is irreplaceable. No one else, even the best of friends, can love us the way our parents do. And even though particular friends cannot be replaced, the love of which friends are capable can be had again, with new friends. When our parents die they take their special love with them and in our more reflective moments we anticipate losing it. Both the anticipation and the actual experience of losing our parents' irreplaceable love imbues the relationship with a poignancy which presses upon us the magnitude of this love's value. Appreciating the full value of our parents' love deepens our overall capacity to feel and appreciate. It increases our depth as people, and this is worth having.

The parent–adult child relationship has a solidity and stability which derives from the permanence of one's status as parent and child. We outgrow childhood, but not being someone's child. ... Friendship is different. We can acquire and lose friends; the status of friend is not permanent for the lives of the parties ....

The stability and strength which come from the permanence of status is buttressed by the lack of choice concerning that status. Children obviously choose neither their parents nor to be anyone's child. Although parents (ideally) choose to have children, they don't choose to have just these children (even when exercising autonomy in the strong sense of shaping the child's nature). Parents choose to create the relationship, but have only limited choice and control over who is party to it. This clearly contrasts with friendship, in which parents and adult children exercise considerable choice and control ....

The permanence of status, supplemented by lack of choice, adds security for both parties. We are vouched safe against the changes that can beset even the best of friendships, changes that partly hinge on the fact that friendship is so keenly owing to choice. For that reason alone friendships are more vulnerable. For example, parents and adult children as well as friends may have to make a great effort to keep their respective relationships strong during extended periods of separation. However, the permanence or irrevocability of the parent–adult child status provides an impetus for "keeping up." It is harder to let the relationship unravel knowing that this is still your parent, this is still your child.

The security found in the parent–adult child relationship is strengthened by the kinds of love which characterize it. Knowing that there is someone who loves them unconditionally can afford adult children comfort against the turbulence of the loves which define some other relationships. The quiet, steadfast love of our parents provides an appropriate ballast against passionate currents of romantic love, for example. For parents, their adult children's gratitude-love provides a similar surety against the vicissitudes of aging and the loss of peer friendships.

The historical core of the parent–child relationship is, finally, expressed aesthetically. This aesthetic expression enhances the relationship in a unique way. I have in mind two types of aesthetic closure which can characterize a parent–adult child relationship as no other. The first might be considered "cyclical," and the second, the closure of nexus.

As they age, parents usually come to depend more and more on their adult children for a variety of assistance. While friends also depend on each other, the reversal or exchange of roles in the parent–child relationship adds a basic aesthetic dimension to this dependence. To nurse or bathe or feed in his old age the person who did this for us in our infancy cuts to the heart of our identity. To play the parent to our parents is to complete a human cycle. From the adult child's standpoint, she is incorporating in herself her own childhood by taking care of the person who nurtured her. When this involves helping our parents round out their lives and die, the cycle is truly completed by reversing the way they helped us begin life.

From the parent's standpoint, the adult child represents a regeneration or recreation of the parent qua parent. The parent can *witness* this simply in his adult child's relationship with grandchildren. However, when his adult child cares for him, the parent directly experiences some of the very virtues he helped cultivate. In a sense, the parent returns to care for himself, externalized and embodied in his adult child. In Aristotelian terms, the craftsman's product is plying the craft on the craftsman himself.

The closure of nexus occurs when a grown child has children of her own. She is then poised between her parents and children. For a time, the grown child is simultaneously child and parent, embodying both. This bringing together of both roles, with the concomitant interactions and emotions discussed above, carries with it a closure different from the cyclical sort. This is the closure of embodying two poles simultaneously, being the locus of an intersection. When this happens, we mediate the relationship between our parents and children. The relation of each to the other is conditioned by us. This yields the closure of participating in and maintaining a continuity. We experience ourselves as the link between our children and parents, as the participating nexus, making their relationship possible.

* * *

The ideal parent–adult child relationship contains valuable qualities which are missing from even the best of friendships. The identification, love, stability, and aesthetic closure enrich the parent–adult child relationship in unique ways. We ought not, therefore, lament the fact that friendship doesn't quite capture what the parent–adult child relationship should aspire to. For even as it is in some respects less than complete friendship, so does it also offer what friendship cannot.

Notes

1 See, for example, Jane English's "What Do Grown Children Owe Their Parents?," in [this volume].
2 By "parents" I mean those who are responsible for rearing the child, including guardians and adoptive parents. However, I shall be taking those who are, in addition, the biological parents as the paradigm because genetic similarity makes a slightly stronger case for some of my claims.
3 I will explicitly refer to "adult" (or "grown") child and "young" child where age is relevant. Where the relationship or status is what matters "child" *simpliciter* will be used.
4 There may, of course, be other obstacles to parent–adult child friendship, such as gender-linked roles, sexism, or agism. But these make no difference to my thesis. My claim is meant to hold in the best of circumstances, in which sexism, for instance, plays no part in the family dynamic.

   Similarly, there are many other significant features of both complete friendship and the ideal parent–adult child relationship which has been put to one side for the purposes of this discussion.
5 This point about the formation of self-concept not being reducible to memory is true in general. Consider for example how cultural forces shape our self-concept. In some cultures a person's sense of self is fundamentally determined by kin or clan membership. In contrast, individualistic societies define the self more by personal accomplishment. In neither case must the individual *remember* the forces of identity-formation for them to condition her self-concept.
6 Similar relations may hold between siblings, other relatives, or childhood friends who continue to see each other as adults. I suspect that, as with parents and children, loving siblings can't quite be friends (but will also experience values missing from friendship). This is an interesting but distinct area of inquiry.
7 The way parents boast about their children (whether young or adult) is evidence of this prideful identification. Parental boasting appears to be about the children and not the parents themselves. However, when parents violate the conventional limits on how much bragging is acceptable, their immodesty is exposed. They are seen as praising themselves in their children.
8 The relationship between parents and their grown children may possess another value based on the resemblance which contributes to their mutual identification. The resemblance affords a unique context for self-knowledge and self-improvement. Because they can see so much of themselves in each other, parents and adult children to some extent hold a mirror up to one another. We are able to discover both virtues and flaws, potentials and deficiencies by interacting with our parents and children. Such discovery may

provide a unique impetus for self-improvement. Seeing our strengths and weaknesses externalized in another gives a concreteness to our self-reflection as well as the resolution to change. In the best of cases, then, we don't merely see ourselves in our parents, but we take the discovery of resemblance as a propadeutic to self-improvement.

9 The sort of unconditional love I ascribe to parents is similar to, but different from agape or "neighbor" love. It is similar to it in that both are independent of the person's characteristics or accomplishments and neither depends on what the person does for the one who loves. Both kinds of love, therefore, "accept" the individual for who he or she is. They differ in that parental love, as indicated, is based on the particular relationship; agape abstracts from any such relationship. Much more could and should be said on this than is appropriate here.

Review and Discussion Questions

1 What are the primary differences between friendship and parent–child relationships, according to Kupfer?
2 Kupfer believes that friendship and parent–child relationships are different kinds of relationships, yet there is no judgment that one is better than another. Do you agree with this analysis? Why or why not?
3 Are there any ideas in this essay that you hadn't considered before? How do you evaluate Kupfer's discussion of them?

READING: PARENTS AND CHILDREN AS FRIENDS

KRISTJÁN KRISTJÁNSSON[*]

Kristján Kristjánsson also asks, "Can parents and their children be friends?" He rejects Kupfer's arguments and concludes that there is no reason to believe that they can't. Kristjánsson is Chair of Character and Virtue Ethics within the School of Education, University of Birmingham, United Kingdom.

1 Introduction

Can parents and their children be friends? The prevailing philosophical view seems to be that they cannot, at least not in any salient and philosophically relevant sense of the term "friendship." Nevertheless, this view will seem counter-intuitive to many laypeople and at least some philosophers. The aim of the present article is to challenge this view; and in order to do so, we must first explore what philosophers tend to mean by "true" or "real" friendship.

Most contemporary philosophical discussions of friendship draw, either explicitly or implicitly, on Aristotle's exploration of friendship as a generically human relation of deep moral significance. In Aristotle's canonical account, all friendship rests on conscious, reciprocated goodwill between two persons. The different reasons and motivations mediating the goodwill, however, call for a distinction

---

[*] Abridged from "Parents and Children as Friends" by Kristján Kristjánsson, *Journal of Social Philosophy* 37(2) (Summer 2006): 250–265. Copyright © 2006 by Blackwell Publishing, Inc. Reprinted by permission of Copyright Clearance Center on behalf of the publisher.

among three kinds of friendship. Of those three, only one—*character friendship*—is true and "complete." The other two—*friendship for utility* and *friendship for pleasure*—constitute lean counterparts of character friendship and can, in fact, only be subsumed under the concept of friendship to the extent that they resemble the true, primary kind. In character friendships, friends love one another because of their respective virtuous characters and wish good for one another, each for the other's own sake. Such friendships last "as long as they are good; and virtue is enduring." In friendships based on utility, by contrast, we love others not for themselves, but only insofar as we can gain some good from them for ourselves; in friendships based on pleasure, we are fond of others not because of their moral characters, but simply because they appear pleasant (e.g., witty or affable) to us. These two inferior types of friendship are easily dissolved, because they are conditional upon coincidental, fleeting, and non-moral characteristics; take away those characteristics, the relevant benefits in question, and you remove the relation of friendship.[1]

In short, in true character friendship, A loves B and vice versa, (1) for B's own sake, (2) for what B really is, and (3) because B has a virtuous character with each of these conditions implying the other two.[2] Because moral virtue is an objective merit and, once gained, an enduring one at that, character friendships tend to be stable and lifelong, come rain or shine. Such friendships are, to be sure, instrumentally and extrinsically valuable in many ways, for they are both highly advantageous and immediately pleasant; but their true value cuts deeper than that, being non-instrumental and intrinsic. The ultimate pleasure derived from them is what Mill would call a higher-quality pleasure or, in Aristotle's terms, a pleasure that completes virtue, not "as some sort of ornament" but rather as "pleasure within itself."[3]

The moral worth of friendship lies in its being a virtue, or involving virtue. As a relationship of virtue, it is at once conducive to and constitutive of the ultimate human *telos* of *eudaimonia*, and is thus "most necessary for our life."[4] This last remark may hardly be considered an overstatement, given the space that Aristotle devotes to his discussion of friendship in the *Nicomachean Ethics*—much more than is devoted to any of the individual moral and intellectual virtues. In Aristotle's schema, the actualization of *eudaimonia* is partly dependent upon moral luck: lack of certain important goods makes it impossible for one to lead a happy life. Lack of friends is one of those goods and perhaps the most salient one, as "having friends seems to be the greatest external good."[5] Virtuous persons without such goods will never be wholly miserable, as long as they remain fully virtuous, but the absence of a life-enhancing relationship such as friendship will "oppress and spoil" their blessedness, and they will not "altogether have the character of happiness."[6]

Aristotle's distinction between "complete" friendship and the two other types, which are only "friendships by similarity,"[7] has commanded such wide-spread philosophical assent because it seems, for one thing, to resonate well with ordinary language. Although the term "friend" is sometimes used indiscriminately and with exaggeration, most people would—if pressed—be more than ready to accept that there are friends and there are friends. More precisely, a distinction between persons who are our "real" or true "friends" (*qua* "kindred spirits," "other selves") and those who are merely our acquaintances or companions (such as drinking buddies and squash partners) will be familiar enough to most people. There is a related distinction in ordinary parlance between "being a friend to" and "being a friend of": My neighbor, the electrician, was a real friend *to me* when the electricity went off in my flat; but although I hold him dear for that, he is not, therefore, necessarily a friend *of mine*.[8] We evidently have good reason to give Emerson's statement—in a discussion of friendship that is scarcely less famous and considerably more poetic than Aristotle's—a sympathetic nod: "I hate the prostitution of the name of friendship to signify modish and worldly alliances."[9]

I assume in what follows that Aristotle, Emerson, and ordinary language are right in that there exists a primary form of "real friendship" that must be distinguished from less complete alliances of advantage and mutual comfort. Moreover, I assume with Aristotle that this primary form is best described as that of "character friendship," possessing, at least broadly, the characteristics that he ascribes to it. Indeed, in subsequent sections, I use the word "friendship," unless otherwise stated, as a short form for "character friendship." ...

In the following section, I use a widely read article by Joseph Kupfer as the springboard of my discussion.[10] In this article, Kupfer argues that parents and their children are incapable of mutual full-blown friendships, even when the children have reached adulthood. ... Kupfer adduces various *structural* (psychological and social) arguments for the impossibility of parent–child friendships, and in Section II, I concentrate on rebutting those arguments with respect to parent–child relationships in general ....

II Structural Barriers to Friendship?

Kupfer's article offers a sustained and systematic attack on the idea that parents and their children can be friends. More precisely, Kupfer marshals a number of arguments that are meant to demonstrate that whereas parents and their children can enjoy relationships rich in qualities that are lacking in the best of friendships, they cannot become the "true" or "complete" friends that they might be with peers. He delineates various obstacles that, in his view, are built into the structure of the parent–child relationship and that prevent it from ever growing out of the one-sided dependency characteristic of the earliest phases of the relationship.[11] In what follows, let us refer to Kupfer's three prime structural arguments as (1) the unequal-autonomy argument, (2) the non-independence argument, and (3) the special-value argument.

According to Kupfer's (1) unequal-autonomy argument, friendship requires equal autonomy in the relationship. Otherwise, there will be unequal influence and power at work, leading to inequality in dependency, with one party relying disproportionately on the other. Furthermore, unequal autonomy is likely to constrain the mutual and full self-disclosure that characterizes true friendships. Because children are less autonomous than parents in the relationship in question, however (i.e., according to Kupfer's understanding of autonomy, less self-determining, less able to choose for themselves on the basis of their own values), such a relationship cannot constitute friendship ....

.... Kupfer can ... be criticized for proposing too restrictive a conception of friendship. If friendship is only possible between persons of equal autonomy (in Kupfer's sense), then various relationships that seem to constitute possible examples of friendship, such as the relationship between the guru/mentor and disciple/student, are excluded from the reckoning. Kupfer's considerations about the impossibility of the parent–child relationship ever growing fully out of the dependency relationship that characterizes its beginnings seem equally applicable to the guru–disciple relationship. However enlightened disciples eventually become, one would have to argue, they might never be able to interact with their old gurus on completely equal footing; yet it would be counter-intuitive to suppose that gurus and their disciples cannot be friends.

Simply to fault Kupfer on the grounds of contrary intuitions may be hasty. In order to do full justice to Kupfer's non-equality argument, we must look more closely at how he elaborates upon it. Of particular importance are two further expressions of the argument: one ontological and the other epistemological. The ontological expression (1a) relates to the nature of one's self-concept; the epistemological one (1b) to one's privileged knowledge of another person. Kupfer's point in (1a) is that our level of autonomy in general depends upon our self-concept. Inevitably, the child's self-concept includes different aspects of the child's history with the parents (*qua* receiver of care). Similarly, the parents' sense of self is informed by the history of unequal autonomy *vis-à-vis* the child (*qua* providers of care, guardians, and protectors). Hence, in its interactions with its parents, the child can never view itself fully as the author of its own being, which means that the condition for full autonomy in the relationship is never satisfactorily met.[12]

But is Kupfer's condition of full autonomy not too strict and demanding? It smacks of the Kantian notion of an autonomous self as necessarily formed and sustained independent of the selves of others and prior to all its contingent ends. ... Our lives as human beings are, by necessity, intertwined and shackled together with the heavy chains of social and psychological interdependence, but this does not bar us from gradually becoming autonomous agents—authors of our own lives. Thus, if my sense of myself requires me to seek recognition from others, and my social existence and social relations are essential rather than contingent parts of my personhood, it is unreasonable to insist that because someone else has helped shaped my identity, I cannot be fully autonomous with regard to that person. To paraphrase Robert Frost's famous lines in "The Star Splitter": If one by one we counted out potential friends for having played a role in shaping our self-concept, it would not take us long to get so we had no friends left to live with.

Kupfer's point in (1b) is that the parent witnesses the child's coming to be. This gives the parent intimate, privileged knowledge of the child's development and character, aspirations and humiliations. Thus, the parent has special access to the child's personal identity which the child does not and cannot enjoy with respect to the parent. This epistemic superiority, then, rules out friendship between the two.[13] Now, I have already challenged the general thesis that a relationship of superiority precludes friendship; the same considerations would apply here. More specifically, we may also question the empirical thesis that the parent is, in fact, typically such an expert on the child's character that the parent has a privileged status with regard to the child. I wonder if, in the complicated juggling act of modern-day child rearing, where the demands of spouse, work, friends, and hobbies vie with those of children for parents' attention, children are not typically more exclusive experts on their parents than vice versa. In the first years of life, the child's full-time job is growing up, and it has ample time to study its parents' characters (and character weaknesses). How often we see small children who have become deftly aware of their parents' little foibles and whims, and having learnt to play up to them, can use them to their advantage. Older children commonly use their privileged knowledge of their parents' characters to woo and manipulate them in a more systematic fashion. If this manipulation process works both ways, rather than merely one way as Kupfer suggests, then his contention that the one-sided privileged knowledge in question precludes the child's autonomy in the parent–child relationship does not go through. I conclude, then, that neither the general (philosophical) part nor the empirical part of Kupfer's unequal-autonomy argument sustains it.

Let us turn next to Kupfer's (2) non-independence argument. Part of the delight in friendship, he says, turns upon the way in which two people discover each other and gradually get to know each other as distinct individuals. However, the relationship between parents and their children cannot progress in this way because their lives have already been entwined since the child's beginning. Hence, they will never be able to encounter and discover each other as beings with independent histories: as true "others." The parents are too "naturally familiar" to the child, and vice versa, for them to become friends.[14]

Some of the things Aristotle has to say about the parent–child relationship may seem to reinforce Kupfer's insights: "For a parent is fond of his children because he regards them as part of himself; and children are fond of a parent because they regard themselves as coming from him." Furthermore, a parent "loves his children as [he loves] himself ... Children love a parent because they regard themselves as coming from him."[15] So on this understanding it is, indeed, the case that parents and children are not true "others." However, the impression that this reinforces Kupfer's argument about the radical difference between the parent–child relationship and friendship is illusory; it does anything but that. Aristotle's point is namely that in *all forms of philia*, be it the loving relationship between a parent and a child or the fondness between two friends, one party is related to the other "in the same way as he is related to himself, since a friend is another self."[16] The notion of the friend or the non-erotically beloved person as "another self" is precisely what gives the idea of *philia* its unity. It is not as if we first learn to love ourselves and then incorporate others under the same umbrella; rather the capacity to love ourselves and the capacity to love others (family members, friends) arise together and cannot be separated.[17]

We hardly need Aristotle to tell us all this. It is a common and familiar—if perhaps not an uncontroversial—claim in modern psychology that all forms of deep affection aim at self-extension; that is to say, they aim at satisfying the human need to overcome our separateness, to leave the prison of our aloneness. In his book on the art of loving, Erich Fromm went as far as to hold that "the desire for interpersonal fusion is the most powerful striving in man."[18] "I *am* Heathcliff," was Cathy's climactic revelation in *Wuthering Heights*. So far is it from being the case that this desire for the collapse of ego boundaries separates both erotic and non-erotic love from friendship, that precisely the opposite seems to hold: In deep friendship, we also seek union with another self in order to form a new whole, a new entirety—or, as Emerson puts it: "The essence of friendship is entireness."[19] If it is true, as Kupfer maintains, that the selves of parents and children are naturally entwined from the beginning, then this should, *ceteris paribus*, facilitate rather than hinder the forming of friendship between them.

Finally, Kupfer argues that we need not lament the fact that the relationship of friendship does not capture the essence of the parent–child relationship, for even if the latter kind of relationship fails to pass muster as friendship, it offers us something that friendship cannot. In other words, Kupfer's (3) special-value argument rests on the assumption that the parent–child relationship produces value that is radically different from that produced by friendship. This unique value allegedly rests on four essential characteristics of the parent–child relationships that it does not share with friendship: (3a) identification, (3b) unconditionality, (3c) permanence, and (3d) aesthetic worth. Let us look at each of these characteristics in turn.

By (3a) "identification," Kupfer means experiencing another person's well-being and suffering as constitutive of one's own well-being and suffering. For instance, parents take pride in their children's achievements as if they were their own achievements. By contrast, "friends are glad for one another and receive pleasure, but they do not seem to take pride *in* one another's achievements."[20] What Kupfer is saying here is basically the natural converse of his earlier point (2) about parent–child non-independence: Just as parents and children cannot, whereas friends can, separate their life histories, so friends cannot, whereas parents and children can, identify with each other's achievements and failures as if they were their own. If the considerations presented above in response to (2) were correct, then Kupfer's general point does not hold good here either: mutual identification is just as much a characteristic of deep friendships as it is of successful parent–child relationships. More specifically, I would question Kupfer's contention about the nature of extended pride. His idea of how people claim value for themselves by identifying with valued others seems much too restrictive. Consider the "*we* are number 1!" chant of ecstatic football fans around the world. The players on the field are not even the personal friends of the fans identifying with them, let alone their parents or children! In the case of our friends, taking pride in their achievements seems even more natural and appropriate—or as Emerson emphatically put it: "I must feel pride in my friend's accomplishments as if they were mine, and a property in his virtues."[21]

One's fondness for one's friends is conditional upon their retaining their identity: their moral character. Although "virtue is enduring," as Aristotle pointed out (see earlier), even the best can become morally corrupt. And does not the Latin proverb tell us that "corruption of the best becomes the worst"? In such cases, one's fondness may appropriately be revoked—the friendship cancelled. However, Kupfer observes, this does not apply to the parent–child relationship: (3b) "parents (ideally) feel an 'unconditional' love for their children: a love that is untouched by accomplishments or failures, kindness or callousness."[22] ... [E]ven if it is true that unconditionality ideally characterizes parent–child relationships but not friendships, this acknowledgment does not demonstrate that parents and children cannot be friends: The value of unconditionality could simply complement the friendship, just as the value of romantic love often complements friendship, by adding new layers of intimacy, without disintegrating the underlying friendship.[23] I return to this point at the end of the present section.

Kupfer's insistence on (3c), the permanency of the parent–child relationship, as opposed to the essential impermanency of friendship, is closely related to the value of unconditionality. Precisely because of the unconditionality of parent–child relationships, they retain their solidity and stability, no matter how functions and needs shift. "Friendship is different. We can acquire and lose friends."[24] If Kupfer is still talking here about true character friendships, this seems to be a frivolous way of describing their onset and closure. For Aristotle, by contrast, the dissolution of such friendships can never be taken light heartedly; whether or not we should cancel a friendship that has gone bad is an agonizing question. Aristotle's conclusion is that we should wait and see, and only give up the friendship when we are sure that the other person has become "incurably vicious." For if "someone can be set right, we should try harder to rescue his character than his property, in so far as character is better and more proper to friendship."[25] Aristotle's notion of the essential permanency of friendships, which can never be treated lightly, seems to be more intuitively plausible than Kupfer's conception. I would submit that in the view of most people, friendships are—to cite Emerson once again—"not glass threads or frostwork, but the solidest thing we know." And even if we may talk of choosing or ending friendships, friends are essentially "self-elected."[26]

The parent–child relationship has, finally, in Kupfer's view, (3d) aesthetic worth that cannot be attributed to mere friendship. What he has in mind here is the aesthetic dimension involved, first, in the "reversal or exchange of roles" when the child nurses the aged parent in the same way as the parent once nursed the helpless child, and, second, in the "closure of nexus" when grown children have children of their own.[27] In aesthetic terms, the craftsman's product finally plies the craft on the craftsman himself. But why can such an aesthetic dimension not be added to friendship as well? Think of the relationship between the guru and the disciple; does it not culminate ideally in the closure at work when the disciple starts paying back the emotional and intellectual debt incurred: when the disciple becomes the giver and the guru the receiver? Or think, more mundanely and typically, of two friends in a situation in which one has been the stronger party, constantly pulling the chestnuts out of the fire for the other, but where a change of fortunes brings about a reversal of roles. Is that not also an aesthetic closure, in Kupfer's sense? I agree with Emerson that friendship adds "rhyme and reason" to our whole life journey—that it aids and comforts us through "all the passages of life and death."[28] Surely that imparts friendship with what Kupfer characterizes as aesthetic worth.

All in all, it seems to me that Kupfer systematically overstates and overdraws the distinction between the values which characterize parent–child relationships and friendships, in order to provide focus for his own thesis that parents and children cannot be friends. Most of the specific values he discusses indicate, as I have argued, the commonalties of parent–child relationships and friendships rather than their dissimilarities. And even if it were correct that the former kind of relationship has some special value that is not reducible to the value of friendship and even incommensurable with it, we cannot conclude that parent–child relationships cannot also be friendships. More plausibly, such value would be surplus value, added on top of the value of friendship. As Klaasen has argued convincingly in the context of the relationship between friendship and romantic love, incommensurability does not imply incompatibility: "While we cannot square a circle, because squares and circles are incommensurable, we can inscribe a circle within a square, or a square within a circle."[29] Well-ordered, loving parent–child relationships might then well—even given the incommensurability of values—*contain* within them friendships between parents and children, without any loss to the essential characteristics of the latter kind of relationship ….

Notes

1 See Aristotle, *Nicomachean Ethics*, trans. T. Irwin (Indianapolis, IN: Hackett, 1985), 209–216 [1155b16–1157b5].
2 See Terence Irwin's commentary, in Aristotle, *Ethics*, 359.
3 Aristotle, *Ethics*, 20–21 [1099a16–18].

4 Ibid., 207 [1155a1–3].
5 Ibid., 257 [1169b7–10].
6 Ibid., 21 and 26 [1099b2–6 and 1100b23–34].
7 Ibid., 215 [1157a31–34].
8 Cf. Elizabeth Telfer, "Friendship," in *Other Selves: Philosophers on Friendship*, ed. M. Pakaluk (Indianapolis, IN: Hackett, 1991), 250–67, 250.
9 Ralph W. Emerson, "Friendship," in *Other Selves*, 220–32, 227.
10 Joseph Kupfer, "Can Parents and Children Be Friends?" [in this volume].
11 Ibid.
12 Ibid.
13 Ibid.
14 Ibid.
15 Aristotle, *Ethics*, 230 [1161b16–29].
16 Ibid., 260 [1170b5–14].
17 Ibid., 253–56 [1168a28–1169b2]. Cf. Talbot Brewer, "Virtues We Can Share: Friendship and Aristotelian Ethical Theory," *Ethics* 115, no. 3 (2005): 721–58.
18 Erich Fromm, *The Art of Loving* (London: George Allen & Unwin, 1957), 18.
19 Emerson, "Friendship," 232.
20 Kupfer, "Friends."
21 Emerson, "Friendship," 222.
22 Kupfer, "Friends."
23 Cf. Johann A. Klaasen, "Friends and Lovers," *Journal of Social Philosophy*, 35, no. 3 (2004): 413–19. For the opposite view, see James Conlon, "Why Lovers Can't Be Friends," in *Philosophical Perspectives on Sex and Love*, ed. R. M. Stewart (New York: Oxford University Press, 1995): 295–99.
24 Kupfer, "Friends."
25 Aristotle, *Ethics*, 244 [1165b17–21].
26 Emerson, "Friendship," 225 and 229.
27 Kupfer, "Friends."
28 Emerson, "Friendship," 227.
29 Klaasen, "Friends and Lovers," 414.

Review and Discussion Questions

1 What is Aristotle's analysis of friendship?
2 What are Kristjánsson's counterarguments to Kupfer?
3 Which author—Kupfer or Kristjánsson—has the better view? Why?

READING: WHAT DO GROWN CHILDREN OWE THEIR PARENTS?

JANE ENGLISH[*]

One way to view the responsibilities of grown children to their parents is to suppose that children owe their parents love, respect, and financial or other help on the basis of past sacrifices parents have made. Jane English rejects this form of argument, claiming instead that friendship is a better model than debts owed for understanding the

---

[*] From Jane English, "What Do Grown Children Owe Their Parents?" in Onora O'Neill and William Ruddick (eds.), *Having Children* (New York: Oxford University Press, 1979). Reprinted by permission.

parent–child relationship. Jane English was Professor of Philosophy at the University of North Carolina.

What do grown children owe their parents? I will contend that the answer is "nothing." Although I agree that there are many things that children ought to do for their parents, I will argue that it is inappropriate and misleading to describe them as things "owed." I will maintain that parents' voluntary sacrifices, rather than creating "debts" to be "repaid," tend to create love or "friendship." The duties of grown children are those of friends and result from love between them and their parents rather than being things owed in repayment for the parents' earlier sacrifices. Thus, I will oppose those philosophers who use the word "owe" whenever a duty or obligation exists. Although the "debt" metaphor is appropriate in some moral circumstances, my argument is that a love relationship is not such a case.

Misunderstandings about the proper relationship between parents and their grown children have resulted from reliance on the "owing" terminology. For instance, we hear parents complain, "You owe it to us to write home (keep up your piano playing, not adopt a hippie lifestyle), because of all we sacrificed for you (paying for piano lessons, sending you to college)." The child is sometimes even heard to reply, "I didn't ask to be born (to be given piano lessons, to be sent to college)." This inappropriate idiom of ordinary language tends to obscure, or even to undermine, the love that is the correct ground of filial obligation.

1 Favors Create Debts

There are some cases, other than literal debts, in which talk of "owing," though metaphorical, is apt. New to the neighborhood, Max barely knows his neighbor, Nina, but he asks her if she will take in his mail while he is gone for a month's vacation. She agrees. If, subsequently, Nina asks Max to do the same for her, it seems that Max has a moral obligation to agree (greater than the one he would have had if Nina had not done the same for him), unless for some reason it would be a burden far out of proportion to the one Nina bore for him. I will call this a *favor*: when A, at B's request, bears some burden for B, then B incurs an obligation to reciprocate. Here the metaphor of Max's "owing" Nina is appropriate. It is not literally a debt, of course, nor can Nina pass this IOU on to heirs, demand payment in the form of Max's taking out her garbage, or sue Max. Nonetheless, since Max ought to perform one act of similar nature and amount of sacrifice in return, the term is suggestive. Once he reciprocates, the debt is "discharged"—that is, their obligations revert to the condition they were in before Max's initial request.

Contrast a situation in which Max simply goes on vacation and, to his surprise, finds upon his return that his neighbor has mowed his grass twice weekly in his absence. This is a voluntary sacrifice rather than a favor, and Max has no duty to reciprocate. It would be nice for him to volunteer to do so, but this would be supererogatory on his part. Rather than a favor, Nina's action is a friendly gesture. As a result, she might expect Max to chat over the back fence, help her catch her straying dog, or something similar—she might expect the development of a friendship. But Max would be chatting (or whatever) out of friendship, rather than in repayment for mown grass. If he did not return her gesture, she might feel rebuffed or miffed but not unjustly treated or indignant, since Max has not failed to perform a duty. Talk of "owing" would be out of place in this case.

It is sometimes difficult to distinguish between favors and nonfavors, because friends tend to do favors for each other, and those who exchange favors tend to become friends. But one test is to ask how Max is motivated. Is it "to be nice to Nina" or "because she did x for me"? Favors are frequently performed by total strangers without any friendship developing. Nevertheless, a temporary obligation is created, even if the chance for repayment never arises. For instance, suppose that Oscar and Matilda, total strangers, are waiting in a long checkout line at the supermarket. Oscar, having forgotten the oregano, asks Matilda to watch his cart for a second. She does. If Matilda now asks Oscar to return the favor while she picks up some tomato sauce, he is obliged to agree. Even if she had not watched his cart, it would be inconsiderate of him to refuse, claiming he was too busy reading the magazines. He may have a duty to help others, but he would not "owe" it to her. But if she had done the same for him, he incurs an additional obligation to help, and talk of "owing" is apt. It suggests an agreement to perform equal, reciprocal, canceling sacrifices.

2 The Duties of Friendship versus Debts

The terms "owe" and "repay" are helpful in the case of favors, because the sameness of the amount of sacrifice on the two sides is important; the monetary metaphor suggests equal quantities of sacrifice. But friendship ought to be characterized by *mutuality* rather than reciprocity: friends offer what they can give and accept what they need, without regard for the total amounts of benefits exchanged. And friends are motivated by love rather than by the prospect of repayment. Hence, talk of "owing" is singularly out of place in friendship.

For example, suppose Alfred takes Beatrice out for an expensive dinner and a movie. Beatrice incurs no obligation to "repay" him with a goodnight kiss or a return engagement. If Alfred complains that she "owes" him something, he is operating under the assumption that she should repay a favor, but, on the contrary, his was a generous gesture done in the hopes of developing a friendship. We hope that he would not want her repayment in the form of sex or attention if this was done to discharge a debt rather than from friendship. Since, if Alfred is prone to reasoning in this way, Beatrice may well decline the invitation or request to pay for her own dinner, his attitude of expecting a "return" on his "investment" could hinder the development of a friendship. Beatrice should return the gesture only if she is motivated by friendship.

Another common misuse of the "owing" idiom occurs when the Smiths have dined at the Joneses' four times, but the Joneses at the Smiths' only once. People often say, "We owe them three dinners." This line of thinking may be appropriate between business acquaintances, but not between friends. After all, the Joneses invited the Smiths not in order to feed them or to be fed in turn, but because of the friendly contact presumably enjoyed by all on such occasions. If the Smiths do not feel friendship toward the Joneses, they can decline future invitations and not invite the Joneses; they owe them nothing. Of course, between friends of equal resources and needs, roughly equal sacrifices (though not necessarily roughly equal dinners) will typically occur. If the sacrifices are highly out of proportion to the resources, the relationship is closer to servility than to friendship.

Another difference between favors and friendship is that after a friendship ends, the duties of friendship end. The party that has sacrificed less owes the other nothing. For instance, suppose Elmer donated a pint of blood that his wife Doris needed during an operation. Years after their divorce, Elmer is in an accident and needs one pint of blood. His new wife, Cora, is also of the same blood type. It seems that Doris not only does not "owe" Elmer blood but that she should actually refrain from coming forward if Cora has volunteered to donate. To insist on donating not only interferes with the newlyweds' friendship, but it belittles Doris and Elmer's former relationship by suggesting that Elmer gave blood in hopes of favors returned instead of simply out of love for Doris. It is one of the heart-rending features of divorce that it attends to quantity in a relationship previously characterized by mutuality. If Cora could not donate, Doris's obligation is the same as that for any former spouse in need of blood; it is not increased by the fact that Elmer similarly aided her. It is affected by the degree to which they are still friends, which in turn may (or may not) have been influenced by Elmer's donation.

In short, unlike the debts created by favors, the duties of friendship do not require equal quantities of sacrifice. Performing equal sacrifices does not cancel the duties of friendship, as it does the debts of favors. Unrequested sacrifices do not themselves create debts, but friends have duties regardless of whether they requested or initiated the friendship. Those who perform favors may be motivated by mutual gain, whereas friends should be motivated by affection. These characteristics of the friendship relation are distorted by talk of "owing."

3 Parents and Children

The relationship between children and their parents should be one of friendship characterized by mutuality rather than one of reciprocal favors. The quantity of parental sacrifice is not relevant in determining what duties the grown child has. The medical assistance grown children ought to offer their ill mothers in old age depends upon the mothers' need, not upon whether they endured a difficult pregnancy, for example. Nor do one's duties to one's parents cease once an equal quantity of sacrifice has been performed as the phrase "discharging a debt" may lead us to think.

Rather, what children ought to do for their parents (and parents for children) depends upon (1) their respective needs, abilities, and resources and (2) the extent to which there is an ongoing friendship between them. Thus, regardless of the quantity of childhood sacrifices, an able, wealthy child has an obligation to help his needy parents more than does a needy child. To illustrate, suppose sisters Cecile and Dana are equally loved by their parents, even though Cecile was an easy child to care for, seldom ill, while Dana was often sick and caused some trouble as a juvenile delinquent. As adults, Dana is a struggling artist living far away, while Cecile is a wealthy lawyer living nearby. When the parents need visits and financial aid, Cecile has an obligation to bear a higher proportion of these burdens than her sister. This results from her abilities rather than from the quantities of sacrifice made by the parents earlier.

Sacrifices have an important causal role in creating an ongoing friendship, which may lead us to assume incorrectly that it is the sacrifices that are the source of the obligation. That the source is the friendship instead can be seen by examining cases in which the sacrifices occurred but the friendship, for some reason, did not develop or persist. For example, if a woman gives up her newborn child for adoption and if no feelings of love ever develop on either side, it seems that the grown child does not have an obligation to "repay" her for her sacrifices in pregnancy. For that matter, if the adopted child has an unimpaired love relationship with the adoptive parents, he or she has the same obligations to help them as a natural child would have.

The filial obligations of grown children are a result of friendship rather than owed for services rendered. Suppose that Vance married Lola despite his parents' strong wish that he marry within their religion and that as a result, the parents refuse to speak to him again. As the years pass, the parents are unaware of Vance's problems, his accomplishments, the birth of his children. The love that once existed between them, let us suppose, has been completely destroyed by this event and thirty years of desuetude. At this point, it seems, Vance is under no obligation to pay his parents' medical bills in their old age, beyond his general duty to help those in need. An additional, filial obligation would only arise from whatever love he may still feel for them. It would be irrelevant for his parents to argue, "But look how much we sacrificed for you when you were young," for that sacrifice was not a favor but occurred as part of a friendship which existed at that time but is now, we have supposed, defunct. A more appropriate message would be, "We still love you, and we would like to renew our friendship."

I hope this helps to set the question of what children ought to do for their parents in a new light. The parental argument, "You ought to do x because we did y for you," should be replaced by, "We love you and you will be happier if you do x," or "We believe you love us, and anyone who loved us would do x." If the parents' sacrifice had been a favor, the child's reply, "I never asked you to do y for me," would have been relevant; to the revised parental remarks, this reply is clearly irrelevant. The child can either do x or dispute one of the parents' claims: by showing that a love relationship does not exist or that love for someone does not motivate doing x or that he or she will not be happier doing x.

Seen in this light, parental requests for children to write home, visit, and offer them a reasonable amount of emotional and financial support in life's crises are well founded, so long as a friendship still exists. Love for others does call for caring about and caring for them. Some other parental requests, such as for more sweeping changes in the child's lifestyle or life goals, can be seen to be insupportable, once we shift the justification from debts owed to love. The terminology of favors suggests the reasoning, "Since we paid for your college education, you owe it to us to make a career of engineering, rather than becoming a rock musician." This tends to alienate affection even further, since the tuition payments are depicted as investments for a return rather than done from love, as though the child's life goals could be "bought." Basing the argument on love leads to different reasoning patterns. The suppressed premise, "If A loves B, then A follows B's wishes as to A's lifelong career" is simply false. Love does not even dictate that the child adopt the parents' values as to the desirability of alternative life goals. So the parents' strongest available argument here is, "We love you, we are deeply concerned about your happiness, and in the long run you will be happier as an engineer." This makes it clear that an empirical claim is really the subject of the debate.

The function of these examples is to draw out our considered judgments as to the proper relation between parents and their grown children and to show how poorly they fit the model of favors. What is relevant is the ongoing friendship that exists between parents and children. Although that relationship developed partly as a result of parental sacrifices for the child, the duties that grown children have to their parents result from the friendship rather than from the sacrifices. The idiom of owing favors to one's parents can actually be destructive if it undermines the role of mutuality and leads us to think in terms of quantitative reciprocal favors.

Review and Discussion Questions

1 What differences does English find between duties to friends and the obligation to repay debts?
2 Why does English advocate the model of friendship rather than of reciprocal favors in describing the parent–child relationship?
3 Does the friendship model exhaust the duties of children? Is the mere fact of a biological connection between parent and child morally irrelevant? Explain.
4 Suppose a parent has not been a friend to the child, but instead has been strict, remote, and uncompromising but also self-sacrificing. Does the adult child then owe the parent nothing?

Essay and Paper Topics for Chapter 11

1 Apply any of the moral theories from Part I to write an essay in which you evaluate the position of two authors from this chapter.
2 Suppose you were the judge and jury to decide which position in the debate between Kupfer and Kristjánsson is most cogent. Summarize the arguments and deliver your verdict, giving reasons to explain your position.
3 Compare English's position with the view of parent–child relationships described by Judith Jarvis Thomson in her article on abortion.
4 Drawing on the essays about friendship, describe what you regard as the ideal relationship between parents (or caretakers more broadly) and their adult children.

Chapter 12

Personal Dimensions of Technology
Friendships, Self-Driving Cars, and Privacy

What is the personal impact of technology on how we think and reason and on how we form and sustain relationships? These topics have taken on new urgency with the advent of personal technologies that influence how we work, how we learn, and how we spend our free time. Some writers emphasize the spectacular potential of these technologies. Others are astonished by what they see as a worrisome degradation of human thought and human relationships. The following essays consider a spectrum of contrasting assessments.

> ### READING: IS GOOGLE MAKING US STUPID? WHAT THE INTERNET IS DOING TO OUR BRAINS
>
> NICHOLAS CARR[*]
>
> Does spending a large amount of time on the Internet and texting affect your abilities and your self-conception? In this essay, Nicholas Carr considers some of the costs of the Internet in terms of how it affects human lives. Nicholas Carr writes about technology, culture, and economics. His books and articles have been translated into over twenty languages.
>
> "Dave, stop. Stop, will you? Stop, Dave. Will you stop, Dave?" So the supercomputer HAL pleads with the implacable astronaut Dave Bowman in a famous and weirdly poignant scene toward the end of Stanley Kubrick's *2001: A Space Odyssey*. Bowman, having nearly been sent to a deep-space death by the malfunctioning machine, is calmly, coldly disconnecting the memory circuits that control its artificial "brain." "Dave, my mind is going," HAL says, forlornly. "I can feel it. I can feel it."
>
> I can feel it, too. Over the past few years I've had an uncomfortable sense that someone, or something, has been tinkering with my brain, re-mapping the neural circuitry, reprogramming the memory. My mind isn't going—so far as I can tell—but it's changing. I'm not thinking the way I used to think. I can feel it most strongly when I'm reading. Immersing myself in a book or a lengthy article used

---

[*] Nicholas Carr, "Is Google Making Us Stupid? What the Internet Is Doing to Our Brains," *The Atlantic* (July/August 2008).

to be easy. My mind would get caught up in the narrative or the turns of the argument, and I'd spend hours strolling through long stretches of prose. That's rarely the case anymore. Now my concentration often starts to drift after two or three pages. I get fidgety, lose the thread, begin looking for something else to do. I feel as if I'm always dragging my wayward brain back to the text. The deep reading that used to come naturally has become a struggle.

I think I know what's going on. For more than a decade now, I've been spending a lot of time online, searching and surfing and sometimes adding to the great databases of the Internet. The Web has been a godsend to me as a writer. Research that once required days in the stacks or periodical rooms of libraries can now be done in minutes. A few Google searches, some quick clicks on hyperlinks, and I've got the telltale fact or pithy quote I was after. Even when I'm not working, I'm as likely as not to be foraging in the Web's info-thickets—reading and writing e-mails, scanning headlines and blog posts, watching videos and listening to podcasts, or just tripping from link to link to link. (Unlike footnotes, to which they're sometimes likened, hyperlinks don't merely point to related works; they propel you toward them.)

For me, as for others, the Net is becoming a universal medium, the conduit for most of the information that flows through my eyes and ears and into my mind. The advantages of having immediate access to such an incredibly rich store of information are many, and they've been widely described and duly applauded. "The perfect recall of silicon memory," *Wired*'s Clive Thompson has written, "can be an enormous boon to thinking." But that boon comes at a price. As the media theorist Marshall McLuhan pointed out in the 1960s, media are not just passive channels of information. They supply the stuff of thought, but they also shape the process of thought. And what the Net seems to be doing is chipping away my capacity for concentration and contemplation. My mind now expects to take in information the way the Net distributes it: in a swiftly moving stream of particles. Once I was a scuba diver in the sea of words. Now I zip along the surface like a guy on a Jet Ski ....

Bruce Friedman, who blogs regularly about the use of computers in medicine, also has described how the Internet has altered his mental habits. "I now have almost totally lost the ability to read and absorb a longish article on the web or in print," he wrote earlier this year. A pathologist who has long been on the faculty of the University of Michigan Medical School, Friedman elaborated on his comment in a telephone conversation with me. His thinking, he said, has taken on a "staccato" quality, reflecting the way he quickly scans short passages of text from many sources online. "I can't read *War and Peace* anymore," he admitted. "I've lost the ability to do that. Even a blog post of more than three or four paragraphs is too much to absorb. I skim it."

Anecdotes alone don't prove much. And we still await the long-term neurological and psychological experiments that will provide a definitive picture of how Internet use affects cognition. But a recently published study of online research habits, conducted by scholars from University College London, suggests that we may well be in the midst of a sea change in the way we read and think. As part of the five-year research program, the scholars examined computer logs documenting the behavior of visitors to two popular research sites, one operated by the British Library and one by a U.K. educational consortium, that provide access to journal articles, e-books, and other sources of written information. They found that people using the sites exhibited "a form of skimming activity," hopping from one source to another and rarely returning to any source they'd already visited. They typically read no more than one or two pages of an article or book before they would "bounce" out to another site. Sometimes they'd save a long article, but there's no evidence that they ever went back and actually read it. The authors of the study report:

> It is clear that users are not reading online in the traditional sense; indeed there are signs that new forms of "reading" are emerging as users "power browse" horizontally through titles, contents pages and abstracts going for quick wins. It almost seems that they go online to avoid reading in the traditional sense.

Thanks to the ubiquity of text on the Internet, not to mention the popularity of text-messaging on cell phones, we may well be reading more today than we did in the 1970s or 1980s, when television was our medium of choice. But it's a different kind of reading, and behind it lies a different kind of thinking—perhaps even a new sense of the self. "We are not only *what* we read," says Maryanne Wolf, a developmental psychologist at Tufts University and the author of *Proust and the Squid: The Story and Science of the Reading Brain*. "We are *how* we read." Wolf worries that the style of reading promoted by the Net, a style that puts "efficiency" and "immediacy" above all else, may be weakening our capacity for the kind of deep reading that emerged when an earlier technology, the printing press, made long and complex works of prose commonplace. When we read online, she says, we tend to become "mere decoders of information." Our ability to interpret text, to make the rich mental connections that form when we read deeply and without distraction, remains largely disengaged.

Reading, explains Wolf, is not an instinctive skill for human beings. It's not etched into our genes the way speech is. We have to teach our minds how to translate the symbolic characters we see into the language we understand. And the media or other technologies we use in learning and practicing the craft of reading play an important part in shaping the neural circuits inside our brains. Experiments demonstrate that readers of ideograms, such as the Chinese, develop a mental circuitry for reading that is very different from the circuitry found in those of us whose written language employs an alphabet. The variations extend across many regions of the brain, including those that govern such essential cognitive functions as memory and the interpretation of visual and auditory stimuli. We can expect as well that the circuits woven by our use of the Net will be different from those woven by our reading of books and other printed works.

Sometime in 1882, Friedrich Nietzsche bought a typewriter—a Malling-Hansen Writing Ball, to be precise. His vision was failing, and keeping his eyes focused on a page had become exhausting and painful, often bringing on crushing headaches. He had been forced to curtail his writing, and he feared that he would soon have to give it up. The typewriter rescued him, at least for a time. Once he had mastered touch-typing, he was able to write with his eyes closed, using only the tips of his fingers. Words could once again flow from his mind to the page.

But the machine had a subtler effect on his work. One of Nietzsche's friends, a composer, noticed a change in the style of his writing. His already terse prose had become even tighter, more telegraphic. "Perhaps you will through this instrument even take to a new idiom," the friend wrote in a letter, noting that, in his own work, his "'thoughts' in music and language often depend on the quality of pen and paper."

"You are right," Nietzsche replied, "our writing equipment takes part in the forming of our thoughts." Under the sway of the machine, writes the German media scholar Friedrich A. Kittler, Nietzsche's prose "changed from arguments to aphorisms, from thoughts to puns, from rhetoric to telegram style."

The human brain is almost infinitely malleable. People used to think that our mental meshwork, the dense connections formed among the 100 billion or so neurons inside our skulls, was largely fixed by the time we reached adulthood. But brain researchers have discovered that that's not the case. James Olds, a professor of neuroscience who directs the Krasnow Institute for Advanced Study at George Mason University, says that even the adult mind "is very plastic." Nerve cells routinely break old connections and form new ones. "The brain," according to Olds, "has the ability to reprogram itself on the fly, altering the way it functions."

As we use what the sociologist Daniel Bell has called our "intellectual technologies"—the tools that extend our mental rather than our physical capacities—we inevitably begin to take on the qualities of those technologies. The mechanical clock, which came into common use in the 14th century, provides a compelling example. In *Technics and Civilization*, the historian and cultural critic Lewis Mumford described how the clock "disassociated time from human events and helped create the belief in an independent world of mathematically measurable sequences." The "abstract framework of divided time" became "the point of reference for both action and thought."

The clock's methodical ticking helped bring into being the scientific mind and the scientific man. But it also took something away. As the late MIT computer scientist Joseph Weizenbaum observed in his 1976 book, *Computer Power and Human Reason: From Judgment to Calculation*, the conception of the world that emerged from the widespread use of timekeeping instruments "remains an impoverished version of the older one, for it rests on a rejection of those direct experiences that formed the basis for, and indeed constituted, the old reality." In deciding when to eat, to work, to sleep, to rise, we stopped listening to our senses and started obeying the clock.

The process of adapting to new intellectual technologies is reflected in the changing metaphors we use to explain ourselves to ourselves. When the mechanical clock arrived, people began thinking of their brains as operating "like clockwork." Today, in the age of software, we have come to think of them as operating "like computers." But the changes, neuroscience tells us, go much deeper than metaphor. Thanks to our brain's plasticity, the adaptation occurs also at a biological level.

The Internet promises to have particularly far-reaching effects on cognition. In a paper published in 1936, the British mathematician Alan Turing proved that a digital computer, which at the time existed only as a theoretical machine, could be programmed to perform the function of any other information-processing device. And that's what we're seeing today. The Internet, an immeasurably powerful computing system, is subsuming most of our other intellectual technologies.

It's becoming our map and our clock, our printing press and our typewriter, our calculator and our telephone, and our radio and TV.

When the Net absorbs a medium, that medium is re-created in the Net's image. It injects the medium's content with hyperlinks, blinking ads, and other digital gewgaws, and it surrounds the content with the content of all the other media it has absorbed. A new e-mail message, for instance, may announce its arrival as we're glancing over the latest headlines at a newspaper's site. The result is to scatter our attention and diffuse our concentration.

The Net's influence doesn't end at the edges of a computer screen, either. As people's minds become attuned to the crazy quilt of Internet media, traditional media have to adapt to the audience's new expectations. Television programs add text crawls and pop-up ads, and magazines and newspapers shorten their articles, introduce capsule summaries, and crowd their pages with easy-to-browse info-snippets. When, in March of this year, *The New York Times* decided to devote the second and third pages of every edition to article abstracts, its design director, Tom Bodkin, explained that the "shortcuts" would give harried readers a quick "taste" of the day's news, sparing them the "less efficient" method of actually turning the pages and reading the articles. Old media have little choice but to play by the new-media rules.

Never has a communications system played so many roles in our lives—or exerted such broad influence over our thoughts—as the Internet does today. Yet, for all that's been written about the Net, there's been little consideration of how, exactly, it's reprogramming us. The Net's intellectual ethic remains obscure.

About the same time that Nietzsche started using his typewriter, an earnest young man named Frederick Winslow Taylor carried a stopwatch into the Midvale Steel plant in Philadelphia and began a historic series of experiments aimed at improving the efficiency of the plant's machinists. With the approval of Midvale's owners, he recruited a group of factory hands, set them to work on various metalworking machines, and recorded and timed their every movement as well as the operations of the machines. By breaking down every job into a sequence of small, discrete steps and then testing different ways of performing each one, Taylor created a set of precise instructions—an "algorithm," we might say today—for how each worker should work. Midvale's employees grumbled about the strict new regime, claiming that it turned them into little more than automatons, but the factory's productivity soared.

More than a hundred years after the invention of the steam engine, the Industrial Revolution had at last found its philosophy and its philosopher. Taylor's tight industrial choreography—his "system," as he liked to call it—was embraced by manufacturers throughout the country and, in time, around the world. Seeking maximum speed, maximum efficiency, and maximum output, factory owners used time-and-motion studies to organize their work and configure the jobs of their workers. The goal, as Taylor defined it in his celebrated 1911 treatise, *The Principles of Scientific Management*, was to identify and adopt, for every job, the "one best method" of work and thereby to effect "the gradual substitution of science for rule of thumb throughout the mechanic arts." Once his system was applied to all acts of manual labor, Taylor assured his followers, it would bring about a restructuring not only of industry but of society, creating a utopia of perfect efficiency. "In the past the man has been first," he declared; "in the future the system must be first."

Taylor's system is still very much with us; it remains the ethic of industrial manufacturing. And now, thanks to the growing power that computer engineers and software coders wield over our intellectual lives, Taylor's ethic is beginning to govern the realm of the mind as well. The Internet is a machine designed for the efficient and automated collection, transmission, and manipulation of information, and its legions of programmers are intent on finding the "one best method"—the perfect algorithm—to carry out every mental movement of what we've come to describe as "knowledge work."

Google's headquarters, in Mountain View, California—the Googleplex—is the Internet's high church, and the religion practiced inside its walls is Taylorism. Google, says its chief executive, Eric Schmidt, is "a company that's founded around the science of measurement," and it is striving to "systematize everything" it does. Drawing on the terabytes of behavioral data it collects through its search engine and other sites, it carries out thousands of experiments a day, according to the *Harvard Business Review*, and it uses the results to refine the algorithms that increasingly control how people find information and extract meaning from it. What Taylor did for the work of the hand, Google is doing for the work of the mind.

The company has declared that its mission is "to organize the world's information and make it universally accessible and useful." It seeks to develop "the perfect search engine," which it defines as something that "understands exactly what you mean and gives you back exactly what you want." In Google's view, information is a kind of commodity, a utilitarian resource that can be mined and processed with industrial efficiency. The more pieces of information we can "access" and the faster we can extract their gist, the more productive we become as thinkers.

Where does it end? Sergey Brin and Larry Page, the gifted young men who founded Google while pursuing doctoral degrees in computer science at Stanford, speak frequently of their desire to turn their search engine into an artificial intelligence, a HAL-like machine that might be connected directly to our brains. "The ultimate search engine is something as smart as people—or smarter," Page said in a speech a few years back. "For us, working on search is a way to work on artificial intelligence." In a 2004 interview with *Newsweek*, Brin said, "Certainly if you had all the world's information directly attached to your brain, or an artificial brain that was smarter than your brain, you'd be better off." Last year, Page told a convention of scientists that Google is "really trying to build artificial intelligence and to do it on a large scale."

Such an ambition is a natural one, even an admirable one, for a pair of math whizzes with vast quantities of cash at their disposal and a small army of computer scientists in their employ. A fundamentally scientific enterprise, Google is motivated by a desire to use technology, in Eric Schmidt's words, "to solve problems that have never been solved before," and artificial intelligence is the hardest problem out there. Why wouldn't Brin and Page want to be the ones to crack it?

Still, their easy assumption that we'd all "be better off" if our brains were supplemented, or even replaced, by an artificial intelligence is unsettling. It suggests a belief that intelligence is the output of a mechanical process, a series of discrete steps that can be isolated, measured, and optimized. In Google's world, the world we enter when we go online, there's little place for the fuzziness of contemplation. Ambiguity is not an opening for insight but a bug to be fixed. The human brain is just an outdated computer that needs a faster processor and a bigger hard drive.

The idea that our minds should operate as highspeed data-processing machines is not only built into the workings of the Internet, it is the network's reigning business model as well. The faster we surf across the Web—the more links we click and pages we view—the more opportunities Google and other companies gain to collect information about us and to feed us advertisements. Most of the proprietors of the commercial Internet have a financial stake in collecting the crumbs of data we leave behind as we flit from link to link—the more crumbs, the better. The last thing these companies want is to encourage leisurely reading or slow, concentrated thought. It's in their economic interest to drive us to distraction.

Maybe I'm just a worrywart. Just as there's a tendency to glorify technological progress, there's a countertendency to expect the worst of every new tool or machine. In Plato's *Phaedrus*, Socrates bemoaned the development of writing. He feared that, as people came to rely on the written word as a substitute for the knowledge they used to carry inside their heads, they would, in the words of one of the dialogue's characters, "cease to exercise their memory and become forgetful." And because they would be able to "receive a quantity of information without proper instruction," they would "be thought very knowledgeable when they are for the most part quite ignorant." They would be "filled with the conceit of wisdom instead of real wisdom." Socrates wasn't wrong—the new technology did often have the effects he feared—but he was shortsighted. He couldn't foresee the many ways that writing and reading would serve to spread information, spur fresh ideas, and expand human knowledge (if not wisdom).

The arrival of Gutenberg's printing press, in the 15th century, set off another round of teeth gnashing. The Italian humanist Hieronimo Squarciafico worried that the easy availability of books would lead to intellectual laziness, making men "less studious" and weakening their minds. Others argued that cheaply printed books and broadsheets would undermine religious authority, demean the work of scholars and scribes, and spread sedition and debauchery. As New York University professor Clay Shirky notes, "Most of the arguments made against the printing press were correct, even prescient." But, again, the doomsayers were unable to imagine the myriad blessings that the printed word would deliver.

So, yes, you should be skeptical of my skepticism. Perhaps those who dismiss critics of the Internet as Luddites or nostalgists will be proved correct, and from our hyperactive, data-stoked minds will spring a golden age of intellectual discovery and universal wisdom. Then again, the Net isn't the alphabet, and although it may replace the printing press, it produces something altogether different. The kind of deep reading that a sequence of printed pages promotes is valuable not just for the knowledge we acquire from the author's words but for the intellectual vibrations those words set off within our own minds. In the quiet spaces opened up by the sustained, undistracted reading of a book, or by any other act of contemplation, for that matter, we make our own associations, draw our own inferences and analogies, foster our own ideas. Deep reading, as Maryanne Wolf argues, is indistinguishable from deep thinking.

If we lose those quiet spaces, or fill them up with "content," we will sacrifice something important not only in our selves but in our culture. In a recent essay, the playwright Richard Foreman eloquently described what's at stake:

> I come from a tradition of Western culture, in which the ideal (my ideal) was the complex, dense and "cathedral-like" structure of the highly educated and articulate personality—a man or woman who carried inside themselves

a personally constructed and unique version of the entire heritage of the West. [But now] I see within us all (myself included) the replacement of complex inner density with a new kind of self—evolving under the pressure of information overload and the technology of the "instantly available."

As we are drained of our "inner repertory of dense cultural inheritance," Foreman concluded, we risk turning into "'pancake people'—spread wide and thin as we connect with that vast network of information accessed by the mere touch of a button."

I'm haunted by that scene in *2001*. What makes it so poignant, and so weird, is the computer's emotional response to the disassembly of its mind: its despair as one circuit after another goes dark, its childlike pleading with the astronaut—"I can feel it. I can feel it. I'm afraid"—and its final reversion to what can only be called a state of innocence. HAL's outpouring of feeling contrasts with the emotionlessness that characterizes the human figures in the film, who go about their business with an almost robotic efficiency. Their thoughts and actions feel scripted, as if they're following the steps of an algorithm. In the world of *2001*, people have become so machinelike that the most human character turns out to be a machine. That's the essence of Kubrick's dark prophecy: as we come to rely on computers to mediate our understanding of the world, it is our own intelligence that flattens into artificial intelligence.

Review and Discussion Questions

1. What is the point of discussing Friedrich Nietzsche's typewriter? Do you agree with the point?
2. According to Carr, how did the invention of the mechanized clock change the metaphors that people used to explain themselves and their sense of identity?
3. What does the Internet do to our cognitive abilities, according to Carr? Do you agree that it "programs" us to be and think in certain ways? Which ways?
4. What is the "ethic of industrial manufacturing," according to Carr? Do you agree that this ethic, given advancing technology, is used to govern people's minds as well?
5. Is there value in mental ambiguity? What is that value?
6. What does "deep reading" and "deep thinking" mean, in your view? What are "pancake people" (in the words of Carr)? Are you one of these? How do you know, either way?
7. What are the ethical implications of the ideas in this article?

READING: FRIENDSHIP IN THE SHADOW OF TECHNOLOGY

LAURENCE THOMAS[*]

How does our use of modern technology affect the quality and condition of friendships? In what ways, if any, should we be concerned about how our use of technology shapes our conception of friendship and the actual experience of interacting with others in friendship? Laurence Thomas explores these questions in this essay. Laurence Thomas is a Professor of Philosophy and Political Science at Syracuse University.

---

[*] Original article written for this book.

Is having 5000 friends an indication of the truly admirable qualities of character that a person has? Or, is the very idea of having that many friends rather incomprehensible? Well, Aristotle held that when it comes to friendship at its very best—companion friendship, as we may say—no individual ever has more than a few companion friends. For he held that not only do companion friends delight in spending time together, but that a companion friend is rather like another self. However, it was more than 2000 years ago that Aristotle put forward his view of friendship; and it might simply be that times have changed, with the reality of Facebook friends (which can be up to 5000) standing as irrefutable evidence of the transformation that has occurred with respect to friendship. Moreover, so this line of thought might continue, an indisputable fact is that owing to technology human beings nowadays can communicate with one another in ways that were both impossible and downright inconceivable when Aristotle advanced his account of friendship.

In Aristotle's day, of course friends had to spend time together, since in effect that was just about the only way in which they could communicate with one another at all. But thanks to technology friends can routinely and frequently communicate with one another, though they are at opposite ends of the earth. There is email; there is Skype; and there are cell phones and social networking sites. Furthermore, people who live in the very same country have text-messaging available to them as a means of direct communication, although their domiciles may be separated by hundreds—if not thousands—of miles. As to Aristotle's idea of a companion friend being like another self, what more do we need as evidence of this than a friend using some form of technology to tell us that she or he agrees with us or is happy for us? Indeed, if a person chooses "Like" on a friend's Facebook page for just the right posting, is that not quite substantial evidence that these two individuals have lots in common? And is that not pretty much what Aristotle meant by the idea that a companion friend is like another self?

Putting all of the above considerations together, it is quite tempting to think that in view of modern communicative personal technology Aristotle's idea of companion friendship is a little outdated. What I shall argue in this essay, however, is that *au contraire* Aristotle's account of companion friendship has mightily withstood the test of time; and that personal communicative technology may very well be an impediment to the realization of friendship at its best. I set the stage by offering a brief story of an experience between two friends.

Here is a small portion of a cell phone conversation that took place about three years ago between Joshua and Neil whose companion friendship goes back many years (where the context for the call is that Neil had just landed in Paris and was calling Joshua to let him know that):

Josh: My father is in the hospital
Neil: Oh my, I must go and see him immediately
Josh: Ok, but I should tell you that my father no longer likes black people
Neil: No problem. I am no longer black.

Joshua and Neil laughed and laughed and laughed together. Although that exchange between them took no more than 12 seconds, it was a most majestic sign of the depth of their longstanding friendship. The very essence of Aristotle's view is that in spending time together friends constantly reinforce and affirm the depth of their friendship and, in particular, they gain much insight into one another's character as well as their own character. Of course, they do so in the obvious respects by helping, encouraging, and being supportive of one another in various ways. However, they also do in entirely spontaneous and unforeseeable ways that are tied to what is unfolding before them at any given moment, where what is so marvelously affirmed on-the-spot is the tremendous depth of their trust in and understanding of one another. And there is no way to know in advance the respect in which that affirmation will be taking place. Neil and Joshua never supposed for even a moment that their ethnic differences were in any way a relevant, let alone negative, factor in their friendship. Just so, the 12-second exchange recounted above was as profound an indication as either of them could have ever wanted that their friendship beautifully transcended their ethnic differences.

It goes without saying that in ways that Aristotle could not possibly have foreseen technology would one day play a pivotal role in the lives of individuals and, in particular, in the way in which communication takes place between individuals. Indeed, this was not seen by many a mere generation ago. One reason why personal communicative technology plays such a pivotal role in the lives of individuals is that they can avail themselves of it 24 hours a day and 7 days a week in order to communicate with one another. What is more, individuals can do so just about wherever they might be. At first glance, then, it looks as if this technology is none other than the great facilitator of friendship precisely because it is the great facilitator of communication. In what follows, we shall see why things are not quite what they appear to be.

1 Communication and Conversation

Significantly, while technology is undoubtedly the greater facilitator of communication, it is not quite the great facilitator of conversation. For example, the very advantage of the cell phone, namely that people can have it with them wherever they are, also turns out to be one of its major liabilities in terms of being a tool for genuine conversation. This is because people tend to be doing something else while talking. Or, they are with other people or the surroundings such as street noise are an impediment to one or both individuals to the conversation being able to hear one another well. Consequently, the undivided attention that was generally characteristic of conversations between two people using that home fixture and "dinosaur" called the landline is far rarer these days with cell phone calls. To be sure, people can arrange to have a cell phone conversation between them, where each will essentially have one another's undivided attention. Typically, though, this will be because there is a specific issue that needs to be discussed; and that gives us a significant difference between the spontaneity of conversation that is characteristic of friendship. Good friends do not have an agenda for conversing with one another. Rather, they simply delight in one another's company and the conversations that flow from being together, whatever the topic turns out to be. Joshua had no idea that Neil was going to call him.

Now, to be sure, people can be distracted at home too. Still, by comparison to the cell phone, the probability drops considerably that a person called on her or his landline will be distracted. The rather interesting point here is this. There is a profound respect in which the landline at home served to nicely supplement friendship precisely because in general if a person spontaneously called to chat with a friend, it was often possible to do so at some length. By contrast, the cell phone does not supplement friendship to the same degree; and the reason for this is none other than the reality that in spontaneously calling a person's cell phone to chat it is not at all out of the question that, owing to the very mobility that comes with the cell phone, the person reached will be in the midst of doing something else or will be in an environment that is not conducive to a good conversation.

The concluding consideration of the preceding paragraph perhaps points to an explanation for why texting and posting on social networking sites have become the preferred mode of communication between so many young people, as opposed to making cell phone calls. As a purely practical matter, it has become increasingly unreasonable owing to the considerations mentioned above to expect that a rich conversation will ensue with a friend if the person is reached on her or his cell phone. So it actually makes more sense to send the individual a text message or to post a comment on the person's Facebook page, since the message is apt to be read with greater attentiveness (when it gets read) than it would be listened to over the cell phone. Then in addition to the fact that individuals can communicate in this way pretty much whenever it pleases them, they can do so in just about any social context whatsoever: while at a concert or a restaurant; while travelling in a car or on public transportation; while waiting at an office or listening to a lecture; and so on. So it would seem that the disadvantage of the decrease in conversation is more than offset by the considerable increase in communication. If that is the case, then it turns out that texting and postings on social networking sites are comparable to the landline telephone after all in that they wonderfully serve to supplement friendship at best. As we shall see in what follows, the comparison fails mightily.

II The Majestic Mutual Configuration

At the outset, it must be acknowledged that receiving a wonderful note from a loved one or a dear friend is typically something that we treasure. In fact, there is little doubt that receiving such a note is generally better than having those words spoken directly to us. This is because in a reflective manner we can mightily savor the words of the note and recall in various ways the remarkable character of the person who wrote them without having to respond in any way whatsoever; and there is something quite marvelous about that. What is also true, of course, is that notes like that generally are appropriate for only special occasions or defining moments in an individual's life. Such notes are not and cannot be an everyday occurrence. What is more, and this gets to the very heart of the matter, such notes are hardly a substitute for salubrious interaction between the two individuals in question. Quite the contrary, such notes are invariably born of that interaction. So if texting and postings on social networking sites are a supplement to friendship, the support for this view cannot come from the significance that special notes have in the life of individuals. I have made it clear that I do not think that they are a supplement to friendship. I now turn to explain why.

The obvious question that needs to be addressed at this point is: why is spending time together so important to friendship—so important that not even a wealth of communication between individuals via texting or postings on social networking sites can compensate for doing so? The answer is very simple, namely that it is only through directly interacting with another on a regular basis that we can get a genuine sense of the quality of character that a person has and the subtle ways in which it may be changing. For it is then and only then that we actually witness how a person behaves and reacts in real time to countless many things that the person does or that occur to the person or that the person directly witnesses: some to be expected and some not to be expected; some intentional and some not; some gracious and some not; some inappropriate and some not; and so on. We witness not only what the person does but the way in which the person does it. Likewise, we witness not just what the person says to various questions and comments in various circumstances but also the way in which the person says it, where this includes tonality, body language, and character of the delivery. And in this regard, our assessment of an individual's character is refined and reinforced over time, resulting in what we might call a reliable composite picture of the individual's character. Two final points are in order here. One is that with face-to-face conversation it is possible for there to be enormous spontaneity, often occasioned by the surroundings of the moment that allow for friends to respond to one another in affirming ways that neither could possibly have anticipated. The other is that in directly witnessing a companion friend's behavior on a regular basis, it turns out that by our own behavior we thereby reveal to the friend the countless ways in which we take delight in and admire her or his character. Obviously, this goes in both directions. Accordingly, in terms of providing a composite picture, friends give to one another an affirmation regarding the qualities of one another's character that neither can give to herself or himself.

With regard to the above considerations, telephone conversations come in second because in a telephone conversation friends do not get to witness one another's body language. Just so, the vocal communication between good friends is most informative precisely because, as has been indicated above, how a person says something bears mightily upon how we understand what the person says; and obviously that can be determined over the telephone. Consider the wealth of assessments that we often articulate about a friend while talking with that person over the phone rightly based upon the tonality and delivery of the person speaking: "Wow, I really got you going with that remark"; "You seem sad"; "I can hear it in your voice" (be it anger or bitterness or joy or sheer disinterest); "You seem distracted"; "You don't sound like yourself"; "I can tell you are really committed to being there"; and so on. And we so often know that the friend is kidding just by the way the friend says something. So it was with how Neil heard Joshua.

Now, all this talk about friends bearing witness to one another's character would be rather mundane but for the ever so sublime truth that, owing to the trust that good friends have in one another, the observations that they make about one another, directly or indirectly, play a fundamental role in each coming to have enormous self-understanding and self-knowledge. For obvious reasons, there are quite significant limits to what we can learn about ourselves from a brief interaction with a stranger, given that the basic forms of politeness are being followed. To be sure, it is hardly trivial to know that we come across as polite. But if that is all that a person knows about herself or himself, then that person's self-knowledge is very limited indeed. Some of the most profound insights that we can have about ourselves are gained through interactions with close friends and only through such interaction. These insights might include for example our ability to be observant when doing so really counts, the extent to which we are secure regarding an important social issue, our capacity to make substantial and sound inferences on the basis of limited information, our ability to show deep warmth without making a person feel uncomfortable, the extent to which our behavior elicits deep feelings of trust on another's part, and so on. Needless to say, no matter how marvelously perceptive a person was yesterday or no matter how well the person behaved yesterday, or no matter how socially malleable an individual was in just the right ways the days before, the excellences of the past do not render irrelevant being excellent in the present. And this simple truth speaks to what is so fundamentally important about the continual interaction between good friends. Thus, the interaction between good friends is not just a rich snapshot of the past. It is also a very rich and informed snapshot of the continual and evolving present. It is against the backdrop of this truth that we have quite substantial grounds for holding that texting and postings on social networking sites do not at all serve to supplement companion friendship.

Again, recall the exchange between Josh and Neil recounted above that endured all of 12 seconds. It is next to impossible to imagine that exchange being such an affirming experience if it had taken place via texting or postings on a social networking site. For one thing, the timing would be off dramatically; and so often in life the timing makes all the difference in the world. For another, there would not be the wonderful experience of mutual laughter between them that served as a deep, deep affirmation of the depth of the friendship. The following three smiley-face emoticons ☺☺☺ in a text message would of course be understood to indicate humor. Just so, it is clear that they (or a dozen more) would not even come close to standing in for Josh and Neil actually experiencing the rich laughter on the part of both that took place between them—the very laughter that served as a superb indication that the bond between them had been majestically underwritten by that 12-second exchange—an exchange which neither Josh nor Neil could ever have anticipated.

There is simply no denying the extraordinary wonders of technology as a vehicle for communicating information. The mistake lies in losing sight of the truth that in so very many instances what matters enormously to human beings is not just that the right information is communicated to us, but also the way in which we experience that information being communicated to us. Perhaps nothing brings this out more than the way in which loving parents say "I love you" to their infant child or, in general, the way in which a child learns a language. It would never occur to anyone to think that an infant child could learn the moral beauty of those three words by parents postings signs of "I love you" throughout the house, pointing at them, and then saying those three words. Precisely what we know is that a child learns the majestic meaning of those words by experiencing parental love when they are uttered to her or him by the parents. Notice, though, that long after the child has learnt their meaning, experiencing parental love when those words are uttered by the parents never becomes a trivial matter. More generally, it is never inconsequential that a person experiences the warm emotions that individuals have toward her or him when they utter words to her or him that are meant to be affirming. This is because emotional displays of warmth reflect the view that not just the correct words are being used but the reality that the corresponding configuration of sentiments is genuinely in place. This is precisely why a pregnant pause during a set of remarks owing to the depth of emotion can be so very riveting. For a gifted speaker, choosing the right words is often easy enough. Exhibiting the right emotional display, however, is another matter entirely. What clearly follows from these considerations is that putting the practice of texting and postings on social networking sites over a one-on-one conversation results in a seriously diminished form of friendship. Indeed, it is doubtful that such a form of friendship can ever achieve the depth of reinforcement that Aristotle's idea of companion friendship occasions. I shall explain why in what follows.

One of the significant features of companion friends is their uniqueness. While no companion friendship may last forever, every companion friendship marks a defining period in a person's life. Nothing ever seems to render inconsequential the time that was spent together. Not even another companion friend. And part of what is forever savored is none other than the time that was spent together. To be sure, they often did things together such as see a movie or attend a conference or show up at a party. But above all they spent time together talking with one another and reacting in front of each to one thing and then another. By way of those shared moments each magnificently contributed to the life of the other. And in that regard neither is ever replaceable. If texting and posting on social networking sites are privileged over conversation as one of the key ways of interacting between friends, a question that very forcefully presents itself is whether by the very nature of things friends become far more replaceable. The question would surely seem to warrant an affirmative answer, because the emotional affirmation that I have described is no longer being constantly underwritten. After all, a person can text a witty message or post a witty remark and yet be entirely indifferent to an individual; and everyone knows this. No doubt this is part of the explanation for why what matters so much to people nowadays is how many friends they have on Facebook, for sincerity and caring on the part of those responding has *de facto* become irrelevant since there is simply no way to monitor or determine such factors using these forms of communication. But this also means that people have set aside entirely or, in any event, seriously diminished the importance of one of the fundamental aspects of friendship described above, namely that of witnessing the visible emotional display that comes with affirming a person in conversation. Last but hardly least, insofar as communication by way of technology is privileged over face-to-face interaction, then the opportunities for the kind of extraordinarily affirming occasions akin to the moment that took place between Josh and Neil diminish precipitously. Taken all together, these considerations result in a configuration of friendship whereby friends are far more replaceable than they were just a decade or two ago. Or to put the matter a quite different way and more correctly: Aristotle's conception of companion friendship is less often realized. A most poignant indication that perhaps friends are becoming replaceable in some important respect is the common occurrence these days of friends having lunch together spending a considerable amount of time texting rather than talking to one another. Indeed, it sometimes occurs that one will be texting while the other is eating, with the one texting utterly oblivious to the reality that the other person is just sitting there eating.

III Conclusion: Keeping It Real

To state the obvious, long before there was personal communicative technology there have been people who are disingenuous and insincere in their interactions with others. Yet, even these individuals realized that the appearance of being genuine generally served them very well. However, it would seem that recent communicative technology has changed the end game, if you will. So very often nowadays that game appears to be none other than receiving and sending bits of information. And this is in keeping with the reality that so much texting and posting takes place in a context that is the very antithesis of an environment that is conducive to genuine reflection. Or, the person is multitasking, as they say, which means that the texting and posting is hardly the person's number one priority; nor is texting or posting content that is indeed meaningful. Against this backdrop, it may very well seem to make far more sense to have 5000 friends the majority of whom one does not know and one could not even recognize if one's life depended upon it, than it does to have two or three friends with whom the interaction has been so very rich that it has served to redefine one's soul for the better. But, alas, this tells us something so very profound, namely that we have lost sight of one of the most fundamental social goods in life, namely companion friendship. It has become commonplace nowadays for friends who eat together to give at least as much priority to texting as they do to conversing with one another, although there is no urgent reason whatsoever to attend to texting. Offhand, this looks awfully egotistical.

To be sure, there is simply no denying the wonders of communicative personal technology. However, friendship at its best will survive only if human beings do not allow themselves to be so reconfigured by technology that they become indifferent to the deep and majestic affirmation that human beings can give to one another by and only by directly interacting with one another. If technology should get the upper-hand, then we who are human may become increasingly more like zombies than human beings. Any two zombies may send one another a million text messages a day. Each, though, will be ever so replaceable by another zombie. Accordingly, whatever they might be, they will not be and could not possibly be the kind of companion friends so masterfully described by Aristotle more than 2000 years ago.

Review and Discussion Questions

1 What is the importance of face-to-face interaction for developing friendship, according to Thomas? Do you agree with this view?
2 Is there an ideal conception of friendship? What is that? In Aristotle's view, what is companion friendship?
3 What does the exchange between Neil and Joshua reveal about the nature and mode of friendship, according to Thomas?
4 Have you ever written a lengthy handwritten note to a friend? According to Thomas, landline phone conversations and writing personal handwritten notes to someone can supplement and strengthen friendship. But cell phone calls and texting are activities that do not work in the same way. What is Thomas's argument and what is your assessment of that argument?
5 Is there an important difference between communication and conversation?
6 What is your own assessment about whether technology enriches or degrades friendships?

READING: SOCIAL NETWORKING SITES AND OUR LIVES

PEW INTERNET AND AMERICAN LIFE PROJECT[*]

Contrary to arguments that criticize the impact of technology on social life, the Pew Internet and American Life Project conducted a study that found that participation in social networking sites seems to improve rather than diminish

---

[*] Keith N. Hampton and others, "Social Networking Sites and Our Lives," Pew Internet and American Life Project, July 16, 2011.

participation in social life more broadly. This study was carried out by the Pew Research Center, a nonpartisan "fact tank" that provides information on the issues, attitudes, and trends shaping America and the world.

There has been a great deal of speculation about the impact of social networking sites (SNS) on users' lives. Some fear that SNS use might diminish human relationships and contact, perhaps increasing social isolation. Others exult that pervasive connectivity using technology will add to people's stores of social capital and lead to other social payoffs.

We tackle these important issues with the results of what we believe is the first national, representative survey of American adults on their use of SNS and their overall social networks. Some 2,255 American adults were surveyed between October 20–November 28, 2010, including 1,787 internet users. There were 975 users of SNS such as Facebook, MySpace, LinkedIn, and Twitter.[1]

In this report, we recognize that there is a great deal of variation in how people use SNS, in the types of platforms that are available, and the types of people that are attracted to different sites. We pull these variables apart and provide a detailed picture of what SNS users look like, which SNS platforms different people use, and the relationship between uses of technology and the size and structure of people's overall social networks. We also examine the amount of support SNS users receive from their social ties, their ability to consider multiple viewpoints, their levels of social trust, and their community, civic, and political participation, and we compare them with users and non-users of other technologies ....

Questions have been raised about the social impact of widespread use of social networking sites (SNS) like Facebook, LinkedIn, MySpace, and Twitter. Do these technologies isolate people and truncate their relationships? Or are there benefits associated with being connected to others in this way? ....

The findings presented here paint a rich and complex picture of the role that digital technology plays in people's social worlds. Wherever possible, we seek to disentangle whether people's varying social behaviors and attitudes are related to the different ways they use social networking sites, or to other relevant demographic characteristics, such as age, gender and social class.

1 The Number of Those Using Social Networking Sites Has Nearly Doubled since 2008 and the Population of SNS Users Has Gotten Older

In this Pew Internet sample, 79% of American adults said they used the internet and nearly half of adults (47%), or 59% of internet users, say they use at least one of SNS. This is close to double the 26% of adults (34% of internet users) who used a SNS in 2008. Among other things, this means the average age of adult SNS users has shifted from 33 in 2008 to 38 in 2010. Over half of all adult SNS users are now over the age of 35. Some 56% of SNS users now are female.

Facebook dominates the SNS space in this survey: 92% of SNS users are on Facebook; 29% use MySpace, 18% used LinkedIn and 13% use Twitter.

There is considerable variance in the way people use various social networking sites: 52% of Facebook users and 33% of Twitter users engage with the platform daily, while only 7% of MySpace and 6% of LinkedIn users do the same.

On Facebook on an average day:

- 15% of Facebook users update their own status.
- 22% comment on another's post or status.
- 20% comment on another user's photos.
- 26% "Like" another user's content.
- 10% send another user a private message.

2 Facebook Users Are More Trusting than Others

We asked people if they felt "that most people can be trusted." When we used regression analysis to control for demographic factors, we found that the typical internet user is more than twice as likely as others to feel that people can be trusted. Further, we found that Facebook users are even more likely to be trusting. We used regression analysis to control for other factors and found that a Facebook user who uses the site multiple times per day is 43% more likely than other internet users and more than three times as likely as non-internet users to feel that most people can be trusted.

3 Facebook Users Have More Close Relationships

The average American has just over two discussion confidants (2.16)—that is, people with whom they discuss important matters. This is a modest, but significantly larger number than the average of 1.93 core ties reported when we asked this same question in 2008. Controlling for other factors we found that someone who uses Facebook several times per day averages 9% more close, core ties in their overall social network compared with other internet users.

4 Facebook Users Get More Social Support than Other People

We looked at how much total support, emotional support, companionship, and instrumental aid adults receive. On a scale of 100, the average American scored 75/100 on a scale of total support, 75/100 on emotional support (such as receiving advice), 76/100 in companionship (such as having people to spend time with), and 75/100 in instrumental aid (such as having someone to help if they are sick in bed).

Internet users in general score 3 points higher in total support, 6 points higher in companionship, and 4 points higher in instrumental support. A Facebook user who uses the site multiple times per day tends to score an additional 5 points higher in total support, 5 points higher in emotional support, and 5 points higher in companionship, than internet users of similar demographic characteristics. For Facebook users, the additional boost is equivalent to about half the total support that the average American receives as a result of being married or cohabitating with a partner.

5 Facebook Users Are Much More Politically Engaged than Most People

Our survey was conducted over the November 2010 elections. At that time, 10% of Americans reported that they had attended a political rally, 23%

reported that they had tried to convince someone to vote for a specific candidate, and 66% reported that they had or intended to vote. Internet users in general were over twice as likely to attend a political meeting, 78% more likely to try and influence someone's vote, and 53% more likely to have voted or intended to vote. Compared with other internet users, and users of other SNS platforms, a Facebook user who uses the site multiple times per day was an additional two and half times more likely to attend a political rally or meeting, 57% more likely to persuade someone on their vote, and an additional 43% more likely to have said they would vote.

6 Facebook Revives "Dormant" Relationships

In our sample, the average Facebook user has 229 Facebook friends. They reported that their friends list contains:

- 22% people from high school
- 12% extended family
- 10% coworkers
- 9% college friends
- 8% immediate family
- 7% people from voluntary groups
- 2% neighbors

Over 31% of Facebook friends cannot be classified into these categories. However, only 7% of Facebook friends are people users have never met in person, and only 3% are people who have met only one time. The remainder is friends-of-friends and social ties that are not currently active relationships, but "dormant" ties that may, at some point in time, become an important source of information.

7 Social Networking Sites Are Increasingly Used to Keep Up with Close Social Ties

Looking only at those people that SNS users report as their core discussion confidants, 40% of users have friended all of their closest confidants. This is a substantial increase from the 29% of users who reported in our 2008 survey that they had friended all of their core confidants.

8 MySpace Users Are More Likely to Be Open to Opposing Points of View

We measured "perspective taking," or the ability of people to consider multiple points of view. There is no evidence that SNS users, including those who use Facebook, are any more likely than others to cocoon themselves in social networks of like-minded and similar people, as some have feared.

Moreover, regression analysis found that those who use MySpace have significantly higher levels of perspective taking. The average adult scored 64/100 on a scale of perspective taking, using regression analysis to control for demographic factors, a MySpace user who uses the site a half dozen times per month tends to score about 8 points higher on the scale.

Conclusion

The report is the first national survey of how the use of social networking sites (SNS) by adults is related to people's overall social networks. The findings suggest that there is little validity to concerns that people who use SNS experience smaller social networks, less closeness, or are exposed to less diversity. We did find that people who are already likely to have large overall social networks—those with more years of education—gravitate to specific SNS platforms, such as LinkedIn and Twitter. The size of their overall networks is no larger (or smaller) than what we would expect given their existing characteristics and propensities.

However, total network size may not be as important as other factors—such as intimacy. Americans have more close social ties than they did two years ago. And they are less socially isolated. We found that the frequent use of Facebook is associated with having more overall close ties.

In addition, we found that only a small fraction of Facebook friends are people whom users have never met or met only once.

We find many outcomes associated with SNS use that cannot be explained by the demographic characteristics of those who uses these services. Facebook users are more trusting than similar Americans. MySpace users have a greater propensity to take multiple viewpoints. Facebook users have more social support, and they are much more politically engaged compared with Americans of a similar age and education.

The likelihood of an American experiencing a deficit in social support, having less exposure to diverse others, not being able to consider opposing points of view, being untrusting, or otherwise being disengaged from their community and American society generally is unlikely to be a result of how they use technology, especially in comparison to common predictors. A deficit of overall social ties, social support, trust, and community engagement is much more likely to result from traditional factors, such as lower educational attainment.

Note

1 The margin of error on the entire survey is plus or minus 3 percentage points, on the internet users is plus or minus 3 percentage points, and for the SNS users is plus or minus 4 percentage points.

Review and Discussion Questions

1 What is the purpose and main findings of this survey?
2 Do these findings agree or conflict with your perceptions of the impact of social networking sites?
3 What are the connections, if any, between democracy, social networking sites, and the way that we think, drawing from the finding in this survey?
4 Is there any evidence that you can gather that either further supports or undercuts the findings in this survey?
5 In your view, how should we evaluate the ethical implications of social networking sites?

READING: WHY ETHICS MATTERS FOR AUTONOMOUS CARS

PATRICK LIN*

Patrick Lin raises intriguing scenarios and questions about the ethics of self-driving cars. Patrick Lin is Professor of Philosophy and Director of the Ethics + Emerging Sciences Group at the California Polytechnic State University at San Luis Obispo.

If motor vehicles are to be truly autonomous and able to operate responsibly on our roads, they will need to replicate—or do better than—the human decision-making process. But some decisions are more than just a mechanical application of traffic laws and plotting a safe path. They seem to require a sense of ethics, and this is a notoriously difficult capability to reduce into algorithms for a computer to follow.

This chapter will explain why ethics matters for autonomous road vehicles, looking at the most urgent area of their programming ....

A Brief Note about Terminology

I will use "autonomous," "self-driving," "driverless," and "robot" interchangeably. These refer primarily to future vehicles that may have the ability to operate without human intervention for extended periods of time and to perform a broad range of actions. I will also use "cars" to refer loosely to all motor vehicles, from a motorcycle to a freight truck; those distinctions do not matter for the discussion here.

Why Ethics Matters

To start, let me offer a simple scenario that illustrates the need for ethics in autonomous cars. Imagine in some distant future, your autonomous car encounters this terrible choice: it must either swerve left and strike an eight-year-old girl, or swerve right and strike an 80-year-old grandmother [33] [Ed. note: this number corresponds to reference list at end]. Given the car's velocity, either victim would surely be killed on impact. If you do not swerve, both victims will be struck and killed; so there is good reason to think that you ought to swerve one way or another. But what would be the ethically correct decision? If you were programming the self-driving car, how would you instruct it to behave if it ever encountered such a case, as rare as it may be?

Striking the grandmother could be the lesser evil, at least to some eyes. The thinking is that the girl still has her entire life in front of her—a first love, a family of her own, a career, and other adventures and happiness—while the grandmother has already had a full life and her fair share of experiences. Further, the little girl is a moral innocent, more so than just about any adult. We might

---

* Excerpted from "Why Ethics Matters for Autonomous Cars" by Patrick Lin, M. Maurer et al. (Hrsg.), *Autonomes Fahren* (2015), DOI 10.1007/978-3-662-45854-9_4. Reprinted with permission. Some references omitted.

agree that the grandmother has a right to life and as valuable a life as the little girl's; but nevertheless, there are reasons that seem to weigh in favor of saving the little girl over the grandmother, if an accident is unavoidable. Even the grandmother may insist on her own sacrifice, if she were given the chance to choose.

But either choice is ethically incorrect, at least according to the relevant professional codes of ethics. Among its many pledges, the Institute of Electrical and Electronics Engineers (IEEE), for instance, commits itself and its 430,000+ members "to treat fairly all persons and to not engage in acts of discrimination based on race, religion, gender, disability, age, national origin, sexual orientation, gender identity, or gender expression" [23]. Therefore, to treat individuals differently on the basis of their age, when age is not a relevant factor, seems to be exactly the kind of discrimination the IEEE prohibits [18, 33].

Age does not appear to be a relevant factor in our scenario as it might be in, say, casting a young actor to play a child's character in a movie. In that movie scenario, it would be appropriate to reject adult actors for the role. Anyway, a reason to discriminate does not necessarily justify that discrimination, since some reasons may be illegitimate. Even if we point to the disparity of life experiences between the old and the young, that difference isn't automatically an appropriate basis for different treatment.

Discriminating on the basis of age in our crash scenario would seem to be the same evil as discriminating on the basis of race, religion, gender, disability, national origin, and so on, even if we can invent reasons to prefer one such group over another. In Germany—home to many influential automotive companies that are working to develop self-driving technologies—the right to life and human dignity is basic and set forth in the first two articles of the very first chapter in the nation's constitution [9]. So it is difficult to see how German law could even allow a company to create a product that is capable to making such a horrific and apparently illegal choice. The United States similarly strives to offer equal protection to all persons, such as stipulated in the fourteenth amendment of its constitution.

If we cannot ethically choose a path forward, then what ought to be done? One solution is to refuse to make a swerve decision, allowing both victims to be struck; but this seems much worse than having only one victim die, even if we are prejudiced against her. Anyway, we can force a decision by modifying the scenario: assume that 10 or 100 other pedestrians would die, if the car continued forward; and swerving would again result in only a single death.

Another solution could be to arbitrarily and unpredictably choose a path, without prejudice to either person [34]. But this too seems ethically troubling, in that we are choosing between lives without any deliberation at all—to leave it to chance, when there are potentially some reasons to prefer one over the other, as distasteful and uncomfortable as those reasons may be. This is a dilemma that is not easily solvable and therefore points to a need for ethics in developing autonomous cars.

...

Crash-Optimization Means Targeting

There may be reasons, by the way, to prefer choosing to run over the eight-year-old girl that I have not yet mentioned. If the autonomous car were most interested in protecting its own occupants, then it would make sense to choose a collision with the lightest object possible (the girl). If the choice were between two vehicles, then the car should be programmed to prefer striking a lighter vehicle (such as a Mini Cooper or motorcycle) than a heavier one (such as a sports utility vehicle (SUV) or truck) in an adjacent lane [18, 34].

On the other hand, if the car were charged with protecting other drivers and pedestrians over its own occupants—not an unreasonable imperative—then it should be programmed to prefer a collision with the heavier vehicle than the lighter one. If vehicle-to-vehicle (V2V) and vehicle-to-infrastructure (V2I) communications are rolled out (or V2X to refer to both), or if an autonomous car can identify the specific models of other cars on the road, then it seems to make sense to collide with a safer vehicle (such as a Volvo SUV that has a reputation for safety) over a car not known for crash-safety (such as a Ford Pinto that's prone to exploding upon impact).

This strategy may be both legally and ethically better than the previous one of jealously protecting the car's own occupants. It could minimize lawsuits, because any injury to others would be less severe. Also, because the driver is the one who introduced the risk to society—operating an autonomous vehicle on public roads—the driver may be legally obligated, or at least morally obligated, to absorb the brunt of any harm, at least when squared off against pedestrians, bicycles, and perhaps lighter vehicles.

The ethical point here, however, is that no matter which strategy is adopted by an original equipment manufacturer (OEM), i.e., auto manufacturer, programming a car to choose a collision with any particular kind of object over another very much resembles a targeting algorithm [33]. Somewhat related to the military sense of selecting targets, crash-optimization algorithms may involve the deliberate and systematic discrimination of, say, large vehicles or Volvos to collide into. The owners or operators of these targeted vehicles bear this burden through no fault of their own, other than perhaps that they care about safety or need an SUV to transport a large family.

Beyond Harm

The problem is starkly highlighted by the following scenario [15, 16, 17, 34]: Again, imagine that an autonomous car is facing an imminent crash, but it could select one of two targets in adjacent lanes to swerve into: either a motorcyclist who is wearing a helmet, or a motorcyclist who is not. It probably doesn't matter much to the safety of the car itself or its occupants whether the motorcyclist is wearing a helmet; the impact of a helmet into a car window doesn't introduce that much more risk that the autonomous car should want to avoid it over anything else. But it matters a lot to the motorcyclist whether s/he is wearing a helmet: the one without a helmet would probably not survive such a collision. Therefore, in this dreadful scenario, it seems reasonable to program a good autonomous car to swerve into the motorcyclist with the helmet.

But how well is justice and public policy served by this crash-optimization design? Motorcyclists who wear helmets are essentially being penalized and discriminated against for their responsible decision to wear a helmet. This may encourage some motorcyclists to not wear helmets, in order to avoid targeting by autonomous cars. Likewise, in the previous scenario, sales may decline for automotive brands known for safety, such as Volvo and Mercedes Benz, insofar as customers want to avoid being the preferred targets of crash-optimization systems.

Some readers may want to argue that the motorcyclist without a helmet ought to be targeted, for instance, because he has acted recklessly and therefore is more deserving of harm. Even if that's the correct design, notice that we are again moving beyond harm in making crash-optimization decisions. We're still talking about justice and other such ethical considerations, and that's the point: it's not just a numbers game.

Programmers in such scenarios, as rare as they may be, would need to design cost-functions—algorithms that assign and calculate the expected costs of various possible options, selecting the one with the lowest costs—that potentially determine who gets to live and who gets to die. And this is fundamentally an ethics problem, one that demands much more care and transparency in reasoning than seems currently offered. Indeed, it is difficult to imagine a weightier and more profoundly serious decision a programmer would ever have to make. Yet, there is little discussion about this core issue to date.

...

Self-Sacrifice

As we can see, real-world accidents can be very complicated. In philosophy and ethics, a familiar method is to simplify the issues through hypothetical scenarios, otherwise known as "thought-experiments." This is similar to everyday science experiments in which researchers create unusual conditions to isolate and test desired variables, such as sending spiders into outer space to see how microgravity affects their ability to spin webs. It is not a good objection to those experiments to say that no spiders exist naturally in space; that misses the point of the experiment.

Likewise, it is no objection to our hypothetical examples that they are outlandish and unlikely to happen in the real world, such as a car that can distinguish an eight-year-old from an 80-year-old (though with improving biometrics, facial recognition technologies, and linked databases, this doesn't seem impossible). Our thought-experiments are still useful in drawing out certain ethical intuitions and principles we want to test.

With that understanding, we can devise hypothetical scenarios to see that reasonable ethical principles can lead to controversial results in the context of autonomous driving. Digging into a standard philosophical toolbox for help with ethical dilemmas, one of the first principles we might reach for is consequentialism: that the right thing to do is whatever leads to the best results, especially in quantified terms [44]. As it applies here, consequentialism suggests that we should strive to minimize harm and maximize whatever it is that matters, such as, the number of happy lives.

In this thought-experiment, your future autonomous car is driving you on a narrow road, alongside a cliff. No one and no technology could foresee that a school bus with 28 children would appear around the corner, partially in your lane [29, 36]. Your car calculates that crash is imminent; given the velocities and distance, there is no possible action that can avoid harming you. What should your robot car do?

A good, standard-issue consequentialist would want to optimize results, that is, maximize the number of happy lives and minimize harm. Assuming that all lives in this scenario are more or less equally happy—for instance, there's no super-happy or super-depressed person, and no very important person who has unusual influence over the welfare of others—they would each count for about the same in our moral calculation. As you like, we may either ignore or account for the issue of whether there is extra value in the life of an innocent child who has more years of happiness ahead of her than an average adult; that doesn't matter much for this scenario.

The robot car's two main choices seem to be: (1) to slam on the brakes and crash into the bus, risking everyone's lives, or (2) to drive off the cliff, sparing the lives of everyone on the bus. Performing a quick expected-utility calculation, if the odds of death to each person (including the adult bus driver) in the accident averaged more than one in 30, then colliding into the bus would yield the expected result of more than one death, up to all 30 persons. (Let's say the actual odds are one in three, which gives an expected result of 10 deaths.) If driving off a cliff meant certain death, or the odds of one in one, then the expected result of that would be exactly one death (your own) and no more. The right consequentialist decision for the robot car—if all we care about is maximizing lives and minimizing deaths—is apparently to drive off the cliff and sacrifice the driver, since it is better that only one person should die rather than more than one, especially 10 or all 30 persons.

This decision would likely be different if, instead of a school bus, your robot car were about to collide with another passenger car carrying only one person. Given the same average odds of death, one in three, the expected number of deaths in a collision would only be 0.67, while the expected number of deaths in driving off a cliff remains at one. In that case, the right consequentialist decision would be to allow the accident to occur, as long as the average odds of death are less than one in two. If, instead of another vehicle, your car were about to collide with a deer, then the decision to stay on the road, despite an ensuing accident, would be even more obvious insofar as we value a deer's life less than a human life.

Back to the school-bus scenario, programming an autonomous car with a consequentialist framework for ethics would seem to imply your sacrifice. But what is most striking about this case might not even be your death or the moral mathematics: if you were in a manually driven car today, driving off the cliff might still be the most ethical choice you could make, so perhaps you would choose certain death anyway, had you the time to consider the options. However, it is one thing for you to willingly make that decision of sacrifice yourself, and quite another matter for a machine to make that decision without your consent or foreknowledge that self-sacrifice was even a possibility. That is, there is an astonishing lack of transparency and therefore consent in such a grave decision, one of the most important that can be made about one's life—perhaps noble if voluntary, but criminal if not.

Thus, reasonable ethical principles—e.g., aiming to save the greatest number of lives—can be stressed in the context of autonomous driving. An operator of an autonomous vehicle, rightly or not, may very well value his own life over that of everyone else's, even that of 29 others; or he may even explicitly reject consequentialism. Even if consequentialism is the best ethical theory and the car's moral calculations are correct, the problem may not be with the ethics but with a lack of discussion about ethics. Industry, therefore, may do well to have such a discussion and set expectations with the public. Users—and news headlines—may likely be more forgiving if it is explained in advance that self-sacrifice may be a justified feature, not a bug.

...

Conclusions

We don't really know what our robot-car future will look like, but we can already see that much work needs to be done. Part of the problem is our lack of imagination. Technology policy expert Peter W. Singer observed, "We are still at the 'horseless carriage' stage of this technology, describing these technologies as what they are not, rather than wrestling with what they truly are" [43].

As it applies here, robots aren't merely replacing human drivers, just as human drivers in the first automobiles weren't simply replacing horses: that would [be] like mistaking electricity as merely a replacement for candles. The impact of automating transportation will change society in radical ways, and technology seems to be accelerating. As Singer puts it, "Yes, Moore's Law is operative, but so is Murphy's Law" [43]. When technology goes wrong—and it will—thinking in advance about ethical design and policies can help guide us responsibility into the unknown.

In future autonomous cars, crash-avoidance features alone won't be enough. An accident may be unavoidable as a matter of physics [12, 13], especially as autonomous cars make their way onto city streets [19, 21, 25], a more dynamic environment than highways. It also could be too dangerous to slam on the brakes, or not enough time to hand control back to the unaware human driver, assuming there's a human in the vehicle at all. Technology errors, misaligned sensors, malicious actors, bad weather, and bad luck can also contribute to imminent collisions. Therefore, robot cars will also need to have crash-optimization strategies that are thoughtful about ethics.

If ethics is ignored and the robotic car behaves badly, a powerful case could be made that auto manufacturers were negligent in the design of their product, and that opens them up to tremendous legal liability, should such an event happen. Today, we see activists campaigning against "killer" military robots that don't yet exist, partly on the grounds that machines should never be empowered to make life-and-death decisions [31, 35]. It's not outside the realm of possibility to think that the same precautionary backlash won't happen to the autonomous car industry, if industry doesn't appear to be taking ethics seriously.

The larger challenge, though, isn't just about thinking through ethical dilemmas. It's also about setting accurate expectations with users and the general public who might find themselves surprised in bad ways by autonomous cars; and expectations matter for market acceptance and adoption. Whatever answer to an ethical dilemma that industry might lean towards will not be satisfying to everyone. Ethics and expectations are challenges common to all automotive manufacturers and tier-one suppliers who want to play in this emerging field, not just particular companies.

Automated cars promise great benefits and unintended effects that are difficult to predict, and the technology is coming either way. Change is inescapable and not necessarily a bad thing in itself. But major disruptions and new harms should be anticipated and avoided where possible. That is the role of ethics in innovation policy: it can pave the way for a better future while enabling beneficial technologies. Without looking at ethics, we are driving with one eye closed.

References

9. Federal ministry of justice and consumer protection: Basic law for the federal Republic of Germany. www.gesetze-im-internet.de/englisch_gg/englisch_gg.html (2014). Accessed 8 July 2014.
12. Fraichard, T.: Will the driver seat ever be empty? Report funded by Inria. http://hal.inria.fr/hal-00965176 (2014). Accessed 8 July 2014.
13. Fraichard, T., and Asama, H.: Inevitable collision states: A step towards safer robots? *Advanced Robotics* 18 (10), 1001–1024 (2004).
15. Goodall, N.J.: Autonomous car ethics. Interview with CBC radio. www.cbc.ca/spark/blog/2014/04/13/autonomous-car-ethics (2014). Accessed 8 July 2014.
16. Goodall, N.J.: Machine ethics and automated vehicles. In: Meyer, G. and Beiker, S. (eds.) *Road vehicle automation*. Springer, Cham (2014).
17. Goodall, N.J.: Ethical decision making during automated vehicle crashes. Transportation Research Record: *Journal of the Transportation Research Board* (forthcoming).
18. Goodall, N.J.: Vehicle automation and the duty to act. In: *Proceedings of the 21st world congress on intelligent transport systems*, 7–11 September 2014, Detroit, Michigan (forthcoming).
19. Google: The latest chapter for the self-driving car: Mastering city street driving. http://googleblog.blogspot.co.at/2014/04/the-latest-chapter-for-self-driving-car.html (2014). Accessed 8 July 2014.
21. Hern, A.: Self-driving cars face a long and winding road to success. *The Guardian*. www.theguardian.com/technology/2014/may/28/self-driving-cars-google-success (2014). Accessed 8 July 2014.
23. IEEE: IEEE code of ethics. www.ieee.org/about/corporate/governance/p7-8.html (2014). Accessed 8 July 2014.
25. Jaffe, E.: The first look at how Google's self-driving car handles city streets. *The Atlantic/CityLab*. www.citylab.com/tech/2014/04/first-look-how-googles-self-driving-car-handles-city-streets/8977 (2014). Accessed 8 July 2014.
29. Lin, P.: The ethics of saving lives with autonomous cars is far murkier than you think. *Wired*. www.wired.com/2013/07/the-surprising-ethics-of-robot-cars (2013). Accessed 8 July 2014.
31. Lin, P.: Why the drone wars matter for automated cars. Lecture presented at Proceedings in Automated Driving, Stanford Law School, 12 December 2013. http://stanford.io/1jeIQuw. Accessed 8 July 2014.
33. Lin, P.: Ethics and autonomous cars: Why ethics matters, and how to think about it. Lecture presented at Daimler and Benz Foundation's Villa Ladenburg Project, Monterey, California, 21 February 2014.
34. Lin, P.: The robot car of tomorrow might just be programmed to hit you. *Wired*. www.wired.com/2014/05/the-robot-car-of-tomorrow-might-just-be-programmed-to-hit-you (2014). Accessed 8 July 2014.
35. Lin, P., Bekey, G., Abney, K.: Autonomous military robotics: risk, ethics, and design. Report funded by the US Office of Naval Research. California Polytechnic State University, San Luis Obispo. http://ethics.calpoly.edu/ONR_report.pdf (2008). Accessed 8 July 2014.
36. Marcus, G.: Moral machines. *New Yorker*. www.newyorker.com/online/blogs/news-desk/2012/11/google-driverless-car-morality.html (2012). Accessed 8 July 2014.
43. Singer, P.W.: The robotic revolution. *Brookings Institution*. www.brookings.edu/research/opinions/2012/12/11-robotics-military-singer (2012). Accessed 8 July 2014.
44. Sinnott-Armstrong, W.: Consequentialism. *Stanford Encyclopedia of Philosophy*. http://plato.stanford.edu/entries/consequentialism (2011). Accessed 8 July 2014.

Review and Discussion Questions

1 Describe the first scenario between the grandmother and the girl, and the reason why Lin introduces this example.
2 What are the complications introduced by the motorcycle example?
3 How should we think through the school-bus scenario, in your view?
4 In what sense are there solutions to the ethical questions raised by the author?

READING: TECHNOLOGY AND NEW CHALLENGES FOR PRIVACY

LESLIE P. FRANCIS[*]

Leslie P. Francis offers a brief survey of the role and importance of privacy in contemporary debates. This introductory essay is part of a special issue on privacy in the *Journal of Social Philosophy*, for which Francis was the guest editor. Leslie P. Francis is Distinguished Professor of Philosophy and Law and the Alfred C. Emery Endowed Professor of Law at the University of Utah.

Within the scope of the past half-century, privacy has been heralded as a core constitutional value and unequivocally pronounced dead. Privacy—now replaced by liberty—was discerned to lie at the core of a set of constitutional protections and thus to support rights to contraception, abortion, removal of life-sustaining treatment, and other intimate decisions such as whom to marry. But constitutional privacy's hegemony was short-lived in the United States at least: subject initially to criticism as conceptually confused, constitutional privacy dissolved into a panoply of values ranging from physical integrity to the contents of suitcases or telephone records. Outside of the law, the rise of the Internet, search engines, social networking, and "big data" brought unprecedented abilities to collect, mine, analyze, and identify information about individuals. Commentators identified what they called the "privacy paradox" of people professing to value privacy but behaving as though they did not.

What, then, is to be made of this apparent rapid rise and fall of privacy? Perhaps privacy is at best contextually understood and supported, assuming different forms and importance depending on the norms in place in particular circumstances.[1] Even so, perhaps important metaphysical, epistemological, and normative issues remain, albeit assuming differing forms in different contexts.

...

[More recently] privacy itself has largely disappeared from the major journals publishing theoretical work in ethics, political philosophy, or social philosophy. Much of the more theoretical discussion of privacy has instead been left to the legal academy, where it intertwines with issues of legal policy ranging from surveillance to debates over wearing the headscarf or burka.[2] Nonetheless, it seems

---

[*] Excerpted from "Introduction: Technology and New Challenges for Privacy" by Leslie P. Francis, *Journal of Social Philosophy* 45(3) (2014): 291–303. Reprinted by permission of Wiley-Blackwell.

fair to conclude that discussion of the philosophical roots of privacy has remained limited, especially after the development of recent capabilities of information technology and surveillance.

The "Privacy Paradox" and Rejections of Privacy

The "privacy paradox" observes that although people profess to value privacy, they act as though they do not. They share information over the Internet, apparently with abandon. Whether this indicates that people really do not value privacy, have conflicting values (for example, between privacy and access to valuable information that requires disclosure, or between privacy and security), or are simply confused is unclear. Some studies indicate confusion. For example, Norberg, Horne, and Horne[3] provide evidence that people are responsive to environmental cues about risk when they make decisions about disclosure. Hoofnagle and colleagues demonstrate that young adults are seriously misinformed about the protections online privacy policies provide to them.[4]

On the other hand, it seems quite clear that at least some people attribute fairly low value to privacy, at least in comparison with other goods to be achieved. A case in point is the Web site for sharing medical information, PatientsLikeMe.[5] This Web site rests on the premise that sharing information about conditions such as amyotrophic lateral sclerosis will accelerate disease understanding, diagnosis, and treatment. Quite a number of patients have eagerly joined in the enterprise. Whether such efforts to slough off or move beyond privacy represent merely strategic questions about risk trade-offs or implicate deeper metaphysical or normative questions is the subject of this issue.

Privacy and the Self: Metaphysical or Socially Constructed?

Understood metaphysically, the self is seen as having characteristics that make it the type of entity that it is. Selves may be atomistic or relational. For example, the self may be understood atomistically as a self-motivating individual. Or, the self may be understood as necessarily related to other selves, so that it would cease to be a self if no other such entities existed. On such metaphysical understandings, the self may have value because of the type of entity that it is—indeed this value may be intrinsic to beings of this very type. In addition, the self may have certain moral claims because it is a being of this type, having the value that it has: for example, rights to protection against extinction, to maintenance of integrity, or to the ability to make a range of choices concerning the self. On relational views, the value and protections may rest in the relationships—of caring, of familial ties, even of all humanity or of humans to nature—rather than in the individuals seen as entirely separate. Thus, metaphysical understandings of the self may justify privacy: the right to be let alone for the atomistic self, or the right to engage in the relationships that are constitutive of the relational self.

By contrast, accounts of the self as socially constructed eschew assumptions about essential characteristics. Instead, understandings of the self are built in context, as are understandings of related concepts such as identity or personhood. Requisites to sustaining selves are also constructed in contexts, so that privacy protections that are critical in one set of circumstances might be irrelevant in others.

For example, in a society that is characterized by high population density, privacy's role in supporting the self and the forms that privacy may take might be quite different than in a sparsely populated setting where people live far from one another. Helen Nissenbaum's account of privacy in context and Ian Brown's work on surveillance and identity elaborate these themes.[6]

Technological developments, moreover, have potentially altered understandings of the very boundaries of the self. Cognitive prostheses such as smart phones, tablets, or sensing devices are in widespread use. Whether and when such devices can be viewed as extensions of individual agency is a matter of serious discussion in the bioethics, disability, and cognitive science literatures.[7] What they portend for privacy poses an additional set of questions, for example if data entered into them or processing systems are located in the cloud, they may be subject to risks of data mining or manipulation.

Privacy and Knowledge

In the middle of the last century, privacy in the sense of access to another's person or mind played a major role in epistemological theorizing. Wittgenstein's argument that a private language is unintelligible set the stage; work in neuroimaging and cognitive science may restructure it. Whether people generally (at least those who are not autistic or cognitively impaired in relevant ways) understand others in terms of a theory of mind, whether cognition is social, and what functional magnetic resonance imaging or other scanning methods measure or model are all complex subjects of current discussion. Of particular relevance to contemporary privacy debates is whether available scanning methods or those likely to be developed allow access in any sense to the subjective states of others. If so, the extent to which it is even possible for people to keep thoughts and feelings hidden will come under challenge. The possibility of remote monitoring of thoughts—unknown to the thinker—may migrate from the realm of science fiction, if what scanners monitor are thoughts at all. Also of relevance is whether data mined from Web searches and other forms of web presence yield information about preferences, interests, or identities.

Privacy and Normativity: Individuals and Politics

In political philosophy, a primary subject of privacy scholarship has been the division between the public and the private. Since John Stuart Mill's argument in *On Liberty* that it is only when individuals' actions threaten/harm others that society may intervene coercively, delineating and defending this private sphere has been core to liberal theory. One noteworthy area of debate has been the family. Liberal political philosophers such as John Rawls ([*A Theory of Justice* (Cambridge, MA: Harvard University Press, 1971)]) saw family structures as a matter of individual choice rather than social justice. On the other side, feminist theorists such as Eva Kittay elucidated both the lack of support for care relationships and the family as a locus of oppression. Conservatives resisted social restrictions on intrafamilial behavior (such as requirements that children receive health care or education) as well as social practices with the potential to influence the structure of families to come such as marriage equality.

...

No single special issue can hope to do justice to this richness of privacy issues and scholarship in relation to new technological developments. However, the articles in this issue represent efforts to come to grips with a variety of the new privacy challenges posed by contemporary possibilities for information acquisition and surveillance.

Notes

1. Helen Nissenbaum, *Privacy in Context* (Stanford, CA: Stanford University Press, 2010), 3.
2. Anita Allen's work is an example. Anita Allen, *Unpopular Privacy* (New York, NY: Oxford University Press, 2011); Anita Allen, *Uneasy Access: Privacy for Women in a Free Society* (Totowa, NJ: Rowman and Littlefield, 1988), 11–34; Anita Allen, "Privacy," in *The Oxford Handbook of Practical Ethics*, ed. H. LaFollette (Oxford: Oxford University Press, 2003), 485–513.
3. Patricia A. Norberg, Daniel Horne, & David Horne, "The privacy paradox: Personal information disclosure intentions versus behaviors," *Journal of Consumer Affairs* 41, no. 1 (2007): 100–126.
4. Chris Jay Hoofnagle et al., *How Different Are Young Adults from Older Adults When It Comes to Information Privacy Attitudes and Policies?* Retrieved July 3, 2014 from http://ssrn.come/abstract=1589864.
5. PatientsLikeMe, www.patientslikeme.com.
6. Nissenbaum, n.1; Ian Brown, *How Will Surveillance and Privacy Technologies Impact on the Psychological Notions of Identity?* Retrieved July 3, 2014, from http://ssrn.com/abstract=2207331.
7. Erik Parens, "Good and bad forms of medicalization," *Bioethics* 27, no. 1 (2013): 28–35; Carl Elliott, "Enhancement technologies and the modern self," *Journal of Medicine and Philosophy* 36 (2011): 364–374; Jonathan Wolff, "Cognitive disability in a society of equals," *Metaphilosophy* 40 (2009): 402–415; Andrew Clark and David Chalmers, "The extended mind," *Analysis* 58, no. 1 (1998): 7–19.

Review and Discussion Questions

1. What is the "privacy paradox?"
2. What does it mean to claim that the self is "socially constructed"? What does this idea contrast against? How do debates about the nature of the self impact debates about the value of privacy?
3. List what you regard as the most important examples of privacy protection that matter to you. Do you regard it as a right to have those protections?
4. In political philosophy, what is the standard distinction between the "public" sphere and the "private" sphere? Does this distinction matter from a moral point of view? How so?

READING: THE BENEFITS OF BEING WATCHED

ANDREW OBERG[*]

Andrew Oberg argues for the benefits of being watched. He is skeptical about the value of privacy. Andrew Oberg is Associate Professor at the University of Kochi, Japan.

---

[*] Excerpted from "The Benefits of Being Watched" by Andrew Oberg, *Ethical Perspectives* 21(4) (2014): 513–538. Reprinted by permission of the Center for Ethics, KU Leuven.

Introduction—The Hornet's Nest

Edward Snowden kicked up quite a storm when he revealed the extent of US surveillance programmes and data mining, turned out to be not only focused on foreign suspects and persons of interest, but the American public as well, and even included some offices and embassies of European governments, not to mention the German Chancellor's personal phone.[1] The cynical amongst us are no doubt unsurprised, but there has been much hand-wringing about an intrusive government sticking its nose where it ought not to by both the press and the populace (Bromwich 2013; Noonan 2013).

One of the reasons Snowden gave for his actions to the *Guardian*, the newspaper that broke the story of the then secret information Snowden wished to make public, was that he didn't "want to live in a society that does these sorts of things … I do not want to live in a world where everything I do and say is recorded" (BBC 2013d). Snowden has mostly presented himself as a thoughtful and morally concerned person, someone driven to try to help right what he feels to be a tremendous wrong, though he has more recently also claimed to have been a spy who worked undercover for both the NSA and CIA (BBC 2014). There is also some evidence that Snowden's document theft was an act of foreign espionage; a former Obama cabinet official has said that it was either a Chinese, a Russian, or a Sino-Russian joint effort, and of the 1.7 million documents taken only a "handful" were related to US domestic surveillance programmes, with the US's General Martin Dempsey (chairman of the Joint Chiefs of Staff) reporting that "The vast majority of those [stolen documents] were related to our military capabilities, operations, tactics, techniques and procedures" (Epstein 2014). Perhaps due to this interesting human element, the temptation remains to turn the discussion into one of the man himself.[2] Yet such would be a dead end and a distraction from the issue that still deserves a very thorough public debate even now that the initial furore has subsided: how should we react to the idea that our phones' metadata, our emails, our text messages, our instant messages, our social media posts, and perhaps even our public conversations might be captured for potential later analysis? I would like us to consider that such a condition would have a good deal of benefits over and beyond the obvious utility of greater safety and security, and will begin by first examining Google Glass and its potential use as an eavesdropping technology and "sousveillance"—surveillance "from below" or the recording done by a participant tool—a separate issue from that revealed by Snowden, but one which seems to touch many of the same intuitive nerves and can perhaps instruct us on how we tend to regard third party observance. We will then move on to look at government surveillance and reach, at the obligations we have to our government and the question of probability vis-à-vis utility, and at some of the arguments against surveillance before finally considering the potential psychological and social boons of having eyes and ears in the sky. Being watched, or rather, the awareness of the possibility of being watched, could very well contribute to making us better community members, better neighbours, better friends and relatives—in short, better human beings. I do not mean to disparage Snowden with the arguments presented here; I simply wish to disagree with his conclusions.

Eyewear or Spyware?

Some of the more visceral complaints voiced against the techniques that are now widely known to be in use have at times confused eavesdropping, intentional or otherwise, with broader surveillance; the two are easily considered aspects of a single unwanted intrusion, but there are important differences involved and so a brief scrutiny of the former and some of the derivative worries that have been expressed about it will follow before we proceed to the latter in the next section. In short, and for the purposes of this article, eavesdropping can be considered the obtaining of information about another by a third party present with at least one of the other parties involved. On the other hand, surveillance is done at a distance and it is not always clear exactly who the observer is. Consider, then, what it would be like being around someone wearing a pair of the new Google Glass devices; these remarkable accessories are equipped with both video and still camera functions, which can be operated by touch or by spoken command and can also share what is being recorded with a third party. When a wearer is using these tools the device is an excellent example of sousveillance, which is a form of tool-dependent eavesdropping. Say, for example, that you are at a birthday celebration that your cousin cannot attend and so in order to share the experience with him or her you turn on your Google Glass camera and give your cousin, sitting in front of his or her home computer, the benefit of being able to see and hear through your eyes and ears, as it were. Situations like these fit the makers' intentions and are of course entirely innocuous; yet what if you were another celebrant, someone with a strong dislike for the aforementioned cousin, and found yourself speaking with the Google Glass wearer unaware of the fact that you were being recorded and broadcast? What if you found yourself launching into a tirade on all of the wrongs the absent cousin has done you over the years, and how it is such a relief not to have to see him or her at the party?

It is a simple example, and perhaps inane, but concerns of this nature are what tend to be aired in commentaries about eavesdropping technologies (Lanchester 2013), a category that surveillance and data mining exceed, yet one that gives us a toe-hold into our intuitions on being observed and on the perceived crossing of personal boundaries ....

... are there really well-grounded causes for unease? And if not, how should we view our concerns for privacy regarding the deeper data mining done by a programme like Prism in the name of national security? Most of us do not like sticking our feet in our mouths as the absent cousin example demonstrates, but if we find ourselves walking down a street one day and someone wearing a pair of the Google Glass devices looks at us, runs a (hypothetical) facial recognition check, gets our name and latest tweet or Facebook post, how are we likely to react? We will, of course, continue down the street, blissfully unaware of what happened. And what will the Google Glass wearer have gained by it? Information that we have already made public anyway. Moreover, sites like Facebook have security features that filter what is viewable by other users according to the type of connection between them, and so as long as those filters are operating properly (Greenwald et al. 2013)[3] our would-be spy with the fancy specs will be kept in the dark about the month's wages that I just lost at the track and griped about in my latest status update. This is not to say that we should not be concerned about surveillance because we now share our lives in a far more public fashion than we used to, rather it is simply meant to point out that how we understand our privacy and the value we assign to it is a shifting paradigm; before we rush to judgement on this and related issues we need to re-examine our own behaviour and attitudes.

The fact that Facebook has such security features demonstrates that its users are, in general, concerned to varying degrees about protecting their privacy even while wanting to publicly discuss their lives. What is also demonstrated by this and other social media sites, however, is that the anxieties voiced about eavesdropping technologies seem to forget that none of us exist in a "cone of silence" and that a great many are willing to share personal information in very public forums. The ability to instantly inform all of our online contacts about what we are feeling, thinking, or doing at that precise moment has changed how many of us feel about what is and is not worth sharing, and based on the sheer volume of what we are sharing (Tsukayama 2013)[4] the pendulum of judgement seems to have clearly swung to one side. Given our eagerness to embrace social media, the worry over potentially being eavesdropped upon, whether by a new means like that just described or something as simple as a friend's co-worker peeking at their monitor, appears to be a risk nearly every user is willing to take. And if we are willing to risk our communications being viewed by third parties, and if those third parties stand to gain little or nothing of importance, then these technologies may not be the peril that some have taken them to be. There is still the danger here, however, of a programme compiling a profile of us without our knowledge, based on what we have made public now and then, here and there, and which could be used against us by those who dislike or disagree with what we have shared. Such would go beyond eavesdropping into surveillance (with its unseen and unknown observer) and the mere risk of such may be a motivating factor in altering one's public behaviour, and is something that the oversight boards and external courts reviewing surveillance programmes will need to remain vigilant about. Nevertheless, if we have overestimated the perils of eavesdropping and/or sousveillance technologies, then is it not also possible that we have become unduly startled by what Snowden has shown us about existing data mining and surveillance techniques? But perhaps we are being too blasé; the important difference between our social media activities and our other communications lies in the fact that what we share in our posts we have chosen to make public whereas programmes like Prism are collecting data that we have not necessarily chosen to share. What then is the root of our apprehension at an unknown other reading an email that is meant to be private, noting whom we have called when, or seeing what we have searched for online?

Prism-Reflected Paranoia?

Eavesdropping as such is of course not what really bothers Snowden and those who agree with his point of view. Their (often unspoken) concern is with the powers that be, not with someone who simply likes what his new toy can do, even if that new toy appears to be a lot like the toys the authorities have. They worry about the reach of government, that government surveillance will lead to censorship or government control, that programmes like Prism are one small step away from the Stasi kicking down the door and dragging us away for airing our opinion on what a shambles cabinet minister Y has made of policy Z. Trading our freedoms for security, they say, is a cost far too high and a slope far too slippery.

Except that it is neither. When faced with the kinds of surveillance now being conducted we are not trading anything for anything else, certainly not our liberties for security.[5] A framework of individual civil liberties such as those that form the backbone of the legal charters of many modern liberal democracies cannot exist in the absence of security, and even in societies so obsessed with the notion of being able to rely on oneself for defence that they are willing to risk being put in harm's way by letting average citizens walk around with a hidden firearm,[6] the police are still present to check liberties in favour of public safety. After all, very few drivers being pulled over for speeding argue that their civic freedoms are being impinged upon. Drivers who speed have broken the law, and when checking for speeders the police do not only point their radar guns at known offenders, but also at many who are well within the permitted limits. Even if we consider speeding to be a very minor offense, it remains an offense; in a similar fashion those who may have been or may be investigated for suspicious behaviour exposed through data mining techniques performed on the guilty and innocent alike will be scrutinized by legal authorities operating in a legal framework to ascertain whether or not any laws are in fact being broken. The information that is being gathered is for a specific purpose (public security and the prevention of acts meant to maim, murder, or disrupt the economic or social life of a chosen location) and even if the legal oversight of programmes like the ones revealed is not as transparent as we might like (Holland and Mason 2013; *The Economist* 2014)[7] it does still exist ....

.... [One] line of thought is often present in the background or even foreground of those arguing against this level of surveillance, namely that the government has no business collecting data on its citizens or anyone else, that its scope does not or should not extend to matters of private communication, and that by engaging in these activities it is overextending its mission by a large margin. Such criticisms are based in a now bygone era: at a time when any one of us could be a hidden enemy combatant or involved in aiding those who are we must realize that the old rules of liberty no longer pertain. What I fear we have failed to come to grips with is that in an age of easy access to explosive devices (or at least the ingredients and know-how for producing them) and even easier access to extremist dogmas advocating mass murder and destruction, we are all under suspicion by default. Guilty until proven innocent is putting it too strongly, but that does get close to the mark, and it is only by our continued good behaviour that we maintain our innocence.[8] We have long had domestic police forces that also gather information surreptitiously on suspect individuals—here too bound by legal oversight—with the aim of achieving greater public safety[9]; the absence of any overt statement of such notwithstanding all of us now fall into that same category, and we must be considered so in order for the programmes that work for the prevention, and not simply *ex post facto* punishment, of violent acts perpetrated against strangers to properly function.

This does not mean that we should advocate *carte blanche* powers to our intelligence services and the risk of scope creep enlarging the range of data that Prism and its associated programmes take is a real one. Towards this end, oversight conducted by governmental organisations outside the intelligence community will remain vital ....

... programmes like Prism, with its aim of, and evident success in, preventing terrorist attacks (reportedly over 50 as of June 2013 [Chandwani 2013])[10] can be seen as beneficial to society and thus potentially earning our support as willing members of society, especially given that with these types of surveillance we are not in fact trading freedom for security.

... like our speeder who has been caught and pulled over, arguments of liberties being violated or personal rejection of the laws of the land where one lives (i.e. not taking up the general and voluntary moral obligation) do not get much traction as long as the programmes involved remain legal. As Anscombe (1981) points out, one cannot withdraw from being under governance the way one can from a club one has joined. One may choose to fight against the legality of these programmes for any number of reasons, but when seen from the perspective of the community they are meant to assist, the motivation to carry on that fight—particularly when rooted in purely individualist concerns—will likely fall away.

...

... the utility of a data mining programme like Prism appears to be sufficiently high to compensate for the encroachments on our privacy that we have been experiencing, particularly given that the data gathering acts do not inconvenience us in any way, nor indeed are they even noticed.

...

Some readers may be wondering at this point why the approach taken so far has not been based on any normative theory or why a particular theory has not been argued for ...

.... Privacy itself is such a notoriously hard concept to pin down that a definition of it on which most scholars can concur has still not been found ....

.... The pragmatists taught us that what is true is what works (Brandom 2011), and although this may be a tenuous position and is certainly one that can be (and has been) argued at some length, when applied to the messy world of surveillance it seems to be a better guide than a collection of hard and fast rules as long as we also follow Lyon's (2001) suggestion of putting the social and embodied person first and in place of an abstracted notion of the individual. Once established, legal oversight and regular review of a programme will also assist in ensuring that the means are being used for their intended ends and can help guard against scope creep and other potential hazards of overreach such as profiling or political harassment.

Ancillary Perks

There is another side to the considerations that we have been reflecting on, and it involves the practice of observation and how it may relate to increasing ethical behaviour. Buddhist meditation has been gaining in popularity in the Western world for some decades now, and one core principle that is common to the practices of all the major schools of Buddhism is mindfulness: the self-monitoring and checking of one's speech and behaviour (and even thoughts) prior to their expression, with adjustments deemed necessary made and/or determinedly ill-advised actions/words/thoughts avoided. A practice of meditation is thought to help increase concentration and thus aid in one's mindful watching of oneself, with the same relationship between the practices also working in the opposite direction. In a similar way, the theistic religions have traditionally taught that God is watching and that one should keep an eye on one's behaviour so as not to transgress God's will; again, the important point that both practices share is the supervision or attentive observation of oneself by oneself. But what does this have to do with prying eyes reading our private emails and noting whom we have talked to when and for how long? The thought that we might be being watched may be the motivation all of us non-Buddhists need to help us watch ourselves, and this could be in conjunction with a belief in a divine observer or in its absence. Would we still say or do what we are about to if we thought that it would be recorded or made available to unintended audiences, either through mere eavesdropping or through surveillance and analysis? And if not, should we continue with saying or doing it at all? Feeling as if we were in Bentham's Panopticon[11] may be a bit unsettling at first, but establishing a habit of keeping an eye on what we say and do may well lead to a deeper consideration of others and the effects we all have on one another.

Just the opposite, however, has been suggested. Westacott writes (2010) that as surveillance grows, the chances of our consciences withering into little more than a reminder that someone may be watching increases, and that this stands in contrast to the ideal of an independent conscience prompting us to do what is right simply because it is right. While I share Westacott's wish for the ideal as he described it, I cannot help but think that the many complex issues and varied situations we find ourselves involved in on a day-to-day basis call for an approach that may have more immediate practical benefits and is a closer match with the evolutionary programming we are equipped with. Empirical evidence has been found indicating that we are much more likely to help strangers when we feel our reputation is on the line, and security cameras and other surveillance techniques do provide us with that sense (Jaffe 2012).[12] Moreover, psychological studies into morality have concluded that natural selection has made us into creatures who care much more about guarding our reputations and garnering support for ourselves and/or our groups than for seeking out the truth or doing the right thing (Haidt 2012). If we are genetically inclined to be highly concerned with what others think of us—and this certainly does appear to be the case—then our social structures and institutions would do well to incorporate this into their designs, to work with our inherent tendencies to achieve the maximum effects possible given available resources. The best among us will want to assist those in need regardless of who may be watching and without thought for personal safety and potential praise or reward, but for the rest of us anything that results in the reinforcement of positive and socially beneficial behaviour must be seen for the boon that it is. And if the religious traditions are right, then in time all of these good habits will become ingrained and we will become better people at least by not doing what we should not do and hopefully by also doing what we should.

…

… Snowden concluded that he did not want to live in a world where what he says and does is recorded (BBC 2013d); my own view is that there are compelling reasons for thinking that just such a world may be a tiny bit better than the one we have now. Whether that recording is done by as simple a method as someone wearing a Google Glass device or as sophisticated a method as those employed by Prism does not seem to matter; if we really do care as much about how others regard us as the research indicates, and if thinking that we are being observed can get us in turn to keep an eye on our own behaviour, then perhaps surveillance is something we should welcome, or at least accept for the advantages it brings ...

Seeing Clearly

The high degree of privacy that we used to enjoy is largely a thing of the past, and judging from the great deal of (often deeply) personal information that many of us, particularly of younger generations, are willing to share on social networks it does not seem to be much missed. Even if our friend with the new Google eyewear is not recording us on the brink of our rant against his or her cousin, or no one is storing our email for later analysis that bitterly complains about our boss's politics and happens to contain a flag word, what would be lost by our restraint? Very little, while a great deal could be gained. The programmes being used for the purposes of national security are not the menace to freedom that many have said they are, nor are they beyond the scope and mandate of the governments we have chosen in the age in which we live and under the threats that we endure. There are real advantages to eavesdropping and surveillance technologies, advantages of both a physically preserving and ethically enhancing nature. To discard them entirely in favour of a vague notion of greater freedom would be a profound mistake.

I should note in closing that the foregoing is not meant as a general defence of the governments and agencies that are engaged in programmes like Prism (BBC 2013b; Eddy 2013; Smith-Spark and Simons 2013),[13] nor of what is or is not being done by them with the data gleaned; those are issues for other discussions that have already been taken up elsewhere and it is my hope that they will continue. The present argument is simply meant as a defence of the tools in question, of the means and not the ends to which they may or may not be put. To my mind, there are a great many benefits to being watched, and they are also the benefits of watching.

Notes

1. For general details about Mr Snowden, see "Profile: Edward Snowden" (2013d); for information on the office and embassy buggings, see Castle (2013) and "French and German Fury Over Claims US Bugged EU Offices" (2013a); on Chancellor Merkel's personal bugging see "Obama 'Not Told of Merkel Phone Bugging'" (2013c); and for a round-up of the type of position Mr Snowden held and what the NSA can access, see McKelvey (2013).
2. It is interesting in this regard to note that the most viewed of any of the *Guardian* pieces on Snowden and the leaks has been the short personal video made by Greenwald and Poitras in which Mr Snowden introduces himself and his motivations. A number of books are due out soon on the man and his story; on this, along with a review supplemented by analysis and commentary of the first of the new books, see Soar (2014).
3. These filters may not apply evenly to all situations, however, and in the specific case of a government wanting access to information such would likely be forthcoming as Microsoft's collusion with the NSA demonstrates, see Greenwald et al. (2013).

4 On its seventh birthday, for example, Twitter reported that its users now send more than 400 million tweets per day; Tsukayama (2013).
5 See "Surveillance and Its Discontents" (*The Wall Street Journal* 2013) for a well-argued summary of this line of thought.
6 A map of the transport rules of concealed firearms between US states, all of which allow the practice of publicly carrying them given differing requirements first being met, can be found here: www.usacarry.com/concealed_carry_permit_reciprocity_maps.html.
7 As part of the political fallout of the leaks, plans for increased transparency of the programmes involved were earlier put forward (see Holland and Mason 2013), followed by President Obama's proposals for changes outlined in his January 17 speech. The final versions of any revisions will need to be decided by the US Congress; "New Rules for Spooks" (2014).
8 It is tempting to draw a parallel here with the situation that many European societies faced vis-à-vis anarchist and other socio-political movements in the 19th century, but there are many important dissimilarities, not the least of which are the far more inclusive and socially mobile conditions of the modern West. Good arguments could be made in the opposite direction, however, and I leave it to the reader to decide just how close our times are to theirs.
9 Or, some might retort, for the purpose of punishing deeds that the state dislikes; an interesting discussion could ensue on this point, but that would be beyond the scope of our present concerns.
10 The authorities likely have good reasons for not sharing all of the details involved, but a public case made for the surveillance that showed concretely how it is helping is probably necessary at this point and in my opinion really should have been offered earlier.
11 Those unfamiliar with the design in question could see the following for a brief explanation: http://en.wikipedia.org/wiki/Panopticon.
12 The Dutch research team, whose evidence provided the basis for the following report, claimed it had found a way to reverse the so-called "bystander effect". If such findings hold out then the secondary effects of security camera networks and other devices could assist in making cities even safer than initially thought or hoped; Jaffe (2012).
13 The French DGSE and the British GCHQ may also be running similar operations and cooperating with the US's, "French PM Ayrault Says Spy Programme Claims 'Inexact'" (2013b); German intelligence services likewise appear to have been involved with the US programme (see Eddy 2013), and although Germany later cancelled its information sharing agreement with the UK and US the move is considered largely symbolic (on the cancellation, see Smith-Spark and Simons 2013). The UK's GCHQ has also allegedly tapped into fibre optic cables carrying international phone and internet traffic and shared their findings with the NSA in a separate programme called Tempora, see Eddy (2013).

Works Cited

Anscombe, G. E. M. 1981. "On the source of the authority of the state." In *The collected philosophical papers of G. E. M. Anscombe, Vol. III: Ethics, religion and politics*, 130–155. Oxford: Blackwell.
BBC. 2013a. "French and German fury over claims US bugged EU offices." *BBC News: US & Canada*, June 30. www.bbc.co.uk/news/world-us-canada-23120955 [accessed July 2, 2013].
BBC. 2013b. "French PM Ayrault says spy programme claims 'inexact'." *BBC News: Europe*, July 5. www.bbc.co.uk/news/world-europe-23201769. [accessed July 7, 2013].
BBC. 2013c. "Obama 'not told of Merkel phone bugging'." *BBC News: US & Canada*, October 27. www.bbc.co.uk/news/world-us-canada-24698142 [accessed February 26, 2014].
BBC. 2013d. "Profile: Edward Snowden." *BBC News: US & Canada*, July 1. www.bbc.co.uk/news/world-us-canada-22837100 [accessed July 2, 2013].

BBC. 2014. "John Kerry tells fugitive Edward Snowden to 'man up'." *BBC News: US & Canada*, May 29. www.bbc.com/news/world-us-canada-27614001 [accessed August 4, 2014].

Brandom, Robert B. 2011. *Perspectives on pragmatism: Classical, recent, and contemporary.* Cambridge, MA: Harvard University Press.

Brin, David. 1998. *The transparent society.* New York, NY: Perseus.

Bromwich, David. 2013. "Diary." *London Review of Books* 35/13: 34–35.

Castle, Stephen. 2013. "Report of U.S. spying angers European allies." *New York Times*, June 30.

Chandwani, Karuna. 2013. "PRISM helped dodge over 50 terror attacks; NSA chief says exposure may pose threat to US security." *International Business Times: World*, June 19.

Eddy, Melissa. 2013. "For allies, tangled web of shared intelligence." *International Herald Tribune*, July 11.

Editorial. 2013. "Surveillance and its discontents." *The Wall Street Journal*, June 17.

Editorial. 2014. "New rules for spooks." *The Economist*, January 25.

Efrati, Amir and Geoffrey A. Fowler. 2013. "Google glass is watching—Now what?" *The Wall Street Journal*, May 20.

Epstein, Edward Jay. 2014. "Was Snowden's heist a foreign spy operation?" *The Wall Street Journal*, May 12.

Finn, Rachel L. and David Wright. 2012. "Unmanned aircraft systems: Surveillance, ethics and privacy in civil applications." *Computer Law & Security Review* 28: 184–194.

Gellman, Barton, Julie Tate and Ashkan Soltani. 2014. "In NSA-intercepted data, those not targeted far outnumber the foreigners who are: Files provided by Snowden show extent to which ordinary web users are caught in the net." *The Washington Post: National Security*, July 5.

Greenwald, Glenn. 2014. *No place to hide: Edward Snowden, the NSA, and the U.S. surveillance state.* New York, NY: Metropolitan.

Greenwald, Glenn, Ewen MacAskill, Laura Poitras, Spencer Ackerman and Dominic Rushe. 2013. "How Microsoft handed the NSA access to encrypted messages." *Guardian*, July 12.

Haidt, Jonathan. 2012. *The righteous mind: Why good people are divided by politics and religion.* New York, NY: Pantheon.

Holland, Steve and Jeff Mason. 2013. "Obama pledges greater transparency in surveillance programs." *Reuters*, August 9. www.reuters.com/article/2013/08/09/us-usasurveillance-obama-idUSBRE9780UY20130809 [accessed August 27, 2013].

Introna, Lucas D. 2003. "Workplace surveillance 'is' unethical and unfair." *Surveillance & Society* 1/2: 210–216.

Jaffe, Eric. 2012. "Surveillance cameras could make us better people." *The Atlantic Cities: Arts & Lifestyle*, June 25.

Kitcher, Philip. 2011. *The ethical project.* Cambridge, MA: Harvard University Press.

Kloc, Joe. 2014. "Review board says PRISM is 'valuable and effective'." *Newsweek: U.S.*, July 3.

Lanchester, John. 2013. "Short cuts." *London Review of Books* 35/10: 22.

Lyon, David. 2001. "Facing the future: Seeking ethics for everyday surveillance." *Ethics and Information Technology* 3: 171–181.

Macnish, Kevin. 2014. "Just surveillance? Towards a normative theory of surveillance." *Surveillance & Society* 12/1: 142–153.

Marx, Gary T. 1998. "Ethics for the new surveillance." *The Information Society* 14: 171–185.

Marx, Gary T. 2014. "Toward an imperial system of surveillance ethics." *Surveillance & Society* 12/1: 171–174.

McKelvey, Tara. 2013. "Rise of the low-level contractor with high-level access." *BBC News: Magazine*, June 11. www.bbc.co.uk/news/magazine-22849158 [accessed July 2, 2013].

Menichelli, Francesca. 2013. "Review of Larsen's setting the watch: Privacy and the ethics of CCTV surveillance (Studies in Penal Theory and Penal Ethics)." *Surveillance & Society* 11/1&2: 213–214.

Mukasey, Michael B. 2014. "The paranoid style." *The Wall Street Journal*, May 19.

Noonan, Peggy. 2013. "Privacy isn't all the U.S. is losing." *The Wall Street Journal*, June 17.

Oberg, Andrew. 2014a. "Freedom, equality, and the self under a moral obligation." *Journal of Regional Development Studies* 17: 31–54.

Oberg, Andrew. 2014b. "This has got nothing to do with George." *Think* 13/37: 47–55.

Simmons, John A. 2002. "Political obligation and authority." In *The Blackwell guide to social and political philosophy*, ed. Robert L. Simon, 17–37. Oxford: Blackwell.

Smith-Spark, Laura and Stefan Simons. 2013. "Germany ends information sharing pact with Britain, United States." *CNN: Europe*, August 3. edition.cnn.com/2013/08/03/world/europe/germany-uk-privacy [accessed August 29, 2013].

Soar, Daniel. 2014. "Incendiary devices." *London Review of Books* 36/4: 9–10.

Tsukayama, Hayley. 2013. "Twitter turns 7: Users send over 400 million tweets per day." *The Washington Post*, March 21.

Westacott, Emrys. 2010. "Does surveillance make us morally better?" *Philosophy Now* 79: 6–9.

USA Carry. n.d. "Concealed carry permit reciprocity maps." *USA Carry*. www.usacarry.com/concealed_carry_permit_reciprocity_maps.html [accessed July 7, 2013].

Wikipedia. n.d. "Panopticon." *Wikipedia: The Free Encyclopedia*. http://en.wikipedia.org/wiki/Panopticon [accessed July 7, 2013].

Wikipedia. n.d. "Sousveillance." *Wikipedia: The Free Encyclopedia*. http://en.wikipedia.org/wiki/Sousveillance [accessed August 4, 2014].

Review and Discussion Questions

1. Oberg disagrees with one of Snowden's conclusions. Which?
2. What is "sousveillance" and why does he introduce this topic when his ultimate target is the type of surveillance techniques that Snowden uncovered?
3. When a police officer clocks your speed, are your privacy rights violated? If not, then is this a good example, as Oberg thinks, for analyzing why privacy is not such a significant concern?
4. What are the benefits of being watched, according to Oberg? Is his view convincing?

READING: PRIVACY, NEUROSCIENCE, AND NEURO-SURVEILLANCE

ADAM D. MOORE[*]

Adam D. Moore defends an account of privacy and why protecting rights to privacy matters. This article is part of a recent special edition in *Res Publica* on neuroethics and brain privacy, which anticipates technology that will enable people to know others' thoughts and feelings. Adam D. Moore is Professor at the Information School at the University of Washington.

Our beliefs, feelings, and the ticker-tape of words, images, and thoughts that make up our streams of consciousness would seem to be inherently private. Nevertheless, modern neuroscience is offering to open up the sanctity of this domain to outside viewing. We may be able to find out what other people think, covertly and without permission. It may be possible to "extract private information about users' memories, prejudices, religious and political beliefs, as well as about their possible

---

[*] Adapted from "Privacy, Neuroscience, and Neuro-Surveillance" by Adam D. Moore, *Res Publica* 23 (2017): 159–177. Reprinted by permission of Springer Science and Business Media. Some references have been omitted.

neurophysiological disorders" (Bonaci et al. 2014, p. 1). Bonaci et al. even highlight the first example of brain "spyware". In this case, recorded electroencephalography (EEG) information was used to extract private information "such as credit card PIN's, dates of birth and locations of residence" (2014, p. 1; Martinovic et al. 2012). Neuromarketing promises to allow companies to better pitch products and services based on information scanned from reward-related areas of the brain (Haynes 2012).

A quick survey of recent articles related to privacy and neuroimaging include titles such as "Scientists Can't Read Your Mind with Brain Scans Yet", "Neuroscience: The Mind Reader", and "Brain Says Guilty! Neural Imaging May Nab Criminals" (Cyranoski 2012; Lewis 2013; Miller 2014). These alarmist titles indicate more of a direction than a description of the current state of brain scanning. Nevertheless, one might wonder to what extent current brain-imaging technology impacts individual privacy rights to thoughts, feelings, dispositions, or biases.

The technology being used, advanced, and refined is dizzyingly wide ranging and complex. From EEG and magnetoencephalography (MEG) to magnetic resonance imaging (MRI) and functional magnetic resonance imaging (fMRI), along with numerous other neuroimaging techniques, there seems to be an ever-growing list of ways to potentially peer into the thoughts of human beings (Hallinan et al. 2014, p. 58). Beyond neuroimaging, brain–computer interfaces (BCIs) are being developed for both medical and non-medical purposes (Bonaci et al. 2014). Moreover, consider predictive analytics focused on human behavior. Machine learning and big-data analysis, along with complex predictive modeling, may be able to determine what someone is thinking simply by looking at human behavior.

While currently limited, modern neuroscience and other technologies are promising access to the sanctuary of our private thoughts (Bonaci et al. 2014; Chekroud et al. 2014; Farah et al. 2008; Fischbach and Mindes 2011; Gligorov and Krieger 2010; Hart et al. 2000; Richmond et al. 2012). But this is something we have always confronted. From Gutenberg's press to photography, videos, and genome mapping, we seem to be constantly pushing further into the private lives of individuals. Justice Douglas, dissenting in the famous privacy case *Osborn v. United States* (1966) noted:

> The time may come when no one can be sure whether his words are being recorded for use at some future time; when everyone will fear that his most secret thoughts are no longer his own … when the most confidential and intimate conversations are always open to eager, prying ears. When that time comes, privacy, and with it liberty, will be gone.
>
> (385)

Socrates once said that "the unexamined life is not worth living"—but he was talking about self-examination, not the public examination of private areas, thoughts, or beliefs.

One common retort that I often hear is something like, "What's so great about privacy?" Scholars lament that privacy is a fuzzy concept—there is no agreed-upon definition. Others claim that, aside from being difficult to define, privacy is culturally relative and has no inherent moral value (see Lever 2012). I have argued against these sentiments (Moore 2003, 2008, 2010). A coherent, defensible definition of privacy can be offered ....

Establishing a Moral Presumption in Favor of Privacy

There are two distinctions that have been widely discussed related to defining privacy. The first is the distinction between descriptive and normative conceptions of privacy. A descriptive or non-normative account describes a state or condition where privacy obtains. An example would be Parent's definition, "[p]rivacy is the condition of not having undocumented personal knowledge about one possessed by others" (Parent 1983, p. 269). A normative account, on the other hand, makes references to moral obligations or claims. For example when DeCew talks about what is of "legitimate concern of others" she includes ethical considerations (DeCew 1997, p. 60).

One way to clarify this distinction is to think of a case where the term "privacy" is used in a non-normative way such as someone saying, "When I was getting dressed at the doctor's office the other day I had some measure of privacy." Here it seems that the meaning is non-normative—the person is reporting that a condition obtained. Had someone breached this zone the person may have said "You should not be here, please respect my privacy!" In this latter case, normative aspects are stressed.

Reductionist and non-reductionist accounts of privacy have also been offered. Reductionists, such as Judith Jarvis Thomson, argue that privacy is derived from other rights such as life, liberty, and property rights—there is no overarching concept of privacy but rather several distinct core notions that have been lumped together (Thomson 1975). Viewing privacy in this fashion might mean jettisoning the idea altogether and focusing on more fundamental concepts. For example, Frederick Davis has argued that,

> [i]f truly fundamental interests are accorded the protection they deserve, no need to champion a right to privacy arises. Invasion of privacy is, in reality, a complex of more fundamental wrongs. Similarly, the individual's interest in privacy itself, however real, is derivative and a state better vouchsafed by protecting more immediate rights.
>
> (Davis 1959, p. 20)

Unlike Davis, the non-reductionist views privacy as related to, but distinct from, other rights or moral concepts.

It is my view that the normative and non-normative distinction is important and crucial for conceptual coherence—it is possible and proper to define privacy along normative and descriptive dimensions. Liberty is also defined descriptively and normatively. We may, for example, define liberty without making any essential references to normative claims. Thomas Hobbes defines liberty as "the absence of external impediment" (Hobbes 1985, p. 189). In this example, as with Hobbes's conception of the state of nature, there no moral "oughts" or "shoulds" present.

Alternatively, J. S. Mill defends a normatively loaded account of liberty opening his classic work *On Liberty* with "The subject of this essay is ... civil, or social liberty: the nature and limits of the power which can be legitimately exercised by society over the individual" (Mill 1859, p. 1). Privacy may also be defined descriptively or normatively.

...

While privacy has been defined in many ways over the last century, I favor what has been called a "control"-based definition of privacy (see Allen 2003; Gavison 1983; Gross 1971; Parker 1974; Parent 1983; Warren and Brandeis 1890; Westin 1967). A right to privacy is a right to control access to, and uses of, places, bodies, and personal information (Moore 2003, 2008, 2010). For example, suppose that Smith wears a glove because he is ashamed of a scar on his hand. If you were to snatch the glove away, you would not only be violating Smith's right to property, since the glove is his to control, but also his right to privacy—a right to restrict access to information about the scar on his hand. Similarly, if you were to focus your x-ray camera on Smith's hand, take a picture of the scar through the glove, and then publish the photograph widely, you would violate a right to privacy. While your x-ray camera might diminish Smith's ability to control the information in question, it does not undermine his right to control access (Moore 2007).

...

A serviceable definition of "personal information" is provided by the European Union Data Directive. Personal information is

> any information relating to an identified or identifiable natural person ... one who can be identified, directly or indirectly, in particular by reference to an identification number or to one or more factors specific to his physical, physiological, mental, economic, cultural or social identity.
> (Directive 95/46/EC of the European Parliament and of the Council [1995] OJ L 281 0031–0050)

For example, information about a specific individual's sexual orientation, medical condition, height, weight, income, home address, phone number, occupation, and voting history would be considered personal information on this account.

...

Turning now to questions of value, there is evidence that the ability to control access to places, bodies, and personal information is important for human wellbeing ....

Cultural universals have been found in every society that has been systematically studied (see Murdock 1955; Nussbaum 2000). Based on the Human Relations Area Files at Yale University, Alan Westin has argued that there are aspects of privacy found in every society—privacy is a cultural universal (Roberts and Gregor 1971; Westin 1967). While privacy may be a cultural universal necessary for the proper functioning of human beings, its form—the actual rules of association and disengagement—is culturally dependent (see Spiro 1971). The kinds of privacy rules found in different cultures will be dependent on a host of variables including climate, religion, technological advancement, and political arrangements. Nevertheless, I think it is important to note that relativism about the forms of privacy—the rules of coming together and leave-taking—does not undermine my claim regarding the objective need for these rules. There is strong evidence that the ability to regulate access to our bodies, capacities, and powers and to sensitive personal information is an essential part of human flourishing or wellbeing.

.... Privacy also preserves groups by providing rules of engagement and disassociation. Without privacy, or what may be called a dissociation ritual, there could be no stable social relations. As social animals, we seek the company of our fellows, but at some point, interaction becomes bothersome and there is a mutual agreement to separate. Thus, having "good fences" would be necessary for having "good neighbors" (Rachels 1975, p. 331).

...

Growing up can be understood as the building of a series of walls—the walls of privacy. "Both animals and humans require, at critical stages of life, specific amounts of space in order to act out the dialogues that lead to the consummation of most of the important acts of life" (Spitz 1964, p. 752). Infants are without privacy. As infants grow into toddlers and begin to communicate with language, they express wishes for separation at times .... Toddlers and small children begin requesting privacy as they start the process of self-initiated development. More robust patterns of disassociation continue as children enter puberty. Finally, as young adults emerge, the walls of privacy harden, and access points are maintained vigorously.

A recent article presents additional compelling evidence that privacy is essential for flourishing and wellbeing (Newell et al. 2015). Children who are monitored by parental solicitation or with the use of rule sets (you have to be home by 7 p.m., no playing with this or that kid, etc.) have the same rate of problematic behavior as kids who are not monitored at all .... However, where there is two-way communication between parents and children, when all are actively participating, including the voluntary sharing of information, there is an associated drop in the behaviors mentioned above. In a follow-up article, Kerr and Stattin conclude, "[I]t appears that the less effective strategy, and the one that has the potential of backfiring, is to try to prevent adolescents from getting into trouble by rigorously controlling their activities and associations" (2000, p. 378; also see Barnes et al. 1994; Eaton et al. 2009; Hare et al. 2011; Kafka and London 1991). There are obvious and strong connections between flourishing or wellbeing and privacy for adolescents ....

Having said something about what a right to privacy is and why it is valuable, we might ask how privacy rights are justified (Moore 2007, 2010). A promising line of argument combines notions of autonomy and respect for persons. A central and guiding principle of Western liberal democracies is that individuals, within certain limits, may set and pursue their own life goals and projects (Lever 2016). Rights to privacy erect a moral boundary that allows individuals the space to order their lives as they see fit ....

Privacy protects us from the prying eyes and ears of governments, corporations, and neighbors. Within the walls of privacy, we may experiment with new ways of living that may not be accepted by the majority. Privacy, autonomy, and sovereignty, it would seem, come bundled together.

A second but related line of argument rests on the claim that privacy rights stand as a bulwark against governmental oppression and totalitarian regimes. If individuals have rights to control personal information and to limit access to themselves within certain constraints, then the kinds of oppression that we have witnessed in the 20th century would be nearly impossible. Put another way, if oppressive regimes are to consolidate and maintain power, then privacy rights, broadly defined, must be eliminated or severely restricted. If this is correct, privacy rights are a core value that limits the forces of oppression (Allen 2011; DeCew 1997; Moore 2010; Nissenbaum and Brunton 2015; Rössler 2005; Schoeman 1992; Westin 1967).

Arguably, any plausible account of human wellbeing or flourishing will have a strong right to privacy as a component. Controlling who has access to us is an essential part of being a happy and free person. This may be why "peeping Toms" are held up as moral monsters—they cross a boundary that should never be crossed without consent.

Each of us has the right to control our own thoughts, hopes, feelings, and plans, as well as a right to restrict access to information about our lives, family, and friends. I would argue that what grounds these sentiments is a right to privacy—a right to maintain a certain level of control over personal information. While complete control of all our personal information is a pipe dream for many of us, simply because the information is already out there and most likely cannot or will not be destroyed, this does not detract from the view of personal information ownership. Through our daily activities, we each create and leave digital footprints that others may follow and exploit—and that we do these things does not obviously sanction the gathering and subsequent disclosure of such information by others.

Whatever kind of information we are considering, there is a gathering point where individuals have control. For example, when we purchase a new car and fill out the loan application, no one would deny that we each have the right to demand that such information not be sold to other companies. I would argue that this is true for any disclosed personal information, whether it be patient questionnaire information, video-rental records, voting information, or credit applications. To agree with this view, one first has to agree that individuals have the right to control their personal information—i.e. binding agreements about controlling information presuppose that one of the parties has the right to control this information.

If all of this is correct, then we have a fairly compelling case in support of the view that individuals have moral claims to control access to and uses of specific places and things, as well as certain kinds of information—i.e. we have established a presumption in favor of privacy (Allen 2011; DeCew 1997; Moore 2010; Nissenbaum 2009; Rössler 2005; Westin 1967).

… privacy rights are not absolute. There may be times when such boundary crossings are justified. But note where the burden of justification rests. To override individual rights to privacy, the burden of proof rests on those who would cross into private domains. Consider how far away this guideline is from current practice. In almost every area of technological advancement, the question is not "should we monitor, track, hoard, aggregate, and search ever-increasing amounts of data", or "will these advancements violate privacy rights?" The guiding principle seems to be a question of "is", not "ought"—of what is possible, not what we should do or allow. We can do these things, so it seems that, almost unthinkingly, we roll them out and worry about the "ought" and "value" issues later. Modern advances in neuro-surveillance appear to be no different. Can does not imply should. If we start with a presumption of privacy, however, these impulses will be muted. The privacy protecting principles outlined below are offered as guidelines so that we do not continue to make these sorts of mistakes.

...

.... Understandably, it is impossible to foresee all the ways privacy may be implicated with advancements in neuroscience. Likewise, it is impossible to know all the ways neuroscience might develop to enhance, rather than undermine, individual privacy rights. By offering these guidelines, my hope is to avoid making the sorts of ethical mistakes that we have made in the past.

Privacy as Property

While numerous authors have considered the strengths and weaknesses of viewing privacy as a kind of property (see Laudon 1996; Lessig 2002; Samuelson 2000), I think there are advantages to this approach. If the definition of privacy that I have offered is compelling, then the correct way to view privacy is as a kind of property claim. Furthermore, if this definition of privacy is connected to moral value, as I have argued, then we will have good reasons for viewing privacy in this way.

...

Viewing privacy as a kind of property right may lead us to take privacy more seriously. Loaning my property to someone almost always comes with the implied idea that the property will be returned. When I let you borrow my car, I have not also given consent for you to use my car whenever you desire. Or consider my science fiction novel. Suppose that after years of effort and numerous failures, I come up with a wonderfully entertaining science fiction story. After talking with me about the novel, you ask for a copy, and I gladly oblige. A few weeks later, I am surprised to learn that you have sold my novel to a venture capitalist. My surprise becomes alarm when the plot is substantially changed for a holiday-season movie adaptation you have licensed. In response to my bitter complaints, you reply that by allowing the initial access, I waived all future downstream claims to the work in question.

Setting aside the intuitions surrounding copyright or incentives to produce, we may arguably challenge the default position assumed in this case. The presumption, it would seem, should run the other direction. Allowing access does not entail forfeiting all future downstream claims to physical or intellectual property. If privacy is on a par with physical or intellectual property, then the presumption that access yields forfeiture of future claims should be rejected in the case of private information, as well.

...

One worry with this analysis of privacy is that it is overly American and stresses American views and values. I think this worry is unfounded. First, a set of non-relative or culturally-based reasons and arguments have been offered for a specific definition of privacy and for why privacy is morally valuable. If these reasons and arguments are compelling, then they would apply in different contexts.

...

Consent, Notice, and Control

Outside of cases where individuals clearly waive access claims, such as taking a walk on a busy street or posting a brain scan on the Web, we should insist on norms of consent and notice. For example, if researchers are going to scan your brain while you are playing a game using a virtual reality helmet, your explicit consent should be obtained. If the information found in your brain scans is to be used, saved, or transmitted, consent should also be obtained. Moreover, if your brain scans are to be used in some new way or for a new purpose, again, explicit consent should be obtained. None of this would sound the least bit controversial if we were talking about using your room or your science fiction novel. Legally requiring consent and notice affords individuals an appropriate level of control over their personal information.

Consider the narrower case of employee monitoring. As postulated earlier, suppose we could view your brain at work and discover that you are prejudiced against women, susceptible to depression, or lacking in empathy. Your boss might find such information useful, especially for the purposes of limiting company exposure to lawsuits, lost sales, or theft.

Justifying surveillance of employees in light of privacy rights begins with what I call thin consent (see Moore 2000). A first step in justifying a kind of monitoring is employee notification. The consent takes the following form: "If your employment is to continue then you must agree to such-and-so kinds of surveillance ...". This is appropriately called "thin consent" because it assumes that jobs are hard to find and the employee in question needs the job. Nevertheless, quitting remains a viable option. An employee cannot consent, even thinly, to surveillance, even brain surveillance, if it is unknown to her. Given a fairly strong presumption in favor of privacy, thin consent would seem obligatory.

...

Probable Cause

In US Fourth Amendment law, probable cause forms the boundaries of acceptable state intrusion into private affairs. It prevents the state from engaging in "fishing expeditions", and limits state action to situations in which officers have a reasonable basis to believe criminal activity has occurred. If an agent of the government can demonstrate that a target has committed, is committing, or will commit a crime, then an independent authority, such as a judge, can issue a warrant or subpoena (Moore 2011, 2016).

With probable cause, a warrant issued from a judge, and sunlight provisions opening up the warrant and the procedure to public scrutiny, we can be confident that security or public interest concerns may be addressed with minimal impact on individual privacy. The probable-cause requirement puts the burden of proof in the appropriate place; invasions of private domains must be justified. The official seeking the warrant would highlight the values involved, along with the privacy interests at stake. Judicial oversight inserts an outside element into the process, providing a check on the enthusiasm of law enforcement officials.

Obviously, I am staunchly opposed to what is known as the "third party doctrine" in the US. According to this doctrine, by voluntarily giving information to third parties, such as phone companies, Internet providers, or banks, individuals relinquish privacy claims and have no "reasonable expectation of privacy" concerning this information. Worse yet, because there is no expectation of privacy, government agents can access this information without a court order. There is no need to apply for a warrant or show probable cause. Because of the third party doctrine, over the past decade there has been an alarming decrease in applications for warrants and a sharp increase in the use of subpoenas (Slobogin 2005).

Related to brain privacy or neuro-surveillance, both physical and informational, I would argue that warrants should be the standard. If a government agent can provide compelling evidence of criminal activity and that access to a suspect's brain scan records is necessary for a criminal investigation, then a warrant should be issued and a search conducted. Access to these documents on a third party server would be excluded without a warrant. Moreover, if access is allowed because a warrant has been issued, the rule of notice should still be followed. The information target should be notified that his or her brain scan information has been accessed by law enforcement.

Conclusion

In 1761 James Otis (1761) noted the long English tradition of "a man's house is his castle". Likewise, addressing the English Parliament, William Pitt wrote,

> The poorest man may in his cottage bid defiance to all the force of the crown. It may be frail—its roof may shake—the wind may blow through it—the storm may enter, the rain may enter—but the King of England cannot enter—all his force dares not cross the threshold of the ruined tenement.
>
> (1763, p. 52)

I would argue that the strength of these sentiments should be applied to neuro-privacy, as well. Allowing limited access to brain scans for specific purposes is not also a license that allows others unfettered access to, or use of, this information. If crossing into the private domain of a person's house requires robust justification, then it would seem a similar justification should be offered to peer into the human mind.

...

References

Allen, Anita. 2003. *Why privacy isn't everything: Feminist reflections on personal accountability.* Lanham, MD: Rowman and Littlefield.

Allen, Anita. 2011. *Unpopular privacy: What must we hide?* Oxford: Oxford University Press.

Barnes, Grace M., Michael P. Farrell, and Sarbani Banerjee. 1994. Family influences on alcohol abuse and other problem behaviors among black and white adolescents in a general population sample. *Journal of Research on Adolescence* 4: 183–201.

Bonaci, Tamara, Ryan Calo, and Howard Jay Chizeck. 2014. App stores for the brain: Privacy & security in brain–computer interfaces. In *2014 IEEE International Symposium on Ethics in Science, Technology and Engineering*, 1–7, 23–24.

Chekroud, Adam M., Jim A. C. Everett, Holly Bridge, and Miles Hewstone. 2014. A review of neuroimaging studies of race-related prejudice: Does amygdala response reflect threat?

Frontiers in Human Neuroscience. 8. http://journal.frontiersin.org/article/10.3389/fnhum.2014.00179/full#B60.

Cyranoski, David. 2012. Neuroscience: The mind reader. www.nature.com/news/neuroscience-the-mind-reader-1.10816.

Davis, Frederick. 1959. What do we mean by 'Right to privacy'? *South Dakota Law Review* 4: 1–24.

DeCew, Judith W. 1997. *In pursuit of privacy: Law, ethics, and the rise of technology.* Ithaca, NY: Cornell University Press.

Douglas, William O. 1966. *Osborn v. United States,* 385 U.S. 323.

Eaton, Nicholas, Robert F. Kruger, Wendy Johnson, Matt McGue, and William G. Iacono. 2009. Parental monitoring, personality, and delinquency: Further support for a reconceptualization of monitoring. *Journal of Research in Personality* 43: 49–59.

Farah, Martha J., Elizabeth M. Smith, Cyrena Gawuga, Dennis Lindsell, and Dean Foster. 2008. Brain imaging and brain privacy: A realistic concern? *Journal of Cognitive Neuroscience* 21(1).

Fischbach, Ruth and Janet Mindes. 2011. Why neuroethicists are needed. In *The Oxford handbook of neuroethics,* eds. Judy Illes, and Barbara J. Sahakian. Oxford: Oxford University Press.

Gavison, Ruth. 1983. Information control: Availability and control. In *Public and private in social life,* eds. S. Benn, and G. Gaus, 113–134. New York, NY: St. Martin's Press.

Gligorov, Nada and Stephen C. Krieger. 2010. Functional neuroimaging, free will, and privacy. In *Healthcare and the effect of technology: developments, challenges and advancements,* ed. Stéfane M. Kabene. Hershey, PA: Medical Information Science Reference.

Gross, Hyman. 1971. Privacy and autonomy. In *Privacy,* eds. John W. Chapman and J. Roland Pennock, 169–181. New York, NY: Atherton Press.

Hallinan, Dara, Michael Friedewald, Philip Schütz, and Paul de Hert. 2014. Neurodata and neuroprivacy: Data protection outdated? *Surveillance and Society* 12(1): 55–72.

Hare, Amanda L., Emily G. Marston, and Joseph P. Allen. 2011. Maternal acceptance and adolescents' emotional communication: A longitudinal study. *Journal of Youth and Adolescence* 40: 744–751.

Hart, Allen J., Paul J. Whalen, Lisa M. Shin, Sean C. McInerney, Hakan Fischer, and L. Scott. 2000. Differential response in the human amygdala to racial outgroup vs ingroup face stimuli. *NeuroReport* 11: 2351–2355.

Haynes, John-Dylan. 2012. Brain reading. In *I know what you're thinking: Brain imaging and mental privacy,* eds. Sarah Richmond, Geraint Rees, and Sarah J. L. Edwards. Oxford: Oxford University Press.

Hobbes, Thomas. 1985. *Leviathan:* 1651. In Penguin classics, ed. C. B. MacPhereson.

Kafka, Randy and Perry London. 1991. Communication in relationships and adolescent substance use: The influence of parents and friends. *Adolescence* 26: 587–598.

Kerr, Margaret and Hakan Stattin. 2000. What parents know, how they know it, and several forms of adolescent adjustment: Further support for a reinterpretation of monitoring. *Journal of Developmental Psychology.* 36: 366–380.

Laudon, Kenneth. 1996. Markets and privacy. *Communications of the ACM* 39: 93–104.

Lessig, Lawrence. 2002. Privacy as property. *Social Research* 69: 247–269.

Lever, Annabelle. 2012. Neuroscience v. privacy? A democratic perspective. In *I know what you're thinking: Brain imaging and mental privacy,* eds. S. Richmond, G. Rees, and S. J. L. Edwards. Oxford: Oxford University Press.

Lever, Annabelle. 2016. Democracy, privacy, and security. In *Privacy, security, and accountability,* ed. Adam D. Moore. Lanham, MD: Rowman and Littlefield International.

Lewis, Tanya. 2013. Brain says guilty! Neural imaging may nab criminals. www.livescience.com/37091-brain-imaging-in-the-courtroom.html.

Martinovic, Ivan, Doug Davies, Mario Frank, Daniele Perito, Tomas Ros, and Dawn Song. 2012. On the feasibility of side-channel attacks with brain–computer interfaces. In *Proceedings of the 21st USENIX conference on security symposium.* Berkeley, CA: USENIX Association.

Mill, John Stuart, 1859. *On liberty.* London: Longman, Roberts & Green.

Miller, Greg. 2014. Scientists can't read your mind with brain scans (yet). www.wired.com/2014/04/brain-scan-mind-reading.
Moore, Adam D. 2000. Employee monitoring and computer technology: Evaluative surveillance v. privacy. *Business Ethics Quarterly* 10(3): 697–709.
Moore, Adam D. 2003. Privacy: Its meaning and value. *American Philosophical Quarterly* 40: 215–227.
Moore, Adam D. 2007. Toward informational privacy rights. *San Diego Law Review* 44: 809–845.
Moore, Adam D. 2008. Defining privacy. *Journal of Social Philosophy* 39: 411–428.
Moore, Adam D. 2010. *Privacy rights: Moral and legal foundations.* University Park, PA: Penn State University Press.
Moore, Adam D. 2011. Privacy, security, and government surveillance: Wikileaks and the new accountability. *Public Affairs Quarterly.* 25.
Moore, Adam D. 2016. *Waiving privacy rights: Responsibility, paternalism, and liberty.* Forthcoming, Brookings Institute Press. https://papers.ssrn.com/sol3/papers.cfm?abstract_id=2673717.
Murdock, George P. 1955. The universals of culture. In *Readings in world anthropology*, eds. E. Adamson Hoebel, Jesse D. Jennings, and Elmer R. Smith. New York, NY: McGraw-Hill.
Newell, Bryce, Cheryl Metoyer, and Adam D. Moore. 2015. Privacy in the family. In *The social dimensions of privacy*, eds. Beate Roessler and Dorota Mokrosinska. Cambridge: Cambridge University Press.
Nissenbaum, Helen. 2009. *Privacy in context: Technology, policy, and the integrity of social life.* Stanford, CA: Stanford University Press.
Nissenbaum, Helen and Finn Brunton. 2015. *Obfuscation: A user's guide for privacy and protest.* Cambridge, MA: MIT Press.
Nussbaum, Martha C. 2000. *Woman and human development: The capabilities approach.* Cambridge: Cambridge University Press.
Otis, James. 1761. In *Opposition to writs of assistance. Delivered before the Superior Court.* Boston, MA.
Parent, W. A. 1983. Privacy, morality, and the law. *Philosophy and Public Affairs* 12: 269–288.
Parker, Richard B. 1974. A definition of privacy. *Rutgers Law Review* 27: 275–296.
Pitt, William (the elder, Earl of Chatham). 1763. Speech in the House of Lords. In *Historical sketches of statesmen who flourished in the time of George III*, vol. 1, by Henry Peter Brougham. London and Glasgow: R. Griffin and Co., 1839.
Rachels, James. 1975. Why privacy is important. *Philosophy and Public Affairs* 4: 323–333.
Richmond, Sara, Geraint Rees, and Sarah J. L. Edwards. 2012. *I know what you're thinking: Brain imaging and mental privacy.* Oxford: Oxford University Press.
Roberts, John M. and Thomas Gregor. 1971. Privacy: A cultural view. In *Privacy*, eds. J. Roland Pennock and John W. Chapman, 199–225. New York, NY: Atherton Press.
Rössler, B. 2005. *The value of privacy* (trans. by Rupert, D. V.). Glasgow and Cambridge, UK: Polity.
Ruback, R. Barry and Timothy S. Carr. 1984. Crowding in a woman's prison. *Journal of Applied Social Psychology* 14: 57–68.
Samuelson, Pamela. 2000. Privacy as intellectual property? *Stanford Law Review.* 52: 1125–1173.
Schoeman, Ferdinand David. 1992. *Privacy and social freedom.* New York, NY: Cambridge University Press.
Slobogin, Christopher. 2005. Subpoenas and privacy. *DePaul Law Review* 54: 805.
Spiro, Herbert J. 1971. Privacy in comparative perspective. In *Privacy*, eds. J. Roland Pennock and John W. Chapman, 121–148. New York, NY: Atherton Press.
Spitz, Rene A. 1964. The derailment of dialogue. *Journal of the American Psychoanalytic Association* 12: 752–775.
Thomson, Judith Jarvis. 1975. The right to privacy. *Philosophy and Public Affairs* 4: 295–314.
Warren, Samuel D. and Louis Brandeis. 1890. The right to privacy. *The Harvard Law Review* 4: 193–220.
Westin, Alan. 1967. *Privacy and freedom.* New York, NY: Atheneum.

Review and Discussion Questions

1. What is the distinction between a descriptive and normative definition of privacy?
2. What is Moore's control-based definition of privacy?
3. Why does privacy matter to people, according to Moore?
4. If Moore is correct about why privacy matters to people, does that fact justify a right to privacy? What additional justifications does he offer?
5. What are some examples that support the idea that privacy is a type of property right? Are there any examples that challenge this connection between privacy and property?
6. What are some examples where consent and notice matter for protecting privacy?
7. What is the concept of "probable cause" and how is that relevant for privacy debates, according to Moore?

Essay and Paper Topics for Chapter 12

1. To what extent does technology have the potential to transform our thinking? In what ways? For better or worse? How do you justify your answer?
2. The Pew study and Thomas's reflections about personal technology seem to directly conflict with each other. Which point of view has the greater insight? Explain.
3. What activities are most important for cultivating the best of friendships? To what extent is the widespread use of current technologies facilitating or impeding the development of these types of friendships?
4. What is the most challenging moral issue for autonomous vehicles and how should that issue be addressed prior to their widespread use?
5. Why does privacy matter? Do current uses of technology violate important conditions for privacy?

Part IV

Political, Social, and Economic Relationships

Chapter 13

The Ideal State

What would the ideal government look like? While the ideals of respecting rights and freedom and of promoting democracy are uncontroversial in the abstract, outside that calm center swirl many disagreements. These differences run deep, to the ultimate justification of government, the limits on its power, the rights of individuals, and the purposes of democratic procedures. Is the ideal state best understood as based on a social contract among free and equal persons, as Locke and other social contract theorists argue, or is the ultimate justification of governmental powers that they enable people to have happy lives? What are the limits on governmental power, including majority rule, that should be respected? The readings in this chapter constitute some of the most important works on those subjects.

READING: THE SECOND TREATISE OF GOVERNMENT

JOHN LOCKE[*]

Born in 1632, John Locke was an important figure in both British and American politics; indeed, there are few, if any, philosophers who were more influential in the development of American political institutions and beliefs than John Locke. Locke's father was a politically influential lawyer who supported Oliver Cromwell and the British Parliament against King Charles I. John Locke was sent to Oxford at fifteen, where he became friendly with noted chemist Robert Boyle as well as other scientists, all of whom exerted an important influence on young John. After graduation, Locke worked as a tutor in Greek. Then, after serving a period as a diplomat, he returned to Oxford to study medicine. Locke was active throughout his life in political and public affairs. At one point, he was forced into exile by the king, but he returned to England after the Glorious Revolution in 1688. He died in 1704 at the age of seventy-two. Locke's influence is evident, among other places, in the U.S. Declaration of Independence. In his *First Treatise of Government*, Locke attacks the divine right of kings; in the *Second Treatise*, from which the following selection is taken, he addresses the legitimate role of government and the limits on governmental power. Locke begins by imagining persons in a state of nature in which each is independently

---

[*] From *The Second Treatise of Government: An Essay Concerning the Origin, Extent and End of Civil Government* (1690).

pursuing his or her own interests. In that situation, he argues, people possess natural moral rights to life, property, and liberty, rights that are not to be transgressed by others. Given the realities of such a state of nature, it is in the interests of people to move toward cooperation and trade and to establish common institutions to provide protection of life and property. Governmental action is severely limited, however, by people's natural rights—a topic to which he devotes considerable attention. Locke also considers the related and important question of how a previously unowned resource may justly become the property of one person.

Of the State of Nature

To understand political power aright, and derive it from its original, we must consider what state all men are naturally in, and that is a state of perfect freedom to order their actions and dispose of their possessions and persons as they think fit, within the bounds of the law of nature, without asking leave, or depending upon the will of any other man.

A state also of equality, wherein all the power and jurisdiction is reciprocal, no one having more than another; there being nothing more evident than that creatures of the same species and rank, promiscuously born to all the same advantages of nature, and the use of the same faculties, should also be equal one amongst another without subordination or subjection, unless the Lord and Master of them all should by any manifest declaration of His will set one above another, and confer on him by an evident and clear appointment an undoubted right to domination and sovereignty.

But though this be a state of liberty, yet it is not a state of license; though man in that state have an uncontrollable liberty to dispose of his person or possessions, yet he has not liberty to destroy himself, or so much as any creature in his possession, but where some nobler use than its bare preservation calls for it. The state of nature has a law of nature to govern it, which obliges everyone; and reason, which is that law, teaches all mankind who will but consult it, that, being all equal and independent, no one ought to harm another in his life, health, liberty, or possessions. For men being all the workmanship of one omnipotent and infinitely wise Maker—all the servants of one sovereign Master, sent into the world by His order, and about His business—they are His property, whose workmanship they are, made to last during His, not one another's pleasure; and being furnished with like faculties, sharing all in one community of nature, there cannot be supposed any such subordination among us, that may authorize us to destroy one another, as if we were made for one another's uses, as the inferior ranks of creatures are for ours. Everyone, as he is bound to preserve himself, and not to quit his station willfully, so, by the like reason, when his own preservation comes not in competition, ought he, as much as he can, to preserve the rest of mankind, and not, unless it be to do justice on an offender, take away or impair the life, or what tends to the preservation of the life, the liberty, health, limb, or goods of another.

And that all men may be restrained from invading others' rights, and from doing hurt to one another, and the law of nature be observed, which willeth the peace and preservation of all mankind, the execution of the law of nature is in that state put into every man's hand, whereby everyone has a right to punish the transgressors of that law to such a degree as may hinder its violation. For the law of nature would, as all other laws that concern men in this world, be in vain if there were nobody that, in the state of nature, had a power to execute that law, and thereby preserve the innocent and restrain offenders. And if anyone in the state of nature may punish another for any evil he has done, everyone may do so. For in that state of perfect equality, where naturally there is no superiority or jurisdiction of one over another, what any may do in prosecution of that law, everyone must needs have a right to do.

And thus in the state of nature one man comes by a power over another; but yet no absolute or arbitrary power, to use a criminal, when he has got him in his hands, according to the passionate heats or boundless extravagance of his own will; but only to retribute to him so far as calm reason and conscience dictate what is proportionate to his transgression, which is so much as may serve for reparation and restraint. For these two are the only reasons why one man may lawfully do harm to another, which is that we call punishment. In transgressing the law of nature, the offender declares himself to live by another rule than that of common reason and equity, which is that measure God has set to the actions of men, for their mutual security; and so he becomes dangerous to mankind, the tie which is to secure them from injury and violence being slighted and broken by him. Which, being a trespass against the whole species, and the peace and safety of it, provided for by the law of nature, every man upon this score, by the right he hath to preserve mankind in general, may restrain, or, where it is necessary, destroy things noxious to them, and so may bring such evil on anyone who hath transgressed that law, as may make him repent the doing of it, and thereby deter him, and by his example others, from doing the like mischief. And in this case, and upon this ground, every man hath a right to punish the offender, and be executioner of the law of nature ....

Besides the crime which consists in violating the law, and varying from the right rule of reason, whereby a man so far becomes degenerate, and declares himself to quit the principles of human nature, and to be a noxious creature, there is commonly injury done, and some person or other, some other man receives damage by his transgression, in which case he who hath received any damage, has, besides the right of punishment common to him with other men, a particular right to seek reparation from him that has done it. And any other person who finds it just, may also join with him that is injured, and assist him in recovering from the offender so much as may make satisfaction for the harm he has suffered.

.... The magistrate, who by being magistrate hath the common right of punishing put into his hands, can often, where the public good demands not the execution of the law, remit the punishment of criminal offenses by his own authority, but yet cannot remit the satisfaction due to any private man for the damage he has received. That he who has suffered the damage has a right to demand in his own name, and he alone can remit. The damnified person has this power of appropriating to himself the goods or service of the offender, by right of self-preservation, as every man has a power to punish the crime, to prevent its being committed again, by the right he has of preserving all mankind, and doing all reasonable things he can in order to that end. And thus it is that every man in the state of nature has a power to kill a murderer, both to deter others from doing the like injury, which no reparation can compensate, by the example of the punishment that attends it from everybody, and also to secure men from the attempts of a criminal who having renounced reason, the common rule and measure God hath given to mankind, hath by the unjust violence and slaughter he hath committed upon one, declared war against all mankind, and therefore may be destroyed as a lion or a tiger, one of those wild savage beasts with whom men can have no society nor security ....

To this strange doctrine—viz, that in the state of nature everyone has the executive power of the law of nature—I doubt not but it will be objected that it is unreasonable for men to be judges in their own cases, that self-love will make men partial to themselves and their friends. And on the other side, that ill-nature, passion, and revenge will carry them too far in punishing others; and hence nothing but confusion and disorder will follow; and that therefore God hath certainly appointed government to restrain the partiality and violence of men. I easily grant that civil government is the proper remedy for the inconveniences of the state of nature, which must certainly be great where men may be judges in their own case, since 'tis easy to be imagined that he who was so unjust as to do his brother an injury, will scarce be so just as to condemn himself for it. But I shall desire those who make this objection, to remember that absolute monarchs are but men, and if government is to be the remedy of those evils which necessarily follow from men's being judges in their own cases, and the state of nature is therefore not to be endured, I desire to know what kind of government that is, and how much better it is than the state of nature, where one man commanding a multitude, has the liberty to be judge in his own case, and may do to all his subjects whatever he pleases, without the least question or control of those who execute his pleasure; and in whatsoever he doth, whether led by reason, mistake, or passion, must be submitted to, which men in the state of nature are not bound to do one to another? And if he that judges, judges amiss in his own or any other case, he is answerable for it to the rest of mankind.

'Tis often asked as a mighty objection, Where are, or ever were there, any men in such a state of nature? To which it may suffice as an answer at present: that since all princes and rulers of independent governments all through the world are in a state of nature, 'tis plain the world never was, nor ever will be, without numbers of men in that state. I have named all governors of independent communities, whether they are or are not in league with others. For 'tis not every compact that puts an end to the state of nature between men, but only this one of agreeing together mutually to enter into one community, and make one body politic; other promises and compacts men may make one with another, and yet still be in the state of nature. The promises and bargains for truck, etc., between the two men in Soldania, in or between a Swiss and an Indian, in the woods of America, are binding to them, though they are perfectly in a state of nature in reference to one another. For truth and keeping of faith belong to men as men, and not as members of society ....

Of Property

Whether we consider natural reason, which tells us that men being once born have a right to their preservation, and consequently to meat and drink and such other things as nature affords for their subsistence; or revelation, which gives us an account of those grants God made of the world to Adam, and to Noah and his sons, 'tis very clear that God, as King David says, Psalm cxv. 16, "has given the earth to the children of men," given it to mankind in common. But this being supposed, it seems to some a very great difficulty how anyone should ever come to have a property in anything. I will not content myself to answer that if it be difficult to make out property upon a supposition that God gave the world to Adam and his posterity in common, it is impossible that any man but one universal monarch should have any property upon a supposition that God gave the world to Adam and his heirs in succession, exclusive of all the rest of his posterity. But I shall endeavor to show how men might come to have a property in several parts of that which God gave to mankind in common, and that without any express compact of all the commoners.

God, who hath given the world to men in common, hath also given them reason to make use of it to the best advantage of life and convenience. The earth and all that is therein is given to men for the support and comfort of their being. And though all the fruits it naturally produces, and beasts it feeds, belong to mankind in common, as they are produced by the spontaneous hand of nature; and nobody has originally a private dominion exclusive of the rest of mankind in any of them as they are thus in their natural state; yet being given for the use of men, there must of necessity be a means to appropriate them some way or other before they can be of any use or at all beneficial to any particular man. The fruit or venison which nourishes the wild Indian, who knows no enclosure, and is still a tenant in common, must be his, and so his, i.e., a part of him, that another can no longer have any right to it, before it can do any good for the support of his life.

Though the earth and all inferior creatures be common to all men, yet every man has a property in his own person; this nobody has any right to but himself. The labor of his body and the work of his hands we may say are properly his. Whatsoever, then, he removes out of the state that nature hath provided and left it in, he hath mixed his labor with, and joined to it something that is his own, and thereby makes it his property. It being by him removed from the common state nature placed it in, it hath by this labor something annexed to it that excludes the common right of other men. For this labor being the unquestionable property of the laborer, no man but he can have a right to what that is once joined to, at least where there is enough, and as good left in common for others.

He that is nourished by the acorns he picked up under an oak, or the apples he gathered from the trees in the wood, has certainly appropriated them to himself. Nobody can deny but the nourishment is his. I ask, then, When did they begin to be his—when he digested, or when he ate, or when he boiled, or when he brought them home, or when he picked them up? And 'tis plain if the first gathering made them not his, nothing else could. That labor put a distinction between them and common; that added something to them more than nature, the common mother of all, had done, and so they became his private right. And will anyone say he had no right to those acorns or apples he thus appropriated, because he had not the consent of all mankind to make them his? Was it a robbery thus to assume to himself what belonged to all in common? If such a consent as that was necessary, man had starved, notwithstanding the plenty God had given him. We see in commons which remain so by compact that 'tis the taking any part of what is common and removing it out of the state nature leaves it in, which begins the property; without which the common is of no use. And the taking of this or that part does not depend on the express consent of all the commoners. Thus the grass my horse has bit, the turfs my servant has cut, and the ore I have dug in any place where I have a right to them in common with others, become my property without the assignation or consent of anybody. The labor that was mine removing them out of that common state they were in, hath fixed my property in them ....

It will perhaps be objected to this, that if gathering the acorns, or other fruits of the earth, etc., makes a right to them, then anyone may engross as much as he will. To which I answer, Not so. The same law of nature that does by this means give us property, does also bound that property too. "God has given us all things richly" (1 Tim. vi. 17), is the voice of reason confirmed by inspiration. But how far has He given it to us? To enjoy. As much as anyone can make use of to any advantage of life before it spoils, so much he may by his labor fix a property in; whatever is beyond this, is more than his share, and belongs to others. Nothing was made by God for man to spoil or destroy. And thus considering the plenty of natural provisions there was a long time in the world, and the few spenders, and to how small a part of that provision the industry of one man could extend itself, and engross it to the prejudice of others—especially keeping within the bounds, set by reason, of what might serve for his use—there could be then little room for quarrels or contentions about property so established ....

Of the Beginning and Ends of Political Societies

Men being, as has been said, by nature all free, equal, and independent, no one can be put out of this estate, and subjected to the political power of another, without his own consent, which is done by agreeing with other men to join and unite into a community for their comfortable, safe, and peaceable living one amongst another, in a secure enjoyment of their properties, and a greater security against any that are not of it. This any number of men may do, because it injures not the freedom of the rest; they are left as they were in the liberty of the state of nature. When any number of men have so consented to make one community or government, they are thereby presently incorporated, and make one body politic, wherein the majority have a right to act and conclude the rest.

For when any number of men have, by the consent of every individual, made a community, they have thereby made that community one body, with a power to act as one body, which is only by the will and determination of the majority. For that which acts any community, being only the consent of the individuals of it, and it being one body must move one way, it is necessary the body should move that way whither the greater force carries it, which is the consent of the majority; or else it is impossible it should act or continue one body, one community, which the consent of every individual that united into it agreed that it should; and so everyone is bound by that consent to be concluded by the majority. And therefore we see that in assemblies empowered to act by positive laws, where no number is set by that positive law which empowers them, the act of the majority passes for the act of the whole, and of course determines, as having by the law of nature and reason the power of the whole.

And thus every man, by consenting with others to make one body politic under one government, puts himself under an obligation to every one of that society, to submit to the determination of the majority, and to be concluded by it; or else this original compact, whereby he with others incorporates into one society, would signify nothing, and be no compact, if he be left free and under no other ties than he was in before in the state of nature. For what appearance would there be of any compact? What new engagement if he were no farther tied by any decrees of the society, than he himself thought fit, and did actually consent to? This would be still as great a liberty as he himself had before his compact, or anyone else in the state of nature hath, who may submit himself and consent to any acts of it if he thinks fit ....

Universal consent is next to impossible ever to be had. ... [So] where the majority cannot conclude the rest, there they cannot act as one body, and consequently will be immediately dissolved again.

Whosoever therefore out of a state of nature unite into a community must be understood to give up all the power necessary to the ends for which they unite into society, to the majority of the community, unless they expressly agreed in any number greater than the majority. And this is done by barely agreeing to unite into one political society, which is all the compact that is, or needs be, between the individuals that enter into or make up a commonwealth ....

Every man being, as has been shown, naturally free, and nothing being able to put him into subjection to any earthly power but only his own consent, it is to be considered what shall be understood to be sufficient declaration of a man's consent to make him subject to the laws of any government. There is a common distinction of an express and a tacit consent, which will concern our present case. Nobody doubts but an express consent of any man entering into any society makes him a perfect member of that society, a subject of that government. The difficulty is, what ought to be looked upon as a tacit consent, and how far it binds i.e., how far anyone shall be looked on to have consented, and thereby submitted to any government, where he has made no expressions of it at all. And to this I say that every man that hath any possession or enjoyment of any part of the dominions of any government doth thereby give his tacit consent, and is as far forth obliged to obedience to the laws of that government during such enjoyment as anyone under it; whether this his possession be of land to him and his heirs for ever, or a lodging only for a week; or whether it be barely traveling freely on the highway; and in effect it reaches as far as the very being of anyone within the territories of that government ....

If man in the state of nature be so free, as has been said; if he be absolute lord of his own person and possessions, equal to the greatest and subject to nobody, why will he part with his freedom? Why will he give up this empire and subject himself to the dominion and control of any other power? To which it is obvious to answer that ... in the state of nature there are many things wanting.

First, there wants an established, settled, known law, received and allowed by common consent to be the standard of right and wrong, and the common measure to decide all controversies between them; for though the law of nature be plain and intelligible to all rational creatures, yet men being biased by their interest, as well as ignorant for want of study of it, are not apt to allow of it as a law binding to them in the application of it to their particular cases.

Secondly, in the state of nature there wants a known and indifferent judge with authority to determine all differences according to the established law; for everyone in that state being both judge and executioner of the law of nature, men being partial to themselves, passion and revenge is very apt to carry them too far and with too much heat in their own cases, as well as negligence and unconcernedness to make them too remiss in other men's.

Thirdly, in the state of nature there often wants power to back and support the sentence when right and to give it due execution. They who by any injustice offended will seldom fail where they are able by force to make good their injustice; such resistance many times makes the punishment dangerous and frequently destructive to those who attempt it.

Thus mankind, notwithstanding all the privileges of the state of nature, being but in an ill condition while they remain in it, are quickly driven into society. ... It is this that makes them so willingly give up every one his single power of punishing, to be exercised by such alone as shall be appointed to it amongst them and by such rules as the community, or those authorized by them to that purpose, shall agree on. And in this we have the original right and rise of both the legislative and executive power, as well as of the governments and societies themselves ....

To understand this the better, it is fit to consider that every man when he at first incorporates himself into any commonwealth, he, by his uniting himself thereunto, annexed also, and submits to the community those possessions which he has or shall acquire that do not already belong to any other government; for it would be a direct contradiction for anyone to enter into society with others for the securing and regulating of property, and yet to suppose his land, whose property is to be regulated by the laws of the society, should be exempt from the jurisdiction of that government to which he himself, and the property of the land, is a subject ....

But since the government has a direct jurisdiction only over the land, and reaches the possessor of it (before he has actually incorporated himself in the society), only as he dwells upon, and enjoys that: the obligation anyone is under, by virtue of such enjoyment, to submit to the government, begins and ends with the enjoyment; so that whenever the owner, who has given nothing but such a tacit consent to the government, will by donation, sale, or otherwise, quit the said possession, he is at liberty to go and incorporate himself into any other commonwealth, or to agree with others to begin a new one ... in any part of the world they can find free and unpossessed ....

The reason why men enter into society is the preservation of their property; and the end why they choose and authorize a legislative is that there may be laws made, and rules set, as guards and fences to the properties of all the members of the society to limit the power and moderate the dominion of every part and member of the society. For since it can never be supposed to be the will of the society that the legislative should have a power to destroy that which everyone designs secure by entering into society, and for which the people submitted themselves to legislators of their own making, whenever the legislators endeavor to take away and destroy the property of the people, or to reduce them to slavery under arbitrary power, they put themselves into a state of war with the people, who are thereupon absolved from any further obedience, and are left to the common refuge which God hath provided for all men against force and violence. Whensoever, therefore, the legislative shall transgress this fundamental rule of society, and either by ambition, fear, folly, or corruption, endeavor to grasp themselves or put into the hands of any other an absolute power over the lives, liberties, and estates of the people, by this breach of trust they forfeit the power the people had put into their hands, for quite contrary ends, and it devolves to the people, who have a right to resume their original liberty, and by the establishment of the new legislative (such as they shall think fit) provide for their own safety and security, which is the end for which they are in society.

Review and Discussion Questions

1 Describe the state of nature as Locke envisions it. In what sense(s) is every person an equal there?
2 How does Locke view nature and humankind's relationship to it?
3 Why are people motivated to leave the state of nature?
4 What justifies or makes legitimate a government? When may citizens revolt, according to Locke?
5 What justifies somebody's taking an unowned resource for his or her own use? What provisos or limitations does Locke place on the acquisition of unowned resources?
6 What would be the danger of not having a single court and police system rather than many? Could such danger or risk justify *forcing* people to pay to support the system? Explain.

READING: LIBERTARIAN JUSTICE

TIBOR R. MACHAN[*]

In this essay, Tibor R. Machan discusses and defends the libertarian theory of justice. After outlining the central tenets of libertarianism, he goes on to discuss the ethical basis of the theory. Libertarianism depends, he argues, on a view of the nature of human beings and of the value of human lives. Machan also addresses some of the most important criticisms of libertarianism, the legitimate role of a libertarian government, and why libertarianism is universal rather than culturally relative. Tibor R. Machan is Emeritus Professor in the Department of Philosophy at Auburn University.

The Nature of Justice

By libertarian justice one would have in mind the account of justice advanced in libertarian political theory. Since what justice is has been and remains in serious, often deep-seated dispute, there are widely different conceptions of it emanating from different schools of political thought, each aiming to be the true or right one. Libertarianism proposes one, as do socialism, fascism, welfare-statism, and so forth.

As to which conception of justice is right or what justice really is, there is a great deal to be said on how that might be determined. In this discussion I shall not be aiming to find a fixed, final, perfect ideal of justice, along lines suggested in some of Plato's dialogues. Nor am I convinced that some consensus is what is wanted, nor that no determination is possible. Instead, it seems to me that a conception that arises from justified and thus most reasonable propositions in various branches of human inquiry, starting with metaphysics and including psychology, economics, and ethics, will constitute the right idea of what justice is. Why

---

[*] Tibor R. Machan, "Libertarian Justice," in James P. Sterba (ed.), *Social and Political Philosophy: Contemporary Perspectives* (London: Routledge, 2001), pp. 93–114. Copyright © 2001 by Tibor R. Machan. Reprinted by permission of the author.

this should be so is a story that is too long to tell here, even though a great deal depends on it.

To do justice is to treat something appropriate to its nature or as it deserves or ought to be treated. Only certain kinds of beings can be said to deserve or be owed justice. (There is no problem about doing justice to a rock or the moon, although some environmentalists argue that the issue does arise *vis-à-vis* trees, and even mountains.)

When we want to learn what it is to do justice to human beings, we must first learn what is due them. That, in turn, depends on what kind of beings they are.

As an analogous case in point, when defenders of animal rights lay out their reasons for why animals have rights, they tell us about the nature of animals. They focus on what kind of beings they are, on what in their nature warrants our ascribing to them and respecting their rights. Justice for the animals consists of treating them in accordance with standards derived from a consideration of their nature.

Libertarian Justice

Libertarians take it that justice consists in establishing and maintaining a political system in which the respect and protection of the right to life, liberty, and property of the human individual are of primary legal significance. They maintain that human beings are essentially creative, inventive, and choosing beings. To be human is then, primarily, to take the initiative via one's thinking mind, which then issues in intentions, deliberations, wants, omissions, and so forth, for all of which one can be responsible.

In particular, the thinking mind of a human being is not a passive, reflexive or reactive but an active faculty. Individual human beings are distinguished by virtue of their capacity to activate their conceptual form of awareness, their thinking, so as to learn how to live and flourish.[1]

We, then, regard and treat human beings appropriately by acknowledging that they do such thinking. We do them *justice* if we don't thwart their rational capacity for creativity, inventiveness, and initiative.

Justice as Liberty

Justice as liberty, in contrast to justice as fairness, order, harmony or welfare, rests on the above view. Human beings are in possession of free will, and need to guide their own lives to excellence or flourishing. The decisive issue about justice, as a guiding principle of a community, has to be human nature.

Before turning to human nature, I wish to spell out the most basic tenets of libertarianism. If these tenets are wrong, then so is libertarianism.

1 Adult human beings (and children derivatively and with proper adjustments) are sovereign over their lives, actions and belongings. They have the rights to life, liberty and property.
2 They have the responsibility in their communities to acknowledge and act in terms of this fact (namely 1 above) *vis-à-vis* all others.

3 They ought to develop institutions that assure the protection of their sovereignty, delegating the required powers to agents (governments, private defense agencies, legal authorities or some such special group) for this purpose.
4 Such delegation of powers must itself occur without the violation of sovereignty or individual rights.
5 The agencies to which the power of protecting rights is delegated must exercise this power for the sole purpose of protecting these rights.
6 All concerns apart from the protection of individual rights must be acted on by members of communities without the violation of those rights.

As with all normative theories, libertarianism has several versions, even though the above tenets are not very complicated. Most libertarian political theorists would not find serious objections against them although their exact terminology may differ.

Libertarianism and Individual Sovereignty

Libertarians uphold the sovereignty of each adult individual in social life. They hold that persons ought to be self-governing and ought not to be ruled by others without their consent.

Libertarians distinguish themselves in the political arena in most Western countries from both the left and the right, both of which enlist government for the purpose of regimenting certain aspects of the individual's life, thus conflicting with the libertarian concern with individual sovereignty or self-rule. This is because, on the one hand, the left is concerned with arranging community life so as to protect the materially worst off from the best off, taking the interests of the two to be in unavoidable conflict. So they regiment economic life and thus undermine the sovereignty with which libertarians are concerned. The right does the same when it comes to their spiritual or mental life, since it sees those elements of human community life as having primary importance. The libertarian, in contrast, sees justification for only those laws that aim at protecting everyone's sovereignty.

Since, however, body and soul aren't ever sharply divided, both the left's and right's administration of justice involves regulating both people's spiritual and their economic activities (e.g. when advertisers are regulated in what they may say in their commercials, and when Sunday blue laws prohibit commerce in liquor, respectively).[2]

So, in the particular areas of their philosophical focus, the left and right both want government to wield powers far beyond what is consistent with libertarianism.

Protecting Rights: the Highest Public Good

The libertarian sees the just function of the legal system and authorities as, first and foremost, to protect individual rights. In this respect the libertarian is more loyal to the (original) vision of the American republic than are republicans, democrats, socialists, conservatives, liberals, communitarians, as well as Islamic, Christian, Hindu or other religious fundamentalists with powerful political agendas. These all seek to impose ways of private conduct, often claiming that there does not even exist a sphere of legitimate privacy in human life.

Libertarians believe that they flesh out the US Declaration of Independence more accurately, consistently and completely than do all others. Why? Because if we really do have the right to our lives, for example, then we may, and even ought to, establish a legal system that protects us against all efforts on the part of either criminals, foreign aggressors or the legal authorities themselves to force us to live our lives in any way other than how we choose to. No official paternalistic intervention, even for the sake of improving some aspect of our lives, is tolerable—be it bans on drug abuse and smoking in private places, or regulation of employment. Adults are off-limits as far as regimenting their lives, actions and goals is concerned. That is what having an *unalienable right* to life, liberty and the pursuit of happiness comes to, nothing less. A proper legal order has as its primary goal to protect these rights.

Cases in Point

Consider the particularly controversial libertarian position that no one has the authority to prevent a sovereign adult citizen from committing or seeking assisted suicide, unless it is demonstrably evident that one is deranged. Or consider the view that adults may not be prohibited from using harmful, debilitating drugs, even ones that may be addictive for someone. Or again that risky activities such as mountain climbing, race car driving, sexual promiscuity, and so forth, should not be prohibited.

In all these cases the libertarian holds the position that adults have the basic right to make the choice to pursue the course they want to pursue, provided they are not "dumping" the damaging results on other persons by violating their rights.

Putting it plainly, libertarians hold that one's right to life implies the final, unqualified authority to decide what happens to one's life. So that if, for example, someone who can assist with suicide is freely, voluntarily invited to help, prohibiting it is wrong and ought to be unlawful.

The right to life, according to libertarianism, means that the individual agent, not other people, should be the one who makes decisions about his or her life, including whether to delegate to someone else who is willing the authority to help with ending it, whether to ruin it with drugs, and so forth.

Rights are principles identified in the field of political theory that spell out "borders" around us, or an individual's sphere of personal authority. This so that the sovereignty of the individual as a moral agent is acknowledged and can be protected in the midst of social life wherein others can choose to encroach upon it. In order to cross those borders, those inside must provide those outside with permission, an action that can then be evaluated as right or wrong for the agent to have carried out.

So if there are basic individual rights then they may not be violated. To have the authority to make someone act as one would want, that person's permission is required. The simplest example is sexual intercourse. Only if someone consents to such interaction may the intercourse commence. But even less drastic instances apply: no public authority may forcibly make one person provide services for another, however vital these services may be. And if the service consists of supplying the person with resources wanted or needed, those too must be obtained with the permission of the owner. Since what is owned, even in great abundance, can be what a person creates or produces, to hold that others in dire need own these resources is to believe that others are due involuntary servitude and even own the agent's life and efforts which create the resources. (We will see shortly that rarely there may be justification for someone to expropriate someone else's resources, though this would not justify claiming that they have a right to them.)

Rights and Sovereignty

A way to appreciate this issue of individual rights is to focus on the right to private property, as we normally understand it. Rights identify borders for all persons or citizens within which actions may be taken free of others' interference, regardless of the moral quality of those actions. Those actions need not be equal in their moral quality, yet none may stop or regulate them against the agent's will.

In the case of universal private property rights, the borders around one's actions are most clearly apprehensible because they often consist of actions *vis-à-vis* objects with clear physical limits. If it is your car, you have the authority to use it, provided no third parties are unavoidably affected. Norman Malcolm tells the following illustrative story about Wittgenstein which makes the above point quite clear:

> When in very good spirits he would jest in a delightful manner. This took the form of deliberately absurd or extravagant remarks uttered in a tone, and with the mien, of affected seriousness. On one walk he "gave" me each tree that we passed, with the reservation that I was not to cut it down or do anything to it, or prevent the previous owners from doing anything to it: with those reservations they were henceforth *mine*.[3]

Ownership without the authority to decide to what use the owned item will be put is meaningless, absurd.

Similarly, if it is your life, somebody who wants to do something to it must gain your permission—as when you authorize a physician to perform a risky operation or a cabby to drive you to the airport. On the other hand if, for example, you don't want to go into the ring with a world champion boxer who wants to fight you, that, too, is properly up to you, not somebody else. If you want to smoke, drink, take drugs, climb mountains or go skiing, provided no one's rights are violated by such actions, you need no one's permission.

What, then, is so fundamental about libertarianism is that it proposes that individuals are the ones who are sovereign over themselves and their belongings, not the legal authorities and not even the majority of the people.

Sovereignty in the present context is that condition under which somebody has the fundamental right to governance and others must ask permission before they intrude on the sphere being governed. Personal or individual sovereignty, which is what is at issue here, concerns self-governance.

Accordingly, in cases wherein some are being governed by others—for example, legal adjudication or a medical procedure—the consent of those who are to be governed is necessary before the government by others than oneself can commence. That is because the lives of those whose governance is at issue are their own, not someone else's—the family's, society's, nation's, race's, ethnic group's, gender's or humanity's—even if one misgoverns oneself, even if one wastes one's life away.

People may offer others advice, write editorials directed at them, send them letters, try to talk with them—in short, they may approach others in peaceful ways. But they have no authority to take over the governance of another's life. Arguably, this is the very idea of civilized life, one catering to persons as citizens and not as subjects.

Libertarianism versus Democracy

Even arguments for democracy—meaning for the rule of many, indeed, the bulk of the people—do not void this individual sovereignty. Why should they? After all, the majority is composed of individuals, and if alone they aren't authorized to intrude on your life, together they aren't either.

Democracy is a method, mainly, of selecting administrators of various, including governmental, tasks. Confined in line with sound moral principles, it may be deployed for the limited purpose of selecting administrators of a legal order that respects and protects individual rights in ways that do not violate those rights. Or it is a method which can be used to reach decisions on a great many issues, provided all those affected have agreed to its use, as in the Rotary or Lions Club.

One must authorize—delegate authority to—legal administrators to do certain things. Only then do they acquire proper authority—as opposed to mere power—to do them. If the authority was not given, then the officials lack it and must stay out of one's life (educational, commercial, scientific, religious, or anything else) as well as one's actions—that is what having the right to liberty means.

I am free in the political sense if I can take various actions without interference from other people. (There are other senses of "freedom" but they are not relevant here.) If I want to pursue a life of productivity, creativity, art, science or education, I may embark on those pursuits and no one may prohibit me from doing so. If one requires the cooperation of others for success with these pursuits, their consent is morally necessary. And if one chooses not to embark upon such pursuits but, instead, chooses to be idle, lazy, imprudent, neglectful toward oneself and one's best interests, including making contributions to one's fellow human beings in need, this, though often morally reprehensible, is also something one has a right to do. No one is to be placed into involuntary servitude to others or even to oneself. Voluntary association is morally and politically essential to free men and women.

The Risks of Liberty

An oft repeated reason for rejecting the libertarian position is that when one is wrong in what one chooses to do, then one has no right to act freely. This is why some kinds of forcible interference, including and especially by government, is thought to be justified. So that, for example, if one chooses to pursue a life of laziness, drug addiction or debauchery, then this may be forcibly prevented.

In answer to this, the libertarian claims that we must accept the risk that goes with being free, including in the marketplace. Yes, some professionals, for example, will not pursue excellence but merely cater to whatever consumers demand. With the authority to run one's life, including one's profession, goes the risk that one may mismanage these.

.... They all need to *choose to* do what is right, not be made to behave correctly, for example, by dint of government regimentation. That is how the libertarian system accords with nature, that is, with the moral—i.e. choice making—nature of the citizens of a country.

Just because no guarantee exists that people will use their liberty so as to do the right thing, it does not follow that none will do it or that making them do it is a valid substitute. And it is unjustifiably cynical to think that those in a free market would not freely choose to pursue excellence while attempting to prepare their wares and services for purchase in the market. The market is viewed as much too demand driven by the likes of Speamann. In fact, however, more often it is because of the desire for excellence that the market provides one with what is desirable. The mutual pursuit of excellence by producer and consumer is more likely what markets amount to, instead of the mutual pursuit of sheer and meager satisfaction.

There are other risks of the protection of individual rights to liberty that have been held to be intolerable by some critics of libertarianism. James P. Sterba has argued in many fora that the risk posed to the innocent poor or helpless who cannot find help in society based on voluntary contributions is morally and ought to be legally intolerable. It asks of these individuals to accept something that is unreasonable to ask anyone to accept, namely, to respect the private property of the very rich even while they are threatened with devastation.[4]

Sterba says that because of this unacceptable situation, the innocent poor or helpless have a right to welfare, namely, to portions of the wealth of those who have enough for themselves not to miss it.

Yet Sterba's case is not a good one because there is no justification for even a good person to deprive another from what belongs to another merely because he may need sustenance. No one has a right to my second kidney, even though I may not need it, or my second eye, even though I could see well enough without it. If indeed I own my wealth, there is no justification for another to take it from me, even if I have plenty or am not making good use of it (as indeed many do with their talents or other assets) ....

[Not] helping others is not doing violence to them because even if one were not alive, those others would be in need. One then cannot be said to have caused the neediness and thus has no obligation to repair it.

Under certain circumstances, however, it would be unreasonable to demand of a desperately needy innocent person that he respect everyone's property rights. Such an emergency can make it reasonable for that person to steal. Yet that would remain stealing, only forgivable or excusable stealing.

To change the legal system in light of this fact falls under the well-known edict that hard cases make bad law. The idea is that when extraordinary circumstances are met with extraordinary choices—for example, cannibalism in the Donner Party or murder in an overloaded lifeboat—the evaluation of that behavior ought not to be generalized to similar behavior in normal circumstances. Indeed, the legal systems of many societies respond to such cases with the instrument of judicial discretion. (Courts sometimes convict rare cases of cannibalism performed under extreme duress, only to later pardon the convict.)

Moreover, there are systemic ways for the innocent poor or helpless to obtain support without the violation of any individual's right to private property. They may not be guarantees, but then neither could welfare from state sources be guaranteed, either in a democracy or any other system. Michael Otsuka has argued that wealth might be obtained for the innocent poor or helpless from punishment of rich criminals.[5] And earlier he maintained that such help could be obtained from resources not owned by anyone.[6]

So not only would it be wrong to adjust a just human community to help the innocent poor or helpless by instituting systematic breaches of private property rights, but it would be unnecessary in order to help such persons.[7] ...

No one may forcibly make another behave the right way—for example, to be generous, charitable, kind, or helpful. It matters not that these are indeed the ways one ought at times to act—for example, generously, charitably, kindly. The primary goal of the ethical life is self-perfection, self-development as a good human being, and so coercively to bring about the generous or helpful behavior of the rich or anyone else is morally and ought to be legally wrong.

The Integrity of Law

The legal authority within a given jurisdiction is a kind of referee whose integrity—whose nature as the referee—would be sacrificed by intruding on the peaceful choices made by the citizenry. The legal authority is only concerned with maintaining peace and the maximum absence of violence against individual rights, and with no one abridging those rights with impunity. That means that if someone's rights are violated, the culprit at least gets punished for the deed.

Neither the legal authorities nor anyone else can always prevent the violation of rights. Just like a referee in a basketball court who cannot always prevent the players from misbehaving. But once they have misbehaved, adverse consequences follow—they must get penalized for it. So similarly, the function of the legal authority, as the libertarian sees it, is to protect against and penalize violators of individual rights.

As adults we all have equal status—not economically, not in terms of our beauty, our background or how nice our parents are but in terms of our rights. "All men are created equal" does not mean that we are created equally wise, smart, wealthy, lucky or beautiful. It means that we are all equally in charge of our lives.

In the case of the US Declaration of Independence, wherein the Lockean libertarian political stance is clearly sketched out, we have an example of how the ideals of the right to negative liberty function. The Declaration could be used by Abraham Lincoln, for example, so as to criticize the Constitution of the United States, which tolerated slavery. Because in the Declaration there was no tolerance of slavery. The Declaration was not a political instrument as the Constitution was and still is, wherein a lot of compromises were and are still being made. The Declaration articulated an unblemished vision of a free society. It made reference to unalienable rights to life, liberty and the pursuit of happiness, and the function of government to secure these rights.

What Governments Are For

The libertarian theory of justice is laid out in the Declaration. Such justice consists of respecting the basic rights to life, liberty and the pursuit of happiness. And government aims to maintaining such justice when it secures those rights, protects them and acts in terms of them. Government is not established to do anything else. Not to manage a post office, build monuments, run Amtrak, conduct AIDS prevention programs, maintain parks, forests and beaches or undertake the education of children. Rather, the distinctive task of government or the legal authorities is to secure the basic rights that individuals have. This arises from the imperative to have one's rights protected, something that most likely requires expertise—due process, for example, is required in the administration of laws.

Libertarianism sees the rule of law secured via the system of constitutional negative rights that function as a system of consistent standards of justice. In contrast to a system of negative and positive rights, which conflict and thus require democratic or some alternative arbitration among basic rights, libertarian justice relies on this system of rights to serve as standards for adjudicating conflicting claims of legality.

We can grasp this distinctiveness of the libertarian polity by recalling that, in contrast, many conservatives and social democrats or modern liberals endorse such public policies as establishing minimum wages, social security systems, licensing of professions, regulations of industry, the "war on drugs," closer unity between government and church, and bans on prostitution, gambling, pornography and other vices. Each of these policies champions an unjustified paternalism and prior restraint ....

The question can be raised of course, do people really have these rights? That is the most controversial political question about the libertarian position on justice. Once we have correctly identified these rights it pretty much follows that the only time someone may use force against another person—which is what the legal authorities such as the courts, police, military, and bureaucracy are professionally trained to do—is in the protection of those rights.

But what if those basic, natural rights are all a fiction, a myth? What if they are—as has been claimed by philosophical luminaries from Jeremy Bentham and Karl Marx to Richard Rorty—nonsense, an ideological invention and just plainly untenable, respectively? Bentham thought very little of them because he distrusted the reasoning found in John Locke in support for basic individual rights. Marx thought they were thinly disguised ideological tools for maintaining the rule of the bourgeoisie. And Rorty just thinks they are culture-bound fictions having no foundations at all.

Rights and Relativism

So, clearly it is prominently maintained, in opposition to libertarian political theory, that the rights spoken of in the Declaration of Independence are contrivances.

This view of rights is close to a similar position on political principles in general, namely, relativism. When one hears it said, for instance, that for the people of Cuba socialism may be a sound system, while for those in the USA it may well not be, one is hearing political relativism. It says that for certain people, related to their special historical situation or particular economic or technological development, it is okay for one party or a dictator to basically run their lives.

Some government officials at the 1996 Vienna conference on human rights, from Africa and Asia, protested the United Nations' endorsement of the very idea of basic individual rights because, they said, that those ideas do not apply to their society. And there is widespread agreement with this idea on the part of many people in university philosophy, political science and history departments ....

Is there an answer to that? Yes there is, as the libertarian sees it.

Apart from metaphysical issues, there could well be certain facts that remain stable or steady in human affairs as long as the species exists as a distinctive kind of entity. If those in the fifth century BC were members of the human species, as were those in the nineteenth, are those in the twenty-first and will be those in the twenty-third century, that fact, of our mutual humanity, could have certain ethical and political implications. Some principles of ethics and politics could then be universalizable, apply throughout the human species, including the idea that each individual is a sovereign over his or her life. It is no easy task to demonstrate that the kind of being we humans are implies certain normative principles, but there is ample evidence that such an inference can be drawn from what we know of humans. If we do indeed have a distinctive nature involving the capacity for creative thought and self-government, a suitable community life would require that these basic facts about us be as fully accommodated as possible.

Of course, not all thinkers through all historical periods have stressed the importance of individual sovereignty. But this does not mean that individual sovereignty was not right back then or is unimportant, only that many thinkers paid little attention to it. There may be many reasons for that.

For example, given that these thinkers were part of a class of people who benefited from treating many others as if those others could be used against—and thus not permitted to follow—their own will, this is not surprising. Pointing out to the world that every individual is equally important is not always in one's vested interest. Leaders of tribes, countries, nations, states and other political units would very likely lose their standing if it were to become widely known that they are not entitled to their special positions. Individualism, a vital component of libertarianism, would most likely be suppressed even if it came to light philosophically. It is, thus, no argument against the universal validity of the position that in many societies it is not prominently embraced and, rather, anti-individualist positions are the dominant traditions.

But, given the fact of some permanent features of human nature, it is true, among other things, that no human being should be made to serve the will of another human being against his or her choice. In other words, that slavery, whether it is full-scale, partial or even minimal, has always been and will always be wrong when it comes to human beings. It is no excuse that in the 1900s or in Athenian Greece, science, economics, sociology or politics were different. Slavery was wrong then and it was wrong 150 years ago and will always be so, as long as those slaves are human beings or have the characteristics of human beings, free will and moral responsibility over their lives. Such a principle could be correct even if not widely embraced—agreement with it isn't what makes it true.

Universalism and Libertarianism

The anti-slavery stance is an example of a universal position that the libertarian embraces. Not that all principles are comparably widely universalizable. For example, how you should dress or keep clean or even rear your kids will change, based on technological, agricultural and other developments. The answers to various particular, special questions are not the same as they were 200 or 3,200 years ago. These answers depend a great deal on the vehicles we drive, the kind of dwellings in which we live. Given these changes, it would be silly to maintain that there is a fundamental principle concerning those details—how we should furnish our apartments and so forth. Those matters depend too much on certain variable aspects of human life. They include a great deal of what makes up various different and equally valid human cultures.

But there are basic principles to which people allude when they say that certain values or principles of conduct do not change. The reason for the libertarian thinking this is right, is that human beings do remain fundamentally the same throughout all those technological and related changes. No matter what the changes may be, our humanity remains intact.

Human Nature and Human Rights

It is this idea of our universal humanity and that certain norms of human interaction follow from it for community life that is implicitly accepted by human rights watch groups going from country to country, examining whether such practices as slavery, forced labor and suppression of dissent exist. It does not matter whether it exists in China, Burundi, the USA or Canada. These human rights watch groups consider certain practices and policies to be inexcusable because of the fundamental humanity of the inhabitants of all these communities.

Underlying the idea of these rights to life, liberty and the pursuit of happiness—or property—is the fact of our human nature. And this nature is understood to be distinctive by virtue of the basic fact of our creative potential and our life-sustaining need to take the initiative in life, as well as the corresponding moral responsibility we have for living our lives properly (whatever that comes to).

For us, unlike for the rest of the animal world, there are very few instincts on which we can rely to guide us in our lives. We must discover how to live and flourish. That's why we need education—we are not born with sufficiently detailed genetically built-in programs that guide us through life the way in which geese, cats or even the higher mammals are, who do the right thing nearly automatically. We must learn that we have very few built-in measures that sustain our lives. We have to learn everything—how to eat, talk, walk, drive and the many, many far more complex tasks that amount to living human lives.

Nearly everything we do to live reasonably successfully has to be learned. So we either make good use of our minds or we don't. Human beings have the capacity to get themselves going or to fail to do so. This is fundamental to them all. Unless they are thwarted in this task by governments, criminals or invading armies, they are free either to pay heed to what their lives require or not to do so and then to act accordingly. And the right condition for their human lives is when others do not prevent them from doing so.

The wilds and the rest of the non-human world—viruses, mad dogs, earthquakes, floods, and so forth—do not always leave us in peace, undisturbed and unharmed, so that we do often face terrible hardship caused by them. However, other persons can and ought to refrain from imposing themselves on us when we do not give our permission for them to do so, namely by consistently respecting our rights. In other words, it is right for us all not to be intruded upon by those who have a choice about how they will act. This will enhance our chances to make the effort to think through the problems that face us and to act so as to reach solutions to those problems. Instead of interacting with others coercively, we will then enjoy the fruits of voluntary cooperative interactions, including competing with others, trading with them and so forth. It is only such a community of others that is suitable to us all, one in which we as adult human beings interact on a voluntary basis.

Libertarianism and Community

By no means does this mean, as some critics of classical liberalism and libertarianism have suggested, that community life is alien to us, quite the contrary. People flourish best among other people. But only if these other people do not thwart their freedom. We not only have the right to but definitely should form clubs, churches, associations, corporations and thus embark on the solutions of all of our problems and the attainment of our aspirations in the company of other persons. But only if this does not involve coercion, compulsion, or some other violation of these other persons' sovereignty.

Conservatives like George Will and modern liberals and communitarians unite against the libertarian, however, on grounds that his view of human beings is too narrow. Will joins Michael Sandel, claiming that

> much damage is done when we define human beings not as social beings—not in terms of morally serious roles (citizen, marriage partner, parent, etc.)—but only with reference to the watery idea of a single, morally empty capacity of "choice." Politics becomes empty; citizenship, too.[8]

But this is a bogus criticism, repeated since Hegel and Marx advanced it in more or less formidable ways, by all those who would forcibly twist the lives of people to follow a vision that they have not freely embraced. Of course, human beings are "social beings." But this does not mean what Marx meant by it, namely, "The human essence is the true collectivity of man."[9] Rather it means that human beings live and flourish most in the company of others. Yet this is something as human beings they must do by choice when they reach maturity, otherwise it isn't a fully human community in which they live. For the social options available to them are numerous, some suitable, some not. And they are responsible for making the right choice about the kind of social unions in which they will partake. And when they are prevented from exercising this choice, as in a totalitarian state, violence is done to them even while those perpetrating the violence claim they are merely reforming the victims by sending them to insane asylums or jailing them for counter-revolutionary conduct.

The condition of freely choosing how to live their own lives is a quintessentially human requirement based on the fact that moral choice cannot be secured from men and women who are coerced to live even in ways that may be best for them. F. A. Hayek made this point as follows:

> That freedom is the matrix required for the growth of moral values—indeed not merely one value among many but the source of all values—is almost self-evident. It is only where the individual has choice, and its inherent responsibility, that he has occasion to affirm existing values, to contribute to their further growth, and then earn moral merit.[10]

Hayek also argued that:

> The growth of what we call civilization is due to this principle of a person's responsibility for his own actions and their consequences, and the freedom to pursue his own ends without having to obey the leader of the band to which he belongs.[11]

Human beings are properly held responsible for assuming various social roles in life—in their marriages, families, polities, etc.—but this responsibility is empty if not chosen by them but imposed on them coercively by, for example, an elite. What Will so cavalierly and callously regards as a "morally empty capacity of 'choice,'" is, in fact, the absolutely indispensable prerequisite of the moral life.

In the making of these and other choices in our lives, we may or may not win the prize of success. There is no guarantee. That is one of the reasons that a libertarian proposes a non-utopian form of community. Such an arrangement does not promise to solve all of our problems. It rests on the recognition that free men and women might not solve their problems or might do so inadequately, incompletely. They may just decide to sit and fiddle their thumbs and watch TV talk shows all day long. There is plenty of evidence and common sense to support this view. There is no guarantee that people will do the right thing when they are free.

Yet it is more likely that they will discover the right thing to do if they are free, than if they are regimented around by others who have their own lives to attend to and, in any case, ought to mind their own business. Free men and women are more likely than those who aren't free to detect the consequences of their own chosen actions and learn from them. Their own lives are more familiar to them than to others; they will experience the adverse consequences of irresponsible conduct, whether via failures within their own lives or from adverse reactions from others who have been injured by them. If a legal system concentrates on retaliation rather than prevention, the lessons it can teach will not only follow the principles of justice but also have a better chance of registering and producing lessons for those who live within its framework. Prior restraint is not only morally and politically objectionable because it does violence to individual sovereignty and involves paternalism, but also because it contributes to what I have dubbed the moral tragedy of the commons. Therein the results of irresponsibility are not tied to those who perpetrate it but are dumped on the community at large, including many who are completely innocent of any wrongdoing.

When government agents force us to pay a minimum wage, tell us how to run our business, and to meet various requirements so as to become doctors, psychologists, or chiropractors, they address an area that we ought to be left to address in our voluntary cooperative groups. These matters are not properly and fruitfully addressed by means of regimentation by others. They are not to be dealt with by petty or major tyrannical policies—that is, by people who wield guns even if they mean well.

That is the most fundamental notion concerning public policy, according to the libertarian. Based on this notion and various details we learn from all fields of knowledge, we can figure out, also, various peaceful ways of dealing with, for example, cloning, education, drug abuse, child raising, mental health, diseases and all kinds of issues with which life confronts us. These are some of the issues not directly dealt with in libertarian theory and must be left for other fields than politics to address. But there is at least one point implied by libertarianism for all areas of social life: coercion—which is to say rights violation—is not suited for any part of it. It is the right to freedom of association for all persons who are not crucially incapacitated that generates this point.

Notes

1. Among philosophers who share crucial elements of this view we can list Socrates, Aristotle, Augustine, Aquinas, Descartes, Spinoza, Kant, Wittgenstein, and, of course, Ayn Rand, who has spawned perhaps the most philosophically potent arguments for libertarian justice. (To be sure, Rand did not call herself a libertarian but, more fundamentally, an objectivist. Yet the conclusions she reached in the sphere of politics are libertarian ones.)
2. Conservatives aren't united so much on doctrine as on ways to think about normative matters. They hold that how we decide our institutions, laws and practices should be grounded in tradition: what has worked in the past, what has been tried and found true.
3. Norman Malcolm, *Ludwig Wittgenstein: A Memoir* (London: Van Nostrand Rinehold Co., 1970) pp. 31–2.
4. Sterba has advanced his views in many forums, including his introduction to a book he edited, *Justice: Alternative Perspectives* (Belmont, CA: Wadsworth Publishing Co., 1991).
5. Michael Otsuka, "Making the Unjust Provide from the Least Well Off," *The Journal of Ethics*, vol. 2 (1998) pp. 247–59.
6. Michael Otsuka, "Self-Ownership and Equality," *Philosophy and Public Affairs*, vol. 27 (1998) pp. 65–92.
7. The only serious exception would be orphaned or severely neglected children, although with the considerable demand for adoptions and the general compassion most people have for children, it doesn't seem likely that unfortunate children would fail to find sufficient support for their flourishing in a free society. (I thank Randall R. Dipert for raising this issue to me.)
8. George Will, "What Courts Are Teaching," *Newsweek*, December 7, 1998, p. 98.
9. Karl Marx, "On the Jewish Question," in D. McLellan (ed.) *Selected Writings* (London: Oxford University Press, 1977) p. 126.
10. F. A. Hayek, "The Moral Element in Free Enterprise," in Mark W. Hendrickson (ed.) *The Morality of Capitalism* (Irvington-on-Hudson, NY: The Foundation for Economic Education, 1992) (originally written for *The Freeman*, 1962).
11. F. A. Hayek, "Socialism and Science," in Chiaki Nishiyama and Kurt R. Leube (eds.) *The Essence of Hayek* (Stanford, CA: Hoover Institution Press, 1984) p. 118.

Review and Discussion Questions

1. What are the key tenets of libertarianism?
2. Why does Machan think that libertarianism is the right political theory, based on the nature of human beings and human values?
3. What is the purpose of governments, according to libertarians?
4. Does Machan claim libertarianism applies to all societies, at all times? Explain.
5. Explain why Machan thinks that while it is sometimes wrong for people to refuse to help each other, it is also wrong for governments or others to *force* people to help.
6. How does Machan answer those who say that libertarianism ignores the fact that people are "social beings"?

READING: ON LIBERTY

JOHN STUART MILL[*]

None of Mill's works has had a greater impact than *On Liberty*; its ideas are often discussed by academics, politicians, and the general public, even by people who have never heard of him. According to letters and other material from Mill's life, *On Liberty* should be thought of as a joint work authored by Mill himself and his longtime friend Harriet Taylor. Mill even said in a letter that there was not a sentence in the book that the two did not go over together many times. (Harriet Taylor also had a major role in his other works, including *The Subjection of Women*.) For a brief description of John Stuart Mill's life, see Introduction to the reading in Chapter 3 "*Utilitarianism*".

In *On Liberty*, Mill examines a fundamental question of political philosophy: What are the limits of society's power over the individual? Mill's answer is that society may interfere with an individual's speech or actions only on the grounds of self-protection. Accordingly, Mill first discusses the history of the fight of the individual against tyrannical government. He then explores the importance of individuality to a person's overall well-being, and, finally, he considers his famous "harm principle," which provides that government is justified in interfering with a citizen's liberty only if there is the threat of harm to others.

Introductory

The subject of this essay is ... civil, or social liberty: the nature and limits of power which can be legitimately exercised by society over the individual. ... The struggle between liberty and authority is the most conspicuous feature in the portions of history with which we are earliest familiar, particularly in that of Greece, Rome, and England. But in old times this contest was between subjects, or some classes of subjects, and the government. By liberty, was meant protection against the tyranny of the political rulers. The rulers were conceived (except in some of the popular governments of Greece) as in a necessarily antagonistic position to the people whom they ruled ....

A time, however, came, in the progress of human affairs, when men ceased to think it a necessity of nature that their governors should be an independent power, opposed in interest to themselves. It appeared to them much better that the various magistrates of the State should be their tenants or delegates, revocable at their pleasure. In that way alone, it seemed, could they have complete security that the powers of government would never be abused to their disadvantage. By degrees this new demand for elective and temporary rulers became the prominent object of the exertions of the popular party, wherever any such party existed; and superseded, to a considerable extent, the previous efforts to limit the power of rulers ....

But in political and philosophical theories, as well as in persons, success discloses faults and infirmities which failure might have concealed from observation. ... It was

---

[*] From John Stuart Mill, *On Liberty* (1859).

now perceived that such phrases as "self-government," and "the power of the people over themselves," do not express the true state of the case. The "people" who exercise the power are not always the same people with those over whom it is exercised; and the "self-government" spoken of is not the government of each by himself, but of each by all the rest. The will of the people, moreover, practically means the will of the most numerous or the most active *part* of the people—the majority, or those who succeed in making themselves accepted as the majority; the people, consequently, may desire to oppress a part of their number, and precautions are as much needed against this as against any other abuse of power. The limitation, therefore, of the power of government over individuals loses none of its importance when the holders of power are regularly accountable to the community, that is, to the strongest party therein ....

The object of this essay is to assert one very simple principle, as entitled to govern absolutely the dealings of society with the individual in the way of compulsion and control, whether the means used be physical force in the form of legal penalties or the moral coercion of public opinion. That principle is, that the sole end for which mankind are warranted, individually or collectively, in interfering with the liberty of action of any of their number, is self-protection. That the only purpose for which power can be rightfully exercised over any member of a civilized community, against his will, is to prevent harm to others. His own good, either physical or moral, is not a sufficient warrant. He cannot rightfully be compelled to do or forbear because it will be better for him to do so, because it will make him happier, because, in the opinions of others, to do so would be wise or even right. These are good reasons for remonstrating with him, or reasoning with him, or persuading him, or entreating him, but not for compelling him or visiting him with any evil in case he do otherwise. To justify that, the conduct from which it is desired to deter him must be calculated to produce evil to someone else. The only part of the conduct of anyone, for which he is amenable to society, is that which concerns others. In the part which merely concerns himself, his independence is, of right, absolute. Over himself, over his own body and mind, the individual is sovereign.

It is, perhaps, hardly necessary to say that this doctrine is meant to apply only to human beings in the maturity of their faculties. We are not speaking of children, or of young persons below the age which the law may fix as that of manhood or womanhood. Those who are still in a state to require being taken care of by others, must be protected against their own actions as well as against external injury. For the same reason, we may leave out of consideration those backward states of society in which the race itself may be considered as in its nonage. The early difficulties in the way of spontaneous progress are so great, and there is seldom any choice of means for overcoming them; and a ruler full of the spirit of improvement is warranted in the use of any expedients that will attain an end, perhaps otherwise unattainable. Despotism is a legitimate mode of government in dealing with barbarians, provided the end be their improvement, and the means justified by actually effecting that end. Liberty, as a principle, has no application to any state of things anterior to the time when mankind have become capable of being improved by free and equal discussion. Until then, there is nothing for them but implicit obedience to an Akbar or a Charlemagne, if they are so fortunate as to find one. But as soon as mankind have attained the capacity of being guided to their own improvement by conviction or persuasion (a period long since reached in all nations with whom we need here concern ourselves), compulsion, either in the direct form or in that of pains and penalties for noncompliance, is no longer admissible as a means to their own good, and justifiable only for the security of others.

It is proper to state that I forgo any advantage which could be derived to my argument from the idea of abstract right, as a thing independent of utility. I regard utility as the ultimate appeal on all ethical questions; but it must be utility in the largest sense, grounded on the permanent interests of a man as a progressive being. These interests, I contend, authorized the subjection of individual spontaneity to external control, only in respect to those actions of each which concern the interest of other people. If anyone does an act hurtful to others, there is a *prima facie* case for punishing him, by law, or, where legal penalties are not safely applicable, by general disapprobation. There are also many positive acts for the benefit of others, which he may rightfully be compelled to perform: such as to give evidence in a court of justice; to bear his fair share in the common defense, or in any other joint work necessary to the interest of the society of which he enjoys the protection; and to perform certain acts of individual beneficence, such as saving a fellow-creature's life, or interposing to protect the defenseless against ill-usage, things which whenever it is obviously a man's duty to do, he may rightfully be made responsible to society for not doing. A person may cause evil to others not only by his actions but by his inaction, and in either case he is justly accountable to them for the injury. The latter case, it is true, requires a much more cautious exercise of compulsion than the former ....

This, then is the appropriate region of human liberty. It comprises, *first*, the inward domain of consciousness; demanding liberty of conscience in the most comprehensive sense; liberty of thought and feeling; absolute freedom of opinion and sentiment on all subjects, practical or speculative, scientific, moral or theological ....

Secondly, the principle requires liberty of tastes and pursuits; of framing the plan of our life to suit our own character; of doing as we like, subject to such consequences as may follow: without impediment from our fellow-creatures, so long as what we do does not harm them, even though they should think our conduct foolish, perverse, or wrong.

Thirdly, from this liberty of each individual, follows the liberty, within the same limits, of combinations among individuals; freedom to unite, for any purpose not involving harm to others: the persons combining being supposed to be of full age, and not forced or deceived.

No society in which these liberties are not, on the whole, respected, is free, whatever may be its form of government; and none is completely free in which they do not exist absolute and unqualified. The only freedom which deserves the name, is that of pursuing our own good in our own way, as long as we do not attempt to deprive others of theirs, or impede their efforts to obtain it. Each is the proper guardian of his own health, whether bodily, or mental and spiritual ....

Of Individuality, as One of the Elements of Well-Being

No one pretends that actions should be as free as opinions. On the contrary, even opinions lose their immunity when the circumstances in which they are expressed are such as to constitute their expression a positive instigation to some mischievous act. An opinion that corn-dealers are starvers of the poor, or that private property is robbery, ought to be unmolested when simply circulated through the press, but may justly incur punishment when delivered orally to an excited mob assembled before the house of a corn-dealer, or when handed about among the same mob in the form of a placard. ... It is desirable, in short, that in things which do not primarily concern others, individuality should assert itself. Where not the person's own character, but the traditions or customs of other people are the rule of conduct, there is wanting one of the principal ingredients of human happiness, and quite the chief ingredient of individual and social progress ....

Few persons, out of Germany, even comprehend the meaning of the doctrine which Wilhelm von Humboldt, so eminent both as a savant and as a politician, made the text of a treatise—that

> the end of man, or that which is prescribed by the eternal or immutable dictates of reason, and not suggested by vague and transient desires, is the highest and most harmonious development of his powers to a complete and consistent whole

that, therefore, the object "towards which every human being must ceaselessly direct his efforts, and on which especially those who design to influence their fellowmen must ever keep their eyes, is the individuality of power and development"; that for this there are two requisites, "freedom, and variety of situations"; and that from the union of these arise "individual vigor and manifold diversity," which combine themselves in "originality." [These quotes from Wilhelm von Humboldt, *The Sphere and Duties of Government* as translated by Joseph Coulthard (1854), available at https://oll.libertyfund.org/Home3/Book.php?recordID=0053—Ed. note] ....

He who lets the world, or his own portion of it, choose his plan of life for him, has no need of any other faculty than the ape-like one of imitation. He who chooses his plan for himself, employs all his faculties. He must use observation to see, reasoning and judgments to foresee, activity to gather materials for decision, discrimination to decide, and when he has decided, firmness and self-control to hold to his deliberate decision. And these qualities he requires and exercises exactly in proportion as the part of his conduct which he determines according to his own judgment and feelings is a large one. It is possible that he might be guided in some good path, and kept out of harm's way, without any of these things. But what will be his comparative worth as a human being? It really is of importance, not only what men do, but also what manner of men they are that do it. Among the works of man which human life is rightly employed in perfecting and beautifying, the first in importance surely is man himself. ... Human nature is not a machine to be built after a model, and set to do exactly the work prescribed for it, but a tree, which requires to grow and develop itself on all sides, according to the tendency of the inward forces which make it a living thing ....

But society has now fairly got the better of individuality. ... In our times, from the highest class of society down to the lowest, everyone lives as under the eye of a hostile and dreaded censorship. Not only in what concerns others, but in what concerns only themselves, the individual or the family do not ask themselves—what do I prefer? or, what would suit my character and disposition? or, what would allow the best and highest in me to have fair play, and enable it to grow and thrive? They ask themselves, what is suitable to my position? what is usually done by persons of my station and pecuniary circumstances? or (worse still) what is usually done by persons of a station and circumstances superior to mine? I do not mean that they choose what is customary in preference to what suits their own inclination. It does not occur to them to have any inclination, except for what is customary. Thus the mind itself is bowed to the yoke: even in what people do for pleasure, conformity is the first thing thought of; they like crowds; they exercise choice only among things commonly done: peculiarity of taste, eccentricity of conduct, are shunned equally with crimes: until by dint of not following their own nature they have no nature to follow: their human capacities are withered and starved: they become incapable of any strong wishes or native pleasures, and are generally without either opinions or feelings of home growth, or properly their own. Now is this, or is it not, the desirable condition of human nature? ....

Of the Limits to the Authority of Society Over the Individual

Though society is not founded on a contract, and though no good purpose is answered by inventing a contract in order to deduce social obligations from it, everyone who receives the protection of society owes a return for the benefit, and the fact of living in society renders it indispensable that each should be bound to observe a certain line of conduct towards the rest. This conduct consists, *first*, in not injuring the interests of one another; or rather certain interests, which either by express legal provision or by tacit understanding, ought to be considered as rights; and *secondly*, in each person's bearing his share (to be fixed on some equitable principle) of the labors and sacrifices incurred for defending the society or its members from injury and molestation. These conditions society is justified in enforcing, at all costs to those who endeavor to withhold fulfillment. Nor is this all that society may do. The acts of an individual may be hurtful to others, or wanting in due consideration for their welfare, without going to the length of violating any of their constituted rights. The offender may then be justly punished by opinion, though not by law. As soon as any part of a person's conduct affects prejudicially the interests of others, society has jurisdiction over it, and the question whether the general welfare will or will not be promoted by interfering with it, becomes open to discussion. But there is no room for entertaining any such question when a person's conduct affects the interests of no persons besides himself, or need not affect them unless they like (all the persons concerned being of full age, and the ordinary amount of understanding). In all such cases, there should be perfect freedom, legal and social, to do the action and stand the consequences.

It would be a great misunderstanding of this doctrine to suppose that it is one of selfish indifference, which pretends that human beings have no business with each other's conduct in life, and that they should not concern themselves about the well-doing or well-being of one another, unless their own interest is involved. Instead of any diminution, there is need of a great increase of disinterested exertion to promote the good of others. But disinterested benevolence can find other instruments to persuade people to their good than whips and scourges, either of the literal or the metaphorical sort. I am the last person to undervalue the self-regarding virtues: they are only second in importance, if even second, to the social. It is equally the business of education to cultivate both. But even education works by conviction and persuasion as well as by compulsion, and it is by the former only that, when the period of education is passed, the self-regarding virtues should be inculcated. Human beings owe to each other help to distinguish the better from the worse, and encouragement to choose the former and avoid the latter. They should be forever stimulating each other to increased exercise of their higher faculties, and increased direction of their feelings and aims towards wise instead of foolish, elevating instead of degrading, objects and contemplations. But neither one person, nor any number of persons, is warranted in saying to another human creature of ripe years, that he shall not do with his life for his own benefit what he chooses to do with it. He is the person most interested in his own well-being: the interest which any other person, except in cases of strong personal attachment, can have in it, is trifling, compared with that which he himself has; the interest which society has in him individually (except as to conduct to others) is fractional, and altogether indirect; while with respect to his own feelings and circumstances, the most ordinary man or woman has means of knowledge immeasurably surpassing those that can be possessed by anyone else. The interference of society to overrule his judgment and purposes in what only regards himself must be grounded on general presumptions; which may be altogether wrong, and even if right, are as likely as not to be misapplied to individual cases, by persons no better acquainted with the circumstances of such cases than those are who look at them merely from without. In this department, therefore, of human affairs, individuality has its proper field of action. In the conduct of human beings towards one another it is necessary that general rules should for the most part be observed, in order that people may know what they have to expect; but in each person's own concerns his individual spontaneity is entitled to free exercise. Considerations to aid his judgment, exhortations to strengthen his will, may be offered to him, even obtruded on him, by others: but he himself is the final judge. All errors which he is likely to commit against advice and warning are far outweighed by the evil of allowing others to constrain him to what they deem his good ....

Though doing no wrong to anyone, a person may so act as to compel us to judge him, and feel to him, as a fool, or as a being of an inferior order; and since this judgment and feeling are a fact which he would prefer to avoid, it is doing him a service to warn him of it beforehand, as of any other disagreeable consequence to which he exposes himself. ... We have a right, also, in various ways, to act upon our unfavorable opinion of anyone, not to the oppression of his individuality, but in the exercise of ours. We are not bound, for example, to seek his society; we have a right to avoid it (though not to parade the avoidance), for we have a right to choose the society most acceptable to us. We have a right, and it may be our duty, to caution others against him, if we think his example or conversation likely to have a pernicious effect on those with whom he associates. We may give others a preference over him in optional good offices, except those which tend to his improvement. In these various modes a person may suffer very severe penalties at the hands of others for faults which directly concern only himself; but he suffers these penalties only in so far as they are the natural and, as it were, the spontaneous consequences of the faults themselves, not because they are purposely inflicted on him for the sake of punishment ....

What I contend for is, that the inconveniences which are strictly inseparable from the unfavorable judgment of others, are the only ones to which a person should ever be subjected for that portion of his conduct and character which concerns his own good, but which does not affect the interest of others in their relations with him. Acts injurious to others require a totally different treatment. Encroachment on their rights; infliction on them of any loss or damage not justified by his own rights; falsehood or duplicity in dealing with them; unfair or ungenerous use of advantages over them; even selfish abstinence from defending them against injury—these are fit objects of moral reprobation, and, in grave cases, of moral retribution and punishment. And not only these acts, but the dispositions which lead to them, are properly immoral, and fit subjects of disapprobation which may rise to abhorrence ....

The distinction here pointed out between the part of a person's life which concerns only himself, and that which concerns others, many persons will refuse to admit. How (it may be asked)—can any part of the conduct of a member of society be a matter of indifference to the other members? No person is an entirely isolated being; it is impossible for a person to do anything seriously or permanently hurtful to himself, without mischief reaching at least to his near connections, and often far beyond them. If he injures his property, he does harm to those who directly or indirectly derived support from it, and usually diminishes, by a greater or less amount, the general resources of the community. If he deteriorates his bodily or mental faculties, he not only brings evil upon all who depended on him for any portion of their happiness, but disqualifies himself for rendering the services which he owes to his fellow-creatures generally; perhaps becomes a burden on their affection or benevolence; and if such conduct were very frequent, hardly an offense that is committed would detract more from the general sum of good. Finally, if by his vices or follies a person does not direct harm to others, he is nevertheless (it may be said) injurious by his example; and ought to be compelled to control himself, for the sake of those whom the sight or knowledge of his conduct might corrupt or mislead.

And even (it will be added) if the consequences of misconduct could be confined to the vicious or thoughtless individual, ought society to abandon to their own guidance those who are manifestly unfit for it? If protection against themselves is confessedly due to children and persons under age, is not society equally bound to afford it to persons of mature years who are equally incapable of self-government? If gambling, or drunkenness, or incontinence, or idleness, or uncleanliness, are as injurious to happiness, and as great a hindrance to improvement, as many or most of the acts prohibited by law, why (it may be asked) should not law, so far as is consistent with practicability and social convenience, endeavor to repress these also? And as a supplement to the unavoidable imperfections of law, ought not opinion at least to organize a powerful police against these vices, and visit rigidly with social penalties those who are known to practice them? There is no question here (it may be said) about restricting individuality, or impeding the trial of new and original experiments in living. The only things it is sought to prevent are things which have been tried and condemned from the beginning of the world until now; things which experience has shown not to be useful or suitable to any person's individuality. There must be some length of time and amount of experience after which a moral or prudential truth may be regarded as established: and it is merely desired to prevent generation after generation from falling over the same precipice which has been fatal to their predecessors.

I fully admit that the mischief which a person does to himself may seriously affect, both through their sympathies and their interests, those nearly connected with him and, in a minor degree, society at large. When, by conduct of this sort, a person is led to violate a distinct and assignable obligation to any other person or persons, the case is taken out of the self-regarding class and becomes amenable to moral disapprobation in the proper sense of the term. If, for example, a man, through intemperance or extravagance, becomes unable to pay his debts, or, having undertaken the moral responsibility of a family, becomes from the same cause incapable of supporting or educating them, he is deservedly reprobated, and might be justly punished; but it is for the breach of duty to his family or creditors, not for the extravagance. If the resources which ought to have been devoted to them, had been diverted from them for the most prudent investment, the moral culpability would have been the same. George Barnwell murdered his uncle to get money for his mistress, but if he had done it to set himself up in business he would equally have been hanged. Again, in the frequent case of a man who causes grief to his family by addiction to bad habits, he deserves reproach for his unkindness or ingratitude; but so he may for cultivating habits not in themselves vicious, if they are painful to those with whom he passes his life, or who from personal ties are dependent on him for their comfort. Whoever fails in the consideration generally due to the interests and feelings of others, not being compelled by some more imperative duty, or justified by allowable self-preference, is a subject of moral disapprobation for that failure, but not for the cause of it, nor for the errors, merely personal to himself, which may have remotely led to it. In like manner, when a person disables himself, by conduct purely self-regarding, from the performance of some definite duty incumbent on him to the public, he is guilty of a social offense. No person ought to be punished simply for being drunk; but a soldier or policeman should be punished for being drunk on duty. Whenever, in short, there is a definite damage, or a definite risk of damage, either to an individual or to the public, the case is taken out of the province of liberty and placed in that of morality or law.

But with regard to the merely contingent or, as it may be called, constructive injury which a person causes to society by conduct which neither violates any specific duty to the public, nor occasions perceptible hurt to any assignable individual except himself, the inconvenience is one which society can afford to bear, for the sake of the greater good of human freedom. If grown persons are to be punished for not taking proper care of themselves, I would rather it were for their own sake than under pretense of preventing them from impairing their capacity or rendering to society benefits which society does not pretend it has a right to exact. But I cannot consent to argue the point as if society had no means of bringing its weaker members up to its ordinary standard of rational conduct, except waiting till they do something irrational, and then punishing them, legally or morally, for it. Society has had absolute power over them during all the early portion of their existence; it has had the whole period of childhood and nonage in which to try whether it could make them capable of rational conduct in life. The existing generation is master both of the training and the entire circumstances of the generation to come; it cannot indeed make them perfectly wise and good, because it is itself so lamentably deficient in goodness and wisdom; and its best efforts are not always, in individual cases, its most successful ones; but it is perfectly well able to make the rising generation, as a whole, as good as, and a little better than, itself. If society lets any considerable number of its members grow up mere children, incapable of being acted on by rational consideration of distant motives, society has itself to blame for the consequences. Armed not only with all the powers of education, but with the ascendancy which the authority of a received opinion always exercises over the minds who are least fitted to judge for themselves, and aided by the *natural* penalties which cannot be prevented from falling on those who incur the distaste or the contempt of those who know them— let not society pretend that it needs, besides all this, the power to issue commands and enforce obedience in the personal concerns of individuals in which, on all principles of justice and policy, the decision ought to rest with those who are to abide the consequences. Nor is there anything which tends more to discredit and frustrate the better means of influencing conduct than a resort to the worse. If there be among those whom it is attempted to coerce into prudence or temperance any of the material of which vigorous and independent characters are made, they will infallibly rebel against the yoke. No such person will ever feel that others have a right to control him in his concerns, such as they have to prevent him from injuring them in theirs; and it easily comes to be considered a mark of spirit and courage to fly in the face of such usurped authority and do with ostentation the exact opposite of what it enjoins, as in the fashion of grossness which succeeded, in the time of Charles II, to the fanatical moral intolerance of the Puritans. With respect to what is said of the necessity of protecting society from the bad example set to others by the vicious or the self-indulgent, it is true that bad example may have a pernicious effect, especially the example of doing wrong to others with impunity to the wrongdoer. But we are now speaking of conduct which, while it does no wrong to others, is supposed to do great harm to the agent himself; and I do not see how those who believe this can think otherwise than that the example, on the whole, must be more salutary than hurtful, since, if it displays the misconduct, it displays also the painful or degrading consequences which, if the conduct is justly censured, must be supposed to be in all or most cases attendant on it.

But the strongest of all the arguments against the interference of the public with purely personal conduct is that, when it does interfere, the odds are that it interferes wrongly and in the wrong place. On questions of social morality, of duty to others, the opinion of the public, that is, of an overruling majority, though often wrong, is likely to be still oftener right, because on such questions they are only required to judge of their own interests, of the manner in which some mode of conduct, if allowed to be practiced, would affect themselves. But the opinion of a similar majority, imposed as a law on the minority, on questions of self-regarding conduct is quite as likely to be wrong as right, for in these cases public opinion means, at the best, some people's opinion of what is good or bad for other people, while very often it does not even mean that—the public, with the most perfect indifference, passing over the pleasure or convenience of those whose conduct they censure and considering only their own preference. There are many who consider as an injury to themselves any conduct which they have a distaste for, and resent it as an outrage to their feelings; as a religious bigot, when charged with disregarding the religious feelings of others, has been known to retort that they disregard his feelings by persisting in their abominable worship or creed. But there is no parity between the feeling of a person for his own opinion and the feeling of another who is offended at his holding it, no more than between the desire of a thief to take a purse and the desire of the right owner to keep it. And a person's taste is as much his own peculiar concern as his opinion or his purse. It is easy for anyone to imagine an ideal public which leaves the freedom and choice of individuals in all uncertain matters undisturbed and only requires them to abstain from modes of conduct which universal experience has condemned. But where has there been seen a public which set any such limit to its censorship? Or when does the public trouble itself about universal experience? In its interferences with personal conduct it is seldom thinking of anything but the enormity of acting or feeling differently from itself ....

Applications

.... It is a proper office of public authority to guard against accidents. If either a public officer or anyone else saw a person attempting to cross a bridge which had been ascertained to be unsafe, and there were no time to warn him of his danger, they might seize him and turn him back, without any real infringement of his liberty; for liberty consists in doing what one desires, and he does not desire to fall into the river. Nevertheless, when there is not a certainty, but only a danger of mischief, no one but the person himself can judge of the sufficiency of the motive which may prompt him to incur the risk; in this case, therefore (unless he is a child, or delirious, or in some state of excitement or absorption incompatible with the full use of the reflecting faculty), he ought, I conceive, to be only warned of the danger; not forcibly prevented from exposing himself to it ....

[However,] in this and most other civilized countries an engagement by which a person should sell himself, or allow himself to be sold, as a slave, would be null and void; neither enforced by law nor by opinion. The ground for thus limiting his power of voluntarily disposing of his own lot in life, is apparent, and is very clearly seen in this extreme case. The reason for not interfering unless for the sake of others, with a person's voluntary acts, is consideration for his liberty. His voluntary choice is evidence that what he so chooses is desirable, or at least endurable, to him, and his good is on the whole best provided for by allowing him to take his own means of pursuing it. But by selling himself for a slave, he abdicates his liberty; he forgoes any future use of it beyond that single act. He therefore defeats, in his own case, the very purpose which is the justification of allowing him to dispose of himself. He is no longer free; but is thenceforth in a position which has no longer the presumption in its favour, that would be afforded by his voluntarily remaining in it. The principle of freedom cannot require that he should be free not to be free. It is not freedom to be allowed to alienate his freedom ....

Review and Discussion Questions

1 Mill argues that the good life involves more than mere contentment. Of what else, specifically, does true well-being consist?
2 What faculties does Mill believe people living truly worthwhile and valuable lives will employ?

3 Mill admits that many acts may affect others, but he insists that unless they also harm others, government may not intervene. How does Mill understand *harm*?
4 Describe how Mill thinks society may try to influence people whose actions are harmless to others, yet either immoral or not in their true interest.
5 What reasons does Mill give to support his claim that people should be free to make their own decisions?
6 Sometimes, Mill says, society is wise not to interfere even though an act is harmful to another. Give an example of such an act; then explain why Mill thinks society should nevertheless not interfere.
7 Explain the connection between individuality and liberty.
8 What does Mill say may be done if somebody is about to walk across an unsafe bridge? Explain.
9 Why may a person not sell himself or herself into slavery, according to Mill? Is this position consistent with the rest of his essay? Explain.

READING: ON REPRESENTATIVE GOVERNMENT

JOHN STUART MILL[*]

Democracy or *democratic government* is sometimes equated with governments that respect rights and freedom. Other times, the term is used more narrowly to refer to the procedures allowing for citizens to participate in the political institutions and in the law-making processes. In this selection, John Stuart Mill discusses that second idea, claiming that democracy's advantages are not limited to its tendency to secure individual rights, liberty, or economic prosperity. Those who live in democratic systems, he argues, are advantaged by the effect of democratic institutions on the character of people, both intellectual and moral. For a description of Mill's life, see Introduction to the reading in Chapter 3 "*Utilitarianism*".

It has long (perhaps throughout the entire duration of British freedom) been a common saying, that if a good despot could be ensured, despotic monarchy would be the best form of government. I look upon this as a radical and most pernicious misconception of what good government is; which, until it can be got rid of, will fatally vitiate all our speculations on government.

The supposition is, that absolute power, in the hands of an eminent individual, would ensure a virtuous and intelligent performance of all the duties of government. Good laws would be established and enforced, bad laws would be reformed; the best men would be placed in all situations of trust; justice would be as well administered, the public burthens would be as light and as judiciously imposed, every branch of administration would be as purely and as intelligently conducted, as the circumstances of the country and its degree of intellectual and moral cultivation would admit. I am willing, for the sake of the argument, to concede all this; but I must point out how great the concession is; how much more is needed to produce even an approximation to these results than is conveyed in the simple

---

[*] From John Stuart Mill, *Considerations on Representative Government* (1861).

expression, a good despot. Their realisation would in fact imply, not merely a good monarch, but an all-seeing one. He must be at all times informed correctly, in considerable detail, of the conduct and working of every branch of administration in every district of the country, and must be able, in the twenty-four hours per day which are all that is granted to a king as to the humblest labourer, to give an effective share of attention and superintendence to all parts of this vast field; or he must at least be capable of discerning and choosing out, from among the mass of his subjects, not only a large abundance of honest and able men, fit to conduct every branch of public administration under supervision and control, but also the small number of men of eminent virtues and talents who can be trusted not only to do without that supervision, but to exercise it themselves over others. So extraordinary are the faculties and energies required for performing this task in any supportable manner, that the good despot whom we are supposing can hardly be imagined as consenting to undertake it, unless as a refuge from intolerable evils, and a transitional preparation for something beyond. But the argument can do without even this immense item in the account. Suppose the difficulty vanquished. What should we then have? One man of superhuman mental activity managing the entire affairs of a mentally passive people. Their passivity is implied in the very idea of absolute power. The nation as a whole and every individual composing it, are without any potential voice in their own destiny. They exercise no will in respect to their collective interests. All is decided for them by a will not their own, which it is legally a crime for them to disobey. What sort of human beings can be formed under such a regimen? What development can wither their thinking or their active faculties attain under it? On matters of pure theory they might perhaps be allowed to speculate, so long as their speculations either did not approach politics, or had not the remotest connection with its practice. On practical affairs they could at most be only suffered to suggest; and even under the most moderate of despots, none but persons of already admitted or reputed superiority could hope that their suggestions would be known to, much less regarded by, those who had the management of affairs. A person must have a very unusual taste for intellectual exercise in and for itself, who will put himself to the trouble of thought when it is to have no outward effect, or qualify himself for functions which he has no chance of being allowed to exercise ....

But the public at large remains without information and without interest on all the greater matters of practice; or, if they have any knowledge of them, it is but a *dilettante* knowledge, like that which people have of the mechanical arts who have never handled a tool. Nor is it only in their intelligence that they suffer. Their moral capacities are equally stunted. Wherever the sphere of action of human beings is artificially circumscribed, their sentiments are narrowed and dwarfed in the same proportion. The food of feeling is action: even domestic affection lives upon voluntary good offices. Let a person have nothing to do for his country, and he will not care for it. It has been said of old, that in a despotism there is at most but one patriot, the despot himself; and the saying rests on a just appreciation of the effects of absolute subjection, even to a good and wise master. ... Leaving things to the Government, like leaving them to Providence, is synonymous with caring nothing about them, and accepting their results, when disagreeable, as visitations of Nature. With the exception, therefore, of a few studious men who take an intellectual interest in speculation for its own sake, the intelligence and sentiments of the whole people are given up to the material interests, and, when these are provided for, to the amusement and ornamentation, of private life. But to say this is to say, if the whole testimony of history is worth anything, that the era of national decline has arrived: that is, if the nation had ever attained anything to decline from. ... And that state does not mean stupid tranquility, with security against change for the worse; it often means being overrun, conquered, and reduced to domestic slavery, either by a stronger despot, or by the nearest barbarous people who retain along with their savage rudeness the energies of freedom.

Such are not merely the natural tendencies, but the inherent necessities of despotic government; from which there is no outlet, unless in so far as the despotism consents not to be despotism ....

There is no difficulty in showing that the ideally best form of government is that in which the sovereignty, or supreme controlling power in the last resort, is vested in the entire aggregate of the community; every citizen not only having a voice in the exercise of that ultimate sovereignty, but being, at least occasionally, called on to take an actual part in the government, by the personal discharge of some public function, local or general.

To test this proposition, it has to be examined in reference to the two branches into which ... the inquiry into the goodness of a government conveniently divides itself, namely, how far it promotes the good management of the affairs of society by means of the existing faculties, moral, intellectual, and active, of its various members, and what is its effect in improving or deteriorating those faculties.

The ideally best form of government, it is scarcely necessary to say, does not mean one which is practicable or eligible in all states of civilisation, but the one which, in the circumstances in which it is practicable and eligible, is attended with the greatest amount of beneficial consequences, immediate and prospective. A completely popular government is the only polity which can make out any claim to this character. It is pre-eminent in both the departments between which the excellence of a political constitution is divided. It is both more favourable to present good government, and promotes a better and higher form of national character, than any other polity whatsoever.

Its superiority in reference to present wellbeing rests upon two principles, of as universal truth and applicability as any general propositions which can be laid down respecting human affairs. The first is, that the rights and interests of every or any person are only secure from being disregarded when the person interested is himself able, and habitually disposed, to stand up for them. The second is, that the general prosperity attains a greater height, and is more widely diffused, in proportion to the amount and variety of the personal energies enlisted in promoting it.

Putting these two propositions into a shape more special to their present application; human beings are only secure from evil at the hands of others in proportion as they have the power of being, and are, self-*protecting*; and they only achieve a high degree of success in their struggle with Nature in proportion as they are self-*dependent*, relying on what they themselves can do, either separately or in concert, rather than on what others do for them.

The former proposition—that each is the only safe guardian of his own rights and interests—is one of those elementary maxims of prudence, which every person, capable of conducting his own affairs, implicitly acts upon, wherever he himself is interested ….

It is an adherent condition of human affairs that no intention, however sincere, of protecting the interests of others can make it safe or salutary to tie up their own hands. Still more obviously true is it, that by their own hands only can any positive and durable improvement of their circumstances in life be worked out. Through the joint influence of these two principles, all free communities have both been more exempt from social injustice and crime, and have attained more brilliant prosperity, than any others, or than they themselves after they lost their freedom. Contrast the free states of the world, while their freedom lasted, with the contemporary subjects of monarchical or oligarchical despotism. … Their superior prosperity was too obvious ever to have been gainsaid: while their superiority in good government and social relations is proved by the prosperity, and is manifest besides in every page of history ….

Thus stands the case as regards present wellbeing: the good management of the affairs of the existing generation. If we now pass to the influence of the form of government upon character, we shall find the superiority of popular government over every other to be, if possible, still more decided and indisputable.

This question really depends upon a still more fundamental one, viz., which of two common types of character, for the general good of humanity, it is most desirable should predominate—the active, or the passive type; that which struggles against evils, or that which endures them; that which bends to circumstances, or that which endeavours to make circumstances bend to itself.

The commonplaces of moralists, and the general sympathies of mankind, are in favour of the passive type. Energetic characters may be admired, but the acquiescent and submissive are those which most men personally prefer. The passiveness of our neighbours increases our sense of security, and plays into the hands of our wilfulness. Passive characters, if we do not happen to need their activity, seem an obstruction the less in our own path. A contented character is not a dangerous rival. Yet nothing is more certain than that improvement in human affairs is wholly the work of the uncontented characters; and, moreover, that it is much easier for an active mind to acquire the virtues of patience than for a passive one to assume those of energy.

Of the three varieties of mental excellence, intellectual, practical, and moral, there never could be any doubt in regard to the first two which side had the advantage. All intellectual superiority is the fruit of active effort. Enterprise, the desire to keep moving, to be trying and accomplishing new things for our own benefit or that of others, is the parent even of speculative, and much more of practical, talent. The intellectual culture compatible with the other type is of that feeble and vague description which belongs to a mind that stops at amusement, or at simple contemplation. The test of real and vigorous thinking, the thinking which ascertains truths instead of dreaming dreams, is successful application to practice. … With respect to practical improvement, the case is still more evident. The character which improves human life is that which struggles with natural powers and tendencies not that which gives way to them. The self-benefiting qualities are all on the side of the active and energetic character: and the habits and conduct which promote the advantage of each individual member of the community must be at least a part of those which conduce most in the end to the advancement of the community as a whole.

But on the point of moral preferability, there seems at first sign to be room for doubt. ... Contentment is always counted among the moral virtues. But it is a complete error to suppose that contentment is necessarily or naturally attendant on passivity of character; and useless it is, the moral consequences are mischievous. Where there exists a desire for advantages not possessed, the mind which does not potentially possess them by means of its own energies is apt to look with hatred and malice on those who do. The person bestirring himself with hopeful prospects to improve his circumstances is the one who feels good-will towards others engaged in, or who have succeeded in, the same pursuit. And where the majority are so engaged, those who do not attain the object have had the tone given to their feelings by the general habit of the country, and ascribe their failure to want of effort or opportunity, or to their personal ill luck. But those who, while desiring what others possess, put no energy into striving for it, are either incessantly grumbling that fortune does not do for them what they do not attempt to do for themselves, or overflowing with envy and ill-will towards those who possess what they would like to have.

There are, no doubt, in all countries really contented characters, who not merely do not seek, but do not desire, what they do not already possess, and these naturally bear no ill-will towards such as have apparently a more favoured lot. But the great mass of seeming contentment is real discontent, combined with indolence or self-indulgence, which, while taking no legitimate means of raising itself, delights in bringing others down to its own level. And if we look narrowing even at the cases of innocent contentment, we perceive that they only win our admiration when the indifference is solely to improvement in outward circumstances, and there is a striving for perpetual advancement in spiritual worth, or at least a disinterested zeal to benefit others. The contented man, or the contented family, who have no ambition to make any one else happier, to promote the good of their country or their neighbourhood, or to improve themselves in moral excellence, excite in us neither admiration nor approval. We rightly ascribe this sort of contentment to mere unmanliness and want of spirit. The content which we approve is an ability to do cheerfully without what cannot be had, a just appreciation of the comparative value of different objects of desire, and a willing renunciation of the less when incompatible with the greater. These, however, are excellences more natural to the character, in proportion as it is actively engaged in the attempt to improve its own or some other lot. He who is continually measuring his energy against difficulties learns what are the difficulties insuperable to him, and what are those which, though he might overcome, the success is not worth the cost. He whose thoughts and activities are all needed for, and habitually employed in, practicable and useful enterprises, is the person of all others least likely to let his mind dwell with brooding discontent upon things either not worth attaining, or which are not so to him. Thus the active, self-helping character is not only intrinsically the best, but is the likeliest to acquire all that is really excellent or desirable in the opposite type.

The striving, go-ahead character of England and the United States is only a fit subject of disapproving criticism on account of the very secondary objects on which it commonly expends its strength. In itself it is the foundation of the best hopes for the general improvement of mankind ....

Now there can be no kind of doubt that the passive type of character is favoured by the government of one or a few, and the active self-helping type by that of the Many. Irresponsible rulers need the quiescence of the ruled more than they need any activity but that which they can compel. Submissiveness to the prescriptions of men as necessities of nature is the lesson inculcated by all governments upon those who are wholly without participation in them. The will of superiors, and the law as the will of superiors, must be passively yielded to. But no men are mere instruments or materials in the hands of their rulers who have will or spirit or a spring of internal activity in the rest of their proceedings: and any manifestation of these qualities, instead of receiving encouragement from despots, has to get itself forgiven by them.

Very different is the state of the human faculties where a human being feels himself under no other external restraint than the necessities of nature, or mandates of society which he has his share in imposing, and which it is open to him, if he thinks them wrong, publicly to dissent from, and exert himself actively to get altered. No doubt, under a government partially popular, this freedom may be exercised even by those who are not partakers in the full privileges of citizenship. But it is a great additional stimulus to any one's self-help and self-reliance when he starts from even ground, and has not to feel that his success depends on the impression he can make upon sentiments and dispositions of a body of whom he is not one. It is a great discouragement to an individual, and a still greater one to a class, to be left out of the constitution; to be reduced to plead from outside the door to the arbiters of their destiny, not taken into consultation within. The maximum of the invigorating effect of freedom upon the character is only obtained when the person acted on either is, or is looking forward to becoming, a citizen as fully privileged as any other. What is still more important than even this matter of feeling is the practical discipline which the character obtains from the occasional demand made upon the citizens to exercise, for a time and in their turn, some social function. It is not sufficiently considered how little there is in most men's ordinary life to give any largeness either to their conceptions or to their sentiments. Their work is a routine: not a labour of love, but of self-interest in the most elementary form, the satisfaction of daily wants; neither the thing done, nor the process of doing it, introduces the mind to thoughts or feelings extending beyond individuals; if instructive books are within their reach, there is no stimulus to read them; and in most cases the individual has no access to any person of cultivation much superior to his own. Giving him something to do for the public, supplies, in a measure, all these deficiencies. If circumstances allow the amount of public duty assigned him to be considerable, it makes him an educated man. Notwithstanding the defects of the social system and moral ideas of antiquity, the practice of the dicastery and the ecclesia raised the intellectual standard of an average Athenian citizen far beyond anything of which there is yet an example in any other mass of men, ancient or modern. The proofs of this are apparent in every page of our great historian of Greece; but we need scarcely look further than to the high quality of the addresses which their great orators deemed best calculated to act with effect on their understanding and will. A benefit of the same kind, though far less in degree, is produced on Englishmen of the lower middle class by their liability to be placed on juries and to serve parish offices; which, though it does not occur to so many, nor is so continuous, nor introduces them to so great a variety of elevated considerations, as to admit of comparison with the public education which every citizen of Athens obtained from her democratic institutions, must make them nevertheless very different beings, in range of ideas and development of faculties, from those who have done nothing in their lives but drive a quill, or sell goods over a counter. Still more salutary is the moral part of the instruction afforded by the participation of the private citizen, if even rarely, in public functions. He is called upon, while so engaged, to weigh interests not his own; to be guided, in case of conflicting claims, by another rule than his private partialities; to apply, at every turn, principles and maxims which have for their reason of existence the common good; and he usually finds associated with him in the same work minds more familiarised than his own with these ideas and operations, whose study it will be to supply reasons to his understanding, and stimulation to his feeling for the general interest. He is made to feel himself one of the public, and whatever is for their benefit to be for his benefit. Where this school of public spirit does not exist, scarcely any sense is entertained that private persons, in no eminent social situation, owe any duties to society, except to obey the laws and submit to the government. There is no unselfish sentiment of identification with the public. Every thought or feeling, either of interest or of duty, is absorbed in the individual and in the family. The man never thinks of any collective interest, of any objects to be pursued jointly with others, but only in competition with them, and in some measure at their expense. A neighbour, not being an ally or an associate, since he is never engaged in any common undertaking for joint benefit, is therefore only a rival. Thus even private morality suffers, while public is actually extinct. Were this the universal and only possible state of things, the utmost aspirations of the lawgiver or the moralist could only stretch to make the bulk of the community a flock of sheep innocently nibbling the grass side by side.

From these accumulated considerations it is evident that the only government which can fully satisfy all the exigencies of the social state is one in which the whole people participate; that any participation, even in the smallest public function, is useful; that the participation should everywhere be as great as the general degree of improvement of the community will allow; and that nothing less can be ultimately desirable than the admission of all to a share in the sovereign power of the state. But since all cannot, in a community exceeding a single small town, participate personally in any but some very minor portions of the public business, it follows that the ideal type of a perfect government must be representative.

Review and Discussion Questions

1 What advantages does representative government have in managing the lives of people, independent of their character?
2 Using the three types of mental excellence, explain why Mill thinks a passive character is less desirable than an active one.
3 How does democratic government tend to promote more active character in people?
4 Mill's view is sometimes criticized on the ground that people are neither well informed nor motivated to participate effectively. Do you think that criticism has merit? Explain.

READING: A THEORY OF JUSTICE

JOHN RAWLS[*]

Political philosophy has experienced a renaissance in recent years, in large part because of the work of John Rawls. His book *A Theory of Justice* has been translated into Japanese, Chinese, and Korean, as well as every major European language. In it, Rawls revives the social contract tradition. The focus of social justice is what he terms society's *basic structure*, by which he means its constitution, its laws, and its economic system, not the justice or injustice of individual acts. Rawls's social contract is hypothetical rather than historical: Correct principles of justice are ones that *would be* chosen in a fair position of equality. That, in turn, requires us to imagine ourselves in an "original position" behind a "veil of ignorance" that prevents us from relying on such morally irrelevant factors as race, gender, social class, or even our particular talents. By forcing ourselves to choose under fair circumstances, he argues, justice is assured. Situated in such a position, he then argues, people would choose to construct their government according to principles that (1) respect basic liberties and (2) allow social and economic inequalities only if they benefit everybody, in particular society's least advantaged, and ensure that everyone is given genuine (fair) equality of opportunity to seek various positions. John Rawls held the James Bryant Conant University Professorship of Philosophy at Harvard University.

The Main Idea of the Theory of Justice

My aim is to present a conception of justice which generalizes and carries to a higher level of abstraction the familiar theory of the social contract as found, say, in Locke, Rousseau, and Kant. In order to do this we are not to think of the original contract as one to enter a particular society or to set up a particular form of government. Rather, the guiding idea is that the principles of justice for the basic structure of society are the object of the original agreement. They are the principles that free and rational persons concerned to further their own interests would accept in an initial position of equality as defining the fundamental terms of their association. These principles are to regulate all further agreements; they specify the kinds of social cooperation that can be entered into and the forms of government that can be established. This way of regarding the principles of justice I shall call justice as fairness.

Thus we are to imagine that those who engage in social cooperation choose together, in one joint act, the principles which are to assign basic rights and duties and to determine the division of social benefits. Men are to decide in advance how they are to regulate their claims against one another and what is to be the foundation charter of their society. Just as each person must decide by rational reflection

---

[*] Reprinted by permission of the publisher from *A Theory of Justice*, Second Edition, by John Rawls (Cambridge, MA: The Belknap Press of Harvard University Press, 1971), pp. 10–19, 52–56, 30–35. Copyright © 1971, 1999 by the President and Fellows of Harvard College. Most footnotes omitted.

what constitutes his good, that is, the system of ends which it is rational for him to pursue, so a group of persons must decide once and for all what is to count among them as just and unjust. The choice which rational men would make in this hypothetical situation of equal liberty, assuming for the present that this choice problem has a solution, determines the principles of justice.

In justice as fairness, the original position of equality corresponds to the state of nature in the traditional theory of the social contract. This original position is not, of course, thought of as an actual historical state of affairs, much less as a primitive condition of culture. It is understood as a purely hypothetical situation characterized so as to lead to a certain conception of justice. Among the essential features of this situation is that no one knows his place in society, his class position or social status, nor does anyone know his fortune in the distribution of natural assets and abilities, his intelligence, strength, and the like. I shall even assume that the parties do not know their conceptions of the good or their special psychological propensities. The principles of justice are chosen behind a veil of ignorance. This ensures that no one is advantaged or disadvantaged in the choice of principles by the outcome of natural chance or the contingency of social circumstances. Since all are similarly situated and no one is able to design principles to favor his particular condition, the principles of justice are the result of a fair agreement or bargain. For given the circumstances of the original position, the symmetry of everyone's relations to each other, this initial situation is fair between individuals as moral persons, that is, as rational beings with their own ends and capable, I shall assume, of a sense of justice. The original position is, one might say, the appropriate initial status quo, and thus the fundamental agreements reached in it are fair. This explains the propriety of the name "justice as fairness": it conveys the idea that the principles of justice are agreed to in an initial situation that is fair. The name does not mean that the concepts of justice and fairness are the same, any more than the phrase "poetry as metaphor" means that the concepts of poetry and metaphor are the same.

Justice as fairness begins, as I have said, with one of the most general of all choices which persons might make together, namely, with the choice of the first principles of a conception of justice which is to regulate all subsequent criticism and reform of institutions. Then, having chosen a conception of justice, we can suppose that they are to choose a constitution and a legislature to enact laws, and so on, all in accordance with the principles of justice initially agreed upon. Our social situation is just if it is such that by this sequence of hypothetical agreements we would have contracted into the general system of rules which defines it. Moreover, assuming that the original position does determine a set of principles (that is, that a particular conception of justice would be chosen), it will then be true that whenever social institutions satisfy these principles those engaged in them can say to one another that they are cooperating on terms to which they would agree if they were free and equal persons whose relations with respect to one another were fair. They could all view their arrangements as meeting the stipulations which they would acknowledge in an initial situation that embodies widely accepted and reasonable constraints on the choice of principles. The general recognition of this fact would provide the basis for a public acceptance of the corresponding principles of justice. No society can, of course, be a scheme of cooperation which men enter voluntarily in a literal sense; each person finds himself placed at birth in some particular position in some particular society, and the nature of this position materially affects his life prospects. Yet a society satisfying the principles of justice as fairness comes as close as a society can to being a voluntary scheme, for it meets the principles which free and equal persons would assent to under circumstances that are fair. In this sense its members are autonomous and the obligations they recognize self-imposed.

One feature of justice as fairness is to think of the parties in the initial situation as rational and mutually disinterested. This does not mean that the parties are egoists, that is, individuals with only certain kinds of interests, say in wealth, prestige, and domination. But they are conceived as not taking an interest in one another's interests. They are to presume that even their spiritual aims may be opposed, in the way that the aims of those of different religions may be opposed. Moreover, the concept of rationality must be interpreted as far as possible in the narrow sense, standard in economic theory, of taking the most effective means to given ends. ... [O]ne must try to avoid introducing into it any controversial ethical elements. The initial situation must be characterized by stipulations that are widely accepted.

In working out the conception of justice as fairness, one main task clearly is to determine which principles of justice would be chosen in the original position. To do this we must describe this situation in some detail and formulate with care the problem of choice which it presents. ... It may be observed, however, that once the principles of justice are thought of as arising from an original agreement in a situation of equality, it is an open question whether the principle of utility would be acknowledged. Offhand it hardly seems likely that persons who view themselves as equals, entitled to press their claims upon one another, would agree to a principle which may require lesser life prospects for some simply for the sake of a greater sum of advantages enjoyed by others. Since each desires to protect his interests, his capacity to advance his conception of the good, no one has a reason to acquiesce in an enduring loss for himself in order to bring about a greater net balance of satisfaction. In the absence of strong and lasting benevolent impulses, a rational man would not accept a basic structure merely because it maximized the algebraic sum of advantages irrespective of its permanent effects on his own basic rights and interests. Thus it seems that the principle of utility is incompatible with the conception of social cooperation among equals for mutual advantage. It appears to be inconsistent with the idea of reciprocity implicit in the notion of a well-ordered society. Or, at any rate, so I shall argue.

I shall maintain instead that the persons in the initial situation would choose two rather different principles: the first requires equality in the assignment of basic rights and duties, while the second holds that social and economic inequalities, for example inequalities of wealth and authority, are just only if they result in compensating benefits for everyone, and in particular for the least advantaged members of society. These principles rule out justifying institutions on the grounds that the hardships of some are offset by a greater good in the aggregate. It may be expedient but it is not just that some should have less in order that others may prosper. But there is no injustice in the greater benefits earned by a few provided that the situation of persons not so fortunate is thereby improved. The intuitive idea is that since everyone's well-being depends upon a scheme of cooperation without which no one could have a satisfactory life, the division of advantages should be such as to draw forth the willing cooperation of everyone taking part in it, including those less well situated. Yet this can be expected only if reasonable terms are proposed. The two principles mentioned seem to be a fair agreement on the basis of which those better endowed, or more fortunate in their social position, neither of which we can be said to deserve, could expect the willing cooperation of others when some workable scheme is a necessary condition of the welfare of all. Once we decide to look for a conception of justice that nullifies the accidents of natural endowment and the contingencies of social circumstances as counters in quest for political and economic advantage, we are led to these principles. They express the result of leaving aside those aspects of the social world that seem arbitrary from a moral point of view ....

The Original Position and Justification

I have said that the original position is the appropriate initial status quo which ensures that the fundamental agreements reached in it are fair. This fact yields the name "justice as fairness." It is clear, then, that I want to say that one conception of justice is more reasonable than another, or justifiable with respect to it, if rational persons in the initial situation would choose its principles over those of the other for the role of justice. Conceptions of justice are to be ranked by their acceptability to persons so circumstanced. Understood in this way the question of justification is settled by working out a problem of deliberation: we have to ascertain which principles it would be rational to adopt given the contractual situation. This connects the theory of justice with the theory of rational choice.

If this view of the problem of justification is to succeed, we must, of course, describe in some detail the nature of this choice problem. A problem of rational decision has a definite answer only if we know the beliefs and interests of the parties, their relations with respect to one another, the alternatives between which they are to choose, the procedure whereby they make up their minds, and so on. ... The concept of the original position, as I shall refer to it, is that of the most philosophically favored interpretation of this initial choice situation for purposes of a theory of justice.

But how are we to decide on the most favored interpretation? ... To justify a particular description of the initial situation, one shows that it incorporates these commonly held presumptions. One argues from widely accepted but weak premises to more specific conclusions. Each of the presumptions should by itself be natural and plausible; some of them may seem innocuous or even trivial. The aim of the contract approach is to establish that taken together they impose significant bounds on acceptable principles of justice ....

One should not be misled, then, by the somewhat unusual conditions which characterize the original position. The idea here is simply to make vivid to ourselves the restrictions that it seems reasonable to impose on arguments for principles of justice, and therefore on these principles themselves. Thus it seems reasonable and generally acceptable that no one should be advantaged or disadvantaged by natural fortune or social circumstances in the choice of principles. [Rawls thus argues in a later section that it is reasonable in the original position to exclude knowledge of "natural talents," such as intelligence as well as inherited wealth and social class, race, and gender, because all of these are "morally arbitrary." Social class and natural talents are not "deserved," and one's "character" also "depends in large part on fortunate family and social circumstances."—Ed.]

It also seems widely agreed that it should be impossible to tailor principles to the circumstances of one's own case. We should ensure further that particular inclinations and aspirations, and persons' conceptions of their good, do not affect the principles adopted. The aim is to rule out those principles that it would be rational to propose for acceptance, however little the chance of success, only if one knew certain things that are irrelevant from the standpoint of justice. For example, if a man knew that he was wealthy, he might find it rational to advance the principle that various taxes for welfare measures be counted unjust; if he knew that he was poor, he would most likely propose the contrary principle. To represent the desired restrictions, one imagines a situation in which everyone is deprived of this sort of information. One excludes the knowledge of those contingencies which sets men at odds and allows them to be guided by their prejudices. In this manner, the veil of ignorance is arrived at in a natural way. This concept should cause no difficulty if we keep in mind the constraints on arguments that it is meant to express. At any time we can enter the original position, so to speak, simply by following a certain procedure, namely, by arguing for principles of justice in accordance with these restrictions.

It seems reasonable to suppose that the parties in the original position are equal. That is, all have the same rights in the procedure for choosing principles; each can make proposals, submit reasons for their acceptance, and so on. Obviously the purpose of these conditions is to represent equality between human beings as moral persons, as creatures having a conception of their good and capable of a sense of justice. The basis of equality is taken to be similarity in these two respects. Systems of ends are not ranked in value; and each man is presumed to have the requisite ability to understand and to act upon whatever principles are adopted. Together with the veil of ignorance, these conditions define the principles of justice as those which rational persons concerned to advance their interests would consent to as equals when none are known to be advantaged or disadvantaged by social and natural contingencies.

There is, however, another side to justifying a particular description of the original position. This is to see if the principles which would be chosen match our considered convictions of justice or extend them in an acceptable way. We can note whether applying these principles would lead us to make the same judgments about the basic structure of society which we now make intuitively and in which we have the greatest confidence; or whether, in cases where our present judgments are in doubt and given with hesitation, these principles offer a resolution which we can affirm on reflection. There are questions which we feel sure must be answered in a certain way. For example, we are confident that religious intolerance and racial discrimination are unjust. We think that we have examined these things with care and have reached what we believe is an impartial judgment not likely to be distorted by an excessive attention to our own interests. These convictions are provisional fixed points which we presume any conception of justice must fit. But we have much less assurance as to what is the correct distribution of wealth and authority. Here we may be looking for a way to remove our doubts. We can check an interpretation of the initial situation, then, by the capacity of its principles to accommodate our firmest convictions and to provide guidance where guidance is needed.

In searching for the most favored description of this situation we work from both ends. ... By going back and forth, sometimes altering the conditions of the contractual circumstances, at others withdrawing our judgments and conforming them to principle, I assume that eventually we shall find a description of the initial situation that both expresses reasonable conditions and yields principles which match our considered judgments duly pruned and adjusted. This state of affairs I refer to as reflective equilibrium. It is an equilibrium because at last our principles and judgments coincide: and it is reflective since we know to what principles our judgments conform and the premises of their derivation. At the moment everything is in order. But this equilibrium is not necessarily stable. It is liable to be upset by further examination of the conditions which should be imposed on the contractual situation and by particular cases which may lead us to revise our judgments. Yet for the time being we have done what we can to render coherent and to justify our convictions of social justice. We have reached a conception of the original position ....

In arriving at the favored interpretation of the initial situation there is no point at which an appeal is made to self-evidence. ... A conception of justice cannot be deduced from self-evident premises or conditions on principles; instead, its justification is a matter of the mutual support of many considerations, of everything fitting together into one coherent view.

A final comment. We shall want to say that certain principles of justice are justified because they would be agreed to in an initial situation of equality. I have emphasized that this original position is purely hypothetical. It is natural to ask why, if this agreement is never actually entered into, we should take any interest in these principles, moral or otherwise. The answer is that the conditions embodied in the description of the original position are ones that we do in fact accept. Or if we do not, then perhaps we can be persuaded to do so by philosophical reflection. Each aspect of the contractual situation can be given supporting grounds. Thus what we shall do is to collect together into one conception a number of conditions on principles that we are ready upon due consideration to recognize as reasonable. These constraints express what we are prepared to regard as limits on fair terms of social cooperation. One way to look at the idea of the original position, therefore, is to see it as an expository device which sums up the meaning of these conditions and helps us to extract their consequences. On the other hand, this conception is also an intuitive notion that suggests its own elaboration, so that led on by it we are drawn to define more clearly the standpoint from which we can best interpret moral relationships. We need a conception that enables us to envision our objective from afar: the intuitive notion of the original position is to do this for us ....

Two Principles of Justice

I shall now state in a provisional form the two principles of justice that I believe would be chosen in the original position. ... The first statement of the two principles reads as follows.

First: each person is to have an equal right to the most extensive scheme of equal basic liberties compatible with a similar scheme of liberties for others.

Second: social and economic inequalities are to be arranged so that they are both (a) reasonably expected to be to everyone's advantage, and (b) attached to positions and offices open to all ....

These principles primarily apply, as I have said, to the basic structure of society and govern the assignment of rights and duties and regulate the distribution of social and economic advantages. Their formulation presupposes that, for the purposes of a theory of justice, the social structure may be viewed as having two more or less distinct parts, the first principle applying to the one, the second principle to the other. Thus we distinguish between the aspects of the social system that define and secure the equal basic liberties and the aspects that specify and establish social and economic inequalities. Now it is essential to observe that the basic liberties are given by a list of such liberties. Important among these are political liberty (the right to vote and to hold public office) and freedom of speech and assembly; liberty of conscience and freedom of thought; freedom of the person, which includes freedom from psychological oppression and physical assault and dismemberment (integrity of the person); the right to hold personal property and freedom from arbitrary arrest and seizure as defined by the concept of the rule of law. These liberties are to be equal by the first principle.

The second principle applies, in the first approximation, to the distribution of income and wealth and to the design of organizations that make use of differences in authority and responsibility. While the distribution of wealth and income need not be equal, it must be to everyone's advantage, and at the same time, positions of authority and responsibility must be accessible to all. One applies the second principle by holding positions open and then, subject to this constraint, arranges social and economic inequalities so that everyone benefits.

These principles are to be arranged in a serial order with the first principle prior to the second. This ordering means that infringements of the basic equal liberties protected by the first principle cannot be justified, or compensated for, by greater social and economic advantages. These liberties have a central range of application within which they can be limited and compromised only when they conflict with other basic liberties. Since they may be limited when they clash with one another, none of these liberties is absolute; but however they are adjusted to form one system, this system is to be the same for all. It is difficult, and perhaps impossible, to give a complete specification of these liberties independently from the particular circumstances—social, economic, and technological—of a given society. The hypothesis is that the general form of such a list could be devised with sufficient exactness to sustain this conception of justice. Of course, liberties not on the list, for example, the right to own certain kinds of property (e.g., means of production) and freedom of contract as understood by the doctrine of laissez-faire are not basic; and so they are not protected by the priority of the first principle. Finally, in regard to the second principle, the distribution of wealth and income, and positions of authority and responsibility, are to be consistent with both the basic liberties and equality of opportunity.

The two principles are rather specific in their content, and their acceptance rests on certain assumptions that I must eventually try to explain and justify. For the present, it should be observed that these principles are a special case of a more general conception of justice that can be expressed as follows.

> All social values—liberty and opportunity, income and wealth, and the social bases of self-respect—are to be distributed equally unless an unequal distribution of any, or all, of these values is to everyone's advantage.

Injustice, then, is simply inequalities that are not to the benefit of all. Of course, this conception is extremely vague and requires interpretation.

As a first step, suppose that the basic structure of society distributes certain primary goods, that is, things that every rational man is presumed to want. These goods normally have a use, whatever a person's rational plan of life. For simplicity, assume that the chief primary goods at the disposition of society are rights, liberties, and opportunities, and income and wealth. ... [and self-respect. (Rawls understands self-respect to involve two related beliefs or attitudes: that one's goals and values are worthy ones, and that one has a reasonable prospect of achieving those worthwhile ends.—Ed.)] These are the social primary goods. Other primary goods such as health and vigor, intelligence and imagination, are natural goods; although their possession is influenced by the basic structure, they are not so directly under its control. Imagine, then, a hypothetical initial arrangement in which all the social primary goods are equally distributed: everyone has similar rights and duties, and income and wealth are evenly shared. This state of affairs provides a benchmark for judging improvements. If certain inequalities of wealth and differences in authority would make everyone better off than in this hypothetical starting situation, then they accord with the general conception.

Now it is possible, at least theoretically, that by giving up some of their fundamental liberties men are sufficiently compensated by the resulting social and economic gains. ... We need not suppose anything so drastic as consenting to a condition of slavery. Imagine instead that people seem willing to forgo certain political rights when the economic returns are significant. It is this kind of exchange which the two principles rule out; being arranged in serial order they do not permit exchanges between basic liberties and economic and social gains except under extenuating circumstances.

For the most part, I shall leave aside the general conception of justice and examine instead the two principles in serial order. The advantage of this procedure is that from the first the matter of priorities is recognized and an effort made to find principles to deal with it. One is led to attend throughout to the conditions under which the absolute weight of liberty with respect to social and economic advantages, as defined by the lexical order of the two principles, would be reasonable. Offhand, this ranking appears extreme and too special a case to be of much interest; but there is more justification for it than would appear at first sight. Or at any rate, so I shall maintain. [Rawls argues that it is rational after a certain level of economic development has been achieved by the society.—Ed.] Furthermore, the distinction between fundamental rights and liberties and economic and social benefits marks a difference among primary social goods that suggests an important division in the social system ....

Now the second principle insists that each person benefit from permissible inequalities in the basic structure. This means that it must be reasonable for each relevant representative man defined by this structure, when he views it as a going concern, to prefer his prospects with the inequality to his prospects without it. One is not allowed to justify differences in income or in positions of authority and responsibility on the ground that the disadvantages of those in one position are outweighed by the greater advantages of those in another. Much less can infringements of liberty be counterbalanced in this way. It is obvious, however, that there are indefinitely many ways in which all may be advantaged when the initial arrangement of equality is taken as a benchmark. How then are we to choose among these possibilities? The principles must be specified so that they yield a determinate conclusion. I now turn to this problem.

The Reasoning Leading to the Two Principles of Justice

I [now] take up the choice between the two principles of justice and the principle of average utility. Determining the rational preference between these two options is perhaps the central problem in developing the conception of justice as fairness as a viable alternative to the utilitarian tradition ....

Now consider the point of view of anyone in the original position. There is no way for him to win special advantages for himself. Nor, on the other hand, are there grounds for his acquiescing in special disadvantages. Since it is not reasonable for him to expect more than an equal share in the division of social primary goods, and since it is not rational for him to agree to less, the sensible thing is to acknowledge as the first step a principle of justice requiring an equal distribution. Indeed, this principle is so obvious given the symmetry of the parties that it would occur to everyone immediately. Thus the parties start with a principle requiring equal basic liberties for all, as well as fair equality of opportunity and equal division of income and wealth.

But even holding firm to the priority of the basic liberties and fair equality of opportunity [By fair equality of opportunity Rawls means that two equally talented children would have the same chance to reach their goals, regardless of socioeconomic background.—Ed.] there is no reason why this initial acknowledgment should be final. Society should take into account economic efficiency and the requirements of organization and technology. If there are inequalities in income and wealth and differences in authority and degrees of responsibility that work to make everyone better off in comparison with the benchmark of equality, why not permit them? One might think that ideally individuals should want to serve one another. But since the parties are assumed to be mutually disinterested, their acceptance of these economic and institutional inequalities is only the recognition of the relations of opposition in which men stand in the circumstances of justice. They have no grounds for complaining of one another's motives. Thus the parties would agree to these differences only if they would be dejected by the bare knowledge or perception that others are better situated; but I suppose that they decide as if they are not moved by envy. Thus the basic structure should allow these inequalities so long as these improve everyone's situation, including that of the least advantaged, provided that they are consistent with equal liberty and fair opportunity. Because the parties start from an equal division of all social primary goods, those who benefit least have, so to speak, a veto. Thus we arrive at the [second, or] difference principle. Taking equality as the basis of comparison, those who have gained more must do so on terms that are justifiable to those who have gained the least.

By some such reasoning, then, the parties might arrive at the two principles of justice in serial order. I shall not try to justify this ordering here, but the following remarks may convey the intuitive idea. I assume that the parties view themselves as free persons who have fundamental aims and interests in the name of which they think it legitimate for them to make claims on one another concerning the design of the basic structure of society. The religious interest is a familiar historical example; the interest in the integrity of the person is another. In the original position the parties do not know what particular forms these interests take, but they do assume that they have such interests and that the basic liberties necessary for their protection are guaranteed by the first principle. Since they must secure these interests, they rank the first principle prior to the second. The case for the two principles can be strengthened by spelling out in more detail the notion of a free person. Very roughly, the parties regard themselves as having a highest-order interest in how all their other interests, including even their fundamental ones, are shaped and regulated by social institutions. They do not think of themselves as inevitably bound to, or as identical with, the pursuit of any particular complex of fundamental interests that they may have at any given time, although they want the right to advance such interests (provided they are admissible). Rather, free persons conceive of themselves as beings who can revise and alter their final ends and who give first priority to preserving their liberty in these matters. Hence, they not only have final ends that they are in principle free to pursue or to reject, but their original allegiance and continued devotion to these ends are to be formed and affirmed under conditions that are free. Since the two principles secure a social form that maintains these conditions, they would be agreed to rather than the principle of utility. Only by this agreement can the parties be sure that their highest-order interest as free persons is guaranteed.

The priority of liberty means that whenever the basic liberties can be effectively established, a lesser or an unequal liberty cannot be exchanged for an improvement in economic well-being. It is only when social circumstances do not allow the effective establishment of these basic rights that one can concede their limitation, and even then these restrictions can be granted only to the extent that they are necessary to prepare the way for the time when they are no longer justified. The denial of the equal liberties can be defended only when it is essential to change the conditions of civilization so that in due course these liberties can be enjoyed. Thus, in adopting the serial order of the two principles, the parties are assuming that the conditions of their society, whatever they are, admit the effective realization of the equal liberties. Or that if they do not, circumstances are nevertheless sufficiently favorable so that the priority of the first principle points out the most urgent changes and identifies the preferred path to the social state in which all the basic liberties can be fully instituted. The complete realization of the two principles in serial order is the long-run tendency of this ordering, at least under reasonably fortunate conditions.

It seems from these remarks that the two principles are at least a plausible conception of justice ....

Equal Liberty of Conscience

.... Turning then to liberty of conscience, it seems evident that the parties must choose principles that secure the integrity of their religious and moral freedom. They do not know, of course, what their religious or moral convictions are or what is the particular content of their moral or religious obligations as they interpret them. Indeed, they do not know that they think of themselves as having such obligations. The possibility that they do suffices for the argument, although I shall make the stronger assumption. Further, the parties do not know how their religious or moral view fares in their society; whether, for example, it is in the majority or the minority. All they know is that they have obligations which they interpret in this way. The question they are to decide is which principle they should adopt to regulate the liberties of citizens in regard to their fundamental religious, moral, and philosophical interests.

Now it seems that equal liberty of conscience is the only principle that the persons in the original position can acknowledge. They cannot take chances with their liberty by permitting the dominant religious or moral doctrine to persecute or to suppress others if it wishes. Even granting (what may be questioned) that it is more probable than not that one will turn out to belong to the majority (if a majority exists), to gamble in this way would show that one did not take one's religious or moral convictions seriously or highly value the liberty to examine one's beliefs. Nor, on the other hand, could the parties consent to the principle of utility. In this case, their freedom would be subject to the calculus of social interests and they would be authorizing its restriction if this would lead to a greater net balance of satisfaction. Of course, as we have seen, a utilitarian may try to argue from the general facts of social life that when properly carried out, the computation of advantages never justifies such limitations, at least under reasonably favorable conditions of culture. But even if the parties were persuaded of this, they might as well guarantee their freedom straightaway by adopting the principle of equal liberty. There is nothing gained by not doing so, and, to the extent that the outcome of the actuarial calculation is unclear, a great deal may be lost. Indeed, if we give a realistic interpretation to the general knowledge available to the parties ... they are forced to reject the utilitarian principle. These considerations have all the more force in view of the complexity and vagueness of these calculations (if we can so describe them) as they are bound to be made in practice.

Moreover, the initial agreement on the principle of equal liberty is final. An individual recognizing religious and moral obligations regards them as binding absolutely in the sense that he cannot qualify his fulfillment of them for the sake of greater means for promoting his other interests. Greater economic and social benefits are not a sufficient reason for accepting less than an equal liberty. It seems possible to consent to an unequal liberty only if there is a threat of coercion which it is unwise to resist from the standpoint of liberty itself. For example, the situation may be one in which a person's religion or his moral view will be tolerated provided that he does not protest, whereas claiming an equal liberty will bring greater repression that cannot be effectively opposed. But from the perspective of the original position, there is no way of ascertaining the relative strength of various doctrines and so these considerations do not arise. The veil of ignorance leads to an agreement on the principles of equal liberty; and the strength of religious and moral obligations as men interpret them seems to require that the two principles be put in serial order, at least when applied to freedom of conscience.

It may be said against the principle of equal liberty that religious sects, say, cannot acknowledge any principle at all for limiting their claims on one another. The duty to religious and divine law being absolute, no understanding among persons of different faiths is permissible from a religious point of view. Certainly men have often acted as if they held this doctrine. It is unnecessary, however, to argue against it. It suffices that if any principle can be agreed to, it must be that of equal liberty. A person may indeed think that others ought to recognize the same beliefs and first principles that he does and that by not doing so they are grievously in error and miss the way to their salvation. But an understanding of religious obligation and of philosophical and moral first principles shows that we cannot expect others to acquiesce in an inferior liberty. Much less can we ask them to recognize us as the proper interpreter of their religious duties or moral obligations.

We should now observe that these reasons for the first principle receive further support once the parties' concern for the next generation is taken into account. Since they have a desire to obtain similar liberties for their descendants, and these liberties are also secured by the principle of equal liberty, there is no conflict of interests between generations.

Review and Discussion Questions

1 What does Rawls mean by the "basic structure" of society?
2 Describe the original position: Behind the veil of ignorance, what do people know and what do they not know?
3 What are "social primary goods"? What role do they play in Rawls's theory?
4 In what sense are the social contractors equal? How does Rawls's theory express the idea that all persons are "created equal"?
5 Why does Rawls term his theory "justice as fairness"? What reasons does Rawls give for using this hypothetical thought experiment of a veil of ignorance?
6 Discuss Rawls's defense of liberty of conscience. How does he answer religious sects that believe others should accept a religious basis of state power?
7 It is sometimes said that Rawls unreasonably assumes people can "forget" their social class, natural talents, and conception of the good when, in fact, they cannot do so. How would Rawls respond to that objection? Are there other circumstances in which we expect people to ignore what they know in making a decision?
8 Does Rawls assume people are in fact concerned only with their own well-being? Explain.

Essay and Paper Topics for Chapter 13

1 Compare the differing conceptions of the social contract presented by Locke and Rawls.
2 In what ways should government promote well-being, if at all?
3 "It is neither possible, nor desirable, to seek complete neutrality between different ideas of human well-being or happiness." Discuss.
4 Compare the views of all of the writers in this chapter on the nature, and the limits, of the duties we owe to each other.

Chapter 14

Protests, Patriotism, and the Rule of Law

Law surrounds us from before we are born until long after we are dead. It limits what we may do to others and what they may do to us. It influences whether we attend school, what our jobs are like, whether we live in peace or fear, and how we die. It also punishes us when we violate it, even though we may sometimes believe the law to be unjust. Essays in this chapter address a range of interrelated problems about legal obligation and the ideal of the rule of law, including the basis of legal obligation, the nature and value of patriotism, whether and under what conditions civil disobedience is justified, the nature and importance of the rule of law, and legitimate and illegitimate uses of police force.

READING: FLAG BURNING AS CONSTITUTIONALLY PROTECTED

TEXAS V. JOHNSON[*]

In 1989, forty-eight states and the U.S. Congress had passed laws banning flag burning. After burning the U.S. flag as an act of political protest, Gregory Lee Johnson was convicted of desecrating a flag in violation of Texas law. The state of Texas, after losing in lower courts, appealed to the U.S. Supreme Court, which had to decide whether Johnson's conviction was consistent with the First Amendment's protection of freedom of speech. By a narrow vote of five to four, the Court again held that the Texas law was unconstitutional. Delivering the opinion of the Court, Justice Brennan argues that the state cannot "prescribe what shall be orthodox" by punishing symbolic actions such as flag burning. The way to preserve the flag's special role in our national life, he argues, is not to punish those who feel differently about this symbol but to persuade them that they are wrong. In their separate dissents, Justice Rehnquist and Justice Stevens reject the idea that the flag is just another symbol toward which it would be unconstitutional to require minimal respect.

Justice Brennan

As in *Spence* [*v. Washington*, a 1974 case on expressive conduct], "[w]e are confronted with a case of prosecution for the expression of an idea through activity,"

---

[*] *Texas v. Johnson* 57 L.W. 4770 (1989).

and "[a]ccordingly, we must examine with particular care the interests advanced by [petitioner] to support its prosecution." ... Johnson was not, we add, prosecuted for the expression of just any idea; he was prosecuted for his expression of dissatisfaction with the policies of this country, expression situated at the core of our First Amendment values.

Moreover, Johnson was prosecuted because he knew that his politically charged expression would cause "serious offense." If he had burned the flag as a means of disposing of it because it was dirty or torn, he would not have been convicted of flag desecration under this Texas law: federal law designates burning as the preferred means of disposing of a flag "when it is in such condition that it is no longer a fitting emblem for display." ...

If we are to hold that a State may forbid flag burning wherever it is likely to endanger the flag's symbolic role, but allow it wherever burning a flag promotes that role—as where, for example, a person ceremoniously burns a dirty flag—we would be saying that when it comes to impairing the flag's physical integrity, the flag itself may be used as a symbol—as a substitute for the written or spoken word or a "short cut from mind to mind"—only in one direction. We would be permitting a State to "prescribe what shall be orthodox" by saying that one may burn the flag to convey one's attitude toward it and its referents only if one does not endanger the flag's representation of nationhood and national unity.

We never before have held that the government may ensure that a symbol be used to express only one view of that symbol or its referents ....

We are fortified in today's conclusion by our conviction that forbidding criminal punishment for conduct such as Johnson's will not endanger the special role played by our flag or the feelings it inspires. To paraphrase Justice [Oliver Wendell] Holmes, we submit that nobody can suppose that this one gesture of an unknown man will change our nation's attitude toward its flag. ... Indeed, Texas's argument that the burning of an American flag "is an act having a high likelihood to cause a breach of peace" ... and its statute's implicit assumption that physical mistreatment of the flag will lead to "serious offense," tend to confirm that the flag's special role is not in danger; if it were, no one would riot or take offense because a flag had been burned.

We are tempted to say, in fact, that the flag's deservedly cherished place in our community will be strengthened, not weakened, by our holding today. Our decision is a reaffirmation of the principles of freedom and inclusiveness that the flag best reflects, and of the conviction that our toleration of criticism such as Johnson's is a sign and source of our strength. Indeed, one of the proudest images of our flag, the one immortalized in our own national anthem, is of the bombardment it survived at Fort McHenry. It is the nation's resilience, not its rigidity, that Texas sees reflected in the flag—and it is that resilience that we reassert today.

The way to preserve the flag's special role is not to punish those who feel differently about these matters. It is to persuade them that they are wrong.

To courageous, self-reliant men, with confidence in the power of free and fearless reasoning applied through the processes of popular government, no danger flowing from speech can be deemed clear and present, unless the incidence of the evil apprehended is so imminent that it may befall before there is opportunity for full discussion. If there be time to expose through discussion the falsehood and fallacies, to avert the evil by the processes of education, the remedy to be applied is more speech, not enforced silence ....

And, precisely because it is our flag that is involved, one's response to the flag burner may exploit the uniquely persuasive power of the flag itself. We can imagine no more appropriate response to burning a flag than waving one's own, no better way to counter a flag burner's message than by saluting the flag that burns, no surer means of preserving the dignity even of the flag that burned than by—as one witness here did—according its remains a respectful burial. We do not consecrate the flag by punishing its desecration, for in doing so we dilute the freedom that this cherished emblem represents.

Johnson was convicted for engaging in expressive conduct. The State's interest in preventing breaches of the peace does not support his conviction because Johnson's conduct did not threaten to disturb the peace. Nor does the State's interest in preserving the flag as a symbol of nationhood and national unity justify his criminal conviction for engaging in political expression. The judgment of the Texas Court of Criminal Appeals is therefore affirmed.

Justice Rehnquist, Dissenting

In holding this Texas statute unconstitutional, the court ignores Justice Holmes's familiar aphorism that "a page of history is worth a volume of logic." ... For more than 200 years, the American flag has occupied a unique position as the symbol of our nation, a uniqueness that justifies a governmental prohibition against flag burning in the way respondent Johnson did here.

In the First and Second World Wars, thousands of our countrymen died on foreign soil fighting for the American cause. At Iwo Jima in the Second World War, United States Marines fought hand to hand against thousands of Japanese. By the time the Marines reached the top of Mount Suribachi, they raised a piece of pipe upright and from one end fluttered a flag. That ascent had cost nearly 6,000 American lives ....

During the Korean War, the successful amphibious landing of American troops at Inchon was marked by the raising of an American flag within an hour of the event ....

The government is simply recognizing as a fact the profound regard for the American flag created by that history when it enacts statutes prohibiting the disrespectful public burning of the flag.

The court concludes its opinion with a regrettably patronizing civics lecture, presumably addressed to members of both houses of Congress, the members of the 48 state legislatures that enacted prohibitions against flag burning and the troops fighting under that flag in Vietnam who objected to its being burned: "The way to preserve the flag's special role is not to punish those who feel differently about these matters. It is to persuade them that they are wrong." ...

The court's role as the final expositor of the Constitution is well established, but its role as a platonic guardian admonishing those responsible to public opinion as if they were truant schoolchildren has no similar place in our system of government. The cry of "no taxation without representation" animated those who revolted against the English Crown to found our nation—the idea that those who submitted to government should have some say as to what kind of laws would be passed.

Surely one of the high purposes of a democratic society is to legislate against conduct that is regarded as evil and profoundly offensive to the majority of people—whether it be murder, embezzlement, pollution, or flag burning.

Our Constitution wisely places limits on powers of legislative majorities to act, but the declaration of such limits by this court "is, at all times, a question of much delicacy, which ought seldom, if ever, to be decided in the affirmative, in a doubtful case." ... Uncritical extension of constitutional protection to the burning of the flag risks the frustration of the very purpose for which organized governments are instituted. The Court decides that the American flag is just another symbol, about which not only must opinions pro and con be tolerated, but for which the most minimal public respect may not be enjoined. The government may conscript men into the armed forces where they must fight and perhaps die for the flag, but the government may not prohibit the public burning of the banner under which they fight. I would uphold the Texas statute as applied in this case.

Justice Stevens, Dissenting

As the court analyzes this case, it presents the question whether the state of Texas, or indeed the federal government, has the power to prohibit the public desecration of the American flag. The question is unique. In my judgment, rules that apply to a host of other symbols, such as state flags, armbands, or various privately promoted emblems of political or commercial identity, are not necessarily controlling. Even if flag burning could be considered just another species of symbolic speech under the logical application of the rules that the Court has developed in its interpretation of the First Amendment in other contexts, this case has an intangible dimension that makes those rules inapplicable.

A country's flag is a symbol of more than "nationhood and national unity." ... It also signifies the ideas that characterize the society that has chosen that emblem as well as the special history that has animated the growth and power of those ideas. The fleurs-de-lis and the tricolor both symbolized "nationhood and national unity," but they had vastly different meanings. The message conveyed by some flags—the swastika, for example—may survive long after it has outlived its usefulness as a symbol of regimented unity in a particular nation.

So it is with the American flag. It is more than a proud symbol of the courage, the determination, and the gifts of nature that transformed 13 fledgling Colonies into a world power. It is a symbol of freedom, of equal opportunity, of religious tolerance, and of good will for other peoples who share our aspirations. The symbol carries its message to dissidents both at home and abroad who may have no interest at all in our national unity or survival.

The value of the flag as a symbol cannot be measured. Even so, I have no doubt that the interest in preserving that value for the future is both significant and legitimate. Conceivably that value will be enhanced by the Court's conclusion that our national commitment to free expression is so strong that even the United States as ultimate guarantor of that freedom is without power to prohibit the desecration of its unique symbol. But I am unpersuaded ....

The case has nothing to do with "disagreeable ideas." ... [I]t involves disagreeable conduct that, in my opinion, diminishes the value of an important national asset.

The court is therefore quite wrong in blandly asserting that respondent "was prosecuted for his expression of dissatisfaction with the policies of this country, expression situated at the core of our First Amendment values." ... Respondent was prosecuted because of the method he chose to express his dissatisfaction with those policies. Had he chosen to spray-paint—or perhaps convey with a motion picture projector—his message of dissatisfaction on the facade of the Lincoln Memorial, there would be no question about the power of the government to prohibit his means of expression. The prohibition would be supported by the legitimate interest in preserving the quality of an important national asset. Though the asset at stake in this case is intangible, given its unique value, the same interest supports a prohibition on the desecration of the American flag.

The ideas of liberty and equality have been an irresistible force in motivating leaders like Patrick Henry, Susan B. Anthony, and Abraham Lincoln, schoolteachers like Nathan Hale and Booker T. Washington, the Philippine Scouts who fought at Bataan, and the soldiers who scaled the bluff at Omaha Beach. If those ideas are worth fighting for—and our history demonstrates that they are—it cannot be true that the flag that uniquely symbolizes their power is not itself worthy of protection from unnecessary desecration.

I respectfully dissent.

Review and Discussion Questions

1 What does Texas argue is the danger in allowing flag burning?
2 What is at the heart of the issue, for Justice Brennan?
3 Why, according to Justice Brennan, might allowing such political protests actually *increase* people's sense of patriotism?
4 Explain the reasoning behind the two dissenting opinions.
5 What is patriotism? Was Johnson's action unpatriotic? How would the different judges answer these questions?

READING: IS PATRIOTISM A VIRTUE?

ALASDAIR MACINTYRE[*]

In this essay, Alasdair MacIntyre argues that classical "liberal" moral theories such as utilitarianism and Kantianism, which rest on familiar Enlightenment ideals of objectivity and impartiality, are deeply mistaken. Because such theories would have us judge actions from an impartial standpoint, it follows that patriotism, rather than being a virtue, would in fact be a moral vice since patriots are partial or biased in favor of their own nation. MacIntyre defends patriotism against this charge by questioning the adequacy of the liberal moral vision. Morality must finally rest, he claims, on the values found in the community in which people live

---

[*] The Lindley Lecture, Department of Philosophy, University of Kansas (1984). Copyright © 1984 by the University of Kansas. Reprinted by permission of the author and the University of Kansas.

rather than on the universal, cross-cultural norms of liberalism. The liberal vision should be replaced, he argues, by the patriot's willingness to exempt his or her nation's projects and practices from criticism. Such an exemption does not mean, however, that the patriot must support any particular policy or even government—but instead that he or she remains committed to the nation viewed as a historic project with a distinctive political and moral identity. Only through such a patriotic stance, he argues, can a satisfactory moral vision be supported, one that maintains the essentially historical connections that constitute a community's identity and provides people's lives with meaning. Alasdair MacIntyre is Emeritus University Professor of Philosophy at Notre Dame University.

I

.... It is quite clear that there are large disagreements about patriotism in our society. And although it would be a mistake to suppose that there are only two clear, simple, and mutually opposed sets of beliefs about patriotism, it is at least plausible to suggest that the range of conflicting views can be placed on a spectrum with two poles. At one end is the view, taken for granted by almost everyone in the nineteenth century, a commonplace in the literary culture of the McGuffey readers, that "patriotism" names a virtue. At the other end is the contrasting view, expressed with sometimes shocking clarity in the nineteen sixties, that "patriotism" names a vice. It would be misleading for me to suggest that I am going to be able to offer good reasons for taking one of these views rather than the other. What I do hope to achieve is a clarification of the issues that divide them.

A necessary first step is to distinguish patriotism, properly so called, from two other sets of attitudes that are all too easily assimilated to it. The first is that exhibited by those who are protagonists of their own nation's causes because, and only because, so they assert, it is their nation which is the champion of some great moral ideal.

In the Great War of 1914–18 Max Weber claimed that Imperial Germany should be supported because its was the cause of *Kultur*, while Emile Durkheim claimed with equal vehemence that France should be supported because its was the cause of *civilization*. And here and now there are those American politicians who claim that the United States deserves our allegiance because it champions the goods of freedom. ... What distinguishes their attitude from patriotism is twofold: first, it is the ideal and not the nation which is the primary object of their regard; and secondly, insofar as their regard for the ideal provides good reasons for allegiance to their country, it provides good reasons for anyone at all to uphold their country's cause, irrespective of their nationality or citizenship.

Patriotism, by contrast, is defined in terms of a kind of loyalty to a particular nation which only those possessing that particular nationality can exhibit. Only Frenchmen can be patriotic about France, while anyone can make the cause of *civilization* their own. But it would be all too easy in noticing this to fail to make a second equally important distinction. Patriotism is not to be confused with a mindless loyalty to one's own particular nation which has no regard at all for the characteristics of that particular nation. Patriotism does generally and characteristically involve a peculiar regard not just for one's own nation but for the particular characteristics and merits and achievements of one's own nation. These latter are indeed valued as merits and achievements and their character as merits and achievements provides reasons supportive of the patriot's attitudes. But the patriot does not value in the same way precisely similar merits and achievements when they are the merits and achievements of some nation other than his or hers. For he or she—at least in the role of patriot—values them not just as merits and achievements but as the merits and achievements of this particular nation ....

II

The presupposition of the thesis [that patriotism is not a virtue] is an account of morality which has enjoyed high prestige in our culture. According to that account, to judge from a moral standpoint is to judge impersonally. It is to judge as any rational person would judge, independently of his or her interests, affections, and social position. And to act morally is to act in accordance with such impersonal judgments. Thus, to think and to act morally involves a moral agent in abstracting him or herself from all social particularity and partiality. The potential conflict between morality so understood and patriotism is at once clear. For patriotism requires me to exhibit peculiar devotion to my nation and you to yours. It requires me to regard such contingent social facts as where I was born and what government ruled over that place at that time, who my parents were, who my great-great-grandparents were, and so on as deciding for me the question of what virtuous action is—at least insofar as it is the virtue of patriotism which is in question. Hence, the moral standpoint and the patriotic standpoint are systematically incompatible ....

For the impersonal moral standpoint, understood as the philosophical protagonists of modern liberalism have understood it, requires neutrality not only between rival and competing interests but also between rival and competing sets of beliefs about the best way for human beings to live. Each individual is to be left free to pursue in his or her own way that way of life which he or she judges to be best; while morality by contrast consists of rules which, just because they are such that any rational person, independently of his or her interests or point of view on the best way for human beings to live, would assent to them, are equally binding on all persons. Hence, in conflicts between nations or other communities over ways of life, the standpoint of morality will once again be that of an impersonal arbiter, adjudicating in ways that give equal weight to each individual person's needs, desires, beliefs about the good and the like, while the patriot is once again required to be partisan.

Notice that in speaking of the standpoint of liberal impersonal morality in the way in which I have done, I have been describing a standpoint whose truth is both presupposed by the political actions and utterances of a great many people in our society and explicitly articulated and defended by most modern moral philosophers and that it has at the level of moral philosophy a number of distinct versions—some with a Kantian flavor, some utilitarian, some contractarian. ... What morality provides is standards by which all actual social structures may be brought to judgment from a standpoint independent of all of them. It is morality so understood that is allegiance, which is not only incompatible with treating patriotism as a virtue but which requires that patriotism—at least in any substantial version—be treated as a vice.

But is this the only possible way to understand morality? As a matter of history, the answer is clearly "No." ...

III

According to the liberal account of morality, *where* and *from whom* I learn the principles of morality are and must be irrelevant both to the question of what the content of morality is and to that of the nature of my commitment to it, as irrelevant as *where* and *from whom* I learn the principles and precepts of mathematics are to the content of mathematics and the nature of my commitment to mathematical truths. By contrast, on the alternative account of morality which I am going to sketch, the questions of *where* and *from whom* I learn my morality turn out to be crucial for both the content and the nature of moral commitment.

On this view, it is an essential characteristic of the morality which each of us acquires that it is learned from, in, and through the way of life of some particular community. ... [T]he form of the rules of morality as taught and apprehended will be intimately connected with specific institutional arrangements. The moralities of different societies may agree in having a precept enjoining that a child should honor his or her parents, but what it is so to honor and indeed what a father is and what a mother is will vary greatly between different social orders. So that what I learn as a guide to my actions and as a standard for evaluating them is never morality as such, but always the highly specific morality of some highly specific social order ....

[It] is not just that I first apprehend the rules of morality in some socially specific and particularized form. ... For central to those goods is the enjoyment of one particular kind of social life lived out through a particular set of social relationships, and thus what I enjoy is the good of *this* particular social life inhabited by me and I enjoy it as what it is. It may well be that it follows that I would enjoy and benefit equally from similar forms of social life in other communities; but this hypothetical truth in no way diminishes the importance of the contention that my goods are as a matter of fact found *here*, among *these* particular people, in *these* particular relationships ....

It follows that *I* find *my* justification for allegiance to these rules of morality in *my* particular community; deprived of the life of that community, *I* would have no reason to be moral. But this is not all. To obey the rules of morality is characteristically and generally a hard task for human beings. Indeed, were it not so, our need for morality would not be what it is. It is because we are continually liable to be blinded by immediate desire, to be distracted from our responsibilities, to lapse into backsliding and because even the best of us may at times encounter quite unusual temptations that it is important to morality that I can only be a moral agent because we are moral agents, that I need those around me to reinforce my moral strengths and assist in remedying my moral weaknesses ....

Indeed, the case for treating patriotism as a virtue is now clear. *If*, first of all, it is the case that I can only apprehend the rules of morality in the version in which they are incarnated in some specific community, and *if*, secondly, it is the case that the justification of morality must be in terms of particular goods enjoyed within the life of particular communities; and *if*, thirdly, it is the case that I am characteristically brought into being and maintained as a moral agent only through the particular kinds of moral sustenance afforded by my community, *then* it is clear that deprived of this community, I am unlikely to flourish as a moral agent. Hence, my allegiance to the community and what it requires of me—even to the point of requiring me to die to sustain its life—could not meaningfully be contrasted with or counterposed to what morality required of me. Detached from my community, I will be apt to lose my hold upon all genuine standards of judgment. Loyalty to that community, to the hierarchy of particular kinship, particular local community, and particular natural community, is on this view a prerequisite for morality. So patriotism and those loyalties cognate to it are not just virtues but central virtues. Everything, however, turns on the truth or falsity of the claims advanced in the three preceding if-clauses ....

What we have here are two rival and incompatible moralities [the morality of liberalism and the morality of patriotism], each of which is viewed from within by its adherents as morality as such, each of which makes its exclusive claim to our allegiance. How are we to evaluate such claims? ...

IV

.... The morality for which patriotism is a virtue offers a form of rational justification for moral rules and precepts whose structure is clear and rationally defensible. The rules of morality are justifiable if, and only if, they are productive of and partially constitutive of a form of shared social life whose goods are directly enjoyed by those inhabiting the particular communities whose social life is of that kind. Hence, qua member of this or that particular community, I can appreciate the justification for what morality requires of me from within the social roles that I live out in my community. By contrast, it may be argued, liberal morality requires of me to assume an abstract and artificial—perhaps even an impossible—stance, that of a rational being as such responding to the requirements of morality, not qua parent or farmer or quarterback but qua rational agent who has abstracted him or herself from all social particularity, who has become not merely Adam Smith's impartial spectator but a correspondingly impartial actor and one who in his impartiality is doomed to rootlessness, to be a citizen of nowhere. How can I justify to myself performing this act of abstraction and detachment?

The liberal answer is clear: such abstraction and detachment is defensible because it is a necessary condition of moral freedom, of emancipation from the bondage of the social, political, and economic status quo. For unless I can stand back from every and any feature of that status quo, including the roles within it which I myself presently inhabit, I will be unable to view it critically and to decide for myself what stance it is rational and right for me to adopt toward it. This does not preclude that the outcome for such a critical evaluation may not be an endorsement of all or some of the existing social order, but even such an endorsement will only be free and rational if I have made it for myself in this way. ... Thus, liberal morality does after all appeal to an overriding good, the good of this particular kind of emancipating freedom. And in the name of this good it is able not only to respond to the question about how the rules of morality are to be justified but also to frame a plausible and potentially damaging objection to the morality of patriotism.

It is of the essence of the morality of liberalism that no limitations are or can be set upon the criticism of the social status quo. No institution, no practice, no loyalty can be immune from being put in question and perhaps rejected. Conversely, the morality of patriotism is one which, precisely because it is framed in terms of the membership of some particular social community with some particular social, political, and economic structure, must exempt at least some fundamental structures of that community's life from criticism. Because patriotism has to be a loyalty that is in some respects unconditional, so in just those respects rational criticism is ruled out. But if so, the adherents of the morality of patriotism have condemned themselves to a fundamentally irrational attitude—since to refuse to examine some of one's fundamental beliefs and attitudes is to insist on accepting them, whether they are rationally justifiable or not, which is irrational—and have imprisoned themselves within that irrationality. What answer can the adherents of the morality of patriotism make to this kind of accusation? The reply must be threefold.

When the liberal moralist claims that the patriot is bound to treat his or her nation's projects and practices in some measure uncritically, the claim is not only that at any one time certain of these projects and practices will be being treated uncritically; it is that some at least must be permanently exempted from criticism. ... What then is exempted? The answer is: the nation conceived *as a project*, a project somehow or other brought to birth in the past and carried on so that a morally distinctive community was brought into being which embodied a claim to political autonomy in its various organized and institutionalized expressions. ... What the patriot is committed to is a particular way of linking a past which has conferred a distinctive moral and political identity upon him or her with a future for the project which is his or her nation which it is his or her responsibility to bring into being. Only this allegiance is unconditional, and allegiance to particular governments or forms of government or particular leaders will be entirely conditional upon their being devoted to furthering that project rather than frustrating or destroying it. Hence, there is nothing inconsistent in a patriot's being deeply opposed to his country's contemporary rulers or plotting their overthrow, as Adam von Trott did ....

.... [I]t does not follow that it cannot provide rational grounds for repudiating many features of that country's present organized social life. The conception of justice engendered by the notion of citizenship within a particular community may provide standards by which particular political institutions are found wanting. ... Yes, the liberal critic of patriotism will respond, this indeed may happen; but it may not and it often will not. Patriotism turns out to be a permanent source of moral danger. And this claim, I take it, cannot in fact be successfully rebutted ....

That the rational protagonist of the morality of patriotism is compelled, if my argument is correct, to concede this does not mean that there is not more to be said in the debate. And what needs to be said is that the liberal morality of impartiality and impersonality turns out also to be a morally dangerous phenomenon in an interestingly corresponding way. For suppose the bonds of patriotism to be dissolved: Would liberal morality be able to provide anything adequately substantial in its place? What the morality of patriotism at its best provides is a clear account of and justification for the particular bonds and loyalties which form so much of the substance of the moral life. It does so by underlining the moral importance of the different members of a group acknowledging a shared history. Each one of us to some degree or other understands his or her life as an enacted narrative, and because of our relationships with others we have to understand ourselves as characters in the enacted narratives of other people's lives. Moreover, the story of each of our lives is characteristically embedded in the story of one or more larger units.

I understand the story of my life in such a way that it is part of the history of my family or of this farm or of this university or of this countryside; and I understand the story of the lives of other individuals around me as embedded in the same larger stories, so that I and they share a common stake in the outcome of that story and in what sort of story it both is and is to be: tragic, heroic, comic.

A central contention of the morality of patriotism is that I will obliterate and lose a central dimension of the moral life if I do not understand the enacted narrative of my own individual life as embedded in the history of my country. For if I do not so understand it, I will not understand what I owe to others or what others owe to me, for what crimes of my nation I am bound to make reparation, for what benefits to my nation I am bound to feel gratitude. Understanding what is owed to and by me and understanding the history of the communities of which I am a part is on this view one and the same thing ....

In modern communities in which membership is understood only or primarily in terms of reciprocal self-interest, only two resources are generally available when destructive conflicts of interest threaten such reciprocity. One is the arbitrary imposition of some solution by force; the other is appeal to the neutral, impartial, and impersonal standards of liberal morality. The importance of this resource is scarcely to be underrated, but how much of a resource is it? The problem is that some motivation has to be provided for allegiance to the standards of impartiality and impersonality which both has rational justification and can outweigh the considerations provided by interest. Since any large need for such allegiance arises precisely and only when and insofar as the possibility of appeals to reciprocity in interests has broken down, such reciprocity can no longer provide the relevant kind of motivation. And it is difficult to identify anything that can take its place. The appeal to moral agents qua rational beings to place their allegiance to impersonal rationality above that to their interests has, just because it is an appeal to rationality, to furnish an adequate reason for so doing. And this is a point at which liberal accounts of morality are notoriously vulnerable. This vulnerability becomes a manifest practical liability at one key point in the social order.

Every political community, except in the most exceptional conditions, requires standing, armed forces for its minimal security. Of the members of these armed forces it must require both that they be prepared to sacrifice their own lives for the sake of the community's security and that their willingness to do so be not contingent upon their own individual evaluation of the rightness or wrongness of their country's cause on some specific issue, measured by some standard that is neutral and impartial relative to the interests of their own community and the interests of other communities. And, that is to say, good soldiers may not be liberals and must indeed embody in their actions a good deal at least of the morality of patriotism. So the political survival of any polity in which liberal morality had secured large-scale allegiance would depend upon there still being enough young men and women who rejected that liberal morality. And in this sense liberal morality tends toward the dissolution of social bonds.

Hence the charge that the morality of patriotism can successfully bring against liberal morality is the mirror image of that which liberal morality can successfully urge against the morality of patriotism. For while the liberal moralist was able to conclude that patriotism is a permanent source of moral danger because of the way it places our ties to our nation beyond rational criticism, the moralist who defends patriotism is able to conclude that liberal morality is a permanent source of moral danger because of the way it renders our social and moral ties too open to dissolution by rational criticism. And each party is in fact in the right against the other ....

Review and Discussion Questions

1. Describe the two (mistaken) conceptions of patriotism that MacIntyre identifies.
2. Describe what it is that "liberal" moral theories have in common, giving examples from other readings.
3. Explain MacIntyre's argument that patriotism (however defined) must be a vice from the perspective of liberal moral theory.
4. MacIntyre outlines an alternative to liberal morality (which is often called communitarianism). Explain the three facts that, he claims, lead naturally to this moral theory as opposed to liberalism.
5. How does MacIntyre think patriotism is based on the nature of value?
6. MacIntyre argues that communitarian morality has an advantage over liberalism when people are asked to join the military and fight. Explain his argument.
7. How do you think a nation could identify its historical project? Can it be done without in some way invoking universal moral standards?
8. Is MacIntyre right in thinking that true patriotism does not rest in the commitment to one's country based on the values it stands for (freedom, for example)?
9. Might MacIntyre's view lead to ethical relativism and thus the conclusion that, for example, the Nazis did not violate human rights? Explain.
10. "MacIntyre has confused a nation/state with a culture." Discuss.

READING: PATRIOTISM AS BAD FAITH

SIMON KELLER[*]

Simon Keller begins his remarks, "Most people think that patriotism is a virtue." But he argues that this view is mistaken and patriotism is more likely a vice to be avoided. He argues that patriotism almost inevitably implies a type of "bad faith." Simon Keller is Professor in the School of History, Philosophy, Political Science, and International Relations at Victoria University of Wellington, Australia.

Most people think that patriotism is a virtue. That, at least, is what is suggested by a quick glance at the political world and the popular media in this and similar countries.[1] Politicians constitute an extreme case—I think that many of them would rather be called cowardly or selfish or corrupt than unpatriotic—but their case is odd only for its extremity.[2] In everyday life, it seems as though you are usually offering a compliment when you call someone a patriot and as though patriotism is usually thought to be something that we should foster in our children and ourselves. Patriotism, in the popular imagination, may not quite rank alongside kindness, justice, temperance, and the like, but it is a virtue nonetheless; it is a character trait that the ideal person would possess.

---

[*] Simon Keller, "Patriotism as Bad Faith," *Ethics* 115 (April 2006): 563–592. Some footnotes omitted.

Recent philosophical discussions of patriotism have usually been framed by the debate over universalism and communitarianism. Universalism—sometimes called "liberal universalism," and closely related to cosmopolitanism—is the view that many of the most important ethical judgments are ideally made from an impartial, detached perspective, free of particular allegiances.[3] Universalists believe that it is possible and often desirable to form ethical judgments not as a member of a particular community but, rather, from the point of view of a neutral and unencumbered observer—simply as one human among many, perhaps, or as a bare rational agent.

Communitarians believe that ethical judgments are properly made from within a tradition, or a community, or a structure of social roles and allegiances.[4] It is a mistake, on this way of looking at things, to expect us to ignore our membership in communities when making ethical judgments. A communitarian is likely to regard as perfectly natural and desirable those moral judgments that are essentially made as a member of this or that community.

The contemporary philosophical debate about patriotism can be represented by a cast of three. First, there is the *communitarian patriot*, whose view is classically presented in Alasdair MacIntyre's article, "Is Patriotism a Virtue?" and whose answer to that question is "Yes!" Someone who lacks a patriotic commitment to his country, says the communitarian patriot, is alienated from the embedded perspective that makes ethics possible and is hence ethically deficient; patriotism is not just a virtue, but a central virtue.

At the other extreme is the *hard universalist*, represented in articles like Paul Gomberg's "Patriotism Is Like Racism."[5] The patriot favors one country and one group of people over others, and such favoritism, says the hard universalist, is abhorrent; no one is inherently more valuable than anyone else, just in virtue of being a citizen of one country rather than another.[6] In the eyes of the hard universalist, patriotism is hence a vice.

Between the communitarian patriot and the hard universalist lies the *soft universalist*. Soft universalism is perhaps the most popular view among philosophers; it is given very clear expression in Marcia Baron's "Patriotism and 'Liberal' Morality."[7] The soft universalist's claim is that a good universalist can also be a patriot, in some attenuated sense at least. Patriotic loyalty, on this way of seeing things, can be consistent with the ethical judgments that are correctly made from the neutral point of view; perhaps individuals are able, in the right circumstances, to have special loyalties to their own countries while still meeting the broader obligations that are evident from the neutral point of view. While the soft universalist might be reluctant to classify patriotism as a virtue, he at least thinks that it is not a vice ....

One reason why the debate over patriotism is a site for the debate between universalists and communitarians is that it is taken to be an illuminating case study, displaying the differing approaches taken by universalists and communitarians to loyalties in general. Some think that it is wrong to try to save your mother rather than a stranger from drowning, when the chances of saving the stranger are slightly higher, but most think that a preference for your mother in such a circumstance is justifiable, even required. But if it is wrong to favor someone just because she is your compatriot, is it not also wrong to favor someone just because she is your mother? If we cannot place patriotism on solid philosophical ground, then won't we have to regard loyalties to family, romantic partners, and friends as equally problematic? ...

It is worth giving further emphasis to the closeness of the analogy that philosophers see between patriotism and other loyalties. MacIntyre treats patriotism as

> one of a class of loyalty-exhibiting virtues (that is, if it *is* a virtue at all), other members of which are marital fidelity, the love of one's own family and kin, friendship, and loyalty to such institutions as schools and cricket or baseball clubs.[8]

.... While it is often admitted that there are more and less extreme forms of patriotism, it is generally accepted that patriotism is an attitude of essentially the same type as our loyalties to family, friends, and the rest, just with a different object.

In the first part of this article, I will dispute that analogy. I will lay out some ways in which loyalties differ and give reasons to think that patriotism is in certain ways unlike other familiar kinds of loyalty. In the second part of the article, I will try to show that the differences between patriotism and other loyalties are of ethical consequence. More precisely, I will argue that patriotism, properly understood, involves a disposition to fall into a kind of bad faith and that this is a reason to think that patriotism is certainly not a virtue and is probably a vice. If I am right, then it is possible to demonstrate the undesirability of patriotism without taking a stand in the debate between universalists and communitarians and without implying anything implausible about the ethical status of other loyalties and allegiances.

I What Is Patriotism?

The Question

A patriot loves, and is loyal to, his own country. In this first part of the article, I am going to make some claims about how the kinds of love and loyalty involved in patriotism differ from other forms of love and loyalty. It cannot be doubted, though, that patriotism can mean different things to people of different times, places, and political inclinations. So what is the point, we might ask, in trying to defend some single account of what patriotism really is? Well, it is not my intention just to stipulate a meaning for "patriotism" or to fight over the use of a word. I aim rather to articulate a conception of patriotism that most of us recognize and share, one that captures the notion of patriotism that dominates in public discourse nowadays ....

Choice

Understanding the nature of some kinds of loyalty involves understanding that the loyalty involved is given by choice and could be transferred to some other object should the subject so decide. Consider, for example, the loyalty that you might have for a political candidate, where you support him not because he grew up on your block or for his raw sexual magnetism, but for his political platform. Typically, in such a case you have a number of candidates to whom you could give your support, and you find a way of deciding between them. Should you judge that your candidate has changed or failed, or should there be a change in your own political opinions, then you have the option of shifting your loyalty to a different candidate.

Other forms of loyalty, like the loyalty that people characteristically have for their parents, are not in this respect subject to choice. This is not to say that you have no option but to be loyal to your parents but, rather, that you cannot choose who is to be the object of your filial loyalty, if anyone is. The only people to whom you can show filial loyalty are your parents (or those who play that institutional role), and you do not, exceptional cases aside, get to decide which people are your parents (or play that role).

In this regard, patriotism is similar to filial loyalty and different from loyalty to a political candidate, because you cannot, in standard cases, decide which country is your own. There might be exceptions. Perhaps when Robert E. Lee was deciding whether to take command of the Union army or the Confederate army, he was deciding whether to be a Northern or a Southern patriot; perhaps someone who has a certain sort of upbringing can find herself able to decide whether to be (say) French or American; and perhaps it is possible for (say) an American to take steps—immigration, naturalization, enculturation—that will eventually lead to her becoming the sort of person who could be (say) a French patriot. Such cases, though, are not representative. An individual who asks herself, "Should I be a patriot?" does not typically face the further question, "If so, then of which country?"

Loyalties Derived and Nonderived

Some loyalties are derived from different, more fundamental loyalties. Your loyalty to a political candidate might be derived from a more fundamental loyalty to certain values and principles, or from a more fundamental loyalty to the candidate's party. You might be loyal to a particular brand of toothpaste because of your deeper loyalty to your hometown, which is where the toothpaste is made. You might maintain your loyalty to the Red Sox out of loyalty to your father, with whom you used to go to the games.

Other loyalties are what we might call nonderived or "first-level" loyalties, or loyalties "in the first instance," meaning that that there are no deeper loyalties of which they can informatively be regarded as manifestations. Loyalties to moral principles might be nonderived loyalties. Often, the loyalties of fans to sports teams are nonderived. My love for the Geelong Football Club is not an expression of my deeper love for something else and does not depend essentially on any value or principle that the club represents; I just find myself loving and caring about the club for its own sake. And filial loyalty, again, is an obvious case of a loyalty that tends to be nonderived. There is just no answer to the question, "In virtue of which more fundamental loyalty do you love your mother?" So far as a hierarchy of loyalties is concerned, this is a place where explanation bottoms out.

Love of country could be derived. Your love of Nepal may stem from your love of climbing, your love of Switzerland from your love of cheese, your love of America from your love of freedom. As philosophers have often pointed out, however, something important about patriotism is missing from loves like these.[9] What is missing is the importance of the patriot's country being *her* country. ... A patriot is loyal to her country in the first instance, not in virtue of a deeper loyalty to something else.

Seriousness

There is a kind of seriousness that is involved in some loyalties but not others. If a loyalty of yours is serious, as I will use the word, then it can demand that you make significant sacrifices for the sake of its object; that you show its object a genuine, non-ironic reverence; and that you allow that loyalty to have some force when making some morally weighty decisions. Some examples, by now familiar, might make the distinction clearer.

I am, as I say, a lover of the Geelong Football Club. My loyalty to the club is passionate, and I allow it to have a significant impact upon my life. The money I spend on club membership and going to the games, the time I spend following news of the club, the impact that the club's performance has upon my mood, are considerable. But my loyalty to Geelong is not serious, in the sense in question ....

Loyalty to a parent, however, is often serious. You might make enormous sacrifices for your parents, take your obligations to them to have a serious moral dimension (you might tell lies or break rules to keep them out of trouble), and show them a reverence that—without extending to singing an anthem or saluting a flag—is certainly not ironic or self-conscious. And all of this may be true even though your non-serious loyalty to a football club is in a sense more passionate and takes up more of your energy than your filial loyalty. The kind of seriousness of loyalties that I am trying to bring out here does not necessarily go along with intensity.

Patriotism, as it is usually understood, characteristically presents itself as a serious loyalty. You can show your patriotism by standing during the national anthem, wearing your country's flag on your lapel or your backpack—in general, by showing an unironic reverence for your country. Patriotism is often cited (or appealed to) as a reason why you do (or should) make significant sacrifices for your country. Many people take patriotism to involve a preparedness, under extreme circumstances, to kill or die for your country; it is at any rate difficult to imagine someone who is a genuine patriot but takes her loyalty to country to generate no morally weighty reasons at all ....

Patriotism and the Qualities of a Country

There is a conception of patriotism according to which it necessarily involves the belief that your country is, objectively, the best or has features that make it superior to all others. Baron recommends a way of thinking about patriotism that, she says, "certainly does not accord with the usual ways of thinking about it in our culture," because it does not require that the patriot see her own country as superior.[10] There are some circles within which it seems to be thought that the way to express your patriotism is to say that yours is the greatest or freest or most beautiful country of all and that someone who said that some different country was a bit better than his would have his patriotism questioned.

We should step back, though, from the idea that being a patriot means taking your own country to be the one that everyone has most reason to admire or that looks most valuable from the neutral point of view. Someone who said, for example,

> I don't think that my own country is by any means the best. There are others I could name that are more beautiful, have greater histories, and stand more resolutely for what is right. But there are many wonderful things about my country, and it's certainly on the whole a good country, so I'm proud to call it my own

could, surely, properly count himself a patriot.

Even the belief that your country is on the whole a good country, however, might not be a requirement of patriotism. There are dissidents who count themselves as patriotic, even while making broad condemnations of their own countries, and who indeed see themselves as expressing their patriotism through their very concern that their countries become better than they are. This is what we might call patriotic dissent, and it is not the same thing as just plain dissent. Distinctively patriotic dissent is made such by its appeal to qualities that the dissenter takes to be central to the identity of the country, but that she thinks it to be losing or ignoring or showing insufficient respect.

Where the (just plain) dissident might say, "This policy needs to be changed, because it does not respect the rule of law, and the rule of law should be respected," the patriotic dissident might add,

> and what makes it especially important that we change the policy is that our country represents and is built upon respect for the rule of law. If we abandon that principle, then we abandon an aspect of our very identity; we cease to be the country that I recognize and love.

Cicero and the patriotic dissidents of late Roman times, for example, attacked their country for failing to live up to its glorious past. Patriotic American dissidents in the sixties complained that America was not being true to the values of freedom and equal rights that lie at its heart. In counting patriotic dissidents as patriots, we are counting those who say things like,

> There are some wonderful things about my country, but those things are being outweighed or overlooked in ways that make my country, on the whole, a pretty awful one at present. As one who understands what is truly valuable about this country, it is my patriotic duty to speak out against its present state.

While the patriotic dissident might be reluctant to say that her country is on the whole a good one, her patriotism does make reference to characteristics of her country that she regards as genuinely, objectively valuable and as playing an important role in making that country what it is. And this, I want to suggest, is a necessary condition for patriotism. Truly patriotic loyalty is entangled with a conception of the beloved country as having certain valuable characteristics, characteristics that make it, in some minimal way at least, genuinely worthy of patriotic loyalty. Patriotism, on the common understanding of the notion, always takes itself to be grounded in the relevant country's possession of certain specified, reasonably determinate qualities that the patriot takes to be genuinely valuable and to make a nontrivial contribution to the country's identity.

One way of grasping this point is to think about how a patriot would respond to the invitation, "Describe your country for me. What is it like?" My suggestion is that when a patriot answers this question—when she expresses her characterization of her own country or her beliefs about what are its most central or defining characteristics—she must call upon some properties that she takes to be good properties for a country to possess. When the patriot thinks about what it is that she loves, or what it is that grounds her loyalty, she must have in mind something that she takes to have value from the neutral point of view. In this respect, patriotic love differs from the love that people characteristically have for their parents. It is missing the point to cite your parents' wonderful characteristics in explaining why you love them, because there are no particular features of your parents (of the type that count as having objective value) in which your love for them is essentially grounded. Not so, I claim, for patriotic love.

Let me say what this rules out. First, it rules out statements like this: "I am a true, genuine patriot, but there is nothing much that I like about my country; there is nothing important about my country for which I feel any affection." Someone who said such a thing would be speaking very strangely ....

.... If I tell you that we are about to be treated to a patriotic discourse or to attend a patriotic event, then you know that what is to come will involve some praise of our country's qualities. The point is not, of course, that this is all that patriotism can be but, rather, that patriotism is a kind of love for country that makes reference to, or latches onto, aspects of a country that are taken to merit pride or approval or affection or reverence. Without that, you don't have patriotism ....

My Country, Right or Wrong?

I think that my claim about how a patriot must view his own country accords with our ordinary understanding of the notion and with most of what philosophers have said about it. It may appear, however, to be out of line with one popular expression of patriotism: the slogan, "My country, right or wrong!" From my experience of talking to people about this slogan, there is a good deal less agreement about its meaning than you would initially expect. I will quickly mention some of the ways in which the slogan might be understood and say how I think they each relate to the attitudes constitutive of patriotism.

Sometimes the slogan is taken to mean, "I'll support what my country does, whether I think it's right or wrong." Sometimes, it is taken to mean, "Right and wrong are not my concerns, I'm just concerned with standing up for my country." Either of these statements is consistent with (though not, of course, required by) patriotism as I have painted it. It is indeed overwhelmingly likely that someone who made either of these statements would be able to say just what it is about his country that makes it merit such devotion; this would involve pointing to certain valuable characteristics of the country, even if not characteristics like "always being right."

Sometimes the slogan is taken to have the meaning it takes when placed in the context of the famous remark of Carl Schurz: "My country right or wrong; if right, to be kept right; and if wrong, to be set right." (Note that this is evidently not where the shorter slogan originates. Schurz was responding to a senator from Wisconsin, who was apparently taunting him by saying, "My country, right or wrong.")[11] This version of the slogan expresses an intention to support the moral flourishing of a country, regardless of its starting point ....

Still, there might be cases under which someone would endorse the slogan simply in light of the country's being her country. This is consistent with her being thoroughly disgusted with and ashamed of her country, with her thinking that there is nothing important to recommend it at all. And that, for reasons I have discussed, just doesn't sound like patriotism. So I am happy to accept that some imaginable exclamations of, "My country, right or wrong" might not be expressions of patriotism—though most of them are.

What Is Patriotism?

Patriotism, I have been trying to show, is not just a loyalty like any other. To be a patriot is to have a serious loyalty to country, one that is not characterized by the phenomenology of choice, is essentially grounded in the country's being yours, and involves reference to (what are taken to be) valuable defining qualities of the country. In one way or another, the features of patriotism just mentioned set it apart from some familiar forms of loyalty to, for example, political candidates, parents, and football clubs. Whether patriotism is thereby set apart from all familiar forms of loyalty is a question to which I will return. (It isn't.) But we have at least opened up the space for an argument against the desirability of patriotism that cannot be translated into an attack upon loyalty in general.

II Against Patriotism

Confessions

When I am watching Geelong play football and the umpire makes a controversial decision, I very quickly form a judgment about whether the decision is right or wrong. If the decision goes the way of the other team, then even though the umpire is right there on the scene and I am a long way away in the stands, I will probably believe that it is the wrong decision. Only when the conclusion is absolutely unavoidable will I believe that the opposing team has been the victim of a bad umpiring decision, and in such cases I will probably still point out that it was about time we got one back. When a fight breaks out or a game turns ugly, I am unlikely to think that a Geelong player is to blame. When I am sitting around talking about football with my friends, I will defend the sorts of views that you would expect a Geelong supporter to defend. If the discussion is about who is the greatest footballer in history, I will put the case for one of Geelong's great players. I will do my best to marshal facts in favor of my claim, and I will sometimes get them wrong; I might say that my favorite player kicked more goals than anyone else who has played in his position, and my sparring partner might produce evidence that this is not in fact the case. But this won't move me from my claim about which club is home to the greatest footballer. Perhaps I will say that the statistic in question is not so important after all, or perhaps I will dispute the evidence, or perhaps I will quickly decide that it is not really him but some other Geelong footballer that deserves the title of the greatest ever. One way or another, I will do my best to hang onto the beliefs that go along with being a supporter of my team.

Even as I express my disgust at the umpire's decision and even as I defend the greatness of my own team's players, my companions and I are aware that my expressed opinions are not really what they present themselves to be. The purported facts to which I appeal in support of my opinions are not really what lead me to hold them. Really, I hold those opinions because I am a Geelong supporter. It would spoil the fun for me or anyone else to point this out, but we nevertheless know it to be the case. That is why my football-related opinions are so easy to predict.

I don't know whether this way of behaving will be familiar to all or most supporters of football teams, but it really is the way things are for me. And my belief-forming habits as a football supporter make me guilty of a mild form of bad faith. "The one who practices bad faith," says Sartre, "is hiding a displeasing truth or presenting as truth a pleasing falsehood."

> I must know in my capacity as deceiver the truth which is hidden from me in my capacity as the one deceived. Better yet I must know the truth very exactly *in order* to conceal it more carefully—and this not at two different moments, which at a pinch would allow us to reestablish a semblance of duality—but in the unitary structure of a single project.[12]

My project is to form and defend Geelong-centric beliefs about the world of football; for these to be the sorts of beliefs that I can defend in conversation, I must take them to be supported by an interpretation of the evidence that is not influenced by the desire to reach one conclusion rather than another, but for them to be the beliefs that I want them to be I must actively interpret the evidence in a biased manner. I want to have certain beliefs, but to ensure that I have those beliefs I must deceive myself about my motivations, without acknowledging the deceit.

The use of Sartrean machinery to evaluate my attitudes toward the Geelong Football Club is more than a little overblown, and that is because my support of Geelong is not a very serious matter. My being a supporter of Geelong, rather than some other team, does not influence any really important decisions of mine or result in any important change in my view of the world. If things do become a little serious—if, for instance, the player I name as the greatest in the game will be rewarded with a brand new car—then I will know that I should try to rise above my biased perspective and take a more reflective point of view. In any event, the point is not to confess to my own bad faith as a football fan, though I do feel better, but to suggest that the same brand of bad faith is displayed by those with the much more serious bundle of attitudes that makes for patriotism.

Bad Faith and Patriotism

A patriot's loyalty to country makes reference to fairly determinate characteristics that play a role in her own conception of her country and that she takes to be the sorts of characteristics that contribute to a country's being a good country. This amounts to the patriot's having beliefs, tied in with her patriotism, about her country's purely descriptive qualities. Some likely candidates are, "My country is a free country," "My country is beautiful in a special and unusual way," "My country stands for equality," "My country is founded on the principle of equal rights for all," "My country is, compared to others, open and tolerant," "In my country, great individuals are able to flourish," "Mine is a country of rolling green fields and friendly farmers," "My country defends just causes on the international stage," and, "My country is brave and unyielding in conflict." Even a patriot, whose loyalty to country is entangled with a belief that her country has valuable qualities, has a somewhat independent conception of the sorts of descriptions that a country must meet, if it is to have valuable qualities.

Each of the beliefs just mentioned is one that the patriot could have about any country, not just her own, and is a belief that could conceivably turn out to be false. It is quite possible to encounter evidence that a country is not really so beautiful, does not really defend just causes on the international stage, in fact contains a preponderance of very grumpy farmers, or is not as open and tolerant as it seemed. When the patriot encounters such evidence with regard to a country that isn't her own, she will, depending on what kind of evidence it is, in certain ways alter her beliefs. Perhaps she will change her mind about whether the country is as she imagined, perhaps she will suspend judgment until further evidence emerges—whatever. But what I want to claim is that she is constitutionally unlikely to respond in the same sorts of ways to evidence that her own country lacks the valuable qualities that she thought it to have and that it is here that her bad faith is to be found.

If the patriot is guilty of the brand of bad faith that I display as a football fan, then that is because she interprets evidence with the goal of sustaining her conception of her country as bearing particular, valuable characteristics. Out of patriotic loyalty, she is motivated to believe that her country has certain features, and she marshals the evidence in ways that support this belief; but she cannot maintain the belief in its full-blooded form if she admits to herself that it is not grounded in an unbiased assessment of the evidence; so she does not make this admission. A patriot might find herself confronted with evidence that her country is guilty of systematic wartime atrocities or that the founders of her country were motivated by a racist ideology, where this is evidence that, were it to concern a different country, would lead her to conclude that the country does not merit affection in the way that she had thought. If she responds in such a way as to avoid drawing the same conclusion about her own country—if she denies the evidence, or starts believing that wartime atrocities and racist ideologies are not so bad after all, or immediately turns her efforts to believing that her country has some different qualities that she can convince herself to think valuable—then we have our instance of bad faith.

All of this presupposes not just that the patriot has certain sorts of beliefs but also that she is motivated to maintain them, even in the face of countervailing evidence. Must the patriot be so motivated?

She will be if she sees her patriotism as a virtue. To see a character trait as a virtue is to see it as one that the ideal person would possess and is hence, in standard cases, to desire to cultivate it in yourself. A society in which patriotism is regarded as a virtue will be one in which people, especially children, are given special encouragement to view their country with pride and reverence and to have the associated descriptive beliefs, supported by the relevant evidence or not. It indeed seems quite plausible to think that this pressure, and the brand of bad faith to which it gives rise, is present in societies that value patriotism. We have all heard claims to the effect that teachers and leaders should present our country's history and political system in a positive light, for fear that people will otherwise fail to love the country in the ways that they should.

The deep source of patriotic bad faith, however, lies in the tension between patriotism's demanding certain sorts of beliefs and its failing to be grounded in or dependent upon those beliefs.[13] The patriot does not direct her patriotic love at her country just because she judges it to have particular valuable qualities, but the kind of loyalty that she has to her country, the kind of fidelity that she shows it, involves an acceptance of that judgment. The patriot is motivated to maintain her belief that her country has valuable features of a certain sort because she has a commitment that is grounded in that country's being her own country. To admit to any such motivation would be to admit that the belief is not formed in response only to the evidence and, hence, to undermine the credibility of the belief and the integrity of the loyalty that depends upon it—and so the motivation cannot be admitted.

The patriot's belief that her country has certain attractive features presents itself as having been formed through an unbiased set of opinions about the nature of her own country plus some neutrally endorsed criteria for what properties of countries count as valuable, but this is not really the full story. Driven by her loyalty to country, the patriot will hide from herself the true nature of the procedure through which she responds to evidence that bears upon the question of what her country is really like.

That is my basic case for the claim that patriotism is connected with bad faith. I need to say much more about the exact content and status of the claim, why it gives reason to think that patriotism is a vice, and where it leaves patriotism as compared to some other kinds of loyalty.

Clarifying the Thesis

My picture of patriotic bad faith relies upon a scenario under which the patriot encounters evidence that challenges her patriotic beliefs or her picture of her country as being characterized by particular valuable qualities. ... There will be cases, however, in which the patriot's conception of her own country is perfectly accurate, and in which she never faces any reason to think otherwise. The patriot might believe that her country is founded upon the values of freedom and equality, and it may indeed be founded upon those values; if so, then she may never need to creatively interpret any evidence to the contrary.

Such a fortunate patriot might never fall into bad faith, because she might never need to hide from herself the truth about how she responds to the evidence about her country that she actually confronts—but she will still be disposed to fall into bad faith, under circumstances that (as it happens) never actually arise. She may never need to hide from herself the truth about how she responds to certain types of evidence, but she would, if such evidence were encountered. So while it is overstating things to say that patriotism inevitably involves bad faith, it still seems true—and this is my official claim—that patriotism involves the disposition to fall into bad faith under some easily imaginable circumstances.

The Strength of the Thesis

…. Can we imagine a genuine patriot …? [Consider] the case of a patriot who seriously and honestly confronts evidence that his country is not as he thought and takes such evidence as a reason to examine and rethink his patriotism. Rather than avoiding consideration of the possibility that his country lacks the characteristics to which his patriotism makes reference, such a patriot is prompted to wonder whether he really ought to have the kind of first-order loyalty to country that he does.

This kind of response requires that the patriot examine himself, not just his country. Most likely, it will lead to the loss of any distinctively patriotic outlook, through a process that I think might be familiar to many readers. It is a process of moving away from an instinctive attitude to your own country of the form "This is my great/beautiful/free/ … country" and toward the recognition that your country, like any other, needs to be critically evaluated and that the patriotic picture of it held by you and others could well be illusory. In coming to this realization, you come to take a perspective upon your country that is too detached to coexist with genuine patriotism. To be a patriot who comes to such a point of view is to throw into question and revise what is likely to be a deeply held element of your way of making sense of the world. It is likely to involve a change, to a greater or lesser extent, in your self-conception; you are likely to cease to take your belonging to your country as a part of your identity in the way that you did. It can be difficult, disillusioning, and traumatic. As such, it is not a process upon which most patriots are likely to embark, and it is a process of reevaluation that patriotic loyalty positively discourages. But it is one way in which a patriot might respond to challenges to his patriotic beliefs, and it need not involve bad faith.

Here, then, is my claim about the nature of the connection between bad faith and patriotism. The patriot can encounter circumstances under which she would, were her patriotism not at stake, revise certain of her beliefs but under which she feels loyal to her country in a way that requires her to keep them. Usually, that loyalty will provide her with a motive to find ways of keeping those beliefs whatever the evidence, and that motive leads to bad faith. It is possible, however, that other elements of a patriot's psychology or circumstances will be such as to outweigh, or prevent the emergence of, that motive—most likely, I think, by prompting the kind of change in perspective described in the previous paragraph. Patriotism is by its nature such as to make the patriot likely to have the disposition to fall into bad faith, but there can be exceptions.

Let me make some comments about the strength of my claim in another dimension. Whether or not you are convinced by the somewhat restrictive construal of patriotism for which I argued in Section I, I want it to be clear that my argument really is supposed to reveal something about a very broad class of loyalties to country, not just about the unthinking, jingoistic forms of patriotism that are so easy to belittle. The claim also applies to patriotic dissidents, and to those whose patriotism is not really political in nature. Among the patriots whom I think likely to be guilty of bad faith are American dissidents who say that flouting international treaties is not just wrong but un-American, American patriots who are viscerally resistant to suggestions that the defenders of the Alamo did not really go down fighting, Australians overseas who tell us that people are friendlier back home, Australian patriots who insist that inner-city Melbourne or outback

Queensland is the real Australia, and so on and on. I am not, of course, saying that the beliefs mentioned in these examples are false, just that the patriots concerned are unlikely to consider the evidence on its merits ....

What's So Bad About Bad Faith?

Assume that I am right in my claim that patriotism involves the disposition to fall into bad faith: where does this leave us with regard to our assessment of patriotism? Is bad faith necessarily a bad thing?

I think that the link between patriotism and bad faith yields a clear presumptive case against patriotism's being a virtue and for its being a vice. The structure and role of patriotic attitudes are such that the patriot is likely to have biased, poorly supported beliefs that play an important role in determining her view of the world. Her resistance to certain sorts of beliefs is likely to lead her to have an inflated view of her own country's value and importance and to dismiss without adequate consideration those who are putting forth reasons to doubt that her country is what she takes it to be. Depending upon what sorts of beliefs ground her patriotism, the patriot is likely to be drawn toward unrealistically rosy pictures of her country's people and history, the principles for which it stands, or the ways in which it operates. All of this could well turn out to be influential when it comes to her making morally significant decisions: decisions about whether to support or fight in a war, about who should get her vote, about whether to make certain significant sacrifices, and so on ....

.... If the conclusion is to be resisted, then some work must be done in patriotism's defense.

Bad Faith and Other Loyalties

I said that I wanted to find a way of arguing against patriotism that did not translate automatically into an attack upon loyalties of all sorts, but there are reasons to suspect that I have not really succeeded ....

Parents are often especially open to evidence that their children have special talents and other valuable characteristics and especially inclined to give their own children the benefit of the doubt. And this, leaving aside tennis parents and the like, can be a very good thing; there certainly doesn't seem to be anything sinister about it. Why think differently about the patriot's tendency to think well of her own country?

I think that things are different when it is countries rather than children that are at issue. The thought that citizens should be inclined to assume the best of their own countries or to give their own countries the benefit of the doubt, is one that I find obviously false and somewhat disturbing. The important point, though, is this. A parent's love for a child is not essentially tied up with a conception of the child as having specified, objectively valuable characteristics. One way to see this is to see that a parent who moves to a more objective point of view is not thereby undermining her love for her child. It makes perfect sense (and is often a good exercise) to say,

> I think that my child has these special qualities that set him apart from others, but I'll admit that I could easily be wrong. I'm biased, after all. But whether

I'm wrong or not makes no difference to my loving my child, and my being prepared to make significant sacrifices for his sake.

Compare this to someone who says, for example, "As a patriot, I think that my country stands for freedom and equality, but I'll admit that I could easily be wrong. I'm biased, after all." It is difficult to hear this statement except as involving the speaker's taking a step back from his own patriotism. It sounds like he is entertaining the possibility that his patriotism is misplaced and wondering whether he really ought to have the serious commitment to country that he does. Patriotic loyalty discourages you from wondering whether the object of your loyalty really has the valuable qualities you think it to have. A parent's love for a child does not.

The case of friendship is more complicated, because there are so many different forms that a friendship can take. It seems true that some (though certainly not all) friendships can be such that loyalty to your friend requires an inclination to believe things about her that you would not, given the same evidence, believe about a stranger. Usually, though, there is a kind of opt-out clause that keeps you from being required to do anything too serious on the basis of such beliefs. Your loyalty to your friend might require you to be inclined to believe that she is a decent enough poet or that she is innocent of the crime of which she has been charged, without requiring you to invest in her self-publishing venture or act as her defense lawyer (without taking a more objective view of things first).[14] Remember also that a friendship is not always a good friendship but can be dysfunctional or destructive or stifling. And when you are required to make serious decisions or sacrifices on the basis of biased beliefs, on pain of being a disloyal friend, you have probably got yourself into a friendship that is not a very good one. If patriotism turns out to be analogous to friendships like these, then that—again—is not good news for patriotism.

My claim is not that patriotism is absolutely unique in being connected, by its nature, to a disposition toward bad faith. My case against patriotism could be made against any loyalty that has the following three features: first, it is not grounded in or answerable to the neutral judgment that its object has certain valuable characteristics; second, it essentially involves the belief that its object does have certain valuable characteristics; and third, it plays a role in the making of important, morally weighty decisions. Another case in which these features are present is that of a certain kind (certainly not the only kind) of loyalty to family, a kind that involves not just a special affection for your family but an endorsement of the values and way of life with which your family is associated. We can all think of cases in which loyalty to family is taken to have a very serious moral dimension and is taken to essentially involve taking your family to be a good or excellent family—where this attitude is required simply in virtue of this family's being your family. Some religious loyalties might be similar. Of such loyalties, and any others like it, I am committed to drawing the conclusion that I have drawn about patriotism (and I think that it is the right conclusion to draw) ….

Conclusion

I have argued that there are reasons to think that patriotism, by virtue of its very nature, is undesirable. Patriotic loyalty is of a kind that requires certain beliefs about its object, without being premised upon an independent judgment that these beliefs are true. As a result, the patriot has a tendency to make judgments about the qualities of her own country in a way quite different from that in which she makes judgments about others, but she is unable within her patriotism to admit to this tendency. That is patriotic bad faith.

Sometimes the disposition to patriotic bad faith is not something that we need be too concerned about. In some cases, it will never be expressed. In others, the motivations underlying it will be very weak. Given, however, the moral seriousness of patriotism and the importance that patriotism tends to hold for those who have it, there is good reason to think that the disposition to patriotic bad faith will usually be more than just an interesting psychological quirk or harmless indulgence. Patriotic bad faith is likely to play a central role in the patriot's construal of the world and of her own moral obligations, and it is likely to lead the patriot to make bad decisions of real consequence ....

More generally, I have tried to show that patriotism is not just another form of loyalty and, indeed, that familiar loyalties differ in several ways that could plausibly be held to be of ethical importance. Whether I am right or wrong in my criticisms of patriotism, neither the universalist nor anyone else should be bullied into endorsing particular kinds of loyalties on pain of being unable to endorse any loyalties at all. The class of loyalties and loves is less unified than it might seem.

Notes

1 I am writing in the United States and thinking of other English-speaking countries with which I am familiar, such as Britain, Australia, New Zealand, and Canada. In some other parts of the world, I am told, the epithet "patriotic" is not so likely to be taken as a compliment.
2 In 2001, the U.S. Congress passed a bill called the USA PATRIOT Act. Even though "USA PATRIOT" is an acronym (for "Uniting and Strengthening America by Providing Appropriate Tools Required to Intercept and Obstruct Terrorism"), it was said that some members of Congress were reluctant to oppose the bill for fear of looking unpatriotic.
3 For a classic statement of liberal universalism, see part 1 of John Rawls, *A Theory of Justice* (Cambridge, MA: Harvard University Press, 1971). Cosmopolitanism is the view that humans' most morally salient characteristics are those connected with their shared humanity; within a cosmopolitan ethical outlook, distinctions are not drawn on the basis of nationality or country of origin. See A. John Simmons, "Human Rights and World Citizenship: The Universality of Human Rights in Kant and Locke," in *Justification and Legitimacy: Essays on Rights and Obligations* (Cambridge: Cambridge University Press, 2001), 179–196; Martha C. Nussbaum, "Patriotism and Cosmopolitanism," published along with numerous replies in *For Love of Country?* (Boston, MA: Beacon, 2002); and Catherine Lu, "The One and Many Faces of Cosmopolitanism," *Journal of Political Philosophy* 8 (2000): 244–267.
4 The version of communitarianism sketched here follows that articulated by Alasdair MacIntyre in "Is Patriotism a Virtue?" the E. H. Lindley Lecture, University of Kansas, 1984, reprinted in *Patriotism*, ed. Igor Primoratz (Amherst, NY: Humanity Books, 2002), 43–58 (future page references are to the Primoratz edition). See also Michael J. Sandel, *Liberalism and the Limits of Justice* (Cambridge: Cambridge University Press, 1982).
5 Paul Gomberg, "Patriotism Is Like Racism," *Ethics* 101 (1990): 144–150.
6 As Nussbaum puts it, "What is it about the national boundary that magically converts people toward whom we are both incurious and indifferent into people to whom we have duties of mutual respect?" ("Patriotism and Cosmopolitanism," 14).
7 Marcia Baron, "Patriotism and 'Liberal' Morality," in *Mind, Value and Culture: Essays in Honor of E. M. Adams*, ed. David Weissbord (Atascadero, CA: Ridgeview, 1989), 269–300. Reprinted with modifications in Primoratz, *Patriotism*, 59–86 (future page

references are to the Primoratz edition). See also Stephen Nathanson, *Patriotism, Morality and Peace* (Lanham, MD: Rowman & Littlefield, 1993).
8 MacIntyre, "Is Patriotism a Virtue?" 44, italics MacIntyre's.
9 See, e.g., MacIntyre, "Is Patriotism a Virtue?" 44; and Igor Primoratz's "Introduction" to *Patriotism*, 10–12. Kleingeld might have a contrasting view. One of the types of patriotism that she discusses, "trait-based patriotism," does appear to be, in the relevant sense, derived (in Primoratz, "Kantian Patriotism," 320–22).
10 Baron, "Patriotism and 'Liberal' Morality," 77.
11 See Hans L. Trefousse, *Carl Schurz: A Biography* (New York: Fordham University Press, 1998), 180.
12 Jean-Paul Sartre, *Being and Nothingness*, trans. Hazel E. Barnes (London: Routledge, 1969), 49.
13 Some awareness of this tension is displayed in the evocative final section of MacIntyre's "Is Patriotism a Virtue?" For a more positive view of the way in which patriotism combines particularity and universal judgments, see Benjamin R. Barber, "Constitutional Faith," in Nussbaum, *For Love of Country?*, 30–37.
14 I explore these issues at greater length in "Friendship and Belief," *Philosophical Papers* 33 (2004): 329–51.

Review and Discussion Questions

1 What are the three positions on patriotism that are part of contemporary philosophical debates?
2 What are the characteristics of being patriotic to one's country, according to Keller?
3 How do these characteristics differ from loyalty to one's family members, in Keller's view?
4 Do you agree or disagree with the statement that you should "support your country, right or wrong"? What does this statement mean? How does Keller analyze it?
5 What is Keller's argument against patriotism? What is bad faith in his view?
6 What is bad about bad faith, according to Keller? Do you agree with his discussion? Why or why not?
7 What is your assessment of Keller's account of patriotism? How does it differ from your own account, if you have one?

READING: FREDERICK DOUGLASS'S PATRIOTISM

BERNARD R. BOXILL[*]

Frederick Douglass was one of the most significant and remarkable figures in American history. Born into slavery, he escaped at age twenty, moved from Massachusetts to England, and then returned to the United States, all the while devoting his life to speaking out against slavery, supporting the abolitionist movement, and fighting for the equality of all persons. He decried the evils of the United States and yet conveyed a deep conviction for this same country. Was he a patriot? In what sense did he (could he) love his country? Was the United States "his country"? In this essay, Bernard Boxill explores the meaning and

---

[*] Bernard Boxill, "Frederick Douglass's Patriotism," *Journal of Ethics* 13 (2009): 301–317. Some footnotes omitted.

significance of patriotism and love of country in light of the extraordinary life and convictions of Frederick Douglass. Bernard Boxill is Professor Emeritus of Philosophy at the University of North Carolina, Chapel Hill.

Although Frederick Douglass disclaimed any patriotism or love of the United States in the years when he considered its constitution to be pro-slavery, I argue that he was in fact always a patriot and always a lover of his country. This conclusion leads me to argue further that patriotism is not as expressly political as many philosophers suppose. Patriots love their country despite its politics and often unreasonably, although in loving their country they are concerned with its politics. The greatest among them freely dedicate themselves selflessly to the improvement of their country, partly because they love it, and partly because they are moved to take on great projects.

I

Early in his career Frederick Douglass often maintained that he had and could have no patriotism. His argument for taking this stand was straightforward: To have patriotism is to love one's country; consequently to have patriotism one must have a country; but he had no country; consequently he had and could have no patriotism.[1] Douglass also used his claim to have no country to reject accusations of being a traitor. Again his argument was straightforward: A traitor is a betrayer of his country; consequently a traitor must have a country; but he had no country; consequently he was not and could not be a traitor.[2]

Around the same time that Douglass was claiming that he had and could have no patriotism he was also often claiming that he did not and could not love the United States.[3] This claim did not follow from his claim to have no patriotism. That claim was based on his claim that he had no country; but it does not imply that he did not and could not love the U.S. One can love a country even if it is not one's country, though one cannot, of course, love it in the way that a patriot loves his country. To support his claim that he did not love the U.S., Douglass therefore had to appeal to a claim that went beyond his claim that the U.S. was not his country. The claim he appealed to was that the U.S. was simply too wicked for him to love.[4]

Douglass expressed these views while he was on his first visit to England. The reasons for this visit are relevant to the present issue so I will recount them briefly. Douglass was born a slave in Maryland. When he was about twenty he escaped from slavery and settled with his wife in New Bedford, Massachusetts, where he eventually came to the attention of William Lloyd Garrison, the great abolitionist. Garrison was impressed by the intelligence and articulateness of the young man and promptly employed him as an anti-slavery lecturer hoping that Douglass would be especially effective in this role because he was a recently escaped slave. But although Douglass went so far as to show his audiences the stripes on his back, many refused to believe that he had ever been a slave because they thought that he spoke too well and too learnedly. To prove that he was what he said he was Douglass wrote and published his first book, *Narrative of the Life of Frederick Douglass an American Slave*, giving specific details of his life as a slave including his master's name and city of residence. As a result, although the book did what it was intended to do and succeeded in proving his claim to have been a slave, it also revealed who he was, thus making it possible for his master Thomas Auld to send slave catchers up North to bring him back to Maryland and slavery. To avert this terrible reversal in his fortunes Douglass fled to England where he would be safe from Auld for the English recognized no one in England as a slave.

When English friends bought his freedom from Auld Douglass promptly returned to the U.S. And a few years later, despite his earlier insistence that he was not and could not be a patriot, that the U.S. was not his country, and that he did not love the U.S., Douglass began to insist that the opposite was true. Specifically he began to claim that the U.S. was his country, that he loved her and that he was a patriot.[5] This change of heart was evidently not because he believed that the U.S. had become less wicked. In his opinion the U.S. was as wicked as ever and perhaps more so. In his view for example the Slave Power appeared to have become more entrenched and more aggressive than ever before, managing to get a new and more obtrusive Fugitive Slave Law passed that gave judges monetary incentives to find any blacks captured in the North to be escaped slaves, thus making every nominally free black person in the U.S. liable to be kidnapped, judged to be an escaped slave, and sent south into slavery. For her increased wickedness Douglass criticized her more harshly than ever, though like most patriots whose patriotism is doubted when they criticize their country, Douglass began to argue that he criticized the U.S. precisely because he was a patriot and loved her as his country; that had he been less of a patriot and less of a lover of his country he would have criticized her less.[6] Interestingly the U.S.'s wickedness had apparently lost its power to prevent Douglass from loving her and from claiming her as his country. This was a radical turnabout. ... What had provoked these metamorphoses?

II

One explanation that leaps to mind appeals to his famous change of mind and heart about the U.S. Constitution. Early on, for example when he was on his first trip to England, and still under the influence of Garrison and Wendell Phillips, Douglass believed firmly that the Constitution was radically pro-slavery.[7] If this belief was correct, then as Douglass often repeated the Constitution did not and could not recognize him as a human being making it understandable for him to disclaim all patriotism, and all love for the U.S. Later on, however, Lysander Spooner, Gerrit Smith and others managed to convince Douglass that Garrison and Phillips were mistaken in claiming that the Constitution was pro-slavery. On their account, and with that account Douglass eventually fully and enthusiastically concurred, the Constitution was really, when properly read and interpreted, radically anti-slavery.[8] Arguably this change of mind about the Constitution could explain Douglass's change of heart and mind about the U.S. ... [But] loving the constitution of a country does not straightforwardly imply loving the country it is the constitution of; neither does it imply being a patriot of that country. An English patriot who was persuaded by the arguments of Spooner and Douglass that the U.S. Constitution was designed to end slavery and secure justice would presumably love that constitution if he loved freedom and justice. But it does not follow that the U.S. would be his country, and even less that he would be a U.S. patriot. England would probably continue to be his country, and he would presumably remain an English patriot. As for loving the U.S. we can fairly speculate that he might well find himself unable to do so, precisely because he thought that its constitution was just. Given that the U.S. supported slavery, despite having a constitution specifically designed to end slavery, he would have to suppose that its government and people were wickedly misreading, misinterpreting, or simply ignoring its constitution. Indeed this was precisely how Douglass responded after he joined Spooner and Smith in defending the Constitution. The more he sang the virtues of the Constitution the more he mourned the vices of the government and the people. In his view the Constitution was good and right, but the people had allowed the Slave Power to get a hold of the government which then disobeyed the Constitution it was pledged to obey; instead of ending slavery as the Constitution demanded, the government with the connivance of the people protected and actually tried to extend slavery. How could he love a country with such a government and such a people?

In addition to being traitors to their own constitution and supporting a crime that it condemned and was designed to put an end to, Douglass added that the country was a country of hypocrites.[9] If the U.S. had changed her Constitution to make it say plainly that she was a slave holding country, she would still, of course, be wicked, but at least she would be honest. But the U.S. did not possess even the questionable virtue of being truthful about her wickedness; she continued the farce of designating herself the home of the free, and of paying tribute to a constitution that was designed to end slavery, all the while betraying its principles, and trying her best to secure and even extend her system of slavery. Douglass felt that this particular aspect of the U.S.'s wickedness to be especially execrable ....

.... Despite having all these reasons not to love the U.S., after he became persuaded of the justice of her constitution, Douglass as we have seen claimed to love the U.S., to hold her as his country, and to be a patriot. If his change of heart about the U.S. Constitution does not plausibly explain his change of heart about the U.S., what does?

III

I have pressed my reservations about the view that Douglass became a patriot because he changed his mind about the U.S. Constitution. Nevertheless, I am persuaded that Douglass spoke truly when he claimed to love the U.S. and to be a patriot. I will now explain why I am so persuaded, and will begin by suggesting that Douglass always did love the U.S., and was always a patriot even in those early days when as a Garrisonian he claimed that her constitution was pro-slavery and consequently that he had no country, could not be a patriot, and could not love the U.S. This suggestion will seem bold and even incredible. I have tried hard but unsuccessfully to find reasons to explain how Douglass could truly claim to be a patriot *after* he had decided that the U.S. Constitution was anti-slavery and *after* presumably he had some reason to love her and consider her his country. How then could I be right that he did love her and that she was his country *before* his change of mind about her constitution, that is, when he still considered her constitution to be pro-slavery?

Douglass's reasons for thinking that the U.S. could not be his country when he believed her constitution to be pro-slavery do not stand up to scrutiny. He seemed to think that the U.S. could not be his country because of something about her political system. Thus, when he claimed to have no country and in particular claimed that the U.S. was not his country, he did so by claiming that the U.S. Constitution, the foundation of the political system, was pro-slavery ....

But even if the laws denied that Douglass was human and on that ground withheld citizenship from him, it does not follow that the U.S. could not be his country. Being the citizen of a country and it being one's country are different things. One can fail to be a citizen of a country, although it is nevertheless one's country. I take this to be the case because although a country must have inhabitants and these inhabitants must have customs and habits and traditions, and perhaps even laws, it need not have citizens. The very idea of citizenship may be unknown in some countries. But it does not follow that in such countries there can be no patriotism. Patriotism is a very old idea. Commentators often note that it is much older than nationalism, but it is also much older than the idea of citizenship. There were patriots, people claiming to love their countries, long before ideas of citizenship were heard of or invented, and consequently long before these people thought or could think of themselves as citizens. Consequently someone could be a patriot, and so have a country, even if he or she was not a citizen of that country. If so, then even if the U.S. Constitution failed to recognize Douglass as a human being, and even if this implied that he was not and could not be a U.S. citizen, it does not follow that he could not have a country, that the U.S. could not be that country, and that he could not be a patriot.

Could the U.S. be Douglass's country if, in addition to denying him citizenship, it proposed also to expel him from within its borders or to deport him and all other black people from the country? Many notable U.S. citizens dreamed of deporting all blacks from the country even after such a project should have been dismissed as not only immoral but also impractical. Beginning with Thomas Jefferson and possibly even earlier, white statesmen and slave holders often claimed to be willing to free their slaves on the condition that the freed slaves would then be expelled from the country.[10] And throughout most of Douglass's life even many opponents of slavery including Lincoln clung to the hope of somehow ridding the country of all blacks.[11] But even deporting and banishing a person from a country does not necessarily mean that it cannot be his country. It is possible for avowed patriots to be stripped of their citizenship and exiled, banished, or deported. And it is possible too for them to continue to truly insist on their patriotism and on their love of the country that exiled them even while they are in exile.

If these remarks are sound the U.S. could have been Douglass's country even if her Constitution denied that he could ever be a citizen. Of course during the period in which he believed that her Constitution denied his humanity, he denied that the U.S. was his country or that he loved her; but this contradicts nothing that I have argued for. My arguments defend my view that the U.S. could conceivably be Douglass's country and that he could conceivably love her even if its Constitution denied his humanity and his citizenship. When Douglass denied that the U.S. was his country or that he loved her he need not have been challenging that view. He might only have been claiming that he found it psychologically impossible to love a country or to consider it to be his country when its fundamental laws treated him as contemptuously as the U.S. Constitution treated him.

But apart from what was conceivable, was Douglass during the period in which he believed that the Constitution denied his humanity in fact a patriot, did he in fact love the U.S., and was she in fact his country? We have so far failed to find reasons to answer this question in the affirmative, but we have been looking for such reasons in the wrong place. Because patriotism is love of one's country, and countries always have some sort of political system or other, the habit has arisen of thinking of patriotism as love of the political system of one's country. And from that habit the further habit has arisen of searching in the political system of a country for the reasons why patriots love their countries. This is why it seemed so natural to try to explain Douglass's love of the U.S. by appealing to his love for its Constitution. But what seemed so natural was mistaken, and the habits on which it was based were supported by mistaken assumptions. As we have seen, patriots often vigorously criticize the political systems of their country. Indeed, they often maintain that they criticize the political system of their country precisely because they are patriots and love their country, and have done this so often that at some times criticism of the political system of one's country has been taken to be the most obvious distinguishing mark if not the essence of the patriot. But if so, then clearly patriotism cannot necessarily involve, though of course it may involve, love of the political system of one's country.

.... The source of a patriot's love of his country need not lie in its political system. Even if Douglass loved the U.S. Constitution when he became persuaded that it was anti-slavery, it does not follow that his love of the Constitution accounts for his love of the U.S.

IV

What does it mean to say that a certain country is one's country? ... One ready answer to this question is that one's country is the country in which one feels most at home. Feeling at home in a country suggests feeling comfortable in it, knowing one's way around in it, and being effortlessly familiar with its language, landscape, customs and mores. But in this sense feeling at home in a country does not mean that it is one's country. Although the metaphor of home for country is highly suggestive, like all metaphors it must be searched for limitations and these must be carefully spelled out. Feeling at home in a country stresses some of the psychological aspects commonly associated with that country being one's country, but the presence of these aspects in particular cases is not sufficient for a country to be one's country. An individual who has lived in a foreign country for a very long time may feel at home in it in the sense just noted, while all the time that he is feeling so much at home, being clear, and being clearly correct, that the country he is in is not his country ....

To see that a country being one's country involves more than the way one feels about it, let us ask what suffices to make a country *not* one's country. Interestingly, hating a country and being its enemy does not suffice. A spy in a country is an enemy of that country and he may hate it, but it may be his country if he is a traitor. A traitor is an enemy of his country, but his country is still his country; indeed he is a traitor just because it is his country. What makes a traitor's country his country, even if he is its enemy? Psychological answers to that question are obviously not enough. Suppose, for example, one said that a traitor's country is his country because it helped to make him the person he is. This answer must be incorrect because when Douglass declared that he could not be a traitor to the U.S. because it was not his country he was not denying the undeniable fact that the U.S. had helped to make him the person he was. His point surely is that he owed the U.S. no gratitude for making him the person he was. Even if it had helped to make him a good person, he owed it no gratitude because it never intended to make him a good person or to help prepare him for a good life; it intended to destroy him. Let us suppose then that a traitor's country may be his country, because even if he is its enemy he owes it a debt of gratitude for caring and nurturing him and for trying even if unsuccessfully to prepare him for a good life.

But when a person says that a county is his country he may mean something more than that he owes it a debt of gratitude for caring and nurturing him and for trying to prepare him for a good life. Here the metaphor of home for country is highly suggestive. Normally, people feel and have obligations of gratitude to their homes, but their homes owe them something too, something more than the acceptance of their gratitude. Specifically, their homes owe them welcome. When you go home you expect to be recognized and welcomed and to be made to feel at home. If you are rejected as an outsider, as a stranger, with no connections to the country, you rightfully feel that you have been betrayed. Memories of early tenderness and care cause normal human beings to feel the strongest love and affection for home. Home, having made her children love her, ought not to betray or even disappoint that love. Just because home has been good to its children it is obligated to welcome them back should they return.

These remarks about home and its obligations to its children apply to standard cases of a country and its obligations to persons rightfully claiming it as its country. People owe obligations to their country because it nurtured and cared for them, and it is obligated to welcome them because by nurturing and caring for them,[12] it made them love it. But this standard case cannot apply to Douglass. As we have noted, the U.S. had not nurtured and cared for him and had not caused him to love her and consequently had not in this way incurred an obligation to welcome him. What then did he mean when he claimed that she was his country? ...

U.S. blacks had made enormous contributions to the well-being and security of the U.S. Not only had they fought valiantly on its side in its war for independence, when they could have sided with the enemy and perhaps changed the outcome of the war; as the distinguished historian Edmund Morgan put it 150 years later,

> the position of the United States in the world depended not only in 1776 but during the span of a long lifetime thereafter on slave labor. To a very large degree it may be said that Americans bought their independence with slave labor.[13]

As a black person Douglass was therefore a member of a group of people who had helped significantly in the building of the U.S.[14] U.S. citizens owed him welcome because they were living and prospering in a house that he and his people had helped to build. No one should be a stranger and an outcast in a place that he and his own kith and kin had spilt their blood and sweat to make.

The U.S. was thus obligated to Douglass, but what about his obligation to her, which is as we have seen implied by his claim that the U.S. was his country?

Normally, as we have seen, this obligation is generated by the debt of gratitude a person owes to the country that intending well by him nurtured and cared for him. Since the U.S. had not intended well by Douglass and had not nurtured and cared for Douglass, the obligation in question, if he had it, must have been generated in some other way. But to say that it is normally generated by a debt of gratitude is only to say what justifies or supports it; it is not to say what it is. Naturally it depends on the amount of the debt, and by "amount" I mean to include both the extent of the benefit received and the goodness of the intentions of those who extended it. A very small debt in this sense generates a correspondingly small obligation. As the debt becomes greater in both of the senses noted, it generates obligations to respect, esteem, defend, and further the good of, perhaps even revere, the benefactor. This is why everyone agrees that we normally owe our greatest debt of gratitude to our mothers who carried us in their bodies, risked their lives so that we could have life, and nursed and cared for us.

Accordingly, as a general rule we naturally expect patriotism to be greatest among those most favored by their countries, and to be least among those least favored or, like Douglass, not favored at all by their countries. But there are exceptions to the rule. A moderate exception is the case of individuals fiercely patriotic to their adopted countries. It shows that a patriot may not owe his country a debt of gratitude for nurturing and caring for him in his infancy. But it is only a moderate exception because it does not show that patriotism need not be founded on a debt of gratitude. Although immigrants were not nurtured by the country that accepts them, they often owe it debts of gratitude for taking them in, recognizing their talents, and giving them opportunities. The case of Alexander Hamilton comes to mind. The more notable exception to the rule in question is of the patriot who owes no debt of gratitude to his country, the case of Douglass, for example. He owed the U.S. nothing. She had done nothing for him, and on the contrary had tried her best to destroy him. She owed him, but he did not owe her. His obligation to her, implied in his claim that she was his country, therefore had to be freely taken on. I can see no other way of accounting for his having such an obligation ....

If individuals can freely take on obligations to countries that owe them nothing, it follows that those who already owe debts of gratitude to their countries can take on obligations to their countries beyond those obligations that their debts already generate. Indeed I think that the most notable cases of patriotism are those of individuals who take on such additional obligations. Strictly speaking, the debt of gratitude that even the most favored individuals owe their countries is fairly limited. For example, we expect and require most natives of a country to be patriotic to the extent of not betraying their countries. But the individuals we single out as great patriots are prepared to do far more than merely not betray their countries. They are prepared to make great kills for their countries even to the extent of being prepared to die for them, and have dedicated a considerable part of their lives and talents to improving, building up, protecting, and defending their countries.

V

So far so good, I think. But since I think that Douglass was a great patriot, the question becomes, why on earth would he dedicate himself to the U.S. in these ways? The fact that he did it freely does not mean that he did it for no reason. So what was Douglass's reason for taking on obligations to the U.S. even beyond the ordinary obligations of those U.S. citizens who had good reasons to be grateful for the good it had done them? A plausible answer to this question, one with which we should already be familiar, is that he took on these obligations after he became convinced that the U.S. Constitution was anti-slavery, and consequently that despite its bad behavior it was oriented in some fundamental way to achieving worthy ends ....

Yet I think that the suggestion is mistaken. Douglass did not dedicate himself to the U.S. when he came to believe that its Constitution was anti-slavery. His dedication to the U.S. preceded that belief. The reason for his dedication to the U.S. lay in the contents of another great document in the U.S. history, one far greater than even a Constitution designed to end slavery. That document is, of course, the Declaration of Independence. Douglass would have agreed with Lincoln that the Declaration of Independence was the "apple of gold," and the Constitution was the "picture of silver subsequently framed around it. The picture was made, not to conceal, or destroy the apple; but to adorn and preserve it."[15] Lincoln meant that the Constitution was a means to the ends of equality and rights enunciated in the second paragraph of the Declaration of Independence. Douglass dedicated himself to the U.S. because he had dedicated himself to those ends and the U.S., let us remember, was the first country that had declared that its reason for existing was to secure those ends, first for its own people, and then through their example for all people. If it failed, if it could not overcome the curse of slavery with which it was born, perhaps no other country would ever dare take up the project again. Trying to make a greedy and selfish people realize that the ideals they had declared were enough to justify their bloody revolution for independence was a great challenge. But great men freely take on great challenges. They do so partly for the fame that meeting these challenges ensures, for "the love of fame is the ruling passion of the noblest minds," as Alexander Hamilton put it, but more substantially because meeting these challenges secures a great end, justifies for them the talents they believe they are blessed with, and gives them a reason for living.

Douglass was a U.S. patriot then because he wanted to join and contribute to the first great struggle to secure the human rights of all human beings. Securing these rights in the U.S. would set the stage for securing them universally. But in addition to being a patriot because being a great man he wanted to take up a great challenge, Douglass also took up that challenge because he loved the U.S. This last point is the hardest of all to establish, but there is evidence for it. Recall the point made earlier in this paper, namely, that Douglass returned promptly to the U.S. when it became safe for him to do so. This was strange behavior from a man denying any patriotism and any love or attachment to the U.S. True enough, with his freedom purchased he would no longer—technically at least—be subject to capture and re-enslavement in the U.S., but the mere fact that one cannot be enslaved in a country hardly seems a compelling reason for hurrying to its shores if one does not love it or feel any connection to it. Further, if he could not be legally enslaved in the U.S. if he returned there, he would certainly be subject to racial insult and discrimination. So again, and more pointedly, why could he have wanted to return there if he felt no attachment to the place? It was not as if he had nowhere else to go. He could easily have stayed in England where he claimed to have suffered no racial discrimination and on the contrary had been welcomed and honored. Indeed he had been invited to stay and to send for his wife and family to join him. With all these inducements to stay in England, why did he decide to return to the U.S.? ...

.... He was returning to the U.S., he maintained, only because three million people identified with him by their complexion as well as many members of his immediate family, including his brothers and sisters and a grandmother remained there in slavery. Douglass passionately maintained that this was indeed his reason for returning to the U.S., but he was not altogether believable. After all, he did not have to go to the U.S. to be rejoined with his family. As we have already seen, he could have brought his family to England to join him, and its members could have lived there with him in freedom. Naturally, he could not bring the three million people identified with him by their color to England to join him; but his going back to the U.S. would not do them much good; certainly it would not free them, and as we have seen he could fight for their freedom in England as effectively as he could in the U.S.

It could be argued perhaps that he did not want to live in ease in England while they remained enslaved in the U.S. and that he returned to it to share in their burdens. But before we make too much of this argument we should note that there were definite limits to Douglass's willingness to share the burdens of slavery with his black brethren. In the first place he escaped from slavery rather than continue to share in those burdens; then he fled the country when it seemed that he would be compelled to share them again; and finally he became willing to return only when he had some assurance that he would not be enslaved if he returned. We cannot therefore dismiss the suspicion that despite her wickedness and her contempt for him Douglass loved the U.S. and that that love accounted in part for his decision to return there.

Why would he want to deny that he loved the U.S.? Consider, first, that there are often few if any "good" reasons for loving. Love is more often explained by its causes than by its reasonableness. Nevertheless, lovers who prize their reasonableness try to deny their love if they can find no good reasons for it. This goes a long way to explain why, when Douglass was a Garrisonian and therefore believed that the Constitution was pro-slavery, he denied that he loved the U.S. This belief, supposing that he loved the U.S., would naturally lead him to think of his love as unreasonable, wrongheaded, and perhaps even perverse. And being a reasonable person, or wanting to prove to himself that he prized being reasonable, Douglass would therefore very naturally want to rid himself of his love of the U.S. that seemed to him to be so unreasonable. But ridding oneself of a love, even of a love one regards as unreasonable, is not an easy thing to do. Often the best that people can do is to deny that they have these loves. Perhaps they believe that denying them will eradicate them. In any case, it would be perfectly natural for Douglass to respond to the question his prized reasonableness would relentlessly put to him, "How can you love the U.S. when her most basic laws deny your very humanity?" with the answer, "I do not love the U.S."

How successful Douglass's efforts to suppress his love of the U.S. were I do not know, but I suspect that they were not very successful. There is an unmistakable hint of desperation in his rhetorical questions,

> How can I love a country that dooms 3,000,000 of my brethren, some of them my own kindred, my own brothers, my own sisters ... How can I, I say, love a country thus cursed, thus bedewed with the blood of my brethren?[16]

But Douglass would admit his love for the U.S. after he became convinced that its Constitution was anti-slavery. At that point loving the U.S. would not appear to be so wrong headed after all. In any case, if Douglass could not bring himself to admit his love for the U.S., two of his comrades in arms, no less implacably opposed to U.S. slavery and racism than he was, and both at some time driven to the desperate point of recommending emigration to escape her wickedness, admitted it. "We love our country, dearly love her," Martin Delany admitted forthrightly, "but she don't love us, and drives us from her embraces."[17] Garnet (1966) was only slightly more circumspect stressing the primordial affective roots of his love of the U.S.:

> the U.S. is my home, my country, and I have no other. I love whatever good there may be in her institutions. I hate her sins. I love the green-hills which my eyes first beheld in my infancy. I love every inch of soil which my feet pressed in my youth ...[18]

And Douglass admitted those affective roots at least even when he claimed to have no patriotism. "I do not know that I ever felt the emotion," he said of patriotism,

> but sometimes thought I had a glimpse of it. When I have been delighted with the little brook that passes by the cottage in which I was born, with the woods and the fertile field, I felt a sort of glow which I suspect resembles a little what they call patriotism.[19]

Notes

1. Douglass (1982a, p. 60).
2. Douglass (1985b, p. 102).
3. Douglass (1982a, p. 60).
4. Douglass (1982a, p. 60).
5. Douglass (1985a, pp. 92–93).
6. Douglass (1985a, pp. 92–93).
7. Douglass (1982b, p. 101).
8. Douglass (1985b, pp. 340–366).
9. Douglass (1982c, p. 269).
10. Jefferson (1982, pp. 137–138).
11. Lincoln (1992, pp. 88–89).
12. Locke (1988, pp. 287–290).
13. Morgan (1972/1973, p. 6).
14. Meyers (2008, p. 178).
15. Cited in Schneider (2006, p. 33).
16. Douglass (1982a, p. 60).
17. Delany (1988, p. 203).
18. Garnet (1966, pp. 201–202).
19. Douglass (1982b, p. 103).

References

Abraham Lincoln. 1992. Eulogy on Henry Clay. At Springfield Illinois, on July 6, 1852. In *Lincoln: Selected speeches and writings*, ed. Gore Vidal, 86, 87. New York: Vintage Books/Library of America Edition.

Edmund S. Morgan. 1972/1973. Slavery and freedom: The American paradox. *The Journal of American History* LIX: 6.

Frederick Douglass. 1982a. Country, conscience, and the anti-slavery cause: An address delivered in New York. New York, on May 11, 1847. In *The Frederick Douglass papers volume 2 1847–1854*, ed. John Blassingame, 60. New Haven, CT: Yale University Press.

Frederick Douglass. 1982b. Love of God, love of man, love of country: An address delivered in Syracuse, New York, on September 24, 1847. In *The Frederick Douglass papers volume 2 1847–1854*, ed. John Blassingame, 102. New Haven, CT: Yale University Press.

Frederick Douglass. 1982c. An antislavery tocsin: An address delivered in Rochester, New York, on December 8, 1850. In *The Frederick Douglass papers volume 2 1847–1854*, ed. John W. Blassingame, 269. New Haven, CT: Yale University Press.

Frederick Douglass. 1985a. We ask only for our rights: An address delivered in Troy, New York, on September 4, 1855. In *The Frederick Douglass papers volume 3 1853–1863*, ed. John Blassingame, 92, 93. New Haven, CT: Yale University Press.

Frederick Douglass. 1985b. The American constitution and the slave: An address delivered in Glasgow, Scotland, on March 26, 1860. In *The Frederick Douglass papers volume 3 1855–1863*, ed. John Blassingame, 340–66. New Haven, CT: Yale University Press.

Henry Highland Garnet. 1966. The past and present condition, and the destiny of the colored race. In *Negro social and political thought 1850–1920*, ed. Howard Brotz. New York: Basic Books.

Igor Primoratz. 2002. Introduction. In *Patriotism*, ed. Igor Primoratz, 10. New York: Humanity Books.

John Locke. 1988. The second treatise of government. In *Locke: Two treatises of government*, ed. Peter Laslett, 287–90. Cambridge: Cambridge University Press.

Martin R. Delany. 1988. *The condition, elevation, emigration, and destiny of the colored people of the United States*. Salem, MA: Ayre Company.

Peter C. Meyers. 2008. *Frederick Douglass: Race and the rebirth of American liberalism*. Lawrence, KS: The University of Kansas Press.

Thomas Jefferson. 1982. *Notes on the State of Virginia*. In ed. William Peden, 137, 138. Chapel Hill, NC: University of North Carolina Press.

Thomas C. Schneider. 2006. *Lincoln's defense of politics*. Columbia, MO: University Press of Missouri.

Review and Discussion Questions

1. Boxill reports that Douglass went through a metamorphosis of sorts: from declaring that he had no country and was not patriotic to a position that the United States was his country and he loved his country. Boxill considers the hypothesis that his changing views are explained by his reinterpretation of the U.S. Constitution. What is this hypothesis?
2. Why does Boxill reject the hypothesis that Douglass's love of country is grounded in his attitude toward the U.S. Constitution?
3. Based on what you know about Douglass's life, was he a patriotic American? How would Keller answer this question?
4. Boxill develops the analogy of country with "home." What is the analogy, what is its significance, and do you find it convincing?
5. If Douglass's patriotism is not explained by his convictions about the political system, then what it does explain, according to Boxill?
6. How, if at all, do Douglass's convictions about the United States affect your sense of patriotism?
7. If Douglass could be construed as patriotic, is he susceptible to Keller's analysis that his patriotism would imply bad faith? Or would Douglass be a case of patriotism in good faith, in Keller's view?

READING: LETTER FROM A BIRMINGHAM JAIL

DR. MARTIN LUTHER KING, JR.*

Dr. Martin Luther King's movement of nonviolent resistance came under attack not only through violence by those who defended racial segregation, but also from the arguments of fellow clergy who supported his goals yet disputed his methods. They wanted him to let the court system work out the issues rather than pursue nonviolent protests that could incite civil disturbance. While sitting in jail, Dr. King extemporaneously penned a response to these clergy. His letter has become one of the most powerful statements of nonviolent civil disobedience ever written. Dr. King was a civil rights leader and Nobel Peace Prize winner. He was assassinated in 1968.

My Dear Fellow Clergymen

While confined here in the Birmingham city jail, I came across your recent statement calling our present activities "unwise and untimely." Seldom, if ever, do I pause to answer criticism of my work and ideas. If I sought to answer all of the criticisms that cross my desk, my secretaries would be engaged in little else in the course of the day, and I would have no time for constructive work. But since I feel that you are men of genuine good will and your criticisms are sincerely set forth, I would like to answer your statement in what I hope will be patient and reasonable terms.

I think I should give the reason for my being in Birmingham, since you have been influenced by the argument of "outsiders coming in." I have the honor of serving as president of the Southern Christian Leadership Conference, an organization operating in every southern state, with headquarters in Atlanta, Georgia. We have some eighty-five affiliate organizations all across the South—one being the Alabama Christian Movement for Human Rights. Whenever necessary and possible we share staff, educational and financial resources with our affiliates. Several months ago our local affiliate here in Birmingham invited us to be on call to engage in a nonviolent direct-action program if such were deemed necessary. We readily consented and when the hour came we lived up to our promises. So I am here, along with several members of my staff, because we were invited here. I am here because I have basic organizational ties here.

Beyond this, I am in Birmingham because injustice is here. Just as the eighth-century prophets left their little villages and carried their "thus saith the Lord" far beyond the boundaries of their home-towns; and just as the Apostle Paul left his little village of Tarsus and carried the gospel of Jesus Christ to practically every hamlet and city of the Graeco-Roman world, I too am compelled to carry the

---

* "Letter from a Birmingham Jail" by Martin Luther King, Jr. Copyright © 1963 by Dr. Martin Luther King, Jr. Copyright renewed 1991 by Coretta Scott King. Reprinted by arrangement with The Heirs to the Estate of Martin Luther King Jr., c/o Writers House as proprietor, New York, NY.

gospel of freedom beyond my particular hometown. Like Paul, I must constantly respond to the Macedonian call for aid.

Moreover, I am cognizant of the interrelatedness of all communities and states. I cannot sit idly by in Atlanta and not be concerned about what happens in Birmingham. Injustice anywhere is a threat to justice everywhere. We are caught in an inescapable network of mutuality, tied in a single garment of destiny. Whatever affects one directly affects all indirectly. Never again can we afford to live with the narrow, provincial "outside agitator" idea. Anyone who lives in the United States can never be considered an outsider anywhere in this country.

You deplore the demonstrations that are presently taking place in Birmingham. But I am sorry that your statement did not express a similar concern for the conditions that brought the demonstrations into being. I am sure that each of you would want to go beyond the superficial social analyst who looks merely at effects, and does not grapple with underlying causes. I would not hesitate to say that it is unfortunate that so-called demonstrations are taking place in Birmingham at this time, but I would say in more emphatic terms that it is even more unfortunate that the white power structure of this city left the Negro community with no other alternative.

In any nonviolent campaign there are four basic steps: (1) collection of the facts to determine whether injustices are alive, (2) negotiation, (3) self-purification, and (4) direct action. We have gone through all of these steps in Birmingham. There can be no gainsaying of the fact that racial injustice engulfs this community.

Birmingham is probably the most thoroughly segregated city in the United States. Its ugly record of police brutality is known in every section of this country. Its unjust treatment of Negroes in the courts is a notorious reality. There have been more unsolved bombings of Negro homes and churches in Birmingham than any city in this nation. These are the hard, brutal and unbelievable facts. On the basis of these conditions Negro leaders sought to negotiate with the city fathers. But the political leaders consistently refused to engage in good faith negotiation.

Then came the opportunity last September to talk with some of the leaders of the economic community. In these negotiating sessions certain promises were made by the merchants—such as the promise to remove the humiliating racial signs from the stores. On the basis of these promises Rev. Shuttlesworth and the leaders of the Alabama Christian Movement for Human Rights agreed to call a moratorium on any type of demonstrations. As the weeks and months unfolded we realized that we were the victims of a broken promise. The signs remained. Like so many experiences of the past we were confronted with blasted hopes, and the dark shadow of a deep disappointment settled upon us. So we had no alternative except that of preparing for direct action, whereby we would present our very bodies as a means of laying our case before the conscience of the local and national community. We were not unmindful of the difficulties involved. So we decided to go through a process of self-purification. We started having workshops on nonviolence and repeatedly asked ourselves the questions, "Are you able to accept blows without retaliating?" "Are you able to endure the ordeals of jail?" We decided to set our direct-action program around the Easter season, realizing that with the exception of Christmas, this was the largest shopping period of the year. Knowing that a strong economic withdrawal program would be the byproduct of direct action, we felt that this was the best time to bring pressure on the merchants for the needed changes. Then it occurred to us that the March election was ahead and so we speedily decided to postpone action until after election day. When we discovered that Mr. Connor was in the run-off, we decided again to postpone action so that the demonstrations could not be used to cloud the issues. At this time we agreed to begin our nonviolent witness the day after the run-off.

This reveals that we did not move irresponsibly into direct action. We too wanted to see Mr. Connor defeated; so we went through postponement after postponement to aid in this community need. After this we felt that direct action could be delayed no longer.

You may well ask, "Why direct action? Why sit-ins, marches, etc.? Isn't negotiation a better path?" You are exactly right in your call for negotiation. Indeed, this is the purpose of direct action. Nonviolent direct action seeks to create such a crisis and establish such creative tension that a community that has constantly refused to negotiate is forced to confront the issue. It seeks so to dramatize the issue that it can no longer be ignored. I just referred to the creation of tension as a part of the work of the nonviolent resister. This may sound rather shocking. But I must confess that I am not afraid of the word *tension*. I have earnestly worked and preached against violent tension, but there is a type of constructive nonviolent tension that is necessary for growth. Just as Socrates felt that it was necessary to create a tension in the mind so that individuals could rise from the bondage of myths and half-truths to the unfettered realm of creative analysis and objective appraisal, we must see the need of having nonviolent gadflies to create the kind of tension in society that will help men to rise from the dark depths of prejudice and racism to the majestic heights of understanding and brotherhood. So the purpose of the direct action is to create a situation so crisis-packed that it will inevitably open the door to negotiation. We, therefore, concur with you in your call for negotiation. Too long has our beloved Southland been bogged down in the tragic attempt to live in monologue rather than dialogue.

One of the basic points in your statement is that our acts are untimely. Some have asked, "Why didn't you give the new administration time to act?" The only answer that I can give to this inquiry is that the new administration must be prodded about as much as the outgoing one before it acts. We will be sadly mistaken if we feel that the election of Mr. Boutwell will bring the millennium to Birmingham. While Mr. Boutwell is much more articulate and gentle than Mr. Connor, they are both segregationists, dedicated to the task of maintaining the status quo. The hope I see in Mr. Boutwell is that he will be reasonable enough to see the futility of massive resistance to desegregation. But he will not see this without pressure from the devotees of civil rights. My friends, I must say to you that we have not made a single gain in civil rights without determined legal and nonviolent pressure. History is the long and tragic story of the fact that privileged groups seldom give up their privileges voluntarily. Individuals may see the moral light and voluntarily give up their unjust posture; but as Reinhold Niebuhr has reminded us, groups are more immoral than individuals.

We know through painful experience that freedom is never voluntarily given by the oppressor; it must be demanded by the oppressed. Frankly, I have never yet engaged in a direct-action movement that was "well-timed," according to the timetable of those who have not suffered unduly from the disease of segregation. For years now I have heard the word "Wait!" It rings in the ear of every Negro with a piercing familiarity. This "Wait" has almost always meant "Never." It has been a tranquilizing thalidomide, relieving the emotional stress for a moment, only to give birth to an ill-formed infant of frustration. We must come to see with the distinguished jurist of yesterday that "justice too long delayed is justice denied." We have waited for more than 340 years for our constitutional and God-given rights. The nations of Asia and Africa are moving with jet-like speed toward the goal of political independence, and we still creep at horse and buggy pace toward the gaining of a cup of coffee at a lunch counter. I guess it is easy for those who have never felt the stinging darts of segregation to say, "Wait." But when you have seen vicious mobs lynch your mothers and fathers at will and drown your sisters and brothers at whim; when you have seen hate-filled policemen curse, kick, brutalize and even kill your black brothers and sisters with impunity; when you see the vast majority of your twenty million Negro brothers smothering in an airtight cage of poverty in the midst of an affluent society; when you suddenly find your tongue twisted and your speech stammering as you seek to explain to your six-year-old daughter why she can't go to the public amusement park that has just been advertised on television, and see tears welling up in her little eyes when she is told that Funtown is closed to colored children, and see the depressing clouds of inferiority begin to form in her little mental sky, and see her begin to distort her little personality by unconsciously developing a bitterness toward white people; when you have to concoct an answer for a five-year-old son asking in agonizing pathos: "Daddy, why do white people treat colored people so mean?"; when you take a cross-country drive and find it necessary to sleep night after night in the uncomfortable corners of your automobile because no motel will accept you; when you are humiliated day in and day out by nagging signs reading "white" and "colored"; when your first name becomes "nigger" and your middle name becomes "boy" (however old you are) and your last name becomes "John," and when your wife and mother are never given the respected title "Mrs."; when you are harried by day and haunted by night by the fact that you are a Negro, living constantly at tiptoe stance never quite knowing what to expect next, and plagued with inner fears and outer resentments; when you are forever fighting a degenerating sense of "nobodiness"; then you will understand why we find it difficult to wait. There comes a time when the cup of endurance runs over, and men are no longer willing to be plunged into an abyss of injustice where they experience the blackness of corroding despair. I hope, sirs, you can understand our legitimate and unavoidable impatience.

You express a great deal of anxiety over our willingness to break laws. This is certainly a legitimate concern. Since we so diligently urge people to obey the Supreme Court's decision of 1954 outlawing segregation in the public schools, it is rather strange and paradoxical to find us consciously breaking laws. One may well ask, "How can you advocate breaking some laws and obeying others?" The answer is found in the fact that there are two types of laws: there are *just* and there are *unjust* laws. I would agree with Saint Augustine that "An unjust law is no law at all."

Now what is the difference between the two? How does one determine when a law is just or unjust? A just law is a man-made code that squares with the moral law or the law of God. An unjust law is a code that is out of harmony with the moral law. To put it in the terms of Saint Thomas Aquinas, an unjust law is a human law that is not rooted in eternal and natural law. Any law that uplifts human personality is just. Any law that degrades human personality is unjust. All segregation statutes are unjust because segregation distorts the soul and damages the personality. It gives the segregator a false sense of superiority, and the segregated a false sense of inferiority. To use the words of Martin Buber, the great Jewish philosopher, segregation substitutes an "I–it" relationship for the "I–thou" relationship, and ends up relegating persons to the status of things. So segregation is not only politically, economically and sociologically unsound, but it is morally wrong and sinful. Paul Tillich has said that sin is separation. Isn't segregation an existential expression of man's tragic separation, an expression of his awful estrangement, his terrible sinfulness? So I can urge men to disobey segregation ordinances because they are morally wrong.

Let us turn to a more concrete example of just and unjust laws. An unjust law is a code that a majority inflicts on a minority that is not binding on itself. This is difference made legal. On the other hand a just law is a code that a majority compels a minority to follow that it is willing to follow itself. This is sameness made legal.

Let me give another explanation. An unjust law is a code inflicted upon a minority which that minority had no part in enacting or creating because they did not have the unhampered right to vote. Who can say that the legislature of Alabama which set up the segregation laws was democratically elected? Throughout the state of Alabama all types of conniving methods are used to prevent Negroes from becoming registered voters and there are some counties without a single Negro registered to vote despite the fact that the Negro constitutes a majority of the population. Can any law set up in such a state be considered democratically structured?

These are just a few examples of unjust and just laws. There are some instances when a law is just on its face and unjust in its application. For instance, I was arrested Friday on a charge of parading without a permit. Now there is nothing wrong with an ordinance which requires a permit for a parade, but when the ordinance is used to preserve segregation and to deny citizens the First Amendment privilege of peaceful assembly and peaceful protest, then it becomes unjust.

I hope you can see the distinction I am trying to point out. In no sense do I advocate evading or defying the law as the rabid segregationist would do. This would lead to anarchy. One who breaks an unjust law must do it *openly, lovingly* (not hatefully as the white mothers did in New Orleans when they were seen on television screaming, "nigger, nigger, nigger"), and with a willingness to accept the penalty. I submit that an individual who breaks a law that conscience tells him is unjust, and willingly accepts the penalty by staying in jail to arouse the conscience of the community over its injustice, is in reality expressing the very highest respect for law.

Of course, there is nothing new about this kind of civil disobedience. It was seen sublimely in the refusal of Shadrach, Meshach and Abednego to obey the laws of Nebuchadnezzar because a higher moral law was involved. It was practiced superbly by the early Christians who were willing to face hungry lions and the excruciating pain of chopping blocks, before submitting to certain unjust laws of the Roman Empire. To a degree academic freedom is a reality today because Socrates practiced civil disobedience.

We can never forget that everything Hitler did in Germany was "legal" and everything the Hungarian freedom fighters did in Hungary was "illegal." It was "illegal" to aid and comfort a Jew in Hitler's Germany. But I am sure that if I had lived in Germany during that time I would have aided and comforted my Jewish brothers even though it was illegal. If I lived in a Communist country today where certain principles dear to the Christian faith are suppressed, I believe I would openly advocate disobeying these anti-religious laws. I must make two honest confessions to you, my Christian and Jewish brothers. First, I must confess that over the last few years I have been gravely disappointed with the white moderate. I have almost reached the regrettable conclusion that the Negro's great stumbling block in the stride toward freedom is not the White Citizens Counciler or the Ku Klux Klanner, but the white moderate who is more devoted to "order" than to justice; who prefers a negative peace which is the absence of tension to a positive peace which is the presence of justice; who constantly says, "I agree with you in the goal you seek, but I can't agree with your methods of direct action"; who paternalistically feels that he can set the timetable for another man's freedom; who lives by the myth of time and who constantly advised the Negro to wait until a "more convenient season." Shallow understanding from people of good will is more frustrating than absolute misunderstanding from people of ill will. Lukewarm acceptance is much more bewildering than outright rejection.

I had hoped that the white moderate would understand that law and order exist for the purpose of establishing justice, and that when they fail to do this they become dangerously structured dams that block the flow of social progress. I had hoped that the white moderate would understand that the present tension of the South is merely a necessary phase of the transition from an obnoxious negative peace, where the Negro passively accepted his unjust plight, to a substance-filled positive peace, where all men will respect the dignity and worth of human personality. Actually, we who engage in nonviolent direct action are not the creators of tension. We merely bring to the surface the hidden tension that is already alive. We bring it out in the open where it can be seen and dealt with. Like a boil that can never be cured as long as it is covered up but must be opened with all its pus-flowing ugliness to the natural medicines of air and light, injustice must likewise be exposed, with all of the tension its exposing creates, to the light of human conscience and the air of national opinion before it can be cured.

In your statement you asserted that our actions, even though peaceful, must be condemned because they precipitate violence. But can this assertion be logically made? Isn't this like condemning the robbed man because his possession of money precipitated the evil act of robbery? Isn't this like condemning Socrates because his unswerving commitment to truth and his philosophical delvings precipitated the misguided popular mind to make him drink the hemlock? Isn't this like condemning Jesus because His unique God-consciousness and never-ceasing devotion to his will precipitated the evil act of crucifixion? We must come to see, as federal courts have consistently affirmed, that it is immoral to urge an individual to withdraw his efforts to gain his basic constitutional rights because the quest precipitates violence. Society must protect the robbed and punish the robber.

I had also hoped that the white moderate would reject the myth of time. I received a letter this morning from a white brother in Texas which said:

> All Christians know that the colored people will receive equal rights eventually, but it is possible that you are in too great of a religious hurry. It has taken Christianity almost two thousand years to accomplish what it has. The teachings of Christ take time to come to earth.

All that is said here grows out of a tragic misconception of time. It is the strangely irrational notion that there is something in the very flow of time that will inevitably cure all ills. Actually time is neutral. It can be used either destructively or constructively. I am coming to feel that the people of ill will have used time much more effectively than the people of good will. We will have to repent in this generation not merely for the vitriolic words and actions of the bad people, but for the appalling silence of the good people. We must come to see that human progress never rolls in on wheels of inevitability. It comes through the tireless efforts and persistent work of men willing to be co-workers with God, and without this hard work time itself becomes an ally of the forces of social stagnation. We must use time creatively, and forever realize that the time is always ripe to do right. Now is the time to make real the promise of democracy, and transform our pending national elegy into a creative psalm of brotherhood. Now is the time to lift our national policy from the quicksand of racial injustice to the solid rock of human dignity.

You spoke of our activity in Birmingham as extreme. At first I was rather disappointed that fellow clergymen would see my nonviolent efforts as those of the extremist. I started thinking about the fact that I stand in the middle of two opposing forces in the Negro community. One is a force of complacency made up of Negroes who, as a result of long years of oppression, have been so completely drained of self-respect and a sense of "somebodiness" that they have adjusted to segregation, and, of a few Negroes in the middle class who, because of a degree of academic and economic security, and because at points they profit by segregation, have unconsciously become insensitive to the problems of the masses. The other force is one of bitterness and hatred, and comes perilously close to advocating violence. It is expressed in the various black nationalist groups that are springing up over the nation, the largest and best known being Elijah Muhammad's Muslim movement. This movement is nourished by the contemporary frustration over the continued existence of racial discrimination. It is made up of people who have lost faith in America, who have absolutely repudiated Christianity, and who have concluded that the white man is an incurable "devil." I have tried to stand between these two forces, saying that we need not follow the "do-nothingism" of the complacent or the hatred and despair of the black nationalist. There is the more excellent way of love and nonviolent protest. I'm grateful to God that, through the Negro church, the dimension of nonviolence entered our struggle. If this philosophy had not emerged, I am convinced that by now many streets of the South would be flowing with floods of blood. And I am further convinced that if our white brothers dismiss as "rabble-rousers" and "outside agitators" those of us who are working through the channels of nonviolent direct action and refuse to support our nonviolent efforts, millions of Negroes, out of frustration and despair, will seek solace and security in black nationalist ideologies, a development that will lead inevitably to a frightening racial nightmare.

Oppressed people cannot remain oppressed forever. The urge for freedom will eventually come. This is what happened to the American Negro. Something within has reminded him of his birthright of freedom; something without has reminded him that he can gain it. Consciously and unconsciously, he has been swept in by what the Germans call the *Zeitgeist*, and with his black brothers of Africa, and his brown and yellow brothers of Asia, South America and the Caribbean, he is moving with a sense of cosmic urgency toward the promised land of racial justice. Recognizing this vital urge that has engulfed the Negro community, one should readily understand public demonstrations. The Negro has many pent-up resentments and latent frustrations. He has to get them out. So let him march sometime; let him have his prayer pilgrimages to the city hall; understand why he must have sit-ins and freedom rides. If his repressed emotions do not come out in these nonviolent ways, they will come out in ominous expressions of violence. This is not a threat; it is a fact of history. So I have not said to my people "get rid of your discontent." But I have tried to say that this normal and healthy discontent can be channelized through the creative outlet of nonviolent direct action. Now this approach is being dismissed as extremist. I must admit that I was initially disappointed in being so categorized.

But as I continued to think about the matter I gradually gained a bit of satisfaction from being considered an extremist. Was not Jesus an extremist in love—"Love your enemies, bless them that curse you, pray for them that despitefully use you." Was not Amos an extremist for justice—"Let justice roll down like waters and righteousness like a mighty stream." Was not Paul an extremist for the gospel of Jesus Christ—"I bear in my body the marks of the Lord Jesus." Was not Martin Luther an extremist—"Here I stand; I can do none other so help me God." Was not John Bunyan an extremist—"I will stay in jail to the end of my days before I make a butchery of my conscience." Was not Abraham Lincoln an extremist—"This nation cannot survive half slave and half free." Was not Thomas Jefferson an extremist—"We hold these truths to be self-evident, that all men are created equal." So the question is not whether we will be extremist but what kind of extremist will we be. Will we be extremists for hate or will we be extremists for love? Will we be extremists for the preservation of injustice—or will we be extremists for the cause of justice? In that dramatic scene on Calvary's hill, three men were crucified. We must not forget that all three were crucified for the same crime—the crime of extremism. Two were extremists for immorality, and thusly fell below their environment. The other, Jesus Christ, was an extremist for love, truth and goodness, and thereby rose above his environment. So, after all, maybe the South, the nation and the world are in dire need of creative extremists.

I had hoped that the white moderate would see this. Maybe I was too optimistic. Maybe I expected too much. I guess I should have realized that few members of a race that has oppressed another race can understand or appreciate the deep groans and passionate yearnings of those that have been oppressed and still fewer have the vision to see that injustice must be rooted out by strong, persistent and determined action. I am thankful, however, that some of our white brothers have grasped the meaning of this social revolution and committed themselves to it.

They are still all too small in quantity, but they are big in quality. Some like Ralph McGill, Lillian Smith, Harry Golden and James Dabbs have written about our struggle in eloquent, prophetic and understanding terms. Others have marched with us down nameless streets of the South. They have languished in filthy roach-infested jails, suffering the abuse and brutality of angry policemen who see them as "dirty nigger-lovers." They, unlike so many of their moderate brothers and sisters, have recognized the urgency of the moment and sensed the need for powerful "action" antidotes to combat the disease of segregation.

Let me rush on to mention my other disappointment. I have been so greatly disappointed with the white church and its leadership. Of course, there are some notable exceptions. I am not unmindful of the fact that each of you has taken some significant stands on this issue. I commend you, Rev. Stallings, for your Christian stance on this past Sunday, in welcoming Negroes to your worship service on a nonsegregated basis. I commend the Catholic leaders of this state for integrating Springhill College several years ago.

But despite these notable exceptions I must honestly reiterate that I have been disappointed with the church. I do not say that as one of the negative critics who can always find something wrong with the church. I say it as a minister of the gospel, who loves the church; who was nurtured in its bosom; who has been sustained by its spiritual blessings and who will remain true to it as long as the cord of life shall lengthen.

I had the strange feeling when I was suddenly catapulted into the leadership of the bus protest in Montgomery several years ago that we would have the support of the white church. I felt that the white ministers, priests and rabbis of the South would be some of our strongest allies. Instead, some have been outright opponents, refusing to understand the freedom movement and misrepresenting its leaders; all too many others have been more cautious than courageous and have remained silent behind the anesthetizing security of the stained-glass windows.

In spite of my shattered dreams of the past, I came to Birmingham with the hope that the white religious leadership of this community would see the justice of our cause, and with deep moral concern, serve as the channel through which our just grievances would get to the power structure. I had hoped that each of you would understand. But again I have been disappointed. I have heard numerous religious leaders of the South call upon their worshippers to comply with a desegregation decision because it is the *law*, but I have longed to hear white ministers say, "Follow this decree because integration is morally *right* and the Negro is your brother." In the midst of blatant injustices inflicted upon the Negro, I have watched white churches stand on the sideline and merely mouth pious irrelevancies and sanctimonious trivialities. In the midst of a mighty struggle to rid our nation of racial and economic injustice, I have heard so many ministers say, "Those are social issues with which the gospel has no real concern," and I have watched so many churches commit themselves to a completely otherworldly religion which made a strange distinction between body and soul, the sacred and the secular.

So here we are moving toward the exit of the twentieth century with a religious community largely adjusted to the status quo, standing as a taillight behind other community agencies rather than a headlight leading men to higher levels of justice.

I have traveled the length and breadth of Alabama, Mississippi and all the other southern states. On sweltering summer days and crisp autumn mornings I have looked at her beautiful churches with their lofty spires pointing heavenward. I have beheld the impressive outlay of her massive religious education buildings. Over and over again I have found myself asking:

> What kind of people worship here? Who is their God? Where were their voices when the lips of Governor Barnett dripped with words of interposition and nullification? Where were they when Governor Wallace gave the clarion call for defiance and hatred? Where were their voices of support when tired, bruised and weary Negro men and women decided to rise from the dark dungeons of complacency to the bright hills of creative protest?

Yes, these questions are still in my mind. In deep disappointment, I have wept over the laxity of the church. But be assured that my tears have been tears of love. There can be no deep disappointment where there is not deep love. Yes, I love the church; I love her sacred walls. How could I do otherwise? I am in the rather unique position of being the son, the grandson and the great-grandson of preachers. Yes, I see the church as the body of Christ. But, oh! How we have blemished and scarred that body through social neglect and fear of being nonconformists.

There was a time when the church was very powerful. It was during that period when the early Christians rejoiced when they were deemed worthy to suffer for what they believed. In those days the church was not merely a thermometer that recorded the ideas and principles of popular opinion; it was a thermostat that transformed the mores of society. Wherever the early Christians entered a town the power structure got disturbed and immediately sought to convict them for being "disturbers of the peace" and "outside agitators." But they went on with the conviction that they were "a colony of heaven," and had to obey God rather than man. They were small in number but big in commitment. They were too God-intoxicated to be "astronomically intimidated." They brought an end to such ancient evils as infanticide and gladiatorial contest.

Things are different now. The contemporary church is often a weak, ineffectual voice with an uncertain sound. It is so often the arch-supporter of the status quo. Far from being disturbed by the presence of the church, the power structure of the average community is consoled by the church's silent and often vocal sanction of things as they are.

But the judgment of God is upon the church as never before. If the church of today does not recapture the sacrificial spirit of the early church, it will lose its authentic ring, forfeit the loyalty of millions, and be dismissed as an irrelevant social club with no meaning for the twentieth century. I am meeting young people every day whose disappointment with the church has risen to outright disgust.

Maybe again, I have been too optimistic. Is organized religion too inextricably bound to the status quo to save our nation and the world? Maybe I must turn my faith to the inner spiritual church, the church within the church, as the true *ecclesia* and the hope of the world. But again I am thankful to God that some noble souls from the ranks of organized religion have broken loose from the paralyzing chains of conformity and joined us as active partners in the struggle for freedom. They have left their secure congregations and walked the streets of Albany, Georgia, with us. They have gone through the highways of the South on tortuous rides for freedom. Yes, they have gone to jail with us. Some have been kicked out of their churches, and lost support of their bishops and fellow ministers. But they have gone with the faith that right defeated is stronger than evil triumphant. These men have been the leaven in the lump of the race. Their witness has been the spiritual salt that has preserved the true meaning of the gospel in these troubled times. They have carved a tunnel of hope through the dark mountain of disappointment.

I hope the church as a whole will meet the challenge of this decisive hour. But even if the church does not come to the aid of justice, I have no despair about the future. I have no fear about the outcome of our struggle in Birmingham, even if our motives are presently misunderstood. We will reach the goal of freedom in Birmingham and all over the nation, because the goal of America is freedom. Abused and scorned though we may be, our destiny is tied up with the destiny of America. Before the Pilgrims landed at Plymouth we were here. Before the pen of Jefferson etched across the pages of history the majestic words of the Declaration of Independence, we were here. For more than two centuries our foreparents labored in this country without wages; they made cotton king; and they built the homes of their masters in the midst of brutal injustice and shameful humiliation— and yet out of a bottomless vitality they continued to thrive and develop. If the inexpressible cruelties of slavery could not stop us, the opposition we now face will surely fail. We will win our freedom because the sacred heritage of our nation and the eternal will of God are embodied in our echoing demands.

I must close now. But before closing I am impelled to mention one other point in your statement that troubled me profoundly. You warmly commended the Birmingham police force for keeping "order" and "preventing violence." I don't believe you would have so warmly commended the police force if you had seen its angry violent dogs literally biting six unarmed, nonviolent Negroes. I don't believe you would so quickly commend the policemen if you would observe their ugly and inhuman treatment of Negroes here in the city jail; if you would watch them push and curse old Negro women and young Negro girls; if you would see them slap and kick old Negro men and young boys; if you will observe them, as they did on two occasions, refuse to give us food because we wanted to sing our grace together. I'm sorry that I can't join you in your praise for the police department.

It is true that they have been rather disciplined in their public handling of the demonstrators. In this sense they have been rather publicly "nonviolent." But for what purpose? To preserve the evil system of segregation. Over the last few years I have consistently preached that nonviolence demands that the means we use must be as pure as the ends we seek. So I have tried to make it clear that it is wrong to use immoral means to attain moral ends. But now I must affirm that it is just as wrong, or even more so, to use moral means to preserve immoral ends. Maybe Mr. Connor and his policemen have been rather publicly nonviolent, as Chief Pritchett was in Albany, Georgia, but they have used the moral means of nonviolence to maintain the immoral end of flagrant racial injustice. T. S. Eliot has said that there is no greater treason than to do the right deed for the wrong reason.

I wish you had commended the Negro sit-inners and demonstrators of Birmingham for their sublime courage, their willingness to suffer and their amazing discipline in the midst of the most inhuman provocation. One day the South will recognize its real heroes. They will be the James Merediths, courageously and with a majestic sense of purpose facing jeering and hostile mobs and the agonizing loneliness that characterizes the life of the pioneer. They will be old, oppressed, battered Negro women, symbolized in a seventy-two-year-old woman of Montgomery, Alabama, who rose up with a sense of dignity and with her people decided not to ride the segregated buses, and responded to one who inquired about her tiredness with ungrammatical profundity: "My feet is tired, but my soul is rested." They will be the young high school and college students, young ministers of the gospel and a host of their elders courageously and nonviolently sitting-in at lunch counters and willingly going to jail for conscience's sake. One day the South will know that when these disinherited children of God sat down at lunch counters they were in reality standing up for the best in the American dream and the more sacred values in our Judeo-Christian heritage, and thusly, carrying our whole nation back to those great wells of democracy which were dug deep by the Founding Fathers in the formulation of the Constitution and the Declaration of Independence.

Never before have I written a letter this long (or should I say a book?). I'm afraid that it is much too long to take your precious time. I can assure you that it would have been much shorter if I had been writing from a comfortable desk, but what else is there to do when you are alone for days in the dull monotony of a narrow jail-cell other than write long letters, think strange thoughts, and pray long prayers?

If I have said anything in this letter that is an overstatement of the truth and is indicative of an unreasonable impatience, I beg you to forgive me. If I have said anything in this letter that is an understatement of the truth and is indicative of my having a patience that makes me patient with anything less than brotherhood, I beg God to forgive me.

I hope this letter finds you strong in the faith. I also hope that circumstances will soon make it possible for me to meet each of you, not as an integrationist or a civil rights leader, but as a fellow clergyman and a Christian brother. Let us all hope that the dark clouds of racial prejudice will soon pass away and the deep fog of misunderstanding will be lifted from our fear-drenched communities and in some not too distant tomorrow the radiant stars of love and brotherhood will shine over our great nation with all of their scintillating beauty.

Yours for the cause of Peace and Brotherhood,
Martin Luther King, Jr.

Review and Discussion Questions

1 What is King's argument?
2 What is King's account of justice? Under what conditions is civil disobedience justified?
3 What is the importance of King's four-step procedure for direct action, which includes the concept of self-purification?
4 Are King's arguments in this essay dependent on a commitment to Christianity? If so, why? If not, then what else grounds the legitimacy of his position? What difference does it make whether his argument is grounded specifically in Christian thinking or not?
5 What are the three most important insights from this letter, in your view?

READING: CRITO

PLATO[*]

Plato was born into an aristocratic family in Athens around 427 B.C. Socrates (470–399 B.C.) was a friend of Plato's family from the time Plato was a schoolboy. Although a young Athenian of Plato's class would normally have pursued a political career, Plato chose philosophy instead. He achieved great fame as Socrates' most talented student and one of the world's greatest philosophers. In 387 B.C., Plato founded the Academy, a school of higher education and research (which existed for more than 900 years), and he was its head until his death in 347 B.C. at the age of eighty. Plato wrote some twenty-five dialogues, including "Crito" and the book-length *Republic*.

"Crito" begins after Socrates has been condemned to death for corrupting the youth of Athens through his teaching. Friends try to convince Socrates to allow them to save his life by breaking him out of jail, but Socrates will agree only if he can be convinced that violating the law would be just. "Crito" thus sets the stage for centuries of debate over the nature and extent of legal obligation. (Socrates, in fact, refused to disobey and was executed.)

Scene: The Prison of Socrates

SOCRATES: Dear Crito, ... I am and always have been one of those natures who must be guided by reason, whatever the reason may be which upon reflection appears to me to be the best; and now that this fortune has come upon me, I cannot put away the reasons which I have before given: the principles which I have hitherto honored and revered I still honor, and unless we can find other and better principles on the instant, I am certain not to agree with you; no, not even if the power of the multitude could inflict many more imprisonments, confiscations, deaths, frightening us like children with hobgoblin terrors. But what will be the fairest way of considering the question? Shall I return to your old argument about the opinions of men, some of which are to be regarded, and others, as we were saying, are not to be regarded? Now were we right in maintaining this before I was condemned? And has the argument which was once good now proved to be talk for the sake of talking; in fact an amusement only, and altogether vanity? That is what I want to consider with your help, Crito: whether, under my present circumstances, the argument appears to be in any way different or not; and is to be allowed by me or disallowed. That argument, which, as I believe, is maintained by many who assume to be authorities, was to the effect, as I was saying, that the opinions of some men are to be regarded, and of other men not to be regarded. Now you, Crito, are a disinterested person

---

[*] Plato, *The Dialogues of Plato*, 3rd ed., translated by Benjamin Jowett (London: Oxford University Press, 1892).

who is not going to die tomorrow—at least, there is no human probability of this, and you are therefore not liable to be deceived by the circumstances in which you are placed. Tell me then, whether I am right in saying that some opinions, and the opinions of some men only, are to be valued, and other opinions and the opinions of other men, are not to be valued. I ask you whether I was right in maintaining this?

CRITO: Certainly ....

SOCRATES: Very good; and is not this true, Crito, of other things which we need not separately enumerate? In the matter of just and unjust, fair and foul, good and evil, which are the subjects of our present consultation, ought we to follow the opinion of the many and to fear them; or the opinion of the one man who has understanding, and whom we ought to fear and reverence more than all the rest of the world: and whom deserting we shall destroy and injure that principle in us which may be assumed to be improved by justice and deteriorated by injustice; is there not such a principle?

CRITO: Certainly there is, Socrates.

SOCRATES: Take a parallel instance: if, acting under the advice of men who have no understanding, we destroy that which is improvable by health and deteriorated by disease—when that has been destroyed, I say, would life be worth having? And that is—the body?

CRITO: Yes.

SOCRATES: Could we live, having an evil and corrupted body?

CRITO: Certainly not.

SOCRATES: And will life be worth having, if that higher part of man be depraved, which is improved by justice and deteriorated by injustice? Do we suppose that principle, whatever it may be in man, which has to do with justice and injustice, to be inferior to the body?

CRITO: Certainly not.

SOCRATES: More honored, then?

CRITO: Far more honored.

SOCRATES: Then, my friend, we must not regard what the many say of us; but what he, the one man who has understanding of just and unjust, will say, and what the truth will say. And therefore you begin in error when you suggest that we should regard the opinion of the many about just and unjust, good and evil, honorable and dishonorable. Well, someone will say, "But the many can kill us."

CRITO: Yes, Socrates; that will clearly be the answer.

SOCRATES: That is true: but still I find with surprise that the old argument is, as I conceive, unshaken as ever. And I should like to know whether I may say the same of another proposition—that not life, but a good life, is to be chiefly valued?

CRITO: Yes, that also remains.

SOCRATES: And a good life is equivalent to a just and honorable one—that holds also?

CRITO: Yes, that holds.

SOCRATES: From these premises I proceed to argue the question whether I ought not to try and escape without the consent of the Athenians: and if I am clearly right in escaping, then I will make the attempt; but if not, I will abstain. The other considerations which you mention, of money and loss of character and the duty of educating children, are, I fear, only the doctrines of the multitude, who would be as ready to call people to life, if they were able, as they are to put them to death and with as little reason. But now, since the argument has thus far prevailed, the only question which remains to be considered is, whether we shall do rightly either in escaping or in suffering others to aid in our escape and paying them in money and thanks, or whether we shall not do rightly; and if the latter, then death or any other calamity which may ensue on my remaining here must not be allowed to enter into the calculation.

CRITO: I think that you are right, Socrates; how then shall we proceed?

SOCRATES: Let us consider the matter together, and do you either refute me if you can, and I will be convinced; or else cease, my dear friend, from repeating to me that I ought to escape against the wishes of the Athenians: for I am extremely desirous to be persuaded by you, but not against my own better judgment. And now please to consider my first position, and do your best to answer me.

CRITO: I will do my best.

SOCRATES: Are we to say that we are never intentionally to do wrong, or that in one way we ought and in another way we ought not to do wrong, or is doing wrong always evil and dishonorable, as I was just now saying, and as has been already acknowledged by us? Are all our former admissions which were made within a few days to be thrown away? And have we, at our age, been earnestly discoursing with one another all our life long only to discover that we are no better than children? Or are we to rest assured, in spite of the opinion of the many, and in spite of consequences whether better or worse, of the truth of what was then said, that injustice is always an evil and dishonor to him who acts unjustly? Shall we affirm that?

CRITO: Yes.

SOCRATES: Then we must do no wrong?

CRITO: Certainly not.

SOCRATES: Nor when injured injure in return, as the many imagine; for we must injure no one at all?

CRITO: Clearly not.

SOCRATES: Again, Crito, may we do evil?

CRITO: Surely not, Socrates.

SOCRATES: And what of doing evil in return for evil, which is the morality of the many—is that just or not?

CRITO: Not just.

SOCRATES: For doing evil to another is the same as injuring him?

CRITO: Very true.

SOCRATES: Then we ought not to retaliate or render evil for evil to anyone, whatever evil we may have suffered from him. But I would have you consider, Crito, whether you really mean what you are saying. For this opinion has never been held, and never will be held, by any considerable number of persons; and those who are agreed and those who are not agreed upon this point have no common ground, and can only despise one another when they see how widely they differ. Tell me, then, whether you agree with and assent to my first principle, that neither injury nor retaliation nor warding off evil by evil is ever right. And shall that be the premise of our argument? Or do you decline and dissent from this? For this has been of old and is still my opinion; but, if you are of another opinion, let me hear what you have to say. If, however, you remain of the same mind as formerly, I will proceed to the next step.

CRITO: You may proceed, for I have not changed my mind.

SOCRATES: Then I will proceed to the next step, which may be put in the form of a question: Ought a man to do what he admits to be right, or ought he to betray the right?

CRITO: He ought to do what he thinks right.

SOCRATES: But if this is true, what is the application? In leaving the prison against the will of the Athenians, do I wrong any? Or rather do I not wrong those whom I ought least to wrong? Do I not desert the principles which were acknowledged by us to be just? What do you say?

CRITO: I cannot tell, Socrates, for I do not know.

SOCRATES: Then consider the matter in this way: Imagine that I am about to play truant (you may call the proceeding by any name which you like), and the laws and the government come and interrogate me: "Tell us, Socrates," they say; "what are you about? Are you going by an act of yours to overturn us—the laws and the whole state, as far as in you lies? Do you imagine that a state can subsist and not be overthrown, in which the decisions of law have no power, but are set aside and overthrown by individuals?" What will be our answer, Crito, to these and the like words? Anyone, and especially a clever rhetorician, will have a good deal to urge about the evil of setting aside the law which requires a sentence to be carried out; and we might reply, "Yes; but the state has injured us and given an unjust sentence." Suppose I say that?

CRITO: Very good, Socrates.

SOCRATES: "And was that our agreement with you?" the law would say; "or were you to abide by the sentence of the state?" And if I were to express astonishment at their saying this, the law would probably add: "Answer, Socrates, instead of opening your eyes: you are in the habit of asking and answering questions. Tell us what complaint you have to make against us which justifies you in attempting to destroy us and the state? In the first place did we not bring you into existence? Your father married your mother by our aid and begat you. Say whether you have any objection to urge against those of us who regulate marriage?" None, I should reply. "Or against those of us who regulate the system of nurture and education of children in which you were trained? Were not the laws, who have the charge of this, right in commanding your father to train you in music and gymnastic?" Right, I should reply, "Well then, since you were brought into the world and nurtured and educated by us, can you deny in the first place that you are our child and slave, as your fathers were before you? And if this is true you are not on equal terms with us; nor can you think that you have a right to do to us what we are doing to you. Would you have any right to strike or revile or do any other evil to a father or to your master, if you had one, when you have been struck or reviled by him, or received some other evil at his hands?—you would not say this? And because we think right to destroy you, do you think that you have any right to destroy us in return, and your country as far as in you lies? And will you, O professor of true virtue, say that you are justified in this? Has a philosopher like you failed to discover that our country is more to be valued and higher and holier far than mother or father or any ancestor, and more to be regarded in the eyes of the gods and of men of understanding? Also to be soothed, and gently and reverently entreated when angry, even more than a father, and if not persuaded, obeyed? And when we are punished by her, whether with imprisonment or stripes, the punishment is to be endured in silence; and if she lead us to wounds or death in battle, thither we follow as is right; neither may anyone yield or retreat or leave his rank, but whether in battle or in a court of law, or in any other place, he must do what his city and his country order him; or he must change their view of what is just: and if he may do no violence to his father or mother, much less may he do violence to his country."

What answer shall we make to this, Crito? Do the laws speak truly, or do they not?

CRITO: I think that they do.

SOCRATES: Then the laws will say: "Consider, Socrates, if this is true, that in your present attempt you are going to do us wrong. For, after having brought you into the world, and nurtured and educated you, and given you and every other citizen a share in every good that we had to give, we further proclaim and give the right to every Athenian, that if he does not like us when he has come of age and has seen the ways of the city, and made our acquaintance, he may go where he pleases and take his goods with him; and none of us laws will forbid him or interfere with him. Any of you who does not like us and the city, and who wants to go to a colony or to any other city, may go where he likes, and take his goods with him. But he who has experience of the manner in which we order justice and administer the state, and still remains, has entered into an implied contract that he will do as we command him. And he who disobeys us is, as we maintain, thrice wrong; first, because in disobeying us he is disobeying his parents; secondly, because we are the authors of his education; thirdly, because he has made an agreement with us that he will duly obey our commands; and he neither obeys them nor convinces us that our commands are wrong; and we do not rudely impose them, but give them the alternative of obeying or convincing us; that is what we offer, and he does neither. These are the sort of accusations to which, as we were saying, you, Socrates, will be exposed if you accomplish your intentions; you, above all other Athenians."

Suppose I ask, why is this? They will justly retort upon me that I above all other men have acknowledged the agreement. "There is clear proof," they will say, "Socrates, that we and the city were not displeasing to you. Of all Athenians you have been the most constant resident in the city, which, as you never leave, you may be supposed to love. For you never went out of the city either to see the games, except once when you went to the Isthmus, or to any other place unless you were on military service; nor did you travel as other men do. Nor had you any curiosity to know other states or their laws: your affections did not go beyond us and our state; we were your special favorites, and you acquiesced in our government of you; and this is the state in which you begat your children, which is a proof of your satisfaction. Moreover, you might, if you had liked, have fixed the penalty at banishment in the course of the trial—the state which refuses to let you go now would have let you go then. But you pretended that you preferred death to exile, and that you were not grieved at death. And now you have forgotten these fine sentiments, and pay no respect to us the laws, of whom you are the destroyer; and are doing what only a miserable slave would do, running away and turning your back upon the compacts and agreements which you made as a citizen. And first of all answer this very question: Are we right in saying that you agreed to be governed according to us in deed, and not in word only?" Is that true or not? How shall we answer that, Crito? Must we not agree?

CRITO: There is no help, Socrates.

SOCRATES: Then will they not say: "You, Socrates, are breaking the covenants and agreements which you made with us at your leisure, not in any haste or under any compulsion or deception, but having had seventy years to think of them, during which time you were at liberty to leave the city, if we were not to your mind, or if our covenants appeared to you to be unfair. You had your choice, and might have gone either to Lacedaemon or Crete, which you often praise for their good government, or to some other Hellenic or foreign state. Whereas you, above all other Athenians, seemed to be so fond of the state, or, in other words, of us her laws (for who would like a state that has no laws), that you never stirred out of her; the halt, the blind, the maimed were not more stationary in her than you were. And now you run away and forsake your agreements. Not so, Socrates, if you will take our advice; do not make yourself ridiculous by escaping out of the city. Listen, then, Socrates, to us who have brought you up. Think not of life and children first, and of justice afterwards, but of justice first, that you may be justified before the princes of the world below. For neither will you nor any that belong to you be happier or holier or juster in this life, or happier in another, if you do as Crito bids. Now you depart in innocence, a sufferer and not a doer of evil; a victim, not of the laws, but of men. But if you go forth, returning evil for evil, and injury for injury, breaking the covenants and agreements which you have made with us, and wronging those whom you ought least to wrong, that is to say, yourself, your friends, your country, and us, we shall be angry with you while you live, and our brethren, and laws in the world below, will receive you as an enemy; for they will know that you have done your best to destroy us. Listen, then, to us and not to Crito."

This is the voice which I seem to hear murmuring in my ears, like the sound of the flute in the ears of the mystic; that voice, I say, is humming in my ears, and prevents me from hearing any other. And I know that anything more which you may say will be vain. Yet speak, if you have anything to say.

CRITO: I have nothing to say, Socrates.

SOCRATES: Then let me follow the intimations of the will of God.

Review and Discussion Questions

1 Elaborate on Socrates' notion that the law is like a parent and so deserves obedience from its citizens.
2 Sometimes we can lead others to expect us to behave in a certain way even though we never overtly promise to do so. Give an example of such behavior, and then discuss whether Socrates has done anything that can fairly be interpreted as leading others to expect him to obey the law.
3 At his trial, Socrates made an argument in his own defense. Is that relevant to the present issue?
4 Obviously, Socrates has benefited from living in Athens and has gladly accepted these benefits. Does that constitute an implied contract to obey?
5 What is gratitude? Does Socrates think part of his obligation to remain and serve his sentence is based on gratitude? Explain.

READING: LEGITIMATE AND ILLEGITIMATE USES OF POLICE FORCE

JOHN KLEINIG[*]

John Kleinig applies Locke's social contract approach to defend his views about the ethics of police enforcement. John Kleinig is Emeritus Professor of Philosophy in the Department of Criminal Justice at the John Jay College and Graduate Center, CUNY.

Whatever status we ultimately accord it, the conceit of a social contract is a useful one. Not only does it offer a philosophical framework for reconciling state power with individual liberty, but it also enables us to understand distributions of state power through the formation of defensive armies and internal policing mechanisms. In fact it does more than that; it helps to structure an argument about the limits of the power it distributes. To state it crudely, the social contract authorizes the ethical, efficient, and conditional transfer of a self-defensive and punitive right that we all possess to a social agency or agencies that have been instituted to secure our basic or fundamental rights.

The argumentative power of the contractualist position lies in the way in which it purports to explain why liberal individuals, concerned about their security, might nonetheless be prepared to entrust to others the authority to employ force to ensure their rights, and to do so in a way that also justifies their decision. And if we see members of the police as legitimate social guarantors (or at least partial guarantors) of a right that we have by virtue of our status as humans, then their use of force can be seen not only as derivative of a broadly human right, but also as limited by the scope of that right.

Undoubtedly we can ask legitimate questions about both the foundational right to the defense of self and others as well as the right to punish those who violate our rights. These questions may be quite radical—such as those of a pacifist kind—or they may focus more on the nature and derivation of the right and its vestedness in civil authorities and their agents. Although I do not want to cast aspersions on the more radical questions, my plan here is to focus narrowly on the basis for the exercise of force on the part of the police, on the constraints to which it should be subject, and the excesses to which it is prone.

John Locke's political philosophy remains a fruitful starting point for this discussion, partly because his foundational commitments still resonate fairly well with the liberal democratic ethos within which I suspect most of our discussion will be conducted, but also because he offers enough detail to enable us to locate policing—or more broadly law enforcement—within a liberal democratic framework.

So, by way of brief introduction, I reiterate the main contours of the Lockean contractualist terrain. Central to it is a particular conception of persons as equally

---

[*] Excerpted from "Legitimate and Illegitimate Uses of Police Force" by John Kleinig, *Criminal Justice Ethics* 33(2) (2014): 83–103. Reprinted by permission of Routledge, Taylor and Francis. Some footnotes omitted.

bearers of rights, whether we characterize these parsimoniously as "life, liberty and property" or more generously, as most of us might be inclined to do in the twenty-first century, and whether we characterize them with Locke as divine endowments or, more in keeping with a secular age, as the concomitants of our human capacity for rational self-government. Although Locke focuses most of his attention on what he sometimes broadly refers to as "property,"[1] he adds that in the state of nature or pre-civil society,

> all men may be restrained from invading others' rights, and from doing hurt to one another, and … the execution of the law of nature [the moral law] is … put into every man's hands, whereby everyone has a right to punish the transgressors of that law to such a degree as may hinder its violation."[2]

…. Humans are not angels. The trust that we can have in our fellows and the trust that they can have in us is limited. Despite our possessing the rational power to discern accurately and disinterestedly the law of nature (or breaches thereof), we do a rather bad job of it in practice and are likely to find ourselves unable to give it practical effect.

…

As is well known, Locke resolves this challenge by suggesting that despite our shortcomings we are rational enough to see the wisdom of joining together in what we know as civil society through the creation of and support for institutions that will enable us to exercise our rights equally and to the fullest. In his account of civil society, Locke seeks to make good on the deficiencies of a state of nature by positing the formation of three institutions that it lacks but that he believes to be essential to the enjoyment of our rights. These are, first, a legislature that is tasked with drawing up societally recognized rules or laws to which all will be subject; second, a judiciary that is administered by impartial judges who will interpret and apply what the legislature has mandated; and finally an executive that gives practical effect to the laws by apprehending those who have violated them and ensuring that the punitive judgments associated with their breach are put into effect. …

It is not immediately apparent who or what comprises Locke's executive. I have often used his brief discussion of it to draw attention to the integral role of a policing institution within civil society. Police are those who are empowered to ensure that rights violators are "brought to justice." Those who threaten or violate the rights of others are apprehended, they answer for their transgressions, and they are punished. But it does not take too much thought to see that identifying Locke's "executive" with the police is an oversimplification. We do not (ordinarily) see it as the role of police to punish rights violators and many of us are indignant when they "take the law into their own hands" and presume themselves to be agents of societal punishment. In any case, what we now call police did not have its modern institutional forms when Locke was writing, and so what he refers to as the "power to back and support the sentence when right, and to give it due execution" ranges over a more diffuse set of societal arrangements than we have in the case of the legislature and judiciary.[3] Insofar as policing constitutes part of that executive function, it was, in Locke's time, fragmented and disorganized. Many prosecutions were private, and police powers were exercised by a mix of private agencies, constables (often local householders in rotation), those who deputized for them, night-watchmen, and associational collectives, with some informal public assistance in the case of street crimes. Although policing as we know it was prefigured in Locke's account, modern policing institutions were not established until 1829 in London and spread from there. Locke's executive encompassed not only the policing function, but also the courts and what we now characterize generally as "corrections." The courts determine guilt and are the venue for sentencing, and correctional institutions of various kinds (for example, prison, probation, and parole) actually implement the punishment.

Nevertheless, what we ask of police is integral to the executive that Locke sees as lacking in the state of nature and the punishment that is visited on rights violators. For, as Locke makes clear, people who violate the rights of others "will seldom fail, where they are able, by force to make good their injustice" and, particularly if they resist, can be dangerous to those who would punish them.[4] So the questions that we are left with are: how do we conceive of the force that is vested in the police, and when does it exceed its proper bounds?

Basic Principles

To the extent that we see police coercive authority as entrusted—an authority that we have conditionally surrendered to others for the securing of our rights—several constraints come to mind. Some are implicit in the account that Locke provides; others are more readily derivable from general moral considerations. ...

Problematic Cases

...

I Police Must Respect Our Status as Moral Agents

I begin with the dignitarian constraint. Various coercive police practices either inherently or easily lend themselves to its violation.

(a) In a landmark Californian case *Rochin v. California*, raiding police believed that Richard Rochin swallowed two drug capsules, thus denying them evidence they wished to obtain. Failing to recover them manually, they took him to an emergency room and had his stomach pumped so that he vomited them up. This behavior was subsequently said to "shock the conscience," "offend even hardened sensibilities," and to be "offensive to human dignity."[5] Apart from determining that this use of force violated the Constitution's due process clause, the Court also likened it to a coerced confession.

(b) Germans are familiar with the case of Wolfgang Daschner, formerly vice president of the Frankfurt police, who, in an effort to discover the whereabouts of a kidnapped boy, had it conveyed to the boy's kidnapper that unless he revealed the child's location, torturous pain would be inflicted on him.[6] The threat succeeded, but the child had already been murdered. Subsequently Daschner and a subordinate were convicted of coercion/instructing to commit coercion, though the mild sentence imposed reflected the Regional

Court's judgment that there were strong mitigating circumstances. Nevertheless, it was thought important to affirm that any police activity designed to humiliate or degrade those on whom it is imposed will transgress a fundamental dignitarian constraint.

(c) Whereas the Rochin and Daschner cases refer to individual incidents, there are some common police practices—such as strip and body-cavity searches—that, though sometimes justified for security or evidentiary reasons, are often conducted in ways or under circumstances that violate dignity. Such searches are inherently inclined to violate dignity, and the dignitarian constraint may be violated not only by how they are conducted, but also how often and by whom they are conducted. Problematic examples abound. Last year, in Florida, a woman motorist was pulled over—allegedly for failing to come to a complete stop at a stop sign—and then strip-searched in public, while several male officers looked on and her children viewed the proceedings through the car window. In a particularly egregious boundary violation, the female officer who conducted the search removed the woman's tampon. No drugs or other contraband were found. The situation here has been aggravated by a recent U.S. Supreme Court decision, *Florence v. Board of Chosen Freeholders*, which held that prior to entering a cell, even for a misdemeanor, police may conduct a strip search, whether or not there is reason to believe that the person is carrying a weapon or contraband. In the 5–4 decision, the majority argued that the interests of security outweighed those of privacy. In the abstract, that may be correct; in practice, however, whether one outweighs the other should be a matter of circumstances and probabilities.

(d) In large U.S. cities, another common practice, especially with high-profile or newsworthy arrestees, is "the perp walk," a post-arrest photo-op that the police stage for media purposes. In the difficult relationships that often exist between police and media, the perp walk helps to moderate what is often felt to be an adversarial relationship. It is, however, often humiliating to those arrested—a public and often shameful announcement of guilt before guilt has been established. The widely disseminated images of guilt—handcuffs, police escort—often outlast the outcome, which may be a prosecutorial decision not to proceed or an acquittal.

2 Police Force Must Be Exercised

Although one can debate measurements or determinations of proportionality and claims of excessive force, the requirement is nevertheless frequently breached.

(a) From talking with police officers I have come to believe that one of the most common uses of excessive force is constituted by the over-tightening of handcuffs when arrests or investigatory stops are made. In some respects the problem of over-tightening is aggravated in the U.S. context, because there is generally no discretion regarding the handcuffing of arrestees. Every arrestee, from a 5-year-old child to a 97-year-old grandmother, is handcuffed, and so the opportunity for custodial over-tightening is ever present. My own view—which needs a defense that I cannot give here—is that the very act of handcuffing may constitute unreasonable or excessive force. If that view appears unreasonable—stories about the consequences of "lax" cuffing practices circulate—then there are probably many situations for which alternatives to metal handcuffs, such as plastic easy cuffs or velcro handcuffs could be used. The excessive tightening of handcuffs may be injurious, but more often it is simply very painful. Injury has been estimated to occur in perhaps 1 in 20 cases and is sometimes aggravated when a person is transported in a police vehicle while handcuffed behind the back. Probably the most common form of injury is superficial radial neuropathy, which may clear up in a week or two but the effects of which can take up to three years to disappear. ... the over-tightening, whether simply painful or more seriously injurious, may have various causes. It may result from struggle, as officers seek to bring a person under control, and if that is the case the cuffs are unlikely to be loosened until the officers feel assured that "a safe controlled environment" has been achieved. Or cuffs may be over-tightened as a result of unintended movements and a failure to double-lock them. But cuffs may also be over-tightened in the wake of an uncontrolled adrenaline rush, or as payback for what is perceived as disrespect. ...

(b) Perhaps the most common context for adrenaline-fueled excessive force is at the conclusion of a chase, whether a high-speed vehicle pursuit or one on foot. The stress involved in pursuing someone who is seeking to evade apprehension is associated with the production of adrenaline, heightened energy, and, frequently, a distortion of perspective and judgment. It is now generally required that police officers who wish to engage in high-speed pursuits get permission to do so and, if they have engaged in them, receive permission to continue. But even when permission is given and the pursuit concludes with an arrest, the adrenaline high and other factors may impair rational judgment and they, too, frequently manifest themselves in arrests involving excessive force.

...

(c) Disrespect—sometimes called "contempt of cop"—is another common cause for unnecessary, excessive, or disproportionate force. Police training often reinforces in police the sense that they possess non-negotiable social authority, manifested in "coming on strong" to take control of a situation, of not backing down ... the sense of authority that is inculcated in police officers—partly as a result of training, partly as an expression of the prevailing police culture—often leads to somewhat thin-skinned responses to any sort of challenge. Legally speaking, only "fighting words" serve to remove First Amendment protections but, practically speaking, a much lower standard operates and results in the use of unreasonable or excessive force. That this conduct occurs cuts to the heart of the First Amendment guarantee of free speech, which, more than anything, is supposed to protect the right to criticize exercises of governmental authority.

"Contempt of cop" arrests can be prompted by even less. Sometimes people may simply want to observe or document police action, while officers take umbrage at the fact that their conduct is being monitored. Refusal to leave or stop monitoring what is occurring may lead to what is in effect a "contempt of cop" arrest.

In many cases, prosecutors do not follow up on charges made as a result of "contempt of cop"; nevertheless, miffed officers or officers who have inadequate alternative grounds for an arrest are able to get some sort of satisfaction from the fact that a disrespectful or challenging person has been taught a lesson and will think twice on a future occasion. Worse still, the person who has been arrested may be haunted by it when applying for a job or grant or other benefit that requires an answer to the question of whether one has ever been arrested. Sealing an arrest record is not always an easy matter.

3 Police Force Must Be Exercised Proportionately

Because of its macho traditions and culture of control, police are more likely to focus on proportionate force than on the least force necessary. Breaches of the principle of the least restrictive alternative are therefore quite common.

(a) Greater inclusiveness in policing, especially the greater involvement of female officers, has provided a context in which that breach has become clearly visible. ... One area in which this challenge has been noticeable is in the use of deadly force. Kenneth Winston reviews situations in which women police officers, faced with potentially deadly threats, have talked down those threats rather than responding to them with the deadly force that might otherwise have been expected and accepted.[7] These officers have sometimes been criticized by their colleagues for their non-violent solutions, as though their alternative approach had evinced cultural weakness rather than moral and tactical strength.

(b) Technological developments in intermediate force have also encouraged excess. Most police departments adopt some form of a "continuum of force" policy that matches situations with considerations of proportionality ("appropriate levels of force"), though officers are often encouraged to increase their use of force by a notch to ensure control over a situation. As intermediate force technologies have improved—increasing the ability of police to exercise control while decreasing the likelihood of lasting injury—the temptation to use more force than necessary has grown. Macing became the technique of choice in the 1980s and 1990s, and now it has been superseded by taser use. Rather than engaging in the harder work of persuading citizens to accede to police demands and thereby acquiring control over a situation, using or threatening to use tasers to ensure conformity has become common. At a certain level I support the development and use of non-injurious control technologies. The development of tasers provides police officers with the opportunity to use less force than a situation might otherwise warrant. Thus, although a person who has a knife or other dangerous object and poses a threat to police officers may be stopped by using deadly force, tasers offer a less costly means of achieving the same end. ... The worry I have is that tasers have come to replace less invasive and more humane ways in which police can assert their social and de jure authority—an authority that ought to be embedded in their epistemological status (their "being authorities") more than their being in power.

4 Practicability: The Force Used Must Be Likely to Achieve Its Ends

Police decision-making is usually based on a judgment of probabilities—the likelihood that use of a particular strategy or tactic will serve legitimate police ends. The danger is that force will be exercised in situations in which the achievement of those ends is at best moot.

(a) I will note only in passing the debate about the usefulness of so-called "enhanced interrogation techniques" in extracting information from those on whom they are practiced. Moreover, police have formally eschewed the use of "third degree" tactics, though they sometimes still operate informally. Other state agencies have shown themselves willing to use them, even though the evidence for their usefulness is spotty or at best ambiguous. Nevertheless, certain other interrogation tactics amount to coercive or excessive force. If, for example, you look at the tactics used in the Central Park Jogger rape case, with the subsequent conviction of five young people, you see combinations of threat, psychological pressure, and trickery that I think qualify as violence. Insofar as the purpose of police interrogation is to serve the end of convicting the guilty (rather than convicting those who are being interrogated) then the interrogational techniques that are sometimes employed compromise the achievement of that end. In practice, there is no clear practical line between persuasion, manipulation, and coercion, and what may be employed in good faith may cross from one to the other. ...

(b) Other forcible interventions have also been of dubious merit. Police profiling has been of questionable usefulness. Admittedly, responding to criminality with limited resources requires that those resources be deployed in an efficient and ethical manner. And developing profiles for investigative purposes is superficially a meritorious task. But it is a task that requires a keen awareness not only of its probabilistic character, but also of the subtleties of relevance. The racial profiling on the New Jersey Turnpike in the 1990s that turned so sour, only to return again with a different profile after 9/11, can serve as an example of the hazards involved in using this criterion for forcible interventions.

...

5 Police Force Must Be Appropriately Motivated

The issue of motivation is more subtle, because police are unlikely to accept—or even recognize—that their professional judgments are affected by inappropriate attitudes, presumptions, or motivations.

(a) The disproportionate use of police force against people of color is often said to reflect a social fact—greater involvement in crime, greater resistance to police—rather than any underlying racial prejudice. I do not wish to argue that police are more likely to be racially prejudiced than the larger population of which they are a part, or that such racial prejudice as they display is more likely to manifest itself in illegitimate exercises of force. Nevertheless, it is hard to ignore the racial disparities in the use of force by police. Even if there is statistical evidence that people of color are more likely to be involved in crime than Caucasians (and there is some controversial evidence to that effect), it does not fully accommodate the disparities, and dominantly white societies have to come to terms with the fact of underlying racial prejudice. That prejudice is not, of course, necessarily constituted along simple color lines, but may show itself in other ways—toward particular ethnicities, particular religious groups, particular socio-economic classes, and so forth.

(b) But police often manifest another problematic motivation—the desire to punish. It may not be articulated in quite that manner. It may be presented as the desire to teach a lesson, to "kick ass," or to "touch up." Sometimes it is consciously intended as a legitimate police response to a social situation, at other times as a "deposit" on what the courts are expected eventually to impose.

   (i) .... As we know, crime-fighting constitutes only a small fraction, probably a minor fraction, of police work. A significant amount of their work is also concerned with maintaining order, and, Gary Sykes argues, in communities that have been ravaged by economic and other changes, and that have not been well served by other social supports so that they now teeter on the brink of disorder, police may well think it appropriate to respond to some of that disorder with a little street justice. This context may seem to connect usefully with notions of police discretion, in which the complexity of social life makes it appropriate that police use their professional judgment about how situations should best be handled.

   .... The complexities of social life do call for situational judgments, and a legalism that feeds every formal infraction into the hopper of the criminal justice system is likely to be inadequately nuanced and inappropriately heavy-handed. This is especially true for cases of loitering with intent, disorderly conduct, vagrancy, and so on. ... Especially in the contexts in which Sykes envisages street justice being administered, we are likely to find it vulnerable to discriminatory or otherwise inappropriate expressions. The point is not to argue for either failure to intervene or for a mechanical application of the law, but rather for responses that are conciliatory more than punitive.

   (ii) .... Street justice usually represents the shortcutting of an extended and somewhat inefficient process. Several factors contribute to this usurpation of the punitive function. The most general is that police often view themselves as crime fighters, as those who bring rights' violators to justice, justice being constituted by punishment. It is easy to slip from the role of crime fighter to that of a societal agent of punishment. The social isolation that police often conceptualize and sometimes help to create for themselves can lead them to think that they are the thin blue line between civilization and barbarism, and that a sometimes unappreciative society depends on their executing justice. This attitude may be reinforced by certain elements within that larger society who tolerate—even approve of—their "kicking ass." Especially in regard to street crimes, there are those who think that informal punishment, summary or street justice, is a legitimate way of expressing appropriate moral umbrage as well as "keeping the streets safe and clean."

> ... the temptation for police to take punishment into their own hands is often reinforced by what they see as a weak or broken criminal justice system. High standards of proof, judicial discretion, and plea bargains that are seen to be "soft on crime," along with a lack of real appreciation for the difficulties and sometimes dangers associated with police work, give rise to practices designed to ensure moral and not only procedural justice. To the extent that police see themselves as the direct agents of punishment rather than, at best, gate-openers to society's punitive or corrective mechanisms, they reverse the direction of the social contract, replacing the rule of law with the rule of men and exceeding their role as societal agents of coercive force.

Some Concluding Reflections

Let me conclude this review of common and problematic exercises of force by police with some additional generalities that sum up my concerns or indicate directions for further development.

1. Although I have not made any attempt to establish this claim here, I would suggest that, except in the most egregious cases, police officers are unlikely to suffer consequences for the excessive use of force. The 1989 decision in Graham v. Connor, that the "reasonable-ness" of the police use of force was not to be judged from the 20/20 perspective of hindsight, has also enabled officers to claim situational support for what might otherwise be seen as illegitimate uses of force.[8]
2. The less likely it is that a use of force will result in significant or visible injury, the greater the temptation to misuse it.
3. Excessive force is more likely to be used on members of minority groups than on others. Although it is sometimes argued that there are benign ways of explaining the disparities, at best such explanations lessen the degree of discrimination rather than serve to dispel the complaint.
4. Where those who are agents of essential institutions misuse the authority those institutions give them, the institutions themselves are diminished and Lockean concerns about the failings of the state of nature are revived. Authority is undermined, and with it the sanction that police have to use the force for which they are equipped.

None of these points is intended to deny the practical as well as moral challenges of translating broad theory into practice. The sketch I provided focuses on excesses in the course of doing the hard work of drawing policy and implementation lines; moreover, it does not attempt to spell out best practices. There, ultimately, the real challenges lie—moving beyond the broad generalities I have provided to a nuanced and case-based application and the equally important task of developing cultural sensitivities that will lead to the wise application of law enforcement discretion. Police occupy a difficult space between order and disorder, moral conformity and immoral opportunism. They are our proxies with regard to practical decisions we are not well prepared to make ourselves. We therefore owe it to them to enable them in their task, while holding them accountable for the decisions they make with the authority we have vested in them. The present article, though not sufficient for the fine-grained determinations that need to be made, nevertheless offers a framework within which it is hoped that those decisions may be fruitfully considered.

Notes

1 "[L]ives, liberties and estates, which I call by the general name, property." Locke, *Second Treatise*, 1689, par. 123. Cf. also par. 87.
2 Ibid., par. 7.
3 Ibid., par. 126.
4 Ibid., par. 126.
5 *Rochin v. California*, 342 U.S. 165 (1952).
6 See Landgericht Frankfurt am Main, "Androhung unmittelbaren Zwangs bei polizeilicher Vernehmung—Fall Daschner." *Neue Juristische Wochenschrift* 58, no. 10 (2005): 692–696; Florian Jessberger, "Bad Torture—Good Torture? What International Criminal Lawyers May Learn from the Recent Trial of Police Officers in Germany." *Journal of International Criminal Justice* 3, no. 5 (2005): 1059–1073; S.C. Greer, "Should Police Threats to Torture Suspects Always Be Severely Punished? Reflections on the Gäfgen Case." *Human Rights Law Review* 11, no. 1 (2011): 67–89.
7 See Kenneth W. Winston, "Teaching with Cases," in *Teaching Criminal Justice Ethics: Strategic Issues*, edited by John Kleinig and Margaret Leland Smith, 145–165. Cincinnati, OH: Anderson, 1997).
8 *Graham v. Connor*, 490 U.S. 386 (1989).

Review and Discussion Questions

1 Does it make sense to say that each individual person has a right to self-defense? Is that the best moral foundation for debating the role and function of policing?
2 How does Kleinig derive his list of constraints on police action from his account of human rights?
3 Does his list of constraints provide a basis to examine and evaluate the most recent police controversies?
4 Kleinig writes, "Police occupy a difficult space between order and disorder, moral conformity and immoral opportunism." Do you agree with this way of framing the difficulties? How would you describe the "space" that the police occupy?

Essay and Paper Topics for Chapter 14

1 Write an essay in which you discuss whether or not you believe there is at least a general, if not an absolute, moral obligation to obey the law, using any of the authors you have read in this chapter.
2 How important is it to cultivate or eliminate patriotic attitudes for becoming a good moral person? Explain your reasoning.
3 What would make the use of police force legitimate? What would make it illegitimate? Draw on any readings in Chapters 13 and 14 to defend your position.
4 Could King's approach to civil disobedience also provide the basis for patriotism, as MacIntyre understands patriotism?
5 Is there a distinction between being a "good" patriot and being a "bad" patriot?

Chapter 15

Democracy
Foundations, Recent Contributions, and Global Challenges

Democratic institutions and norms have had an unsteady history: contested, rejected, celebrated, and built piece by piece; destroyed at some moments, sustained in others. The first two readings address the question: What are the ultimate foundations for understanding why democracy matters? The next reading suggests ways to envision political institutions that are not necessarily democratic for a changing and imperfect world. The last three readings address a range of important questions, including: what is the relationship between tradition and democracy? What are the requirements of democracy from a global perspective? What are social movements and what is their proper role in a democracy?

READING: GETTYSBURG ADDRESS (1863)

ABRAHAM LINCOLN

Abraham Lincoln served as President of the United States from 1861 until his assassination in 1865. He led the United States through the Civil War. This address marks the commemoration of the Battle of Gettysburg, a decisive victory for the Union. Lincoln delivered this speech less than six months after the battle—a speech that has become one of the most significant documents in American history.

Four score and seven years ago our fathers brought forth on this continent, a new nation, conceived in Liberty, and dedicated to the proposition that all men are created equal.

Now we are engaged in a great civil war, testing whether that nation, or any nation so conceived and so dedicated, can long endure. We are met on a great battle-field of that war. We have come to dedicate a portion of that field, as a final resting place for those who here gave their lives that that nation might live. It is altogether fitting and proper that we should do this.

But, in a larger sense, we cannot dedicate—we cannot consecrate—we cannot hallow—this ground. The brave men, living and dead, who struggled here, have consecrated it, far above our poor power to add or detract. The world will little note, nor long remember what we say here, but it can never forget what they did here. It is for us the living, rather, to be dedicated here to the unfinished work which they who fought here have thus far so nobly advanced. It is rather for us to be here dedicated to the great task remaining before us—that from these honored dead we take increased devotion to that cause for which they gave the last full measure of devotion—that we here highly resolve that these dead shall not have died in vain—that this nation, under God, shall have a new birth of freedom—and that government of the people, by the people, for the people, shall not perish from the earth.

Review and Discussion Questions

1 Explain the meaning of this expression: "of the people, by the people, for the people."
2 Combining this with the Declaration of Independence, do these two documents contain all the essential concepts for understanding the grounding of democracy?
3 What is the relationship between democracy and war?

READINGS: WHAT JUSTIFIES DEMOCRACY? AND RULE OVER NONE II: SOCIAL EQUALITY AND THE JUSTIFICATION OF DEMOCRACY

NIKO KOLODNY[*]

In a two-part series of articles, Niko Kolodny argues that the ultimate justification for democracy is grounded in realizing the social equality of human beings. This position may be thought to contrast against answers that ground democracy in liberty, happiness, or other values. Niko Kolodny is Professor of Philosophy at the University of California, Berkeley.

Ordinary political discourse, at least in the West, scarcely questions that we are to live in a democracy, where social decisions will ultimately be controlled by some principle of "one person, one vote." As fierce as debates over law or policy may be, those debates take place against a background assumption that, in the end, the question will be resolved by democratic means ....

.... Democracy has a straightforward justification or, indeed, justifications. There is a powerful instrumental case for democracy. It seems plausible that, at least over the long run, democracy better secures individual liberty and broadly shared prosperity than the alternatives. Moreover, democracy seems to have more intrinsic virtues. It is a particularly fitting response to persistent disagreement. It treats people fairly. It does not insult them. It realizes a form of autonomy. It provides avenues for civic engagement. Indeed, where explicit justifications of democracy are offered—and there have been notable proposals in recent years—they typically rest, in the end, on one or more of these considerations.

However, I doubt that any of these considerations represents even a *pro tanto* justification of democracy of the right kind—at least not unless it rests on some prior,

---

[*] Excerpted from "What Justifies Democracy" and "Rule Over None II: Social Equality and the Justification of Democracy" by Niko Kolodny, *Philosophy & Public Affairs* 42(3) (2014). Reprinted by permission of Wiley-Blackwell. Some footnotes omitted.

independent justification. [In his first article, Kolodny critiques these justifications as insufficient. We pick up the discussion with his defense of his own account—Ed. note.]

...

[T]he justification of democracy rests instead on the fact that democracy is a particularly important constituent of a society in which people are related to one another as social equals, as opposed to social inferiors or superiors. The concern for democracy is rooted in a concern not to have anyone else above—or, for that matter, below—one ... I do not expect readers to find this account especially inventive or surprising. The aim is instead to come to terms with something that lies more or less in plain view, something that we are prone to look past, in the search for a more involved, hidden explanation.

While this justification of democracy might help to reconcile us to our own ideals, it might seem, at first, detached from any live controversy. After all, our political culture has more or less settled that, whether or not we do live in a democracy, we are supposed to. However, even if it is not a live controversy whether to live in a democracy, it remains a live controversy, debated almost without cease, what kind of democracy to live in. What sort of electoral system should we have? Should we allow money to influence political outcomes? From left, right, and center, we hear pleas to count this or that institution as more or less "democratic" than some alternative, in a sense about which we are supposed to care. The practical point of asking what justifies democracy is to know when such pleas should be taken seriously. Accordingly, the latter sections of this article ask to what extent this justification of democracy, rooted in relations of social equality, constrains what sort of democracy we should have.

...

Preliminaries: Justifying Democracy

To "justify democracy" would be to answer the following questions:

1 Institutions: Why should we want, or establish, or maintain democratic institutions? Why do we, in general, have reason to try, over the long run, to make political decisions democratically?
2 Authority: Why does the fact that a political decision was made democratically contribute, *pro tanto*, to my being morally required, as an official or a citizen of the relevant polity, to implement or comply with it?
3 Legitimacy: Why does the fact that a political decision was made democratically contribute, *pro tanto*, to its being permissible to implement it, even despite its treating me, as a citizen of the relevant polity, in distinctively "political" ways that, at least in other contexts, are objectionable, such as using force against me, threatening to use force against me, or coercing me?

...

Preliminaries: The Instrumental Argument for Democracy

To be sure, a large part of the justification of democracy is simply instrumental. For a variety of reasons, something like the following seems plausible:

Reliability Thesis: As things actually are, or could reasonably be expected to be, some democratic procedure of decision making is *more substantively reliable* than any nondemocratic procedure. That is, there is some democratic procedure such that if people, in general, try, over the long run, to follow it, then the substantive good will be better served than if they were to try to follow any nondemocratic procedure.

However, this instrumental argument seems incomplete in two ways. First, even if unlikely (and clichéd), we can imagine that the will of a benevolent dictator was, or the calculations of a bureau of technocrats were, more substantively reliable. Nevertheless, there seems to be a familiar "democratic" objection to such procedures. A common reply is that such procedures are ruled out by an *Equality Constraint*, which says, roughly, that if a procedure gives anyone a say, it should give everyone an equal say ....

Second, suppose that the Reliability Thesis is true. Even so, why does it follow ... that any particular decision that might issue from that procedure is authoritative (roughly, morally binding) or legitimate (roughly, permissible to implement)? Suppose someone could bring about substantively better results by disregarding the democratic decision. What reason does she have against this? The Reliability Thesis may answer Institutions: whether to establish and sustain democratic institutions in general and over the long run. But it is less clear how it answers Legitimacy or Authority, which have to do with the normative standing of particular decisions that issue from those institutions. Call this the *Bridging Problem*.

My thesis, in brief, is that the value of relations of social equality supports an Equality Constraint and a solution to the Bridging Problem. But what are relations of social equality?

Here it may help to start negatively: with what relations of social equality are not. I take it that we intuitively grasp the notion of relations of social superiority and inferiority: that, in virtue of how a society is structured, some people can be—in a sense that is perfectly familiar, even if its analysis is elusive—"above" and others "below." We know the paradigms. The servant is "subordinate" to the lord of the manor, the slave "subordinate" to the master, and so on. If asked to place various social groups in a hierarchy, we do this with ease. The plebian is "lower than" the patrician, the untouchable "lower than" the Brahmin, and so on. We know what Alexis de Tocqueville found so conspicuously absent when he wrote of being struck by the "equality of conditions" (among white men) of Jacksonian America.[1] We know how to follow the subtle negotiations among different "stations" that preoccupy so many European novels well into the twentieth century. Social inequality—the presence of social inferiority and superiority—is what social scientists would describe as "stratification," or what might otherwise be described as "distinctions in rank or status," "hierarchy," or "subordination." To some extent, it is the analogue—irrevocably transformed by symbol and self-consciousness—of "pecking order" in other social animals. This analogy may help to explain the primitive depth and inarticulateness of our consciousness about relations of social superiority and inferiority. And I take it that whereas human beings are instinctively conscious of relations of social inferiority and superiority, we, at least here and now, are not simply conscious of these relations, but are moreover disquieted by them, see them as a problem. The paradigms provoke in us a sense of unease.

But what in these paradigms provokes this unease? What are relations of social superiority and inferiority, exactly? The main negative point is that it is *not* simply a matter of how *stuff* is allocated ....

.... Imagine a society administered by a class of ascetic warriors, selected at an early age, by a battery of aptitude tests, to make laws for the laypeople and to regulate justice among them. Imagine that they scrupulously distribute means in the way just described. Of course, by hypothesis, they have greater means of certain kinds, such as the opportunity to perform their administrative role. However, suppose that, by way of compensation, they deprive themselves of many personal liberties and material comforts that civilians enjoy. Arguably—to the extent the worth of various means is commensurable at all—they are not even advantaged, on balance, in the distribution of overall means. Yet there is an obvious sense in which they constitute a superior social stratum, occupy a higher position in the hierarchy. This is surely one of the first things that would register on a visitor to their shores.

.... It seems to have to do with the following:

(i) Some having greater relative power (whether formal or legal, or otherwise) over others ....
(ii) Some having greater relative de facto authority (whether formal or legal, or otherwise) over others, in the sense that their commands or requests are generally, if not exceptionlessly, complied with ....
(iii) Some having attributes (for example, race, lineage, wealth, perceived divine favor) that generally attract greater *consideration* than the corresponding attributes of others.

...

.... This account of social inequality is only a first approximation .... This preliminary account simply tells us where to look: not at who has what, but instead at who enjoys power or authority over, or greater consideration in comparison with, whom.

...

So much, for the moment, for what relations of social inequality are. I argue—or, rather, I propose for consideration, since it is not the sort of claim that admits of much articulate argument—that we have reason to avoid relations of social superiority and inferiority for their own sake ... in a way that deliberately avoids ... asymmetries in power, authority, and consideration ....

...

Suppose, then, that—whether from sincere conviction or only from a polite gameness—the reader grants a concern for social equality. The question is then why equal opportunity to influence political decisions should be a particularly important component of social equality.

...

Returning to the paradigms that provoke anxiety about social inequality, we can observe, first, that one way of avoiding, or at least moderating, what would otherwise be a relation of social inferiority is being able to escape it at will. If one can exit a slave "contract" at will, either because, as one knows, one can void it at will, or because it is already void (that is, will not be enforced by third parties), then it is not clear in what sense one really is a slave. More generally, what seems to matter for relations of social inferiority and superiority is not so much equality in *actual* power, authority, and consideration, but instead equality of opportunity for power, authority, and consideration, where equality of opportunity is understood not as equal ex ante chances, but instead as *ongoing freedom (both formal and informal) to exit relations of inequality.*

.... The point is ... that the freer one is to exit what would otherwise be a relation of social inferiority, the less it seems a relation of social inferiority in the first place.

However, one typically cannot escape the effects of political decisions at will, or at least not without high cost or difficulty. By contrast, escaping subjection to the decisions of nonpolitical associations (at least in nonslaveholding or nonfeudal societies) can be freer. Of course, it need not be freer.[2] But, in that case, worries about social inequality in those nonpolitical relations intuitively *do not* seem out of place. This is not an objection to the account, but rather an implication of it: that disparities of power in employment, or in the family, may be as threatening to social equality as disparities of political power when, like political power, they cannot be voluntarily escaped.

... if we do have equal influence over political decisions, and those decisions have final authority over nonpolitical decisions, then that itself contributes to moderating the threat of social inequality .... The threat to social equality that hierarchy would otherwise pose, one might say, is moderated by the fact that whatever hierarchy there may be is ultimately regulated or authorized from a standpoint of equality ....

Finally, although there are many kinds of power that one person can have over another, the power to subject another to physical force—to literally "push another around"—is especially important to relations of social superiority and inferiority.

... political decisions characteristically involve force, for example, through commands ultimately backed by threats of force.

The thesis, then, is that it is a particularly important component of relations of social equality among individuals that they enjoy equal opportunity for influence over the political decisions to which they are subject ....

What is "equal opportunity to influence" political decisions? Note, first, that it is a matter of influence, not correspondence. One enjoys influence to the extent that the decision is reached by a process that is positively sensitive to one's choice or judgment, such as by a fair vote. By contrast, one enjoys correspondence with a political decision just when the decision is the one that matches one's choice or judgment ....

Second, what matters is one's equal relative influence with others, not the absolute extent of one's influence ....

Third, what matters is opportunity for influence, not the exercise of this opportunity ....

Fourth, what matters is, specifically, equality of opportunity for *informed* influence. Suppose an asymmetry in influence over a decision would threaten social inequality between us. It scarcely defuses the threat that while both of us can, in a suitably objective sense, influence the decision, I know how to influence it in accord with my judgments, but you do not: your attempts at influence are, from your perspective, more or less random. To take an extreme case, a disparity of knowledge of this kind could be what makes you my slave; I know the code that unlocks your chains, whereas you can only enter numbers at random.

Finally, what matters is equal opportunity not only for informed influence, but also for autonomous influence: influence knowingly in accord with judgments that are themselves reached by free reflection on what one takes to be relevant reasons. It scarcely defuses the threat of social equality if I can manipulate the judgments that underlie your vote.

How, then, do we ensure equal opportunity for informed, autonomous influence over political decisions among people who do have ongoing social relations?

One possibility, in principle, would be anarchism: that no political decisions are made at all. Perhaps we can imagine a state of nature where no one has final de facto authority over anyone …. It is hard to see why there would be relations of social inferiority and superiority under such conditions, at least with respect to the making of political decisions. So there is no argument, here, that social equality requires the state, only, as we will see, that it is compatible with the state.

Let us, however, make the entirely safe, factual assumption that more substantial political decisions will be made. Then one possibility, already broached in passing, is to ensure that no individual has any opportunity for influence over those decisions.

To some extent this is realized by the "rule of law," which is often tellingly contrasted with the rule of men. To the extent that the greater power, authority, and consideration (the "majesty" of the law) really do reside in the law, and not in any individual, none of us is ruled by any other one of us. Indeed, I suspect that this is the source of much of the appeal of the ideal of the rule of law: not simply its regularity or predictability, but also its impersonality.

The difficulty is that the rule of law, on its own, is insufficient. The laws themselves must come from somewhere. And if the laws come from only some of us, then the rule of law will seem merely like a particularly efficient and self-disciplined way of subordinating the rest of us ….

…. To a great extent, the accumulated body of law to which we are subject was made by those no longer living. In this way, we are subject to political decisions of the dead ….

The difficulty, of course, is that this inheritance, as rich as it may be, is neither perfectly prescient nor perfectly self-interpreting …. New decisions will need to be made, and old decisions will have to be disambiguated.

This can be done without giving any of us any opportunity for influence, such as by lottery, or it can be done by giving each of us some positive, but equal, opportunity for influence, such as by voting. The concern for social equality thus functions as an Equality Constraint …

A Solution to the Bridging Problem and Answers to Legitimacy and Authority

…. Suppose, to take the case of Authority, I face a choice on some particular occasion of implementing either the democratic decision or a substantively superior decision ….

.... If I were to disregard the democratic decision, then I would be depriving others of equal opportunity to influence this very decision ... I would be, by depriving others of that equal influence, relating to them as a social superior, at least in that instance. If others have a claim on me to avoid relations of social superiority, then they have at least that claim on me to implement the democratic decision.

Similar reasoning might help to explain Legitimacy ... when a decision has substantive defects, what positive reason remains to overcome my objection? To this challenge, the answer is that if the decision was democratically made, then that is a positive reason that at least countervails against, even if it does not ultimately prevail over, my objection ....

.... If I have equal opportunity with every other individual to influence political decisions, then the mere fact that I am subjected to those decisions does not subordinate me to any other individual ....

Which Democracy? Representation

.... It remains to be seen to what extent, and in which ways, this justification of democracy constrains what sort of democracy we should have.

... in ordinary, nonpolitical contexts, if a person, or group, as "principal," delegates to another person, as "agent," certain powers (for example, to make certain decisions, to bargain on behalf of the principal's aims), this need not imply the social inferiority of the individual principal (or the members of the group principal) to the agent. Examples of such agents are lawyers, doctors, accountants, and financial planners. Moreover, this extends to political contexts as well. As just observed, legislatures regularly delegate decisions to subsidiary officers or bodies (among other things, by passing laws that do so). Again, no question of the social inferiority of the legislature, or its members, to the delegate arises in these cases ....

The suggestion, then, is that the relationship between the citizenry and official—say, representative in the legislature—might be one of such delegation. If so, then the electorate, or individual constituents belonging to it, need not be socially inferior to the representative. The representative can be, qua representative, a "public servant," in the full sense of the phrase. No doubt, many of our actual representatives only pay lip service to the idea that they are public servants. But, at least at first glance, that seems a failing of reality to live up to the democratic ideal, not necessarily a failing of the democratic ideal itself.

...

Which Democracy? Persistent Minorities

.... Why, though, are persistent minorities cause for concern?

One cause for concern is obvious and, in the real world, of the utmost seriousness. The existence of persistent minorities may be expected to lead to outcomes that are substantively bad, and bad, in particular, because they disadvantage members of those minorities. When it is said that under polarization, "minority group interests" are not "represented," the root concern is often just that outcomes will tend to treat *members* of those groups—the *people* with those interests—badly in substantive terms.

This may be a compelling reason to alter our electoral system, within the wide latitude permitted by equal a priori chances, in ways that can be expected to produce substantively better outcomes. Take Lani Guinier's example of an "at large" vote on which songs will be played at the high school prom, which has the predictable effect that every song will be, say, "classic rock" and no song will be "urban contemporary." In this case, a "proportional party list" system would produce a better substantive outcome—a fairer distribution of musical enjoyment between classic rock and urban contemporary listeners—than "winner-take-all."

...

The other possible complaint is not against the presence of a persistent minority as such. It is instead against the manipulation of formal procedures that often attends a persistent minority: where voting rules are changed, or districts are gerrymandered, to favor a specific person, group, or party. Take Guinier's example in which a board responded to the election of a member from an ethnic minority by replacing a requirement for certain motions from a single member's say to two members' say, effectively depriving the new board member of the power to make such motions. And racial or partisan gerrymandering of districts, albeit within equal population constraints, seems structurally equivalent. In such cases, the rule being followed is to select whatever equal chances rule is most likely to ratify the choices or judgments of one's own group. And such self-referential riders are, as we noted earlier, at odds with social equality: with a willingness to concede to others as much influence as one enjoys over common affairs.

...

Which Democracy? Informal Opportunity for Influence

.... As far as social equality is concerned, inequalities of influence over political decisions resulting from informal conditions are (at least in the first instance) no less threatening than inequalities of influence over political decisions built into formal procedures ... informal inequalities are not directly established or endorsed by the state's public pronouncements, and they are largely hidden from view.

As we noted earlier, social equality requires equal opportunity to knowingly influence political decisions in line with one's judgments .... Having the means to persuade others seems as much an opportunity to influence a decision as being able to cast a ballot oneself.

.... Achieving equality of access to relevant information, as many theorists have suggested, presents daunting practical challenges.[3] The very division of labor seems to militate against it. In any moderately complex society, some will be paid to acquire relevant political information, whereas others will have to acquire it, if they acquire it at all, in their spare time. Likewise, achieving equality of access to the levers of indirect influence, presumably through subsidies ("floors") or limits ("ceilings") on campaign finance and expenditure, also presents serious practical challenges.

Although it would be a mistake to minimize these practical challenges, there are limits to what philosophy (at least of the kind being pursued in this article) can say about them. However, there is a more immediate theoretical objection to the idea of equal opportunity for indirect influence, which philosophy ought to be able to address. Intuitively, it matters what form indirect influence takes. Granted, it may be objectionable if Expert has more opportunity than Crank to make his case to Hearer, because of factors that do not depend on Hearer's autonomous judgment ... his free reflection on what he takes to be relevant reasons. For example, it may be objectionable that Expert, but not Crank, has access to a printing press. But it hardly seems objectionable that Expert has a greater capacity to affect Hearer's vote simply because Hearer will, upon free reflection, take the considerations that Expert offers to be better reasons. The *Difference Intuition*, to give it a name, is that while "judgment-independent" inequalities in opportunity for informal influence may be problematic, "judgment-dependent" inequalities—which merely result from the influenced person exercising his judgment—certainly are not.

... Crank cannot claim that, simply because Hearer makes up his mind to disregard Crank's reasons, Crank has been deprived of equal opportunity for influence .... In sum, the very idea of equality of opportunity requires us to distinguish between judgment-dependent and judgment-independent inequalities, and to see the latter, but not the former, as compromising that equality of opportunity.

... using an unjust share of wealth to buy an expensive car is not nearly as troubling as using it to buy a Senate seat, with all that that implies for one's influence over the lives of others. Instead, I suspect, the core of the concern about the effect of disparities of wealth on our politics is a concern about a few wielding inordinate power with respect to the many, in a way that seems simply incompatible with a society of equals, a society in which none rules over any other.

Notes

1 Alexis de Tocqueville, *Democracy in America*, vol. 1 (1835).
2 Moreover, the freedom to exit any particular relation of subordination to any particular superior may not suffice for what matters for social equality: a freedom to exit all such relations. It might be like the relation between the proletarian and the capitalist class depicted by Marx. Or it might be like the relation between women and men, in a society where each woman has the right to divorce her current husband, but is expected to be subservient wife of some husband.
3 See Joseph Schumpeter, *Capitalism, Socialism, and Democracy* (New York: Harper and Brothers, 1950); and Anthony Downs, *An Economic Theory of Democracy* (New York: Harper and Row, 1957).

Review and Discussion Questions

1 What is social equality, for Kolodny?
2 Do you agree that this idea is the best way to understand why democracy is justified?
3 For Kolodny, why is democracy so important for political life but not as necessary for other activities, such as family life?
4 What is wrong with gerrymandering, according to Kolodny's analysis?
5 What is the point of the Expert/Crank discussion near the end of the essay?

READING: ARE CHARTER CITIES LEGITIMATE?

RAHUL SAGAR[*]

Rahul Sagar defends the concept of charter cities even if they lack a democratic structure. This article presses questions of what makes a political structure democratic and what matters most for assessing whether a political order is justified. Rahul Sagar is Global Network Associate Professor of Political Science at New York University at Abu Dhabi.

Poverty and underdevelopment are among the most pressing problems of our time. It has been persuasively argued that transfers of wealth and knowledge alone cannot solve these problems—it is also necessary to put in place political and legal institutions that will stimulate growth and development. But how to establish such institutions in the least developed parts of the world where regimes are often "extractive" and have no desire to see change?

Revolution is difficult, and often accompanied by instability and violence, as recent events in the Middle East show. Nor can those living under oppressive regimes easily move to more desirable locations, as the travails of illegal migrants journeying to America and Europe remind us daily. It is entirely reasonable to demand that the developed world permit greater inward migration, especially in the form of guest worker programs. Yet the numbers involved are staggering—a recent survey suggests that 640 million adults worldwide would like to migrate, principally to North America and Western Europe. This raises serious concerns about the cultural and financial implications, and hence about the political viability, of proposals that would permit sizable inflows.

These constraints explain the appeal of Paul Romer's much-discussed proposal to create charter cities—that is, "model" cities featuring economic and social institutions conducive to growth and development that are open to all willing to migrate there.[1] This proposal has been lauded as "the world's quickest shortcut to economic development." More recently, it has been cited as an answer to the migrant crisis confronting Europe. Romer's proposal has not been universally welcomed though. It has also been sharply criticized as being contrary to liberal democratic norms and as verging on neo-colonialism. How valid are these criticisms? I argue below that these criticisms can be rebutted ....

The Concept

The charter city concept obviously has a material aspect. A charter city must be large enough to accommodate "millions of residents" because this is the scale at which "the services and amenities of modern urban life become feasible."[2] "A good target size," according to Romer, "is 1,000 square kilometers, roughly the size of Hong Kong and Singapore."[3] An additional requirement—a "necessity" in

---

[*] Excerpted from "Are Charter Cities Legitimate?" by Rahul Sagar, *The Journal of Political Philosophy* 24(4) (2016): 509–529. Reprinted by permission of Wiley-Blackwell. Some footnotes omitted.

fact—is "access to the sea" because "as long as a charter city can ship goods back and forth on container ships, it can thrive even if its neighbors turn hostile or unstable."[4]

From a moral and legal perspective, central to this concept is the notion of being chartered. This term can be understood in two senses. In the first sense a city is chartered when its establishment is an act of law rather than force. It is founded, that is, by a grant from the relevant legal authority, in this case the sovereign entity that controls the territory in question. This definition distinguishes a charter city from a colonial possession acquired through coercion or fraud ....

A charter city is also chartered in the sense of having a charter that "pre-specifies the broad rules that would apply there."[5] Romer keeps these rules minimal on the grounds that one size cannot fit all. Because "a city's governance structure could vary significantly depending on where it is established," he writes, we must "leave broad scope for experiments and let competition and choice determine which experiments persist." The principles he requires every charter to protect are legal equality and individual choice. A charter must contain "a commitment to the equal treatment of all residents under the law"—in other words, it must protect the rule of law. Further, it must guarantee "choice, backed by both voluntary entry and free exit for all residents, employers, and investors."[6] Romer also emphasizes that charter cities must ensure probity—for instance, by creating an oversight body armed with the right to audit and dismiss corrupt officials. These details aside, Romer permits great flexibility. He does not, for example, explicitly require charter cities to be liberal democratic, though some discussions reference eventual "transitions" to democracy.

Why believe that the principles outlined above will be upheld? It is one thing to make a promise—for instance, that there will be no expropriation—and quite another to enforce such a promise, especially in underdeveloped parts of the world, where the willingness and ability to enforce such norms and rules may be weak or even non-existent. Freedom of movement could conceivably serve a disciplining function in this context, with violations of the rule of law being punished by a debilitating exodus. But what guarantee is there that even this fundamental right will be upheld—what is to stop, for instance, unlawful detention in labor camps?

Romer addresses this problem of political risk—or the questionable credibility of a charter city's political and legal commitments—with the striking proposal that foreign nations serve as guarantors for the city's charter. The idea is that a city could, for instance, contract out the training and auditing of its police force to Sweden or make respected external jurisdictions such the United Kingdom the final authority on judicial matters.[7] A move in this direction would, he argues, give the city's institutions "instant credibility of enforcement."[8]

.... As I understand it, a charter city involves an *irrevocable* grant of authority —that is, the authority vested in it cannot be lawfully taken away without its consent. A charter city is, in other words, a *free* or *self-governing* entity, at least within the bounds of the authority transferred to it ....

So understood there are no contemporary examples of a charter city. This is not surprising since, historically, sovereigns have ceded territory only under the threat of violence, and the territory so ceded has rarely, if ever, been permitted to govern itself. The closest historical analogies to the charter city as conceived here are the Shanghai International Settlement, the Tangier International Zone, and British Hong Kong ....

Moral Objections

Having clarified what a charter city is, we are now ready to consider the moral objections lodged against it .... The first concerns the thinness of the guarantees a charter is required to enshrine ... charter city residents may have no reliable way of expressing and defending their interests ....

Romer's response has been to emphasize the centrality of individual choice. A charter city protects individual choice by guaranteeing the freedom of movement, effectively allowing individuals to vote with their feet ....

A more fundamental objection is that the individuals migrating to such cities may be doing so out of necessity rather than genuinely "free" choice. Imagine, for instance, the case of a woman living in rural Philippines. Her family falls on hard times and her choices are to either enter the sex trade or to migrate to a charter city where female workers earn less than men. Assume she chooses the latter. In this case it could be argued that while it is true that this Filipino woman has migrated to the charter city voluntarily, her choice should not be seen as legitimating the rules of the city because, were the possibility open to her, she would prefer to migrate to a country that ensures equal pay for equal work.

Defending Technocracy

"The legitimacy of any system of power," David Beetham writes, "lies in the degree to which it is acknowledged as rightful, both by those involved with and subject to it and by third parties whose support and recognition it may depend on." Although this definition is "a widely agreed-on one," he adds, "much else about the subject is strongly contested."[9]

One such disagreement concerns whether a regime must be liberal democratic in order to be legitimate. The conventional view, which hardly needs elaboration, is that in view of the equality and autonomy of individuals a regime is legitimate only when those over whom it rules have consented to be subject to its laws and commands. To ensure that such consent is given freely, citizens must enjoy the procedural and substantive securities associated with liberal democracy.

Romer does not challenge the conventional view. He merely broadens the mechanism by which consent can be given—he wants us to accept that people can also vote with their feet. I have already explained why this claim is problematic—namely, migration may be involuntary or coerced in various subtle ways. Consent theory more generally is vulnerable to a similar challenge. A number of scholars, including John Simmons, Allen Buchanan, and Russell Hardin, have pointed out that few, if any, regimes can satisfy consent theory because social and political inequalities raise a question mark over the quality of consent that citizens can offer ....

.... Hence I want to focus on a positive question: is consent, as expressed through the procedures of liberal democracy, the only reasonable standard of legitimacy? To put the question in context: must a charter city be liberal democratic in order to be legitimate?

...

Rawls ... argues in *The Law of Peoples* that because not all societies wish to be liberal, and because self-determination is "an important good for a people," it is inappropriate to require every society to become liberal democratic in order for its rulers to be deemed legitimate.[10] In his view a regime that diverges from liberal democratic norms is legitimate when it is "decent"—that is, it eschews aggression, respects basic rights, pursues the common good, upholds the rule of law, and consults with citizens. The legitimacy of such a regime, he argues, lies in the fact that it genuinely furthers and represents the principled interests and collective aspirations of its citizens.

.... The central problem is that Rawls permits the common good to be defined in terms of adherence to communal values. In practice, complex modern societies are not likely to actually share a common understanding of their tradition and culture. A deeper issue is that a tradition or culture may condone unequal treatment on grounds that are not acceptable to internal dissidents or foreign observers. For instance, Rawls allows the imaginary republic of Kazanistan (the archetypal decent regime discussed in *The Law of Peoples*) to legally discriminate against women and minorities if this is what its communal values genuinely demand. Why should dissidents and observers view such use of political power as rightful? ...

Rawls's response to this challenge is to underscore the importance of the political institutions characteristic of a decent regime. In such a regime public officials must respect "the right to express political dissent" and are obliged "to give a conscientious reply" to critical views. Otherwise citizens will, he warns, come to "their duties and obligations as mere commands imposed by force."[11] Such consultations give citizens the means by which to challenge and reform the prevailing conception of the common good. In the event should we find in a place like Kazanistan little or no criticism of the lower status accorded to women and minorities, then we will have reason to conclude that such laws really do embody the values of citizens (rather than the sentiments of some narrow sect or group of clerics). This outcome may distress liberals, Rawls observes, but if we truly value self-determination, then we ought to treat as legitimate a regime that enacts and enforces such laws.

Rawls's claim falls apart, however, when we reflect on the basis of public consultations. To wit, suppose internal dissidents and foreign observers challenge the inferior status accorded to women and minorities as irrational or contrary to the values and traditions of that society. Who judges this claim and on what basis? When the common good is defined along communal lines, the right to ascertain what it amounts to will presumably be invested in traditional or religious authorities. These authorities will simply respond that, interpreted "correctly," the relevant scriptures or records justify the subordination of women and minorities. Since such claims are not open to empirical investigation and falsification, from the perspective of dissidents and observers, the regime will appear to be issuing illegitimate commands rather than embodying their interests and aspirations.

... explanation for why legitimacy need not be tied to liberal democracy draws on consequentialist notions relating to performance or output or service. On this view a non-democratic regime can be legitimate when it generates, for those over whom it exercises power, more desirable consequences than any plausible alternative could .... We come together, as the opening line of Aristotle's *Politics* underlines, not merely to survive, but to live well. I agree then with Rawls that in order to be legitimate, a non-democratic regime must further some common good. However, for the reasons outlined immediately above, I think Rawls makes a mistake when he permits the common good to be defined in communal terms. In order to establish in the eyes of all concerned that it is in fact pursuing the common good, a regime must pursue a conception of it founded on reason rather than revelation.

The consequentialist account presented above is typically challenged by pointing to pervasive moral and political disagreement. Such disagreement is thought to make democracy attractive, as it constitutes a fair means by which to resolve our differences. I see the force of this challenge when we seek to identify a full-blown account of the Good. In this case, the quest for an impartial identification of the Good can lead to *ipsedixistism* ("it is true because I say so").[12] But is it not possible to identify a minimal conception of the common good on which there is in fact widespread agreement? Arguably, there are interests—encapsulated under the term *well-being*—that we recognize as important regardless of our substantive moral theories. By this I refer to an individual's interests, starting with physical security and sustenance, continuing on to the exercise of basic functions, and then finally on to the cultivation of broader intellectual and emotional capabilities. The activities, documents, and statements of national governments, international institutions, and civil society groups confirm that such objectives are widely desired. If so, then a regime that is able to secure such goods will enjoy "output legitimacy" (to use Fritz Scharpf's widely cited term).[13]

This claim will quickly invite objections. It will be pointed out that there are likely to be disputes over how well-being ought to be conceived and measured. But we can sidestep this difficulty by means of a reformulation: a charter city must pursue a *plausible* conception of well-being—that is, a conception endorsed by a wide range of disinterested observers. In this sense a plausible conception of well-being is human development as reported in the United Nations Human Development Report (HDR), which tracks indicators such as per capita income, infant mortality, literacy, and life expectancy, as well as measures of inequality. There are other indices that we could also employ—tracking outcomes in areas as varied as law enforcement, social equity, and service provision—effectively creating an index of plausible indices.

A second objection will be that if international agreement on the importance of human development can serve as the basis for requiring charter cities to pursue these objectives, then why should the near-universal ratification of the International Covenant on Civil and Political Rights not be viewed as also requiring them to enshrine a broad spectrum of political and civil liberties? ....

... the relevant observation is that individuals' interests are hierarchical in nature, and that when these interests come into conflict, it is appropriate to prioritize the more fundamental among them. In environments where poverty and inequality have fostered violence, exploitation, and instability, individuals may be willing to forego political and civil liberties should this be necessary to secure more fundamental interests such as order, security, and an escape from poverty and stagnation.

Is this a *bourgeois* argument that privileges material outcomes at the expense of freedom? It will seem so to those who shout "give me liberty or give me death," but not to the sizable number who evidently prefer effective administration—a preference structure made clear by the risky endeavors of illegal immigrants, and even by the endeavors of skilled migrants who leave their home countries to take up "guest worker" positions overseas. In both cases we see individuals—especially those migrating from democracies such as India and the Philippines to non-democracies like

Hong Kong and Qatar—choosing to forego political and civil liberties in order to secure livelihoods and improve their living standards.

A third objection will be that absent the procedural and substantive securities associated with liberal democracy, power will be abused. But such an absolute statement is belied by experience. One would be hard-pressed to claim, for instance, that over the past half century Hong Kong has experienced grave abuses of power (whereas racial minorities in the United States do routinely claim to have experienced abuse and received no redress). Similarly a one-party dominant system in Singapore has not prevented the country from routinely coming at the top of Transparency International's Corruption Perceptions Index (the United States, by contrast, usually ranks much lower).

.... As liberties protect fundamental interests, restrictions are justified only when they are necessary to protect higher order interests. This formulation is hardly unusual. It expresses the well-known idea that while political and civil liberties should not be subject to the fluctuations of a bare utilitarian calculus, when the exercise of a right has the potential to negatively affect even more valuable interests, such as sustenance and stability, a process of balancing will have to ensue, and may lead to the curtailing of that right. This logic should be familiar to liberal societies. It is, after all, how they justify their own divergences from liberal democratic norms when, for example, they curtail speech or maintain secrecy in the name of national security. In acting this way liberal societies acknowledge a hierarchy of interests. The justification for a charter city's divergence from liberal democratic norms rests on the same reasoning. Crucially, since the legitimacy of a charter city depends on the furthering of well-being, public reasoning and deliberation on rights violations become meaningful in a way that they cannot be on Rawls's account, since the debate in this instance is based on reason rather than revelation.

Notes

1 For an overview see Paul Romer, 'Charter Cities,' Urbanization Project; available at http://tinyurl.com/ophzzvy.
2 Brandon Fuller and Paul Romer, *Success and the City: How Charter Cities Could Transform the Developing World*, Macdonald-Laurier Institute, April, 2012, p. 4, available at http://tinyurl.com/m7ynq7g.
3 Ibid., p. 7.
4 Paul Romer, 'For richer, for poorer,' *Prospect*, February 2010, pp. 5–6.
5 Fuller and Romer, *Success and the City*, p. 7.
6 Ibid.
7 Romer, 'For richer, for poorer,' p. 4; Fuller and Romer, *Success and the City*, p. 15.
8 Fuller and Romer, *Success and the City*, p. 7.
9 David Beetham, 'Legitimacy,' in *International Encyclopedia of Political Science*, eds. Bertrand Badie, Dirk Berg-Schlosser, and Leonardo Morlino (Thousand Oaks, CA: Sage, 2011), p. 1415.
10 Rawls, *The Law of Peoples* (Cambridge, MA: Harvard University Press, 2001), p. 85.
11 Ibid., p. 66.
12 Ken Binmore, 'A Utilitarian Theory of Political Legitimacy,' in *Economics, Values, and Organization*, eds. Avner Ben-Ner and Louis Putterman (Cambridge: Cambridge University Press, 1998), pp. 101–132, at pp. 104–7.
13 Fritz Scharpf, *Governing in Europe: Effective and Democratic?* (Oxford: Oxford University Press, 1999), pp. 7–14.

Review and Discussion Questions

1 Would Kolodny support the creation of charter cities? In what ways would he critique Sagar's analysis?
2 If people have an exit option from charter cities, then is that condition sufficient to establish that those who remain consent to the arrangement? What is Sagar's analysis?
3 Can a political system be legitimate without determining whether people consent to it? How does Sagar respond? What is his conception of "output legitimacy" and what is the role of this idea in his argument?
4 Do you agree with the significance that Sagar places on the distinction between reason and revelation relevant to organizing and justifying a political community?

READING: POLITICAL MORALITY AND THE AUTHORITY OF TRADITION

STEVEN WALL[*]

Steven Wall defends the importance of being connected to a political tradition, whether or not it has a history that fulfills the full range of democratic ideals. He asks us to consider whether and in what sense tradition has its own value. Steven Wall is Professor of Philosophy at the University of Arizona.

Traditions are important to people, or at least to many of us. They help to order our lives and to give them meaning. They tie us to the past and extend our concerns into the future .... A political tradition is authoritative for people if it guides them in their political activity, giving them reasons that they would not otherwise have. By understanding these reasons, and their grounds, we can come to understand the moral significance of political traditions. Attention to the authority of political traditions, in turn, will illuminate how the political morality of societies depends on their past. That political morality is so dependent on the past is an important and neglected truth of political conservatism, one that I hope here to bring into sharper focus ....

...

Political traditions are "formed ways of acting" that have been transmitted from the past.[1] While they are constituted in part by ideas and habits of thought, they exist in practice. Political traditions are traditions of behavior, not simply traditions of thought. Importantly, traditions of behavior exist only if their adherents view them as a source of reasons. A group of friends who live apart may vacation together at the same location every year. This pattern of behavior would not be a tradition unless it was seen by the members of the group as providing them with reasons to do so. The reason-providing character of traditions is crucial to their existence, but it is also puzzling. For, on the one hand, the bare fact that something has been done in the past is not a good reason to keep doing it. But, on the

---

[*] Excerpted from "Political Morality and the Authority of Tradition" by Steven Wall, *The Journal of Political Philosophy* 24(2) (2016): 137–161. Reprinted by permission of Wiley-Blackwell. Some footnotes omitted.

other, if there are good reasons to do what was done in the past, then—or so it seems—we can simply advert to these reasons to explain why we should continue to do so. The puzzle is not a deep one, however. The fact that something has been done in the past can be a partial reason for continuing to do it. One function of traditions is to coordinate behavior to help people do what they have reason to do, but would not be able to do, or do as well, without the coordination. The group of friends in my example may rely on a tradition to help them coordinate their plans. They may know that without it they would not vacation together or would do so less often. That they have a practice of vacationing together is then a reason for them to continue doing so, but it is only a partial reason. A complete statement of their reason would need to include the reason provided by the value of their friendship and the value of taking vacations together as a way of preserving it.

Political traditions are distinctive in a number of ways. Some traditions of behavior are short-lived, but political traditions stretch across generations of people. They direct attention backwards to past generations and forward to future ones. By so doing, they impart continuity to the politics of a society. They give a society an image of itself as a continuous self-governing entity with a distinctive character expressed in time.

Political traditions are also more encompassing than other traditions. When a political tradition exists in a political society, there is a sense in which all the members of the society are subject to it. It is, after all, a tradition of their society.[2] This fact complicates the point I made above about the reason-giving character of traditions. Adhering to a tradition of behavior requires that one see a reason to comply with it; but people can be subject to a tradition, even when they acknowledge no such reason.

Political traditions include legal traditions, and the legal traditions of a society make up much of its political traditions. But political traditions should not be identified too tightly with legal traditions. For one thing, legal practices may reflect a political tradition of a society, but not every element of the tradition may be reflected in the law. For example, a political society may have a political tradition of decentralized government. This tradition may be expressed in the constitutional structure and the legal decisions of the society, but it may also include ideals that are not themselves part of the law …

…. Among the defenders of political tradition (and traditions generally), there is a tendency to trace the traditions back to a founding moment at which their authority was established. Founders of the tradition are then depicted as supremely wise or divinely inspired. We can call this *sacred traditionalism*, since the authority of the established practices is grounded ultimately in their sacred origins ….

Political traditions decay and die. A living political tradition is widely practiced and its authority is widely recognized. Still, the adherents of a living political tradition can be expected to disagree about what it embodies. As many writers have observed, traditions involve conflict as well as continuity. In this respect, the adherents of a living political tradition participate in a historically extended argument about its character and its intimations.

…. Consider an abstract universal principle. The principle requires governments to treat their citizens with equal concern, for example. Now suppose, as is plausible, that there is more than one articulation of that principle that, considered abstractly, has a claim to rational acceptance. Here the political traditions of a society can play a role in favoring some articulations over others, thereby helping to *specify* the tradition-independent principle for that society. Second, consider a case in which a universal principle does not determine what ought to be done in a particular situation. The principle holds that claims to legitimately acquired property must be honored, for example. Circumstances will arise in which the claims to legitimately acquired property come into conflict. Decisions then will need to be made as to which claims ought to prevail, and many of these decisions will be left open by the universal principle. Different political societies, as a consequence, have room to resolve these conflicts differently; and in so doing they can establish their own tradition-dependent principles, principles that typically will be expressed in the law, for reaching determinate results. Here, we can say, tradition-dependent principles *complete* tradition-independent principles. Finally, consider a case in which two or more purportedly universal principles provide conflicting directives in a particular situation and in which neither principle takes priority over the other. One principle holds that undeserved inequalities in wealth are unjust, whereas a second holds that inequalities in wealth that contribute to significant perfectionist achievement are just. The two principles will conflict in a range of circumstances, and there may exist, in the abstract, no determinate ranking of them. If so, different societies will have leeway to adopt decisions on these matters which lead to the establishment of different tradition-dependent principles of economic justice that give greater or lesser weight to one of the two principles. Here, we can say, tradition-dependent principles *establish an ordering* of the conflicting directives expressed by tradition-independent principles.

Tradition-dependent principles, in these and other ways, supplement universal principles and thereby make political morality more determinate for political societies. Once a political tradition has been established, then those who are subject to it have reason to follow the tradition-dependent principles that inform the tradition.[3] The reason follows from the societal need for a reasonably determinate political morality. Even when people know that different patterns of behavior could have been adopted, and different principles could have played the concretizing roles—specifying, completing, and ordering tradition-independent values—that the established tradition-dependent principles play in their society, they cannot claim the established principles altogether lack authority for them. It remains the case, however, that those who are merely subject to a political tradition do not have reason to wholeheartedly accept its authority. While they may have reason to follow the tradition in the near term, they may have no reason to support its continued existence into the future. Thus to understand fully the authority of political traditions, we must take up the standpoint of those who adhere to them. We must explain how the adherents of these traditions could have reason to preserve them, even when alternatives are available (if not immediately, then in due course) and even when these alternatives could perform the functions for which the traditions are needed as well, or perhaps better, than the established ones.

This explanatory challenge will occupy us for much of the remainder of this article ....

The explanation I offer appeals to the value of self-determination. Self-determination, of course, is variously understood. To clarify what I have in mind, I proceed indirectly. In time-honored fashion, I build on an analogy between the structure of the polity and that of the soul. For there are important parallels between the self-determination of a person and that of a political society ....

Self-determination is an ideal for agents who both need to act and confront a problem. The problem is that reason, which guides them in their actions insofar as they are rational, underdetermines what they must do. If reason completely determined what each agent must do on every occasion, there would be no problem of self-determination and there would be no ideal that represents a valuable response to that problem.

People are self-determining to the extent that they fashion their character by choosing projects and assuming commitments from a range of desirable alternatives. Self-determining people become one kind of person rather than another by the decisions they make, by the facts that they acknowledge about themselves, and by the ways in which these decisions and acknowledgements constrain their future .... Holding others things constant, people who lead good lives will lead better lives if they realize this ideal than if they do not.

... on what basis are we to make self-determining choices? This question takes us to the heart of the problem of self-determination. We must find a way to reconcile the necessity of reason with the contingency of choice. That reconciliation is needed to make sense of both the self-determination of persons and—as will emerge—political societies. I now introduce two ideas that are crucial to the reconciliation we seek. These are the ideas of a *framework commitment* and a *policy of self-management*.

Framework commitments, once assumed, help to fix and make more definite what we have reason to do over significant stretches of our life. They structure future practical reasoning and, to a large extent, set the conditions for the success of the lives we lead. For many people the choice of a career is prime example of such a commitment. Other examples include decisions to get married or to have children or to take up substantial goals. Having adopted a framework commitment, a person will have reasons to do things to further it that she would not have if she had not adopted the commitment ....

Framework commitments require people in their practical reasoning to assign weight to certain considerations that when judged from an uncommitted standpoint would not have the same significance. Policies of self-management help agents to do this, and they are often part and parcel of framework commitments ....

In assuming framework commitments and adopting policies of self-management, agents fashion a character over time. Their self-fashioned character, in turn, concretizes, completes, and orders the demands of reason that apply to them. The necessity of reason is not flouted, but its demands are fixed, at least in significant part, by the contingent choices they make. Further, in selecting some framework commitments and self-management policies over others, agents are free from the demands of practical reason in the specific sense I have specified. Their choices and decisions are neither determined by reason nor groundless or arbitrary.

...

Just as individual people confront the problem of self-determination, so too do collective agents. The collective agent that concerns us presently is that of a political society extended across generations. The problem of self-determination for an agent of this kind has the same general form as that which confronts an individual agent. The agent must act, but reason underdetermines what it must do. To be self-determining, political societies need to adopt societal analogues of framework commitments and policies of self-management. The practices and patterns of thought that constitute political traditions play this role. By establishing political traditions, and pursuing their intimations in practice, a society fashions a more determinate political morality for itself, one that reveals its character and structures its collective practical reasoning over time.

...

Recall that political traditions include legal traditions. The law of a modern society is structured by a constitution. And the establishment of a constitution is a societal framework commitment, if anything is. Constitutions pervasively shape the future political decisions of a society. Moreover, and importantly, constitutions do not merely establish relations and domains of authority. They also articulate political aspirations, often expressed in abstract language. By so doing, they assign significance to some values over others. The content of these aspirations is then filled in as the society develops and its constitutional practice unfolds.

.... For example, the constitutional practice of free speech in the United States is fundamentally structured by the commitment expressed in the 1st Amendment to the US Constitution. That commitment establishes that freedom of speech is a basic liberty, but it does not specify how that liberty is to be regulated or how it is to be balanced against other concerns. Constitutional practice fills in these details ....

The commitments and policies of constitutional practice are societal analogues to the framework commitments and policies of self-management that structure personal self-determination. The same can be said of non-legal political traditions. A political society may have a history of supporting excellence in the arts. This may be a source of pride for its members, and they may view themselves as under an obligation to continue this tradition ....

Societal framework commitments, and the policies that guide their pursuit, extend across time, tying different generations of members to common projects. When the members of the society accept its traditions, they can view these commitments as ones they have assumed. For this reason, the members can say that for *us* to be self-determining we must pursue the commitments we have adopted. The fact that their society has this tradition then explains why they have a reason to preserve it. The reason is grounded in the value of the self-determination of the society to which they belong and identify with. In this way, the collective self-determination of a society can contribute to the self-determination of its members.

.... With both personal and collective self-determination, it is important that people identify with the commitments that structure their decision-making. But this does not mean that the commitments must have originated in a self-conscious choice. Indeed, the way in which a commitment is sustained over time is often more important than how it originated.

Still, self-determining people must know they could have gone down different paths, and that the traditions they adhere to were not the only possible traditions their society could have adopted. This awareness of the contingency of the commitments that structure self-determination helps to explain why the account I have presented is not excessively conservative. It is true that for some it will be unthinkable that they could reject the commitments and policies that have shaped their lives. But for others the commitments will not be viewed as necessary in this way. Those who adhere to a political tradition certainly do not need not think that they are just stuck with it ....

Notwithstanding these points, there remains a conservative dimension to self-determination as I have described it. To respond well to the problem of self-determination, one must adopt some commitments and policies. Once adopted, these commitments help to fix what one has reason to do and what one needs to do to lead a successful life. In this way, past commitments acquire a default justificatory status. One has reason to retain them, unless some compelling reason emerges that calls for their revision or abandonment. Agents, whether individual or collective, that continually move from one set of commitments and policies to another lack the stability necessary for self-determination.

.... The political traditions of a society, including its constitutional structure, consist of established practices that set the basic terms of political interaction for the society .... Normally, to participate in the politics of their society, citizens must work within the framework established by these practices. And that framework can be accepted by those who disagree, and disagree sharply, over the best understanding of the principles embodied in it.

The required consensus, then, is modest. It remains true that many members of modern societies take no interest in politics. Others participate in politics solely to advance their own interests. On my account, these members will not be participants in the self-determination of their society. And if the political life of a society becomes little more than interest group competition, then it will not have the moral dimension necessary for self-determination.

The political self-determination that adherence to tradition makes possible is, accordingly, an achievement, and a fragile one. A society that does not care about its past may still comply with traditional practices insofar as they constitute solutions to coordination problems, but it will not be seen by those who live in it as an enterprise that binds its past, present, and future members to a shared project of self-governance ....

The account of political self-determination I have been discussing may seem unrealistic .... In real world societies, much of the past is shrouded in mystery and selective remembrance. Historians speak of "imagined communities"[4] and "invented traditions."[5] Further, the myths and distortions can privilege the interests of some members over others. So political societies that are successful in establishing the conditions necessary for self-determination may do so by distorting or manufacturing the understanding of past practice in objectionable ways.

.... In addressing this concern, two related issues need to be distinguished. The first issue concerns accuracy. We can ask how accurate a society's understanding of its past must be for its self-determination to be genuine .... The second issue concerns manipulation. Traditions may be invented, or the understanding of their nature and history distorted, because doing so serves the interests of those in power, who seek to legitimate their rule.

Both issues point to the need for an authenticity condition on genuine self-determination. Formulating such a condition is a challenging task. If the only reason people identify with the political traditions of their society is that those in power have deliberately brought this about, and have done so to benefit from it, then the manufactured identification is not the kind of identification that plausibly serves self-determination. We can say, a bit more generally, although still imprecisely, that if the members of a political society could not continue to identify with their traditions in light of an awareness of how this identification had come about, then this identification will not serve their self-determination.

.... Political societies that suppress free discussion over the nature and value of their established practices cannot appeal to the value of self-determination in defense of these traditions, since they do not honor the conditions necessary for its authentic expression.[6] This suggests that the real divide may not be between genuine and "invented" traditions, but rather between traditions that persist under conditions of free inquiry and those that must be maintained by force or indoctrination.

Still, the accuracy issue remains ....

.... Some images [of society] will require too much falsification of past practice, too much forgetting about what the society has actually committed itself to, and if these images come to dominate a society's understanding of itself, then the value of its self-determination, and by extension its contribution to the self-determination of its members, will be put in doubt. Here the traditions may continue to play the role of concretizing political morality for the society in question, and the traditions and the false image of them may give the society a distinctive character, but the resulting self-determination will be fantasy.

It is important not to exaggerate this valid point, however. In both the personal and the collective case, it is a mistake to insist on fully accurate self-understandings. Indeed, some misrepresentations of the past—so long as they are not the product of self-deception and have not been produced by the manipulative interventions of others—may even augment self-determination. Stewards of a tradition who have exaggerated ideas about its past, ideas that invest the tradition with exceptional worth, may be more effective as agents in extending the tradition forward in valuable ways. Further, distortion of memory is endemic to human life, and recall of the past is always selective. A plausible ideal of self-determination will not demand a psychologically unrealistic degree of truthfulness.

...

Political traditions bind societies to their past, but the past, on any honest reading, is replete with injustice and unreasonableness. Is not a defense of the authority of political tradition, in effect, an effort to preserve injustice? The question is more complex than it first appears ... in this section I assume that unjust practices should never be preserved ....

.... For Dworkin, integrity asks citizens to conceive of their law as expressing a coherent and attractive moral vision ....

.... The proponent of a political tradition must be able to construct an account of the tradition that shows it to have intimations—to use Oakeshott's term—that can be pursued without requiring one to flout justice. Adherents to a political tradition need not agree on the account that best accomplishes this task ....

I do not wish to exaggerate the coherence required for self-determination. Self-determining people can assume commitments that reflect different concerns, and their lives can include tensions between commitments that must be worked out in practice. Likewise, to be self-determining societies need not have political traditions that express one overarching purpose. These traditions need only be sufficiently coherent to guide present and future political activity.

...

The deference to tradition I have been defending cannot be rejected on the grounds that it serves as a justification for preserving unjust arrangements. Still, justice is not the only virtue of political institutions and it would be a mistake to rule out altogether the possibility that unjust established practices have a valid claim to conservation ....

.... Value, including the value of justice, comes in degrees. A very unjust established practice may have no claim to conservation, but it does not follow that a substantially, but not perfectly, just established practice has no claim to conservation. Consider, once again, the parallel with personal self-determination. A person can adopt framework commitments that are worthwhile, but not as good as they could have been. Having adopted these commitments, the conditions of his self-determination over time are made more definite. His success in self-determination now may require him to continue with the course he has embarked upon, even if he realizes that he could have made better choices at the beginning. Of course, this is not always the case. Sometimes the right thing to do is to abandon plans and start over. But not always. Sometimes the value of self-determination will justify the decision to stay true to the framework commitments one has assumed. Valuable self-determination is a valuable achievement, and it does not lose its value simply because a more perfect achievement was possible.

Does this point carry over to the self-determination of political societies?

.... Those who identify with a valuable political tradition will want to preserve it, and they, in all likelihood, will want to preserve it, even if a more valuable political tradition could be conceived as a replacement. They must, of course, believe that the tradition is valuable and that it coheres reasonably well with tradition-independent principles, but they need not think that it is better than all alternatives.

...

Notes

1 The phrase is from John G. A. Pocock, *Political Thought and History* (Cambridge: Cambridge University Press, 2009), p. 187.
2 Two caveats: (1) members of a society can be subject to the same tradition, even as they develop competing understandings of it; and (2) members of multinational societies, with territorially distinct subunits, can be subject to some political traditions to which other members are not subject.
3 Assuming, of course, that the principles do not flout universal, tradition-independent, principles of political morality.
4 Benedict Anderson, *Imagined Communities* (New York: Verso, 1983).
5 See Eric Hobsbawm and Terence Ranger, eds, *The Invention of Tradition* (Cambridge: Cambridge University Press, 1983).
6 China comes to mind. Chinese political thought is deeply traditional, but the Chinese state has systematically suppressed free debate over its political practices. For this reason, the account of tradition's authority that I have been developing does not apply to it. For an argument that Confucian political thought is consistent with human rights, including free speech and discussion, see Joseph Chan, *Confucian Perfectionism* (Princeton, NJ: Princeton University Press, 2013).

Review and Discussion Questions

1 What are the characteristics of a political tradition, according to Wall?
2 Why are political traditions important for Wall?
3 What is self-determination? Why does Wall introduce this idea? To address what challenge?

4 In what sense is it appropriate to describe Wall as a "conservative"?
5 For Wall, what is the best way to value and assess one's political traditions?
6 How would Wall assess Sagar's discussion of reason and revelation?
7 How would you compare and contrast the grounding that Kolodny, Sagar, and Wall offer for democracy and political society?

READING: TRANSNATIONAL LEGAL SITES AND DEMOCRACY-BUILDING

SEYLA BENHABIB[*]

Seyla Benhabib believes that democratic ideals apply beyond the nation-state and not only in theory. She argues that legal processes are already connecting people and their political dialogues across national boundaries as part of creating and building global democratic institutions. Seyla Benhabib is the Eugene Meyer Professor of Political Science and Philosophy at Yale University.

The Return of Cosmopolitanism

Until recently, the term "cosmopolitanism" lay buried in the study of ideas of the eighteenth century; by the nineteenth century, historians were already struggling with the rise of nationalism. Cosmopolitanism seemed a forgotten expression from a discredited European and North American Enlightenment.

The last two decades have seen a remarkable revival of interest in cosmopolitanism across a wide variety of fields, ranging from law to cultural studies, from philosophy to international politics, and even to city planning and urban studies. Undoubtedly, the most important reason for this shift in our sensibilities and cognitions is the confluence of epoch-making transformations referred to as globalization and the end of the "West-phalian-Keynesian-Fordist" paradigm by many; as the spread of neo-liberal capitalism by some; and as the rise of multiculturalism and the rest's displacing the West by still others. Cosmopolitanism has become a place-holder for thinking beyond the confusing present towards a possible and viable future.

However, far from espousing cosmopolitanism, there are growing forces in our world who see themselves in the midst of a "global civil war" between Islam and Europe or the West more generally. Each side provokes the other into a series of intensified confrontations: after the 11 September 2001 attacks against the US, came the subway bombings in Madrid of 2004 and in London of 2007. Add to them the Danish caricature controversy over the representation of the Prophet Mohammed (2005), the murder of Theo van Gogh in the Netherlands by a Moroccan militant, and the French "scarf affair" (1989–2004), forbidding Muslim schoolgirls to attend public French schools with the *hijab*, and the list

---

[*] Excerpted from "Transnational Legal Sites and Democracy-Building: Reconfiguring Political Geographies" by Seyla Benhabib, *Philosophy and Social Criticism* 39 (2013): 471–486. Reprinted by permission of Sage Publications, Inc. Some footnotes omitted.

grows longer. The most recent and tragic iteration of these events occurred in Norway with the massacre by Anders Behring Breivik on 22 July 2011 of over 70 young people, among them many immigrants. After this event, dark clouds once more gathered over the chances of cultural coexistence and religious tolerance. Viewed against this background, cosmopolitan ideals seem like pious wishes at best and naive appeasements of dark forces of our civilization at worst. Carl Schmitt is the theorist *du jour* and the left and the right find satisfaction in the language of the eternal confrontation between "friend and foe" in politics.

Is cosmopolitanism then the naive privileged attitude of globe-trotting and world-hugging elites, removed from the concerns of ordinary citizens? I contend that "cosmopolitanism" denotes no such privileged attitude but, rather, that it suggests a field of unresolved contrasts: between particularistic attachments and universalist aspirations; between the multiplicity of human laws and the ideals of a rational order that would be common to all human cities; and between belief in the unity of humankind and the healthy agonisms and antagonisms generated by human diversity.

Cosmopolitans become naive only if they forget these tensions and contrasts and embrace instead a Pollyannaish, ceaseless affirmation of global oneness and unity. As David J. Depew wisely observes,

> Cosmopolitanism, then, *considered as a positive ideal*, whether formally or materially, generates antinomies that undermine its internal coherence .... Considered, however, *as a critical ideal*, these difficulties largely disappear. The resulting conception of cosmopolitanism [is] a negative ideal aimed at blocking false totalization.[1] (emphases added)

As a critical ideal, cosmopolitanism has a moral, a cultural and a legal dimension: morally, the cosmopolitan tradition is committed to viewing each individual as equally entitled to moral respect and concern; legally, cosmopolitanism considers each individual as a legal person entitled to the protection of her or his human rights in virtue of that person's moral personality and not on account of citizenship or other membership status. Culturally, cosmopolitanism insists on the hybridity of cultures and their continuous interaction with and learning from one another.

In this article, I wish to focus on one aspect of cosmopolitanism, namely its legal dimension. I wish to highlight the radical transformations that have occurred in the world society of states and in the conceptualization of cosmopolitan human rights in international law after 1948. I will contend that many of these legal developments are leading us to the emergence of transnational legal and political sites of struggle. Furthermore, these new sites have created new "political geographies" which, in turn, have important effects on democracy-building measures within states.

Legal Cosmopolitanism

It is now widely accepted that since the Universal Declaration of Human Rights in 1948, we have entered a phase in the evolution of global civil society which is characterized by a transition from *international* to *cosmopolitan* norms of justice. While norms of international law emerge either through what is recognized as customary international law or through treaty obligations to which states and their representatives are signatories, cosmopolitan norms accrue to individuals considered as moral and legal persons in a world-wide civil society ... their peculiarity is that these covenants bind signatory states and their representatives to treat their citizens and residents in accordance with certain norms, even when states later wish, as is often the case, to engage in actions that contradict these terms and violate the obligations generated by these treaties themselves ....

The best-known of the human rights agreements which have been signed by a majority of the world's states since the 1948 Universal Declaration on Human Rights (UDHR) are as follows: the United Nations Convention on the Prevention and Punishment of the Crime of Genocide, adopted by Resolution 260 (III) A of the UN General Assembly on 9 December 1948 (ch. II); the 1951 Convention on Refugees (which entered into force in 1954); the International Covenant on Civil and Political Rights (ICCPR; signed in 1966 and entered into force in 1976, with 167 countries out of 195 being party to it as of 2012); the International Covenant on Economic, Social and Cultural Rights (ICESCR; entered into force the same year and with 160 member parties as of 2012); the Convention on the Elimination of All Forms of Discrimination Against Women (CEDAW; signed in 1979 and entered into force in 1981, with 99 signatories and 187 state parties as of 2012); the International Convention on the Elimination of All Forms of Racial Discrimination (entered into force on 12 March 1969, with 86 signatories and 175 parties as of 2012); the Convention Against Torture and Other Cruel, Inhuman or Degrading Treatment or Punishment (entered into force 26 June 1987, with 78 signatories and 150 parties as of 2012). These are some of the best-known among many other treaties and conventions.

The skeptic will ask: But what does all this really mean? What possible significance can these multilateral human rights covenants have, if states continuously and brazenly violate them, manipulate them to serve their own ends and the like? Are they not mere words at worst or aspirational ideals at best that have little traction in influencing and limiting state conduct? Do these developments add to a novel, enforceable and justiciable legal world order? Doesn't the process of formulating *RUDs*—reservations, understandings and declarations to which states are entitled—take the bite out of the human rights treaties in particular and make them merely convenient smoke-screens for states to hide behind?

While skeptical doubts about state behavior and an international state-system that remains beset by violence, civil wars and proxy wars cannot be set aside, I remain convinced that something has changed profoundly in the grammar and syntax of the language of international law, sovereignty and human rights. Just as repeated use may imperceptibly change grammar and syntax in a language—consider, for example, the frequent use of contractions such as "he's" for "he is" in English— legal practice, institutionalization and adjudication by courts may change legal doctrine. In an earlier work, I described such processes of transformation in the international domain through the use of another metaphor: we are like travelers navigating a new terrain with the help of old maps; while the terrain has radically changed, our maps have not. Thus, we stumble upon streams we did not know existed, and we have to climb hills we had never dreamt of.[2]

... I have the impression that law and legal scholarship today ... are anticipating a world that is yet to be born, *"une vérité à faire"*. Legal scholarship has become

a constitutive element in a new world that is yet to come, but which we, as contemporaries, can only grasp with the help of various metaphors.
...

Human Rights, Constitutional Rights and Democratic Iterations: The Leyla Sahin Case

What I wish to do in the following is to analyze the well-known case of "*Leyla Sahin*" in front of the European Court of Human Rights ....

Leyla Sahin and her attorneys lodged a case with the European Commission of Human Rights against the Republic of Turkey for preventing her from pursuing her university studies because she wore the *hijab*. They claimed that Turkey had thereby violated her rights and freedoms under articles 8, 9, 10 and 14, and under article 12, protocol 1. On 29 June 2004 the chamber ruled that there had been no violation ....

Upon appeal by the applicant on 27 September 2004 the case was then referred to the Grand Chamber of the ECtHR and was accepted. The facts of the case are as follows: Leyla Sahin was born in 1973 and had lived in Vienna since 1999, because she had decided to pursue her medical studies in Vienna University instead of in Turkey. In 1997, as a fifth-year student at the Faculty of Medicine at Bursa University, she had then enrolled at the Cerrahpasa Faculty of Medicine in Istanbul. In the spring of 1998, in accordance with a circular of the vice-chancellor of Istanbul University which forbade the wearing of the *hijab* on the part of women and of having beards on the part of male students, she was denied access to an examination on oncology, to attend lectures in neurology and other exams and classes. When she requested the Istanbul Administrative Court that this circular be set aside because it violated her rights under the Turkish Constitution, the court affirmed the prerogative of the vice-chancellor to pass such a regulation in order to maintain "public order" and denied her appeal.

The Grand Chamber found that while Istanbul University regulations restricting the wearing of the Islamic headscarf and measures taken thereupon had interfered with the applicant's right to manifest her religion, it also held that such interference was prescribed by law and pursued one of the aims set out in paragraph 2 of article 9 of the convention. This crucial paragraph reads:

> Freedom to manifest one's religion or beliefs shall be subject only to such limitations as are prescribed by law and are necessary in a democratic society in the interests of public safety, for the protection of public order, health or morals, or for the protection of the rights and freedoms of others.[3]

The ECtHR Grand Chamber considered the actions of the Turkish university authorities to be "justified in principle and proportionate to the aims pursued," and as "being necessary in a democratic society". The Court held *16 to 1* that there had been no violation of article 9 of the Convention; and ruled likewise concerning article 2, protocol 1, in a 9 to 1 vote. It also held unanimously that there had been no violations of articles 8, 10 and 14.

This decision contains a survey of most laws and regulations concerning the wearing of the *hijab* in the 47 member countries of the Council of Europe, and comes to the conclusion that there is no established standard across countries in this regard. In evaluating the actions of the Republic of Turkey, the court invokes the now-famous criterion of "margin of appreciation" which takes into consideration the member countries' arguments about what they consider to be necessary for maintaining "public safety, for the protection of public order, health or morals, or for the protection of the rights and freedoms of others" in a democratic society. Siding with states' rights to "place restrictions on freedom to manifest one's religion or belief", in order to reconcile the interests of various groups, the court goes on to assert that "Pluralism, tolerance and broadmindedness are hallmarks of a 'democratic society'", but fails to clarify how or why exactly these values would have been endangered by women wearing the Muslim *hijab* in institutions of higher learning. It is stated that wearing the *hijab* would negatively affect the rights of Turkey's non-practicing Muslims as well as other minorities but very little is said about who these minorities are and their rights. Furthermore, the court asserts that this religious symbol was hard to reconcile with "gender equality" and that "the wearing of the Islamic headscarf could not easily be reconciled with the message of tolerance, respect for others and, above all, equality and non-discrimination that all teachers in a democratic society should convey to their pupils" (para. 111).

While it would be foolish to deny concerns about the place of toleration for non-Muslims within the context of traditional Islamic thought as well as of Islamist ideology, what is remarkable about these assertions is their paternalism, their unclarified political assumptions, and their views about Islam and gender equality in general. And these are exactly the issues that led Judge Tulkens to her dissent. She writes:

> The first concerns the argument the majority uses to justify the width of the margin, namely the diversity of practice between States on the issue of regulating the wearing of religious symbols in educational institutions, thus, the lack of a European consensus in this sphere. The comparative law materials [she continues] "do not allow this conclusion as in none of the member States *has the ban on the wearing of religious symbols extended to university education, which is intended for young adults, who are less amenable to pressure.*"[4]

...

Judge Tulkens then takes aim at the political assumptions guiding the ECtHR's decision: "While everyone agrees on the need to prevent radical Islamism, a serious objection may nevertheless be made to such reasoning. Merely wearing the headscarf cannot be associated with fundamentalism .... Not all women who wear the headscarf are fundamentalists." Finally, with respect to *equality*, she asks: "However, what, in fact, is the connection between the ban and sexual equality? The judgment does not say." Citing a decision of the German Constitutional Court, she maintains that wearing the headscarf has no single meaning, and crucially: "What is lacking in this debate is the opinion of women, both those who wear the headscarf and those who choose not to" (para. 11).

The European Court of Human Rights did not resolve the Leyla Sahin case in a manner that many, including myself, who see the wearing of the *hijab* as a fundamental human right, would have wished. The cosmopolitan interpretation of article 9 of the ICCPR would have implied a different outcome than the subordination of women's political agency and their freedom to manifest their religion to the guarantees of an unquestioned norm of public safety. Nevertheless, Judge Tulken's dissent and the arguments she brought to light concerning the court's hidden assumptions created a space for "democratic iterations".

Transnational Legal Spheres and Democratic Iterations

.... As I considered in an earlier article,[5] the debate about the *hijab* of Muslim girls is a transnational phenomenon, engaging both European countries, such as France, Germany and Turkey, and also others in a judicial dialogue across borders.

Just as the judges of the Turkish Constitutional Court consider it necessary to uphold the ban on the wearing of the headscarves in universities for the sake of maintaining secularism and public order, judges on the German Constitutional Court, members of the French Stasi Commission and judges of the ECtHR concur with them. But in Turkey, France, or Germany, as well as on the bench of the ECtHR, there are also those who see such a high-handed defense of secularism as violating human rights to freedom of religious expression, the principles of pluralism and tolerance for the rights of others in a democratic society. There are no clear demarcations of the "inside" from the "outside" here. The conversation is a transnational as well as a translegal one ....

More importantly, through the confrontations and negotiations between state power, legislative and administrative instances and the girls and women wearing the headscarves and their supporters, the meaning of the symbol itself is undergoing changes: for the girls and women involved, the headscarf and the turban are no longer simply expressions of Muslim humility but symbols of an embattled identity and signs of public defiance. The wearing of the headscarf itself politicizes them and transforms some of them from being "docile objects" into increasingly confrontational citizens.

...

.... Since the contextualization of human rights norms entails processes of public practical reason, and since states cannot simply hide behind the shield of sovereignty, what we are looking at is a *transnational conversation of practical reason*s that move back and forth between the moral and the legal concept of human rights and their supporting arguments.

Returning to the Leyla Sahin case discussed above, if we consider Judge Tulken's dissenting challenge, we can see that she uncovers several assumptions concerning gender equality and the headscarf, the autonomy of university students, and the meanings of secularism in liberal democracies that the other judges of the ECtHR either take for granted or simply leave unexplained. The "authority of good reasons", exercised by the ECtHR, is here upended by the "power of better reasons" voiced by the dissent. And neither are Judge Tulken's arguments confined to the ECtHR case alone: they can be extended and are extended by democratic citizens and stakeholders, whether or not they are familiar with her specific formulations, to the public arena of debate in their own societies ....

Notes

1 David. J. Depew, 'Narrativism, Cosmopolitanism, and Historical Epistemology,' *CLIO* 14 (4) (1985): 357–78 (375).
2 Seyla Benhabib, *The Rights of Others: Aliens, Residents and Citizens, the John Seeley Lectures* (Cambridge: Cambridge University Press, 2004), p. 6.
3 http://con-ventions.coe.int/Treaty/EN/Treaties/Html/005.htm
4 Para. 3, Dissent; emphases added.
5 Seyla Benhabib, 'The Return of Political Theology: The Scarf Affair in Comparative Constitutional Perspective in France, Germany and Turkey,' in *Benhabib, Dignity in Adversity*, pp. 166–84; originally published in *Philosophy & Social Criticism* 36(3–4) (2010): 451–471.

Review and Discussion Questions

1 What are the three dimensions of cosmopolitanism, according to Benhabib?
2 Describe the case of Leyla Sahin.
3 What about this case illustrates a process of global democracy-building that Benhabib describes as a "new world yet to come"?
4 What is the relationship between transnational legal conversation and the creation of global democracy, if any?
5 Does Benhabib's analysis suggest the creation of a global political tradition in Wall's sense?
6 How does the development of transnational legal systems relate to Kolodny's justification of democracy?

READING: SOCIAL MOVEMENTS

AVERY KOLERS[*]

Avery Kolers analyzes the nature of social movements. His essay focuses on basic questions about what constitutes a social movement and ethical challenges that arise when participating in social movements. Avery Kolers is Professor of Philosophy and Director of the Social Change Program at the University of Louisville.

Lysistrata forces warring armies to make peace by organizing the women of Greece to deny sex to their husbands and seize the Acropolis. The women's action constitutes a "rational attempt by excluded groups to mobilize sufficient political leverage to advance collective interests through noninstitutionalized means" (McAdam, 1999: 36–7). By participating, they discover a power and discipline they did not know they were capable of, earning newfound respect and self-respect as political agents rather than a "herd of weaklings" (Aristophanes, 1981: 335).

Under what conditions would we say that the Greek women's protest had become a social movement—what proportion of the group would have to maintain solidarity, over how many struggles, with what general focus? How do the actions of individual participants and groups sit with philosophical theories of action, of moral justification, and of democracy?

---

[*] Adapted from "Social Movements" by Avery Kolers, *Philosophy Compass* 10(11) (2016): 580–590. Reprinted by permission of Wiley-Blackwell. Notes omitted.

...

This overview first engages the ontological issues around the concept and nature of social movements and social action, both individual and collective. It then moves to the problems of ethics and political philosophy raised by the existence and behavior of social movements. Finally, it turns to metaphilosophical questions, such as how much revision of basic philosophical commitments is required by the reality of social movements.

...

What Is a Social Movement?

The sociological definition cited above—"rational attempts by excluded groups to mobilize sufficient political leverage to advance collective interests through noninstitutionalized means"—is grounded in the "political process" model of social movements (McAdam, 1999: 36). Charles Tilly and Sidney Tarrow develop a related "contentious politics" model, defining a social movement as a "sustained campaign of claim making, using repeated performances that advertise the claim, based on organizations, networks, traditions, and solidarities that sustain these activities," and specifying that in social movements the government is involved as either a maker or target of claims (Tilly & Tarrow, 2015: 11). Yet this approach has been challenged from other perspectives, on grounds of whether all the criteria are necessary conditions. For instance, some social movements seem not to engage governments, but target social norms and cultural values rather than, or prior to, policy (Staggenborg, 2008: 100). Moreover, many sociologists argue that power is not located solely in the government, but is distributed among multiple centers, any of which might be the site of social movements; nor need movements be composed of members of "excluded" groups. These considerations ground an alternative "multi-institutional politics" approach (Armstrong & Bernstein, 2008).

For philosophers, these sociological disputes raise ontological questions. First are questions of group constitution, persistence, and agency. Movements are composed of individuals yet differ somehow from "groups," "organizations," and "networks"—which are puzzling in their own right. When do a number of persons, for instance, constitute a network, or networks a movement? Further, "traditions" and "solidarities" seem to add layers of subjectivity and valuation. Individuals participate in social movements by formally or informally joining organizations or networks that are constituent parts of a movement. Yet neither individuals nor sub-groups nor networks become groups or movements all at once, or all to the same degree. Being "sustained" over time adds further complexity; a pair of events might be separated by decades, feature different individuals and distinct demands, and target different power centers. What then unifies them into a single "campaign"? A deeper puzzle is that social movements seem to come in waves or cycles—e.g., "the Sixties"—that obey macro-level regularities but are unpredictable and whimsical at micro and meso levels (Staggenborg, 2008).

...

A further challenge for action theory is that at least some social movements arguably cannot be specified without reference to the social identity of their members. The US civil rights movement, for instance, is essentially an *African-American-led* movement. The feminist movement, the labor movement, and others similarly seem mischaracterized unless the role of persons with particular identities or structural locations is made explicit. If we want to understand the movement, it seems we need a way to characterize movements by connecting triads of *identities, interests*, and *aims*: for example, African Americans, civil rights, and equal treatment in public institutions; women, feminism, and reproductive freedom; workers, the labor movement, and economic security. Shared social identities, however, are hard enough to characterize in the first place, and such triads generate a dilemma of *essentialism* and *authenticity* (Young, 1997; Shelby, 2005). Essentialism is the error of supposing that all members of a social group are unified by a particular shared identity or set of experiences or interests—for example, the assumption that feminism is built on a foundation of "sisterhood" or a shared "women's experience." ... Moreover, accounts of social identities typically abjure any supposedly shared interests. On the contrary: groups share identities despite a radical diversity of interests. And if it is impossible to characterize identity groups in a way that fixes their interests or still less their aims, then any movement's claim to be pressing political claims *for* or *on behalf* of a social group faces the challenge of showing that it is articulating the group's "authentic" interests. If the group is characterized independently of the interests, there will be no unanimity; but if the interests are given priority, then the social group dissolves and we are back to characterizing movements merely in terms of goals.

...

Social movements change public attitudes not primarily by making factual assertions, but by manipulating the salience and presentation of information. Movements create spectacular events to move public opinion on their focal issues. Persuasion by spectacle may be effective, but is obviously epistemically suspect, as are manifestos accompanying such spectacles. To be sure, both the requirement of justifying one's spectacle, and the existence of counter-movements, media, or official responses, can serve as "checks" on the veracity of claims made in these ways. But—as is evident in the climate change and gun-rights "debates" in the contemporary US (Brulle 2014)—clashes of movements do not reliably yield true information, nor should we expect that the truth "lies somewhere in between." The "market of ideas" is hardly *free*, as credibility and even the ability to be heard depend on control of social resources rather than the quality of the reasons one gives (Fricker, 2009). Social movements thus cannot be guaranteed to enhance the epistemic situation of the populace in general. Nor does debate *within* social movements necessarily work through reasoned deliberation. Charisma, rhetoric, and unnoticed cues are at least as important as truth or justification (Blee, 2013), and demographic features of groups can drive polarization or moderation irrespective of where the truth may lie (Sunstein, 2002). Ascribing beliefs to "the movement" brings back the dilemma of essentialism and authenticity. And all of these epistemologically suspect features of social movements are amplified by the internet and social media (Gainous & Wagner, 2011).

.... Even when they misdiagnose their problems, social movements often have genuine grievances, and their inaccurate attempts to articulate these grievances might be an essential part of understanding reality. For instance, downwardly mobile white supremacists have evidently misunderstood the *causes* of their plight, but their frustration might nonetheless have a real material basis that would otherwise be ignored or misunderstood by mainstream and credentialed observers

(Faludi; Kimmel). Social movements thus do essential work in not just revealing attitudes but in alerting others to genuine social problems and spurring creativity both in understanding those problems and in devising win-win solutions. Creativity and problem-solving are epistemic virtues. Hence false assertions can be epistemically productive.

Furthermore, although some movement groups internally reproduce the epistemic injustice of the broader society, social movements can embody distributed knowing and collective reasoning, using decentralized epistemic practices to generate a more accurate picture of reality than is available to any one member or brain trust, let alone to outsiders in more privileged social locations (Ganz, 2000). Hence in the context of social movements, the individualistic focus of reliabilism, foundationalism, and coherentism might be less helpful than feminist epistemologies and attempts to dissolve epistemic injustice by taking activists' testimony seriously.

The Ethics and Politics of Social Movements

It is easy to cheer on Lysistrata and her comrades as they compel their husbands to end the interminable war. But in reality, social movements often challenge widespread social norms and moral convictions. Even when movements are right to challenge these conventions, their choice of tactics and rhetoric may be wrong; and anyway, their rightness will not be evident to all. They might violate the law or alienate the broader populace. What role, then, do social movements have in democracy? Are movements compatible with public deliberation? And supposing they are, how should individuals be involved? Are we required to join the struggle, or may we stand back for reasons of caution or competing priorities?

Democracy and Social Movement

There has perhaps never been a social movement that could count among its galvanized members anything close to a majority of the population. When movements succeed, then, we might ascribe that to volume or coercion rather than numbers or arguments. Social movements might even cause elected officials to misread what matters to most people, or what the median voter wants, and hence movements risk engendering minority rule. Do social movements, then, have a legitimate role in democracy?

The answer to that question depends on what democracy is, and what justifies it. One plausible approach is structural and partly consequentialist: democratic governance—featuring popular sovereignty, responsible government, an independent judiciary, and a list of protected freedoms—characterizes the just society (Rawls, 1999). On this approach, social movements might constitute "democratic feedback" through which institutions self-correct (Gilbert, 1999). That movements are not majoritarian is, then, no mark against them, since, like the independent judiciary, social movements might serve as a countermajoritarian check on tyrannical majorities. A similar case could be made for movements as counterweights when any one tendency of a democratic society, no matter how healthy or essential in its own right, crowds out other values. Conflict might be essential to a longer-term equilibrium (Hampshire, 2000; Levy, 2014; Mouffe, 2013).

Deliberative democrats, on the other hand, treat deliberation, rather than social structures, as essential to democracy. The giving of reasons is the essence of political speech, and for one reason or another—be it equality, freedom, or political quality—properly structured deliberation justifies democracy (Christiano, 2008; Cohen, 2009; Estlund, 2008). Social movements, however, violate basic deliberative norms, and thus seem to be democratically suspect. Yet as Iris Marion Young shows, deliberative democrats risk begging crucial questions by imagining that all stakeholders are included as equal citizens and are equally able to articulate their interests in shared public forums. This universal inclusion is grossly absent from real democracies, and has been advanced, insofar as it has, only thanks to oppositional movements that violated deliberative norms (Young, 2001).

Most theorists of deliberative democracy do embrace a role for "contestation," at least as an aspect of nonideal theory. The question then becomes whether we envision a more just future when contestation is no longer required. If so, then, as is sometimes said of affirmative-action policies, the goal of social movements should be their own obsolescence. Most democratic theorists do not, however, envision the obsolescence of social movements but their incorporation within a democratic culture, often through civil society organizations (Cohen, 2009: 62; Dryzek, 2000).

Social movements thus pose a dilemma to both our conception and justification of democracy. The more open deliberation is to contentious politics, the less plausible deliberation is as a justificatory ideal; but the more ideally we conceive of democratic deliberation, the less space it has for the social movements that have brought us nearly every expansion of democratic rights, including democracy itself.

Let us assume, however, that social movements as such are compatible with democracy. The next question is how individuals should respond to social movement organizations' calls to action. Is there any affirmative moral reason to join or avoid social movements?

There are two general answers to this question. The first regards participation as an *option*: a lifestyle choice, at most supererogatory. The second treats activism as sometimes an *obligation*, and hence participation as at least sometimes morally required.

The option model maps onto the behavior and attitudes of most people in contemporary liberal states. Liberals argue that political participation is only one permissible project, and has no pride of place (Kymlicka, 1989). Some people like politics, others like sports, and everyone may do their own thing. Indeed, those who are uninformed or misinformed might even be required *not* to participate (Brennan). Yet the lifestyle model faces the immediate objection that if someone is treated unjustly, then inaction partly constitutes the injustice. Hence King (1986: 295), attacks the "white moderate" as a greater obstacle to justice than "the Ku Klux Klanner." If King is right, then activism is at least sometimes required by justice ....

...

Finally, beyond all these questions about the morality of *becoming involved*, there remain questions of responsibility for actions carried out by movements and by individuals acting—or so they think—*for* movements. When, for instance, is a strike appropriate? A hunger strike? Is violence ever permissible? When may individual activists act entrepreneurially, and when should they await and comply with the dictates of an organization's formalized decision procedure? When are movements accountable for individual actions, and vice versa? These questions take the applied ethics of social movements rather far afield, and moral philosophers have only recently begun to engage these questions in depth.

Social *justice* movements make genuine demands upon each of us, especially but not exclusively those who are complicit in structural injustices. How we ought to respond to these demands is one of the most urgent moral questions that we face.

Deep philosophical questions remain: questions regarding the ontology of social movements and protest cycles; the justification of the beliefs we gain from social movements; their role or even admissibility in deliberative democracy; and the morality of individual participation ….

A case could be made for … embracing eliminativism about social movements. Perhaps they are mere narrative constructs that help people think of themselves as playing a role in historical change. To wit, sociologists have been unable to develop a *predictive* theory of social movements—either of their rise and fall, or of their breakthroughs and failures. Perhaps, then, the wrong question is being asked.

Yet to deny that social movements are real would be to leave a massive explanatory gap in our understanding of ourselves and our social world. If nothing is yet available to fill this gap, we might instead revisit the philosophical commitments that seem to create it—commitments on the nature of collective action, the justification of belief, the elements of justice, democratic deliberation, and the ethical life. There may be more things on the streets than are dreamt of in our philosophy.

Works Cited

Alcoff, L. M. and E. Potter, Eds. *Feminist Epistemologies*. New York: Routledge, 1992.
Appiah, K. A. 'Race, Culture, Identity: Misunderstood Connections.' *Color Conscious: The Political Morality of Race*. Eds. K. A. Appiah and A. Gutmann. Princeton, NJ: Princeton University Press, 1998.
Aristophanes. *The Complete Plays*. Ed. M. Hadas. New York: Bantam, 1981.
Armstrong, E. A. and M. Bernstein. 'Culture, Power, and Institutions: A Multi-Institutional Politics Approach to Social Movements.' *Sociological Theory* 26 (2008): 75–99.
Baron, M. 'Kantian Ethics.' *Three Methods of Ethics*. Eds. M. Baron, P. Pettit, and M. Slote. Malden, MA: Blackwell Publishing, 1997, 3–91.
Barry, C. and K. MacDonald. 'How Should We Think about Individual Consumer Responsibility to Address Labour Injustices?' *Global Justice and International Labour Rights*. Eds. Y. Dahan, H. Lerner, and F. Milman-Sivan. New York: Cambridge University Press, 2016.
Blee, K. 'How Options Disappear: Causality and Emergence in Grassroots Activist Groups.' *American Journal of Sociology* 119.3 (2013): 655–681.
Blum, L. A. *Moral Perception and Particularity*. New York: Cambridge University Press, 1994.
Bratman, M. *Shared Agency*. New York: Oxford University Press, 2014.
Brulle, R. J. 'Institutionalizing Delay: Foundation Funding and the Creation of U.S. Climate Change Counter-Movement Organizations.' *Climatic Change* 122.4 (2014): 681–694.
Carastathis, A. 'The Concept of Intersectionality in Feminist Theory.' *Philosophy Compass* 9.5 (2014): 304–314.
Christiano, T. *The Constitution of Equality*. New York: Oxford University Press, 2008.
Cohen, J. *Philosophy, Politics, Democracy*. Cambridge, MA: Harvard University Press, 2009.
Crenshaw, K. 'Demarginalizing the Intersection of Race and Sex: A Black Feminist Critique of Antidiscrimination Doctrine, Feminist Theory and Antiracist Politics.' *University of Chicago Legal Forum* 139 (1989): 139–167.
Dryzek, J. *Deliberative Democracy and Beyond*. New York: Oxford University Press, 2000.
Estlund, D. *Democratic Authority*. Princeton, NJ: Princeton University Press, 2008.

Fricker, M. *Epistemic Injustice*. New York: Oxford University Press, 2009.
Gainous, J. and K. M. Wagner. *Rebooting American Politics: The Internet Revolution*. Lanham, MD: Rowman & Littlefield, 2011.
Ganz, M. 'Resources and Resourcefulness: Strategic Capacity in the Unionization of California Agriculture, 1959–1966.' *American Journal of Sociology* 105.4 (2000): 1003–1062.
Gilbert, A. *Must Global Politics Constrain Democracy?* Princeton, NJ: Princeton University Press, 1999.
Gilbert, M. *A Theory of Political Obligation*. New York: Oxford University Press, 2008.
Glasgow, J. and J. M. Woodward. 'Basic Racial Realism.' *Journal of the American Philosophical Association* 1 (2015): 449–466.
Goldman, A. I. *Knowledge in a Social World*. New York: Oxford University Press, 1999.
Hampshire, S. *Justice Is Conflict*. Princeton, NJ: Princeton University Press, 2000.
Haslanger, S. *Resisting Reality: Social Construction and Social Critique*. New York: Oxford University Press, 2012.
Jamieson, D. 'When Utilitarians Should Be Virtue Theorists.' *Utilitas* 19.2 (2007): 160–183.
Kant, I. *Groundwork for the Metaphysics of Morals*. Ed. L. Denis. Peterborough, Ontario: Broadview Press, 2005.
King, M. L. Jr. 'Letter from Birmingham City Jail.' *A Testament of Hope: The Essential Writings and Speeches of Martin Luther King, Jr.* Ed. J. M. Washington. San Francisco, CA: HarperSanFrancisco, 1986. 289–302.
Kolers, A. *A Moral Theory of Solidarity*. New York: Oxford University Press, 2016.
Kutz, C. *Complicity*. New York: Cambridge University Press, 2000.
Kymlicka, W. 'Liberal Individualism and Liberal Neutrality.' *Ethics* 99.4 (1989): 883–905.
Levy, J. *Rationalism, Pluralism, and Freedom*. New York: Oxford University Press, 2014.
Lugones, M. *Pilgrimages/Peregrinajes: Theorizing Coalition against Multiple Oppressions*. Lanham, MD: Rowman & Littlefield, 2003.
Lukes, S. 'Methodological Individualism Reconsidered.' *British Journal of Sociology* 19.2 (1968): 119–129.
McAdam, D. *Political Process and the Development of Black Insurgency, 1930–1970*, 2nd ed. Chicago, IL: University of Chicago Press, 1999.
Medina, J. *The Epistemology of Resistance*. New York: Oxford University Press, 2012.
Mills, C. 'But What Are You Really?' *Mills, Blackness Visible*. Ithaca, NY: Cornell University Press, 1998.
Mohanty, C. T. *Feminism without Borders: Decolonizing Theory, Practicing Solidarity*. Durham, NC: Duke University Press, 2003.
Mouffe, C. *Agonistics*. New York: Verso Press, 2013.
Oberschall, A. *Social Conflict and Social Movements*. Englewood Cliffs, NJ: Prentice-Hall, 1973.
Owen, D. 'Reasons and Practices of Reasoning: On the Analytic/Continental Distinction in Political Philosophy.' *European Journal of Political Theory* 15 (2016): 172–188.
Pettit, P. 'The Consequentialist Perspective.' *Three Methods of Ethics*. Eds. M. Baron, P. Pettit, and M. Slote. Malden, MA: Blackwell Publishing, 1997. 92–174.
Rawls, J. *A Theory of Justice*, revised ed. Cambridge, MA: Belknap/Harvard University Press, 1999.
Schlosberg, D. *Defining Environmental Justice*. New York: Oxford University Press, 2007.
Schmitt, F., ed. *Socializing Epistemology*. Lanham, MD: Rowman & Littlefield, 1994.
Shapiro, S. 'Massively Shared Agency.' *Rational and Social Agency: The Philosophy of Michael Bratman*. Eds. M. Vargas and G. Yaffe. New York: Oxford University Press, 2014. 257–293.
Shelby, T. *We Who Are Dark: Philosophical Foundations of Black Solidarity*. Cambridge, MA: Harvard University Press, 2005.
Shrader-Frechette, K. 'Human Rights and Duties to Alleviate Environmental Justice: The Domestic Case.' *Journal of Human Rights* 6 (2007): 107–130.
Singer, P. 'Famine, Affluence, and Morality.' *Philosophy & Public Affairs* 1 (1972): 229–243.
Staggenborg, S. *Social Movements*. New York: Oxford University Press, 2008.
Sunstein, C. 'The Law of Group Polarization.' *Journal of Political Philosophy* 10 (2002): 175–195.

Tilly, C. and S. Tarrow. *Contentious Politics*, 2nd ed. New York: Oxford University Press, 2015.
Weir, A. *Identities and Freedom*. New York: Oxford University Press, 2011.
Young, I. M. *Justice and the Politics of Difference*. Princeton, NJ: Princeton University Press, 1991.
Young, I. M. 'Gender as Seriality.' *Intersecting Voices: Dilemmas of Gender, Political Philosophy, and Policy*. Princeton, NJ: Princeton University Press, 1997. 12–37.
Young, I. M. 'Activist Challenges to Deliberative Democracy.' *Political Theory* 29 (2001): 670–690.
Young, I. M. *Responsibility for Justice*. New York: Oxford University Press, 2011.

Review and Discussion Questions

1 What is a social movement?
2 Are social movements important for democracy? Why? What is the relationship between the two ideas?
3 Select a social movement that matters to you. Characterize what makes it a social movement. Assess the accuracy of its claims and who is making those claims. What, if anything, was accomplished by this movement? How were its activities related to, or an expression of, democracy?
4 If you were part of a social movement that included activities that you disagreed with, at what point do you become complicit in those activities?

Essay and Paper Topics for Chapter 15

1 Compare and contrast Lincoln's and Kolodny's understanding of the foundations of democracy.
2 Under what conditions, if any, might the value of tradition legitimately override the value of promoting democracy?
3 Must social movements that promote democratic institutions be internally organized on democratic principles? Explain.
4 Is advocating global democracy an inevitable conclusion given a commitment to the value of democracy at the level of the nation-state?
5 Are there morally viable forms of government other than democracy? Explain.

Chapter 16

Liberty
Free Speech and Drug Use

When, and why, can government restrict people's liberty? The readings to follow examine this question in relation to debates about free speech and drug use. What is the value of free speech? Should the government be able to restrict hateful and offensive speech? Are there good reasons to protect the speech rights of corporations distinct from the speech rights of people? Regarding drug use, are legal restrictions legitimate or should drug use be decriminalized? The readings that follow address these questions and more, including the purposes of freedom of speech, notable Supreme Court cases bearing on free speech protections, the nature of harm, and debates about drug use and addiction.

> ### READING: OF THE LIBERTY OF THOUGHT AND DISCUSSION
>
> JOHN STUART MILL
>
> In the following selection, taken from his classic work *On Liberty*, John Stuart Mill provides what may be the best-known and most widely quoted defense of freedom of conscience and speech ever written. Arguing that along with other liberties, protecting freedom of conscience and speech is of vital social importance, Mill vigorously upholds freedom of opinion, regardless of whether the belief is true or false. Indeed, he argues, it is especially important that false and evil opinions be freely expressed. For a brief description of John Stuart Mill's life, see the introduction to *Utilitarianism* (Chapter 3). Other selections from *On Liberty* are reprinted in Chapter 13.
>
> The time, it is to be hoped, is gone by, when any defense would be necessary of the "liberty of the press" as one of the securities against corrupt or tyrannical government. No argument, we may suppose, can now be needed against permitting a legislature or an executive, not identified in interest with the people, to prescribe opinions to them, and determine what doctrines or what arguments they shall be allowed to hear …. Let us suppose … that government is entirely at one with the people, and never thinks of exerting any power of coercion unless in agreement with what it conceives to be their voice. But I deny the right of the people to exercise such coercion, either by themselves or by their government. The power itself is illegitimate. The best government has no more title to it than the worst. It is as noxious, or more noxious, when

exerted in accordance with public opinion than when in opposition to it. If all mankind minus one were of one opinion, mankind would be no more justified in silencing that one person than he, if he had the power, would be justified in silencing mankind. Were an opinion a personal possession of no value except to the owner, if to be obstructed in the enjoyment of it were simply a private injury, it would make some difference whether the injury was inflicted only on a few persons or on many. But the peculiar evil of silencing the expression of an opinion is that it is robbing the human race, posterity as well as the existing generation—those who dissent from the opinion, still more than those who hold it. If the opinion is right, they are deprived of the opportunity of exchanging error for truth; if wrong, they lose, what is almost as great a benefit, the clearer perception and livelier impression of truth produced by its collision with error.

It is necessary to consider separately these two hypotheses, each of which has a distinct branch of the argument corresponding to it. We can never be sure that the opinion we are endeavoring to stifle is a false opinion; and if we were sure, stifling it would be an evil still.

First, the opinion which it is attempted to suppress by authority may possibly be true. Those who desire to suppress it, of course, deny its truth; but they are not infallible. They have no authority to decide the question for all mankind and exclude every other person from the means of judging. To refuse a hearing to an opinion because they are sure that it is false is to assume that *their* certainty is the same thing as *absolute* certainty. All silencing of discussion is an assumption of infallibility. Its condemnation may be allowed to rest on this common argument, not the worse for being common.

Unfortunately for the good sense of mankind, the fact of their fallibility is far from carrying the weight in their practical judgment which is always allowed to it in theory; for while everyone well knows himself to be fallible, few think it necessary to take any precautions against their own fallibility, or admit the supposition that any opinion of which they feel very certain may be one of the examples of the error to which they acknowledge themselves to be liable ....

The objection likely to be made to this argument would probably take some such form as the following. There is no greater assumption of infallibility in forbidding the propagation of error than in any other thing which is done by public authority on its own judgment and responsibility. ...

There is no such thing as absolute certainty, but there is assurance sufficient for the purposes of human life. We may, and must, assume our opinion to be true for the guidance of our own conduct; and it is assuming no more when we forbid bad men to pervert society by the propagation of opinions which we regard as false and pernicious.

I answer, that it is assuming very much more. There is the greatest difference between presuming an opinion to be true because, with every opportunity for contesting it, it has not been refuted, and assuming its truth for the purpose of not permitting its refutation. Complete liberty of contradicting and disproving our opinion is the very condition which justifies us in assuming its truth for purposes of action; and on no other terms can a being with human faculties have any rational assurance of being right ....

Let us now pass to the second division of the argument, and dismissing the supposition that any of the received opinions may be false, let us assume them to be true and examine into the worth of the manner in which they are likely to be held when their truth is not freely and openly canvassed. However unwillingly a person who has a strong opinion may admit the possibility that his opinion may be false, he ought to be moved by the consideration that, however true it may be, if it is not fully, frequently, and fearlessly discussed, it will be held as a dead dogma, not a living truth ....

If the cultivation of the understanding consists in one thing more than in another, it is surely in learning the grounds of one's own opinions. Whatever people believe, on subjects on which it is of the first importance to believe rightly, they ought to be able to defend against at least the common objections. ... The greatest orator, save one, of antiquity, has left it on record that he always studied his adversary's case with as great, if not still greater, intensity than even his own. What Cicero practiced as the means of forensic success requires to be imitated by all who study any subject in order to arrive at the truth. He who knows only his own side of the case knows little of that. His reasons may be good, and no one may have been able to refute them. But if he is equally unable to refute the reasons on the opposite side, if he does not so much as know what they are, he has no ground for preferring either opinion. The rational position for him would be suspension of judgment, and unless he contents himself with that, he is either led by authority or adopts, like the generality of the world, the side to which he feels most inclination. Nor is it enough that he should hear the arguments of adversaries from his own teachers, presented as they state them, and accompanied by what they offer as refutations. That is not the way to do justice to the arguments or bring them into real contact with his own mind. He must be able to hear them from persons who actually believe them, who defend them in earnest and do their very utmost for them. He must know them in their most plausible and persuasive form; he must feel the whole force of the difficulty which the true view of the subject has to encounter and dispose of, else he will never really possess himself of the portion of truth which meets and removes that difficulty. ...

The fact ... is that not only the grounds of the opinion are forgotten in the absence of discussion, but too often the meaning of the opinion itself. The words which convey it cease to suggest ideas, or suggest only a small portion of those they were originally employed to communicate. Instead of a vivid conception and a living belief, there remain only a few phrases retained by rote; or, if any part, the shell and husk only of the meanings is retained, the finer essence being lost. The great chapter in human history which this fact occupies and fills cannot be too earnestly studied and meditated on ....

We have hitherto considered only two possibilities: that the received opinion may be false, and some other opinion, consequently, true; or that, the received opinion being true, a conflict with the opposite error is essential to a clear apprehension and deep feeling of its truth. But there is a commoner case than either of these: when the conflicting doctrines, instead of being one true and the other false, share the truth between them, and the nonconforming opinion is needed to supply the remainder of the truth of which the received doctrine embodies only a part. Popular opinions, on subjects not palpable to sense, are often true, but seldom or never the whole truth. They are a part of the truth, sometimes a greater, sometimes a smaller part, but exaggerated, distorted, and disjointed from the truths by which they ought to be accompanied and limited. Heretical opinions, on the other hand, are generally some of these suppressed and neglected truths, bursting the bonds which kept them down, and either seeking reconciliation with the truth contained in the common opinion, or fronting it as enemies, and setting themselves up, with similar exclusiveness, as the whole truth. The latter case is hitherto the most frequent, as, in the human mind, one-sidedness has always been the rule, and many-sidedness the exception. ... Such being the partial character of prevailing opinions, even when resting on a true foundation, every opinion which embodies somewhat of the portion of truth which the common opinion omits ought to be considered precious, with whatever amount of error and confusion that truth may be blended ....

We have now recognized the necessity to the mental well-being of mankind (on which all their other well-being depends) of freedom of opinion, and freedom of the expression of opinion, on four distinct grounds, which we will now briefly recapitulate:

First, if any opinion is compelled to silence, that opinion may, for aught we can certainly know, be true. To deny this is to assume our own infallibility.

Secondly, although the silenced opinion be an error, it may, and very commonly does, contain a portion of truth; and since the general or prevailing opinion on any subject is rarely or never the whole truth, it is only by the collision of adverse opinions that the remainder of the truth has any chance of being supplied.

Thirdly, even if the received opinion be not only true, but the whole truth; unless it is suffered to be, and actually is, vigorously and earnestly contested, it will, by most of those who receive it, be held in the manner of a prejudice, with little comprehension or feeling of its rational grounds. And not only this, but fourthly, the meaning of the doctrine itself will be in danger of being lost or enfeebled, and deprived of its vital effect on the character and conduct: the dogma becoming a mere formal profession, inefficacious for good, but cumbering the ground and preventing the growth of any real and heartfelt conviction from reason or personal experience.

Review and Discussion Questions

1 What values or purposes does Mill think are served by freedom of speech?
2 Why does Mill think that false speech should be tolerated or even encouraged?
3 Explain why Mill thinks those who would censor speech are assuming, falsely, that they are "infallible."
4 How does Mill respond to those who say that "offensive" speech may be banned?
5 Describe how Mill's discussion of free speech fits into his larger discussion of liberty and individuality in *On Liberty*.
6 Suppose somebody defends censorship of Nazi propaganda based on the claim that unless their ideas are suppressed, Nazis might eventually gain power, as occurred in post-World War I Germany. How would Mill respond to such an argument? Is that response sound? Explain.

READING: POWERS IN PUBLIC: REACTIONS, RESPONSES, AND RESISTANCE TO OFFENSIVE PUBLIC SPEECH

LAURA BETH NIELSEN[*]

Laura Beth Nielsen compares the legal status and practice of begging against the legal status and practice of racist and sexist speech. She considers how the law treats these types of speech differently. She also considers how people typically respond to offensive public speech. Laura Beth Nielsen is Research Professor at the American Bar Foundation as well as Professor of Sociology and Director of the Center for Legal Studies at Northwestern University.

Everyone who has spent time in public places has been part of a speech interaction initiated by a stranger. White women and people of color regularly encounter offensive racist and sexually suggestive speech in public places (Davis 1994; Duneier 1999; Feagin and Sikes 1994; Girdner 1980; Gardner 1995; Nielsen 2002; Nielsen 2004). Empirical evidence proves and commentary suggests that such speech is harmful to its targets (Delgado 1993; Feagin and Sikes 1994; Feagin 1991, MacKinnon 1993; Nielsen 2002; Nielsen 2004). This chapter considers the claim that offensive public speech, like other forms of "undesirable" speech, is "best" countered with more speech.

Despite notable exceptions (Delgado and Stefanie 1994; Delgado and Yun 1995; MacKinnon 1993; Matsuda et al. 1993; Meiklejohn 1948), many legal scholars advocate unfettered free speech, claiming that individuals who are offended or harmed by speech can (and should) counter these bad effects with various kinds of "more speech" (Abel 1998; Chevigny 1988; Post 1990; Post 1993; Volokh 1992). But what exactly might that entail? And how realistic is it to expect the target to engage the speaker?

The popular and jurisprudential preference for "more speech" places the burden of response on the individual target of the such speech—but, as we shall see, only for *some* forms of speech and not others. In this essay, I argue that the jurisprudential preference for more speech has serious flaws ....

All Speech Is NOT Protected Equally

At first blush, begging may seem like an odd comparison for racist and sexist speech. I include the study of begging (or panhandling) in my research primarily to show that all public speech is *not* protected (or conversely, restricted) equally. By including begging with sexist and racist speech. I make no *normative* judgment about begging's relative harm or offense to ordinary citizens in public. However, law's treatment of begging provides insight into the legal and social construction of public places. Moreover, law's treatment of begging raises a number of theoretically driven, but empirically unexamined, questions. Unless we consider a form of unsolicited street speech that tends to target white men, we could not compare

---

[*] Excerpted from "Powers in Public: Reactions, Responses, and Resistance to Offensive Public Speech" by Laura Beth Nielsen, *Speech and Harm* (2012): 148–173. Reprinted with permission. Some footnotes omitted.

the treatment of more or less privileged groups in First Amendment jurisprudence. Also, by including begging, we can gain some leverage in examining how law defines "offensive" public speech and consider what individuals consider "offensive" in their everyday lives.

Hate speech, especially in public places, continues to pose a fundamental jurisprudential problem in American society. Law itself, in the form of judicial opinion and political debate, and most legal scholars largely view the problem of street harassment acontextually—that is, for the most part, the social context (public space) in which such interactions occur is absent from consideration and analysis. Attempts to regulate race-related speech, including racist hate speech, generally have met unsympathetic responses by the courts and by advocates of free speech. Restrictions on sexually suggestive or sexually explicit speech are largely accepted in the workplace and in education, but are not considered viable for public spaces. Meanwhile, restrictions on begging in public places are constitutionally ambiguous but continue to be upheld. These conflicts continue to unfold in legal battles over hate speech codes, restrictions on begging and loitering, as well as other restrictions on public speech and behavior.

A full doctrinal analysis of this disparity is beyond the scope of this paper, but it is important to understand that courts largely allow (with some notable exceptions) the regulation of begging, but strike down restrictions on racist speech and have provided little guidance on sexist speech outside the workplace. Although speech in public spaces enjoys the highest degree of First Amendment protection by the courts (*Hague v. CIO*, 1939), many cities and states have and enforce laws which specifically prohibit begging and which routinely survive constitutional scrutiny ....

One notable example is the New York City Transit Authority's prohibition on begging within the confines of the New York City Transit Authority (including Grand Central Station). When challenged by homeless advocates and civil libertarians, the Second Circuit Court of Appeals upheld the restriction. The *Young* Court determined that the ordinance restricted a type of speech that does not merit full constitutional protection and went on to articulate a compelling state interest in protecting commuters who must use this space for transportation. Relying on a survey conducted by the Transit Authority, commuters felt annoyed and sometimes threatened by the beggars in "the *very real* context of the New York City subway," in which people with *legitimate* business are intimidated, harassed, and threatened (*Young*, p. 159; emphasis added). In a populist appeal, the Court asserted that the subway is the "primary means of transportation for literally millions of people of modest means, including hard-working men and women, students and elderly pensioners" (*Young*, p. 153). Moreover, ample alternative channels were left open to beggars in New York City, according to the *Young* Court, because panhandlers could beg in any of the streets and sidewalks of the city.

In contrast, laws, ordinances, and codes aimed at restricting racist speech have been passed in a variety of settings, but they have also been struck down. Hate speech regulation has been written into city ordinances (e.g. St. Paul, Minn., Legis. Code § 292.02 (1990)), workplace environments (Post 1990), as well as both public (*Doe v. University of Michigan*, 1989, or *UMW Post Inc. v. Board of Regents of the University of Wisconsin System*, 1991) and private institutions of higher learning (*Corry v. Stanford*, 1995). Only restrictions on racist speech in the workplace have been upheld, although not every situation has been legally tested. Restrictions on racist speech in institutions of higher learning and city ordinances have been struck down on the grounds that they are content-based, which the courts treat as a fundamental constitutional flaw.

...

Of the three types of public discourse that concern me here (begging, race-related public speech, and gender-related public speech), gender-related public speech is the least doctrinally developed. Although verbal harassment on the basis of sex is prohibited by federal anti-discrimination laws in the workplace by Title VII of the Civil Rights Act of 1964, restrictions on gender-related speech in public have not been passed or challenged at the Supreme Court level. Although speech restrictions in the workplace now are widely accepted (but see Volokh 1992), the idea that women should not suffer unreasonable sexual advances by people with power over them was, until very recently, not widely accepted. In recent years, however, prohibitions on sexual harassment in the workplace have become accepted in the law, and even in society more generally. But harassing gender-related speech in public remains a novel and untested legal issue.

First Amendment doctrine about unsolicited speech between strangers in public places is confused at best. Statutes that are clearly content-based which mention "asking for money" are treated as though they are content-neutral (and therefore are subjected to a less burdensome constitutional standard as in *Smith v. Ft. Lauderdale*, 1999). Statutes designed to prohibit various kinds of speech that might disturb public order including racist speech are universally struck down (as content-based and therefore unjustifiable as in *Cony v. Stanford*, 1995). Why?

I suggest that the difference embodies judgment about the perceived social value of the target of the speech in question. What happens in fact is that speech which targets people of higher social status (e.g. begging) is successfully regulated, and speech that targets people on the basis of their race and/or gender is struck down. My perhaps simplistic, but factually accurate, analysis of this is that the law protects people from harassment and annoyance only when they are of a certain social status. As I see it, the law favors the powerful, and courts are hostile to the claims of people of color.

Scholars of Critical Race Theory have posited a more subtle version of this argument, according to which judges are sympathetic to claims they can understand (Delgado and Stefancic 1997; Delgado and Yun 1995; Lederer and Delgado 1995). Unfortunately, the relatively homogenous composition of the judiciary prevents those who have actually experienced the harms of hate speech (e.g. white women and people of color) from being in a position to decide such matters ...

To observe that courts tend to give cursory treatment to some harms or subjective experiences of threat and not others is not necessarily to advocate for a different outcome. Rather, it merely points to the ways in which life experience frames how individual decision-makers decide that some words are *merely* offensive, while others are obviously and necessarily threatening. As I have argued, in the United States, we treat our problematic public speech differently. When it is targeted toward those with more social capital, courts are more likely to intervene.

And what advice do judges give to targets of unsolicited speech they abhor? More speech. In legal opinion and commentary, the remedy to troubling speech (when the law does not intervene) is for the deliberative process to take place. We are supposed to engage in a "free trade of idea" (*Abrams v. U.S.*, 1919) saying, "the best test of truth is the power of the thought to get itself accepted in the competition of the market" (*ibid.*). The idea that more speech is the answer to some forms of troubling speech also was famously declared by Justice Brandeis in his concurring opinion in *Whitney v. California* (1927). Brandeis wrote, "[i]f there be time to expose through discussion the falsehood and fallacies, to avert the evil by process of education the remedy to be applied is more speech, not enforced silence" (at 377). Indeed, both formal law and ordinary citizens claim that it is not proper for law to intervene in offensive public speech encounters, at least those that revolve around racist and sexist speech (Nielsen 2004). The jurisprudentially preferred solution for the problem of offensive speech (of some varieties) is *more speech*.

This formulation of the problem (that an offensive idea has been inserted into the marketplace of ideas) crowds out other formulations of what precisely may be problematic about being the target of racist or sexist speech in public places. For example, a target might feel threatened, objectified, or dehumanized. In the course of day-to-day life, targets of racist or sexist speech are reminded of their subordinate social status or their status as sex objects. Framing the problem of offensive speech as skewing a "marketplace of ideas" makes the remedy of more speech seem sensible. After all, markets are thought to run well when they are unregulated and the power of a good product/idea will prevail in the end. Thus, rather than looking to the courts to prevent the offensive speech from entering the marketplace, consumers of ideas are expected to reject the bad ones, insert the better ones, and eventually prevail.

Unfortunately, judicial prescriptions for more speech are typically vague. Should a target of offensive speech (or consumer ideas in a marketplace) respond immediately? Should she hold a protest or rally at a later time to condemn the idea? We do not know precisely what is imagined by the judiciary's instruction to engage in "more speech," but in what follows, we see what some individual targets think and do when unexpectedly confronted with offensive speech in public places.

In some contexts, more speech may be just what is called for. Organized counter-speech is documented and advocated as a remedy in the face of organized racist hate speech as when the Nazis marched through Skokie (Abel 1998; Downs 1985), and in a policed public environment, counter-speech may be effective and safe. But what of the victim of individual, targeted hate speech in public? What kind of speech effectively counters the "truth" of a racial epithet or sexual slur? And how likely are those who are made its target likely to respond? I'll consider some of these questions in the next section.

"More Speech" Relies on Faulty Empirical Assumptions

This section of the paper uses empirical data to answer the question: (How) do ordinary citizens respond when they are made the target of offensive public speech?[1] In other words, does the judicially recommended response actually happen on the streets? If so when, and if not, why not? In what follows, I consider race-related public speech, gender-related public speech, and begging, in that order.

...

Responding to Race-Related Speech in Public Places

Race-related speech may be the most troubling kind of public speech, but, for the most part, targets of racist speech do not counter it. By far the most common response to problematic race-related public speech (i.e. racist speech, racist hate speech) between strangers in public is to ignore it. Targets say they typically, "do nothing," "laugh it off," "ignore it," or, "ignore it and leave" when they are targeted. This woman's story about being called a "white bitch" was common; she was subjected to a race-related comment and ignored it.

> And there was some strike somewhere ... and we had taken a boat ride, and when we got off, the strikers ... didn't accost us physically, but verbally. And they hollered at us about all being white rich bitches who were supported by their husbands who never worked a day in their lives.
> Q: And how did you respond to that?
> A: ... I didn't respond ... you know.
> Q: Just keep walking?
> A: I just keep walking and acting like I'm deaf [laugh]
> (54-year-old white woman, homemaker, interview #05)

There are a variety of reasons why targets report that they are unwilling to engage in counter-speech. Many report being fearful for their safety, as these quotations illustrate:

> And I was at a gas station, and a guy came out, and didn't talk to me directly, but I knew he was talking about me. I was seated in the car, and the driver who was beside me was white, and the guy just said, kind of in the air, "I can see the driver's the only human being around here." Implying I was not a human being.
> Q: Uh huh. And did you respond to that in any way?
> A: No, I didn't, because I was afraid.
> (21-year-old Filipino woman, student, interview #75)

> [W]ith racist comments, I think it combines more things. You feel threatened ....
> (24-year-old white woman, child advocate, interview #51)

...

Fear is not the only reason to ignore such speech. A number of interviewees reported ignoring such speech because the speaker is ignorant, and targets believe that it is not their job to educate or debate with speakers. This is combined with the idea that such an interaction would ultimately not change the attitudes of the speaker at all ....

More speech does, of course, occur, though rarely. In fact, only 16 of 100 respondents indicated that they had *ever* responded verbally to a racist comment. The evidence suggests that men are more likely to respond verbally, though one woman talked about how she "corrects" people who make racist or race-insensitive remarks.

> I don't like hearing racist remarks. You know, and I don't tolerate them. If I hear them, I say something ... I'm ... not gonna let shit slide, excuse my

French. I feel strongly, you know, that if people stop tolerating racist remarks, people would stop making them. Now, I think I'm a perfect example, because those van drivers, for example ... they know better. They know that if they say—start—if they say, "Chink," I'm going to call them on it, if they even say, "Oriental," I'm going to educate them. I'll say, "Excuse." I'll do it very diplomatically ... "Chinamen," for example, I'll say, "You shouldn't do that, it's just [like] ... somebody black being called a nigger. Don't do that. It's offensive. Maybe you don't know that," or I'll say ... something like that. Or I'll say, "You shouldn't call Asians oriental—there are oriental rugs and vases, but not people." You know? And people will usually accept it. They'll say, "Oh, oh, I didn't know that," or something like that.

    (59-year-old African-American woman, volunteer worker, interview #85)

Other people responded less politely:

A: ... [T]hree friends and I were all walking, and then this guy said, "Oh, one more of you and you're a gang," or something like that. Or whatever.
Q: And how did you respond to that?
A: I—I really—I didn't really care. I—but my friends ... responded with some vulgar language.
    (18-year-old African-American man, gas station attendant, interview #31)

...

Reactions to Gender-Related Speech in Public Places

Women repeatedly make the point that they are capable of dealing with some problematic gender-related public speech—in particular, offensive sexually suggestive speech—on their own ....

Although all 63 women interviewed claimed to have been the target of offensive, sexually suggestive speech by a stranger in a public place, the most common response was to simply ignore it. Of the 63 women interviewed, 27 (about 43%) said that ignoring offensive sexually suggestive speech was their primary response, although there were many reasons given for ignoring the speech.

Some women ignore such speech because they fear the consequences of any other response.

I know just last week, I was in the BART Station at Montgomery and there was, um, I think a homeless man who came up to me and said, "I hate women, they're all sluts" ... That probably sticks in my mind the most ....
Q: Um, what did you say to the guy who, um, informed you that all women are sluts?
A: Um, I just turned around; I didn't say anything. I was pretty scared of him.
    (24-year-old white woman, student, interview #10)

A: [Men will say things] like, "Hey, baby, you look real good," or "Ooh, come back here and talk to me," or you know, "Let's go somewhere and be alone," that kind of stuff.

Q: And how do you typically respond to this type of comment?
A: It depends. *If I don't feel threatened, then I usually say something* like, you know, "Does your mother know you're here—talking to women this way?" or "How would you feel if someone talked to your girlfriend this way?" or something like that. *If I feel threatened, I just pretend like I didn't hear it and I keep going.*
(29-year-old white woman, interview #16, emphasis mine)

Notice that both respondents here make a calculation about their personal safety, and the second respondent also makes a reference to the women in the speaker's life ....

Occasionally, however, women's decision to ignore comments is a form of hidden resistance, or at least defiance. For example, some women ignore these comments because they think that the man seeks a response.

...

Women also fail to respond because they are ashamed. When a man shouted loudly that one woman had nice legs, she "Just kept on walking. I acted like I didn't hear it. I was embarrassed" (43-year-old African-American woman, project manager, interview #45).

...

When women do respond to offensive sexually suggestive speech in public places, their responses often are ambiguous. Some report offering an obscene gesture; some glare or act rudely; and others mention having a husband or boyfriend. These responses do not critically engage with the (offensive) message of the speech in question. This is not to suggest that women have an obligation to be more forthcoming and to jeopardize their safety for the sake of combating sexism. Instead, the purpose of illustrating women's reactions, responses, and resistance is to demonstrate that the seemingly simple "more speech" solution is not so simple after all. Targets have a difficult time "handling it" when it comes to responding to such speech.

Begging

In contrast to the other types of problematic public speech, targets of begging are not reluctant to respond to panhandlers. When the initial speech is deemed appropriate, targets often respond by saying something benign such as "no thank you" or, "not today." Even when the initial speech is perceived to be inappropriate, targets are nevertheless considerably more likely to respond verbally than are targets of race-related or gender-related public speech. Of course, the same considerations about personal safety are present in targets' calculations about whether to respond to begging. However, respondents do not report as many complicated, calculated ways of dealing with it as they do with the other forms of offensive public speech. Far more subjects simply respond to begging, indicating that this type of speech is less intimidating than the other forms of street speech discussed above.

How State Action Supports "More Speech" in Response to Begging

As we have seen, targets of begging are considerably more likely to speak back than targets of either race-related or gender-related public speech. While there may be many reasons for this, I suggest that one reason is the existence of various formal mechanisms that discourage begging. I shall argue that these mechanisms support speaking back in the case of begging. Furthermore, the absence of such mechanisms in the cases of race-related and gender-related public speech actually function to discourage speaking back in those cases.

Most large cities in the United States have ordinances prohibiting begging ....

...

In some of the nation's largest cities, at least, these ordinances and others like them are designed to prevent homeless people from annoying other citizens, and are enforced with vigor and regularity ....

.... Other formal, extra-legal mechanisms designed to resist begging in public places include awareness and education programs. These programs provide referrals to homeless people in the form of pamphlets listing locations of soup kitchens, homeless shelters, as well as city, county, state, and federal aid agencies. Similar pamphlets are distributed to potential donors to educate them about the options available for charitable donation, including donations to non-profit and religious groups that help the homeless. For example, in New York City, part of the anti-panhandling movement was to convince targets that by giving cash to panhandlers, they would be preventing the person from getting help (Lessig 1995).

That there are such formal and informal state policies prohibiting (or discouraging) begging suggests that such policies are necessary and this, in turn, suggests that it is simply not viable to expect the targets of such speech to combat it with "more speech". Moreover, by formally discouraging begging, these policies send a social message that begging is inappropriate and this, in turn, supports those inclined to refuse the panhandler's request for money.

These formal and informal mechanisms set up by the state (in the form of speech regulations) and by business and business interests (such as voucher and competition programs) support targets in speaking back if they are troubled by begging. Although there are these formal mechanisms that support speaking back in the case of begging, there are no such mechanisms for those seeking to resist race-related and gender-related public speech. In such cases, we are on our own.

Conclusion: Law and Power in Sidewalk Social Encounters

...

One interpretation of these data is that targets respond to problematic public speech when they are really offended by it. Some First Amendment scholars whose model for combating racist and sexist speech involves "more speech" may take heart in these results, claiming that they are evidence that simply allowing more speech is effective. Those who really are bothered by such speech will respond.

This interpretation, however, ignores the effects such speech has on many of its targets. All targets, whether they reported responding to such speech or not, said that they weighed their options very carefully when deciding how and whether to respond, and that the most important factor that determined their response was their own safety in the situation. So, these comments engender fear for physical safety, just as many critical race scholars have claimed (Delgado and Yun 1995). And since women are more likely to fear for their physical safety when they are made targets of sexually suggestive speech than are man-targets, "more speech" disproportionately burdens women by requiring that they overcome their fears for their safety more often than men. This is in addition to the burden placed by the "more speech" idea in the first instance.

...

Overt state power may seem absent in these fleeting but pervasive street encounters, but it is not. State power, through law, works to normalize and justify such interactions when they are race- or gender-related. The false but tacit assumption that "more speech" is both easy and simple, coupled with the assumption that any proposed regulation of problematic race- or gender-related speech would not survive judicial scrutiny, provides powerful normative reasons for people to oppose the legal regulation of such speech. When the offensive public speech is begging, and the targets include the more privileged members of society, by contrast, the state intervenes. Thus, state power is implicated because for certain kinds of public speech (problematic gender- or race-related speech), but not others (begging), the judicially preferred solution, "more speech", requires the burden to be borne by the target, with no help from the state. Law, as an institution and as official ideology, treats such offensive public speech as a problem with which its targets must live.

Note

1 The research involved ethnography of public places and in-depth interviews with 100 subjects drawn from public places including a suburb, a small city, and a large city in California. I conducted the ethnography in subway stations, public thoroughfares, and outside places of business, varying the time of day and night and day of the week when I conducted observations. I then randomly chose people from the public places where I conducted observations to interview at a later time. Those interviews, lasting about an hour each, were tape-recorded, transcribed, and analyzed using NVivo, a qualitative data analysis software program. The final sample was 63 percent women and 37 percent men; 51 percent white, 27 percent AfricanAmerican, 6 percent Hispanic, and 16 percent Asian/Pacific Islander. Over 50 percent of subjects were between the ages of 18 and 34, but the sample includes people in their 50s, 60s, and 70s. The research is described in detail in Nielsen, Laura Beth. 2004. *License to Harass: Law, Hierarchy, and Offensive Public Speech*. Princeton: Princeton University Press.

References

Abel, Richard L. 1998. *Speaking Respect, Respecting Speech*. Chicago, IL: University of Chicago Press.

Chevigny, Paul 1988. *More Speech: Dialogue Rights and Modern Liberty*. Philadelphia, PA: Temple University Press.

Davis, Diedre 1994. "The Harm That Has No Name: Street Harassment, Embodiment, and African-American Women," *U.C.L.A. Women's Law Journal* 4.

Delgado, Richard 1993. "Words That Wound: A Tort Action for Racial Insults Epithets, and Name Calling," in *Words That Wound: Critical Race Theory: Assaultive Speech, and the First Amendment*, ed. Charles R. Lawrence, Mari J. Matsuda, Richard Delgado, and Kimberle W. Crenshaw. Boulder, CO: Westview Press.

Delgado, Richard, and Jean Stefancic 1997. *Must We Defend Nazis? Hate Speech, Pornography, and the New First Amendment*. New York: New York University Press.

Delgado, Richard, and Jean Stefanie 1994. "Hateful Speech, Loving Communities: Why Our Notion of 'A Just Balance' Changes So Slowly," *California Law Review* 82.

Delgado, Richard, and David Yun 1995. "'The Speech We Hate': First Amendment Totalism, the ACLU, and the Principle of Dialogic Politics," *Arizona State Law Journal* 27: 1281.

Downs, Donald 1985. *Nazis in Skokie: Freedom, Community, and the First Amendment*. Notre Dame, IN: University of Notre Dame Press.

Duneier, Mitchell 1999. *Sidewalk*. New York: Farrar, Straus, and Giroux.

Feagin, Joe R. 1991. "The Continuing Significance of Race: Antiblack Discrimination in Public Places," *American Sociological Review* 56: 101–16.

Feagin, Joe R., and Melvin P. Sikes 1994. *Living with Racism: The Black Middle Class Experience*. Boston, MA: Beacon Press.

Gardner, Carol Brooks 1980. "Passing By: Street Remarks, Address Rights, and Urban Women," *Sociological Inquiry* 50.

Gardner, Carol Brooks 1995. *Passing By: Gender and Public Harassment*. Berkeley, CA: University of California Press.

Lederer, Laura, and Richard Delgado (eds.) 1995. *The Price We Pay: The Case Against Racist Speech, Hate Propaganda, and Pornography*. New York: Hill and Wang.

Lessig, Lawrence 1995. "Understanding Changed Readings: Fidelity and Theory," *Stanford Law Review* 47: 395.

MacKinnon, Catharine 1993. *Only Words*. Cambridge, MA: Harvard University Press.

Matsuda, Mari, Charles R. Lawrence, Richard Delgado, and Kimberle William Crenshaw 1993. *Words That Wound: Critical Race Theory, Assaultive Speech, and the First Amendment*. Boulder, CO: Westview Press.

Meiklejohn, Alexander 1948. *Free Speech and Its Relation to Government*. New York: Harper Brothers Publishers.

Nielsen, Laura Beth 2002. "Subtle, Pervasive, Harmful: Racist and Sexist Remarks in Public as Hate Speech," *Journal of Social Issues* 58: 265–80.

Nielsen, Laura Beth 2004. *License to Harass: Law, Hierarchy, and Offensive Public Speech*. Princeton, NJ: Princeton University Press.

Post, Robert 1990. "Racist Speech, Democracy, and the First Amendment," *William and Mary Law Review* 32: 267–327.

Post, Robert 1993. "Meiklejohn's Mistake: Individual Autonomy and the Reform of Public Discourse," *University of Colorado Law Review* 64.

Volokh, Eugene 1992. "Freedom of Speech and Workplace Harassment," *University of California Law Review* 39: 1791.

Review and Discussion Questions

1 What are some examples of the ways that all speech is not protected equally, according to Nielsen?

2 What explains the difference between begging regulations relating to racist and sexist speech, according to Nielsen?

3 What is Nielsen's response to the position that the best way to combat offensive speech is more speech?

4 Why are people who are confronted with begging more likely to respond verbally than those accosted with sexist or racist speech, according to Nielsen?

5 Does Nielsen's analysis support increased regulation of hate speech or not, in your view?

READING: THE SOCIAL BENEFITS OF PROTECTING HATE SPEECH AND EXPOSING SOURCES OF PREJUDICE

MARCUS SCHULZKE[*]

Marcus Schulzke argues that protecting hate speech provides a range of social benefits as part of a marketplace of ideas. He takes for granted that hate speech expresses ideas that are unjustified and offensive but argues that exposing these ideas has value. These important benefits would be lost if hate speech were suppressed. Marcus Schulzke is a Lecturer in the Department of Politics at the University of York, United Kingdom.

Introduction

Because it must be balanced against other rights and potential consequences, the right to free speech needs to have some limitations. The challenge is determining how to frame the right in a way that protects individual liberties and the goods that free speech helps to secure, while also preventing speech from interfering with the exercise of other rights or inflicting harm. Hate speech, which I define as speech that is meant to offend, exclude, intimidate, or discriminate against members of a group based on the members' race, religion, sex, sexual orientation, nationality, or ethnicity, is one type of speech that could potentially warrant suppression on the grounds that it is harmful.

Those who favor the prohibition of hate speech on consequentialist grounds tend to rely on two central claims: that hate speech inflicts serious harms and that it lacks any redeeming value that could outweigh those harms (Brownmiller 1975; Dworkin 1981; Feinberg 1985; MacKinnon 1993; Matsuda 1993; Langton 1993; Fish 1994; Lederer and Delgado 1995; Haworth 1998; O'Connor 2002; Waldron 2012; Ishani Maitra 2012). Among the harms most commonly attributed to hate speech are that it is offensive (Wolfson 1997), silences marginalized groups (MacKinnon 1993; Langton 1993; Levin 2010), contaminates society (O'Connor 2002; Waldron 2012), and promotes aggressive actions (Brownmiller 1975; Dworkin 1981; MacKinnon 1993). Although there are grounds for doubting the likelihood of these harms, and for questioning whether offense in particular qualifies as a type of harm, I will assume that the first half of the consequentialist argument against hate speech is correct and that hate speech can potentially harm its targets as well as bystanders. Specifically, I accept that speech may be harmful in an immediate sense if it causes fear, guilt, anxiety and other negative emotions, or in a cumulative sense when it contributes to low self-esteem and feelings of subordination among members of the targeted group (Delgado 1993; Matsuda 1993).

My goal is to show that, regardless of the merits of the first component of the consequentialist argument against hate speech—that is to say, regardless of

---

[*] Excerpted from "The Social Benefits of Protecting Hate Speech and Exposing Sources of Prejudice" by Marcus Schulzke, *Res Publica* 22 (2016): 225–242. Reprinted by permission of Springer Science and Business Media. Notes omitted.

whether or not hate speech is in some way harmful—it is incorrect to think that permitting hate speech lacks any valuable consequences that could help to justify the infliction of harm. Even if proponents of restricting hate speech are correct in thinking that hate speech has no *inherent* value, protecting it may have socially beneficial consequences. The social benefits of protecting hate speech become clear when one considers how the use of hate speech exposes those with hateful beliefs to public evaluation. Restricting hate speech silences prejudice without directly addressing its underlying causes ....

I argue that people who are legally permitted to engage in hate speech have more opportunities to expose themselves as hateful people to other members of society; they are free to put their beliefs on display for others to judge. This has two benefits. First, allowing the exposure of prejudice through hate speech can facilitate trust between members of society. Hate speech users demonstrate that they are untrustworthy, especially in positions of authority, responsibility, or influence, in which they might be able to covertly act on their prejudices. This is extremely valuable for societies whose members must frequently trust each other with little information about others' beliefs and few opportunities to discover prejudices that are not stated openly. Second, permitting hate speech facilitates efforts to combat prejudice by allowing hate speech users to make themselves targets of persuasion and refutation. This helps to promote the deliberative goals that are commonly linked to the right to free speech. My argument advances a conception of free speech as a social good that helps to form what Holmes (1919) called a "marketplace of ideas." Although hate speech may be harmful in some ways, it can benefit this marketplace by promoting the kind of open exchange of ideas that can facilitate incremental progress towards a more tolerant society.

...

It is important to make several qualifications at the outset. First, my argument for protecting hate speech is meant for liberal democratic societies with reasonably high standards of human rights and a commitment to the rule of law. It may not apply in places where marginalized groups cannot be adequately protected if hate speech users decide to act on their beliefs. There are critical differences between hateful speech and hateful actions, such as violence, physical coercion, and the deliberate cultivation of institutional biases. My argument will be motivated by the goal of showing that hate speech exposes those who may engage in hateful actions, especially covert hateful actions, and that it may do so in ways that may prevent or mitigate those actions' effects. Second, my argument is not meant to apply in repressive or authoritarian societies in which the state either engages in discrimination or protects those who do, as such states may use hate speech to legitimize repression and violence. Finally, I am not arguing that hate speech or the opinions expressed in it are beneficial in themselves. I assume that hate speech is usually, if not always, used to express ideas that are unjustified, hostile, and deliberately offensive. In fact, my argument presupposes that hate speech has these negative characteristics. My contention is that the social value of permitting hate speech follows directly from its ability to expose undesirable beliefs and attitudes to public scrutiny.

...

Facilitating Social Trust

Trust between strangers is vital to social life. We must trust others to follow traffic rules, to not steal from us, to respect our bodily integrity, and to act according to their particular roles. It would be impossible to have a stable social existence without being able to rely on others to treat us in relatively predictable and fair ways. I will call this generalized trust that others will act in appropriate ways and perform their prescribed roles "social trust," to emphasize that it is essential for social life and that it is often directed generally at other members of society or institutions and not exclusively at acquaintances. Although it is a fairly abstract concept, the effects of social trust are evidenced in many ways, such as the stabilizing role it plays in political associations (Tilly 2005; Maloy 2009) the extent to which liberal institutions and policies depend on it for legitimacy (Miller 1988a, b, 2000), and the fact that social institutions of any kind would collapse without some degree of trust between the people who collectively sustain them (Searle 1995, 2010; Toumela 2013).

...

Protecting hate speech provides a mechanism of preserving social trust because it affords people and institutions that are prejudiced opportunities to expose their beliefs to public scrutiny. When a person or institution engages in hate speech, or any other type of speech for that matter, the speaker makes beliefs and attitudes visible to others. This gives others a greater capacity for making informed judgments about who holds prejudices that should disqualify them from performing certain roles—or prejudices that should at least be taken into account when deciding what degree of trust is warranted ....

By my account, states are justified in permitting speech that offends or even inflicts some harm in the interest of generating greater openness about prejudices, as well as to secure the many other benefits associated with expansive free speech rights (Holmes 1919; Mill 1989; Dworkin 1978; Schauer 1982; Post 1990; Raz 1991; Sunstein 1993; Sumner 2004). Permitting hate speech serves as a mechanism for making incremental progress toward more tolerant attitudes. It brings attitudes that impede that progress into focus and allows them to be addressed before they may disrupt public trust that is founded on a presumption that people will generally treat each other fairly, especially when acting in official capacities.

...

Openness is even more important for members of the marginalized groups that are the targets of hate speech. They are at a heightened risk of being victims of discrimination and therefore stand to gain the most from knowing which other members of society may act in discriminatory ways. They have a particularly strong interest in uncovering prejudices among those performing important political and social roles, who may help to perpetuate institutional discrimination ....

My argument not only applies to people acting within the government but to any people and institutions that wield influence. Over the past decade there have been dozens of instances of public figures and corporations expressing intolerance in ways that indirectly empowered members of the public to make more informed decisions about where to place their trust. Celebrities like Mel Gibson, Michael Richards, and Paula Dean have made racist comments that provoked widespread condemnation. Powerful business leaders like LA Clippers owner Donald Sterling and Papa John's International CEO John Schnatter faced a similar fate when their racist comments were recorded. News commentators and writers, such as Don Imus and David Irving, have discredited themselves and cast doubt on their reliability as sources of information. Companies like Chick-fil-A and Urban Outfitters have expressed homophobia and racism, thereby allowing conscientious consumers to avoid buying their products. These and other hateful comments, which could plausibly be considered harmful according to the definition I offered in the introduction, may have been facilitated by protections on hate speech that made the speakers less guarded about revealing their prejudices.

Some of the best evidence of the benefits of exposing prejudice comes from the struggle to eliminate racism from American law enforcement, which has become particularly important in recent years following a long series of incidents in which police have killed or seriously injured unarmed black men. A persistent challenge when it comes to prosecuting police officers is determining whether they attacked because of reasonable concerns about their safety or whether they acted because of anti-black prejudices. In many instances, the difficulty of distinguishing between these motives has helped to protect police officers from prosecution.

Evidence of police officers engaging in hate speech has been extremely useful in two ways. First, when these comments come from officers who have physically injured or killed black people, or who may have helped to cover up racially motivated attacks, the comments provide evidence of racist motives that can strengthen the case against them (Lowery and Kindy 2015). Second, when police officers who have not been involved in attacks are discovered making racist comments they may be removed (Gambino 2015). The harms associated with hate speech are counterbalanced by the benefits of cultivating a climate in which police officers with racist attitudes may be more easily discovered before they can act on their prejudices, especially if they may act covertly or excuse their actions with appeals to self-defense. Dismissing these officers helps to restore trust in law enforcement by showing a concerted effort to purge those whose beliefs make them unfit for their roles.

...

Suppressing hate speech may force those who would engage in it to hide their enmity, but the mere concealment of prejudice is not much of a victory for tolerance. Those who are prejudiced are apt to maintain their hateful opinions even when they cannot be expressed, and to maintain them in private where they cannot be seen or challenged by more enlightened members of their societies. If hate speech is not protected, then it may not be clear where prejudice exists, who it is directed at, or how deep a problem it is ....

When people are permitted to state their prejudices openly, without fear of legal repercussions, they make themselves clearer targets for attempts at persuasion and make their misguided views manifest to bystanders. Convincing those with deep prejudices that they are wrong is extremely difficult under any circumstances, and certainly cannot be an easy matter just because hate speech is protected. Many people with intense hatred of other groups might be unwilling to consider counterarguments, making them impossible to persuade. Nevertheless, unsuccessful efforts at persuasion may still be valuable for bystanders. If hate speech is as vacuous and clearly objectionable as those who favor restricting it claim that it is (Fish 1994;

Haworth 1998; Young 2011), then any public debate in which those who engage in hate speech must defend their beliefs should end with those beliefs being decisively refuted. Bystanders, especially those who might be susceptible to becoming prejudiced, can profit from seeing public debate that refutes the dubious facts sustaining prejudices and that demonstrates how little evidence there is to support hateful belief systems. And bystanders only have the opportunity to see that hateful beliefs are founded on flawed evidence if those who are prejudiced are first able to make themselves targets of refutation.

...

Deliberation and Hate Groups

...

Group expressions of hate are another means by which hateful people, whose prejudices might otherwise remain covert, expose their beliefs to other members of society. Expressions of hatred become clear embodiments of prejudices that might otherwise lack a clear location. This gives activists referents of counter-organizing, thereby transforming expressions of hatred into more opportunities for combatting prejudice. Protests and other symbolic acts of hate speech often inspire opponents to stage counter-protests or to engage in other forms of contestation that promote tolerance, build solidarity among opponents of discrimination, and show hate groups the strength of the opposing point of view (Gillion 2013; McAdam et al. 2001). Moreover, in addition to showing the victims of hate that they have support, counter-protests and other forms of expression against hate groups offer those who are targeted a chance to become more than just victims of prejudice. They may redefine themselves through their acts of resistance as activists and take part in the public struggle against those who engage in hate speech.

...

The first potential counterargument one might raise against my central thesis is that the free use of hate speech may convince some people to become prejudiced or create a general atmosphere of hostility. Waldron (2012, p. 96), the critic of protecting hate speech who gives the most plausible account of hate speech's potential social costs, raises this concern when he discusses the possibilities that hate speech may be contagious or that it may cause social pollution akin to environmental pollution. He argues that hate speech "creates something like an environmental threat to social peace, a sort of slow-acting poison, accumulating here and there, word by word" (2012, p. 4). By this reasoning, my argument about protecting hate speech could be seen as creating the risk that hate speech usage, and prejudice itself, will spread or accumulate. However, there is good reason to reject Waldron's account of hate speech contagion.

...

If the ideas expressed in hate speech are clearly false and lack any benefits that would make it valuable on consequentialist grounds, then it is implausible to think that hate speech can be persuasive for audiences that are not already predisposed to intolerance. It is likewise implausible to think that such valueless speech, which comes from "a few crazies" (Waldron 2012, p. 195), will be capable of poisoning an entire society. This is especially true if opponents of prejudice actively combat hateful views and demonstrate the wrongness of those who publicly reveal their prejudices. Thus, I maintain that the risk of vacuous hate speech perpetuating prejudices is fairly small based on the logic of the arguments made in support of restricting this type of speech ....

Second, one could argue that even if hate speech is not persuasive, its usage could embolden those who would otherwise remain silent to announce, or even act on, their own hateful beliefs. This danger is particularly strong in places where a majority of people adhere to the intolerant beliefs espoused in hate speech. In a predominately intolerant society one could not expect to realize the advantages of hate speech that I have identified, as members of such a society might not exclude hate speech users from positions of authority or organize opposition against them.

My argument does presuppose a society that is generally tolerant, and in which most people do not share the beliefs being expressed through hate speech .... Thus, while I admit that the second potential counterargument would succeed in showing that my thesis does not hold true in all contexts, it does not refute it in the context of the fairly tolerant liberal democratic society that is also assumed by those who support restricting hate speech.

Third, one could argue that hate speech is dangerous because it may inspire those with hateful ideas to take action when they would not do so otherwise. The danger here is that there might be an intensification of existing prejudices to the point of threats or violence. Any speech that goes beyond insulting, offending, and intimidating, to express actionable threats should not be protected, and my argument for permitting hate speech does not extend to such cases. Threats and violence may reveal hateful people's beliefs, just as speech does, but those kinds of actions are apt to inflict far more serious harms than speech—harms that will probably not be counterbalanced by the goods associated with an expansive free speech right. Thus, hate speech should be protected, but efforts to act on prejudices beyond speech alone should be severely punished.

Conclusion

...

I do not claim that hateful ideas are in any way good in themselves or that the content expressed in hate speech has any value. As I have emphasized, my argument assumes that the prejudices underlying hate speech are unambiguously harmful and misguided. My point is that the wrongness of prejudice is the reason that it is so important to publicly expose those who perpetuate it. The benefits that I attribute to hate speech are not derived from prejudice itself or from attempts to offend. Rather, these benefits come from making private attitudes public in ways that may facilitate incremental progress toward greater tolerance for members of marginalized groups. Thus, all efforts should be made to end hate speech by altering the prejudices that give rise to it, but so long as prejudice exists, it should not be hidden.

References

Brownmiller, Susan. 1975. *Against our will: Men, women and rape*. New York: Ballantine.
Delgado, Richard. 1993. Words that wound: A tort action for racial insults epithets, and name calling, in *Words That Wound: Critical Race Theory: Assaultive Speech, and the First*

Amendment, ed. Charles R. Lawrence, Mari J. Matsuda, Richard Delgado, and Kimberle W. Crenshaw. Boulder, CO: Westview Press.

Dworkin, Andrea. 1981. *Pornography: Men possessing women*. London: The Women's Press.

Dworkin, Ronald. 1978. *Taking rights seriously*. Cambridge, MA: Harvard University Press.

Feinberg, Joel. 1985. *Offense to others: The moral limits of the criminal law*. New York: Oxford University Press.

Fish, S. 1994. *There's no such thing as free speech ... and it's a good thing too*. New York: Oxford University Press.

Gambino, Lauren. 2015. San Francisco police chief calls for officers' firing after racist text allegations. *The Guardian*. www.theguardian.com/us-news/2015/apr/04/san-francisco-police-officers-firing-racist-homophobic-text-messages.

Gillion, D.Q. 2013. *The political power of protest: Minority activism and shifts in public policy*. New York: Cambridge University Press.

Haworth, Alan. 1998. *Free speech*. New York: Routledge.

Holmes, Oliver Wendel. 1919. *Abrams v. United States*, 250 U.S. 616, 630.

Ishani Maitra, Mary Kate McGowan. 2012. Introduction and overview. In *Speech and harm: Controversies over free speech*, ed. Mary Kate McGowan & Ishani Maitra. New York: Oxford University Press.

Langton, Rae. 1993. Speech acts and unspeakable acts. *Philosophy & Public Affairs* 22(4): 293–330.

Lederer, Laura, and Richard Delgado (eds.) 1995. *The price we pay: The case against racist speech, hate propaganda, and pornography*. New York: Hill and Wang.

Levin, Abigail. 2010. *The cost of free speech: Pornography, hate speech, and their challenge to liberalism*. New York: Palgrave Macmillan.

Lowery, Wesley, and Kimberly Kindy. 2015. These are the racially charged e-mails that got 3 Ferguson police and court officials fired. *The Washington Post*. www.washingtonpost.com/news/post-nation/wp/2015/04/03/these-are-the-racist-e-mails-that-got-3-ferguson-police-and-court-officials-fired.

MacKinnon, Catharine 1993. *Only words*. Cambridge, MA: Harvard University Press.

Maloy, J.S. 2009. Two concepts of trust. *The Journal of Politics* 71(2): 492–505.

Matsuda, Mari. 1993. Public response to racist speech: Considering the victim's story. In *Words that wound: Critical race theory, assaultive speech, and the First Amendment*, ed. M. Matsuda, C. Lawrence, R. Delgao, and K. Crenshaw. Boulder, CO: Westview Press.

McAdam, D., Sidney Tarrow, and Charles Tilly. 2001. *Dynamics of contention*. New York: Cambridge University Press.

Mill, John Stuart. 1989 [1859]. On liberty in J. S. Mill: *'On liberty' and other writings*, ed. Stefan Collini, 1–116. New York: Cambridge University Press.

Miller, David. 1988a. The ethical significance of nationality. *Ethics* 98(4): 647–662.

Miller, David. 2000. *Citizenship and national identity*. Malden, MA: Blackwell.

O'Connor, Peg. 2002. *Oppression and responsibility: A Wittgensteinian approach to social practices and moral theory*. University Park, PA: Pennsylvania State University Press.

Post, Robert C. 1990. Racist speech, democracy, and the First Amendment. *William and Mary Law Review* 32: 267–327.

Raz, Joseph. 1991. Free expression and personal identification. *Oxford Journal of Legal Studies* 11(3): 303–324.

Schauer, Frederick. 1982. *Free speech: A philosophical enquiry*. New York: Cambridge University Press.

Searle, John R. 1995. *The construction of social reality*. New York: Simon & Schuster.

Searle, John R. 2010. *Making the social world: The structure of human civilization*. New York: Oxford University Press.

Sumner, L.W. 2004. *The hateful and the obscene: Studies in the limits of free expression*. Toronto: University of Toronto Press.

Sunstein, Cass R. 1993. *Democracy and the problem of free speech*. New York: The Free Press.

Toumela, Raimo. 2013. *Social ontology: Collective intentionality and group agents*. New York: Oxford University Press.

Tilly, Charles. 2005. *Trust and rule*. New York: Cambridge University Press.

Waldron, Jeremy. 2012. *The harm in hate speech*. Cambridge, MA: Harvard University Press.

Wolfson, Nicholas. 1997. *Hate speech, sex speech, free speech*. Westport, CT: Praeger.
Young, Caleb. 2011. Does freedom of speech include hate speech? *Res Publica* 17: 385–403.

Review and Discussion Questions

1 What does the phrase "marketplace of ideas" mean?
2 What is the relationship between social trust and protecting hate speech, according to Schulzke?
3 Are Schulzke's examples of celebrities, powerful business leaders, and the police convincing? What is the point?
4 What are three counterarguments to Schulzke's views and his responses to those arguments?

READING: ORGANIZED PROTESTS AND FREE SPEECH

SNYDER V. PHELPS (WESTBORO BAPTIST CHURCH)*

Albert Snyder's son was killed in the line of duty, serving in Iraq. During the funeral service, Fred Phelps and six other Westboro Baptist parishioners (a church that Phelps founded twenty years before) picketed the funeral, carrying signs with messages such as "God Hates the USA/Thank God for 9/11," "America Is Doomed," "Thank God for Dead Soldiers," "God Hates Fags," "You're Going to Hell," "God Hates You," and "Priests Rape Boys." Phelps had notified authorities in advance of his plan to picket and complied with police instructions. Snyder filed suit against Phelps for emotional distress. In an 8–1 decision, the Court held that Phelps was protected against tort liability based on the First Amendment on free speech.

CHIEF JUSTICE ROBERTS delivered the opinion of the court.

A jury held members of the Westboro Baptist Church liable for millions of dollars in damages for picketing near a soldier's funeral service.

The picket signs reflected the church's view that the United States is overly tolerant of sin and that God kills American soldiers as punishment. The question presented is whether the First Amendment shields the church members from tort liability for their speech in this case.

I

A

Fred Phelps founded the Westboro Baptist Church in Topeka, Kansas, in 1955. The church's congregation believes that God hates and punishes the United States for its tolerance of homosexuality, particularly in America's military. The church frequently communicates its views by picketing, often at military funerals. In the

---

* *Snyder v. Phelps*, 562 U.S. 443

more than 20 years that the members of Westboro Baptist have publicized their message, they have picketed nearly 600 funerals ....

Marine Lance Corporal Matthew Snyder was killed in Iraq in the line of duty. Lance Corporal Snyder's father selected the Catholic church in the Snyders' hometown of Westminster, Maryland, as the site for his son's funeral. Local newspapers provided notice of the time and location of the service.

Phelps became aware of Matthew Snyder's funeral and decided to travel to Maryland with six other Westboro Baptist parishioners (two of his daughters and four of his grandchildren) to picket. On the day of the memorial service, the Westboro congregation members picketed on public land adjacent to public streets near the Maryland State House, the United States Naval Academy, and Matthew Snyder's funeral. The Westboro picketers carried signs that were largely the same at all three locations. They stated, for instance: "God Hates the USA/Thank God for 9/11," "America Is Doomed," "Don't Pray for the USA," "Thank God for IEDs," "Thank God for Dead Soldiers," "Pope in Hell," "Priests Rape Boys," "God Hates Fags," "You're Going to Hell," and "God Hates You."

The church had notified the authorities in advance of its intent to picket at the time of the funeral, and the picketers complied with police instructions in staging their demonstration. The picketing took place within a 10- by 25-foot plot of public land adjacent to a public street, behind a temporary fence. ... That plot was approximately 1,000 feet from the church where the funeral was held. Several buildings separated the picket site from the church. ... The Westboro picketers displayed their signs for about 30 minutes before the funeral began and sang hymns and recited Bible verses. None of the picketers entered church property or went to the cemetery. They did not yell or use profanity, and there was no violence associated with the picketing ....

The funeral procession passed within 200 to 300 feet of the picket site. Although Snyder testified that he could see the tops of the picket signs as he drove to the funeral, he did not see what was written on the signs until later that night, while watching a news broadcast covering the event ....

II

To succeed on a claim for intentional infliction of emotional distress in Maryland, a plaintiff must demonstrate that the defendant intentionally or recklessly engaged in extreme and outrageous conduct that caused the plaintiff to suffer severe emotional distress. ... The Free Speech Clause of the First Amendment—"Congress shall make no law ... abridging the freedom of speech"—can serve as a defense in state tort suits, including suits for intentional infliction of emotional distress ....

Whether the First Amendment prohibits holding Westboro liable for its speech in this case turns largely on whether that speech is of public or private concern, as determined by all the circumstances of the case. ... The First Amendment reflects "a profound national commitment to the principle that debate on public issues should be uninhibited, robust, and wide-open." *New York Times Co.* v. *Sullivan*, 376 U.S. 254, 270 (1964). That is because "speech concerning public affairs is more than self-expression; it is the essence of self-government." *Garrison* v. *Louisiana*, 379 U.S. 64, 74-75 (1964). Accordingly, "speech on public issues occupies the highest rung of the hierarchy of First Amendment values, and is entitled to special protection." *Connick* v. *Myers*, 461 U.S. 138, 145 (1983) (internal quotation marks omitted).

"'[N]ot all speech is of equal First Amendment importance,'" however, and where matters of purely private significance are at issue, First Amendment protections are often less rigorous. *Hustler, supra*, at 56 (quoting *Dun & Bradstreet, supra*, at 758); see *Connick, supra*, at 145–147. That is because restricting speech on purely private matters does not implicate the same constitutional concerns as limiting speech on matters of public interest: "[T]here is no threat to the free and robust debate of public issues; there is no potential interference with a meaningful dialogue of ideas"; and the "threat of liability" does not pose the risk of "a reaction of self-censorship" on matters of public import. *Dun & Bradstreet, supra*, at 760 (internal quotation marks omitted) ....

Speech deals with matters of public concern when it can "be fairly considered as relating to any matter of political, social, or other concern to the community," *Connick, supra*, at 146 .... The arguably "inappropriate or controversial character of a statement is irrelevant to the question whether it deals with a matter of public concern." *Rankin* v. *McPherson*, 483 U.S. 378, 387 (1987).

Our opinion in *Dun & Bradstreet*, on the other hand, provides an example of speech of only private concern. In that case we held, as a general matter, that information about a particular individual's credit report "concerns no public issue." 472 U.S., at 762 ....

The "content" of Westboro's signs plainly relates to broad issues of interest to society at large, rather than matters of "purely private concern." *Dun & Bradstreet, supra*, at 759. The placards read "God Hates the USA/Thank God for 9/11," "America Is Doomed," "Don't Pray for the USA," "Thank God for IEDs," "Fag Troops," "Semper Fi Fags," "God Hates Fags," "Maryland Taliban," "Fags Doom Nations," "Not Blessed Just Cursed," "Thank God for Dead Soldiers," "Pope in Hell," "Priests Rape Boys," "You're Going to Hell," and "God Hates You." App. 3781–3787. While these messages may fall short of refined social or political commentary, the issues they highlight—the political and moral conduct of the United States and its citizens, the fate of our Nation, homosexuality in the military, and scandals involving the Catholic clergy—are matters of public import. The signs certainly convey Westboro's position on those issues, in a manner designed, unlike the private speech in *Dun & Bradstreet*, to reach as broad a public audience as possible. And even if a few of the signs—such as "You're Going to Hell" and "God Hates You"—were viewed as containing messages related to Matthew Snyder or the Snyders specifically, that would not change the fact that the overall thrust and dominant theme of Westboro's demonstration spoke to broader public issues.

Apart from the content of Westboro's signs, Snyder contends that the "context" of the speech—its connection with his son's funeral—makes the speech a matter of private rather than public concern. The fact that Westboro spoke in connection with a funeral, however, cannot by itself transform the nature of Westboro's speech. Westboro's signs, displayed on public land next to a public street, reflect the fact that the church finds much to condemn in modern society. Its speech is "fairly characterized as constituting speech on a matter of public concern," *Connick*, 461 U.S., at 146, and the funeral setting does not alter that conclusion ....

Snyder goes on to argue that Westboro's speech should be afforded less than full First Amendment protection "not only because of the words" but also because the church members exploited the funeral "as a platform to bring their message to a broader audience." Brief for Petitioner 44, 40. There is no doubt that Westboro chose to stage its picketing at the Naval Academy, the Maryland State House, and Matthew Snyder's funeral to increase publicity for its views and because of the relation between those sites and its views—in the case of the military funeral, because Westboro believes that God is killing American soldiers as punishment for the Nation's sinful policies.

Westboro's choice to convey its views in conjunction with Matthew Snyder's funeral made the expression of those views particularly hurtful to many, especially to Matthew's father. The record makes clear that the applicable legal term —"emotional distress"—fails to capture fully the anguish Westboro's choice added to Mr. Snyder's already incalculable grief. But Westboro conducted its picketing peacefully on matters of public concern at a public place adjacent to a public street. Such space occupies a "special position in terms of First Amendment protection." *United States* v. *Grace*, 461 U.S. 171, 180 (1983). "[W]e have repeatedly referred to public streets as the archetype of a traditional public forum," noting that "'[t]ime out of mind' public streets and sidewalks have been used for public assembly and debate." *Frisby* v. *Schultz*, 487 U.S. 474, 480 (1988).[1] ...

The record confirms that any distress occasioned by Westboro's picketing turned on the content and viewpoint of the message conveyed, rather than any interference with the funeral itself. A group of parishioners standing at the very spot where Westboro stood, holding signs that said "God Bless America" and "God Loves You," would not have been subjected to liability. It was what Westboro said that exposed it to tort damages.

Given that Westboro's speech was at a public place on a matter of public concern, that speech is entitled to "special protection" under the First Amendment. Such speech cannot be restricted simply because it is upsetting or arouses contempt ....

IV

Our holding today is narrow. We are required in First Amendment cases to carefully review the record, and the reach of our opinion here is limited by the particular facts before us. As we have noted, "the sensitivity and significance of the interests presented in clashes between First Amendment and [state law] rights counsel relying on limited principles that sweep no more broadly than the appropriate context of the instant case." *Florida Star* v. *B. J. F.*, 491 U.S. 524, 533 (1989).

Westboro believes that America is morally flawed; many Americans might feel the same about Westboro. Westboro's funeral picketing is certainly hurtful and its contribution to public discourse may be negligible. But Westboro addressed matters of public import on public property, in a peaceful manner, in full compliance with the guidance of local officials. The speech was indeed planned to coincide with Matthew Snyder's funeral, but did not itself disrupt that funeral, and Westboro's choice to conduct its picketing at that time and place did not alter the nature of its speech.

Speech is powerful. It can stir people to action, move them to tears of both joy and sorrow, and—as it did here—inflict great pain. On the facts before us, we cannot react to that pain by punishing the speaker. As a Nation we have chosen a different course—to protect even hurtful speech on public issues to ensure that we do not stifle public debate. That choice requires that we shield Westboro from tort liability for its picketing in this case.

The judgment of the United States Court of Appeals for the Fourth Circuit is affirmed.

It is so ordered.

Note

1 The dissent is wrong to suggest that the Court considers a public street "a free-fire zone in which otherwise actionable verbal attacks are shielded from liability." *Post*, at 10–11. The fact that Westboro conducted its picketing adjacent to a public street does not insulate the speech from liability, but instead heightens concerns that what is at issue is an effort to communicate to the public the church's views on matters of public concern. That is why our precedents so clearly recognize the special significance of this traditional public forum.

Justice Alito, Dissenting

Our profound national commitment to free and open debate is not a license for the vicious verbal assault that occurred in this case. Petitioner Albert Snyder is not a public figure. He is simply a parent whose son, Marine Lance Corporal Matthew Snyder, was killed in Iraq. Mr. Snyder wanted what is surely the right of any parent who experiences such an incalculable loss: to bury his son in peace. But respondents, members of the Westboro Baptist Church, deprived him of that elementary right. They first issued a press release and thus turned Matthew's funeral into a tumultuous media event. They then appeared at the church, approached as closely as they could without trespassing, and launched a malevolent verbal attack on Matthew and his family at a time of acute emotional vulnerability. As a result, Albert Snyder suffered severe and lasting emotional injury. The Court now holds that the First Amendment protected respondents' right to brutalize Mr. Snyder. I cannot agree.

I

Respondents and other members of their church have strong opinions on certain moral, religious, and political issues, and the First Amendment ensures that they have almost limitless opportunities to express their views. They may write and distribute books, articles, and other texts; they may create and disseminate video and audio recordings; they may circulate petitions; they may speak to individuals and groups in public forums and in any private venue that wishes to accommodate them; they may picket peacefully in countless locations; they may appear on television and speak on the radio; they may post messages on the Internet and send out e-mails. And they may express their views in terms that are "uninhibited," "vehement," and "caustic." *New York Times Co. v. Sullivan*, 376 U.S. 254, 270 (1964).

It does not follow, however, that they may intentionally inflict severe emotional injury on private persons at a time of intense emotional sensitivity by launching vicious verbal attacks that make no contribution to public debate. To protect against such injury, "most if not all jurisdictions" permit recovery in tort for the intentional infliction of emotional distress (or IIED). *Hustler Magazine, Inc. v. Falwell*, 485 U.S. 46, 53 (1988).

This is a very narrow tort with requirements that "are rigorous, and difficult to satisfy." W. Keeton, D. Dobbs, R. Keeton, & D. Owen, Prosser and Keeton on Law of Torts §12, p. 61 (5th ed. 1984). To recover, a plaintiff must show that the conduct at issue caused harm that was truly severe.

.... A plaintiff must also establish that the defendant's conduct was "'so outrageous in character, and so extreme in degree, as to go beyond all possible bounds of decency, and to be regarded as atrocious, and utterly intolerable in a civilized community.'" Id., at 567, 380 A. 2d, at 614 (quoting Restatement (Second) of Torts §46, Comment d).

Although the elements of the IIED tort are difficult to meet, respondents long ago abandoned any effort to show that those tough standards were not satisfied here. ... Instead, they maintained that the First Amendment gave them a license to engage in such conduct. They are wrong.

II

.... This Court has recognized that words may "by their very utterance inflict injury" and that the First Amendment does not shield utterances that form "no essential part of any exposition of ideas, and are of such slight social value as a step to truth that any benefit that may be derived from them is clearly outweighed by the social interest in order and morality." *Chaplinsky v. New Hampshire*, 315 U.S. 568, 572 (1942); see also *Cantwell v. Connecticut*, 310 U.S. 296, 310 (1940) ("[P]ersonal abuse is not in any proper sense communication of information or opinion safeguarded by the Constitution"). When grave injury is intentionally inflicted by means of an attack like the one at issue here, the First Amendment should not interfere with recovery.

III

In this case, respondents brutally attacked Matthew Snyder, and this attack, which was almost certain to inflict injury, was central to respondents' well-practiced strategy for attracting public attention.

On the morning of Matthew Snyder's funeral, respondents could have chosen to stage their protest at countless locations. They could have picketed the United States Capitol, the White House, the Supreme Court, the Pentagon, or any of the more than 5,600 military recruiting stations in this country. They could have returned to the Maryland State House or the United States Naval Academy, where they had been the day before. They could have selected any public road where pedestrians are allowed. (There are more than 4,000,000 miles of public roads in the United States.[1]) They could have staged their protest in a public park. (There are more than 20,000 public parks in this country.[2]) They could have chosen any Catholic church where no funeral was taking place. (There are nearly 19,000 Catholic churches in the United States.[3]) But of course, a small group picketing at any of these locations would have probably gone unnoticed.

The Westboro Baptist Church, however, has devised a strategy that remedies this problem. As the Court notes, church members have protested at nearly 600 military funerals. *Ante*, at 1. They have also picketed the funerals of police officers,[4] firefighters,[5] and the victims of natural disasters,[6] accidents,[7] and shocking crimes.[8] And in advance of these protests, they issue press releases to ensure that their protests will attract public attention.[9]

This strategy works because it is expected that respondents' verbal assaults will wound the family and friends of the deceased and because the media is irresistibly drawn to the sight of persons who are visibly in grief. The more outrageous the funeral protest, the more publicity the Westboro Baptist Church is able to obtain. Thus, when the church recently announced its intention to picket the funeral of a 9-year-old girl killed in the shooting spree in Tucson—proclaiming that she was "better off dead"[10]—their announcement was national news,[11] and the church was able to obtain free air time on the radio in exchange for canceling its protest.[12] Similarly, in 2006, the church got air time on a talk radio show in exchange for canceling its threatened protest at the funeral of five Amish girls killed by a crazed gunman.[13] ...

Even if those who attended the funeral were not alerted in advance about respondents' intentions, the meaning of these signs would not have been missed. Since respondents chose to stage their protest at Matthew Snyder's funeral and not at any of the other countless available venues, a reasonable person would have assumed that there was a connection between the messages on the placards and the deceased. Moreover, since a church funeral is an event that naturally brings to mind thoughts about the afterlife, some of respondents' signs—e.g., "God Hates You," "Not Blessed Just Cursed," and "You're Going to Hell"—would have likely been interpreted as referring to God's judgment of the deceased.

Other signs would most naturally have been understood as suggesting—falsely— that Matthew was gay. Homosexuality was the theme of many of the signs. There were signs reading "God Hates Fags," "Semper Fi Fags," "Fags Doom Nations," and "Fag Troops." Id., at 3781–3787. Another placard depicted two men engaging in anal intercourse. A reasonable bystander seeing those signs would have likely concluded that they were meant to suggest that the deceased was a homosexual. ...

Justice Breyer provides an apt analogy to a case in which the First Amendment would permit recovery in tort for a verbal attack:

> [S]uppose that A were physically to assault B, knowing that the assault (being newsworthy) would provide A with an opportunity to transmit to the public his views on a matter of public concern. The constitutionally protected nature of the end would not shield A's use of unlawful, unprotected means. And in some circumstances the use of certain words as means would be similarly unprotected.
>
> (*Ante*, at 1 (concurring opinion))

This captures what respondents did in this case. Indeed, this is the strategy that they have routinely employed—and that they will now continue to employ—inflicting severe and lasting emotional injury on an ever growing list of innocent victims.

IV

The Court concludes that respondents' speech was protected by the First Amendment for essentially three reasons, but none is sound.

First—and most important—the Court finds that "the overall thrust and dominant theme of [their] demonstration spoke to" broad public issues. *Ante*, at 8. As I have attempted to show, this portrayal is quite inaccurate; respondents' attack on Matthew was of central importance. But in any event, I fail to see why actionable speech should be immunized simply because it is interspersed with speech that is protected. The First Amendment allows recovery for defamatory statements that are interspersed with nondefamatory statements on matters of public concern, and there is no good reason why respondents' attack on Matthew Snyder and his family should be treated differently.

Second, the Court suggests that respondents' personal attack on Matthew Snyder is entitled to First Amendment protection because it was not motivated by a private grudge, see *ante*, at 9, but I see no basis for the strange distinction that the Court appears to draw. Respondents' motivation—"to increase publicity for its views," ibid.—did not transform their statements attacking the character of a private figure into statements that made a contribution to debate on matters of public concern. Nor did their publicity-seeking motivation soften the sting of their attack. And as far as culpability is concerned, one might well think that wounding statements uttered in the heat of a private feud are less, not more, blameworthy than similar statements made as part of a cold and calculated strategy to slash a stranger as a means of attracting public attention.

Third, the Court finds it significant that respondents' protest occurred on a public street, but this fact alone should not be enough to preclude IIED liability. To be sure, statements made on a public street may be less likely to satisfy the elements of the IIED tort than statements made on private property, but there is no reason why a public street in close proximity to the scene of a funeral should be regarded as a free-fire zone in which otherwise actionable verbal attacks are shielded from liability. If the First Amendment permits the States to protect their residents from the harm inflicted by such attacks—and the Court does not hold otherwise—then the location of the tort should not be dispositive. A physical assault may occur without trespassing; it is no defense that the perpetrator had "the right to be where [he was]." See *ante*, at 11. And the same should be true with respect to unprotected speech. Neither classic "fighting words" nor defamatory statements are immunized when they occur in a public place, and there is no good reason to treat a verbal assault based on the conduct or character of a private figure like Matthew Snyder any differently.

.... At funerals, the emotional well-being of bereaved relatives is particularly vulnerable. ... Exploitation of a funeral for the purpose of attracting public attention "intrud[es] upon their ... grief," ibid., and may permanently stain their memories of the final moments before a loved one is laid to rest. Allowing family members to have a few hours of peace without harassment does not undermine public debate. I would therefore hold that, in this setting, the First Amendment permits a private figure to recover for the intentional infliction of emotional distress caused by speech on a matter of private concern. ...

VI

Respondents' outrageous conduct caused petitioner great injury, and the Court now compounds that injury by depriving petitioner of a judgment that acknowledges the wrong he suffered. In order to have a society in which public issues can be openly and vigorously debated, it is not necessary to allow the brutalization of innocent victims like petitioner. I therefore respectfully dissent.

Notes

1. See Dept. of Transp., Federal Highway Administration, Highway Statistics 2008, Table HM-12M, www.fhwa.dot.gov/policyinformation/statistics/2008/hm12m.cfm (all Internet materials as visited February 25, 2011, and available in Clerk of Court's case file).
2. See Trust for Public Land, 2010 City Park Facts, www.tpl.org/content_documents/City Park-Facts_2010.pdf.
3. See United States Conference of Catholic Bishops, Catholic Information Project, www.usccb.org/comm/cip.shtml#toc4.
4. See www.godhatesfags.com/fliers/20110124_St-Petersburg-FL-Dead-Police.pdf.
5. See www.godhatesfags.com/fliers/20110120_Dead-Volunteer-Firefighter-Connecting_the_Dots-Baltimore-MD.pdf.
6. See www.godhatesfags.com/fliers/20110104_Newburg-and-Rolla-MO-Tornado-Connecting-the-Dots.pdf.
7. See www.godhatesfags.com/fliers/20101218_Wichita-KS-Two-Dead-Wichita-Bikers.pdf.
8. See www.godhatesfags.com/fliers/20110129_Tampa-FL-God-Sent-Military-Mom-Shooter-to-Kill-Kids.pdf.
9. See nn. 5–9, supra.
10. See www.godhatesfags.com/fliers/20110109_AZ-Shooter-Connecting-the-Dots-Day-2.pdf.
11. See, e.g., Stanglin, "Anti-Gay Church Group Plans to Picket Tucson Funerals", *USA Today*, January 10, 2011, http://content.usatoday.com/communities/ondeadline/post/2011/01/anti-gay-church-group-plans-topicket-tucston-funerals/1; Mohanani, Group to Picket 9-Year-Old Tucson Victim's Funeral, *Palm Beach Post*, January 11, 2011, www.palmbeachpost.com/news/nation/group-to-picket-9-year-old-tucsonvictims-1177921.html; Mehta & Santa Cruz, Tucson Rallies to Protect Girl's Family from Protesters, *Los Angeles Times*, January 11, 2011, http://articles.latimes.com/2011/jan/11/nation/la-na-funeral-protest-20110112; Medrano, Funeral Protest: Arizona Rallies to Foil Westboro Baptist Church, *Christian Science Monitor*, January 11, 2011, www.csmonitor.com/USA/2011/0111/Funeral-protest-Arizona-rallies-tofoil-Westboro-Baptist-Church.
12. See Santa Cruz & Mehta, "Westboro Church Agrees Not to Take Protest to Shooting Victims' Funerals", *Los Angeles Times*, January 13, 2011, http://articles.latimes.com/2011/jan/13/nation/la-na-funeralprotest-20110113; www.godhatesfags.com/fliers/20110112_AZ-Shooter-Mike-Gallagher-Radio-Exchange.pdf.
13. See Steinberg, "Air Time Instead of Funeral Protest", *N.Y. Times*, October 6, 2006, p. A14.

Review and Discussion Questions

1 The majority of the Court claims that the ability to sue for emotional distress depends significantly on whether the speech is a public or private concern. What

is the distinction between a public and private concern, and why should that be relevant to this debate about free speech?

2 If the speech had been interpreted as private, should someone be able to sue for damages? Explain your reasoning.

3 Did Phelps's free speech cause harm to Snyder? If not, why not? If so, how is this harm any different (in a legally relevant sense) from physical assault, which is routinely prohibited by law?

4 What is Alito's dissent? Which position do you support? Why?

READING: NAZI MARCHES

VILLAGE OF SKOKIE V. NATIONAL SOCIALIST PARTY[*]

Skokie, Illinois, was the home of more than forty thousand Jews and five to seven thousand survivors of Nazi concentration camps. When the National Socialist Party (the American Nazi Party) tried to march in Skokie, the village won an injunction preventing various forms of conduct. An appeals court modified that injunction but allowed the ban on displaying the swastika to stand. Here the Supreme Court of Illinois considers an appeal by the Nazi leader, Frank Collin, of the lower court's ban. (The U.S. Supreme Court later refused to reconsider this decision of the Illinois Supreme Court.)

Per Curiam: [D]efendant Frank Collin, who testified that he was "party leader," stated that on or about March 20, 1977, he sent officials of the plaintiff village a letter stating that the party members and supporters would hold a peaceable, public assembly in the village on May 1, 1977, to protest the Skokie Park District's requirement that the party procure $350,000 of insurance prior to the party's use of the Skokie public parks for public assemblies. The demonstration was to begin at 3 P.M., last 20 to 30 minutes, and consist of 30 to 50 demonstrators marching in single file, back and forth, in front of the village hall. The marchers were to wear uniforms which include a swastika emblem or armband. They were to carry a party banner containing a swastika emblem and signs containing such statements as "White Free Speech," "Free Speech for the White Man," and "Free Speech for White America." The demonstrators would not distribute handbills, make any derogatory statements directed to any ethnic or religious group, or obstruct traffic. They would cooperate with any reasonable police instructions or requests.

At the hearing on plaintiff's motion for an "emergency injunction" a resident of Skokie testified that he was a survivor of the Nazi holocaust. He further testified that the Jewish community in and around Skokie feels the purpose of the march in the "heart of the Jewish population" is to remind the two million survivors "that we are not through with you" and to show "that the Nazi threat is not over, it can

---

[*] *Village of Skokie v. National Socialist Party* 373 N.E. 2d 21 (Il I. 1978).

happen again." Another resident of Skokie testified that as the result of defendants' announced intention to march in Skokie, 15 to 18 Jewish organizations, within the village and surrounding area, were called and a counterdemonstration of an estimated 12,000 to 15,000 people was scheduled for the same day. There was opinion evidence that defendants' planned demonstration in Skokie would result in violence ....

In defining the constitutional rights of the parties who come before this court, we are, of course, bound by the pronouncements of the United States Supreme Court in its interpretation of the United States Constitution. The decisions of that court, particularly *Cohen v. California* ... in our opinion compel us to permit the demonstration as proposed, including display of the swastika.

"It is firmly settled that under our Constitution the public expression of ideas may not be prohibited merely because the ideas are themselves offensive to some of their hearers" ... and it is entirely clear that the wearing of distinctive clothing can be symbolic expression of a thought or philosophy. The symbolic expression of thought falls within the free speech clause of the First Amendment ... and the plaintiff village has the heavy burden of justifying the imposition of a prior restraint upon defendants' right to freedom of speech .... The village of Skokie seeks to meet this burden by application of the "fighting words" doctrine first enunciated in *Chaplinsky v. New Hampshire* (1942) .... That doctrine was designed to permit punishment of extremely hostile personal communication likely to cause immediate physical response, "no words being 'forbidden except such as have a direct tendency to cause acts of violence by the persons to whom, individually, the remark is addressed'." ... In *Cohen* the Supreme Court restated the description of fighting words as "those personally abusive epithets which, when addressed to the ordinary citizen, are, as a matter of common knowledge, inherently likely to provoke violent reaction." ... Plaintiff urges, and the appellate court has held, that the exhibition of the Nazi symbol, the swastika, addresses to ordinary citizens a message which is tantamount of fighting words. Plaintiff further asks this court to extend *Chaplinsky*, which upheld a statute punishing the use of such words, and hold that the fighting words doctrine permits a prior restraint on defendants' symbolic speech. In our judgment we are precluded from doing so.

In *Cohen*, defendant's conviction stemmed from wearing a jacket bearing the words "Fuck the Draft" in a Los Angeles County courthouse corridor. The Supreme Court for reasons we believe applicable here refused to find that the jacket inscription constituted fighting words. That court stated:

> The constitutional right of free expression is powerful medicine in a society as diverse and populous as ours. It is designed and intended to remove governmental restraints from the arena of public discussion, putting the decision as to what views shall be voiced largely into the hands of each of us, in the hope that use of such freedom will ultimately produce a more capable citizenry and more perfect polity and in the belief that no other approach would comport with the premise of individual dignity and choice upon which our political system rests ....
>
> To many, the immediate consequence of this freedom may often appear to be only verbal tumult, discord, and even offensive utterance. These are, however, within established limits, in truth necessary side effects of the broader

enduring values which the process of open debate permits us to achieve. That the air may at times seem filled with verbal cacophony is, in this sense not a sign of weakness but of strength. We cannot lose sight of the fact that, in what otherwise might seem a trifling and annoying instance of individual distasteful abuse of a privilege, these fundamental societal values arc truly implicated ... "[S]o long as the means are peaceful, the communication need not meet standards of acceptability" ....

Against this perception of the constitutional policies involved, we discern certain more particularized considerations that peculiarly call for reversal of this conviction. First, the principle contended for by the State seems inherently boundless. How is one to distinguish this from any other offensive word? Surely the State has no right to cleanse public debate to the point where it is grammatically palatable to the most squeamish among us. Yet no readily ascertainable general principle exists for stopping short of that result were we to affirm the judgment below. For, while the particular four-letter word being litigated here is perhaps more distasteful than most others of its genre, it is nevertheless often true that one man's vulgarity is another's lyric. Indeed, we think it is largely because governmental officials cannot make principled distinctions in this area that the Constitution leaves matters of taste and style so largely to the individual. ...

Finally, and in the same vein, we cannot indulge the facile assumption that one can forbid particular words without also running a substantial risk of suppressing ideas in the process. Indeed, governments might soon seize upon the censorship of particular words as a convenient guise for banning the expression of unpopular views. We have been able, as noted above, to discern little social benefit that might result from running the risk of opening the door to such grave results.

The display of the swastika, as offensive to the principles of a free nation as the memories it recalls may be, is symbolic political speech intended to convey to the public the beliefs of those who display it. It does not, in our opinion, fall within the definition of "fighting words," and that doctrine cannot be used here to overcome the heavy presumption against the constitutional validity of a prior restraint.

Nor can we find that the swastika, while not representing fighting words, is nevertheless so offensive and peace threatening to the public that its display can be enjoined. We do not doubt that the sight of this symbol is abhorrent to the Jewish citizens of Skokie, and that the survivors of the Nazi persecutions, tormented by their recollections, may have strong feelings regarding its display. Yet it is entirely clear that this factor does not justify enjoining defendants' speech. The *Cohen* court spoke to this subject.

> Finally, in arguments before this Court much has been made of the claim that Cohen's distasteful mode of expression was thrust upon unwilling or unsuspecting viewers, and that the State might therefore legitimately act as it did in order to protect the sensitive from otherwise unavoidable exposure to appellant's crude form of protest. Of course, the mere presumed presence of unwitting listeners or viewers does not serve automatically to justify curtailing all speech capable of giving offense .... While this Court has recognized that

government may properly act in many situations to prohibit intrusion into the privacy of the home of unwelcome views and ideas which cannot be totally banned from the public dialogue we have at the same time consistently stressed that "we are often 'captives' outside the sanctuary of the home and subject to objectionable speech." The ability of government, consonant with the Constitution, to shut off discourse solely to protect others from hearing it is, in other words, dependent upon a showing that substantial privacy interests are being invaded in an essentially intolerable manner. Any broader view of this authority would effectively empower a majority to silence dissidents simply as a matter of personal predilections.

Rockwell v. Morris ... also involved an American Nazi leader, George Lincoln Rockwell, who challenged a bar to his use of a New York City park to hold a public demonstration where anti-Semitic speeches would be made. Although approximately 2½ million Jewish New Yorkers were hostile to Rockwell's message, the court ordered that a permit to speak be granted, stating:

> A community need not wait to be subverted by street riots and storm troopers; but, also, it cannot, by its policemen or commissioners, suppress a speaker, in prior restraint, on the basis of news reports, hysteria, or inference that what he did yesterday, he will do today. Thus, too, if the speaker incites others to immediate unlawful action he may be punished in a proper case, stopped when disorder actually impends; but this is not to be confused with unlawful action from others who seek unlawfully to suppress or punish the speaker.
>
> So, the unpopularity of views, their shocking quality, their obnoxiousness, and even their alarming impact is not enough. Otherwise, the preacher of any strange doctrine could be stopped; the anti-racist himself could be suppressed, if he undertakes to speak in "restricted" areas; and one who asks that public schools be open indiscriminately to all ethnic groups could be lawfully suppressed, if only he chose to speak where persuasion is needed most.

In summary, as we read the controlling Supreme Court opinions, use of the swastika is a symbolic form of free speech entitled to First Amendment protections. Its display on uniforms or banners by those engaged in peaceful demonstrations cannot be totally precluded solely because that display may provoke a violent reaction by those who view it. Particularly is this true where, as here, there has been advance notice by the demonstrators of their plans so that they have become, as the complaint alleges, "common knowledge" and those to whom sight of the swastika banner or uniforms would be offensive are forewarned and need not view them. A speaker who gives prior notice of his message has not compelled a confrontation with those who voluntarily listen.

As to those who happen to be in a position to be involuntarily confronted with the swastika, the following observations from *Erznoznik v. City of Jacksonville* ... are appropriate:

> The plain, if at all times disquieting, truth is that in our pluralistic society, constantly proliferating new and ingenious forms of expression, "we are inescapably captive

audiences for many purposes." ... Much that we encounter offends our esthetic, if not our political and moral, sensibilities. Nevertheless, the Constitution does not permit government to decide which types of otherwise protected speech are sufficiently offensive to require protection for the unwilling listener or viewer. Rather, absent the narrow circumstances described above [home intrusion or captive audience], the burden normally falls upon the viewer to "avoid further bombardment of [his] sensibilities simply by averting [his] eyes."

Review and Discussion Questions

1 Describe the factual background and legal issues in this case.
2 The court relied on an earlier U.S. Supreme Court case, *Cohen v. California*, in deciding this one. What happened in *Cohen*? Why does the court think it is relevant to *Skokie*?
3 What do you think the intention of the Nazis was in deciding to march in Skokie, if not to win political converts to their cause? Should the court have considered their purposes? Why or why not?
4 How does the court distinguish this case from *Chaplinsky* and the fighting words exception?
5 It is sometimes said that had the court ruled otherwise, it would be put on a slippery slope of trying to balance the offensiveness of speech against the First Amendment rights of the speaker, with the result that important political acts such as civil rights marches would have been jeopardized. Do you agree? Explain.

READING: DO CORPORATIONS HAVE FREEDOM OF SPEECH?

CITIZENS UNITED V. FEDERAL ELECTION COMMISSION*

Citizens United is a nonprofit corporation that, within thirty days of a primary election, wished to pay for the release of a documentary film highly critical of Hillary Clinton. The corporation sought declaratory and injunctive relief by the Federal Election Commission (FEC) from a federal law that prohibited corporations and unions from using general treasury funds for speech that is an "electioneering communication" shortly before an election. The FEC denied the relief, which led to this case. In a landmark 5–4 decision, the Supreme Court held that the law restricting corporate speech is unconstitutional, violating the First Amendment protection of free speech. The excerpts below focus on the central argument of the case: how the Court should interpret the First Amendment in relation to corporate speech. There are two other debates in this case that are not included in the passages below. First, the following excerpts mention but bypass much of the contentious disagreement and analysis about the relevance of previous cases for deciding the current case. This debate centered around interpreting the significance of *First*

---

* *Citizens United v. Federal Election Commission*, 558 U.S. 310

National Bank of Boston v. Bellotti and *Austin v. Michigan Chamber of Commerce*. Second, although the Court struck down the law that curtailed corporate speech, the Court upheld the legal requirement that corporations must disclose what groups or persons are making the speech and they must clarify that the communication is not authorized or made by the political candidate.

JUSTICE KENNEDY delivered the opinion of the Court ....

The First Amendment provides that "Congress shall make no law ... abridging the freedom of speech." ...

The law before us is an outright ban, backed by criminal sanctions. Section 441b makes it a felony for all corporations—including nonprofit advocacy corporations—either to expressly advocate the election or defeat of candidates or to broadcast electioneering communications within 30 days of a primary election and 60 days of a general election. Thus, the following acts would all be felonies under §441b: The Sierra Club runs an ad, within the crucial phase of 60 days before the general election, that exhorts the public to disapprove of a Congressman who favors logging in national forests; the National Rifle Association publishes a book urging the public to vote for the challenger because the incumbent U.S. Senator supports a handgun ban; and the American Civil Liberties Union creates a Web site telling the public to vote for a Presidential candidate in light of that candidate's defense of free speech. These prohibitions are classic examples of censorship ....

Speech is an essential mechanism of democracy, for it is the means to hold officials accountable to the people. ... The right of citizens to inquire, to hear, to speak, and to use information to reach consensus is a precondition to enlightened self-government and a necessary means to protect it. The First Amendment "'has its fullest and most urgent application' to speech uttered during a campaign for political office." *Eu v. San Francisco County Democratic Central Comm.*, 489 U.S. 214, 223 (1989) (quoting *Monitor Patriot Co. v. Roy*, 401 U.S. 265, 272 (1971)) ....

For these reasons, political speech must prevail against laws that would suppress it, whether by design or inadvertence. Laws that burden political speech are "subject to strict scrutiny," which requires the Government to prove that the restriction "furthers a compelling interest and is narrowly tailored to achieve that interest." *WRTL*, 551 U.S., at 464 (opinion of Roberts, C. J.). While it might be maintained that political speech simply cannot be banned or restricted as a categorical matter, see *Simon & Schuster*, 502 U.S., at 124 (Kennedy, J., concurring in judgment), the quoted language from *WRTL* provides a sufficient framework for protecting the relevant First Amendment interests in this case. We shall employ it here.

Premised on mistrust of governmental power, the First Amendment stands against attempts to disfavor certain subjects or viewpoints. See, *e.g., United States v. Playboy Entertainment Group, Inc.*, 529 U.S. 803, 813 (2000) (striking down content-based restriction). Prohibited, too, are restrictions distinguishing among different speakers, allowing speech by some but not others. See *First Nat. Bank of Boston v. Bellotti*, 435 U.S. 765, 784 (1978). As instruments to censor, these categories are interrelated: Speech restrictions based on the identity of the speaker are all too often simply a means to control content.

Quite apart from the purpose or effect of regulating content, moreover, the Government may commit a constitutional wrong when by law it identifies certain preferred speakers. By taking the right to speak from some and giving it to others, the Government deprives the disadvantaged person or class of the right to use speech to strive to establish worth, standing, and respect for the speaker's voice. The Government may not by these means deprive the public of the right and privilege to determine for itself what speech and speakers are worthy of consideration. The First Amendment protects speech and speaker, and the ideas that flow from each ....

We find no basis for the proposition that, in the context of political speech, the Government may impose restrictions on certain disfavored speakers. Both history and logic lead us to this conclusion ....

* * *

This protection has been extended by explicit holdings to the context of political speech. See, *e.g., Button*, 371 U.S., at 428–429; *Grosjean v. American Press Co.*, 297 U.S. 233, 244 (1936). Under the rationale of these precedents, political speech does not lose First Amendment protection "simply because its source is a corporation." *Bellotti, supra*, at 784; see *Pacific Gas & Elec. Co. v. Public Util. Comm'n of Cal.*, 475 U.S. 1, 8 (1986) (plurality opinion). ... The Court has thus rejected the argument that political speech of corporations or other associations should be treated differently under the First Amendment simply because such associations are not "natural persons." *Id.*, at 776; see *id.*, at 780, n. 16. Cf. *id.*, at 828 (Rehnquist, J., dissenting) ....

Bellotti ... rested on the principle that the Government lacks the power to ban corporations from speaking.

Bellotti did not address the constitutionality of the State's ban on corporate independent expenditures to support candidates. In our view, however, that restriction would have been unconstitutional under *Bellotti*'s central principle: that the First Amendment does not allow political speech restrictions based on a speaker's corporate identity. See *ibid.*

Thus the law stood until *Austin*. *Austin* "uph[eld] a direct restriction on the independent expenditure of funds for political speech for the first time in [this Court's] history." 494 U.S., at 695 (Kennedy, J., dissenting). There, the Michigan Chamber of Commerce sought to use general treasury funds to run a newspaper ad supporting a specific candidate. Michigan law, however, prohibited corporate independent expenditures that supported or opposed any candidate for state office. A violation of the law was punishable as a felony. The Court sustained the speech prohibition.

To bypass *Buckley* and *Bellotti*, the *Austin* Court identified a new governmental interest in limiting political speech: an antidistortion interest. *Austin* found a compelling governmental interest in preventing "the corrosive and distorting effects of immense aggregations of wealth that are accumulated with the help of the corporate form and that have little or no correlation to the public's support for the corporation's political ideas." 494 U.S., at 660 ....

* * *

The Court is thus confronted with conflicting lines of precedent: a pre-*Austin* line that forbids restrictions on political speech based on the speaker's corporate identity and a post-*Austin* line that permits them ....

In its defense of the corporate-speech restrictions in §441b, the Government notes the antidistortion rationale on which *Austin* and its progeny rest in part, yet it all but abandons reliance upon it. It argues instead that two other compelling interests support *Austin*'s holding that corporate expenditure restrictions are constitutional: an anticorruption interest, see 494 U.S., at 678 (Stevens, J., concurring), and a shareholder-protection interest, see *id.*, at 674–675 (Brennan, J., concurring). We consider the three points in turn.

* * *

As for *Austin*'s antidistortion rationale, the Government does little to defend it. See Tr. of Oral Arg. 45–48 (September 9, 2009). And with good reason, for the rationale cannot support §441b.

If the First Amendment has any force, it prohibits Congress from fining or jailing citizens, or associations of citizens, for simply engaging in political speech. If the antidistortion rationale were to be accepted, however, it would permit Government to ban political speech simply because the speaker is an association that has taken on the corporate form. The Government contends that *Austin* permits it to ban corporate expenditures for almost all forms of communication stemming from a corporation. See Part II–E, *supra*; Tr. of Oral Arg. 66 (September 9, 2009); see also *id.*, at 26–31 (March 24, 2009). If *Austin* were correct, the Government could prohibit a corporation from expressing political views in media beyond those presented here, such as by printing books. The Government responds "that the FEC has never applied this statute to a book," and if it did, "there would be quite [a] good as-applied challenge." Tr. of Oral Arg. 65 (September 9, 2009). This troubling assertion of brooding governmental power cannot be reconciled with the confidence and stability in civic discourse that the First Amendment must secure.

Political speech is "indispensable to decision-making in a democracy, and this is no less true because the speech comes from a corporation rather than an individual." *Bellotti*, 435 U.S., at 777 (footnote omitted). ... *Austin* sought to defend the antidistortion rationale as a means to prevent corporations from obtaining "an unfair advantage in the political marketplace" by using "resources amassed in the economic marketplace." 494 U.S., at 659 (quoting *MCFL, supra*, at 257). But *Buckley* rejected the premise that the Government has an interest "in equalizing the relative ability of individuals and groups to influence the outcome of elections." 424 U.S., at 48 ....

It is irrelevant for purposes of the First Amendment that corporate funds may "have little or no correlation to the public's support for the corporation's political ideas." *Id.*, at 660 (majority opinion). All speakers, including individuals and the media, use money amassed from the economic marketplace to fund their speech. The First Amendment protects the resulting speech, even if it was enabled by economic transactions with persons or entities who disagree with the speaker's ideas ....

Austin's antidistortion rationale would produce the dangerous, and unacceptable, consequence that Congress could ban political speech of media corporations. ... Thus, under the Government's reasoning, wealthy media corporations could have their voices diminished to put them on par with other media entities. There is no precedent for permitting this under the First Amendment.

The media exemption discloses further difficulties with the law now under consideration. There is no precedent supporting laws that attempt to distinguish between corporations which are deemed to be exempt as media corporations and those which are not. ... With the advent of the Internet and the decline of print and broadcast media, moreover, the line between the media and others who wish to comment on political and social issues becomes far more blurred.

The law's exception for media corporations is, on its own terms, all but an admission of the invalidity of the antidistortion rationale. And the exemption results in a further, separate reason for finding this law invalid: Again by its own terms, the law exempts some corporations but covers others, even though both have the need or the motive to communicate their views. The exemption applies to media corporations owned or controlled by corporations that have diverse and substantial investments and participate in endeavors other than news. So even assuming the most doubtful proposition that a news organization has a right to speak when others do not, the exemption would allow a conglomerate that owns both a media business and an unrelated business to influence or control the media in order to advance its overall business interest. At the same time, some other corporation, with an identical business interest but no media outlet in its ownership structure, would be forbidden to speak or inform the public about the same issue. This differential treatment cannot be squared with the First Amendment ....

The censorship we now confront is vast in its reach. The Government has "muffle[d] the voices that best represent the most significant segments of the economy." *McConnell, supra*, at 257–258 (opinion of SCALIA, J.). And "the electorate [has been] deprived of information, knowledge and opinion vital to its function." *CIO*, 335 U.S., at 144 (Rutledge, J., concurring in result). By suppressing the speech of manifold corporations, both for-profit and non-profit, the Government prevents their voices and viewpoints from reaching the public and advising voters on which persons or entities are hostile to their interests. Factions will necessarily form in our Republic, but the remedy of "destroying the liberty" of some factions is "worse than the disease." The Federalist No. 10, p. 130 (B. Wright ed. 1961) (J. Madison). Factions should be checked by permitting them all to speak, see *ibid.*, and by entrusting the people to judge what is true and what is false.

The purpose and effect of this law is to prevent corporations, including small and nonprofit corporations, from presenting both facts and opinions to the public ....

When Government seeks to use its full power, including the criminal law, to command where a person may get his or her information or what distrusted source he or she may not hear, it uses censorship to control thought. This is unlawful. The First Amendment confirms the freedom to think for ourselves.

* * *

What we have said also shows the invalidity of other arguments made by the Government. For the most part relinquishing the antidistortion rationale, the Government falls back on the argument that corporate political speech can be banned in order to prevent corruption or its appearance ....

... [W]e conclude that independent expenditures, including those made by corporations, do not give rise to corruption or the appearance of corruption ....

The appearance of influence or access, furthermore, will not cause the electorate to lose faith in our democracy. By definition, an independent expenditure is political speech presented to the electorate that is not coordinated with a candidate. See *Buckley, supra*, at 46. The fact that a corporation, or any other speaker, is willing to spend money to try to persuade voters presupposes that the people have the ultimate influence over elected officials. This is inconsistent with any suggestion that the electorate will refuse "'to take part in democratic governance'" because of additional political speech made by a corporation or any other speaker ....

.... If elected officials succumb to improper influences from independent expenditures; if they surrender their best judgment; and if they put expediency before principle, then surely there is cause for concern. We must give weight to attempts by Congress to seek to dispel either the appearance or the reality of these influences. The remedies enacted by law, however, must comply with the First Amendment; and, it is our law and our tradition that more speech, not less, is the governing rule. An outright ban on corporate political speech during the critical preelection period is not a permissible remedy. Here Congress has created categorical bans on speech that are asymmetrical to preventing *quid pro quo* corruption.

* * *

The Government contends further that corporate independent expenditures can be limited because of its interest in protecting dissenting shareholders from being compelled to fund corporate political speech. This asserted interest, like *Austin*'s antidistortion rationale, would allow the Government to ban the political speech even of media corporations. See *supra*, at 35–37. Assume, for example, that a shareholder of a corporation that owns a newspaper disagrees with the political views the newspaper expresses. See *Austin*, 494 U.S., at 687 (Scalia, J., dissenting). Under the Government's view, that potential disagreement could give the Government the authority to restrict the media corporation's political speech. The First Amendment does not allow that power. There is, furthermore, little evidence of abuse that cannot be corrected by shareholders "through the procedures of corporate democracy." *Bellotti*, 435 U.S., at 794; see *id.*, at 794, n. 34.

Those reasons are sufficient to reject this shareholder-protection interest; and, moreover, the statute is both underinclusive and overinclusive. As to the first, if Congress had been seeking to protect dissenting shareholders, it would not have banned corporate speech in only certain media within 30 or 60 days before an election. A dissenting shareholder's interests would be implicated by speech in any media at any time. As to the second, the statute is overinclusive because it covers all corporations, including nonprofit corporations and for-profit corporations with only single shareholders. As to other corporations, the remedy is not to restrict speech but to consider and explore other regulatory mechanisms. The regulatory mechanism here, based on speech, contravenes the First Amendment.

* * *

We need not reach the question whether the Government has a compelling interest in preventing foreign individuals or associations from influencing our Nation's political process. Cf. 2 U.S. C. §441e (contribution and expenditure ban applied to "foreign national[s]"). Section 441b is not limited to corporations or associations that were created in foreign countries or funded predominantly by foreign shareholders. Section 441b therefore would be overbroad even if we assumed, *arguendo*, that the Government has a compelling interest in limiting foreign influence over our political process. See *Broadrick*, 413 U.S., at 615.

* * *

... Political speech is so ingrained in our culture that speakers find ways to circumvent campaign finance laws. See, *e.g., McConnell*, 540 U.S., at 176–177 ("Given BCRA's tighter restrictions on the raising and spending of soft money, the incentives ... to exploit [26 U.S. C. §527] organizations will only increase"). Our Nation's speech dynamic is changing, and informative voices should not have to circumvent onerous restrictions to exercise their First Amendment rights. Speakers have become adept at presenting citizens with sound bites, talking points, and scripted messages that dominate the 24-hour news cycle. Corporations, like individuals, do not have monolithic views. On certain topics corporations may possess valuable expertise, leaving them the best equipped to point out errors or fallacies in speech of all sorts, including the speech of candidates and elected officials.

Rapid changes in technology—and the creative dynamic inherent in the concept of free expression—counsel against upholding a law that restricts political speech in certain media or by certain speakers. See Part II–C, *supra*. Today, 30-second television ads may be the most effective way to convey a political message. See *McConnell, supra*, at 261 (opinion of Scalia, J.). Soon, however, it may be that Internet sources, such as blogs and social networking Web sites, will provide citizens with significant information about political candidates and issues. Yet, §441b would seem to ban a blog post expressly advocating the election or defeat of a candidate if that blog were created with corporate funds. See 2 U.S. C. §441b(a); *MCFL, supra*, at 249. The First Amendment does not permit Congress to make these categorical distinctions based on the corporate identity of the speaker and the content of the political speech ....

* * *

When word concerning the plot of the movie *Mr. Smith Goes to Washington* reached the circles of Government, some officials sought, by persuasion, to discourage its distribution. See Smoodin, "Compulsory" Viewing for Every Citizen: *Mr. Smith* and the Rhetoric of Reception, 35 Cinema Journal 3, 19, and n. 52 (Winter 1996) (citing Mr. Smith Riles Washington, Time, October 30, 1939, p. 49); Nugent, Capra's Capitol Offense, N. Y. Times, October 29, 1939, p. X5. Under *Austin*, though, officials could have done more than discourage its distribution—they could have banned the film. After all, it, like *Hillary*, was speech funded by a corporation that was critical of Members of Congress. *Mr. Smith Goes to Washington* may be fiction and caricature; but fiction and caricature can be a powerful force.

Modern-day movies, television comedies, or skits on Youtube.com might portray public officials or public policies in unflattering ways. Yet if a covered transmission during the blackout period creates the background for candidate endorsement or opposition, a felony occurs solely because a corporation, other than an exempt media corporation, has made the "purchase, payment, distribution, loan, advance, deposit, or gift of money or anything of value" in order to engage in political speech. 2 U. S. C. §431(9)(A)(i). Speech would be suppressed in the realm where its necessity is most evident: in the public dialogue preceding a real election. Governments are often hostile to speech, but under our law and our tradition it seems stranger than fiction for our Government to make this political speech a crime. Yet this is the statute's purpose and design.

Some members of the public might consider *Hillary* to be insightful and instructive; some might find it to be neither high art nor a fair discussion on how to set the Nation's course; still others simply might suspend judgment on these points but decide to think more about issues and candidates. Those choices and assessments, however, are not for the Government to make.

> The First Amendment underwrites the freedom to experiment and to create in the realm of thought and speech. Citizens must be free to use new forms, and new forums, for the expression of ideas. The civic discourse belongs to the people, and the Government may not prescribe the means used to conduct it.
>
> *McConnell, supra*, at 341 (opinion of Kennedy, J.)

The judgment of the District Court is reversed with respect to the constitutionality of 2 U. S. C. §441b's restrictions on corporate independent expenditures. The judgment is affirmed with respect to BCRA's disclaimer and disclosure requirements. The case is remanded for further proceedings consistent with this opinion.

It is so ordered.

JUSTICE SCALIA, with whom JUSTICE ALITO joins, and with whom JUSTICE THOMAS joins in part, concurring.

I join the opinion of the Court.[1]

I write separately to address Justice Stevens' discussion of *"Original Understandings,"* post, at 34 (opinion concurring in part and dissenting in part) (hereinafter referred to as the dissent). This section of the dissent purports to show that today's decision is not supported by the original understanding of the First Amendment. The dissent attempts this demonstration, however, in splendid isolation from the text of the First Amendment. It never shows why "the freedom of speech" that was the right of Englishmen did not include the freedom to speak in association with other individuals, including association in the corporate form ....

The dissent says that when the Framers "constitutionalized the right to free speech in the First Amendment, it was the free speech of individual Americans that they had in mind." *Post*, at 37. That is no doubt true. All the provisions of the Bill of Rights set forth the rights of individual men and women—not, for example, of trees or polar bears. But the individual person's right to speak includes the right to speak *in association with other individual persons*. Surely the dissent does not believe that speech by the Republican Party or the Democratic Party can be censored because it is not the speech of "an individual American." It is the speech of many individual Americans, who have associated in a common cause, giving the leadership of the party the right to speak on their behalf. The association of individuals in a business corporation is no different—or at least it cannot be denied the right to speak on the simplistic ground that it is not "an individual American."

But to return to, and summarize, my principal point, which is the conformity of today's opinion with the original meaning of the First Amendment. The Amendment is written in terms of "speech," not speakers. Its text offers no foothold for excluding any category of speaker, from single individuals to partnerships of individuals, to unincorporated associations of individuals, to incorporated associations of individuals—and the dissent offers no evidence about the original meaning of the text to support any such exclusion. We are therefore simply left with the question whether the speech at issue in this case is "speech" covered by the First Amendment. No one says otherwise. A documentary film critical of a potential Presidential candidate is core political speech, and its nature as such does not change simply because it was funded by a corporation. Nor does the character of that funding produce any reduction whatever in the "inherent worth of the speech" and "its capacity for informing the public," *First Nat. Bank of Boston* v. *Bellotti*, 435 U.S. 765, 777 (1978). Indeed, to exclude or impede corporate speech is to muzzle the principal agents of the modern free economy. We should celebrate rather than condemn the addition of this speech to the public debate.

Note

1 JUSTICE THOMAS does not join Part IV of the Court's opinion.

Justice Stevens, with whom Justice Ginsburg, Justice Breyer, and Justice Sotomayor join, concurring in part and dissenting in part. ...

The basic premise underlying the Court's ruling is its iteration, and constant reiteration, of the proposition that the First Amendment bars regulatory distinctions based on a speaker's identity, including its "identity" as a corporation. ... The conceit that corporations must be treated identically to natural persons in the political sphere is not only inaccurate but also inadequate to justify the Court's disposition of this case.

In the context of election to public office, the distinction between corporate and human speakers is significant. Although they make enormous contributions to our society, corporations are not actually members of it. They cannot vote or run for office. Because they may be managed and controlled by nonresidents, their interests may conflict in fundamental respects with the interests of eligible voters. The financial resources, legal structure, and instrumental orientation of corporations raise legitimate concerns about their role in the electoral process. Our lawmakers have a compelling constitutional basis, if not also a democratic duty, to take measures designed to guard against the potentially deleterious effects of corporate spending in local and national races. ...

* * *

The Court's ruling threatens to undermine the integrity of elected institutions across the Nation. ...

... The ruling rests on several premises. First, the Court claims that *Austin* and *McConnell* have "banned" corporate speech. Second, it claims that the First Amendment precludes regulatory distinctions based on speaker identity, including the speaker's identity as a corporation. Third, it claims that *Austin* and *McConnell* were radical outliers in our First Amendment tradition and our campaign finance jurisprudence. Each of these claims is wrong.

The So-Called "Ban"

Pervading the Court's analysis is the ominous image of a "categorical ba[n]" on corporate speech .... This characterization is highly misleading, and needs to be corrected.

In fact it already has been. Our cases have repeatedly pointed out that, "[c]ontrary to the [majority's] critical assumptions," the statutes upheld in *Austin* and *McConnell* do "not impose an absolute ban on all forms of corporate political spending." *Austin*, 494 U.S., at 660; see also *McConnell*, 540 U.S., at 203–204; Beaumont, 539 U.S., at 162–163. For starters, both statutes provide exemptions for PACs, separate segregated funds established by a corporation for political purposes ....

Under BCRA, any corporation's "stockholders and their families and its executive or administrative personnel and their families" can pool their resources to finance electioneering communications .... A significant and growing number of corporations avail themselves of this option; during the most recent election cycle, corporate and union PACs raised nearly a billion dollars. Administering a PAC entails some administrative burden, but so does complying with the disclaimer, disclosure, and reporting requirements that the Court today upholds ... and no one has suggested that the burden is severe for a sophisticated for-profit corporation ....

So let us be clear: Neither *Austin* nor *McConnell* held or implied that corporations may be silenced; the FEC is not a "censor"; and in the years since these cases were decided, corporations have continued to play a major role in the national dialogue. Laws such as §203 target a class of communications that is especially likely to corrupt the political process, that is at least one degree removed from the views of individual citizens, and that may not even reflect the views of those who pay for it. Such laws burden political speech, and that is always a serious matter, demanding careful scrutiny. But the majority's incessant talk of a "ban" aims at a straw man.

Identity-Based Distinctions

The second pillar of the Court's opinion is its assertion that "the Government cannot restrict political speech based on the speaker's ... identity." ... Like its paeans to unfettered discourse, the Court's denunciation of identity-based distinctions may have rhetorical appeal but it obscures reality...

.... [I]n a variety of contexts, we have held that speech can be regulated differentially on account of the speaker's identity, when identity is understood in categorical or institutional terms. The Government routinely places special restrictions on the speech rights of students,[1] prisoners,[2] members of the Armed Forces,[3] foreigners,[4] and its own employees.[5] When such restrictions are justified by a legitimate governmental interest, they do not necessarily raise constitutional problems.[6] In contrast to the blanket rule that the majority espouses, our cases recognize that the Government's interests may be more or less compelling with respect to different classes of speakers ....

The free speech guarantee thus does not render every other public interest an illegitimate basis for qualifying a speaker's autonomy; society could scarcely function if it did. It is fair to say that our First Amendment doctrine has "frowned on" certain identity-based distinctions, *Los Angeles Police Dept. v. United Reporting Publishing Corp.*, 528 U.S. 32, 47, n. 4 (1999) (Stevens, J., dissenting), particularly those that may reflect invidious discrimination or preferential treatment of a politically powerful group. But it is simply incorrect to suggest that we have prohibited all legislative distinctions based on identity or content. Not even close.

The election context is distinctive in many ways, and the Court, of course, is right that the First Amendment closely guards political speech. But in this context, too, the authority of legislatures to enact viewpoint-neutral regulations based on content and identity is well settled. We have, for example, allowed state-run broadcasters to exclude independent candidates from televised debates .... We have upheld statutes that prohibit the distribution or display of campaign materials near a polling place .... Although we have not reviewed them directly, we have never cast doubt on laws that place special restrictions on campaign spending by foreign nationals .... And we have consistently approved laws that bar Government employees, but not others, from contributing to or participating in political activities. See n. 45, *supra*. These statutes burden the political expression of one class of speakers, namely, civil servants. Yet we have sustained them on the basis of longstanding practice and Congress' reasoned judgment that certain regulations which leave "untouched full participation ... in political decisions at the ballot box," *Civil Service Comm'n v. Letter Carriers*, 413 U.S. 548, 556 (1973) (internal quotation marks omitted), help ensure that public officials are "sufficiently free from improper influences," id., at 564, and that "confidence in the system of representative Government is not ... eroded to a disastrous extent," id., at 565.

The same logic applies to this case with additional force because it is the identity of corporations, rather than individuals, that the Legislature has taken into account. As we have unanimously observed, legislatures are entitled to decide "that the special characteristics of the corporate structure require particularly careful regulation" in an electoral context. NRWC, 459 U.S., at 209–210.[7] Not only has the distinctive potential of corporations to corrupt the electoral process long been recognized, but within the area of campaign finance, corporate spending is also "furthest from the core of political expression, since corporations' First Amendment speech and association interests are derived largely from those of their members and of the public in receiving information," Beaumont, 539 U.S., at 161, n. 8 (citation omitted). Campaign finance distinctions based on corporate identity tend to be less worrisome, in other words, because the "speakers" are not natural persons, much less members of our political community, and the governmental interests are of the highest order. Furthermore, when corporations, as a class, are distinguished from noncorporations, as a class, there is a lesser risk that regulatory distinctions will reflect invidious discrimination or political favoritism.

If taken seriously, our colleagues' assumption that the identity of a speaker has no relevance to the Government's ability to regulate political speech would lead to some remarkable conclusions. Such an assumption would have accorded the propaganda broadcasts to our troops by "Tokyo Rose" during World War II the same protection as speech by Allied commanders. More pertinently, it would appear to afford the same protection to multinational corporations controlled by foreigners as to individual Americans: To do otherwise, after all, could "'enhance the relative voice'" of some (i.e., humans) over others (i.e., nonhumans). *Ante*, at 33 (quoting Buckley, 424 U.S., at 49).[8] Under the majority's view, I suppose it may be a First Amendment problem that corporations are not permitted to vote, given that voting is, among other things, a form of speech.[9]

In short, the Court dramatically overstates its critique of identity-based distinctions, without ever explaining why corporate identity demands the same treatment as individual identity. Only the most wooden approach to the First Amendment could justify the unprecedented line it seeks to draw.

* * *

.... The Court invokes "ancient First Amendment principles," *ante*, at 1 (internal quotation marks omitted), and original understandings, *ante*, at 37–38, to defend today's ruling, yet it makes only a perfunctory attempt to ground its analysis in the principles or understandings of those who drafted and ratified the Amendment. Perhaps this is because there is not a scintilla of evidence to support the notion that anyone believed it would preclude regulatory distinctions based on the corporate form ....

.... Unlike our colleagues, they had little trouble distinguishing corporations from human beings, and when they constitutionalized the right to free speech in the First Amendment, it was the free speech of individual Americans that they had in mind. While individuals might join together to exercise their speech rights, business corporations, at least, were plainly not seen as facilitating such associational or expressive ends. Even "the notion that business corporations could invoke the First Amendment would probably have been quite a novelty," given that "at the time, the legitimacy of every corporate activity was thought to rest entirely in a concession of the sovereign." Shelledy, Autonomy, Debate, and Corporate Speech, 18 Hastings Const. L. Q. 541, 578 (1991); cf. *Trustees of Dartmouth College* v. *Woodward*, 4 Wheat. 518, 636, ... it seems to me implausible that the Framers believed "the freedom of speech" would extend equally to all corporate speakers, much less that it would preclude legislatures from taking limited measures to guard against corporate capture of elections ....

The truth is we cannot be certain how a law such as BCRA §203 meshes with the original meaning of the First Amendment. I have given several reasons why I believe the Constitution would have been understood then, and ought to be understood now, to permit reasonable restrictions on corporate electioneering, and I will give many more reasons in the pages to come. The Court enlists the Framers in its defense without seriously grappling with their understandings of corporations or the free speech right, or with the republican principles that underlay those understandings.

In fairness, our campaign finance jurisprudence has never attended very closely to the views of the Framers, see *Randall* v. *Sorrell*, 548 U.S. 230, 280 (2006)

(Stevens, J., dissenting), whose political universe differed profoundly from that of today. We have long since held that corporations are covered by the First Amendment, and many legal scholars have long since rejected the concession theory of the corporation. But "historical context is usually relevant," ibid. (internal quotation marks omitted), and in light of the Court's effort to cast itself as guardian of ancient values, it pays to remember that nothing in our constitutional history dictates today's outcome. To the contrary, this history helps illuminate just how extraordinarily dissonant the decision is ....

* * *

.... I come at last to the interests that are at stake. The majority recognizes that *Austin* and *McConnell* may be defended on anticorruption, antidistortion, and shareholder protection rationales. *Ante*, at 32–46. It badly errs both in explaining the nature of these rationales, which overlap and complement each other, and in applying them to the case at hand.

The Anticorruption Interest

.... Corruption can take many forms. Bribery may be the paradigm case. But the difference between selling a vote and selling access is a matter of degree, not kind. And selling access is not qualitatively different from giving special preference to those who spent money on one's behalf. Corruption operates along a spectrum, and the majority's apparent belief that quid pro quo arrangements can be neatly demarcated from other improper influences does not accord with the theory or reality of politics. It certainly does not accord with the record Congress developed in passing BCRA, a record that stands as a remarkable testament to the energy and ingenuity with which corporations, unions, lobbyists, and politicians may go about scratching each other's backs—and which amply supported Congress' determination to target a limited set of especially destructive practices ....

.... Corporations, as a class, tend to be more attuned to the complexities of the legislative process and more directly affected by tax and appropriations measures that receive little public scrutiny; they also have vastly more money with which to try to buy access and votes. See Supp. Brief for Appellee 17 (stating that the Fortune 100 companies earned revenues of $13.1 trillion during the last election cycle). Business corporations must engage the political process in instrumental terms if they are to maximize shareholder value. The unparalleled resources, professional lobbyists, and single-minded focus they bring to this effort, I believed, make quid pro quo corruption and its appearance inherently more likely when they (or their conduits or trade groups) spend unrestricted sums on elections.

It is with regret rather than satisfaction that I can now say that time has borne out my concerns. The legislative and judicial proceedings relating to BCRA generated a substantial body of evidence suggesting that, as corporations grew more and more adept at crafting "issue ads" to help or harm a particular candidate, these nominally independent expenditures began to corrupt the political process in a very direct sense. The sponsors of these ads were routinely granted special access after the campaign was over; "candidates and officials knew who their friends were," *McConnell*, 540 U.S., at 129. Many corporate independent expenditures, it seemed, had become essentially interchangeable with direct contributions in their capacity to generate quid pro quo arrangements. In an age in which money and television ads are the coin of the campaign realm, it is hardly surprising that corporations deployed these ads to curry favor with, and to gain influence over, public officials ....

.... Starting today, corporations with large war chests to deploy on electioneering may find democratically elected bodies becoming much more attuned to their interests. The majority both misreads the facts and draws the wrong conclusions when it suggests that the BCRA record provides "only scant evidence that independent expenditures ... ingratiate," and that, "in any event," none of it matters. Ibid. ...

Austin and Corporate Expenditures

Just as the majority gives short shrift to the general societal interests at stake in campaign finance regulation, it also overlooks the distinctive considerations raised by the regulation of corporate expenditures. The majority fails to appreciate that *Austin*'s antidistortion rationale is itself an anticorruption rationale, see 494 U.S., at 660 (describing "a different type of corruption"), tied to the special concerns raised by corporations. Understood properly, "antidistortion" is simply a variant on the classic governmental interest in protecting against improper influences on officeholders that debilitate the democratic process. It is manifestly not just an "'equalizing'" ideal in disguise ....

I Antidistortion

The fact that corporations are different from human beings might seem to need no elaboration, except that the majority opinion almost completely elides it. *Austin* set forth some of the basic differences. Unlike natural persons, corporations have "limited liability" for their owners and managers, "perpetual life," separation of ownership and control, "and favorable treatment of the accumulation and distribution of assets ... that enhance their ability to attract capital and to deploy their resources in ways that maximize the return on their shareholders' investments." 494 U.S., at 658–659. Unlike voters in U.S. elections, corporations may be foreign controlled ....

It might also be added that corporations have no consciences, no beliefs, no feelings, no thoughts, no desires. Corporations help structure and facilitate the activities of human beings, to be sure, and their "personhood" often serves as a useful legal fiction. But they are not themselves members of "We the People" by whom and for whom our Constitution was established.

These basic points help explain why corporate electioneering is not only more likely to impair compelling governmental interests, but also why restrictions on that electioneering are less likely to encroach upon First Amendment freedoms. One fundamental concern of the First Amendment is to "protec[t] the individual's interest in self-expression." *Consolidated Edison Co. of N. Y. v. Public Serv. Comm'n of N. Y.*, 447 U.S. 530, 534, n. 2 (1980); ....

It is an interesting question "who" is even speaking when a business corporation places an advertisement that endorses or attacks a particular candidate. Presumably it is not the customers or employees, who typically have no say in such matters. It cannot realistically be said to be the shareholders, who tend to be far removed from the day-to-day decisions of the firm and whose political preferences may be opaque to management. Perhaps the officers or directors of the corporation have the best claim to be the ones speaking, except their fiduciary duties generally prohibit them from using corporate funds for personal ends. Some individuals associated with the corporation must make the decision to place the ad, but the idea that these individuals are thereby fostering their self-expression or cultivating their critical faculties is fanciful. It is entirely possible that the corporation's electoral message will conflict with their personal convictions. Take away the ability to use general treasury funds for some of those ads, and no one's autonomy, dignity, or political equality has been impinged upon in the least ....

.... [S]ome corporations have affirmatively urged Congress to place limits on their electioneering communications. These corporations fear that officeholders will shake them down for supportive ads, that they will have to spend increasing sums on elections in an ever-escalating arms race with their competitors, and that public trust in business will be eroded. See id., at 10–19. A system that effectively forces corporations to use their shareholders' money both to maintain access to, and to avoid retribution from, elected officials may ultimately prove more harmful than beneficial to many corporations. It can impose a kind of implicit tax.

In short, regulations such as §203 and the statute upheld in *Austin* impose only a limited burden on First Amendment freedoms not only because they target a narrow subset of expenditures and leave untouched the broader "public dialogue," *ante*, at 25, but also because they leave untouched the speech of natural persons ....

.... The legal structure of corporations allows them to amass and deploy financial resources on a scale few natural persons can match .... In a state election such as the one at issue in *Austin*, the interests of nonresident corporations may be fundamentally adverse to the interests of local voters. Consequently, when corporations grab up the prime broadcasting slots on the eve of an election, they can flood the market with advocacy that bears "little or no correlation" to the ideas of natural persons or to any broader notion of the public good, 494 U.S., at 660. The opinions of real people may be marginalized. "The expenditure restrictions of [2 U.S. C.] §441b are thus meant to ensure that competition among actors in the political arena is truly competition among ideas." MCFL, 479 U.S., at 259.

In addition to this immediate drowning out of noncorporate voices, there may be deleterious effects that follow soon thereafter. Corporate "domination" of electioneering, *Austin*, 494 U.S., at 659, can generate the impression that corporations dominate our democracy. When citizens turn on their televisions and radios before an election and hear only corporate electioneering, they may lose faith in their capacity, as citizens, to influence public policy. A Government captured by corporate interests, they may come to believe, will be neither responsive to their needs nor willing to give their views a fair hearing. The predictable result is cynicism and disenchantment: an increased perception that large spenders "'call the tune'" and a reduced "'willingness of voters to take part in democratic governance.'" *McConnell*, 540 U.S., at 144 (quoting Shrink Missouri, 528 U.S., at 390) ....

The majority's unwillingness to distinguish between corporations and humans similarly blinds it to the possibility that corporations' "war chests" and their special "advantages" in the legal realm, *Austin*, 494 U.S., at 659, may translate into special advantages in the market for legislation. When large numbers of citizens have a common stake in a measure that is under consideration, it may be very difficult for them to coordinate resources on behalf of their position. The corporate form, by contrast, "provides a simple way to channel rents to only those who have paid their dues, as it were. If you do not own stock, you do not benefit from the larger dividends or appreciation in the stock price caused by the passage of private interest legislation." Sitkoff, Corporate Political Speech, Political Extortion, and the Competition for Corporate Charters, 69 U. Chi. L. Rev. 1103, 1113 (2002). Corporations, that is, are uniquely equipped to seek laws that favor their owners, not simply because they have a lot of money but because of their legal and organizational structure. Remove all restrictions on their electioneering, and the door may be opened to a type of rent seeking that is "far more destructive" than what noncorporations are capable of. Ibid. It is for reasons such as these that our campaign finance jurisprudence has long appreciated that "the 'differing structures and purposes' of different entities 'may require different forms of regulation in order to protect the integrity of the electoral process.'" NRWC, 459 U.S., at 210 (quoting California Medical Assn., 453 U.S., at 201) ....

.... In the real world, we have seen, corporate domination of the airwaves prior to an election may decrease the average listener's exposure to relevant viewpoints, and it may diminish citizens' willingness and capacity to participate in the democratic process.

None of this is to suggest that corporations can or should be denied an opportunity to participate in election campaigns or in any other public forum (much less that a work of art such as Mr. Smith Goes to Washington may be banned), or to deny that some corporate speech may contribute significantly to public debate. What it shows, however, is that *Austin*'s "concern about corporate domination of the political process," 494 U.S., at 659, reflects more than a concern to protect governmental interests outside of the First Amendment. It also reflects a concern to facilitate First Amendment values by preserving some breathing room around the electoral "marketplace" of ideas, *ante*, at 19, 34, 38, 52, 54, the marketplace in which the actual people of this Nation determine how they will govern themselves. The majority seems oblivious to the simple truth that laws such as §203 do not merely pit the anticorruption interest against the First Amendment, but also pit competing First Amendment values against each other. There are, to be sure, serious concerns with any effort to balance the First Amendment rights of speakers against the First Amendment rights of listeners. But when the speakers in question are not real people and when the appeal to "First Amendment principles" depends almost entirely on the listeners' perspective, *ante*, at 1, 48, it becomes necessary to consider how listeners will actually be affected.

In critiquing *Austin*'s antidistortion rationale and campaign finance regulation more generally, our colleagues place tremendous weight on the example of media corporations. See *ante*, at 35–38, 46; *ante*, at 1, 11 (opinion of Roberts, C. J.);

ante, at 6 (opinion of Scalia, J.). Yet it is not at all clear that *Austin* would permit §203 to be applied to them. The press plays a unique role not only in the text, history, and structure of the First Amendment but also in facilitating public discourse; as the *Austin* Court explained, "media corporations differ significantly from other corporations in that their resources are devoted to the collection of information and its dissemination to the public," 494 U.S., at 667. Our colleagues have raised some interesting and difficult questions about Congress' authority to regulate electioneering by the press, and about how to define what constitutes the press. But that is not the case before us. Section 203 does not apply to media corporations, and even if it did, Citizens United is not a media corporation. There would be absolutely no reason to consider the issue of media corporations if the majority did not, first, transform Citizens United's as-applied challenge into a facial challenge and, second, invent the theory that legislatures must eschew all "identity"-based distinctions and treat a local nonprofit news outlet exactly the same as General Motors. This calls to mind George Berkeley's description of philosophers: "[W]e have first raised a dust and then complain we cannot see." Principles of Human Knowledge/Three Dialogues 38, 3 (R. Woolhouse ed. 1988) ....

2 Shareholder Protection

There is yet another way in which laws such as §203 can serve First Amendment values. Interwoven with *Austin*'s concern to protect the integrity of the electoral process is a concern to protect the rights of shareholders from a kind of coerced speech: electioneering expenditures that do not "reflec[t] [their] support." 494 U.S., at 660–661. When corporations use general treasury funds to praise or attack a particular candidate for office, it is the shareholders, as the residual claimants, who are effectively footing the bill. Those shareholders who disagree with the corporation's electoral message may find their financial investments being used to undermine their political convictions.

The PAC mechanism, by contrast, helps assure that those who pay for an electioneering communication actually support its content and that managers do not use general treasuries to advance personal agendas. Ibid. It "'allows corporate political participation without the temptation to use corporate funds for political influence, quite possibly at odds with the sentiments of some shareholders or members.'" *McConnell*, 540 U.S., at 204 (quoting Beaumont, 539 U.S., at 163). A rule that privileges the use of PACs thus does more than facilitate the political speech of like-minded shareholders; it also curbs the rent seeking behavior of executives and respects the views of dissenters ....

If and when shareholders learn that a corporation has been spending general treasury money on objectionable electioneering, they can divest. Even assuming that they reliably learn as much, however, this solution is only partial. The injury to the shareholders' expressive rights has already occurred; they might have preferred to keep that corporation's stock in their portfolio for any number of economic reasons; and they may incur a capital gains tax or other penalty from selling their shares, changing their pension plan, or the like. The shareholder protection rationale has been criticized as underinclusive, in that corporations also spend money on lobbying and charitable contributions in ways that any particular shareholder might disapprove. But those expenditures do not implicate the selection of public officials, an area in which "the interests of unwilling ... corporate shareholders [in not being] forced to subsidize that speech" "are at their zenith." *Austin*, 494 U.S., at 677 (Brennan, J., concurring). And in any event, the question is whether shareholder protection provides a basis for regulating expenditures in the weeks before an election, not whether additional types of corporate communications might similarly be conditioned on voluntariness ....

.... At bottom, the Court's opinion is thus a rejection of the common sense of the American people, who have recognized a need to prevent corporations from undermining self-government since the founding, and who have fought against the distinctive corrupting potential of corporate electioneering since the days of Theodore Roosevelt. It is a strange time to repudiate that common sense. While American democracy is imperfect, few outside the majority of this Court would have thought its flaws included a dearth of corporate money in politics.

I would affirm the judgment of the District Court.

Notes

1 See, e.g., *Bethel School Dist. No. 403* v. *Fraser.* 478 U.S. 675, 682 (1986) ("[T]he constitutional rights of students in public school are not automatically coextensive with the rights of adults in other settings").
2 See, e.g., *Jones* v. *North Carolina Prisoners' Labor Union, Inc.*, 433 U.S. 119, 129 (1977) ("In a prison context, an inmate does not retain those First Amendment rights that are inconsistent with his status as a prisoner or with the legitimate penological objectives of the corrections system" (internal quotation marks omitted)).
3 See, e.g., *Parker* v. *Levy*, 417 U.S. 733, 758 (1974) ("While the members of the military are not excluded from the protection granted by the First Amendment, the different character of the military community and of the military mission requires a different application of those protections").
4 See, e.g., 2 U.S. C. §441e(a)(1) (foreign nationals may not directly or indirectly make contributions or independent expenditures in connection with a U.S. election).
5 See, e.g., *Civil Service Comm'n* v. *Letter Carriers*, 413 U.S. 548 (1973) (upholding statute prohibiting Executive Branch employees from taking "any active part in political management or in political campaigns" (internal quotation marks omitted)); *Public Workers* v. *Mitchell*, 330 U.S. 75 (1947) (same); *United States* v. *Wurzbach*, 280 U.S. 396 (1930) (upholding statute prohibiting federal employees from making contributions to Members of Congress for "any political purpose whatever" (internal quotation marks omitted)); Ex parte Curtis, 106 U.S. 371 (1882) (upholding statute prohibiting certain federal employees from giving money to other employees for political purposes).
6 The majority states that the cases just cited are "inapposite" because they "stand only for the proposition that there are certain governmental functions that cannot operate without some restrictions on particular kinds of speech." *Ante*, at 25. The majority's creative suggestion that these cases stand only for that one proposition is quite implausible. In any event, the proposition lies at the heart of this case, as Congress and half the state legislatures have concluded, over many decades, that their core functions of administering elections and passing legislation cannot operate effectively without some narrow restrictions on corporate electioneering paid for by general treasury funds.
7 They are likewise entitled to regulate media corporations differently from other corporations "to ensure that the law 'does not hinder or prevent the institutional press from reporting on, and publishing editorials about, newsworthy events.'" *McConnell*, 540 U.S., at 208 (quoting *Austin v. Michigan Chamber of Commerce*, 494 U.S. 652. 668 (1990)).

8 The Court all but confesses that a categorical approach to speaker identity is untenable when it acknowledges that Congress might be allowed to take measures aimed at "preventing foreign individuals or associations from influencing our Nation's political process." *Ante*, at 46–47. Such measures have been a part of U.S. campaign finance law for many years. The notion that Congress might lack the authority to distinguish foreigners from citizens in the regulation of electioneering would certainly have surprised the Framers, whose "obsession with foreign influence derived from a fear that foreign powers and individuals had no basic investment in the well-being of the country." Teachout, The Anti-Corruption Principle, 94 Cornell L. Rev. 341, 393, n. 245 (2009) (hereinafter Teachout); see also U.S. Const., Art. I, §9. cl. 8 ("[N]o Person holding any Office of Profit or Trust ... shall, without the Consent of the Congress, accept of any present, Emolument, Office, or Title, of any kind whatever, from any King, Prince, or foreign State"). Professor Teachout observes that a corporation might be analogized to a foreign power in this respect, "inasmuch as its legal loyalties necessarily exclude patriotism." Teachout 393, n. 245.

9 See A. Bickel, The Supreme Court and the Idea of Progress 59–60 (1978); A. Meiklejohn, Political Freedom: The Constitutional Powers of the People 39–40 (1965); Tokaji, First Amendment Equal Protection: On Discretion, Inequality, and Participation, 101 Mich. L. Rev. 2409, 2508–2509 (2003). Of course, voting is not speech in a pure or formal sense, but then again neither is a campaign expenditure; both are nevertheless communicative acts aimed at influencing electoral outcomes. Cf. Strauss, Corruption, Equality, and Campaign Finance Reform, 94 Colum. L. Rev. 1369, 1383–1384 (1994) (hereinafter Strauss).

Review and Discussion Questions

1 Why does the majority believe that corporate speech ought to be protected by the First Amendment?
2 Does the majority make a good case that speech should not be proscribed based on the identity of the speaker? If you grant this point, does it follow that corporate speech thereby can't be proscribed?
3 How does the minority defend the constitutionality of restrictions on corporate speech against the position of the majority?
4 How does the minority defend the anti-distortion, anti-corruption, and shareholder-protection arguments supporting restrictions on corporate speech?

READING: THE ETHICS OF SMOKING

ROBERT E. GOODIN[*]

Unlike the next author, who doubts whether alcohol and other drugs cause people to lose control, Robert Goodin claims that tobacco's addictive nature means people do not voluntarily choose to smoke and therefore do not freely accept its risks. Beyond these "Kantian-style" questions about consent, he argues, lie other, more utilitarian issues about the social costs of smoking. Goodin describes those costs and then responds to two familiar arguments that defenders of smoking have

---

[*] Abridged from "The Ethics of Smoking" by Robert E. Goodin *Ethics* 99, no. 3 (1989).

offered in an attempt to show that smoking is not, in fact, economically costly. He concludes with a discussion of three proposals: mandatory warnings, bans, and "medicalization"—that is, making tobacco a prescription drug. Robert E. Goodin is Distinguished Professor of Philosophy at the Australian National University.

1 Do Smokers Voluntarily Accept the Risks?

Given what we know of the health risks from smoking, we may well be tempted to ban cigarette manufacturers from continuing to manufacture their product on the grounds that we are preventing them from causing illness to others in the same way that we prevent other manufacturers from releasing pollutants into the atmosphere, thereby causing danger to members of the community.

That would be to move too quickly. As Dworkin (1972/1983, p. 22) continues,

> The difference is ... that in the former but not the latter case the harm is of such a nature that it could be avoided by those individuals affected, if they so chose. The incurring of the harm requires the active cooperation of the victim. It would be a mistake in theory and hypocritical in practice to assert that our interference in such cases is just like our interference in standard cases of protecting others from harm.

Courts have been as sensitive to this distinction as moral philosophers, appealing to the venerable legal maxim, *volenti non fit injuria*, to hold that through their voluntary assumption of the risk smokers have waived any claims against cigarette manufacturers. In perhaps one of the most dramatic cases (given the well-established synergism between smoking and asbestos inhalation) the Fifth Circuit refused to enjoin cigarette manufacturers as codefendants in a suit against Johns-Manville, saying that "the danger is to the smoker who willingly courts it."[1]

Certainly there is, morally speaking, a world of difference between the harms that others inflict upon you and the harms that you inflict upon yourself. The question is simply whether, in the case of smoking, the active cooperation of the smoker really is such as to constitute voluntary acceptance of the consequent risks of illness and death. This question is decomposable into two further ones. The first concerns the question of whether smokers knew the risks. The second concerns the question of whether, even if smoking in full knowledge of the risks, they could be said to have "accepted" the risks in a sense that was fully voluntary.

The first is essentially a question of "informed consent." People can be held to have consented only if they knew to what they were supposedly consenting. In the personalized context of medical encounters, this means that each and every person being treated is told, in terms he or she understands, by the attending physician what the risks of the treatment might be (Gorovitz 1982, Chap. 3). For largely anonymous transactions in the market, such personalized standards are inappropriate. Instead, we are forced to infer consent from what people know or should have known (in the standard legal construct, what a "reasonable" person should have been expected to know) about the product. And in the anonymous world of the market, printed warnings necessarily take the place of face-to-face admonitions.

Cigarette manufacturers, in defending against product liability suits, have claimed on both these grounds that smokers should be construed as having consented to the risks that they have run. They claim, first, that any "reasonable" person should have known, and the "ordinary consumer" did indeed know, that smoking was an "inherently dangerous" activity. Their interrogatories constantly seek to establish that plaintiffs had, in their youth, consorted with people calling cigarettes "coffin nails," and so on. Manufacturers claim, second, that printing of government-mandated health warnings on cigarette packets from 1966 onward has constituted further explicit warning to users.

Now, of course, there are some risks (e.g., Buerger's disease, a circulatory condition induced, often in quite young people, by smoking that can result in amputation of limbs) of which smokers were never warned, by grandmother, or government health warnings either. Indeed, the warnings of both folk wisdom and cigarette packets in the 1960s and 1970s at least were desperately non-specific; and there is a more general question whether an all-purpose warning that "X may be hazardous to your health," without specifying just how likely X is to cause just what sorts of harms, is adequate warning to secure people's informed consent at all.

Furthermore, cigarette manufacturers take back through their advertising what is given by way of warnings.[2] The problem is not so much one of literally deceptive advertising—though there is evidence of that, too (U.S. FTC 1981, 1984, 1985) as it is one of the widespread use of deceptively healthy imagery (U.S. FTC 1981, pp. 428a, 491a). The printed warnings may say "smoking kills," but the advertising images are the very picture of robust good health. Cowboys, sports, and the great outdoors figure centrally in the ads. The U.S. Federal Trade Commission has continually warned Congress that "current practices and methods of cigarette advertising" have the effect of "reducing anxieties about the health risks posed by cigarette smoking" (U.S. FTC 1984, p. 5), "negat[ing] the effect of health warnings because they imply that smoking is a habit which is compatible with performing various outdoor activities and having a strong healthy body" (U.S. FTC 1985, p. 5).[3] The point is not that advertising bypasses consumers' capacity to reason and somehow renders them unfree to choose intelligently whether or not to consume the product. The point is, rather, that tobacco companies in effect are giving out and, more important, consumers are receiving—conflicting information. The implicit health claims of the advertising imagery conflict with the explicit health warnings and thus undercut any *volenti* or informed-consent defense companies might try to mount on the basis of those warnings.

Despite tobacco companies' best efforts, however, nearly everyone—smokers included—knows, in broad outline, the health risks that smoking entails. In a 1978 Gallup poll, only 24 percent of heavy smokers claimed they were unaware of or did not believe the evidence that smoking is hazardous. How that recalcitrant residual should be handled is a hard question. Having smoked thousands of packets containing increasingly stern warnings, and having been exposed to hundreds of column inches of newspaper reporting and several hours of broadcasting about smoking's hazards, they are presumably incorrigible in their false beliefs in this regard. Providing them with still more information is likely to prove pointless.

Ordinarily it is not the business of public policy to prevent people from relying on false inferences from full information which would harm only themselves. Sometimes, however, it is. One such case comes when the false beliefs would lead to decisions that are "far-reaching, potentially dangerous, and irreversible"—as, for example, with people who believe that when they jump out of a tenth-story window they will float upward (Dworkin 1972/1983, p. 31).

We are particularly inclined toward intervention when false beliefs with such disastrous results are traceable to familiar, well-understood forms of cognitive defect. One is "wishful thinking": smokers believing the practice is safe because they smoke rather than smoking because they believe it to be safe (Pears 1984). There is substantial evidence that smokers believe, groundlessly, that they are less vulnerable to smoking-related diseases; there is also evidence that they came to acquire those beliefs, and to "forget" what they previously knew about the dangers of smoking, after they took up the habit (Leventhal, Glynn, and Fleming 1987). Another cognitive defect is the "anchoring" fallacy (Kahneman, Slovic, and Tversky 1982): people smoke many times without any (immediately perceptible) bad effects; and ... extrapolating from their own experience, they therefore quite reasonably but quite wrongly conclude that smoking is safe for them. Yet another phenomenon, sometimes regarded as a cognitive defect, is "time-discounting": since young smokers will not suffer the full effects of smoking-related diseases for some years to come, they may puff away happily now with little regard for the consequences if they attach relatively little importance to future pains relative to present pleasures in their utility functions (Fuchs 1982). All of these cognitive defects point to relatively weak forms of irrationality. In and of themselves, they would not be enough to justify interference with people's liberty, perhaps. But when they lead people to make decisions that are far-reaching, potentially dangerous, and irreversible, perhaps intervention would be justified.

Interfering with people's choices in such cases is paternalistic, admittedly. But there are many different layers of paternalism. What is involved here is a relatively weak form of paternalism, working within the individual's own theory of the good and merely imposing upon him better means of achieving his own ends.[4] It is one thing to stop people who want to commit suicide from doing so but quite another to stop people who want to live from acting in a way that they falsely believe to be safe. Smokers who deny the health risks fall into that latter, easier category.

The larger and harder question is how to deal with the great majority of smokers who, knowing the risks, continue smoking anyway. Of course, it might be said that they do not really know the risks. Although most acknowledge that smoking is "unhealthy," in some vague sense, few know exactly what chances they run of exactly what diseases. In one poll, 49 percent of smokers did not know that smoking causes most cases of lung cancer, 63 percent that it causes most cases of bronchitis, and 85 percent that it causes most cases of emphysema. Overestimating badly the risks of dying in other, more dramatic ways (car crashes, etc.), people badly underestimate the relative risks of dying in the more mundane ways associated with smoking—thus allowing them to rationalize further their smoking behavior as being "not all that dangerous," compared to other things that they are also doing.[5] Besides all that, there is the distinction between "knowing intellectually" some statistic and "feeling in your guts" its full implications. Consent counts—morally, as well as legally—only if it is truly informed consent, only if people know what it is to which they are consenting. That, in turn, requires not only that we can state the probabilities but also that we "appreciate them in an emotionally genuine manner" (Dworkin 1972/1983, p. 30). There is reason to believe that smokers do not.

It may still be argued that, as long as people had the facts, they can and should be held responsible if they chose not to act upon them when they could have done so. It may be folly for utilitarian policymakers to rely upon people's such imperfect responses to facts for purposes of constructing social welfare functions and framing public policies around them. But there is the separate matter of who ought to be blamed when some self-inflicted harm befalls people. There, arguably, responsibility ought to be on people's own shoulders (Knowles 1977; Wikler 1987). Arguably, we ought to stick to that judgment, even if people were "pressured" into smoking by the bullying of aggressive advertising or peer pressure.

What crucially transforms the "voluntary acceptance" argument is evidence of the addictive nature of cigarette smoking. Of course, saying that smoking is addictive is not to say that no one can ever give it up. Many have done so. By the same token, though, more than 70 percent of American service-men addicted to heroin in Vietnam gave it up when returning to the United States; yet we still rightly regard heroin as an addictive drug. The test of addictiveness is not impossibility but rather difficulty of withdrawal ....

To establish a substance as addictive, we require evidence of "physical need" for the substance among its users. That evidence is necessary to prove smoking is an addiction rather than just a "habit" (U.S. DHEW 1964, chaps. 13–14), a psychological dependence, or a matter of mere sociological pressure (Daniels 1985, p. 159)—none of which would undercut, in a way that addictiveness does, claims that the risks of smoking are voluntarily incurred. That physical link has now been established, though. Particular receptors for the active ingredients of tobacco smoke have been discovered in the brain; the physiological sites and mechanisms by which nicotine acts on the brain have now been well mapped, and its tendency to generate compulsive, repetitive behavior in consequence has been well established. Such evidence—summarized in the surgeon general's 1988 report—has been one of the crucial factors leading the World Health Organization and the American Psychiatric Association to classify "nicotine dependence" as an addiction.

None of that evidence proves that it would be literally impossible for smokers to resist the impulse to smoke. Through extraordinary acts of will, they might. Nor does any of that evidence prove that it is literally impossible for them to break their dependence altogether. Many have. Recall, however, that the issue is not one of impossibility but rather of how hard people should have to try before their will is said to be sufficiently impaired that their agreement does not count as genuine consent.

The evidence suggests that nicotine addicts have to try very hard indeed. This is the second crucial fact to establish in proving a substance addictive.[6] Central among the WHO/APA criteria for diagnosing nicotine dependence is the requirement of evidence of "continuous use of tobacco for at least one month with ... unsuccessful attempts to stop or significantly reduce the amount of tobacco use on a permanent basis." A vast majority of smokers do indeed find themselves in this position. The surgeon general reports that 90 percent of regular smokers have tried to quit. Another 1975 survey found that 84 percent of smokers had attempted to stop but that only 36 percent of them had succeeded in maintaining their changed behavior for a whole year.[7]

Such evidence of smokers trying and failing to stop is rightly regarded as central to the issue of addiction, philosophically as well as diagnostically. Some describe free will in terms of "second-order volitions"—desires about desires—controlling "first-order" ones (Frankfurt 1971). Others talk of one's "evaluational structure" controlling one's "motivational structure," so one strives to obtain something if and only if one thinks it of value (Watson 1975, 1977). Addiction—the absence of free will—is thus a matter of first-order volitions winning out over second-order ones and surface desires prevailing over the agent's own deeper values. In the case of smoking, trying to stop can be seen as a manifestation of one's second-order volitions or one's deeper values and failing to stop as evidence of the triumph of first-order surface desires over them. The same criteria the WHO/APA use to diagnose nicotine dependence also establish the impairment of the smoker's free will, philosophically.

Various policy implications follow from evidence of addictiveness. One might be that over-the-counter sales of cigarettes should be banned. If the product is truly addictive, then we have no more reason to respect a person's voluntary choice (however well informed) to abandon his future volition to an addiction than we have for respecting a person's voluntary choice (however well informed) to sell himself into slavery (Mill 1859/1975, pp. 126–27). I am unsure how far to press this argument. After all, we do permit people to bind their future selves (through contracts, e.g.). But if it is the size of the stakes or the difficulty of breaking out of the bonds that makes the crucial difference, then acquiring a lethal and hard-to-break addiction is much more like a slavery contract than it is like an ordinary commercial commitment.

In any case, addictiveness thus defined makes it far easier to justify interventions that on their face appear paternalistic. In some sense, they would then be not paternalistic at all. Where people "wish to stop smoking, but do not have the requisite willpower ... we are not imposing a good on someone who rejects it. We are simply using coercion to enable people to carry out their own goals" (Dworkin 1972/1983, p. 32). It is, of course, genuinely difficult to decide which is the "authentic" self: with whom should we side, when the person who asks us to help him "enforce rules on himself" repudiates the rules at the time they need to be enforced? But at least we have more of a warrant for interference in such cases than if we were never asked for assistance at all. Much of the assistance we render in such situations will necessarily be of a very personal nature and outside the scope of public policy. There is nonetheless a substantial role for public policy in these realms. Banning or restricting smoking in public places (especially the workplace) can contribute crucially to an individual's own efforts at smoking cessation, for example.

The force of the addiction findings ... is to undercut the claim that there is any continuing consent to the risks involved in smoking. There might have been consent in the very first instance—in smoking your first cigarette. But once you were hooked, you lost the capacity to consent in any meaningful sense on a continuing basis. As Hume (1760) says, to consent implies the possibility of doing otherwise; and addiction substantially deprives you of the capacity to do other than continue smoking. So once you have become addicted to nicotine, your subsequent smoking cannot be taken as indicating your consent to the risks.

If there is to be consent at all, then, it can only be consent in the very first instance, that is, when you first began to smoke. That, in turn, seriously undercuts the extent to which cigarette manufacturers can rely upon *volenti* or informed-consent defenses in product liability litigation and its moral analogues. Many of those now dying from tobacco-induced diseases started smoking well before warnings began appearing on packets in 1966; their consent to the risks of smoking could only have been based on "common knowledge" and "folk wisdom."

That is a short-term problem, though, since that cohort of smokers will eventually die off. The more serious, continuing problem is this. A vast majority of smokers began smoking in their early to middle teens. Evidence suggests that "of those teenagers who smoke more than a single cigarette only 15 percent avoid becoming regular dependent smokers"; and a great majority, perhaps up to 95 percent, of regular adult smokers are thought to have been addicted before they were twenty-one years of age. Being below the age of consent, they were incapable of consenting in the first instance;[8] and being addicted by the time they reached the age of consent they were incapable of consenting later, either.

2 Do the Benefits Outweigh the Costs?

In addition to Kantian-style questions about informed consent, there are utilitarian-style questions of overall social welfare to be considered in this connection. Presumably it is in these latter terms that public health measures are ordinarily justified. We do not leave it to the discretion of consumers, however well informed, whether or not to drink grossly polluted water, ingest grossly contaminated foods, or inject grossly dangerous drugs. We simply prohibit such things, on grounds of public health, by appeal to utilitarian calculations of one sort or another.

To some extent, the same considerations that lead us to believe such measures are justified on grounds of social utility might also give us grounds for presuming people's (at least hypothetical) consent to them, also. To some extent, we can appeal to externality arguments to justify the measures: contagious diseases and costly cures affect the community as a whole. But to some extent, the justification of public health measures must be baldly paternalistic, turning on the benefits accruing to the person himself from avoiding diseases that he might otherwise cavalierly court.

All those considerations are in play in the case of smoking. Paternalistic elements have been canvassed above. There are contagion effects, too: being among smokers exerts strong social pressure upon people to start smoking and makes it difficult for people to stop; and these contagion effects are particularly pronounced among young people, whose smoking behavior is strongly affected by that of parents and peers. As regards externalities, smoking is believed to cause at least half of residential fires, harming family and neighbors as well as the smokers themselves; treating smoking-induced illnesses is costly, and even in the United States some 40 percent of those costs are borne by the public; premature deaths cost the economy productive members and entail pain and suffering for family and friends; and so on.

Dealing just in those nonquantified terms of human costs, smoking must surely stand indicted. The U.S. surgeon general says it is the "chief, single, avoidable cause of death in our society and the most important public health problem of our time." Cigarettes kill 25 percent of their users, even when used as their manufacturers intended they be used. Suppose a toaster or lawnmower had a similar record. It would be whipped off the market forthwith. On utilitarian grounds, there would seem to be no reason why cigarettes should be treated any differently.

For those preferring hard, solid numbers, economists (focusing principally upon medical costs and lost productivity) calculate that smoking costs the American economy on net $52–$62 billion per year. By that reckoning, too, there is clearly a case to answer against smoking, on grounds of social utility.

There are, in fact, rejoinders available on two levels. One is a microlevel argument couched in terms of benefits to smokers themselves from the practice. The other is a macrolevel argument, querying the real costs to society from the practice.

The first style of argument … is that cost-benefit calculations should take into account whatever subjective pleasures smokers derive from the practice. In the boldest statement of this very standard microeconomic proposition, Buchanan (1970) argues that if fully informed people would be willing to buy the product in preference to all others on the market, then we would be making them worse off (in preference—which for him equates to welfare terms) by banning that product from the market ….

The … way around the microeconomic argument … starts from the observation that cigarette sales are substantially price inelastic [i.e., sales do not go up and down much as prices fluctuate—Ed. note]. Estimates of just how inelastic vary. But much evidence suggests that even rather large increases in the price of the product (induced, e.g., by increased excise taxes) result in only slight decreases in sales to adult consumers. We might infer either of two conclusions from that fact. One would be that there is an enormous "consumer's surplus" (subjective benefit, net of subjective cost) that smokers enjoy, which even large taxes would not extinguish. Price inelasticity would then be taken as evidence that there are substantial subjective gains to consumers from smoking, which ought to be set off against the calculated social costs in any utilitarian decision procedure. Which would predominate we cannot say in advance. But other things being equal, utilitarians ought to be more inclined to allow smoking the more satisfaction consumers derive from it.

Alternatively, we might infer from price inelasticity that people are indeed addicted to the product. Present users will pay any price for cigarettes for the same reason they will pay any price for heroin: they cannot help themselves. Most of them would rather not, according to surveys. Most wish they were not hooked but backslide every time they try to get unhooked.

There is, admittedly, a bit of a problem in determining what should count as a "benefit" to addicts. In one sense, they benefit from having their habits serviced—certainly they would suffer in some obvious sense otherwise. So in a way, the implication of the addiction interpretation would be much the same as that of the consumer surplus interpretation, that is, present users benefit, as indicated by their willingness to pay, from smoking. In another way, however, they would benefit—even in terms of subjective preferences—if they were to stop. In the same terms, others would benefit if they were never to start.

Addictive substances are not ordinary economic goods. Ordinarily, cultivating new tastes (acquiring a taste for fine foods, e.g.) is thought to make you better off—able to derive more pleasure—than before. With addictions, however, you are worse off, even in your own eyes, than before; whatever momentary pleasures you derive from servicing the addiction, you would prefer to stop but find that you cannot. Thus, we should do whatever we can to prevent new addicts, who would be subjectively worse off once addicted than they were before. As regards existing addicts, there may be a utilitarian case for continuing to service their habits, though even they would be subjectively better off in the long run if they could be helped to break the habit.

Whereas the first rejoinder to the utilitarian argument for curbing smoking alleges an underestimate of consumer benefits from smoking, a second rejoinder alleges an overestimate of net social costs. The less interesting versions of this argument point to the tobacco industry's contribution to the aggregate economy—but a contribution of $3.3 billion to the Gross National Product, set off against the $52–$62 billion cost estimates described above, leaves the industry's account well in the red.

A more interesting version of this argument alleges that the above procedures overstate true social costs. As regards the narrow question of health care costs, everyone dies of something sooner or later. For an accurate assessment of the medical costs of smoking-related diseases, then, we must deduct the costs that would have been incurred had the people killed by smoking died of something else later (Wikler 1978/1983, p. 46). In terms of hospital bed days and overall medical expenditure, over the course of their lives as a whole, there is some evidence to suggest that there may be no significant difference between smokers and nonsmokers.

Similarly, perhaps we need not worry too much about externalities, in the sense of the unfair imposition of burdens on others. Smokers could be refused treatment in public hospital beds and made to pay their own way. They could be required to carry complete insurance against smoking-related diseases; and to avoid unfairness to coinsureds, we could further require that risks to smokers be pooled only with those of other smokers (Wikler 1978/1983, p. 49), as is increasingly done by insurance companies for purely commercial reasons anyway. Alternatively, and perhaps more practically, "users of cigarettes and alcohol ... could be made to pay an excise tax, the proceeds of which would cover the costs of treatment for lung cancer and other resulting illnesses" (Wikler 1978/1983, p. 49).

In those narrow terms, at least, smokers already more than pay their own way. In the United Kingdom, the cigarette tax accounts for over 8 percent of total government revenue. It has been estimated that in Ontario it takes only 8 percent of tobacco tax revenues to pay for all public health care expenditure on smoking-related disease. Even in the United States, if we count only the share of health care costs borne by the federal government, that is almost exactly counterbalanced by the federal excise tax on cigarettes—although there, as in those other cases as well, matters would look very different if we were to count total costs to the economy and society (e.g., lost productivity) as well as just medical costs borne by the government.

In other ways, too, smokers save us money by dying early. Just think:

> Smoking tends to cause few problems during a person's productive years and then to kill the individual before the need to provide years of social security and pension payments. From this perspective, the truly burdensome individual

may be the unreasonably fit senior citizen who lives on for thirty years after retirement, contributing to the bankruptcy of the social security system, and using up savings that would have reverted to the public purse via inheritance taxes, had an immoderate lifestyle brought an early death.

(Wikler 1978/1983, p. 46)

In the eyes of many, this will appear to be a reductio ad absurdum. What it seems to suggest is nothing less than a thinly veiled form of not-altogether-voluntary euthanasia. Many suppose it is unjust, if not necessarily uneconomic, to encourage people to die off promptly upon their ceasing to be productive members of the work force (cf. Battin 1987).

What this is a reductio of, however, is not the utilitarian calculus but rather an economic calculus that serves as such a poor proxy for it. Most people who are already retired would wish to enjoy a long and happy retirement; most people still in the workforce would wish the same for themselves and, indeed, for their elders. Those preferences, too, must be factored into any proper calculus of social utility. Once they are, early deaths induced by smoking are almost certain to turn out to be costs rather than benefits in the broader social scale of values.

3 Policy Options

Publicity

Mandatory health warnings on cigarette packages and advertisements, and public health campaigns more generally, are [a] popular government response to smoking. Some thirty-eight countries now require such warnings. Among the more important reasons for the popularity of this strategy is that health warnings and public information campaigns are seen as the least paternalistic forms of government intervention. Mill (1859/1975, p. 118) himself holds that "labelling [a] drug with some word expressive of its dangerous character, may be enforced without violation of liberty," since presumably "the buyer cannot wish not to know that the thing he possesses has poisonous qualities." In this judgment, Mill has been followed by a host of more recent commentators.

No doubt publicizing health risks reduces smoking. Publication of the two great official reports—by the Royal College of Physicians in 1962 and the surgeon general in 1964—produced long-term drops in cigarette consumption by between 7 percent and 14 percent. The antismoking television advertisements, allowed under the Fairness Doctrine in the United States until the 1970 legislation banning television advertising of cigarettes altogether, seemed to have an effect almost twice as strong.

There are reasons to believe that health campaigns cannot work in isolation from other policy initiatives, though. Specifically, allowing cigarette advertising undercuts health messages by inducing newspapers and magazines to engage in self-censorship of health reports that might offend their tobacco sponsors. Thus, a publicity campaign might not really succeed unless coupled with something stronger: an advertising ban. Otherwise the message simply might not get carried effectively.

Bans

There are, in fact, various regulatory options under this general heading. Most modestly, we might ban cigarette advertising, either in particular settings (e.g., on television) or in general. More dramatically, we might ban sales of cigarettes, either to a certain group (e.g., children) or in general. Most dramatically, we might ban use of tobacco, either in particular settings (e.g., where there is a particular fire hazard, as in elevators, theaters, and subways, or where there are synergistic effects with other substances in the immediate vicinity, such as asbestos) or in general.

These are separable policy options, any one of which can be pursued independently of any other. From 1975, Norway has banned advertising but not sale of cigarettes. Similarly, we can ban sale without banning consumption. (Most states allow you to eat game birds and fish you shoot or catch yourself but not to sell them.) Though there is no modern experience of a general ban on sale or use of tobacco, advertising bans are reasonably common: fifteen countries have total bans, and another twelve have strong partial bans.

Advertising bans can be particularly helpful in reducing cigarette consumption among adolescents, with whom we should be especially concerned on grounds of "informed consent." There is good evidence that cigarette advertising in general, and sport sponsorship in particular, appeals to children. Conversely, banning advertising of cigarettes in Norway in 1975 led to a sharp decline in the percentage of teenagers who subsequently became daily smokers.

Against bans on the use or sale of tobacco, the Prohibition analogy is standardly urged. Already we have evidence of substantial "bootlegging" (or "buttlegging") of cigarettes between states with low cigarette taxes and those with high ones. Any more serious ban on sale or use of tobacco would no doubt lead to even more illicit activity of this sort. Even accepting such slippage, however, this strategy is still bound to reduce smoking substantially. Whether more would be lost in terms of respect for the law than would be gained in terms of public health remains an open question.

Medicalization

If smoking tobacco is addictive, then perhaps a medical rather than legal or economic response is indicated. The idea here would be to make tobacco a prescription drug, available to registered users only.[9] The model would be methadone maintenance programs for heroin addicts, perhaps. The aim in making tobacco a prescription drug would be to respond humanely to the needs of present addicts, while discouraging new users. Again, it would be impossible to stop all new users—they can always smoke the cigarettes of registered users illicitly, unless we require registered users to smoke only in the clinics. But again, such a policy would have a strong tendency in the desired direction.

Notes

1 *Johns-Manville Sales Corp. v. International Association of Machinists, Machinists Local 1609,* 621 F.2d 756 at 759 (5th Cir. 1980).

2 Warnings that "smoking may be dangerous," when conjoined with pictures of people enjoying dangerous sports (white-water rafting, etc.), perversely serve to make smoking more attractive; warnings that "smoking may complicate pregnancy," when conjoined with sexually provocative photos in a magazine devoted to casual sex without procreation, again perversely undercut the health warnings.
3 Literally, of course, it is—at least broadly speaking and in the short run. But in the medium to long term, participation even in purely recreational sport (not to mention serious sport, where peak performance is required) is impaired by the consequences of smoking. Insofar as young smokers are encouraged in the belief that they can always quit, should smoking become a problem later, that is a false belief (as shown by the addiction evidence, discussed below); and advertisements carrying any such implications once again would count as clearly deceptive advertising.
4 One of a person's ends—continued life—at least. Perhaps the person has other ends ("relaxation," or whatever) that are well served by smoking, and insofar as "people taking risks actually value the direct consequences associated with them ... it is more difficult to intrude paternalistically" (Daniels 1985, p. 158, 163). But assuming that smoking is not the only means to the other ends—not the only way to relax, etc.—the intrusion is only minimally difficult to justify.
5 Logically, it would be perfectly possible for people both to underestimate the extent of the risk and simultaneously to overreact to it. People might suppose the chances of snakebite are slight but live in mortal fear of it nonetheless. Psychologically, however, the reverse seems to happen. People's subjective probability estimates of an event's likelihood increase the more they dread it and the more "psychologically available" the event therefore is to them (Kahneman, Slovic, and Tversky 1982). Smoking-related diseases, in contrast, tend to be "quiet killers" of which people have little direct or indirect experience, which tend to be underreported in newspapers and which act on people one at a time rather than catastrophically killing many people at once (Lichtenstein et al. 1978, p. 567). Smoking-related diseases being psychologically less available to people in these ways, they underestimate their frequency dramatically—by a factor of eight, in the case of lung cancer, according to one study (Slovic, Fischhoff, and Lichtenstein 1982, p. 469).
6 There are other physical needs that we would have trouble renouncing—such as our need for food—that we would be loath to call "addictions." Be that as it may, we would also be loath, for precisely those reasons, to say that we "eat of our own free will" (we would have no hesitation [in saying] that someone who makes a credible threat of preventing us from eating has "coerced" us, etc.). Since involuntariness and impairment of free will are what is really at issue here, those thus do seem to be the aspects of addictiveness that matter in the present context.
7 The graphs mapping the relapse rate after a given period of time are almost identical for nicotine and for heroin, although it might be wrong to make too much of that fact. (Perhaps heroin addicts find both that it is harder to give up and that they have more reason to do so: then relapse rates would appear the same, even though heroin is more addictive in the sense of being harder to give up.) Pointing to the addiction evidence, U.S. federal courts have decided that "smoking can be an involuntary act for some persons" and that Social Security disability benefits may not therefore be routinely withheld from victims of smoking-related diseases on the grounds that they are suffering from voluntarily self-inflicted injuries (*Gordon v. Schweiker*, 725 F.2d 231, 236 [1984]).
8 Strictly speaking, ability to consent is not predicated—legally or morally—upon attaining some arbitrary age but, rather, upon having attained the capacity to make reasoned choices in the matter at hand. The level of understanding manifested by teenagers about smoking clearly suggests that their decision to start smoking cannot be deemed an informed choice, however (Leventhal, Glynn, and Fleming 1987).
9 Ironically, nicotine-containing chewing gum is a controlled prescription drug in the United States, United Kingdom, Sweden, and Canada, whereas wet snuff (whose risks are, if anything, greater) is freely available over the counter to adult purchasers. Czechoslovakia now requires consumers of twenty or more cigarettes per day to

register with the medical service that monitors respiratory diseases, perhaps as a first step in this "medicalization" direction (*Daily Express,* London, February 17, 1986).

References

Battin, Margaret P. "Age Rationing and the Just Distribution of Health Care: Is There a Duty to Die?" *Ethics* 97 (1987): 317–40.
Buchanan, James M. "In Defense of Caveat Emptor." *University of Chicago Law Review* 38 (1970): 64–73.
Daniels, Norman. *Just Health Care.* Princeton, NJ: Princeton University Press, 1985.
Dworkin, Gerald. "Paternalism." *Monist* 56, no. 1 (1972): 64–84. Reprinted in Sartorius, ed., 1983, 19–34.
Frankfurt, Harry G. "Freedom of the Will and the Concept of a Person." *Journal of Philosophy* 68 (1971): 5–20.
Fuchs, Victor R. "Time Preference and Health: An Exploratory Study." In *Economic Aspects of Health,* ed. Victor R. Fuchs, 93–120. Chicago, IL: University of Chicago Press, 1982.
Gorovitz, Samuel. *Doctors' Dilemmas.* New York: Oxford University Press, 1982.
Hume, David. "Of the Original Contract." In *Essays, Literary, Moral and Political.* London: A. Millar, 1760.
Kahneman, D., P. Slovic, and A. Tversky, eds. *Judgment under Uncertainty.* Cambridge: Cambridge University Press, 1982.
Knowles, John H. "The Responsibility of the Individual." *Daedalus* 106, no. 1 (1977): 57–80.
Leventhal, Howard, Kathleen Glynn, and Raymond Fleming, "Is the Smoking Decision an 'Informed Choice'?" *Journal of the American Medical Association* 257 (1987): 3373–76.
Lichtenstein, S., P. Slovic, B. Fischhoff, M. Layman, and B. Combs. "Judged Frequency of Lethal Events." *Journal of Experimental Psychology (Human Learning and Memory)* 4 (1978): 551–78.
Mill, John Stuart. On Liberty. In *Three Essays,* ed. Richard Wollheim, 1–141. Oxford: Oxford University Press, 1975 (1859).
Pears, David. *Motivated Irrationality.* Oxford: Clarendon, 1984.
Slovic, P., B. Fischhoff, and S. Lichtenstein, "Fact vs. Fears: Understanding Perceived Risks." In Kahneman, Slovic, and Tversky, eds., 1982, 463–89.
United States Department of Health, Education and Welfare (U.S. DHEW). Smoking and Health. Report of the Advisory Committee to the Surgeon General of the Public Health Service. Washington, DC: Government Printing Office, 1964.
United States Federal Trade Commission (U.S. FTC). Staff Report on the Cigarette Advertising Investigation, Matthew L. Meyers, chairman. Public version. Washington, DC: FTC, 1981.
U.S. FTC. A Report to the Congress Pursuant to the Federal Cigarette Labelling and Advertising Act. Washington, DC: Government Printing Office, 1984.
U.S. FTC. A Report to the Congress Pursuant to the Federal Cigarette Labelling and Advertising Act. Washington, DC: Government Printing Office, 1985.
Watson, Gary. "Free Agency." *Journal of Philosophy* 72 (1975): 205–20.
Watson, Gary. "Skepticism about Weakness of Will." *Philosophical Review* 86 (1977): 316–39.
Wikler, Daniel. "Persuasion and Coercion for Health: Ethical Issues in Government Efforts to Change Life-styles." *Health and Society* (now *Milbank Quarterly*) 56 (1978): 303–38. Reprinted in Sartorius, ed., 1983, 35–59.
Wikler, Daniel. "Personal Responsibility for Illness." In *Health Care Ethics,* ed. D. van de Veer and T. Regan, 326–58. Philadelphia, PA: Temple University Press, 1987.

Review and Discussion Questions

1 What role do ads play in encouraging smoking, according to Goodin?
2 Describe the three "cognitive defects" that Goodin thinks are relevant in assessing smoking.
3 In what "weak" sense does Goodin agree that interfering with smoking is paternalistic?

4 Describe how Goodin responds to those who say people voluntarily accept the risks of smoking.
5 What are the costs of smoking, according to Goodin?
6 How does Goodin respond to those who claim the benefits of smoking are often underestimated?
7 How does Goodin respond to those who claim that the costs of smoking are often overestimated?
8 What response does Goodin give to each of the three policy options?

READING: ADDICTION AND DRUG POLICY

DANIEL SHAPIRO[*]

Much of the debate surrounding drug legalization revolves around the nature of drug addiction and the extent to which it is possible for addicts to quit. In this essay, Daniel Shapiro attacks what he terms the "standard view" that heroin and cocaine are inherently addictive. Instead, he claims, we should see drug use not in terms of pharmacology and addictive potency but rather in terms of how the experience is interpreted, focusing specifically on the "setting" and the "set" of drug use. He then discusses cigarette smoking and how its pharmacological effects, social setting, and personal set interact, and concludes with a brief answer to his student-critics. Daniel Shapiro is Professor of Philosophy at West Virginia University.

Most people think that illegal drugs, such as cocaine and heroin, are highly addictive. Usually their addictiveness is explained by pharmacology: their chemical composition and its effects on the brain are such that, after a while, it's hard to stop using them. This view of drug addiction—I call it the standard view—underlies most opposition to legalizing cocaine and heroin. James Wilson's (1990) arguments are typical: legalization increases access, and increased access to addictive drugs increases addiction. The standard view also underlies the increasingly popular opinion, given a philosophical defense by Robert Goodin (1989), that cigarette smokers are addicts in the grip of a powerful drug.

However, the standard view is false: pharmacology, I shall argue, does not by itself do much to explain drug addiction. I will offer a different explanation of drug addiction and discuss its implications for the debate about drug legalization.

Problems with the Standard View

We label someone as a drug addict because of his behavior. A drug addict uses drugs repeatedly, compulsively, and wants to stop or cut back on his use but finds it's difficult to do so; at its worst, drug addiction dominates or crowds out other

---

[*] This is a slightly revised version of a paper originally published in an earlier edition. Copyright © 2003 Daniel Shapiro. Reprinted by permission.

activities and concerns. The standard view attempts to explain this compulsive behavior by the drug's effects on the brain. Repeated use of an addictive drug induces cravings and the user comes to need a substantial amount to get the effect she wants, i.e., develops tolerance. If the user tries to stop, she then suffers very disagreeable effects, called withdrawal symptoms. (For more detail on the standard view, see American Psychiatric Association 1994, 176–81.)

Cravings, tolerance, and withdrawal symptoms: do these explain drug addiction? A craving or strong desire to do something doesn't *make* one do something: one can act on a desire or ignore it *or* attempt to extinguish it. Tolerance explains why the user increases her intake to get the effect she wants, but that doesn't explain why she would find it difficult to *stop wanting* this effect. Thus, the key idea in the standard view is really withdrawal symptoms, because that is needed to explain the difficulty in extinguishing the desire to take the drug or to stop wanting the effects the drug produces. However, for this explanation to work, these symptoms have to be really bad, for if they aren't, why not just put up with them as a small price to pay for getting free of the drug? However, withdrawal symptoms aren't *that* bad. Heroin is considered terribly addictive, yet pharmacologists describe its withdrawal symptoms as like having a bad flu for about a week: typical withdrawal symptoms include fever, diarrhea, sneezing, muscle cramps, and vomiting (Kaplan 1983, 15, 19, 35). While a bad flu is quite unpleasant, it's not so bad that one has little choice but to take heroin rather than experience it. Indeed, most withdrawal symptoms for any drug cease within a few weeks, yet most heavy users who relapse do so after that period and few drug addicts report withdrawal symptoms as the reason for their relapse (Peele 1985, 19–20, 67; Schacter 1982, 436–44; Waldorf, Reinarman, and Murphy 1991, 241).

Thus, cravings, tolerance, and withdrawal symptoms cannot explain addiction. An additional problem for the standard view is that most drug users, whether they use legal or illegal drugs, do not become addicts, and few addicts remain so permanently. (Cigarette smokers are a partial exception, which I discuss later.) Anonymous surveys of drug users by the Substance Abuse and Mental Health Services Administration indicate that less than 10 percent of those who have tried powder cocaine use it monthly (National Household Survey of Drug Abuse 2001, tables H1 and H2). Furthermore, most monthly users are not addicts; a survey of young adults, for example (Johnston, O'Malley, and Bachman for the National Institute on Drug Abuse 1996, 84–5), found that less than 10 percent of monthly cocaine users used it daily. (Even a daily user need not be an addict; someone who drinks daily is not thereby an alcoholic.) The figures are not appreciably different for crack cocaine (Erickson, Edward, Smart, and Murray 1994, 167–74, 231–32, Morgan and Zimmer 1997, 142–44) and only slightly higher for heroin (Husak 1992, 125; Sullum 2003, 228). These surveys have been confirmed by longitudinal studies—studies of a set of users over time—which indicate that moderate and/or controlled use of these drugs is the norm, not the exception, and that even heavy users do not inevitably march to addiction, let alone remain permanent addicts (Waldorf, Reinarman, and Murphy 1991; Erickson, Smart, and Murray 1994; Zinberg 1984, 111–34, 152–71). The standard view has to explain the preeminence of controlled use by arguing that drug laws reduce access to illegal drugs. However, I argue below that even with easy access to drugs most people use them responsibly, and so something other than the law and pharmacology must explain patterns of drug use.

An Alternative View

I will defend a view of addiction summed up by Norman Zinberg's book, *Drug, Set, and Setting* (1984). "Drug" means pharmacology; "set" means the individual's mindset, his personality, values, and expectations; and "setting" means the cultural or social surroundings of drug use. This should sound like common sense. Humans are interpretative animals, and so what results from drug use depends not just on the experience or effects produced by the drug but *also* on the interpretation of that experience or effects. And how one interprets or understands the experience depends on one's individuality and the cultural or social setting. I begin with setting. Hospital patients that get continuous and massive doses of narcotics rarely get addicted or crave the drugs after release from the hospital (Peele 1985, 17; Falk 1996, 9). The quantity and duration of their drug use pales in significance compared with the setting of their drug consumption: subsequent ill effects from the drug are rarely interpreted in terms of addiction. A study of Vietnam veterans, the largest study of untreated heroin users ever conducted, provides more dramatic evidence of the role of setting. Three-quarters of Vietnam vets who used heroin in Vietnam became addicted, but after coming home, only half of heroin users in Vietnam continued to use, and of those only 12 percent were addicts (Robins, Helzer, Hesselbrock, and Wish 1980). Wilson also mentions this study and says that the change was because heroin is illegal in the U.S. (1990, 22), and while this undoubtedly played a role, so did the difference in social setting: Vietnam, with its absence of work and family, as well as loneliness and fear of death, helped to promote acceptance of heavy drug use.

Along the same lines, consider the effects of alcohol in different cultures. In Finland, for example, violence and alcohol are linked, for sometimes heavy drinkers end up in fights; in Greece, Italy, and other Mediterranean countries, however, where almost all drinking is moderate and controlled, there is no violence-alcohol link (Peele 1985, 25). Why the differences? Humans are social or cultural animals, not just products of their biochemistry, and this means, in part, that social norms or rules play a significant role in influencing behavior. In cultures where potentially intoxicating drugs such as alcohol are viewed as supplements or accompaniments to life, moderate and controlled use will be the norm—hence, even though Mediterranean cultures typically consume large amounts of alcohol, there is little alcoholism—while in cultures where alcohol is also viewed as a way of escaping one's problems, alcoholism will be more prevalent, which may explain the problem in Finland and some other Scandinavian cultures. In addition to cultural influences, most people learn to use alcohol responsibly by observing their parents. They see their parents drink at a ball game or to celebrate special occasions or with food at a meal, but rarely on an empty stomach; they learn it's wrong to be drunk at work, to drink and drive; they learn that uncontrolled behavior with alcohol is generally frowned upon; they absorb certain norms and values such as "know your limit," "don't drink alone," "don't drink in the morning," and so forth. They learn about rituals which reinforce moderation, such as the phrase "let's have a drink." These informal rules and rituals teach most people how to use alcohol responsibly (Zinberg 1987, 258–62).

While social controls are harder to develop with illicit drugs—accurate information is pretty scarce, and parents feel uncomfortable teaching their children about controlled use—even here sanctions and rituals promoting moderate use exist. For example, in a study of an eleven-year follow-up of an informal network of middle-class cocaine users largely connected through ties of friendship, most of whom were moderate users, the authors concluded that:

> Rather than cocaine overpowering user concerns with family, health, and career, we found that the high value most of our users placed upon family, health, and career achievement ... mitigated against abuse and addiction. Such group norms and the informal social controls that seemed to stem from them (e.g., expressions of concern, warning about risks, the use of pejorative names like "coke hog," refusal to share with abusers) mediated the force of pharmacological, physiological, and psychological factors which can lead to addiction.
>
> (Murphy 1989: 435)

Even many heavy cocaine users are able to prevent their use from becoming out of control (or out of control for significant periods of time) by regulating the time and circumstances of use (not using during work, never using too late at night, limiting use on weekdays), using with friends rather than alone, employing fixed rules (paying bills before spending money on cocaine), etc. (Waldorf, Reinarman, and Murphy 1991). Unsurprisingly, these studies of controlled cocaine use generally focus on middle-class users: their income and the psychological support of friends and family put them at less of a risk of ruining their lives by drug use than those with little income or hope (Peele 1991, 159–60).

I now examine the effects of set on drug use, that is, the effect of expectations, personality, and values. Expectations are important because drug use occurs in a pattern of ongoing activity, and one's interpretation of the drug's effects depends upon expectations of how those effects will fit into or alter those activities. Expectations explain the well-known placebo effect: if people consume something they mistakenly believe will stop or alleviate their pain, it often does. Along the same lines, in experiments with American college-age men, aggression and sexual arousal increased when these men were told they were drinking liquor, even though they were drinking 0 proof, while when drinking liquor and told they were not, they acted normally (Peele 1985, 17). The role of expectations also explains why many users of heroin, cocaine, and other psychoactive drugs do not like or even recognize the effects when they first take it and have to be taught to or learn how to appreciate the effects (Peele 1985, 13–14; Waldorf, Reinarman, and Murphy 1991, 264; Zinberg 1984, 117). The importance of expectations means that those users who view the drug as overpowering them will tend to find their lives dominated by the drug, while those who view it as an enhancement or a complement to certain experiences or activities will tend not to let drugs dominate or overpower their other interests (Peele 1991, 156–58, 169–70).

As for the individual's personality and values, the predictions of common sense are pretty much accurate. Psychologically healthy people are likely to engage in controlled, moderate drug use, or if they find themselves progressing to uncontrolled use, they tend to cut back. On the other hand, drug addicts of all kinds tend to have more psychological problems before they started using illicit drugs (Peele

1991, 153–54, 157, Zinberg 1984, 74–76.) People who are motivated to control their own lives will tend to make drug use an accompaniment or an ingredient in their lives, not the dominant factor. Those who place a high value on responsibility, work, family, productivity, etc., will tend to fit drug use into their lives rather than letting it run their lives (Waldorf, Reinarman, and Murphy 1991, 267; Peele 1991, 160–66). That's why drug use of all kinds, licit or illicit, tends to taper off with age: keeping a job, raising a family, and so forth leave limited time or motivation for uncontrolled or near continuous drug use (Peele 1985, 15). And it's why it's not uncommon for addicts to explain their addiction by saying that they drifted into the addict's life; with little to compete with their drug use, or lacking motivation to substitute other activities or interests, drug use comes to dominate their lives (DeGrandpre and White 1996, 44–46). Those with richer lives, or who are motivated on an individual and/or cultural level to get richer lives, are less likely to succumb to addiction. To summarize: even with easy access to intoxicating drugs, most drug users don't become addicts, or if they do, don't remain addicts for that long, because most people have and are motivated to find better things to do with their lives. These better things result from their individual personality and values and their social or cultural setting.

Cigarette Smoking and the Role of Pharmacology

I've discussed how set and setting influence drug use, but where does pharmacology fit in? Its role is revealed by examining why it is much harder to stop smoking cigarettes—only half of smokers that try to stop smoking succeed in quitting—than to stop using other substances. (For more detail in what follows, see Shapiro 1994 and the references cited therein.)

Smokers smoke to relax; to concentrate; to handle anxiety, stress, and difficult interpersonal situations; as a way of taking a break during the day; as a social lubricant; as a means of oral gratification—and this is a partial list. Since smoking is a means to or part of so many activities, situations, and moods, stopping smoking is a major life change and major life changes do not come easily. Part of the reason smoking is so integrated into people's lives is pharmacological. Nicotine's effects on the brain are mild and subtle: it doesn't disrupt your life. While addicts or heavy users of other drugs such as cocaine, heroin, or alcohol *also* use their drugs as a means to or part of a variety of activities, situations, and moods, most users of these drugs are not lifelong addicts or heavy users, because these drugs are not so mild and heavy use has a stronger tendency over time to disrupt people's lives.

The pharmacology of smoking, however, cannot be separated from its social setting. Smoking doesn't disrupt people's lives in part because it is legal. Even with increasing regulations, smokers still can smoke in a variety of situations (driving, walking on public streets, etc.), while one cannot use illegal drugs except in a furtive and secretive manner. Furthermore, the mild effects of nicotine are due to its mild potency—smokers can carefully control their nicotine intake, getting small doses throughout the day—and its mild potency is due partly to smoking being legal. Legal drugs tend to have milder potencies than illegal ones for two reasons. First, illegal markets create incentives for stronger potencies, as sellers will favor concentrated forms of a drug that can be easily concealed and give a big bang for the buck. Second, in legal markets different potencies of the same drug openly compete, and over time the weaker ones come to be preferred—consider the popularity of low tar/nicotine cigarettes and wine and beer over hard liquor.

Thus, pharmacology and setting interact: smoking is well integrated into people's lives because the nicotine in cigarettes has mild pharmacological effects and because smoking is legal, and nicotine has those mild effects in part because smoking is legal. Pharmacology also interacts with what I've been calling set. The harms of smoking are slow to occur, are cumulative, and largely affect one's health, not one's ability to perform normal activities (at least prior to getting seriously ill). Furthermore, to eliminate these harms requires complete smoking cessation; cutting back rarely suffices (even light smokers increase their chances of getting lung cancer, emphysema, and heart disease). Thus, quitting smoking requires strong motivation, since its bad effects are not immediate and it does not disrupt one's life. Add to this what I noted earlier, that stopping smoking means changing one's life, and it's unsurprising that many find it difficult to stop.

Thus, it is a mistake to argue, as Goodin did, that the difficulty in quitting is mainly explicable by the effects of nicotine. Smokers are addicted to smoking, an *activity*, and their being addicted to it is not reducible to their being addicted to a *drug*. If my explanation of the relative difficulty of quitting smoking is correct, then the standard view of an addictive drug is quite suspect. That view suggests that knowledge of a drug's pharmacology provides a basis for making reasonable predictions about a drug's addictiveness. However, understanding nicotine's effects upon the brain (which is what Goodin stressed in his explanation of smokers' addiction) does not tell us that it's hard to stop smoking; we only know that once we add information about set and setting. Generalizing from the case of smoking, all we can say is:

> The milder the effects upon the brain, the easier for adults to purchase, the more easily integrated into one's life, and the more the bad effects are cumulative, slow-acting and only reversible upon complete cessation, the more addictive the drug.

Besides being a mouthful, this understanding of drug addiction requires introducing the *interaction* of set and setting with pharmacology to explain the addictiveness potential of various drugs. It is simpler and less misleading to say that people tend to *addict themselves* to various substances (and activities), this tendency varying with various cultural and individual influences.

Conclusion

My argument undercuts the worry that legalizing cocaine and heroin will produce an explosion of addiction because people will have access to inherently and powerfully addictive drugs. The standard view that cocaine and heroin are inherently addictive is false, because no drug is *inherently* addictive. The desire of most people to lead responsible and productive lives in a social setting that rewards such desires is what controls and limits most drug use. Ironically, if cocaine and heroin in a legal market would be as disruptive as many drug prohibitionists fear, then that is an excellent reason why addiction would not explode under legalization—drug use that tends to thrive is drug use that is woven into, rather than disrupts, responsible people's lives.

Addendum

After I wrote this article, some of my students raised the following objection. I argue that drug addiction that disrupts people's lives would not thrive under legalization because most people's desire and ability to lead responsible lives would break or prevent such addiction. However, suppose that legalization of cocaine and heroin makes the use of those drugs similar to the use of cigarettes—small, mild doses throughout the day which are well integrated into people's lives. If legalization brings it about that those who addict themselves to these drugs are like those who addict themselves to smoking—their addiction does not disrupt their lives, but is integrated into it—wouldn't that mean that addiction to these drugs would become as prevalent as cigarette addiction?

It is possible that legalizing heroin and cocaine would make its use similar to the current use of cigarettes. However, if this happened, the main worry about heroin and cocaine addiction would be gone. We would not have a problem of a large increase in the number of people throwing away or messing up their lives. At worst, if legalizing cocaine and heroin produced as bad health effects as cigarette smoking does (which is dubious—see Carnwath and Smith 2002, 137–39; Morgan and Zimmer 1997, 131, 136, 141), then we would have a new health problem. Of course, someone might argue that one should not legalize a drug which could worsen the health of a significant percentage of its users, even if that use does not mess up most of its users' lives. It is beyond the scope of this paper to evaluate such arguments (however, see Shapiro 1994), but notice that the implications of my essay cut against the claim that these health risks were not voluntarily incurred. Since one's drug use partly depends on one's values and personality, then to the extent that one can be said to be responsible for the choices influenced by one's values and personality, then to that extent those who addict themselves to a certain drug can be said to have voluntarily incurred the risks involved in that drug use.

References

American Psychiatric Association. 1994. *Diagnostic and Statistical Manual of Mental Disorders*. 4th ed. Washington, DC: American Psychiatric Association.
Carnwath, T., and I. Smith. 2002. *Heroin Century*. London: Routledge.
DeGrandpre, R., and E. White. 1996. "Drugs: In Care of the Self." *Common Knowledge* 3: 27–48.
Erickson, P., E. Edward, R. Smart, and G. Murray. 1994. *The Steel Drug: Crack and Cocaine in Perspective*. 2nd ed. New York: MacMillan.
Falk, J. 1996. "Environmental Factors in the Instigation and Maintenance of Drug Abuse." In W. Bickel and R. DeGrandpre, eds., *Drug Policy and Human Nature*. New York: Plenum Press.
Goodin, R. 1989. "The Ethics of Smoking." *Ethics* 99: 574–624.
Husak, D. 1992. *Drugs and Rights*. New York: Cambridge University Press.
Johnston, L. D., P. M. O'Malley, and J. G. Bachman. 1996. *Monitoring the Future Study, 1975–1994: National Survey Results on Drug Use*. Volume II: College Students and Young Adults. Rockville, MD: National Institute on Drug Abuse.
Kaplan, J. 1983. *The Hardest Drug: Heroin and Public Policy*. Chicago, IL: University of Chicago Press.
Morgan, J., and L. Zimmerman. 1997. "The Social Pharmacology of Smokeable Cocaine: Not All It's Cracked Up to Be." In C. Reinarman and H. Levine, eds., *Crack in America: Demon Drugs and Social Justice*. Berkeley, CA: University of California Press.

Peele, S. 1985. *The Meaning of Addiction: Compulsive Experience and Its Interpretation.* Lexington, MA: DC Heath and Company.

Peele, S. 1991. *The Diseasing of America: Addiction Treatment Out of Control.* Boston, MA: Houghton Mifflin Company.

Robins, L., J. Helzer, M. Hesselbrock, and E. Wish. 1980. "Vietnam Veterans Three Years After Vietnam: How Our Study Changed Our View of Heroin." In L. Brill and C. Winick, eds., *The Yearbook of Substance Use and Abuse.* Vol. 2. New York: Human Sciences Press.

Schacter, S. 1982. "Recidivism and Self-Cure of Smoking and Obesity." *American Psychologist* 37: 436–44.

Shapiro, D. 1994. "Smoking Tobacco: Irrationality, Addiction and Paternalism." *Public Affairs Quarterly* 8: 187–203.

Sullum, J. 2003. *Saying Yes: In Defense of Drug Use.* New York: Tarcher/Putnam.

Waldorf, D., C. Reinarman, and S. Murphy. 1991. *Cocaine Changes: The Experience of Using and Quitting.* Philadelphia, PA: Temple University Press.

Wilson, J. 1990. "Against the Legalization of Drugs." *Commentary* 89: 21–28.

Zinberg, N. 1984. *Drug, Set, and Setting.* New Haven, CT: Yale University Press.

Zinberg, N. 1987. "The Use and Misuse of Intoxicants." In R. Hamowy, ed., *Dealing with Drugs.* Lexington, MA: DC Heath and Company.

Review and Discussion Questions

1 What does Shapiro mean by the standard view of addiction?
2 Describe the objections Shapiro raises against the standard view of addiction.
3 The alternative view of addiction rests on the interaction of set, setting, and pharmacology. Explain this alternative understanding of addiction.
4 Describe Shapiro's understanding of the role of tobacco's pharmacological effects in smoking.
5 What are the policy implications of Shapiro's conclusions?
6 How does Shapiro respond to Goodin's view that smokers do not consent to the harm of smoking resulting from their addiction?

READING: THE ETHICS OF ADDICTION: AN ARGUMENT IN FAVOR OF LETTING AMERICANS TAKE ANY DRUG THEY WANT

THOMAS SZASZ[*]

Relying explicitly on John Stuart Mill's discussion of liberty, Thomas Szasz discusses the legalization of drugs. After reviewing the historical effects of prohibition, he argues that such policies lead to socially harmful consequences and also fail to respect the legitimate control citizens may exercise over their own lives. A decent regard for individual liberty demands that government respect its citizens' right to "life, liberty, and the pursuit of highs." Thomas Szasz is a psychiatrist and the author of many books.

---

[*] "The Ethics of Addiction: An Argument in Favor of Letting Americans Take Any Drug They Want" by Thomas Szasz, *Harper's Magazine*, April 1972. Copyright © 1972 by Harper's Magazine. All rights reserved. Reproduced from the April issue by special permission.

To avoid clichés about "drug abuse," let us analyze its official definition. According to the World Health Organization,

> Drug addiction is a state of periodic or chronic intoxication detrimental to the individual and to society, produced by the repeated consumption of a drug (natural or synthetic). Its characteristics include: (1) an overpowering desire or need (compulsion) to continue taking the drug and to obtain it by any means, (2) a tendency to increase the dosage, and (3) a psychic (psychological) and sometimes physical dependence on the effects of the drug.

Since this definition hinges on the harm done to both the individual and society, it is clearly an ethical one. Moreover, by not specifying what is "detrimental," it consigns the problem of addiction to psychiatrists who define the patient's "dangerousness to himself and others."

Next, we come to the effort to obtain the addictive substance "by any means." This suggests that the substance must be prohibited or is very expensive and is hence difficult for the ordinary person to obtain (rather than that the person who wants it has an inordinate craving for it). If there were an abundant and inexpensive supply of what the "addict" wants, there would be no reason for him to go to "any means" to obtain it. Thus by the WHO's definition, one can be addicted only to a substance that is illegal or otherwise difficult to obtain. This surely removes the problem of addiction from the realm of medicine and psychiatry and puts it squarely into that of morals and law.

In short, drug addiction or drug abuse cannot be defined without specifying the proper and improper uses of certain pharmacologically active agents. The regular administration of morphine by a physician to a patient dying of cancer is the paradigm of the proper use of a narcotic; whereas even its occasional self-administration by a physically healthy person for the purpose of "pharmacological pleasure" is the paradigm of drug abuse.

I submit that these judgments have nothing whatever to do with medicine, pharmacology, or psychiatry. They are moral judgments. Indeed, our present views on addiction are astonishingly similar to some of our former views on sex. Until recently, masturbation—or self-abuse, as it was called—was professionally declared, and popularly accepted, as both the cause and the symptom of a variety of illnesses. Even today, homosexuality—called a "sexual perversion"—is regarded as a disease by medical and psychiatric experts as well as by "well-informed" laymen. [The American Psychiatric Association removed homosexuality as a mental disorder in 1973—Ed. note.]

To be sure, it is now virtually impossible to cite a contemporary medical authority to support the concept of self-abuse. Medical opinion holds that whether a person masturbates or not is medically irrelevant and that engaging in the practice or refraining from it is a matter of personal morals or lifestyle. On the other hand, it is virtually impossible to cite a contemporary medical authority to oppose the concept of drug abuse. Medical opinion holds that drug abuse is a major medical, psychiatric, and public health problem; that drug addiction is a disease similar to diabetes, requiring prolonged (or lifelong) and careful, medically supervised treatment; and that taking or not taking drugs is primarily, if not solely, a matter of medical responsibility.

Thus the man on the street can only believe what he hears from all sides—that drug addiction is a disease, "like any other" which has now reached "epidemic proportions" and whose "medical" containment justifies the limitless expenditure of tax monies and the corresponding aggrandizement and enrichment of noble medical warriors against this "plague."

Propaganda to Justify Prohibition

Like any social policy, our drug laws may be examined from two entirely different points of view: technical and moral. Our present inclination is either to ignore the moral perspective or to mistake the technical for the moral.

Since most of the propagandists against drug abuse seek to justify certain repressive policies because of the alleged dangerousness of various drugs, they often falsify the facts about the true pharmacological properties of the drugs they seek to prohibit. They do so for two reasons: first, because many substances in daily use are just as harmful as the substances they want to prohibit: second, because they realize that dangerousness alone is never a sufficiently persuasive argument to justify the prohibition of any drug, substance, or artifact. Accordingly, the more they ignore the moral dimensions of the problem, the more they must escalate their fraudulent claims about the dangers of drugs.

To be sure, some drugs are more dangerous than others. It is easier to kill oneself with heroin than with aspirin. But it is also easier to kill oneself by jumping off a high building than a low one. In the case of drugs, we regard their potentiality for self-injury as justification for their prohibition; in the case of buildings, we do not.

Furthermore, we systematically blur and confuse the two quite different ways in which narcotics may cause death: by a deliberate act of suicide or by accidental overdosage.

Every individual is capable of injuring or killing himself. This potentiality is a fundamental expression of human freedom. Self-destructive behavior may be regarded as sinful and penalized by means of informal sanctions. But it should not be regarded as a crime or (mental) disease, justifying or warranting the use of the police powers of the state for its control.

Therefore, it is absurd to deprive an adult of a drug (or of anything else) because he might use it to kill himself. To do so is to treat everyone the way institutional psychiatrists treat the so-called suicidal mental patient: they not only imprison such a person but take everything away from him—shoelaces, belts, razor blades, eating utensils, and so forth—until the "patient" lies naked on a mattress in a padded cell—lest he kill himself. The result is degrading tyrannization.

Death by accidental overdose is an altogether different matter. But can anyone doubt that this danger now looms so large precisely because the sale of narcotics and many other drugs is illegal? Those who buy illicit drugs cannot be sure what drug they are getting or how much of it. Free trade in drugs, with governmental action limited to safeguarding the purity of the product and the veracity of the labeling, should reduce the risk of accidental overdose with "dangerous drugs" to the same levels that prevail, and that we find acceptable, with respect to other chemical agents and physical artifacts that abound in our complex technological society.

This essay is not intended as an exposition on the pharmacological properties of narcotics and other mind-affecting drugs. However, I want to make it clear that in my view, *regardless* of their danger, all drugs should be "legalized" (a misleading term I employ reluctantly as a concession to common usage). Although I recognize that some drugs—notably heroin, the amphetamines, and LSD, among those now in vogue—may have undesirable or dangerous consequences, I favor free trade in drugs for the same reason the Founding Fathers favored free trade in ideas. In an open society, it is none of the government's business what idea a man puts into his mind; likewise, it should be none of the government's business what drug he puts into his body.

Withdrawal Pains from Tradition

It is a fundamental characteristic of human beings that they get used to things: one becomes habituated, or "addicted," not only to narcotics, but to cigarettes, cocktails before dinner, orange juice for breakfast, comic strips, and so forth. It is similarly a fundamental characteristic of living organisms that they acquire increasing tolerance to various chemical agents and physical stimuli: the first cigarette may cause nothing but nausea and headache; a year later, smoking three packs a day may be pure joy. Both alcohol and opiates are "addictive" in the sense that the more regularly they are used, the more the user craves them and the greater his tolerance for them becomes. Yet none of this involves any mysterious process of "getting hooked." It is simply an aspect of the universal biological propensity for *learning,* which is especially well developed in man. The opiate habit, like the cigarette habit or food habit, can be broken—and without any medical assistance—provided the person wants to break it. Often he doesn't. And why, indeed, should he, if he has nothing better to do with his life? Or, as happens to be the case with morphine, if he can live an essentially normal life while under its influence?

Actually, opium is much less toxic than alcohol. Just as it is possible to be an "alcoholic" and work and be productive, so it is (or, rather, it used to be) possible to be an opium addict and work and be productive. According to a definitive study published by the American Medical Association in 1929,

> [M]orphine addiction is not characterized by physical deterioration or impairment of physical fitness. ... There is no evidence of change in the circulatory, hepatic, renal, or endocrine functions. When it is considered that these subjects had been addicted for at least five years, some of them for as long as twenty years, these negative observations are highly significant.

In a 1928 study, Lawrence Kolb, an Assistant Surgeon General of the United States Public Health Service, found that of 119 persons addicted to opiates through medical practice,

> [Ninety] had good industrial records and only 29 had poor ones. ... Judged by the output of labor and their own statements, none of the normal persons had [his] efficiency reduced by opium. Twenty-two of them worked regularly while taking opium for twenty-five years or more; one of them, a woman aged 81 and still alert mentally, had taken 3 grains of morphine daily for 65

years. [The usual therapeutic dose is one-quarter grain, three to four grains being fatal for the nonaddict.] She gave birth to and raised six children, and managed her household affairs with more than average efficiency. A widow, aged 66, had taken 17 grains of morphine daily for most of 37 years. She is alert mentally, does physical labor every day, and makes her own living.

I am not citing this evidence to recommend the opium habit. The point is that we must, in plain honesty, distinguish between pharmacological effects and personal inclinations. Some people take drugs to help them function and conform to social expectations; others take them for the very opposite reason, to ritualize their refusal to function and conform to social expectations. Much of the "drug abuse" we now witness—perhaps nearly all of it—is of the second type. But instead of acknowledging that "addicts" are unfit or unwilling to work and be "normal," we prefer to believe that they act as they do because certain drugs—especially heroin, LSD, and the amphetamines—make them "sick." If only we could get them "well," so runs this comforting view, they would become "productive" and "useful" citizens. To believe this is like believing that if an illiterate cigarette smoker would only stop smoking, he would become an Einstein. With a falsehood like this, one can go far. No wonder that politicians and psychiatrists love it.

The concept of free trade in drugs runs counter to our cherished notion that everyone must work and idleness is acceptable only under special conditions. ... [Drug users] are, in principle at least, capable of working and supporting themselves. But they refuse: they "drop out"; and in doing so, they challenge the most basic values of our society.

The fear that free trade in narcotics would result in vast masses of our population spending their days and nights smoking opium or mainlining heroin, rather than working and taking care of their responsibilities, is a bugaboo that does not deserve to be taken seriously. Habits of work and idleness are deep-seated cultural patterns. Free trade in abortions has not made an industrious people like the Japanese give up work for fornication. Nor would free trade in drugs convert such a people from hustlers to hippies. Indeed, I think the opposite might be the case: it is questionable whether, or for how long, a responsible people can tolerate being treated as totally irresponsible with respect to drugs and drug-taking. In other words, how long can we live with the inconsistency of being expected to be responsible for operating cars and computers but not for operating our own bodies?

Although my argument about drug-taking is moral and political, and does not depend upon showing that free trade in drugs would also have fiscal advantages over our present policies, let me indicate briefly some of its economic implications.

The war on addiction is not only astronomically expensive; it is also counterproductive. On April 1, 1967, New York State's narcotics addiction control program, hailed as "the most massive ever tried in the nation," went into effect. "The program, which may cost up to $400 million in three years," reported the *New York Times*, "was hailed by Governor Rockefeller as 'the start of an unending war.'" Three years later, it was conservatively estimated that the number of addicts in the state had tripled or quadrupled. New York State Senator John Hughes reports that the cost of caring for each addict during this time was $12,000 per year (as against $4,000 per year for patients in state mental hospitals). ... The salaries of the medical bureaucrats in charge of these programs are similarly attractive. In short, the detection and rehabilitation of addicts is good business. We now know that the spread of witchcraft in the late Middle Ages was due more to the work of witchmongers than to the lure of witchcraft. Is it not possible that the spread of addiction in our day is due more to the work of addictmongers than to the lure of narcotics?

Let us see how far some of the monies spent on the war on addiction could go in supporting people who prefer to drop out of society and drug themselves. Their "habit" itself would cost next to nothing: free trade would bring the price of narcotics down to a negligible amount ....

I am not advocating that we spend our hard-earned money in this way. I am only trying to show that free trade in narcotics would be more economical for those of us who work, even if we had to support legions of addicts, than is our present program of trying to "cure" them. Moreover, I have not even made use, in my economic estimates, of the incalculable sums we would save by reducing crimes now engendered by the illegal traffic in drugs.

The Right of Self-Medication

Clearly, the argument that marijuana—or heroin, methadone, or morphine—is prohibited because it is addictive or dangerous cannot be supported by facts. For one thing, there are many drugs, from insulin to penicillin, that are neither addictive nor dangerous but are nevertheless also prohibited; they can be obtained only through a physician's prescription. For another, there are many things, from dynamite to guns, that are much more dangerous than narcotics (especially to others) but are not prohibited. As everyone knows, it is still possible in the United States to walk into a store and walk out with a shotgun. We enjoy this right not because we believe that guns are safe but because we believe even more strongly that civil liberties are precious. At the same time, it is not possible in the United States to walk into a store and walk out with a bottle of barbiturates, codeine, or other drugs.

I believe that just as we regard freedom of speech and religion as fundamental rights, so we should also regard freedom of self-medication as a fundamental right. Like most rights, the right of self-medication should apply only to adults, and it should not be an unqualified right. Since these are important qualifications, it is necessary to specify their precise range.

John Stuart Mill said (approximately) that a person's right to swing his arm ends where his neighbor's nose begins. And Oliver Wendell Holmes said that no one has a right to shout "Fire!" in a crowded theater. Similarly, the limiting condition with respect to self-medication should be the inflicting of actual (as against symbolic) harm on others.

Our present practices with respect to alcohol embody and reflect this individualistic ethic. We have the right to buy, possess, and consume alcoholic beverages. Regardless of how offensive drunkenness might be to a person, he cannot interfere with another person's "right" to become inebriated so long as that person drinks in the privacy of his own home or at some other appropriate location, and so long as he conducts himself in an otherwise law-abiding manner. In short, we have a right to be intoxicated—in private. Public intoxication is considered an offense to others and is therefore a violation of the criminal law. It makes sense that what is a "right" in one place may become, by virtue of its disruptive or disturbing effect on others, an offense somewhere else.

The right to self-medication should be hedged in by similar limits. Public intoxication, not only with alcohol but with any drug, should be an offense punishable by the criminal law. Furthermore, acts that may injure others—such as driving a car—should, when carried out in a drug-intoxicated state, be punished especially strictly and severely. The right to self-medication must thus entail unqualified responsibility for the effects of one's drug-intoxicated behavior on others. For unless we are willing to hold ourselves responsible for our own behavior, and hold others responsible for theirs, the liberty to use drugs (or to engage in other acts) degenerates into a license to hurt others.

Such, then, would be the situation of adults, if we regarded the freedom to take drugs as a fundamental right similar to the freedom to read and worship. What would be the situation of children? Since many people who are now said to be drug addicts or drug abusers are minors, it is especially important that we think clearly about this aspect of the problem.

I do not believe, and I do not advocate, that children should have a right to ingest, inject, or otherwise use any drug or substance they want. Children do not have the right to drive, drink, vote, marry, or make binding contracts. They acquire these rights at various ages, coming into their full possession at maturity, usually between the ages of eighteen and twenty-one. The right to self-medication should similarly be withheld until maturity.

In short, I suggest that "dangerous" drugs be treated, more or less, as alcohol is treated now. Neither the use of narcotics nor their possession should be prohibited, but only their sale to minors. Of course, this would result in the ready availability of all kinds of drugs among minors—though perhaps their availability would be no greater than it is now but would only be more visible and hence more easily subject to proper controls. This arrangement would place responsibility for the use of all drugs by children where it belongs: on parents and their children. This is where the major responsibility rests for the use of alcohol. It is a tragic symptom of our refusal to take personal liberty and responsibility seriously that there appears to be no public desire to assume a similar stance toward other "dangerous" drugs.

Consider what would happen should a child bring a bottle of gin to school and get drunk there. Would the school authorities blame the local liquor stores as pushers? Or would they blame the parents and the child himself? There is liquor in practically every home in America and yet children rarely bring liquor to school. Whereas marijuana, Dexedrine, and heroin—substances children usually do not find at home and whose very possession is a criminal offense—frequently find their way into the school.

Our attitude toward sexual activity provides another model for our attitude toward drugs. Although we generally discourage children below a certain age from engaging in sexual activities with others, we do not prohibit such activities by law. What we do prohibit by law is the sexual seduction of children by adults. The "pharmacological seduction" of children by adults should be similarly punishable. In other words, adults who give or sell drugs to children should be regarded as offenders. Such a specific and limited prohibition—as against the kinds of generalized prohibitions that we had under the Volstead Act or have now with respect to countless drugs—would be relatively easy to enforce. Moreover, it would probably be rarely violated, for there would be little psychological interest and no economic profit in doing so.

The True Faith: Scientific Medicine

What I am suggesting is that while addiction is ostensibly a medical and pharmacological problem, actually it is a moral and political problem. We ought to know that there is no necessary connection between facts and values, between what is and what ought to be. Thus, objectively quite harmful acts, objects, or persons may be accepted and tolerated—by minimizing their dangerousness. Conversely, objectively quite harmless acts, objects, or persons may be prohibited and persecuted—by exaggerating their dangerousness. It is always necessary to distinguish—and especially so when dealing with social policy—between description and prescription, fact and rhetoric, truth and falsehood.

In our society, there are two principal methods of legitimizing policy: social tradition and scientific judgment. More than anything else, time is the supreme ethical arbiter. Whatever a social practice might be, if people engage in it, generation after generation, that practice becomes acceptable.

Many opponents of illegal drugs admit that nicotine may be more harmful to health than marijuana; nevertheless, they urge that smoking cigarettes should be legal but smoking marijuana should not be, because the former habit is socially accepted while the latter is not. This is a perfectly reasonable argument. But let us understand it for what it is—a plea for legitimizing old and accepted practices and for illegitimizing novel and unaccepted ones. It is a justification that rests on precedent, not evidence.

The other method of legitimizing policy, ever more important in the modern world, is through the authority of science. In matters of health, a vast and increasingly elastic category, physicians play important roles as legitimizers and illegitimizers. This, in short, is why we regard being medicated by a doctor as drug use and self-medication (especially with certain classes of drugs) as drug abuse.

This, too, is a perfectly reasonable arrangement. But we must understand that it is a plea for legitimizing what doctors do because they do it with "good therapeutic" intent; and for illegitimizing what laymen do because they do it with bad self-abusive ("masturbatory" or mind-altering) intent. This justification rests on the principles of professionalism, not of pharmacology. Hence we applaud the systematic medical use of methadone and call it "treatment for heroin addiction" but decry the occasional nonmedical use of marijuana and call it "dangerous drug abuse."

Our present concept of drug abuse articulates and symbolizes a fundamental policy of scientific medicine—namely, that a layman should not medicate his own body but should place its medical care under the supervision of a duly accredited physician. Before the Reformation, the practice of True Christianity rested on a similar policy—namely, that a layman should not himself commune with God but should place his spiritual care under the supervision of a duly accredited priest. The self-interests of the church and of medicine in such policies are obvious enough. What might be less obvious is the interest of the laity: by delegating responsibility for the spiritual and medical welfare of the people to a class of authoritatively accredited specialists, these policies—and the practices they ensure—relieve individuals from assuming the burdens of responsibility for themselves. As I see it, our present problems with drug use and drug abuse are just one of the consequences of our pervasive ambivalence about personal autonomy and responsibility.

I propose a medical reformation analogous to the Protestant Reformation: specifically, a "protest" against the systematic mystification of man's relationship to his body and his professionalized separation from it. The immediate aim of this reform would be to remove the physician as intermediary between man and his body and to give the layman direct access to the language and contents of the pharmacopoeia. If man had unencumbered access to his own body and the means of chemically altering it, it would spell the end of medicine, at least as we now know it. This is why, with faith in scientific medicine so strong, there is little interest in this kind of medical reform. Physicians fear the loss of their privileges: laymen, the loss of their protections.

Finally, since luckily we still do not live in the utopian perfection of "one world," our technical approach to the "drug problem" has led, and will undoubtedly continue to lead, to some curious attempts to combat it.

Here is one such attempt: the American government is now pressuring Turkey to restrict its farmers from growing poppies (the source of morphine and heroin). If turnabout is fair play, perhaps we should expect the Turkish government to pressure the United States to restrict its farmers from growing corn and wheat. Or should we assume that Muslims have enough self-control to leave alcohol alone, but Christians need all the controls that politicians, policemen, and physicians can bring to bear on them to enable them to leave opiates alone?

Life, Liberty, and the Pursuit of Highs

Sooner or later we shall have to confront the basic moral dilemma underlying this problem: Does a person have the right to take a drug, any drug—not because he needs it to cure an illness but because he wants to take it?

The Declaration of Independence speaks of our inalienable right to "life, liberty, and the pursuit of happiness." How are we to interpret this? By asserting that we ought to be free to pursue happiness by playing golf or watching television but not by drinking alcohol or smoking marijuana or ingesting pep pills?

The Constitution and the Bill of Rights are silent on the subject of drugs. This would seem to imply that the adult citizen has, or ought to have, the right to medicate his own body as he sees fit. Were this not the case, why should there have been a need for a constitutional amendment to outlaw drinking? But if ingesting alcohol was, and is now again, a constitutional right, is ingesting opium or heroin or barbiturates or anything else not also such a right? If it is, then the Harrison Narcotic Act is not only a bad law but is unconstitutional as well, because it prescribes in a legislative act what ought to be promulgated in a constitutional amendment.

The questions remain: as American citizens, should we have the right to take narcotics or other drugs? If we take drugs and conduct ourselves as responsible and law-abiding citizens, should we have a right to remain unmolested by the government? Lastly, if we take drugs and break the law, should we have a right to be treated as persons accused of crime rather than as patients accused of mental illness?

These are fundamental questions that are conspicuous by their absence from all contemporary discussions of problems of drug addiction and drug abuse. The result is that instead of debating the use of drugs in moral and political terms, we define our task as the ostensibly narrow technical problem of protecting people from poisoning themselves with substances for whose use they cannot possibly assume responsibility. This, I think, best explains the frightening national consensus against personal responsibility for taking drugs and for one's conduct while under their influence ....

To me, unanimity on an issue as basic and complex as this means a complete evasion of the actual problem and an attempt to master it by attacking and overpowering a scapegoat—"dangerous drugs" and "drug abusers." There is an ominous resemblance between the unanimity with which all "reasonable" men—and especially politicians, physicians, and priests—formerly supported the protective measures of society against witches and Jews and that with which they now support them against drug addicts and drug abusers.

After all is said and done, the issue comes down to whether we accept or reject the ethical principle John Stuart Mill so clearly enunciated:

> The only purpose [he wrote in *On Liberty*] for which power can be rightfully exercised over any member of a civilized community, against his will, is to prevent harm to others. His own good, either physical or moral, is not a sufficient warrant. He cannot rightfully be compelled to do or forbear because it will make him happier, because in the opinions of others, to do so would be wise, or even right. ... In the part [of his conduct] which merely concerns himself, his independence is, of right, absolute. Over himself, over his own body and mind, the individual is sovereign.[1]

By recognizing the problem of drug abuse for what it is—a moral and political question rather than a medical or therapeutic one—we can choose to maximize the sphere of action of the state at the expense of the individual, or of the individual at the expense of the state. In other words, we could commit ourselves to the view that the state, the representative of many, is more important than the individual; that it therefore has the right, indeed the duty, to regulate the life of the individual in the best interests of the group. Or we could commit ourselves to the view that individual dignity and liberty are the supreme values of life, and that the foremost duty of the state is to protect and promote these values.

In short, we must choose between the ethic of collectivism and individualism and pay the price of either—or of both.

Note

1 Mill, John Stuart (1859). *On Liberty*. Oxford, UK: Oxford University. pp. 21–22.

Review and Discussion Questions

1 Describe the "myths" that Szasz says surround drug addiction.
2 What, specifically, does Szasz propose should be done about drug laws? What motivates him to make that proposal?
3 Is this proposal one that Mill would accept? Why?
4 How does Szasz understand addiction? Do you agree with Szasz's analysis? Explain.

5 This article was written in 1972. What lessons can be learned from the events since then? Would Szasz be likely to feel vindicated or refuted by recent history? Explain.
6 Is Szasz right that the Constitution's silence about drugs suggests a right to take them? Explain.

Essay and Paper Topics for Chapter 16

1 Should the United States legalize drug use? Draw on any arguments presented in this chapter to build your case.
2 Compare and contrast Mill's discussion of liberty with Nielsen's discussion of free speech. To what extent do they express similar commitments? To what extent do they disagree with each other?
3 After summarizing the views, build a case for supporting either the majority decision or the dissenting position in Citizens United.
4 Is there a viable distinction between speech and action? Explain.
5 Apply ideas from Mill, Nielsen, and Schulzke to analyze whether *Snyder v. Phelps* and *Skokie* were good decisions.

Chapter 17

Economic Justice
Markets and Property

Economic and business relationships raise a host of challenging debates. Markets presuppose a property rights system. How is it possible to assess whether markets and the related property system are legitimate or just? The first four readings consider different answers to that question. The fifth reading considers a Supreme Court case about the right to private property set against the governmental power to take private property through eminent domain. This case challenges us to consider how society should balance individualist and collective perspectives. The last two articles debate the moral responsibilities of one of the most powerful and influential sets of institutions in contemporary economies: corporations. Taken together, these readings examine some of the most profound moral issues that are raised by economic relationships in our world today.

READING: OF JUSTICE

DAVID HUME[*]

In this essay, which is from his *An Enquiry Concerning the Principles of Morals* (another selection of which was reprinted in Chapter 2), David Hume discusses why economic justice is necessary given the scarcity of resources, the reasons why property should be protected, and the importance of utility in deciding these issues.

That Justice is so useful to society, and consequently that *part* of its merit, at least, must arise from that consideration, it would be a superfluous undertaking to prove. That public utility is the *sole* origin of justice, and that reflections on the beneficial consequences of this virtue are the *sole* foundation of its merit; this proposition, being more curious and important, will better deserve our examination and enquiry.

    Let us suppose that nature has bestowed on the human race such profuse *abundance* of all *external* conveniences, that, without any uncertainty in the event, without any care or industry on our part, every individual finds himself fully provided with whatever his most voracious appetites can want, or luxurious imagination wish or desire. His natural beauty, we shall suppose, surpasses all acquired ornaments: the

---

[*] David Hume. 1751. *An Enquiry Concerning the Principles of Morals*.

perpetual clemency of the seasons renders useless all clothes or covering; the raw herbage affords him the most delicious fare; the clear fountain, the richest beverage. No laborious occupation required: no tillage: no navigation. Music, poetry, and contemplation form his sole business: conversation, mirth, and friendship his sole amusement.

It seems evident that, in such a happy state, every other social virtue would flourish, and receive tenfold increase; but the cautious, jealous virtue of justice would never once have been dreamed of. For what purpose make a partition of goods, where every one has already more than enough? Why give rise to property, where there cannot possibly be any injury? Why call this object mine, when upon the seizing of it by another, I need but stretch out my hand to possess myself to what is equally valuable? Justice, in that case, being totally useless, would be an idle ceremonial, and could never possibly have place in the catalogue of virtues.

We see, even in the present necessitous condition of mankind, that, wherever any benefit is bestowed by nature in an unlimited abundance, we leave it always in common among the whole human race, and make no subdivisions of right and property. Water and air, though the most necessary of all objects, are not challenged as the property of individuals; nor can any man commit injustice by the most lavish use and enjoyment of these blessings. In fertile extensive countries, with few inhabitants, land is regarded on the same footing.

Again; suppose, that, though the necessities of the human race continue the same as at present, yet the mind is so enlarged, and so replete with friendship and generosity, that every man has the utmost tenderness for every man, and feels no more concern for his own interest than for that of his fellows; it seems evident, that the use of justice would, in this case, be suspended by such an extensive benevolence, nor would the divisions and barriers of property and obligation have ever been thought of. Why should I bind another, by a deed or promise, to do me any good office, when I know that he is already prompted, by the strongest inclination, to seek my happiness, and would, of himself, perform the desired service; except the hurt, he thereby receives, be greater than the benefit accruing to me? ....

To make this truth more evident, let us reverse the foregoing suppositions; and carrying everything to the opposite extreme, consider what would be the effect of these new situations. Suppose a society to fall into such want of all common necessaries, that the utmost frugality and industry cannot preserve the greater number from perishing, and the whole from extreme misery; it will readily, I believe, be admitted, that the strict laws of justice are suspended, in such a pressing emergence, and give place to the stronger motives of necessity and self-preservation. Is it any crime, after a shipwreck, to seize whatever means or instrument of safety one can lay hold of, without regard to former limitations of property? Or if a city besieged were perishing with hunger; can we imagine, that men will see any means of preservation before them, and lose their lives, from a scrupulous regard to what, in other situations, would be the rules of equity and justice? The use and tendency of that virtue is to procure happiness and security, by preserving order in society: but where the society is ready to perish from extreme necessity, no greater evil can be dreaded from violence and injustice;

and every man may now provide for himself by all the means, which prudence can dictate, or humanity permit ....

Thus, the rules of equity or justice depend entirely on the particular state and condition in which men are placed, and owe their origin and existence to that utility, which results to the public from their strict and regular observance. Reverse, in any considerable circumstance, the condition of men: Produce extreme abundance or extreme necessity: Implant in the human breast perfect moderation and humanity, or perfect rapaciousness and malice: By rendering justice totally *useless*, you thereby totally destroy its essence, and suspend its obligation upon mankind. The common situation of society is a medium amidst all these extremes. We are naturally partial to ourselves, and to our friends; but are capable of learning the advantage resulting from a more equitable conduct. Few enjoyments are given us from the open and liberal hand of nature; but by art, labor, and industry, we can extract them in great abundance. Hence the ideas of property become necessary in all civil society: Hence justice derives its usefulness to the public: And hence alone arises its merit and moral obligation.

These conclusions are so natural and obvious, that they have not escaped even the poets, in their descriptions of the felicity attending the golden age or the reign of Saturn. The seasons, in that first period of nature, were so temperate, if we credit these agreeable fictions, that there was no necessity for men to provide themselves with clothes and houses, as a security against the violence of heat and cold: The rivers flowed with wine and milk: The oaks yielded honey; and nature spontaneously produced her greatest delicacies. Nor were these the chief advantages of that happy age. Tempests were not alone removed from nature; but those more furious tempests were unknown to human breasts, which now cause such uproar, and engender such confusion. Avarice, ambition, cruelty, selfishness, were never heard of: Cordial affection, compassion, sympathy, were the only movements with which the mind was yet acquainted. Even the punctilious distinction of *mine* and *thine* was banished from among the happy race of mortals, and carried with it the very notion of property and obligation, justice and injustice ....

If we examine the *particular* laws, by which justice is directed, and property determined; we shall still be presented with the same conclusion. The good of mankind is the only object of all these laws and regulations. Not only is it requisite, for the peace and interest of society, that men's possessions should be separated; but the rules, which we follow, in making the separation, are such as can best be contrived to serve farther the interests of society. ... Render possessions ever so equal, men's different degrees of art, care, and industry will immediately break that equality. Or if you check these virtues, you reduce society to the most extreme indigence; and instead of preventing want and beggary in a few, render it unavoidable to the whole community ....

Who sees not, for instance, that whatever is produced or improved by man's art or industry ought, for ever, to be secured to him, in order to give encouragement to such *useful* habits and accomplishments? That the property ought to also descend to children and relations, for the same *useful* purpose? That it may be alienated by consent, in order to beget that commerce and intercourse, which is so *beneficial* to human society? And that all contracts and promises ought carefully to be fulfilled, in order to secure mutual trust and confidence, by which the general *interest* of mankind is so much promoted? ....

Examine the writers on the laws of nature; and you will always find, that, whatever principles they set out with, they are sure to terminate here at last, and to assign, as the ultimate reason for every rule which they establish, the convenience and necessities of mankind.

What is man's property? Anything which it is lawful for him, and for him alone, to use. *But what rule have we by which we can distinguish these objects?* Here we must have recourse to statutes, customs, precedents, analogies, and a hundred other circumstances; some of which are constant and inflexible, some variable and arbitrary. But the ultimate point, in which they all professedly terminate, is the interest and happiness of human society ....

All birds of the same species in every age and country, built their nests alike: in this we see the force of instinct. Men, in different times and places, frame their houses differently: here we perceive the influence of reason and custom. A like inference may be drawn from comparing the instinct of generation and the institution of property.

How great soever the variety of municipal laws, it must be confessed, that their chief outlines pretty regularly concur; because the purposes, to which they tend, are everywhere exactly similar. In like manner, all houses have a roof and walls, windows and chimneys; though diversified in their shape, figure, and materials. The purposes of the latter, directed to the conveniences of human life, discover not more plainly their origin from reason and reflection, than do those of the former, which points all to a like end ....

The convenience, or rather necessity, which leads to justice is so universal, and everywhere points so much to the same rules, that the habit takes place in all societies; and it is not without some scrutiny, that we are able to ascertain its true origin. The matter, however, is not so obscure, but that even in common life we have every moment recourse to the principle of public utility, and ask, *What must become of the world, if such practices prevail? How could society subsist under such disorders?* Were the distinction or separation of possessions entirely useless, can any one conceive, that it ever should have obtained in society?

Thus we seem, upon the whole, to have attained a knowledge of the force of that principle here insisted on, and can determine what degree of esteem or moral approbation may result from reflections on public interest and utility. The necessity of justice to the support of society is the sole foundation of that virtue.

Review and Discussion Questions

1 Hume imagines possible worlds in which available resources are different from our own world and in which human beings are different. What are those worlds?
2 What is the point Hume makes about property by describing our actual world and how it might have been different?
3 Explain how Hume thinks property rights should be determined in society. What justifies private property, according to Hume?

READING: THE ENTITLEMENT THEORY

ROBERT NOZICK*

Like John Locke, Robert Nozick begins with a strong commitment to prepolitical individual rights—rights that may not be transgressed by others, either as individuals or collectively as the state. Commonly called *negative rights*, they constitute "side constraints" on the actions of others, ensuring a person's freedom from interference in the pursuit of his or her own life. These rights are negative because they require only that others refrain from acting in certain ways; in particular, that they refrain from interfering with us. Beyond this, no one is obliged to do anything positive for us; we have no right, for example, to require others to provide us with satisfying work or with any material goods we might need. Each individual is to be seen as autonomous and responsible and should be left to fashion his or her own life free from the interference of others—as long as this is compatible with the right of others to do the same. Only the acknowledgment of this almost absolute right to be free from coercion, argues Nozick, fully respects the distinctiveness of persons, each with a unique life to lead. This framework of individual rights and corresponding duties constitutes the basis of what power the government may legitimately have. In Nozick's view, the only morally legitimate state is the so-called night-watchman state, one whose functions are restricted to protecting the negative rights of citizens; that is, to protecting them against force, theft, fraud, and so on. In the selection that follows, Nozick is especially concerned with rejecting the claim that a larger state is necessary in order to achieve a just economic distribution.

In contrast to theories he calls *end-state* and *patterned*, Nozick proposes the *entitlement theory of justice*. According to this theory, a distribution is just if it arises from a prior just distribution by just means. For example, as Locke also argued, unowned resources may be acquired originally by one's taking something from nature, subject to certain provisos. And, once legitimately owned, there are a number of ways of legitimately transferring justly acquired objects—gifts and voluntary exchange are among them, theft and blackmail are not. There is, however, no pattern to which a just distribution should conform. In the absence of force and fraud, people may do what they wish with their holdings. They have a right to acquire and dispose of their property as they see fit, and individuals are entitled to their personal talents and characteristics and to whatever property they can obtain with them, as long as the negative rights of others are not violated in the process. Taxation for purposes of redistribution, he then argues, is on a par with forced labor. In the final section, "The Tale of the Slave," Nozick creates an imaginary series of events meant to illustrate and extend his argument that taking property is tantamount to slavery. Robert Nozick was the Joseph Pellegrino University Professor at Harvard University.

---

* Selected excerpts from pages 149–157, 160–163, and 290–292 from *Anarchy, State, and Utopia* by Robert Nozick. Copyright © 1974 by Basic Books, Inc. Reprinted by permission of Basic Books, a member of Perseus Books, L.L.C. Footnotes omitted.

The term "distributive justice" is not a neutral one. Hearing the term "distribution," most people presume that some thing or mechanism uses some principle or criterion to give out a supply of things. Into this process of distributing shares some error may have crept. So it is an open question, at least, whether *re*distribution should take place; whether we should do again what has already been done once, though poorly. However, we are not in the position of children who have been given portions of pie by someone who now makes last-minute adjustments to rectify careless cutting. There is no *central* distribution, no person or group entitled to control all the resources, jointly deciding how they are to be doled out. What each person gets, he gets from others who give to him in exchange for something, or as a gift. In a free society, diverse persons control different resources, and new holdings arise out of the voluntary exchanges and actions of persons. There is no more a distributing or distribution of shares than there is a distributing of mates in a society in which persons choose whom they shall marry. The total result is the product of many individual decisions which the different individuals involved are entitled to make. ... We shall speak of people's holdings; a principle of justice in holdings describes (part of) what justice tells us (requires) about holdings.

The Entitlement Theory

The subject of justice in holdings consists of three major topics. The first is the *original acquisition of holdings,* the appropriation of unheld things. This includes the issues of how unheld things may come to be held; the process, or processes, by which unheld things may come to be held; the things that may come to be held by these processes; the extent of what comes to be held by a particular process; and so on. We shall refer to the complicated truth about this topic, which we shall not formulate here, as the principle of justice in acquisition. The second topic concerns the *transfer of holdings* from one person to another. By what processes may a person transfer holdings to another? How may a person acquire a holding from another who holds it? Under this topic come general descriptions of voluntary exchange, and gift and (on the other hand) fraud, as well as reference to particular conventional details fixed upon in a given society. The complicated truth about this subject (with place-holders for conventional details) we shall call the principle of justice in transfer. (And we shall suppose it also includes principles governing how a person may divest himself of a holding, passing it into an unheld state.)

If the world were wholly just, the following inductive definition would exhaustively cover the subject of justice in holdings.

1 A person who acquires a holding in accordance with the principle of justice in acquisition is entitled to that holding.
2 A person who acquires a holding in accordance with the principle of justice in transfer, from someone else entitled to the holding, is entitled to the holding.
3 No one is entitled to a holding except by (repeated) applications of 1 and 2.

The complete principle of distributive justice would say simply that a distribution is just if everyone is entitled to the holdings they possess under the distribution.

A distribution is just if it arises from another just distribution by legitimate means. The legitimate means of moving from one distribution to another are specified by the principle of justice in transfer. The legitimate first "moves" are specified by the principle of justice in acquisition. Whatever arises from a just situation by just steps is itself just. The means of change specified by the principle of justice in transfer preserve justice ....

Not all actual situations are generated in accordance with the two principles of justice in holdings: the principle of justice in acquisition and the principle of justice in transfer. Some people steal from others or defraud them or enslave them, seizing their product and preventing them from living as they choose, or forcibly exclude others from competing in exchanges. None of these are permissible modes of transition from one situation to another. And some persons acquire holdings by means not sanctioned by the principle of justice in acquisition. The existence of past injustice (previous violations of the first two principles of justice in holdings) raises the third major topic under justice in holdings: the *rectification of injustice in holdings*. If past injustice has shaped present holdings in various ways, some identifiable and some not, what now, if anything, ought to be done to rectify these injustices? What obligations do the performers of injustice have toward those whose position is worse than it would have been had the injustice not been done? Or than it would have been had compensation been paid promptly? How, if at all, do things change if the beneficiaries and those made worse off are not the direct parties in the act of injustice, but, for example, their descendants? Is an injustice done to someone whose holding was itself based upon an unrectified injustice? How far back must one go in wiping clean the historical slate of injustices? What may victims of injustice permissibly do in order to rectify the injustices being done to them, including the many injustices done by persons acting through their government? I do not know of a thorough or theoretically sophisticated treatment of such issues. Idealizing greatly, let us suppose theoretical investigation will produce a principle of rectification. This principle uses historical information about previous situations and injustices done in them (as defined by the first two principles of justice and rights against interference) and information about the actual course of events that flowed from these injustices until the present, and it yields a description (or descriptions) of holdings in the society. The principle of rectification presumably will make use of its best estimate of subjunctive information about what would have occurred (or a probability distribution over what might have occurred, using the expected value) if the injustice had not taken place. If the actual description of holdings turns out not to be one of the descriptions yielded by the principle, then one of the descriptions yielded must be realized.

The general outlines of the theory of justice in holdings are that the holdings of a person are just if he is entitled to them by the principles of justice in acquisition and transfer, or by the principle of rectification of injustice (as specified by the first two principles). If each person's holdings are just, then the total set (distribution) of holdings is just ....

Historical Principles and End-Result Principles

The general outlines of the entitlement theory illuminate the nature and defects of other conceptions of distributive justice. The entitlement theory of justice in distribution is *historical;* whether a distribution is just depends upon how it came about. In contrast, *current time-slice principles* of justice hold that the justice of a distribution is determined by how things are distributed (who has what) as judged by some *structural* principle(s) of just distribution. A utilitarian who judges between any two distributions by seeing which has the greater sum of utility and, if the sums tie, applies some fixed equality criterion to choose the more equal distribution, would hold a current time-slice principle of justice ....

Most persons do not accept current time-slice principles as constituting the whole story about distributive shares. They think it relevant in assessing the justice of a situation to consider not only the distribution it embodies but also how that distribution came about. If some persons are in prison for murder or war crimes, we do not say that to assess the justice of the distribution in the society we must look only at what this person has and that person has and that person has ... at the current time. We think it relevant to ask whether someone did something so that he *deserved* to be punished, deserved to have a lower share. Most will agree to the relevance of further information with regard to punishments and penalties. Consider also desired things. One traditional socialist view is that workers are entitled to the product and full fruits of their labor; they have earned it; a distribution is unjust if it does not give the workers what they are entitled to. Such entitlements are based upon some past history. No socialist holding this view would find it comforting to be told that because the actual distribution A happens to coincide structurally with the one he desires D, A therefore is no less just than D; it differs only in that the "parasitic" owners of capital receive under A what the workers are entitled to under D and the workers receive under A what the owners are entitled to under D, namely very little. This socialist rightly, in my view, holds onto the notions of earning, producing, entitlement, desert, and so forth, and he rejects current time-slice principles that look only to the structure of the resulting set of holdings. (The set of holdings resulting from what? Isn't it implausible that how holdings are produced and come to exist has no effect at all on who should hold what?) His mistake lies in his view of what entitlements arise out of what sorts of productive processes.

We construe the position we discuss too narrowly by speaking of *current* time-slice principles. Nothing is changed if structural principles operate upon a time sequence of current time-slice profiles and, for example, give someone more now to counterbalance the less he has had earlier. ... Henceforth, we shall refer to such unhistorical principles of distributive justice, including the current time-slice principles, as *end-result principles* or *end-state principles*.

In contrast to end-result principles of justice, *historical principles* of justice hold that past circumstances or actions of people can create differential entitlements or differential deserts to things ....

Patterning

The entitlement principles of justice in holdings that we have sketched are historical principles of justice. To better understand their precise character, we shall distinguish them from another subclass of the historical principles. Consider, as an example, the principle of distribution according to moral merit. This principle requires that total distributive shares vary directly with moral merit; no person should have a greater share than anyone whose moral merit is greater. (If moral merit could be not merely ordered but measured on an interval or ratio scale, stronger principles could be formulated.) Or consider the principle that results by substituting "usefulness to society" for "moral merit" in the previous principle. ... The principle of distribution in accordance with moral merit is a patterned historical principle, which specifies a patterned distribution. "Distribute according to IQ," is a patterned principle that ... is not historical, however, in that it does not look to any past actions creating differential entitlements to evaluate a distribution; it requires only distributional matrices whose columns are labeled by IQ scores. The distribution in a society, however, may be composed of such simple patterned distributions, without itself being simply patterned. Different sectors may operate different patterns, or some combination of patterns may operate in different proportions across a society. A distribution composed in this manner, from a small number of patterned distributions, we also shall term "patterned." And we extend the use of "pattern" to include the overall designs put forth by combinations of end-state principles.

Almost every suggested principle of distributive justice is patterned; to each according to his moral merit or needs or marginal product or how hard he tries or the weighted sum of the foregoing, and so on. The principle of entitlement we have sketched is *not* patterned. There is no one natural dimension or weighted sum or combination of a small number of natural dimensions that yields the distributions generated in accordance with the principle of entitlement. The set of holdings that results when some persons receive their marginal products, others win at gambling, others receive a share of their mate's income, others receive gifts from foundations, others receive interest on loans, others receive gifts from admirers, others receive returns on investment, others make for themselves much of what they have, others find things, and so on, will not be patterned ....

How Liberty Upsets Patterns

It is not clear how those holding alternative conceptions of distributive justice can reject the entitlement conception of justice in holdings. For suppose a distribution favored by one of these nonentitlement conceptions is realized. Let us suppose it is your favorite one and let us call this distribution D_1; perhaps everyone has an equal share, perhaps shares vary in accordance with some dimension you treasure. Now suppose that Wilt Chamberlain is greatly in demand by basketball teams, being a great gate attraction. [Chamberlain was a dominating NBA basketball star of the 1960s and early 1970s—Ed. note.] (Also suppose contracts run only for a year, with players being free agents.) He signs the following sort of contract with a team: in each home game, twenty-five cents from the price of each ticket of admission goes to him. (We ignore the question of whether he is "gouging" the owners, letting them look out for themselves.) The season starts, and people cheerfully attend his team's games; they buy their tickets, each time dropping a separate twenty-five cents of their admission price into a special box with Chamberlain's name on it. They are excited about seeing him play; it is worth the total admission price to them. Let us suppose that in one season one million persons attend his home games, and Wilt Chamberlain winds up with $250,000, a much larger sum than the average income and larger even than anyone else has. Is he entitled to this income? Is this new distribution, D_2, unjust? If so, why? There is *no* question about whether each of the people was entitled to the control over the resources they held in D_1; because that was the distribution (your favorite) that (for the purposes of argument) we assumed was acceptable. Each of these persons chose to give twenty-five cents of their money to Chamberlain. They could have spent it on going to the movies or on candy bars or on copies of *Dissent* magazine or of *Monthly Review*. But they all, at least one million of them, converged on giving it to Wilt Chamberlain in exchange for watching him play basketball. If D_1 was a just distribution and people voluntarily moved from it to D_2, transferring parts of their shares they were given under D_1 (what was it for if not to do something with?), isn't D_2 also just? If the people were entitled to dispose of the resources to which they were entitled (under D_1), didn't this include their being entitled to give it to, or exchange it with, Wilt Chamberlain? Can anyone else complain on grounds of justice? Each other person already has his legitimate share under D_1 Under D_1, there is nothing that anyone has that anyone else has a claim of justice against. After someone transfers something to Wilt Chamberlain, third parties *still* have their legitimate shares; *their* shares are not changed. By what process could such a transfer among two persons give rise to a legitimate claim of distributive justice on a portion of what was transferred by a third party who had no claim of justice on any holding of the others *before* the transfer?

.... We might imagine the exchanges occurring in a socialist society after hours. [Suppose] Wilt Chamberlain decides to put in *overtime* to earn additional money. (First his work quota is set; he works time over that.) Or imagine it is a skilled juggler people like to see who puts on shows after hours.

Why might someone work overtime in a society in which it is assumed their needs are satisfied? Perhaps because they care about things other than needs. I like to write in books that I read and to have easy access to books for browsing at odd hours. It would be very pleasant and convenient to have the resources of Widener Library in my backyard. No society, I assume, will provide such resources close to each person who would like them as part of his regular allotment (under D_1). Thus, persons either must do without some extra things that they want or be allowed to do something extra to get some of these things. On what basis could the inequalities that would eventuate be forbidden? Notice also that small factories would spring up in a socialist society, unless forbidden. I melt down some of my personal possessions (under D_1) and build a machine out of the material. I offer you, and others, a philosophy lecture once a week in exchange for your cranking the handle on my machine, whose products I exchange for yet other things, and so on. (The raw materials used by the machine are given to me by others who possess them under D_1 in exchange for hearing lectures.) Each person might participate to gain things over and above their allotment under D_1 Some persons even might want to leave their job in socialist industry and work full time in this private sector. ... Here I wish merely to note how private property even in means of production would occur in a socialist society that did not forbid people to use as they wished some of the resources they are given under the socialist distribution D_1. The socialist society would have to forbid capitalist acts between consenting adults.

The general point illustrated by the Wilt Chamberlain example and the example of the entrepreneur in a socialist society is that no end-state principle or distributional-patterned principle of justice can be continuously realized without continuous interference with people's lives. Any favored pattern would be transformed into one unfavored by the principle, by people choosing to act in various ways; for example, by people exchanging goods and services with other people or giving things to other people, things the transferrers are entitled to under the favored distributional pattern. To maintain a pattern one must either continually interfere to stop people from transferring resources as they wish to or continually (or periodically) interfere to take from some persons resources that others for some reason chose to transfer to them ....

Redistribution and Property Rights

Apparently, patterned principles allow people to choose to spend upon themselves, but not upon others, those resources they are entitled to (or rather, receive) under some favored distributional pattern D_1. For if each of several persons chooses to expend some of his D_1 resources upon one other person, then that other person will receive more than his D_1 share, distributing the favored distributional pattern. Maintaining a distributional pattern is individualism with a vengeance! Patterned distributional principles do not give people what entitlement principles do, only better distributed. For they do not give the right to choose what to do with what one has; they do not give the right to choose to pursue an end involving (intrinsically, or as a means) the enhancement of another's position. To such views, families are disturbing; for within a family occur transfers that upset the favored distributional pattern. Either families themselves become units to which distribution takes place, the column-occupiers (on what rationale?), or loving behavior is forbidden. We should note in passing the ambivalent position of radicals toward the family. Its loving relationships are seen as a model to be emulated and extended across the whole society at the same time that it is denounced as a suffocating institution to be broken and condemned as a focus of parochial concerns that interfere with achieving radical goals. Need we say that it is not appropriate to enforce across the wider society the relationships of love and care appropriate within a family, relationships which are voluntarily undertaken?[1] Incidentally, love is an interesting instance of another relationship that is historical, in that (like justice) it depends upon what actually occurred. An adult may come to love another because of the other's characteristics; but it is the other person, and not the characteristics, that is loved. The love is not transferable to someone else with the same characteristics, even to one who "scores" higher for these characteristics. And the love endures through changes of the characteristics that give rise to it. One loves the particular person one actually encountered. Why love is historical, attaching to persons in this way and not to characteristics, is an interesting and puzzling question.

Proponents of patterned principles of distributive justice focus upon criteria for determining who is to receive holdings; they consider the reasons for which someone should have something and also the total picture of holdings. Whether or not it is better to give than to receive, proponents of patterned principles ignore giving altogether. In considering the distribution of goods, income, and so forth, their theories are theories of recipient justice; they completely ignore any right a person might have to give something to someone. Even in exchanges where each party is simultaneously giver and recipient, patterned principles of justice focus only upon the recipient role and its supposed rights. Thus discussions tend to focus on whether people (should) have a right to inherit, rather than on whether people (should) have a right to bequeath or on whether persons who have a right to hold also have a right to choose that others hold in their place. I lack a good explanation of why the usual theories of distributive justice are so recipient oriented; ignoring givers and transferrers and their rights is of a piece with ignoring producers and their entitlements. But why is it *all* ignored?

Patterned principles of distributive justice necessitate *re*distributive activities. The likelihood is small that any actual freely-arrived-at set of holdings fits a given pattern; and the likelihood is nil that it will continue to fit the pattern as people exchange and give. From the point of view of an entitlement theory, redistribution is a serious matter indeed, involving, as it does, the violation of people's rights. (An exception is those takings that fall under the principle of the rectification of injustices.) From other points of view, also, it is serious.

Taxation of earnings from labor is on a par with forced labor.[2] Some persons find this claim obviously true: taking the earnings of *n* hours labor is like taking *n* hours from the person; it is like forcing the person to work *n* hours for another's purpose. Others find the claim absurd. But even these, *if* they object to forced labor, would oppose forcing unemployed hippies to work for the benefit of the needy. And they would also object to forcing each person to work five extra hours each week for the benefit of the needy. But a system that takes five hours' wages in taxes does not seem to them like one that forces someone to work five hours, since it offers the person forced a wider range of choice in activities than does taxation in kind with the particular labor specified. (But we can imagine a gradation of systems of forced labor, from one that specifies a particular activity to one that gives a choice among two activities to … and so on up.) Furthermore, people envisage a system with something like a proportional tax on everything above the amount necessary for basic needs. Some think this does not force someone to work extra hours, since there is no fixed number of extra hours he is forced to work and since he can avoid the tax entirely by earning only enough to cover his basic needs. This is a very uncharacteristic view of forcing for those who *also* think people are forced to do something *whenever* the alternatives they face are considerably worse. However, *neither* view is correct. The fact that others intentionally intervene, in violation of a side constraint against aggression, to threaten force to limit the alternatives, in this case to paying taxes or (presumably the worse alternative) bare subsistence, makes the taxation system one of forced labor and distinguishes it from other cases of limited choices which are not forcings.

The man who chooses to work longer to gain an income more than sufficient for his basic needs prefers some extra goods or services to the leisure and activities he could perform during the possible nonworking hours: whereas the man who chooses not to work the extra time prefers the leisure activities to the extra goods or services he could acquire by working more. Given this, if it would be illegitimate for a tax system to seize some of a man's leisure (forced labor) for the purpose of serving the needy, how can it be legitimate for a tax system to seize some of a man's goods for that purpose? Why should we treat the man whose happiness requires certain material goods or services differently from the man whose preferences and desires make such goods unnecessary for his happiness? Why should the man who prefers seeing a movie (and who has to earn money for a ticket) be open to the required call to aid the needy, while the person who prefers looking at a sunset (and hence need earn no extra money) is not? Indeed, isn't it surprising that redistributionists choose to ignore the man whose pleasures are so easily attainable without extra labor, while adding yet another burden to the poor unfortunate who must work for his pleasures? If anything, one would have expected the reverse. Why is the person with the nonmaterial or nonconsumption desire allowed to proceed unimpeded to his most favored feasible alternative, whereas the man whose pleasures or desires involve material things and who must work for extra money (thereby serving whomever considers his activities valuable enough to pay him) is constrained in what he can realize? Perhaps there is no difference in principle. And perhaps some think the answer concerns merely administrative convenience. (These questions and issues will not disturb those who think that forced labor to serve the needy or to realize some favored end-state pattern is acceptable.) In a fuller discussion we would have (and want) to extend our argument to include interest, entrepreneurial profits, and so on. Those who doubt that this extension can be carried through, and who draw the line here at taxation of income from labor, will have to state rather complicated patterned *historical* principles of distributive justice, since end-state principles would not distinguish *sources* of income in any way. It is enough for now to get away from end-state principles and to make clear how various patterned principles are dependent upon particular views about the sources or the illegitimacy or the lesser legitimacy of profits, interest, and so on; which particular views may well be mistaken.

What sort of right over others does a legally institutionalized end-state pattern give one? The central core of the notion of a property right in X, relative to which other parts of the notion are to be explained, is the right to determine what shall be done with X; the right to choose which of the constrained set of options concerning X shall be realized or attempted. The constraints are set by other principles or laws operating in the society; in our theory, by the Lockean rights people possess (under the minimal state). My property rights in my knife allow me to leave it where I will, but not in your chest. I may choose which of the acceptable options involving the knife is to be realized. This notion of property helps us to understand why earlier theorists spoke of people as having property in themselves and their labor. They viewed each person as having a right to decide what would become of himself and what he would do and as having a right to reap the benefits of what he did ....

When end-result principles of distributive justice are built into the legal structure of a society, they (as do most patterned principles) give each citizen an enforceable claim to some portion of the total social product; that is, to some portion of the sum total of the individually and jointly made products. This total product is produced by individuals laboring, using means of production others have saved to bring into existence, by people organizing production or creating means to produce new things or things in a new way. It is on this batch of individual activities that patterned distributional principles give each individual an enforceable claim. Each person has a claim to the activities and the products of other persons, independently of whether the other persons enter into particular relationships that give rise to these claims, and independently of whether they voluntarily take these claims upon themselves, in charity or in exchange for something.

Whether it is done through taxation on wages or on wages over a certain amount or through seizure of profits or through there being a big *social pot* so that it's not clear what's coming from where and what's going where, patterned principles of distributive justice involve appropriating the actions of other persons. Seizing the results of someone's labor is equivalent to seizing hours from him and directing him to carry on various activities. If people force you to do certain work, or unrewarded work, for a certain period of time, they decide what you are to do and what purposes your work is to serve apart from your decisions. This process whereby they take this decision from you makes them a *part owner* of you; it gives them a property right in you, just as having such partial control and power of decision, by right, over an animal or inanimate object would be to have a property right in it.

End-state and most patterned principles of distributive justice institute (partial) ownership by others of people and their actions and labor. These principles involve a shift from the classical liberals' notion of self-ownership to a notion of (partial) property rights in *other* people ....

May a person emigrate from a nation that has institutionalized some end-state or patterned distributional principle? .... Consider a nation having a compulsory scheme of minimal social provision to aid the neediest (or one organized so as to maximize the position of the worst-off group); no one may opt out of participating in it. (None may say, "Don't compel me to contribute to others and don't provide for me via this compulsory mechanism if I am in need.") Everyone above a certain level is forced to contribute to aid the needy. But if emigration from the country were allowed, anyone could choose to move to another country that did not have compulsory social provision but otherwise was (as much as possible) identical. In such a case, the person's *only* motive for leaving would be to avoid participating in the compulsory scheme of social provision. And if he does leave, the needy in his initial country will receive no (compelled) help from him. What rationale yields the result that the person be permitted to emigrate yet forbidden to stay and opt out of the compulsory scheme of social provision? If providing for the needy is of overriding importance, this does militate against allowing internal opting out; but it also speaks against allowing external emigration. (Would it also support, to some extent, the kidnapping of persons living in a place without compulsory social provision, who could be forced to make a contribution to the needy in your community?) ....

The Tale of the Slave

Consider the following sequence of cases, which we shall call *The Tale of the Slave*, and imagine it is you.

1   There is a slave completely at the mercy of his brutal master's whims. He often is cruelly beaten, called out in the middle of the night, and so on.
2   The master is kindlier and beats the slave only for stated infractions of his rules (not fulfilling the work quota and so on). He gives the slave some free time.
3   The master has a group of slaves, and he decides how things are to be allocated among them on nice grounds, taking into account their needs, merit, and so on.
4   The master allows his slaves four days on their own and requires them to work only three days a week on his land. The rest of the time is their own.
5   The master allows his slaves to go off and work in the city (or anywhere they wish) for wages. He requires only that they send back to him three-sevenths of their wages. He also retains the power to recall them to the plantation if some emergency threatens his land and to raise or lower the three-sevenths amount

required to be turned over to him. He further retains the right to restrict the slaves from participating in certain dangerous activities that threaten his financial return, for example, mountain climbing, cigarette smoking.

6 The master allows all of his 10,000 slaves, except you, to vote, and the joint decision is made by all of them. There is open discussion, and so forth, among them, and they have the power to determine to what uses to put whatever percentage of your (and their) earnings they decide to take, what activities may legitimately be forbidden to you, and so on.

Let us pause in this sequence of cases to take stock. If the master [in case 6] contracts this transfer of power so that he cannot withdraw it, you have a change of master. You now have 10,000 masters instead of just one; rather you have one 10,000-headed master. Perhaps the 10,000 even will be kindlier than the benevolent master in case 2. Still, they are your master. However, still more can be done. A kindly single master (as in case 2) might allow his slave(s) to speak up and try to persuade him to make a certain decision. The 10,000-headed master can do this too.

7 Though still not having the vote, you are at liberty (and are given the right) to enter into the discussions of the 10,000 to try to persuade them to adopt various policies and to treat you and themselves in a certain way. They then go off to vote to decide upon policies covering the vast range of their powers.
8 In appreciation of your useful contributions to discussion, the 10,000 allow you to vote if they are deadlocked; they commit themselves to this procedure. After the discussion you mark your vote on a slip of paper, and they go off and vote. In the eventuality that they divide evenly on some issue, 5,000 for and 5,000 against, they look at your ballot and count it. This has never yet happened; they have never yet had the occasion to open your ballot. (A single master also might commit himself to letting his slave decide any issue concerning about which he, the master, was absolutely indifferent.)
9 They throw your vote in with theirs. If they are exactly tied, your vote carries the issue. Otherwise it makes no difference to the electoral outcome.

The question is: which transition from case 1 to case 9 made it no longer the tale of a slave?

Notes

1 One indication of the stringency of Rawls's difference principle is its inappropriateness as a governing principle even within a family of individuals who love one another. Should a family devote its resources to maximizing the position of its least well off and least talented child, holding back the other children or using resources of their education and development only if they will follow a policy through their lifetimes of maximizing the position of their least fortunate sibling? Surely not. How then can this even be considered as the appropriate policy for enforcement in the wider society? ....
2 I am unsure as to whether the arguments I present below show that such taxation merely is forced labor; so that "is on a par with" means "is one kind of." Or alternatively, whether the arguments emphasize the great similarities between such taxation and forced labor, to show it is plausible and illuminating to view such taxation in the light of forced labor.

Review and Discussion Questions

1. Why does Nozick think that the notion of "distributive justice" is misleading?
2. What are the three topics that Nozick thinks constitute the subject of justice in holdings?
3. Distinguish historical from end-result principles.
4. What is a patterned principle?
5. Using the Wilt Chamberlain example, explain Nozick's argument that no patterned principle is compatible with freedom.
6. In what way does Nozick think taxation is comparable to forced labor?
7. What does Nozick mean by "self-ownership," and how is it relevant to entitlements?
8. Explain *The Tale of the Slave*, indicating the point Nozick is making with the parable.
9. How would you answer the question at the end of Nozick's essay?

READING: INEQUALITY AND OTHER PROBLEMS WITH NOZICK'S LIBERTARIANISM

JOHN RAWLS[*]

More than twenty years after writing *A Theory of Justice*, John Rawls published *Political Liberalism*, an extended and reconsidered account of his earlier views. In this excerpt Rawls criticizes libertarian ideas about markets, particularly Nozick's famous formulation. Rawls argues that the major institutions in society, not individual relationships, are the first subject of justice. He calls these institutions the "basic structure" of society and includes a society's constitution, federal and state laws, capitalist institutions, financial markets, and the family as examples of society's major institutions. Rawls explains why he believes that justice ought to be concerned primarily with the rules of society's basic structure and why Nozick's entitlement theory, based on the nonviolation of individual rights, is inadequate as an account of economic justice. John Rawls held the James Bryant Conant University Professorship of Philosophy at Harvard University.

Libertarianism Has No Special Role for the Basic Structure

A completely general theory like utilitarianism is not the only kind of view that rejects the idea that special first principles are required for the basic structure. Consider for example the libertarian theory, which holds that only a minimal state limited to the narrow functions of protection against force, theft, fraud, enforcement of contracts, and so on, is justified; and that any state with more comprehensive powers violates the rights of individuals. For our purposes here, perhaps the main features of this theory are these:[1]

The aim is to see how the minimal state could have arisen from a perfectly just situation by a series of steps each of which is morally permissible and violates no

---

[*] Abridged from pp. 262–271, "Libertarianism Has No Special Role for the Basic Structure," in *Political Liberalism* by John Rawls. Copyright © 1993 by Columbia University Press. Reprinted by permission of Columbia University Press.

one's rights. If we can see how this could happen when everyone acts as they ought and why a no more extensive state could arise, then we shall have justified the minimal state, provided of course that the moral theory that identifies the initial situation as just, and defines the permissible departures from it, is correct. To this end, we assume that a state of nature once existed in which there was relative abundance and the actual configuration of people's holdings raised no moral questions. The existing configuration was just and all were adequately provided for. This state of nature is also characterized by the absence of any institution (such as the state) that enforces certain rules and thereby establishes an institutional basis for people's expectations as to how others will act.

Next, a libertarian theory defines certain basic principles of justice that govern the acquisition of holdings (the appropriation of previously unheld things) and the transfer of holdings from one person (or association) to another. Then a just configuration of holdings is defined recursively: a person is entitled to hold whatever is acquired in accordance with the principles of justice in acquisition and transfer, and no one is entitled to something except by repeated application of these principles. If one starts from a state of nature in which the existing array of holdings is just, and if everyone always acts subsequently in accordance with justice in acquisition and transfer, then all later configurations are likewise said to be just. It is maintained that the principles of just acquisition and transfer preserve the justice of holdings throughout the whole sequence of historical transactions, however extended in time. The only way injustice is thought to arise is from deliberate violations of these principles, or from error and ignorance of what they require and the like.

Finally, and most relevant for our purposes here, a great variety of associations and modes of cooperation may form depending upon what individuals actually do and what agreements are reached. No special theory is needed to cover these transactions and joint activities: the requisite theory is already provided by the principles of justice in acquisition and transfer, suitably interpreted in the light of certain provisos. All forms of legitimate social cooperation are, then, the handiwork of individuals who voluntarily consent to them; there are no powers or rights lawfully exercised by associations, including the state, that are not rights already possessed by each individual acting alone in the initial just state of nature.

One noteworthy feature of this doctrine is that the state is just like any other private association. The state comes about in the same way as other associations and its formation in the perfectly as-if just historical process is governed by the same principles.[2] Of course, the state serves certain characteristic purposes, but this is true of associations generally. Moreover, the relation of individuals to the state (the legitimate minimal state) is just like their relation with any private corporation with which they have made an agreement. Thus political allegiance is interpreted as a private contractual obligation with, so to speak, a large and successful monopolistic firm: namely, the locally dominant protection agency. There is in general no uniform public law that applies equally to all persons, but rather a network of private agreements; this network represents the procedures the dominant protection agency (the state) has agreed to use with its clients, as it were, and these procedures may differ from client to client depending on the bargain each was in a position to make with the dominant agency. No one can be compelled to enter into such an agreement and everyone always has the option of becoming an independent: we have the choice of being one of the state's clients, just as we do in the case of other associations. While the libertarian view makes important use of the notion of agreement, it is not a *social* contract theory at all; for a social contract theory envisages the original compact as establishing a system of common public law which defines and regulates political authority and applies to everyone as citizen. Both political authority and citizenship are to be understood through the conception of the social contract itself. By viewing the state as a private association the libertarian doctrine rejects the fundamental ideas of the contract theory, and so quite naturally it has no place for a special theory of justice for the basic structure. ... The problem here is to show why the basic structure has a special role and why it is reasonable to seek special principles to regulate it.

The Importance of Background Justice

I shall begin by noting several considerations that might lead us to regard the basic structure as the first subject of justice, at least when we proceed within the framework of a Kantian social contract theory.

The first consideration is this: suppose we begin with the initially attractive idea that social circumstances and people's relationships to one another should develop over time in accordance with free agreements fairly arrived at and fully honored.

Straightaway we need an account of when agreements are free and the social circumstances under which they are reached are fair. In addition, while these conditions may be fair at an earlier time, the accumulated results of many separate and ostensibly fair agreements, together with social trends and historical contingencies, are likely in the course of time to alter citizens' relationships and opportunities so that the conditions for free and fair agreements no longer hold. The role of the institutions that belong to the basic structure is to secure just background conditions against which the actions of individuals and associations take place. Unless this structure is appropriately regulated and adjusted, an initially just social process will eventually cease to be just, however free and fair particular transactions may look when viewed by themselves ....

There are four points to emphasize in these familiar observations: first, we cannot tell by looking only at the conduct of individuals and associations in the immediate (or local) circumstances whether, from a social point of view, agreements reached are just or fair. For this assessment depends importantly on the features of the basic structure, on whether it succeeds in maintaining background justice. Thus whether wage agreements are fair rests, for example, on the nature of the labor market: excess market power must be prevented and fair bargaining power should obtain between employers and employees. But in addition, fairness depends on underlying social conditions, such as fair opportunity, extending backward in time and well beyond any limited view.

Second, fair background conditions may exist at one time and be gradually undermined even though no one acts unfairly when their conduct is judged by the rules that apply to transactions within the appropriately circumscribed local situation. The fact that everyone with reason believes that they are acting fairly and scrupulously honoring the norms governing agreements is not sufficient to preserve background justice. This is an important though obvious point: when our social world is pervaded by duplicity and deceit we are tempted to think that law and government are necessary only because of the propensity of individuals to act unfairly. But, to the contrary, the tendency is rather for background justice to be eroded even when individuals act fairly: the overall result of separate and independent transactions is away from and not toward background justice. We might say: in this case the invisible hand guides things in the wrong direction and favors an oligopolistic configuration of accumulations that succeeds in maintaining unjustified inequalities and restrictions on fair opportunity. Therefore, we require special institutions to preserve background justice, and a special conception of justice to define how these institutions are to be set up.

The preceding observation assumes, thirdly, that there are no feasible and practicable rules that it is sensible to impose on individuals that can prevent the erosion of background justice. This is because the rules governing agreements and individual transactions cannot be too complex, or require too much information to be correctly applied; nor should they enjoin individuals to engage in bargaining with many widely scattered third parties, since this would impose excessive transaction costs. ... All of this is evident enough if we consider the cumulative effects of the purchase and sale of landed property and its transmission by bequest over generations. It is obviously not sensible to impose on parents (as heads of families) the duty to adjust their own bequests to what they estimate the effects of the totality of actual bequests will be on the next generation, much less beyond.

Thus, fourth and finally, we arrive at the idea of a division of labor between two kinds of social rules, and the different institutional forms in which these rules are realized. The basic structure comprises first the institutions that define the social background and includes as well those operations that continually adjust and compensate for the inevitable tendencies away from background fairness, for example, such operations as income and inheritance taxation designed to even out the ownership of property. This structure also enforces through the legal system another set of rules that govern the transactions and agreements between individuals and associations (the law of contract, and so on). The rules relating to fraud and duress, and the like, belong to these rules, and satisfy the requirements of simplicity and practicality. They are framed to leave individuals and associations free to act effectively in pursuit of their ends and without excessive constraints.

To conclude: we start with the basic structure and try to see how this structure itself should make the adjustments necessary to preserve background justice. What we look for, in effect, is an institutional division of labor between the basic structure and the rules applying directly to individuals and associations and to be followed by them in particular transactions. If this division of labor can be established, individuals and associations are then left free to advance their ends more effectively within the framework of the basic structure, secure in the knowledge that elsewhere in the social system the necessary corrections to preserve background justice are being made.

How the Basic Structure Affects Individuals

Further reflections also point to the special role of the basic structure ....

Now everyone recognizes that the institutional form of society affects its members and determines in large part the kind of persons they want to be as well as the kind of persons they are. The social structure also limits people's ambitions and hopes in different ways; for they will with reason view themselves in part according to their position in it and take account of the means and opportunities they can realistically expect. So an economic regime, say, is not only an institutional scheme for satisfying existing desires and aspirations but a way of fashioning desires and aspirations in the future. More generally, the basic structure shapes the way the social system produces and reproduces over time a certain form of culture shared by persons with certain conceptions of their good.

Again, we cannot view the talents and abilities of individuals as fixed natural gifts. To be sure, even as realized there is presumably a significant genetic component. However, these abilities and talents cannot come to fruition apart from social conditions, and as realized they always take but one of many possible forms. Developed natural capacities are always a selection, a small selection at that, from the possibilities that might have been attained. In addition, an ability is not, for example, a computer in the head with a definite measurable capacity unaffected by social circumstances. Among the elements affecting the realization of natural capacities are social attitudes of encouragement and support and the institutions concerned with their training and use. Thus even a potential ability at any given time is not something unaffected by existing social forms and particular contingencies over the course of life up to that moment. So not only our final ends and hopes for ourselves but also our realized abilities and talents reflect, to a large degree, our personal history, opportunities, and social position. There is no way of knowing what we might have been had these things been different.

Finally, the preceding considerations must be viewed together with the fact that the basic structure most likely permits significant social and economic inequalities in the life prospects of citizens depending on their social origins, their realized natural endowments, and the chance opportunities and accidents that have shaped their personal history ....

The nature of inequalities in life prospects can be clarified by contrasting them with other inequalities. Thus imagine a university in which there are three ranks of faculty and everyone stays in each rank the same length of time and receives the same salary. Then while there are inequalities of rank and salary at any given time, there is no inequality in life prospects between faculty members. The same may be true when members of an association adopt a rotation scheme for filling certain more highly privileged or rewarded positions, perhaps because they involve taking greater responsibility. If the scheme is designed so that, barring accidents, death, and the like, all serve the same time in these positions, there are again no inequalities in life prospects.

What the theory of justice must regulate is the inequalities in life prospects between citizens that arise from social starting positions, natural advantages, and historical contingencies. Even if these inequalities are not in some cases very great, their effect may be great enough so that over time they have significant cumulative consequences. The Kantian form of the contract doctrine focuses on these inequalities in the basic structure in the conviction that these inequalities are the most fundamental ones: once suitable principles are found to govern them and the requisite institutions are established, the problem of how to regulate other inequalities can be much more easily resolved.

Notes

1. I follow the account in Robert Nozick, *Anarchy, State, and Utopia* (New York: Basic Books, 1974).
2. I distinguish here and elsewhere below between an as-if historical and an as-if nonhistorical process (or procedure). In both cases the process is hypothetical in the sense that the process has not actually occurred, or may not have occurred. But as-if historical processes can occur: they are not thought to be excluded by fundamental social laws or natural facts. Thus on the libertarian view, if everyone were to follow the principles of justice in acquisition and transfer, and they can follow them, then the as-if historical process leading to the formation of the state would be realized. By contrast, an as-if nonhistorical process, for example, the procedure leading up to the agreement in the original position, cannot take place ....

Review and Discussion Questions

1. Suppose that a society exists in which no one's rights are violated on an individual level. What is Rawls's argument that injustice could still occur over time?
2. What is objectionable about serious inequalities in life prospects created by the basic structure in society? How do you think Nozick would respond to this problem?
3. Rawls refers to a division of labor between two kinds of social rules. What is he talking about, and why does he believe that this distinction is important?

READING: MONEY AND COMMODITIES

MICHAEL WALZER[*]

In this selection from his book *Spheres of Justice*, Walzer begins with a discussion of the types of goods that cannot be bought or sold, suggesting that selling these goods could undermine some important values. He then considers the question of ownership more broadly and examines what occurs when market power becomes illegitimately applied to other spheres of life, such as gaining political power. Walzer's overall political philosophy is that social life divides into distinct spheres, such as markets, politics, family, and religion, and that each sphere has its own principles for deciding what counts as legitimate success in that sphere. These principles are not then reducible to any single overall principle that regulates all spheres of life, as suggested by utilitarianism or any other "monistic" account of the good. Rather, Walzer is a pluralist about the goods of life. The key to a just society, he maintains, is that power and success in one sphere not be used to seize power or success in another sphere. One of his examples is that wealth attained through market success should not, for that reason, enable a student to earn an "A" in a class. Education has its own criteria for success distinct from those of the marketplace; justice requires understanding and respecting the criteria distinctive to that sphere. Professor Walzer is Emeritus Professor at the Institute for Advanced Study in Princeton.

---

[*] Abridged from Chapter 4 in *Spheres of Justice* by Michael Walzer. Copyright © 1983 by Basic Books, Inc. Reprinted by permission of Basic Books, a member of the Perseus Books, L.L.C. Footnotes omitted.

Money and Commodities

What Money Can't Buy—Blocked Exchanges

Let me try to suggest the full set of blocked [market] exchanges in the United States today. I will rely in part on the first chapter of Arthur Okun's *Equality and Efficiency,* where Okun draws a line between the sphere of money and what he calls "the domain of rights."[1] Rights of course, are proof against sale and purchase, and Okun revealingly recasts the Bill of Rights as a series of blocked exchanges. But it's not only rights that stand outside the cash nexus. Whenever we ban the use of money, we do indeed establish a right—namely, that this particular good be distributed in some other way. But we must argue about the meaning of the good before we can say anything more about its rightful distributions. ... Blocked exchanges set limits on the dominance of wealth.

1. Human beings cannot be bought and sold. The sale of slaves, even of oneself as a slave, is ruled out. This is an example of what Okun calls "prohibitions on exchanges born of desperation."[2] There are many such prohibitions, but the others merely regulate the labor market, and I will list them separately. This one establishes what is and is not marketable: not persons or the liberty of persons but only their labor power and the things they make. (Animals are marketable because we conceive them to be without personality, even though liberty is undoubtedly a value for some of them.) Personal liberty is not, however, proof against conscription or imprisonment; it is proof only against sale and purchase.

2. Political power and influence cannot be bought and sold. Citizens cannot sell their votes or officials their decisions. Bribery is an illegal transaction. It hasn't always been so; in many cultures, gifts from clients and suitors are a normal part of the remuneration of office holders. But here the gift relationship will only work—that is, fit into a set of more or less coherent meanings—when "office" hasn't fully emerged as an autonomous good and when the line between public and private is hazy and indistinct. It won't work in a republic, which draws the line sharply: Athens, for example, had an extraordinary set of rules designed to repress bribery; the more offices the citizens shared, the more elaborate the rules became.

3. Criminal justice is not for sale. It is not only that judges and juries cannot be bribed but that the services of defense attorneys are a matter of communal provision—a necessary form of welfare given the adversary system.

4. Freedom of speech, press, religion, assembly: none of these require money payments; none of them are available at auction; they are simply guaranteed to every citizen. It's often said that the exercise of these freedoms costs money, but that's not, strictly speaking, the case: talk and worship are cheap; so is the meeting of citizens; so is publication in many of its forms. Quick access to large audiences is expensive, but that is another matter, not of freedom itself but of influence and power.

5. Marriage and procreation rights are not for sale. Citizens are limited to one spouse and cannot purchase a license for polygamy. And if limits are ever set on the number of children we can have, I assume that these won't take the form [of] licenses to give birth that can be traded on the market.

6   The right to leave the political community is not for sale. The modern state has, to be sure, an investment in every citizen, and it might legitimately require that some part of that investment be repaid, in work or money, before permitting emigration. The Soviet Union adopted a policy of this sort, chiefly as a mechanism to bar emigration altogether. Used differently, it seems fair enough, even if it then has differential effects on successful and unsuccessful citizens. But the citizens can claim, in their turn, that they never sought the health care and education that they received (as children, say) and owe nothing in return. That claim underestimates the benefits of citizenship but nicely captures its consensual character. And so it is best to let them go once they have fulfilled those obligations in kind (military service) that are fulfilled in any case by young men and women who aren't yet fully consenting citizens. No one can buy his way out of these.

7   And so, again, exemptions from military service, from jury duty, and from any other form of communally imposed work cannot be sold by the government or bought by citizens—for reasons I have already given.

8   Political offices cannot be bought; to buy them would be a kind of simony, for the political community is like a church in this sense, that its services matter a great deal to its members and wealth is no adequate sign of a capacity to deliver those services. Nor can professional standing be bought, insofar as this is regulated by the community, for doctors and lawyers are our secular priests; we need to be sure about their qualifications.

9   Basic welfare services like police protection or primary and secondary schooling are purchasable only at the margins. A minimum is guaranteed to every citizen and doesn't have to be paid for by individuals. If policemen dun shopkeepers for protection money, they are acting like gangsters, not like policemen. But shopkeepers can hire security guards and night watchmen for the sake of a higher level of protection than the political community is willing to pay for. Similarly, parents can hire private tutors for their children or send them to private schools. The market in services is subject to restraint only if it distorts the character, or lowers the value, of communal provision. (I should also note that some goods are partially provided, hence partially insulated from market control. The mechanism here is not the blocked but the subsidized exchange—as in the case of college and university education, many cultural activities, travel generally, and so on.)

10 Desperate exchanges, "trades of last resort," are barred, though the meaning of desperation is always open to dispute. The eight-hour day, minimum wage laws, health and safety regulations: all these set a floor, establish basic standards, below which workers cannot bid against one another for employment. Jobs can be auctioned off, but only within these limits. This is a restraint of market liberty for the sake of some communal conception of personal liberty, a reassertion, at lower levels of loss, of the ban on slavery.

11 Prizes and honors of many sorts, public and private, are not available for purchase. The Congressional Medal of Honor cannot be bought, nor can the Pulitzer Prize or the Most Valuable Player Award, or even the trophy given by a local Chamber of Commerce to the "businessman of the year." Celebrity is certainly for sale, though the price can be high, but a good name is not. Prestige, esteem, and status stand somewhere between these two. Money is

implicated in their distribution; but even in our own society, it is only sometimes determinative.

12 Divine grace cannot be bought—and not only because God doesn't need the money. His servants and deputies often do need it. Still, the sale of indulgences is commonly thought to require reform, if not Reformation.

13 Love and friendship cannot be bought, not on our common understanding of what these two mean. Of course, one can buy all sorts of things—clothing, automobiles, gourmet foods, and so on—that make one a better candidate for love and friendship or more self-confident in the pursuit of lovers and friends. Advertisers commonly play on these possibilities, and they are real enough.

.... But the direct purchase is blocked, not in the law but more deeply, in our shared morality and sensibility. Men and women marry for money, but this is not a "marriage of true minds." Sex is for sale, but the sale does not make for "a meaningful relationship." People who believe that sexual intercourse is morally tied to love and marriage are likely to favor a ban on prostitution—just as, in other cultures, people who believed that intercourse was a sacred ritual would have deplored the behavior of priestesses who tried to make a little money on the side. Sex can be sold only when it is understood in terms of pleasure and not exclusively in terms of married love or religious worship.

14 Finally, a long series of criminal sales are ruled out. Murder, Inc., cannot sell its services; blackmail is illegal; heroin cannot be sold, nor can stolen goods or goods fraudulently described or adulterated milk or information thought vital to the security of the state. And arguments go on about unsafe cars, guns, inflammable shirts, drugs with uncertain side effects, and so on. All these are useful illustrations of the fact that the sphere of money and commodities is subject to continuous redefinition.

I think that this is an exhaustive list, though it is possible that I have omitted some crucial category. In any case, the list is long enough to suggest that if money answereth all things, it does so, as it were, behind the backs of many of the things and in spite of their social meanings. The market where exchanges of these sorts are free is a black market, and the men and women who frequent it are likely to do so sneakily and then to lie about what they are doing.

What Money Can Buy

What is the proper sphere of money? What social goods are rightly marketable? The obvious answer is also the right one; it points us to a range of goods that have probably always been marketable, whatever else has or has not been: all those objects, commodities, products, services, beyond what is communally provided, that individual men and women find useful or pleasing, the common stock of bazaars, emporiums, and trading posts ....

The market produces and reproduces inequalities; people end up with more or less, with different numbers and different kinds of possessions. There is no way to ensure that everyone is possessed of whatever set of things marks the "average American," for any such effort will simply raise the average. Here is a sad version of the pursuit of happiness: communal provision endlessly chasing consumer demand. Perhaps there is some point beyond which the fetishism of commodities will lose its grip. Perhaps, more modestly, there is some lower point at which individuals are safe against any radical loss of status. That last possibility suggests the value of partial redistributions in the sphere of money, even if the result is something well short of simple equality. But it also suggests that we must look outside that sphere and strengthen autonomous distributions elsewhere. There are, after all, activities more central to the meaning of membership than owning and using commodities.

Our purpose is to tame "the inexorable dynamic of a money economy," to make money harmless—or at least to make sure that the harms experienced in the sphere of money are not mortal, not to life and not to social standing [as equal citizens] either. But the market remains a competitive sphere, where risk is common, where the readiness to take risks is often a virtue, and where people win and lose. An exciting place: for even when money buys only what it should buy, it is still a very good thing to have. It answereth some things that nothing else can answer. And once we have blocked every wrongful exchange and controlled the sheer weight of money itself, we have no reason to worry about the answers the market provides. Individual men and women still have reason to worry and so they will try to minimize their risks or to share them or spread them out or to buy themselves insurance. In the regime of complex equality, certain sorts of risks will regularly be shared, because the power to impose risks on others, to make authoritative decisions in factories and corporations, is not a marketable good. This is only one more example of a blocked exchange; I will take it up in detail later. Given the right blocks, there is no such thing as a maldistribution of consumer goods. It just doesn't matter, from the standpoint of complex equality, that you have a yacht and I don't ....

The Marketplace

There is a stronger argument about the sphere of money, the common argument of the defenders of capitalism: that market outcomes matter a great deal because the market, if it is free, gives to each person exactly what he deserves. The market rewards us all in accordance with the contributions we make to one another's well-being. The goods and services we provide are valued by potential consumers in such-and-such a way, and these values are aggregated by the market, which determines the price we receive. And that price is our desert, for it expresses the only worth our goods and services can have, the worth they actually have for other people. But this is to misunderstand the meaning of desert. Unless there are standards of worth independent of what people want (and are willing to buy) at this or that moment in time, there can be no deservingness at all. We would never know what a person deserved until we saw what he had gotten. And that can't be right.

Imagine a novelist who writes what he hopes will be a best-seller. He studies his potential audience, designs his book to meet the current fashion. Perhaps he had to violate the canons of his art in order to do that, and perhaps he is a novelist for whom the violation was painful. He has stooped to conquer. Does he now deserve the fruits of his conquest? Does he deserve a conquest that bears fruit? His novel appears, let's say, during a depression when no one has money for books and very few copies are sold; his reward is small. Has he gotten less than he deserves? (His fellow writers smile at his disappointment; perhaps that's what he deserves.) Years later, in better times, the book is reissued and does well. Has its author become more deserving? Surely desert can't hang on the state of the economy. There is too much luck involved here; talk of desert makes little sense. We would do better to say simply that the writer is entitled to his royalties, large or small ....

Notes

1 Arthur Okun, *Equality and Efficiency: The Big Tradeoff* (Washington, DC, 1975), pp. 6ff.
2 Ibid., p. 20.

Review and Discussion Questions

1 Is Walzer arguing that these market exchanges are *actually* blocked in our society or that we all believe that they *should* be blocked, or both? Assess each of his specific claims.
2 "There are no legitimate reasons for prohibiting market exchanges between consenting adults." Assess this statement.
3 Based on what moral ideas, if any, should market trade be permitted? Based on what moral ideas, if any, should market trade be blocked?

READING: PROPERTY RIGHTS AND EMINENT DOMAIN

KELO V. CITY OF NEW LONDON[*]

Your home may be your castle, but can government ever take your home without your consent if you are compensated? The U.S. Constitution allows for these takings if they serve some specified public use, such as roads or parks. But how far should this power extend and how broadly should government be able to interpret what "public use" means? In this controversial case that aroused widespread public and legislative reaction, the U.S. Supreme Court decided that private property can be confiscated for the public use of economic development, even if one's home is not blighted or otherwise in disrepair.

Justice Stevens Delivered the Opinion of the Court

In 2000, the city of New London approved a development plan that, in the words of the Supreme Court of Connecticut, was "projected to create in excess of 1,000 jobs, to increase tax and other revenues, and to revitalize an economically distressed city, including its downtown and waterfront areas." 268 Conn. 1, 5, 843 A. 2d 500, 507 (2004). In assembling the land needed for this project, the city's development agent has purchased property from willing sellers and proposes to use the power of eminent domain to acquire the remainder of the property from

---

[*] *Kelo v. City of New London, Connecticut, et al.* 545 U.S. (2005). Some footnotes omitted.

unwilling owners in exchange for just compensation. The question presented is whether the city's proposed disposition of this property qualifies as a "public use" within the meaning of the Takings Clause of the Fifth Amendment to the Constitution.[1]

I

The city of New London (hereinafter City) sits at the junction of the Thames River and the Long Island Sound in southeastern Connecticut. Decades of economic decline led a state agency in 1990 to designate the City a "distressed municipality." In 1996, the Federal Government closed the Naval Undersea Warfare Center, which had been located in the Fort Trumbull area of the City and had employed over 1,500 people. In 1998, the City's unemployment rate was nearly double that of the State, and its population of just under 24,000 residents was at its lowest since 1920.

These conditions prompted state and local officials to target New London, and particularly its Fort Trumbull area, for economic revitalization. To this end, respondent New London Development Corporation (NLDC), a private nonprofit entity established some years earlier to assist the City in planning economic development, was reactivated. In January 1998, the State authorized a $5.35 million bond issue to support the NLDC's planning activities and a $10 million bond issue toward the creation of a Fort Trumbull State Park. In February, the pharmaceutical company Pfizer Inc. announced that it would build a $300 million research facility on a site immediately adjacent to Fort Trumbull ....

.... The development plan encompasses seven parcels. Parcel 1 is designated for a waterfront conference hotel at the center of a "small urban village" that will include restaurants and shopping. ... A pedestrian "riverwalk" will originate here. ... Parcel 2 will be the site of approximately 80 new residences organized into an urban neighborhood. ... This parcel also includes space reserved for a new U.S. Coast Guard Museum. Parcel 3, which is located immediately north of the Pfizer facility, will contain at least 90,000 square feet of research and development office space. Parcel 4A is a 2.4-acre site that will be used either to support the adjacent state park ... or to support the nearby marina. Parcel 4B will include a renovated marina. ... Parcels 5, 6, and 7 will provide land for office and retail space, parking, and water-dependent commercial uses. 1 App. 113.

The NLDC intended the development plan to capitalize on the arrival of the Pfizer facility and the new commerce it was expected to attract. In addition to creating jobs, generating tax revenue, and helping to "build momentum for the revitalization of downtown New London," *id.*, at 92, the plan was also designed to make the City more attractive and to create leisure and recreational opportunities on the waterfront and in the park.

The city council approved the plan in January 2000, and designated the NLDC as its development agent in charge of implementation. See Conn. Gen. Stat. §8–188 (2005). The city council also authorized the NLDC to purchase property or to acquire property by exercising eminent domain in the City's name. §8–193. The NLDC successfully negotiated the purchase of most of the real estate in the 90-acre area, but its negotiations with petitioners failed. As a consequence, in November 2000, the NLDC initiated the condemnation proceedings that gave rise to this case.[2]

II

Petitioner Susette Kelo has lived in the Fort Trumbull area since 1997. She has made extensive improvements to her house, which she prizes for its water view. Petitioner Wilhelmina Dery was born in her Fort Trumbull house in 1918 and has lived there her entire life. Her husband Charles (also a petitioner) has lived in the house since they married some 60 years ago. In all, the nine petitioners own 15 properties in Fort Trumbull—4 in parcel 3 of the development plan and 11 in parcel 4A. Ten of the parcels are occupied by the owner or a family member; the other five are held as investment properties. There is no allegation that any of these properties is blighted or otherwise in poor condition; rather, they were condemned only because they happen to be located in the development area ....

III

Two polar propositions are perfectly clear. On the one hand, it has long been accepted that the sovereign may not take the property of A for the sole purpose of transferring it to another private party B, even though A is paid just compensation. On the other hand, it is equally clear that a State may transfer property from one private party to another if future "use by the public" is the purpose of the taking; the condemnation of land for a railroad with common-carrier duties is a familiar example. Neither of these propositions, however, determines the disposition of this case.

As for the first proposition, the City would no doubt be forbidden from taking petitioners' land for the purpose of conferring a private benefit on a particular private party. ... Nor would the City be allowed to take property under the mere pretext of a public purpose, when its actual purpose was to bestow a private benefit. The takings before us, however, would be executed pursuant to a "carefully considered" development plan ....

On the other hand, this is not a case in which the City is planning to open the condemned land—at least not in its entirety—to use by the general public. ... But ... this "Court long ago rejected any literal requirement that condemned property be put into use for the general public." *Id.*, at 244. Indeed, while many state courts in the mid-19th century endorsed "use by the public" as the proper definition of public use, that narrow view steadily eroded over time. Not only was the "use by the public" test difficult to administer (*e.g.*, what proportion of the public need have access to the property? at what price?), but it proved to be impractical given the diverse and always evolving needs of society.[3] Accordingly, when this Court began applying the Fifth Amendment to the States at the close of the 19th century, it embraced the broader and more natural interpretation of public use as "public purpose." ...

The disposition of this case therefore turns on the question whether the City's development plan serves a "public purpose." ...

Viewed as a whole, our jurisprudence has recognized that the needs of society have varied between different parts of the Nation, just as they have evolved over time in response to changed circumstances. Our earliest cases in particular embodied a strong theme of federalism, emphasizing the "great respect" that we owe to state legislatures and state courts in discerning local public needs ....

IV

Those who govern the City were not confronted with the need to remove blight in the Fort Trumbull area, but their determination that the area was sufficiently distressed to justify a program of economic rejuvenation is entitled to our deference. The City has carefully formulated an economic development plan that it believes will provide appreciable benefits to the community, including—but by no means limited to—new jobs and increased tax revenue. ... Because that plan unquestionably serves a public purpose, the takings challenged here satisfy the public use requirement of the Fifth Amendment.

To avoid this result, petitioners urge us to adopt a new bright-line rule that economic development does not qualify as a public use. Putting aside the unpersuasive suggestion that the City's plan will provide only purely economic benefits, neither precedent nor logic supports petitioners' proposal. Promoting economic development is a traditional and long accepted function of government ....

Petitioners contend that using eminent domain for economic development impermissibly blurs the boundary between public and private takings. Again, our cases foreclose this objection. Quite simply, the government's pursuit of a public purpose will often benefit individual private parties ....

[P]etitioners maintain that for takings of this kind we should require a "reasonable certainty" that the expected public benefits will actually accrue. Such a rule, however, would represent an even greater departure from our precedent.

> When the legislature's purpose is legitimate and its means are not irrational, our cases make clear that empirical debates over the wisdom of takings—no less than debates over the wisdom of other kinds of socioeconomic legislation—are not to be carried out in the federal courts.
>
> (*Midkiff*, 467 U.S., at 242)

Just as we decline to second-guess the City's considered judgments about the efficacy of its development plan, we also decline to second-guess the City's determinations as to what lands it needs to acquire in order to effectuate the project.

> It is not for the courts to oversee the choice of the boundary line nor to sit in review on the size of a particular project area. Once the question of the public purpose has been decided, the amount and character of land to be taken for the project and the need for a particular tract to complete the integrated plan rests in the discretion of the legislative branch.
>
> (*Berman*, 348 U.S., at 35–36)

In affirming the City's authority to take petitioners' properties, we do not minimize the hardship that condemnations may entail, notwithstanding the payment of just compensation. We emphasize that nothing in our opinion precludes any State from placing further restrictions on its exercise of the takings power. Indeed, many States already impose "public use" requirements that are stricter than the federal baseline. Some of these requirements have been established as a matter of state constitutional law, while others are expressed in state eminent domain statutes that carefully limit the grounds upon which takings may be exercised. As the submissions of the parties and their *amici* make clear, the necessity and wisdom of using eminent domain to promote economic development are certainly matters of legitimate public debate. This Court's authority, however, extends only to determining whether the City's proposed condemnations are for a "public use" within the meaning of the Fifth Amendment to the Federal Constitution. Because over a century of our case law interpreting that provision dictates an affirmative answer to that question, we may not grant petitioners the relief that they seek.

The judgment of the Supreme Court of Connecticut is affirmed.

It is so ordered.

Notes

1 "[N]or shall private property be taken for public use, without just compensation." U.S. Const., Amdt. 5. That Clause is made applicable to the States by the Fourteenth Amendment. See *Chicago, B. & Q. R. Co. v. Chicago*, 166 U. S. 226 (1897).
2 In the remainder of the opinion we will differentiate between the City and the NLDC only where necessary.
3 From upholding the Mill Acts (which authorized manufacturers dependent on power-producing dams to flood upstream lands in exchange for just compensation), to approving takings necessary for the economic development of the West through mining and irrigation, many state courts either circumvented the "use by the public" test when necessary or abandoned it completely. See Nichols, *The Meaning of Public Use in the Law of Eminent Domain*, 20 B. U. L. Rev. 615, 619–624 (1940) (tracing this development and collecting cases). For example, in rejecting the "use by the public" test as overly restrictive, the Nevada Supreme Court stressed that "[m]ining is the greatest of the industrial pursuits in this state. All other interests are subservient to it. Our mountains are almost barren of timber, and our valleys could never be made profitable for agricultural purposes except for the fact of a home market having been created by the mining developments in different sections of the state. The mining and milling interests give employment to many men, and the benefits derived from this business are distributed as much, and sometimes more, among the laboring classes than with the owners of the mines and mills. ... The present prosperity of the state is entirely due to the mining developments already made, and the entire people of the state are directly interested in having the future developments unobstructed by the obstinate action of any individual or individuals." *Dayton Gold & Silver Mining Co.*, 11 Nev at 409–410, 1876 WL, at 11.

Review and Discussion Questions

1 Who has the better argument: Justice Stevens or the dissenters?
2 Many commentators noted that this decision united liberals and conservatives in opposition to the social implications of this decision. How might this be so?
3 Under what conditions can a community legitimately exert authority over what is otherwise someone's private property?

READING: THE SOCIAL RESPONSIBILITY OF BUSINESS IS TO INCREASE ITS PROFITS

MILTON FRIEDMAN[*]

The following essay has greatly influenced public culture. Milton Friedman provides the moral argument that corporations ought to maximize profits within the law. Calls for corporations to pursue social responsibilities are not only bad ideas but immoral. Note that Friedman is not apologizing for "the way it is"; he is providing his account of the ideal model for business responsibility. Milton Friedman was a Nobel Laureate economist at the University of Chicago.

When I hear businessmen speak eloquently about the "social responsibilities of business in a free-enterprise system," I am reminded of the wonderful line about the Frenchman who discovered at the age of 70 that he had been speaking prose all his life. The businessmen believe that they are defending free enterprise when they declaim that business is not concerned "merely" with profit but also with promoting desirable "social" ends; that business has a "social conscience" and takes seriously its responsibilities for providing employment, eliminating discrimination, avoiding pollution and whatever else may be the catchwords of the contemporary crop of reformers. In fact they are—or would be if they or anyone else took them seriously—preaching pure and unadulterated socialism. Businessmen who talk this way are unwitting puppets of the intellectual forces that have been undermining the basis of a free society these past decades.

The discussions of the "social responsibilities of business" are notable for their analytical looseness and lack of rigor. What does it mean to say that "business" has responsibilities? Only people can have responsibilities. A corporation is an artificial person and in this sense may have artificial responsibilities, but "business" as a whole cannot be said to have responsibilities, even in this vague sense. The first step toward clarity in examining the doctrine of the social responsibility of business is to ask precisely what it implies for whom.

Presumably, the individuals who are to be responsible are businessmen, which means individual proprietors or corporate executives. Most of the discussion of social responsibility is directed at corporations, so in what follows I shall mostly neglect the individual proprietors and speak of corporate executives.

In a free-enterprise, private-property system, a corporate executive is an employee of the owners of the business. He has direct responsibility to his employers. That responsibility is to conduct the business in accordance with their desires, which generally will be to make as much money as possible while conforming to the basic rules of the society, both those embodied in law and those embodied in ethical custom. Of course, in some cases his employers may have a different objective. A group of persons might establish a corporation for an eleemosynary purpose—for example, a hospital or a school. The manager of

---

[*] "The Social Responsibility of Business Is to Increase Its Profits" by Milton Friedman, *The New York Times Magazine*, September 13, 1970, p. SM 17. Copyright © 1970 by Milton Friedman. Reprinted by permission of The New York Times Company.

such a corporation will not have money profit as his objective but the rendering of certain services.

In either case, the key point is that, in his capacity as a corporate executive, the manager is the agent of the individuals who own the corporation or establish the eleemosynary institution, and his primary responsibility is to them.

Needless to say, this does not mean that it is easy to judge how well he is performing his task. But at least the criterion of performance is straightforward, and the persons among whom a voluntary contractual arrangement exists are clearly defined.

Of course, the corporate executive is also a person in his own right. As a person, he may have many other responsibilities that he recognizes or assumes voluntarily—to his family, his conscience, his feelings of charity, his church, his clubs, his city, his country. He may feel impelled by these responsibilities to devote part of his income to causes he regards as worthy, to refuse to work for particular corporations, even to leave his job, for example, to join his country's armed forces. If we wish, we may refer to some of these responsibilities as "social responsibilities." But in these respects he is acting as a principal, not an agent; he is spending his own money or time or energy, not the money of his employers or the time or energy he has contracted to devote to their purposes. If these are responsibilities, they are the social responsibilities of individuals, not of business.

What does it mean to say that the corporate executive has a "social responsibility" in his capacity as businessman? If this statement is not pure rhetoric, it must mean that he is to act in some way that is not in the interest of his employers. For example, that he is to refrain from increasing the price of the product in order to contribute to the social objective of preventing inflation, even though a price increase would be in the best interests of the corporation. Or that he is to make expenditures on reducing pollution beyond the amount that is in the best interests of the corporation or that is required by law in order to contribute to the social objective of improving the environment. Or that, at the expense of corporate profits, he is to hire "hardcore" unemployed instead of better qualified available workmen to contribute to the social objective of reducing poverty.

In each of these cases, the corporate executive would be spending someone else's money for a general social interest. Insofar as his actions in accord with his "social responsibility" reduce returns to stockholders, he is spending their money. Insofar as his actions raise the price to customers, he is spending the customers' money. Insofar as his actions lower the wages of some employees, he is spending their money.

The stockholders or the customers or the employees could separately spend their own money on the particular action if they wished to do so. The executive is exercising a distinct "social responsibility," rather than serving as an agent of the stockholders or the customers or the employees, only if he spends the money in a different way than they would have spent it.

But if he does this, he is in effect imposing taxes, on the one hand, and deciding how the tax proceeds shall be spent, on the other.

This process raises political questions on two levels: principle and consequences. On the level of political principle, the imposition of taxes and the expenditure of tax proceeds are governmental functions. We have established elaborate constitutional, parliamentary, and judicial provisions to control these functions, to assure that taxes are imposed so far as possible in accordance with the preferences and desires of the public—after all, "taxation without representation" was one of the battle cries of the American Revolution. We have a system of checks and balances to separate the legislative function of imposing taxes and enacting expenditures from the executive function of collecting taxes and administering expenditure programs and from the judicial function of mediating disputes and interpreting the law.

Here the businessman—self-selected or appointed directly or indirectly by stockholders—is to be simultaneously legislator, executive, and jurist. He is to decide whom to tax by how much and for what purpose, and he is to spend the proceeds—all this guided only by general exhortations from on high to restrain inflation, improve the environment, fight poverty and so on and on.

The whole justification for permitting the corporate executive to be selected by the stockholders is that the executive is an agent serving the interests of his principal. This justification disappears when the corporate executive imposes taxes and spends the proceeds for "social" purposes. He becomes in effect a public employee, a civil servant, even though he remains in name an employee of a private enterprise. On grounds of political principle, it is intolerable that such civil servants—insofar as their actions in the name of social responsibility are real and not just window-dressing—should be selected as they are now. If they are to be civil servants, then they must be elected through a political process. If they are to impose taxes and make expenditures to foster "social" objectives, then political machinery must be set up to make the assessment of taxes and to determine through a political process the objectives to be served.

This is the basic reason why the doctrine of "social responsibility" involves the acceptance of the socialist view that political mechanisms, not market mechanisms, are the appropriate way to determine the allocation of scarce resources to alternative uses.

On the grounds of consequences, can the corporate executive in fact discharge his alleged "social responsibilities?" On the other hand, suppose he could get away with spending the stockholders' or customers' or employees' money. How is he to know how to spend it? He is told that he must contribute to fighting inflation. How is he to know what action of his will contribute to that end? He is presumably an expert in running his company—in producing a product or selling it or financing it. But nothing about his selection makes him an expert on inflation. Will his holding down the price of his product reduce inflationary pressure? Or, by leaving more spending power in the hands of his customers, simply divert it elsewhere? Or, by forcing him to produce less because of the lower price, will it simply contribute to shortages? Even if he could answer these questions, how much cost is he justified in imposing on his stockholders, customers, and employees for this social purpose? What is his appropriate share and what is the appropriate share of others?

And, whether he wants to or not, can he get away with spending his stockholders', customers' or employees' money? Will not the stockholders fire him? (Either the present ones or those who take over when his actions in the name of social responsibility have reduced the corporation's profits and the price of its stock.) His customers and his employees can desert him for other producers and employers less scrupulous in exercising their social responsibilities.

This facet of "social responsibility" doctrine is brought into sharp relief when the doctrine is used to justify wage restraint by trade unions. The conflict of interest is naked and clear when union officials are asked to subordinate the interest of their members to some more general purpose. If the union officials try to enforce wage restraint, the consequence is likely to be wildcat strikes, rank-and-file revolts, and the emergence of strong competitors for their jobs. We thus have the ironic phenomenon that union leaders—at least in the U.S.—have objected to Government interference with the market far more consistently and courageously than have business leaders.

The difficulty of exercising "social responsibility" illustrates, of course, the great virtue of private competitive enterprise—it forces people to be responsible for their own actions and makes it difficult for them to "exploit" other people for either selfish or unselfish purposes. They can do good—but only at their own expense.

Many a reader who has followed the argument this far may be tempted to remonstrate that it is all well and good to speak of Government's having the responsibility to impose taxes and determine expenditures for such "social" purposes as controlling pollution or training the hard-core unemployed, but that the problems are too urgent to wait on the slow course of political processes, that the exercise of social responsibility by businessmen is a quicker and surer way to solve pressing current problems.

Aside from the question of fact—I share Adam Smith's skepticism about the benefits that can be expected from "those who affected to trade for the public good"—this argument must be rejected on grounds of principle. What it amounts to is an assertion that those who favor the taxes and expenditures in question have failed to persuade a majority of their fellow citizens to be of like mind and that they are seeking to attain by undemocratic procedures what they cannot attain by democratic procedures. In a free society, it is hard for "evil" people to do "evil," especially since one man's good is another's evil.

I have, for simplicity, concentrated on the special case of the corporate executive, except only for the brief digression on trade unions. But precisely the same argument applies to the newer phenomenon of calling upon stockholders to require corporations to exercise social responsibility (the recent G.M. crusade for example). In most of these cases, what is in effect involved is some stockholders trying to get other stockholders (or customers or employees) to contribute against their will to "social" causes favored by the activists. Insofar as they succeed, they are again imposing taxes and spending the proceeds.

The situation of the individual proprietor is somewhat different. If he acts to reduce the returns of his enterprise in order to exercise his "social responsibility," he is spending his own money, not someone else's. If he wishes to spend his money on such purposes, that is his right, and I cannot see that there is any objection to his doing so. In the process, he, too, may impose costs on employees and customers. However, because he is far less likely than a large corporation or union to have monopolistic power, any such side effects will tend to be minor.

Of course, in practice, the doctrine of social responsibility is frequently a cloak for actions that are justified on other grounds rather than a reason for those actions.

To illustrate, it may well be in the long-run interest of a corporation that is a major employer in a small community to devote resources to providing amenities to that community or to improving its government. That may make it easier to attract desirable employees, it may reduce the wage bill or lessen losses from pilferage and sabotage or have other worthwhile effects. Or it may be that, given the laws about the deductibility of corporate charitable contributions, the stockholders can contribute more to charities they favor by having the corporation make the gift than by doing it themselves, since they can in that way contribute an amount that would otherwise have been paid as corporate taxes.

In each of these—and many similar—cases, there is a strong temptation to rationalize these actions as an exercise of "social responsibility." In the present climate of opinion, with its wide-spread aversion to "capitalism," "profits," the "soulless corporation," and so on, this is one way for a corporation to generate goodwill as a by-product of expenditures that are entirely justified in its own self-interest.

It would be inconsistent of me to call on corporate executives to refrain from this hypocritical window-dressing because it harms the foundations of a free society. That would be to call on them to exercise a "social responsibility"! If our institutions, and the attitudes of the public make it in their self-interest to cloak their actions in this way, I cannot summon much indignation to denounce them. At the same time, I can express admiration for those individual proprietors or owners of closely held corporations or stockholders of more broadly held corporations who disdain such tactics as approaching fraud.

Whether blameworthy or not, the use of the cloak of social responsibility, and the nonsense spoken in its name by influential and prestigious businessmen, does clearly harm the foundations of a free society. I have been impressed time and again by the schizophrenic character of many businessmen. They are capable of being extremely farsighted and clear-headed in matters that are internal to their businesses. They are incredibly short-sighted and muddle-headed in matters that are outside their businesses but affect the possible survival of business in general. This short-sightedness is strikingly exemplified in the calls from many businessmen for wage and price guidelines or controls or income policies. There is nothing that could do more in a brief period to destroy a market system and replace it by a centrally controlled system than effective governmental control of prices and wages.

The short-sightedness is also exemplified in speeches by businessmen on social responsibility. This may gain them kudos in the short run. But it helps to strengthen the already too prevalent view that the pursuit of profits is wicked and immoral and must be curbed and controlled by external forces. Once this view is adopted, the external forces that curb the market will not be the social consciences, however highly developed, of the pontificating executives; it will be the iron fist of Government bureaucrats. Here, as with price and wage controls, businessmen seem to me to reveal a suicidal impulse.

The political principle that underlies the market mechanism is unanimity. In an ideal free market resting on private property, no individual can coerce any other, all cooperation is voluntary, all parties to such cooperation benefit or they need not participate. There are no values, no "social" responsibilities in any sense other than the shared values and responsibilities of individuals. Society is a collection of individuals and of the various groups they voluntarily form.

The political principle that underlies the political mechanism is conformity. The individual must serve a more general social interest—whether that be determined by a church or a dictator or a majority. The individual may have a vote and say in what is to be done, but if he is overruled, he must conform. It is appropriate for some to require others to contribute to a general social purpose whether they wish to or not.

Unfortunately, unanimity is not always feasible. There are some respects in which conformity appears unavoidable, so I do not see how one can avoid the use of the political mechanism altogether.

But the doctrine of "social responsibility" taken seriously would extend the scope of the political mechanism to every human activity. It does not differ in philosophy from the most explicitly collectivist doctrine. It differs only by professing to believe that collectivist ends can be attained without collectivist means. That is why, in my book *Capitalism and Freedom*, I have called it a "fundamentally subversive doctrine" in a free society, and have said that in such a society,

> there is one and only one social responsibility of business—to use its resources and engage in activities designed to increase its profits so long as it stays within the rules of the game, which is to say, engages in open and free competition without deception or fraud.
> ([Chicago, IL: University of Chicago Press, 1962, p. 133])

Review and Discussion Questions

1 What is the full range of responsibilities that corporations ought to follow, according to Friedman?
2 Summarize what you take to be the strongest arguments in favor of Friedman's position.
3 If you disagree with his position, what is the most compelling argument that corporations ought to do more than what Friedman outlines?
4 What relationship between government and business is implied by this argument?

READING: RETHINKING THE SOCIAL RESPONSIBILITY OF BUSINESS: A DEBATE

JOHN MACKEY AND MILTON FRIEDMAN*

Years after his original publication on corporate social responsibility, and shortly before he died at age ninety-four, Milton Friedman participated in this written exchange with John Mackey, the founder and CEO of grocery chain Whole Foods Market. Friedman maintained the correctness of his basic position in the face of years of intense scrutiny. John Mackey, on the other hand, argues that Friedman misses the most important points about the nature of business enterprise and, more significantly, fails to understand the future of capitalism. Friedman responds that there is no fundamental disagreement between their views, but Mackey insists

---

* Abridged from "Rethinking the Social Responsibility of Business: A Reason Debate Featuring Milton Friedman, Whole Foods' John Mackey, and Cypress Semiconductor's TJ Rodgers," *Reason*, October 2005, pp. 29–37. Copyright © 2005. Reprinted by permission of *Reason*.

that the disagreement is deep and real. Mackey is the CEO of Whole Foods Market.

Putting Customers Ahead of Investors
John Mackey

In 1970 Milton Friedman wrote that "there is one and only one social responsibility of business—to use its resources and engage in activities designed to increase its profits so long as it stays within the rules of the game, which is to say, engages in open and free competition without deception or fraud." That's the orthodox view among free market economists: that the only social responsibility a law-abiding business has is to maximize profits for the shareholders.

I strongly disagree. I'm a businessman and a free market libertarian, but I believe that the enlightened corporation should try to create value for *all* of its constituencies. From an investor's perspective, the purpose of the business is to maximize profits. But that's not the purpose for other stakeholders—for customers, employees, suppliers, and the community. Each of those groups will define the purpose of the business in terms of its own needs and desires, and each perspective is valid and legitimate.

My argument should not be mistaken for a hostility to profit. I believe I know something about creating shareholder value. When I co-founded Whole Foods Market 27 years ago, we began with $45,000 in capital; we only had $250,000 in sales our first year. During the last 12 months we had sales of more than $4.6 billion, net profits of more than $160 million, and a market capitalization over $8 billion.

But we have not achieved our tremendous increase in shareholder value by making shareholder value the primary purpose of our business. In my marriage, my wife's happiness is an end in itself, not merely a means to my own happiness; love leads me to put my wife's happiness first, but in doing so I also make myself happier. Similarly, the most successful businesses put the customer first, ahead of the investors. In the profit-centered business, customer happiness is merely a means to an end: maximizing profits. In the customer-centered business, customer happiness is an end in itself, and will be pursued with greater interest, passion, and empathy than the profit-centered business is capable of.

Not that we're only concerned with customers. At Whole Foods, we measure our success by how much value we can create for all six of our most important stakeholders: customers, team members (employees), investors, vendors, communities, and the environment ....

There is, of course, no magical formula to calculate how much value each stakeholder should receive from the company. It is a dynamic process that evolves with the competitive marketplace. No stakeholder remains satisfied for long. It is the function of company leadership to develop solutions that continually work for the common good.

Many thinking people will readily accept my arguments that caring about customers and employees is good business. But they might draw the line at believing a company has any responsibility to its community and environment. To donate time and capital to philanthropy, they will argue, is to steal from the investors.

After all, the corporation's assets legally belong to the investors, don't they? Management has a fiduciary responsibility to maximize shareholder value; therefore, any activities that don't maximize shareholder value are violations of this duty. If you feel altruism towards other people, you should exercise that altruism with your own money, not with the assets of a corporation that doesn't belong to you.

This position sounds reasonable. A company's assets do belong to the investors, and its management does have a duty to manage those assets responsibly. In my view, the argument is not *wrong* so much as it is too narrow.

First, there can be little doubt that a certain amount of corporate philanthropy is simply good business and works for the long-term benefit of the investors. For example: In addition to the many thousands of small donations each Whole Foods store makes each year, we also hold five 5 percent Days throughout the year. On those days, we donate 5 percent of a store's total sales to a nonprofit organization. While our stores select worthwhile organizations to support, they also tend to focus on groups that have large membership lists, which are contacted and encouraged to shop our store that day to support the organization. This usually brings hundreds of new or lapsed customers into our stores, many of whom then become regular shoppers. So a 5 percent Day not only allows us to support worthwhile causes, but is an excellent marketing strategy that has benefited Whole Foods investors immensely.

That said, I believe such programs would be completely justifiable even if they produced no profits and no P.R. This is because I believe the entrepreneurs, not the current investors in a company's stock, have the right and responsibility to define the purpose of the company. It is the entrepreneurs who create a company, who bring all the factors of production together and coordinate it into viable business. It is the entrepreneurs who set the company strategy and who negotiate the terms of trade with all of the voluntarily cooperating stakeholders—including the investors. At Whole Foods we "hired" our original investors. They didn't hire us.

We first announced that we would donate 5 percent of the company's net profits to philanthropy when we drafted our mission statement, back in 1985. Our policy has therefore been in place for over 20 years, and it predates our IPO by seven years. All seven of the private investors at the time we created the policy voted for it when they served on our board of directors. When we took in venture capital money back in 1989, none of the venture firms objected to the policy. In addition, in almost 14 years as a publicly traded company, almost no investors have ever raised objections to the policy. How can Whole Foods' philanthropy be "theft" from the current investors if the original owners of the company unanimously approved the policy and all subsequent investors made their investments after the policy was in effect and well publicized?

The shareholders of a public company own their stock voluntarily. If they don't agree with the philosophy of the business, they can always sell their investment, just as the customers and employees can exit their relationships with the company if they don't like the terms of trade. If that is unacceptable to them, they always have the legal right to submit a resolution at our annual shareholders meeting to change the company's philanthropic philosophy. A number of our company policies have been changed over the years through successful shareholder resolutions.

Another objection to the Whole Foods philosophy is where to draw the line. If donating 5 percent of profits is good, wouldn't 10 percent be even better? Why not donate 100 percent of our profits to the betterment of society? But the fact that Whole Foods has responsibilities to our community doesn't mean that we don't have any responsibilities to our investors. It's a question of finding the appropriate balance and trying to create value for all of our stakeholders. Is 5 percent the "right amount" to donate to the community? I don't think there is a right answer to this question, except that I believe 0 percent is too little. It is an arbitrary percentage that the co-founders of the company decided was a reasonable amount and which was approved by the owners of the company at the time we made the decision. Corporate philanthropy is a good thing, but it requires the legitimacy of investor approval. In my experience, most investors understand that it can be beneficial to both the corporation and to the larger society.

That doesn't answer the question of *why* we give money to the community stakeholder. For that, you should turn to one of the fathers of free-market economics, Adam Smith. *The Wealth of Nations* was a tremendous achievement, but economists would be well served to read Smith's other great book, *The Theory of Moral Sentiments*. There he explains that human nature isn't just about self-interest. It also includes sympathy, empathy, friendship, love, and the desire for social approval. As motives for human behavior, these are at least as important as self-interest. For many people, they are more important.

When we are small children we are egocentric, concerned only about our own needs and desires. As we mature, most people grow beyond this egocentrism and begin to care about others—their families, friends, communities, and countries. Our capacity to love can expand even further: to loving people from different races, religions, and countries—potentially to unlimited love for all people and even for other sentient creatures. This is our potential as human beings, to take joy in the flourishing of people everywhere. Whole Foods gives money to our communities because we care about them and feel a responsibility to help them flourish as well as possible.

The business model that Whole Foods has embraced could represent a new form of capitalism, one that more consciously works for the common good instead of depending solely on the "invisible hand" to generate positive results for society. The "brand" of capitalism is in terrible shape throughout the world, and corporations are widely seen as selfish, greedy, and uncaring. This is both unfortunate and unnecessary, and could be changed if businesses and economists widely adopted the business model that I have outlined here.

To extend our love and care beyond our narrow self-interest is antithetical to neither our human nature nor our financial success. Rather, it leads to the further fulfillment of both. Why do we not encourage this in our theories of business and economics? Why do we restrict our theories to such a pessimistic and crabby view of human nature? What are we afraid of?

Making Philanthropy Out of Obscenity
Milton Friedman

> By pursuing his own interest [an individual] frequently promotes that of the society more effectually than when he really intends to promote it.

> I have never known much good done by those who affected to trade for the public good.
>
> (Adam Smith, *The Wealth of Nations*)

The differences between John Mackey and me regarding the social responsibility of business are for the most part rhetorical. Strip off the camouflage, and it turns out we are in essential agreement. Moreover, his company, Whole Foods Market, behaves in accordance with the principles I spelled out in my 1970 *New York Times Magazine* article.

With respect to his company, it could hardly be otherwise. It has done well in a highly competitive industry. Had it devoted any significant fraction of its resources to exercising a social responsibility unrelated to the bottom line, it would be out of business by now or would have been taken over ....

I believe Mackey's flat statement that "corporate philanthropy is a good thing" is flatly wrong. Consider the decision by the founders of Whole Foods to donate 5 percent of net profits to philanthropy. They were clearly within their rights in doing so. They were spending their own money, using 5 percent of one part of their wealth to establish, thanks to corporate tax provisions, the equivalent of a 501c(3) charitable foundation, though with no mission statement, no separate by-laws, and no provision for deciding on the beneficiaries. But what reason is there to suppose that the stream of profit distributed in this way would do more good for society than investing that stream of profit in the enterprise itself or paying it out as dividends and letting the stockholders dispose of it? The practice makes sense only because of our obscene tax laws, whereby a stockholder can make a larger gift for a given after-tax cost if the corporation makes the gift on his behalf than if he makes the gift directly. That is a good reason for eliminating the corporate tax or for eliminating the deductibility of corporate charity, but it is not a justification for corporate charity.

Whole Foods Market's contribution to society—and as a customer I can testify that it is an important one—is to enhance the pleasure of shopping for food. Whole Foods has no special competence in deciding how charity should be distributed. Any funds devoted to the latter would surely have contributed more to society if they had been devoted to improving still further the former.

Finally, I shall try to explain why my statement that "the social responsibility of business [is] to increase its profits" and Mackey's statement that "the enlightened corporation should try to create value for *all* of its constituencies" are equivalent.

Note first that I refer to *social* responsibility, not financial, or accounting, or legal. It is social precisely to allow for the constituencies to which Mackey refers. Maximizing profits is an end from the private point of view; it is a means from the social point of view. A system based on private property and free markets is a sophisticated means of enabling people to cooperate in their economic activities without compulsion; it enables separated knowledge to assure that each resource is used for its most valued use, and is combined with other resources in the most efficient way.

Of course, this is abstract and idealized. The world is not ideal. There are all sorts of deviations from the perfect market—many, if not most, I suspect, due to government interventions. But with all its defects, the current largely free-market, private-property world seems to me vastly preferable to a world in which a large fraction of resources is used and distributed by 501c(3)s and their corporate counterparts.

Profit Is the Means, Not End

John Mackey

Let me begin my response to Milton Friedman by noting that he is one of my personal heroes. His contributions to economic thought and the fight for freedom are without parallel, and it is an honor to have him critique my article.

Friedman says "the differences between John Mackey and me regarding the social responsibility of business are for the most part rhetorical." But are we essentially in agreement? I don't think so. We are thinking about business in entirely different ways.

Friedman is thinking only in terms of maximizing profits for the investors. If putting customers first helps maximize profits for the investors, then it is acceptable. If some corporate philanthropy creates goodwill and helps a company "cloak" its self-interested goals of maximizing profits, then it is acceptable (although Friedman also believes it is "hypocritical"). In contrast to Friedman, I do not believe maximizing profits for the investors is the only acceptable justification for all corporate actions. The investors are not the only people who matter. Corporations can exist for purposes other than simply maximizing profits.

As for who decides what the purpose of any particular business is, I made an important argument that Friedman doesn't address: "I believe the entrepreneurs, not the current investors in a company's stock, have the right and responsibility to define the purpose of the company." Whole Foods Market was not created solely to maximize profits for its investors, but to create value for all of its stakeholders. I believe there are thousands of other businesses similar to Whole Foods (Medtronic, REI, and Starbucks, for example) that were created by entrepreneurs with goals beyond maximizing profits, and that these goals are neither "hypocritical" nor "cloaking devices" but are intrinsic to the purpose of the business.

I will concede that many other businesses, such as T.J. Rodgers' Cypress Semiconductor, have been created by entrepreneurs whose sole purpose for the business is to maximize profits for their investors. Does Cypress therefore have any social responsibility besides maximizing profits if it follows the laws of society? No, it doesn't. Rodgers apparently created it solely to maximize profits, and therefore all of Friedman's arguments about business social responsibility become completely valid. Business social responsibility should not be coerced; it is a voluntary decision that the entrepreneurial leadership of every company must make on its own. Friedman is right to argue that profit making is intrinsically valuable for society, but I believe he is mistaken that all businesses have only this purpose.

While Friedman believes that taking care of customers, employees, and business philanthropy are means to the end of increasing investor profits, I take the exact opposite view: Making high profits is the means to the end of fulfilling Whole Foods' core business mission. We want to improve the health and well-being of everyone on the planet through higher-quality foods and better nutrition, and we can't fulfill this mission unless we are highly profitable. High profits are necessary to fuel our growth across the United States and the world. Just as people cannot live without eating, so a business cannot live without profits. But most people don't live to eat, and neither must businesses live just to make profits.

Toward the end of his critique Friedman says his statement that "the social responsibility of business [is] to increase its profits" and my statement that "the enlightened corporation should try to create value for all of its constituencies" are "equivalent." He argues that maximizing profits is a private end achieved through social means because it supports a society based on private property and free markets. If our two statements are equivalent, if we really mean the same thing, then I know which statement has the superior "marketing power." Mine does.

Both capitalism and corporations are misunderstood, mistrusted, and disliked around the world because of statements like Friedman's on social responsibility. His comment is used by the enemies of capitalism to argue that capitalism is greedy, selfish, and uncaring. It is right up there with William Vanderbilt's "the public be damned" and former G.M. Chairman Charlie Wilson's declaration that "what's good for the country is good for General Motors, and vice versa." If we are truly interested in spreading capitalism throughout the world (I certainly am), we need to do a better job marketing it. I believe if economists and business people consistently communicated and acted on my message that "the enlightened corporation should try to create value for all of its constituencies," we would see most of the resistance to capitalism disappear.

Friedman also understands that Whole Foods makes an important contribution to society besides simply maximizing profits for our investors, which is to "enhance the pleasure of shopping for food." This is why we put "satisfying and delighting our customers" as a core value whenever we talk about the purpose of our business. Why don't Friedman and other economists consistently teach this idea? Why don't they talk more about all the valuable contributions that business makes in creating value for its customers, for its employees, and for its communities? Why talk only about maximizing profits for the investors? Doing so harms the brand of capitalism.

As for Whole Foods' philanthropy, who does have "special competence" in this area? Does the government? Do individuals? Libertarians generally would agree that most bureaucratic government solutions to social problems cause more harm than good and that government help is seldom the answer. Neither do individuals have any special competence in charity. By Friedman's logic, individuals shouldn't donate any money to help others but should instead keep all their money invested in businesses, where it will create more social value.

The truth is that there is no way to calculate whether money invested in business or money invested in helping to solve social problems will create more value. Businesses exist within real communities and have real effects, both good and bad, on those communities. Like individuals living in communities, businesses make valuable social contributions by providing goods and services and employment. But just as individuals can feel a responsibility to provide some philanthropic support for the communities in which they live, so too can a business. The responsibility of business toward the community is not infinite, but neither is it zero. Each enlightened business must find the proper balance between all of its constituencies: customers, employees, investors, suppliers, and communities.

Review and Discussion Questions

1 What are Friedman and Mackey disagreeing about?
2 What do they agree about?
3 Who has the better argument? Why?
4 Is there an important position about corporate responsibility that is not represented by either Friedman or Mackey? What additional insights are relevant to this debate?

Essay and Paper Topics for Chapter 17

1. "Consumers and stockholders are the people who bear primary moral responsibility for creating economic justice, not corporate management." Assess, drawing on readings from this or the last chapter.
2. How does the debate about corporate responsibility relate to the debate about whether and to what extent corporations should have a right to speak in Chapter 16?
3. Compare and contrast the positions of Hume, Nozick, and Rawls.
4. Develop two examples to illustrate appropriate and inappropriate exercises of eminent domain. What are your underlying principles of economic justice that justify this distinction?
5. Should people be able to trade voluntarily for anything that they want? Draw on Walzer's analysis to develop general principles that inform how you answer that question.

Chapter 18

Race, Gender, and Affirmative Action

What do racial and gender equality require? Do women live in a world of male domination and oppression? In an ideal society, how would people think about racial and ethnic differences? Essays in this chapter offer a variety of perspectives on these controversial and much-discussed issues. We start with *Brown v. Board of Education*, the famous decision that rejected the idea of "separate but equal" as it applied to the long-standing practice of racial segregation. The next reading examines how we should think about the challenges that inner cities face. This chapter also considers two Supreme Court cases on affirmative action in higher education and an analysis of reverse discrimination. The next readings in this chapter are perhaps the most important early work on women's rights and equality. Other readings explore the strengths and weaknesses of this early vision of sexual equality, including the alternative "dominance" approach advocated by some feminists and the connections between neutrality and sexual equality. The essays also discuss how an ideal society should treat such differences. Should identity politics be encouraged or should law be color blind?

READING: SEPARATE BUT EQUAL?

BROWN V. BOARD OF EDUCATION*

This case is by nearly any account one of the most dramatic and significant Supreme Court decisions in U.S. history. In a single decision, the Court ruled unconstitutional the long-standing and deeply embedded institution of racial segregation.

Mr. Chief Justice Warren Delivered the Opinion of the Court

These cases come to us from the States of Kansas, South Carolina, Virginia, and Delaware. They are premised on different facts and different local conditions, but a common legal question justifies their consideration together in this consolidated opinion. [347 U.S. 483, 487]

In each of the cases, minors of the Negro race, through their legal representatives, seek the aid of the courts in obtaining admission to the public schools of

---

* *Brown v. Board of Education*, 347 U.S. 483 (1954).

their community on a nonsegregated basis. In each instance, [347 U.S. 483, 488] they had been denied admission to schools attended by white children under laws requiring or permitting segregation according to race. This segregation was alleged to deprive the plaintiffs of the equal protection of the laws under the Fourteenth Amendment. In each of the cases other than the Delaware case, a three-judge federal district court denied relief to the plaintiffs on the so-called "separate but equal" doctrine announced by this Court in Plessy v. Ferguson, 163 U.S. 537. Under that doctrine, equality of treatment is accorded when the races are provided substantially equal facilities, even though these facilities be separate. In the Delaware case, the Supreme Court of Delaware adhered to that doctrine, but ordered that the plaintiffs be admitted to the white schools because of their superiority to the Negro schools.

The plaintiffs contend that segregated public schools are not "equal" and cannot be made "equal," and that hence they are deprived of the equal protection of the laws. Because of the obvious importance of the question presented, the Court took jurisdiction ....

In the first cases in this Court construing the Fourteenth Amendment, decided shortly after its adoption, the Court interpreted it as proscribing all state-imposed discriminations against the Negro race. The doctrine of [347 U.S. 483, 491] "separate but equal" did not make its appearance in this Court until 1896 in the case of Plessy v. Ferguson, supra, involving not education but transportation. American courts have since labored with the doctrine for over half a century. In this Court, there have been six cases involving the "separate but equal" doctrine in the field of public education. In Cumming v. County Board of Education, 175 U.S. 528, and Gong Lum v. Rice, 275 U.S. 78, the validity of the doctrine itself was not challenged. In more recent cases, all on the graduate school [347 U.S. 483, 492] level, inequality was found in that specific benefits enjoyed by white students were denied to Negro students of the same educational qualifications. Missouri ex rel. Gaines v. Canada, 305 U.S. 337; Sipuel v. Oklahoma, 332 U.S. 631; Sweatt v. Painter, 339 U.S. 629; McLaurin v. Oklahoma State Regents, 339 U.S. 637. In none of these cases was it necessary to re-examine the doctrine to grant relief to the Negro plaintiff. And in Sweatt v. Painter, supra, the Court expressly reserved decision on the question whether Plessy v. Ferguson should be held inapplicable to public education.

In the instant cases, that question is directly presented. Here, unlike Sweatt v. Painter, there are findings below that the Negro and white schools involved have been equalized, or are being equalized, with respect to buildings, curricula, qualifications and salaries of teachers, and other "tangible" factors. Our decision, therefore, cannot turn on merely a comparison of these tangible factors in the Negro and white schools involved in each of the cases. We must look instead to the effect of segregation itself on public education.

In approaching this problem, we cannot turn the clock back to 1868 when the Amendment was adopted, or even to 1896 when Plessy v. Ferguson was written. We must consider public education in the light of its full development and its present place in American life throughout [347 U.S. 483, 493] the Nation. Only in this way can it be determined if segregation in public schools deprives these plaintiffs of the equal protection of the laws.

Today, education is perhaps the most important function of state and local governments. Compulsory school attendance laws and the great expenditures for education both demonstrate our recognition of the importance of education to our democratic society. It is required in the performance of our most basic public responsibilities, even service in the armed forces. It is the very foundation of good citizenship. Today it is a principal instrument in awakening the child to cultural values, in preparing him for later professional training, and in helping him to adjust normally to his environment. In these days, it is doubtful that any child may reasonably be expected to succeed in life if he is denied the opportunity of an education. Such an opportunity, where the state has undertaken to provide it, is a right which must be made available to all on equal terms.

We come then to the question presented: Does segregation of children in public schools solely on the basis of race, even though the physical facilities and other "tangible" factors may be equal, deprive the children of the minority group of equal educational opportunities? We believe that it does.

In Sweatt v. Painter, supra, in finding that a segregated law school for Negroes could not provide them equal educational opportunities, this Court relied in large part on "those qualities which are incapable of objective measurement but which make for greatness in a law school." In McLaurin v. Oklahoma State Regents, supra, the Court, in requiring that a Negro admitted to a white graduate school be treated like all other students, again resorted to intangible considerations: "... his ability to study, to engage in discussions and exchange views with other students, and, in general, to learn his profession." [347 U.S. 483, 494] Such considerations apply with added force to children in grade and high schools. To separate them from others of similar age and qualifications solely because of their race generates a feeling of inferiority as to their status in the community that may affect their hearts and minds in a way unlikely ever to be undone. The effect of this separation on their educational opportunities was well stated by a finding in the Kansas case by a court which nevertheless felt compelled to rule against the Negro plaintiffs:

> Segregation of white and colored children in public schools has a detrimental effect upon the colored children. The impact is greater when it has the sanction of the law; for the policy of separating the races is usually interpreted as denoting the inferiority of the negro group. A sense of inferiority affects the motivation of a child to learn. Segregation with the sanction of law, therefore, has a tendency to [retard] the educational and mental development of negro children and to deprive them of some of the benefits they would receive in a racial[ly] integrated school system.
>
> (87 A.2d 862, 865 (1952))

Whatever may have been the extent of psychological knowledge at the time of Plessy v. Ferguson, this finding is amply supported by modern authority. Any language [347 U.S. 483, 495] in Plessy v. Ferguson contrary to this finding is rejected.

We conclude that in the field of public education the doctrine of "separate but equal" has no place. Separate educational facilities are inherently unequal. Therefore, we hold that the plaintiffs and others similarly situated for whom the actions have been brought are, by reason of the segregation complained of, deprived of the equal protection of the laws guaranteed by the Fourteenth Amendment. This disposition makes unnecessary any discussion whether such segregation also violates the Due Process Clause of the Fourteenth Amendment.

Because these are class actions, because of the wide applicability of this decision, and because of the great variety of local conditions, the formulation of decrees in these cases presents problems of considerable complexity. On reargument, the consideration of appropriate relief was necessarily subordinated to the primary question—the constitutionality of segregation in public education. We have now announced that such segregation is a denial of the equal protection of the laws. In order that we may have the full assistance of the parties in formulating decrees, the cases will be restored to the docket, and the parties are requested to present further argument on Questions 4 and 5 previously propounded by the Court for the reargument this Term. The Attorney General [347 U.S. 483, 496] of the United States is again invited to participate. The Attorneys General of the states requiring or permitting segregation in public education will also be permitted to appear as amici curiae upon request to do so by September 15, 1954, and submission of briefs by October 1, 1954.

It is so ordered.

Review and Discussion Questions

1 Why can't "separate but equal" be equal, according to the Supreme Court?
2 In your view, are there any conditions, racial or otherwise, that could establish separate but equal practices compatible with a moral ideal of equality? Why or why not?
3 Why does equal protection under the law matter? What is wrong with living in a society without it?

READING: RETHINKING THE PROBLEM OF THE GHETTO

TOMMIE SHELBY[*]

Tommie Shelby argues that the plight of inner cities in America is a problem of justice for all citizens, not a technical problem of urban management. He advocates a form of ghetto abolitionism. This excerpt includes a portion of his Introduction and the Epilogue from his book *Dark Ghettos: Injustice, Dissent, and Reform*. Tommie Shelby is the Caldwell Titcomb Professor of African and African American Studies and of Philosophy at Harvard University.

From New York City to Los Angeles, poor black neighborhoods blot the metropolitan landscapes of the United States. Social scientists, ordinary observers, and inhabitants of these stigmatized neighborhoods often refer to them as "ghettos."[1] In addition to concentrated poverty, these communities typically have a number of troubling characteristics—high rates of racial segregation, violence, street crime,

---

[*] Excerpted from *Dark Ghettos: Injustice, Dissent, and Reform*, by Tommie Shelby (Boston, MA: Belknap Press, 2016). Reprinted with permission of Harvard University Press. Some footnotes omitted.

joblessness, teenage pregnancy, family instability, school dropouts, welfare receipt, and drug abuse. Such neighborhoods emerged decades ago, after countless black Americans abandoned rural southern areas for industrializing cities in the wake of Reconstruction's collapse. Despite the efforts of the Civil Rights movement and various federal antipoverty initiatives over the years, ghettos are still a dreadful reality.

Why do ghettos persist? Some charge that the government has yet to create an opportunity structure that would enable those born or raised in ghettos to escape poverty. Others point to the attitudes and conduct of ghetto denizens, arguing that the black poor should make better choices and stop blaming the government or racism for hardships they have effectively imposed on themselves. Some split the difference, insisting that the public, through government action, should create more opportunity *and* that the urban poor should make more responsible choices.

This long-standing and contentious debate has reached an impasse over what best explains the persistence of ghetto conditions (the dysfunctional behavior of the black poor or structural obstacles to upward mobility) and over what kinds of state interventions (if any) would be most cost-effective in solving the problem. However, I urge that we re-frame the debate, that we not view it primarily in terms of behavior versus structure or the strengths and weaknesses of particular antipoverty measures, but in terms of what justice requires and how we, individually and collectively, should respond to injustice.

Many view ghettos and their occupants as a "social problem" to be axed, and they espouse policy approaches that take the following form. Describe some salient and disconcerting features of ghettos (the prevalence of impoverished single-mother families and youth violence). Identify the linchpin that keeps ghettos in place (joblessness or aggregation). And then propose a cost-effective solution that would remove this linchpin (a jobs program or an integration initiative) with the expectation that ghettos will, eventually, fade away as a result. I call this the *medical model*. The primary aim of those working within this framework is to increase the material welfare of people living in ghettos through narrowly targeted and empirically grounded interventions into their lives.

Yet from the standpoint of justice, this approach has serious limitations and pitfalls. Just as physicians take basic human anatomy as given when treating patients, policymakers working within the medical model treat the background structure of society as given and focus only on alleviating the burdens of the disadvantaged. When it comes to the ghetto poor, this generally means attempting to integrate them into an existing social system rather than viewing their unwillingness to fully operate as a sign that the system itself needs fundamental reform. In short, features of society that could and should be altered often get little scrutiny. This is the problem of *status quo bias*.

In addition, the technocratic reasoning of the medical model marginalizes the political agency of those it aims to help. The ghetto poor are regarded as passive victims in need of assistance rather than as political allies in what should be a collective effort to secure justice for all. The everyday, sometimes unusual, and often misunderstood choices of those in these disadvantaged communities are viewed, when seen through the lens of the medical model, as at best devoid of moral content or political intent and at worst pathological. Indeed, status quo bias invites us to see dysfunction where perhaps lies resistance to injustice. Call this the problem of *downgraded agency*.

Furthermore, focusing on the problems of the disadvantaged can divert attention from or obscure the numerous ways in which the advantaged unfairly benefit from an unjust social structure. Keep in mind that the privileged have a tendency to believe that they have earned all their advantages while the disadvantaged have brought their hardships on themselves. Narrowly focusing on "fighting poverty" might seem progressive. But it can also serve to quiet the grievances of those most distressed while preserving a stratified social order that would still be marred by serious injustices, illegitimate privileges, and ill-gotten gains. Call this the *unjust-advantage blind spot problem*.

To avoid these limits and pitfalls, I advocate thinking about ghettos through a *systemic-injustice* framework. When we take up the problem using this model, both government and ordinary citizens are viewed as having a duty to ensure that the social system of cooperation we all participate in is just. The presence of ghettos in American cities is a strong indication that just background conditions do not prevail. Reflection on ghettos, then, serves not only to focus our energies on relieving the immense burdens the ghetto poor carry but also to make us think, as fellow citizens, about the fairness of the overall social structure we inhabit and maintain. Were the more affluent in society to think about the matter this way, they would view the ghetto poor, not simply as disadvantaged people in need of their help or government intervention, but as fellow citizens with an equal claim on a just social structure. They might then come to recognize that achieving social justice will require not only eschewing their paternalistic (and sometimes positive attitudes) towards the black poor but also relinquishing their unjust advantages.

...

Epilogue: Renewing Ghetto Abolitionism

The ghetto should be abolished. Like American slavery and Jim Crow segregation, the ghetto should never have come into existence. In calling for its abolition, I'm not suggesting that black neighborhoods should be proscribed or that their poor black inhabitants should be dispersed. There is nothing wrong with the existence of predominantly black urban communities and, in light of the long-standing predicament of black people in the United States, there is much to be said in favor of such neighborhoods. The problem is that too many black neighborhoods lack needed resources, are offered only inadequate public services and substandard schools, are beset with violent street crime, and are home to many stigmatized and unjustly disadvantaged people with little spatial or economic mobility.

Abolishing the ghetto should not be seen simply as a matter of overcoming racial prejudice or reviving the War on Poverty. It should instead be viewed as an aggressive attempt at fundamental reform of the basic structure of our society. We, as residents of the United States, are all implicated in the perpetuation of ghettos. The ghetto is not "their" problem but ours, privileged and disadvantaged alike. The ghetto is a sign that our social order is profoundly unjust. It is a sign obscured by a host of legitimating ideologies—racist, sexist, economic, moral, religious, and nationalist. Insofar as we uphold that order, we are complicit in the oppression of our fellow citizens and, for some at least, contributing to our own oppression. Our duty of justice calls for response.

In recent reform efforts, disadvantaged ghetto denizens are too often viewed more as unruly chess pieces than as moral agents and allies. Yet the myriad ways in which they register dissent—sometimes subtle, sometimes overt—suggest that many act defiantly out of a sense of justice. Their noncompliance with societal expectations—refusing to delay childbearing, to marry, to accept low-paying and demeaning jobs, to respect the law, and to submit to other "mainstream" norms—can be a healthy expression of self-respect and a morally rooted opposition to the status quo, not mere nihilism or despair. Even though some of their defiant acts of transgression may add to their burdens (and annoy, anger, and frighten the affluent), they are not unjustified and certainly don't warrant condemnation. Instead this rebellion should draw our attention to the failures of reciprocity embedded in the social institutions and informal practices that constitute the structure of our society. Of course not everything the ghetto poor do and say merits approbation, and some of their conduct is, frankly, harmful wrongdoing and should therefore be discouraged and sometimes punished. But there is much to be learned from the impure dissent that emanates from American ghettos, whether this dissent takes the form of hip hop expression or more implicit modes of communication. These valuable elements should be seen as part of a political ethic that we might label *ghetto abolitionism*.

Calls for the abolition of ghettos date back to the Civil Rights movement. The movement to end Jim Crow was based primarily in the South, where blacks were not fully urbanized, explicit segregation laws were enforced, and blacks lacked an effective right to vote or run for public office. It took years of organized protest, skillful political maneuvering, and the Civil Rights Act (1964) and the Voting Rights Act (1965) to abolish the Jim Crow regime (though its negative effects are still felt today). Meanwhile, in cities like Los Angeles, New York City, Philadelphia, Detroit, Chicago, Newark, and Baltimore, blacks had been locked in the ghetto for decades, despite the absence of explicit segregation laws and notwithstanding the freedom to participate in electoral politics. It was in these cities (and others) that early calls for the abolition of the ghetto rang out—in the fiery speeches of black militants; in the verse, essays, plays, and books by intellectuals and artists; in the boycotts and union organizing of working-class people, and in destructive urban riots. These campaigns for social justice highlighted the plight of the oppressed in poor black urban communities, and demanded not only civil rights and an end to institutional racism, but also economic justice and a fair criminal justice system.

Consider the Black Panther Party's "Ten Point Program." It called for the political empowerment of black communities, a full-employment economy and guaranteed income for the involuntarily jobless, reparations for years of labor exploitation, decent and affordable housing, quality education for all, universal health care, and fundamental criminal justice reform. The group recruited in ghettos, capturing the attention and raising the consciousness of poor black youth. Indeed, Huey Newton, cofounder of the Party, argued that the "lumpenproletariat"—the unemployable element of the working class with no assets or marketable skills who therefore often turn to the underground economy for income—had revolutionary potential. Whatever one thinks of the ideology, tactics, or leadership of the Black Panthers, it cannot be denied that they mobilized to abolish ghettos on grounds of systemic injustice. Ghetto abolitionism, for these black radicals, was a collective effort, one that included the ghetto poor as allies, to (in my terms) fundamentally change the basic structure of U.S. society.

After the demise of the Black Power movement, the emergence of a relatively large black middle class (most of whom no longer live in ghetto neighborhoods), and the substantial increase of black elected officials (including many mayors of large U.S. cities), demands for the abolition of the ghetto have been less insistent and more muted. The call must be renewed. Perhaps that's what we're seeing in the recent Black Lives Matter movement to end unjustified police violence and racial profiling and in the youth-led uprisings in Ferguson and Baltimore. These welcome developments echo the fifty-year-old Black Panther Party demand for "an immediate end to POLICE BRUTALITY and MURDER of Black people." Such defiant protest is an essential element of ghetto abolitionism, though it must move beyond a focus on racism and the police to a broader campaign focused on economic justice.

I join the call for ghetto abolition, and this book—which is insufficient as a solution to all of the complex problems of the ghetto—is meant as an answer to the call. It is a contribution to the intellectual arm of a collective effort that reaches back at least to Du Bois's *The Philadelphia Negro* (1899). I offer no new political strategies or policy proposals. Others are better equipped for those tasks. What I have offered is a dense set of values and principles that should inform the next ghetto abolition movement (a nonideal theory of corrective justice with its accompanying political ethics). I've offered a way of conceptualizing the problem (as one of basic justice rather than black poverty). And I've defended a philosophical framework for responding to the problem (a systemic-injustice model rather than the medical model that now reigns in policy circles and among black elites). Let me close by briefly commenting on each of these ideas.

Ghetto abolitionism, when viewed within the systemic-injustice framework and in accordance with liberal-egalitarian principles, would help more than just the ghetto poor. It would help all who are unjustly disadvantaged. It not only attacks racism in all its forms, but calls for more robust enforcement of antidiscrimination law. It opposes class-based stratification, demanding a more equitable sharing of the benefits of social cooperation, technological advance, and economic growth. It insists on equal and extensive liberty for all, from freedom of expression and association to the right to an unconditional social minimum and to participate as equals in collective self-governance.

Ghetto abolitionism must be a grassroots effort, at least initially. It aims to change minds, to extend the bonds of solidarity, to mobilize and organize, and ultimately to influence public policy, from local ordinances to federal law. Liberal-egalitarian policy, when in corrective practice mode, is not limited to antipoverty initiatives but seeks more comprehensive social reform. When it embraces ghetto abolitionism, as it should, such policy eschews the medical model of social problem solving and fully embraces the systemic-injustice paradigm. Fundamental questions about the basic structure of society are not avoided and considerations of civic reciprocity are kept clearly and constantly in view.

Given the duty to ease the burdens of the oppressed, policy efforts must lighten the load on the ghetto poor while we work diligently to bring about a fully just society. These efforts must respect the moral and political agency of ghetto denizens, however. This means, for instance, not treating residential integration as a policy goal. The ghetto poor should be economically empowered and protected from housing discrimination so that they have real freedom to choose their neighborhood communities. Reproductive freedom should be respected. And while some wrongful procreation among the ghetto poor may exist, a stingy welfare regime should not be used to deter it, as this would only compound the economic injustices faced by many black women. No doubt poor families would be better off if they had two adult co-parents to share the workload. But the public lacks legitimate tools to do any more than recommend this familial arrangement. As there is nothing wrong with single-mother families (provided they receive the public support they are due), the state isn't justified in maintaining a highly punitive child-support regime on the basis of paternity alone. Nor is the state a suitable matchmaker for the oppressed, and many who share a biological child would do better—for themselves and their children—by not sharing a household.

Policymakers should certainly expand employment opportunities for the jobless. But the employment options and wages for low-skilled workers would need to be significantly improved and workfare requirements dropped altogether if the state is to avoid pushing the black poor into exploitative and demeaning forms of servitude. While voluntary job training and skills enhancement programs are welcome, a state that has created and allowed the ghetto to persist lacks the moral standing to act as an aggressive agent of cultural reform in the lives of its most embattled citizens.

In view of the serious injustices that disfigure the basic structure of society, sinking it below any reasonable standard for tolerable injustice, the ghetto poor owe neither loyalty nor obedience to the state. Even the state's enforcement rights are in jeopardy in light of racialized mass incarceration and unnecessary (and often malicious) violence in law enforcement practice. Criminal justice reform has to be a priority. Due process is a constitutional essential that underwrites the state's moral right to punish criminal offenders, and some who commit violent acts in ghettos must be contained to protect the weak and vulnerable in those communities.

As my title indicates, this book is partly inspired by and a tribute to Kenneth B. Clark's important but neglected work *Dark Ghetto: Dilemmas of Social Power* (1965). Clark is best known for his role in convincing the U.S. Supreme Court that school segregation negatively affects black south, which led to "separate but equal" public policy being declared unconstitutional. He also conducted the noted series of televised interviews "The Negro and the American Promise," which featured Martin Luther King Jr., Malcolm X, and James Baldwin. The interviews were later transcribed and collected in the book *The Negro Provost*, wherein Clark, reflecting on the political ethics of blacks in America, concludes: "The Negro has no more or less virtues or frailties than those found in other human beings. He is an individual who relies as much in courage and cowardice or ambivalence as do other human beings. He reacts to injustices and cruelties with the same patterns of accommodation, intimidation, rebellion, or philosophy as do others."[2]

Although Clark's *Dark Ghetto* is rooted in psychology and my book is a work of philosophy, I am entering the long-overdue conversation his book initiated but that was never fully taken up. The post-civil-rights scholarly and public discussion of ghetto communities was shaped more by another work, made public the same year: Daniel Patrick Moynihan's "The Negro Family: The Case for National Action."

I prefer Clark's treatise, not because Moynihan uses the inflammatory word "pathology" to describe features of black life in ghetto communities. Clark uses the word even more frequently and to refer to precisely the same phenomena (welfare dependency, single-mother families, nonmarital births, broken homes, disorder, delinquency, addiction, violence, and crime). I don't prefer *Dark Ghetto* because Moynihan "blames the victim" and Clark does not. Clark is actually much more critical of the conduct of ghetto denizens. I don't side with Clark because he is black and Moynihan white, or because Clark spent many years living in a ghetto and Moynihan did not. No doubt Clark's racial identity and past residence in a ghetto community give him greater standing (among blacks and whites alike) to be bold when assessing the actions and attitudes of the ghetto poor—a privilege that, arguably, I am exercising myself. But my claims rest on no presumption of epistemic privilege in virtue of my race or class background. Finally, my fondness for Clark over Moynihan is not because one is a "liberal" and the other a "radical," as both were avowed liberals. Rather, I am drawn to Clark's study because it seems to me to better exhibit the systemic-injustice model than Moynihan's infamous but influential sort.

I do not endorse *all* of Clark's particular theoretical conclusions. I don't agree that dependence on public support is pathological or an unfair burden on the public, for instance. Nor do I think reliance on public support is a threat to personal dignity. I do not accept his patriarchal conception of the family or of male gender identity. And I'm not inclined to see integration as a solution to black disadvantage. Yet I believe that Clark's book falls into fewer pits than Moynihan's report, rooted as Moynihan's was in the medical model approach to social problems.

Moynihan does insist that U.S. society has not provided substantive equal opportunity for all blacks and should seek racial parity in socioeconomic well-being. But he conceptualizes the problem of the ghetto as primarily one of "family instability," which, he claims, perpetuates the cycle of poverty and its associated dysfunctional conduct. He takes the linchpin of this problem to be high rates of male unemployment, which calls for an antipoverty strategy of enhancing job opportunities and increasing labor force participation. While he acknowledges the significance of past racial injustice in creating unstable black families, he says, "At this point, the present tangle of pathology is capable of perpetuating itself without assistance from the white world."[3] Drawing attention to his implicit reliance on the medical model of reform isn't to indict Moynihan. After all, as assistant secretary of labor at the time, he was attempting to persuade the Johnson administration to take proactive measures to address racial inequality. He wasn't addressing the general public or trying to spur or support a social movement for wide-ranging egalitarian reform. Nevertheless, the differences between his approach and Clark's are striking and important.

Clark consistently structures his explanatory claims around questions of social justice. He does not avoid making judgments of value or tackling controversial moral questions. He insists that objectivity in social inquiry is not equivalent to value neutrality. And he speaks freely about empirical facts and social justice without attempting to reduce matters of value to matters of fact, without treating values as merely subjective, and without regarding disagreements about justice as intractable or irresolvable. He recognizes, and this is key, that the only way forward is to give both scientific research and ethical reflection their due.

Grasping the importance of listening to the voices of the ghetto poor, Clark's prologue, titled "The Cry of the Ghetto," consists of thirty-two quotes from ghetto denizens, male and female and of all ages, who reflect on their plight and register their strong dissent from the status quo, condemning racism and discrimination, economic inequality and exploitation, lack of access to decent education, police brutality and harassment, inadequate protection from violence, political marginalization, media representations of black life, and American imperialism. In Clark's text, the ghetto poor are treated as agents of social change, as playing a central role in rebuilding their communities, and as taking the lead in reform efforts.

However, Clark does not romanticize the ghetto poor. He suggests, for example, that the ghetto outlaw persona is often mere pretense. He aims that self-esteem is sometimes acquired, perversely, through violent conduct. He notes the rampant political cynicism in ghetto communities. He believes that some ostensible dissent is nothing more than catharsis and posturing. Clark highlights the challenge of maintaining self-esteem and self-respect under ghetto conditions and the challenge of maintaining black solidarity in the face of internal class division. Yet he holds that the preservation of self-respect despite pervasive injustice is a prerequisite for any successful campaign for justice. In some acts of delinquency, he sees rebellion against oppression. For instance, he argues that dropping out of school is sometimes a defiant affirmation of self-respect in response to the condescension, low expectations, and criticism of teachers. And he believes it would be productive to enlist delinquents and criminal offenders in the collective project of solving community problems.

Clark regards unemployment and underemployment as problems, but emphasizes the fact that poor blacks are often restricted to menial service jobs that pay poverty-level wages. Joblessness as such is not therefore the linchpin. It is the quality of the jobs available and the low wages that call out for remedy. To prevent urban riots, Clark suggests creating decent jobs and reducing socioeconomic inequality. This would require fundamental change, a dramatic movement toward a more just society, rather than mere work programs and social services for the poor. Indeed, Clark appreciates how the single-minded focus on "helping" disadvantaged blacks obscures and evades the fact that the ghetto poor are in "need" because they live under a social structure that is unjust and that has shaped their personalities, conduct, and ambitions. This benefactor stance also conceals the fact that there are people with a vested interest in leaving the basic structure more or less as it is. Social work and philanthropy are inadequate and insulting responses to the problems of the ghetto, because they are rooted in benevolence rather than justice and opt to leave black communities dependent upon the goodwill of others rather than empowering them.

Clark invokes with approval the *internal colonization thesis*—the Black Power claim that the "white power structure" functions as a mother country over its black ghetto colonies. The analogy is not perfect, but it has the virtue of making vivid social relationships of domination and exploitation. Clark also focuses on the privileges of affluent whites, their tendency to rationalize their complicity in injustice, and their role in perpetuating ghetto conditions. And he even notes how some black leaders in the ghetto—clergy, informal spokespersons, and elected representatives—exploit the status quo for personal gain.

Finally, one of the things that Clark appreciates is that the modern American ghetto is not only appropriate for social-scientific study but also ripe for philosophical reflection:

> To understand Harlem, one must seek the truth and one must dare to accept and understand the truths one does find. One must understand its inconsistencies, its contradictions, its paradoxes, its ironies, its comic and its tragic face, its cruel and its self-destructive forces, and its desperate surge for life. And above all one must understand its humanity. The truth of the dark ghetto is not merely a truth about Negroes; it reflects the deeper torment and anguish of the total human predicament.[4]

My book is "political" in the way some academic books are and political philosophy must be. While it is not a social-scientific study, it is informed, indeed deeply shaped, by such studies and offers an interpretation of their moral significance. But this book is also a philosophical meditation on life in America's ghettos. I was searching, and continue to search, for those deeper, elusive, and more general "truths" behind the familiar facts about poor black neighborhoods. I hope my empathy for the plight of disadvantaged ghetto denizens is evident. But though moved by a sense of identification and solidarity with them, I have tried to remain objective and self-critical throughout.

A philosophical treatise on the ghetto might seem foolhardy, arrogant, and quixotic. The issues are tremendously complex. The topic is so big that no lone individual can be expected to say anything about it that is at once true, significant, and comprehensive. The relevant empirical and philosophical literature is vast, more than one can master in a lifetime of study. And the subject is highly controversial, where emotions run hot and enemies (and strange bedfellows) are easily made. So it might seem wiser (or safer) for a philosopher to dip his or her toe in these dark waters rather than dive right in. Yet here I am, soaked from head to foot.

Though I have been developing its arguments for more than ten years, this book is not, as Kenneth Clark claimed his *Dark Ghetto* to be, a "study of the total phenomenon of the ghetto." There are relevant issues—concerning education, democracy, and health, for example—that I have not addressed. I feel compelled, however, to make my current thinking public, trusting that readers will understand that all interdisciplinary work (particularly across the humanities–social science divide) has limitations of scope and depth. My hope is that other scholars, seeing merit in my approach, will be moved to supplement, build on, and correct these initial efforts. I don't expect mine to be the last word.

Notes

1 For an informative history of the concept ghetto in social science and policy, see Mitchell Duneier, *Ghetto: The Invention of a Place, the History of an Idea* (New York: Farrar, Straus and Giroux, 2016).
2 Kenneth B. Clark, *The Negro Protest: James Baldwin, Malcolm X, Martin Luther King talk with Kenneth B. Clark* (Boston, MA: Beacon Press, 1963), 51–52.
3 Moynihan, "The Negro Family," 48–51, 65–73, 93.
4 Kenneth B. Clark, *Dark Ghetto: Dilemmas of Social Power*, 2nd edition (Middletown, CT: Wesleyan University Press, 1989), xxxix.

> **Review and Discussion Questions**
>
> 1 What is the contrast between the medical model and Shelby's systemic-injustice framework?
> 2 What are the problems of "status quo bias," "downgraded agency," and "unjust-advantage blind spot"?
> 3 Shelby writes that "The ghetto should be abolished." What does he mean by that?
> 4 Do you agree with Shelby's approach for thinking about inner cities?

> **READING: AFFIRMATIVE ACTION IN HIGHER EDUCATION**
>
> GRUTTER V. BOLLINGER[*]
>
> Not since the famous *Regents of the University of California v. Bakke* case in 1978 has the Supreme Court attempted a comprehensive reassessment of affirmative action policies in U.S. colleges and law schools. Then, in 2003, the Court produced two affirmative action decisions in one day. Like the nation as whole, the Court was divided, by a 5–4 decision in *Grutter v. Bollinger* and a 6–3 decision in *Gratz v. Bollinger*. Both decisions produced strong sentiments and arguments about the role of affirmative action in American life. In *Grutter v. Bollinger*, the Court found that the University of Michigan's use of race as a factor for law school admissions was constitutionally permissible.
>
> ## Justice O'Connor Delivered the Opinion of the Court
>
> This case requires us to decide whether the use of race as a factor in student admissions by the University of Michigan Law School (Law School) is unlawful ....
>
> **II**
>
> *A*
>
> We last addressed the use of race in public higher education over 25 years ago. In the landmark *Bakke* case, we reviewed a racial set-aside program that reserved 16 out of 100 seats in a medical school class for members of certain minority groups. 438 U.S. 265 (1978). The decision produced six separate opinions, none of which commanded a majority of the Court ....
>
> Since this Court's splintered decision in *Bakke*, Justice Powell's opinion announcing the judgment of the Court has served as the touchstone for constitutional analysis of race-conscious admissions policies. Public and private universities across the Nation have modeled their own admissions programs on Justice Powell's views on permissible race-conscious policies ....

---

[*] *Grutter v. Bollinger*, 539 U.S. (2003).

.... [F]or the reasons set out below, today we endorse Justice Powell's view that student body diversity is a compelling state interest that can justify the use of race in university admissions.

B

The Equal Protection Clause provides that no State shall "deny to any person within its jurisdiction the equal protection of the laws." U.S. Const., Amdt. 14, §2. Because the Fourteenth Amendment "protect[s] *persons*, not *groups*," all "governmental action based on race—a *group* classification long recognized as in most circumstances irrelevant and therefore prohibited—should be subjected to detailed judicial inquiry to ensure that the *personal* right to equal protection of the laws has not been infringed." *Adarand Constructors, Inc.* v. *Peña*, 515 U.S. 200, 227 (1995) (emphasis in original; internal quotation marks and citation omitted). We are a "free people whose institutions are founded upon the doctrine of equality." *Loving* v. *Virginia*, 388 U.S. 1, 11 (1967) (internal quotation marks and citation omitted). It follows from that principle that "government may treat people differently because of their race only for the most compelling reasons." *Adarand Constructors, Inc.* v. *Peña*, 515 U.S., at 227 ....

Strict scrutiny is not "strict in theory, but fatal in fact." *Adarand Constructors, Inc.* v. *Peña, supra*, at 237 (internal quotation marks and citation omitted). Although all governmental uses of race are subject to strict scrutiny not all are invalidated by it ....

When race-based action is necessary to further a compelling governmental interest, such action does not violate the constitutional guarantee of equal protection so long as the narrow-tailoring requirement is also satisfied ....

III

A

With these principles in mind, we turn to the question whether the Law School's use of race is justified by a compelling state interest ....

[T]he Law School asks us to recognize, in the context of higher education, a compelling state interest in student body diversity ....

The Law School's educational judgment that such diversity is essential to its educational mission is one to which we defer ....

We have long recognized that, given the important purpose of public education and the expansive freedoms of speech and thought associated with the university environment, universities occupy a special niche in our constitutional tradition ....

As part of its goal of "assembling a class that is both exceptionally academically qualified and broadly diverse," the Law School seeks to "enroll a 'critical mass' of minority students." Brief for Respondents Bollinger et al. 13. ... the Law School's concept of critical mass is defined by reference to the educational benefits that diversity is designed to produce.

These benefits are substantial. As the District Court emphasized, the Law School's admissions policy promotes "cross-racial understanding," helps to break down racial stereotypes, and "enables [students] to better understand persons of different races." App. to Pet. for Cert. 246a. These benefits are "important and laudable," because "classroom discussion is livelier, more spirited, and simply more enlightening and interesting" when the students have "the greatest possible variety of backgrounds." *Id.*, at 246a, 244a.

The Law School's claim of a compelling interest is further bolstered by its *amici*, who point to the educational benefits that flow from student body diversity. In addition to the expert studies and reports entered into evidence at trial, numerous studies show that student body diversity promotes learning outcomes, and "better prepares students for an increasingly diverse workforce and society, and better prepares them as professionals." Brief for American Educational Research et al. *Amici Curiae* 3; ...

These benefits are not theoretical but real, as major American businesses have made clear that the skills needed in today's increasingly global marketplace can only be developed through exposure to widely diverse people, cultures, ideas, and viewpoints. ... What is more, high-ranking retired officers and civilian leaders of the United States military assert that, "[b]ased on [their] decades of experience," a "highly qualified, racially diverse officer corps ... is essential to the military's ability to fulfill its principle mission to provide national security." Brief for Julius W. Becton, Jr. et al. as *Amici Curiae* 27. ... We agree that "[i]t requires only a small step from this analysis to conclude that our country's other most selective institutions must remain both diverse and selective." *Ibid.*

We have repeatedly acknowledged the overriding importance of preparing students for work and citizenship, describing education as pivotal to "sustaining our political and cultural heritage" with a fundamental role in maintaining the fabric of society. *Plyler v. Doe*, 457 U.S. 202, 221 (1982). This Court has long recognized that "education ... is the very foundation of good citizenship." *Brown v. Board of Education*, 347 U.S. 483, 493 (1954) .... Effective participation by members of all racial and ethnic groups in the civic life of our Nation is essential if the dream of one Nation, indivisible, is to be realized.

Moreover, universities, and in particular, law schools, represent the training ground for a large number of our Nation's leaders ....

.... Access to legal education (and thus the legal profession) must be inclusive of talented and qualified individuals of every race and ethnicity, so that all members of our heterogeneous society may participate in the educational institutions that provide the training and education necessary to succeed in America.

The Law School does not premise its need for critical mass on "any belief that minority students always (or even consistently) express some characteristic minority viewpoint on any issue." Brief for Respondent Bollinger et al. 30. To the contrary, diminishing the force of such stereotypes is both a crucial part of the Law School's mission, and one that it cannot accomplish with only token numbers of minority students. Just as growing up in a particular region or having particular professional experiences is likely to affect an individual's views, so too is one's own, unique experience of being a racial minority in a society, like our own, in which race unfortunately still matters. The Law School has determined, based on its experience and expertise, that a "critical mass" of underrepresented minorities is necessary to further its compelling interest in securing the educational benefits of a diverse student body.

B

Even in the limited circumstance when drawing racial distinctions is permissible to further a compelling state interest, government is still "constrained in how it may pursue that end: [T]he means chosen to accomplish the [government's] asserted purpose must be specifically and narrowly framed to accomplish that purpose." *Shaw v. Hunt*, 517 U.S. 899, 908 (1996) (internal quotation marks and citation omitted) ....

Since *Bakke*, we have had no occasion to define the contours of the narrow-tailoring inquiry with respect to race-conscious university admissions programs. That inquiry must be calibrated to fit the distinct issues raised by the use of race to achieve student body diversity in public higher education ....

We find that the Law School's admissions program bears the hallmarks of a narrowly tailored plan. As Justice Powell made clear in *Bakke*, truly individualized consideration demands that race be used in a flexible, nonmechanical way. It follows from this mandate that universities cannot establish quotas for members of certain racial groups or put members of those groups on separate admissions tracks. See *id.*, at 315–316. Nor can universities insulate applicants who belong to certain racial or ethnic groups from the competition for admission. *Ibid.* Universities can, however, consider race or ethnicity more flexibly as a "plus" factor in the context of individualized consideration of each and every applicant. *Ibid.*

We are satisfied that the Law School's admissions program, like the Harvard plan described by Justice Powell, does not operate as a quota. Properly understood, a "quota" is a program in which a certain fixed number or proportion of opportunities are "reserved exclusively for certain minority groups." *Richmond v. J. A. Croson Co., supra*, at 496 (plurality opinion) ....

That a race-conscious admissions program does not operate as a quota does not, by itself, satisfy the requirement of individualized consideration. When using race as a "plus" factor in university admissions, a university's admissions program must remain flexible enough to ensure that each applicant is evaluated as an individual and not in a way that makes an applicant's race or ethnicity the defining feature of his or her application. The importance of this individualized consideration in the context of a race-conscious admissions program is paramount ....

... With respect to the use of race itself, all underrepresented minority students admitted by the Law School have been deemed qualified. By virtue of our Nation's struggle with racial inequality, such students are both likely to have experiences of particular importance to the Law School's mission, and less likely to be admitted in meaningful numbers on criteria that ignore those experiences. See App. 120.

The Law School does not, however, limit in any way the broad range of qualities and experiences that may be considered valuable contributions to student body diversity. ... All applicants have the opportunity to highlight their own potential diversity contributions through the submission of a personal statement, letters of recommendation, and an essay describing the ways in which the applicant will contribute to the life and diversity of the Law School.

What is more, the Law School actually gives substantial weight to diversity factors besides race. The Law School frequently accepts nonminority applicants with grades and test scores lower than underrepresented minority applicants (and other nonminority applicants) who are rejected. See Brief for Respondents Bollinger et al. 10; App. 121–122. This shows that the Law School seriously weighs many other diversity factors besides race that can make a real and dispositive difference for nonminority applicants as well. By this flexible approach, the Law School sufficiently takes into account, in practice as well as in theory, a wide variety of characteristics besides race and ethnicity that contribute to a diverse student body ....

.... We are satisfied that the Law School adequately considered race-neutral alternatives currently capable of producing a critical mass without forcing the Law School to abandon the academic selectivity that is the cornerstone of its educational mission.

We acknowledge that "there are serious problems of justice connected with the idea of preference itself." *Bakke*, 438 U.S., at 298 (opinion of Powell, J.). Narrow tailoring, therefore, requires that a race-conscious admissions program not unduly harm members of any racial group ....

We are satisfied that the Law School's admissions program does not. Because the Law School considers "all pertinent elements of diversity," it can (and does) select nonminority applicants who have greater potential to enhance student body diversity over underrepresented minority applicants. See *Bakke, supra*, at 317 (opinion of Powell, J.) ....

We are mindful, however, that "[a] core purpose of the Fourteenth Amendment was to do away with all governmentally imposed discrimination based on race." *Palmore* v. *Sidoti*, 466 U.S. 429, 432 (1984). Accordingly, race-conscious admissions policies must be limited in time. This requirement reflects that racial classifications, however compelling their goals, are potentially so dangerous that they may be employed no more broadly than the interest demands. Enshrining a permanent justification for racial preferences would offend this fundamental equal protection principle. We see no reason to exempt race-conscious admissions programs from the requirement that all governmental use of race must have a logical end point ....

In the context of higher education, the durational requirement can be met by sunset provisions in race-conscious admissions policies and periodic reviews to determine whether racial preferences are still necessary to achieve student body diversity ....

The requirement that all race-conscious admissions programs have a termination point "assure[s] all citizens that the deviation from the norm of equal treatment of all racial and ethnic groups is a temporary matter, a measure taken in the service of the goal of equality itself." *Richmond* v. *J. A. Croson Co.*, 488 U.S., at 510 (plurality opinion) ....

We take the Law School at its word that it would "like nothing better than to find a race-neutral admissions formula" and will terminate its race-conscious admissions program as soon as practicable ....

It has been 25 years since Justice Powell first approved the use of race to further an interest in student body diversity in the context of public higher education. Since that time, the number of minority applicants with high grades and test scores has indeed increased. See Tr. of Oral Arg. 43. We expect that 25 years from now, the use of racial preferences will no longer be necessary to further the interest approved today.

.... The judgment of the Court of Appeals for the Sixth Circuit, accordingly, is affirmed.

It is so ordered.

Justice Scalia, with Whom Justice Thomas Joins, Concurring in Part and Dissenting in Part

I join the opinion of the Chief Justice. As he demonstrates, the University of Michigan Law School's mystical "critical mass" justification for its discrimination by race challenges even the most gullible mind. The admissions statistics show it to be a sham to cover a scheme of racially proportionate admissions.

I also join Parts I through VII of Justice Thomas's opinion.[1] I find particularly unanswerable his central point: that the allegedly "compelling state interest" at issue here is not the incremental "educational benefit" that emanates from the fabled "critical mass" of minority students, but rather Michigan's interest in maintaining a "prestige" law school whose normal admissions standards disproportionately exclude blacks and other minorities. If that is a compelling state interest, everything is.

I add the following: The "educational benefit" that the University of Michigan seeks to achieve by racial discrimination consists, according to the Court, of "'cross-racial understanding,'" *ante*, at 18, and "'better prepar[ation of] students for an increasingly diverse workforce and society,'" *ibid.*, all of which is necessary not only for work, but also for good "citizenship," *ante*, at 19. This is not, of course, an "educational benefit" on which students will be graded on their Law School transcript (Works and Plays Well with Others: B+) or tested by the bar examiners (TS: Describe in 500 words or less your cross-racial understanding). For it is a lesson of life rather than law—essentially the same lesson taught to (or rather learned by, for it cannot be "taught" in the usual sense) people three feet shorter and twenty years younger than the full-grown adults at the University of Michigan Law School, in institutions ranging from Boy Scout troops to public-school kindergartens. If properly considered an "educational benefit" at all, it is surely not one that is either uniquely relevant to law school or uniquely "teachable" in a formal educational setting. *And therefore:* If it is appropriate for the University of Michigan Law School to use racial discrimination for the purpose of putting together a "critical mass" that will convey generic lessons in socialization and good citizenship, surely it is no less appropriate—indeed, *particularly* appropriate—for the civil service system of the State of Michigan to do so. There, also, those exposed to "critical masses" of certain races will presumably become better Americans, better Michiganders, better civil servants. And surely private employers cannot be criticized—indeed, should be praised—if they also "teach" good citizenship to their adult employees through a patriotic, all-American system of racial discrimination in hiring. The nonminority individuals who are deprived of a legal education, a civil service job, or any job at all by reason of their skin color will surely understand.

Unlike a clear constitutional holding that racial preferences in state educational institutions are impermissible, or even a clear anticonstitutional holding that racial preferences in state educational institutions are OK, today's *Grutter-Gratz* split double header seems perversely designed to prolong the controversy and the litigation. Some future lawsuits will presumably focus on whether the discriminatory scheme in question contains enough evaluation of the applicant "as an individual," *ante*, at 24, and sufficiently avoids "separate admissions tracks" *ante*, at 22, to fall under *Grutter* rather than *Gratz*. Some will focus on whether a university has gone beyond the bounds of a "good faith effort" and has so zealously pursued its "critical mass" as to make it an unconstitutional *de facto* quota system, rather than merely "a permissible goal." *Ante*, at 23 (quoting *Sheet Metal Workers* v. *EEOC*, 478 U.S. 421, 495 (1986) (O'Connor, J., concurring in part and dissenting in part)). Other lawsuits may focus on whether, in the particular setting at issue, any educational benefits flow from racial diversity. (That issue was not contested in *Grutter*; and while the opinion accords "a degree of deference to a university's academic decisions," *ante*, at 16, "deference does not imply abandonment or abdication of judicial review," *Miller-El* v. *Cockrell*, 537 U.S. 322, 340 (2003).) Still other suits may challenge the bona fides of the institution's expressed commitment to the educational benefits of diversity that immunize the discriminatory scheme in *Grutter*. (Tempting targets, one would suppose, will be those universities that talk the talk of multiculturalism and racial diversity in the courts but walk the walk of tribalism and racial segregation on their campuses—through minority-only student organizations, separate minority housing opportunities, separate minority student centers, even separate minority-only graduation ceremonies.) And still other suits may claim that the institution's racial preferences have gone below or above the mystical *Grutter*-approved "critical mass." Finally, litigation can be expected on behalf of minority groups intentionally short changed in the institution's composition of its generic minority "critical mass." I do not look forward to any of these cases. The Constitution proscribes government discrimination on the basis of race, and state-provided education is no exception.

Justice Thomas, with Whom Justice Scalia Joins as to Parts I–VII, Concurring in Part and Dissenting in Part

Frederick Douglass, speaking to a group of abolitionists almost 140 years ago, delivered a message lost on today's majority:

> "[I]n regard to the colored people, there is always more that is benevolent, I perceive, than just, manifested towards us. What I ask for the negro is not benevolence, not pity, not sympathy, but simply *justice*. The American people have always been anxious to know what they shall do with us. ... I have had but one answer from the beginning. Do nothing with us! Your doing with us has already played the mischief with us. Do nothing with us! If the apples will not remain on the tree of their own strength, if they are worm-eaten at the core, if they are early ripe and disposed to fall, let them fall! ... And if the negro cannot stand on his own legs, let him fall also. All I ask is, give him a chance to stand on his own legs! Let him alone! ... [Y]our interference is doing him positive injury." What the Black Man Wants: An Address Delivered in Boston, Massachusetts, on January 26, 1865, reprinted in 4 The Frederick Douglass Papers 59, 68.
> (J. Blassingame & J. McKivigan eds. 1991) (emphasis in original)

Like Douglass, I believe blacks can achieve in every avenue of American life without the meddling of university administrators. Because I wish to see all students succeed whatever their color, I share, in some respect, the sympathies of those who sponsor the type of discrimination advanced by the University of Michigan Law School (Law School). The Constitution does not, however, tolerate institutional devotion to the status quo in admissions policies when such devotion ripens into racial discrimination. Nor does the Constitution countenance the unprecedented deference the Court gives to the Law School, an approach inconsistent with the very concept of "strict scrutiny."

No one would argue that a university could set up a lower general admission standard and then impose heightened requirements only on black applicants. Similarly, a university may not maintain a high admission standard and grant exemptions to favored races. The Law School, of its own choosing, and for its own purposes, maintains an exclusionary admissions system that it knows produces racially disproportionate results. Racial discrimination is not a permissible solution to the self-inflicted wounds of this elitist admissions policy.

The majority upholds the Law School's racial discrimination not by interpreting the people's Constitution, but by responding to a faddish slogan of the cognoscenti ....

.... The Constitution abhors classifications based on race, not only because those classifications can harm favored races or are based on illegitimate motives, but also because every time the government places citizens on racial registers and makes race relevant to the provision of burdens or benefits, it demeans us all ....

II

Unlike the majority, I seek to define with precision the interest being asserted by the Law School before determining whether that interest is so compelling as to justify racial discrimination. The Law School maintains that it wishes to obtain "educational benefits that flow from student body diversity," (Brief for Respondents Bollinger et al. 14.) This statement must be evaluated carefully, because it implies that both "diversity" and "educational benefits" are components of the Law School's compelling state interest ....

Undoubtedly there are other ways to "better" the education of law students aside from ensuring that the student body contains a "critical mass" of underrepresented minority students. Attaining "diversity," whatever it means,[2] is the mechanism by which the Law School obtains educational benefits, not an end of itself. The Law School, however, apparently believes that only a racially mixed student body can lead to the educational benefits it seeks ....

III

A

A close reading of the Court's opinion reveals that all of its legal work is done through one conclusory statement: The Law School has a "compelling interest in securing the educational benefits of a diverse student body." ...

.... Today, the Court insists on radically expanding the range of permissible uses of race to something as trivial (by comparison) as the assembling of a law school class. I can only presume that the majority's failure to justify its decision by reference to any principle arises from the absence of any such principle. See Part VI, *infra*.

B

Under the proper standard, there is no pressing public necessity in maintaining a public law school at all and, it follows, certainly not an elite law school. Likewise, marginal improvements in legal education do not qualify as a compelling state interest.

IV

The interest in remaining elite and exclusive that the majority thinks so obviously critical requires the use of admissions "standards" that, in turn, create the Law School's "need" to discriminate on the basis of race. ... The Court never explicitly holds that the Law School's desire to retain the status quo in "academic selectivity" is itself a compelling state interest, and, as I have demonstrated, it is not. See Part III-B, *supra*. Therefore, the Law School should be forced to choose between its classroom aesthetic and its exclusionary admissions system—it cannot have it both ways.

With the adoption of different admissions methods, such as accepting all students who meet minimum qualifications, see Brief for United States as *Amicus Curiae* 13–14, the Law School could achieve its vision of the racially aesthetic student body without the use of racial discrimination. The Law School concedes this, but the Court holds, implicitly and under the guise of narrow tailoring, that the Law School has a compelling state interest in doing what it wants to do. I cannot agree ....

A

.... In my view, there is no basis for a right of public universities to do what would otherwise violate the Equal Protection Clause.

.... The majority's broad deference to both the Law School's judgment that racial aesthetics leads to educational benefits and its stubborn refusal to alter the status quo in admissions methods finds no basis in the Constitution or decisions of this Court.

B

The Court's deference to the Law School's conclusion that its racial experimentation leads to educational benefits will, if adhered to, have serious collateral consequences. The Court relies heavily on social science evidence to justify its deference. ... The Court never acknowledges, however, the growing evidence that racial (and other sorts) of heterogeneity actually impairs learning among black students ....

The majority grants deference to the Law School's "assessment that diversity will, in fact, yield educational benefits," *ante*, at 16. It follows, therefore, that an HBC's [Historically Black Colleges] assessment that racial homogeneity will yield educational benefits would similarly be given deference.[3] An HBC's rejection of white applicants in order to maintain racial homogeneity seems permissible, therefore, under the majority's view of the Equal Protection Clause. ... Contained within today's majority opinion is the seed of a new constitutional justification for a concept I thought long and rightly rejected—racial segregation ....

V

Putting aside the absence of any legal support for the majority's reflexive deference, there is much to be said for the view that the use of tests and other measures to "predict" academic performance is a poor substitute for a system that gives every applicant a chance to prove he can succeed in the study of law. The rallying cry that in the absence of racial discrimination in admissions there would be a true meritocracy ignores the fact that the entire process is poisoned by numerous exceptions to "merit." For example, in the national debate on racial discrimination in higher education admissions, much has been made of the fact that elite institutions utilize a so-called "legacy" preference to give the children of alumni an advantage in admissions. This, and other, exceptions to a "true" meritocracy give the lie to protestations that merit admissions are in fact the order of the day at the Nation's universities. The Equal Protection Clause does not, however, prohibit the use of unseemly legacy preferences or many other kinds of arbitrary admissions procedures. What the Equal Protection Clause does prohibit are classifications made on the basis of race. So while legacy preferences can stand under the Constitution, racial discrimination cannot.[4] I will not twist the Constitution to invalidate legacy preferences or otherwise impose my vision of higher education admissions on the Nation. The majority should similarly stay its impulse to validate faddish racial discrimination the Constitution clearly forbids.

In any event, there is nothing ancient, honorable, or constitutionally protected about "selective" admissions. The University of Michigan should be well aware that alternative methods have historically been used for the admission of students, for it brought to this country the German certificate system in the late-19th century. See H. Wechsler, The Qualified Student 16–39 (1977) (herein-after Qualified Student). Under this system, a secondary school was certified by a university so that any graduate who completed the course offered by the school was offered admission to the university ....

Certification was replaced by selective admissions in the beginning of the 20th century, as universities sought to exercise more control over the composition of their student bodies. Since its inception, selective admissions has been the vehicle for racial, ethnic, and religious tinkering and experimentation by university administrators. The initial driving force for the relocation of the selective function from the high school to the universities was the same desire to select racial winners and losers that the Law School exhibits today. Columbia, Harvard, and others infamously determined that they had "too many" Jews, just as today the Law School argues it would have "too many" whites if it could not discriminate in its admissions process. See Qualified Student 155–168 (Columbia); H. Broun & G. Britt, Christians Only: A Study in Prejudice 53–54 (1931) (Harvard).

.... [N]o modern law school can claim ignorance of the poor performance of blacks, relatively speaking, on the Law School Admissions Test (LSAT). Nevertheless, law schools continue to use the test and then attempt to "correct" for black underperformance by using racial discrimination in admissions so as to obtain their aesthetic student body. The Law School's continued adherence to measures it knows produce racially skewed results is not entitled to deference by this Court ....

Having decided to use the LSAT, the Law School must accept the constitutional burdens that come with this decision. The Law School may freely continue to employ the LSAT and other allegedly merit-based standards in whatever fashion it likes. What the Equal Protection Clause forbids, but the Court today allows, is the use of these standards hand-in-hand with racial discrimination. An infinite variety of admissions methods are available to the Law School. Considering all of the radical thinking that has historically occurred at this country's universities, the Law School's intractable approach toward admissions is striking.

The Court will not even deign to make the Law School try other methods, however, preferring instead to grant a 25-year license to violate the Constitution. And the same Court that had the courage to order the desegregation of all public schools in the South now fears, on the basis of platitudes rather than principle, to force the Law School to abandon a decidedly imperfect admissions regime that provides the basis for racial discrimination.

VI

The absence of any articulated legal principle supporting the majority's principal holding suggests another rationale. I believe what lies beneath the Court's decision today are the benighted notions that one can tell when racial discrimination benefits (rather than hurts) minority groups, see *Ada-rand*, 515 U.S., at 239 (Scalia, J., concurring in part and concurring in judgment), and that racial discrimination is necessary to remedy general societal ills ....

... I must contest the notion that the Law School's discrimination benefits those admitted as a result of it ....

The Law School tantalizes unprepared students with the promise of a University of Michigan degree and all of the opportunities that it offers. These overmatched students take the bait, only to find that they cannot succeed in the cauldron of competition. And this mismatch crisis is not restricted to elite institutions. ... While these students may graduate with law degrees, there is no evidence that they have received a qualitatively better legal education (or become better lawyers) than if they had gone to a less "elite" law school for which they were better prepared. And the aestheticists will never address the real problems facing "underrepresented minorities,"[5] instead continuing their social experiments on other people's children ....

It is uncontested that each year, the Law School admits a handful of blacks who would be admitted in the absence of racial discrimination. See Brief for Respondents Bollinger et al. 6. Who can differentiate between those who belong and those who do not? The majority of blacks are admitted to the Law School because of discrimination, and because of this policy all are tarred as undeserving. This problem of stigma does not depend on determinacy as to whether those stigmatized are actually the "beneficiaries" of racial discrimination. When blacks take positions in the highest places of government, industry, or academia, it is an open question today whether their skin color played a part in their advancement. The question itself is the stigma—because either racial discrimination did play a role, in which case the person may be deemed "otherwise unqualified," or it did not, in which case asking the question itself unfairly marks those blacks who would succeed without discrimination ....

The Court also holds that racial discrimination in admissions should be given another 25 years before it is deemed no longer narrowly tailored to the Law School's fabricated compelling state interest ....

Indeed, the very existence of racial discrimination of the type practiced by the Law School may impede the narrowing of the LSAT testing gap. An applicant's LSAT score can improve dramatically with preparation, but such preparation is a cost, and there must be sufficient benefits attached to an improved score to justify additional study. Whites scoring between 163 and 167 on the LSAT are routinely rejected by the Law School, and thus whites aspiring to admission at the Law School have every incentive to improve their score to levels above that range. See App. 199 (showing that in 2000, 209 out of 422 white applicants were rejected in this scoring range). Blacks, on the other hand, are nearly guaranteed admission if they score above 155. *Id.*, at 198 (showing that 63 out of 77 black applicants are accepted with LSAT scores above 155). As admission prospects approach certainty, there is no incentive for the black applicant to continue to prepare for the LSAT once he is reasonably assured of achieving the requisite score. It is far from certain that the LSAT test-taker's behavior is responsive to the Law School's admissions policies.[6] Nevertheless, the possibility remains that this racial discrimination will help fulfill the bigot's prophecy about black underperformance—just as it confirms the conspiracy theorist's belief that "institutional racism" is at fault for every racial disparity in our society ....

* * *

.... [T]he majority has placed its *imprimatur* on a practice that can only weaken the principle of equality embodied in the Declaration of Independence and the Equal Protection Clause. "Our Constitution is color-blind, and neither knows nor tolerates classes among citizens." *Plessy* v. *Ferguson*, 163 U.S. 537, 559 (1896) (Harlan, J., dissenting). It has been nearly 140 years since Frederick Douglass asked the intellectual ancestors of the Law School to "[d]o nothing with us!" and the Nation adopted the Fourteenth Amendment. Now we must wait another 25 years to see this principle of equality vindicated ....

Justice Kennedy, Dissenting

The separate opinion by Justice Powell in *Regents of Univ. of Cal.* v. *Bakke* is based on the principle that a university admissions program may take account of race as one, non-predominant factor in a system designed to consider each applicant as an individual, provided the program can meet the test of strict scrutiny by the judiciary. 438 U.S. 265, 289–291, 315–318 (1978). This is a unitary formulation. If strict scrutiny is abandoned or manipulated to distort its real and accepted meaning, the Court lacks authority to approve the use of race even in this modest, limited way. The opinion by Justice Powell, in my view, states the correct rule for resolving this case. The Court, however, does not apply strict scrutiny ....

The Court, in a review that is nothing short of perfunctory, accepts the University of Michigan Law School's assurances that its admissions process meets with constitutional requirements. The majority fails to confront the reality of how the Law School's admissions policy is implemented. The dissenting opinion by The

Chief Justice, which I join in full, demonstrates beyond question why the concept of critical mass is a delusion used by the Law School to mask its attempt to make race an automatic factor in most instances and to achieve numerical goals indistinguishable from quotas ....

About 80 to 85 percent of the places in the entering class are given to applicants in the upper range of Law School Admissions Test scores and grades. An applicant with these credentials likely will be admitted without consideration of race or ethnicity. With respect to the remaining 15 to 20 percent of the seats, race is likely outcome determinative for many members of minority groups. That is where the competition becomes tight and where any given applicant's chance of admission is far smaller if he or she lacks minority status. At this point the numerical concept of critical mass has the real potential to compromise individual review.

The Law School has not demonstrated how individual consideration is, or can be, preserved at this stage of the application process given the instruction to attain what it calls critical mass. In fact the evidence shows otherwise ....

To be constitutional, a university's compelling interest in a diverse student body must be achieved by a system where individual assessment is safeguarded through the entire process. There is no constitutional objection to the goal of considering race as one modest factor among many others to achieve diversity, but an educational institution must ensure, through sufficient procedures, that each applicant receives individual consideration and that race does not become a predominant factor in the admissions decision-making. The Law School failed to comply with this requirement ....

If universities are given the latitude to administer programs that are tantamount to quotas, they will have few incentives to make the existing minority admissions schemes transparent and protective of individual review. The unhappy consequence will be to perpetuate the hostilities that proper consideration of race is designed to avoid. The perpetuation, of course, would be the worst of all outcomes. Other programs do exist which will be more effective in bringing about the harmony and mutual respect among all citizens that our constitutional tradition has always sought. They, and not the program under review here, should be the model, even if the Court defaults by not demanding it.

It is regrettable the Court's important holding allowing racial minorities to have their special circumstances considered in order to improve their educational opportunities is accompanied by a suspension of the strict scrutiny which was the predicate of allowing race to be considered in the first place. If the Court abdicates its constitutional duty to give strict scrutiny to the use of race in university admissions, it negates my authority to approve the use of race in pursuit of student diversity. The Constitution cannot confer the right to classify on the basis of race even in this special context absent searching judicial review. For these reasons, though I reiterate my approval of giving appropriate consideration to race in this one context, I must dissent in the present case.

Notes

1 Part VII of Justice Thomas's opinion describes those portions of the Court's opinion in which I concur. See *post*, at 27–31.
2 "[D]iversity," for all of its devotees, is more a fashionable catchphrase than it is a useful term, especially when something as serious as racial discrimination is at issue. Because

the Equal Protection Clause renders the color of one's skin constitutionally irrelevant to the Law School's mission, I refer to the Law School's interest as an "aesthetic." That is, the Law School wants to have a certain appearance, from the shape of the desks and tables in its classrooms to the color of the students sitting at them.

I also use the term "aesthetic" because I believe it underlines the ineffectiveness of racially discriminatory admissions in actually helping those who are truly underprivileged. Cf. *Orr v. Orr*, 440 U.S. 268, 283 (1979) (noting that suspect classifications are especially impermissible when "the choice made by the State appears to redound ... to the benefit of those without need for special solicitude"). It must be remembered that the Law School's racial discrimination does nothing for those too poor or uneducated to participate in elite higher education and therefore presents only an illusory solution to the challenges facing our Nation.

3 For example, North Carolina A&T State University, which is currently 5.4 percent white, College Admissions Data Handbook 643, could seek to reduce the representation of whites in order to gain additional educational benefits.
4 Were this Court to have the courage to forbid the use of racial discrimination in admissions, legacy preferences (and similar practices) might quickly become less popular—a possibility not lost, I am certain, on the elites (both individual and institutional) supporting the Law School in this case.
5 For example, there is no recognition by the Law School in this case that even with their racial discrimination in place, black *men* are "underrepresented" at the Law School. See ABA–LSAC Guide 426 (reporting that the Law School has 46 black women and 28 black men). Why does the Law School not also discriminate in favor of black men over black women, given this underrepresentation? The answer is, again, that all the Law School cares about is its own image among know-it-all elites, not solving real problems like the crisis of black male underperformance.
6 I use the LSAT as an example, but the same incentive structure is in place for any admissions criteria, including undergraduate grades, on which minorities are consistently admitted at thresholds significantly lower than whites.

Review and Discussion Questions

1 What about Michigan Law School's admissions process does Justice O'Connor identify as most important for determining the constitutionality of the case?
2 What is Justice Scalia's argument?
3 Justice Thomas begins with a quote from Frederick Douglass. What is the argument in that quote? Do you agree with it? Why or why not?
4 What is Justice Kennedy's dissent?
5 In your view, what explains the deep division in this decision?
6 What is the best argument presented across all the opinions?

READING: AFFIRMATIVE ACTION IN HIGHER EDUCATION

GRATZ V. BOLLINGER[*]

In contrast to its decision in *Grutter*, the Supreme Court found in this case that the undergraduate admissions procedure at the University of Michigan that awarded points to a candidate for a minority classification was unconstitutional.

---

[*] *Gratz and Hamacher v. Bollinger* 539 U.S. (2003).

Chief Justice Rehnquist Delivered the Opinion of the Court ....

B

Petitioners argue, first and foremost, that the University's use of race in undergraduate admissions violates the Fourteenth Amendment. Specifically, they contend that this Court has only sanctioned the use of racial classifications to remedy identified discrimination, a justification on which respondents have never relied. Brief for Petitioners 15–16. Petitioners further argue that "diversity as a basis for employing racial preferences is simply too open-ended, ill-defined, and indefinite to constitute a compelling interest capable of supporting narrowly-tailored means." *Id.*, at 17–18, 40–41. But for the reasons set forth today in *Grutter* v. *Bollinger, post*, at 15–21, the Court has rejected these arguments of petitioners.

Petitioners alternatively argue that even if the University's interest in diversity can constitute a compelling state interest, the District Court erroneously concluded that the University's use of race in its current freshman admissions policy is narrowly tailored to achieve such an interest ....

It is by now well established that "all racial classifications reviewable under the Equal Protection Clause must be strictly scrutinized." *Adarand Constructors, Inc.* v. *Peña*, 515 U.S. 200, 224 (1995) ....

To withstand our strict scrutiny analysis, respondents must demonstrate that the University's use of race in its current admission program employs "narrowly tailored measures that further compelling governmental interests." *Id.*, at 227. ... We find that the University's policy, which automatically distributes 20 points, or one-fifth of the points needed to guarantee admission, to every single "underrepresented minority" applicant solely because of race, is not narrowly tailored to achieve the interest in educational diversity that respondents claim justifies their program ....

Justice Powell's opinion in *Bakke* emphasized the importance of considering each particular applicant as an individual, assessing all of the qualities that individual possesses, and in turn, evaluating that individual's ability to contribute to the unique setting of higher education ....

The current LSA policy does not provide such individualized consideration. The LSA's policy automatically distributes 20 points to every single applicant from an "underrepresented minority" group, as defined by the University. The only consideration that accompanies this distribution of points is a factual review of an application to determine whether an individual is a member of one of these minority groups ....

Also instructive in our consideration of the LSA's system is the example provided in the description of the Harvard College Admissions Program, which Justice Powell both discussed in, and attached to, his opinion in *Bakke*. The example was included to "illustrate the kind of significance attached to race" under the Harvard College program. *Id.*, at 324. It provided as follows:

> "The Admissions Committee, with only a few places left to fill, might find itself forced to choose between A, the child of a successful black physician in an academic community with promise of superior academic performance, and B, a black who grew up in an innercity ghetto of semi-literate parents whose

academic achievement was lower but who had demonstrated energy and leadership as well as an apparently abiding interest in black power. If a good number of black students much like A but few like B had already been admitted, the Committee might prefer B; and vice versa. If C, a white student with extraordinary artistic talent, were also seeking one of the remaining places, his unique quality might give him an edge over both A and B. Thus, the critical criteria are often individual qualities or experience *not dependent upon race but sometimes associated with it*."

Ibid. (emphasis added)

This example further demonstrates the problematic nature of the LSA's admissions system. Even if student C's "extraordinary artistic talent" rivaled that of Monet or Picasso, the applicant would receive, at most, five points under the LSA's system. See App. 234-235. At the same time, every single underrepresented minority applicant, including students A and B, would automatically receive 20 points for submitting an application. Clearly, the LSA's system does not offer applicants the individualized selection process described in Harvard's example. Instead of considering how the differing backgrounds, experiences, and characteristics of students A, B, and C might benefit the University, admissions counselors reviewing LSA applications would simply award both A and B 20 points because their applications indicate that they are African-American, and student C would receive up to 5 points for his "extraordinary talent."[1]

... Nothing in Justice Powell's opinion in *Bakke* signaled that a university may employ whatever means it desires to achieve the stated goal of diversity without regard to the limits imposed by our strict scrutiny analysis.

We conclude, therefore, that because the University's use of race in its current freshman admissions policy is not narrowly tailored to achieve respondents' asserted compelling interest in diversity, the admissions policy violates the Equal Protection Clause of the Fourteenth Amendment.[2] ...

It is so ordered.

Justice O'Connor, Concurring.[3]

I

Unlike the law school admissions policy the Court upholds today in *Grutter v. Bollinger, post*, p. 1, the procedures employed by the University of Michigan's (University) Office of Undergraduate Admissions do not provide for a meaningful individualized review of applicants. ... the selection index, by setting up automatic, predetermined point allocations for the soft variables, ensures that the diversity contributions of applicants cannot be individually assessed. This policy stands in sharp contrast to the law school's admissions plan, which enables admissions officers to make nuanced judgments with respect to the contributions each applicant is likely to make to the diversity of the incoming class.

.... [T]he current system, as I understand it, is a nonindividualized, mechanical one. As a result, I join the Court's opinion reversing the decision of the District Court.

Justice Thomas, Concurring

I join the Court's opinion because I believe it correctly applies our precedents, including today's decision in *Grutter* v. *Bollinger, post*. For similar reasons to those given in my separate opinion in that case, see *post* (opinion concurring in part and dissenting in part), however, I would hold that a State's use of racial discrimination in higher education admissions is categorically prohibited by the Equal Protection Clause.

Justice Souter, with Whom Justice Ginsburg Joins as to Part II, Dissenting ....

II

The cases now contain two pointers toward the line between the valid and the unconstitutional in race-conscious admissions schemes. *Grutter* reaffirms the permissibility of individualized consideration of race to achieve a diversity of students, at least where race is not assigned a preordained value in all cases. On the other hand, Justice Powell's opinion in *Regents of Univ. of Cal.* v. *Bakke*, 438 U.S. 265 (1978), rules out a racial quota or set-aside, in which race is the sole fact of eligibility for certain places in a class. Although the freshman admissions system here is subject to argument on the merits, I think it is closer to what *Grutter* approves than to what *Bakke* condemns, and should not be held unconstitutional on the current record.

The record does not describe a system with a quota like the one struck down in *Bakke*, which "insulate[d]" all nonminority candidates from competition from certain seats. *Bakke, supra*, at 317 (opinion of Powell, J.) ....

Subject to one qualification to be taken up below, this scheme of considering, through the selection index system, all of the characteristics that the college thinks relevant to student diversity for every one of the student places to be filled fits Justice Powell's description of a constitutionally acceptable program: one that considers "all pertinent elements of diversity in light of the particular qualifications of each applicant" and places each element "on the same footing for consideration, although not necessarily according them the same weight." *Bakke, supra*, at 317. In the Court's own words, "each characteristic of a particular applicant [is] considered in assessing the applicant's entire application." *Ante*, at 23 ....

The one qualification to this description of the admissions process is that membership in an underrepresented minority is given a weight of 20 points on the 150-point scale. On the face of things, however, this assignment of specific points does not set race apart from all other weighted considerations. Nonminority students may receive 20 points for athletic ability, socioeconomic disadvantage, attendance at a socioeconomically disadvantaged or predominantly minority high school, or at the Provost's discretion; they may also receive 10 points for being residents of Michigan, 6 for residence in an underrepresented Michigan county, 5 for leadership and service, and so on.

The Court nonetheless finds fault with a scheme that "automatically" distributes 20 points to minority applicants because "[t]he only consideration that accompanies this distribution of points is a factual review of an application to determine whether an individual is a member of one of these minority groups." *Ante*, at 23. The objection goes to the use of points to quantify and compare characteristics, or to the number of points awarded due to race, but on either reading the objection is mistaken.

The very nature of a college's permissible practice of awarding value to racial diversity means that race must be considered in a way that increases some applicants' chances for admission. Since college admission is not left entirely to inarticulate intuition, it is hard to see what is inappropriate in assigning some stated value to a relevant characteristic, whether it be reasoning ability, writing style, running speed, or minority race. Justice Powell's plus factors necessarily are assigned some values. The college simply does by a numbered scale what the law school accomplishes in its "holistic review," *Grutter, post*, at 25; the distinction does not imply that applicants to the undergraduate college are denied individualized consideration or a fair chance to compete on the basis of all the various merits their applications may disclose ....

Without knowing more about how the Admissions Review Committee actually functions, it seems especially unfair to treat the candor of the admissions plan as an Achilles' heel. In contrast to the college's forthrightness in saying just what plus factor it gives for membership in an underrepresented minority, it is worth considering the character of one alternative thrown up as preferable, because supposedly not based on race. Drawing on admissions systems used at public universities in California, Florida, and Texas, the United States contends that Michigan could get student diversity in satisfaction of its compelling interest by guaranteeing admission to a fixed percentage of the top students from each high school in Michigan. Brief for United States as *Amicus Curiae* 18; Brief for United States as *Amicus Curiae* in *Grutter* v. *Bollinger*, O. T. 2002, No. 02-241, pp. 13-17.

While there is nothing unconstitutional about such a practice, it nonetheless suffers from a serious disadvantage.[4] It is the disadvantage of deliberate obfuscation. The "percentage plans" are just as race conscious as the point scheme (and fairly so), but they get their racially diverse results without saying directly what they are doing or why they are doing it. In contrast, Michigan states its purpose directly and, if this were a doubtful case for me, I would be tempted to give Michigan an extra point of its own for its frankness. Equal protection cannot become an exercise in which the winners are the ones who hide the ball.

Justice Ginsburg, with Whom Justice Souter Joins, *Dissenting*.[5]

I

Educational institutions, the Court acknowledges, are not barred from any and all consideration of race when making admissions decisions. ... [W]e are not far distant from an overtly discriminatory past, and the effects of centuries of law-sanctioned inequality remain painfully evident in our communities and schools.

In the wake "of a system of racial caste only recently ended," *id.*, at 273 (Ginsburg, J., dissenting), large disparities endure. Unemployment, poverty, and access to health care vary disproportionately by race. Neighborhoods and schools remain racially divided. African-American and Hispanic children are all too often educated in poverty-stricken and underperforming institutions. Adult African-Americans and Hispanics generally earn less than whites with equivalent levels of education. Equally credentialed job applicants receive different receptions depending on their race. Irrational prejudice is still encountered in real estate markets and consumer transactions ....

The Constitution instructs all who act for the government that they may not "deny to any person ... the equal protection of the laws." Amdt. 14, § 1. In implementing this equality instruction, as I see it, government decision-makers may properly distinguish between policies of exclusion and inclusion ....

Our jurisprudence ranks race a "suspect" category, "not because [race] is inevitably an impermissible classification, but because it is one which usually, to our national shame, has been drawn for the purpose of maintaining racial inequality." *Norwalk Core* v. *Norwalk Redevelopment Agency*, 395 F. 2d 920, 931–932 (CA2 1968) (footnote omitted). But where race is considered "for the purpose of achieving equality," *id.*, at 932, no automatic proscription is in order. ... Contemporary human rights documents draw just this line; they distinguish between policies of oppression and measures designed to accelerate *de facto* equality ....

The mere assertion of a laudable governmental purpose, of course, should not immunize a race-conscious measure from careful judicial inspection ....

II

Examining in this light the admissions policy employed by the University of Michigan's College of Literature, Science, and the Arts (College), and for the reasons well stated by Justice Souter, I see no constitutional infirmity. See *ante*, at 3–8 (dissenting opinion). Like other top-ranking institutions, the College has many more applicants for admission than it can accommodate in an entering class. App. to Pet. for Cert. 108a. Every applicant admitted under the current plan, petitioners do not here dispute, is qualified to attend the College. *Id.*, at 111a. The racial and ethnic groups to which the College accords special consideration (African-Americans, Hispanics, and Native-Americans) historically have been relegated to inferior status by law and social practice; their members continue to experience class-based discrimination to this day, see *supra*, at 1–4. There is no suggestion that the College adopted its current policy in order to limit or decrease enrollment by any particular racial or ethnic group, and no seats are reserved on the basis of race. ... Nor has there been any demonstration that the College's program unduly constricts admissions opportunities for students who do not receive special consideration based on race ....

The stain of generations of racial oppression is still visible in our society, see Krieger, 86 Calif. L. Rev., at 1253, and the determination to hasten its removal remains vital. One can reasonably anticipate, therefore, that colleges and universities will seek to maintain their minority enrollment—and the networks and opportunities thereby opened to minority graduates—whether or not they can do so in full candor through adoption of affirmative action plans of the kind here at issue. Without recourse to such plans, institutions of higher education may resort to camouflage. For example, schools may encourage applicants to write of their cultural traditions in the essays they submit, or to indicate whether English is their second language. Seeking to improve their chances for admission, applicants may highlight the minority group associations to which they belong, or the Hispanic surnames of their mothers or grandparents. In turn, teachers' recommendations may emphasize who a student is as much as what he or she has accomplished. ... If honesty is the best policy, surely Michigan's accurately described, fully disclosed College affirmative action program is preferable to achieving similar numbers through winks, nods, and disguises.[6]

* * *

For the reasons stated, I would affirm the judgment of the District Court.

Notes

1. Justice Souter is therefore wrong when he contends that "applicants to the undergraduate college are [not] denied individualized consideration." *Post*, at 6. As Justice O'Connor explains in her concurrence, the LSA's program "ensures that the diversity contributions of applicants cannot be individually assessed." *Post*, at 4.
2. Justice Ginsburg in her dissent observes that "[o]ne can reasonably anticipate ... that colleges and universities will seek to maintain their minority enrollment ... whether or not they can do so in full candor through adoption of affirmative action plans of the kind here at issue." *Post*, at 7–8. She goes on to say that "[i]f honesty is the best policy, surely Michigan's accurately described, fully disclosed College affirmative action program is preferable to achieving similar numbers through winks, nods, and disguises." *Post*, at 8. These observations are remarkable for two reasons. First, they suggest that universities—to whose academic judgment we are told in *Grutter* v. *Bollinger, post*, at 16, we should defer—will pursue their affirmative-action programs whether or not they violate the United States Constitution. Second, they recommend that these violations should be dealt with, not by requiring the universities to obey the Constitution, but by changing the Constitution so that it conforms to the conduct of the universities.
3. Justice Breyer joins this opinion, except for the last sentence.
4. Of course it might be pointless in the State of Michigan, where minorities are a much smaller fraction of the population than in California, Florida, or Texas. Brief for Respondents Bollinger et al. 48–49.
5. Justice Breyer joins Part I of this opinion.
6. Contrary to the Court's contention, I do not suggest "changing the Constitution so that it conforms to the conduct of the universities." *Ante*, at 27, n. 22. In my view, the Constitution, properly interpreted, permits government officials to respond openly to the continuing importance of race. See *supra*, at 4–5. Among constitutionally permissible options, those that candidly disclose their consideration of race seem to me preferable to those that conceal it.

Review and Discussion Questions

1. What is the difference between these two cases such that one approach to affirmative action was found constitutional, while the other approach was unconstitutional?
2. Why must race classifications be strictly scrutinized, according to the Court?
3. Is diversity a legitimate educational goal, and is affirmative action a morally permissible means to reach that goal? (Define what you mean by affirmative action.)
4. What is Justice Ginsburg's dissent in this decision? How do you think Justice Thomas would respond to it?
5. Do these combined cases offer moral clarity regarding the role of affirmative action in the United States? Explain why or why not.

READING: REVERSE DISCRIMINATION

JAMES RACHELS[*]

In this essay, James Rachels considers affirmative action from two perspectives. First, he asks whether it is a wise policy. Is society better off giving preferences to minorities than it would be if it didn't? Rachels then considers the claim that under certain circumstances, affirmative action is required by considerations of justice. James Rachels was University Professor at the University of Alabama at Birmingham.

Is it right to give preferential treatment to blacks, women, or members of other groups who have been discriminated against in the past? I will approach this issue by considering the deserts of the individuals involved. [Rachels earlier argued in this essay that past actions, especially effort, are important factors in distributing punishment, rewards, and other goods. By respecting past effort, he contends, we show respect for the autonomous choices of those who both win and lose.—Ed. note.] "Reverse discrimination" is not a particularly good label for the practices in question because the word "discrimination" has come to have such unsavory connotations. Given the way that word is now used, to ask whether reverse *discrimination* is justified already prejudices the question in favor of a negative answer. But in other ways the term is apt: the most distinctive thing about reverse discrimination is that it *reverses* past patterns, so that those who have been discriminated against are now given preferential treatment. At any rate, the label is now part of our common vocabulary, so I will stay with it.

The following example incorporates the essential elements of reverse discrimination. The admissions committee of a certain law school assesses the qualifications of applicants by assigning numerical values to their college grades, letters of recommendation, and test scores according to some acceptable formula. (The better the grades, etc., the higher the numerical values assigned.) From past experience, the committee judges that a combined score of 600 is necessary for a student to have a reasonable chance of succeeding in the school's program. Thus, in order to be minimally qualified for admission, an applicant must score at least 600. However, because there are more qualified applicants than places available, many who score over 600 are nevertheless rejected.

Against this background two students, one black and one white, apply for admission. The black student's credentials are rated at 700, and the white student's credentials are rated at 720. So although both exceed the minimum requirement by a comfortable margin, the white student's qualifications are somewhat better. But the white applicant is rejected and the black applicant is accepted. The officials of the school explain that this decision is part of a policy designed to bring more blacks into the legal profession. The scores of the white applicants are generally

---

[*] From James Rachels, "What People Deserve," originally printed in John Arthur and William H. Shaw, eds., *Justice and Economic Distribution* (Upper Saddle River, NJ: Prentice Hall, 1978). Reprinted by permission of the estate of James Rachels.

higher than those of the blacks, so some blacks with lower scores must be admitted in order to have a fair number of black students in the entering class ....

Now a number of arguments can be given in support of the law school's policy and other policies like it. Black people have been, and still are, the victims of racist discrimination. One result is that they are poorly represented in the professions. In order to remedy this it is not enough that we simply stop discriminating against them. For so long as there are not enough "role models" available—i.e., black people visibly successful in the professions, whom young blacks can recognize as models to emulate—young blacks cannot be expected to aspire to the professions and prepare for careers in the way that young whites do. It is a vicious cycle: while there are relatively few black lawyers, relatively few young blacks will take seriously the possibility of becoming lawyers, and so they will not be prepared for law school. But if relatively few young blacks are well-prepared for law school, and admissions committees hold them to the same high standards as the white applicants, there will be relatively few black lawyers. Law school admissions committees may try to help set things right, and break this cycle, by temporarily giving preferential treatment to black applicants.

Moreover, although many people now recognize that racist discrimination is wrong, prejudice against blacks is still widespread. One aspect of the problem is that a disproportionate number of blacks are still poor and hold only menial jobs, while the most prestigious jobs are occupied mostly by whites. So long as this is so, it will be easy for the white majority to continue with their old stereotyped ideas about black people. But if there were more black people holding prestigious jobs, it would be much more difficult to sustain the old prejudices. So in the long run law school admissions policies favoring black applicants will help reduce racism throughout the society.

I believe these arguments, and others like them, show that policies of reverse discrimination can be socially useful, although this is certainly a debatable point. For one thing, the resentment of those who disapprove of such policies will diminish their net utility. For another, less qualified persons will not perform as well in the positions they attain. However, I will not discuss these issues any further. I will concentrate instead on the more fundamental question of whether policies of reverse discrimination are unjust. After all, the rejected white student may concede the utility of such policies and nevertheless still complain that he has been treated unjustly. He may point out that he has been turned down simply because of his race. If he had been black and had had exactly the same qualifications, he would have been accepted. This, he may argue, is equally as unjust as discriminating against black people on account of their race. Moreover, he can argue that even if black people have been mistreated, he was not responsible for it, and so it is unfair to penalize him for it now. These are impressive arguments and if they cannot be answered, the rightness of reverse discrimination will remain in doubt regardless of its utility.

I will argue that whether the white applicant has been treated unjustly depends on why he has better credentials than the black, that is, it depends on what accounts for the 20-point difference in their qualifications.

Suppose, for example, that his higher qualifications are due entirely to the fact that he has worked harder. Suppose the two applicants are equally intelligent and have had the same opportunities. But the black student has spent a lot of time enjoying himself, going to the movies, and so forth, while the white student has passed by such pleasures to devote himself to his studies. If *this* is what accounts for the difference in their qualifications, then it seems that the white applicant really has been treated unjustly. For he has earned his superior qualifications; he deserves to be admitted ahead of the black student because he has worked harder for it.

But now suppose a different explanation is given as to why the white student has ended up with a 20-point advantage in qualifications. Suppose the applicants are equally intelligent and they have worked equally hard. However, the black student has had to contend with obstacles which his white competitor has not had to face. For example, his early education was at the hands of ill-trained teachers in crowded, inadequate schools, so that by the time he reached college he was far behind the other students and despite his best efforts he never quite caught up. If *this* is what accounts for the difference in qualifications, things look very different. For now the white student has not earned his superior qualifications. He has done nothing to deserve them. His record is, of course, the result of things he's done, just as the black student's record is the result of things the black student has done. But the fact that he has a *better* record than the black student is not due to anything he has done. That difference is due only to his good luck in having been born into a more advantaged social position. Surely he cannot deserve to be admitted into law school ahead of the black simply because of *that*.

Now in fact black people in the United States have been, and are, systematically discriminated against, and it is reasonable to believe that this mistreatment does make a difference to black people's ability to compete with whites for such goods as law school admission. Therefore, at least some actual cases probably do correspond to the description of my example. Some white students have better qualifications for law school only because they have not had to contend with the obstacles faced by their black competitors. If so, their better qualifications do not automatically entitle them to prior admission.

Thus, it is not the fact that the applicant is black that matters. What is important is that as a result of past discriminatory practices, he has been unfairly handicapped in trying to achieve the sort of academic standing required for admission. If he has a claim to "preferential" treatment now, it is for *that* reason.

It follows that, even though a system of reverse discrimination might involve injustice for some whites, in many cases no injustice will be done. In fact, the reverse is true: If no such system is employed—if, for example, law school admissions are granted purely on the basis of "qualifications"—*that* may involve injustice for the disadvantaged who have been unfairly handicapped in the competition for qualifications.

It also follows that the most common arguments against reverse discrimination are not valid. The white student in our example cannot complain that he is being rejected simply because he is white. The effect of the policy is only to *neutralize an advantage* that he has had because he is white, and that is very different.[1] Nor will it do any good for the white to complain that while blacks may have suffered unjust hardships, *he* is not responsible for it and so should not be penalized for it. The white applicant is not being penalized, or being made to pay reparations, for the wrongs that have been done to blacks. He is simply not being allowed to *profit* from the fact that those wrongs were done by now besting the black in a competition that is "fair" only if we ignore the obstacles which one competitor, but not the other, has had to face.

Note

1 See George Sher, "Justifying Reverse Discrimination in Employment," *Philosophy and Public Affairs* 4, no. 2 (Winter 1975); 159–170. Sher also argues that "reverse discrimination is justified insofar as it neutralizes competitive disadvantages caused by past privations" (p. 165). I have learned a lot from Sher's paper.

Review and Discussion Questions

1 What are the potential advantages of affirmative action that Rachels identifies?
2 What are the potential costs to society of affirmative action, according to Rachels?
3 Describe the factors that could mean that preference in hiring or admission is deserved as a matter of justice.
4 "Reverse discrimination only serves to prevent some people from cashing in on an unfair system; it's rather like awarding a prize to a horse that came in second but would have won had the race been fair." Would Rachels agree or disagree with this statement? Explain.
5 "Since many minorities enjoy education and economic advantages while many whites are poor and suffer educational and other disadvantages, Rachels has not shown that preference based on race or gender is justified." Do you agree? Explain.

READING: THE SUBJECTION OF WOMEN

JOHN STUART MILL AND HARRIET TAYLOR[*]

As noted in the introduction to Mill's essay on utilitarianism, John Stuart Mill and Harriet Taylor enjoyed a lengthy and profoundly rewarding relationship. Her influence on Mill was extraordinary; indeed, there are many who believe it was she, as much or more than he, who was responsible for the following essay. In any event, this is a prescient essay on the subject of women's rights, and even today, more than a century later, it speaks to many issues still very much at the forefront of our discussions of sexual equality.

Mill and Taylor begin with an analysis of the situation faced by women, along with the possible causes of their plight. They then respond to those who would argue that the observed differences between the sexes are natural and those who believe that women willingly accept their lot. They conclude with a discussion of the various reasons why women's equality should be advanced.

It is interesting to note that before Mill and Taylor were married, Mill signed an agreement renouncing all of the powers the law would normally bestow on him, asserting instead that his prospective wife was to retain the same rights to her property and personal freedom as if they had never married. When she died, Mill

---

[*] From John Stuart Mill and Harriet Taylor, *The Subjection of Women* (1869).

bought a house near the graveyard in France where Taylor was buried in order to spend his last years near his wife. The description of an ideal marriage appearing near the end of the essay mirrors Mill's own description of their relationship. (Because the essay was originally published under Mill's name alone, it is written using the first-person singular. Nonetheless, we have included Taylor as coauthor, as we believe Mill might have wished.)

Chapter I

The object of this Essay is to explain as clearly as I am able, the grounds of an opinion which I have held from the very earliest period when I had formed any opinions at all on social or political matters, and which, instead of being weakened or modified, has been constantly growing stronger by the progress of reflection and the experience of life: That the principle which regulates the existing social relations between the two sexes—the legal subordination of one sex to the other—is wrong in itself, and now one of the chief hindrances to human improvement; and that it ought to be replaced by a principle of perfect equality, admitting no power or privilege on the one side, no disability on the other ....

The generality of a practice is in some cases a strong presumption that it is, or at all events once was, conducive to laudable ends. This is the case, when the practice was first adopted, or afterwards kept up, as a means to such ends, and was grounded on experience of the mode in which they could be most effectually attained. If the authority of men over women, when first established, had been the result of a conscientious comparison between different modes of constituting the government of society; if, after trying various other modes of social organization —the government of women over men, equality between the two, and such mixed and divided modes of government as might be invented—it had been decided, on the testimony of experience, that the mode in which women are wholly under the rule of men, having no share at all in public concerns, and each in private being under the legal obligation of obedience to the man with whom she has associated her destiny, was the arrangement most conducive to the happiness and well being of both; its general adoption might then be fairly thought to be some evidence that, at the time when it was adopted, it was the best: though even then the considerations which recommended it may, like so many other primeval social facts of the greatest importance, have subsequently, in the course of ages, ceased to exist. But the state of the case is in every respect the reverse of this. In the first place, the opinion in favour of the present system, which entirely subordinates the weaker sex to the stronger, rests upon theory only; for there never has been trial made of any other: so that experience, in the sense in which it is vulgarly opposed to theory, cannot be pretended to have pronounced any verdict. And in the second place, the adoption of this system of inequality never was the result of deliberation, or forethought, or any social ideas, or any notion whatever of what conduced to the benefit of humanity or the good order of society. It arose simply from the fact that from the very earliest twilight of human society, every woman (owing to the value attached to her by men, combined with her inferiority in muscular strength) was found in a state of bondage to some man. Laws and systems of polity always begin by recognising the relations they find already existing between individuals. They convert what was a mere physical fact into a legal right, give it the sanction of society, and principally aim at the substitution of public and organized means of asserting and protecting these rights, instead of the irregular and lawless conflict of physical strength. Those who had already been compelled to obedience became in this manner legally bound to it. ... But this dependence, as it exists at present, is not an original institution, taking a fresh start from considerations of justice and social expediency—it is the primitive state of slavery lasting on, through successive mitigations and modifications occasioned by the same causes which have softened the general manners, and brought all human relations more under the control of justice and the influence of humanity. It has not lost the taint of its brutal origin. No presumption in its favour, therefore, can be drawn from the fact of its existence. ... The inequality of rights between men and women has no other source than the law of the strongest.

But, it will be said, the rule of men over women differs from all these others in not being a rule of force: it is accepted voluntarily; women make no complaint, and are consenting parties to it. In the first place, a great number of women do not accept it. Ever since there have been women able to make their sentiments known by their writings (the only mode of publicity which society permits to them), an increasing number of them have recorded protests against their present social condition ....

All causes, social and natural, combine to make it unlikely that women should be collectively rebellious to the power of men. They are so far in a position different from all other subject classes, that their masters require something more from them than actual service. Men do not want solely the obedience of women, they want their sentiments. All men, except the most brutish, desire to have, in the woman most nearly connected with them, not a forced slave but a willing one, not a slave merely, but a favourite. They have therefore put everything in practice to enslave their minds. The masters of all other slaves rely, for maintaining obedience, on fear; either fear of themselves, or religious fears. The masters of women wanted more than simple obedience, and they turned the whole force of education to effect their purpose. All women are brought up from the very earliest years in the belief that their ideal of character is the very opposite to that of men; not self-will, and government by self-control, but submission, and yielding to the control of others. All the moralities tell them that it is the duty of women, and all the current sentimentalities that it is their nature, to live for others; to make complete abnegation of themselves, and to have no life but in their affections. And by their affections are meant the only ones they are allowed to have—those to the men with whom they are connected, or to the children who constitute an additional and indefeasible tie between them and a man. When we put together three things—first, the natural attraction between opposite sexes; secondly, the wife's entire dependence on the husband, every privilege or pleasure she has being either his gift, or depending entirely on his will; and lastly, that the principal object of human pursuit, consideration, and all objects of social ambition, can in general be sought or obtained by her only through him, it would be a miracle if the object of being attractive to men had not become the polar star of feminine education and formation of character. And, this great means of influence over the minds of women having been acquired, an instinct of selfishness made men avail themselves of it to the utmost as a means of holding women in subjection, by representing to them meekness, submissiveness, and resignation of all individual will into the hands of a man, as an essential part of sexual attractiveness. Can it be doubted that any of the other yokes which mankind have succeeded in breaking, would have subsisted till now if the same means had existed, and had been as sedulously used, to bow down their minds to it? ...

Neither does it avail anything to say that the *nature* of the two sexes adapts them to their present functions and position, and renders these appropriate to them. Standing on the ground of common sense and the constitution of the human mind, I deny that any one knows, or can know, the nature of the two sexes, as long as they have only been seen in their present relation to one another ....

One thing we may be certain of—that what is contrary to women's nature to do, they never will be made to do by simply giving their nature free play. The anxiety of mankind to interfere in behalf of nature, for fear lest nature should not succeed in effecting its purpose, is an altogether unnecessary solicitude ....

Chapter 2

.... Marriage being the destination appointed by society for women, the prospect they are brought up to, and the object which it is intended should be sought by all of them, except those who are too little attractive to be chosen by any man as his companion; one might have supposed that everything would have been done to make this condition as eligible to them as possible, that they might have no cause to regret being denied the option of any other. Society, however, both in this, and, at first, in all other cases, has preferred to attain its object by foul rather than fair means: but this is the only case in which it has substantially persisted in them even to the present day. Originally women were taken by force, or regularly sold by their father to the husband ....

[Today] the wife is the actual bondservant of her husband: no less so, as far as legal obligation goes, than slaves commonly so called. She vows a life-long obedience to him at the altar, and is held to it all through her life by law. Casuists may say that the obligation of obedience stops short of participation in crime, but it certainly extends to everything else. She can do no act whatever but by his permission, at least tacit. She can acquire no property but for him; the instant it becomes hers, even if by inheritance, it becomes *ipso facto* his. In this respect the wife's position under the common law of England is worse than that of slaves in the laws of many countries. ... The two are called "one person in law," for the purpose of inferring that whatever is hers is his, but the parallel inference is never drawn that whatever is his is hers; the maxim is not applied against the man, except to make him responsible to third parties for her acts, as a master is for the acts of his slaves or of his cattle. I am far from pretending that wives are in general no better treated than slaves; but no slave is a slave to the same lengths, and in so full a sense of the word, as a wife is. Hardly any slave, except one immediately attached to the master's person, is a slave at all hours and all minutes; in general he has, like a soldier, his fixed task, and when it is done, or when he is off duty, he disposes, within certain limits, of his own time, and has a family life into which the master rarely intrudes. "Uncle Tom" under his first master had his own life in his "cabin," almost as much as any man whose work takes him away from home, is able to have in his own family. But it cannot be so with the wife. Above all, a female slave has (in Christian countries) an admitted right, and is considered under a moral obligation, to refuse to her master the last familiarity. Not so the wife: however brutal a tyrant she may unfortunately be chained to—though she may know that he hates her, though it may be his daily pleasure to torture her, and though she may feel it impossible not to loathe him—he can claim from her and enforce the lowest degradation of a human being, that of being made the instrument of an animal function contrary to her inclinations. While she is held in this worst description of slavery as to her own person, what is her position in regard to the children in whom she and her master have a joint interest? They are by law his children. He alone has any legal rights over them. Not one act can she do towards or in relation to them, except by delegation from him. Even after he is dead she is not their legal guardian, unless he by will has made her so. He could even send them away from her, and deprive her of the means of seeing or corresponding with them, until this power was in some degree restricted by Serjeant Talfourd's Act. This is her legal state. And from this state she has no means of withdrawing herself. If she leaves her husband, she can take nothing with her, neither her children nor anything which is rightfully her own. If he chooses, he can compel her to return, by law, or by physical force; or he may content himself with seizing for his own use anything which she may earn, or which may be given to her by her relations ....

When we consider how vast is the number of men, in any great country, who are little higher than brutes, and that this never prevents them from being able, through the law of marriage, to obtain a victim, the breadth and depth of human misery caused in this shape alone by the abuse of the institution swells to something appalling. ... I grant that the wife, if she cannot effectually resist, can at least retaliate; she, too, can make the man's life extremely uncomfortable, and by that power is able to carry many points which she ought, and many which she ought not, to prevail in. But this instrument of self-protection—which may be called the power of the scold, or the shrewish sanction—has the fatal defect, that it avails most against the least tyrannical superiors, and in favour of the least deserving dependents. It is the weapon of irritable and self-willed women; of those who would make the worst use of power if they themselves had it, and who generally turn this power to a bad use ....

But how, it will be asked, can any society exist without government? In a family, as in a state, some one person must be the ultimate ruler. Who shall decide when married people differ in opinion? Both cannot have their way, yet a decision one way or the other must be come to.

It is not true that in all voluntary association between two people, one of them must be absolute master: still less that the law must determine which of them it shall be ....

It is quite true that things which have to be decided every day, and cannot adjust themselves gradually, or wait for a compromise, ought to depend on one will: one person must have their sole control. But it does not follow that this should always be the same person. The natural arrangement is a division of powers between the two; each being absolute in the executive branch of their own department, and any change of system and principle requiring the consent of both ....

The real practical decision of affairs, to whichever may be given the legal authority, will greatly depend, as it even now does, upon comparative qualifications. The mere fact that he is usually the eldest, will in most cases give the preponderance to the man; at least until they both attain a time of life at which the difference in their years is of no importance. There will naturally also be a more potential voice on the side, whichever it is, that brings the means of support ....

After what has been said respecting the obligation of obedience, it is almost superfluous to say anything concerning the more special point included in the general one—a woman's right to her own property; for I need not hope that this treatise can make any impression upon those who need anything to convince them that a woman's inheritance or gains ought to be as much her own after marriage as before. The rule is simple: whatever would be the husband's or wife's if they were not married, should be under their exclusive control during marriage ....

When the support of the family depends, not on property, but on earnings, the common arrangement, by which the man earns the income and the wife superintends the domestic expenditure, seems to me in general the most suitable division of labour between the two persons. If, in addition to the physical suffering of bearing children, and the whole responsibility of their care and education in early years, the wife undertakes the careful and economical application of the husband's earnings to the general comfort of the family; she takes not only her fair share, but usually the larger share, of the bodily and mental exertion required by their joint existence. If she undertakes any additional portion, it seldom relieves her from this, but only prevents her from performing it properly. The care which she is herself disabled from taking of the children and the household, nobody else takes; those of the children who do not die, grow up as they best can, and the management of the household is likely to be so bad, as even in point of economy to be a great drawback from the value of the wife's earnings. In an otherwise just state of things, it is not, therefore, I think, a desirable custom, that the wife should contribute by her labour to the income of the family. In an unjust state of things, her doing so may be useful to her, by making her of more value in the eyes of the man who is legally her master; but, on the other hand, it enables him still farther to abuse his power, by forcing her to work, and leaving the support of the family to her exertions, while he spends most of his time in drinking and idleness. The *power* of earning is essential to the dignity of a woman, if she has not independent property. But if marriage were an equal contract, not implying the obligation of obedience; if the connection were no longer enforced to the oppression of those to whom it is purely a mischief, but a separation, on just terms (I do not now speak of a divorce), could be obtained by any woman who was morally entitled to it; and if she would then find all honourable employments as freely open to her as to men; it would not be necessary for her protection, that during marriage she should make this particular use of her faculties. Like a man when he chooses a profession, so, when a woman marries, it may in general be understood that she makes choice of the management of a household, and the bringing up of a family, as the first call upon her exertions, during as many years of her life as may be required for the purpose; and that she renounces, not all other objects and occupations, but all which are not consistent with the requirements of this. The actual exercise, in a habitual or systematic manner, of outdoor occupations, or such as cannot be carried on at home, would by this principle be practically interdicted to the greater number of married women. But the utmost latitude ought to exist for the adaptation of general rules to individual suitabilities; and there ought to be nothing to prevent faculties exceptionally adapted to any other pursuit, from obeying their vocation notwithstanding marriage: due provision being made for supplying otherwise any falling-short which might become inevitable, in her full performance of the ordinary functions of mistress of a family. These things, if once opinion were rightly directed on the subject, might with perfect safety be left to be regulated by opinion, without any interference of law.

Chapter 3

On the other point which is involved in the just equality of women, their admissibility to all the functions and occupations hitherto retained as the monopoly of the stronger sex, I should anticipate no difficulty in convincing any one who has gone with me on the subject of the equality of women in the family. I believe that their disabilities elsewhere are only clung to in order to maintain their subordination in domestic life. ... It is not sufficient to maintain that women on the average are less gifted than men on the average, with certain of the higher mental faculties, or that a smaller number of women than of men are fit for occupations and functions of the highest intellectual character. It is necessary to maintain that no women at all are fit for them, and that the most eminent women are inferior in mental faculties to the most mediocre of the men on whom those functions at present devolve. ... Is there so great a superfluity of men fit for high duties, that society can afford to reject the service of any competent person? Are we so certain of always finding a man made to our hands for any duty or function of social importance which falls vacant, that we lose nothing by putting a ban upon one-half of mankind, and refusing beforehand to make their faculties available, however distinguished they may be? And even if we could do without them, would it be consistent with justice to refuse to them their fair share of honour and distinction, or to deny to them the equal moral right of all human beings to choose their occupation (short of injury to others) according to their own preferences, at their own risk? Nor is the injustice confined to them: it is shared by those who are in a position to benefit by their services ....

But (it is said) there is anatomical evidence of the superior mental capacity of men compared with women: they have a larger brain. I reply, that in the first place the fact itself is doubtful. It is by no means established that the brain of a woman is smaller than that of a man. ... Next, I must observe that the precise relation which exists between the brain and the intellectual powers is not yet well understood, but is a subject of great dispute. ... It would not be surprising —it is indeed an hypothesis which accords well with the differences actually observed between the mental operations of the two sexes—if men on the average should have the advantage in the size of the brain, and women in activity of cerebral circulation. The results which conjecture, founded on analogy, would lead us to expect from this difference of organization, would correspond to some of those which we most commonly see. In the first place, the mental operations of men might be expected to be slower. They would neither be so prompt as women in thinking, nor so quick to feel. Large bodies take more time to get into full action. On the other hand, when once got thoroughly into play, men's brains would bear more work. It would be more persistent in the line first taken; it would have more difficulty in changing from one mode of action to another, but, in the one thing it was doing, it could go on longer without loss of power or sense of fatigue. And do we not find that the things in which men most excel women are those which require most plodding and long hammering at a single thought, while women do best what must be done rapidly? A woman's brain is sooner fatigued, sooner exhausted; but given the degree of exhaustion, we should expect to find that it would recover itself sooner. I repeat that this speculation is entirely hypothetical ....

Let us take, then, the only marked case which observation affords, of apparent inferiority of women to men, if we except the merely physical one of bodily strength. No production in philosophy, science, or art, entitled to the first rank, has been the work of a woman. Is there any mode of accounting for this, without supposing that women are naturally incapable of producing them?

In the first place, we may fairly question whether experience has afforded sufficient grounds for an induction. It is scarcely three generations since women, saving very rare exceptions, have begun to try their capacity in philosophy, science, or art. It is only in the present generation that their attempts have been at all numerous; and they are even now extremely few, everywhere but in England and France. It is a relevant question, whether a mind possessing the requisites of first-rate eminence in speculation or creative art could have been expected, on the mere calculation of chances, to turn up during that lapse of time, among the women whose tastes and personal position admitted of their devoting themselves to these pursuits ....

Chapter 4

There remains a question, not of less importance than those already discussed, and which will be asked the most importunately by those opponents whose conviction is somewhat shaken on the main point. What good are we to expect from the changes proposed in our customs and institutions? Would mankind be at all better off if women were free? If not, why disturb their minds, and attempt to make a social revolution in the name of an abstract right? ...

To which let me first answer, [there is] the advantage of having the most universal and pervading of all human relations regulated by justice instead of injustice. The vast amount of this gain to human nature, it is hardly possible, by any explanation or illustration, to place in a stronger light than it is placed by the bare statement, to any one who attaches a moral meaning to words. All the selfish propensities, the self-worship, the unjust self-preference, which exist among mankind, have their source and root in, and derive their principal nourishment from, the present constitution of the relation between men and women. Think what it is to a boy, to grow up to manhood in the belief that without any merit or any exertion of his own, though he may be the most frivolous and empty or the most ignorant and stolid of mankind, by the mere fact of being born a male he is by right the superior of all and every one of an entire half of the human race. ... What must be the effect on his character, of this lesson? And men of the cultivated classes are often not aware how deeply it sinks into the immense majority of male minds. For, among right-feeling and well-bred people, the inequality is kept as much as possible out of sight; above all, out of sight of the children. As much obedience is required from boys to their mother as to their father: they are not permitted to domineer over their sisters, nor are they accustomed to see these postponed to them, but the contrary; the compensations of the chivalrous feeling being made prominent, while the servitude which requires them is kept in the background ....

The second benefit to be expected from giving to women the free use of their faculties, by leaving them the free choice of their employments, and opening to them the same field of occupation and the same prizes and encouragements as to other human beings, would be that of doubling the mass of mental faculties available for the higher service of humanity. ... This great accession to the intellectual power of the species, and to the amount of intellect available for the good management of its affairs, would be obtained, partly, through the better and more complete intellectual education of women ....

The opinion of women would then possess a more beneficial, rather than a greater, influence upon the general mass of human belief and sentiment. I say a more beneficial, rather than a greater influence; for the influence of women over the general tone of opinion has always, or at least from the earliest known period, been very considerable ....

The wife's influence tends, as far as it goes, to prevent the husband from falling below the common standard of approbation of the country. It tends quite as strongly to hinder him from rising above it. The wife is the auxiliary of the common public opinion. A man who is married to a woman his inferior in intelligence, finds her a perpetual dead weight, or, worse than a dead weight, a drag, upon every aspiration of his to be better than public opinion requires him to be. It is hardly possible for one who is in these bonds, to attain exalted virtue ....

Though it may stimulate the amatory propensities of men, it does not conduce to married happiness, to exaggerate by differences of education whatever may be the native differences of the sexes. If the married pair are well-bred and well-behaved people, they tolerate each other's tastes; but is mutual toleration what people look forward to, when they enter into marriage? ...

What marriage may be in the case of two persons of cultivated faculties, identical in opinions and purposes, between whom there exists that best kind of equality, similarity of powers and capacities with reciprocal superiority in them—so that each can enjoy the luxury of looking up to the other, and can have alternately the pleasure of leading and of being led in the path of development—I will not attempt to describe. To those who can conceive it, there is no need; to those who cannot, it would appear the dream of an enthusiast. But I maintain, with the profoundest conviction, that this, and this only, is the ideal of marriage; and that all opinions, customs, and institutions which favour any other notion of it, or turn the conceptions and aspirations connected with it into any other direction, by whatever pretences they may be coloured, are relics of primitive barbarism. The moral regeneration of mankind will only really commence, when the most fundamental of the social relations is placed under the rule of equal justice, and when human beings learn to cultivate their strongest sympathy with an equal in rights and in cultivation.

Review and Discussion Questions

1 Describe the situation of English women at the time Mill and Taylor were writing.
2 To what do the authors attribute the situation of women?
3 How do Mill and Taylor answer the claim that women are naturally inferior? That they willingly accept their status?

4 What are the authors' reasons for concluding that the situation they described was intolerable.
5 What do Mill and Taylor see as the ideal marriage? Do you agree? Explain.
6 How does Mill's discussion of well-being described in *On Liberty* inform this essay on women and their plight?
7 Discuss the following statement: There has been more progress in women's equality since the 1950s than from the time Mill and Taylor wrote until the 1950s.

READING: SEXUAL EQUALITY AND DISCRIMINATION: DIFFERENCE VS. DOMINANCE

WILL KYMLICKA[*]

According to Will Kymlicka, sex discrimination is commonly interpreted as the arbitrary or irrational use of gender in the awarding of benefits or positions. That is, sex discrimination is unequal treatment that cannot be justified by reference to some sexual difference. This "difference approach" to discrimination perceives sexual equality in terms of the ability of women to compete under gender-neutral rules for various roles and positions. The problem, Kymlicka argues, is that these roles and positions may be defined in such a way as to make men more suited to them, even under gender-neutral competition. Will Kymlicka is Professor of Philosophy and Canada Research Chair in Political Philosophy at Queen's University in Kingston, Ontario.

Until well into this century, most male theorists on all points of the political spectrum accepted the belief that there was a "foundation in nature" for the confinement of women to the family, and for the "legal and customary subjection of women to their husbands" within the family (Okin 1979: 200).[1] Restrictions on women's civil and political rights were said to be justified by the fact that women are, by nature, unsuited for political and economic activities outside the home. Contemporary theorists have progressively abandoned this assumption of women's natural inferiority. They have accepted that women, like men, should be viewed as "free and equal beings," capable of self-determination and a sense of justice, and hence free to enter the public realm. And liberal democracies have progressively adopted antidiscrimination statutes intended to ensure that women have equal access to education, employment, political office, etc.

But these antidiscrimination statutes have not brought about sexual equality. In the United States and Canada, the extent of job segregation in the lowest-paying occupations is increasing. ... Moreover, domestic violence and sexual assault are increasing, as are other forms of violence and degradation aimed at women. Catharine MacKinnon summarizes her survey of the effects of equal rights in the United States by saying that "sex equality law has been utterly ineffective at

---

[*] From *Contemporary Political Philosophy: An Introduction* by Will Kymlicka. © Will Kymlicka 1990. Reprinted by permission.

getting women what we need and are socially prevented from having on the basis of a condition of birth: a chance at productive lives of reasonable physical security, self-expression, individuation, and minimal respect and dignity" (MacKinnon 1987: 32).

Why is this? Sex discrimination, as commonly interpreted, involves the arbitrary or irrational use of gender in the awarding of benefits or positions. On this view, the most blatant forms of sex discrimination are those where, for example, someone refuses to hire a woman for a job even though gender has no rational relationship to the task being performed. MacKinnon calls this the "difference approach" to sexual discrimination, for it views as discriminatory unequal treatment that cannot be justified by reference to some sexual difference.

Sex discrimination law of this sort was modelled on race discrimination law. And just as race equality legislation aims at a "color-blind" society, so sex equality law aims at a sex-blind society. A society would be non-discriminatory if race or gender never entered into the awarding of benefits. Of course, while it is conceivable that political and economic decisions could entirely disregard race, it is difficult to see how a society could be entirely sex blind. A society which provides for pregnancy benefits, or for sexually segregated sports, takes sex into account, but this does not seem unjust. And while racially segregated washrooms are clearly discriminatory, most people do not feel that way about sex-segregated washrooms. So the "difference approach" accepts that there are legitimate instances of differential treatment of the sexes. These are not discriminatory, however, so long as there is a genuine sexual difference which explains and justifies the differential treatment. Opponents of equal rights for women often invoked the specter of sexually integrated sports (or washrooms) as evidence that sex equality is misguided. But defenders of the difference approach respond that the cases of legitimate differentiation are sufficiently rare, and the cases of arbitrary differentiation so common, that the burden of proof rests on those who claim that sex is a relevant ground for assigning benefits or positions.

This difference approach, as the standard interpretation of sex equality law in most Western countries, has had some successes. Its "moral thrust" is to "grant women access to what men have access to," and it has indeed "gotten women some access to employment and education, the public pursuits, including academic, professional, and blue-collar work, the military, and more than nominal access to athletics" (MacKinnon 1987: 33, 35). The difference approach has helped create gender-neutral access to, or competition for, existing social benefits and positions.

But its successes are limited, for it ignores the gender inequalities which are built into the very definition of these positions. The difference approach sees sex equality in terms of the ability of women to compete under gender-neutral rules for the roles that men have defined. But equality cannot be achieved by allowing men to build social institutions according to their interests and then ignoring the gender of the candidates when deciding who fills the roles in these institutions. The problem is that the roles may be defined in such a way as to make men more suited to them, even under gender-neutral competition.

Consider that fact that most jobs "require that the person, gender neutral, who is qualified for them will be someone who is not the primary caretaker of a preschool child" (MacKinnon 1987: 37). Given that women are still expected to take care of children in our society, men will tend to do better than women in competing for such jobs. This is not because women applicants are discriminated against. Employers may pay no attention to the gender of the applicants or may in fact wish to hire more women. The problem is that many women lack a relevant qualification for the job—i.e., being free from child-care responsibilities. There is gender neutrality, in that employers do not attend to the gender of applicants, but there is no sexual equality, for the job was defined under the assumption that it would be filled by men who had wives at home taking care of the children. The difference approach insists that gender should not be taken into account in deciding who should have a job, but it ignores the fact "that day one of taking gender into account was the day the job was structured with the expectation that its occupant would have no child care responsibilities" (MacKinnon 1987: 37).

Whether or not gender neutrality yields sexual equality depends on whether and how gender was taken into account earlier. As Janet Radcliffe Richards says,

> If a group is kept out of something for long enough, it is overwhelmingly likely that activities of that sort will develop in a way unsuited to the excluded group. We know for certain that women have been kept out of many kinds of work, and this means that the work is quite likely to be unsuited to them. The most obvious example of this is the incompatibility of most work with the bearing and raising of children; I am firmly convinced that if women had been fully involved in the running of society from the start they would have found a way of arranging work and children to fit each other. Men have had no such motivation, and we can see the results.
>
> (Radcliffe Richards 1980: 113–14)

This incompatibility that men have created between child-rearing and paid labor has profoundly unequal results for women. The result is not only that the most valued positions in society are filled by men, while women are disproportionately concentrated into lower-paying part-time work, but also that many women become economically dependent on men. Where most of the "household income" comes from the man's paid work, the woman who does the unpaid domestic work is rendered dependent on him for access to resources. The consequences of this dependence have become more apparent with the rising divorce rate. While married couples may share the same standard of living during marriage, regardless of who earns the income, the effects of divorce are catastrophically unequal. In California, men's average standard of living goes up 42 percent after divorce, women's goes down 73 percent, and similar results have been found in other states (Okin 1979: 161). However, none of these unequal consequences of the incompatibility of child care and paid work are discriminatory, according to the difference approach, for they do not involve arbitrary discrimination. The fact is that freedom from child-care responsibilities is relevant to most existing jobs, and employers are not being arbitrary in insisting on it. Because it is a relevant qualification, the difference approach says that it is not discriminatory to insist upon it, regardless of the disadvantages it creates for women. Indeed, the difference approach sees the concern with child-care responsibilities, rather than irrelevant criteria like gender, as evidence that sex discrimination has been eliminated. It cannot see that the relevance of child-care responsibilities is itself a profound source of sexual inequality, one that has arisen from the way men have historically structured the economy to suit their interests.

So before we decide whether gender should be taken into account, we need to know how it has already been taken into account. And the fact is that almost all important roles and positions have been structured in gender-biased ways:

> Virtually every quality that distinguishes men from women is already affirmatively compensated in this society. Men's physiology defines most sports, their needs define auto and health insurance coverage, their socially-designed biographies define workplace expectations and successful career patterns, their perspectives and concerns define quality in scholarship, their experiences and obsessions define merit, their objectification of life defines art, their military service defines citizenship, their presence defines family, their inability to get along with each other–their wars and rulerships—defines history, their image defines god, and their genitals define sex. For each of their differences from women, what amounts to an affirmative action plan is in effect, otherwise known as the structure and values of American society.
>
> (MacKinnon 1987: 36)

All of this is "gender neutral," in the sense that women are not arbitrarily excluded from pursuing the things society defines as valuable. But it is sexist, because the things being pursued in a gender-neutral way are based on men's interests and values. Women are disadvantaged, not because chauvinists arbitrarily favor men in the awarding of jobs but because the entire society systematically favors men in the defining of jobs, merits, etc.

Indeed, the more society defines positions in a gendered way, the less the difference approach is able to detect an inequality. Consider a society which restricts access to contraception and abortion, which defines paying jobs in such a way as to make them incompatible with child-bearing and child-rearing, and which does not provide economic compensation for domestic labor. Every woman who faces an unplanned pregnancy, and who cannot both raise children and work for wages, is rendered economically dependent on someone who is a stable income-earner (i.e. a man). In order to ensure that she acquires this support, she must become sexually attractive to men. Knowing that this is their likely fate, many girls do not try as hard as boys to acquire employment skills which can only be exercised by those who avoid pregnancy. Where boys pursue personal security by increasing their employment skills, girls pursue security by increasing their attractiveness to men. This, in turn, results in a system of cultural identifications in which masculinity is associated with income-earning and femininity is defined in terms of sexual and domestic service for men and the nurturing of children. So men and women enter marriage with different income-earning potential, and this disparity widens during marriage, as the man acquires valuable job experience. Since the woman faces greater difficulty supporting herself outside of the marriage, she is more dependent on maintaining the marriage, which allows the man to exercise greater control within it.

In such a society, men as a group exercise control over women's general life chances (through political decisions about abortion and economic decisions concerning job requirements), and individual men exercise control over economically vulnerable women within marriages. Yet there need be no arbitrary discrimination. All of this is gender neutral, in that one's gender does not necessarily affect how one is treated by those in charge of distributing contraception, jobs, or domestic pay. But whereas the difference approach takes the absence of arbitrary discrimination as evidence of the absence of sexual inequality, it may in fact be evidence of its pervasiveness. It is precisely because women are dominated in this society that there is no need for them to be discriminated against. Arbitrary discrimination in employment is not only unnecessary for the maintenance of male privilege, it is unlikely to occur, for most women will never be in a position to be arbitrarily discriminated against in employment. Perhaps the occasional woman can overcome the social pressures supporting traditional sex roles. But the greater the domination, the less the likelihood that any women will be in a position to compete for employment, and hence the less room for arbitrary discrimination. The more sexual inequality there is in society, the more that social institutions reflect male interests, the less arbitrary discrimination there will be.

None of the contemporary Western democracies correspond exactly to this model of a patriarchal society, but they all share some of its essential features. And if we are to confront these forms of injustice, we need to reconceptualize sexual inequality as a problem not of arbitrary discrimination but of domination. As MacKinnon puts it,

> to require that one be the same as those who set the standard—those which one is already socially defined as different from—simply means that sex equality is conceptually designed never to be achieved. Those who most need equal treatment will be the least similar, socially, to those whose situation sets the standard as against which one's entitlement to be equally treated is measured. Doctrinally speaking, the deepest problems of sex inequality will not find women 'similarly situated' to men. Far less will practices of sex inequality require that acts be intentionally discriminatory.
>
> (MacKinnon 1987: 44)

The subordination of women is not fundamentally a matter of irrational differentiation on the basis of sex but of male supremacy, under which gender differences are made relevant to the distribution of benefits to the systematic disadvantage of women (MacKinnon 1987: 42; Frye 1983: 38).

Since the problem is domination, the solution is not only the absence of discrimination but the presence of power. Equality requires not only equal opportunity to pursue male-defined roles but also equal power to create female-defined roles or to create androgynous roles men and women have an equal interest in filling. The result of such empowerment could be very different from our society or from the equal opportunity to enter male institutions that is favored by contemporary sex-discrimination theory. From a position of equal power, we would not have created a system of social roles that defines "male" jobs as superior to "female" jobs. For example, the roles of male and female health practitioners were redefined by men against the will of women in the field. With the professionalization of medicine, women were squeezed out of their traditional health care roles as midwives and healers and relegated to the role of nurse—a position which is subservient to, and financially less rewarding than, the role of doctor. That redefinition would not have happened had women been in a position of equality and will have to be rethought now if women are to achieve equality.

Note

1 In accepting this prevailing view that there is "a Foundation in Nature" for the rule of the husband "as the abler and the stronger" (Locke, in Okin 1979: 200), classical liberals created a serious contradiction for themselves. For they also argued that all humans are by nature equal, that nature provides no grounds for an inequality of rights. This, we have seen, was the point of their state-of-nature theories. ... Why should the supposed fact that men are "abler and stronger" justify unequal rights for women when, as Locke himself says, "differences in excellence of parts or ability" do not justify unequal rights? One cannot both maintain equality amongst men as a class, on the grounds that differences in ability do not justify different rights, and also exclude women as a class, on the grounds that they are less able. If women are excluded on the grounds that the average woman is less able than the average man, then all men who are less able than the average man must also be excluded. As Okin puts it, "If the basis of his individualism was to be firm, he needed to argue that individual women were equal with individual men, just as weaker men were with stronger ones" (Okin 1979: 199).

References

Frye, M. 1983. *The Politics of Reality: Essays in Feminist Theory* (Crossing Press, Trumansburg).
MacKinnon, C. 1987. *Feminism Unmodified: Discourses on Life and Law* (Harvard University Press, Cambridge, MA).
Okin, S. 1979. *Women in Western Political Thought* (Princeton University Press, Princeton, NJ).
Radcliffe Richards, J. 1980. *The Skeptical Feminist: A Philosophical Enquiry* (Routledge and Kegan Paul, London).

Review and Discussion Questions

1 Why does Kymlicka think antidiscrimination laws have not achieved sex equality?
2 What is the difference approach to sex equality? Give an example of this approach.
3 What is the dominance approach to sex equality? How does it differ from the difference approach?
4 What specific proposals would be necessary to achieve genuine sex equality?
5 How would Mill and Taylor respond to this essay?

READING: SOCIAL MOVEMENTS AND THE POLITICS OF DIFFERENCE

IRIS MARION YOUNG[*]

In this essay, Iris Marion Young offers a wide-ranging and important discussion of the significance of group differences and personal identity to contemporary politics. Beginning with a critique of Wasserstrom's assimilationist ideal, she goes on to outline an alternative "relational" ideal and defend the "politics of difference"

---

[*] Abridged from "Social Movements and the Politics of Difference," in *Justice and the Politics of Difference* by Iris Marion Young. Copyright © 1990 by Princeton University Press. Reprinted by permission of Princeton University Press. Some references omitted.

as the best means to achieve genuine emancipation. Iris Marion Young was Professor of Political Science at the University of Chicago.

In this chapter I criticize an ideal of justice that defines liberation as the transcendence of group difference, which I refer to as an ideal of assimilation. This ideal usually promotes equal treatment as a primary principle of justice. Recent social movements of oppressed groups challenge this ideal. [Young earlier defined "oppression" as institutional processes that prevent people from developing "skills and capacities necessary for the good life" and "domination" as "constraints on political self-determination."—Ed. note.] Many in these movements argue that a positive self-definition of group difference is in fact more liberatory.

I endorse this politics of difference and argue that at stake is the meaning of social difference itself. Traditional politics that excludes or devalues some persons on account of their group attributes assumes an essentialist meaning of difference; it defines groups as having different natures. An egalitarian politics of difference, on the other hand, defines difference more fluidly and relationally as the product of social processes.

An emancipatory politics that affirms group difference involves a reconception of the meaning of equality. The assimilationist ideal assumes that equal social status for all persons requires treating everyone according to the same principles, rules, and standards. A politics of difference argues, on the other hand, that equality as the participation and inclusion of all groups sometimes requires different treatment for oppressed or disadvantaged groups. To promote social justice, I argue, social policy should sometimes accord special treatment to groups ....

Competing Paradigms of Liberation

In "On Racism and Sexism," Richard Wasserstrom develops a classic statement of the ideal of liberation from group-based oppression as involving the elimination of group-based difference itself. A truly nonracist, nonsexist society, he suggests, would be one in which the race or sex of an individual would be the functional equivalent of eye color in our society today. While physiological differences in skin color or genitals would remain, they would have no significance for a person's sense of identity or how others regard him or her. No political rights or obligations would be connected to race or sex, and no important institutional benefits would be associated with either. People would see no reason to consider race or gender in policy or everyday interactions. In such a society, social group differences would have ceased to exist.

Wasserstrom contrasts this ideal of assimilation with an ideal of diversity much like the one I will argue for, which he agrees is compelling. He offers three primary reasons, however, for choosing the assimilationist ideal of liberation over the ideal of diversity. First, the assimilationist ideal exposes the arbitrariness of group-based social distinctions which are thought natural and necessary. By imagining a society in which race and sex have no social significance, one sees more clearly how pervasively these group categories unnecessarily limit possibilities for some in existing society. Second, the assimilationist ideal presents a clear and unambiguous standard of equality and justice. According to such a standard, any group-related differentiation or discrimination is suspect. Whenever laws or rules, the division of labor, or other social practices allocate benefits differently according to group membership, this is a sign of injustice. The principle of justice is simple: treat everyone according to the same principles, rules, and standards. Third, the assimilationist ideal maximizes choice. In a society where differences make no social difference people can develop themselves as individuals, unconstrained by group norms and expectations.

There is no question that the ideal of liberation as the elimination of group difference has been enormously important in the history of emancipatory politics. The ideal of universal humanity that denies natural differences has been a crucial historical development in the struggle against exclusion and status differentiation. It has made possible the assertion of the equal moral worth of all persons and thus the right of all to participate and be included in all institutions and positions of power and privilege. The assimilationist ideal retains significant rhetorical power in the face of continued beliefs in the essentially different and inferior natures of women, Blacks, and other groups.

The power of this assimilationist ideal has inspired the struggle of oppressed groups and the supporters against the exclusion and denigration of these groups, and continues to inspire many. Periodically in American history, however, movements of the oppressed have questioned and rejected this "path to belonging." ... Instead they have seen self-organization and the assertion of a positive group cultural identity as a better strategy for achieving power and participation in dominant institutions. Recent decades have witnessed a resurgence of this "politics of difference," not only among racial and ethnic groups but also among women, gay men and lesbians, old people, and the disabled ....

None of the social movements asserting positive group specificity is in fact a unity. All have group differences within them. The Black movement, for example, includes middle-class Blacks and working-class Blacks, gays and straight people, men and women, and so it is with any other group. The implications of group differences within a social group have been most systematically discussed in the women's movement. Feminist conferences and publications have generated particularly fruitful, though often emotionally wrenching, discussions of the oppression of racial and ethnic blindness and importance of attending to group differences among women. ... From such discussions emerged principled efforts to provide autonomously organized forums for Black women, Latinas, Jewish women, lesbians, differently abled women, old women, and any other women who see reason for claiming that they have as a group a distinctive voice that might be silenced in a general feminist discourse. Those discussions, along with the practices feminists instituted, structure discussion and interaction among differently identified groups of women and offer some beginning models for the development of a heterogeneous public. Each of the other social movements has also generated discussion of group differences that cut across their identities, leading to other possibilities of coalition and alliance.

Emancipation through the Politics of Difference

Implicit in emancipatory movements asserting a positive sense of group difference is a different ideal of liberation, which might be called democratic cultural pluralism. In this vision the good society does not eliminate or transcend group difference. Rather, there is equality among socially and culturally differentiated groups who mutually respect one another and affirm one another in their differences. What are the reasons for rejecting the assimilationist ideal and promoting a politics of difference?

.... Some deny the reality of social groups. For them, group difference is an invidious fiction produced and perpetuated in order to preserve the privilege of the few. Others, such as Wasserstrom, may agree that social groups do now exist and have real social consequences for the way people identify themselves and one another but assert that such social group differences are undesirable. The assimilationist ideal involves denying either the reality or the desirability of social groups.

Those promoting a politics of difference doubt that a society without group differences is either possible or desirable. Contrary to the assumption of modernization theory, increased urbanization and the extension of equal formal rights to all groups has not led to a decline in particularist affiliations. If anything, the urban concentration and interactions among groups that modernizing social processes introduce tend to reinforce group solidarity and differentiation. Attachment to specific traditions, practices, languages, and other culturally specific forms is a crucial aspect of social existence. People do not usually give up their social group identifications, even when they are oppressed.

Whether eliminating social group difference is possible or desirable in the long run, however, is an academic issue. Today and for the foreseeable future societies are certainly structured by groups, and some are privileged while others are oppressed. New social movements of group specificity do not deny the official story's claim that the ideal of liberation as eliminating difference and treating everyone the same has brought significant improvement in the status of excluded groups. Its main quarrel is with the story's conclusion, namely, that since we have achieved formal equality, only vestiges and holdovers of differential privilege remain, which will die out with the continued persistent assertion of an ideal of social relations that makes differences irrelevant to a person's life prospects. The achievement of formal equality does not eliminate social differences, and rhetorical commitment to the sameness of persons makes it impossible even to name how those differences presently structure privilege and oppression.

Though in many respects the law is now blind to group differences, some groups continue to be marked as deviant, as the Other. In everyday interactions, images, and decisions, assumptions about women, Blacks, Hispanics, gay men and lesbians, old people, and other marked groups continue to justify exclusion, avoidance, paternalism, and authoritarian treatment. Continued racist, sexist, homophobic, ageist, and ableist institutions and behavior create particular circumstances for these groups, usually disadvantaging them in their opportunity to develop their capacities. Finally, in part because they have been segregated from one another and in part because they have particular histories and traditions, there are cultural differences among social groups—differences in language, style of living, body comportment and gestures, values, and perspectives on society.

Today in American society, as in many other societies, there is widespread agreement that no person should be excluded from political and economic activities because of ascribed characteristics. Group differences nevertheless continue to exist, and certain groups continue to be privileged. Under these circumstances, insisting that equality and liberation entail ignoring difference has oppressive consequences in three respects.

First, blindness to difference disadvantages groups whose experience, culture, and socialized capacities differ from those of privileged groups. The strategy of assimilation aims to bring formerly excluded groups into the mainstream. So assimilation always implies coming into the game after it is already begun, after the rules and standards have already been set, and having to prove oneself according to those rules and standards. In the assimilationist strategy, the privileged groups implicitly define the standards according to which all will be measured. Because their privilege involves not recognizing these standards as culturally and experientially specific, the ideal of a common humanity in which all can participate without regard to race, gender, religion, or sexuality poses as neutral and universal. The real differences between oppressed groups and the dominant norm, however, tend to put them at a disadvantage in measuring up to these standards, and for that reason assimilationist policies perpetuate their disadvantage ....

Second, the ideal of a universal humanity without social group differences allows privileged groups to ignore their own group specificity. Blindness to difference perpetuates cultural imperialism by allowing norms expressing the point of view and experience of privileged groups to appear neutral and universal. The assimilationist ideal presumes that there is a humanity in general, an unsituated group-neutral human capacity for self-making that left to itself would make individuality flower, thus guaranteeing that each individual will be different. ... Because there is no such unsituated group-neutral point of view, the situation and experience of dominant groups tend to define the norms of such a humanity in general. Against such a supposedly neutral humanist ideal, only the oppressed groups come to be marked with particularity; they, and not the privileged groups, are marked, objectified as the Others.

Thus, third, this denigration of groups that deviate from an allegedly neutral standard often produces an internalized devaluation by members of those groups themselves. When there is an ideal of general human standards according to which everyone should be evaluated equally, then Puerto Ricans or Chinese Americans are ashamed of their accents or their parents, Black children despise the female-dominated kith and kin networks of their neighborhoods, and feminists seek to root out their tendency to cry or to feel compassion for a frustrated stranger. The aspiration to assimilate helps produce the self-loathing and double consciousness characteristic of oppression. The goal of assimilation holds up to people a demand that they "fit," be like the mainstream, in behavior, values, and goals. At the same time, as long as group differences exist, group members will be marked as different—as Black, Jewish, gay—and thus as unable simply to fit. When participation is taken to imply assimilation, the oppressed person is caught in an irresolvable dilemma: to participate means to accept and adopt an identity one is not, and to try to participate means to be reminded by oneself and others of the identity one is.

A more subtle analysis of the assimilationist ideal might distinguish between a conformist and a transformational ideal of assimilation. In the conformist ideal, status quo institutions and norms are assumed as given and disadvantaged groups who differ from those norms are expected to conform to them.

A transformational ideal of assimilation, on the other hand, recognizes that institutions as given express the interests and perspective of the dominant groups. Achieving assimilation therefore requires altering many institutions and practices in accordance with neutral rules that truly do not disadvantage or stigmatize any person, so that group membership really is irrelevant to how persons are treated. Wasserstrom's ideal fits a transformational assimilation, as does the group-neutral ideal advocated by some feminists (Taub and Williams 1985). Unlike the conformist assimilationist, the transformational assimilationist may allow that group-specific policies, such as affirmative action, are necessary and appropriate means for transforming institutions to fit the assimilationist ideal. Whether conformist or transformational, however, the assimilationist ideal still denies that group difference can be positive and desirable; thus, any form of the ideal of assimilation constructs group difference as a liability or disadvantage.

Under these circumstances, a politics that asserts the positivity of group difference is liberating and empowering. In the act of reclaiming the identity the dominant culture has taught them to despise and affirming it as an identity to celebrate, the oppressed remove double consciousness. I am just what they say I am—a Jewboy, a colored girl, a fag, a dyke, or a hag—and proud of it. No longer does one have the impossible project of trying to become something one is not under circumstances where the very trying reminds one of who one is. This politics asserts that oppressed groups have distinct cultures, experiences, and perspectives on social life with humanly positive meaning, some of which may even be superior to the culture and perspectives of mainstream society. The rejection and devaluation of one's culture and perspective should not be a condition of full participation in social life.

Asserting the value and specificity of the culture and attributes of oppressed groups, moreover, results in a relativizing of the dominant culture. When feminists assert the validity of feminine sensitivity and the positive value of nurturing behavior, when gays describe the prejudice of heterosexuals as homophobic and their own sexuality as positive and self-developing, when Blacks affirm a distinct Afro-American tradition, then the dominant culture is forced to discover itself for the first time as specific: as Anglo, European, Christian, masculine, straight. In a political struggle where oppressed groups insist on the positive value of their specific culture and experience, it becomes increasingly difficult for dominant groups to parade their norms as neutral and universal and to construct the values and behavior of the oppressed as deviant, perverted, or inferior. By puncturing the universalist claim to unity that expels some groups and turns them into the Other, the assertion of positive group specificity introduces the possibility of understanding the relation between groups as merely difference instead of exclusion, opposition, or dominance.

The politics of difference also promotes a notion of group solidarity against the individualism of liberal humanism. Liberal humanism treats each person as an individual, ignoring differences of race, sex, religion, and ethnicity. Each person should be evaluated only according to her or his individual efforts and achievements. With the institutionalization of formal equality, some members of formerly excluded groups have indeed succeeded, by mainstream standards. Structural patterns of group privilege and oppression nevertheless remain.

When political leaders of oppressed groups reject assimilation they are often affirming group solidarity. Where the dominant culture refuses to see anything but the achievement of autonomous individuals, the oppressed assert that we shall not separate from the people with whom we identify in order to "make it" in a white Anglo male world. The politics of difference insists on liberation of the whole group of Blacks, women, and American Indians and that this can be accomplished only through basic institutional changes. These changes must include group representation in policymaking and an elimination of the hierarchy of rewards that forces everyone to compete for scarce positions at the top.

Thus, the assertion of a positive sense of group difference provides a standpoint from which to criticize prevailing institutions and norms. Black Americans find in their traditional communities, which refer to their members as "brother" and "sister," a sense of solidarity absent from the calculating individualism of white professional capitalist society. Feminists find in the traditional female values of nurturing a challenge to a militarist worldview, and lesbians find in their relationships a confrontation with the assumption of complementary gender roles in sexual relationships. From their experience of a culture tied to the land, American Indians formulate a critique of the instrumental rationality of European culture that results in pollution and ecological destruction. Having revealed the specificity of the dominant norms which claim universality and neutrality, social movements of the oppressed are in a position to inquire how the dominant institutions must be changed so that they will no longer reproduce the patterns of privilege and oppression.

From the assertion of positive difference the self-organization of oppressed groups follows. Both liberal humanist and leftist political organizations and movements have found it difficult to accept this principle of group autonomy. In a humanist emancipatory politics, if a group is subject to injustice, then all those interested in a just society should unite to combat the powers that perpetuate that injustice. If many groups are subject to injustice, moreover, then they should unite to work for a just society. The politics of difference is certainly not against coalition, nor does it hold that, for example, whites should not work against racial injustice or men against sexist injustice. This politics of group assertion, however, takes as a basic principle that members of oppressed groups need separate organizations that exclude others, especially those from more privileged groups. Separate organization is probably necessary in order for these groups to discover and reinforce the positivity of their specific experience, to collapse and eliminate double consciousness. In discussions within autonomous organizations, group members can determine their specific needs and interests. Separation and self-organization risk creating pressures toward homogenization of the groups themselves, creating new privileges and exclusions. ... But contemporary emancipatory social movements have found group autonomy an important vehicle for empowerment and the development of a group-specific voice and perspective.

Integration into the full life of the society should not have to imply assimilation to dominant norms and abandonment of group affiliation and culture. If the only alternative to the oppressive exclusion of some groups defined as Other by dominant ideologies is the assertion that they are the same as everybody else, then they will continue to be excluded because they are not the same.

Some might object to the way I have drawn the distinction between an assimilationist ideal of liberation and a radical democratic pluralism. They might claim that I have not painted the ideal of a society that transcends group differences fairly, representing it as homogeneous and conformist. The free society envisaged by liberalism, they might say, is certainly pluralistic. In it persons can affiliate with whomever they choose; liberty encourages a proliferation of lifestyles, activities, and associations. While I have no quarrel with social diversity in this sense, this vision of liberal pluralism does not touch on the primary issues that give rise to the politics of difference. The vision of liberation as the transcendence of group difference seeks to abolish the public and political significance of group difference while retaining and promoting both individual and group diversity in private, or nonpolitical, social contexts. ... [But] this way of distinguishing public and private spheres, where the public represents universal citizenship and the private, individual differences tends to result in group exclusion from the public. Radical democratic pluralism acknowledges and affirms the public and political significance of social group differences as a means of ensuring the participation and inclusion of everyone in social and political institutions.

Bibliography

Bastian, Ann, et al. *Choosing Equality: The Case for Democratic Schooling* (Philadelphia, PA: Temple University Press, 1986).

Boxill, Bernard. *Blacks and Social Justice* (Totowa, NJ: Rowman and Allenheld, 1984).

Canter, Norma V. "Testimony from Mexican American Legal Defense and Education Fund." *Congressional Digest* (March 1987).

Karst, Kenneth. "Paths to Belonging: The Constitution and Cultural Identity." *North Carolina Law Review* 64 (1986): 303–77.

Littleton, Christine. "Reconstructing Sexual Equality." *California Law Review* 75 (July 1987): 1279–1377.

Sears, David O., and Leonia Huddy. "Bilingual Education: Symbolic Meaning and Support Among Non-Hispanics." Paper presented at the annual meeting of the American Political Science Association, Chicago, September 1987.

Taub, Nadine, and Wendy Williams. "Will Equality Require More than Assimilation, Accommodation or Separation from the Existing Social Structure?" *Rutgers Law Review* 31 (1985): 825–44.

Wasserstrom, Richard. "On Racism and Sexism," in *Philosophy and Social Issues* (Notre Dame, IN: Notre Dame University Press, 1980).

Review and Discussion Questions

1 How does Young characterize Wasserstrom's ideal of assimilation? Is it an accurate description of his position? Explain.
2 What objections does Young raise against the ideal of assimilation?
3 What is the difference between the conformist and the transformational versions of assimilation?
4 Compare Young's idea of dominance with John Stuart Mill's discussion of individuality, well-being, and liberty. Does Young oppose all universalist ideals?
5 Discuss whether Young has confused two different categories: cultural groups and groups that suffer oppression.

READING: FREEDOM, CONDITIONING, AND THE REAL WOMAN

JANET RADCLIFFE RICHARDS[*]

In this essay, Janet Radcliffe Richards argues that we are free to the extent that others' desires do not keep us from realizing our own and that freedom is valuable as an end in itself. Some feminists, however, seem to doubt this. Contending that women have been conditioned by male society, they believe that a truly liberated woman is not one who is free to choose without restraints but rather a woman who makes certain choices. In response, Radcliffe Richards argues that the fact that women are as they are because of social influences does not show that their choices are not their own. She explores carefully the relation between freedom and conditioning and discusses the ways in which conditioning ought to be properly attacked. Janet Radcliffe Richards is Professor of Practical Philosophy at Oxford University.

A Defense of Liberty

Here [is my understanding] of freedom as a possession: you are free to the extent that other people's desires do not come between you and your own. Another, apparently rival, account will appear later in the chapter, but for now we shall concentrate on this one. If this is freedom, what is its value?

One obvious and common defense of freedom is that it is a means to happiness. People who approve of freedom say that it leads to happiness because we are made unhappy if we know that other people control what we do or because we know better than anyone else what we want and will be made happiest by being left to decide for ourselves or because freedom leads to strength and self-reliance which in turn lead to happiness. Other people are doubtful about these arguments and say that, on the contrary, too much freedom makes people unhappy. People do not really know what is best for them, it is argued, so they may be happier if other people make the decisions. Midge Decter, for instance, in her arguments against Women's Liberation, says that what is making women dissatisfied is not a lack of freedom but a surfeit of it.[1]

All these arguments are of course important, but here they are beside the point. Here the issue is not whether freedom is an effective means to some *other* end like happiness, but whether it is good *as an end in itself*. Can we argue that freedom is good irrespective of whether it leads to happiness or anything else we value? And if so, how valuable is it in comparison with these other things?

In some sense there can be very little argument on subjects like this one, because with questions of ultimate values there does not seem to be any common ground for discussion between people who disagree. If people really, in the last analysis, value different things, there is nothing more to be said. However, it is possible to do something not unlike arguing. It does seem possible to make it clear by illustration that a great many people, whether they realize it or not, do in fact

---

[*] From Janet Radcliffe Richards, *The Skeptical Feminist* (Harmondsworth, UK: Penguin, 1982). Reprinted by permission.

value freedom as an end in itself and that many value it even more than happiness ....

Suppose, for instance, you were an outstandingly gifted but miserably neurotic artist or musician and someone offered you a drug which would make you happy but would result in your losing all your ability. There are already drugs along these lines, but we are to think of one so entirely effective that once having taken it the patient would not even regret having lost the desire or ability to compose or paint. Suppose also that you had complete faith in its efficacy and in the intentions of the person who offered it. Would you take it? Some people would no doubt be very happy to, but there must be many who in such a situation would rather remain unhappy than achieve happiness at the cost of losing a skill they valued far more than any prospect of happiness.

Suppose, again, you lived in a country with a political regime you disliked intensely, with no way of escaping and not much hope of making things more to your liking. Suppose also that the government had a program of "re-education" which you believed would be completely effective and which would make you entirely happy with the political situation afterward. Would you be willing to undergo this program? Many people would certainly not. They would rather remain unhappy than be so radically changed. Or suppose that you were very dissatisfied with your life as it was. Would you welcome the opportunity (to take a classic example) to become a satisfied pig? Again, probably not.

Of course these thought experiments are all rather artificial. They presuppose impossibilities, and anyway are not specific enough: whether we should be willing to become satisfied pigs would probably depend a good deal on the degree of our unhappiness as human beings. Nevertheless, the arguments are useful because they do suggest that to many people there are things which are more important than happiness.

So far, of course, this does not prove that anyone prefers *freedom* to happiness because the discussion has only been about which of two things we should take if we were in a position to choose, and as long as there is a question of choice some freedom is built into the example. All this shows is that there are occasions where people would choose to cling to what might be called their identities rather than lose them for the sake of happiness. No doubt they would like happiness as well, but given the necessity of choice, happiness might well be abandoned first. However, it is possible to look at the question of freedom by considering similar cases which involve other people.

Why is it, for instance, that so many people object to Soviet dissidents' being put in psychiatric hospitals? Of course there are several reasons. We may not think the "treatment" will work, and we may not like the system the patients' minds are being changed to fit. However, even supposing we did approve of the political system, and supposing we did believe that after treatment the dissidents would fit happily into Russian society and regard their former activities and attitudes as absurd, would we then approve of the practice? Probably not. We might be happy for people to be offered such treatment if they wanted it but still think that they should be allowed to choose for themselves whether they would rather be altered and made happy or remain unhappy but still themselves. And if we think that it is more important to give people this choice than to force happiness on them, it means we are in favour of freedom and regard it as more important than happiness.

There are many other examples of this sort of attitude. For instance, most of us would be shocked by this advertisement described by Sheila Rowbotham:[2] "There was a picture of a young mother with a pram in front of a big block of flats and the heading 'She can't change her environment but you can change her mood with Serenid-D.'" There are all kinds of reasons for being upset about putting people on happiness drugs, including being afraid of side effects and long-term consequences. Nevertheless, part of the objection is to the idea of making women happy *without fulfilling their desires*. If we were concerned only with happiness for people we should not worry about putting them on effective happiness drugs. If happiness is all that matters, there is nothing intrinsically wrong with brainwashing or forcible medication or giving people sedatives and tranquilizers instead of coping with their emotional problems. Most of us do care about allowing people to determine the course of their own lives, rather than having other people make them happy in ways they do not want. Since there can hardly be a feminist in existence who would regard it as an acceptable solution to women's problems that someone should invent some kind of medication or special process of re-education which would make women happy in their present lot but had to be administered against their wills, we must think that most feminists value freedom more than happiness for women. The firm feminist rejection of male paternalism comes not only through the recognition that men's apparent concern for women's well-being is by some curious coincidence remarkably well adapted to the interests of men. Even if men's dominance were wholly good for women, we should still reject its being forced on them. As Kant said, "paternalism is the worst despotism imaginable." And as Mill said, "the only purpose for which power can be rightfully exercised over any member of a civilized community, against his will, is to prevent harm to others. His own good, either physical or moral, is not a sufficient warrant."[3]

There is probably no way of arguing with any feminist who disagrees with all this, as doubtless some must. However, the principle of freedom will be taken as fundamental to feminism throughout this book, and where it produces statements with which feminists disagree, at least it will be obvious where the disagreement stems from. Freedom is being taken as a fundamental good in its own right, and a thing of which we should, therefore, all have as much as possible. How much each individual should have when the claims of other people are taken into consideration is a question of distributive justice ....

Inner Freedom

Two main propositions have been argued for in the previous two sections. One is that we are free to the extent that we can do as we like (which means that we are not properly described as free or not-free, only as more or less free). The other is that freedom, understood in this way, is good in itself. We should all have as much of it as possible, and if our freedom is to be curtailed it is to be for the sake only of other people, not ourselves.

However, we now have to look at the question of whether feminists do indeed think that freedom is a good thing and want it for women. If freedom is the ability to fulfill one's desires, and if feminists do want it for women, they should surely be trying to make the world as much as possible as women would like it to be. However, it is a most conspicuous fact about some feminists that they seem to include among their aims things which not only men find objectionable but which women do too. There are all kinds of things which women seem to want and have no wish to change and yet which many feminists apparently want to abolish. Traditional marriage and division of labor seem to be happily chosen by many women; many enjoy making themselves attractive to men and giving men certain kinds of service in return for being protected by them. Many would rather look after a home and family than do anything else. And many, with the appearance of total freedom, choose to enter beauty competitions (which are watched as willingly by millions more women) or to become striptease artists, "hostesses" of various sorts, and prostitutes.

Of course, you can argue here that some of these apparently free choices are not very free at all, because choosing the best of a bad lot does not give women what they really want. They probably would not choose to become housewives or prostitutes if better things were readily available to them. There is much truth in that, no doubt, but it does not provide the slightest reason for taking away the best there is and leaving these women with something which must, in their eyes, be still worse. The true liberator can always be recognized by her wanting to increase the options open to the people who are to be liberated, and there is never any justification for taking a choice away from a group you want to liberate unless it is demonstrable beyond all reasonable doubt that removing it will bring other, more important, options into existence. To give women freedom we must give them more choice, and then if they really do not want the things they are choosing now, like homes and families, those things will just die out without our having to push them.

Of course, there are many feminists who do want to increase the options open to women. Consider, for instance, the program for the picketing of a Miss America Pageant, which stated "There will be ... Lobbying Visits to the contestants urging our sisters to reject the Pageant Farce and join us. ... We do not plan heavy disruptive tactics."[4] That was genuinely liberating. The women entering the competition might not have thought of other routes to success, or they might not have realized that there were groups of people where different things were valued. However, that is, or at least seems (it is not always easy to know how literally things are to be taken), a very different matter from the demonstrations at the Miss World competition in London where feminist protestors would apparently have liked to disrupt the whole proceedings. To prevent women from doing what they have chosen to do is not to be concerned with their freedom. Nevertheless, that does seem to be the aim of some feminists.

But that is not the end of the matter. This kind of feminist need not accept yet the accusation that she is not really offering women freedom. In general, when the liberators of women or anyone else take the view that they know better than the beneficiaries of their efforts what should be done for them, they will argue that these people are *conditioned,* and therefore not in a state of mind to be able to choose freely no matter how many alternatives are open to them. *That* is why the liberators sometimes have to make choices on their behalf.

This kind of view certainly has intuitive plausibility about it. However, it does present many problems, and in particular the immediate one of seeming to call for (at least) a modification of the account of freedom so far given. It has been argued so far that an individual's freedom is a function mainly of how many choices there are available. If we are to accept, however, that it may sometimes be acceptable to restrict such choices in the name of freedom, on the grounds that the person to be liberated is conditioned and therefore unable to choose, a new element seems to have entered into the idea of liberty. It seems that to be free it is not enough to have a wide range of options open. As well as, or perhaps even instead of, having such options, the free individual must be in a certain state of mind. Freedom must be at least in part an internal thing.

There certainly is no doubt that some such view is widespread in feminism. Perhaps the most striking indication of it is the use of the word "liberated" when applied to women. To the outsider as well as to the feminist, a liberated woman is not one who is free to choose among a great many options but one who makes *certain kinds of choices*; she is not a woman with a tolerant and helpful husband who encourages her to achieve all her ambitions but one who would not stand any nonsense from her husband if he tried any.

Now there is indeed a long philosophical tradition of saying that true freedom does not consist in being in an environment which permits you to do as you please but consists (at least partly, depending on the theory) in being in a particular state of mind. Theories like these still do keep to the basic idea of freedom as the satisfaction of desire, but it is differently interpreted and analyzed. There are innumerable variants on the theme, but we need consider only two, and without too much detail.

The first and more extreme, is the idea that freedom is contained entirely within the mind of the free person, with outside circumstances irrelevant. According to this view, you are truly free when your desires have been so adjusted that you desire nothing you cannot get. According to the Stoic idea, for instance, if the slave reaches total tranquility of mind while the master is in the grips of unrealized desire, the slave is the freer of the two. And in Christianity, the reason for saying that perfect freedom is to be found in the service of God is that once the Christian has achieved a state of mind in which nothing is desired but to do the will of God, that desire need never be unfulfilled: the will of God can be done in any circumstances whatever. This extreme idea of freedom is not much found in feminism, although there are traces of it. The woman who determines that she will no longer care about things which previously obsessed her, like the approval of men, may be looking for freedom in this way. If she ceases to care about what men think, she can act to please herself rather than men and so lessen the extent of her unfulfilled desire.

The second, more moderate, view of internal freedom is one more commonly found in feminism. This idea is that being in the right state of mind is not enough on its own to make you free: to be free you also need the kind of freedom we have been discussing ... which involves being able to do as you like. However, that is not enough on its own, and a necessary condition of your choosing freely is that you should be in the right state of mind before deciding among the options which are open to you. There are all kinds of variants on this idea, but common to them all is something like the view that each individual has a *true self* which should be doing the choosing but that its activities are obstructed by various contaminants which have got into the person in some way and which prevent real choice as effectively as obstructions in the environment do. Plato, for instance, thought that there were parts of the soul and that the lower parts were always trying to pull the highest part from its chosen path. A common idea in religion is that the uncontaminated soul would choose what was good but that evil powers may take possession of it and force evil choices. More recently, there is the psychoanalytic idea that you cannot be truly free without getting rid of the neuroses which come between yourself and your real desires. Of course, an idea along these lines is very common in feminism. The domination of men has been so complete that the male has entered women's souls, making them choose on behalf of men and against their own interests. That they think themselves free is beside the point: all that shows is how well the work of conditioning has been done.

Now it is quite clear that however difficult all this may be to work out in detail, there is something in it. It is also true that (risky as it may sound) it is *sometimes* reasonable to override people's immediate wishes in the cause of their greater freedom, even when the earlier definition of freedom is taken and we say that people are free to the extent that they can do as they like. For instance, if a friend wanted to achieve something which was very important to her, and we knew beyond any doubt that she was setting about it the wrong way but could not persuade her to change, we might override her immediate wishes because we wanted her to get something which we knew she wanted more. Or again, since freedom is not simply a matter of how many immediate choices there are, but also of *scope* of choice, we might override some trivial choice to make sure that there was a greater range of choices later on. This is always being done in the case of children. Parents are not (necessarily) working against their children's freedom if, for instance, they do not let the children decide which schools they should go to. If a school is so much better than another that it will allow the children far more important choices later on in life, it is in the interests of the children's freedom that they should not be allowed to choose now.

Nevertheless, it is obvious that if we are going to take this sort of line, we have to take *great care*. If women's wishes are to be ignored in the name of their freedom, on the grounds that they are conditioned, it is essential to know exactly what is meant by conditioning, why it is supposed to impair freedom, to what extent it is legitimate to ignore what people want if they are conditioned, and how to distinguish women who are conditioned from the ones who are not. If we do not take care, we run the risk of planning a scheme in which the only freedom women get is the freedom to do what their liberators want them to do.

That is a tempting line anyway. As an early feminist, Margaret Rhondda, said, "The passion to decide to look after your fellowmen, to do good to them in your way, is far more common than the desire to put into everyone's hand the power to look after themselves."[5] The danger becomes intensified a thousand times when you can do this but still be able to convince yourself that you are offering freedom because the whole issue has been obscured under more or less indiscriminate accusations of conditioning. If the idea of conditioning is to be used to enhance freedom, and not as a general device by which a liberation movement can do as it likes in the name of freedom, it must be pinned down more precisely.

Conditioning and the Real Woman

There is one point which must be made quite clear before going any further. The conditioning which was referred to in the previous section is supposed to be a sort of thing which is *actually a constraint* on a woman; something which comes between herself and her true desires. Now the word "conditioning" is one which is extremely commonly used in feminism, in all kinds of circumstances, and what must on no account be presumed is that whenever the word is used the so-called conditioned desires, attitudes, and responses are things, which actually do prevent the real woman from fulfilling her real desires.

In feminist contexts, the usual ground for making an accusation of conditioning is to point to the social root of the habit of mind in question (which is, of course, always one which is disapproved of). Women want to make themselves beautiful only because society has made them want to; they think that their mission in life is to be mothers because everyone has been drumming it into them since the age of two; they lack ambition because they have been brought up from birth to think that the female is the natural servant of the male and on no account to compete with him. This may all be true. However, to establish that a woman is conditioned in *that* sense of the word is nothing like enough to show that she is conditioned in the very different sense of having something in her personality which gets between herself and the fulfillment of her real desires and therefore that these environmentally produced characteristics limit her freedom.

The reason why conditioning in the sense of "coming from a (disapproved of) social influence" cannot be the same as conditioning in the sense of "getting in the way of the true woman's desires" is obvious from the discussion of the nature of woman. ... You cannot distinguish between the woman as she now is and what is supposed to be the "true" woman by pointing to the way society has shaped her. It is absolutely inevitable that the adult woman should be as she is partly as a result of social influence, and it is a thing we cannot possibly object to unless we are to suggest that people should be sent to grow up among wolves (and anyway there are social pressures even among wolves). We cannot say of social pressures *in general* that they turn the woman into something which is not her true self; on the contrary, they cannot be anything other than a contribution to what she actually is.

Of course we may not *like* the way women are at present, and if we do not we can argue that their upbringing ought to be changed. Very obviously, for instance, feminists are bound to disapprove of any upbringing which is so much at odds with women's intrinsic natures that they are bound to be unhappy. They can also reasonably object to women's being brought up to depend on men in the achievement of what they want, because that is unreliable and their success in life should be more firmly based. They can disapprove of women's being encouraged to see their main aim in life as relationships with men and all their ambitions directed toward pleasing men in one way or another because it is undignified and they want women to be dignified. They can say that women ought not to be brought up to confine their interests and activities to domestic matters and concentrate their energies on trivia because they would prefer them to be well-educated, ambitious, and serious-minded. Since there is no neutral way to bring children up (they must be surrounded by influences of one kind or another), we have a good deal of choice about how adults eventually turn out. We certainly could make women other than they are now, and it is not surprising that feminists would like to see a good many changes.

On the other hand, none of this provides any reason at all for saying that women as they are now, with the desires they have now, are not *free*. We may think it a good thing that women should be brought up to be happy, dignified, independent, serious, and useful, but, once again, everything is what it is. Happiness is happiness, dignity is dignity, independence is independence: none of these things is freedom. Even though there may be some difficulty about finding a definitive account of freedom, there are limits to what we can reasonably decide to adopt, and it really would be travesty of the language (as well as potentially treacherous) to say that people were not free just because we did not like the way they were or that in making them into something we liked better we should be giving them freedom. We may argue with perfect justice that women are as they are because of social influences, but that is not enough to show that the choices they are making are not their own real choices. And if by "conditioned" we want to mean "not in a state to make free choices," we must mean something more than "influenced by social pressures we disapprove of."

Of course we can still, if we want to, say that "conditioned" does just refer to socially induced characteristics in women, rather than aspects of a woman's character which somehow do get in the way of her real desires. However, this is dangerous. The word has now such deeply entrenched connotations of interference with freedom that if we take a definition which does not include those connotations, we open the floodgates to mistakes and double dealing. I shall therefore take it that "conditioning" is properly used only when it does refer to a real restriction on freedom. The problem is, now that we have decided that a woman brought up one way is no less her real self than a woman brought up any other way, to work out what form conditioning might take.

Freedom and Conditioning

Since we are trying to distinguish the social pressures which condition a woman from the ones which simply form her character, one obvious starting point is the fact that from the point of view of each individual there is a great difference between different kinds of social pressure. Whereas some are congenial and easily conformed to, others are not: some social pressures push people toward doing things for which they have an intrinsic dislike.

Nevertheless, people often go along even with these, because doing so is less unpleasant than suffering the social consequences of resistance. So a woman who has no natural interest in beauty may make herself as beautiful as she can; or one who is not interested in children may do her best to absorb herself in the concerns of a family; or a woman by nature apt to explore jungles may become a secretary, because that is the feminine thing to do and that way she will get social approval. None of this shows conditioning. The environment is constricting, but nevertheless a woman who makes the best choice among the limited set available to her is behaving perfectly rationally and choosing in her own interest, and as long as she is doing that the only restrictions on her freedom are external, not internal.

However, what happens to these women who go along with uncongenial social pressures when liberators appear on the scene and suggest to them that the world would be a better place if women did not spend so much time on their appearance or that children are not necessarily the ideal object of every woman's devotion? Or what happens if they find themselves in a situation where the uncongenial social pressures are beginning to lessen and following their natural inclinations would bring down less social censure?

If they thoroughly understand the situation in which they have grown up there may be no difficulty. They may instantly join in the campaign to change the things which are alien to their natures or at least take advantage of any changes which come about. But this may well not happen. Usually when children are subjected to pressures in growing up, they do not think separately about what they would like to do and what adult pressures and encouragements compel them to do; they just get into habits of doing what produces the least unacceptable consequences. The result is that when the situation changes, or when there is some prospect of its changing, they may not rush to embrace the new but cling to the habits they have grown up with. Probably they do not understand that their present preferences came about by the forcible suppression of their natural (that is, inherent) inclinations, but even if they do they may well have difficulty in ridding themselves of the habits they have gathered. These habits may then come between the adults and their real desires.

A simple analogy can be drawn from an entirely different context. When you learn to drive, you rapidly pick up the skills of braking and steering, and your responses to various situations become so automatic that you can usually do the right thing without thinking. But you may well learn these habits without knowing much about how braking and steering work, and the result is that the first time you skid, you react in the way you always have reacted when the car moves too fast in the wrong direction by braking as hard as possible and hauling the steering wheel round. The consequences are exactly the opposite of what you want. In order to avoid the situation in future, you have to do two things. The first is to understand the theory, so that you know under what conditions the usual methods will and will not work, and the second is to free yourself of your habitual actions.

As a motorist you have very definite desires (to move in particular directions), but you yourself may interfere with their fulfillment through ignorance or bad habits or both. Much the same may happen with women. Their failure to understand the situation they are in and the persistence of deeply entrenched habits may get in the way of what they want to do. And where this happens we can say that a woman's state of mind is obstructing her desires, *without having to resort to dubious theories about hidden desires in the core of her imaginary real self.*

Failure to understand the nature of the world and the structure of possibilities within it acts against women in all kinds of ways. For instance, many women (if not all) are by nature as inclined as men to seek fame and fortune, but the traditional restricted upbringing of a woman means that in most cases there is only a limited number of forms in which she is capable of casting this ambition: she may think as a matter of course that success for a woman must take the form of being pursued by men, envied by women, and renowned for beauty. But if that is the only way in which she can imagine making an impact on the world, she is likely to have condemned herself to failure before even setting out. Few women succeed in being renowned for beauty, and anyway beauty does not last. Or she may have more specific ambitions and look for political power but may automatically presume that political success for a woman must take the form of being the wife of a politician, and in that case her potential for success is restricted from the start by the casting of her ambitions in a form which sets a low upper limit on possible success. If women squeeze their desires into a conventionally feminine mold they are likely to be doomed to failure from the first. But even if they succeed in it, [they] may still fail because of habits of mind which interfere: perhaps she cannot avoid feeling that she ought to take care with her dress or feeling guilty if she lets her husband do his fair share of the housework, however clearly she may understand the unreasonableness of such feelings. Her ingrained habits of mind prevent the fulfillment of her strongest desires.

This analysis seems to provide a very good account of what it is to be conditioned, and there is no difficulty at all about seeing it as an internal lack of freedom: something about the woman which prevents her from doing as she really wants. One aspect of conditioning is *ignorance,* probably the greatest curtailer of freedom there is, because if someone does not know or fully grasp that the world contains certain possibilities, as far as that person is concerned they might just as well not exist. The other aspect is the inability to change unwelcome aspects of oneself, which is as much a restriction on the fulfillment of desire as the inability to change anything in the outside world. If you want to be more beautiful or run faster or be stronger or be able to charm people but cannot do whatever it is, you are as curtailed in your desires as you would be through not having money or influence or a car or tools for a trade.

The upshot of all this is that feminists are indeed right in thinking that lack of freedom can be internal: a woman may be in a state where her own mind prevents her from achieving what she really wants (a matter which must not be confused with her mind preventing what she would have wanted if she had been someone else). However, although the comparisons drawn in the last paragraph between internal and external restrictions on freedom do show that freedom can be limited by aspects of the mind, what they also show at the same time is that there is no intrinsic difference between external and internal lack of freedom; they are essentially the same sort of thing. Internal lack of freedom does not consist in being in a special state of mind or having a particular set of desires, only in having within oneself (rather than in surrounding circumstances) the things which prevent fulfillment of desire. This means that, in fact, there is no problem about reconciling the concept of internal freedom with the first account of freedom given in this chapter. The only acceptable interpretation of "internal freedom" (the only account of it which does not involve calling something quite different by the name of freedom or presuming that the real woman is something uninfluenced by society) is one which makes it essentially a matter of being unimpeded in one's desires by one's own ignorance and habits. This is important. Once it is clear, people will be less likely to be confused by the vague way in which "conditioned" is often used or lured into thinking that if women have socially induced desires which the liberators disapprove of, they are necessarily not free.

The Attack on Conditioning

When women are really conditioned, their preconceptions and immediate desires do get in the way of what, in some perfectly obvious way, they really want. If they are conditioned, therefore, it does seem that other people may be justified in overriding their immediate desires in order to produce not what the liberators think they should want but what they actually do want.

However, there is an obvious danger in taking this attitude, because the only case in which it would be reasonable to override a woman's wishes in the name of her freedom would be where it was absolutely certain that she was conditioned and equally certain what she really wanted and how it could be brought about. And the simple fact of the matter is that it is virtually impossible even to approach certainty in cases like this, let alone reach it. It is very hard to tell when, and to what extent, people are conditioned.

The main reason why this must be so is probably obvious from what has gone before. The point is that it is quite impossible to tell conditioned women from unconditioned ones[6] by their preferences. The pressures on women to be beautiful and maternal and domestic and deferential to men have no doubt left in many women habits of mind which will prevent their ever achieving what they really want to achieve, but we are not entitled to presume that the pressures which produced these mental blocks in some women did the same for all. For the women to whom these pressures were congenial, as they must have been for some, the desires produced became their own most basic desires and not obstacles to the fulfillment of others. If a woman is interested mainly in dress or nursery design, it is no doubt true to say that it can be attributed to her background to some extent: if she had been brought up differently she would have had different interests. However, these may be genuinely hers and ideally suited to her nature. The "conditioned" responses may be genuinely her own. It is therefore impossible to tell whether or not a woman is conditioned just by knowing about her likes and dislikes or about her formative influences.

What that means is that the only attack which can be safely mounted against conditioning must be directed to its source. It is too dangerous to try to "free" women who are regarded as conditioned by forcing them to do what the prevailing feminist ideology presumes they must want because with that method there is always the danger of ignoring women's real wishes. They may not be conditioned at all. The only thing to do is start from the beginning and try, even at this late stage, to remove the cause of the trouble and give conditioned women a chance to become unconditioned in a way which runs no risk of damaging those who are not, because it still leaves women to make their own choices.

There are two stages to this process, corresponding to the two aspects of conditioning. The first is to increase understanding of how the present state of things came about and how it works, so that women who have been doing what does not suit them can understand why, and at the same time [learn] what alternatives are possible. The second is to make help available to women who decide as a result of this that they do want to change their habits.

There are all kinds of ways in which advances could be made on these two fronts. The key to the first is *diversity*. Women must be exposed to kinds of new influences and information (in addition to the old, of course, not instead of them) to make them fully aware of the possibilities the world contains. Some people, no doubt, will try to turn the freedom argument against this procedure by saying that if people have new alternatives thrust before them they are *forced to choose,* and that in itself is an infringement of liberty because people ought to have the freedom not to choose if that is what they would prefer. However, that argument cannot possibly work. This is because it is true as a matter of *logic* that people cannot be the ultimate determiners of their own degree of freedom. Whatever anyone chooses to do, that choice comes from among alternatives which already exist, and those alternatives were not themselves chosen. Since, therefore, the ultimate degree of freedom is always out of the hands of the individual, we are right to insist that the choice given should always be as great as possible. We cannot, in the name of liberty for women, force them to do anything against their wills or bring about states of society they do not like, but we are bound to give them more knowledge of possibilities.

The second part of the attack on conditioning is to reinforce this for women who do decide that they would like to change their lives by giving them every help in overcoming unwelcome habits of mind: help ranging from the support of other women who understand the position to full-scale psychotherapy. As long as this was directed to bringing about what women themselves wanted, and not to persuading them into something they did not want, it would be genuinely liberating.

Still, however energetically we pursued such a program, we should have to be hopelessly optimistic to think that we should actually eliminate all existing conditioning as a result of it, and perhaps this seems to justify the wish of some feminists to make a firm attack on the symptoms of conditioning rather than going in this gentle way for its cause. However much we may want freedom for women, they could argue, even the freedom to stay conditioned, can we allow them this freedom if the price of it is to trap other women in the same bonds? Can we allow a conditioned mother to bring up her daughter in the same way? Surely for the sake of the daughters we ought to be willing to run the risk of attacking directly what we believe to be the mother's conditioned desires, even though we may run some risk of going against their real wishes? Surely we should work directly against bad influences, and deliberately get rid of (for instance), beauty competitions, sexist literature in schools, and anything else we think objectionable, whatever the conditioned mothers may think of the matter?

However, even though conditioned mothers will certainly tend to bring up conditioned daughters, and although we certainly cannot allow that, this conclusion is not the proper one to draw. The way to prevent the daughters from becoming conditioned is not to keep them out of the range of influence of the things which are believed to have conditioned their mothers, because it was not *being in the range of those influences* which did the harm, but *being out of the range of others*. If we bring the daughters up on a diet of so-called nonsexist literature (much of what is around at present is actually *female* sexist) to think that there should be no sex roles, that does not free them from conditioning: it only brings them up with a different sort. If to get feminist approval a little girl is forced to sneer at the idea of beauty competitions, she is as much coerced as her mother was by parents who expected her to look pleased when she was given dolls and pretty party frocks. Once again, whether or not a girl is conditioned cannot be judged by which slogans she grows up chanting, because in theory she could be conditioned into chanting any.

The solution to the problem, as always with questions of freedom, is once again diversity. We can perhaps summarize the conditioned mothers and those of daughters who are to be rescued from conditioning by proposing a solution to the widely debated problem of how free a parent should be to determine a child's education. We can put it this way. Within practicable limits, the parent should be allowed to say that the child *must* learn certain things and have lessons from people of particular political, moral, or religious views. On the other hand, no parent should have the right to *prevent* the child's learning anything (going to scripture classes in the wrong religion or having sex education) or being exposed to other people's views. The education authorities should have a positive duty to diversify influences, since in that way the parent's wishes are respected but the child's freedom is not impaired. That should be what feminists want. As Germaine Greer said of a similar problem, "Censorship is the weapon of the opposition, not ours."[7]

Notes

1 Midge Decter, *The New Chastity and Other Arguments Against Women's Liberation* (New York: Coward, McCann & Geoghegan, 1972), 51.
2 Sheila Rowbotham, *Woman's Consciousness, Man's World* (London: Pelican Books, 1973), 75–6.
3 John Stuart Mill, "On Liberty," in *The Essential Works of John Stuart Mill* (Bantam Martix; Martix edition (1965)), ed. M. Lerner, 263.
4 "No More Miss America!" in *Sisterhood Is Powerful*, ed. R. Morgan (New York: Random House, 1970), 584.
5 Margaret Rhondda, quoted in S. Firestone, *The Dialectic of Sex* (New York: William Morrow and Company, 1970), 20.
6 More accurately, of course, *more* or *less* conditioned and in certain ways rather than just in general. Throughout arguments of this sort it must not be forgotten that freedom is a matter of degree.
7 Germaine Greer, *The Female Eunuch* (New York: McGraw-Hill, 1971), 309.

Review and Discussion Questions

1 How does Radcliffe Richards define freedom? What is the alternative, inner way of understanding freedom that she discusses?
2 In what ways does Radcliffe Richards agree with those who advocate inner freedom?
3 How does Radcliffe Richards distinguish pressures that condition—that is, restrict freedom—from those that merely play a part in the general formation of a person?
4 Why is Radcliffe Richards skeptical of those who argue that women who dress for men or participate in beauty pageants are not truly free? What solutions does Radcliffe Richards think will help ensure that women are not, in fact, choosing in accord with conditioning rather than choosing freely?
5 Explain how censorship can damage women's freedom, according to Radcliffe Richards. How can education help women?
6 How would Radcliffe Richards respond to Catharine MacKinnon, who argues that women's choices are structured and that marriage, prostitution, and sexual harassment are indistinguishable? Explain.

Essay and Paper Topics for Chapter 18

1 Looking at the world today, was *Brown v. Board of Education* a success or a failure or neither? How do you assess the moral significance of the level of racial segregation that you see today?
2 In what ways does Shelby's analysis provide a good framework or not for understanding and responding to the problems of inner cities?

3 How would an ideal society treat racial differences? What is race?
4 What is sexual oppression? How can we know it, or know when it has disappeared?
5 Randall Kennedy, an African American law professor at Harvard, has written that identity politics is "mere superstition and prejudice. ... I eschew racial pride," says Kennedy, "because of my conception of what should properly be the object of pride for an individual: something that he or she has accomplished. I can feel pride in a good deed I have done or a good effort I have made. I cannot feel pride in some state of affairs that is independent of my contribution to it. I did not achieve my racial designation" (*Atlantic Monthly*, May 1997, p. 56). Do you agree? Explain, indicating how you think other authors you have read in this chapter might respond.
6 Discuss Mill/Taylor, Young, and Radcliffe Richards on the questions of the nature of freedom and whether contemporary women are, in fact, truly free.
7 Affirmative action is sometimes defended as an attempt to compensate for society's failure to provide equality of opportunity. Is that a sound argument for such policies? Explain.
8 Describe the ideal educationally diverse campus. Which characteristics make the environment diverse in your vision? How close do actual campuses come to reaching the ideal that you identify?
9 Drawing on the arguments in both court cases, do you believe that affirmative action, such as Michigan Law School process, is generally a good or bad idea?
10 Is racial reconciliation possible in the United States? Discuss.
11 Are race and gender equality separate issues? Discuss.

Chapter 19

Immigration, National Boundaries, and Multiculturalism

Societies are increasingly diverse and multicultural. Such societies raise a variety of urgent questions and problems. Should nations allow open borders for free immigration or should they, for various reasons, prohibit or restrict the ability of persons to immigrate? The first three readings address this question. Consider next all the multiple cultures that develop within a society. Should society evolve through a vision of a melting pot or some idea of cultural preservation, or are these compatible ideals? To what extent are our identities tied to our distinctive cultural groups, and to what extent are they freely chosen? The final three writings explore these questions.

READING: AN OVERVIEW OF THE ETHICS OF IMMIGRATION

JOSEPH H. CARENS[*]

Joseph Carens is a leading scholar in the ethics of immigration. In this essay, Carens develops principles for immigration policy that he believes should limit discretion for being able to restrict immigration. He further defends the aspiration for a world with open borders. Joseph Carens is Professor at the University of Toronto and Fellow of the Royal Society of Canada.

What are the ethical issues raised by immigration? How does immigration affect our understanding of democracy and citizenship? I explore these questions in the context of three presuppositions. First, I am concerned primarily with immigration into the rich democratic states of Europe and North America. I leave open the question of the extent to which this analysis extends to other states.

Second, I presuppose a commitment to democratic principles .... [These] refer to the broad moral commitments that undergird and justify contemporary political institutions and policies throughout North America and Europe—things like the ideas that all human beings are of equal moral worth, that disagreements should normally be resolved through the principle of majority rule, that

[*] Excerpted from "An Overview of the Ethics of Immigration" by Joseph H. Carens, *Critical Review of International Social and Political Philosophy* 17(5) (2014): 538–559. Reprinted with permission of Routledge, Taylor & Francis.

we have a duty to respect the rights and freedoms of individuals, that legitimate government depends upon the consent of the governed, that all citizens should be equal under the law, that coercion should only be exercised in accordance with the rule of law, that people should not be subject to discrimination on the basis of characteristics like race, religion, or gender, that we should respect norms like fairness and reciprocity in our policies, and so on. These ideas can be interpreted in many different ways, and they can even conflict with one another. Nevertheless, on a wide range of topics, like the question of whether it is morally acceptable to force someone to convert from one religion to another, there is no serious disagreement among those who think of themselves as democrats. Many of the questions raised by immigration are interconnected, and a commitment to democratic principles greatly constrains the kinds of answers we can offer to these questions.

Third, for most of my analysis, I am simply going to assume that states normally have a moral right to exercise considerable discretionary control over immigration. I will call this the conventional view. Most of the normative claims that I advance in this article qualify the conventional view but do not challenge it in a fundamental way. At the end of the article, however, I want to step back and offer a fundamental challenge to the conventional view.

...

Sovereignty and Self-Determination

Some people think that it is a mistake even to talk about the ethics of immigration. Immigration and citizenship should be seen as political issues, not moral ones, they say (Hailbronner 1989). On this view, respect for state sovereignty and democratic self-determination preclude any moral assessments of a state's immigration and citizenship policies.

This sort of attempt to shield immigration and citizenship policies from moral scrutiny is misguided. Consider some examples of past policies that almost everyone today would regard as unjust: the Chinese Exclusion Act of the late nineteenth century that barred people of Chinese descent from naturalization in the United States; the denaturalization policies adopted in the 1930s by many European states (including Germany's infamous Nuremberg Laws); and Canadian and Australian policies of excluding potential immigrants on the basis of race.

To criticize such policies as morally wrong does not entail a rejection of state sovereignty or democratic self-determination. We should distinguish the question of who ought to have the authority to determine a policy from the question of whether a given policy is morally acceptable. We can think that an agent has the moral right to make a decision and still think that the decision itself is morally wrong. That applies just as much to a collective agent like a democratic state as it does to individuals. Moral criticism of the Chinese Exclusion Act or the Nuremberg Laws or the White Australia Policy does not imply that some other state should have intervened to change those policies or that there should be an overarching authority to compel states to act morally.

...

Access to Citizenship

Who should be granted citizenship and why? I propose the following principles. Anyone born in a state with a reasonable prospect of living there for an extended period should acquire citizenship at birth. Anyone raised in a state for an extended part of her formative years should acquire citizenship automatically over time (or, at the least, acquire an absolute and unqualified right to citizenship). Anyone who comes to a society as an adult immigrant and lives there legally for an extended period ought to acquire a legal right to naturalization—ideally with no further requirements but at most upon meeting certain modest standards regarding language acquisition and knowledge of the receiving society ...

To understand why settled immigrants and their descendants have a moral right to citizenship, we have to think about why the descendants of citizens have a moral claim to citizenship. Consider what we might call the normal case: children who are born to parents who are citizens of the state where their children are born and who live in that state as well. In other words, the baby's parents are resident citizens. Every democratic state grants citizenship automatically to such children at birth. It may seem intuitively obvious that this practice makes moral sense, but I want to make the underlying rationale explicit, and that rationale is not self-evident. Birthright citizenship is not a natural phenomenon. It is a political practice, even when it concerns the children of resident citizens. Would it be morally wrong for a democratic state not to grant citizenship at birth to the children of its own resident citizens, and, if so, why?

We are embodied creatures. Most of our activities take place within some physical space. In the modern world, the physical spaces in which people live are organized politically primarily as territories governed by states. The state can and should recognize even a baby as a person and a bearer of rights. Beyond that, the state where she lives inevitably structures, secures, and promotes her relationships with other human beings, including her family, in various ways.

When a baby is born to parents who are resident citizens, it is reasonable to expect that she will grow up in that state and receive her social formation there and that her life chances and choices will be affected in central ways by that state's laws and policies. She cannot exercise political agency at birth, but she will be able to do so as an adult. If she is to play that role properly, she should see herself prospectively in it as she is growing up. She needs to know that she is entitled to a voice in the community where she lives and that her voice will matter. In addition, political communities are an important source of identity for many, perhaps most, people in the modern world. A baby born to resident citizens is likely to develop a strong sense of identification with the political community in which she lives and in which her parents are citizens. She is likely to see herself and be seen by others as someone who belongs in that community. All of these circumstances shape her relationship with the state where she is born from the outset. They give her a fundamental interest in being recognized immediately as a member of the political community. Granting her citizenship at birth is a way of recognizing that relationship and giving it legal backing.

If you accept the rationale just offered for birthright citizenship for the children of resident citizens, you can see why that practice makes moral sense, indeed why it is morally required of democratic states, given the way the world is organized politically today. But the same rationale applies, for the most part, to a child of immigrants who is born in a state where her parents have settled permanently. She, too, is likely to grow up in the state, to receive her social formation there, and to have her life chances and choices deeply affected by the state's policies. If these are reasons why the children of resident citizens should get citizenship at birth, they are also reasons why the children of settled immigrants should get citizenship at birth. So, too, with the cultivation of political agency, the child of immigrants should be taught from the beginning that she is entitled to a voice in the community where she lives and that her voice will matter. And so, too, with political identity. Like the child of resident citizens, the child of immigrants has a deep interest in seeing herself and in being seen by others as someone who belongs in the political community in which she lives.

Settled immigrants may leave, returning to their country of origin or going elsewhere and taking their children with them, but that is also true of resident citizens. This possibility does not provide a good enough reason to treat the child's membership in the political community as a contingent matter.

…

Now consider immigrants who arrive as young children. From both a sociological and a moral perspective, these children are very much like the children born in the state to immigrant parents. They belong, and that belonging should be recognized by making them citizens.

All of the reasons why children should get citizenship as a birthright if they are born in a state after their parents have settled there are also reasons why children who settle in a state at a young age should acquire that state's citizenship ….

Finally, what about immigrants who arrive as adults? The moral claims that adult immigrants have to citizenship rest on two distinct but related foundations: social membership and democratic legitimacy (Baubock 1994, Rubio-Marín 2000). Their moral claims to citizenship on the basis of social membership are similar in many respects to the moral claims that their children have, namely that human beings become members of a society over time. Immigrants who arrive in a state as adults have received their social formation elsewhere. For that reason, they do not have quite as obvious a claim to be members of the community as their children who grow up within the state and who may even be born there. Nevertheless, living in a community also makes people members. As adult immigrants settle into their new home, they become involved in a dense network of social associations. They acquire interests and identities that are tied up with other members of the society. Their choices and life chances, like those of their children, become shaped by the state's laws and policies. The longer they live there, the stronger their claims to social membership become. At some point, a threshold is passed. They have been there long enough that they simply are members of the community with a strong moral claim to have that membership officially recognized by the state by its granting of citizenship, or at least a right to citizenship if they want it.

The principles of democratic legitimacy give rise to a second basis for adult immigrants to assert a moral claim to citizenship. It is a fundamental democratic principle that everyone should be able to participate in shaping the laws by which she is to be governed and in choosing the representatives who actually make the laws, once she has reached an age where she is able to exercise independent agency. Full voting rights and the right to seek high public office are normally reserved for citizens, and I will simply assume that practice here. Therefore, to meet the requirements of democratic legitimacy, every adult who lives in a democratic political community on an ongoing basis should be a citizen, or, at the least, should have the right to become a citizen if she chooses to do so. Prior to this point, I have not emphasized the democratic legitimacy argument because I have been talking about the citizenship claims of young children who are not old enough to vote or to participate formally in politics, though they have the same sort of claim prospectively as it were, and the democratic legitimacy argument would apply to them if they reached adult-hood without receiving citizenship.

Inclusion

Even if immigrants and their descendants have appropriate access to the legal status of citizenship, they can still be marginalized economically, socially, and politically. If citizens of immigrant origin are excluded from the economic and educational opportunities that others enjoy, if they are viewed with suspicion and hostility by their fellow citizens, if their concerns are ignored and their voices not heard in political life, they are not really included in the political community. They may be citizens in a formal sense but they are not really citizens in a fuller, more meaningful sense of the term. They are not likely to see themselves or be seen by others as genuine members of the community. In many important ways, they will not belong.

That is clearly wrong from a democratic perspective. No one thinks that democratic equality requires citizens to be equal in every respect, but the democratic ideal of equal citizenship clearly entails much more than the formal equality of equal legal rights. It requires a commitment to some sort of genuine equality of opportunity in economic life and in education, to freedom from domination in social and political life, to an ethos of mutual respect, compromise, and fairness. Democratic theorists have long worried about the tyranny of majorities over minorities in democracies. Citizens of immigrant origin are one important sort of vulnerable minority. So, democratic principles require the substantive, not merely formal, inclusion of citizens of immigrant origin.

...

The deep connection between democratic principles and respect for difference is one reason why pronouncements about the "death of multiculturalism" seem so inappropriate from an ethical perspective. Multiculturalism is a term that can be used in many different ways, but often the social, cultural, and religious diversity that people attribute to multiculturalism is simply the unavoidable consequence of respecting the individual rights and freedoms that democratic states are supposed to provide to all their members (such as rights to religious freedom and rights to live one's life as one chooses so long as one is not harming others). It is dismaying how often contemporary democratic states are willing to override their own principles out of fear and anxiety about differences of culture and identity, as, for example, in the banning of various forms of religious dress and religious architecture.

Democratic justice requires even more than respect for individual rights, however .... What is at issue here is the way people behave, especially public officials but also ordinary citizens. The value of legal citizenship and formal equality is greatly reduced if the representatives of the state and the rest of the citizenry treat immigrants as outsiders who do not really belong and who have somehow acquired a status that is undeserved.

Immigrants bring change with them. That is inevitable. It is not grounds for constructing the immigrants as a threat or a problem. What is needed instead is some sort of mutual adaptation between citizens of immigrant origin and the majority in the state where the immigrants have settled.

This mutual adaptation will inevitably be asymmetrical. Citizens with deep roots in the society are always in the majority, and that matters in a democracy. They have a legitimate interest in maintaining most of the established institutions and practices. Formal and informal norms are pervasive in any complex modern society .... To a considerable extent, it is reasonable to expect that citizens of immigrant origin will learn how things work in the receiving society and reasonable to expect that they will conform to these formal and informal norms. This applies even more to their children. The children of immigrants grow up in the state to which their parents have moved. As we have seen, they should grow up as citizens, and, if the educational system functions properly, they should acquire all of the social tools required to function effectively in the society, including mastery of the official language and many other social capacities as well. This does not mean, however, that the children of immigrants can be expected to be like the children of the majority in every respect or that the immigrants themselves have to conform to every established practice.

... If citizens of immigrant origin have reasons for wanting things to be done differently, they deserve a hearing and their interests must be considered. Sometimes practices can be changed without any real loss to anyone else beyond the adjustment to the change. Sometimes it may be appropriate to leave existing rules or practices in place and provide exemptions for immigrants. Instead of pretending that the social order is culturally neutral or that it is acceptable to expect citizens of immigrant origin simply to conform to the majority, what is needed is what I have called elsewhere a conception of justice as evenhandedness, i.e. a sensitive balancing of considerations that takes the interests of citizens of immigrant origin seriously and gives them weight without assuming that those interests will always prevail (Carens 2000).

...

Irregular Migrants

Now consider immigrants who have settled without authorization, whom I will call irregular migrants. What legal rights, if any, should they have?

...

At first blush, it may appear puzzling to suggest that irregular migrants should have any legal rights. Since they are violating the state's law by settling and working without authorization, why should the state be obliged to grant them any legal rights at all? A moment's reflection, however, makes us aware that irregular migrants are entitled to at least some legal rights. Unlike medieval regimes, modern democratic states do not make criminals into outlaws—people entirely outside the pale of the law's protection. Irregular migrants are clearly entitled to the protection of their basic human rights. The right to security of one's person and property is a good example. The police are supposed to protect even irregular migrants from being robbed and killed. People do not forfeit their right to be secure in their persons and their possessions simply in virtue of being present without authorization. The right to a fair trial and the right to emergency health care are other examples.

The fact that people are legally entitled to certain rights does not mean that they actually are able to make use of those rights. It is a familiar point that irregular migrants are so worried about coming to the attention of the authorities that they are often reluctant to pursue the legal protections and remedies to which they are formally entitled, even when their most basic human rights are at stake. This creates a serious normative problem for democratic states. It makes no moral sense to provide people with purely formal legal rights under conditions that make it impossible for people to exercise those rights effectively.

What is to be done? There is at least a partial solution to this problem. States can and should build a firewall between immigration law enforcement on the one hand and the protection of basic human rights on the other. We ought to establish as a firm legal principle that no information gathered by those responsible for protecting and realizing basic human rights can be used for immigration enforcement purposes. We ought to guarantee that people will be able to pursue their basic rights without exposing themselves to apprehension and deportation. For example, if irregular migrants are victims of a crime or witnesses to one, they should be able to go to the police, report the crime, and serve as witnesses without fear that this will increase the chances of their being apprehended and deported by immigration officials. If they need emergency health care, they should be able to seek help without worrying that the hospital will disclose their identity to those responsible for enforcing immigration laws.

I cannot develop the details here, but roughly the same pattern of argument applies to many other areas of legal rights. The children of irregular migrants should be entitled to a free and compulsory education in the public schools (because that sort of education should be regarded as a basic human right for anyone living within a society). There should be a firewall between the provision of these educational services and the enforcement of immigration laws. Irregular migrants should be legally entitled to their pay if they work and should be legally entitled to the same rights and protections with regard to working conditions as other workers, because these rights and protections reflect a particular democratic state's minimum standards for acceptable working conditions within its territory. Again, these rights can only be effective if they are backed up by a firewall with respect to immigration enforcement.

As the list of rights grows, one might ask whether there are any rights that authorized immigrants have to which the unauthorized immigrants are not entitled. Given the initial assumption about the state's right to control its borders, I would say that irregular migrants are not normally morally entitled to receive the benefits of income support programs, and, of course, they are not morally entitled to stay. Even these constraints are not absolute, however. The longer one stays in a society, the stronger one's claim to membership. That applies even in the case of those who have settled without authorization. When people settle in a country, they form connections and attachments that generate strong moral claims over time. After a while, the conditions of admission become irrelevant.

...

Non-Discrimination in Admissions

Let me turn now to questions about who should get in. In what ways, if any, is the state's right to control admissions morally constrained? As with citizenship, people sometimes say that control over immigration is a fundamental feature of sovereignty and self-determination and so cannot be subject to any normative constraints external to the community's will. But no one really believes this if pressed. Democracies are not entitled to a moral carte blanche. One obvious constraint on immigration policies is the principle of non-discrimination. No one today would claim that a democratic state could legitimately bar African and Asian immigrants just because of their racial or ethnic origins, though this is precisely what Canada, the United States, and Australia did quite openly in the past. To exclude immigrants on the basis of race or ethnicity is a fundamental violation of democratic principles. The same principle applies to religion. There is no possible justification within a democratic framework for excluding people because of their religion. Today, of course, it is Islam that is the focus of exclusion, though religion is often intertwined here with race and ethnicity. Many people in Europe and North America are afraid of Muslims (as, in years past, they were afraid of Catholics and Jews). Western states know that open discrimination against Muslims is incompatible with their principles, and that is precisely why, if they do seek to exclude Muslim immigrants, they usually try to conceal what they are doing. They do not openly announce these exclusions (as they did in their racially exclusive policies in the past), but find other pretexts and justifications—couched in neutral terms but designed to have particular effects. As the old saying goes, hypocrisy is the tribute that vice pays to virtue.

...

Family Reunification

Democratic states are morally obliged to admit the immediate family members of citizens and residents ....

.... No one should be forced by the state to choose between home and family. Whatever the state's general interest in controlling immigration, that interest cannot plausibly be construed to require a complete ban on the admission of non-citizens, and cannot normally be sufficient to justify restrictions on family reunification. I add the qualifier "normally" because even basic rights are rarely absolute, and the right to family reunification cannot be conceived as absolute. States do not have an obligation to admit people whom they have good reason to regard as a threat to national security, for example, even if they are family members. But the right of people to live with their family clearly sets a moral limit to the state's right simply to set its admissions policy as it chooses. Some special justification is needed to override the claim to family reunification, not merely the usual calculation of state interests.

...

Refugees

Now consider refugees. For these purposes, let's just define refugees in broad terms as people forced to flee their home countries with no reasonable prospect of returning there in the foreseeable future. They need new homes. Who should provide those homes? What obligations do we have, if any, to admit refugees?

Note first that my discussion of refugees does not challenge the conventional view about the state's right to exercise discretionary control over immigration under normal circumstances. Rather it presupposes that view. The claim in this section is that refugees are a special case that qualifies the conventional view rather than rejecting it altogether.

In exploring our obligation to admit refugees, let's distinguish between refugees whose plight we are responsible for and refugees whose plight we are not responsible for. Clearly, we have a moral responsibility to find homes and permanent solutions for refugees who have had to flee their homes because of our actions. Americans—whether supporters or opponents of the war—recognized this in the wake of the Vietnam War and took in hundreds of thousands of refugees from Vietnam, Cambodia, and Laos. Americans have the same sort of obligation towards refugees from Iraq and Afghanistan, especially those who have been forced to flee because their lives are in danger as a result of their cooperation with Americans. This issue should have nothing to do with whether one supports or opposes these wars. It is deep moral failure that Americans have done so little in this regard.

All rich countries have responsibilities for refugee flows that we can already foresee. We should already be starting to think about who ought to take in ecological refugees—people forced to flee their homes because of global warming and the resulting changes in their physical environment. Clearly, the rich industrial states bear a major responsibility for the changes that are already taking place. It is our responsibility, not those of geographically proximate states, to find a place for these people to live. Given the divergence between what justice requires and what serves our interests in this case, I am not optimistic about the likelihood of our meeting our responsibilities, but that is no reason not to acknowledge them in a philosophical inquiry like this one.

Even if our own state is not responsible for the circumstances that led a particular group of refugees to flee, we may still have moral obligations to respond to their needs and to offer them a new place to live. The failures of democratic states to respond to the plight of Jews fleeing Hitler is one of the great shames of modern history. The Holocaust was an important part of the impetus behind the creation of the modern refugee regime, a regime that promised that no refugee would be turned away, that refugees would be able to find new homes.

Some will object that many people claim to be refugees when they are really just economic migrants, looking for a better life. There is no doubt that some of the people who seek refugee status, perhaps even many of them, would not qualify under the provisions of the Geneva Convention or other existing refugee legislation. It is also the case, however, that the rich industrial states have systematically tried to prevent everyone who might be able to file a plausible refugee claim from coming. All rich states have imposed visa requirements and carrier sanctions that are entirely indiscriminate in their exclusions (Gibney 2006). When people do arrive seeking protection, they are often met with narrow legal interpretations that deny them refugee status even though officials cannot send them back where they came from because they know that they would be in danger. They wind up in limbo for years. This is a profound moral failure, but I confess that the gap between our interests and our moral duties is so great here that I despair of a feasible solution.

Open Borders

.... Now let's explore the possibility of a direct challenge to the conventional view. Why might someone think that a commitment to democratic principles should lead rich states to open their borders much more fully?

Borders have guards and the guards have guns. This is an obvious fact of political life but one that is easily hidden from view—at least from the view of those of us who are citizens of affluent Western democracies. If we see the guards and guns at all, we find them reassuring because we think of them as there to protect us rather than to keep us out. To Africans in small, leaky vessels seeking to avoid patrol boats while they cross the Mediterranean to southern Europe or to Mexicans willing to risk death from heat and exposure in the Arizona desert to evade the fences and border patrols, it is quite different. To these people, the borders, guards, and guns are all too apparent, their goal of exclusion all too real. What justifies the use of force against such people? Perhaps borders and guards can be justified as a way of keeping out terrorists, armed invaders, or criminals. But most of those trying to get in are not like that. They are ordinary, peaceful people, seeking only the opportunity to build decent, secure lives for themselves and their families. On what moral grounds can we keep out these sorts of people? What gives anyone the right to point guns at them?

To most people, the answer to this question will seem obvious. The power to admit or exclude non-citizens is inherent in sovereignty and essential for any political community. Every state has the legal and moral right to exercise that right in pursuit of its own national interest and of the common good of the members of its community, even if that means denying entry to peaceful, needy foreigners. States may choose to be generous in admitting immigrants, but, in most cases at least, they are under no obligation to do so.

I want to challenge that view. In principle, I argue, borders should generally be open and people should normally be free to leave their country of origin and settle in another, subject only to the sorts of constraints that bind current citizens in their new country. The argument is strongest when applied to the migration of people from poor, developing countries to Europe and North America, but it applies more generally.

Citizenship in Western democracies is the modern equivalent of feudal privilege—an inherited status that greatly enhances one's life chances. Like feudal birthright privileges, the privileges that flow from birthright citizenship in Western democracies are hard to justify when one thinks about them closely. To be born a citizen of an affluent state in Europe or North America is like being born into the nobility (even though most of us belong to the lesser nobility). To be born a citizen of a poor country in Asia or Africa is (for most) like being born into the peasantry in the Middle Ages (even if there are a few rich peasants). In this context, limiting entry to the rich states is a way of protecting a birthright privilege. Reformers in the late Middle Ages objected to the way feudalism restricted freedom, including the freedom of individuals to move from one place to another in search of a better life—a constraint that was crucial to the maintenance of the feudal system. But modern practices of citizenship and state control over borders tie people to the land of their birth almost as effectively. If the feudal practices were wrong, what justifies the modern ones?

My starting point is an assumption of human moral equality, a commitment to the equal moral worth of all human beings. This does not entail the sort of cosmopolitanism that requires every agent to consider the interests of all human beings before acting or that insists that every policy or institution be assessed directly in terms of its effects on all human beings. It does, however, entail a commitment to justification through reason-giving and reflection that does not simply presuppose the validity of conventional moral views or the legitimacy of existing arrangements or our entitlement to what we have.

Freedom of movement is both an important liberty in itself and a prerequisite for other freedoms. So, we should start with a presumption for free migration. Restrictions on migration, like any use of force, need to be defended. Nevertheless, freedom of movement is only one important human interest, and it may conflict with others. There is no reason to assume that all important human freedoms are fully compatible with one another or with other basic human interests. Restrictions on particular freedoms may sometimes be justified because they will promote liberty overall or because they will promote other important human concerns, but we cannot justify restrictions on the freedom of others simply by saying that the restrictions are good for us. We have to show that they somehow take everyone's legitimate claims into account, that we are not violating our fundamental commitment to equal moral worth.

A commitment to equal moral worth may not require us to treat people identically in every way, but it does require us to respect basic human freedoms. People should be free to pursue their own projects and to make their own choices about how they live their lives so long as this does not interfere with the legitimate claims of other individuals to do likewise. To enjoy this general sort of freedom, people have to be free to move where they want (subject to the same restraints as others with regard to respect for private property, the use of public property, etc.). The right to go where you want is itself an important human freedom. It is precisely this freedom, and all that this freedom makes possible, that is taken away by imprisonment. Thus, conventional immigration controls improperly limit the freedom of non-citizens who are not threatening the basic rights and freedoms of citizens.

A commitment to equal moral worth requires some sort of basic commitment to equal opportunity. Access to social positions should be determined by an individual's actual talents and capacities, not limited on the basis of arbitrary native characteristics (such as class, race, or sex). But freedom of movement is essential for equality of opportunity. You have to be able to move to where the opportunities are in order to take advantage of them. Again, the conventional pattern of border controls greatly restricts opportunities for potential immigrants.

Finally, a commitment to equal moral worth entails some commitment to the reduction of existing economic, social, and political inequalities, partly as a means of realizing equal freedom and equal opportunity and partly as a desirable end in itself. Freedom of movement would contribute to a reduction of political, social, and economic inequalities. There are millions of people in poor states today who long for the freedom and economic opportunity they could find in Europe and North America. Many of them take great risks to come. If the borders were open, millions more would move. The exclusion of so many poor and desperate people seems hard to justify from a perspective that takes seriously the claims of all individuals as free and equal moral persons.

I have no illusions about the likelihood of rich states actually opening their borders. The primary motivation for this open borders argument is my sense that it is of vital importance to gain a critical perspective on the ways in which our collective choices are constrained, even when we cannot do anything to alter those constraints. Social institutions and practices may be deeply unjust and yet so firmly established that, for all practical purposes, they must be taken as background givens in deciding how to act in the world at a particular moment in time. For example, feudalism and slavery were unjust social arrangements that were deeply entrenched in places in the past. In those contexts, there was no real hope of transcending them in a foreseeable future. Yet, criticism was still appropriate.

Even if we have to take such arrangements as givens for purposes of immediate action in a particular context, we should not forget about our assessment of their fundamental character. Otherwise, we wind up legitimating what should only be endured. Of course, most people in democratic states think that the institutions they inhabit have nothing in common with feudalism and slavery from a normative perspective. The social arrangements of democratic states, they suppose, are just—or nearly so. It is precisely that complacency that the open borders argument is intended to undermine. For I imagine (or at least hope) that in a century or two people will look back upon our world with bafflement or shock. Just as we wonder about the moral blindness of feudal aristocrats and Southern slave owners, future generations may ask themselves how democrats today could have possibly failed to see the deep injustice of a world so starkly divided between haves and have nots and why we felt so complacent about this division, so unwilling to do what we could to change it.

The argument for open borders provides one way of bringing this deep injustice of the modern world into view. It is only a partial perspective, to be sure, because even if borders were open that would not address all of the underlying injustices that make people want to move. But it is a useful perspective because our responsibility for keeping people from immigrating is clear and direct, whereas our responsibility for poverty and oppression elsewhere often is not as obvious, at least to many people. We have to use overt force to prevent people from moving. We need borders with barriers and guards with guns to keep out people whose only goal is to work hard to build a decent life for themselves and their children. And that is something we could change. At the least, we could let many more people in. Our refusal to do so is a choice we make, and one that keeps many of them from having a chance at a decent life.

References

Carens, J.H., 2000. *Culture, citizenship, and community: A contextual exploration of justice as evenhandedness*. Oxford: Oxford University Press.

Gibney, M., 2006. A thousand little Guantanamos: Western states and measures to prevent the arrival of refugees. In: K. Tunstall, ed. *Migration, displacement, asylum: The Oxford Amnesty Lectures 2004*. Oxford: Oxford University Press, 139–160.

Hailbronner, K., 1989. Citizenship and nationhood in Germany. In: William Rogers Brubaker, ed. *Immigration and the politics of citizenship in Europe and North America: Membership and rights in international migration*. Aldershot: Edward Elgar.

Rubio-Marín, R., 2000. *Immigration as a democratic challenge*. Cambridge: Cambridge University Press.

Review and Discussion Questions

1. What are Carens' presuppositions and why do they matter for his argument?
2. Why does it make sense, morally, for newborns of citizens to be automatically granted citizenship, according to Carens? Why is this question important?
3. What types of rights and opportunities should legal immigrants have, according to Carens, and for what reasons?
4. What should be the legal rights of unauthorized (or "irregular") immigrants?
5. What are Carens' positions regarding the rights of states to endorse immigration policies that discriminate based on race or religion, refugee policy, and family reunifications?
6. What is Carens' argument about open borders?

READING: IMMIGRATION AND DEMOCRATIC PRINCIPLES: ON CARENS' ETHICS OF IMMIGRATION

SARAH SONG[*]

Sarah Song argues that Carens' account of immigration does not take sufficient account of the reasons why nations have legitimate reasons to control their immigration policies and restrict the flow of immigrants. She supports the idea of a collective right to self-determination, which casts doubt on the ideal of open borders. Sarah Song is Professor of Law and Associate Professor of Political Science at the University of California, Berkeley.

.... Carens has done more than any other political theorist or philosopher to develop the normative perspective of prospective migrants from within the liberal democratic tradition, but he has not sufficiently engaged with the other side of the argument. That is, what is at stake for the immigrant-receiving country that might justify its claim to control immigration? In particular, he has not sufficiently explored the value of political community and the principle of collective self-determination.

...

An open borders immigration policy is radically utopian, so one might associate it with a radical cosmopolitan vision of justice. Cosmopolitans hold that all human beings have equal moral worth and are entitled to equal concern and respect. Radical cosmopolitans hold the further assumption that particular human relationships—to family, friends, and compatriots—never provide independent reasons for action or suffice by themselves to generate special responsibilities. Responsibilities to one's associates are justifiable only if they can be justified by reference to the interests of all human beings viewed as moral equals. Yet Carens explicitly distances himself from cosmopolitans who think "the only thing that really matters is the protection of human rights" (p. 161). Instead, he allows for "membership-specific rights" to

---

[*] Adapted from "Immigration and Democratic Principles: On Carens' Ethics of Immigration" by Sarah Song, *Journal of Applied Philosophy* 33(4) (2016): 450–456. Reprinted with permission. The page numbers throughout this reading refer to the following book: Joseph Carens, *The Ethics of Immigration* (Oxford: Oxford University Press, 2013).

which only members of a political community are entitled in contrast to "general human rights" to which everyone is entitled ....

.... Social membership is not based on ancestry or identity but on residence and time spent living in a place. As a normative matter, it serves as the basis for claiming membership-specific rights. It is "normatively prior to" and "more fundamental" than citizenship in the sense that it "provides the foundation upon which moral claims to citizenship normally rest" (p. 160). So social membership serves as the ground for claiming citizenship and other modes of belonging in the political community, but what grounds social membership itself?

.... It is the political community, not a social group or network, to which immigrants seek inclusion in the range of cases Carens discusses in the first part of the book. His theory of social membership presupposes the value and moral relevance of the political community .... What is special about the relationship among members of a political community as opposed to other kinds of community? There are at least two distinctive features of the relationship among members of a political community: it is typically not voluntary and it involves shared subjection to the coercive power of the state. These two features raise the familiar question of the legitimacy of political authority. Linking the question of political legitimacy to Carens' discussion of immigration gives us a way to justify political community as the ground of social membership: it is not only that noncitizen migrants have "rich networks of relationships in the place where they live" (social membership claim) but also that they are subject to the coercive power of the state under which they live (political legitimacy claim).[1]

...

The Principle of Collective Self-Determination

...

I believe a compelling argument can be developed for the political community's *pro tanto* right to control immigration, based on the idea of collective self-determination. In contrast to *conclusory* reasons for action, which require us to act regardless of other considerations in play, *pro tanto* reasons are "genuine reasons for action", but they do not necessarily override competing reasons that may also be in play.[2] So, to say I have the right of freedom of movement is not to say I have an absolute right of free movement. For example, my freedom to move about typically stops at the tip of your nose and the border of your private land, unless I can make the case that there is a basic human interest that will be served by my interfering with your body or property. Similarly, to say that the state has a *pro tanto* right to control immigration recognises it has genuine and compelling reasons for controlling immigration, but they must be weighed against competing considerations. I will say more about this below.

What grounds the state's right to control immigration is the right of collective self-determination .... Collective self-determination has an internal and external dimension. Internally, collective self-determination is the idea of popular sovereignty—that a group of people ought to have independent political control over significant aspects of its common life. We can find its external dimension expressed in international law where it used to be viewed as applying only to specific territories—first, the defeated European powers and later, the overseas trust territories and colonies—and it was understood primarily as a right of secession. The idea of collective self-determination has evolved in international law to be understood as a right of all peoples to participate in processes of collective governance.[3]

What grounds the principle of self-determination itself? One strategy of justification begins with the premise that is central to Carens' case for open borders—the moral equality of persons—and seeks to derive the value of collective self-determination from it. This strategy anticipates the objection that collective self-determination is inherently incompatible with respecting human rights and responds that self-determination can be derived from the premise that all persons *qua* persons should be treated with equal concern and respect. This approach is rooted in value individualism: that individual human beings have intrinsic value and that collective entities like the state derive their value from their contributions to the lives of individuals. One might argue that the right of self-determination should be added to the list of basic human rights on the grounds that it is required to respect the moral equality of persons, for one of two reasons. The first is offered by proponents of a human right to democracy: respecting the moral equality of persons requires recognising a right to democratic self-governance. The claim here is that moral equality requires that all persons be regarded as equal participants in significant political decisions to which they are subject. A second reason starts from the premise of the moral equality of all persons but offers an instrumental argument for recognising a legal right to democracy in international law: democratic governance is so instrumentally valuable for the protection of human rights that it ought to be required for any government to be considered legitimate.

While I share the value individualism underlying these moral equality arguments, they fail to capture something fundamental about the right of self-determination: it is an irreducibly *collective* right. The right of self-determination is irreducibly collective in at least two senses. First, the agent is a collective agent—"we the people"—that is not reducible to the mere aggregation of individual members of a political community. Second, the freedom of self-determination is a collective freedom. This is what Rousseau called "moral liberty" or "obedience to the law one has prescribed for oneself". Moral liberty "alone makes man truly the master of himself" and it is only possible "in the civil state".[4] Rousseau adds another dimension to our understanding of the value of political community: it is only through political community that collective self-determination is possible. The challenge is to provide an account of the relationship of the collective and its individual members such that we can say we have a collective agent that also respects the freedom and equality of individuals.[5]

My point here is that there is a compelling argument for the state's *pro tanto* right to control immigration that is based on the principle of collective self-determination. Recognising such a right is not to say that there should be "closed borders" instead of "open borders" but rather that members of the political community have the right to shape the terms of membership and belonging within constraints, which are themselves defined by democratic principles. We can appeal to the sorts of considerations … I think we can defend the state's right to control immigration while also arguing that the right should be exercised in ways that allow for the admission of refugees and others fleeing violence and war, family reunification policies, the legalisation of irregular migrants, and other policies that Carens defends in the first part of the book.

I greatly admire the clarity, rigor, and wide-ranging scope of Carens' book. And given how controversial and complicated a topic immigration is, I also admire how he wrote the book not only for a scholarly audience but also for "ordinary men and women in North America and Europe who think of themselves as people who believe in democracy and individual rights and who want to understand the challenges posed by immigration into their societies" (p. 3). I think the first part of Carens' book is a model of democratic persuasion. In addressing ordinary men and women in North America and Europe, he implicitly accords a kind of standing to "we the people" in democratic political communities as having the power to shape the future of their communities. If we take seriously the principle of collective self-determination, we are able to see that this power is not merely a convention but a legitimate power of "we the people".

Notes

1 See Sarah Song, "The Significance of Territorial Presence and the Rights of Immigrants" in S. Fine & L. Ypi (eds) *Migration in Political Theory: The Ethics of Movement and Membership* (Oxford: Oxford University Press, 2016).
2 Charles R. Beitz, *The Idea of Human Rights* (Oxford: Oxford University Press, 2009), pp. 116–17.
3 Thomas M. Franck, "Emerging Right to Democratic Governance", *American Journal of International Law* 86 (1992), pp. 46–91, at pp. 54–5.
4 Rousseau, *Social Contract*, Book I, Chapter 8, 151.
5 I draw on Rousseau to address this challenge in Song forthcoming op. cit.

Review and Discussion Questions

1 Describe one way that Song's arguments are similar to Carens' arguments and one way in which her views differ.
2 What is the distinction between an individual right and a collective right?
3 How do you suppose Carens would respond to Song? His actual response can be found at Joseph Carens, "The Ethics of Immigration Revisited: Response to Brock, Fabre, Risse, Song," *Journal of Applied Philosophy* 3(4) (November 2016): 464–466. This special edition offers further analysis and debate of Carens' ideas as presented in his book *The Ethics of Immigration* (Oxford University Press, 2013).

READING: IMMIGRATION AND FREEDOM OF ASSOCIATION

CHRISTOPHER HEATH WELLMAN[*]

Christopher Heath Wellman defends the presumptive right of legitimate states to close borders to immigrants, based on the right of the freedom of association. Christopher Heath Wellman is Professor of Philosophy at Washington University in St. Louis.

In this article I appeal to freedom of association to defend a state's right to control immigration over its territorial borders. Without denying that those of us in wealthy

---

[*] Excerpted from "Immigration and Freedom of Association" by Christopher Heath Wellman, *Ethics* 119 (2008): 109–141. Reprinted by permission of University of Chicago Press. Some footnotes omitted.

societies may have extremely demanding duties of global distributive justice, I ultimately reach the stark conclusion that every legitimate state has the right to close its doors to all potential immigrants, even refugees desperately seeking asylum from incompetent or corrupt political regimes that are either unable or unwilling to protect their citizens' basic moral rights.

...

The Case for the Right to Closed Borders

To appreciate the presumptive case in favor of a state's right to control its borders that can be built upon the right to freedom of association, notice both that (1) freedom of association is widely thought to be important and that (2) it includes the right not to associate and even, in many cases, the right to disassociate.

That freedom of association is highly valued is evident from our views on marriage and religion. In the past, it was thought appropriate for one's father to select one's marital partner or for one's state to determine the religion one practiced, but, thankfully, those times have (largely) passed. Today, virtually everyone agrees that we are entitled to marital and religious freedom of association; we take it for granted that each individual has a right to choose his or her marital partner and the associates with whom he or she practices his or her religion. Put plainly, among our most firmly settled convictions is the belief that each of us enjoys a morally privileged position of dominion over our self-regarding affairs, a position which entitles us to freedom of association in the marital and religious realms.

Second, notice that freedom of association includes a right to reject a potential association and (often) a right to disassociate ....

In the case of matrimony, for instance, this freedom involves more than merely having the right to get married. One fully enjoys freedom of association only if one may choose whether or not to marry a second party who would have one as a partner. Thus, one must not only be permitted to marry a willing partner whom one accepts; one must also have the discretion to reject the proposal of any given suitor and even to remain single indefinitely if one so chooses .... We understand religious self-determination similarly: whether, how, and with whom I attend to my humanity is up to me as an individual. If I elect to explore my religious nature in community with others, I have no duty to do so with anyone in particular, and I have no right to force others to allow me to join them in worship.

In light of our views on marriage and religious self-determination, the case for a state's right to control immigration might seem straight-forward: just as an individual has a right to determine whom (if anyone) he or she would like to marry, a group of fellow-citizens has a right to determine whom (if anyone) it would like to invite into its political community. And just as an individual's freedom of association entitles one to remain single, a state's freedom of association entitles it to exclude all foreigners from its political community. There are at least two reasons that this inference from an individual's to a state's right to freedom of association might strike some as problematic, however. First, presumably there are morally relevant differences between individuals and groups, and these differences might explain why only individuals can have a right to self-determination. Second, even if it is possible for groups to have rights, presumably the interests a group of citizens might have in controlling immigration are nowhere near as important as an individual's interest in having a decisive say regarding whom he or she marries. Let us consider these two issues in turn.

In response to concerns about the differences between individuals and groups, let me begin by highlighting some commonly held convictions which illustrate that we typically posit at least a presumptive group right to freedom of association. Think, for instance, of the controversy that has surrounded groups like the Boy Scouts of America or the Augusta National Golf Club, both of which have faced considerable public pressure and even legal challenges regarding their rights to freedom of association. In particular, some have contested the Boy Scouts' right to exclude homosexuals and atheists, while others have criticized Augusta National's exclusion of women.[1] These cases raise a number of thorny issues. We need not adjudicate either of these conflicts here, however, because the requisite point for our purposes is a minimal one. Specifically, notice that even those who insist that the Boy Scouts should be legally forced to include gays and atheists or that Augusta National cannot justify their continued exclusion of women typically concede that there are weighty reasons in favor of allowing these groups to determine their own membership. That is, even activists lobbying for intervention usually acknowledge that there are reasons to respect these groups' rights to autonomy; the activists claim only that the prima facie case in favor of group self-determination is liable to be outweighed in sufficiently compelling instances (e.g., when society as a whole discriminates against women or privileges theism and heterosexuality over atheism and homosexuality). The key point, of course, is that questioning Augusta National's group right to determine its own membership does not require one to deny that groups have a presumptive right to freedom of association because one could simply assert that this presumptive right is vulnerable to being overridden. And because I seek at this stage to defend only a presumptive case in favor of a state's right to control its own borders, it is enough to note how uncontroversial it is to posit a group's right to freedom of association.

.... Even if one agrees that legitimate states can have rights to self-determination, though, one might still question the argument sketched above on the grounds that the intimacy of marriage makes freedom of association immeasurably more important in the marital context than in the political realm. After all, in the vast majority of cases, fellow citizens will never even meet one another.

I concede that freedom of association is much more important for individuals in the marital context than for groups of citizens in the political realm, but my argument does not rely upon these two types of freedom of association being equally important. Notice, for instance, that being able to choose the associates with whom one worships is also less important than having discretion over one's marital partner, but no one concludes from this that we need not respect freedom of association in the religious realm. It is important to recognize that I seek at this stage to establish only that there is a prima facie case in favor of each legitimate state's right to control immigration (it will be the burden of the remainder of this article to show that competing considerations are not as weighty as one might think) ....

What is more, for several reasons it seems clear that control over membership in one's state is extremely important. To see this, think about why people might care about the membership rules for their golf club. It is tempting to think that club members would be irrational to care about who else are (or could become) members; after all, they are not forced to actually play golf with those members they dislike. But this perspective misses something important. Members of golf clubs typically care about the membership rules because they care about how the club is organized and the new members have a say in how the club is organized. Some members might want to dramatically increase the number of members, for instance, because the increased numbers will mean that each individual is required to pay less. Other members might oppose expanding the membership because of concerns about the difficulty of securing desirable tee times, the wear and tear on the course, and the increased time it takes to play a round if there are more people on the course at any given time.

And if there is nothing mysterious about people caring about who are (or could become) members of their golf clubs, there is certainly nothing irrational about people being heavily invested in their country's immigration policy. Again, to note the lack of intimacy among compatriots is to miss an important part of the story. It is no good to tell citizens that they need not personally (let alone intimately) associate with any fellow citizens they happen to dislike because fellow citizens nonetheless remain political associates; the country's course will be charted by the members of this civic association. The point is that people rightly care very deeply about their countries, and, as a consequence, they rightly care about those policies which will affect how these political communities evolve. And since a country's immigration policy affects who will share in controlling the country's future, it is a matter of considerable importance.

These examples of the golf club and the political state point toward a more general lesson that is worth emphasizing: because the members of a group can change, an important part of group self-determination is having control over what the "self" is. In other words, unlike individual self-determination, a significant component of group self-determination is having control over the group which in turn gets to be self-determining. It stands to reason, then, that if there is any group whose self-determination we care about, we should be concerned about its rules for membership. This explains why freedom of association is such an integral part of the self-determination to which some groups (including legitimate states) are entitled. If so, then anyone who denies that we should care about the freedom of association of nonintimate groups would seem to be committed to the more sweeping claim that we should not care about the self-determination of any nonintimate groups. But, unless one implausibly believes that we should care only about intimate groups, then why should we suppose that only the self-determination of intimate groups matters? Thus, people rightly care deeply about their political states, despite these states being large, anonymous, and multicultural, and, as a consequence, people rightly care about the rules for gaining membership in these states. Or, put another way, the very same reasoning which understandably leads people to jealously guard their state's sovereignty also motivates them to keep an eye on who can gain membership in this sovereign state.

A second, less obvious, reason to care about immigration policy has to do with one's duties of distributive justice. As I will argue in the next section, it seems reasonable to think that we have special distributive responsibilities to our fellow citizens. If this is right, then in the same way that one might be reluctant to form intimate relationships because of the moral freight attached, one might want to limit the number of people with whom one shares a morally significant political relationship. Thus, just as golf club members can disagree about the costs and benefits of adding new members, some citizens might want to open the doors to new immigrants (e.g., in order to expand the labor force), while others would much rather forgo these advantages than incur special obligations to a greater number of people.

Finally, rather than continue to list reasons why citizens ought to care about issues of political membership, let me merely point out that citizens today obviously do care passionately about immigration. I do not insist that the current fervor over political membership is entirely rational, but it is worth noting that anyone who submits that freedom of association in this context is of no real importance is committed to labeling all those who care about this issue as patently irrational. Thus, even though the relationship among citizens does not involve the morally relevant intimacy of that between marital partners, the considerations quickly canvassed above, as well as the behavior of actual citizens, indicate that we need not conclude that control over immigration is therefore of negligible significance. If so, then neither the observation that (1) individual persons are importantly disanalogous to political states nor the fact that (2) freedom of association is much more important for individuals in the marital context than for groups of citizens in the political realm should lead us to abandon our initial comparison between marriage and immigration. As a consequence, we have no reason to abandon the claim that, like autonomous individuals, legitimate political regimes are entitled to a degree of self-determination, one important component of which is freedom of association. In sum, the conclusion initially offered only tentatively can now be endorsed with greater conviction: just as an individual has a right to determine whom (if anyone) he or she would like to marry, a group of fellow-citizens has a right to determine whom (if anyone) it would like to invite into its political community. And just as an individual's freedom of association entitles him or her to remain single, a state's freedom of association entitles it to exclude all foreigners from its political community.

.... I doubt that any one-size-fits-all immigration policy exists, and I, qua philosopher, have no special qualification to comment on the empirical information that would be relevant to fashioning the best policy for any given state. However, if anything, I am personally inclined toward more open borders. My parents were born and raised in different countries, so I would not even be here to write this article if people were not free to cross political borders. What is more, my family and I have profited enormously from having lived and worked in several different countries, so it should come as no surprise that I believe that, just as few individuals flourish in personal isolation, open borders are typically (and within limits) best for political communities and their constituents. Still, just as one might defend the right to divorce without believing that many couples should in fact separate, I defend a legitimate state's right to control its borders without suggesting that strict limits on immigration would necessarily maximize the interests of either the state's constituents or humanity as a whole. My aim is merely to show that whatever deontological reasons there are to respect freedom of association count in favor of allowing political communities to set their own immigration policy.

...

The Egalitarian Case for Open Borders

Egalitarians survey the vast inequalities among states and then allege that it is horribly unjust that people should have such dramatically different life prospects simply because they are born in different countries. The force of this view is not difficult to appreciate. Given that one's country of birth is a function of brute luck, it seems grossly unfair that one's place of birth would so profoundly affect one's life prospects. Some believe that the solution is clear: political borders must be opened, so that no one is denied access to the benefits of wealthy societies ....

Even the most zealous critics of inequality typically recommend neither that we must abolish marriage nor that wealthy couples must literally open up their marriages to the less well off. Instead, it is standard to keep separate our rights to freedom of association and our duties of distributive justice, so that wealthy people are able to marry whomever they choose and then are required to transfer a portion of their wealth to others no matter whom (or even whether) they marry .... Indeed, consider this: despite the enormous disagreement about what type of responsibilities the likes of Bill Gates and Warren Buffet have in virtue of their staggering wealth, no one alleges that, unlike the rest of us, these billionaires are required to marry poor spouses. And just as our domestic redistribution of wealth among individuals has not led us to prohibit marriage, global redistribution does not require us to open all political borders. Instead, even if we presume that wealthy societies have extensive distributive duties, these duties are distinct and can be kept separate from the societies' rights to freedom of association. To reiterate: if wealthy couples need not open up their marriages to those less well off, why think that wealthy countries must open their borders to less fortunate immigrants? Just as relatively wealthy families are required merely to transfer some of their wealth to others, why cannot wealthy countries fully discharge their global distributive duties without including the recipients in their political union, simply by transferring the required level of funds abroad?

Thus, no matter how substantial their duties of distributive justice, wealthier countries need not open their borders ....

As implausible as it might initially seem, I suggest that, even in cases of asylum seekers desperately in need of a political safe haven, a state is not required to take them in. I adopt this stance not because I am unmoved by the plight of asylum seekers but because I am not convinced that the only way to help victims of political injustice is by sheltering them in one's political territory. In my view, these people might also be helped in something like the fashion in which wealthy societies could choose to assist impoverished foreigners: by, as it were, exporting justice. Admittedly, one cannot ship justice in a box, but one can intervene, militarily if necessary, in an unjust political environment to ensure that those currently vulnerable to the state are made safe in their homelands.[2] Let me be clear: I am not suggesting that this is always easy or even advisable, nor do I assert that states are necessarily obligated to take this course of action. I claim instead that where asylum seekers are genuinely left vulnerable because their government is either unable or unwilling to protect their basic rights, then their government is illegitimate, it has no claim to political self-determination, and thus it stands in no position to protest if a third party were to intervene on behalf of (some of) its constituents ....

.... I would like to emphasize that ... most of us in affluent societies have pressing restitutive, Samaritan, and egalitarian duties to do considerably more to help the masses of people in the world tragically imperiled by poverty, and I even think that one good way to provide this assistance is to allow more immigrants from poorer countries. If sound, the arguments of this section establish merely that egalitarian considerations do not by themselves generate a moral duty which requires wealthy countries to open their borders ... [Wellman defends his argument against libertarian objections as well, which are not included in this excerpt. In a separate section, he also argues that state discretion is not unlimited: he argues against the ability of a state to set discriminatory policies that would violate the rights of equal citizenship to those who are already citizens—Ed. note.]

...

Conclusion

In this article I have tried first to construct a presumptive case in favor of a state's right to set its own immigration policy and then to defend this prima facie case against the formidable arguments that have been made on behalf of open borders. If my arguments are sound, then we should conclude that ... legitimate states are entitled to reject all potential immigrants, even those desperately seeking asylum from corrupt governments.

Notes

1 Some also object to the Boy Scouts' refusal to admit girls.
2 Of course, interventions will typically take time, and in these cases the intervening state should not return the refugees to their home state (at least without protecting them) until the intervention is successfully completed.

Review and Discussion Questions

1 What is the right to freedom of association? Is Wellman correct that this right implies a right to dissociate from others?
2 What is the analogy between the freedom to marry and choose one's religion and the state's right to control immigration? Is this a good analogy? Explain.
3 According to Wellman, why does it matter whether or not a state has a right to determine its immigration policy?
4 What is the egalitarian case for open borders, and how does Wellman respond to that position?

READING: MULTICULTURALISM: A LIBERAL PERSPECTIVE

JOSEPH RAZ[*]

In this essay, Joseph Raz weighs the value of a multicultural society along with three objections that are often made against it: that local cultures often violate the freedom of their own members; that rights should not be extended to cultures that are not

---

[*] Abridged from pp. 177–191, "Multiculturalism: A Liberal Perspective," in *Ethics in the Public Domain* by Joseph Raz. Copyright © 2001. Reprinted by permission of Oxford University Press, UK.

themselves tolerant of other cultures; and that a commitment to multiculturalism undermines the common culture necessary to sustain a national government and its commitments to its citizens. Raz's discussion of these questions leads him to inquire into the importance of culture for people's well-being, the ways in which cultures are transformed as they come in contact with others in a liberal state, and the reasons why it is difficult—but not impossible—to assess the value of different cultures. Joseph Raz is the Thomas M. Macioce Professor of Law at Columbia Law School.

1 The Case for Multiculturalism

.... Liberalism is more than just a political morality. It is a political morality which arises out of a view of the good of people, a view which emphasizes the value of freedom to individual well-being. Liberalism upholds the value for people of being in charge of their life, charting its course by their own successive choices. Much liberal thought has been dedicated to exploring the ways in which restrictions on individual choices, be they legal or social, can be removed and obstacles to choice—due to poverty, lack of education, or other limitations on access to goods—overcome. An aspect of freedom which has fallen into disrepute in some circles used to be known as the difference between freedom and license. Freedom, said Spinoza, Kant, and others, is conduct in accord with rational laws. License is arbitrary choice in disregard of reason. There is no denying that the slogan that freedom is not license was often abused, and abused to impose unreasonable restrictions on freedom. I believe, however, that, when correctly understood, this view is right. Moreover, once it is reinstated and its implications are understood, the justification of multiculturalism becomes obvious.

To a considerable degree, the claim that freedom is action in accordance with reason is no more than a consequence of the fact that freedom presupposes the availability of options to choose from and that options—all except the very elementary ones—have an internal structure, an inner logic, and we can exercise our freedom by choosing them only if we comply with their inner reason. A simple illustration will make the point. One cannot play chess by doing what one wants, say, by moving the rook diagonally. One can only play chess by following the rules of chess. Having to do so may look like a limitation of his freedom to a child. But that is the tempting illusion of license. In fact, complying with the rules of chess and of other options is a precondition of freedom, an inescapable part of its realization.

Of course, games are unlike the practice of medicine or law, the profession of teaching, or the role of parents, spouses, friends, etc. Relative to the options which make up the core of our lives, they are simple, relatively one-dimensional, and tend to be governed by relatively explicit rules. The options which make the core of our lives are complex and multidimensional, rely on complex unstated conventions, and allow extensive room for variation and improvisation. One doctor's bedside manner is not like another's. But there are things which every doctor should do, one way or another, and others no doctor may do. And so on.

Freedom depends on options which depend on rules which constitute those options. The next stage in the argument shows that options presuppose a culture. They presuppose shared meanings and common practices. Why so? the child may ask; why must I play chess as it is known to our culture, rather than invent my own game? Indeed, the wise parent will answer, there is nothing to stop you from inventing your own game. But—the philosophically bemused parent will add—this is possible because inventing one's own games is an activity recognized by our culture with its own form and meaning. What you cannot do is invent everything in your life. Why not? the child will persist, as children do. The answer is essentially that we cannot be children all the time. It is impossible to conduct one's life on the basis of explicit and articulated rules to govern all aspects of one's conduct. The density of our activities, their multiplicity of dimensions and aspects, make it impossible to consider and decide deliberately on all of them. A lot has to be done, so to speak, automatically. But to fit into a pattern that automatic aspect of behavior has to be guided, to be directed and channelled into a coherent meaningful whole. Here then is the argument.

The core options which give meaning to our lives—the different occupations we can pursue, the friendships and relationships we can have, the loyalties and commitments which we attract and develop, the cultural, sporting, or other interests we develop—are all dense webs of complex actions and interactions. They are open only to those who master them, but their complexity and the density of their details defy explicit learning or comprehensive articulation. They are available only to those who have or can acquire practical knowledge of them, that is, knowledge embodied in social practices and transmitted by habituation.

So far I have been talking of social practices which constitute options as if they come one by one. The reality is, and practically speaking has to be, different. Social practices are interlaced with each other. Those constituting language are also elements of all others; the practices of parenting and other social relationships intersect. Not only do many people naturally move from one role to another, but even where such transitions are not expected, the different family roles are at least in part defined by analogy and contrast to each other. Similarly with occupations. Our common ways of distinguishing groups of them, such as the professions, clerical jobs, those belonging to trade and commerce, or the caring professions, are each marked by common and overlapping practices. Such conglomerations of interlocking practices which constitute the range of life options open to one who is socialized in them is what cultures are. Small wonder, therefore, that membership in cultural groups is of vital importance to individuals.

Only through being socialized in a culture can one tap the options which give life a meaning. By and large one's cultural membership determines the horizon of one's opportunities, of what one may become, or (if one is older) what one might have been. Little surprise that it is in the interest of every person to be fully integrated in a cultural group. Equally plain is the importance to its members of the prosperity, cultural and material, of their cultural group. Its prosperity contributes to the richness and variety of the opportunities the culture provides access to. This is the first of three ways in which full membership in a cultural group and its prosperity affect one's own prospects in life.

The second is the fact that sameness of culture facilitates social relations and is a condition of rich and comprehensive personal relationships.[1] One particular relationship is especially sensitive to this point. Erotic attraction, economic or certain raw emotional needs can often help overcome even the greatest cultural gaps. But in one's relations with one's children and with one's parents, a common culture is an essential condition for the tight bonding we expect and desire. A policy which forcibly detaches children from the culture of their parents not only undermines the stability of society by undermining people's ability to sustain long-term intimate relations, it also threatens one of the deepest desires of most parents, the desire to understand their children, share their world, and remain close to them.

The third way in which being a member of a prosperous cultural community affects individual well-being takes us to a further dimension not yet considered. For most people, membership in their cultural group is a major determinant of their sense of who they are; it provides a strong focus of identification; it contributes to what we have come to call their sense of their own identity. This is not really surprising: given that one's culture sets the horizon of one's opportunities, it is natural to think of it as constituting one's identity. I am what I am, but equally I am what I can become or could have been. To understand a person, we need to know not just what he is but how he came to be what he is, i.e., to understand what he might have been and why he is some of those things and not others. In this way, one's culture constitutes (contributes to) one's identity. Therefore, slighting one's culture, persecuting it, holding it up for ridicule, slighting its value, etc., affects members of that group. Such conduct hurts them and offends their dignity. This is particularly offensive if it has the imprimatur of one's state or of the majority of official culture of one's country.

So this is the case for multiculturalism. It is a case which recognizes that cultural groups are not susceptible to reductive analysis in terms of individual actions or states of mind. Cultural, and other, groups have a life of their own. But their moral claim to respect and to prosperity rests entirely on their vital importance to the prosperity of individual human beings. This case is a liberal case, for it emphasizes the role of cultures as a precondition for, and a factor which gives shape and content to, individual freedom. Given that dependence of individual freedom and well-being on unimpeded membership in a respected and prosperous cultural group, there is little wonder that multiculturalism emerges as a central element in any decent liberal political program for societies inhabited by a number of viable cultural groups.

II The Dialectics of Pluralism

The Unstable Tensions of Competitive Pluralism

One of the difficulties in making multiculturalism politically acceptable stems from the enmity between members of different cultural groups, especially when they inhabit one and the same country. Such enmity is quite universal. When relations between two communities are at their most amicable, they are accompanied by disapproval of the other culture, be it for its decadence, its vulgarity, its lack of sense of humor, its treatment of women, or something else. It would be comforting to think that such enmity is sometimes justified and that in the other cases it is due to ignorance and bigotry which can be eradicated. I believe, however, that this optimism is unwarranted and that conflict is endemic to multiculturalism.

It is, in fact, endemic to value pluralism in all its forms. Belief in value pluralism is the view that many different activities and forms of life which are incompatible are valuable. Two values are incompatible if they cannot be realized or pursued to the fullest degree in a single life. In this sense, value pluralism is a familiar mundane phenomenon. One cannot be both a sprinter and a long-distance runner, both valuable activities, for they require the development of different physical abilities and also tend to suit different psychological types. Philosophers do not make good generals and generals do not make good philosophers. One cannot pursue both the contemplative and the active life, and so on and so forth.

The plurality and mutual exclusivity of valuable activities and forms or styles of life is a commonplace. It becomes philosophically significant the moment one rejects a still-pervasive belief in the reducibility of all values to one value which serves as a common denominator to the multiplicity of valuable ways of life. In our day and age, with its sometimes creeping, sometimes explicit subjectivism, the reduction is most commonly to the value of feeling happy, or having one's desires satisfied. Value pluralism is the doctrine which denies that such a reduction is possible. It takes the plurality of valuable activities and ways of life to be ultimate and ineliminable. This radically changes our understanding of pluralism. On a reductive-monistic view, when one trades the pleasures (and anxieties) of a family life for a career as a sailor, one is getting, or hoping to get, the same thing one is giving up, be it happiness, pleasure, desire satisfaction, or something else. So long as one plans correctly and succeeds in carrying out one's plans, there is no loss of any kind. One gives up the lesser pleasure one would derive from family life for the greater pleasure of life at sea. If value pluralism is correct, this view is totally wrong. What one loses is of a different kind from what one gains. Even in success there is a loss, and quite commonly there is no meaning to the judgment that one gains more than one loses. When one was faced with valuable options and successfully chose one of them, then one simply chose one way of life rather than another, both being good and not susceptible to comparison of degree.

Theoretically the plurality of valuable ways of life asserted by pluralism need not manifest itself in the same society. We may value the different cultures of Classical Greece without its opportunities and ways of life being options for us. But typically in our day and age, pluralism exists within every society, indeed within every culture. That generates conflict between competing and incompatible activities and ways of life. When valuable alternatives we do not pursue are remote and unavailable, they do not threaten our commitment to and confidence in the values manifested in our own life. But when they are available to us and pursued by others in our vicinity, they tend to be felt as a threat. I chose A over B, but was I right? Skills and character traits cherished by my way of life are a handicap for those pursuing one or another of its alternatives. I value long contemplation and patient examination; these are the qualities I require to succeed in my chosen course. Their life requires impetuosity, swift responses, and decisive action. People whose life requires these excellences despise the slow contemplative types as indecisive. They almost have to. To succeed in their chosen way they have to be committed to it and to believe that the virtues it requires should be cultivated at the expense of those which are incompatible with them. They therefore cannot regard those others as virtues for them. By the same token, it is only natural that they will value in others what they choose to emulate themselves. Hence, a variety of dismissive attitudes to the virtues of the competing ways of life. People who chose my way of life are in a similar position, only with contrary commitments.

Conflict is endemic. Of course, pluralists can step back from their personal commitments and appreciate in the abstract the value of other ways of life and their attendant virtues. But this acknowledgement coexists with, and cannot replace, the feelings of rejection and dismissiveness toward what one knows is in itself valuable. Tension is an inevitable concomitant of accepting the truth of value pluralism. And it is a tension without stability, without a definite resting-point of reconciliation of the two perspectives, the one recognizing the validity of competing values and the one hostile to them. There is no point of equilibrium, no single balance which is correct and could prevail to bring the two perspectives together. One is forever moving from one to the other from time to time.

The Transforming Effect of Multiculturalism

.... [T]he whole idea of multiculturalism is to encourage communities to sustain their own diverse cultures. But while this is so, and while it is of the essence of multiculturalism that different communities should enjoy their fair share of opportunities and resources to maintain their cultures and develop them in their own way, multiculturalism as I see it is not inherently opposed to change, not even to change which is induced by coexistence with other cultural groups. On the contrary, as we will see in what follows, multiculturalism insists that members of the different groups in a society should be aware of the different cultures in their society and learn to appreciate their strengths and respect them. This in itself leads to inevitable developments in the constituent cultures, especially those which have developed in relative isolation and ignorance of other cultures.

Furthermore, multiculturalism calls on all the constituent communities in a society to tolerate each other. Some of these communities have a culture which is itself intolerant, or whose toleration of others is inadequate. Such cultures will face a great pressure for change in a multicultural society.

Finally, as we will see, multiculturalism insists on a right of exit, that is, the right of each individual to abandon his cultural group. Many cultures do all they can to stop their members from drifting away or leaving their communities. On this front again they will find themselves under pressure to change in a liberal multicultural society.

This tension in multiculturalism, between a policy of protecting a plurality of cultures and recognizing and sometimes encouraging change in them, may surprise some. But it should not. Liberal multiculturalism does not arise out of conservative nostalgia for some pure exotic cultures. It is not a policy of conserving, fossilizing some cultures in their pristine state. Nor is it a policy fostering variety for its own sake. It recognizes that change is inevitable in today's world. It recognizes that fossilized cultures cannot serve their members well in contemporary societies, with their generally fast rate of social and economic change. Liberal multiculturalism stems from a concern for the well-being of the members of society. That well-being presupposes, as we saw, respect for one's cultural group and its prosperity. But none of this is opposed to change.

Change is resisted most when it is seen as a result of hostility of the majority, or of the dominant culture, to minority cultures. It is also resisted when it arouses fear that one's culture will disappear altogether by being diluted and then assimilated by others. It is to be hoped that in a country where multiculturalism is practiced by the government and accepted by the population, the first fear will be generally felt to be unfounded. The second is less easily laid to rest. Furthermore, it has to be admitted that liberal multiculturalism is not opposed in principle to the assimilation of one cultural group by others. In some countries, some of the constituent cultures may lose their vitality and be gradually absorbed by others. So long as the process is not coerced, does not arise out of lack of respect for people and their communities, and is gradual, there is nothing wrong in it. The dying of cultures is as much part of normal life as the birth of new ones. But the process is much slower and rarer than those who trumpet their fears of the death of their cultures proclaim. What they most commonly have in mind is resistance to change, masquerading, innocently or otherwise, as a fight for survival.

In these remarks, I display again the nonutopian character of the liberal multiculturalism which I advocate. It is nonutopian in rejecting any ideal which wishes to arrest the course of time, the pressures for change, some moment of perfection. Indeed, it refuses to have any truck with notions of perfection. Furthermore, it is nonutopian in seeing as endemic the continuation of conflict between cultures and, within every one of them, between those favoring change and those resisting it.

Do Not Take Cultures at Their Own Estimation

Finally, the earlier discussion has already brought into the open the most fundamental dialectical element in liberal multiculturalism. While it respects a variety of cultures, it refuses to take them at their own estimation. It has its own reasons for respecting cultures .... These are likely to vary from the reasons provided in most cultures for their value. For example, religious cultures will justify themselves in theological terms. The justification of those very same cultures in the eyes of liberal multiculturalism is humanistic, not theological. In particular, multiculturalism urges respect for cultures which are not themselves liberal cultures—very few are. As we shall see, it does so while imposing liberal protection of individual freedom on those cultures. This in itself brings it into conflict with the cultures it urges governments to respect. The conflict is inevitable because liberal multiculturalism recognizes and respects those cultures because and to the extent that they serve true values. Since its respect of cultures is conditional and granted from a point of view outside many of them, there is little surprise that it finds itself in uneasy alliance with supporters of those cultures, sometimes joining them in a common front while at others turning against them to impose ideals of toleration and mutual respect, or to protect the members of those very cultures against oppression by their own group.

.... The truth is that multiculturalism, while endorsing the perpetuation of several cultural groups in a single political society, also requires the existence of a common culture in which the different coexisting cultures are embedded. This is a direct result of the fact that it speaks for a society in which different cultural groups coexist in relative harmony, sharing in the same political regime. First, coexistence calls for the cultivation of mutual toleration and respect. This affects in a major way first and foremost the education of the young in all the constituent groups in the society. All of them will enjoy education in the cultural traditions of their communities. But all of them will also be educated to understand and respect the traditions of the other groups in the society. This will also apply to the majority group, where such a group exists. Its young will learn the traditions of minority groups in the society. Cultivation of mutual respect and toleration, of knowledge of the history and traditions of one's country with all its communities, will provide one element of a common culture.

A second element will result from the fact that members of all communities will interact in the same economic environment. They will tap the same job market, the same market for services and for goods. Some communities may be overrepresented in some sectors of the market, as either consumers of goods and services or their producers and providers. But by and large they will inhabit the same economy. This means that they will have to possess the same mathematical, literary, and other skills required for effective participation in the economy.

Finally, members of all cultural groups will belong to the same political society. They will all be educated and placed to enjoy roughly equal access to the sources of political power and to decision-making positions. They will have to acquire a common political language, and common conventions of conduct, to be able to compete effectively for resources and to be able to protect their group as well as individual interests in a shared political arena. A common political culture will be the third major component of a common culture that will be generated in liberal multicultural societies ....

It remains the case that, while the liberal common culture of pluralistic societies remains to be developed, a swift social change toward multiculturalism may well severely test the existing bonds of solidarity in a society and threaten disintegration or a backlash of rabid nationalism. This, while it does not pose an objection of principle to liberal multiculturalism, requires great caution in the method and speed with which multicultural policies are implemented.

III Final Words

Multiculturalism, in the sense of the existence within the same political society of a number of sizeable cultural groups wishing and in principle able to maintain their distinct identity, is with us to stay. Insofar as one can discern the trend of historical events, it is likely to grow in size and importance. Liberal multiculturalism, as I called it, as a normative principle affirms that in the circumstances of contemporary industrialist or post-industrialist societies, a political attitude of fostering and encouraging the prosperity, cultural and material, of cultural groups within a society, and respecting their identity, is justified by considerations of freedom and human dignity. These considerations call on governments to take action which goes beyond that required by policies of toleration and nondiscrimination. While incorporating policies of nondiscrimination, liberal multiculturalism transcends the individualistic approach which they tend to incorporate and recognizes the importance of unimpeded membership in a respected and flourishing cultural group for individual well-being.

This doctrine has far-reaching ramifications. It calls on us to reconceive society, changing its self-image. We should learn to think of our societies as consisting not of a majority and minorities but of a plurality of cultural groups. Naturally such developments take a long period to come to fruition, and they cannot be secured through government action alone, as they require a widespread change in attitude ....

The more concrete policies, which become appropriate gradually, as developments justify, include measures like the following.

1. The young of all cultural groups should be educated, if their parents so desire, in the culture of their groups. But all of them should also be educated to be familiar with the history and traditions of all the cultures in the country and an attitude of respect for them should be cultivated.
2. The different customs and practices of the different groups should, within the limits of toleration we have explored earlier, be recognized in law and by all public bodies in society, as well as by private companies and organizations which serve the public, be it as large employers, providers of services, or otherwise. At the moment, petty intolerance is rife in many countries. In Britain, people still have to fight to be allowed to wear traditional dress to school or to work, to give one example.
3. It is crucial to break the link between poverty, undereducation, and ethnicity. So long as certain ethnic groups are so overwhelmingly overrepresented among the poor, ill-educated, unskilled, and semi-skilled workers, the possibilities of cultivating respect for their cultural identity, even the possibility of members of the group being able to have self-respect and to feel pride in their cultures, are greatly undermined.
4. There should be a generous policy of public support for autonomous cultural institutions, such as communal charities, voluntary organizations, libraries, museums, theatre, dance, musical or other artistic groups. Here (as in education) the policy calls for allocation of public resources. In the competition for them, the size of the groups concerned is an important factor. It works in two ways. By and large, it favors the larger groups with a more committed membership. But it also calls for disproportionate support for small groups which are strong enough to pass the viability test. Given that the overheads are significant, the per capita cost of support for small viable cultural groups is greater than for large ones.
5. Public space, streets, squares, parks, shopping arcades, etc. (as well as air space on television) should accommodate all the cultural groups. Where they differ in their aesthetic sense, in their preferences for colors, patterns, smells, music, noise, and speed, the solution may involve dividing some public spaces between them, as often happens without direction in ethnic neighborhoods, while preserving others as common to all.

Of course, all such measures are designed to lead to relatively harmonious coexistence of nonoppressive and tolerant communities. They therefore have their limits. But it is important not to use false standards as tests of the limits of toleration. The fact that the Turkish government does not tolerate certain practices of the Kurds, let us say, in Turkey is no reason why the Kurds from Turkey should not be allowed to continue with [those] practices when they settle in Europe. Similarity, the fact that tolerating certain practices of immigrant communities will lead to a change in the character of some neighborhoods or public spaces in one's country is no reason for suppressing them. The limits of toleration are in denying communities the right to repress their own members, in discouraging intolerant attitudes to outsiders, in insisting on making exit from the community a viable option for its members. Beyond that, liberal multiculturalism will also require all groups to allow their members access to adequate opportunities for self-expression and participation in the economic life of the country and the cultivation of the attitudes and skills required for effective participation in the political culture of the community.

The combined effect of such policies is that liberal multiculturalism leads not to the abandonment of a common culture but to the emergence of a common culture which is respectful toward all the groups of the country and hospitable to their prosperity.

Notes

1 Please do not understand this point as suggesting that people belonging to two nations, or two social classes, say a Frenchman and a Dutch person, cannot be friends. What I am suggesting is that there is a considerable common cultural background to people from diverse but culturally neighbouring groups.

Review and Discussion Questions

1 What is the case for multiculturalism? What does it have to do with the importance of membership?
2 In what way does multiculturalism both protect cultures and also encourage change in them?
3 Describe how Raz thinks majority cultures should deal with inferior cultures that oppress their members.
4 How can solidarity be maintained in a multicultural society?
5 Is Raz right in thinking that meanings depend on how a culture understands something but also that there are genuinely inferior cultures? Explain.

READING: REASON BEFORE IDENTITY

AMARTYA SEN[*]

In this essay, Amartya Sen begins with an event that raised for him the issue of his own identity and the idea that one's identity is a complicated, complex, and important question. He resists both those who see people's identity as vacuous and their actions as self-interested as well as those who suggest identity is controlled by society and people's social identities. Communitarians, he argues, put too much emphasis on the role of identity and too little on people's ability to reason and shape their identities in ways they choose. Given the possibilities of alternative identities, people can exercise choice; they are not born into an identity or forced to discover a preexisting identity. He concludes with a discussion of the potentially dangerous consequences flowing from those who ignore or underemphasize the role reasoning plays in identity. Amartya Sen is Thomas W. Lamont University Professor and Professor of Economics and Philosophy at Harvard University.

Recently, when I was returning from a short trip abroad, the Immigration Officer at Heathrow, who examined my Indian passport, posed a philosophical question of

---

[*] Abridged from *Reason Before Identity* by Amartya Sen. Copyright © 1999. Reprinted by permission of Oxford University Press, UK.

some intricacy. Referring to my address, viz. Master's Lodge, Trinity College, Cambridge, he asked me whether the Master was a close friend of mine. This gave me pause since it compelled me, of course, to examine whether ... I could legitimately claim to be a friend of myself. On reflection, I came to the conclusion that I was a friend—indeed, a close friend (a view corroborated further by the fact that when I say silly things I can immediately see that, with friends like me, I don't need any enemies). Since all this took some time to resolve, the Immigration Officer wanted to know why exactly I hesitated: was there some impropriety involved in my being in Britain?

Well, that practical issue was eventually resolved, but the conversation was a reminder, if one were needed, that identity can be a complicated matter. There is, of course, no great problem in convincing oneself that an object is identical with itself; Wittgenstein has even offered the view that "there is no finer example of a useless proposition."[1] And yet it is not trivial to ask what relations obtain between an object and itself, other than being identical, and also how two identical objects relate to each other.

When we shift our attention from the notion of *being identical* to that of *sharing an identity* and to the idea of *identifying* oneself with others of a particular group, which is central to some of the common uses of the idea of identity, the complexity increases further. It is this difficult problem—of social identity and its role and implications—with which this talk is concerned.

.... While economists have typically been over-skeptical of the role of social identity, it is possible to see evidence of "underskepticism" (if I may coin such a phrase) in some social analysis, concerning the precise reach of social identity and its allegedly overpowering influence. There is, in particular, a fundamental question about how our identities emerge—whether by choice or by passive recognition—and how much reasoning can enter into the development of identity. This question is important in many contexts, including the assessment of communitarian conceptions of rationality (and the corresponding critique of communicable reasoning) and of ethics (including universalizable theories of justice).

Indeed, communitarianism in various forms—strong as well as mild—has been in the ascendancy over the last few decades in contemporary social, political, and moral theorizing, and the dominant and compelling role of social identity in governing behavior as well as knowledge has been forcefully championed. In fact, the advocacy of communitarian perspectives has grown with a relentlessness that bears comparison with the progress of global warming and the depletion of the ozone layer. In many up-to-date theories, social identity figures prominently as the principal determinant of people's understanding of the world, their modes of reasoning and conceptions of rationality, their behavioral norms and practices, and their personal moralities and political commitments. And when these theories of people's perceptions and behavior are combined, as they are in some theories, with the view that the nature of rationality, knowledge, and morality must be entirely parasitic on the subjects' perceptions, the determining role of social identities is, then, given a commanding role in the disciplines of epistemology and ethics.

In the more demanding versions, these theories are amazingly assertive. We are told that we cannot invoke any criterion of rational behavior other than those that obtain in the community to which the people involved belong. Any reference to rationality yields the retort "*which* rationality?" or "*whose* rationality?" It is also argued not only that the explanation of a person's moral judgments must be based on the values and norms of the community of which the person is a part, but also that these judgments can be ethically assessed *only within* those values and norms (a denial of the claims of competing norms on the attention of the person). Various versions of these far-reaching claims have been forcefully aired and powerfully advocated in theories that give social identity a masterful role.

In the political context, this approach has had the effect of rejecting intercultural normative judgments about behavior and institutions, and sometimes even of undermining the possibility of cross-cultural exchange and understanding. The political aspects can be explicit and transparent or they may be implicit and indirect but nevertheless influential, for example in the defense of particular customs and traditions on such matters as women's unequal social position or the use of particular modes of traditional punishment. There is a tendency here to split up the large world into little islands that are not within normative reach of each other ....

Delineating Roles and Choice Over Identities

I would now like to turn to a different but related issue concerning the need for choice and reasoning in social identity. In examining this need, it is useful to consider two rather different ways in which social identity can be important: its *delineating* role and its *perceptual* function. The latter—the perceptual function—is concerned with the way a member of a community may perceive the world, understand reality, accept norms, and argue about what is to be done. This is a big issue, and I shall take it up after I have considered the other role of social identity, that of delineation.

The delineating role of social identity can be an important part of an adequate formulation of any idea of the social good and even in defining the reach and limits of social concern and appropriate conduct. Any formulation of the notion of the social good cannot but raise the question: good of *which* group of individuals? This is a demarcational requirement concerning the domain of social choice. In any diagnosis of the social good, there is the question as to who is to be included in that aggregative exercise, and this task cannot be divorced from the exercise of social identification. The converse may also hold, and, as Charles Taylor has observed in an illuminating discussion of the role of political identity, "the identification of the citizen with the republic as a common enterprise is essentially the recognition of a common good."[2]

It is not hard to see that delineation leaves room for choice and reasoning. To insist on a particular canonical group identity without reasoned support would beg the question: Why focus on this group only rather than another, of which the person may also be a member? For any particular map of group partitioning, two distinct questions can be raised. First, a person may ask whether the lines may be redrawn on the same map. Should a person see herself as European and not just Italian or just German? Or as Irish, and not just Irish Catholic or Irish Protestant? There are substantial issues to discuss here.

Second, there are different maps and different procedures of partitioning people. A person can simultaneously have the identity of being, say, an Italian, a woman, a feminist, a vegetarian, a novelist, a fiscal conservative, a jazz fan, and a Londoner. The possibility of such multiple identities is obvious enough, and their varying context-dependent relevance is no less evident. If this person gets involved in the promotion of classical jazz throughout the world, her identity as a jazz lover may be more relevant than her identity as a Londoner, which however may be more crucial when she makes a telling criticism of the way London transport is organized. The context dependence of relevant identity is elegantly illustrated in a scene in Tom Stoppard's play *Jumpers,* when Inspector Bones, investigating a murder, asks the professor of philosophy, extremely suspiciously, who the assembled people are, to which the philosopher replies: "Logical positivists, mainly."[3]

Given plural delineations, alternative identities can compete for relevance, even in a given context. For example, in considering a problem of London transport, a person's loyalties as a Londoner keen on improving the transport of her city may conflict with her convictions as a fiscal conservative keen on keeping public expenses severely under control. Sometimes the conflicts of identities involving attitudes to rather grander issues may take a more extensive form. For example, being born in a particular country, or within a particular culture, need not eliminate the possibility of adapting a perspective or a loyalty that is very different from that of the bulk of the people in that country or in that culture.

Discovery or Choice?

Communitarian approaches often tend to acquire persuasive power by making a definitive communal identity a matter of self-realization, not of choice. As Michael Sandel presents this claim with admirable clarity, "community describes just what they *have* as fellow citizens but also what they *are,* not a relationship they choose (as in a voluntary association) but an attachment they discover, not merely an attribute but a constituent of their identity."[4] In this reading—what Sandel calls the "constitutive" conception of community—identity comes before reasoning for choice: "the self came by its ends," as he puts it, "not by choice but by reflection, as knowing (or inquiring) subject to object of (self-) understanding."[5] On this view, a person's identity is something he or she detects rather than determines. Social organization can then be seen, as Crowley puts it, as attempts to "create opportunities for men to give voice to what they have *discovered* about themselves and the world and to persuade others of its worth."[6]

It is, however, difficult to imagine that we can really have no substantial choice between alternative identifications and must just "discover" our identity. It is hard to rule out the possibility that we are constantly making these choices. Often such choices are quite explicit, like when Mohandas Gandhi deliberately decides to give priority to his identification with Indians seeking independence from British rule over his identity as a trained barrister pursuing English legal justice, or when E. M. Forster famously concludes, "if I had to choose between betraying my country and betraying my friend, I hope I should have the guts to betray my country."[7] Quite often, however, the choice is implicit and obscure, and less grandly defended, but it may be no less real for that reason.

At this point, I should make a few clarificatory explanations to prevent misunderstandings of what is being claimed. First, the importance of choice does not entail that any choice we make must be once-for-all and permanent. Indeed, our loyalties and self-definitions often oscillate, in ways that are well illustrated by Albert Hirschman's analysis of "shifting involvements."[8] As Emma Rothschild notes, such oscillation may be "a continuous and prized quality of civil society."[9] Choosing can be, to quite an extent, a repeated process.

Second, it is not my purpose to claim that the choices we have are quite unrestricted. There are limits to what we can choose to identify with, and perhaps stronger limits still in persuading others to take us as something other than what they take us to be. A Jewish person in Nazi Germany could have longed to be taken as a gentile to escape persecution or extermination, and an African American facing a lynch mob could have sought a different characterization. But these redefinitions may not be within the person's feasible options. In fact, the persons involved may not even be able to see themselves as gentile or white, even if they were inclined to choose to try to do this. The real options we have about our identity are always limited by our looks, our circumstances, and our background and history.

It is, however, not news that choices are always within certain constraints, and any choice theorist knows that characterizing the constraints faced by the chooser is the first step in understanding any choice that is being made. The point at issue is whether choices exist at all and to what extent they are substantial. The claim that I am presenting here is that they can be quite substantial.

There is a third issue to be addressed here. We can, of course, "discover" our identity in the sense that we may find out that we have a connection or a descent of which we were previously unaware. A person may discover that he is Jewish ....

To recognize this is not the same as making identity just a matter of discovery, even when the person discovers something very important about herself. There are still issues of choice to be faced. The person who discovers that she is Jewish would still have to decide what importance to give to that identity compared with other competing identities—of nationality, class, political belief, and so on. ... Choices have to be made even when discoveries occur.

Responsibility and Herd Behavior

Indeed, I would argue that the belief that we have no choice on these matters is not only mistaken but may have very pernicious implications that extend far beyond communitarian critiques, or for that matter the soundness of liberal theories of justice. If choices do exist and yet it is assumed that they are not there, the use of reasoning may well be replaced by uncritical acceptance of conformist behavior, no matter how rejectable they may be. Typically, such conformism may have conservative implications, protecting old customs and practices from intelligent scrutiny. Indeed, traditional inequalities, such as unequal treatment of women in sexist societies, often survive by making the respective identities, which may include subservient roles of the traditional underdog, matters for unquestioning acceptance rather than reflective examination. But the unquestioned presumptions are merely unquestioned—not unquestionable.

Many past practices and assumed identities have crumbled in response to questioning and scrutiny. Traditions can shift even within a particular country and culture. It is perhaps worth recollecting that John Stuart Mill's *The Subjection of Women*, published in 1874, was taken by many of his British readers to be the ultimate proof of his eccentricity; as a matter of fact, interest on the subject was so little that this is the only book of Mill's on which his publisher lost money.

However, the unquestioning acceptance of a social identity may not always have conservative implications. It can also involve a radical *shift* in identity—accepted as a piece of alleged "discovery" rather than as reasoned choice. Some of my own disturbing memories as I was entering my teenage years in India in the mid-1940s relate to the massive identity shift that followed divisive politics. People's identities as Indians, as Asians, or as members of the human race seemed to give way—quite suddenly—to sectarian identification with Hindu, Muslim, or Sikh communities. The broadly Indian of January was rapidly and unquestioningly transformed into the narrowly Hindu or finely Muslim of March. The carnage that followed had much to do with unreasoned herd behavior by which people, as it were, "discovered" their new divisive and belligerent identities and failed to subject the process to critical examination. The same people were suddenly different.

If some of us today continue to be suspicious of the communitarian approach, despite its attractive features, including the focus on within-group solidarity and on benign affection for others in the group, there is some historical reason for it. Indeed, within-group solidarity can go hand in hand with between-group discord. I believe that similarly unreasoned identity shifts have occurred and are continuing to occur in different parts of the world—in the former Yugoslavia, in Rwanda, in Congo, in Indonesia—in varying forms, with devastating effects. There is something deeply debilitating about denying choice when choice exists, for it is an abdication of responsibility to consider and assess how one should think and what one should identify with. It is a way of falling prey to unreasoned shifts in alleged self-knowledge based on a false belief that one's identity is to be discovered and accepted rather than examined and scrutinized.

This issue is important also in preventing what Anthony Appiah has called "new tyrannies" in the form of newly asserted identities, which may have important political roles but can also tyrannize by eliminating the claims of other identities that we may also have reason to accept and respect. Appiah considers this particularly in the context of the identity of being black—an African American—which has certainly been an important political ingredient in seeking racial justice but which can also be oppressive if it is taken to be the only identity a black person has, with no room being given to other claims. Appiah puts the issue thus:

> In policing this imperialism of identity—an imperialism as visible in racial identities as anywhere else—it is crucial to remember always that we are not simply black or white or yellow or brown, gay or straight or bisexual, Jewish, Christian, Moslem, Buddhist, or Confucian but we are also brothers and sisters; parents and children; liberals, conservatives, and leftists; teachers and lawyers and auto-makers and gardeners; fans of the Padres and the Bruins; amateurs of grunge rock and lovers of Wagner; movie buffs; MTV-holics, mystery-readers; surfers and singers; poets and pet-lovers; students and teachers; friends and lovers. Racial identity can be the basis of resistance to racism—and though we have made great progress, we have further still to go—let us not let our racial identities subject us to new tyrannies.[10]

To deny plurality, choice, and reasoning in identity can be a source of repression, new *and* old, as well as a source of violence and brutality. The need for delineation, important as it is, is perfectly compatible with the recognition of plurality, of conflicting loyalties, of demands of justice and mercy, as well as of affection and solidarity. Choice is possible and important in individual conduct and social decisions, even if we remain oblivious of it.

Perceptions and Culture

I turn now to the perceptual function of social identity. There can be little doubt that the communities or cultures to which a person belongs can have a major influence on the way he or she sees a situation or views a decision. In any explanatory exercise, note has to be taken of local knowledge, rational norms, and particular perceptions and values that are common in a specific community. The empirical case for this recognition is obvious enough.

Does this recognition undermine the role of choice and reasoning? Can this be an argument in the direction of the "discovery" view of identity? How can we reason, the argument may run, about our identity, since *the way we reason* must be independent of what identity we have? We cannot really reason before an identity is established.

I believe this argument is mistaken, but it is important to examine it with some care. It is perfectly obvious that one cannot reason from nowhere. But this does not imply that no matter what the antecedent associations of a person is, they must remain unrejectable and permanent. The alternative to the "discovery" view is not choice from positions "unencumbered" with any identity (as communitarian expositions often seem to imply), but choices that continue to exist in any encumbered position one happens to occupy. Choice does not require jumping out of nowhere into somewhere.

It is certainly true that the way we reason can well be influenced by our knowledge, by our presumptions, and by our attitudinal inclinations regarding what constitutes a good or a bad argument. This is not in dispute. But it does not follow from this that we can reason only within a particular cultural tradition, with a specific identity.

First, even though certain basic cultural attitudes and beliefs may *influence* the nature of our reasoning, they are unlikely to *determine* it fully. There are various influences on our reasoning, and we need not lose our ability to consider other ways of reasoning just because we identify with, and have been influenced by membership of, a particular group. Influence is not the same thing as complete determination, and choices do remain despite the existence—and importance—of cultural influences.

Second, the so-called cultures need not involve any *uniquely* defined set of attitudes and beliefs that can shape our reasoning. Indeed, many of these "cultures" contain very considerable internal variations, and different attitudes and beliefs may be entertained within the same broadly defined culture. For example, Indian traditions are often taken to be intimately associated with religion, and indeed in many ways they are, and yet Sanskrit and Pali have larger literatures on systematic atheism and agnosticism than perhaps in any other classical language—Greek, Roman, Hebrew, or Arabic.

An adult and competent person has the ability to question what has been taught to her—even day in and day out. While circumstances may not encourage a person to do such questioning, the ability to doubt and to question is within each person's capacity. Indeed, it is not absurd to claim that being able to doubt is one of the things that make us human beings, rather than unquestioning animals. I remember with some warmth and amusement a Bengali poem of early nineteenth century, by Raja Ram Mohan Ray, which I encountered as a child: "Just imagine how terrible the day of your death will be; others will go on speaking, and you will not be able to contradict." There is perhaps some plausibility in that characterization of the central feature of death. I may not go so far as to argue for the slogan "dubito ergo sum" but that thought is not very distant either.

These points are so elementary that they would be embarrassing to assert had the opposite not been frequently presumed, either explicitly or by implication. In the context of cultural debates applied to the West itself, it is in fact most uncommon to dispute any of these rather obvious claims. It is hardly ever presumed that just because a person is born English or comes from an Anglican background or from a Conservative family or has been educated in a religious school, she must inescapably think and reason *within* the general attitudes and beliefs of the respective groups. When, however, other cultures are considered, say in Africa or Asia, the constraints imposed by the respective cultures are taken to be much more binding and restrictive. Since the assumption of tradition-given constraints is very often presented by advocates of cultural pluralism and by exponents of the importance of a multicultural world (an ideal that has, for very good reasons, a widespread appeal and plausibility), the assumed constraints are frequently seen not as something that would limit and restrict the freedom of the individual to choose how she would want to live but as a positive assertion of the importance of cultural authenticity and genuineness. The constrained individuals are then seen as heroic resisters of Westernization and defenders of native tradition.

This kind of reading leads to at least two different questions. First, if the presumption of the lack of choice about identity were entirely correct, how could it be appropriate to see in the traditionalism of the people involved a deliberate defense of local culture? If people have a real choice and choose not to depart from their local tradition, then in their traditionalism—*thus chosen*—we may be able to read a deliberate defense and even perhaps a heroic resistance. But how can that conclusion be sustained if, as is standardly assumed, the people had no choice anyway? The status of reasoned choice cannot be thrust upon conformity without reasoning. The linkage with choice and reasoning is important not only for reformers but also for traditionalists resisting reform.

Second, what evidence is there that people born in a non-Western tradition lack the ability to develop any other form of identity? The opportunity to consider any alternative may not, of course, arise, and then ignorance and unfamiliarity may prevent any actual act of choice. An Afghan girl today, kept out of school and away from knowledge of the outside world, may indeed not be able to reason freely. But that does not establish an *inability* to reason, only a lack of opportunity to do so.

I would argue that important as the perceptual role of community and identity may be, it cannot be presumed that the possibility of reasoned choice is ruled out by these influences. This is not to deny that the influences that operate on a person may well be, in practice, very restrictive. They certainly can restrain and limit. But to see in them a heroic defense of traditionalism, rather than a bondage of unreason, would be a mistake.

Notes

1. "A thing is identical with itself."—There is no finer example of a useless proposition, which yet is connected with a certain play of the imagination: Anthony Kenny, ed., *The Wittgenstein Reader* (Oxford: Blackwell, 1994), p. 102.
2. Charles Taylor, *Philosophical Arguments* (Cambridge, MA: Harvard University Press, 1995), pp. 191–92.
3. Tom Stoppard, *Jumpers* (London: Faber & Faber, 1972), p. 41.
4. Michael Sandel, *Liberalism and the Limits of Justice* (Cambridge: Cambridge University Press, 1982), p. 150. This is Sandel's statement of a radical communitarian position. He offers less radical versions as well.
5. Ibid., p. 152; the parentheses are Sandel's own.
6. B. Crowley, *The Self, the Individual and the Community* (Oxford: Clarendon Press, 1987), p. 295.
7. E. M. Forster, *Two Cheers for Democracy.* (New York: Harcourt, Brace, 1951).
8. Albert Hirschman, *Shifting Involvements* (Princeton, NJ: Princeton University Press, 1982).
9. Emma Rothschild, "The Quest for World Order," *Daedalus* 124 (Summer 1995), p. 81.
10. K. Anthony Appiah, "Race, Culture, Identity: Misunderstood Connections" in K. Anthony Appiah and Amy Gutman, *Color Consciousness: The Political Morality of Race* (Princeton, NJ: Princeton University Press, 1996), pp. 103–4.

Review and Discussion Questions

1. How has economic theory assumed identity is irrelevant for understanding people's actions?
2. What shapes people's understanding of the world, according to communitarians?
3. What is the difference between the delineating and perceptual roles of social identity? How does delineation allow for choice?
4. Why does Sen deny that people lack the ability to choose their identities? In what respects are the choices restricted?
5. In what sense do people discover their identities, and in what way is that not true?
6. What are the dangerous implications of the communitarians' emphasis on the discovery of identity and of their de-emphasis on the importance of reason?
7. Discuss the perceptual function of social identity. Does it weaken the importance of reason in favor of the idea that identities are discovered? Explain.

READING: ASSIMILATION AND CULTURAL IDENTITY

WISCONSIN V. YODER[*]

This well-known case arose in response to a Wisconsin law requiring all children to be sent to school until the age of sixteen. The Amish parents of two children, ages fourteen and fifteen, refused to comply, arguing that compulsory school attendance beyond eighth grade violated their constitutional right of "free exercise" of religion protected by the First Amendment to the U.S. Constitution. The case went all the way to the Supreme Court, and the Court overturned the law, upholding the right of the Amish parents to guide the religious future and education of their children.

---

[*] *Wisconsin v. Yoder*, 406 U.S. 205 (1972).

In his dissenting opinion, Justice Douglas discusses problems associated with allowing parents to impose their religious notions on children as well as the possible effects of the Court's ruling on the children's educational development.

Mr. Chief Justice Burger

On complaint of the school district administrator for the public schools, respondents [Mr. and Mrs. Yoder] were charged, tried, and convicted of violating the compulsory-attendance law in Green County Court and were fined the sum of $5 each. Respondents defended on the ground that the application of the compulsory-attendance law violated their rights under the First and Fourteenth Amendments. The trial testimony showed that respondents believed, in accordance with the tenets of Old Order Amish communities generally, that their children's attendance at high school, public or private, was contrary to the Amish religion and way of life. ... The State stipulated that respondents' religious beliefs were sincere.

In support of their position, respondents presented as expert witnesses scholars on religion and education whose testimony is uncontradicted. They expressed their opinions on the relationship of the Amish belief concerning school attendance to the more general tenets of their religion, and described the impact that compulsory high school attendance could have on the continued survival of Amish communities as they exist in the United States today ....

Amish beliefs require members of the community to make their living by farming or closely related activities. Broadly speaking, the Old Order Amish religion pervades and determines the entire mode of life of its adherents ....

Amish objection to formal education beyond the eighth grade is firmly grounded in these central religious concepts. They object to the high school, and higher education generally, because the values they teach are in marked variance with Amish values and the Amish way of life; they view secondary school education as an impermissible exposure of their children to a "worldly" influence in conflict with their beliefs. The high school tends to emphasize intellectual and scientific accomplishments, self-distinction, competitiveness, worldly success, and social life with other students. Amish society emphasizes informal learning-through-doing; a life of "goodness," rather than a life of intellect; wisdom, rather than technical knowledge; community welfare, rather than competition; and separation from, rather than integration with, contemporary worldly society.

Formal high school education takes [Amish children] away from their community, physically and emotionally, during the crucial and formative adolescent period of life. During this period, the children must acquire Amish attitudes favoring manual work and self-reliance and the specific skills needed to perform the adult role of an Amish farmer or housewife. They must learn to enjoy physical labor. ... And, at this time in life, the Amish child must also grow in his faith and his relationship to the Amish community if he is to be prepared to accept the heavy obligations imposed by adult baptism ....

The Amish do not object to elementary education through the first eight grades as a general proposition because they agree that their children must have basic skills in the "three Rs" in order to read the Bible, to be good farmers and citizens, and to be able to deal with non-Amish people when necessary in the course of daily affairs. They view such a basic education as acceptable because it does not significantly expose their children to worldly values or interfere with their development in the Amish community during the crucial adolescent period ....

On the basis of such considerations, [an expert] testified that compulsory high school attendance could not only result in great psychological harm to Amish children, because of the conflicts it would produce, but would also, in his opinion, ultimately result in the destruction of the Old Order Amish church community as it exists in the United States today ....

In order for Wisconsin to compel school attendance beyond the eighth grade against a claim that such attendance interferes with the practice of a legitimate religious belief, it must appear either that the State does not deny the free exercise of religious belief by its requirement, or that there is a state interest of sufficient magnitude to override the interest claiming protection under the Free Exercise Clause ....

A way of life, however virtuous and admirable, may not be interposed as a barrier to reasonable state regulation of education if it is based on purely secular considerations; to have the protection of the Religion Clauses, the claims must be rooted in religious belief. Although a determination of what is a "religious" belief or practice entitled to constitutional protection may present a most delicate question, the very concept of ordered liberty precludes allowing every person to make his own standards on matters of conduct in which society as a whole has important interests. Thus, if the Amish asserted their claims because of their subjective evaluation and rejection of the contemporary secular values accepted by the majority, much as Thoreau rejected the social values of his time and isolated himself at Walden Pond, their claims would not rest on a religious basis. Thoreau's choice was philosophical and personal rather than religious, and such belief does not rise to the demands of the Religion Clauses.

Giving no weight to such secular considerations, however, we see that the record in this case abundantly supports the claim that the traditional way of life of the Amish is not merely a matter of personal preference, but one of deep religious conviction, shared by an organized group, and intimately related to daily living. That the Old Order Amish daily life and religious practice stem from their faith is shown by the fact that it is in response to their literal interpretation of the Biblical injunction from the Epistle of Paul to the Romans, "be not conformed to this world."

Their way of life in a church-oriented community, separated from the outside world and "worldly" influences, their attachment to nature and the soil, is a way inherently simple and uncomplicated, albeit difficult to preserve against the pressure to conform. Their rejection of telephones, automobiles, radios, and television, their mode of dress, of speech, their habits of manual work do indeed set them apart from much of contemporary society; these customs are both symbolic and practical ....

The State advances two primary arguments in support of its system of compulsory education. It notes, as Thomas Jefferson pointed out early in our history, that some degree of education is necessary to prepare citizens to participate effectively and intelligently in our open political system if we are to preserve freedom and independence. Further, education prepares individuals to be self-reliant and self-sufficient participants in society. We accept these propositions.

However, the evidence adduced by the Amish in this case is persuasively to the effect that an additional one or two years of formal high school for Amish children in place of their long-established program of informal vocational education would do little to serve those interests ....

It is one thing to say that compulsory education for a year or two beyond the eighth grade may be necessary when its goal is the preparation of the child for life in modern society as the majority live, but it is quite another if the goal of education be viewed as the preparation of the child for life in the separated agrarian community that is the keystone of the Amish faith ....

Whatever their idiosyncrasies as seen by the majority, the Amish community has been a highly successful social unit within our society, even if apart from the conventional "mainstream."

Its members are productive and very law-abiding members of society; they reject public welfare in any of its usual modern forms ....

This case involves the fundamental interest of parents, as contrasted with that of the State, to guide the religious future and education of their children. The history and culture of Western civilization reflect a strong tradition of parental concern for the nurture and upbringing of their children. This primary role of the parents in the upbringing of their children is now established beyond debate as an enduring American tradition ....

To be sure, the power of the parent, even when linked to a free exercise claim, may be subject to limitation if it appears that parental decisions will jeopardize the health or safety of the child, or have a potential for significant social burdens. But in this case, the Amish have introduced persuasive evidence undermining the arguments the State has advanced to support its claims in terms of the welfare of the child and society as a whole.

Mr. Justice Douglas, Dissenting in Part

The Court's analysis assumes that the only interests at stake in the case are those of the Amish parents on the one hand, and those of the State on the other. The difficulty with this approach is that, despite the Court's claim, the parents are seeking to vindicate not only their own free exercise claims, but also those of their high-school-age children ....

No analysis of religious-liberty claims can take place in a vacuum. If the parents in this case are allowed a religious exemption, the inevitable effect is to impose the parents' notions of religious duty upon their children. Where the child is mature enough to express potentially conflicting desires, it would be an invasion of the child's rights to permit such an imposition without canvassing his views. ... As the child has no other effective forum, it is in this litigation that his rights should be considered. And, if an Amish child desires to attend high school, and is mature enough to have that desire respected, the State may well be able to override the parents' religiously motivated objections.

This issue has never been squarely presented before today. Our opinions are full of talk about the power of the parents over the child's education. ... And we have in the past analyzed similar conflicts between parent and State with little regard for the views of the child ....

Recent cases, however, have clearly held that the children themselves have constitutionally protectible interests.

These children are "persons" within the meaning of the Bill of Rights. ... While the parents, absent dissent, normally speak for the entire family, the education of the child is a matter on which the child will often have decided views. He may want to be a pianist or an astronaut or an oceanographer. To do so he will have to break from the Amish tradition ....

If a parent keeps his child out of school beyond the grade school, then the child will be forever barred from entry into the new and amazing world of diversity that we have today ....

[In the cases in which the Court held anti-polygamy laws constitutional,] action which the Court deemed to be antisocial could be punished even though it was grounded on deeply held and sincere religious convictions. What we do today, at least in this respect, opens the way to give organized religion a broader base than it has ever enjoyed.

In another way, however, the Court retreats when in reference to Henry Thoreau it says his "choice was philosophical and personal rather than religious, and such belief does not rise to the demands of the Religion Clauses." That is contrary to what we held in *United States* v. *Seeger*, where we were concerned with the meaning of the words "religious training and belief" in the Selective Service Act, which were the basis of many conscientious objector claims. We said:

> Within that phrase would come all sincere religious beliefs which are based upon a power or being, or upon a faith, to which all else is subordinate or upon which all else is ultimately dependent. The test might be stated in these words: A sincere and meaningful belief which occupies in the life of its possessor a place parallel to that filled by the God of those admittedly qualifying for the exemption comes within the statutory definition. This construction avoids imputing to Congress an intent to classify different religious beliefs, exempting some and excluding others, and is in accord with the well-established congressional policy of equal treatment for those whose opposition to service is grounded in their religious tenets.

Review and Discussion Questions

1 Describe the legal issue in this case. Is culture also relevant? Why or why not?
2 Does Justice Burger seem to rely more on religious freedom or the rights of parents over children or the value of Amish culture? Explain.
3 On what basis does Justice Douglas dissent?
4 Does Justice Burger think the Constitution should be "neutral" among different religions? Explain.
5 Children will eventually have the right to make decisions for themselves in many areas, independent of what government or others may think. Can parents sometimes damage their children's future right to self-determination? Explain, giving examples.
6 Whose interests are at stake here: those of parents, children, or the Amish culture and religion?

Essay and Paper Topics for Chapter 19

1. It is often said that the United States is "a nation of immigrants," but it is sometimes the children of these immigrants who try to restrict the flow of future immigrants. Is this irrational, unethical? Draw on readings from this chapter as you assess this question.
2. What is the best way to address immigration pressures from Mexico into the United States and what underlying philosophical principles guide this analysis? Integrate any relevant readings across the textbook for developing your discussion.
3. Using the authors in this chapter or elsewhere, discuss the advantages and disadvantages of a multicultural society.
4. What do you believe are the most important determinants of your identity? To what extent does that influence your understanding of the value of a multicultural society? Analyze Sen's approach to those questions as you develop your own responses.

Appendix

The Bill of Rights and the Fourteenth Amendment

A Transcription

The following text is a transcription of the first ten amendments to the Constitution in their original form, as well as the first section of the Fourteenth Amendment. The first ten amendments were ratified December 15, 1791, and form what is known as the "Bill of Rights." The Fourteenth Amendment was passed by Congress June 13, 1866 and ratified July 9, 1868.

Amendment I

Congress shall make no law respecting an establishment of religion, or prohibiting the free exercise thereof; or abridging the freedom of speech, or of the press; or the right of the people peaceably to assemble, and to petition the Government for a redress of grievances.

Amendment II

A well regulated Militia, being necessary to the security of a free State, the right of the people to keep and bear Arms, shall not be infringed.

Amendment III

No Soldier shall, in time of peace be quartered in any house, without the consent of the Owner, nor in time of war, but in a manner to be prescribed by law.

Amendment IV

The right of the people to be secure in their persons, houses, papers, and effects, against unreasonable searches and seizures, shall not be violated, and no Warrants shall issue, but upon probable cause, supported by Oath or affirmation, and particularly describing the place to be searched, and the persons or things to be seized.

Amendment V

No person shall be held to answer for a capital, or otherwise infamous crime, unless on a presentment or indictment of a Grand Jury, except in cases arising in the land or naval forces, or in the Militia, when in actual service in time of War or public danger; nor shall any person be subject for the same offence to be twice put in jeopardy of life or limb; nor shall be compelled in any criminal case to be a witness against himself, nor be deprived of life, liberty, or property, without due process of law; nor shall private property be taken for public use, without just compensation.

Amendment VI

In all criminal prosecutions, the accused shall enjoy the right to a speedy and public trial, by an impartial jury of the State and district wherein the crime shall have been committed, which district shall have been previously ascertained by law, and to be informed of the nature and cause of the accusation; to be confronted with the witnesses against him; to have compulsory process for obtaining witnesses in his favor, and to have the Assistance of Counsel for his defence.

Amendment VII

In Suits at common law, where the value in controversy shall exceed twenty dollars, the right of trial by jury shall be preserved, and no fact tried by a jury, shall be otherwise re-examined in any Court of the United States, than according to the rules of the common law.

Amendment VIII

Excessive bail shall not be required, nor excessive fines imposed, nor cruel and unusual punishments inflicted.

Amendment IX

The enumeration in the Constitution, of certain rights, shall not be construed to deny or disparage others retained by the people.

Amendment X

The powers not delegated to the United States by the Constitution, nor prohibited by it to the States, are reserved to the States respectively, or to the people.

Amendment XIV

Section 1

All persons born or naturalized in the United States, and subject to the jurisdiction thereof, are citizens of the United States and of the State wherein they reside. No State shall make or enforce any law which shall abridge the privileges or immunities of citizens of the United States; nor shall any State deprive any person of life, liberty, or property, without due process of law; nor deny to any person within its jurisdiction the equal protection of the laws.